June 23–25, 2014
Prague, Czech Republic

Association for Computing Machinery

Advancing Computing as a Science & Profession

SPAA'14

Proceedings of the

26th ACM Symposium on Parallelism in Algorithms and Architectures

Sponsored by:

ACM SIGACT & ACM SIGARCH

Supporters:

Oracle Labs, Akamai, and Intel

**Association for
Computing Machinery**

Advancing Computing as a Science & Profession

The Association for Computing Machinery
2 Penn Plaza, Suite 701
New York, New York 10121-0701

Notice to Past Authors of ACM-Published Articles

ACM intends to create a complete electronic archive of all articles and/or other material previously published by ACM. If you have written a work that has been previously published by ACM in any journal or conference proceedings prior to 1978, or any SIG Newsletter at any time, and you do NOT want this work to appear in the ACM Digital Library, please inform permissions@acm.org, stating the title of the work, the author(s), and where and when published.

ISBN: 978-1-4503-2821-0 (Digital)

ISBN: 978-1-4503-3111-1 (Print)

Additional copies may be ordered prepaid from:

ACM Order Department
PO Box 30777
New York, NY 10087-0777, USA

Phone: 1-800-342-6626 (USA and Canada)
+1-212-626-0500 (Global)
Fax: +1-212-944-1318
E-mail: acmhelp@acm.org
Hours of Operation: 8:30 am – 4:30 pm ET

Printed in the USA

Foreword

This volume consists of papers that were presented at the *26th ACM Symposium on Parallelism in Algorithms and Architectures (SPAA'14)*, held on June 23-25, 2014, at Charles University in Prague, Czech Republic.

It was sponsored by the ACM Special Interest Groups on Algorithms and Computation Theory (SIGACT) and Computer Architecture (SIGARCH) and organized in cooperation with the European Association for Theoretical Computer Science (EATCS). Financial support was provided by Akamai, Intel, and Oracle Labs.

The 30 regular presentations that appeared at the conference were selected by the program committee after an electronic discussion. For the first time this included an author response period. The regular presentations were selected out of 122 submitted abstracts. The mix of selected papers reflects the unique nature of SPAA in bringing together the theory and practice of parallel computing. SPAA defines parallelism very broadly to encompass any computational device or scheme that can perform multiple operations or tasks simultaneously or concurrently. However this year shows a continued move back to SPAA's roots – an overwhelming majority of the papers are concerned with parallel processing in a more narrow sense. Strongly represented subjects include scheduling/load balancing, graph algorithms, and transactional memory. Many papers combine theoretical with practical results. Revised and expanded versions of a few best selected papers will be considered for publication in a special issue of the ACM "Transactions on Parallel Computing".

In addition to the regular presentations, this volume includes 12 brief announcements. The committee's decisions in accepting brief announcements were based on the perceived interest of these contributions, with the goal that they serve as bases for further significant advances in parallelism in computing. Extended versions of the SPAA brief announcements may be published later in other conferences or journals.

Finally, this year, there were two invited talks by Fabian Kuhn and Bruce M. Maggs.

The program committee would like to thank all who submitted papers and who helped the committee in the review process. The names of these external reviewers appear later in the proceedings. As the program chair of SPAA 2014, I would very much like to thank the program committee for all of their hard work during the paper selection process. The authors, the external reviewers, and the program committee together made it possible to come up with a great collection of papers for the conference.

Peter Sanders
Karlsruhe Institute of Technology
SPAA 2014 Program Chair

Table of Contents

Session 7: Automatic Complexity Analysis and Streaming

Keynote Address II

Session 8: Distributed Systems

Session 9: Lower Bounds

Session 10: Randomness

SPAA 2014 Organization

General Chair: Guy Blelloch, *Carnegie Mellon University, USA*

Program Chair: Peter Sanders, *Karlsruhe Institute of Technology, Germany*

SPAA Secretary: Christian Scheideler, *University of Paderborn, Germany*

Local Arrangements Chair: Petr Kolman, *Charles University in Prague, Czech Republic*

Publicity Chair: Jeremy Fineman, *Georgetown University*

Treasurer: David Bunde, *Knox College, USA*

Steering Committee: Guy Blelloch, *Carnegie Mellon University, USA*
David Culler, *UC Berkeley, USA*
Frank Dehne, *Carleton University, USA*
Pierre Fraigniaud, *University of Paris-Sud, France*
Phil Gibbons, *Intel Research, USA*
Maurice Herlihy, *Brown University, USA*
Tom Leighton, *MIT and Akamai Technologies*, USA
Charles Leiserson, *MIT, USA*
Fabrizio Luccio, *University of Pisa, Italy*
Friedhelm Meyer auf der Heide, *University of Paderborn, Germany*
Gary Miller, *Carnegie Mellon University, USA*
Burkhard Monien, *University of Paderborn, Germany*
Franco Preparata, *Brown University, USA*
Vijaya Ramachandran, *University of Texas, Austin, USA*
Arnold Rosenberg, *University of Massachusetts Amherst and Colorado State University, USA*
Paul Spirakis, *CTI and University of Liverpool, Greece*
Uzi Vishkin, *University of Maryland, USA*

Reviewers (continued):

Sascha Hunold	Vitaly Osipov
Riko Jacob	Preeti Panda
Navendu Jain	Matthew Patitz
Klaus Jansen	Boaz Patt-Shamir
Łukasz Jeż	Kolin Paul
Daniel Jung	Richard Peng
Jörg Keller	Erez Petrank
Pierre Kelsen	Greg Plaxton
Thomas Kesselheim	Pavel Podlipyan
Amal Khabou	Matteo Pontecorvi
Arindam Khan	Rajeev Raman
Peter Kling	Abhiram Ranade
Nicholas Knight	Sören Riechers
Yusuke Kobayashi	Jason Riedy
Moritz Kobitzsch	Torvald Riegel
Bojana Kodric	Paolo Romano
Annamaria Kovacs	Michał Różański
Evangelos Kranakis	Gopalan Sajith
Sven Krumke	Smruti Sarangi
Fabian Kuhn	Thomas Sauerwald
Janardhan Kulkarni	Nitin Saxena
Subodh Kumar	Jan Christoph Schlegel
Johannes Langguth	Grant Schoenebeck
Luigi Laura	Christian Schulz
Pascal Lenzner	Alexander Setzer
Alejandro Lopez-Ortiz	Bhabani Sinha
Zvi Lotker	Edgar Solomonik
Victor Luchangco	Michael Spear
Euripides Markou	Jochen Speck
Russell Martin	Anand Srivastav
Henning Meyerhenke	Grzegorz Stachowiak
Maged Michael	Thim Strothmann
Mark Moir	Håkan Sundell
Adam Morrison	Kavitha Telikepalli
Luca Moscardelli	Mikkel Thorup
Miguel Mosteiro	Sebastien Tixeuil
Ingo Müller	Rob van Stee
Andrei Negoescu	David Veith
Ofer Neiman	Uzi Vishkin
Calvin Newport	Lisa Wagner
Dang Nguyen	Rolf Wanka
Ioannis Nikolakopoulos	Volker Weichert
Dimitrios Nikolopoulos	Martin Wimmer
Adrian Ogierman	Prudence W.H. Wong
Lorenzo Orecchia	Elli Zavou

SPAA 2014 Sponsors & Supporters

Sponsors:

Supporters:

Oracle Labs

A Distributed Perspective on Graph Connectivity and Cuts

Fabian Kuhn
Dept. of Computer Science
University of Freiburg
Georges-Köhler-Allee 106
79110 Freiburg, Germany

Abstract

Edge and vertex connectivity, as well as edge and vertex cuts are among the most basic and fundamental concepts in graph theory. In particular, they are naturally significant in a networking context as they are a measure for the rate at which information can be transferred across a network. While in a traditional, sequential setting, there is a rich literature (in particular on problems related to edge connectivity and edge cuts), until recently, much less was known from a distributed algorithms point of view. In my talk, I will discuss and give partial answers to some of the following basic questions. Using distributed algorithms, how fast can we compute or approximate the edge or vertex connectivity and is it possible to efficiently find small cuts in a network? Assuming, we have a network with good connectivity properties, to what extent is it possible to exploit this in order to speed up distributed computations? Where such properties can be exploited, are there network structures that allow to make use of good connectivity in a structured (and somewhat canonical) way and can we construct such structures in a distributed manner?

Categories and Subject Descriptors

G.2.2 [**Discrete Mathematics**]: Graph Theory – *graph algorithms, network problems*

General Terms

Algorithms, Theory

Keywords

edge connectivity, vertex connectivity, edge cuts, vertex cuts, distributed algorithms

Short Bio

Fabian Kuhn received his M.Sc. degree in computer science in 2001 and his Ph.D. degree in 2005 from ETH Zurich in Switzerland. He then spent time as a postdoctoral researcher at Microsoft Research, at ETH Zurich, and at MIT. In the following, he was an assistant professor at the University of Lugano, Switzerland and in 2012, he joined the University of Freiburg, Germany as a full professor. Fabian Kuhn's research interests in particular include the complexity of graph-theoretic problems in a distributed context and the algorithmic foundations of mobile and wireless networks.

SPAA'14, June 23–25, 2014, Prague, Czech Republic.
ACM 978-1-4503-2821-0/14/06.
http://dx.doi.org/10.1145/2612669.2612728

On Dynamic Bin Packing for Resource Allocation in the Cloud

Yusen Li
Multi-plAtform Game
Innovation Centre (MAGIC)
Nanyang Technological
University
Singapore
s080007@e.ntu.edu.sg

Xueyan Tang
Parallel and Distributed
Computing Centre
Nanyang Technological
University
Singapore
asxytang@ntu.edu.sg

Wentong Cai
Parallel and Distributed
Computing Centre
Nanyang Technological
University
Singapore
astwcai@ntu.edu.sg

ABSTRACT

Dynamic Bin Packing (DBP) is a variant of classical bin packing, which assumes that items may arrive and depart at arbitrary times. Existing works on DBP generally aim to minimize the maximum number of bins ever used in the packing. In this paper, we consider a new version of the DBP problem, namely, the MinTotal DBP problem which targets at minimizing the total cost of the bins used over time. It is motivated by the request dispatching problem arising in cloud gaming systems. We analyze the competitive ratios of the commonly used First Fit, Best Fit, and Any Fit packing (the family of packing algorithms that open a new bin only when no currently opened bin can accommodate the item to be packed) algorithms for the MinTotal DBP problem. We show that the competitive ratio of Any Fit packing cannot be better than the max/min item interval length ratio μ. The competitive ratio of Best Fit packing is not bounded for any given μ. For First Fit packing, if all the item sizes are smaller than $\frac{W}{k}$ (W is the bin capacity and $k > 1$ is a constant), it has a competitive ratio of $\frac{k}{k-1} \cdot \mu + \frac{6k}{k-1} + 1$. For the general case, First Fit packing has a competitive ratio of $2\mu + 13$. We also propose a Modified First Fit packing algorithm that can achieve a competitive ratio of $\frac{8}{7}\mu + \frac{55}{7}$ when μ is not known and can achieve a competitive ratio of $\mu + 8$ when μ is known.

Categories and Subject Descriptors

C.2.4 [**Computer-Communication Networks**]: Distributed Systems; G.2.1 [**Discrete Mathematics**]: Combinatorics—*Combinatorial algorithms*

Keywords

Dynamic bin packing; cloud gaming; request dispatching; approximation algorithms; worst case bounds

1. INTRODUCTION

Bin packing is a classical combinatorial optimization problem which has been studied extensively [13, 11]. In the classical bin packing problem, given a set of items, the objective is to pack the items into a minimum number of bins such that the total size of the items in each bin does not exceed the bin capacity. Dynamic bin packing (DBP) is a generalization of the classical bin packing problem [12]. In the DBP problem, each item has a size, an arrival time and a departure time. The item stays in the system from its arrival to its departure. The objective is to pack the items into bins to minimize the maximum number of bins ever used over time. Dynamic bin packing has been widely used to model the resource consolidation problems in cloud computing [19, 25].

In this paper, we consider a new version of the DBP problem, which is called the MinTotal DBP problem. In this problem, we assume that each bin used has a cost that is proportional to the duration of its usage, i.e., the period from its opening (when the first item is put into the bin) to its close (when all the items in the bin depart). The objective is to pack the items into bins to minimize the total cost of packing over time. We focus on the online version of the problem, where the items must be assigned to bins as they arrive without any knowledge of their departure times and future item arrivals. The arrival time and the size of an item are only known when the item arrives and the departure time is only known when the item departs. The items are not allowed to move from one bin to another once they have been assigned upon arrivals.

The MinTotal DBP problem considered in this paper is primarily motivated by the request dispatching problem arising in cloud gaming systems. In a cloud gaming system, computer games run on powerful cloud servers, while players interact with the games via networked thin clients [17]. The cloud servers run the game instances, render the 3D graphics, encode them into 2D videos, and stream them to the clients. The clients then decode and display the video streams. This approach frees players from the overhead of setting up games, the hardware/software incompatibility problems, and the need for upgrading their computers regularly. Cloud gaming is a promising application of the rapidly expanding cloud computing infrastructure, and it has attracted a great deal of interests among entrepreneurs and researchers [22]. Several companies have offered cloud gaming services, such as OnLive [3], StreamMyGame [4], and GaiKai [2]. The cloud gaming market has been forecasted to reach 8 billion US dollars in 2017 [1].

Running each game instance demands a certain amount of GPU resources and the resource requirement can be different for running different games. In a cloud gaming system, when a playing request is received by the service provider, it needs to be dispatched to a game server that has enough GPU resources to run the game instance of this request. Several game instances can share the same game server as long as the server's GPU resources are not saturated. Each game instance keeps running in the system until the user stops playing the game. In general, the migration of game instances from one game server to another is not preferable due to large migration overheads and interruption to game play. In order to provide a good user experience, the gaming service provider needs to maintain a set of game servers with powerful GPUs for rendering the game instances. Constant workload fluctuation in cloud gaming makes the provisioning of game servers a challenging issue. The on-demand resource provisioning services in public clouds like Amazon EC2 provide an attractive solution. With these services, game service providers can rent virtual machines on demand to serve as game servers and pay for the resources according to their running hours. This frees game service providers from the complex process of planning, purchasing, and maintaining hardware. This approach has been adopted by many cloud gaming service providers like Gaikai and OnLive [26]. In the cloud gaming systems that use public clouds, one natural and important issue is how to dispatch the playing requests to game servers (i.e., virtual machines) so that the total cost of renting the game servers is minimized. The online MinTotal DBP problem we have defined exactly models this issue, where the game servers and playing requests correspond to the bins and items respectively.

For online bin packing, Any Fit packing algorithms have been extensively studied since they are simple and make decisions based on the current system state only. Any Fit packing refers to the family of packing algorithms that open a new bin only when no currently opened bin can accommodate the item to be packed. First Fit and Best Fit are two commonly used Any Fit packing algorithms. First Fit packing attempts to put a new item into the earliest opened bin that can accommodate the item. Best Fit attempts to assign a new item to the bin with smallest residual capacity that can accommodate the item. In this paper, we analyze the performance of the First Fit, Best Fit and Any Fit packing algorithms for the MinTotal DBP problem. We assume that an infinite number of bins are available for packing and all the bins have the same capacity and the same cost.

The contributions of this paper are as follows. We prove that the competitive ratio of Any Fit packing cannot be better than the max/min item interval length ratio μ. The competitive ratio of Best Fit packing is not bounded for any given μ. We show that for the case where all the item sizes are smaller than $\frac{W}{k}$ (W is the bin capacity and $k > 1$ is a constant), First Fit packing has a competitive ratio of $\frac{k}{k-1} \cdot \mu + \frac{6k}{k-1} + 1$. For the general case, First Fit packing has a competitive ratio of $2\mu + 13$. In addition, we propose a Modified First Fit packing algorithm which classifies and assigns items according to their sizes. Modified First Fit packing can achieve a competitive ratio of $\frac{8}{7}\mu + \frac{55}{7}$ when μ is not known and can achieve a competitive ratio of $\mu + 8$ when μ is known.

The rest of this paper is structured as follows. The related work is summarized in Section 2. Section 3 introduces the system model, notations and packing algorithms. In Sections 4.1 to 4.3, the competitive ratios of First Fit, Best Fit, and Any Fit packing for the MinTotal DBP problem are analyzed. Then, the Modified First Fit packing algorithm is proposed and its competitive ratio for the MinTotal DBP problem is analyzed in Section 4.4. Finally, conclusions are made and future work is discussed in Section 5.

2. RELATED WORK

Cloud gaming systems have been implemented for both commercial use and research studies [17, 3, 4]. However, most of the existing work has focused on measuring the performance of cloud gaming systems [10, 24]. To the best of our knowledge, the resource management issues of cloud gaming have never been studied. The MinTotal DBP problem studied in this paper is related to a variety of research topics including the classical bin packing problem and its variations, as well as the interval scheduling problem.

The classical bin packing problem aims to put a set of items into the least number of bins. The problem and its variations have been studied extensively in both the offline and online versions [11, 15]. It is well known that the offline version of the classical bin packing problem is NP-hard already [16]. For the online version, each item must be assigned to a bin without the knowledge of subsequent items. The items are not allowed to move from one bin to another. So far, the best upper bound on the competitive ratio for classical online bin packing is 1.58889, which is achieved by the HARMONIC++ algorithm proposed in [23]. The best known lower bound for any online packing algorithm is 1.54037 [5].

Dynamic bin packing is a variant of the classical bin packing problem [12]. It generalizes the problem by assuming that items may arrive and depart at arbitrary times. The objective is to minimize the maximum number of bins ever used in the packing. Coffman et al. [12] showed that the First Fit packing algorithm has a competitive ratio between 2.75 to 2.897 and no online algorithm can achieve a competitive ratio smaller than 2.5. Joseph et al. [9] proved that the lower bound 2.5 on the competitive ratio also holds when the offline algorithm does not repack. Ivkovic et al. [18] studied an even more general problem called the fully dynamic bin packing problem, where the migration of items is allowed. They proposed an online algorithm that achieves a competitive ratio of 1.25. Chan et al. [8] studied dynamic bin packing of unit fractions items (i.e., each item has a size $\frac{1}{w}$ for some integer $w \geq 1$). They showed that Any Fit packing algorithms have a tight competitive ratio of 3. They also proved that no online algorithm can achieve a competitive ratio better than 2.428. Classical dynamic bin packing does not consider bin usage costs and focuses simply on minimizing the maximum number of bins ever used. In contrast, the MinTotal DBP problem considered in this paper aims to minimize the total cost of the bins used in the packing.

The interval scheduling problem is also related to our problem [20]. The classical interval scheduling problem considers a set of jobs, each associated with a weight and an interval over which the job should be executed. Each machine can process only a single job at any time. Given a fixed number of machines, the objective is to schedule a feasible subset of jobs whose total weight is maximized [6].

Michele et al. [14] have extended the classical model to a more general version, which is called interval scheduling with bounded parallelism. In this model, each machine can process $g > 1$ jobs simultaneously. If there is a job running on a machine, the machine is called busy. The objective is to assign the jobs to the machines such that the total busy time of the machines is minimized. It was proved that the problem to minimize the total busy time is NP-hard for $g \geq 2$ and a 4-competitive offline algorithm was proposed. George et al. [21] considered two special instances: clique instances (the intervals of all jobs share a common time point) and proper instances (the intervals of all jobs are not contained in one another), and provided constant factor approximation algorithms. However, the interval scheduling problem differs from our problem because the ending time of a job is known at the time of its assignment in interval scheduling, whereas in our MinTotal DBP model, the departure time is not known at the time of item assignment. Furthermore, our MinTotal DBP problem does not assume that all the items have the same size, so the number of items that can be packed into a bin is not fixed.

3. PRELIMINARIES

3.1 Notations and Definitions

We first define the notations used in this paper. Each item r to pack is associated with a 3-tuple $(a(r), d(r), s(r))$, where $a(r)$, $d(r)$ and $s(r)$ denote the arrival time, the departure time and the size of r respectively. Let $I(r)$ denote the time interval $[a(r), d(r)]$ in which item r stays in the system (assume that $d(r) > a(r)$ is always true). We say that item r is *active* during this interval. The interval length of item r is represented by $len(I(r)) = d(r) - a(r)$. For any list of items $\mathcal{R}$, we define the span of $\mathcal{R}$ as $span(\mathcal{R}) = len(\bigcup_{r \in \mathcal{R}} I(r))$, i.e., the length of time in which at least one item in $\mathcal{R}$ is active. Figure 1 shows an example of the span. Let $u(r) = s(r) \cdot len(I(r))$ denote the *resource demand* of item r. For any list of items $\mathcal{R}$, we define the total resource demand of $\mathcal{R}$ as $u(\mathcal{R}) = \sum_{r \in \mathcal{R}} u(r)$.

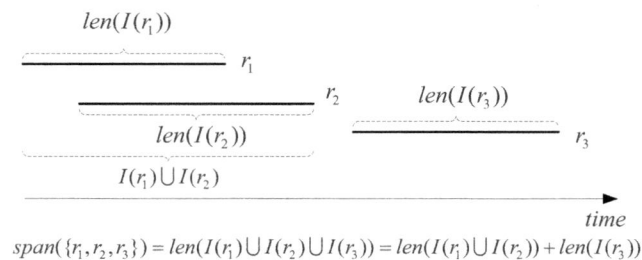

$$span(\{r_1, r_2, r_3\}) = len(I(r_1) \bigcup I(r_2) \bigcup I(r_3)) = len(I(r_1) \bigcup I(r_2)) + len(I(r_3))$$

Figure 1: Span of an item list

At any time, the set of all the items in an opened bin is called the *bin configuration*. The total size of the items in an opened bin is called the *level* of the bin. To represent bin configurations, we denote by $x|_y$ a total size of x that is composed of items with size y each. For example, $1|_{\frac{1}{3}}$ means a total size 1 constituted by 3 items of size $\frac{1}{3}$ each. Then, a bin configuration can be represented in the form of $\langle x_1|_{y_1}, x_2|_{y_2}, ..., x_k|_{y_k} \rangle$. For example, $\langle \frac{1}{2}|_{\frac{1}{2}}, \frac{2}{5}|_{\frac{1}{10}} \rangle$ represents

Table 1: Summary of Key Notations

Notation	Definition
$a(r)$	the arrival time of an item r
$d(r)$	the departure time of an item r
$s(r)$	the size of an item r
$I(r)$	the time interval of $[a(r), d(r)]$
$len(I(r))$	the length of $I(r)$, $len(I(r)) = d(r) - a(r)$
$u(r)$	the resource demand of an item r, $u(r) = s(r) \cdot len(I(r))$
$span(\mathcal{R})$	the span of an item list $\mathcal{R}$, $span(\mathcal{R}) = len(\bigcup_{r \in \mathcal{R}} I(r))$
$u(\mathcal{R})$	the total resource demand of an item list $\mathcal{R}$, $u(\mathcal{R}) = \sum_{r \in \mathcal{R}} u(r)$
W	the bin capacity
C	the bin cost rate
$x\vert_y$	a total size of x that is composed of items with size y each
$\langle x_1\vert_{y_1}, ..., x_k\vert_{y_k} \rangle$	a bin configuration
$A(\mathcal{R}, t)$	the number of opened bins at time t by algorithm A in packing an item list $\mathcal{R}$
$A_{total}(\mathcal{R})$	the total cost incurred by algorithm A in packing $\mathcal{R}$ over the packing period, $A_{total}(\mathcal{R}) = \int_{\min_{r \in \mathcal{R}} a(r)}^{\max_{r \in \mathcal{R}} d(r)} A(\mathcal{R}, t) \cdot C \, dt$
$OPT(\mathcal{R}, t)$	the number of bins needed by optimally repacking the active items in an item list $\mathcal{R}$ at time t
$OPT_{total}(\mathcal{R})$	$OPT_{total}(\mathcal{R}) = \int_{\min_{r \in \mathcal{R}} a(r)}^{\max_{r \in \mathcal{R}} d(r)} OPT(\mathcal{R}, t) \cdot C \, dt$

a bin with a level of $\frac{9}{10}$, which packs one item of size $\frac{1}{2}$ and 4 items of size $\frac{1}{10}$ each.

Let W and C denote the bin capacity and cost rate respectively. Let $n(t)$ denote the number of opened bins at time t. Given a list of items $\mathcal{R}$ to pack, we refer to the period from the first item arrival to the last item departure, i.e., $[\min_{r \in \mathcal{R}} a(r), \max_{r \in \mathcal{R}} d(r)]$ as the *packing period*. The MinTotal DBP problem targets at minimizing the total cost of the bins used over the packing period, i.e.,

$$\text{minimize} \int_{\min_{r \in \mathcal{R}} a(r)}^{\max_{r \in \mathcal{R}} d(r)} n(t) \cdot C \, dt$$

The above notations are summarized in Table 1.

3.2 Packing Algorithms

As aforementioned, we consider the commonly used First Fit, Best Fit, and Any Fit packing algorithms in this paper. Their formal definitions are given below.

- **First Fit (FF)**: Each time when a new item arrives, First Fit packing tries to put it into the earliest opened bin that can accommodate it. If none of the opened bins has enough residual capacity to accommodate the new item, then a new bin is opened. When all the items in a bin depart, the bin is closed.

- **Best Fit (BF)**: Each time when a new item arrives, Best Fit packing tries to put it into the best opened bin, i.e., the one with the smallest residual capacity after adding the item. If no opened bin has sufficient residual capacity to accommodate the new item, then a new bin is opened. When all the items in a bin depart, the bin is closed.

- **Any Fit (AF)**: Each time when a new item arrives, Any Fit packing can put the item into any opened bin that can accommodate it if one exists. If no opened bin has adequate residual capacity to accommodate the new item, then a new bin is opened. When all the items in a bin depart, the bin is closed. It is easy to see that First Fit and Best Fit are special cases of Any Fit packing.

The performance of an online algorithm is normally measured by its competitive ratio, i.e., the worst-case ratio between the cost of the solution constructed by the algorithm and the cost of an optimal solution [7]. In our MinTotal DBP problem, for an online packing algorithm A, let $A(\mathcal{R}, t)$ denote the number of opened bins at time t by A in packing a list of items $\mathcal{R}$. The total cost incurred by A in packing $\mathcal{R}$ over the packing period is given by

$$A_{total}(\mathcal{R}) = \int_{\min_{r \in \mathcal{R}} a(r)}^{\max_{r \in \mathcal{R}} d(r)} A(\mathcal{R}, t) \cdot C \, dt$$

Let $OPT(\mathcal{R}, t)$ denote the minimum achievable number of bins into which all the active items at time t can be repacked. Define

$$OPT_{total}(\mathcal{R}) = \int_{\min_{r \in \mathcal{R}} a(r)}^{\max_{r \in \mathcal{R}} d(r)} OPT(\mathcal{R}, t) \cdot C \, dt$$

In the MinTotal DBP problem, we shall analyze the worst-case ratio of $A_{total}(\mathcal{R})$ to $OPT_{total}(\mathcal{R})$. The worst-case ratio is defined as the positive value α such that the following relation holds for any instance of the problem [12]:

$$A_{total}(\mathcal{R}) \le \alpha \cdot OPT_{total}(\mathcal{R})$$

4. THE COMPETITIVE RATIOS

In this section, we analyze the competitive ratios of the packing algorithms for the MinTotal DBP problem. First, for a given item list $\mathcal{R}$, we have the following obvious bounds for the total cost of any packing algorithm A.

Bound (b.1) $A_{total}(\mathcal{R}) \ge \frac{u(\mathcal{R}) \cdot C}{W}$

Bound (b.2) $A_{total}(\mathcal{R}) \ge span(\mathcal{R}) \cdot C$

Bound (b.3) $A_{total}(\mathcal{R}) \le \sum_{r \in \mathcal{R}} len(I(r)) \cdot C$

Bound (b.1) is derived by assuming that no bin capacity is wasted at any time. Bound (b.2) is derived from the fact that at least one bin must be in use at any time when there is at least one active item. Bound (b.3) is derived by assuming that each item is assigned to a new bin.

For any item list $\mathcal{R}$, let $\mu = \frac{\max_{r \in \mathcal{R}} len(I(r))}{\min_{r \in \mathcal{R}} len(I(r))}$ denote the max/min item interval length ratio, where $\max_{r \in \mathcal{R}} len(I(r))$ is the maximum interval length among all the items $r \in \mathcal{R}$ and $\min_{r \in \mathcal{R}} len(I(r))$ is the minimum interval length among all the items $r \in \mathcal{R}$.

4.1 A Lower Bound for Any Fit Packing

First, we have the following result for Any Fit packing.

THEOREM 1. *For the MinTotal DBP problem, the competitive ratio of Any Fit packing has a lower bound given by the max/min item interval length ratio μ.*

PROOF. Without loss of generality, suppose $W = 1$. Let Δ be the minimum item interval length and $\mu\Delta$ be the maximum item interval length. Let k be an integer. At time 0, let k^2 items of size $\frac{1}{k}$ arrive. Any Fit packing needs to open k bins to pack these items. At time Δ, let some items depart such that each opened bin has only one item left. At time $\mu\Delta$, all the remaining items leave the system.

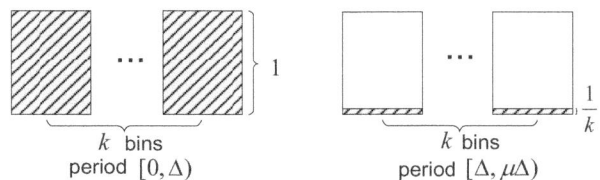

Figure 2: Bin configurations in Any Fit packing

As shown in Figure 2, there are always k opened bins in Any Fit packing from time 0 to $\mu\Delta$. Therefore, the total cost of Any Fit packing is $AF_{total}(\mathcal{R}) = k\mu\Delta \cdot C$. From time Δ to $\mu\Delta$, there are only k active items in the system which can in fact be packed into one bin. Therefore, $OPT_{total}(\mathcal{R}) = k\Delta \cdot C + (\mu - 1)\Delta \cdot C$. It follows that

$$\frac{AF_{total}(\mathcal{R})}{OPT_{total}(\mathcal{R})} = \frac{k\mu\Delta \cdot C}{k\Delta \cdot C + (\mu - 1)\Delta \cdot C} = \frac{k\mu}{k + \mu - 1} \quad (1)$$

According to (1), given any small value ϵ, we can always find an integer k such that $\frac{AF_{total}(\mathcal{R})}{OPT_{total}(\mathcal{R})} > \mu - \epsilon$. Therefore, the competitive ratio of Any Fit packing is at least μ and the theorem is proven.[1] $\square$

4.2 Best Fit Packing

Next, we have the following result for Best Fit packing.

THEOREM 2. *For the MinTotal DBP problem, Best Fit packing has no bounded competitive ratio for any given max/min item interval length ratio μ.*

PROOF. Without loss of generality, suppose $W = 1$. Let k be an integer. Let Δ be the minimum item interval length and $\mu\Delta$ be the maximum item interval length. Suppose that all the items have the same size ε, which is a sufficiently small value and $\frac{1}{\varepsilon}$ is an integer.

At time 0, let $\frac{k}{\varepsilon}$ items arrive. Best Fit packing needs to open k bins to pack all these items since their total size is k. Denote these k bins by $b_1, b_2, ..., b_k$. At time Δ, for each bin b_i, let some items depart to form the bin configuration $\langle (\frac{1}{k} - i \cdot \varepsilon)|_\varepsilon \rangle$ at b_i.

Then, let items arrive and depart according to the following iterative process. In the jth ($j \ge 1$) iteration, k groups of items arrive sequentially in the period $[j\mu\Delta - \delta, j\mu\Delta]$, where δ is a very small variable. The items in each group arrive at the same time and the mth group has $\frac{\frac{1}{k} - (j \cdot k + m) \cdot \varepsilon}{\varepsilon}$ items. By using Best Fit packing, the items in the first group (i.e., $m = 1$) will be assigned to b_1 since b_1 is the bin with the highest level in the system. After the items in the first group are packed, before the second group of items arrive, let all the "old" items in b_1 (the items arrived before time $j\mu\Delta - \delta$) depart. The new configuration of b_1

---

[1] In fact, this example and the lower bound μ are applicable to any online packing algorithm.

will become $\langle(\frac{1}{k} - (jk+1) \cdot \varepsilon)|_\varepsilon\rangle$. Then, the second group will be assigned to bin b_2, and so on so forth. In general, the items in the mth group will be packed in b_m since b_m is the bin with the highest level in the system when the mth group of items arrive. Before the $(m+1)$th group of items arrive, let the "old" items in b_m depart to form the configuration $\langle(\frac{1}{k} - (jk+m) \cdot \varepsilon)|_\varepsilon\rangle$ at b_m. Figure 3 shows the bin configurations in the first few iterations.

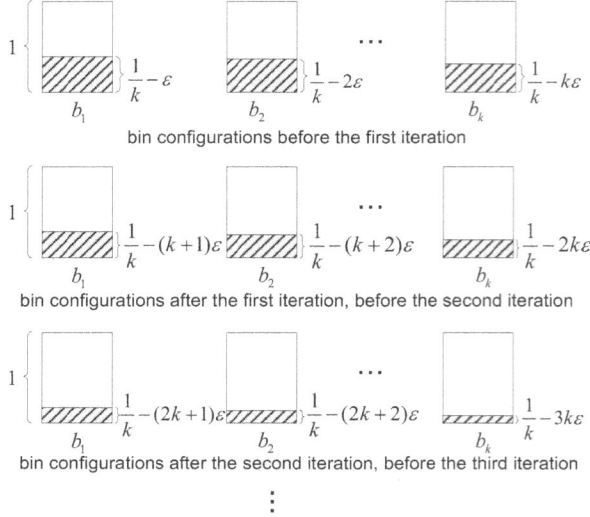

Figure 3: Bin configurations in Best Fit packing

Consider the time interval $[0, n\mu\Delta]$ in the above packing process, where n is an integer. Since there are always k bins in the system, the total cost incurred by Best Fit packing is $BF_{total}(\mathcal{R}) = kn\mu\Delta \cdot C$. On the other hand, the total resource demand in the period $[0, \Delta]$ is $k\Delta$. After time Δ, except the periods $[j\mu\Delta - \delta, j\mu\Delta]$ (for each $1 \leq j \leq n$), all the active items in the system can be packed into one bin at any time. For the periods $[j\mu\Delta - \delta, j\mu\Delta]$, at most two bins are required to pack all the active items. Therefore,

$$OPT_{total}(\mathcal{R}) \leq k\Delta \cdot C + (n\mu\Delta - \Delta - n\delta) \cdot C + n\delta \cdot 2C$$
$$= k\Delta \cdot C + (n\mu\Delta - \Delta) \cdot C + n\delta \cdot C$$

It follows that

$$\frac{BF_{total}(\mathcal{R})}{OPT_{total}(\mathcal{R})} \geq \frac{kn\mu\Delta \cdot C}{k\Delta \cdot C + (n\mu\Delta - \Delta) \cdot C + n\delta \cdot C}$$
$$= \frac{kn\mu\Delta}{k\Delta + (n\mu\Delta - \Delta) + n\delta}$$

It can be proved that when $n \geq \frac{(k-1)\Delta}{\mu\Delta - \delta}$, we have

$$\frac{BF_{total}(\mathcal{R})}{OPT_{total}(\mathcal{R})} \geq \frac{k}{2} \qquad (2)$$

Inequality (2) implies that the ratio $\frac{BF_{total}(\mathcal{R})}{OPT_{total}(\mathcal{R})}$ can be made arbitrarily large as k goes towards infinity. Therefore, Best Fit has no bounded competitive ratio for any given max/min item interval length ratio μ and the theorem is proven. $\square$

4.3 First Fit Packing

Now, we study the competitive ratio of First Fit packing. We start by analyzing two particular cases in which all the item sizes are "large" and "small" respectively. First, we have the following result for the case of "large" items.

THEOREM 3. *For the MinTotal DBP problem, for any item list $\mathcal{R}$, if the item size $s(r) \geq \frac{W}{k}$ ($k > 1$ is a constant) for all the items $r \in \mathcal{R}$, the total cost of First Fit packing is at most $k \cdot OPT_{total}(\mathcal{R})$.*

PROOF. According to Bound (b.3), the total cost of any packing algorithm is at most $C \cdot \sum_{r \in \mathcal{R}} len(I(r))$. If all the item sizes are larger than or equal to $\frac{W}{k}$, we have

$$C \cdot \sum_{r \in \mathcal{R}} len(I(r)) = C \cdot \sum_{r \in \mathcal{R}} \frac{u(r)}{s(r)}$$
$$\leq C \cdot \frac{\sum_{r \in \mathcal{R}} u(r)}{\frac{W}{k}}$$
$$\leq k \cdot C \cdot \frac{u(\mathcal{R})}{W} \qquad (3)$$
$$\leq k \cdot OPT_{total}(\mathcal{R})$$

The last step is based on Bound (b.1). Hence, the theorem is proven. $\square$

Next, we analyze the case of "small" items. It serves as the basis for analyzing the competitive ratio of First Fit packing in the general case, as well as for designing a Modified First Fit packing algorithm in Section 4.4 with improved competitive ratios.

Consider an item list $\mathcal{R}$ in which each item $r \in \mathcal{R}$ has a size $s(r) < \frac{W}{k}$ ($k > 1$ is a constant). Let Δ be the minimum item interval length and $\mu\Delta$ be the maximum item interval length. Suppose a total of m bins $b_1, b_2, ..., b_m$ are used in First Fit packing to pack $\mathcal{R}$. For each bin b_i, let I_i denote the usage period of b_i, i.e., the period from the time when b_i is opened to the time when b_i is closed. Let I_i^- and I_i^+ denote the left and right endpoints of I_i respectively, then I_i can be represented by $[I_i^-, I_i^+]$. Denote the length of I_i by $len(I_i)$, then $len(I_i) = I_i^+ - I_i^-$. Without loss of generality, assume that the bins are indexed in the temporal order of their openings, i.e., $I_1^- \leq I_2^- \leq \cdots \leq I_m^-$.

Let $\mathcal{R}_i$ denote the set of items that are assigned to b_i in First Fit packing, then we have $I_i = \bigcup_{r \in \mathcal{R}_i} I(r)$. The total cost of First Fit packing is given by

$$FF_{total}(\mathcal{R}) = C \cdot \sum_{i=1}^{m} len(I_i)$$

For each bin b_i, let E_i be the latest closing time of all the bins that are opened before b_i, i.e., $E_i = \max\{I_j^+ | 1 \leq j < i\}$. We divide period I_i into two parts. Let I_i^L denote the period $[I_i^-, \min\{I_i^+, E_i\}]$. If $E_i \leq I_i^-$, define $I_i^L = \emptyset$. Let $I_i^R = I_i - I_i^L$ be the remaining period. For the first opened bin b_1, we define E_1 to be the start of the packing period so that $I_1^L = \emptyset$ and $I_1^R = I_1$. Figure 4 shows an example of these definitions. According to the definitions, we have $len(I_i) = len(I_i^L) + len(I_i^R)$ and it follows that

$$FF_{total}(\mathcal{R}) = C \cdot \sum_{i=1}^{m} \left(len(I_i^L) + len(I_i^R) \right) \qquad (4)$$

Obviously, for any two different bins b_i and b_j, $I_i^R \cap I_j^R = \emptyset$. It is also easy to see that $span(\mathcal{R}) = len(\bigcup_{i=1}^{m} I_i^R)$. There-

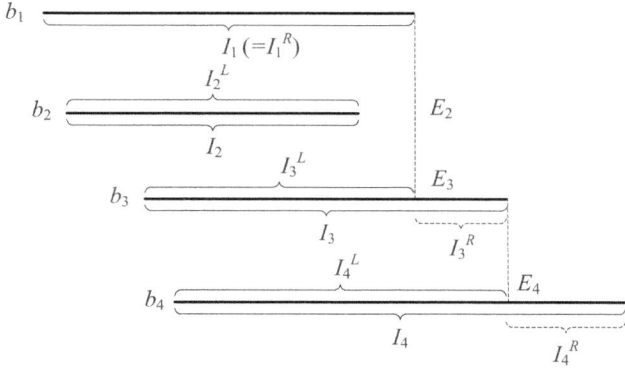

Figure 4: An example of usage periods

fore,

$$span(\mathcal{R}) = \sum_{i=1}^{m} len(I_i^R) \tag{5}$$

According to (4) and (5), we have

$$FF_{total}(\mathcal{R}) = C \cdot \left(\sum_{i=1}^{m} len(I_i^L) \right) + C \cdot span(\mathcal{R}) \tag{6}$$

For each period I_i^L, if its length $len(I_i^L) > (\mu + 2)\Delta$, we split I_i^L into $\lceil \frac{len(I_i^L)}{(\mu+2)\Delta} \rceil$ sub-periods by inserting splitter points that are multiples of $(\mu + 2)\Delta$ before the end of I_i^L, i.e., at times $\min\{I_i^+, E_i\} - k \cdot (\mu + 2)\Delta$, for $k = 1, 2, \ldots, \lceil \frac{len(I_i^L)}{(\mu+2)\Delta} \rceil - 1$. After splitting, if the length of the first sub-period is shorter than 2Δ, we merge the first two sub-periods into one. Then, we label all the sub-periods in the temporal order by $I_{i,1}, I_{i,2}, I_{i,3}, \ldots$, i.e., their left endpoints satisfy $I_{i,1}^- < I_{i,2}^- < I_{i,3}^- < \cdots$. Figure 5 shows an example of the period split and mergence.

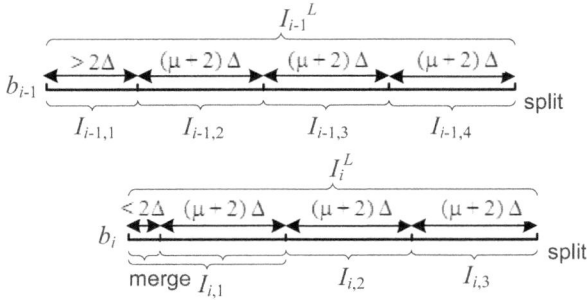

Figure 5: An example of period split and mergence

Note that if the length of I_i^L does not exceed $(\mu + 2)\Delta$, I_i^L is not split. In this case, we define $I_{i,1} = I_i^L$. The above splitting and merging process implies the following features:

Feature (f.1) $len(I_{i,j}) \leq (\mu + 4)\Delta$ for any i and j.

Feature (f.2) $len(I_{i,j}) = (\mu + 2)\Delta$ for any $j \geq 2$ and any i.

Feature (f.3) For any i, if there exists a sub-period $I_{i,j}$ where $j \geq 2$, then the length of the first sub-period $len(I_{i,1}) \geq 2\Delta$.

Let $\mathcal{I}^L$ denote the set of all the sub-periods produced by the above splitting and merging process from all I_i^L's. Define $len(\mathcal{I}^L) = \sum_{I_{i,j} \in \mathcal{I}^L} len(I_{i,j})$. It is obvious that

$$\sum_{i=1}^{m} len(I_i^L) = len(\mathcal{I}^L) \tag{7}$$

For each period $I_{i,j}$, it can be shown that at least one new item must be packed into bin b_i during $I_{i,j} = [I_{i,j}^-, I_{i,j}^+]$. In fact, if $len(I_{i,j}) \geq (\mu + 2)\Delta$, there must be at least one new item packed into b_i during $[I_{i,j}^-, I_{i,j}^- + \mu\Delta]$. This is because all the items packed into b_i before $I_{i,j}^-$ would have departed by time $I_{i,j}^- + \mu\Delta$ since $\mu\Delta$ is the maximum item interval length. Thus, if no new item is packed into b_i during $[I_{i,j}^-, I_{i,j}^- + \mu\Delta]$, b_i would become empty and be closed by time $I_{i,j}^- + \mu\Delta$. On the other hand, if $len(I_{i,j}) < (\mu + 2)\Delta$, according to Feature (f.2), $I_{i,j}$ must be the first sub-period in I_i^L, i.e., $j = 1$. Since b_i is opened at time $I_i^- = I_{i,1}^-$, at least one new item is packed into b_i at time $I_{i,1}^-$.

Let $t_{i,j}$ denote the time point when the "earliest" item (among all the items that are newly packed into b_i in period $I_{i,j}$) is packed into b_i in $I_{i,j}$. We refer to $t_{i,j}$ as the *reference point* of $I_{i,j}$. The above analysis implies that:

Feature (f.4) For each period $I_{i,1}$, it holds that $t_{i,1} = I_{i,1}^-$.

Feature (f.5) For each period $I_{i,j}$, it holds that $I_{i,j}^- \leq t_{i,j} \leq I_{i,j}^- + \mu\Delta$.

It is also easy to infer that there must exist at least one bin b_k satisfying $k < i$ and $t_{i,j} < I_k^+$. Otherwise, $t_{i,j}$ would not be contained in any period I_k where $k < i$. That is, b_i would be the opened bin with the lowest index at time $t_{i,j}$. According to the previous definitions, $t_{i,j}$ would then belong to I_i^R, which contradicts that $t_{i,j}$ is in $I_{i,j}$ (a sub-period of I_i^L). Among all the bins b_k satisfying $k < i$ and $t_{i,j} < I_k^+$, we define the last opened bin (the bin with the highest index) as the *reference bin* of $I_{i,j}$, and denote it by $b^\dagger(I_{i,j})$. We define the period $[t_{i,j} - \Delta, t_{i,j} + \Delta]$ associated with bin $b^\dagger(I_{i,j})$ as the *reference period* of $I_{i,j}$, and denote it by $p^\dagger(I_{i,j})$. Figure 6 shows an example of reference bins and reference periods.

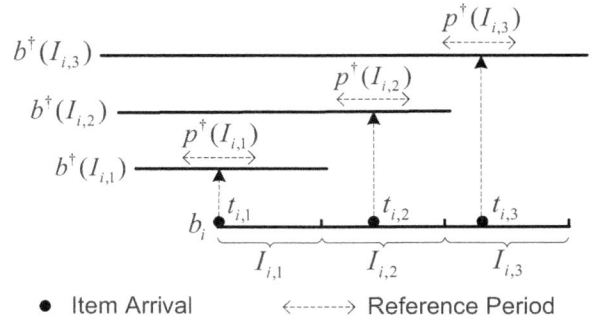

- Item Arrival   ←------→ Reference Period

Figure 6: An example of reference bins and periods

Since there is a new item packed into b_i at time $t_{i,j}$ and the item size is smaller than $\frac{W}{k}$, the reference bin $b^\dagger(I_{i,j})$ must have a level higher than $W - \frac{W}{k}$ at time $t_{i,j}$ according to the First Fit packing algorithm. That is, the total size of the items in $b^\dagger(I_{i,j})$ at time $t_{i,j}$ is larger than $W - \frac{W}{k}$. Recall that each of these items resides in the system for at least Δ time (the minimum item interval length). Thus, each of them must stay in bin $b^\dagger(I_{i,j})$ for at least Δ time during the reference period $p^\dagger(I_{i,j}) = [t_{i,j} - \Delta, t_{i,j} + \Delta]$. Denote by $u(p^\dagger(I_{i,j}))$ the total resource demand of the items in bin $b^\dagger(I_{i,j})$ over period $p^\dagger(I_{i,j})$. It follows that

$$u(p^\dagger(I_{i,j})) \geq \left(W - \frac{W}{k} \right) \cdot \Delta \qquad (8)$$

We define that two reference periods intersect if and only if they are associated with the same bin and their time intervals overlap. Then, for any two different periods I_{i_1,j_1} and I_{i_2,j_2}, their reference periods intersect if and only if $b^\dagger(I_{i_1,j_1}) = b^\dagger(I_{i_2,j_2})$ and $|t_{i_1,j_1} - t_{i_2,j_2}| < 2\Delta$. Next, we analyze whether two reference periods will intersect according to the five cases classified by Table 2.

Table 2: Case Classification

	$j_1 \geq 2, j_2 \geq 2$	$j_1 = 1, j_2 \geq 2$ or $j_1 \geq 2, j_2 = 1$	$j_1 = 1, j_2 = 1$
$i_1 = i_2$	Case I	Case II	—
$i_1 \neq i_2$	Case III	Case IV	Case V

For Cases I, II, III and IV, we have the following lemma.

LEMMA 1. *The reference periods of I_{i_1,j_1} and I_{i_2,j_2} do not intersect in Cases I, II, III and IV.*

PROOF. For convenience, denote $I_{i_1,j_1} = [I_{i_1,j_1}^-, I_{i_1,j_1}^+]$ and $I_{i_2,j_2} = [I_{i_2,j_2}^-, I_{i_2,j_2}^+]$.

For Case I, since $j_1 \geq 2$ and $j_2 \geq 2$, it follows from Feature (f.2) that $len(I_{i_1,j_1}) = len(I_{i_2,j_2}) = (\mu + 2)\Delta$. Without loss of generality, suppose $j_1 < j_2$. Since $i_1 = i_2$, it follows that $I_{i_1,j_1}^+ \leq I_{i_2,j_2}^-$. According to Features (f.2) and (f.5), we have $t_{i_1,j_1} \leq I_{i_1,j_1}^- + \mu\Delta = I_{i_1,j_1}^+ - 2\Delta$ and $t_{i_2,j_2} \geq I_{i_2,j_2}^- \geq I_{i_1,j_1}^+$. As a result, $t_{i_2,j_2} - t_{i_1,j_1} \geq 2\Delta$. Therefore, the two reference periods cannot intersect.

For Case II, without loss of generality, suppose $j_1 = 1$ and $j_2 \geq 2$. Since $i_1 = i_2$, we have $I_{i_1,j_1}^+ \leq I_{i_2,j_2}^-$. According to Feature (f.4), $t_{i_1,j_1} = I_{i_1,j_1}^-$. It also follows from Feature (f.3) that $len(I_{i_1,j_1}) = I_{i_1,j_1}^+ - I_{i_1,j_1}^- \geq 2\Delta$. Moreover, based on Feature (f.5), we have $t_{i_2,j_2} \geq I_{i_2,j_2}^- \geq I_{i_1,j_1}^+$. Thus, $t_{i_2,j_2} - t_{i_1,j_1} = t_{i_2,j_2} - I_{i_1,j_1}^- \geq I_{i_1,j_1}^+ - I_{i_1,j_1}^- \geq 2\Delta$. Therefore, the two reference periods cannot intersect.

For Case III, without loss of generality, suppose $i_1 < i_2$. If $b^\dagger(I_{i_1,j_1}) \neq b^\dagger(I_{i_2,j_2})$, the two reference periods must not intersect according to the definition. If $b^\dagger(I_{i_1,j_1}) = b^\dagger(I_{i_2,j_2})$, it must hold that $t_{i_2,j_2} \geq I_{i_1}^+ \geq I_{i_1,j_1}^+$. This is because otherwise, the reference bin of I_{i_2,j_2} would be b_{i_1}, which cannot be the same as $b^\dagger(I_{i_1,j_1})$. Moreover, since $j_1 \geq 2$, it follows from Features (f.2) and (f.5) that $t_{i_1,j_1} \leq I_{i_1,j_1}^- + \mu\Delta = I_{i_1,j_1}^+ - 2\Delta$. Thus, we have $t_{i_2,j_2} - t_{i_1,j_1} \geq 2\Delta$. Therefore, the two reference periods cannot intersect.

For Case IV, without loss of generality, suppose $j_1 = 1$ and $j_2 \geq 2$. According to Feature (f.4), $t_{i_1,j_1} = I_{i_1,j_1}^-$. If $i_1 < i_2$, it follows that $I_{i_1,j_1}^- = I_{i_1}^- \leq I_{i_2}^-$. Since $j_2 \geq 2$, Feature (f.3) implies that $t_{i_2,j_2} \geq I_{i_2,j_2}^- \geq I_{i_2}^- + 2\Delta$. Therefore, $t_{i_2,j_2} - t_{i_1,j_1} = t_{i_2,j_2} - I_{i_1,j_1}^- \geq t_{i_2,j_2} - I_{i_2}^- \geq 2\Delta$. If $i_1 > i_2$, for the case where $b^\dagger(I_{i_1,j_1}) \neq b^\dagger(I_{i_2,j_2})$, the two reference periods

must not intersect according to the definition. For the case where $b^\dagger(I_{i_1,j_1}) = b^\dagger(I_{i_2,j_2})$, it must hold that $t_{i_1,j_1} \geq I_{i_2}^+ \geq I_{i_2,j_2}^+$. This is because otherwise, the reference bin of I_{i_1,j_1} would be b_{i_2}, which cannot be the same as $b^\dagger(I_{i_2,j_2})$. Since $j_2 \geq 2$, based on Features (f.2) and (f.5), we have $t_{i_2,j_2} \leq I_{i_2,j_2}^- + \mu\Delta = I_{i_2,j_2}^+ - 2\Delta$. As a result, $t_{i_1,j_1} - t_{i_2,j_2} \geq 2\Delta$. Thus, the two references periods cannot intersect. $\square$

Now, we examine Case V. First, we have the following lemma.

LEMMA 2. *In Case V, suppose $i_1 < i_2$, if the reference periods of I_{i_1,j_1} and I_{i_2,j_2} intersect, the length of I_{i_1,j_1} must be shorter than 2Δ.*

PROOF. In Case V, according to Feature (f.4), we have $t_{i_1,j_1} = I_{i_1,j_1}^-$ and $t_{i_2,j_2} = I_{i_2,j_2}^-$. Assume on the contrary that the length of I_{i_1,j_1} is equal to or longer than 2Δ, i.e., $I_{i_1,j_1}^+ - I_{i_1,j_1}^- \geq 2\Delta$. If the two reference periods of I_{i_1,j_1} and I_{i_2,j_2} intersect, we have $b^\dagger(I_{i_1,j_1}) = b^\dagger(I_{i_2,j_2})$. This implies $t_{i_2,j_2} \geq I_{i_1}^+ \geq I_{i_1,j_1}^+$ because otherwise, the reference bin of I_{i_2,j_2} would be b_{i_1}, which cannot be the same as $b^\dagger(I_{i_1,j_1})$. Since $I_{i_1,j_1}^+ - t_{i_1,j_1} = I_{i_1,j_1}^+ - I_{i_1,j_1}^- \geq 2\Delta$, it follows that $t_{i_2,j_2} - t_{i_1,j_1} \geq 2\Delta$, which contradicts that the two reference periods intersect. Thus, the length of I_{i_1,j_1} must be shorter than 2Δ. $\square$

Based on the above analysis, the intersection between reference periods can only happen in Case V, i.e., among the reference periods of $I_{i,1}$'s. We divide $\mathcal{I}^L$ into two subsets: $\mathcal{I}_I^L$ and $\mathcal{I}_U^L$. $\mathcal{I}_I^L$ contains the periods in $\mathcal{I}^L$ whose reference periods intersect with at least one other reference period. $\mathcal{I}_U^L$ contains the periods in $\mathcal{I}^L$ whose reference periods do not intersect with any other reference period. It is apparent that $\mathcal{I}_I^L \cap \mathcal{I}_U^L = \emptyset$ and

$$len(\mathcal{I}^L) = len(\mathcal{I}_I^L) + len(\mathcal{I}_U^L) \qquad (9)$$

For any period $I_{i,j} \in \mathcal{I}_I^L$, we must have $j = 1$. Consider two different periods $I_{i,1} \in \mathcal{I}_I^L$ and $I_{k,1} \in \mathcal{I}_I^L$. Suppose $i < k$. If their reference periods intersect, we call $I_{i,1}$ the "front-intersect" period of $I_{k,1}$ and call $I_{k,1}$ the "back-intersect" period of $I_{i,1}$. We then have the following lemma.

LEMMA 3. *For each period $I_{i,1} \in \mathcal{I}_I^L$, there is at most one "front-intersect" period and at most one "back-intersect" period of $I_{i,1}$.*

PROOF. Assume on the contrary that there are two "back-intersect" periods of $I_{i,1}$, which are denoted by $I_{k,1}$ and $I_{h,1}$. It follows that $i < k$ and $i < h$. Without loss of generality, suppose $k < h$. Then, we have $t_{h,1} \geq I_k^+$ (otherwise, the reference bin of $I_{h,1}$ would be b_k and cannot be the same as $b^\dagger(I_{i,1})$) and $t_{k,1} \geq I_i^+$ (otherwise, the reference bin of $I_{k,1}$ would be b_i and cannot be the same as $b^\dagger(I_{i,1})$). According to Feature (f.4), $t_{i,1} = I_{i,1}^-$ and $t_{k,1} = I_{k,1}^-$. Since the minimum item interval length is Δ, we have $I_k^+ \geq I_k^- + \Delta = I_{k,1}^- + \Delta$ and $I_i^+ \geq I_i^- + \Delta = I_{i,1}^- + \Delta$. Therefore, $t_{h,1} - t_{i,1} \geq I_k^+ - t_{i,1} \geq \Delta + I_{k,1}^- - t_{i,1} = \Delta + t_{k,1} - t_{i,1} \geq \Delta + I_i^+ - t_{i,1} = \Delta + I_i^+ - I_{i,1}^- \geq 2\Delta$. It contradicts the assumption that $I_{h,1}$ is a "back-intersect" period of $I_{i,1}$. Thus, $I_{i,1}$ can have at most one "back-intersect" period. The proof for the "front-intersect" case is similar. $\square$

Next, we construct pairs for the periods in $\mathcal{I}_I^L$ according to the following rule. Consider each period $I_{i,1} \in \mathcal{I}_I^L$ in the ascending order of i. If $I_{i,1}$ has not been added into any pair and $I_{i,1}$ has a "back-intersect" period (denoted by $I_{i',1}$), we construct a pair $(I_{i,1}, I_{i',1})$. We name the pair as a *joint-period* composed of $(I_{i,1}, I_{i',1})$ (where $i < i'$), and define the reference period of the joint-period as the reference period of $I_{i,1}$, i.e., $p^\dagger(I_{i,1})$. Note that a period in $\mathcal{I}_I^L$ that has no "back-intersect" period might not be added into any pair. We name such period as a *single period*. An example of the pairing process is shown in Figure 7.

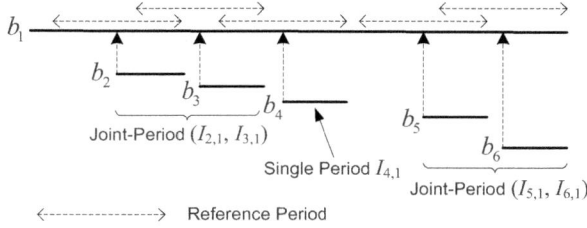

Figure 7: An example of pairing

LEMMA 4. *The reference periods of all the joint-periods and single-periods do not intersect.*

PROOF. We first show that the reference periods of any two joint-periods do not intersect. Assume on the contrary that the reference period of a joint-period composed of $(I_{i,1}, I_{i',1})$ (where $i < i'$) intersects with the reference period of another joint-period composed of $(I_{k,1}, I_{k',1})$ (where $k < k'$). Without loss of generality, suppose $i < k$. Then, $I_{i,1}$ would have two "back-intersect" periods $I_{k,1}$ and $I_{i',1}$, which contradicts Lemma 3.

We then show that the reference period of any single period does not intersect with the reference period of any joint-period. Assume on the contrary that the reference period of a single period $I_{k,1}$ intersects with the reference period of a joint-period composed of $(I_{i,1}, I_{i',1})$ (where $i < i'$). If $k < i$, it implies that $I_{k,1}$ has a "back-intersect" period $I_{i,1}$, which contradicts our pairing rule. If $k > i$, it implies that $I_{i,1}$ has two "back-intersect" periods $I_{k,1}$ and $I_{i',1}$, which contradicts Lemma 3.

Furthermore, it is obvious that the reference periods of any two single periods do not intersect. Therefore, in summary, the reference periods of all the joint-periods and single periods do not intersect. □

Note that according to Feature (f.1) and Lemma 2, the total length of the two periods constituting a joint-period should be shorter than $(\mu+4)\Delta + 2\Delta = (\mu+6)\Delta$. Let $\mathcal{I}_I^L(J)$ denote the set of all the joint-periods, and $|\mathcal{I}_I^L(J)|$ be the number of joint-periods in $\mathcal{I}_I^L(J)$. Let $\mathcal{I}_I^L(S)$ denote the set of all the single periods, and $|\mathcal{I}_I^L(S)|$ be the number of single periods in $\mathcal{I}_I^L(S)$. It follows that $len(\mathcal{I}_I^L) \le |\mathcal{I}_I^L(J)| \cdot (\mu+6)\Delta + |\mathcal{I}_I^L(S)| \cdot (\mu+4)\Delta$.

Let $|\mathcal{I}_U^L|$ be the number of periods in $\mathcal{I}_U^L$. Since each period in $\mathcal{I}_U^L$ is at most $(\mu+4)\Delta$ long (Feature (f.1)), we have $len(\mathcal{I}_U^L) \le |\mathcal{I}_U^L| \cdot (\mu+4)\Delta$. Therefore, it follows from (9) that

$$
\begin{aligned}
len(\mathcal{I}^L) &\le |\mathcal{I}_I^L(J)| \cdot (\mu+6)\Delta + |\mathcal{I}_I^L(S)| \cdot (\mu+4)\Delta \\
&\quad + |\mathcal{I}_U^L| \cdot (\mu+4)\Delta \\
&\le \left(|\mathcal{I}_I^L(J)| + |\mathcal{I}_I^L(S)| + |\mathcal{I}_U^L|\right) \cdot (\mu+6)\Delta
\end{aligned}
$$

According to (6) and (7), we have

$$
\begin{aligned}
FF_{total}(\mathcal{R}) &\le C \cdot \left(|\mathcal{I}_I^L(J)| + |\mathcal{I}_I^L(S)| + |\mathcal{I}_U^L|\right) \cdot (\mu+6)\Delta \\
&\quad + C \cdot span(\mathcal{R}) \quad (10)
\end{aligned}
$$

On the other hand, according to the previous analysis, the reference periods of all the periods in $\mathcal{I}_U^L$, the joint-periods in $\mathcal{I}_I^L(J)$ and the single periods in $\mathcal{I}_I^L(S)$ do not intersect. Thus, based on (8), the total resource demand $u(\mathcal{R})$ satisfies

$$
u(\mathcal{R}) \ge \left(|\mathcal{I}_I^L(J)| + |\mathcal{I}_I^L(S)| + |\mathcal{I}_U^L|\right) \cdot \left(W - \frac{W}{k}\right) \cdot \Delta \quad (11)
$$

According to (10) and (11), we have

$$
FF_{total}(\mathcal{R}) \le \frac{C \cdot (\mu+6)}{W \cdot (1 - \frac{1}{k})} \cdot u(\mathcal{R}) + C \cdot span(\mathcal{R}) \quad (12)
$$

Moreover, we have the following bounds for $OPT_{total}(\mathcal{R})$: $OPT_{total}(\mathcal{R}) \ge \frac{C \cdot u(\mathcal{R})}{W}$ (this is derived by assuming that no bin capacity is wasted at any time) and $OPT_{total}(\mathcal{R}) \ge C \cdot span(\mathcal{R})$ (this is derived from the fact that at least one bin must be in use at any time when there is at least one active item). It follows that

$$
FF_{total}(\mathcal{R}) \le \left(\frac{k}{k-1} \cdot \mu + \frac{6k}{k-1} + 1\right) \cdot OPT_{total}(\mathcal{R})
$$

Therefore, we have the following result.

THEOREM 4. *For the MinTotal DBP problem, for any item list $\mathcal{R}$, if the item size $s(r) < \frac{W}{k}$ ($k > 1$ is a constant) for all the items $r \in \mathcal{R}$, the total cost of First Fit packing is at most $(\frac{k}{k-1} \cdot \mu + \frac{6k}{k-1} + 1) \cdot OPT_{total}(\mathcal{R})$.* □

Next, we consider the general case for First Fit packing. We follow the above analysis for Theorem 4. Let $b_1, b_2, ..., b_m$ denote the bins used in First Fit packing to pack an item list $\mathcal{R}$. For each bin b_i, its usage period I_i is divided into two parts I_i^L and I_i^R. Then, we perform split and mergence on all I_i^L's to produce the set of sub-periods $\mathcal{I}^L$. $\mathcal{I}^L$ is further divided into two subsets $\mathcal{I}_I^L$ and $\mathcal{I}_U^L$ based on the intersections between periods. From $\mathcal{I}_I^L$, we construct the set of joint-periods $\mathcal{I}_I^L(J)$ and the set of single periods $\mathcal{I}_I^L(S)$. According to (10), the total cost of First Fit packing is at most

$$
C \cdot \left(|\mathcal{I}_I^L(J)| + |\mathcal{I}_I^L(S)| + |\mathcal{I}_U^L|\right) \cdot (\mu+6)\Delta + C \cdot span(\mathcal{R}) \quad (13)
$$

where $|\mathcal{I}_I^L(J)|$, $|\mathcal{I}_I^L(S)|$ and $|\mathcal{I}_U^L|$ are the sizes of sets $\mathcal{I}_I^L(J)$, $\mathcal{I}_I^L(S)$ and $\mathcal{I}_U^L$ respectively.

Consider a period $I_{i,j}$ in $\mathcal{I}_U^L \cup \mathcal{I}_I^L(S)$ or a joint-period composed of $(I_{i,j}, I_{i',j'})$ in $\mathcal{I}_I^L(J)$. Recall that its reference period $p^\dagger(I_{i,j})$ is the period $[t_{i,j} - \Delta, t_{i,j} + \Delta]$ associated with the reference bin $b^\dagger(I_{i,j})$. Let $p^\ddagger(I_{i,j})$ denote the same period $[t_{i,j} - \Delta, t_{i,j} + \Delta]$ associated with bin b_i. We refer to $p^\ddagger(I_{i,j})$ as the *auxiliary period* of $I_{i,j}$. Figure 8 shows an example of auxiliary periods.

In the above analysis for Theorem 4, we have shown that a new item must be packed into b_i at time $t_{i,j}$. According to the First Fit packing algorithm, after this item is packed, the total level of bins b_i and $b^\dagger(I_{i,j})$ should be higher than W (the bin capacity). Otherwise, the new item would have been packed into $b^\dagger(I_{i,j})$ instead. Moreover, since Δ is the minimum item interval length, all the items in bin b_i at time $t_{i,j}$ must reside in the system for at least Δ time during the auxiliary period $p^\ddagger(I_{i,j})$, and all the items in bin $b^\dagger(I_{i,j})$

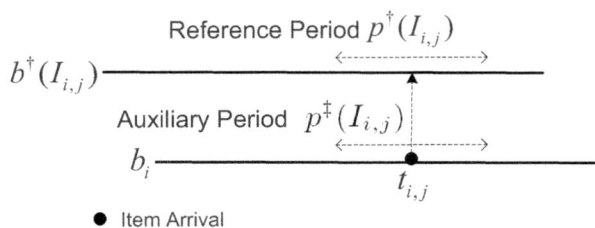

Figure 8: An example of auxiliary periods

at time $t_{i,j}$ must reside in the system for at least Δ time during the reference period $p^{\dagger}(I_{i,j})$. It follows that the total resource demand of the items in bin b_i over $p^{\ddagger}(I_{i,j})$ and the items in bin $b^{\dagger}(I_{i,j})$ over $p^{\dagger}(I_{i,j})$ satisfies

$$u(p^{\dagger}(I_{i,j})) + u(p^{\ddagger}(I_{i,j})) \geq W \cdot \Delta \qquad (14)$$

According to the previous analysis, all the reference periods of those in $\mathcal{I}_U^L \cup \mathcal{I}_I^L(J) \cup \mathcal{I}_I^L(S)$ do not intersect with each other. Next, we examine the intersections among the auxiliary periods.

LEMMA 5. *The auxiliary periods of two different periods I_{i_1,j_1} and I_{i_2,j_2} do not intersect.*

PROOF. If $i_1 \neq i_2$, the auxiliary periods $p^{\ddagger}(I_{i_1,j_1})$ and $p^{\ddagger}(I_{i_2,j_2})$ do not intersect since they are associated with different bins. If $i_1 = i_2$, without loss of generality, suppose $j_1 < j_2$. According to the analysis on Cases I and II in Lemma 1, it must hold that $t_{i_2,j_2} - t_{i_1,j_1} \geq 2\Delta$. Therefore, $p^{\ddagger}(I_{i_1,j_1})$ and $p^{\ddagger}(I_{i_2,j_2})$ cannot intersect. $\square$

Since all the reference periods of those in $\mathcal{I}_U^L \cup \mathcal{I}_I^L(J) \cup \mathcal{I}_I^L(S)$ do not intersect and all the auxiliary periods of those in $\mathcal{I}_U^L \cup \mathcal{I}_I^L(J) \cup \mathcal{I}_I^L(S)$ do not intersect either, any time point associated with each bin can be shared by at most one reference period and one auxiliary period. Therefore, it follows from (14) that

$$u(\mathcal{R}) \geq \frac{1}{2}\big(|\mathcal{I}_I^L(J)| + |\mathcal{I}_I^L(S)| + |\mathcal{I}_U^L|\big) \cdot W \cdot \Delta \qquad (15)$$

According to (13) and (15), we have

$$
\begin{aligned}
FF_{total}(\mathcal{R}) &\leq \frac{2C \cdot (\mu + 6)}{W} \cdot u(\mathcal{R}) + C \cdot span(\mathcal{R}) \\
&\leq 2 \cdot (\mu + 6) \cdot OPT_{total}(\mathcal{R}) + OPT_{total}(\mathcal{R}) \\
&\leq (2\mu + 13) \cdot OPT_{total}(\mathcal{R})
\end{aligned}
$$

Therefore, we have the following result.

THEOREM 5. *For the MinTotal DBP problem, First Fit packing has a competitive ratio of $2\mu + 13$.* $\square$

4.4 A Modified First Fit Packing Algorithm

The analysis in the previous section shows that the competitive ratio of First Fit packing for the MinTotal DBP problem is much related to the item sizes. Inspired by Theorem 3 and Theorem 4, we propose a new Modified First Fit packing algorithm that can achieve improved competitive ratios.

- **Modified First Fit (MFF)**: Define a variable $k > 1$. The items with sizes equal to or larger than $\frac{W}{k}$ are classified as large items. The items with sizes smaller

than $\frac{W}{k}$ are classified as small items. Modified First Fit packing uses the classical First Fit algorithm to pack the large items and the small items separately.

Given an item list $\mathcal{R}$, let $\mathcal{R}^L$ denote the set of all the large items and $\mathcal{R}^S$ denote the set of all the small items. Then, $s(r) \geq \frac{W}{k}$ for all $r \in \mathcal{R}^L$, and $s(r) < \frac{W}{k}$ for all $r \in \mathcal{R}^S$. According to (3) in the proof of Theorem 3, we have

$$MFF_{total}(\mathcal{R}^L) \leq k \cdot \frac{C \cdot u(\mathcal{R}^L)}{W}$$

According to (12) in the analysis of Theorem 4, we have

$$MFF_{total}(\mathcal{R}^S) \leq \frac{C \cdot (\mu + 6)}{W \cdot (1 - \frac{1}{k})} \cdot u(\mathcal{R}^S) + C \cdot span(\mathcal{R}^S)$$

Note that $u(\mathcal{R}^L) \leq u(\mathcal{R})$, $u(\mathcal{R}^S) \leq u(\mathcal{R})$, and $span(\mathcal{R}^S) \leq span(\mathcal{R})$. Thus, it follows that

$$
\begin{aligned}
MFF_{total}(\mathcal{R}) &= MFF_{total}(\mathcal{R}^L) + MFF_{total}(\mathcal{R}^S) \\
&\leq k \cdot \frac{C \cdot u(\mathcal{R}^L)}{W} + \frac{C \cdot (\mu + 6)}{W \cdot (1 - \frac{1}{k})} \cdot u(\mathcal{R}^S) + C \cdot span(\mathcal{R}^S) \\
&\leq \max\left\{k, \frac{\mu + 6}{1 - \frac{1}{k}}\right\} \cdot \frac{C \cdot u(\mathcal{R})}{W} + C \cdot span(\mathcal{R})
\end{aligned}
$$

If the max/min item interval length ratio μ is not known, we can set $k = 8$ in Modified First Fit packing. In this case,

$$\max\left\{k, \frac{\mu + 6}{1 - \frac{1}{k}}\right\} = \max\left\{8, \frac{8}{7}\mu + \frac{48}{7}\right\}$$

Since $\mu \geq 1$, we have $\frac{8}{7}\mu + \frac{48}{7} \geq 8$. Therefore,

$$
\begin{aligned}
MFF_{total}(\mathcal{R}) &\leq \left(\frac{8}{7}\mu + \frac{48}{7}\right) \cdot \frac{C \cdot u(\mathcal{R})}{W} + C \cdot span(\mathcal{R}) \\
&\leq \left(\frac{8}{7}\mu + \frac{55}{7}\right) \cdot OPT_{total}(\mathcal{R})
\end{aligned}
$$

Therefore, when μ is not known, Modified First Fit packing can achieve a competitive ratio of $\frac{8}{7}\mu + \frac{55}{7}$ for the MinTotal DBP problem.

In certain applications such as cloud gaming, it is possible to estimate the max/min item interval length ratio μ according to the statistics of historical playing data. If μ is known, it can be derived that when $k = \mu + 7$, $\max\left\{k, \frac{\mu + 6}{1 - \frac{1}{k}}\right\}$ achieves the smallest value which is given by $\mu + 7$. Therefore, we have

$$
\begin{aligned}
MFF_{total}(\mathcal{R}) &\leq (\mu + 7) \cdot \frac{C \cdot u(\mathcal{R})}{W} + C \cdot span(\mathcal{R}) \\
&\leq (\mu + 8) \cdot OPT_{total}(\mathcal{R})
\end{aligned}
$$

Therefore, when μ is known, Modified First Fit packing can achieve a competitive ratio of $\mu + 8$ for the MinTotal DBP problem.[2]

5. CONCLUSIONS

In this paper, we have studied the MinTotal Dynamic Bin Packing problem that aims to minimize the total cost of the bins used over time. We have analyzed the competitive ratios of the commonly used First Fit, Best Fit and Any Fit packing algorithms for this problem. It is shown that the competitive ratio of Any Fit packing cannot be better than

---

[2]Since μ is known, Modified First Fit packing in this case is a semi-online algorithm.

the max/min item interval length ratio μ. Best Fit packing has no bounded competitive ratio even for any given μ. In a special case where all the item sizes are smaller than $\frac{W}{k}$ (W is the bin capacity and $k > 1$ is a constant), First Fit packing has a competitive ratio of $\frac{k}{k-1}\mu + \frac{6k}{k-1} + 1$. For the general case, First Fit packing has a competitive ratio of $2\mu+13$. We have also proposed a Modified First Fit packing algorithm which classifies and assigns items according to their sizes. We have shown that Modified First Fit packing can achieve a competitive ratio of $\frac{8}{7}\mu + \frac{55}{7}$ when μ is not known and can achieve a competitive ratio of $\mu + 8$ when μ is known. In the future work, we would like to further investigate the constrained Dynamic Bin Packing problem in which each item is allowed to be assigned to only a subset of bins to cater for the interactivity constraints of dispatching playing requests among distributed clouds in cloud gaming.

6. ACKNOWLEDGMENTS

This research is supported by Multi-plAtform Game Innovation Centre (MAGIC), funded by the Singapore National Research Foundation under its IDM Futures Funding Initiative and administered by the Interactive & Digital Media Programme Office, Media Development Authority.

7. REFERENCES

[1] Distribution and monetization strategies to increase revenues from cloud gaming. http://www.cgconfusa.com/report/documents/Content-5minCloudGamingReportHighlights.pdf.

[2] Gaikai. http://www.gaikai.com/.

[3] Onlive. http://www.onlive.com/.

[4] Streammygame. http://www.streammygame.com/smg/index.php.

[5] J. Balogh, J. Békési, and G. Galambos. New lower bounds for certain classes of bin packing algorithms. *Approximation and Online Algorithms (Lecture Notes in Computer Science, Volume 6534)*, pages 25–36, 2011.

[6] A. Bar-Noy, R. Bar-Yehuda, A. Freund, J. S. Naor, and B. Schieber. A unified approach to approximating resource allocation and scheduling. *Journal of the ACM*, 48(5):735–744, Sept. 2001.

[7] A. Borodin and R. El-Yaniv. *Online computation and competitive analysis*, volume 53. Cambridge University Press Cambridge, 1998.

[8] J. W.-T. Chan, T.-W. Lam, and P. W. Wong. Dynamic bin packing of unit fractions items. *Theoretical Computer Science*, 409(3):521–529, 2008.

[9] W.-T. Chan, P. W. Wong, and F. C. Yung. On dynamic bin packing: An improved lower bound and resource augmentation analysis. *Computing and Combinatorics*, pages 309–319, 2006.

[10] K.-T. Chen, Y.-C. Chang, P.-H. Tseng, C.-Y. Huang, and C.-L. Lei. Measuring the latency of cloud gaming systems. In *Proceedings of the 19th ACM International Conference on Multimedia*, pages 1269–1272. ACM, 2011.

[11] E. G. Coffman, J. Csirik, G. Galambos, S. Martello, and D. Vigo. Bin packing approximation algorithms: Survey and classification. *Handbook of Combinatorial Optimization (second ed.)*, pages 455–531, 2013.

[12] E. G. Coffman, Jr, M. R. Garey, and D. S. Johnson. Dynamic bin packing. *SIAM Journal on Computing*, 12(2):227–258, 1983.

[13] E. G. Coffman, Jr., M. R. Garey, and D. S. Johnson. Approximation algorithms for bin packing: A survey. *Approximation Algorithms for NP-hard Problems*, pages 46–93, 1997.

[14] M. Flammini, G. Monaco, L. Moscardelli, H. Shachnai, M. Shalom, T. Tamir, and S. Zaks. Minimizing total busy time in parallel scheduling with application to optical networks. In *Proceedings of the 23th IEEE International Symposium on Parallel and Distributed Processing*, pages 1–12. IEEE, 2009.

[15] G. Galambos and G. J. Woeginger. On-line bin packingąła restricted survey. *Zeitschrift für Operations Research*, 42(1):25–45, 1995.

[16] M. R. Gary and D. S. Johnson. Computers and intractability: A guide to the theory of np-completeness, 1979.

[17] C.-Y. Huang, C.-H. Hsu, Y.-C. Chang, and K.-T. Chen. Gaminganywhere: an open cloud gaming system. In *Proceedings of the 4th ACM Multimedia Systems Conference*, pages 36–47. ACM, 2013.

[18] Z. Ivkovic and E. L. Lloyd. Fully dynamic algorithms for bin packing: Being (mostly) myopic helps. *SIAM Journal on Computing*, 28(2):574–611, 1998.

[19] J. W. Jiang, T. Lan, S. Ha, M. Chen, and M. Chiang. Joint vm placement and routing for data center traffic engineering. In *Proceedings of the 31th IEEE International Conference on Computer Communications*, pages 2876–2880. IEEE, 2012.

[20] E. L. Lawler, J. K. Lenstra, A. H. Rinnooy Kan, and D. B. Shmoys. Sequencing and scheduling: Algorithms and complexity. *Handbooks in Operations Research and Management Science*, 4:445–522, 1993.

[21] G. B. Mertzios, M. Shalom, A. Voloshin, P. W. Wong, and S. Zaks. Optimizing busy time on parallel machines. In *Proceedings of the 26th IEEE International Parallel and Distributed Processing Symposium*, pages 238–248. IEEE, 2012.

[22] P. E. Ross. Cloud computing's killer app: Gaming. *IEEE Spectrum*, 46(3):14–14, 2009.

[23] S. S. Seiden. On the online bin packing problem. *Journal of the ACM*, 49(5):640–671, 2002.

[24] C. Sharon, W. Bernard, G. Simon, C. Rosenberg, et al. The brewing storm in cloud gaming: A measurement study on cloud to end-user latency. In *Proceedings of the 11th ACM Annual Workshop on Network and Systems Support for Games*, 2012.

[25] A. Stolyar. An infinite server system with general packing constraints. *arXiv preprint arXiv:1205.4271*, 2012.

[26] C. Zhang, Z. Qi, J. Yao, M. Yu, and H. Guan. vgasa: Adaptive scheduling algorithm of virtualized gpu resource in cloud gaming. *IEEE Transactions on Parallel and Distributed Systems*, accepted to appear, 2014.

On the Online Fault-Tolerant Server Consolidation Problem

Khuzaima Daudjee
University of Waterloo
Waterloo, Canada
kdaudjee@uwaterloo.ca

Shahin Kamali
University of Waterloo
Waterloo, Canada
s3kamali@uwaterloo.ca

Alejandro López-Ortiz
University of Waterloo
Waterloo, Canada
alopez-o@uwaterloo.ca

ABSTRACT

In the server consolidation problem, the goal is to minimize the number of servers needed to host a set of clients. The clients appear in an online manner and each of them has a certain load. The servers have uniform capacity and the total load of clients assigned to a server must not exceed this capacity. Additionally, to have a fault-tolerant solution, the load of each client should be distributed between at least two different servers so that failure of one server avoids service interruption by migrating the load to the other servers hosting the respective second loads. In a simple setting, upon receiving a client, an online algorithm needs to select two servers and assign half of the load of the client to each server. We analyze the problem in the framework of competitive analysis. First, we provide upper and lower bounds for the competitive ratio of two well known heuristics which are introduced in the context of tenant placement in the cloud. In particular, we show their competitive ratios are no better than 2. We then present a new algorithm called Horizontal Harmonic and show that it has an improved competitive ratio which converges to 1.59. The simplicity of this algorithm makes it a good choice for use by cloud service providers. Finally, we prove a general lower bound that shows any online algorithm for the online fault-tolerant server consolidation problem has a competitive ratio of at least 1.42.

Categories and Subject Descriptors

F.2 [**Analysis of Algorithms and Problem Complexity**]: Miscellaneous; F.1.2 [**Modes of Computation**]: Online computation

Keywords

Server Consolidation, Online Bin Packing, and Competitive Analysis

1. INTRODUCTION

Server consolidation is an essential concept for efficient use of computer resources by means of reducing the number of required active servers. Certain applications involve a large number of *clients* which appear in a sequential, online manner. Each client requires a certain amount of resources which is referred to as the *load* of

the client. Servers have uniform *capacity*, which is the maximum load that they can supply so that their performance is not compromised. It is naturally assumed that the load of any client is no larger than the server capacity. At the time a client appears, one or more servers should be selected to host the client. If more than one server is selected, the load of the client is uniformly distributed among them [10]. An efficient algorithm reduces the number of active servers by smart selection of the hosting servers for each client. Reducing the number of servers is essential to avoid *server sprawl* situation in which there are numerous under-utilized active servers which consume more resources than required by the workload. Preventing server sprawl is particularly important for saving on the energy-related costs which account for 70 to 80 percent of a data center's ongoing operational costs [4]. In a dynamic setting, the server consolidation problem is *online* in the sense that at the time of selecting servers for a client, an algorithm does not know the load of future clients.

The server consolidation problem is closely related to the bin packing problem. In the classical bin packing problem, the input is a sequence of *items* which should be packed into a minimum number of *bins*. Bins are assumed to have uniform capacity of 1, and each item has a *size* which is no more than 1. In the context of server consolidation, items and bins respectively represent clients and servers, and the size of an item represents a client's load. In a valid packing, the total size of items assigned to each bin, termed as the *level* of the bin, is no more than 1, i.e., the servers are not overloaded. In this paper, we interchangeably use terms 'client' and 'item', as well as terms 'server' and 'bin'. Note that in the classical bin packing problem, in contrast to the server consolidation problem, items cannot be divided between two bins and each item is 'packed' on a single bin (server).

One application area of server consolidation is in multi-tenant database systems [5, 10]. Here, each client represents a *tenant* which is a process (e.g., an enterprise application) with a certain load. The load indicates the processing time or memory requirement of the tenant. In multi-tenant systems, similar to many other server consolidation applications, it is desirable to have a *fault-tolerant* solution so that failing or removing a server does not interrupt the service. To achieve such a guarantee, there should be more than one copy or *replica* of each tenant in the system. When a tenant is replicated in k servers, its load is uniformly distributed among the k replicas. It is preferable to have a small number of replicas for each tenant since more replicas require complex management and the problem becomes more constrained [10]. Assuming a single server can handle the load of a tenant, having two replicas for a tenant is sufficient to protect the system against failure of a single server. Hence, taking the same approach of [10], we assume each

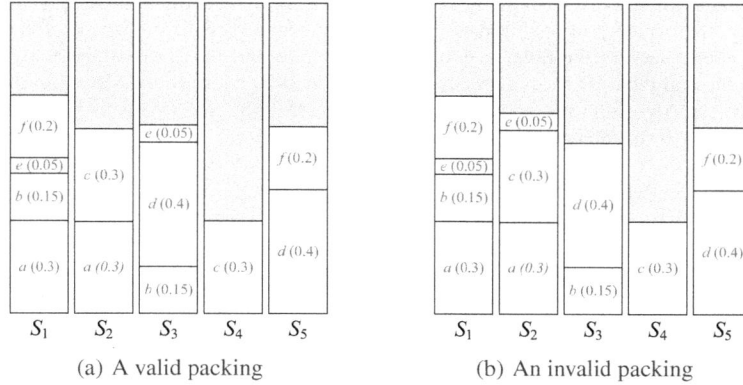

(a) A valid packing	(b) An invalid packing

Figure 1: Two packings associated with a sequence of items $\sigma = \langle a = 0.6, b = 0.3, c = 0.6, d = 0.8, e = 0.1, f = 0.4 \rangle$**. Each item has a blue and a red replica. The packing on the left is a valid packing; if any server fails, the load redirected to other servers does not cause an overflow. The packing on the right is not valid since if server** S_2 **fails, the shared items between the first two servers (i.e.,** a **and** e**) will add an extra load of size** $0.3 + 0.05 = 0.35$ **to server** S_1**. The total size of replicas in that server will be** $0.7 + 0.35 = 1.05$**, which is more that the unit capacity of servers.**

tenant has two replicas, which we refer to as *blue* and *red* replicas. The blue and red replicas of an item a both have size $a/2$.

The two replicas associated with an item should be hosted on different servers so that in case of one server's failure, the tenant's load can be directed to the tenant replica on the other hosting server. This requires a reserved capacity in each server S_x so that in case of a failure of any other server $S_{x'}$ ($x' \neq x$), the additional load imposed on S_x (due to the items which are hosted by both servers) does not cause an overflow in S_x. To be more precise, let T denote the total load of items which have one replica in S_x and one in $S_{x'}$. There is a load of $T/2$ on each server associated with these items which we denote by $L_{(x,x')}$. In case $S_{x'}$ fails, this load is redirected to S_x, i.e., the load of S_x is increased by $L_{(x,x')}$. Consequently, to maintain all items (tenants) after a failure, it is required to have a reserved capacity of $L_{(x,x')}$ in S_x. This can be translated into the bin packing language as follows:

DEFINITION 1. *An instance of the online fault-tolerant server consolidation problem (alternatively called online fault-tolerant bin packing problem) is defined by a sequence* $\sigma = \langle a_1, a_2, \ldots, a_n \rangle$ *of items (clients) which should be placed in a minimum number of bins (servers); here* a_i *denotes the size (load) of the item. Bins have uniform capacity of 1 and item sizes are in the range* $(0, 1]$ *(i.e.,* $a_i \in (0, 1]$*). Items are revealed in an online manner. Upon receiving an item* $a_i (1 \leq i \leq n)$*, an algorithm should place two replicas of* a_i*, each having a size of* $a_i/2$*, into two different bins. These two replicas are 'partners' of each other and are referred to as blue and red replicas. An online algorithm needs to maintain a 'valid packing' after serving each item. In a valid packing, no two replicas of the same item are placed in the same bin. Moreover, for each bin* S_x *in a valid packing, we have* $L_x + L_{(x,x')} \leq 1$ *(* $x \neq x'$ *); here* L_x *is the total size of replicas placed in* S_x *(level of* S_x*), i.e.,* $L_x = \sum a_j (a_j \in S_x)$*, and* $L_{(x,x')}$ *is the total size of replicas in* S_x *which have their partner in* $S_{x'}$*, i.e.,* $L_{(x,x')} = 1/2 \sum a_j (a_j \in S_x$ *and* $a_j \in S_{x'})$ *(see Figure 1).*

Competitive analysis is the standard method for comparing online algorithms and in particular bin packing algorithms [12]. The competitive ratio of an algorithm is defined as the maximum ratio between the cost of an online algorithm and that of OPT for serving the same sequence, where OPT is an optimal *offline* algorithm that

can see the whole sequence in advance. In this paper, by competitive ratio, we mean *asymptotic* competitive ratio where the number of opened bins by OPT is arbitrarily large. For the results related to the *absolute* competitive ratio, we refer the reader to [2, 3].

1.1 Previous Work and Contribution

The classical bin packing problem has been extensively studied in the past few decades. The problem is known to be NP-hard [6] and numerous online and offline heuristics have been proposed for it. The online heuristics include Next-Fit (NF), First-Fit (FF), Best-Fit (BF), and the Harmonic-based class of algorithms. NF maintains a single *open* bin and places an item in that bin; in case the item does not fit, it *closes* the bin and opens a new one. The competitive ratio of NF is known to be 2. FF keeps a list of bins in the order they are opened, places an item in the first bin that has enough space, and opens a new bin if necessary. BF performs similarly to FF, except that the bins are ordered in increasing order of their remaining capacity. FF and BF have the same competitive ratio of 1.7 [8]. Harmonic-based algorithms are based on the idea of packing items of similar sizes together in a bin. For Harmonic$_K$, an item has type i ($1 \leq i \leq K - 1$) if it is in the range $(\frac{1}{i+1}, \frac{1}{i}]$, and type K if it is in the range $(0, \frac{1}{K}]$. The algorithm applies the NF strategy for items of each type separately. The classical Harmonic algorithm has a competitive ratio of approximately 1.69 [9]. The best Harmonic-based algorithm (in terms of competitive analysis) is the best existing online bin packing algorithm and has a competitive ratio of at most 1.59 [11]. It is also known that no online algorithm can have a competitive ratio better than 1.54 [1].

The bin packing problem has been widely used as a model for server consolidation [7, 13, 14]. However, these approaches do not provide fault-tolerant solutions; moreover, the proposed strategies are offline and not suitable for dynamic environments where clients are coming in an online manner.

The fault-tolerant server consolidation problem as defined in Section 1 has been recently introduced in [10]. In the same paper, two strategies were introduced for the problem and their average performance was evaluated in a real-world system. The first strategy is referred to as the *Mirroring Algorithm* . This algorithm treats blue and red replicas separately using the Best Fit packing rule. Since two replicas of the same item have equal sizes, the packings associated with blue and red replicas are the same, i.e., they mirror each other. To achieve a valid packing, the capacity of each bin is assumed to be 0.5. This is because when a server (bin) fails, its entire load is redirected to the mirrored bin and the total load is doubled. We theoretically analyze the Mirroring Algorithm and show an upper bound of 3 and a lower bound of $2.\bar{6}$ for the competitive ratio of this algorithm.

In [10], a second strategy is introduced which we refer to as the *Interleaving Algorithm* . This algorithm also applies BF strategy to place replicas. In doing so, it considers a *legal capacity* for each bin as the total capacity of the bin (i.e., 1) minus the level of the bin and the maximum load redirected to the bin in case of another bin's failure. More precisely, the legal capacity of a bin S_x is $1 - L_x - \max_{x'} L_{(x,x')}$, where L_x is the total size of replicas in S_x, and $L_{(x,x')}$ is the total size of replicas in S_x which have their partner in bin $S_{x'}$ (see Definition 1). For placing the first replica of an item (the blue replica), the algorithm considers a fraction μ of the legal capacity and applies the Best Fit strategy to place the replica in a bin which has enough (but minimum) capacity. Here, μ is a parameter of the algorithm which is a positive value no more than 1. For placing the red replica, the actual legal capacity is considered and again the Best Fit strategy is applied to place the replica in a bin other than that of its partner. We provide upper and lower bound for the competitive ratio of the Interleaving Algorithm. Our results indicate that, in terms of competitive ratio, Interleaving Algorithm does not provide a big improvement over Mirroring Algorithm. In particular, for the suggested value of $\mu = 0.85$ in [10], we show that the competitive ratio of the algorithm is in the range $(2, 3.71)$.

We introduce a new algorithm called *Horizontal Harmonic* (HH). The algorithm is inspired by the Harmonic algorithm for the bin packing problem [9] and defines K classes for replicas based on their sizes; here, K is a parameter of the algorithm and is a constant around 30. We show that the competitive ratio of this algorithm converges to 1.59 for large values of K. For small values of K, the competitive ratio of HH is still better than existing algorithms, e.g., when $K = 30$, the competitive ratio of HH is 1.625. Hence, in the worst case, Horizontal Harmonic outperforms its counterparts. The algorithm is simple and runs in linear time which is better than the existing algorithms which run in $O(n \log n)$ time.

We also prove a general lower bound on the competitive ratio of any online algorithm for the fault-tolerant server consolidation problem. We show the competitive ratio of any online algorithm is at least $10/7 > 1.428$.

1.2 A Shifting Technique

We introduce a *shifting lemma* which will be used in a few occasions in our lower bound arguments. An offline algorithm (particularly OPT) can use this technique to achieve a packing in which each pair of bins host replicas of at most one shared item. Consider a long sequence of replicas with a constant number of different sizes, and assume item sizes are larger than a constant value. Consequently, each bin contains a constant number of replicas and there are a constant number of *bin types*. We say that two bins have the same type if the multi-sets formed by the sizes of the hosted replicas are the same for both bins.

LEMMA 1. *Consider a packing of the blue replicas of a long sequence into X bins so that each bin contains a constant number of replicas, and there are a constant number of bin types. Assume there is an empty space of size greater than or equal to the size of the largest replica in each bin. To achieve a valid packing, an offline algorithm OFF can place the red replicas into $X + c$ bins, where c is a constant integer.*

PROOF. Note that if the empty space of a bin is less than the size of the largest replica in the bin, the packing is not valid (in case of the failure of the bin hosting the partner of the largest replica, the bin will be overloaded). To achieve a valid packing, when placing the red replicas, OFF ensures that any two bins share replicas of at most one item. As a result, if any bin fails, the redirected load to any other bin B is smaller than the size of the largest replica hosted on B, which is indeed smaller than the reserved space in B.

To place the red replicas, OFF considers a fixed ordering of the blue replicas inside all bins, e.g., assume the blue replicas are placed in decreasing order of their sizes. Consider a bin type u and let c_u denote the number of replicas in such a bin type (c_u is a constant). OFF partitions the bins of type u into groups of size c_u; the last group might include less bins. The bins in each group include c_u^2 blue replicas (except potentially the last group). OFF opens c_u new bins to place the red partners of these replicas in the following manner: if a blue replica x is placed as the jth replica in the ith bin in a group ($0 \le i, j \le c - 1$), then OFF places the red partner of x as the ith replica in the $(j + i) \bmod c_u$-th bin among the bins opened for the red partners (see Figure 2.)

We show that in the resulting packing, no two bins share replicas of more than one item. Assume otherwise, i.e., assume two blue replicas hosted by a blue bin have their red replicas placed in the same red bin. This implies $(i + j) \bmod c_u = (i + j') \bmod c_u$, where i is the index of the blue bin in its group and j and j' are the indices of the two replicas inside the bin (w.l.o.g assume $j' > j$). So we will have $i + j = i + j' - k\, c_u$ for some positive integer k. This implies $j' \ge k\, c_u$ which contradicts the fact that there are c_u replicas in each bins.

For each group of c_u bins of type u in the packing of blue replicas, c_u bins are opened for the red replicas. The only exception is the last group of blue bins which might include as few as one bin while OFF opens c_u red bins for this group. Since c_u is a constant, for each bin type, a constant number of extra bins are opened. There are a constant number of bin types; hence, the total number of opened bins for the red replicas is at most a constant value more than the number of bins in the packing of blue replica. □

Figure 2: The shifting technique results in the same packings for the blue and the red replicas in a way that any two bins share replicas of at most one item. In this example, a bin with four different item sizes is considered. For each set of four bins hosting the blue replicas, four bins are opened for placing the red replicas. The red partners of the replicas in the first blue bin are distributed among these four bins; the same holds for the red replicas of other bins. In the resulting packing, the reserved space in each bin is equal to the size of the largest replica hosted on the bin.

2. ANALYSIS OF EXISTING ALGORITHMS

In this section, we provide upper and lower bounds for the competitive ratio of existing algorithms for the fault-tolerant server consolidation problem.

2.1 Mirroring Algorithm

The Mirroring Algorithm places blue and red replicas of all items separately using the Best-Fit strategy. In case of a bin's failure, its entire load goes to the mirrored server. To achieve a valid packing, the capacity of each bin is assumed to be 0.5. Figure 3 shows a packing associated with the Mirroring Algorithm. We first provide an upper bound for the competitive ratio of the Mirroring Algorithm. In the following lemma, we consider a sequence of *replicas* in which each item is presented as two replicas of the same size.

LEMMA 2. *For any sufficiently long sequence σ of replicas, the cost of the Mirroring Algorithm is at most 3 times more than that of* OPT *(within an additive constant).*

PROOF. Let σ_1 denote a subsequence of σ formed by replicas smaller than or equal to $1/4$ and σ_2 denote the set of replicas larger than $1/4$. Also, let W_1 denote the total size of replicas in σ_1 and L_2 denote the number of replicas in σ_2, i.e., the length of σ_2. To prove the lemma we show that $\mathrm{OPT}(\sigma) > W_1 + 3L_2/8$ and $\mathrm{MIR}(\sigma) \leq 3W_1 + L_2 + c$, where $\mathrm{MIR}(\sigma)$ is the cost of the Mirroring Algorithm for serving σ and c is a constant value. Note that these two inequalities guarantee that $\mathrm{MIR}(\sigma) < 3 \times \mathrm{OPT}(\sigma) + c$.

The cost of an optimal packing is no less than the total size of all replicas in the sequence plus the required reserved space in the bins of an optimal packing. Let X denote the number of bins in an optimal packing which include a replica in σ_2 (i.e., a replica larger than $1/4$). Since at most two replicas of σ_2 can be hosted on the same bin (otherwise the reserved space will be less than the size of any of these replicas), we have $X \geq L_2/2$. For each bin which includes a replica of size larger than $1/4$, a reserved space of size larger than $1/4$ is required. Hence, the total reserved space in an optimal packing is more than $X/4 \geq L_2/8$. The total size of replicas in σ_1 is W_1 and the total size of replicas in σ_2 is at least $L_2/4$. Hence, the total size of replicas in σ is at least $W_1 + L_2/4$. Consequently, we have $\mathrm{OPT}(\sigma) > W_1 + L_2/4 + L_2/8 = W_1 + 3L_2/8$.

Let m_1 (resp. m_2) denote the number of bins in the packing of the Mirroring Algorithm which do not include (resp. include) a replica of size larger than $1/4$. So, we have $\mathrm{MIR}(\sigma) = m_1 + m_2$. Clearly $m_2 \leq L_2$ since the number of bins opened for replicas of size larger than $1/4$ cannot be more than the number of these replicas. We show $m_1 \leq 3W_1$. Let σ_s denote the set of blue replicas in σ which are placed in bins without a replica larger than $1/4$, and let Y denote the number of such bins. Since the red replicas are excluded, we have $Y = m_1/2$. Let W_s denote the total size of replicas in σ_s; note that $W_s \leq W_1/2$. The algorithm applies the Best Fit strategy to place the replicas in σ_s into bins of size $1/2$. The number of opened bins does not change if we double the size of replicas and capacity of bins at the same time; hence, the number of bins opened for replicas in σ_s (i.e., Y) is equal to the number of bins that the Best Fit algorithm opens for the same sequence as σ_s in which replicas sizes are doubled. Doubling replicas' sizes in σ_s results in a sequence in which each replica has a size at most equal to $1/2$. The cost of the Best Fit for serving such a sequence is at most 1.5 times the total size of the sequence (within an additive constant) [2]. Hence, $Y \leq 1.5 \times 2W_s + c' \leq 3 \times W_1/2 + c'$ for some constant c'. So, we have $m_1 = 2Y \leq 3W_1 + c$ and $\mathrm{MIR}(\sigma) = m_1 + m_2 \leq 3W_1 + L_2 + c$, where $c = 2c'$. $\square$

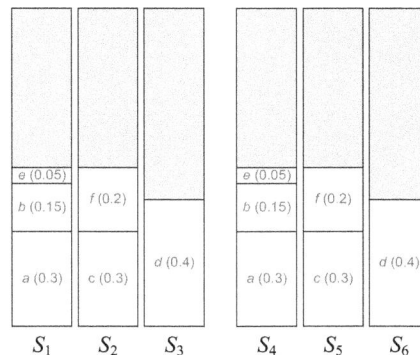

Figure 3: The packing of the Best-Fit Mirroring algorithm when applied on sequence $\langle\, a = 0.6, b = 0.3, c = 0.6\,, d = 0.8, e = 0.1, f = 0.2\,\rangle$.

Next, we provide a lower bound for the competitive ratio of the Mirroring Algorithm algorithm:

LEMMA 3. *There are arbitrary long sequences for which the cost of the Mirroring Algorithm is at least $8/3$ times more than that of* OPT *for serving the same sequence (within an additive constant).*

PROOF. Consider the following sequence σ of $n = 4m$ items where m is a large integer. The sequence starts with m items of size $\frac{1}{6} - 8\epsilon$, followed by m items of size $\frac{1}{3} + 2\epsilon$, and ends with $2m$ items have size $\frac{1}{2} + 2\epsilon$. So, the sequence of blue (and red) *replicas* has the following form:

$$\sigma_{blue} = \langle\, \underbrace{\frac{1}{12} - 4\epsilon, \ldots, \frac{1}{12} - 4\epsilon}_{m}, \underbrace{\frac{1}{6} + \epsilon, \ldots, \frac{1}{6} + \epsilon}_{m}, \underbrace{\frac{1}{4} + \epsilon, \ldots, \frac{1}{4} + \epsilon}_{2m}\,\rangle$$

We show that the cost of the Mirroring Algorithm for serving σ is $16m/3$ while the cost of OPT is at most $2m + c$ where c is a non-negative constant independent of m. The ratio between these values approaches $8/3$ for large values of m.

For the Mirroring Algorithm, we only consider the cost of the packing associated with the blue replicas; the actual cost is twice this cost. To pack the first m blue replicas, the algorithm places 6 replicas of size $1/12 - 4\epsilon$ in the same bin. The level of each bin will be $1/2 - 24\epsilon$ and the remaining capacity would be 24ϵ (recall that the level of a bin cannot be more than $1/2$ in a valid packing for the Mirroring Algorithm). Hence, no other replica will be placed in these bins and they can be thought as being closed; the algorithm opens $m/6$ bins for placing the first m replicas. Similarly, the algorithm places two replicas of size $1/6 + \epsilon$ in the same bin and opens $m/2$ bins for these replicas. Finally, the algorithm opens a bin for each replica of size $1/4 + \epsilon$ (having two replicas of that size results in a level larger than $1/2$). In total, the number of opened bins for the blue replicas is $m/6 + m/2 + 2m = 8m/3$. Adding to this the number of mirrored bins for the red replicas, the total cost of the Mirroring Algorithm will be $16m/3$ (see Figure 4(a)).

Next, we describe an offline algorithm OFF which places blue and red replicas separately. For placing the blue replicas, OFF places two replicas of size $1/4 + \epsilon$ together with one replica of size $1/6 + \epsilon$ and one replica of size $1/12 - 4\epsilon$ in the same bin. Note that the level of such a bin will be $3/4 - \epsilon$, and there is an empty space of size equal to the largest replica placed in the bin. OFF opens m bins to place the blue replicas. Since there is only one bin type with four replicas in each bin in the packing of blue

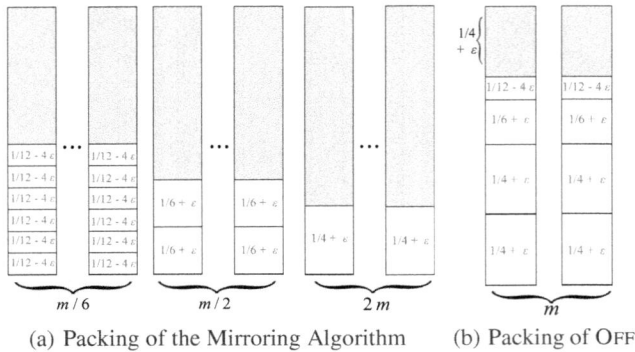

$m/6$ $m/2$ $2m$ m

(a) Packing of the Mirroring Algorithm   (b) Packing of OFF

Figure 4: Packings of the Mirroring Algorithm and OFF for placing the blue replicas of σ. The packing of the Mirroring Algorithm for the red replicas is a mirror of its packing for the blue replicas, while OFF applies the shifting technique for placing the red replicas.

replicas, OFF can apply the shifting technique (Lemma 1) to place the red replicas in $m + c$ bins for some constant c. Consequently, the cost of OPT is no more than $2m + c$ (see Figure 4(b)). $\square$

From Lemmas 2 and 3 we get the following theorem:

THEOREM 1. *The competitive ratio of the Mirroring Algorithm for the fault-tolerant server consolidation problem is at least $8/3 = 2.\bar{6}$ and at most 3.*

2.2 Interleaving Algorithm

In the Interleaving Algorithm, in contrast to the Mirroring Algorithm, the blue and red replicas of different items are 'mixed', i.e., a bin can include blue replicas of some items and red replicas of some other items. To place the blue replicas, the algorithms considers a fraction $\mu \leq 1$ of the legal capacity and applies the Best Fit strategy (the suggested parameter in [10] is $\mu = 0.85$). Recall that the legal capacity of a bin is its actual capacity (its left space) minus the maximum load that might be redirected to the bin in case of another bin's failure. For placing the red replicas, the entire legal capacity of the bins is considered and the Best Fit strategy is applied to place the replica in an bin which does not include its partner. This way, more replicas are assigned to a single bin and the average cost decreases when compared to the Mirroring Algorithm. However, for many sequences, the Mirroring Algorithm and the Interleaving Algorithm result in almost similar packings. This is particularly the case when replicas' sizes are relatively small. In what follows, we provide upper and lower bound for the competitive ratio of the Interleaving Algorithm.

LEMMA 4. *For any sufficiently long sequence σ, the cost of the Interleaving Algorithm is at most $4/\mu - 1$ times that of OPT (within an additive constant).*

PROOF. The structure of the proof is similar to that of Lemma 2. Let σ_1 denote a subsequence of σ formed by replicas smaller than or equal to $\mu/4$ and σ_2 denote the set of replicas larger than $\mu/4$. Also, let W_1 denote the total size of σ_1 and L_2 denote the number of replicas in σ_2 (i.e., the length of σ_2). We prove that $\text{OPT}(\sigma) > W_1 + L_2\mu/(4-\mu)$ while $\text{IA}(\sigma) \leq 8W_1/3 + L_2 + c$, where $\text{IA}(\sigma)$ is the cost of the Interleaving Algorithm algorithm and c is a constant value. These two prove a competitive ratio of

at most $\max(4/\mu - 1, 8/3)$ for the Interleaving Algorithm. Note that for $\mu \leq 1$, we have $4/\mu - 1 \geq 8/3$.

The cost of OPT is no less than the total size of all replicas in the sequence plus the required reserved space in the bins of an optimal packing. Let X denote the number of bins in an optimal packing which include a replica of σ_2. Also, let $i \geq 5$ denote an integer so that $1/i < \mu/4 \leq 1/(i-1)$. Hence, at most $(i-2)$ replicas of σ_2 can be hosted on the same bin; otherwise, the reserved space will be less than the size of any of these replicas. So we have $X \geq L_2/(i-2)$. For each bin which includes a replica of size larger than $\mu/4$, a reserved space of size more than $\mu/4$ is required. Hence, the total reserved space in an optimal packing is more than $X \times (\mu/4) \geq L_2\mu/(4(i-2)) > L_2\mu^2/(16-4\mu)$. The last inequality holds because $i - 2 \leq (4-\mu)/\mu$. The total size of replicas in σ_1 is W_1 and the total size of replicas in σ_2 is more than $L_2 \times (\mu/4)$. Hence, the total size of replicas in σ is lower bounded by $W_1 + L_2 \times \mu/4$. Consequently, we have $\text{OPT}(\sigma) > W_1 + L_2\mu/4 + L_2\mu^2/(16-4\mu)) = W_1 + L_2\mu/(4-\mu)$.

Let m_1 (resp. m_2) denote the number of bins in the packing of the Interleaving Algorithm algorithm which do not include (resp. include) a replica of size larger than $\mu/4$. So, we have $IA(\sigma) = m_1 + m_2$. Clearly $m_2 \leq L_2$. We show $m_1 \leq 8W_1/3 + c$. Among the bins which include only replicas of size smaller than or equal to $\mu/4$, consider the last bin opened by the Interleaving Algorithm. If the first replica in such a bin is a blue replica, by definition of the Interleaving Algorithm algorithm, for any previously opened bin B we have $\mu \times cap(B) < \mu/4$ where $cap(B)$ is the legal capacity of B. If the first replica in the last bin is a red replica, we will have $cap(B) < \mu/4$ which also gives $\mu \times cap(B) < \mu/4$ (the only exception might be the bin which includes the partner of the red replica). Recall that the legal capacity of B is the remaining space of B minus the maximum total size of replicas which are shared between B and any other bin B'. From this definition we get $cap(B) \geq 1 - 2 \, level(B)$; consequently, we have $\mu \times (1 - 2 \, level(B)) < \mu/4$ and $level(B) \geq 3/8$. So, the level of all bins which include only replicas of size at most $\mu/4$, except potentially a constant number of them, is at least $3/8$. The total size of all replicas in these bins is at most W_1; hence, the number of these bins (m_1) is at most $8W_1/3 + c$. Consequently, the cost of the Interleaving Algorithm is at most $8W_1/3 + L_2 + c$. $\square$

Note that when μ converges to zero, the above upper bound does not provide a non-trivial worst-case guarantee for the performance of the Interleaving Algorithm algorithm. In fact, for small values of μ, the algorithm is not competitive at all (i.e., does not have a constant competitive ratio). This is because, when μ is sufficiently small, the algorithm opens a new bin for placing each blue replica while an optimal offline algorithm can efficiently place these replicas together in same bins. In what follows, we prove a general lower bound for the competitive ratio of the Interleaving Algorithm algorithm which holds for all values of μ.

LEMMA 5. *There are arbitrary long sequences for which the cost of the Interleaving Algorithm is at least $2 - \epsilon^*$ times more than that of OPT, in which ϵ^* is a small constant positive value.*

PROOF. Consider an input sequence σ with the following subsequence of *replicas* in which $\epsilon_m = \epsilon^*/8$ and $\epsilon_i = \epsilon_{i+1} \times \frac{\mu}{2\mu+1}$ $(1 \leq i \leq m - 1)$. Here, m is an arbitrary integer which defines the length of the sequence.

$$\sigma = \langle \underbrace{\epsilon_1, \ldots, \epsilon_1}_{n_1}, \underbrace{\epsilon_2, \ldots, \epsilon_2}_{n_2}, \ldots, \underbrace{\epsilon_m, \ldots, \epsilon_m}_{n_m} \rangle$$

We define the values of n_i ($1 \leq i \leq m$) to be $\lfloor \frac{\mu - \epsilon_i}{2\mu\epsilon_i} \rfloor$. Let W denote the total size of replicas in σ. To prove the lemma, we show that in the final packing of the Interleaving Algorithm for σ, the level of all bins is smaller than or equal to 1/2, while there is an offline packing in which the level of all bins is at least $1 - 4\epsilon_m$. This implies that the cost of the Interleaving Algorithm is at least $2W$ while the cost of OPT is at most $W/(1 - 4\epsilon_m)$. Consequently, the competitive ratio of the Interleaving Algorithm is at least $2(1 - 4\epsilon_m) = 2 - \epsilon^*$.

To place the first two replicas of size ϵ_1, the Interleaving Algorithm opens 2 bins. We argue that it places the rest of replicas with size ϵ_1 in these two bins. After placing t items of size ϵ_1 in each of these bins ($t \leq n_1 - 1$), the level of the bins will be $t \times \epsilon_1$ and their legal capacity will be $1 - 2t\epsilon_1$. For placing the next two replicas (the next item), the Interleaving Algorithm compares ϵ_1 with either a fraction μ of the legal capacity (for the blue replica) or the actual legal capacity (for the red replica). In both cases, ϵ_1 is smaller because we have $\mu \times (1 - 2t\epsilon_1) > \mu(1 - 2n_1\epsilon_1) \geq \epsilon_1$. Consequently, the first n_1 replicas will be placed into two bins. Next, we show that after placing n_1 replicas, there is no enough space for any other replica in these bins. For any consequent replica ϵ_j ($j > 1$), we have $\epsilon_j \geq \epsilon_1(2 + 1/\mu)$. This gives the following:

$$\epsilon_1(2 + \frac{1}{\mu}) \leq \epsilon_j \Rightarrow 1 - 2\epsilon_1(\frac{1}{2\epsilon_1} - \frac{1}{2\mu} - 1) \leq \epsilon_j \Rightarrow$$

$$1 - 2\epsilon_1 \lfloor \frac{1}{2\epsilon_1} - \frac{1}{2\mu} \rfloor < \epsilon_j \Rightarrow 1 - 2\epsilon_1 n_1 < \epsilon_j$$

Consequently, ϵ_j is larger than the legal capacity of the two bins and placing it in any of these two bins results in an invalid packing. Hence, the two bins opened for ϵ_1 can be assumed as being closed after placing the n_1 replicas of this size. Consequently the Interleaving Algorithm opens a new pair of bins for the next replicas which have size ϵ_2.

Replacing ϵ_1 and n_1 with respectively ϵ_i and n_i in the above argument, one can show that the Interleaving Algorithm opens a pair of bins for each group of replicas of size ϵ_i ($1 \leq i \leq m$) and closes the bins after placing these replicas. Consequently, in the packing of the Interleaving Algorithm, each bin has a mirrored bin. The level of these bins cannot be more than 1/2 in a valid packing. As a result, the cost of the Interleaving Algorithm bins for placing σ cannot be less than $W/2$.

Consider an offline algorithm OFF that places blue and red replicas separately using NF strategy. For blue replicas, the algorithm assumes a capacity of $1 - 2\epsilon_m$ for each bin. This way, the level of each bin (except possibly one) will be more than $1 - 3\epsilon_m$ and OFF opens M bins for the blue replicas where $M < W/(2 \times (1 - 3\epsilon_m)) + 1$. Note that M grows with m. To place the red replicas, OFF again assumes a capacity of $1 - 2\epsilon_m$ for each bin and applies NF on a different permutation of input. The red partners of blue replicas that are placed in the same bin are partitioned into a set of *multi-replicas*. Each multi-replica includes a multiset of red replicas whose total size is a constant value between ϵ_m and $2\epsilon_m$. The permutation is defined in rounds. Each round includes exactly one multi-replica from red replicas of each of the M blue bins. Since the size of multi-replicas is constant and the value of M grows with m, each round involves opening more than one bin (assuming m is large). Hence, no two multi-replicas of the same blue bin are placed in the same red bin. Moreover, the total size of shared replicas between two bins is no more than the size of multi-replicas, which is no more than $2\epsilon_m$. Hence, the total redirected load in case of a bin's failure is no more than the reserved space. Finally, the level of all red bins (except possibly one) is more than $1 - 4\epsilon_m$ as the size of multi-replicas is at most $2\epsilon_m$. Consequently, the cost of OFF

(and hence, OPT) is at most $W/(1 - 4\epsilon_m) + c$ where c is a constant. To conclude, the competitive ratio of the Interleaving Algorithm is at least $2(1 - 4\epsilon_m) = 2 - \epsilon^*$. □

From Lemmas 4 and 5, we get the following result:

THEOREM 2. *The competitive ratio of the Interleaving Algorithm with parameter μ for the fault-tolerant server consolidation problem is at least $2 - \epsilon$ and at most $4/\mu - 1$, where ϵ is a small constant positive value.*

Note that for the suggested value of $\mu = 0.85$, the competitive ratio of Interleaving Algorithm is in the range $(2 - \epsilon, 3.71)$.

3. Horizontal Harmonic Algorithm

In this section we introduce the Horizontal Harmonic (HH) algorithm which is inspired by the Harmonic algorithm for the bin packing problem. Similar to the Harmonic algorithm, HH is based on placing replicas of almost equal sizes in the same bins. It define *classes* for replicas based on their sizes and treats replicas of each class separately. The algorithm has a parameter K which defines the number of classes. We assume K is a constant around 30. The replicas with sizes in the range $(\frac{1}{i+2}, \frac{1}{i+1}]$ belong to class i, where $1 \leq i < K$ (note that the size of a replica is at most 1/2). The replicas which have size in the range $(0, \frac{1}{K+1}]$ belong to class K.

For placing the blue replicas from class $i < K$, Horizontal Harmonic places i replicas in the same bin; this way, an empty space of size $\frac{1}{i+1}$ is reserved for the load of one replica of the same class in case of another bin's failure. One can think of placing the blue replicas as vertically stacking them into bins, one bin after another. For placing the red replicas of class i, the algorithm opens i bins. If the blue replica of an items x is placed as the jth replica in its bin, the red replica is placed in the jth bin among the i open bins for the red replicas. This ensures that two bins share replicas of at most one item. Consequently, the reserved space for one bin is sufficient for having a valid packing (see Figure 5).

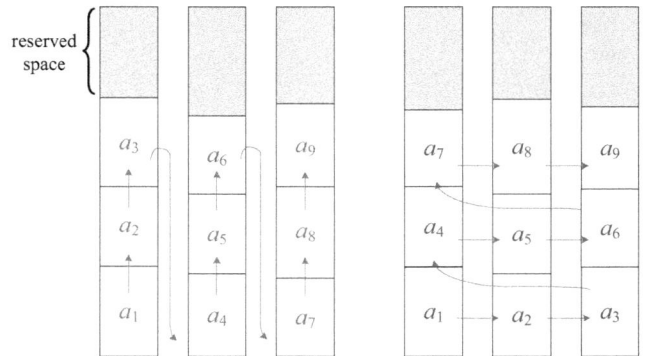

Figure 5: The main idea behind the Horizontal Harmonic algorithm is to apply Harmonic algorithm on the blue replicas, while horizontally placing the red replicas of type i in i different bins. This ensures that no two bins share replicas of more than one item. In this example, it is assumed that items arrive as $\langle a_1, a_2, \ldots, a_9 \rangle$. The replicas have type 3, i.e., their size is in the range $(\frac{1}{5}, \frac{1}{4}]$. Three replicas are placed in each bin while an empty space of size $\frac{1}{4}$ is reserved in each bin. The size of the reserved space is an upper bound for the size of replicas in this class.

For placing the replicas in class K, the algorithm considers the largest integer α_K so that $\alpha_K^2 + \alpha_K \leq K$, i.e., $\alpha_k = \lfloor \frac{\sqrt{4K+1}-1}{2} \rfloor$. This ensures that $\frac{1}{\alpha_K} - \frac{1}{\alpha_K+1} \geq \frac{1}{K}$; consequently, the algorithm can group set of replicas of class K into *multi-replicas* with total size in the range $(\frac{1}{\alpha_K+1}, \frac{1}{\alpha_K}]$. The algorithm treats these multi-replicas similar to the way that it treats replicas of class $\alpha_K - 1$, i.e., it places $\alpha_K - 1$ multi-replicas in the same bin. In what follows, when there is no risk of confusion, we replace α_K with α. Algorithm 1 illustrates the details of the algorithm.

Algorithm 1: Horizontal Harmonic with parameter K

---

input : A sequence $\sigma = \langle a_1, a_2, \ldots, a_n \rangle$ of items (clients)
output: A fault-tolerant packing of σ

$\alpha \leftarrow \lfloor (\sqrt{4K+1}-1)/2 \rfloor$; // used for the replicas of class K
$mrSize \leftarrow 0$; // multi-replica size
for $j \leftarrow 1$ *to* K **do**
    $blueBins_j, redBins_j \leftarrow$ arrays of j empty bins
    // $bIndex_j$ (resp. $rIndx_j$) is the index of the current blue (red) bin among the j open blue (red) bins of type j
    $bIndx_j, rIndx_j \leftarrow 1$
    // set the number of replicas (multi-replicas) that fit in a bin of type j (capacity of the bin)
    if $j < K$ **then** $cap_j \leftarrow j$ **else** $cap_j \leftarrow \alpha - 1$
end
for $i \leftarrow 1$ *to* n **do**
    $a_{\text{blue}}, a_{\text{red}} \leftarrow a_i/2$; // size of the replicas
    $j \leftarrow \lfloor 1/a_{\text{blue}} \rfloor - 1$; // the class of the current replica
    if $rIndx_j > cap_j$ **then**
        $rIndx_j \leftarrow 1$; $bIndx_j \leftarrow bIndx_j + 1$
        if $bIndx_j > cap_j$ **then**
            $blueBins_j, redBins_j \leftarrow$ arrays of j empty bins
            $bIndx_j, rIndx_j \leftarrow 1$
    place a_{blue} into bin $blueBins_j[\text{bIndx}_j]$
    place a_{red} into bin $redBins_j[\text{bIndx}_j]$
    if $j < K$ **then** $rIndx_j \leftarrow rIndx_j + 1$
    else
        $mrSize \leftarrow mrSize + a_{\text{blue}}$
        if $mrSize > 1/(\alpha+1)$ **then**
            $rIndx_j \leftarrow rIndx_j + 1$; $mrSize \leftarrow 0$
    end
end

Horizontal Harmonic Algorithm guarantees that two bins do not share replicas of more than one item. At the same time, it guarantees that each bin has a certain level (used space). These properties intuitively justify the advantage of the algorithm over the algorithms which are based on the Best Fit strategy. Horizontal Harmonic is simple and runs in linear time. This gives another advantage to the algorithm compared to the existing algorithms which are based on the BF and run in time $\Theta(n \lg n)$.

LEMMA 6. *The competitive ratio of* HH *with* $K \geq 30$ *classes is at most*

$$\chi = 1.5 + 1/12 \times \max\left(\frac{\alpha+1}{\alpha-1}, \frac{13}{11} \right)$$

PROOF. Consider a sequence σ of sufficiently large length. We would like to show $\text{HH}_K(\sigma) \leq \chi \text{OPT}(\sigma)$. To do so, we assign *weights* to replicas in σ based on their class. The weight of a replica which belongs to class $i < K$ is equal to $1/i$; the weight of a replica x in class K is $\frac{x(\alpha+1)}{\alpha-1}$. Recall that $\alpha = \lfloor \frac{\sqrt{4K+1}-1}{2} \rfloor$. Furthermore, we define *density* of a replica as the ratio between the weight and the size of the replica. See Table 1 for a summary of weight and density of replicas in different classes.

To prove the lemma we show I) the total weight of replicas in any bin of HH, except possibly a constant number of them, is at least 1. II) the total weight of replicas in a bin of OPT is at most χ. These two respectively imply that $\text{HH}(\sigma) \leq \omega(\sigma) + c$ and $\text{OPT}(\sigma) \geq \omega(\sigma)/\chi$ in which $\omega(\sigma)$ is the total weight of replicas in σ. We will have $\text{HH}(\sigma) \leq \chi \text{OPT}(\sigma) + c$ which completes the proof.

Proving (I) is relatively easy. Consider a bin of HH associated with replicas of class j ($j < K$). HH places j replicas of this class in the same bin (except possibly the $2j$ most recently opened bins of the class). Consequently, the total weight of replicas is $j \times 1/j = 1$ for all bins of class j (except the mentioned ones). The replicas of class K are accumulated and the associated multi-replicas are treated like replicas of class $\alpha - 1$. The level of these bins is at least $\frac{\alpha-1}{\alpha+1}$ and consequently the total weight of replicas in such bins is 1 (again, with the exception of the last $2\alpha - 2$ most recently opened bins of class K). To summarize, the weight of all bins of HH, except a constant number of them in each class, is at least 1. Since K is a constant, statement (I) follows.

To prove (II), we show that to achieve maximum weight, a bin B_{opt} should include a replica of class 1 with weight $1/3 + \epsilon$ and a replica of class 2 with weight $1/4 + \epsilon$, where ϵ is a sufficiently small positive value. Let B_1 denote a bin which includes three replicas of sizes $1/3 + \epsilon$, $1/4 + \epsilon$, and $1/13 + \epsilon$. Note that there is enough space for the largest replica (i.e., $1/3 + \epsilon$ in case of a bin's failure. The total weight of replicas in B_1 is $\omega(B_1) = 1 + 1/2 + 1/11 > 1.59$.

Assume B_{opt} does not include a replica of class 1. Consider the case that the largest replica in B_{opt} belongs to class $i \in \{2, 3, 4\}$. The level of the bin is less than $(i+1)/(i+2)$ (otherwise, there will not be enough space in case of failure of the bin hosting the partner of largest replica). Since $K \geq 30$, we have $\alpha \geq 5$ and the density of replicas in class K will be less than 3/2. Since the items of class i (or higher) have density larger than $(i+2)/i$, the density of all replicas in the bin is less than $(i+2)/i$; this implies that the total weight of the bin cannot be more than $(i+1)/(i+2) \times (i+2)/i = (i+1)/i < \omega(B_1)$. If the largest replica belongs to class 5 or higher, the density of all replicas in the bin will be less than 3/2 and consequently the weight of the bin is less than $3/2 < \omega(B_1)$.

Hence, to achieve the maximum weight, B_{opt} should include a replica of class 1. If such a replica has size more than $1/3 + \epsilon$, one can replace it with $1/3 + \epsilon$ and fill the resulted space with replicas of size ϵ to achieve a new bin with weight more than B_{opt}. Hence, to achieve the maximum weight, a bin b_{opt} should include a replica of size $1/3 + \epsilon$. This implies that there should be an empty space of size $1/3 + \epsilon$ in B_{opt}, i.e., the level of B_{opt} cannot be more than $2/3 - \epsilon$ and there will be an empty space of size $1/3 - 2\epsilon$ to be filled with other replicas. We claim that a replica of class two with size $1/4 + \epsilon$ should be in B_{opt}. Consider otherwise; then the density of replicas (except the one with type 1) in B_{opt} is less than 5/3 and the total weight of all replicas in B_{opt} will be less than $1 + (1/3 - 2\epsilon) \times 5/3 < \omega(B_1)$. So, there is a replica of class two in B_{opt}. As before, this replica cannot have size more than $1/4 + \epsilon$ (otherwise, it can be reduced to a replica of size $1/4 + \epsilon$).

So, to achieve maximum weight, B_{opt} should have replicas of sizes $1/3 + \epsilon$ and $1/4 + \epsilon$. Note that the weight of these two replicas is $1 + 1/2 = 1.5$. There will be an available space of size $1/12 - 3\epsilon$. Only replicas of class greater or equal to 11 can fill this empty space (i.e., replicas with size smaller than $1/12$). As Table 1 indicates, all these replicas have density smaller than $\max\{\frac{\alpha+1}{\alpha-1}, \frac{13}{11}\}$. Consequently, the weight of B_{opt} cannot be more than $\chi = 1.5 + 1/12 \times \max\left(\frac{\alpha+1}{\alpha-1}, \frac{13}{11} \right)$. $\square$

Class	Replica Size	No. Replicas in a Bin	Bin Level	Replica Weight	Replica Density
1	$x \in (\frac{1}{3}, \frac{1}{2}]$	1	$> \frac{1}{3}$	1	< 3
2	$x \in (\frac{1}{4}, \frac{1}{3}]$	2	$> \frac{1}{2}$	$\frac{1}{2}$	< 2
...	...	...	...	...	...
$i < K$	$x \in (\frac{1}{i+2}, \frac{1}{i+1}]$	i	$> \frac{i}{i+2}$	$\frac{1}{i}$	$< \frac{i+2}{i}$
...	...	...	...	...	...
$K-1$	$x \in (\frac{1}{K+1}, \frac{1}{K}]$	$K-1$	$> \frac{K-1}{K+1}$	$\frac{1}{K-1}$	$< \frac{K+1}{K-1}$
K	$x \in (0, \frac{1}{K+1}]$	N/A	$> \frac{\alpha-1}{\alpha+1}$	$\frac{x(\alpha+1)}{\alpha-1}$	$< \frac{\alpha+1}{\alpha-1}$

Table 1: Characteristics of replicas and bins for each class of Horizontal Harmonic.

The following two lemmas provide lower bounds for the competitive ratio of HH. To analyze the algorithm, define $\beta_1 = 3$, $\beta_2 = 4$ and $\beta_{i+1} = \beta_i(\beta_i - 1) + 1$ $(i \geq 2)$.

LEMMA 7. *The competitive ratio of* HH *with* $K \geq 5$ *classes is at least* $\sum_{i=1}^{K-1} 1/(\beta_i - 2) > 1.597$.

PROOF. Consider the following sequence of replicas (blue and red replicas are included in the sequence and n is an even integer):

$$\sigma = \langle \underbrace{\frac{1}{3}+\epsilon, \ldots, \frac{1}{3}+\epsilon}_{n}, \underbrace{\frac{1}{4}+\epsilon, \ldots, \frac{1}{4}+\epsilon}_{n}, \ldots, \underbrace{\frac{1}{\beta_K}+\epsilon, \ldots, \frac{1}{\beta_K}+\epsilon}_{n} \rangle$$

HH classifies replicas by their sizes and places $\beta_i - 2$ replicas of size $\frac{1}{\beta_i} + \epsilon$ in the same bin (seeFigure 6(a)). Consequently, the number of opened bins will be $n \times \sum_{1}^{K-1} 1/(\beta_i - 2) + c$, where c is a constant.

To place the blue replicas, an offline algorithm OFF includes all replicas of different sizes in the same bin. As illustrated in Figure 6(b), there will be an empty space of size larger than $1/3 + \epsilon$ in such a bin. The total size of replicas plus the reserved space will be $\frac{2}{3} + \frac{1}{4} + \ldots + \frac{1}{\beta_K} < 1$. This way, OFF opens $n/2$ bins for placing the blue replicas. Note that there are a constant number of replica sizes and bin types in the packing of the blue replicas. Hence, OFF can apply the shifting lemma (Lemma 1) to place the red replicas in $n/2 + c'$ bins. In total, OFF opens $n + c'$ bins for packing σ. Consequently, the ratio between the cost of HH and that of OPT for serving σ is at least $\sum_{i=1}^{K-1} 1/(\beta_i - 2)$ for large values of n. □

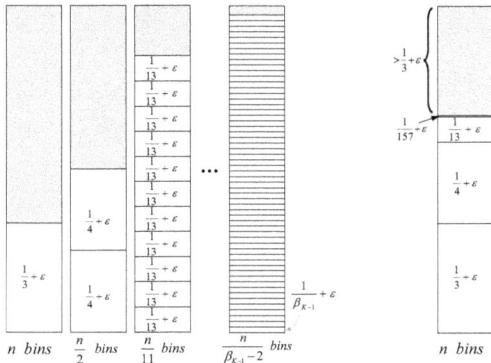

(a) The packing of the HH   (b) The packing of OFF

Figure 6: Lower bound argument for the Horizontal Harmonic algorithm.

LEMMA 8. *The competitive ratio of* HH *with* K *classes is at least* $1.5 + \frac{\alpha+1-3\epsilon'}{(\alpha-1)(12+\epsilon')}$ *in which* ϵ' *is an arbitrary small constant value.*

PROOF. Consider the following sequence of replicas (blue and red replicas are included in the sequence and n is an even integer):

$$\sigma = \langle \underbrace{\frac{1}{3}+\epsilon, \ldots, \frac{1}{3}+\epsilon}_{n}, \underbrace{\frac{1}{4}+\epsilon, \ldots, \frac{1}{4}+\epsilon}_{n}, \underbrace{\epsilon, \ldots, \epsilon}_{n \times (\frac{1}{12\epsilon}-3)} \rangle$$

Here, we have $\epsilon = \epsilon'/(12\alpha + 12)$. HH opens one bin for each replica of size $1/3 + \epsilon$, and one bin for each two replicas of size $1/4 + \epsilon$. To place replicas of size ϵ, it accumulates them to form multi-replicas of size no more than $\frac{1}{\alpha+1} + \epsilon$. The number of replicas in a multi-replica is upper-bounded by $\frac{1}{(\alpha+1)\epsilon} + 1$ and there will be at least $n \times (\frac{1}{12\epsilon} - 3)/(\frac{1}{(\alpha+1)\epsilon} + 1) = n \times \frac{\alpha+1-3\epsilon'}{12+\epsilon'}$ multi-replicas. The algorithm places $\alpha - 1$ multi-replicas in the same bin; hence, it opens at least $n \times \frac{\alpha+1-3\epsilon'}{(12+\epsilon')(\alpha-1)}$ bins for replicas of size ϵ. In total, HH opens at least $n \times (1.5 + \frac{\alpha+1-3\epsilon'}{(12+\epsilon')(\alpha-1)})$ for packing σ.

An offline algorithm OFF can place one blue replica of size $1/3 + \epsilon$, one blue replica of size $1/4 + \epsilon$, and $1/12\epsilon - 3$ blue replicas of size ϵ in the same bin. Note that there is an empty space of size $\frac{1}{3} + \epsilon$ in each bin. The total size of the replicas plus the reserved space will be $\frac{2}{3} + 2\epsilon + \frac{1}{4} + \epsilon + (\frac{1}{12\epsilon} - 3) \times \epsilon = 1$. Consequently, OFF places all blue replicas in at most $n/2$ bins. Since ϵ is a constant, there will be a constant number of replicas in each bin; hence, OFF can apply the shifting lemma to place the red replicas in $n/2 + c$ bins for some constant c. In total, OFF opens $n + c$ bins for placing σ; consequently, the ratio between the cost of two algorithms is at least $1.5 + \frac{\alpha+1-3\epsilon'}{(\alpha-1)(12+\epsilon')}$. □

From Lemmas 6, 7, and 8 we get the following theorem.

THEOREM 3. *The competitive ratio of* HH *with* K *classes* $(K \geq 30)$ *is at least* $\max(1.597, l^* - \epsilon)$ *and at most* $\max(1.599, l^*)$, *where* $l^* = 1.5 + \frac{\alpha+1}{12(\alpha-1)}$, ϵ *is an arbitrary small constant value, and* $\alpha = \lfloor \frac{\sqrt{4K+1}-1}{2} \rfloor$.

The bounds in the above theorem are tight for small values of K, e.g., for the suggested value of $K = 30$, the upper and lower bounds for the competitive ratio of HH almost match at 1.625. Note that when $K \to \infty$ we have $\alpha \to \infty$ and consequently the competitive ratio of HH converges to a value between 1.597 and 1.599.

4. GENERAL LOWER BOUND

In this section, we show that the competitive ratio of any online algorithm for the fault-tolerant server consolidation problem is at least 1.37. In the proof, we build sequences which contain only items of sizes $1/6 - 6\epsilon$, $1/2 + 2\epsilon$, and $2/3 + 2\epsilon$, where ϵ is a sufficiently small constant. The replicas for these items have sizes

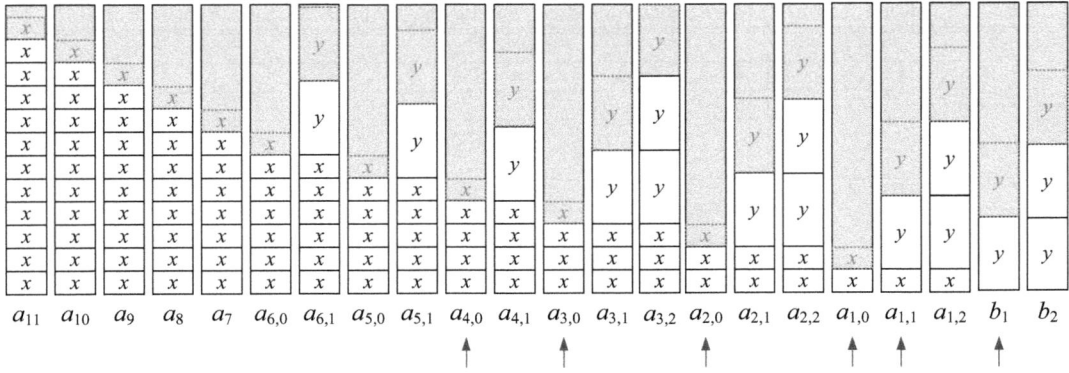

Figure 7: Potential bins after serving $\sigma_1\sigma_2$. Note that in a fault-tolerant packing, each bin needs to have an empty space of size at least equal to the largest hosted replica. Bins which have enough space for a replica of size z are indicated by arrows.

$x = 1/12 - 3\epsilon$, $y = 1/4 + \epsilon$, and $z = 1/3 + \epsilon$, respectively. In what follows, we consider a sequence of replicas rather than items. Consider a sequence $\sigma = \sigma_1\sigma_2\sigma_3$ in which σ_1, σ_2, and σ_3 are composed of n replicas of respectively sizes x, y, and z. Here, n is a sufficiently large even integer. We compare the cost of any online algorithm $\mathbb{A}$ with that of OPT after serving sequences σ_1, $\sigma_1\sigma_2$, and $\sigma_1\sigma_2\sigma_3$.

LEMMA 9. *Consider the sequence $\sigma = \sigma_1\sigma_2\sigma_3$ as defined above. We have* $\text{OPT}(\sigma_1) = n/11 + c_1$, $\text{OPT}(\sigma_1\sigma_2) \le n/2 + c_2$, *and* $\text{OPT}(\sigma_1\sigma_2\sigma_3) \le n + c_3$, *where c_1, c_2, and c_3 are constants.*

PROOF. We present an offline algorithm OFF which places blue and red replicas separately. The algorithm places the blue replicas in a way that the size of the reserved space in each bin is just equal to the size of largest replica in that bin. To ensure a valid packing, OFF applies the shifting lemma (Lemma 1) to place the red replicas.

For serving σ_1, OFF places 11 blue replicas of size x in each bin. Hence, it opens at most $n/2 \times 1/11 + 1$ bins for placing the blue replicas of σ_1 (note that there are $n/2$ blue replicas in σ_1). There will be an empty space of size larger than $1/12$ in case of a bin's failure. Using the shifting technique, OFF places the red replicas in the same number of bins (within an additive constant). Consequently, we have $\text{OPT}(\sigma_1) \le n/11 + c_1$ for some constant c_1. For packing $\sigma_1\sigma_2$, OFF places two blue replicas of size x with two blue replica of size y in the same bin. The total size of the replicas in the bin will be $2(1/12 - 3\epsilon) + 2(1/4 + \epsilon) = 2/3 - 4\epsilon$; hence there is enough space for another replica of size y. OFF opens at most $n \times 1/4 + 1$ bins for the blue replicas. Again, it applies the shifting technique for placing the red replicas in the same number of bins (within an additive constant). The total number of bins in such an offline solution will be $n/2 + c_2$ for some constant c_2. Finally, to place the blue replicas of $\sigma_1\sigma_2\sigma_3$, OFF places one replica of size x, one replica of size y, and one replica of size z in each bin. The size of the replicas in each bin will be $1/12 - 3\epsilon + 1/4 + \epsilon + 1/3 + \epsilon = 2/3 - \epsilon$; hence there is an empty space of size $1/3 + \epsilon$ in case of a bin's failure. The number of opened bins for the blue replicas will be $3n/2 \times 1/3 = n/2$. Using the shifting technique, the red replicas can be packed in the same number of bins (again, within an additive constant). Hence, the total number of bins will be $n + c_3$ for some constant c_3. □

The above lemma helps us prove the following theorem:

THEOREM 4. *The competitive ratio of any online algorithm $\mathbb{A}$ for the fault-tolerant server consolidation problem is at least $10/7$.*

PROOF. Consider the packing of $\mathbb{A}$ after serving $\sigma_1\sigma_2$. At this point the algorithm has placed n replicas of size x and n replicas of size y. Figure 7 shows all possible bins which include replicas of sizes x and y. Note that if a bin includes more than 6 replicas of size x, then there is no space for a replica of size y (to host a replica of size y, a bin requires a space of size $2y > 1/2$). Similarly, if a bin contains more than three replicas of size x, then it includes no more than one replica of size y. For $1 \le i \le 6$, let $a_{i,j}$ denote the number of bins which include i replicas of size x and j replicas of size y ($j \in \{0, 1, 2\}$). Also, for $7 \le i \le 11$, let a_i denote the number of bins which only include i replicas of size x. Finally, let b_1 (resp. b_2) denote the number of bins which include only one (resp. two) replicas of size y (and no replica of size x). Define the following variables:

$$
\begin{cases}
S_1 = a_{1,1} \\
S_2 = a_{1,2} + a_{2,2} + a_{3,2} \\
S_3 = a_{1,0} + a_{2,0} + a_{3,0} + a_{4,0} \\
S_4 = \quad\quad a_{2,1} + a_{3,1} + a_{4,1} \\
S_5 = \quad\quad\quad\quad\quad\quad\quad a_{5,1} + a_{6,1} \\
S_6 = \quad\quad\quad\quad\quad\quad\quad a_{5,0} + a_{6,0} + \sum_{i=7}^{12} a_i
\end{cases}
$$

The cost of $\mathbb{A}$ for serving σ_1 is equal to the number of bins which include a replica of size x. So, we have:

$$\mathbb{A}(\sigma_1) = \sum_{i=1}^{6} S_i \tag{1}$$

Counting the number of replicas of size x we get:

$$n \le S_1 + 3S_2 + 4S_3 + 4S_4 + 6S_5 + 11S_6 \tag{2}$$

Similarly, for serving $\sigma_1\sigma_2$ we have:

$$\mathbb{A}(\sigma_1\sigma_2) = \sum_{i=1}^{6} S_i + b_1 + b_2 \tag{3}$$

And counting the number of replicas of size y we get:

$$n = S_1 + 2S_2 + S_4 + S_5 + b_1 + 2b_2 \tag{4}$$

20

$$
\begin{aligned}
(n/11 + c_1) \times r_A &\geq S_1 + S_2 + S_3 + S_4 + S_5 + S_6 \\
(n/2 + c_2) \times r_A &\geq S_1 + S_2 + S_3 + S_4 + S_5 + S_6 + b_1 + b_2 \\
(n + c_3) \times r_A &\geq \quad\;\; S_2 + S_3 + S_4 + S_5 + S_6 \qquad\; + b_2 + n \\
-\tfrac{3}{11}n &\geq -\tfrac{3}{11}S_1 - \tfrac{9}{11}S_2 - \tfrac{12}{11}S_3 - \tfrac{12}{11}S_4 - \tfrac{18}{11}S_5 - 3S_6 \\
-n &= -S_1 - 2S_2 \qquad\; - S_4 - S_5 \qquad - b_1 - 2b_2 \\
\hline
\tfrac{35}{22}n \times r_A - \tfrac{14}{11}n + r_A(c_1+c_2+c_3) &\geq \tfrac{8}{11}S_1 + \tfrac{2}{11}S_2 + \tfrac{10}{11}S_3 + \tfrac{10}{11}S_4 + \tfrac{4}{11}S_5 \qquad + n
\end{aligned}
\tag{6}
$$

Next, we count the number of opened bins that potentially can host a replica of size z. First, if a bin contains more than 4 replicas of size x, it cannot include a replica of size z; otherwise, its level will be at least $5/12 + 1/3 - 14\epsilon$ and its empty space will be at most $1/4 + 14\epsilon$ which is not enough for another replica of size z. With similar arguments, a bin which contains two replicas of size y cannot host a replica of size z and the same holds for a bin with one replica of size y and more than one replica of size x. Furthermore, no two replicas of size z can be placed in the same bin. Hence, the number of bins which can host a replica of size z is at most $a_{1,0} + a_{1,1} + a_{2,0} + a_{3,0} + a_{4,0} + b_1 = S_1 + S_3 + b_1$. Except those replicas which can be placed in these bins, for any other replica in σ_3 a new bin should be opened. Hence, we have:

$$\mathbb{A}(\sigma_1\sigma_2\sigma_3) \geq S_2 + S_4 + S_5 + S_6 + b_2 + n \tag{5}$$

Let r_A denote the competitive ratio of $\mathbb{A}$. By Lemma 9, we have $\mathbb{A}(\sigma_1) \leq r_A \times \text{OPT}(\sigma_1) = r_A \times (n/11 + c_1)$. Similarly, $\mathbb{A}(\sigma_1\sigma_2) \leq r_A \times (n/2 + c_2)$ and $\mathbb{A}(\sigma_1\sigma_2\sigma_3) \leq r_A \times (n + c_3)$. Here, c_1, c_2 and c_3 are some constant values. From Equations (1),(2),(3),(4), and (5), we respectively get the system of equations in (6). Since all values of S_i $(1 \leq i \leq 6)$ are positive, summing all equations in that system, we get $35/22 \times r_A \geq 25/11 - c/n$ where c is a constant. This implies that r_A is lower bounded by $10/7$ for large values of n. $\square$

5. DISCUSSION

We studied the online server consolidation problem as a fault-tolerant variant of the online bin packing problem. An application of this problem is earlier studied for tenant placement in the Cloud [10]. We investigated the theoretical aspects of the problem under the framework of competitive analysis. We provided upper and lower bounds for the competitive ratios of the two heuristics introduced in [10]. We then presented Horizontal Harmonic as an alternative to these heuristics. This algorithm is simple and runs in linear time which makes it faster than its counterparts. The competitive ratio of Horizontal Harmonic is no more than 1.625 which is better than the other algorithms whose competitive ratios are lower-bounded by 2. Finally, we proved a general lower bound of $10/7 > 1.42$ for the competitive ratio of any online algorithm. Note that there is a gap between this lower bound and the best upper bound (given by Horizontal Harmonic). Closing this gap seems difficult, considering the fact that there is still a gap between the best upper and lower bound for the classical online bin packing problem. We conjecture that both upper and lower bounds for the online fault-tolerant server consolidation problem can be improved and leave it as a future work.

An extension of the bin packing problem, called vector packing problem, has been used to address the server consolidation problem where the load of a client is defined by a vector rather than a single value [13]. Fields of this vector represents the amount of different resources required by the client. In order to maintain high performance, a server should not be overload with respect to any of these fields. The ideas in this paper might be extended to provide a fault-tolerant vector packing algorithm. Other directions for future work include considering absolute competitive ratio, variable sized bins (i.e., different types of servers) and studying settings in which there are incompatibility constraints where some items are not allowed to be placed together in the same bin.

6. REFERENCES

[1] J. Balogh, J. Békési, and G. Galambos. New lower bounds for certain classes of bin packing algorithms. *Theoret. Comput. Sci.*, 440–441:1–13, 2012.

[2] E. G. Coffman, M. R. Garey, and D. S. Johnson. Approximation algorithms for bin packing: A survey. In D. Hochbaum, editor, *Approximation algorithms for NP-hard Problems*. PWS Publishing Co., 1997.

[3] E. G. Coffman Jr., J. Csirik, G. Galambos, S. Martello, and D. Vigo. Bin packing approximation algorithms: survey and classification. In P. M. Pardalos, D.-Z. Du, and R. L. Graham, editors, *Handbook of Combinatorial Optimization*, pages 455–531. Springer, 2013.

[4] CyrusOne executive report. Build vs. buy: Addressing capital constraints in the data center. 2013.

[5] A. J. Elmore, S. Das, A. Pucher, D. Agrawal, A. El Abbadi, and X. Yan. Characterizing tenant behavior for placement and crisis mitigation in multitenant dbmss. In *ACM SIGMOD '13*, pages 517–528, 2013.

[6] M. R. Garey and D. S. Johnson. *Computers and Intractability: A Guide to the theory of of NP-Completeness*. Freeman and Company, 1979.

[7] R. Gupta, S. K. Bose, S. Sundarrajan, M. Chebiyam, and A. Chakrabarti. A two stage heuristic algorithm for solving the server consolidation problem with item-item and bin-item incompatibility constraints. In *IEEE SCC'98*, pages 39–46, 2008.

[8] D. S. Johnson, A. Demers, J. D. Ullman, M. R. Garey, and R. L. Graham. Worst-case performance bounds for simple one-dimensional packing algorithms. *SIAM J. Comput.*, 3:256–278, 1974.

[9] C. C. Lee and D. T. Lee. A simple online bin packing algorithm. *J. ACM*, 32:562–572, 1985.

[10] J. Schaffner, T. Januschowski, M. Kercher, T. Kraska, H. Plattner, M. J. Franklin, and D. Jacobs. RTP: Robust tenant placement for elastic in-memory database clusters. In *ACM SIGMOD '13*, pages 773–784, 2013.

[11] S. S. Seiden. On the online bin packing problem. *J. ACM*, 49:640–671, 2002.

[12] D. Sleator and R. E. Tarjan. Amortized efficiency of list update and paging rules. *Commun. ACM*, 28:202–208, 1985.

[13] B. Speitkamp and M. Bichler. A mathematical programming approach for server consolidation problems in virtualized data centers. *IEEE T. Services Comput.*, 3(4):266–278, 2010.

[14] C. Subramanian, A. Vasan, and A. Sivasubramaniam. Reducing data center power with server consolidation: Approximation and evaluation. In *HiPC '10*, pages 1–10, 2010.

Competitively Scheduling Tasks with Intermediate Parallelizability

Sungjin Im
Electrical Engineering and
Computer Science
University of California
Merced, CA 95344
sim3@ucmerced.edu

Benjamin Moseley
Toyota Technological Institute
Chicago, IL 60637
moseley@ttic.edu

Kirk Pruhs
Dept. of Computer Science
University of Pittsburgh
Pittsburgh, PA 15260
kirk@cs.pitt.edu

Eric Torng
Dept. of Computer Science
and Engineering
Michigan State University
East Lansing, MI 48824
torng@msu.edu

ABSTRACT

We introduce a scheduling algorithm Intermediate-SRPT, and show that it is $O(\log P)$-competitive with respect to average waiting time when scheduling jobs whose parallelizability is intermediate between being fully parallelizable and sequential. Here the parameter P denotes the ratio between the maximum job size to the minimum. We also show a general matching lower bound on the competitive ratio. Our analysis builds on an interesting combination of potential function and local competitiveness arguments.

Categories and Subject Descriptors

F.2.2 [**Nonnumerical Algorithms and Problem**]: Sequencing and scheduling

General Terms

Algorithms, Theory

Keywords

Scheduling, Parallelization, Speedup curves.

1. INTRODUCTION

Due to the effects of Moore's law, around a decade ago chip makers such as Intel hit a thermal wall, where the cost of cooling became prohibitive if all switches were devoted to a single high speed processor. In response the chip makers abruptly switched to predominantly producing multiprocessor chips [11]. The advantage of multiprocessor chips is

that k processors with speed s/k would use only about $1/k^2$ fraction of the dynamic power of a single speed s processor (assuming the standard cube-root rule relationship between dynamic power and speed), but potentially would have the same processing capability; of course, fully utilizing the processing capability of a multiprocessor is a grand challenge. Our focus here is on one of these challenges, namely the scheduling of tasks.

One (not universally accepted) vision of the future is articulated by Anant Agarwal, CEO of Tilera [12].:

> "I would like to call it a corollary of Moore's Law that the number of cores will double every 18 months."

Tilera currently produces products with order of 10^2 processors [1], and products with order of 10^3 processors are in research and development [2]. In such settings, there will likely often be more processors than tasks, and thus a scheduler would have to partition the processors among the tasks. To achieve optimal performance, the scheduler must consider the parellizability of tasks when partitioning and scheduling. For example, whereas some highly parallel tasks might be sped up almost linearly when assigned additional processors and thus benefit greatly from being given more processors, other highly sequential tasks might not be sped up at all when assigned additional processors. In between these two extremes lie perhaps the majority of tasks which have intermediate levels of parallelizability.

The initial motivating questions for the research that we report on here are:

> What is the best algorithm to schedule jobs with intermediate parallelizability, and what worst-case relative error guarantee does this algorithm give?

Under standard assumptions (which we will elaborate on momentarily) it is clear how to optimally schedule n fully parallelizable tasks on m processors: all m processors are allocated to the task with the least amount of unprocessed work. Let us call this algorithm Parallel-SRPT. Further it is known how to schedule n fully sequential tasks on m processors in an optimally competitive way: the up to m

tasks with the least unprocessed work are each allocated one processor. Let us call this algorithm Sequential-SRPT. For sequential jobs with sizes are between 1 and P, Sequential-SRPT is $O(\log P)$-competitive, with respect to the objective of average waiting time [10]. Further, this competitive ratio is best possible for online algorithms [10].

It was previously not known how to schedule jobs of intermediate parallelizability in an optimally competitive way, and it was not clear a priori what the best scheduling policy would be. Presumably the "right" algorithm should agree with Parallel-SRPT when jobs are fully parallelizable, and agree with Sequential-SRPT when the jobs are sequential. After a moment's reflection, the most obvious property that both Parallel-SRPT and Sequential-SRPT share is that they schedule jobs in such a way as to maximize the rate of reduction of the fractional number of unfinished jobs, under the assumption that the original size of each job was its current size. So perhaps the most natural candidate for the best algorithm to schedule tasks with intermediate parallelizability would again be to assume that the remaining unfinished work of each job was its original work, and then greedily maximize the rate that the fractional number of unfinished jobs is being reduced by. Quite surprisingly (at least to us) we show in Section 3 that the competitive ratio of this natural hybrid algorithm is large.

Our main result is a less obvious algorithm (though still simple and natural), which we call Intermediate-SRPT, that we show is optimally competitive for all intermediate levels of parallelizability. We now describe the Intermediate-SRPT algorithm, introduce our natural model for intermediate parallelizability, state our upper bound on the competitive ratio of the Intermediate-SRPT algorithm, and finally state our general matching lower bound on the competitive ratio of any algorithm.

Intermediate-SRPT Algorithm Description: If there are at least m tasks, the m tasks with the least unprocessed work are each allocated one processor (this is like Sequential-SRPT). If there are strictly fewer than m tasks, the processors are evenly partitioned among the tasks (this is essentially the Round Robin or Processor Sharing Algorithm).

Modeling Intermediate Parallelizability: We assume that for each job j there exists an $\alpha_j \in (0,1)$ such that the speedup curve for job j is $\Gamma_j(x) = x$ for $x \leq 1$, and $\Gamma_j(x) = x^{\alpha_j}$ for $x \geq 1$. The speedup curve gives the rate that work is processed if the job is allocated x processors. Note that $\alpha_j = 0$ corresponds to a sequential job and $\alpha_j = 1$ corresponds to a fully parallelizable job. We believe speed-up curves of the form x^{α_j} give a natural way of interpolating intermediate degrees of parallelizability without being grounded in any specific machine model.

THEOREM 1. *For jobs of intermediate parallelizability, the algorithm Intermediate-SRPT has competitive ratio $O(1) \cdot 4^{1/(1-\alpha)} \log P$ with respect to average waiting time, where $\alpha = \max_j \alpha_j$. In particular, this holds for the special case that each $\alpha_j = \alpha$.*

THEOREM 2. *For all $\alpha \in [0,1)$, the competitive ratio of every algorithm with respect to average waiting time, restricted to instances with tasks with speedup curves of the form $\Gamma_j(x) = x$ for $x \leq 1$, and $\Gamma_j(x) = x^\alpha$ for $x \geq 1$, is $\Omega(\log P)$.*

Taken together, these results show (again somewhat surprisingly to us) that scheduling jobs that are even slightly less than fully parallelizable is more like scheduling sequential jobs than like scheduling fully parallelizable jobs. The lower bound for the natural hybrid algorithm shows that its "error" is that it will sometimes allocate too many processors to one job. This is the right strategy if the jobs are fully parallelizable, but can lead to a large relative error if the jobs are even a bit less than fully parallelizable. The algorithm Intermediate-SRPT corrects this error by functioning as Sequential-SRPT when the system is underloaded, and sharing the processors equally when the system is overloaded. Theorem 1 and Theorem 2 together establish that the optimal competitive ratio jumps from 1 to $\Theta(\log P)$ the instant $\alpha < 1$.

Theorem 1 is proved in Section 2. Theorem 2, is proved in Section 4. But first, we review standard modeling assumptions and notation, and review the most closely related papers in the literature.

1.1 Standard Modeling Assumptions and Notation

There are m identical unit-speed processors. Each task/job j has three characteristics: a release time r_j when it arrives in the system, a size or work amount $p_j \in [1, P]$ specifying the amount of processing that has to be performed on job j to finish it, and a speed-up curve $\Gamma_j(x)$ specifying the rate at which work on job j is processed if assigned x processors. A job is fully parallelizable if $\Gamma_j(x) = x$, and is sequential if $\Gamma_j(x) = x$ for $x \leq 1$, and $\Gamma_j(x) = 1$ for $x \geq 1$. A job j has intermediate parallelizability if there exists an $\alpha \in (0,1)$ such that the speed-up curve for j is $\Gamma_j(x) = x$ for $x \leq 1$, and $\Gamma_j(x) = x^\alpha$ for $x \geq 1$. If $p_j(t)$ is the amount of unprocessed work on job j at time t, then the fractional number of jobs at time t is $\sum_j \frac{p_j(t)}{p_j}$.

The flow/waiting/response time for job j in a schedule S is $F_j^S = C_j^S - r_j$ which is the length of time between when the job is released and when the job is completed in schedule S, and the average flow/waiting/response time of the schedule is $\sum_j F_j^S / n$. Within the context of this paper, the competitive (approximation/worst-case) ratio of an online scheduling algorithm A is the maximum over all inputs I with job sizes in the range $[1, P]$, of the ratio between total flow time for the schedule produces by A on I and the optimal flow time for instance I (this is essentially just a measure of worst-case relative error).

1.2 Related Literature

The speedup curves models was introduced into the literature in [5], who showed that equally partitioning the processors among the jobs is 2-competitive for total waiting time if jobs have arbitrary speedup curves and all jobs are released at the same time.

The other standard way to measure the quality of an online scheduling algorithm, beside competitive ratio, is resource/speed augmentation analysis [9, 13]. An online algorithm A is s-speed c-competitive if for all inputs I, the cost for A on I with s-speed processors is at most c times the optimal cost for I on speed 1 processors. An algorithm is scalable if it is $(1 + \epsilon)$-speed $O(1)$-competitive for all fixed constant $\epsilon > 0$.

[4] showed that partitioning the processors equally amongst the jobs is $(2+\epsilon)$-speed $O(1)$-competitive with respect to average waiting time for jobs with arbitrary speedup curves. [6] showed that the algorithm that partitions the processors equally amongst the latest arriving jobs is scalable.

[3] gives essentially optimally competitive algorithms for scheduling jobs with arbitrary speedup curves in a setting of identical speed scalable processors where the objective is total waiting time plus energy (in this setting one essentially gets speed augmentation for free). As [3] focused on non-clairvoyant scheduling algorithms, the competitive ratios were super-constant. [7] shows a scalable algorithm is achievable when the scheduler has access to a job's parallelizability. [14, 16] give essentially optimally competitive algorithms for scheduling jobs with arbitrary speedup curves for the objective of maximum waiting time. [17] considers scheduling jobs with arbitrary speedup curves and with precedence constraints.

[10] also shows that the competitive ratio with respect to average waiting time of Sequential-SRPT is $O(\log \frac{n}{m})$, and give a general matching lower bound for all online algorithms.

There is a large literature on online scheduling. One good survey for providing background on related results is [15].

2. ANALYSIS OF INTERMEDIATE-SRPT

Our goal in this section is to prove Theorem 1, which upper bounds the competitive ratio for the Intermediate-SRPT algorithm.

2.1 Analysis Overview

Our analysis will be based on a somewhat novel combination of potential function and local competitiveness arguments. Let $A(t)$ and $OPT(t)$ be the unfinished jobs at time t in the algorithm's and optimal solution's schedules, respectively. In Subsection 2.3, we will define a potential function $\Phi(t)$ that satisfies the following standard properties:

- Boundary Condition: $\Phi(0) = \Phi(\infty) = 0$.

- Discontinuous Changes Condition: the potential function can only decrease when a job arrives, or is completed by our algorithm or the optimal solution.

- Continuous Changes Condition: at any time t when no job arrives or completes, $|A(t)| + \frac{d}{dt}\Phi(t) \leq c|OPT(t)|$.

By integrating over time, one can see that the existence of such a potential function suffices to show that the algorithm is c-competitive for the total flow time objective. We refer the reader to [8] for details.

The novelty in our analysis lies in proving the Continuous Changes Condition. Most analyses based on potential functions rely on resource (speed) augmentation to prove this condition. We will partition time into overloaded and underloaded times. Let $\mathcal{O}$ denote the set of overloaded times t when $A(t) \geq m$, and $\mathcal{U}$ denote the set of underloaded times when $A(t) < m$. Theorem 1 then follows easily from the following three lemmas. Intuitively Lemma 1 shows that during the overloaded times, the unfinished jobs for the algorithm can be charged to the unfinished jobs for optimal at that time (a local competitiveness argument). Intuitively Lemma 2 shows that during the overloaded times, the increase in the potential function can be charged to the unfinished jobs for optimal at that time. Together Lemma 1

and Lemma 2 show that the Continuous Changes Condition holds at overloaded times. Lemma 3 then shows that the Continuous Change Condition holds at underloaded times.

LEMMA 1. *At all times $t \in \mathcal{O}$,*
$$|A(t)| \leq m(3 + \log P) + 2|OPT(t)|$$

LEMMA 2. *At all times $t \in \mathcal{O}$,*
$$\frac{d}{dt}\Phi(t) \leq O(1)4^{1/(1-\alpha)} \log P \; |OPT(t)|$$

LEMMA 3. *At all times $t \in \mathcal{U}$,*
$$|A(t)| + \frac{d}{dt}\Phi(t) \leq O(1)2^{1/(1-\alpha)} \; |OPT(t)|$$

In Subsection 2.2, we prove Lemma 1. In Subsection 2.3, we define the potential function Φ and prove the Boundary Condition, and the Discontinuous Changes Condition. In subsection 2.4 we prove Lemma 2. In subsection 2.5 we prove Lemma 3.

2.2 Local Competitiveness During Overloaded Times

This section is devoted to proving Lemma 1 and is an adaptation of a similar result from [10]. We will need to define additional notation. At any time, we classify jobs based on remaining length. A job whose remaining length is in $[2^k, 2^{k+1})$ is in class k for integer $0 \leq k \leq k_{max} = \lfloor \log P \rfloor$. Note that the number of initial job classes is $\lceil \log P \rceil$. We define one special class -1 to denote jobs whose remaining length is strictly less than 1.

For scheduling algorithm S, let $\delta^S(t)$ denote the number of jobs that are alive at time t in schedule S and $V^S(t)$ denote the total volume of this schedule, where the volume is defined to be the sum of remaining lengths of jobs that are still alive. Note that $\delta^A(t) = |A(t)|$ and $\delta^{OPT}(t) = |OPT(t)|$. We define the volume difference $\Delta V(t) = V^A(t) - V^{OPT}(t)$. For function $f \in \{V, \Delta V, \delta\}$, we define $f_{\geq h, \leq k}(t)$ to be the function f restricted to jobs in class at least h and at most k. We similarly define $f_{=k}(t)$. In Lemma 4 we bound the volume by which our algorithm can be behind optimal, and then use this Lemma in the proof of Lemma 5, which bounds the number of jobs by which our algorithm can be behind optimal. It is easy to see that Lemma 1 immediately follows from Lemma 5 and the observation that the number of jobs in class -1 is at most m.

LEMMA 4. *For any time $t \in \mathcal{O}$,*
$$\Delta V_{\leq k}(t) \leq m2^{k+1}$$

PROOF. First, for time t, we define time t' to be the earliest time such that $[t', t) \in \mathcal{O}$. Next, we define t_k to be the latest time in $[t', t)$ prior to time t in which a job of class strictly higher than k was processed by some machine. If there is no such time t_k, then we set $t_k = t'$.

We first observe that $\Delta V_{\leq k}(t_k) \leq m2^{k+1}$. By the definition of t_k, it follows that for any time $t_k - \epsilon$ for any $\epsilon > 0$, $\delta^A_{\leq k}(t_k - \epsilon) \leq m - 1$. It may be the case that some job enters class k at time t_k by the algorithm's processing, but this only means that $\delta^A_{\leq k}(t_k) \leq m$ when restricted to jobs that arrived strictly prior to time t_k. The volume of such jobs is restricted to at most $m2^{k+1}$ because each such job has a maximum remaining length of 2^{k+1}. Finally, jobs that arrive

24

at time t_k do not affect $\Delta V_{\leq k}(t_k)$ since such jobs increase both $V_{\leq k}^{OPT}(t)$ and $V_{\leq k}^A(t)$.

We next observe that $\Delta V_{\leq k}(t) \leq \Delta V_{\leq k}(t_k)$. This follows because by the definition of $\mathcal{O}$, each machine is processing one job during $[t_k, t]$ and by the definition of t_k, each job processed cannot be in a class larger than k. Thus, our algorithm completes as much work on jobs in classes at most k during this time period as OPT and the result follows. □

LEMMA 5. *For any time $t \in \mathcal{O}$,*

$$\delta_{\geq 0, \leq k_{max}}^A(t) \leq m(k_{max} + 2) + 2\delta_{\leq k_{max}}^{OPT}(t)$$

PROOF. We formulate $\delta_{\geq 0, \leq k_{max}}^A(t)$ as follows:

$$
\begin{aligned}
\sum_{k=0}^{k_{max}} \delta_{=k}^A(t) &\leq \sum_{k=0}^{k_{max}} \frac{V_k^A(t)}{2^k} \\
&= \sum_{k=0}^{k_{max}} \frac{\Delta V_{=k}(t) + V_{=k}^{OPT}(t)}{2^k} \\
&= \sum_{k=0}^{k_{max}} \frac{\Delta V_{\leq k}(t) - \Delta V_{\leq k-1}(t)}{2^k} + \frac{V_{=k}^{OPT}(t)}{2^k} \\
&\leq \frac{\Delta V_{\leq k_{max}}(t)}{2^{k_{max}}} + \sum_{k=0}^{k_{max}-1} \frac{\Delta V_{\leq k}(t)}{2^{k+1}} \\
&\quad - \frac{\Delta V_{\leq -1}(t)}{2^0} + 2\delta_{\geq 0, \leq k_{max}}^{OPT}(t) \\
&\leq 2m + \sum_{k=0}^{k_{max}-1} m + \delta_{\leq -1}^{OPT}(t) + 2\delta_{\geq 0, \leq k_{max}}^{OPT}(t) \\
&\leq m(k_{max} + 2) + 2\delta_{\leq k_{max}}^{OPT}(t).
\end{aligned}
$$

The first inequality follows since 2^k is the minimum remaining length of any job in class k. The fourth inequality follows by assuming the jobs in δ_k^{OPT} have remaining length 2^{k+1}. The fifth inequality follows from the previous lemma, observing that we can eliminate the negative term and add a positive term $\delta_{\leq -1}^{OPT}(t)$. □

2.3 Potential Function Analysis

In this section, we define the potential function Φ, and then we prove the Boundary Condition and the Discontinuous Changes Condition.

Definition of the Potential Function: Let $p_i^A(t)$ and $p_i^{OPT}(t)$ denote the remaining processing time of job i in the algorithm's and optimal solution's schedules at time t, respectively. Let $z_i(t) = \max\{p_i^A(t) - p_i^{OPT}(t), 0\}$. Recall that $A(t)$ and $OPT(t)$ denote the unfinished jobs in the algorithm's and optimal solution's schedules, respectively. Let $\mathtt{rank}(i, t) = \min\{m, \sum_{j \in A(t), r_j \leq r_i} 1\}$ where without loss of generality we assume that each job arrives at a unique time. Note that $\mathtt{rank}(i, t) \leq m$ for all i and t. We define the potential function as follows:

$$\Phi(t) = 16 \sum_{i \in A(t)} \frac{z_i(t)}{\Gamma_i(m/\mathtt{rank}(i, t))}$$

Throughout the analysis, the following simple lemma will be useful.

PROPOSITION 1. *For any B and C where $B \geq C$ and any job j, it is the case that $\frac{\Gamma_j(B)}{\Gamma_j(B)} \leq \frac{B}{C}$.*

PROOF. The proposition follows immediately by the assumption that Γ_j is a concave function and $\Gamma_j(0) = 0$. □

Boundary Condition: It is easy to see that $\Phi(0) = \Phi(\infty) = 0$ from the definition of the potential function Φ.

Discontinuous Changes Condition: First consider when a job arrives at time t. In this case there is no change in the potential function. This is because the $\mathtt{rank}$ for every job remains the same for all jobs that arrive before time t. Further, for the job i that arrives at this time, $z_i(t) = 0$. Thus, there is no change in the potential. Next observe that optimal completing a job has no effect on the potential. Now consider the case where the algorithm completes some job i at time t. In this case, the potential function can only decrease. To see that this is the case, consider any job $j \in A(t)$. If $r_j < r_i$, then there is no change in job j's term in the potential function. However, if $r_j > r_i$ then $\mathtt{rank}(j, t)$ may decrease by at most one. Since Γ_j is non-decreasing, $\Gamma_j(m/\mathtt{rank}(j, t))$ can only increase for a job j where $r_j \geq r_i$. Since this is in the denominator of the term in the potential function corresponding to job j and $z_j(t)$ is non-negative, the potential function can only decrease.

2.4 Potential Function Change During Overloaded Times

In this subsection we prove Lemma 2. If $|A(t)| \geq 10m \log P$, then Lemma 2 immediately follows from Lemmas 6 and 7. If $40 \cdot 4^{1/(1-\alpha)} \log P |OPT(t)| \geq |A(t)|$, then Lemma 2 immediately follows from Lemma 7. If $m \leq |A(t)| \leq 10m \log P$ and $40 \cdot 4^{1/(1-\alpha)} \log P |OPT(t)| \leq |A(t)|$ (which in turn implies that $|OPT(t)| \leq \frac{1}{4} \cdot \frac{1}{4^{1/(1-\alpha)}} m$), then Lemma 2 immediately follows from Lemmas 8 and 9.

First we consider the case where the algorithm has a large number of jobs compared to m.

LEMMA 6. *If $|A(t)| \geq 10m \log P$, then $|OPT(t)| \geq |A(t)|/2 - 2m \log P \geq |A(t)|/4$.*

PROOF. The lemma immediately follows from Lemma 1 by noticing that $t \in \mathcal{O}$. □

LEMMA 7. *At all times t, the rate of increase in the potential due to optimal processing the jobs is at most $16(|A(t)| + |OPT(t)|)$.*

PROOF. Let $q_i^{OPT}(t)$ be the number of machines assigned to job i by OPT at time t. The change in the potential due to optimal processing the jobs can then be bounded as follows:

$$
\begin{aligned}
&16 \sum_{i \in OPT(t)} \frac{\Gamma_i(q_i^{OPT}(t))}{\Gamma_i(m/\mathtt{rank}(i, t))} \\
&\leq 16 \sum_{i \in OPT(t)} \frac{\Gamma_i(q_i^{OPT}(t))}{\Gamma_i(m/|A(t)|)} \quad \text{[Since } \Gamma_i \text{ is non-decreasing]} \\
&\leq 16|OPT(t)| + 16 \sum_{i \in OPT(t)} \frac{q_i^{OPT}(t)}{m/|A(t)|} \quad \text{[By Proposition 1]} \\
&= 16|OPT(t)| + 16|A(t)| \sum_{i \in OPT(t)} \frac{q_i^{OPT}(t)}{m} \\
&\leq 16(|A(t)| + |OPT(t)|)
\end{aligned}
$$

The second inequality holds since for each job i with $\frac{q_i^{OPT}(t)}{m/|A(t)|} \leq 1$, it is the case that $\frac{\Gamma_i(q_i^{OPT}(t))}{\Gamma_i(m/|A(t)|)} \leq 1$. □

LEMMA 8. *At any time t where $|OPT(t)| \leq m$, the rate of increase in the potential due to optimal processing the jobs is at most $16m^\alpha |OPT(t)|^{1-\alpha}$.*

PROOF. As before, let $q_i^{OPT}(t)$ be the number of machines assigned to job i by OPT at time t. Let Γ be a function such that $\Gamma(x) = x$ for $0 \leq x \leq 1$ and $\Gamma(x) = x^\alpha$ for $x \geq 1$. Recall that $\texttt{rank}(i,t) \leq m$ for all i and t from the definition of $\texttt{rank}$. The change in the potential due to optimal processing the jobs can then be bounded as follows:

$$16 \sum_{i \in OPT(t)} \frac{\Gamma_i(q_i^{OPT}(t))}{\Gamma_i(m/\texttt{rank}(i,t))}$$

$$\leq \quad 16 \sum_{i \in OPT(t)} \frac{\Gamma_i(q_i^{OPT}(t))}{\Gamma_i(m/m)} \quad \text{[Since } \Gamma_i \text{ is non-decreasing]}$$

$$= \quad 16 \sum_{i \in OPT(t)} \Gamma_i(q_i^{OPT}(t)) \quad \text{[Since } \Gamma_i(1) = 1\text{]}$$

$$\leq \quad 16 \sum_{i \in OPT(t)} \Gamma(q_i^{OPT}(t))$$

$$\leq \quad 16|OPT(t)|(m/|OPT(t)|)^\alpha \quad \text{[Due to the concavity of } \Gamma\text{]}$$

$$= \quad 16m^\alpha |OPT(t)|^{1-\alpha}$$

□

LEMMA 9. *At any time t where $m \leq |A(t)| \leq 10m \log P$ and $|OPT(t)| \leq \frac{1}{4} \cdot \frac{1}{4^{1/(1-\alpha)}} m$, the rate of increase in the potential due to the algorithm processing jobs is at most $-4m$.*

PROOF. When $|A(t)| \geq m$ the algorithm assigns the shortest m jobs each on a unique machine. Let $A'(t)$ denote these m jobs. Notice that $z_i(t)$ decreases at a rate of one for each job in $A'(t) \setminus OPT(t)$. Thus, we have that the change in the potential due to the algorithm is at most:

$$-16 \sum_{i \in A'(t) \setminus OPT(t)} \frac{1}{\Gamma_i(m/\texttt{rank}(i,t))}$$

$$\leq \quad -16 \sum_{i \in A'(t) \setminus OPT(t)} \frac{\texttt{rank}(i,t))}{m}$$

$$\leq \quad -\frac{16}{m} \sum_{i=1}^{|A'(t) \setminus OPT(t)|} i$$

$$\leq \quad -\frac{16}{m} \frac{(3m/4)^2}{2}$$

$$\leq \quad -4m$$

The first inequality easily follows from Proposition 1 and by observing that $m/\texttt{rank}(i,t)) \geq 1$ since $\texttt{rank}(i,t) \leq m$. The second to last inequality holds since $|OPT(t)| \leq (1/4)m$ and $|A'(t)| = m$. □

2.5 Underloaded Times

Our goal in this subsection is to prove Lemma 3. Let t be a time such that $|A(t)| \leq m$. If $|OPT(t)| \geq \frac{1}{16}|A(t)|$, then Lemma 3 immediately follows from Lemma 7; the potential can only decrease when the algorithm processes jobs. Hence we assume that $|OPT(t)| \leq \frac{1}{16}|A(t)|$.

First we bound the increase in the potential function due to the processing of optimal. Again, let $q_i^{OPT}(t)$ be the number of processors assigned to job i at time t by OPT. The increase in the potential is at most the following.

$$16 \sum_{i \in OPT(t)} \frac{\Gamma_i(q_i^{OPT}(t))}{\Gamma_i(m/\texttt{rank}(i,t))}$$

$$\leq \quad 16 \sum_{i \in OPT(t)} \frac{\Gamma_i(q_i^{OPT}(t))}{\Gamma_i(m/|A(t)|)} \quad \text{[Since } \Gamma_i \text{ is non-decreasing]}$$

$$\leq \quad 16|OPT(t)| + 16 \sum_{i \in OPT(t), q_i^{OPT}(t) \geq m/|A(t)|} \frac{(q_i^{OPT}(t))^{\alpha_i}}{(m/|A(t)|)^{\alpha_i}}$$

$$\leq \quad 16|OPT(t)| + 16 \sum_{i \in OPT(t)} \frac{(q_i^{OPT}(t))^\alpha}{(m/|A(t)|)^\alpha}$$

The second to last inequality holds for the following reason. Consider any job i such that $\frac{q_i^{OPT}(t)}{(m/|A(t)|)^{\alpha_i}} \leq 1$. Then we have $\frac{(q_i^{OPT}(t))^{\alpha_i}}{(m/|A(t)|)^{\alpha_i}} \leq 1$. Hence the total contribution of such jobs is at most $16|OPT(t)|$. Since our goal is to bound the total change of the potential plus $|A(t)|$ by $|OPT(t)|$, we will ignore $16|OPT(t)|$, and proceed with our string of inequalities.

$$16 \sum_{i \in OPT(t)} \frac{(q_i^{OPT}(t))^\alpha}{(m/|A(t)|)^\alpha} \quad \leq \quad 16 \sum_{i \in OPT(t)} \frac{(m/|OPT(t)|)^\alpha}{(m/|A(t)|)^\alpha}$$

$$= \quad 16|OPT(t)| \frac{(m/|OPT(t)|)^\alpha}{(m/|A(t)|)^\alpha}$$

$$\leq \quad 16|OPT(t)|^{1-\alpha}|A(t)|^\alpha$$

$$\leq \quad 16\left(\frac{1}{2^{\alpha+2}}|A(t)| + 2^{\frac{\alpha+2}{1-\alpha}\alpha}|OPT(t)|\right)$$

The first inequality is immediate from the fact that $0 \leq \alpha < 1$. The last inequality can be easily shown by considering two cases whether $|A(t)| \geq 2^{\frac{\alpha+2}{1-\alpha}}|OPT(t)|$ or not.

Now we consider the decrease in the potential function due to the algorithm processing jobs. When $|A(t)| < m$ then the algorithm gives each job equal share of every processor. Thus, for all $i \in A(t) \setminus OPT(t)$ it is the case that $z_i(t)$ decreases at a rate of $\Gamma_i(m/|A(t)|)$. Thus, we have the decrease due to the algorithm is as follows.

$$-16 \sum_{i \in A(t) \setminus OPT(t)} \frac{\Gamma_i(m/|A(t)|)}{\Gamma_i(m/\texttt{rank}(i,t))}$$

$$\leq \quad -16 \sum_{i \in A(t) \setminus OPT(t), \texttt{rank}(i,t) \geq |A(t)|/2} \frac{\Gamma_i(m/|A(t)|)}{\Gamma_i(2m/|A(t)|)}$$

$$\leq \quad -16(|A(t) \setminus OPT(t)| - |A(t)|/2)(1/2)^\alpha$$

$$\leq \quad -16(1 - \frac{1}{2} - \frac{1}{16})|A(t)|(1/2)^\alpha$$

$$\leq \quad -6|A(t)|(1/2)^\alpha$$

So far we have shown that

$$\frac{d}{dt}\Phi(t) \quad \leq \quad 16\left(\frac{1}{2^{\alpha+2}}|A(t)| + 2^{\frac{\alpha+2}{1-\alpha}\alpha}|OPT(t)|\right) - 6|A(t)|(1/2)^\alpha$$

$$\leq \quad -|A(t)| + O(1)2^{1/(1-\alpha)}|OPT(t)|$$

This completes the proof.

3. LOWER BOUND FOR GREEDY ALGORITHM

In this section, we prove that the following natural greedy hybrid of Parallel-SRPT and Sequential-SRPT has a super-logarithmic lower bound on its competitive ratio.

Description of Greedy Algorithm: At all times allocate processors to jobs in such a way as to maximize the instantaneous rate at which the fractional number of unfinished jobs would be decreased, if it was the case that the original work of each job was its remaining unprocessed work. Using a simple exchange argument one can prove that if each job j has a speedup curve of the form $\Gamma_j(x) = x^\alpha$ for $\alpha \in (0, 1)$, then this policy can be implemented in the following greedy way: We arbitrarily number the processors from 1 to m. At each decision point, the machines schedule jobs in order from machine 1 to machine m. When it is machine i's turn to schedule a job, let $p(i, j)$ be the number of processors from 1 to $i - 1$ that have been assigned to job j. Processor i chooses job j that maximizes $\frac{\Gamma(p(i,j)+1) - \Gamma(p(i,j))}{p_j(t)}$.

LEMMA 10. *This Greedy algorithm has a competitive ratio that is $\Omega(\max\{P, n^{1/3}\})$.*

PROOF. Let $\epsilon = 1 - \alpha$. Consider an input instance where $m - m^{1-\epsilon}$ jobs of size m are released at time 0. From time 0 to time $m - \frac{1}{m^{1-\epsilon}}$, one job of size 1 is released every $\frac{1}{m^{1-\epsilon}}$ time units. Finally, at time $m + 1$, we release a job of size 1 every $\frac{1}{m^{1-\epsilon}}$ time units for $X = m^2$ time units (a total of $X m^{1-\epsilon}$ jobs are released in this final phase).

This greedy algorithm will devote all m machines to the 1 job of size 1 and complete it just as the next size 1 job arrives. This follows by considering the last processor m. It balances the choice of $\frac{m^{1-\epsilon} - (m-1)^{1-\epsilon}}{1}$ versus $\frac{1}{m}$. Given that $\epsilon > 0$, it will always choose to assign the machine to the size 1 job.

At time m, this greedy algorithm will still have all $m - m^{1-\epsilon}$ jobs of size m remaining. In this next unit of time, it can only complete at most m units of work on these $m - m^{1-\epsilon}$ jobs; in particular, it cannot finish any of these jobs and cannot reduce the processing time to less than 1. After time $m + 1$, it will assign all m processors to the newly arrived job until the stream ends. The total flow time incurred will thus be m for the jobs of size 1 released prior to time m, X for the jobs of size 1 released after time $m + 1$, and $(m - m^{1-\epsilon} + 1)(X + m + 1)$ for the jobs of size m up to the end of the long stream. We ignore the flow time incurred to complete these long jobs after the end of the stream. The dominant term is $(m - m^{1-\epsilon})X$ for the size m jobs during the long stream.

On the other hand, an alternative algorithm (not necessarily optimal but simple to conceptualize) will assign $m - m^{1-\epsilon}$ machines to the size m jobs from time 0 to time m completing them by time m. On the remaining $m^{1-\epsilon}$ machines, it assigns one machine to each job of size 1 as that job arrives. Because it operates efficiently, each such machine will complete its assigned size 1 job exactly 1 time unit later. During this time, each job will complete just as its machine is needed to schedule the next arriving size 1 job because the number of jobs that arrive during 1 unit of time is exactly $m^{1-\epsilon}$. By time $m + 1$, this algorithm will have completed all of these jobs and will now devote all m machines to the stream of size 1 jobs that arrive completing each one just as the next arrives. Before time $m + 1$, this algorithm incurs a total time of $m^{2-\epsilon}$ for the size 1 jobs since each of these jobs is scheduled immediately on one processor. The large jobs each complete within m time units of arrival for a total flow time of $m^2 - m^{2-\epsilon}$. Finally, during the stream of length X, each job incurs a flow time of $\frac{1}{m^{1-\epsilon}}$ for a total flow time of X.

The $\Omega(P)$ bound follows from the observation that $P = m$. The $\Omega(n^{1/3})$ bound follows from the observation that $n = \Theta(m^{3-\epsilon})$. $\square$

4. GENERAL LOWER BOUND

Our goal in this section is to prove Theorem 2, which gives a logarithmic lower bound on the competitive ratio of any algorithm. This lower bound is an adaptation of the lower bound proof from [10]. The proof is slightly more complex because online algorithms can exploit the fact that the jobs have intermediate parallelizability to catch up on jobs that they should have finished earlier.

We construct a family of input instances parameterized by α where each instance is composed of two parts. In the first part, jobs are released in phases. Each phase has long jobs and short jobs that force the online algorithm to choose between completing almost all of the short jobs before the halfway point of a phase or completing all the jobs in the phase by the end of the phase. The family of input instances is structured such that any deterministic online algorithm on at least one instance in the family must face a time T where it has at least $\Omega(m \log P)$ unfinished jobs whereas the optimal algorithm at the same moment in time will have at most $m/2$ unfinished jobs. The second part of the input instance starts at time T and presents a stream of m jobs of size 1 for P^2 consecutive starting times.

We formally define the family of input instances as follows. First, we need to define the following terms. Let $\epsilon = 1 - \alpha$. We define a length reduction factor $r = 1/2(1 - \frac{1}{2^\epsilon})$; the length of the long jobs will be multiplied by r (equivalently divided by a factor of $1/r$) in each phase of the input instance. We choose the number of machines m such that $\frac{1}{2} \frac{2^\epsilon - 1}{2^\epsilon + 1} m$ is an integer. We choose the longest job length P such that the maximum number of phases $L = 1/2 \log_{\frac{1}{r}} P$ is an integer and $\log_{\frac{1}{r}}^2 P < \frac{1}{4} \frac{2^\epsilon - 1}{2^\epsilon + 1} P^{1/2}$.

The first part has at most $L = 1/2 \log_{\frac{1}{r}} P$ phases numbered from 0 to $L - 1$. Each phase $0 \leq i \leq L - 1$ has a phase length $p_i = P r^i$ and a start time $s_i = \sum_{j=0}^{i-1} p_j$. During phase i, $m/2$ long jobs of length p_i are released at time s_i, and m short jobs of length 1 are released at times $s_i + j$ for $0 \leq j \leq p_i/2 - 1$.

The adversary begins by releasing the jobs in phase 0 starting at time $s_0 = 0$. In general, suppose the adversary has released the jobs in phase i starting at time s_i where $i \leq L - 1$. The adversary decides at time $s_i + p_i/2$ whether or not to (i) begin the second part of the input instance at time $s_i + p_i/2$ or (ii) to release the next set of jobs starting at time s_{i+1} as follows. If the online algorithm has at least $m \log_{\frac{1}{r}} P$ remaining work from length 1 jobs released in phase i at time $s_i + p_i/2$, then the adversary begins the second part of the input instance at time $s_i + p_i/2$. Otherwise, if $i < L - 1$, then the adversary releases the jobs in phase $i + 1$ starting at time s_{i+1}. If $i = L - 1$, then the adversary starts the second part of the input instance at time $s_i + p_i$. This leaves us with two possible cases. In the first case, the adversary starts the second part of the input instance at some time $T = s_i + p_i/2$ where $0 \leq i \leq L-1$. In the second case, the adversary starts the second part of the input instance at time $T = s_{L-1} + p_{L-1}$.

We now argue that for both cases, the optimal flow time is bounded by $O(mP^2)$. As in [10], we define a notion of a standard schedule for phase i that has the goal of completing all jobs released in phase i by time $s_i + p_i$. Each of the $m/2$ long jobs are processed non-preemptively by one machine for the entire phase. For the m length 1 jobs released at time $s_i + k$ where $0 \leq k \leq p_i/2 - 1$, $m/2$ of them are completed by using $m/2$ machines at time $s_i + k$ and the other $m/2$ are completed using $m/2$ machines at time $s_i + k + p_i/2$. The total flow time of this standard schedule for phase i is $2mp_i + m/2(p_i/2)^2$.

We now show that the optimal flow time is $O(mP^2)$ for the first case by giving a specific schedule with flow time $O(mP^2)$. The standard schedule is used for all phases up to but not including phase i. For phase i, the $m/2$ long jobs are ignored and each length 1 job is assigned its own machine immediately upon arrival. Thus, by time $T = s_i + p_i/2$, only the $m/2$ long jobs of phase i remain. For time $T + k$ where $0 \leq k \leq P^2 - 1$, the m jobs of length 1 released at time $T + k$ are each assigned their own machine and completed by time $T + k + 1$. Finally, at time $T + P^2$, each of the $m/2$ long jobs of size p_{L-1} are assigned to 2 machines and completed by time $T + P^2 + p_i/2^\alpha$. Clearly, the overall flow time for this feasible schedule is $O(mP^2)$.

We now show that the optimal flow time is $O(mP^2)$ for the second case by giving a specific schedule with flow time $O(mP^2)$. The standard schedule is used for all phases. Thus, by time $T = s_{L-1} + p_{L-1}/2$, no jobs remain. For time $T + k$ where $0 \leq k \leq P^2 - 1$, the m jobs of length 1 released at time $T + k$ are each assigned their own machine and completed by time $T + k + 1$. Clearly, the overall flow time for this feasible schedule is $O(mP^2)$.

We now show that the online flow time for both cases is at least $\Omega(mP^2 \log_{\frac{1}{r}} P)$. By the definition of the first case, the online algorithm has at least $m \log_{\frac{1}{r}} P$ remaining work from the length 1 jobs released in phase i at time $T = s_i + p_i/2$. Thus, the online algorithm has at least $m \log_{\frac{1}{r}} P$ unfinished jobs from time T to time $T + P^2$. Using only the flow time from this time interval, we see that the online algorithm incurs a total flow time of at least $mP^2 \log_{\frac{1}{r}} P$ and the theorem follows for this case.

We now consider the second case. In our analysis, we opt for simplicity rather than proving the most accurate bound. The first key observation is that in phase i for $0 \leq i \leq L-1$, online completes at least $mp_i/2 - m \log_{\frac{1}{r}} P$ of the total available work from the length 1 jobs by time $s_i + p_i/2$, the halfway point of phase i. This means that at most $m \log_{\frac{1}{r}} P$ work can be completed on the long jobs, possibly from earlier phases, during the time interval $[s_i, s_i + p_i/2]$.

We will prove that at time T, the amount of unfinished work from the $m/2$ long jobs from phase i for $0 \leq i \leq L-1$ is at least $\frac{1}{2} \frac{2^\epsilon - 1}{2^\epsilon + 1} \frac{m}{2} p_i$. This implies that the number of long jobs with remaining length at least 1 from phase i at time T is at least $\frac{1}{2} \frac{2^\epsilon - 1}{2^\epsilon + 1} \frac{m}{2}$. Given that there are $L = 1/2 \log_{\frac{1}{r}} P$ phases, we have that the total number of jobs with remaining length at least 1 at time T is at least $L \frac{1}{2} \frac{2^\epsilon - 1}{2^\epsilon + 1} \frac{m}{2} =$

$\frac{1}{2} (\log_{\frac{1}{r}} P) \frac{1}{2} \frac{2^\epsilon - 1}{2^\epsilon + 1} \frac{m}{2}$ which is $\Omega(m \log_{\frac{1}{r}} P)$. Thus, the total flow time incurred in interval $[T, T + P^2]$ is $\Omega(mP^2 \log_{\frac{1}{r}} P)$.

Consider the $m/2$ long jobs from phase i. From our previous observation, we can complete at most $(L - i)m \log_{\frac{1}{r}} P \leq \frac{m}{2} \log_{\frac{1}{r}} \log_{\frac{1}{r}} P \leq \frac{1}{2} \frac{2^\epsilon - 1}{2^\epsilon + 1} \frac{m}{2} P^{1/2} \leq \frac{1}{2} \frac{2^\epsilon - 1}{2^\epsilon + 1} \frac{m}{2} p^i$ work on these $m/2$ jobs during the first half of phases i to $L - 1$. During the second half of phases i to $L - 1$, the best we can do is devote 2 machines to each job for the entire second half of these phases; note that we ignore the processing required by any unfinished length 1 jobs from phase i in the second half of phase i. Given that the phase lengths form a geometric progression with multiplicative factor r, the total time available in these second halves of phases is strictly less than $\frac{p_i}{2} \frac{1}{1-r}$. Thus, the total amount of work that can be completed in the second half of these phases is strictly less than $\frac{m}{2} 2^\alpha \frac{p_i}{2} \frac{1}{1-r}$ which is equal to $\frac{m}{2} \frac{2}{2^\epsilon + 1} p_i$. Thus, considering only the second half of these phases, there is strictly more than $\frac{2^\epsilon - 1}{2^\epsilon + 1} \frac{m}{2} p_i$ unfinished work for these $m/2$ long jobs from phase i at time T. Taking into account how much work can be done in the first half of these phases, we see that the total unfinished work on the $m/2$ long jobs from phase i at time T is at least $\frac{1}{2} \frac{2^\epsilon - 1}{2^\epsilon + 1} \frac{m}{2} p^i$, and the theorem follows for the second case.

Acknowledgment

Sungjin Im's work was supported in part by NSF Award CCF-1008065, and was partially done while the author was at Duke. Kirk Pruhs' work was supported in part by NSF grants CCF-1115575, CNS-1253218, and an IBM Faculty Award.

5. REFERENCES

[1] http://www.tilera.com/.

[2] http://projects.csail.mit.edu/angstrom/.

[3] Ho-Leung Chan, Jeff Edmonds, and Kirk Pruhs. Speed scaling of processes with arbitrary speedup curves on a multiprocessor. *Theory Comput. Syst.*, 49(4):817–833, 2011.

[4] Jeff Edmonds. Scheduling in the dark. *Theor. Comput. Sci.*, 235(1):109–141, 2000.

[5] Jeff Edmonds, Jarek Gryz, Dongming Liang, and Renée J. Miller. Mining for empty spaces in large data sets. *Theor. Comput. Sci.*, 296(3):435–452, 2003.

[6] Jeff Edmonds and Kirk Pruhs. Scalably scheduling processes with arbitrary speedup curves. *ACM Transactions on Algorithms*, 8(3):28, 2012.

[7] Kyle Fox, Sungjin Im, and Benjamin Moseley. Energy efficient scheduling of parallelizable jobs. In *SODA*, pages 948–957, 2013.

[8] Sungjin Im, Benjamin Moseley, and Kirk Pruhs. A tutorial on amortized local competitiveness in online scheduling. *SIGACT News*, 42(2):83–97, 2011.

[9] Bala Kalyanasundaram and Kirk Pruhs. Speed is as powerful as clairvoyance. *J. ACM*, 47(4):617–643, 2000.

[10] Stefano Leonardi and Danny Raz. Approximating total flow time on parallel machines. *Journal of Computer and Systems Sciences*, 73(6):875–891, 2007.

[11] John Markoff. Intel's big shift after hitting technical wall. *New York Times*, May 2004.

[12] Rick Merritt. CPU designers debate multi-core future. *EE Times*, February 2008.

[13] Cynthia A. Phillips, Clifford Stein, Eric Torng, and Joel Wein. Optimal time-critical scheduling via resource augmentation. *Algorithmica*, 32(2):163–200, 2002.

[14] Kirk Pruhs, Julien Robert, and Nicolas Schabanel. Minimizing maximum flowtime of jobs with arbitrary parallelizability. In *WAOA*, pages 237–248, 2010.

[15] Kirk Pruhs, Jiri Sgall, and Eric Torng. *Handbook of Scheduling: Algorithms, Models, and Performance Analysis*, chapter Online Scheduling. 2004.

[16] Julien Robert and Nicolas Schabanel. Non-clairvoyant batch sets scheduling: Fairness is fair enough. In *ESA*, pages 741–753, 2007.

[17] Julien Robert and Nicolas Schabanel. Non-clairvoyant scheduling with precedence constraints. In *SODA*, pages 491–500, 2008.

Experimental Analysis of Space-Bounded Schedulers

Harsha Vardhan Simhadri
Carnegie Mellon University,
Lawrence Berkeley Lab
harshas@lbl.gov

Guy E. Blelloch
Carnegie Mellon University
guyb@cs.cmu.edu

Jeremy T. Fineman
Georgetown University
jfineman@cs.georgetown.edu

Phillip B. Gibbons
Intel Labs Pittsburgh
phillip.b.gibbons@intel.com

Aapo Kyrola
Carnegie Mellon University
akyrola@cs.cmu.edu

ABSTRACT

The running time of nested parallel programs on shared memory machines depends in significant part on how well the scheduler mapping the program to the machine is optimized for the organization of caches and processors on the machine. Recent work proposed "space-bounded schedulers" for scheduling such programs on the multi-level cache hierarchies of current machines. The main benefit of this class of schedulers is that they provably preserve locality of the program at every level in the hierarchy, resulting (in theory) in fewer cache misses and better use of bandwidth than the popular work-stealing scheduler. On the other hand, compared to work-stealing, space-bounded schedulers are inferior at load balancing and may have greater scheduling overheads, raising the question as to the relative effectiveness of the two schedulers in practice.

In this paper, we provide the first experimental study aimed at addressing this question. To facilitate this study, we built a flexible experimental framework with separate interfaces for programs and schedulers. This enables a head-to-head comparison of the relative strengths of schedulers in terms of running times and cache miss counts across a range of benchmarks. (The framework is validated by comparisons with the Intel® Cilk^{TM} Plus work-stealing scheduler.) We present experimental results on a 32-core Xeon® 7560 comparing work-stealing, hierarchy-minded work-stealing, and two variants of space-bounded schedulers on both divide-and-conquer micro-benchmarks and some popular algorithmic kernels. Our results indicate that space-bounded schedulers reduce the number of L3 cache misses compared to work-stealing schedulers by 25–65% for most of the benchmarks, but incur up to 7% additional scheduler and load-imbalance overhead. Only for memory-intensive benchmarks can the reduction in cache misses overcome the added overhead, resulting in up to a 25% improvement in running time for synthetic benchmarks and about 20% improvement for algorithmic kernels. We also quantify runtime improvements

varying the available bandwidth per core (the "bandwidth gap"), and show up to 50% improvements in the running times of kernels as this gap increases 4-fold. As part of our study, we generalize prior definitions of space-bounded schedulers to allow for more practical variants (while still preserving their guarantees), and explore implementation tradeoffs.

Categories and Subject Descriptors

D.3.4 [**Processors**]: Runtime environments

Keywords

Thread schedulers, space-bounded schedulers, work stealing, cache misses, multicores, memory bandwidth

1. INTRODUCTION

Writing nested parallel programs using fork-join primitives on top of a unified memory space is an elegant and productive way to program parallel machines. Nested parallel programs are portable, sufficiently expressive for many algorithmic problems [28, 5], relatively easy to analyze [22, 3], and supported by many programming languages including OpenMP [25], Cilk++ [17], Intel® TBB [18], Java Fork-Join [21], and Microsoft TPL [23]. The unified memory address space hides from programmers the complexity of managing a diverse set of physical memory components like RAM and caches. Processor cores can access memory locations without explicitly specifying their physical location. Beneath this interface, however, the real cost of accessing a memory address from a core can vary widely, depending on where in the machine's cache/memory hierarchy the data resides at time of access. Runtime thread schedulers can play a large role in determining this cost, by optimizing the timing and placement of program tasks for effective use of the machine's caches.

Machine Models and Schedulers. Robust schedulers for mapping nested parallel programs to machines with certain kinds of simple cache organizations such as single-level shared and private caches have been proposed. They work well both in theory [10, 11, 8] and in practice [22, 24]. Among these, the *work-stealing scheduler* is particularly appealing for private caches because of its simplicity and low overheads, and is widely deployed in various run-time systems such as Cilk++. The *PDF scheduler* [8] is suited for shared caches and practical versions of this schedule have been studied. The cost of these schedulers in terms of cache

ACM acknowledges that this contribution was authored or co-authored by an employee, contractor or affiliate of the national government of United States. As such, the Government retains a nonexclusive, royalty-free right to publish or reproduce this article, or to allow others to do so, for Government purposes only.
SPAA'14, June 23–25, 2014, Prague, Czech Republic.
Copyright is held by the owner/author(s). Publication rights licensed to ACM.
ACM 978-1-4503-2821-0/14/06 ...$15.00.
http://dx.doi.org/10.1145/2612669.2612678.

misses or running times can be bounded by the locality cost of the programs as measured in certain abstract program-centric cost models [10, 1, 6, 7, 29].

However, modern parallel machines have multiple levels of cache, with each cache shared amongst a subset of cores (*e.g.*, see Fig. 1(a)). A parallel memory hierarchy (PMH) as represented by a tree of caches [2] (Fig. 1(b)) is a reasonably accurate and tractable model for such machines [16, 14, 6]. Because previously studied schedulers for simple machine models may not be optimal for these complex machines, recent work has proposed a variety of hierarchy-aware schedulers [16, 14, 27, 15, 6] for use on such machines. For example, hierarchy-aware work-stealing schedulers such as PWS and HWS schedulers [27] have been proposed, but no theoretical bounds are known.

To address his gap, *space-bounded schedulers* [14, 15] have been proposed and analyzed. To use space-bounded schedulers, the computation needs to annotate each function call with the size of its memory footprint. The scheduler then tries to match the memory footprint of a subcomputation to a cache of appropriate size in the hierarchy and then run the subcomputation fully on the cores associated with that cache. Note that although space annotations are required, the computation can be oblivious to the size of the caches and hence is portable across machines. Under certain conditions these schedulers can guarantee good bounds on cache misses at every level of the hierarchy and running time in terms of some intuitive program-centric metrics. Cole and Ramachandran [15] presented such schedulers with strong asymptotic bounds on cache misses and runtime for highly balanced computations. Our follow-on work [6] presented slightly generalized schedulers that obtain similarly strong bounds for unbalanced computations.

Our Results: The First Experimental Study of Space-Bounded Schedulers. While space-bounded schedulers have good theoretical guarantees on the PMH model, there has been no experimental study to suggest that these (asymptotic) guarantees translate into good performance on real machines with multi-level caches. Existing analyses of these schedulers ignore the overhead costs of the scheduler itself and account only for the program run time. Intuitively, given the low overheads and highly-adaptive load balancing of work-stealing in practice, space-bounded schedulers would seem to be inferior on both accounts, but superior in terms of cache misses. This raises the question as to the relative effectiveness of the two types of schedulers in practice.

This paper presents the first experimental study aimed at addressing this question through a head-to-head comparison of work-stealing and space-bounded schedulers. To facilitate a fair comparison of the schedulers on various benchmarks, it is necessary to have a framework that provides separate modular interfaces for writing portable nested parallel programs and specifying schedulers. The framework should be light-weight, flexible, provide fine-grained timers, and enable access to various hardware counters for cache misses, clock cycles, etc. Prior scheduler frameworks, such as the Sequoia framework [16] which implements a scheduler that closely resembles a space-bounded scheduler, fall short of these goals by (i) forcing a program to specify the specific sizes of the levels of the hierarchy it is intended for, making it non-portable, and (ii) lacking the flexibility to readily support work-stealing or its variants.

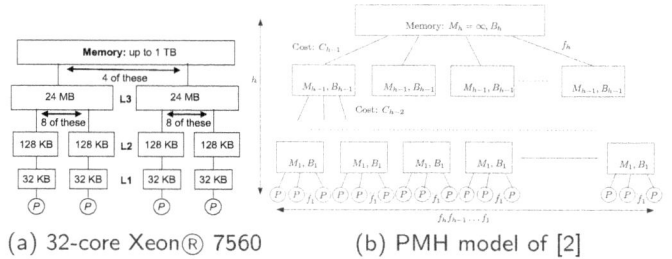

(a) 32-core Xeon® 7560   (b) PMH model of [2]

Figure 1: Memory hierarchy of a current generation architecture from Intel®, plus an example abstract parallel hierarchy model. Each cache (rectangle) is shared by all cores (circles) in its subtree.

This paper describes a scheduler framework that we designed and implemented, which achieves these goals. To specify a (nested-parallel) program in the framework, the programmer uses a Fork-Join primitive (and a Parallel-For built on top of Fork-Join). To specify the scheduler, one needs to implement just three primitives describing the management of tasks at Fork and Join points: **add**, **get**, and **done**. Any scheduler can be described in this framework as long as the schedule does not require the preemption of sequential segments of the program. A simple work-stealing scheduler, for example, can be described with only 10s of lines of code in this framework. Furthermore, in this framework, program tasks are completely managed by the schedulers, allowing them full control of the execution.

The framework enables a head-to-head comparison of the relative strengths of schedulers in terms of running times and cache miss counts across a range of benchmarks. (The framework is validated by comparisons with the commercial Cilk™ Plus work-stealing scheduler.) We present experimental results on a 32-core Intel® Nehalem series Xeon® 7560 multicore with 3 levels of cache. As depicted in Fig. 1(a), each L3 cache is shared (among the 8 cores on a socket) while the L1 and L2 caches are exclusive to cores. We compare four schedulers—work-stealing, priority work-stealing (PWS) [27], and two variants of space-bounded schedulers—on both divide-and-conquer micro-benchmarks (scan-based and gather-based) and popular algorithmic kernels such as quicksort, sample sort, matrix multiplication, and quad trees.

Our results indicate that space-bounded schedulers reduce the number of L3 cache misses compared to work-stealing schedulers by 25–65% for most of the benchmarks, while incurring up to 7% additional overhead. For memory-intensive benchmarks, the reduction in cache misses overcomes the added overhead, resulting in up to a 25% improvement in running time for synthetic benchmarks and about 20% improvement for algorithmic kernels. To better understand how the widening gap between processing power (cores) and memory bandwidth impacts scheduler performance, we quantify runtime improvements over a 4-fold range in the available bandwidth per core and show further improvements in the running times of kernels (up to 50%) as the bandwidth gap increases.

Finally, as part of our study, we generalize prior definitions of space-bounded schedulers to allow for more practical variants, and explore implementation tradeoffs, e.g., in a key parameter of such schedulers. This is useful for engineering space-bounded schedulers, which were previously described only at a high level suitable for theoretical analyses, into a form suitable for real machines.

Contributions. The contributions of this paper are:

- A modular framework for describing schedulers, machines as tree of caches, and nested parallel programs (Section 3). The framework is equipped with timers and counters. Schedulers that are expected to work well on tree of cache models such space-bounded schedulers and certain work-stealing schedulers are implemented.

- A precise definition for the class of space-bounded schedulers that retains the competitive cache miss bounds expected for this class, but also allows more schedulers than previous definitions (which were motivated mainly by theoretical guarantees [15, 6]) (Section 4). We describe two variants, highlighting the engineering details that allow for low overhead.

- The first experimental study of space-bounded schedulers, and the first head-to-head comparison with work-stealing schedulers (Section 5). On a common multi-core machine configuration (4 sockets, 32 cores, 3 levels of caches), we quantify the reduction in L3 cache misses incurred by space-bounded schedulers relative to both work-stealing variants on synthetic and non-synthetic benchmarks. On bandwidth-bound benchmarks, an improvement in cache misses translates to improvement in running times, although some of the improvement is eroded by the greater overhead of the space-bounded scheduler.

2. DEFINITIONS

We start with a recursive definition of nested parallel computation, and use it to define what constitutes a schedule. We will then define the parallel memory hierarchy (PMH) model—a machine model that reasonably accurately represents shared memory parallel machines with deep memory hierarchies. This terminology will be used later to define schedulers for the PMH model.

Computation Model, Tasks and Strands. We consider computations with nested parallelism, allowing arbitrary dynamic nesting of fork-join constructs including parallel loops, but no other synchronizations. This corresponds to the class of algorithms with series-parallel dependence graphs (see Fig. 2(left)).

Nested parallel computations can be decomposed into "tasks", "parallel blocks" and "strands" recursively as follows. As a base case, a **strand** is a serial sequence of instructions not containing any parallel constructs or subtasks. A **task** is formed by serially composing $k \geq 1$ strands interleaved with $(k-1)$ "parallel blocks", denoted by $\mathsf{t} = \ell_1; \mathsf{b}_1; \ldots; \ell_k$. A **parallel block** is formed by composing in parallel one or more tasks with a fork point before all of them and a join point after (denoted by $\mathsf{b} = \mathsf{t}_1 \| \mathsf{t}_2 \| \ldots \| \mathsf{t}_k$). A parallel block can be, for example, a parallel loop or some constant number of recursive calls. The top-level computation is a task. We use the notation $\mathsf{L}(\mathsf{t})$ to indicate all strands that are recursively included in a task.

Our computation model assumes all strands share a single memory address space. We say two strands are **concurrent** if they are not ordered in the dependence graph. Concurrent reads (*i.e.*, concurrent strands reading the same memory location) are permitted, but not data races (*i.e.*, concurrent

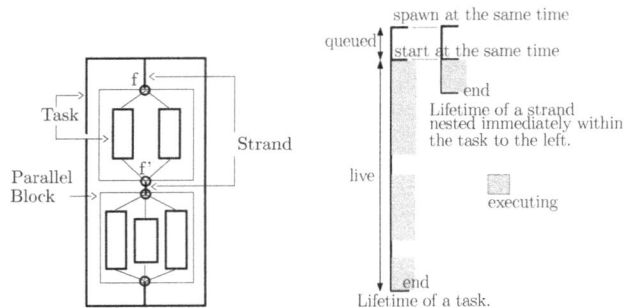

Figure 2: (left) **Decomposing the computation: tasks, strands and parallel blocks.** f, f' **are corresponding fork and join points.** (right) **Timeline of a task and its first strand, showing the difference between being** *live* **and execution.**

strands that read or write the same location with at least one write). For every strand ℓ, there exists a task $\mathsf{t}(\ell)$ such that ℓ is nested immediately inside $\mathsf{t}(\ell)$. We call this the **task of strand** ℓ.

Schedule. We now define what constitutes a valid schedule for a nested parallel computation on a machine. These definitions will enable us to precisely define space-bounded schedulers later on. We restrict ourselves to non-preemptive schedulers—schedulers that cannot migrate strands across cores once they begin executing. Both work-stealing and space-bounded schedulers are non-premptive. We use P to denote the set of cores on the machine, and L to denote the set of strands in the computation. A non-preemptive schedule defines three functions for each strand ℓ.

- **Start time:** $start : \mathsf{L} \to \mathbb{Z}$, where $start(\ell)$ denotes the time the first instruction of ℓ begins executing;

- **End time:** $end : \mathsf{L} \to \mathbb{Z}$, where $end(\ell)$ denotes the (post-facto) time the last instruction of ℓ finishes; and

- **Location:** $proc : \mathsf{L} \to P$, where $proc(\ell)$ denotes the core on which the strand is executed. Note that $proc$ is well defined because of the non-preemptive policy for strands.

We say that a strand ℓ is **live** at any time τ with $start(\ell) \leq \tau < end(\ell)$.

A non-preemptive schedule must also obey the following constraints on the ordering of strands and timing:

- (*ordering*): For any strand ℓ_1 ordered by the fork-join dependence graph before ℓ_2: $end(\ell_1) \leq start(\ell_2)$.

- (*processing time*): For any strand ℓ, $end(\ell) = start(\ell) + \gamma_{\langle \text{schedule}, \text{machine} \rangle}(\ell)$. Here γ denotes the processing time of the strand, which may vary depending on the specifics of the machine and the history of the schedule. The schedule alone does not control this value.

- (*non-preemptive execution*): No two strands may be live on the same core at the same time, i.e., $\ell_1 \neq \ell_2, proc(\ell_1) = proc(\ell_2) \implies [start(\ell_1), end(\ell_1)) \cap [start(\ell_2), end(\ell_2)) = \emptyset$.

We extend the same notation and terminology to tasks. The start time $start(\mathsf{t})$ of a task t is a shorthand for $start(\mathsf{t}) = start(\ell_s)$, where ℓ_s is the first strand in t. Similarly $end(\mathsf{t})$ denotes the end time of the last strand in t. The function $proc$, however, is undefined for tasks as a task's contained strands may execute on different cores.

When discussing specific schedulers, it is convenient to consider the time a task or strand first becomes available to execute. We use the term *spawn time* to refer to this time, which is the instant at which the preceding fork or join finishes. Naturally, the spawn time is no later than the start time, but a schedule may choose not to execute the task or strand immediately. We say that the task or strand is *queued* during the time between its spawn time and start time and *live* during the time between its start time and end time. Fig. 2(right) illustrates the spawn, start and end times of a task and its initial strand. The task and initial strand are spawned and start at the same time by definition. The strand is continuously executed until it ends, while a task goes through several phases of execution and idling before it ends.

Machine Model: Parallel Memory Hierarchy (PMH). Following prior work addressing multi-level parallel hierarchies [2, 12, 4, 13, 31, 9, 14, 6], we model parallel machines using a tree-of-caches abstraction. For concreteness, we use a symmetric variant of the parallel memory hierarchy (PMH) model [2] (see Fig. 1(b)), which is consistent with many other models [4, 9, 12, 13, 14]. A PMH consists of a height-h tree of memory units, called *caches*. The leaves of the tree are at level-0 and any internal node has level one greater than its children. The leaves (level-0 nodes) are cores, and the level-h root corresponds to an infinitely large main memory. As described in [6] each level in the tree is parameterized by four parameters: the size of the cache M_i at level i, the block size B_i used to transfer to the next higher level, the cost of a cache miss C_i which represents the combined costs of latency and bandwidth, and the fanout f_i (number of level $i-1$ caches below it).

3. EXPERIMENTAL FRAMEWORK

We implemented a C++ based framework with the following design objectives in which nested parallel programs and schedulers can be built for shared memory multicore machines. The implementation, along with a few schedulers and algorithms, is available on the web page http://www.cs.cmu.edu/~hsimhadr/sched-exp. Some of the code for the threadpool module has been adapted from an earlier implementation of threadpool [20].

Modularity: The framework separates the specification of three components—programs, schedulers, and description of machine parameters—for portability and fairness. The user can choose any of the candidates from these three categories. Note, however, some schedulers may not be able to execute programs without scheduler-specific hints (such as space annotations).

Clean Interface: The interface for specifying the components should be clean, composable, and the specification built on the interface should be easy to reason about.

Hint Passing: While it is important to separate program and schedulers, it is useful to allow the program to pass hints (extra annotations on tasks) to the scheduler to guide its decisions.

Minimal Overhead: The framework itself should be lightweight with minimal system calls, locking and code complexity. The control flow should pass between the functional modules (program, scheduler) with negligible time spent outside. The framework should avoid generating background memory traffic and interrupts.

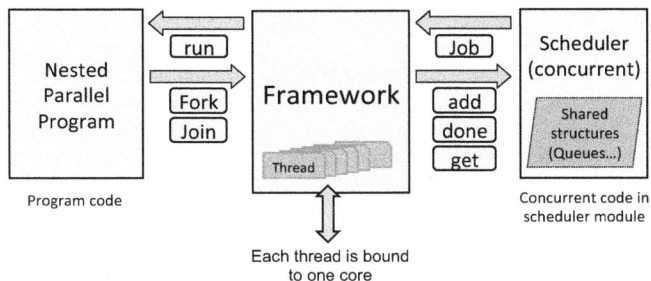

Figure 3: Interface for the program and scheduling modules.

Timing and Measurement: It should enable fine-grained measurements of the various modules. Measurements include not only clock time, but also insightful hardware counters such as cache and memory traffic statistics. In light of the earlier objective, the framework should avoid OS system calls for these, and should use direct assembly instructions.

3.1 Interface

The framework has separate interfaces for the program and the scheduler.

Programs: Nested parallel programs, with no other synchronization primitives, are composed from tasks using `fork` and `join` constructs. A `parallel_for` primitive built with `fork` and `join` is also provided. Tasks are implemented as instances of classes that inherit from the `Job` class. Different kinds of tasks are specified as classes with a method that specifies the code to be executed. An instance of a class derived from `Job` is a task containing a pointer to a strand nested immediately within the task. The control flow of this function is sequential with a terminal `fork` or `join` call. (This interface could be readily extended to handle non-nested parallel constructs such as futures [30] by adding other primitives to the interface beyond `fork` and `join`.)

The interface allows extra annotations on a task such as its size, which is required by space-bounded schedulers. Such tasks inherit a derived class of `Job` class, the extensions in the derived class specifying the annotations. For example, the class `SBJob` suited for space-bounded schedulers is derived from `Job` by adding two functions—`size(uint block_size)` and `strand_size(uint block_size)`—that allow the annotations of the job size.

Scheduler: The scheduler is a concurrent module that handles queued and live tasks (as defined in Section 2) and is responsible for maintaining its own queues and other internal shared data structures. The module interacts with the framework that consists of a thread attached to each processing core on the machine, through an interface with three call-back functions.

- `Job* get (ThreadIdType)`: This is called by the framework on behalf of a thread attached to a core when the core is ready to execute a new strand, after completing a previously live strand. The function may change the internal state of the scheduler module and return a (possibly null) `Job` so that the core may immediately begin executing the strand. This function specifies *proc* for the strand.
- `void done(Job*,ThreadIdType)` This is called when a core finishes the execution of a strand. The scheduler

is allowed to update its internal state to reflect this completion.

- void add(Job*,ThreadIdType): This is called when a fork or join is encountered. In case of a fork, this call-back is invoked once for each of the newly spawned tasks. For a join, it is invoked for the continuation task of the join. This function decides where to enqueue the job.

Other auxiliary parameters to these call-backs have been dropped from the above description for clarity and brevity. The Job* argument passed to these functions may be instances of one of the derived classes of Job* that carry additional information helpful to the scheduler. Appendix A presents an example of a work-stealing scheduler implemented in this scheduler interface.

Machine configuration: The interface for specifying machine descriptions accepts a description of the cache hierarchy: number of levels, fanout at each level, and cache and cache-line size at each level. In addition, a mapping between the logical numbering of cores on the system to their left-to-right position as a leaf in the tree of caches must be specified. For example, Fig. 4 is a description of one Nehalem-EX series 4-socket × 8-core machine (32 physical cores) with 3 levels of caches as depicted in Fig. 1(a).

3.2 Implementation

The runtime system initially fixes a POSIX thread to each core. Each thread then repeatedly performs a call (get) to the scheduler module to ask for work. Once assigned a task and a specific strand inside it, the thread completes the strand and asks for more work. Each strand either ends in a fork or a join. In either scenario, the framework invokes the done call back. For a fork, the add call-back is invoked to let the scheduler add new tasks to its data structures.

All specifics of how the scheduler operates (*e.g.*, how the scheduler handles work requests, whether it is distributed or centralized, internal data structures, where mutual exclusion occurs, etc.) are relegated to scheduler implementations. Outside the scheduling modules, the runtime system includes no locks, synchronization, or system calls (except during the initialization and cleanup of the thread pool), meeting our design objective.

3.3 Measurements

Active time and overheads: Control flow on each thread moves between the program and the scheduler modules. Fine-grained timers in the framework break down the execution time into five components: (i) active time—the time spent executing the program, (ii) add overhead, (iii) done overhead, (iv) get overhead, and (v) empty queue overhead. While active time depends on the number of instructions and the communication costs of the program, add, done and get overheads depend on the complexity of the scheduler, and the number of times the scheduler code is invoked by forks and joins. The empty queue overhead is the amount of time the scheduler fails to assign work to a thread (get returns null), and reflects on the load balancing capability of the scheduler. In most of the results in Section 5, we usually report two numbers: active time averaged over all threads and the average overhead, which includes measures (ii)–(v). Note that while we might expect this partition of time to be independent, it is not so in practice—the background coher-

```
int num_procs=32;
int num_levels = 4;
int fan_outs[4] = {4,8,1,1};
long long int sizes[4] = {0, 3*(1<<22), 1<<18, 1<<15};
int block_sizes[4] = {64,64,64,64};
int map[32] = {0,4,8,12,16,20,24,28,
               2,6,10,14,18,22,26,30,
               1,5,9,13,17,21,25,29,
               3,7,11,15,19,23,27,31};
```

Figure 4: Specification entry for a 32-core Xeon® machine depicted in Fig. 1(a).

ence traffic generated by the scheduler's bookkeeping may adversely affect active time. The timers have very little overhead in practice—less than 1% in most of our experiments.

Measuring hardware counters: Modern multicores are equipped with hardware counters that can provide various performance statistics such as the number of cache misses at various levels. Such counters, however, are somewhat challenging to use. Appendix B details the specific methodology we used for the Intel® Nehalem architecture.

4. SCHEDULERS

In this section, we will define the class of space-bounded schedulers and describe the schedulers we compare using our framework.

4.1 Space-bounded Schedulers

Space-bounded schedulers are designed to achieve good cache performance on PMHs and use the sizes of tasks and strands to choose a schedule (*start*, *end*, *proc*) mapping the hierarchy of tasks in a nested parallel program to the hierarchy of caches. They have been described previously in [14] and [6]. The definitions in [14] are not complete in that they do not specify how to handle "skip level" tasks (described below). Our earlier definition [6] handled skip level tasks, but was more restrictive than necessary, ruling out practical variants, as discussed below. Here, we provide a broader definition for the class of space-bounded schedulers that allows for practical variants, while retaining the strong analytical bounds on cache misses that are the hallmark of the class of space-bounded schedulers. Specifically, our new definition provides more flexibility in the scheduling of strands by (i) allowing each strand to have its own size, and (ii) accounting for strand sizes differently from task sizes.

Informally, a space-bounded schedule satisfies two properties: (i) *Anchored:* Each task t gets "anchored" to a smallest possible cache that is larger than its size—strands within t can only be scheduled on cores in the tree rooted at the cache; and (ii) *Bounded:* At any point in time, the sum of the sizes of all tasks and strands occupying space in a cache is at most the size of the cache. These two conditions (when formally defined) are sufficient to imply strong bounds on the number of cache misses at every level in the tree of caches. A good space-bounded scheduler would also handle load balancing subject to anchoring constraints to quickly complete execution.

More formally, a space-bounded scheduler is parameterized by a global *dilation* parameter $0 < \sigma \le 1$ and machine parameters $\{M_i, B_i, C_i, f_i\}$. We will need the following terminologies for the definition (which are both simplified and generalized from [6]).

Chowdhury et. al. [14] also suggest two other approaches to scheduling: CGC (coarse-grained contiguous) and CGC-on-SB (which combines CGC with space bounded schedulers). CGC is designed to keep nearby blocks of iterations close together so they are run on the same cache. This can be simulated in our framework by grouping iterations recursively (which is what we do). This means that our approach will not have constant critical path length for certain algorithms, but experimentally we are using a modest number of cores. CGC-on-SB is primarily a mechanism for skipping levels in the cache. Our variant of space-bounded scheduler already allows for level skipping.

Task Size and Strand Size: The size of a task (strand) is defined as a function of cache-line size B, independent of the scheduler. Let $loc(\mathsf{t}; B)$ denote the set of distinct cache lines touched by instructions within a task t. Then $S(\mathsf{t}; B) = |loc(\mathsf{t}; B)| \cdot B$ denotes the *size* of t. The size of a strand is defined in the same way. While results in [6] show that it is not necessary for the analytical bounds that strands be allowed to have their own size, we found that the flexibility it enables is an important running time optimization.[1] Note that even strands immediately nested within the same task may have different sizes.

Cluster: For any cache X_i, its *cluster* is the set of caches and cores nested below X_i. Let $P(X_i)$ denote the set of cores in X_i's cluster.

Befitting Cache: Given a particular cache hierarchy and dilation parameter $\sigma \in (0, 1]$, we say that a level-i cache *befits* a task t if $\sigma M_{i-1} < S(\mathsf{t}, B_i) \leq \sigma M_i$.

Maximal Task: We say that a task t with parent task t' is *level-i maximal* if and only if a level-i cache befits t but not t', i.e., $\sigma M_{i-1} < S(\mathsf{t}, B_i) \leq \sigma M_i < S(\mathsf{t}', B_i)$.

Anchored: A task t with strand set $\mathsf{L}(t)$ is said to be *anchored* to level-i cache X_i (or equivalently to X_i's cluster) if and only if (i) it is executed entirely in the cluster, i.e., $\{proc(\ell) | \ell \in \mathsf{L}(t)\} \subseteq P(X_i)$, and (ii) the cache befits the task. Anchoring prevents the migration of tasks to a different cluster or cache. The advantage of anchoring a task to a befitting cache is that once it loads its working set, it can reuse the working set without the risk of losing it from the cache. If a task is not anchored anywhere, for notational convenience we assume it is anchored at the root of the tree.

Cache-occupying tasks: The definition depends on whether the cache is inclusive or non-inclusive. For a level-i inclusive cache X_i and time τ, the set of *cache-occupying tasks* for a cache X_i at time τ, denoted by $\mathsf{Ot}(X_i, \tau)$, is the union of (a) the maximal tasks live at time τ that are anchored to X_i, and (b) the maximal tasks live at time τ that are anchored to any cache below X_i in the hierarchy whose immediate parents are anchored to a cache above X_i in the hierarchy. The tasks in (b) are called "skip level" tasks. For a non-inclusive cache, only type (a) tasks are included in $\mathsf{Ot}(X_i, \tau)$. Tasks in $\mathsf{Ot}(X_i, \tau)$ are the tasks that consume space in the cache at time τ. Note that we need account only for *maximal* tasks because any non-maximal task t' is anchored to the same cache as its closest enclosing maximal task t and $loc(\mathsf{t}'; B) \subseteq loc(\mathsf{t}; B)$.

Cache-occupying strands: The set of *cache-occupying strands* for a cache X_i at time τ, denoted by $\mathsf{Ol}(X_i, \tau)$, is the set of strands $\{\ell\}$ such that (a) ℓ is live at time τ (b) ℓ is executed below X_i, i.e., $proc(\ell) \in P(X_i)$, and (c) ℓ's task is anchored strictly above X_i.

A *space-bounded scheduler* for a particular cache hierarchy is a scheduler parameterized by $\sigma \in (0, 1]$ that satisfies the following two properties:

- *Anchored:* Every subtask (recursively) of the root task is anchored to a **befitting** cache.
- *Bounded:* At every time τ, for every level-i cache X_i, the sum of the sizes of cache-occupying tasks and strands is at most M_i:

$$\Sigma_{\mathsf{t} \in \mathsf{Ot}(X_i, \tau)} S(\mathsf{t}, B_i) + \Sigma_{\ell \in \mathsf{Ol}(X_i, \tau)} S(\ell, B_i) \leq M_i.$$

A key property of the definition of space-bounded schedulers in [6] is that for any PMH and any level i, one can upper bound the number of level-i cache misses incurred by executing a task on the PMH by $Q^*(\mathsf{t}; \sigma M_i, B_i)$, where Q^* is the cache complexity as defined in the Parallel Cache-Oblivious (PCO) model in [6]. Roughly speaking, the cache complexity Q^* of a task t in terms of a cache of size M and line size B is defined as follows. Decompose the task into a collection of maximal subtasks that fit in M space, and "glue nodes" – instructions outside these subtasks. For a maximal size M task t', the PCO cache complexity $Q^*(\mathsf{t}'; M; B)$ is defined to be the number of distinct cache lines it accesses, counting accesses to a cache line from unordered instructions multiple times. The model then pessimistically counts all memory instructions that fall outside of a maximal subtask (i.e., glue nodes) as cache misses. The total cache complexity of an algorithm is the sum of the complexities of the maximal subtasks, and the memory accesses outside of maximal subtasks. Note that Q^* is a *program-centric* or *machine-independent* metric, capturing the inherent locality in a parallel algorithm [7, 29].

THEOREM 1. *Consider a PMH and any dilation parameter $0 < \sigma \leq 1$. Let t be a task anchored to the root of the tree. Then the number of level-i cache misses incurred by executing t with any space-bounded scheduler is at most $Q^*(\mathsf{t}; \sigma M_i, B_i)$, where Q^* is the cache complexity as defined in the Parallel Cache-Oblivious (PCO) model in [6].*

The proof is a simple adaptation of the proof in [6] to account for our more general definition. At a high level, the argument is that for any cache X_i, the cache-occupying tasks and strands for X_i bring in their working sets into the cache X_i exactly once because the boundedness property prevents cache overflows. Thus a replacement policy that keeps these working sets in the cache until they are no longer needed will incur no additional misses; because the PMH model assumes an ideal replacement policy, it will perform at least as well.

In the course of our experimental study, we found that the following minor modification to the boundedness property of space-bounded schedulers improves their performance. Namely, we introduce a new parameter $\mu \in (0, 1]$ ($\mu = 0.2$ in our experiments) and modify the boundedness property to be such that at every time τ, for every level-i cache X_i:

$$\Sigma_{\mathsf{t} \in \mathsf{Ot}(X_i, \tau)} S(\mathsf{t}, B_i) + \Sigma_{\ell \in \mathsf{Ol}(X_i, \tau)} \min\{\mu M_i, S(\ell, B_i)\} \leq M_i,$$

The minimum term with μM_i is to allow several large strands to be explored simultaneously without their space measure

---

[1] On the other hand, it does require additional size information on programs—thus we view it as optional: Any strand whose size is not specified is assumed by default to be the size of its enclosing task.

taking too much of the space bound. This helps the scheduler to quickly traverse the higher levels of recursion in the DAG and reveal parallelism so that the scheduler can achieve better load balance.

Given this modified boundedness condition, it is easy to show that the bound in Theorem 1 becomes $Q^*(\mathbf{t}; \mu\sigma M_i, B_i)$.

Note that while setting σ to 1 yields the best bounds on cache misses, it also makes load balancing harder. As we will see later, a lower value for σ like 0.5 allows greater scheduling flexibility.

4.2 Schedulers implemented

Space-bounded schedulers: SB and SB-D. We implemented a space-bounded scheduler by constructing a tree of caches based on the specification of the target machine. Each cache is assigned one logical queue, a counter to keep track of "occupied" space and a lock to protect updates to the counter and queue. Cores can be considered to be leaves of the tree; when a scheduler call-back is issued to a thread, that thread can modify an internal node of the tree after gathering all locks on the path to the node from the core it is mapped onto. This scheduler accepts Jobs which are annotated with task and strand sizes. When a new Job is spawned at a fork, the add call-back enqueues it at the cluster where its parent was anchored. For a new Job spawned at a join, add enqueues it at the cluster where the Job that called the corresponding fork of this join was anchored.

A basic version of such a scheduler would implement logical queues at each cache as one queue. However, this presents two problems: (i) It is difficult to separate tasks in queues by the level of cache that befits it, and (ii) a single queue might be a contention hotspot. To solve problem (i), behind each logical queue, we use separate "buckets" for each level of cache below to hold tasks that befit those levels. Cores looking for a task at a cache go through these buckets from the top (heaviest tasks) to bottom. We refer to this variant as the **SB** scheduler. To solve problem (ii) involving queueing hotspots, we replace the top bucket with a distributed queue—one queue for each child cache—like in the work-stealing scheduler. We refer to the **SB** scheduler with this modification as the **SB-D** scheduler.

Work-Stealing scheduler: WS. A basic work-stealing scheduler based on Cilk++ [11] is implemented and is referred to as the **WS** scheduler. Since the Cilk++ runtime system is built around work-stealing and deeply integrated and optimized exclusively for it, we focus our comparison on the **WS** implementation in our framework for fairness and to allow us to implement variants. The head-to-head micro-benchmark study in Section 5 between our **WS** implementation and Cilk^{TM} Plus (the commercial version of Cilk++) suggests that, for these benchmarks, **WS** well-represents the performance of Cilk++'s work-stealing. We associate a double-ended queue (dequeue) of ready tasks with each core. The function add enqueues new tasks (or strands) spawned on a core to the bottom of its dequeue. When in need of work, the core uses get to remove a task from the bottom of its dequeue. If its dequeue is empty, it chooses another dequeue uniformly at random, and *steals* the work by removing a task from the *top* of that core's dequeue. The only contention in this type of scheduler is on the distributed dequeues—there is no other centralized data structure.

To implement the dequeues, we employed a simple two-locks-per-dequeue approach, one associated with the owning core, and the second associated with all cores currently attempting to steal. Remote cores need to obtain the second lock before they attempt to lock the first. Contention is thus minimized for the common case where the core needs to obtain only the first lock before it asks for work from its own dequeue.

Priority Work-Stealing scheduler: PWS. Unlike in the basic **WS** scheduler, cores in the **PWS** scheduler [27] choose victims of their steals according to the "closeness" of the victims in the socket layout. Dequeues at cores that are closer in the cache hierarchy are chosen with a higher probability than those that are farther away to improve scheduling locality while retaining the load balancing properties of **WS** scheduler. On our 4 socket machines, we set the probability of an intra-socket steal to be 10 times that of an inter-socket steal.

5. EXPERIMENTS

The goal of our experimental study is to compare the performance of the four schedulers on a range of benchmarks, varying the available memory bandwidth. Our primary metrics are runtime and L3 (last level) cache misses. We have found that the cache misses on other levels do not vary significantly among the schedulers (within 5%). We will also validate our work-stealing implementation via a comparison with the commercial Cilk^{TM} Plus scheduler. Finally, we will quantify the overheads for space-bounded schedulers and study the performance impact of the key parameter σ for space-bounded schedulers.

5.1 Benchmarks

We use seven benchmarks in our study. The first two are synthetic micro-benchmarks that mimic the behavior of memory-intensive divide-and-conquer algorithms. Because of their simplicity, we use these benchmarks to closely analyze the behavior of the schedulers under various conditions and verify that we get the expected cache behavior on a real machine. The remaining five benchmarks are a set of popular algorithmic kernels.

Recursive repeated map (RRM): This benchmark takes two n-length arrays A and B and a point-wise map function that maps elements of A to B. In our experiments each element of the arrays is a double and the function simply adds one. RRM first does a parallel point-wise map from A to B, and repeats the same operation multiple times. It then divides A and B into two by some ratio (e.g., 50/50) and recursively calls the same operation on each of the two parts. The base case of the recursion is set to some constant at which point the recursion terminates. The input parameters are the size of the arrays n, number of repeats r, the cut ratio f, and the base-case size. We set $r = 3$ (the number of repeats in quicksort), and $f = 50\%$ in the experiments unless mentioned otherwise. RRM is a memory intensive benchmark because there is very little work done per memory operation. However, once a recursive call fits in a cache (i.e., the cache size is at least $16n$ bytes for subproblem size n), all remaining accesses are cache hits.

Recursive repeated gather (RRG): This benchmark is similar to RRM but instead of doing a simple map it does a gather. In particular at any given level of the recursion it takes three n-length arrays A, B and I and for each location i sets $B[i] = A[I[i] \mod n]$. The values in I are random integers. As with RRM after repeating r times it splits the arrays in two and repeats on each part. RRG is even more memory intensive than RRM because its accesses are random instead of linear. Again, however, once a recursive call fits in a cache all remaining accesses are cache hits.

Quicksort: This is a parallel quicksort algorithm that both parallelizes the partitioning and the recursive calls, using a median-of-3 pivot selection strategy. It switches to a version which parallelizes only the recursive calls for $n < 128K$ and a serial version for $n < 16K$. These parameters worked well for all the schedulers. We note that our quicksort is about 2x faster than the Cilk code found in the Cilk+ guide [22]. This is because it does the partitioning in parallel. It is also the case that the divide does not exactly partition the data evenly, because it depends on how well the pivot divides the data. For an input of size n the program has cache complexity $Q^*(n; M, B) = O(\lceil n/B \rceil \log_2(n/M))$ and therefore is reasonably memory intensive.

Samplesort: This is cache-optimal parallel Sample Sort algorithm described in [9]. The algorithm splits the input of size n into $\sqrt{n}$ subarrays, recursively sorts each subarray, "block transposes" them into $\sqrt{n}$ buckets and recursively sorts these buckets. For this algorithm, $Q^*(n; M, B) = O(\lceil n/B \rceil \log_{2+(M/B)} n/B)$ making it relatively cache friendly, and optimally cache oblivious even.

Aware samplesort: This is a variant of sample-sort that is aware of the cache sizes. In particular it moves elements into buckets that fit into the L3 cache and then runs quicksort on the buckets. This is the fastest sort we implemented and is in fact faster than any other sort we found for this machine. In particular it is about 10% faster than the PBBS sample sort [28].

Quad-tree: This generates a quad tree for a set of n points in two dimensions. This is implemented by recursively partitioning the points into four sets along the mid line of each of two dimensions. When the number of points is less than 16K we revert to a sequential algorithm.

Matrix multiplication: This benchmark is an 8-way recursive matrix multiplication. To allow for an in-place implementation, four of the recursive calls are invoked in parallel followed by the other four. Matrix multiplication has cache complexity $Q^*(n; M, B) = (\lceil n^2/B \rceil \times \lceil n/\sqrt{M} \rceil)$. The ratio of instructions to cache misses is therefore very high, about $B\sqrt{M}$, making this is a very compute-intensive benchmark. We switch to serial Intel® Math Kernel Library's `cblas_dgemm` matrix multiplication for sizes of $\leq 128 \times 128$ to make use of the floating point SIMD operations.

5.2 Experimental Setup

The benchmarks were run on a 4-socket 32-core Xeon® 7560 machine (Nehalem-EX architecture), as described in Fig. 1(a) and Fig. 4, using each of the four schedulers. Each core uses 2-way hyperthreading. The last level cache on each socket is a 24MB L3 cache that is shared by eight cores. Each of the four sockets on the machine has memory links to distinct DRAM modules. The sockets are connected with the Intel® QPI interconnect. Memory requests from a socket to a DRAM module connected to another socket pass through the QPI, the remote socket, and the remote memory link. To prevent excessive TLB cache misses, we use Linux hugepages of size 2MB to pre-allocate the space required by the algorithms. We configured the system to have a pool of 10,000

huge pages by setting `vm.nr_hugepages` to that value using `sysctl`. We used the `hugectl` tool to execute memory allocations with hugepages.

Monitoring L3 cache. We focus on L3 cache misses, the most expensive cache level before DRAM on our machine. While we will report runtime subdivided into application code and scheduler code, such partitioning was not possible for L3 misses because of software limitations. Even if it were possible to count them separately, it would be difficult to interpret the results because of the non-trivial interference between the data cached by the program and by the scheduler. Further details can be found in Appendix B.

Controlling bandwidth. As part of our study, we will quantify runtime improvements varying the available memory bandwidth per core (the "bandwidth gap"). We control the memory bandwidth available to the program as follows. Because the QPI has high bandwidth, if we treat the RAM as a single functional module, the bandwidth between the L3 and the RAM depends on the number of memory links used, which in turn depends on the mapping of pages to DRAM modules. If all the pages used by a program are mapped to DRAM modules connected to one socket, the program effectively utilizes one-fourth of the memory bandwidth. On the other hand, an even distribution of pages to DRAM modules across the sockets provides the full bandwidth to the program. The `numactl` tool can be used to control this mapping.

Code. We use the same code for the applications/algorithms for all benchmarks, except for the CilkPlus code, which we kept as close as possible. The code always includes the space annotations, but those annotations are ignored by the schedulers that do not need them. The code was compiled with a CilkPlus fork of `gcc 4.8.0` compiler.

5.3 Results

We use $\sigma = 0.5$ and $\mu = 0.2$ in the **SB** and **SB-D** schedulers, after some experimentation with the parameters, unless otherwise noted. All numbers reported in this paper are the average of at least 10 runs with the smallest and largest readings across runs removed. The results are not sensitive to this particular choice of reporting.

Synthetic benchmarks. Fig. 5 and Fig. 6 show the number of L3 cache misses of RRM and RRG, respectively, along with their active times and scheduling overheads on 64 hyperthreads at different bandwidth values. In addition to the four schedulers discussed in Section 4.2 (**WS**, **PWS**, **SB** and **SB-D**), we include the CilkPlus work-stealing scheduler in these plots to validate our **WS** implementation. We could not separate overhead from time in CilkPlus because it does not supply such information.

These plots show that the space-bounded schedulers incur roughly 42–44% fewer L3 cache misses than the work-stealing schedulers. As expected, the number of L3 misses does not significantly depend on the available bandwidth. On the other hand, the active time is most influenced by the number of instructions in the benchmark (constant across schedulers) and the costs incurred by L3 misses. The extent to which improvements in L3 misses translates to an improvement in active time depends on the memory bandwidth given to the program. When the bandwidth is low (25%), the active times are almost directly proportional to

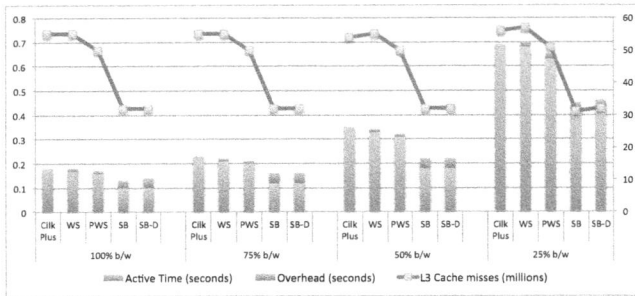

Figure 5: RRM on 10 million double elements, varying the memory bandwidth. Left axis is running time in seconds. Right axis is L3 misses in millions.

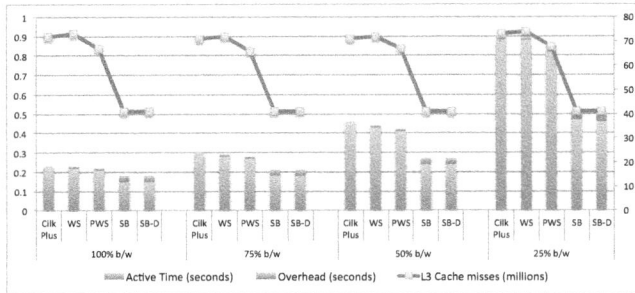

Figure 6: RRG on 10 million double elements, varying the memory bandwidth. Left axis is running time in seconds. Right axis is L3 misses in millions.

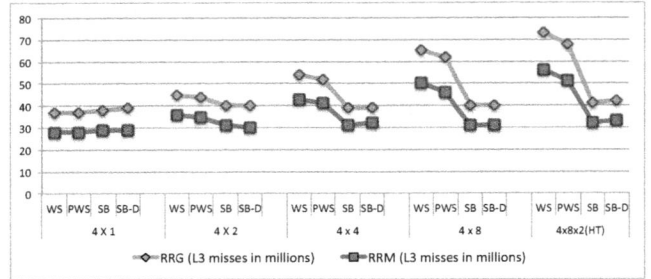

Figure 7: L3 cache misses for RRM and RRG, varying the number of cores used per socket.

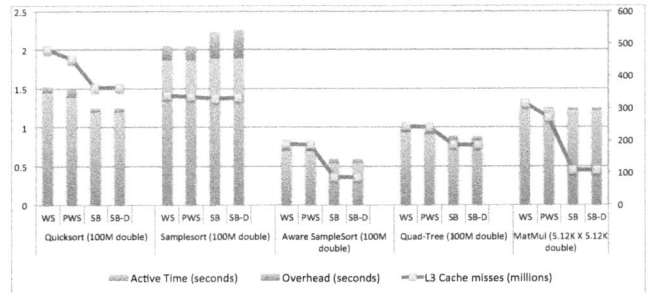

Figure 8: Active times, overheads, and L3 cache misses for the 5 benchmark algorithms at full bandwidth.

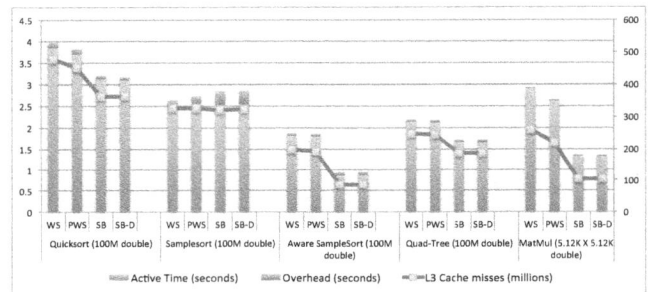

Figure 9: Active times, overheads, and L3 cache misses for the 5 benchmark algorithms at 25% bandwidth.

the number of L3 cache misses, while at full bandwidth, the active times are far less sensitive to misses.

The differences in L3 cache costs of space-bounded and work-stealing schedulers roughly corresponds to the difference between the cache complexity of the program with a cache of size σM_3 (M_3 being the size of L3) and a cache of size $M_3/16$ (because eight cores with sixteen hyperthreads share an L3 cache). In other words, space-bounded schedulers share the cache constructively while work-stealing schedulers effectively split the cache between the cores. To see this, consider our RRM benchmark. Each Map operation that does not fit in L3 touches $2 \times 10^7 \times 8 = 160$ million bytes of data, and RRM has to unfold four levels of recursion before it fits in $\sigma M_3 = 0.5 \times 24\text{MB} = 12\text{MB}$ space with space-bounded schedulers. Therefore, since the cache line size $B_3 = 64$ bytes, space-bounded schedulers incur about $(160 \times 10^6 \times 3 \times 4)/64 = 30 \times 10^6$ cache misses, which matches closely with the results in Fig. 5. On the other hand, the number of cache misses of the **WS** scheduler (55 million) corresponds to unfolding about 7 levels of recursions, three more than with space-bounded schedulers. Loosely speaking, this means that the recursion has to unravel to one-sixteenth the size of L3 before work-stealing schedulers start preserving locality.

To support this observation, we ran the RRM and RRG benchmarks varying the number of cores per socket; the results are in Fig. 7. The number of L3 cache misses when using the **SB** and **SB-D** schedulers do not change with the number of cores, because cores constructively share the L3 cache independent of their number. However, when using the **WS** and **PWS** schedulers, the number of L3 misses is highly dependent on the number of cores: when fewer cores are active on each socket, there is lesser contention for space in the shared L3 cache. Thus, again the experimental results coincide with the theoretical analysis.

These experiments indicate that the advantages of space-bounded schedulers over work-stealing schedulers improve as (i) the number of cores per socket goes up, and (ii) the bandwidth per core goes down. At 8 cores there is a 30–35% reduction in L3 cache misses. At 64 cores we would expect (by the analysis) over a 60% reduction.

Algorithms. Fig. 8 and Fig. 9 show the active times, scheduling overheads, and L3 cache misses of the five algorithmic kernels at 100% and 25% bandwidth, respectively, with 64 hyperthreads. These plots show that the space-bounded schedulers incur significantly fewer L3 cache misses on 4 of the 5 benchmarks, with up to 65% on matrix multiply. The cache-oblivious sample sort is the sole benchmark

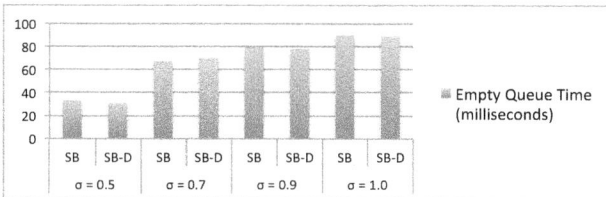

Figure 10: Empty queue times for Quad-tree.

with little difference in L3 cache misses across schedulers. Given the problem size $n = 10^8$ doubles and sample sort's $\sqrt{n}$-way recursion, all subtasks after one level of recursion are much smaller than the L3 cache. Thus, all four schedulers avoid overflowing the cache. Because of their added overhead relative to work-stealing, the space-bounded schedulers are 7% slower for this benchmark.

As with the synthetic benchmarks, the sensitivity of active time to L3 cache misses depends on whether the algorithm is memory-intensive enough to stress the bandwidth. Matrix Multiplication, although benefitting from space-bounded schedulers in terms of cache misses, shows no significant improvement in active time at full bandwidth because it is very compute intensive. However, when the machine bandwidth is reduced to 25%, Matrix Multiplication is bandwidth bound and the space-bounded schedulers are about 50% faster than work-stealing. The other three benchmarks—Quicksort, Aware Samplesort and Quad-tree—are memory intensive and see improvements of up to 25% in running time at full bandwidth (Fig. 8). At 25% bandwidth, the improvement is even more significant and up to 40% (Fig. 9).

Load balance and the dilation parameter σ. The choice of σ, determining which tasks are maximal, is an important parameter affecting the performance of space-bounded schedulers, especially their ability to load balance. If σ were set to 1, it is likely that one task that is about the size of the cache gets anchored to the cache, leaving little room for other tasks or strands. This adversely affects load balance, and we would expect to see greater empty queue times. On the other hand, if σ were set to a lower value like 0.5, then each cache can allow more than one task or strand to be simultaneously anchored, leading to better load balance. Fig. 10 gives an example algorithm (Quad-tree) demonstrating this. If σ is too low (closer to 0), then the number of levels of recursion until the space-bounded schedulers preserve locality would increase, resulting in less effective use of shared caches.

Comparison of scheduler variants. Looking at the results, we find that while **PWS** can reduce the number of cache misses by up to 10% compared to standard **WS**, it has negligible impact on running times for the benchmarks studied. Similarly, while **SB-D** is designed to remove a serial bottleneck in the **SB** scheduler, the runtime (and cache miss) performance of the two are nearly identical. This is because our benchmarks call the scheduler sufficiently infrequently so that the performance difference of each invocation is not noticeable in the overall running time.

6. CONCLUSION

We developed a framework for comparing schedulers, and deployed it on a 32-core machine with 3 levels of caches. We used it to compare four schedulers, two each of work-stealing and space-bounded types. As predicted by theory, we did notice that space-bounded schedulers demonstrate some, or even significant, improvement over work-stealing schedulers in terms of cache miss counts on shared caches for most benchmarks. In memory-intensive benchmarks with low instruction count to cache miss count ratios, an improvement in L3 miss count because of space-bounded schedulers can improve running time, despite their added overheads. On the other hand, for compute-intensive benchmarks or benchmarks with highly optimized cache complexities, work-stealing schedulers are slightly faster, because of their low scheduling overhead. Improving the overhead of space-bounded schedulers further could make the case for space-bounded schedulers stronger and is an important direction for future work.

Our experiments were run on an Intel® multicore with (only) 8 cores per socket, 32 cores total, and one level of shared cache (the L3). The experiments make it clear that as the core count per socket goes up (as is expected with each new generation), the advantages of space-bounded schedulers should increase due to the increased benefit of avoiding cache conflicts among the many unrelated threads sharing the limited on-chip cache capacity. As the core count per socket goes up, the available bandwidth per core decreases, again increasing space-bounded schedulers' advantage. We also anticipate a greater advantage for space-bounded schedulers over work-stealing schedulers when more cache levels are shared and when the caches are shared amongst a greater number of cores. Such studies are left to future work, when such multicores become available. On the other hand, compute-intensive benchmarks will likely continue to benefit from the lower scheduling overheads of work-stealing schedulers, for the next few generations of multicores, if not longer.

Acknowledgements

This work is supported in part by the National Science Foundation under grant numbers CCF-1018188, CCF-1314633, CCF-1314590, the Intel Science and Technology Center for Cloud Computing (ISTC-CC), the Department of Energy under the Dynamic Exascale Global Address Space (DE-GAS) programming environments project, and a Facebook Graduate Fellowship.

7. REFERENCES

[1] U. A. Acar, G. E. Blelloch, and R. D. Blumofe. The data locality of work stealing. *Theory Comp. Sys.*, 35(3), 2002.

[2] B. Alpern, L. Carter, and J. Ferrante. Modeling parallel computers as memory hierarchies. In *Programming Models for Massively Parallel Computers*, 1993.

[3] G. E. Blelloch. Programming parallel algorithms. *Communications of the ACM*, 39(3), 1996.

[4] G. E. Blelloch, R. A. Chowdhury, P. B. Gibbons, V. Ramachandran, S. Chen, and M. Kozuch. Provably good multicore cache performance for divide-and-conquer algorithms. In *SODA*, 2008.

[5] G. E. Blelloch, J. T. Fineman, P. B. Gibbons, and J. Shun. Internally deterministic parallel algorithms can be fast. In *PPoPP*, 2012.

[6] G. E. Blelloch, J. T. Fineman, P. B. Gibbons, and H. V. Simhadri. Scheduling irregular parallel computations on hierarchical caches. In *SPAA*, 2011.

[7] G. E. Blelloch, J. T. Fineman, P. B. Gibbons, and H. V. Simhadri. Program-centric cost models for locality. In *MSPC*, 2013.

[8] G. E. Blelloch, P. B. Gibbons, and Y. Matias. Provably efficient scheduling for languages with fine-grained parallelism. *JACM*, 46(2), 1999.

[9] G. E. Blelloch, P. B. Gibbons, and H. V. Simhadri. Low-depth cache oblivious algorithms. In *SPAA*, 2010.

[10] R. D. Blumofe, M. Frigo, C. F. Joerg, C. E. Leiserson, and K. H. Randall. An analysis of dag-consistent distributed shared-memory algorithms. In *SPAA*, 1996.

[11] R. D. Blumofe and C. E. Leiserson. Scheduling multithreaded computations by work stealing. *JACM*, 46(5), 1999.

[12] R. A. Chowdhury and V. Ramachandran. The cache-oblivious gaussian elimination paradigm: theoretical framework, parallelization and experimental evaluation. In *SPAA*, 2007.

[13] R. A. Chowdhury and V. Ramachandran. Cache-efficient dynamic programming algorithms for multicores. In *SPAA*, 2008.

[14] R. A. Chowdhury, F. Silvestri, B. Blakeley, and V. Ramachandran. Oblivious algorithms for multicores and network of processors. In *IPDPS*, 2010.

[15] R. Cole and V. Ramachandran. Efficient resource oblivious algorithms for multicores. *Arxiv preprint arXiv.11034071*, 2011.

[16] K. Fatahalian, D. R. Horn, T. J. Knight, L. Leem, M. Houston, J. Y. Park, M. Erez, M. Ren, A. Aiken, W. J. Dally, et al. Sequoia: Programming the memory hierarchy. In *Supercomputing*, 2006.

[17] Intel. Intel Cilk++ SDK programmer's guide. https://www.clear.rice.edu/comp422/resources/Intel_Cilk++_Programmers_Guide.pdf, 2009.

[18] Intel. Intel Thread Building Blocks reference manual. http://software.intel.com/sites/products/documentation/doclib/tbb_sa/help/index.htm\#reference/reference.htm, 2013. Version 4.1.

[19] Intel. Performance counter monitor (PCM). http://www.intel.com/software/pcm, 2013. Version 2.4.

[20] R. Kriemann. Implementation and usage of a thread pool based on posix threads. www.hlnum.org/english/projects/tools/threadpool/doc.html, 2004.

[21] D. Lea. A java fork/join framework. In *ACM Java Grande*, 2000.

[22] C. Leiserson. The Cilk++ concurrency platform. *J. Supercomputing*, 51, 2010.

[23] Microsoft. Task Parallel Library. http://msdn.microsoft.com/en-us/library/dd460717.aspx, 2013. .NET version 4.5.

[24] G. J. Narlikar. Scheduling threads for low space requirement and good locality. In *SPAA*, 1999.

[25] OpenMP Architecture Review Board. OpenMP API. http://www.openmp.org/mp-documents/spec30.pdf, May 2008. v 3.0.

[26] Perfmon2. libpfm. http://perfmon2.sourceforge.net/, 2012.

[27] J.-N. Quintin and F. Wagner. Hierarchical work-stealing. In *EuroPar*, 2010.

[28] J. Shun, G. E. Blelloch, J. T. Fineman, P. B. Gibbons, A. Kyrola, H. V. Simhadri, and K. Tangwongsan. Brief announcement: the problem based benchmark suite. In *SPAA*, 2012.

[29] H. V. Simhadri. *Program-Centric Cost Models for Locality and Parallelism*. PhD thesis, CMU, 2013.

[30] D. Spoonhower, G. E. Blelloch, P. B. Gibbons, and R. Harper. Beyond nested parallelism: tight bounds on work-stealing overheads for parallel futures. In *SPAA*, 2009.

[31] L. G. Valiant. A bridging model for multi-core computing. In *ESA*, 2008.

APPENDIX

A. WORK STEALING SCHEDULER

Fig. 11 provides an example of a work-stealing scheduler implemented using the scheduler interface presented in Section 3.1. The Job* argument passed to the **add** and **done** functions may be instances of one of the derived classes of Job* that carry additional information helpful to the scheduler.

```
void WS_Scheduler::add (Job *job, int thread_id) {
  _local_lock[thread_id].lock();
  _job_queues[thread_id].push_back(job);
  _local_lock[thread_id].unlock();
}
int
WS_Scheduler::steal_choice (int thread_id) {
  return (int)((((double)rand())/((double)RAND_MAX))
            *_num_threads);
}
Job* WS_Scheduler::get (int thread_id) {
  _local_lock[thread_id].lock();
  if (_job_queues[thread_id].size() > 0) {
    Job * ret = _job_queues[thread_id].back();
    _job_queues[thread_id].pop_back();
    _local_lock[thread_id].unlock();
    return ret;
  } else {
    _local_lock[thread_id].unlock();
    int choice = steal_choice(thread_id);
    _steal_lock[choice].lock();
    _local_lock[choice].lock();
    if (_job_queues[choice].size() > 0) {
      Job * ret = _job_queues[choice].front();
      _job_queues[choice].erase(_job_queues[choice].begin());
      ++_num_steals[thread_id];
      _local_lock[choice].unlock();
      _steal_lock[choice].unlock();
      return ret;
    }
    _local_lock[choice].unlock();
    _steal_lock[choice].unlock();
  }
  return NULL;
}
void WS_Scheduler::done (Job *job, int thread_id,
                bool deactivate) {}
```

Figure 11: WS scheduler implemented in scheduler interface

B. MEASURING HARDWARE COUNTERS

Multicore processors based on newer architectures like Intel® Nehalem-EX and Sandybridge contain numerous functional components such as cores (which includes the CPU and lower level caches), DRAM controllers, bridges to the inter-socket interconnect (QPI) and higher level cache units (L3). Each component is provided with a performance monitoring unit (PMU)—a collection of hardware registers that can track statistics of events relevant to the component.

For instance, while the core PMU on Xeon® 7500 series (our experimental setup, see Fig. 1(a)) is capable of providing statistics such as the number of instructions, L1 and L2 cache hit/miss statistics, and traffic going in and out, it is unable to monitor L3 cache misses (which constitute a significant portion of active time). This is because L3 cache is a separate unit with its own PMU(s). In fact, each Xeon® 7560 die has eight L3 cache banks on a bus that also connects DRAM and QPI controllers (see Fig. 12). Each L3 bank is connected to a core via buffered queues. The address space is hashed onto the L3 banks so that a unique bank is responsible for each address. To collect L3 statistics such as L3 misses, we monitor PMUs (called C-Boxes on Nehalem-EX) on all L3 banks and aggregate the numbers in our results.

Software access to core PMUs on most Intel® architectures is well supported by several tools including the Linux kernel, the Linux perf tool, and higher level APIs such as libpfm [26]. We use the libpfm library to provide fine-grained access to the core PMU. However, access to *uncore* PMUs—complex architecture-specific components like the C-Box—is not supported by most tools. Newer Linux kernels (3.7+) are incrementally adding software interfaces to these PMUs at the time of this writing, but we are only able to make program-wide measurements using this interface rather than fine-grained measurements. For accessing uncore counters, we adapt the Intel® PCM 2.4 tool [19].

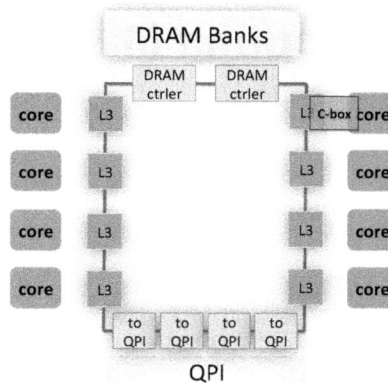

Figure 12: Layout of 8 cores and L3 cache banks on a bidirectional ring in Xeon® 7560. Each L3 bank hosts a performance monitoring unit called C-box that measures traffic into and out of the L3 bank.

To count L3 cache misses, the uncore counters in the C-boxes were programmed using the Intel® PCM tool to count misses that occur due to any reason (LLC_MISSES - event code: 0x14, umask: 0b111) and L3 cache fills in any coherence state (LLC_S_FILLS - event code: 0x16, umask: 0b1111). Both the numbers concur up to three significant digits in most cases. Therefore, only the L3 cache miss numbers are reported in this paper.

On Computing Maximal Independent Sets of Hypergraphs in Parallel

Ioana O. Bercea
Department of Computer
Science
University of Maryland
College Park, MD, USA
ioana@cs.umd.edu

Navin Goyal
Microsoft Research India
Bangalore, India
navingo@microsoft.com

David G. Harris
Department of Applied
Mathematics
University of Maryland
College Park, MD, USA
davidgharris29@hotmail.com

Aravind Srinivasan
Department of Computer
Science and UMIACS
University of Maryland
College Park, MD, USA
srin@cs.umd.edu

ABSTRACT

Whether or not the problem of finding maximal independent sets (MIS) in hypergraphs is in *(R)NC* is one of the fundamental problems in the theory of parallel computing. Unlike the well-understood case of MIS in graphs, for the hypergraph problem, our knowledge is quite limited despite considerable work. It is known that the problem is in *RNC* when the edges of the hypergraph have constant size. For general hypergraphs with n vertices and m edges, the fastest previously known algorithm works in time $O(\sqrt{n})$ with poly(m, n) processors. In this paper we give an EREW PRAM algorithm that works in time $n^{o(1)}$ with poly(m, n) processors on general hypergraphs satisfying $m \leq n^{\frac{\log^{(2)} n}{8(\log^{(3)} n)^2}}$ where $\log^{(2)} n = \log \log n$ and $\log^{(3)} n = \log \log \log n$. Our algorithm is based on a sampling idea that reduces the dimension of the hypergraph and employs the algorithm for constant dimension hypergraphs as a subroutine.

Categories and Subject Descriptors

G.2.2 [**Discrete Mathematics**]: Hypergraphs—*Independent Sets*; F.1.2 [**Computation by Abstract Devices**]: Parallelism and concurrency; F.2.2 [**Analysis of Algorithms and Problem Complexity**]: Computations on discrete structures; G.1.0 [**Numerical Analysis**]: Parallel algorithms

Keywords

hypergraphs; independent sets;randomized algorithms; parallel algorithms

SPAA'14, June 23–25, 2014, Prague, Czech Republic.
Copyright 2014 ACM 978-1-4503-2821-0/14/06.
http://dx.doi.org/10.1145/2612669.2612670 ...$15.00.

1. INTRODUCTION

Fast parallel algorithms for constructing maximal independent sets (MIS) in graphs are well studied and very efficient algorithms are now known (see, e.g., [3] for a brief survey). These algorithms serve as a primitive in numerous applications. The more general problem of fast parallel MIS in hypergraphs is also well studied but is not so well understood. Let us first formally state the problem before describing what is known about it.

A *hypergraph* $H = (V, E)$ is a set of vertices V and a collection of edges $e \in E$ such that $e \subseteq V$. The *dimension* of a hypergraph is the maximum edge size. Let n be the number of vertices, m the number of edges and d the dimension of the hypergraph. A subset of vertices of H is called *independent* in H if it contains no edge. We call an independent set *maximal* if it is not contained in a larger independent set. Karp and Ramachandran [3] asked whether the problem of finding an MIS in hypergraphs is in NC. While the general problem remains open, progress has been made on some special classes of hypergraphs. We now briefly survey some of the previous work; further references can be found in the papers mentioned below.

In a seminal paper, Beame and Luby [2] gave an algorithm (called the BL algorithm henceforth) and showed that the problem is in RNC for hypergraphs with edges of size at most 3 ([2] claimed that their algorithm was in RNC for all constant dimension hypergraphs; this however turned out to be erroneous). This algorithm is similar to some of the MIS algorithms for graphs and is based on independently marking vertices and unmarking if all vertices in an edge get marked. Kelsen [5] extended the analysis of the BL algorithm to hypergraphs with constant dimension (the dimension can actually be super-constant; we state the precise bound later in the paper where we use this fact). Luczak and Szymanska [7] showed that the problem is in RNC for linear hypergraphs (linear hypergraphs satisfy $|e \cap e'| \leq 1$ for all distinct edges e, e'). Beame and Luby [2] also gave another appealing algorithm based on random permutations which they conjectured to work in RNC for the general problem. Shachnai and Srinivasan [9] made progress towards the analysis of this algorithm. For general hypergraphs, Karp, Upfal and Wigderson [4] gave an algorithm with running time $O(\sqrt{n})$ and poly(m, n) processors (their algorithm actually works in a harder model of computation where the hypergraph is accessible only via an oracle, but it can be adapted to run in time $O(\sqrt{n}) \cdot (\log n + \log m)$ with high probability on mn processors).

Our contribution.

We give a parallel algorithm that we call the SBL (*sampling* BL) algorithm. The algorithm works on hypergraphs that do not have too many edges but no other restrictions and works in time $O(n^{o(1)})$. This is the first parallel algorithm that works on general hypergraphs with a relatively weak restriction on the cardinality of the edge set and a running time of $o(\sqrt{n})$.

More precisely,

THEOREM 1. *The* SBL *algorithm finds a maximal independent set in hypergraphs with n vertices and m edges and* $m \leq n^{\frac{\log^{(2)} n}{8(\log^{(3)} n)^2}}$. *It runs in time* $O(n^{2/\log^{(3)} n})$ *on EREW PRAM with* poly(m, n) *processors.*

The parameters above have been chosen to keep the computation in the analysis simple and there is some flexibility in their choice.

Our algorithm crucially uses BL as a subroutine. However, we need to use it on hypergraphs with slightly superconstant dimensions. Kelsen's original analysis [5] of BL is formulated for constant dimension hypergraphs. A slight modification of this analysis, specifically in the potential function used to describe progress being made in each round, allows it to be applicable without the assumption that the dimension is $O(1)$. We present this modification. We also discuss two additional improvements that can be made to Kelsen's analysis of the BL algorithm, which could be of independent interest: (1) Kelsen developed concentration inequalities for polynomials in independent random variables. Since then much stronger versions of such inequalities have become available [6, 8]. We employ one such inequality and obtain an improved upper bound which we later use in the analysis. (2) We also show that a significantly larger marking probability can be employed, without affecting the runtime negatively. Unfortunately, both of the above modifications do not lead to a significant improvement in the final running time of the algorithm. Nevertheless, we hope that this identifies the main bottlenecks in Kelsen's approach and will be useful for the future work.

Organization.

The next section is devoted to the SBL algorithm. Section 3 delves into Kelsen's analysis of the BL algorithm. We note that there is a large overlap with Kelsen's paper in Sec. 3 owing to the fact that we are mainly talking about modifications to his analysis and this requires us to restate many of his results and proofs to make the paper somewhat self-contained.

2. SBL **ALGORITHM**

We now explain the SBL algorithm which mainly uses the BL algorithm as a subroutine. Denote the input hypergraph by $H = (V, E)$. Intuitively, we can think of the BL algorithm as iteratively coloring the vertices in V red or blue; at the

end of the run of the algorithm the blue vertices will form the final MIS. The idea of our algorithm is to randomly sample a subset V' of vertices by independently marking each vertex in V with probability p (to be carefully chosen). With high probability, the hypergraph $H' = (V', E')$, where $E' = \{e \in E : e \subseteq V'\}$ is the set of edges with all vertices marked, has dimension at most d, where d is suitably small (if H' has an edge with size more than d then we declare failure and start over). We then apply the BL algorithm to H' to get a red-blue coloring of its vertices, where blue vertices form an MIS in H'. This coloring will be the permanent coloring of the vertices of H'. Going back to H, we remove the edges of H that have a red vertex as these edges cannot be all blue in any completion of the coloring of H'. For the remaining edges, we remove their blue vertices and thus get a hypergraph on $V \setminus V'$. We repeat the above process on this updated hypergraph until the number of edges becomes at most $1/p^2$. At this point we can just use the algorithm that takes time linear in the number of vertices or alternatively the Karp–Upfal–Wigderson algorithm [4] which we shall call KUW. The vertices in the MIS returned by this last call will again be colored blue, while the rest will be colored red.

Algorithm 1 SBL

Input: A hypergraph $H = (V, E)$
Output: A maximal independent set $I \subseteq V$

1: Let $p = 1/n^{\alpha}$ and $d = \frac{\log^{(2)} n}{4 \log^{(3)} n}$ where $n = |V|$ and $\alpha = 1/\log^{(3)} n$.
2: $I \leftarrow \emptyset$
3: **if** $\max_{e \in E} |e| > d$ **then**
4:    **while** $|V| \geq 1/p^2$ **do**
5:       *Invariant:* If I' is an IS in H', then $I \cup I'$ will be an IS in H.
6:       Select vertices independently at random with probability p
7:       Let V' be the collection of such selected vertices, $E' = \{e \in E : e \subseteq V'\}$ and $H' = (V', E')$.
8:       **if** $\max_{e' \in E'} |e'| > d$ **then**
9:          FAIL
10:       **else**
11:          Run $I' =$BL(H')
12:          Update $I = I \cup I'$, $V = V \setminus V'$
13:          **for all** $e \in E$ **do**
14:             **if** $e \cap (V' \setminus I') \neq \emptyset$ **then**
15:                $E \leftarrow E \setminus e$.
16:          **for all** $e \in E$ **do**
17:             $e \leftarrow e \setminus I'$.
18:    Run $I' =$ KUW(H).
19:    Update $I = I \cup I'$.
20: **else**
21:    Run $I =$BL(H).
22: Return I.

2.1 **Correctness of** SBL

We claim that in the final coloring produced by the SBL algorithm, the set of blue vertices forms an MIS in the original hypergraph H. Let H_i be the hypergraph being colored in round i, where by round we mean one iteration of the **while** loop or the last call we make either to BL or KUW. We use the fact that the set I' returned either by BL or KUW is indeed an MIS in H_i, so every violation of independence or maximality in H_i leads to a contradiction.

If the final set of blue vertices is not independent then there is some round i of SBL in which some edge e became fully blue. This means that a nonempty subset e' of e must be an edge in the hypergraph H_i, since $e \setminus e'$ is fully blue and e' is not yet colored. But now round i cannot color e' fully blue because it finds an MIS in H_i—a contradiction.

If the final set of blue vertices is not maximal, then it means that some red vertex can be recolored blue without violating independence. Let v be such a vertex and suppose that it was colored red in round i. Then in H_i, there exists a hyperedge e' such that recoloring v blue will make it fully blue which in turn would lead to some edge e in H being fully blue—a contradiction.

2.2 Analysis of SBL

We use the BL algorithm as a subroutine and use the following theorem about its performance:

THEOREM 2. *On a hypergraph with n vertices, m edges and dimension $d \leq \frac{\log^{(2)} n}{4 \log^{(3)} n}$, the BL algorithm terminates after $O((\log n)^{(d+4)!})$ time with probability at least $1 - 1/n^{\Theta(\log n \log^{(2)} n)}$. It uses $\mathrm{poly}(m, n)$ processors and can be implemented on EREW PRAM.*

The above result is essentially the same as the corresponding statement in [5] when $d = O(1)$. As mentioned before, the proof follows from a slight modification of the potential function of [5]; it appears in Section 3.1.

In the analysis of the running time below we will focus on the number of rounds of SBL algorithm. The time for each round of SBL is dominated by the time for running BL in that round. Specifically, notice that the only other call we make is to KUW(H) when the number of vertices in H is less than $1/p^2 = n^{2/\log^{(3)} n}$. In the worst case, the runtime of the algorithm is linear in the number of vertices, so we get an additional factor of $O(n^{2/\log^{(3)} n})$ in our overall runtime.

We begin by setting values of the parameters used in the algorithm:

- $p := 1/n^\alpha$,
- $m := n^\beta$,
- $\alpha := 1/\log^{(3)} n$,
- $\beta := \frac{\log^{(2)} n}{8(\log^{(3)} n)^2}$.

We will use the following form of the Chernoff bound (see, e.g., [1]).

LEMMA 1. *Let X be a random variable taking value 1 with probability $p \in [0, 1]$ and value 0 with probability $1 - p$. Then the sum $X_1 + \ldots + X_n$ of i.i.d. copies of X for $a > 0$ satisfies*

$$\Pr[(X_1 + \ldots + X_n) \leq pn - a] \leq e^{-a^2/2pn}.$$

There are three kinds of events (A, B, and C) that can happen during the execution of the SBL algorithm resulting in failure or high running time. We will show that the union of these events has small probability by upper bounding each event separately and then applying the union bound. We use $\Pr[B] \leq \Pr[A] + \Pr[B|\neg A]$ and similarly for $\Pr[C]$, resulting in the bound

$$\Pr[A \lor B \lor C] \leq 3\Pr[A] + \Pr[B|\neg A] + \Pr[C|\neg A]. \quad (1)$$

1. With high probability in each round, the fraction of vertices colored is substantial and thus the number of rounds is small.

2. The probability that a large hyperedge is ever fully marked in a round is small and thus all our applications of BL algorithm are valid.

3. The probability that a run of BL algorithm fails in some round is small.

We now prove these three claims.

(1) Denote the number of marked vertices in round i of SBL by n_i; thus $n_1 = n$, and in round i, the BL algorithm is invoked on a hypergraph with $n_i - n_{i+1}$ vertices (the set of marked vertices). Then, for each i, by Lemma 1 we have:

$$\Pr[(n_i - n_{i+1}) \leq pn_i/2] \leq e^{-pn_i/8} \leq e^{-1/(8p)}.$$

The inequality above holds because SBL algorithm maintains that $n_i \geq 1/p^2$ and so $pn_i \geq 1/p$ for all i. If the above event holds in each round, then the smallest r satisfying $(1 - p/2)^r \leq \frac{1}{p^2 n}$ is an upper bound on the number of rounds. Setting $r := \frac{2 \log n}{p}$ gives an upper bound on the number of rounds. Then the probability of the event not holding in some round becomes $\frac{2 \log n}{p} \cdot e^{-1/8p} \leq \frac{1}{n^{\log n}}$, for sufficiently large n.

(2) Conditioning on the number of rounds being upper bounded by r, the probability that an edge of size at least $d + 1$ is fully marked in some round is at most $rmp^{(d+1)}$. If we want this probability to be upper bounded by $1/n$ then we can take

$$d := \frac{\log(rmn)}{\log(1/p)} - 1.$$

Substituting the values of r, p, m as chosen above we get:

$$
\begin{aligned}
d &= \frac{\log 2 + \log^{(2)} n}{\log 1/p} + \frac{\log m}{\log 1/p} + \frac{\log n}{\log 1/p} \\
&= \frac{(\log 2 + \log^{(2)} n) \log^{(3)} n}{\log n} + \frac{\beta(\log^{(3)} n)(\log n)}{\log n} + \frac{\log^{(3)} n \log n}{\log n} \\
&\leq 2\beta \cdot \log^{(3)} n \\
&= \frac{\log^{(2)} n}{4 \log^{(3)} n},
\end{aligned}
$$

where the inequality holds for all sufficiently large n.

(3) Theorem 2 gives that the probability of failure of BL algorithm in round i is at most $\frac{1}{n_i^{\Theta(\log n_i \log^{(2)} n_i)}}$. Using $n_i \geq 1/p^2$, this probability is at most $\frac{1}{n^{\log n}}$ for sufficiently large n. Hence, conditioning on the number of rounds being upper bounded by r, the probability of any one round failing is upper bounded by $r \cdot \frac{1}{n^{\log n}} \leq \frac{1}{n^{(\log n)/2}}$.

Thus the total probability of failure using (1) is at most $\frac{3}{n^{\log n}} + \frac{1}{n} + \frac{1}{n^{(\log n)/2}} \leq 2/n$, for sufficiently large n.

Now we account for the time taken by the algorithm. The first round takes time at most $(\log pn)^{d^d}$ (with high prob.), and the subsequent rounds have the same upper bound. Thus the total time is bounded by $r(\log pn)^{d^d}$ (here we are upper bounding $(d+4)!$ somewhat crudely by d^d which holds for all sufficiently large n). For our choice of d above we can upper bound this by

$$r(\log n)^{d^d} \le r(\log n)^{(\log n)^{1/4}} = \frac{2 \log n}{p} (\log n)^{(\log n)^{1/4}} =$$

$$2n^{1/\log^{(3)} n} (\log n)^{(\log n)^{1/4}+1} \le n^{2/\log^{(3)} n},$$

for sufficiently large n.

This completes the analysis.

3. ANALYSIS OF BL

In this section, we present a streamlined analysis of BL and show that it can accommodate for a larger d while maintaining the running time of $O((\log n)^{(d+4)!})$.

Before we describe the improvements in the analysis, we give a brief overview of the algorithm. In the first step, each vertex is marked independently at random with some probability p. After the marking step, for any edge that is fully marked, we unmark all its vertices. We add the remaining marked vertices to the independent set and perform a cleanup operation in which we update the vertex and edge set (by trimming them), remove singleton edges and discard all edges that now contain smaller edges as subsets. We then recurse on this new hypergraph. For a pseudocode of the algorithm we refer the reader to Appendix A.

Like usual, the general strategy in upper bounding the number of rounds necessary for the algorithm to finish, is to define an appropriate quantity and show that progress is being made in each round. Intuitively, we can pick one of several such quantities (the number of vertices, the maximum degree of a vertex, the number of edges etc.) and show that it is reduced by a constant fraction every couple of rounds. The trouble comes from the fact that, in the case of hypergraphs and of the BL algorithm in particular, none of these quantities are easy to track. For example, the probability that a vertex gets discarded in one round depends on whether it was marked but never participated in a fully marked edge. When it comes to the degree of a vertex, more evolved measures are needed than in the classical graph case, since now, several vertices can participate together in multiple edges. In this context, we define some essential notation. Let $H = (V, E)$ be a hypergraph with dimension d. For $\emptyset \ne x \subseteq V$ and an integer j with $1 \le j \le d - |x|$, we define the number of edges of size $|x| + j$ that include x as a subset:

$$N_j(x, H) = \{y \subseteq V : x \cup y \in E \wedge x \cap y = \emptyset \wedge |y| = j\}.$$

We also define the normalized degree of x with respect to dimension $|x| + j$ edges

$$d_j(x, H) = (|N_j(x, H)|)^{1/j}.$$

The maximum normalized degree with respect to dimension i edges then becomes

$$\Delta_i(H) = \max\{d_{i-|x|}(x, H) : x \subseteq V \wedge 0 < |x| < i\}.$$

Finally, the maximum normalized degree is defined as

$$\Delta(H) = \max\{\Delta_i(H) : 2 \le i \le d\}.$$

At this point, notice that, as noted in [5], the main bottleneck in the analysis is the migration of higher dimensional edges to lower dimensional ones. Specifically, in each round, we need to account for the decrease in $N_j(x, H)$ due to edges of size $|x| + j$ decreasing in size, but also for the potential

increase due to edges of size $|x| + k$, $k > j$ becoming edges of size $|x| + j$. In order to upper bound such an increase, [5] develops a bound on the upper tail of sums of dependent random variables defined on the edges of a hypergraph. We mention the general bound here and defer the description of its application to later in the paper.

In order to state the result, we need to describe the probabilistic setting: we consider a hypergraph $H = (V(H), E(H))$ with $n(H)$ vertices, $m(H)$ edges and dimension $dim(H)$. We also consider a weight function w on its edges $w(e) > 0$ for any edge e. The random variables C_v will correspond to each vertex being colored independently at random with probability p for the color blue and $1 - p$ for the color red. Alternatively, the random variable will take the value 1 with probability p and value 0 with probability $1 - p$. The random variable whose upper tail we will bound will be expressed as the polynomial $S(H, w, p)$. The terms of this polynomial will correspond to an edge e being fully colored blue $C_e = \prod_{v \in e} C_v$. The weights $w(e)$ will become the corresponding coefficients. The polynomial $S(H, w, p)$ then represents the sum of all the weighted edges being colored blue:

$$S(H, w, p) = \sum_{e \in E(H)} w(e) \cdot C_e.$$

Unlike general concentration bounds, we will not compare $S(H, w, p)$ just against its expectation. We will, instead, consider the expected values of all partial derivatives of the polynomial $S(H, w, p)$ with respect to subsets of vertices. Specifically, for a given $x \subseteq V(H)$, we will consider quantities of the form

$$P(H, w, p, x) = \sum_{\substack{e \in E(H) \\ x \subseteq e}} w(e) \cdot p^{|e| - |x|}.$$

Essentially, this term represents the expected sum of the weighted edges around x that are colored all blue, given that x is already colored blue. Notice that this is the same setting used by more recent and considerably better concentration inequalities (e.g. [6],[8]) to describe their results and in that sense, Kelsen's bound is surprisingly advanced. We then define:

$$D(H, w, p) = \max\{P(H, w, p, x) : x \subseteq V(H)\}.$$

Notice that $D(H, w, p)$ is greater than the expectation of $S(H, w, p)$. The final result follows:

THEOREM 3. *(Theorem 1 in [5]) Let (H, w) be a weighted hypergraph with $dim(H) = d > 0$ and $n(H) = n \ge 3$. For $0 < p \le 1$ and $\delta > 1$, we have*

$$\Pr[S(H, w, p) > k(H) \cdot D(H, w, p)] < p(H)$$

where

$$k(H) = (\log n + 2)^{2^d - 1} \cdot \delta^{2^{d-1}} \quad and$$
$$p(H) = (2^d \cdot \lceil \log n \rceil \cdot m(H))^{d-1} \cdot \log n \cdot (\tfrac{4e}{\delta - 1})^{(\delta - 1)/4}.$$

We are now ready to describe the complete analysis. In order to prove **Theorem 2**, we present a succinct version of the analysis that emphasizes the main ingredients of the proof and our contribution. For full details of the original analysis, we refer the reader to the papers of Beame and Luby [2] and Kelsen [5]. In the following subsection, we will revisit some of the tools used and show that the analysis goes through even when we consider a higher sampling probability.

3.1 Theorem 2

The main purpose of **Theorem 2** is to show that the analysis follows even when we allow $d \leq \frac{\log^{(2)} n}{4 \log^{(3)} n}$. We start by setting the initial sampling probability to $p = 1/(a\Delta)$ where $a = 2^{d+1}$. The first crucial step is lower bounding the probability that a particular set of vertices X is added to the independent set. We begin by defining random variables C_v for when a vertex v is initially marked (i.e. $C_v = 1$ when the v is marked and 0 otherwise) and E_v for when a vertex is unmarked later due its participation in fully marked edges (i.e. $E_v = 1$ when v is unmarked, 0 otherwise). We also define the random variable $A_v = C_v \wedge \neg E_v$ to stand for when the vertex v gets added to the independent set. This notion can be extended to subsets of vertices, by defining $C_X = \bigwedge_{v \in X} C_v$ and $E_X = \bigvee_{v \in X} E_v$, and $A_X = C_X \wedge \neg E_X$. Notice that

$$\Pr[A_X] = \Pr[C_X] \cdot (1 - \Pr[E_X | C_X]).$$

Lemma 1 from [2] shows that $\Pr[A_X] > 1/2 \cdot p^{|X|}$ by proving that $\Pr[E_X | C_X] < 1/2$.

LEMMA 2. *(Lemma 1 in [2])* Given a hypergraph $H = (V, E)$ of dimension d, and a set of vertices $X \subseteq V$ with $|X| < d$ such that no $e \subset X$ is an edge, we have $\Pr[E_X | C_X] < 1/2$. *(I.e. given that X is marked, it will be added to the IS with probability $> 1/2$.)*

We will use the preceding lemma to ensure that progress is being made at each stage of the algorithm. Specifically, we will focus our attention on those sets X that have a large degree with respect to edges of size $|X| + j$. To this extent, *Lemma 2* in [2]) shows that if such a large degree set exists, then one of the edges that contains it is likely to decrease and turn X into an edge by itself. Once that event occurs, the degree of X becomes 0.

LEMMA 3. *(Lemma 2 in [2])* For any set of vertices X and j such that $|X| + j \leq d$, if $d_j(X, H) \geq \epsilon\Delta$, then

$$Pr[\exists Y \in N_j(X, H) : A_Y] \geq \frac{1}{4}(\epsilon/a)^j,$$

where $a = 2^{d+1}$.

We now discuss the last ingredient of the proof: the upper bound on the migration of edges from higher dimensions to lower dimensions. Notice that the previous lemma is not enough to show that the degree of X will become 0 in a polylogarithmic number of stages. This is because over each stage, $d_j(X, H)$ can actually increase through the migration of edges from $N_k(X, H)$ where $k > j$. In this context, we employ **Theorem 3**. The hypergraph H' we construct consists of all the vertices in H and has as edges all subsets of size $k - j$ of the elements in $N_k(X, H)$, i.e all the potential ways in which an edge of size $|X| + k$ can lose $k - j$ vertices and become an edge of size $|X| + j$ around X. Formally, let $X_{j,k}$ be the edge set:

$$X_{j,k} = \{Y : Y \subseteq V(H') \wedge |Y| = k - j \wedge \exists Z \in N_k(X, H'), Y \subseteq Z\}.$$

The random variables C_v correspond to the situation in which a vertex v gets marked, with probability p. The weight w' of each edge $Y \in X_{j,k}$ represents the number of edges of size $|X| + j$ around X that would be formed if Y were to be fully added to the MIS. Formally:

$$w'(Y) = |N_j(X \cup Y, H')|.$$

The polynomial $S(H', w', p)$ then becomes an upper bound on the potential increase in $N_j(X, H)$ due to edges in $N_k(X, H)$. Notice that, in our case, H' has dimension at most $d - 1 < \frac{\log^{(2)} n}{4(\log^{(3)} n)}$, but by choosing $\delta = \log^2 n$, we can arrive at a cleaner formulation of *Theorem 1* from [5]:

COROLLARY 1. *(Corollary 1 in [5])* Fix a $d > 0$ and a real number p, $0 < p \leq 1$. For any weighted hypergraph (H', w) of dimension at most d with at most n vertices,

$$\Pr[S(H', w', p) > (\log n)^{2^{d+1}} \cdot D(H', w', p)] < \frac{1}{n^{\Theta(\log n \cdot \log \log n)}}.$$

When it comes to $D(H', w', p)$, we can bound it by something more meaningful in our context:

LEMMA 4. *(Lemma 3 in [5])* Let H', w' and p be defined as above. Then:

$$D(H', w', p) \leq (\Delta_{|X|+k}(H))^j.$$

Notice that the same bound applies when we consider the increase in the normalized degree $d_j(X, H')$ and since $\Delta_{|X|+k}(H) \leq \Delta$, we obtain the following *Corollary 3* from [5]:

COROLLARY 2. *(Corollary 3 in [5])* With high probability, for $2 \leq j \leq d$, the maximum increase in $d_{j-|X|}(X, H)$ for any non-empty $X \subseteq V$ during a single stage of the algorithm is less than

$$\sum_{k > j} (\log n)^{2^{k-j+1}} \cdot \Delta_k(H).$$

Notice that this bound is meaningful in comparison with the trivial bound we would obtain by considering the worst case scenario of *all* higher dimensional edges migrating down:

$$\left(\sum_{k > j} \Delta_k(H)^{k - |X|}\right)^{1/(j - |X|)} \geq \sum_{k > j} \Delta_k(H),$$

since $\Delta_k(H)$ could be as high as n.

At this point in the analysis, we can describe the behaviour of each individual $d_j(X, H)$ by a lower bound on the probability that it diminishes when it is too large (**Lemma 3**) and an upper bound on how much it can increase in each stage (**Corollary 2**). We would like to be able to somehow compare these quantities with a universal threshold that we can show will eventually decrease. The trouble comes from expressing the latter of the quantities in terms of this universal threshold: if we compare each $\Delta_k(H)$ to the threshold in the same way (suppose by saying that it is smaller than $1/2$ of the threshold value), we obtain a trivial upper bound on the increase in $\Delta_j(H)$. A solution to this problem would be to define an individual threshold for each $\Delta_k(H)$ separately and relate all of these back to a universal threshold. In this context, [5] defines the values $v_i(H)$ inductively by $v_d(H) = \Delta_d(H)$ and:

$$v_i(H) = \max\{\Delta_i(H), (\log n)^{f(i)} \cdot v_{i+1}(H)\},$$

for $2 \leq i < d$, where f is a carefully chosen function (to be defined later) that accommodates for the increase in $\Delta_j(H)$ due to migration from higher edges. Essentially, $v_i(H)$ tries to take into account the most significant term in the increased $\Delta_i(H)$: it is either the $\Delta_i(H)$ from the previous round or the most significant term from larger edges offset by a scaling factor $(\log n)^{f(i)} \cdot v_{i+1}(H)$. These individual thresholds relate to the universal threshold by considering the quantities $T_j = v_2(H)/(\log n)^{F(j-1)}$, where $F(i) = \sum_{j=2}^{i} f(j)$ for $2 \le i \le d$. Notice that for any hypergraph H', $v_i(H') \le v_2(H')/(\log n)^{F(j-1)}$. The rest of the analysis focuses on showing that the universal threshold $v_2(H)$ is reduced by a constant fraction every several rounds.

Let $H_s = (V(H_s), E(H_s))$ be the hypergraph used in stage s of the algorithm and let $v_i = v_i(H_{s_0})$ be the values of these potential functions at the start of a fixed stage of the algorithm. Similarly, let T_j be defined with respect to v_j. The main technical lemma is the following:

LEMMA 5. *(Lemma 4 in [5]) Let r be an arbitrary positive constant. Then, with high probability, at any stage s with $s_0 \le s \le s_0 + (\log n)^r$, we have*

$$v_2(H_s) \le v_2 \cdot (1 + o(1)).$$

In fact, [5] proves that something stronger holds with high probability:

$$v_j(H_s) \le T_j \cdot (1 + \lambda(n)),$$

where $\lambda(n) = 2 \cdot \log^{(2)} n / \log n$.

The main argument is by induction on $d - j$ and we will not reproduce it entirely. We will, instead, give the general intuition and focus on the parts of the argument that could change if we allow d to be non-constant. Notice that $v_j(H_s) = \max\{\Delta_j(H_s), (\log n)^{f(j)} \cdot v_{j+1}(H_s)\}$. By induction,

$$(\log n)^{f(j)} \cdot v_{j+1}(H_s) \le (\log n)^{f(j)} \cdot T_{j+1} \cdot (1 + \lambda(n))$$
$$\le T_j \cdot (1 + \lambda(n)).$$

So we only need to focus on showing that

$$\Delta_j(H_s) \le T_j \cdot (1 + \lambda(n)),$$

with high probability. The tactic is to show that, if $\Delta_j(H_s)$ ever becomes greater than $\frac{1}{2} \cdot T_j \cdot (1 + \lambda(n))$, then in q_j consecutive stages it will decrease with high probability, taking into account the potential migration of edges during those stages. Specifically, suppose there exists an $x \subseteq V(H_s)$ such that

$$d_{j-|x|}(x, H_s) \ge \frac{1}{2} \cdot T_j \cdot (1 + \lambda(n)).$$

One can show that this implies that

$$d_{j-|x|}(x, H_s) \ge \frac{\Delta(H_s)}{2(\log n)^{F(j-1)}}.$$

At this point, we can apply **Lemma 3** with $\epsilon = \frac{1}{2(\log n)^{F(j-1)}}$ and get that

$$\Pr[d_{j-|x|}(x, H_{s+1}) > 0] \le$$
$$1 - \frac{1}{2^{d(d+1)} \cdot (\log n)^{F(j-1)(j-1)}}.$$

In other words, the probability that in the next round we still have a high normalized degree is small. Notice that if we repeat the argument for

$$q_j = 2^{d(d+1)} \cdot (\log \log n) \cdot (\log n)^{F(j-1)(j-1)+2}$$

stages, we have that this remains true with probability at most $1/n^{\Theta(\log n \log \log n)}$. This is the first place in which we differ from the conventional analysis in [5] since we cannot ignore the $2^{d(d+1)}$ factor because it is not constant any more.

The only step left missing is to guarantee that the increase in $d_{j-|x|}(x, H_s)$ during those q_j stages is not large. We apply **Corollary 2** and get that the total increase is $q_j \cdot \sum_{k>j} (\log n)^{2^{k-j+1}} \cdot \Delta_k(H_s)$. We want to show that such an increase is smaller than $\lambda(n) \cdot T_j$ and since by the inductive assumption we have that $\Delta_k(H_s) \le T_k \cdot (1 + \lambda(n))$, we are left to show that

$$q_j \cdot \sum_{k>j} (\log n)^{2^{k-j+1}} \cdot T_k \cdot (1 + \lambda(n)) \le \lambda(n) \cdot T_j.$$

After some calculation, plugging in the values of q_j and $\lambda(n)$, this can be shown to reduce itself to:

$$2^{d(d+1)} \cdot \sum_{k>j} (\log n)^{2^{k-j+1} + F(j-1) \cdot j - F(k-1) + 2} \le$$
$$\frac{2}{\log n + 2 \log \log n}.$$

It is at this point that the definition of f comes into play. [5] define $f(2) = 7$ and $f(i) = (i-1) \cdot \sum_{j=2}^{i-1} f(i) + 7$ for $i > 2$. We then get that $F(i) = i \cdot F(i-1) + 7$ for $i \ge 2$ and $F(1) = 0$. Notice that this definition of F does not allow us to make the above argument. Consider the case when $k = j + 1$. Then

$$2^{k-j+1} + F(j-1) \cdot j - F(k-1) + 2 = -1$$

and the claim becomes

$$2^{d(d+1)} \le \frac{\log n}{\log n + 2 \log \log n}.$$

This is not true for the larger value of d we are considering. Notice that this was not an issue in the original analysis, because $2^{d(d+1)}$ was a constant in the case they were considering.

In order for the claim to be true, a different definition of f is required. Specifically, we define the recurrence relationship to be

$$f(i) = (i-1) \cdot \sum_{j=2}^{i-1} f(i) + d^2.$$

In this context, we obtain that $F(i) = i \cdot F(i-1) + d^2$. The claim then becomes:

$$2^{d(d+1)} \cdot \sum_{k>j} (\log n)^{2^{k-j+1} + 2 - d^2 + F(j) - F(k-1)} \le$$
$$\frac{2}{\log n + 2 \log \log n}.$$

We will now show that the claim is true for this new definition of f.

We will begin by first noticing that, for any j, the highest term in the sum is achieved for $k = j + 1$. Formally:

LEMMA 6. *For any $k > j + 1$ and any $j \ge 2$, we have*

$$2^{k-j+1} + 2 - d^2 + F(j) - F(k-1) \le 6 - d^2.$$

The proof is done by showing that the terms are decreasing as a function of k and therefore, the maximum is achieved for the lowest possible value of k: $j + 1$.

As a consequence, the entire left hand side of the inequality can be upper bounded by

$$2^{d(d+1)} \cdot (d-j) \cdot \frac{1}{(\log n)^{d^2-6}} \cdot$$

By taking $2^{d(d+1)} \leq e^{d(d+1)}$ and $d - j < \log \log n$, it would be enough to show

$$e^{d(d+1)} \cdot \frac{1}{(\log n)^{d^2-6}} \leq \frac{1}{\log^2 n} \cdot$$

In other words, we can show that

$$d(d+1) \leq (\log \log n) \cdot (d^2 - 8).$$

One can check that this inequality holds for $d < \frac{\log^{(2)} n}{4 \log^{(3)} n}$.

At this point, we have shown that the total increase in $d_{j-|x|}(x, H_s)$ during those stages is upper bounded with high probability by $\lambda(n) \cdot T_j$. Moreover, notice that after q_j stages, $\Delta_j(H)$ will not exceed $T_j \cdot \frac{1+3\lambda(n)}{2}$ and hence, after q_d stages, we have that, with high probability,

$$v_j(H_{s_1}) \leq T_j \cdot \frac{1+3\lambda(n)}{2}$$

for any $2 \leq j \leq d$ and $s_0 \leq s_1 \leq s_0 + (\log n)^{q_j}$. In fact, going back to the start of the algorithm, $v_2(H)$ is reduced by a constant factor, with high probability, every q_d stages. Hence, after $O(\log n \cdot q_d)$ stages, we have that $v_2(H) = 0$ and therefore, $V(H) = 0$ and the algorithm terminates.

Now we are left to prove that

$$\log n \cdot q_d \leq (\log n)^{(d+4)!}.$$

Notice that

$$q_d \leq (\log^{(2)} n)^2 \cdot (\log n)^{F(d-1)(d-1)+2}$$
$$\leq (\log n)^{F(d-1)(d-1)+3}$$
$$\leq (\log n)^{(d+4)!-1}$$

where the last inequality can be verified by inductively proving that $F(i) \leq d^2 \cdot (i+2)!$ for all i.

3.2 Larger sampling probability

In the attempt to provide insight into what happens with BL when we consider larger dimensions, we can show that the original lemmas from [2] hold even when the sampling probability is considerably larger: $p = 1/(5d \cdot \Delta)$ versus $1/(2^{d+1} \cdot \Delta)$.

Consider the extension of Lemma 1 from [2]:

LEMMA 7. *Given a hypergraph $H = (V, E)$ with dimension d, let $p = 1/(a\Delta)$ where $a = 5d$. Then for any set of vertices $X \subseteq V$ with $|X| < d$ such that no $e \subset X$ is an edge, we have that $\Pr[E_X|C_X] < 1/2$.*

PROOF. Let $f(X) = \Pr[E_X|C_X]$. Notice that $f(X) = \Pr[\exists e \in E, e \cap X \neq \emptyset : C_{e-X}]$. Consider a vertex $t \notin X$. Then we have

$$f(X \cup \{t\}) = \Pr[\exists e \in E, e \cap (X \cup \{t\}) \neq \emptyset : C_{e-(X \cup \{t\})}]$$
$$= \Pr[(\exists e \in E, e \cap X \neq \emptyset : C_{e-X}) \vee$$
$$(\exists e \in E, e \cap X = \emptyset, t \in e : C_{e-\{t\}})]$$
$$\leq \Pr[(\exists e \in E, e \cap X \neq \emptyset : C_{e-X})] +$$
$$\Pr[(\exists e \in E, e \cap X = \emptyset, t \in e : C_{e-\{t\}})]$$
$$\leq f(X) + \Pr[(\exists e \in E, e \cap X = \emptyset, t \in e : C_{e-\{t\}})]$$
$$\leq f(X) + \Pr[(\exists e \in E, t \in e : C_{e-\{t\}})]$$
$$\leq f(X) + f(\{t\}).$$

Notice that we can upper bound $f(\{t\})$ using the union bound. Specifically,

$$f(\{t\}) \leq \sum_{k=1}^{d-1} |N_k(\{t\}, H)| \cdot p^k \leq \sum_{k=1}^{d-1} d_k(\{t\}, H)^k \cdot p^k$$
$$\leq \sum_{k=1}^{d-1} \Delta^k(H) \cdot p^k \leq \sum_{k=1}^{d-1} \frac{1}{a^k} < \frac{1}{a-1}$$

Overall, we get that

$$f(X) \leq \sum_{t \in X} f(\{t\}) < \frac{|X|}{a-1} < \frac{d}{a-1} \leq \frac{1}{2}.$$

$\square$

This carries over when we consider Lemma 2 in [2]:

LEMMA 8. *Let $a = 5d$. For any set of vertices X and j such that $|X| + j \leq c$, if $d_j(X, H) \geq \epsilon\Delta$, then*

$$Pr[\exists Y \in N_j(X, H) : A_Y] \geq \frac{1}{4}(\epsilon/a)^j.$$

PROOF. Notice that we need a lower bound on $\Pr[\exists Y \in N_j(X, H)$ s.t. $A_Y]$ and hence, we cannot use the union bound as usual. Instead, we will lower bound this event by another one. Specifically, we will require that there is a *unique* $Y \in N_j(X, H)$ such that A_Y. In this context, we can decompose the event into disjoint elements:

$$\Pr[\exists! Y \in N_j(X, H), A_Y] = \sum_{Y \in N_j(X, H)} \Pr[A_Y \wedge \neg(\exists Z \in N_j(X, H) \setminus \{Y\} : A_Z)].$$

We also have

$$\Pr[A_Y \wedge \neg(\exists Z \in N_j(X, H) \setminus \{Y\} : A_Z)] =$$
$$\Pr[A_Y] \cdot (1 - \Pr[(\exists Z \in N_j(X, H) \setminus \{Y\} : A_Z)|A_Y]).$$

Now we can apply the union bound and get

$$\Pr[\exists Z \in N_j(X, H) \setminus \{Y\} : A_Z|A_Y] \leq \sum_{\substack{Z \in N_j(X, H) \\ Z \neq Y}} \Pr[A_Z|A_Y].$$

Putting everything together, we get

$$\Pr[\exists Y \in N_j(X, H), A_Y] \geq$$
$$\sum_{Y \in N_j(X, H)} \Pr[A_Y] \cdot (1 - \sum_{\substack{Z \in N_j(X, H) \\ Z \neq Y}} \Pr[A_Z|A_Y]).$$

In other words, we are left with showing an upper bound on $\sum_{\substack{Z \in N_j(X, H) \\ Z \neq Y}} \Pr[A_Z|A_Y].$

Notice the following argument from [2]:

$$\Pr[A_Z|A_Y] = \frac{\Pr[A_Y \wedge A_Z]}{\Pr[A_Y]}$$
$$\leq \frac{\Pr[C_Y \wedge C_Z]}{\Pr[A_Y]}$$
$$\leq 2 \cdot \frac{\Pr[C_Y \wedge C_Z]}{\Pr[C_Y]}$$
$$\leq 2 \cdot \Pr[C_Z|C_Y] = 2 \cdot \Pr[C_{Z-Y}],$$

where the second to last inequality uses the previous lemma in the sense that:

$$\begin{aligned}
\Pr[A_Y] &= \Pr[C_Y \wedge \neg E_Y] \\
&= \Pr[C_Y] \cdot \Pr[\neg E_Y | C_Y] \\
&= \Pr[C_Y] \cdot (1 - \Pr[E_Y | C_Y]) \\
&\geq \frac{1}{2} \Pr[C_Y].
\end{aligned}$$

We therefore get that

$$\begin{aligned}
\sum_{\substack{Z \in N_j(X,H) \\ Z \neq Y}} \Pr[A_Z | A_Y] &\leq 2 \cdot \sum_{\substack{Z \in N_j(X,H) \\ Z \neq Y}} \Pr[C_{Z-Y}] \\
&\leq 2 \cdot \sum_{S \subset Y} \sum_{\substack{Z \in N_j(X,H) \\ Y \cap Z = S}} \Pr[C_{Z-S}] \\
&\leq 2 \cdot \sum_{S \subset Y} (1/a)^{j-|S|} \\
&\leq \frac{1}{2}.
\end{aligned}$$

The last inequality is true because

$$\begin{aligned}
\sum_{S \subset Y} (1/a)^{j-|S|} &= \sum_{l=0}^{j-1} \binom{j}{l} (1/a)^{j-l} \\
&= (1 + 1/a)^j - 1 \\
&\leq (1 + 1/a)^d - 1 \\
&\leq ((1 + 1/a)^a)^{d/a} - 1 \\
&\leq e^{d/a} - 1.
\end{aligned}$$

For $d/a \leq 1/5$ we get that $e^{d/a} - 1 \leq 1/4$ and the previous inequality follows. At this point, we get

$$\sum_{\substack{Z \in N_j(X,H) \\ Z \neq Y}} \Pr[A_Z | A_Y] \leq 1/2.$$

Overall, we have

$$\begin{aligned}
\Pr[\exists Y \in N_j(X,H) : A_Y] &\geq \sum_{Y \in N_j(X,H)} \Pr[A_Y] \cdot (1 - \frac{1}{2}) \\
&\geq \frac{1}{4} \cdot \sum_{Y \in N_j(X,H)} \Pr[C_Y] \\
&\geq \frac{1}{4} \cdot |N_j(X,H)| \cdot p^j \\
&\geq \frac{1}{4} \cdot d_j(X,H)^j \cdot (1/a\Delta)^j \\
&\geq \frac{1}{4} \cdot (\epsilon/a)^j.
\end{aligned}$$

□

The next step of the proof that we are going to improve is the bound that Kelsen gives on the maximum potential increase in edges in one round, using the same setting as in the original analysis but employing the Kim-Vu concentration bound [6]. We obtain an analogue of *Corollary 2* in [5]:

COROLLARY 3. *For $X \subseteq V$, and $1 \leq j < k \leq d - |X|$, we have*

$$\Pr[S(X,j,k) > (1 + a_{k-j}\lambda^{k-j}) \cdot (\Delta_{|X|+k}(H))^j] \leq 2e^2 e^{-\lambda} n^{k-j-1},$$

where $a_{k-j} = 8^{k-j}(k-j)!^{1/2}$.

Notice that we upper bounded the term $D(H', w', p)$ by $(\Delta_{|X|+k}(H))^j$, just like [5]. Simple algebra can show that this result follows even for the new value of a. Choosing $\lambda = \Theta(\log^2 n)$, we get that an analogue of Corollary 3 in [5]:

COROLLARY 4. *With high probability, for $2 \leq j \leq d$, the maximum increase in $d_{j-|X|}(X,H)$ for any non-empty $X \subseteq V$ during a single stage of the algorithm is less than:*

$$\sum_{k>j} (\log n)^{2(k-j)} \cdot \Delta_k(H).$$

Notice that the bound of $(\log n)^{2(k-j)}$ is much smaller than the one of $(\log n)^{2^{k-j+1}}$ in [5].

3.3 Discussion

In context of these improvements, the natural next step is to investigate what effect they have on the overall running time of BL. We show that, under the current set up of the potential function, no improvement is possible. Specifically, we show that the function F must be roughly exponential for the argument to follow, despite the obvious improvements.

Notice that in our previous attempt to call BL on a hypergraph with super-constant dimension, the main issue was showing that the increase in q_j rounds was upper bounded by $T_j \cdot \lambda(n)$. Incorporating all of the new improvements, we get that the claim formally looks like:

$$(5d)^d \cdot \sum_{k>j} (\log n)^{2(k-j)+F(j-1)\cdot j-F(k-1)+2} \leq \frac{2}{\log n + 2 \log \log n}.$$

We proved this claim by showing that the largest term in the sum was upper bounded by $\frac{1}{(\log n)^{d^2-6}}$. We check the minimal conditions that f must satisfy in order for the new claim to be true by precisely looking at this largest term in the case when $k = j+1$ for a fixed $2 \leq j \leq d$. Notice that, first of all, this will be the largest term when we allow F to satisfy $F(k-1) > F(j) + 2(k-j-2)$ for all $k > j$. Given that, the term will be:

$$(\log n)^{4+F(j-1)\cdot j-F(j)}.$$

Notice that, in order for the claim to be true, this term needs to be smaller than

$$\frac{1}{(5d)^d} \cdot \frac{2}{\log n + 2 \log \log n}.$$

In order for this to happen, we must have that

$$(\log n)^{4+F(j-1)\cdot j-F(j)} \leq \frac{1}{\log n}.$$

This, in turn, requires that

$$F(j) \geq F(j-1) \cdot j + 5.$$

4. CONCLUSION

In this paper, we build on the RNC algorithm for computing an MIS in constant dimension hypergraphs to get an $n^{o(1)}$ algorithm on general hypergraphs when the number of edges is upper bounded by $n^{\frac{\log^{(2)} n}{8(\log^{(3)} n)^2}}$. In order to perform the analysis, we prove that the subroutine algorithm can be adapted to run on a larger dimension while maintaining an appropriate running time. We also present independent improvements to the analysis of the latter and identify the main bottleneck in the approach that affects the final runtime most significantly. For example, notice that the factor of j in the above inequality $F(j) \geq F(j-1) \cdot j + 5$ originated from **Lemma 3**. Specifically, [2] lower bound the probability that $d_j(X) > \epsilon\Delta$ becomes 0 in the next iteration, as a function of $(\epsilon/a)^j$. A refinement of that result could potentially lead to a weaker restriction on F and hence, a smaller running time.

Acknowledgments.

Authors David G. Harris and Aravind Srinivasan were supported in part by **NSF Award CNS-1010789**. We thank the anonymous SPAA reviewers for useful and extensive comments on a previous version of this paper.

5. REFERENCES

[1] Noga Alon and Joel Spencer. *The Probabilistic Method.* John Wiley, 1992.

[2] P. Beame and M. Luby. Parallel search for maximal independence given minimal dependence. In *Proceedings of the first annual ACM-SIAM symposium on Discrete algorithms*, pages 212–218. Society for Industrial and Applied Mathematics, 1990.

[3] Richard M. Karp and Vijaya Ramachandran. Parallel algorithms for shared-memory machines. In *Handbook of Theoretical Computer Science, Volume A: Algorithms and Complexity (A)*, pages 869–942. 1990.

[4] R.M. Karp, E. Upfal, and A. Wigderson. The complexity of parallel search. *J. Comput. Syst. Sci.*, 36(2):225–253, 1988.

[5] Pierre Kelsen. On the Parallel Complexity of Computing a Maximal Independent Set in a Hypergraph. *Fourth annual ACM symposium on Theory of computing*, 3:339–350, 1992.

[6] Jeong Han Kim and Van H. Vu. Concentration of multivariate polynomials and its applications. *Combinatorica*, 20(3):417–434, 2000.

[7] Tomasz Luczak and Edyta Szymanska. A parallel randomized algorithm for finding a maximal independent set in a linear hypergraph. *J. Algorithms*, 25(2):311–320, 1997.

[8] Warren Schudy and Maxim Sviridenko. Concentration and moment inequalities for polynomials of independent random variables. In *SODA*, pages 437–446, 2012.

[9] Hadas Shachnai and Aravind Srinivasan. Finding large independent sets in graphs and hypergraphs. *SIAM J. Discrete Math.*, 18(3):488–500, 2004.

APPENDIX

A. BL ALGORITHM

We give the pseudocode of the BL algorithm as initially described in [2].

Algorithm 2 BL

Input: A hypergraph $H = (V, E)$
Output: A maximal independent set $I \subseteq V$.

1: Calculate $\Delta(H)$ as defined in Section 3.
2: Let $d = \max\{|e| : e \in E\}$ and $p = 1/(2^{d+1}\Delta)$.
3: $H' = (V', E') \leftarrow H = (V, E)$.
4: $I \leftarrow \emptyset$.
5: **while** $V' \neq \emptyset$ **do**
6:     Select vertices independently at random with probability p.
7:     Let I' be the collection of such selected vertices.
8:     **for all** $e \in E'$ such that $e \subseteq I'$ **do**
9:         $I' \leftarrow I' \setminus e$.
10:     $I \leftarrow I \cup I'$.
11:     $V' \leftarrow V' \setminus I'$.
12:     **for all** $e \in E'$ **do**
13:         $e \leftarrow e \setminus I'$.
14:     **for all** $e, e' \in E'$ **do**
15:         **if** $e \subseteq e'$ **then**
16:             $E' \leftarrow E' \setminus e$.
17:     **for all** $e = \{v\} \in E'$ **do**
18:         $E' \leftarrow E' \setminus e$.
19:         $V' \leftarrow V' \setminus \{v\}$.
20: Return I.

Hierarchical Graph Partitioning

Mohammadtaghi Hajiaghayi *
University of Maryland
College Park, MD
hajiagha@cs.umd.edu

Theodore Johnson
AT&T Research Laboratory
Florham Park, NJ
johnsont@research.att.com

Mohammad Reza Khani *
University of Maryland
College Park, MD
khani@cs.umd.edu

Barna Saha
AT&T Research Laboratory
Florham Park, NJ
barna@research.att.com

ABSTRACT

One of the important optimization questions in highly parallel systems is the problem of assigning computational resources to communicating tasks. While scheduling tasks/operators, tasks assigned to nearby resources (e.g. on the same CPU core) have low communication costs, whereas tasks assigned to distant resources (e.g. on different server racks) have high communication costs. An optimal solution of task to resource assignment minimizes the communication cost of the task ensemble while satisfying the load balancing requirements. We model such an optimization question of minimizing communication cost as a new class of graph partitioning problems called *hierarchical graph partitioning*.

In hierarchical graph partitioning we are given a graph $G = (V, E)$, vertices representing the tasks and edges representing the communication among the vertices. We are also given vertex demands $d : V(G) \rightarrow \mathbb{R}^+$ denoting the processing load of each task and edge weights $w : E(G) \rightarrow \mathbb{R}^+$ denoting the amount of communication and our goal is to decompose G into k parts/servers of nearly equal weight (for load balancing) and minimize the total cost of the edges being cut (communication cost). However, unlike traditional k-balanced graph partitioning where the cost of an edge cut is independent of the parts containing the two respective end vertices, here the cost varies with the distance of the servers corresponding to the two parts. Since, the servers are generally arranged in a hierarchy, distance is given by a tree metric. In this paper, we initiate the study of hierarchical graph partitioning problem and give efficient algorithms with approximation guarantee. Hierarchical graph partitioning is a significant generalization of graph partitioning problem and faithfully captures several practical scenarios that have served as major motivating applications for graph partitioning.

*supported in part by NSF CAREER award 1053605, ONR YIP award N000141110662, DARPA/AFRL award FA8650-11-1-7162.

Categories and Subject Descriptors

G.2.2 [**Mathematics of Computing**]: Graph Theory—*Graph algorithms*

Keywords

Approximation algorithms; Graph Partitioning

1. INTRODUCTION

The research in this paper is motivated by practical problems encountered in optimizing a parallelized data stream processing system such as TidalRace at AT&T [13]. Such a system consists of a collection of streaming inputs, a collection of streaming outputs, and a DAG of processing tasks between the inputs and outputs. A modern commodity server will have 64 or more cores available for executing these tasks, often configured with four CPU sockets, eight cores per CPU socket, and two virtual cores per actual core through the use of hyperthreading. A modern parallelized operating system such as Linux will schedule a ready task on any available CPU core. Although a modern operating system will exhibit some locality preferences in its scheduling decisions, we found that we could significantly improve performance (i.e., maximum throughput) by *pinning* tasks to particular cores, and thus ensure that tasks execute on cores with warm memory caches. We further observed that we could further improve performance by pinning tasks with high communication volumes on *nearby* cores.

Tasks which are pinned to the same core (or pair of hyperthreaded cores) have a low communication cost because they share L1 through L3 caches. Ideally, we would pin all strongly communicating tasks to the same core. However, we face a scheduling constraint: a task has a CPU demand, which we can describe as a fraction of the CPU core that it will use. If we try to oversubscribe a CPU core's resources, the tasks pinned to that core will not be able to keep up with their workload and will drop data in an uncontrolled fashion.

Tasks on more "distant" cores have higher communication costs. For example, task pinned to cores on the same CPU socket will share the same L3 cache, while tasks pinned to cores on different sockets share only the same memory backplane. Our goal is therefore to pin tasks to cores in a way that does not oversubscribe any core but which minimizes overall communication costs.

The stream optimization problem can also be seen in the context of task placement in distributed steaming systems such as IBM's Infosphere Stream of Facebook's Storm [12].

We study the hierarchical graph partitioning problem which models the optimization problem of minimizing communication cost while placing communicating tasks in such distributed environment. Hierarchical graph partitioning is a generalization of the well-studied k-Balanced Graph Partitioning (k-BGP) problem. In the k-BGP, the given graph is broken into k parts with nearly equal number of vertices such that the edges across the parts are minimized. When $k = 2$, one obtains the famous *Minimum Bisection problem*; this NP Hard problem has played an instrumental role in the study and development of approximation algorithms [3, 6, 10, 20, 26]. However, in these problems, one assumes a uniform metric, that is the cost of cutting an edge is same independent of which parts the two end points belong to. This model is not realistic in distributed streaming system where natural hierarchy is observed among the resources.

The hierarchical graph partitioning (HGP) problem is defined as follows. We are given a hierarchy tree (H) with k leaves that correspond to CPU cores with same capacity to which we assign tasks. Each non-leaf node represents a group. For example, in task scheduling, a set of leaves with common parent corresponds to a set of cores having the same CPU socket. Apart from H, we are given a graph $G = (V, E)$, $|V| = n$, where each node $v \in V$ has a demand $d(v)$ and each edge $e = (u, v)$ in E has weight $w(e)$. Our goal is to assign each node of G to a leaf of H such that the following holds.

Let us denote the root of H as r_H and define the *level* of a node to be the number of edges in the unique path between the node and r_H. If a node is at level j in H we refer to it as a Level-(j) node. We assume that H is regular at each level meaning that every Level-(j) node has exactly $\mathrm{DEG}^{(j)}$ children and the height of H is h. Such regularity assumption captures the most common modern scenarios.

Each level j in H is assigned with cost multiplier $cm(j)$ where $cm(i) \geq cm(i+1)$ for all $i \in \{0, \ldots, h-1\}$, For two leaves a_H and b_H of H, let $\mathrm{LCA}_H(a_H, b_H)$ be the level of the lowest common ancestor of a_H and b_H. A solution to the HGP problem is a function $p : V(G) \to \mathrm{LEAVES}(H)$ which assigns each node of G to a leaf in H such that

$$\forall l \in \mathrm{LEAVES}(H), \quad \sum_{v : p(v) = l} d(v) \leq 1,$$

which minimizes cost $c(p)$ where

$$c(p) = \sum_{u, v \in V(G), u \neq v} cm\left(\mathrm{LCA}_H(p(u), p(v))\right) \cdot w((u, v)). \quad (1)$$

Here we assume that the capacity of leaves of H is normalized to one. Note that the k-BGP problem is the special case of HGP where H has height 1 in which $cm(0) = 1$ and $cm(1) = 0$ and each node of G has demand $\frac{k}{n}$.

1.1 Related Works

The *minimum bisection* (MBS) is a central problem in design and analysis of approximation algorithms. An (α, β)-bicriteria approximation algorithm for this problem gives a solution whose cut size is at most α times the size of an optimal solution but violates the size constraint of each section by at most factor β. The $(O(\log n), 1.5)$ bi-criteria approximation by Leighton and Rao [20], as well as the improvement to $(O(\sqrt{\log n}), 1.5)$ by Arora et al. [3], are seminal papers. Recent work by Räcke [26] obtains an elegant $O(\log n)$ (true) approximation for this problem improving upon the previous bound of $O(\log^{1.5} n)$ by Feige and Krauthgamer

[10]. Finally, different inapproximability results shown in the sequence of papers [6, 16, 18] relate MBS to the unique games conjecture and to refuting random 3SAT formulas, and have transformed the area.

The k-BGP appears as a natural generalization of MBS and has also been an active area of study. No true approximation that does not violate the "balanced" constraint is possible unless P=NP [1]. Leighton et al. [21] and Simon and Teng [27] achieved an $(O(\log k \log n), 2)$-bicriteria approximation. Later works improved the first criterion of the approximation to $O(\log n)$ [9] and finally to $O(\sqrt{\log k \log n})$ [19]. However, all these came at a price of factor 2 violation in the balanced constraint. The first improvement in that regard was achieved by Andreev and Räcke [1] who showed a $O(\frac{1}{\epsilon^2} \log^{1.5} n, (1 + \epsilon))$ approximation bound that was finally improved to $O(\log n, (1 + \epsilon))$ by Feldmann and Foschini [11].

Metric embedding problems are another class of closely related problems to HGP. The metric labeling problem is a generalization of graph partitioning problem where in addition there is a cost for labeling vertices to parts. Starting from the seminal paper of Kleinberg and Tardos [17], there has been a long line of works considering several variants of the problem. Naor and Schwartz [23] introduced balanced metric labeling in which each label has a capacity l, and additionally the semimetric on the labels is uniform. Naor and Schwartz [23] gave an $(O(\log n), O(\min\{l, \log k\}))$- bicriteria approximation algorithm for the problem. Capacitated metric labeling is a generalization of balanced metric labeling where labels can have arbitrary capacity and the metric may not be uniform. When the number of labels is fixed Andrews et al. [2] gave a $O(\log n)$ approximation algorithm for capacitated metric labeling.

The HGP problem is also expensively studied from the non-theory perspective and different heuristics have been proposed. Walshaw and Cross [31] develop algorithms for what they call the mapping problem, which is similar to the HGP problem, except it allows mapping an arbitrary task graph G onto an arbitrary architecture graph. The cost function used is identical. Another approach called "dual recursive bipartitioning" to the mapping problem was developed in Pellegrini [24]. The technique uses recursive bisection of both the task graph and the processor graph while minimizing a similar cost function. More recently, Moulitsas and Karypis [22] work on a class of algorithms called "Architecture-Aware Partitioning Algorithms", in which the task graph is mapped onto nodes of an arbitrary architecture graph. Their algorithm starts with an initial partition and iteratively refine the partition in order to minimize objective functions such as communication time or total time. A hierarchical architecture graph for mapping tasks has also been studied in several other works [5, 28, 29]. There are a number of commonly-used graph partitioning softwares used for HGP type problems such as Zoltan[8], SCOTCH [25], JOSTLE [30], Para-PART [7], etc. For a survey in graph partitioning problems see [4, 15].

1.2 Results and Techniques

In this section we precisely introduce our result and give a summary of our techniques. There is no true approximation algorithm which does not violate the capacity constraint of the leaves of H for HGP as such bounds are not realizable even for k-BGP, which is the special case of HGP when $h = 1$, unless P=NP [1]. Therefore we need bicriteria approximations.

Definition 1 *An (α, β)-bicriteria approximation algorithm for the HGP problem gives a solution which violates the capacity of the*

leaves of H by at most factor β and has cost at most α times the cost of an optimal solution which has no capacity violation.

Our main result is the following.

Theorem 1 *For any positive real value ϵ there is an $(O(\log n), (1 + \epsilon) \cdot (1 + h))$-bicriteria approximation algorithm for HGP when height h is constant.*

The factor $(1+\epsilon)$ blow out in the capacity constraint is the standard consequence of rounding the demands of the nodes of G which is similar to the Knapsack problem. As one may notice height of tree H is the source of difficulty in our algorithm as we require it to be constant and there is $(1 + h)$ factor in the second criterion. Remember that MBS and k-BGP are the special cases of HGP when height h is equal to one. In the following we argue that the usual techniques used in MBS and k-BGP cannot be generalized for HGP even when h is equal to two. In fact we show that when h is equal to two the states of the dynamic programs used in the two problems can be exponential and hence we expect increasing height h makes HGP significantly harder. At the best of our knowledge this is the first paper which deals with such a multiple hierarchy partitioning problem in a theoretical setting. Finally we note that the $O(\log n)$ factor loss in the cost, the first criterion, is the standard consequence of embedding G into a distribution of trees.

The general framework for solving packing problems such as MBS and k-BGP has two steps. The first step is to embed the graph into a distribution of trees using Räcke's hierarchal decomposition for congestion minimization [26]. The embedding guarantees that the cut size of each subset of nodes in the graph is closely approximated with the expected cut size of the corresponding nodes in the distribution of trees. Using this property it can be proved that solving the packing problem for trees suffices to solve the problem for general graphs but with an extra $O(\log n)$ factor blow up in the approximation factor. The second step is to solve the packing problem for trees using a dynamic program. The main idea of the dynamic program is to solve the same problem for each sub-tree of the tree and combine them to get the final result. For example in the k-BGP problem it is only important to keep track of how much each partition is filled when solving the problem for each sub-tree. Therefore, two sub-problems can be combined if no partition overflows using the state of the partitions in each sub-problem. If the capacity of each partition is $\frac{n}{k}$ then there are at most $\frac{n}{k}$ different states for each partition. By allowing a rounding error of ϵ we can assume that there are at most $\frac{1}{\epsilon}$ different states for each partition. Therefore, if for each state s we keep how many partitions are in state s, the overall states of all the partitions can be kept in $k^{1/\epsilon}$.

Our algorithm also has the same two steps. In the first step we extend the paradigm of [2, 26] to round the graph into a probability distribution of decomposition trees for the case when we have multiple levels. The main genuine idea of this paper is dealing with the second step. The standard techniques described above for the second step is not applicable to HGP even when there are only two levels in the hierarchy tree as the number of different states can be exponential in n. Our main idea here is to relax the problem in a way which causes the violation in the capacity constraints but makes the problem tractable. We explain this idea more carefully in the following.

First we describe the standard framework which is usually used for the bin packing type problems first introduced in [14]. We show that although this framework can be applied well to the k-BGP problem, it does not work for the HGP problem. Consider the problem in which we want to pack n items $a_1, a_2, \ldots, a_n$ each has demand one into m bins all with the same size B. The idea of

the framework of Hochbaum and Shmoys [14] is to maintain the state of the bins after packing the first n' items by a B-dimensional vector $\boldsymbol{\alpha}$ whose ith entry specifies how many bins are filled with exactly i items. Hence, the problem can be solved efficiently by a dynamic programming over subproblems $bp(\boldsymbol{\alpha}, n')$ which returns true if the first n' items can be packed into the bins such that $\sum_i \boldsymbol{\alpha}(i)$ is equal to m. Because there are exponentially many different values (m^B) for $\boldsymbol{\alpha}$, instead of solving for the exact portion each bin is packed; for each bin they maintain if it is filled in the range $[(1 + \epsilon)^{j-1} \cdot \epsilon \cdot B, (1 + \epsilon)^j \cdot \epsilon \cdot B)$ for $j \in O(\log_{1+\epsilon} \frac{1}{\epsilon})$ where ϵ is a fixed constant. This way there are only $O(\log_{1+\epsilon} \frac{1}{\epsilon})$ different states for each bin which is a constant number. Therefore the total number of different values for $\boldsymbol{\alpha}$ is $m^{(\log_{1+\epsilon} \frac{1}{\epsilon})}$ and hence polynomial in the size of the input but they violate the capacities by factor $(1 + \epsilon)$.

We can apply this framework to the HGP problem and maintain the states of the leaves of H. However, even for the case when height of H is two there is a major issue. Suppose H has height 2 and each Level-(1) H-node has $\text{DEG}^{(1)}$ children which are leaves of H, all having the same capacity. In order to maintain the state of each leaf we need to maintain how much it is filled and moreover to which Level-(1) H-node it belongs.

In order to avoid the above subtlety we define *mirror functions*. Let $\text{SUB}(a_H)$ be the subtree induced by node a_H in tree H. For a solution $p : V(G) \rightarrow \text{LEAVES}(H)$ we define its *mirror function* $\mathcal{P} : V(H) \rightarrow 2^{V(G)}$ where for each H-node $a_H \in V(H)$

$$\mathcal{P}(a_H) = \{v \in V(G) | p(v) \in \text{SUB}(a_H)\}. \tag{2}$$

We show that cost of solution p can be rewritten using mirror function $\mathcal{P}$ as

$$c(\mathcal{P}) = \sum_{j=1}^{h} \sum_{a_H^{(j)} \in V(H)} w(\text{CUT}(\mathcal{P}(a_H^{(j)}))) \cdot \frac{cm(j-1) - cm(j)}{2}. \tag{3}$$

where $a_H^{(j)}$ is a Level-(j) H-node and $\text{CUT}(\mathcal{P}(a_H^{(j)}))$ is the minimum cut separating $\mathcal{P}(a_H^{(j)})$ form the rest of the leaves. This way, cost of p depends only on $\text{CUT}(\mathcal{P}(a_H))$ for $a_H \in V(H)$.

Suppose we want to solve HGP for rooted tree T. We build a partial mirror function $\mathcal{P}_v$ for each node $v \in V(T)$ where $\mathcal{P}_v$ is the same function as $\mathcal{P}$ except it maps H-nodes to the leaves only at $\text{SUB}(v)$. Building a mirror function is also hard. Lets fix a Level-(j) H-node $a_H^{(j)}$ for which we want to find $\mathcal{P}_v(a_H^{(j)})$. In fact not only we have to find $\mathcal{P}_v(a_H^{(j)})$ we need to partition this set into at most $\text{DEG}^{(j)}$ subsets and assign them to the children of $a_H^{(j)}$. First we relax the condition that $\mathcal{P}_v(a_H^{(j)})$ has to be partitioned into at most $\text{DEG}^{(j)}$ subsets by allowing it to be partitioned into any number of subsets as far as the total demand of each of them is $\text{CP}^{(j+1)}$. Using the relaxed condition we prove a few structural results which at the end shows that there exists an optimal mirror function $\mathcal{P}$ where for each node v and each level j, there is at most one Level-(j) H-node $a_H^{(j)}$ (we refer to $\mathcal{P}(a_H^{(j)})$ as an (v, j)-active set) such that neither $\mathcal{P}(a_H^{(j)}) \cap \text{SUB}(v) = \emptyset$ nor $\mathcal{P}(a_H^{(j)}) \subseteq \text{SUB}(v)$ holds.

From the above conditions we note that it is just enough to maintain the status of (v, j)-active set for each Level-(j). We use a dynamic programming to find the best solution which has at most one (v, j)-active set at each Level-(j). The dynamic programming is involved since we need to keep the consistency among all the levels.

2. PRELIMINARY

In this section we introduce the required definitions which we use throughout the paper. We use subscript H in order to refer to nodes or edges of H but we drop the subscript for nodes or edges of G. We also note that proofs that are omitted due to page constraint can be found in a full version of the paper.

We call cost multiplier cm is normalized if $cm(h) = 0$. The following lemma proves that an α-approximation algorithm for HGP with a normalized cost multipliers can be changed to an algorithm with at most the same approximation factors for HGP with a general cost multipliers.

Lemma 1 *Let ALG be an α-approximation algorithm for HGP which works only for normalized cost multipliers. Using ALG we can find algorithm ALG' which is an α-approximation algorithm for HGP working for any cost multiplier.*

In the rest of the paper we assume that the cost multiplier cm is normalized and hence $cm(h) = 0$.

For a subset of nodes $P \subseteq V(G)$, we define $\text{CUT}(P)$ to be the set of all edges that have one endpoint in P and one endpoint in $V(G) \setminus P$. We use $w(\text{CUT}(P))$ to refer to the sum of the weights of the edges in $\text{CUT}(P)$. We use $\text{SUB}(a_H)$ to denote the subtree rooted at node a_H in tree H.

Recall the definition of mirror function $\mathcal{P}$ from Section 1.2. In the following lemma we show that the cost of solution p and mirror function $\mathcal{P}$ are the same.

Lemma 2 *The cost assigned to solution p (shown in Equation (1)) is equal to the cost of its mirror function $\mathcal{P}$ (shown in Equation (3)).*

Working with mirror function $\mathcal{P}$ as opposed to p has the benefit that it exploits better the fact that graph H is a tree. In fact we can build a solution to the HGP problem by building a mirror function as follows. At the start all the nodes in G are assigned to the Level-(1) node of H (which is root r_H) and hence $\mathcal{P}(r_H) = V(G)$. After that, we partition nodes of G into smaller sets which we refer to them as Level-(2) sets. We assign each Level-(2) set to a Level-(2) node of H. Afterward, we take each Level-(2) set and partition it into smaller sets (Level-(3) sets) and assign them to the Level-(3) nodes of H. In the rest of the paper we work only with mirror functions and refer to them as solutions to the HGP problem.

3. HGP ON TREES

First we formally define the HGP problem on Trees (HGPT) where the objective is to partition only the leaves of a tree. Remember that the hierarchal separation tree H is $\text{DEG}^{(j)}$ regular at each Level-(j), *i.e.*, each H-node at Level-(j) has exactly $\text{DEG}^{(j)}$ children. Moreover the capacity of each Level-(h) H-node is one. We assign capacity $\text{CP}^{(j)}$ to each Level-(j) H-node ($a_H^{(j)}$) which is the total capacity of all the leaves in $\text{SUB}(a_H^{(j)})$. Because H is regular at each level we have $\text{CP}^{(j)} = \prod_{j'=j}^{h} \text{DEG}^{(j')}$. Remember that cm is the cost multiplier for the different layers of hierarchical separation H.

Definition 2 *Let T be a tree rooted at r where each leaf v of T represents a job with demand $0 < d(v) \leq 1$. The function $p : \text{LEAVES}(T) \to \text{LEAVES}(H)$ where $\forall a_H \in \text{LEAVES}(H)$, $\sum_{v:p(v)=a_H} d(v) \leq 1$ is a solution to the HGPT problem.*

Remember form Section 2 that from a mirror function $\mathcal{P}$ we can uniquely define its corresponding solution p to HGP and its cost is the same as p. Therefore, we refer to the mirror functions as solutions.

We note that solving HGP for only the leaves of a tree (as we defined in Definition 2) is more general than solving it for all its nodes. The later can be reduced to the former by adding a dummy leaf for each node and connecting them by an edge of infinity weight. As no partition separates a node from its dummy node, any solution partitioning only leaves in the modified tree can be transformed to a solution which partitions all the nodes in the original tree with the same cost. Moreover, every solution which partitions the nodes in the original tree defines a corresponding solution in the leaves of the modified graph with the same cost. Therefore, the optimal cost is the same in both trees.

Let tree T be the communication graph where each of its leaves v corresponds to a job and has demand $d(v)$. Remember that $\text{CP}^{(j)}$ is the capacity of each Level-(j) H-node and that each Level-(j) H-node has exactly $\text{DEG}^{(j)}$ children. Here we have $\text{CP}^{(h)} = 1$ and $\text{CP}^{(j)} = \prod_{i=j}^{h-1} \text{DEG}^{(i)}$ since H is $\text{DEG}^{(j)}$ regular at each Level-(j).

An intuitive way of seeing a solution to the HGPT problem is the following. At the start we have a single set which is equal to $\text{LEAVES}(T)$ we assign this set to r_H ($\mathcal{P}(r_H) = \text{LEAVES}(T)$). Now we need to partition $\mathcal{P}(r_H)$ into $\text{DEG}^{(1)}$ sets and assign each of them to a children of r_H such that the total demand of each set is at most $\text{CP}^{(1)}$. Then we partition the set assigned to each children ($a_H^{(1)}$) of r_H into $\text{DEG}^{(2)}$ sets each with total demand $\text{CP}^{(2)}$ and assign them to the children of $a_H^{(1)}$. More formally, at iteration j for each Level-(j) H-node $a_H^{(j)}$ we partition $\mathcal{P}(a_H^{(j)})$ into $\text{DEG}^{(j)}$ sets each with total demand at most $\text{CP}^{(j+1)}$. Let $\mathcal{S}^{(j)}$ be a collection containing all the sets that are assigned to the Level-(j) nodes of H. In the following we show that knowing only $\mathcal{S}^{(j)}$ for $0 \leq j \leq h$ is enough to rebuild a solution to the HGPT problem since H is $\text{DEG}^{(j)}$ regular at each Level-(j) and each Level-(j) H-node has capacity $\text{CP}^{(j)}$.

First, we formally redefine a solution to the HGPT problem as follows.

Definition 3 *A solution to the HGPT problem is a family of collections $\mathcal{S}^{(0)}, \mathcal{S}^{(1)}, \ldots, \mathcal{S}^{(h)}$. We refer to $\mathcal{S}^{(j)}$ as the Level-(j) collection where each $S^{(j)} \in \mathcal{S}^{(j)}$ is a subset of $\text{LEAVES}(T)$. We refer to each $S^{(j)} \in \mathcal{S}^{(j)}$ as the Level-(j) set. We need to have the following properties.*

1. *There is exactly one Level-(0) set in $\mathcal{S}^{(0)}$.*

2. *For $j \in [h]$, all the Level-(j) sets form a partition of $\text{LEAVES}(T)$. i.e., no two Level-(j) sets intersect and $\bigcup_{S^{(j)} \in \mathcal{S}^{(j)}} S^{(j)} = \text{LEAVES}(T)$.*

3. *The total demand of each Level-(j) set is at most $\text{CP}^{(j)}$.*

4. *For $j \in [h-1]$, each Level-(j) set is a refinement of at most $\text{DEG}^{(j)}$ Level-($j+1$) sets, ie each Level-(j) set is exactly equal to the union of at most $\text{DEG}^{(j)}$ Level-($j+1$) sets from $\mathcal{S}^{(j+1)}$.*

Note that $\bigcup_{j=0}^{h} \mathcal{S}^{(j)}$ forms a laminar family for $\text{LEAVES}(T)$. The cost of this solution is $\sum_{j=1}^{h} \sum_{S^{(j)} \in \mathcal{S}^{(j)}} w_T(\text{CUT}_T(S^{(j)})) \cdot \frac{cm(j-1)-cm(j)}{2}$. where $\text{CUT}_T(S)$ for $S \subseteq \text{LEAVES}(T)$ is the minimum weight set of edges which separates the leaves in S from the rest of the leaves in T

The following lemma shows that Definition 2 and Definition 3 are the same.

Lemma 3 *For each solution defined by Definition 2 we have a corresponding solution defined by Definition 3 with the same cost and for each solution defined by Definition 3 we have a corresponding solution defined by Definition 2 with the same cost.*

In this section we prove the following theorem about the HGPT problem.

Theorem 2 *There is an algorithm for the HGP problem on trees which finds a solution partitioning the leaves of the tree with optimal cost and violates the capacity of H-nodes at most by a factor of $(1 + h) \cdot (1 + \epsilon)$ where ϵ is an arbitrary small positive value.*

The structure of our proof is as follows. We relax the HGPT problem by removing bound $\text{DEG}^{(j)}$ on the total number of subsets form Constraint 4 of Definition 3. The optimal cost of the relaxed HGPT problem is less than the optimal cost of HGPT as there are less constraints. We solve the relaxed HGPT problem in polynomial time by a dynamic programming. Finally we show that we can change a solution to the relaxed HGPT problem to a solution of HGPT by violating the demand constraint (Constraint 3 in Definition 3) by a factor of at most $(1 + j)$, *i.e.*, each Level-(j) set has the total demand of at most $(1 + j) \cdot \text{CP}^{(j)}$.

Definition 4 *A solution to the Relaxed Hierarchal Graph Partitioning on Tree (RHGPT) problem is a family of collections $\mathcal{S}^{(0)}, \mathcal{S}^{(1)}, \ldots, \mathcal{S}^{(h)}$, where*

1. *There is exactly one Level-(0) set in $\mathcal{S}^{(0)}$.*

2. *For $j \in [h]$, all the Level-(j) sets form a partition of $\text{LEAVES}(T)$, i.e., no two Level-(j) sets intersect and $\bigcup_{S^{(j)} \in \mathcal{S}^{(j)}} S^{(j)} = \text{LEAVES}(T)$.*

3. *The total demand of each Level-(j) set is at most $CP^{(j)}$.*

4. *For $j \in [h - 1]$, each Level-(j) set is a refinement of Level-$(j + 1)$ sets (there is no constraint on the number of them), ie, each Level-(j) set is exactly equal to the union of some of Level-$(j + 1)$ sets from $\mathcal{S}^{(j+1)}$.*

The cost of this solution is $\sum_{j=1}^{h} \sum_{S^{(j)} \in \mathcal{S}^{(j)}} w_T(\text{CUT}_T(S^{(j)})) \cdot \frac{cm(j-1) - cm(j)}{2}$.

Remember that $\text{CUT}_T(S)$ for $S \subseteq \text{LEAVES}(T)$ is the minimum weight set of edges which separates the leaves in S from the rest of the leaves in T and if there are multiple such sets we select the one which minimizes the number of nodes that are connected to S. If there are still multiple such sets we select the one which comes lexicographically first. Let $T \setminus \text{CUT}_T(S)$ be the forest obtained form T after removing $\text{CUT}_T(S)$ from T.

Definition 5 *The* mirror set *of $\text{CUT}_T(S)$ where $S \subseteq \text{LEAVES}(T)$ which we denote by $N(S)$ to be the set of all nodes that are in the connected components of $T \setminus \text{CUT}_T(S)$ which have at least one node of S.*

Note that $N(S)$ contains at least nodes of S. We are not going to find $N(S)$ but we use this definition to prove structural properties about solutions of HGPT.

Let $\mathcal{S}^{(0)}, \mathcal{S}^{(1)}, \ldots, \mathcal{S}^{(h)}$ be an arbitrary solution to the RHGPT problem and $S^{(j)} \in \mathcal{S}^{(j)}$. We prove the following two lemmas about the structure of mirror set $N(S^{(j)})$.

Lemma 4 *For $j \in \{1, \ldots, h\}$, for any two distinct sets $S_1^{(j)}, S_2^{(j)} \in \mathcal{S}^{(j)}$ we have $N(S_1^{(j)}) \cap N(S_2^{(j)}) = \emptyset$.*

Lemma 5 *For $j \in [h - 1]$, for any two sets $S^{(j)} \in \mathcal{S}^{(j)}$ and $S^{(j+1)} \in \mathcal{S}^{(j+1)}$ where $S^{(j+1)} \subseteq S^{(j)}$ we have $N(S^{(j+1)}) \subseteq N(S^{(j)})$.*

In the following we define a class of special solutions to the RHGPT problem which are easily tractable by dynamic programming.

Definition 6 *A nice solution to the RHGPT problem is a solution $s = (\mathcal{S}^{(0)}, \mathcal{S}^{(1)}, \ldots, \mathcal{S}^{(h)})$ where for each node $v \in V(T)$ and each level $j \in [h]$ the following holds.*

1. *There is at most one set $(S_v^{(j)} \in \mathcal{S}^{(j)})$ for which $v \in N(S_v^{(j)})$ we refer to this set if it exists as the (v, j)-active set.*

2. *For all sets $S_v^{(j)'} \in \mathcal{S}^{(j)}$ other than the (v, j)-active set $(S_v^{(j)'} \neq S_v^{(j)})$ we have either $N(S_v^{(j)'}) \subseteq \text{SUB}(v)$ or $N(S_v^{(j)'}) \cap \text{SUB}(v) = \emptyset$.*

Using Lemma 4 and Lemma 5 we can prove the following theorem.

Theorem 3 *There exists an optimal solution $(\mathcal{S}^{(0)}, \mathcal{S}^{(1)}, \ldots, \mathcal{S}^{(h)})$ to the RHGPT problem which is a nice solution.*

PROOF. First we note that any solution $s = (\mathcal{S}^{(0)}, \mathcal{S}^{(1)}, \ldots, \mathcal{S}^{(h)})$ has at most one (v, j)-active set for any $(v, j) \in V(T) \times [h]$. Because for any $S_{v,1}^{(j)}, S_{v,2}^{(j)} \in \mathcal{S}^{(j)}$, by Lemma 4 mirror sets $N(S_{v,1}^{(j)})$ and $N(S_{v,2}^{(j)})$ are disjoint which implies that the mirror set of at most one set of $\mathcal{S}^{(j)}$ contains v. Therefore the Condition 1 of a nice solution in Definition 6 holds for any solution s.

Let $s = (\mathcal{S}^{(0)}, \mathcal{S}^{(1)}, \ldots, \mathcal{S}^{(h)})$ be a solution to RHGPT.

Definition 7 *For each node $v \in V(T)$ and each level $j \in [h]$ we call $S_v^{(j)} \in \mathcal{S}^{(j)}$ a (v, j)-bad set if $S_v^{(j)}$ is not the (v, j)-active set and neither $N(S_v^{(j)}) \subseteq \text{SUB}(v)$ nor $N(S_v^{(j)}) \cap \text{SUB}(v) = \emptyset$. We denote the sum of the total number of (v, j)-bad sets over all $v \in V(T)$ and $j \in [h]$ by $BS(s)$.*

Note that if we prove that there exists an optimal solution s^* for which $BS(s^*)$ is zero then both the conditions of Definition 6 hold and the proof of the theorem follows.

Let solution $s = (\mathcal{S}^{(0)}, \mathcal{S}^{(1)}, \ldots, \mathcal{S}^{(h)})$ be an optimal solution to RHGPT that has the minimum $BS(.)$ number. We prove by contradiction that for each node $v \in V(T)$ and each level $j \in [h]$ there is no (v, j)-bad set $S_v^{(j)}$ in s. Assume otherwise, let $j \in [h]$ be the maximum level number for which there exists node $v \in V(T)$ such that there is at least one (v, j)-bad set $(S_v^{(j)})$.

Since $S_v^{(j)}$ is not the (v, j)-active set, $N(S_v^{(j)})$ does not include v. Moreover $N(S_v^{(j)}) \cap \text{SUB}(v) \neq \emptyset$ and $N(S_v^{(j)}) \not\subseteq \text{SUB}(v)$. In the following we show that we can divide $S_v^{(j)}$ to two subsets $N(S_v^{(j)}) \cap \text{SUB}(v)$ and $N(S_v^{(j)}) \setminus \text{SUB}(v)$ to obtain a new solution which has less (v, j)-bad sets than s while having the same cost.

Let U_1 be $S_v^{(j)} \cap \text{SUB}(v)$ and U_2 be $S_v^{(j)} \setminus \text{SUB}(v)$.

Observation 1 *All the following facts hold for sets U_1 and U_2 (see Figure 1).*

1. $N(U_1) \subseteq \text{SUB}(v) - \{v\}$.

2. $N(U_2) \subseteq (T \setminus \text{SUB}(v))$.

3. $N(S_v^{(j)}) = N(U_1) \cup N(U_2)$.

4. $\text{CUT}_T(S_v^{(j)}) = \text{CUT}_T(U_1) \cup \text{CUT}_T(U_2)$

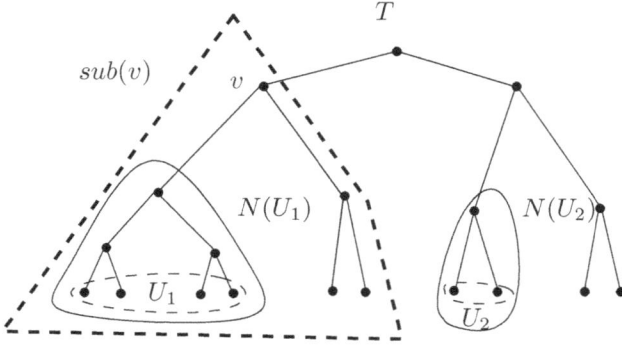

Figure 1: Dividing $N(S_v^{(j)})$ into U_1 and U_2.

We build solution $\hat{s} = (\mathcal{S}^{\hat{(0)}}, \mathcal{S}^{\hat{(1)}}, \ldots, \mathcal{S}^{\hat{(h)}})$ from s as follows. For $k \in [h] - \{j\}$ we have $\mathcal{S}^{\hat{(k)}} = \mathcal{S}^{(k)}$. Collection $\mathcal{S}^{\hat{(j)}}$ is the same as $\mathcal{S}^{(j)}$ except that we replace set $S_v^{(j)}$ with U_1 and U_2. In the full paper we show the following three claims: (1) $\hat{s}$ is a valid solution, (2) $BS(\hat{s})$ is less than $BS(s)$, and (3) $\hat{s}$ has the same cost as s and hence is an optimal solution. Existence of $\hat{s}$ contradicts with the fact that s is an optimal solution to RHGPT with minimum $BS(.)$. Therefore s does not have any (v,j)-bad set for any $(v,j) \in V(T) \times [h]$. $\square$

In the following we prove that the best nice solution can be found with dynamic programming which combined with Theorem 3 implies that we can find an optimal solution to the RHGPT problem.

Theorem 4 *We can find the best nice solution to the RHGPT problem by dynamic programming while violating the capacity constraints of Level-(j) sets (item 3 of Definition 4) by factor $(1 + \epsilon)$ for arbitrary small positive value ϵ.*

We can assume that each node of T has at most two children by repeating the following procedure. If node v of T has f_v children where $f_v > 2$, we create a binary tree of $f_v - 1$ dummy nodes where dummy nodes are connected to each other with the edges of weight infinity. If a dummy node has less than two children in addition to its child we connect it to children of v with the same weight as the edge between v and the children.

Remember that the processing demand of each node $v \in \text{LEAVES}(T)$ is $0 < d(v) \leq 1$. Let $0 < \epsilon$ be a sufficiently small constant. First we scale all the demands by factor ϵ/n and work with the new demand function d' where $d'(v) = \lfloor \frac{d(v)}{\epsilon/n} \rfloor$ for each leaf $v \in \text{LEAVES}(T)$. Note that the maximum value of d' is $\frac{n}{\epsilon}$ since $0 < d(v) \leq 1$. We also assume that the capacity of each Level-(j) H-node is scaled by factor ϵ/n. Note that the rounding error of the floor function in d' for each leaf is ϵ/n. As we can pack at most n nodes into one H-node, the total rounding error for each H-node is at most ϵ. Let $D = \sum_{v \in \text{LEAVES}(T)} d'(v)$ be the total

demand of the leaves which is upper bounded by $\frac{n^2}{\epsilon}$ since we have at most n leaves. Here we develop an algorithm whose running time is polynomial in D and hence is polynomial in n and $\frac{1}{\epsilon}$.

We try to run the dynamic programming over the nodes of T in the sense that we define a subproblem for each $v \in V(T)$ and solve the subproblem by the solutions of subproblems defined for children of v.

Let $v \in V(T)$ be an arbitrary node in T and $s = (\mathcal{S}^{(0)}, \mathcal{S}^{(1)}, \ldots, \mathcal{S}^{(h)})$ be a nice solution. We define the induced family of collection $(s_v = (\mathcal{S}_v^{(0)}, \mathcal{S}_v^{(1)}, \ldots, \mathcal{S}_v^{(h)}))$ of s in v to be the family of collections where each set $S^{(j)} \in \mathcal{S}^{(j)}$ is replaced with $S^{(j)} \cap V(\text{SUB}(v))$ in $\mathcal{S}_v^{(j)}$ and if $S^{(j)} \cap V(\text{SUB}(v)) = \emptyset$ we completely remove $S^{(j)}$ from $\mathcal{S}_v^{(j)}$. Intuitively s_v is the reflection of s (in the sense that we only include nodes of $\text{SUB}(v)$) over the subtree $\text{SUB}(v)$.

Remember that for any nice solution $s = (\mathcal{S}^{(0)}, \mathcal{S}^{(1)}, \ldots, \mathcal{S}^{(h)})$ and each level $j \in [h]$ there is at most one (v, j)-active set (see Figure 2). This means that for all other Level-(j) sets ($S^{(j)} \in \mathcal{S}^{(j)}$) either mirror set $N(S^{(j)})$ and $\text{CUT}_T(S^{(j)})$ is fully in $\text{SUB}(v)$ or fully outside $\text{SUB}(v)$. For each Level-(j) set $S^{(j)}$ that is not the (v, j)-active set either $S^{(j)}$ retains all its elements or does not appear at all when induced to v form the Level-(j) collection of s_v.

Seeing from the opposite direction, in order to rebuild Level-(j) collection $\mathcal{S}^{(j)}$ from Level-(j) induced collection $\mathcal{S}_v^{(j)}$ we need to only add some new leaves to the (v, j)-active set of $\mathcal{S}_v^{(j)}$ while all the other sets of $\mathcal{S}_v^{(j)}$ remain intact, moreover, we might add some new sets of leaves to $\mathcal{S}^{(j)}$. This leads to an important property that we can replace the induced family of collection s_v over nodes of $\text{SUB}(v)$ with any other induced family of collection s'_v (again over nodes of $\text{SUB}(v)$) in solution s and obtain a valid solution as far as the total demand of the (v, j)-active set of s_v is the same as the (v, j)-active set of s'_v. We prove this property more formally later and show that this property results in the fact that an optimal solution is also an optimal induced family of collection over any node $v \in V(T)$. Therefore, we are able to show that the optimal induced family of collection for each node v can be found by considering the optimal induced family of collections over the children of v which is the main idea of our dynamic programming.

The following is a corollary of Lemma 5.

Corollary 1 *Let s be a nice solution of RHGPT. If for level $j \in [h]$ set $S^{(j)} \in \mathcal{S}^{(j)}$ is the (v, j)-active set then there exists set $S^{(j-1)} \in \mathcal{S}^{(j-1)}$ which is the $(v, j-1)$-active set and $S^{(j)} \subseteq S^{(j-1)}$.*

Let us denote the total demand of the (v, j)-active set of s by $D_v^{(j)}$ for any $j \in [h]$, i.e., if $S^{(j)}$ is the (v, j)-active set we have $D_v^{(j)} = \sum_{v \in S^{(j)}} d'(v)$ for any $j \in [h]$. From Corollary 1 we can conclude that $D_v^{(j)} \geq D_v^{(j+1)}$ for any $j \in [h-1]$.

In the following definition we formally define a subproblem defined over subtree of v and the set of its valid solutions for any $v \in V(T)$. In fact, when solving for $\text{SUB}(v)$ we not only hierarchically partition leaves of $\text{SUB}(v)$, we also find a mirror set N_v which also shows how to cut the subset of the leaves from the rest. We will show that the only important information we need to retain when solving for the sub problem defined over $\text{SUB}(v)$ is the size of the (v, j)-active set for any $j \in [h]$ therefore we only have the h-tuple $(D_v^{(1)}, D_v^{(2)}, \ldots, D_v^{(h)})$ in the signature of the subproblem. We force the conditions of a RHGPT solution (Definition 4), conditions of a nice solution (Definition 6, and conditions implied by Corollary 1 to the valid solutions of the subproblem.

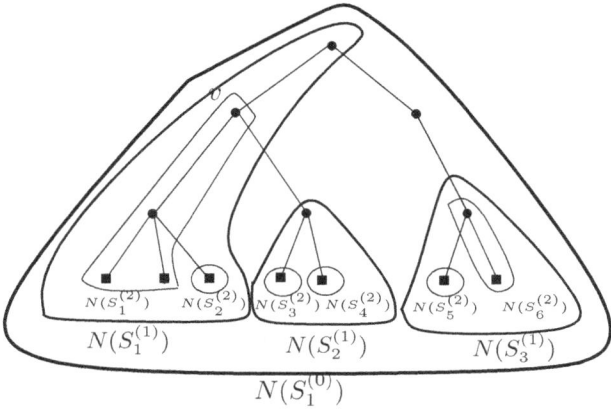

Figure 2: The mirror set $N(.)$ for all the sets in the collections of solution s. Here s has three collections $\mathcal{S}^{(0)}, \mathcal{S}^{(1)}, \mathcal{S}^{(2)}$ where $\mathcal{S}^{(0)} = \{S_1^{(0)}\}$, $\mathcal{S}^{(1)} = \{S_1^{(1)}, S_2^{(1)}, S_3^{(1)}\}$, and $\mathcal{S}^{(2)} = \{S_1^{(2)}, S_2^{(2)}, S_3^{(2)}, S_4^{(2)}, S_5^{(2)}, S_6^{(2)}\}$. Set $S_1^{(0)}$ is the $(v,0)$- active set, $S_1^{(1)}$ is the $(v,1)$-active set, and set $S_1^{(2)}$ is the $(v,2)$-active set. Set $S_1^{(0)}$ is the $(v,0)$-active set, set $S_1^{(1)}$ is the $(v,1)$-active set, and set $S_1^{(2)}$ is the $(v,2)$-active set.

Definition 8 *For a node* $v \in V(T)$ *an a h-tuple* $(D_v^{(1)}, \ldots, D_v^{(h)}) \in \underbrace{[D] \times [D] \times \ldots \times [D]}_{h}$ *(remember D is the upper bound on the total demand) which we refer to as signature, the goal of the subproblem $SP(v, (D^{(1)}, \ldots, D^{(h)}))$ is to find pair (s_v, N_v) where s_v is a family of collections $\left(\mathcal{S}_v^{(0)}, \mathcal{S}_v^{(1)}, \ldots, \mathcal{S}_v^{(h)} \right)$ and $N_v : \bigcup_j \mathcal{S}^{(j)} \to 2^{V(\mathrm{SUB}(v))}$ is a mirror set. The partial solution (s_v, N_v) has to satisfy the following conditions.*

1. *s_v has to be a solution to the RHGPT problem defined over $\mathrm{LEAVES}(\mathrm{SUB}(v))$, i.e., all the conditions of Definition 4 hold over leaves of $\mathrm{SUB}(v)$ for s_v.*

2. *For each $S_v^{(j)} \in \mathcal{S}_v^{(j)}$ for any $j \in [h]$ set $N_v(S_v^{(j)})$ has to contain only $S_v^{(j)}$ from the leaves in $\mathrm{SUB}(v)$. From $N_v(S_v^{(j)})$ we can derive cut function $\mathrm{CUT}_v : \bigcup_j \mathcal{S}^{(j)} \to 2^{E(\mathrm{SUB}(v))}$ where $\mathrm{CUT}_v(S_v^{(j)})$ is the set of all the edges that have exactly one endpoint in $N_v(S_v^{(j)})$.*

3. *For $j \in \{1, \ldots, h\}$, for any two distinct sets $S_1^{(j)}, S_2^{(j)} \in \mathcal{S}_v^{(j)}$ we have $N_v(S_1^{(j)}) \cap N_v(S_2^{(j)}) = \emptyset$.*

4. *For $j \in [h-1]$, for any two sets $S_v^{(j)} \in \mathcal{S}_v^{(j)}$ and $S_v^{(j+1)} \in \mathcal{S}_v^{(j+1)}$ where $S_v^{(j+1)} \subseteq S_v^{(j)}$ we have $N_v(S_v^{(j+1)}) \subseteq N_v(S_v^{(j)})$.*

5. *s_v and N_v have to be nice, i.e., for any $j \in [h]$ and any $u \in \mathrm{SUB}(v)$ we have:*

   (a) *There is at most one set $(A_u^{(j)} \in \mathcal{S}_v^{(j)})$ for which $u \in N_v(A_u^{(j)})$ we refer to this set if it exists as the (u,j)-active set of s_v.*

   (b) *For all sets $S_v^{(j)} \in \mathcal{S}_v^{(j)}$ other than the (u,j)-active set $(S_v^{(j)} \neq A_u^{(j)})$ we have either $N_v(S_v^{(j)}) \subseteq \mathrm{SUB}(v)$ or $N_v(S_v^{(j)}) \cap \mathrm{SUB}(v) = \emptyset$. Note that if $D_v^{(j)} = 0$ then*

there is no (v,j)-active set and hence v is not in any mirror set of Level-(j) sets of $\mathcal{S}_v^{(j)}$.

6. *Size of the (v,j)-active set of s_v has to be $D_v^{(j)}$, i.e., $\sum_{u \in A_v^{(j)}} d'(u) = D_v^{(j)}$ for any $j \in [h]$.*

cost of (s_v, N_v) which is denoted by $c_v(s_v, N_v)$ is

$$\sum_{j=1}^{h} \sum_{S_v^{(j)} \in \mathcal{S}_v^{(j)}} w(\mathrm{CUT}_v(S_v^{(j)})) \cdot \frac{cm(j-1) - cm(j)}{2}.$$

Note that Corollary 1 implies that a signature $(D^{(1)}, \ldots, D^{(h)})$ is valid if $D^{(j)} > D^{(j+1)}$ for $j \in [h-1]$. Another property that $(D^{(1)}, \ldots, D^{(h)})$ has to have in order to be a valid signature is to not violate the Level-(j) H-nodes capacity $(\mathrm{CP}^{(j)})$. In other words, $D^{(j)} \leq \mathrm{CP}^{(j)}$ for all $j \in [h]$. Therefore, if signature $(D^{(1)}, \ldots, D^{(h)})$ is not valid then we return an empty solution with infinity cost for the subproblem $SP(v, (D^{(1)}, \ldots, D^{(h)}))$.

Remember that r is the root of T, therefore if (s_r, N_r) is a non-empty solution to subproblem $SP(r, (.))$ then s_r is a solution to RHGPT over T by Condition 1 in Definition 8.

Corollary 2 *Let (s_r, N_r) be a non-empty solution to subproblem $SP(r, (.))$ then $c_r(s_r, N_r) \geq c(s_r)$.*

Corollary 3 *Let s^* be an optimal nice solution to the RHGPT problem, $N(.)$ be the mirror set as defined in Definition 5, and for any $j \in [h]$ $D_r^{(j)}$ be the size of the (r,j)-active set of s^*. Then, (s^*, N) is a valid solution for subproblem $SP(r, (D_r^{(0)}, \ldots, D_r^{(h)}))$ and $c_r(s^*, N) = c_T(s^*)$.*

From corollaries 2 and 3 we conclude that there exists $(D_r^{(1)*}, \ldots, D_r^{(h)*}) \in [D] \times \ldots \times [D]$ such that the cost of the optimal solution to $SP(r, (D_r^{(1)*}, \ldots, D_r^{(h)*}))$ is the same as the cost of the optimal solution to the RHGPT problem. Therefore, we can find the optimal solution to the RHGPT problem by solving $SP(r, (D_r^{(1)}, \ldots, D_r^{(h)}))$ for any $(D_r^{(1)}, \ldots, D_1^{(h)}) \in [D] \times \ldots \times [D]$ and take the solution which has the minimum cost. In the appendix, we show how to solve $SP(v, (D_v^{(1)}, \ldots, D_v^{(h)}))$ for any $v \in V(T)$ and $(D_v^{(1)}, \ldots, D_v^{(h)}) \in [D] \times \ldots \times [D]$ using dynamic programming.

Dynamic Programming:. **Base case.** If v is a leaf then for subproblem $SP(v, (d'(v), \ldots, d'(v)))$ we return a solution whose cost is zero and $\{v\}$ is the only set in each collection $\mathcal{S}^{(j)}$ which is also the (v,j)-active set for any $j \in [h]$. For any other signatures in subproblem $SP(v, .)$ we return an empty solution with infinity cost.

Recursive Step. In the following we show that $SP(v, (D_v^{(1)}, \ldots, D_v^{(h)}))$ is solvable for any $(D_v^{(1)}, \ldots, D_v^{(h)})$ knowing the solution to the subproblems of the children of v. Therefore, we can start from the leaves of T and recursively solve subproblem SP till reach to root r.

Here we assume that v has two children v_1 and v_2. The case when v has only one child is easier. Let $(D_v^{(1)}, \ldots, D_v^{(h)}) \in [D] \times \ldots \times [D]$ be an arbitrary valid signature we focus on solving subproblem $SP(v, (D_v^{(1)}, \ldots, D_v^{(h)}))$.

We define induce function INDUCE which takes a solution to $SP(v, (D_v^{(1)}, \ldots, D_v^{(h)}))$ and a child of v and induce the solution to the subtree defined over the given child. More formally, let (s_v, N_v) be an optimal solution for $SP(v, (D_v^{(1)}, \ldots, D_v^{(h)}))$ then $\textsc{induce}(v_1, s_v, N_v)$ is equal to (s_1, N_1). Here $s_1 = (\mathcal{S}_1^{(0)}, \mathcal{S}_1^{(1)}, \ldots, \mathcal{S}_1^{(h)})$ is the family of collections where for each set $S_v^{(j)} \in \mathcal{S}_v^{(j)}$ if $S_v^{(j)} \cap V(\textsc{sub}(v_1)) \neq \emptyset$ we add $S_v^{(j)} \cap V(\textsc{sub}(v_1))$ to $\mathcal{S}_1^{(j)}$ with mirror set $N_1(S_v^{(j)} \cap V(\textsc{sub}(v_1))) = N_v(S_v^{(j)}) \cap V(\textsc{sub}(v_1))$.

The important property we have about $SP(v, (D_v^{(1)}, \ldots, D_v^{(h)}))$ is that there exist an optimal solution which is also an optimal solution when induced to v_1 or v_2.

Lemma 6 *There exists an optimal solution (s_v^*, N_v^*) to $SP(v, (D_v^{(1)}, \ldots, D_v^{(h)}))$, $(D_1^{(1)}, \ldots, D_1^{(h)}), (D_2^{(1)}, \ldots, D_2^{(h)}) \in [D] \times \ldots \times [D]$ such that $\textsc{induce}(v_1, s_v^*, N_v^*)$ is an optimal solution to $SP(v_1, (D_1^{(1)}, \ldots, D_1^{(h)}))$ and $\textsc{induce}(v_2, s_v^*, N_v^*)$ is an optimal solution to $SP(v_2, (D_2^{(1)}, \ldots, D_2^{(h)}))$.*

From Lemma 6 we know that there exists an optimal solution for v which is an optimal solution for subproblems defined for both children v_1 and v_2 when induced to them. Therefore, in order to solve $SP(v, (D_v^{(1)}, \ldots, D_v^{(h)}))$, we loop over all the signatures $(D_1^{(0)}, \ldots, D_1^{(h)}), (D_2^{(0)}, \ldots, D_2^{(h)}) \in [D] \times \ldots \times [D]$ and solve subproblems $SP(v_1, (D_1^{(0)}, \ldots, D_1^{(h)}))$ and $SP(v_2, (D_2^{(0)}, \ldots, D_2^{(h)}))$ and merge their optimal solutions. Note that in the merging process the edge vv_1 which connects v to its children might be in the $\textsc{cut}_T$ of some Level-(j) sets and hence adds additional cost to the merged solution (the same thing can happen for vv_2). In the following we show carefully that the extra cost of merging two solutions of children of v only depends on the signatures of the solutions.

Let (s_1, N_1) be a solution for node v_1 with signature D_1^h and (s_2, N_2) be a solution for node v_2 with signature D_2^h. Suppose we want to merge these two solutions and obtain solution (s_v, N_v) for v such that it has signature D_v^h.

Consider a specific level number $j \in [h]$. Let the Level-(j) collection of s_1 be $\mathcal{S}_1^{(j)}$ and the Level-(j) collection of s_2 be $\mathcal{S}_2^{(j)}$ which we want to join and obtain the Level-(j) collection $(\mathcal{S}_v^{(j)})$ of s_v. Note that all the sets of $\mathcal{S}_1^{(j)}$ will remain intact when merging with $\mathcal{S}_2^{(j)}$ except the (v_1, j)-active set (see Condition 5 of Definition 8). In fact the only two sets that could merge together in $\mathcal{S}_v^{(j)}$ are the (v_1, j)-active set of $\mathcal{S}_1^{(j)}$ and the (v_2, j)-active set of $\mathcal{S}_2^{(j)}$. From the signatures of solutions we know that the size of (v_1, j)-active set is $D_1^{(j)}$ and the size of (v_2, j)-active set is $D_2^{(j)}$

For node v_1 (the case for v_2 is the same) and each level number j_1 we have two choices: (1) either we cut edge vv_1 (edge vv_1 is included in $\textsc{cut}_T$ of Level-(j_1) (v_1, j_1)-active set of s_1) and pay $w(vv_1) \cdot \frac{cm(j_1-1)-cm(j_1)}{2}$ or (2) we do not cut vv_1 at level j_1. In the former the (v_1, j_1)-active set of v_1 which has total demand of $D_1^{(j)}$ is closed and is not part of the (v, j_1)-active set of v. In the later if the (v_1, j_1)-active set has a non-zero total demand ($D_1^{(j)} \neq 0$) then it is part of the (v, j_1)-active set, moreover, as the (v, j_1)-active set of v is a subset of all (v, k)-active sets for $k < j_1$ we cannot cut vv_1 for all the other lower levels. In other words, for node v_1 we need to decide about level j_1 where we cut edge vv_1 for all the levels $k > j_1$ and keep edge vv_1 for all levels $k \leq j_1$. This leads to definition of consistency between two signatures associated with children of v as follows.

Definition 9 *A valid signature $(D_1^{(1)}, \ldots, D_1^{(h)})$ is (j_1, j_2)-consistent with signature $(D_2^{(1)}, \ldots, D_2^{(h)})$ regarding signature*

$(D^{(1)}, \ldots, D^{(h)})$ *if the following holds. For each $k \leq \min(j_1, j_2)$ we have $D^{(k)} = D_1^{(k)} + D_2^{(k)}$. For each $k > \max(j_1, j_2)$ we have $D^{(k)} = 0$. If $j_1 \geq j_2$ then for each $j_2 < k \leq j_1$ we have $D^{(k)} = D_1^{(k)}$ otherwise for each $j_1 < k \leq j_2$ we have $D^{(k)} = D_2^{(k)}$.*

Now we explain how to merge the partial solutions of two children of v to get a partial solution to v. Remember $s_1 = (\mathcal{S}_1^{(0)}, \ldots, \mathcal{S}_1^{(0)})$ is a partial solution in node v_1 with signature $(D_1^{(1)}, \ldots, D_1^{(h)})$ and $s_2 = (\mathcal{S}_2^{(0)}, \ldots, \mathcal{S}_2^{(0)})$ is a partial solution in v_2 with signature $(D_2^{(1)}, \ldots, D_2^{(h)})$. Assume that $(D_1^{(1)}, \ldots, D_1^{(h)})$ and $(D_2^{(1)}, \ldots, D_2^{(h)})$ are (j_1, j_2)-consistent with regard to $(D^{(1)}, \ldots, D^{(h)})$. Without loss of generality assume $j_1 \leq j_2$. The output of function $merge(s_{v_1}, j_1, s_{v_2}, j_2)$ is a partial solution $s_v = (\mathcal{S}_v^{(0)}, \ldots, \mathcal{S}_v^{(0)})$ for v where

- For $k > j_2$ we have $\mathcal{S}^{(k)} = \mathcal{S}_1^{(k)} \cup \mathcal{S}_2^{(k)}$ and there is no (v, k)-active set (size of the (v, k)-active set is zero).

- For $j_1 < k \leq j_2$ we have $\mathcal{S}^{(k)} = \mathcal{S}_1^{(k)} \cup \mathcal{S}_2^{(k)}$ and the (v, k)-active set is the (v_2, k)-active set of s_2.

- For $k \leq j_1$ lets $S_1^{(k)}$ be the (v_1, k)-active set of s_1 and $S_2^{(k)}$ be the (v_2, j_2)-active set of s_2 then $\mathcal{S}^{(k)} = \mathcal{S}_1^{(k)} \cup \mathcal{S}_2^{(k)}$ in which we replace $S_1^{(k)}$ and $S_2^{(k)}$ with $S_1^{(k)} \cup S_2^{(k)}$. The (v, k)-active set in this case is $S_1^{(k)} \cup S_2^{(k)}$.

Note that for each level $k > j_1$ if size of (v_1, k)-active set of s_1 ($D_1^{(k)}$) is larger than zero then we cut edge (vv_1) and pay $w(vv_1) \cdot \frac{cm(k-1)-cm(k)}{2}$; a similar argument holds for v_2. The partial cost of s_v is

$$
\begin{aligned}
c(s_v) = \; & c(s_1) + c(s_2) \\
& + \sum_{k : k > j_1 \wedge D_1^{(k)} \neq 0} w(vv_1) \cdot \frac{cm(k-1)-cm(k)}{2} \\
& + \sum_{k : k > j_2 \wedge D_2^{(k)} \neq 0} w(vv_1) \cdot \frac{cm(k-1)-cm(k)}{2} \quad (4)
\end{aligned}
$$

Now we prove the following claim to show how we can find an optimal partial solution for v given optimal partial solutions of its children.

Claim 1 *Let v be a node in T which has two children v_1 and v_2. We can find an optimal solution for subproblem $SP(v, (D^{(1)}, \ldots, D^{(h)}))$ if for any signature $(D_1^{(1)}, \ldots, D_1^{(h)})$ we know an optimal solution to $SP(v_1, (D_1^{(1)}, \ldots, D_1^{(h)}))$ and for any signature $(D_2^{(1)}, \ldots, D_2^{(h)})$ we know an optimal solution to $SP(v_2, (D_2^{(1)}, \ldots, D_2^{(h)}))$.*

PROOF. We run Dynamic Program (DP) algorithm as follows

1. Initialize s_v with an empty solution with cost infinity.

2. For each valid signature $(D_1^{(1)}, \ldots, D_1^{(h)}), (D_2^{(1)}, \ldots, D_2^{(h)}) \in \underbrace{[D] \times [D] \times \ldots \times [D]}_{h}$ and each $j_1, j_2 \in [h]$.

   (a) $s_1 = SP(v_1, (D_1^{(1)}, \ldots, D_1^{(h)}))$.

   (b) $s_2 = SP(v_2, (D_2^{(1)}, \ldots, D_2^{(h)}))$.

(c) if $c(s_1)$ and $c(s_2)$ are not infinity and $(D_1^{(1)}, \ldots, D_1^{(h)})$ and $(D_2^{(1)}, \ldots, D_2^{(h)})$ are (j_1, j_2)-consistent with regard to $(D^{(1)}, \ldots, D^{(h)})$ then:

  i. $s_v' = merge(s_1, j_1, s_2, j_2)$.
  ii. if $c(s_v') < c(s_v)$ then
     A. $s_v = s_v'$.

3. Return s_v.

Finally note that the running time of DP is D^{2h+2}. $\quad\square$

Note that we have in total $O(n)$ nodes and D^h different signatures where solving each subproblem SP takes $O(D^{2h+2})$. Therefore the total running time is $O(n \cdot D^{3h+2})$.

Finally in the following theorem, we show that we can transform any solution to the RHGPT problem to a solution of HGPT by violating the demand capacities.

Theorem 5 *Any solution to the RHGPT problem (Definition 4) can be transformed to a solution of HGPT (Definition 3) without increasing the cost by violating the demand capacities of each Level-(j) set (Constraint 3 in Definition 3) by a factor of $(1 + j)$.*

We apply the procedure of Theorem 5 to the solution of Theorem 4 which gives violation factor $(1 + \epsilon)(1 + h)$ in capacity and since cost is preserved optimally, we get the result stated in Theorem 2.

4. HGP ON ARBITRARY GRAPHS

We embed G into a probability distribution π of p decomposition trees $T_1, T_2, \ldots, T_p$ using Räecke's congestion minimization embedding [26]. A decomposition tree (T) comes along with a node mapping function $m_V : V(T) \to V(G)$ and an edge mapping function $m_E : E(T) \to E^*(G)$. Function m_V maps each vertex of T to a node in G such that it induces a bijection between the leaves of T and the nodes in G. Function m_E maps each edge $e_T = (u_T, v_T)$ of T to a corresponding path in G that connects $m_V(u_t)$ to $m_V(v_T)$. Let function m_V' be the reverse of m_V on the leaves of T which maps each node in G to a leaf in T.

Let u_T and v_T be two neighboring nodes in T with edge $e_T = (u_T, v_T)$ between them. The weight of edge e_T is defined as $w_T(u_T, v_T) = \sum_{m'(u) \in V_{u_T}, m'(v) \in V_{v_T}} w(u, v)$ where V_{u_T}, and V_{v_T} denote the two sets in the partition created by edge e_T over LEAVES(T).

Let P_T be an arbitrary subset of leaves in T. We use $m(P_T)$ to refer to a set of nodes in G where $u \in m(P_T)$ if and only if $m'(u) \in P_T$. We define CUT$_T(P_T)$ where $P_T \subseteq$ LEAVES(T) to be the minimum weight set of edges which separates the leaves in P_T from the rest of the leaves in T. In other words, if we remove the edges of CUT$_T(P_T)$ from T then there will be no path between any leaf in P_T and any leave outside of P_T. If there are multiple such sets we select the one which minimizes the number of nodes that are connected to P_T. If there are still multiple such sets we select the one which comes lexicographically first. (We use this property in the next section when we design our algorithm). The following proposition is a direct result of the way we set the weight of each edge in decomposition tree T.

Proposition 1 *Let P_T be a subset of leaves of decomposition tree T then we have $w_T(\text{CUT}_T(P_T)) \geq w(\text{CUT}(m(P_T)))$.*

A flow $(\mathcal{F}_{s,t})$ between source node s and target t is a set of paths where each path $p_{s,t}$ starts from s, ends at t, and carries $f_{s,t}^p$ amount of flow. Here $\mathcal{F}_{s,t}$ carries the total flow of $\sum_{p \in \mathcal{F}_{s,t}} f_{s,t}^p$. A multi-commodity flow $(\mathcal{MF})$ is the set of $\binom{n}{2}$ flows, one flow for each pair of nodes $\{u, v\}$ in G. The congestion imposed by $\mathcal{MF}$ on G is defined as $max_e\, Load_{\mathcal{MF}}(e)/w(e)$ where $Load_{\mathcal{MF}}(e)$ is the total amount of flow that passes through edge e.

Similar to the edges and nodes we define functions m and m' in order to map a multi-commodity flow from decomposition tree T to G and vice versa. For a given multi-commodity flow $\mathcal{MF}$ in G we can obtain the corresponding multi-commodity flow $\mathcal{MF}_T = m'(\mathcal{MF}_T)$ in decomposition tree T by routing the total flow between each pair of nodes u and v in $\mathcal{MF}$ in the unique path between $m_V'(u)$ and $m_V'(v)$. Similarly, for a given multi-commodity flow $\mathcal{MF}_T$ in decomposition tree T we can obtain the corresponding multi-commodity flow $\mathcal{MF} = m(\mathcal{MF}_T)$ in G by routing all the flow passing through each edge e_T through the path $m_E(e_T)$ in G.

The main contribution of Räecke [26] on embedding graph G into a convex combination of decomposition trees is the following theorem.

Theorem 6 ([26]) *For a graph G there exists a convex combination of $p = O(|E| \log n)$ decomposition trees $T_1, \ldots, T_p$ where each tree T_i has a multiplier λ_i with $\sum_{i=1}^p \lambda_i = 1$ such that the following holds. Suppose we are given a multi-commodity flow $\mathcal{MF}_i$ for each tree T_i with congestion at most C. Then if we map all the multi-commodity flows $\mathcal{MF}_i$ on G when scaled by multiplier λ_i, results in a multi-commodity flow $\mathcal{MF} = \sum_{i=1}^p \lambda_i m_{T_i}(\mathcal{MF}_i)$ in G with congestion at most $O(\log n \cdot C)$.*

Our goal is to use the above theorem to show by solving HGP efficiently in decomposition trees we can obtain an $O(\log n)$-approximation algorithm for HGP in G. Before we start we define a solution to the HGP problem in a decomposition tree. Note that there is a bijection between leaves of a decomposition tree and nodes of G. Therefore we are only interested in assigning leaves of a decomposition trees to the H-nodes.

Definition 10 *For a decomposition tree T, mirror function $\mathcal{P}_T$ is a solution to the HGP problem in T where for each $a_H^{(j)} \in V(H)$ we have $\mathcal{P}_T(a_H^{(j)})$ is a subset of leaves of T. The cost of solution $\mathcal{P}_T$ in T is*

$$C_T(\mathcal{P}_T) = \sum_{a_H^{(j)} \in V(H)} w_T(\text{CUT}_T(\mathcal{P}_T(a_H^{(j)}))) \cdot \frac{cm(j-1) - cm(j)}{2}.$$

Let $\mathcal{P}_T$ be a solution to the HGP in decomposition tree T assigning each of LEAVES(H) to a subset of leaves of T. Similar to multi-commodity flows we use function m_V to map solution $\mathcal{P}_T$ to a solution in G. Let $\mathcal{P} = m(\mathcal{P}_T)$ be a solution for HGP in G where each $a_H \in V(H)$ is assigned to set $m(\mathcal{P}_T(a_H))$, more formally, $\mathcal{P} : V(H) \to 2^{V(G)}$ where $\mathcal{P}(a_H) = \{m_V(v_T) \in V(G) | v_T \in \mathcal{P}_T(a_H)\}$. It can be shown that the cost of a solution in decomposition tree T, $C_T(\mathcal{P}_T)$, is larger than its corresponding solution in G, $C(m(\mathcal{P}_T))$.

Theorem 7 *Let $T_1, \ldots, T_p$ where $p = O(|E| \log n)$ be the set of decomposition trees specified in Theorem 6. Let $\mathcal{P}_i^*$ be the optimum solution of HGP over the leaves of tree T_i and $\mathcal{P}^*$ be an optimal solution to the HGP problem in G. Then the cost of solution $m(\mathcal{P}_q^*)$ where $q = \arg \min_i C_{T_i}(\mathcal{P}_i^*)$ is at most $\beta \cdot C(\mathcal{P}^*)$ where $\beta = O(\log n)$ in Theorem 6.*

We run the algorithm of Theorem 2 on each decomposition tree specified in Theorem 7 and select the solution with the best cost. Therefore, Theorem 1 which is our main result follows.

5. ACKNOWLEDGMENTS

The authors would like to thank anonymous reviewers for all their useful comments.

References

[1] K. Andreev and H. Räcke. Balanced graph partitioning. In *SPAA*, pages 120–124, 2004.

[2] M. Andrews, M. Hajiaghayi, H. Karloff, and A. Moitra. Capacitated metric labeling. In *SODA*, pages 976–995, 2011.

[3] S. Arora, S. Rao, and U. Vazirani. Expander flows, geometric embeddings and graph partitioning. *J. ACM*, 56 (2):5:1–5:37, 2009.

[4] C.-E. Bichot and P. Siarry. *Graph partitioning*. John Wiley & Sons, 2013.

[5] S. Y. Chan, T. C. Ling, and E. Aubanel. The impact of heterogeneous multi-core clusters on graph partitioning: an empirical study. *Cluster Computing*, 15(3):281–302, 2012.

[6] S. Chawla, R. Krauthgamer, R. Kumar, Y. Rabani, and D. Sivakumar. On the hardness of approximating multicut and sparsest-cut. *Comput. Complex.*, 15(2):94–114, 2006.

[7] J. Chen and V. E. Taylor. Parapart: parallel mesh partitioning tool for distributed systems. *Concurrency: Practice and Experience*, 12(2-3):111–123, 2000.

[8] K. Devine, E. Boman, R. Heaphy, B. Hendrickson, and C. Vaughan. Zoltan data management services for parallel dynamic applications. *Computing in Science & Engineering*, 4(2):90–96, 2002.

[9] G. Even, J. S. Naor, S. Rao, and B. Schieber. Fast approximate graph partitioning algorithms. In *SODA*, pages 639–648, 1997.

[10] U. Feige and R. Krauthgamer. A polylogarithmic approximation of the minimum bisection. *SIAM J. Comput.*, 31(4):1090–1118, 2002.

[11] A. E. Feldmann and L. Foschini. Balanced Partitions of Trees and Applications. In *STACS*, volume 14, pages 100–111, 2012.

[12] B. Gedik, H. Andrade, K.-L. Wu, P. S. Yu, and M. Doo. Spade: the system s declarative stream processing engine. In *SIGMOD*, pages 1123–1134, 2008.

[13] L. Golab and T. Johnson. Data stream warehousing. In *SIGMOD*, pages 949–952, 2013.

[14] D. s. Hochbaum and D. B. Shmoys. A polynomial approximation scheme for scheduling on uniform processors: Using the dual approximation approach. *SIAM J. Comput.*, 17(3):539–551, 1988.

[15] T. Hoefler, E. Jeannot, G. Mercier, and J. Žilinskas. An overview of topology mapping algorithms and techniques in high-performance computing. *High-Performance Computing on Complex Environments*, pages 73–94, 2014.

[16] S. A. Khot and N. K. Vishnoi. The unique games conjecture, integrality gap for cut problems and embeddability of negative type metrics into $\ell 1$. In *FOCS*, pages 53–62, 2005.

[17] J. Kleinberg and E. Tardos. Approximation algorithms for classification problems with pairwise relationships: metric labeling and markov random fields. *J. ACM*, 49(5):616–639, 2002.

[18] R. Krauthgamer and Y. Rabani. Improved lower bounds for embeddings into l1. In *SODA*, pages 1010–1017, 2006.

[19] R. Krauthgamer, J. S. Naor, and R. Schwartz. Partitioning graphs into balanced components. In *SODA*, pages 942–949, 2009.

[20] T. Leighton and S. Rao. Multicommodity max-flow min-cut theorems and their use in designing approximation algorithms. *J. ACM*, 46(6):787–832, Nov. 1999.

[21] T. Leighton, F. Makedon, and S. Tragoudas. Approximation algorithms for vlsi partition problems. In *IEEE International Symposium on Circuits and Systems*, pages 2865–2868 vol.4, 1990.

[22] I. Moulitsas and G. Karypis. *Architecture aware partitioning algorithms*. Springer, 2008.

[23] J. Naor and R. Schwartz. Balanced metric labeling. In *STOC*, pages 582–591. ACM, 2005.

[24] F. Pellegrini. Static mapping by dual recursive bipartitioning of process architecture graphs. In *Scalable High-Performance Computing Conference, 1994., Proceedings of the*, pages 486–493. IEEE, 1994.

[25] F. Pellegrini and J. Roman. Scotch: A software package for static mapping by dual recursive bipartitioning of process and architecture graphs. In *High-Performance Computing and Networking*, pages 493–498. Springer, 1996.

[26] H. Räcke. Optimal hierarchical decompositions for congestion minimization in networks. In *STOC*, pages 255–264. ACM, 2008.

[27] H. D. Simon and S.-H. Teng. How good is recursive bisection? *SIAM J. Sci. Comput.*, 18(5):1436–1445, 1997.

[28] J. D. Teresco, J. Faik, and J. E. Flaherty. Hierarchical partitioning and dynamic load balancing for scientific computation. In *Applied Parallel Computing. State of the Art in Scientific Computing*, pages 911–920. Springer, 2006.

[29] J. L. Traff. Implementing the mpi process topology mechanism. In *Supercomputing, ACM/IEEE 2002 Conference*, pages 28–28. IEEE, 2002.

[30] C. Walshaw and M. Cross. Parallel optimisation algorithms for multilevel mesh partitioning. *Parallel Computing*, 26 (12):1635–1660, 2000.

[31] C. Walshaw and M. Cross. Multilevel mesh partitioning for heterogeneous communication networks. *Future generation computer systems*, 17(5):601–623, 2001.

Simple Parallel and Distributed Algorithms for Spectral Graph Sparsification

Ioannis Koutis
Computer Science Department
University of Puerto Rico-Rio Piedras
ioannis.koutis@upr.edu

ABSTRACT

We describe a simple algorithm for spectral graph sparsification, based on iterative computations of weighted spanners and uniform sampling. Leveraging the algorithms of Baswana and Sen for computing spanners, we obtain the first distributed spectral sparsification algorithm. We also obtain a parallel algorithm with improved work and time guarantees. Combining this algorithm with the parallel framework of Peng and Spielman for solving symmetric diagonally dominant linear systems, we get a parallel solver which is much closer to being practical and significantly more efficient in terms of the total work.

Categories and Subject Descriptors

F.2 [**Theory of Computation**]: Analysis of Algorithms and Problem Complexity

Keywords

Parallel algorithms; Distributed algorithms; Spectral Sparsification; SDD linear systems.

1. INTRODUCTION

The efficient transformation of dense instances of graph problems to nearly equivalent sparse instances is a powerful tool in algorithm design. Spectral sparsifiers are sparse graphs that preserve within an $1+\epsilon$ factor the quadratic form $x^T L_G x$, where L_G is the Laplacian of G and ϵ is a parameter of choice. They were introduced by Spielman and Teng [24] as a basic component of the first nearly-linear time solvers for linear systems on symmetric diagonally dominant (SDD) matrices [1]. Such linear system solvers are a key algorithmic primitive with numerous applications [17, 25].

The Spielman and Teng sparsification algorithm produces sparsifiers with $O(n \log^c n/\epsilon^2)$ edges for some fairly large constant c, where n is the number of vertices in the graph.

---

[1] A symmetric matrix A is SDD if for all i, $A_{ii} \geq \sum_{j \neq i} |A_{ij}|$.

SPAA'14, June 23–25, 2014, Prague, Czech Republic.
Copyright 2014 ACM 978-1-4503-2821-0/14/06 ...$15.00.
http://dx.doi.org/10.1145/2612669.2612676 .

At a high level their algorithm is based on graph decompositions into edge-disjoint sets that get sparsified independently via uniform sampling. As noted in [22] the algorithm can be parallelized if the original partitioning subroutine is substituted by a more recent one due to Orecchia and Vishnoi [20].

Peng and Spielman [22] recently presented a novel algebraic framework for solving SDD systems. It enables the use of parallel sparsification algorithms for constructing parallel solvers. Combined with the parallelized Spielman and Teng sparsification algorithm, or a more recent approach due to Peng (Section 3.4, [21]), this algebraic framework yields the first 'truly' parallel SDD solver that does near-linear work and runs in polylogarithmic time.

The new parallel solver leaves something to be desired: its work is by several logarithmic factors larger than that of the fastest known sequential algorithm that runs in $\tilde{O}(m \log n)$ time[2]; here m is the number of non-zero entries in the matrix [16]. This motivates our study on parallel and distributed sparsification algorithms.

Background on spectral sparsification. Besides yielding the SDD solver, the work of Spielman and Teng spurred further research on spectral sparsification as a stand-alone problem. Spielman and Srivastava [23] showed that it is possible to produce a sparsifier with $O(n \log n/\epsilon^2)$ edges in near-linear time. Their approach is based on viewing the graph as an electrical resistive network, where one can define the effective resistance of an edge as the potential difference that must be applied between its two endpoints in order to send one unit of electrical flow from the one vertex to the other. The sparsifier is computed by sampling edges with probabilities proportional to the their effective resistances. Spielman and Srivastava also showed that $O(\log n)$ calls to a solver for SDD linear systems can produce sufficiently good approximations to all effective resistances, allowing for a near-linear time implementation of their sampling scheme. This development was followed by works on slower but more sparsity-efficient spectral sparsification algorithms [2, 10] and on sparsification in the semi-streaming model [8].

The work of Spielman and Srivastava opened the way to the near-$m \log n$ time solver in [15, 16]. This fast solver utilizes an 'incremental sparsification' algorithm that produces a very mildly sparser spectral approximation to the input graph. A direct by-product of this fast solver was the acceleration of the Spielman-Srivastava sparsification scheme. Their scheme was further improved in [12, 11], yielding an $\tilde{O}(m)$ solver for slightly non-sparse graphs; the solver com-

---

[2] We use $\tilde{O}()$ to hide a $poly(\log \log n)$ factor.

bines in an intricate recursive way slower solvers with spectral sparsifiers.

Recent efforts aim to obtain simpler algorithms via alternative approaches. In particular, there has been an interest in combinatorial algorithms that rely less on the power of algebra to achieve similar results [7, 9]. We do not insist that these simpler algorithms are asymptotically as efficient as their algebraic counterparts. In practice there are many phenomena, subtler than asymptotic behavior or even hidden constants, that affect the performance of linear system solvers, and different ideas may lead to better implementations. In particular, there are implementations that exhibit great empirical performance on sparse matrices [13, 19]; solve-free techniques for spectral sparsification have the potential of extending the applicability of these implementations to dense matrices.

The first combinatorial alternative to the spectral sparsification algorithm of Spielman and Teng was given by Kapralov and Panigrahi [7]. A novel feature of their work is the introduction of spanners in the context of spectral graph sparsification. The algorithm is based on tightly approximating effective resistances; more concretely, they define 'robust connectivities' of edges and show they are good upper bounds to the effective resistances, on average. Approximate robust connectivities are then used for sampling; the result follows from an application of the 'oversampling' Lemma of [15] which shows that extra sampling can compensate for the the lack of accuracy in the estimates for the effective resistances; this extra sampling yields the slightly more dense sparsifier. The algorithm generates a sparsifier with $O(n \log^4 n/\epsilon^4)$ edges in $O(m \log^4 n)$ time but it doesn't parallelize mostly due to the use of distance oracles by Thorup and wick [26].

For a more thorough review of the sparsification literature, we refer the reader to the excellent article by Batson et al. [3].

In this work. We describe a simple parallel and distributed algorithm that exposes a closer connection between spanners and sparsification. Using only iterated computations of weighted spanners and uniform sampling the algorithm produces a sparsifier with $O(n \log^3 n \log^3 \rho/\epsilon^2 + m/\rho)$ edges, where ρ is a **sparsification factor** of choice.

The idea behind the algorithm is simple. In order to reduce the number of edges by a factor of ρ, we compute $O(\log^2 n \log^2 \rho/\epsilon^2)$ edge-disjoint spanners of the graph that allow us to certify upper bounds for the effective resistances of the rest of the edges. The upper bounds enable uniformly sampling-away about half of the remaining edges while spectrally preserving the graph within a $(1 + \epsilon/(4 \log \rho))$ factor. The process is applied iteratively, and after $O(\log \rho)$ rounds we get a graph that $(1 + \epsilon)$-approximates the input graph and has $O(n \log^3 n \log^3 \rho + m/\rho)$ edges. The total work is $O(m \log^2 n \log^3 \rho/\epsilon^2)$.

We use our parallel sparsification algorithm to obtain a solver for SDD linear systems that works in polylogarithmic time and does $\tilde{O}((m \log^2 n + n \log^5 n \log^5 \kappa)(\log(1/\tau)))$ work, where τ is a standard measure of tolerance in the error of the approximate solution, and κ is the condition number of the input system.

2. BACKGROUND

Laplacians. Given a weighted graph $G = (V, E, w > 0)$ where $V = \{1, \ldots, n\}$, its Laplacian L_G is the matrix defined by:

(i) $L_G(i, j) = -w_{ij}$ for $i \neq j$ and (ii) $L_G(i, i) = \sum_{j \neq i} w_{ij}$.

Throughout the paper we will n, m to denote the number of vertices and edges of a graph respectively. We will apply algebraic operators on graphs in a standard way. Specifically, given two graphs $G_1 = (V, E, w_1)$ and $G_1 = (V, E, w_2)$ we denote by $G_1 + G_2$ the graph $(V, E, w_1 + w_2)$. Also given a scalar a we let $aG_1 = (V, E, aw_1)$.

Spectral approximation. We say that a graph H, (β/α)-approximates a graph G if:

$$\alpha(x^T L_H x) \leq x^T L_G x \leq \beta(x^T L_H x).$$

Finally, if for all vectors x we have $x^T L_{G_2} x \leq x^T L_{G_1} x$ we will write $G_2 \preceq G_1$.

Stretch. Let p be a path joining the two endpoints of an edge $e \in E$. The stretch $st_p(e)$ of an edge e, is equal to

$$w_e \sum_{e' \in p} (1/w_{e'}).$$

We also define the stretch of e over a graph H as

$$st_H(e) = \min_{p \in H} st_p(e).$$

Spanners. A $\log n$-spanner of a graph G is a subgraph H of G such that for all edges $e \in E$

$$st_H(e) \leq 2 \log n.$$

In the rest of the paper we will use the term spanner to mean a $\log n$-spanner. Every graph contains a spanner with $O(n \log n)$ edges that can be computed efficiently in the CRCW PRAM model and the synchronous distributed model. Concretely, we adapt here Theorems 5.4 and 5.1 respectively, from Baswana and Sen [1].

THEOREM 1. *Given a graph G, a spanner for G of expected size $O(n \log n)$ can be constructed with $O(m \log n)$ work in $\tilde{O}(\log n)$ time with high probability. The algorithm runs in the CRCW PRAM model.*

THEOREM 2. *Given a graph G, a spanner for G of expected size $O(n \log n)$ can be constructed in the synchronous distributed model in $O(\log^2 n)$ rounds and $O(m \log n)$ communication complexity. Moreover, the length of each message communicated is $O(\log n)$.*

Here we define an object that plays a key role in our algorithm.

DEFINITION 1. *Let G be a graph and $H_1, \ldots, H_t$ be subgraphs of G such that H_i is a spanner for the graph $G - \sum_{j=1}^{i-1} H_j$. We call $H = \sum_{j=1}^{t} H_j$ a t-bundle spanner. We call the H_i's the components of H.*

Effective Resistance. A graph can be viewed as an electrical resistive network, with each edge corresponding to a resistor having resistance $r_e = 1/w_e$. The effective resistance $R_{u,v}[G]$ between two vertices u and v in G is defined as the potential difference that has to be applied on u and v in order to drive one unit of current through the network. For instance, in the case of a path p the effective resistance between the two endpoints of p is equal to

$R_e[p] = \sum_{e' \in p}(1/w_{e'})$; this is the well known formula for resistors connected in series.

Now let us recall a simple fact about paths connected 'in parallel', i.e. paths that are vertex-disjoint with the exception of their shared endpoints u and v. Let $p_1, \ldots, p_t$ be paths connected in parallel. Let $P = \sum_{i=1}^t p_i$. For the effective resistance between u and v, in the graph P consisting of the union of the paths, we have

$$R_{u,v}[P] = \left(\sum_{i=1}^t (R_{u,v}[p_i])^{-1} \right)^{-1}. \quad (2.1)$$

The following Lemma has a key role in our sparsification algorithm.

LEMMA 1. *Let G be a graph and H be a t-bundle spanner of G. For every edge e of G which is not in H, we have*

$$w_e R_e[G] \leq \log n/t.$$

PROOF. Let $H_1, \ldots, H_t$ be the components of H. If H' is any subgraph of G then by Rayleigh's monotonicity law [5] the effective resistance of e is at most equal to the effective resistance between the two endpoints of e in H'. In particular, fix an arbitrary edge e not in H. For each i we know by definition that it contains a path p_i such that

$$w_e \sum_{e' \in p_i} (1/w_{e'}) \leq 2 \log n.$$

As we discussed above $\sum_{e' \in p_u}(1/w_{e'})$ is equal to the resistance between the two endpoints of e in p. This implies that the effective resistance of e over p_i satisfies

$$R_e[p_i] \leq 2 \log n/w_e.$$

Now we observe that by definition the paths p_i connect in parallel the two endpoints of e. Let $P = \sum_{j=1}^t p_j$. By invoking equality 2.1 and combining with the last inequality we get that

$$\begin{aligned} (R_e[P])^{-1} &= \left(\sum_{i=1}^t (R_e[p_i])^{-1} \right) \\ &\geq tw_e/(2\log n). \end{aligned}$$

which implies

$$R_e[P] \leq \log n/(tw_e).$$

Finally, we have $R_e[G] \leq R_e[P]$ by Rayleigh's monotonicity law, since P is a subgraph of G. $\square$

Let B_e be the $n \times n$ Laplacian of the unweighted edge e (which is zero everywhere except a 2x2 submatrix). Looking at the effective resistance algebraically, it is well understood that:

$$B_e \preceq R_e[G]G.$$

Then the above lemma implies the following.

COROLLARY 1. *Let G be a graph and H be a t-bundle spanner of G. For every edge e of G which is not in H, we have*

$$w_e B_e \preceq \frac{\log n}{t} G.$$

3. PARALLEL SPARSIFICATION

3.1 Parallel t-bundle Spanner Construction

A t-bundle spanner can be computed iteratively in the obvious way: in the ith iteration we compute a spanner H_i for $G - \sum_{j=1}^{i-1} H_j$. Edges in $\sum_{j=1}^{i-1} H_j$ can declare themselves out of the ith iteration in the parallel or distributed model. Thus extending the algorithms of Baswana and Sen is easy, and we get the following corollaries.

COROLLARY 2. *On input of a graph G, a t-bundle spanner for G of expected size $O(tn \log n)$ can be constructed with $O(tm \log n)$ work in $\tilde{O}(t \log n)$ time, with high probability. The algorithm runs in the CRCW PRAM model.*

COROLLARY 3. *On input of a graph G, a t-bundle spanner for G of expected size $O(tn \log n)$ can be constructed in the synchronous distributed model in $O(t \log^2 n)$ rounds and $O(tm \log n)$ communication complexity. Moreover, the length of each message communicated is $O(\log n)$.*

3.2 Sampling for Parallel Sparsification

We will sparsify graphs using sampling. The Spielman-Srivastava scheme fixes the number of samples and for each sample one edge is selected according to a fixed probability distribution and gets added to the sparsifier [23]. In Algorithm1 we use a slightly different sampling scheme, sampling each edge independently with a fixed probability.

Algorithm 1 PARALLELSAMPLE

Input: Graph G, parameter ϵ

Output: Graph $\tilde{G}$

1: Compute a $(24 \log^2 n/\epsilon^2)$-bundle spanner H for G
2: Let $\tilde{G} := H$
3: For each edge $e \notin H$ with probability $1/4$ add e to $\tilde{G}$ with weight $4w_e$
4: Return $\tilde{G}$

We will need a Theorem due to Tropp [27], and more specifically its following variant [6].

THEOREM 3. *Let $Y_1, \ldots, Y_k$ be independent positive semi-definite matrices of size $n \times n$. Let $Y = \sum_i Y_i$. Let $Z = E[Y]$. Suppose $Y_i \preceq RZ$. Then for all $\epsilon \in [0, 1]$*

$$Pr\left[\sum_i Y_i \preceq (1-\epsilon)Z \right] \leq n \cdot exp(-\epsilon^2/2R)$$

$$Pr\left[\sum_i Y_i \succeq (1+\epsilon)Z \right] \leq n \cdot exp(-\epsilon^2/3R).$$

We have the following Theorem.

THEOREM 4. *The output $\tilde{G}$ of algorithm PARALLELSAMPLE on input G and ϵ satisfies with probability $1 - 1/n^2$ the following:*

(a) $(1-\epsilon)G \preceq \tilde{G} \preceq (1+\epsilon)G$.

(b) The expected number of edges in $\tilde{G}$ is at most

$$O(n \log^3 n/\epsilon^2 + m/2).$$

PARALLELSAMPLE *can be implemented in the CWCR PRAM model to use* $O(m \log^3 n/\epsilon^2)$ *work in* $\tilde{O}(\log^3 n/\epsilon^2)$ *time. In the synchronous distributed model,* PARALLELSAMPLE *can be implemented to run in* $O(\log^4 n/\epsilon^2)$ *rounds, with* $O(m \log^3 n/\epsilon^2)$ *communication complexity, using messages of size* $O(\log n)$.

PROOF. The work, parallel time, and communication complexity guarantees for PARALLELSAMPLE follow directly from the Corollaries 2 and 3, by letting $t = O(\log^2 n/\epsilon^2)$.

Now let B_e be the $n \times n$ Laplacian of the unweighted edge e. For each edge $e \notin H$ we let Y_e be the random variable defined as follows:

$$
\begin{aligned}
Y_e &= 0, &&\text{with probability } 3/4, \\
&= 4w_e B_e &&\text{with probability } 1/4.
\end{aligned}
$$

Also we let

$$H_i = \lfloor \epsilon^2/(6 \log n) \rfloor H,$$

for $i = 1, \ldots, (\lfloor \epsilon^2/(6 \log n) \rfloor)^{-1}$. We apply Theorem 3 to the random matrix that is formed by summing the H_i's and the Y_e's. For the output of the algorithm, we clearly have

$$\tilde{G} = \sum_{e \notin H} Y_e + \sum_i H_i = \sum_{e \notin H} Y_e + H.$$

We also have that $E[\tilde{G}] = G$. Using $H \preceq G$, for each i we have

$$H_i = \lfloor \epsilon^2/(6 \log n) \rfloor H \preceq \epsilon^2/(6 \log n)G.$$

In addition for each $e \notin H$, we have

$$Y_i \preceq 4w_e B_e \preceq \epsilon^2/(6 \log n)G.$$

The last inequality follows by setting $t = 24 \log^2 n/\epsilon^2$ in Corollary 1. Thus the condition of Theorem 3 is satisfied for $R = \epsilon^2/(6 \log n)$, which substituted in the bounds of the Theorem proves that (a) holds with probability at least $1 - 1/2n^2$. For (b), observe that the expected number of edges in H is $O(n \log^3 n/\epsilon^2)$ as stated in Corollaries 2 and 3. The expected numbers of edges outside H is $m/4$ and a simple application of Chernoff's inequality implies that the number is at most $m/2$ with probability at least $1 - 1/2n^2$. Hence a union bound gives that both (a) and (b) hold with probability at least $1 - 1/n^2$. □

3.3 The Algorithm

The main sparsification routine is presented in Algorithm 2.

Algorithm 2 PARALLELSPARSIFY

Input: Graph G, parameters ϵ, ρ

Output: Graph $\tilde{G}$

1: Set $G_0 := G$
2: For $i = 1 : \lceil \log \rho \rceil$
3: Set $G_i := $ PARALLELSPARSIFY$(G_{i-1}, \epsilon/\lceil \log \rho \rceil)$
4: Return $G_{\lceil \log \rho \rceil}$

We prove the following Theorem.

THEOREM 5. *The output* $\tilde{G}$ *of algorithm* PARALLELSPAR-SIFY *on input* G *and* ϵ, ρ *satisfies*

$$(1 - \epsilon)G \preceq \tilde{G} \preceq (1 + \epsilon)G$$

with high probability. The expected number edges in G *is at most*

$$O(n \log^3 n \log^3 \rho/\epsilon^2 + m/\rho).$$

The algorithm does $O(m \log^2 n \log^3 \rho/\epsilon^2)$ *work and runs in* $O(\log^3 n \log^3 \rho/\epsilon^2)$ *time in the CRCW mode. In the synchronous distributed model, it can be implemented to run in* $O(\log^4 n \log^3 \rho/\epsilon^2)$ *rounds with* $O(m \log^3 n \log^3 \rho/\epsilon^2)$ *communication complexity, using messages of size* $O(\log n)$.

PROOF. We can show using induction and Theorem 4 that graph G_t satisfies

$$(1 - \epsilon/\log \rho)^t G \preceq G_t \preceq (1 + \epsilon/\log \rho)^t G.$$

with probability $(1 - 1/n^2)^t$ and the expected number of edges in it is at most

$$O(nt \log^3 n \log^2 \rho/\epsilon^2 + m/2^t).$$

Since $t \leq \lceil \log \rho \rceil$, we get the desired spectral inequality. The parallel and distributed implementations are straightforward. The total work (and communication complexity) is dominated by the work performed in the first iteration, since the size of the graphs decrease geometrically. The claims on the parallel and distributed implementations then follow from Theorem 4. □

4. IMPROVED PARALLEL SDD SOLVER

The Peng-Spielman parallel framework. Peng and Spielman [22] gave the first solver for symmetric diagonally dominant (SDD) linear system that does near-linear work in polylogarithmic time. We shortly review the basic ideas behind their solver in order to highlight how our sparsification routine can be plugged into it, thus deriving work and time guarantees for a more efficient solver.

Let D be a diagonal matrix and A be the adjacency matrix of a graph with positive weights. The main idea in [22] is a reduction of the input SDD linear system with matrix $M_1 = D - A$, to a linear system with matrix $\tilde{M}_1 = D - AD^{-1}A$ which is also shown to be SDD. Matrix $\tilde{M}_1$ is actually never formed explicitly because it can be too dense, as all vertices that are within a distance of 2 in graph A form now a clique in graph $AD^{-1}A$. The **first** step to remedying this problem is replacing $\tilde{M}_1$ with a $(1 + \epsilon/2)$-approximation $\hat{M}_1$ that has $O(n + m \log n/\epsilon^2)$ edges and doesn't contain these cliques, but replaces them with sparse graphs. As shown in Corollary 6.4 of [22] this can be done in in $O(\log n)$ time and $O(n + m \log^2 n/\epsilon^2)$ work. The **second** step is further sparsifying $\tilde{M}_1$ down to $O(n \log^c n/\epsilon^2)$ non-zeros (for some fairly large constant c), using the parallelized Spielman-Teng sparsification algorithm. This step forms a matrix M_2 which is a $(1 + \epsilon)$-approximation of $\tilde{M}_1$, and also an SDD matrix which is of the form $D' - A'$.

This construction is repeated recursively, producing an 'approximate inverse chain' for M_1:

$$\{M_1, M_2, \ldots, M_d\}.$$

The depth d of the chain needs to be $O(\log \kappa)$ where κ is the condition number of M_1, i.e. the ratio of its largest to its smallest non-zero eigenvalue. This is because for $d = O(\kappa)$ the condition number of M_d is very close to 1, i.e. M_d is essentially the identity matrix, and no further reductions are required. The $(1 + \epsilon)$ approximations incurred by the construction of M_{i+1} from M_i compound in a multiplicative fashion. So, in order to keep the total approximation bounded we need to pick, $\epsilon = \Theta(1/\log \kappa)$.

As shown in Theorem 4.5 of [22] an approximate inverse chain can be used to produce an approximate solution for the system in $O(d \log n)$ depth and total work proportional to the total number of non-zero entries in the matrices that constitute the chain.

The solver. We now outline the construction of a parallel SDD solver that uses our improved parallel sparsification algorithm. We can think of all matrices in the approximate inverse chain as Laplacians, and we will refer to them as graphs. For simplicity, we will use $\tilde{O}$ to suppress polylogarithmic factors in n and κ. Also, we note that the spectral approximation bounds hold with high probability, and the claims on the number of edges of the sparsifiers hold in expectation; we won't further discuss randomization for the sake of brevity.

Recall that in the construction of the approximate inverse chain, one has to set $\epsilon = \Theta(1/\log \kappa)$. Given that, observe also that the 'threshold of applicability' of Theorem 5 is when the graph M_i has more than $\tilde{O}(n \log^3 n \log^2 \kappa)$ edges, whenever the sparsification factor ρ is of polylogarithmic size. Let us denote by m' this threshold. Whenever sparsification of $\tilde{M}_i$ is not possible, we simply let $M_{i+1} = \tilde{M}_i$, as implicitly done in [22].

When constructing M_{i+1} from M_i, the number of edges goes up by a factor of $O(\log n \log^2 \kappa)$, in the first step that constructs $\tilde{M}_i$. In order to keep the total size of the inverse approximate chain and thus the work of the solver bounded, we only need to bring the graph back to its original size, if it exceeds m'. Besides its stronger guarantees, a relative advantage of our routine is that we can use it to sparsify the input graph by any factor ρ, rather than aim for a very sparse graph as Peng and Spielman [22] propose. So, using Theorem 5 the graph can be sparsified down to $O(m' + m)$ edges, by setting $\rho = O(\log n \log^2 \kappa)$. The total work is $\tilde{O}((m'+m) \log^2 n \log^2 \kappa)$. Hence the total size of the approximate inverse chain is $\tilde{O}((m' + m) \log \kappa)$, and the total work required for its construction is $\tilde{O}((m' + m) \log^2 n \log^3 \kappa)$.

We can improve the dependence on m by constructing the chain not for the input matrix M, but for a 2-approximation M' of it, which has $\tilde{O}(n \log^3 n + m/\log^2 n \log^3 \kappa)$ edges. This can be constructed by invoking Theorem 5, with $\epsilon = 1/2$ and $\rho = O(\log^2 n \log^3 \kappa)$. The total work for this step is $\tilde{O}(m \log^2 n)$. It is well understood that this approximate chain for M' can be used as a preconditioner for M (in the same way its own chain would be used) incurring only a constant factor in the work and time guarantees.

Combining the above with Theorem 4.5 of [22], we get the following Theorem.

THEOREM 6. *On input of a linear system $Mx = b$, where M is an SDD matrix of dimension n with m non-zeros, a vector x' that satisfies $\|b - M^+ x\|_M < \epsilon$ can be constructed with probability at least $1/2$ in polylogarithmic time and $\tilde{O}(m \log^2 n + m' \log^5 n \log^5 \kappa)$ work.*

5. CONCLUDING REMARKS

Remark 1. Multigrid algorithms provably do linear work in logarithmic time, for certain very special classes of SDD systems that arise from the discretization of partial differential equations [4]. The algebra underlying multigrid is quite different than that used by Peng and Spielman; in contrast with their algorithm, the spectral approximation does not accumulate multiplicatively in the multigrid 'chain'. This imposes a much less demanding constraint for the approximation quality between two subsequent levels, which can be

constant, rather than $O(1/\log \kappa)$. Much of the efficiency of these specialized multigrid algorithms stems from this fact. It remain open whether something similar is possible for general SDD matrices, In particular, it is still open whether there is an $O(n)$-work $O(\log n)$ time algorithm for regular weighted two-dimensional grids that are 'affinity' graphs of images. Experimental evidence [18] seems to suggest that the possibility cannot be dismissed.

Remark 2. It can be shown that low-stretch trees can replace spanners in our construction, reducing the size of the sparsifiers by an $O(\log n)$ factor. The potential advantage of such an algorithm would be that it provides a sparsifier which is expressed naturally as a sum of trees.

Remark 3. While a significant improvement over the solver presented in [22], the total work of our parallel algorithm remains high (in terms of the logarithmic factors) especially for sparse graphs. We conjecture that more improvements are possible, and will probably have to use a different algebraic framework (see Remark 1). Within the Peng and Spielman framework, it seems plausible that improvements can come from replacing the t-bundle by a sparser object; this presents us an interesting problem. The number of logarithmic factors can be probably somewhat decreased by reducing the dimension n, potentially by using a two-level 'Steiner preconditioning' scheme [14].

Remark 4. We wish emphasize the simplicity and implementability of our algorithm as a stand-alone sparsification routine, relative to the other two known solve-free algorithms by Spielman and Teng [24] and Kapralov and Panigrahi [7]. Comparing to the latter, our algorithm has also the 'right' dependency on ϵ ($1/\epsilon^2$ vs $1/\epsilon^4$) and is flexible with the sparsification factor ρ.

Acknowledgments.

This work was supported by NSF CAREER award CCF-1149048.

6. REFERENCES

[1] Surender Baswana and Sandeep Sen. A simple and linear time randomized algorithm for computing sparse spanners in weighted graphs. *Random Struct. Algorithms*, 30(4):532 563, 2007.

[2] Joshua D. Batson, Daniel A. Spielman, and Nikhil Srivastava. Twice-Ramanujan sparsifiers. In *Proceedings of the 41st Annual ACM Symposium on Theory of Computing*, pages 255 262, 2009.

[3] Joshua D. Batson, Daniel A. Spielman, Nikhil Srivastava, and Shang-Hua Teng. Spectral sparsification of graphs: theory and algorithms. *Commun. ACM*, 56(8):87 94, 2013.

[4] James H. Bramble. *Multigrid Methods*. Chapman and Hall, 1993.

[5] Peter G. Doyle and J. Laurie Snell. Random walks and electric networks, 2000.

[6] N. Harvey. Matrix Concentration. http://www.cs.rpi.edu/~drinep/RandNLA/slides/ Harvey_RandNLA@FOCS_2012.pdf, 2012.

[7] Michael Kapralov and Rina Panigrahy. Spectral sparsification via random spanners. In *Proceedings of the 3rd Innovations in Theoretical Computer Science Conference*, ITCS '12, pages 393 398, New ork, N , USA, 2012. ACM.

[8] Jonathan A. Kelner and Alex Levin. Spectral sparsification in the semi-streaming setting. In

Proceeding of the 28th International Symposium on Theoretical Aspects of Computer Science, STACS, pages 440 451, 2011.

[9] Jonathan A. Kelner, Lorenzo Orecchia, Aaron Sidford, and eyuan Allen hu. A Simple, Combinatorial Algorithm for Solving SDD Systems in Nearly-Linear Time. *CoRR*, abs/1301.6628, 2013.

[10] Alexandra Kolla, ury Makarychev, Amin Saberi, and Shang-Hua Teng. Subgraph sparsification and nearly optimal ultrasparsifiers. In *Proceedings of the 42nd ACM Symposium on Theory of Computing, (STOC)*, pages 57 66, 2010.

[11] Ioannis Koutis, Alex Levin, and Richard Peng. Faster spectral sparsification and numerical algorithms for sdd matrices. *CoRR*, abs/1209.5821, 2012.

[12] Ioannis Koutis, Alex Levin, and Richard Peng. Improved spectral sparsification and numerical algorithms for SDD matrices. In *Proceedings of the 29th International Symposium on Theoretical Aspects of Computer Science, STACS*, pages 266 277, 2012.

[13] Ioannis Koutis and Gary Miller. The combinatorial multigrid solver. Conference Talk, March 2009.

[14] Ioannis Koutis and Gary L. Miller. Graph partitioning into isolated, high conductance clusters: Theory, computation and applications to preconditioning. In *Symposiun on Parallel Algorithms and Architectures (SPAA)*, 2008.

[15] Ioannis Koutis, Gary L. Miller, and Richard Peng. Approaching optimality for solving SDD systems. In *FOCS '10: Proceedings of the 51st Annual IEEE Symposium on Foundations of Computer Science*. IEEE Computer Society, 2010.

[16] Ioannis Koutis, Gary L. Miller, and Richard Peng. A nearly $m \log n$ solver for SDD linear systems. In *FOCS '11: Proceedings of the 52nd Annual IEEE Symposium on Foundations of Computer Science*. IEEE Computer Society, 2011.

[17] Ioannis Koutis, Gary L. Miller, and Richard Peng. A fast solver for a class of linear systems. *Commun. ACM*, 55(10):99 107, October 2012.

[18] Dilip Krishnan, Raanan Fattal, and Richard Szeliski. Efficient preconditioning of Laplacian matrices for computer graphics. *ACM Trans. Graph.*, 32(4):142, 2013.

[19] Oren E. Livne and Achi Brandt. Lean Algebraic Multigrid (LAMG): Fast Graph Laplacian Linear Solver. *SIAM J. Scientific Computing*, 34(4), 2012.

[20] Lorenzo Orecchia and Nisheeth K. ishnoi. Towards an SDP-based approach to spectral methods: A nearly-linear-time algorithm for graph partitioning and decomposition. In Dana Randall, editor, *SODA*, pages 532 545. SIAM, 2011.

[21] Richard Peng. *Algorithm design using spectral graph theory*. PhD thesis, Carnegie Mellon University, 2013.

[22] Richard Peng and Daniel A. Spielman. An efficient parallel solver for SDD linear systems. *CoRR*, abs/1311.3286, 2013.

[23] Daniel A. Spielman and Nikhil Srivastava. Graph sparsification by effective resistances. In *Proceedings of the 40th Annual ACM Symposium on Theory of Computing (STOC)*, pages 563 568, 2008.

[24] Daniel A. Spielman and Shang-Hua Teng. Nearly-linear time algorithms for graph partitioning, graph sparsification, and solving linear systems. In *Proceedings of the 36th Annual ACM Symposium on Theory of Computing (STOC)*, pages 81 90, June 2004.

[25] Shang-Hua Teng. The laplacian paradigm: emerging algorithms for massive graphs. In *Proceedings of the 7th annual conference on Theory and Applications of Models of Computation*, TAMC'10, pages 2 14, Berlin, Heidelberg, 2010. Springer- erlag.

[26] Mikkel Thorup and Uri wick. Approximate distance oracles. *J. ACM*, 52(1):1 24, 2005.

[27] Joel A Tropp. User-friendly tail bounds for sums of random matrices. *Foundations of Computational Mathematics*, 12(4):389 434, 2012.

Brief Announcement: Few Buffers, Many Hot Spots, and No Tree Saturation (with High Probability)

Bradley C. Kuszmaul
MIT CSAIL
bradley@mit.edu

William Kuszmaul
MIT PRIMES
william.kuszmaul@gmail.com

ABSTRACT

In a multistage network, hotspots induce tree saturation. The known solutions employ a variety of techniques, including combining (which works only for certain kinds of messages), feedback damping (which appears to provide low utilization in the absence of hot spots), and large numbers of buffers. In practice, the approach used today is to provide large numbers of buffers: in a P-processor system, the rule of thumb appears to be to provide $10P$ buffers, but $10P$ buffers may be too expensive for systems containing 10^5 or more processors. Even employing $\Omega(P)$ buffers does not appear to provide any guarantees, however. This paper shows that by organizing the switches so that the messages addressed to a particular processor can use only certain of the buffers, many hotspots can be tolerated with few buffers. For example, a switch with $O(\log P)$ buffers can tolerate a single hotspot with probability 1, and allows the first few hotspots to have a large number of buffers before being declared a hotspot. A switch with B buffers will block a given non-hotspot message with probability less than $O(1/s)$ if there are $O(B/\log s)$ hotspots, and can handle a factor of $O(\ln \ln s)$ more hotspots before the probability becomes a constant. A similar approach can also be used to improve caching behavior in a multithreaded system in which one of the threads tries to consume all of the cache.

Large-scale computing systems typically employ multistage interconnection networks to interconnect their processors. These systems can suffer from *hotspot contention*, however [7]. Hotspots arise when source processors collectively send too many messages to a particular destination processor—the destination processor falls behind trying to receive messages, and the messages back up into the network filling up buffers in the switches leading to the destination. Then the switches leading to those switches fill up, and eventually the congestion propagates backward through the network, forming a tree rooted at the hot destination of routing nodes with full buffers. This saturation pattern is sometimes called *tree saturation* [7]. Hotspots require very little nonuniform traffic and onset can be very fast and can take a long time to alleviate [4]. Data center and supercom-

SPAA'14, June 23–25, 2014, Prague, Czech Republic.
ACM 978-1-4503-2821-0/14/06.
http://dx.doi.org/10.1145/2612669.2612708.

puter switches urgently need effective congestion management to avoid performance problems [1].

Tree saturation becomes a bigger problem as a system grows to encompass more and more processors. Tree saturation originally was understood as a problem even on networks containing as few as 100 processors [7], but a series of techniques has mitigated tree saturation, at least on networks with as many as thousands of processors. These techniques can be divided into three categories: *message combining* [3], *feedback* [9] , and *buffering* [2, 11]. None of these approaches appear to be in use in modern switches. Combining does not solve the problem for general messages. Feedback is difficult to tune [12]. Here we focus on buffering approaches.

Dias and Kumar [2] do provide a guarantee against hotspots via careful buffer management. Their scheme enforces a rule that each input port may buffer only one message destined to a given processor. They simulated 4 buffers per input port with a 2×2 switch, and found in the face of a single hot spot, the network behaved reasonably well. Although they simulated only one hot spot, their approach can clearly handle more than one hot spot. Given B buffers per input port, a network can tolerate up to B hot spots before non-hotspot traffic is blocked. Our simulation results indicate that it can tolerate $O(B)$ hot spots with good performance, which is not surprising, since it is known that for random routing, only a few buffers are needed per input port.

Today's networks simply employ many buffers, and offer no guarantees in the face of hotspots. For example, Bechtolsheim [1, 6] indicates that for a network containing P processors, a switch should contain enough buffering to hold $10P$ messages. He also points out that the implied memory requirements seem too large to be practical for the next generation of switches.

Using $\Omega(P)$ buffers per switch seems expensive and inefficient. It seems expensive, since with, say 10^6 processors and Ethernet jumbo frames of 10,240 bytes, each switch requires 10GB of memory for P buffers per switch, or perhaps 100GB if we want $10P$ buffers per switch. It seems inefficient since most of those buffers will not be in use most of the time.

We propose a new buffer management technique called a *dampening switch*. The idea of a dampening switch is that if there are few hotspots, then each hotspot can use many buffers, but as the number of hotspots increases, the switch reduces the number of buffers that each hotspot may use. This is in contrast to the switch of [2], which permits a hotspot to use only one buffer per switch.

For the purposes of analyzing these switches, we model a hotspot as a processor that has stopped receiving messages. We model the switching network as a store-and-forward network, so that we can think of each in-transit message residing in exactly one buffer. Real hotspots come and go, and real networks employ cut-through routing, but that does not qualitatively change our results. Any buffer containing a message destined to a hotspot is said to be *claimed* by that hotspot.

We have designed two kind of dampening switches: *counting dampeners* and *hashed dampeners*. The idea of a counting dampener is to count the number of messages destined to each processor and limit the total number of buffers claimed by by hotspots. The idea of a hashed dampener is restrict each destination processor to a set of buffers using a hash function. In this case, the total number of buffers claimed by a hotspot is limited by the combinatorics of the hashing.

The switch operates by accepting messages across its input links. If messages to particular destination processor exceed their buffer quota, then the switch sends link-level flow control information stopping messages destined to that processor. If all the buffers fill up, then the switch sends link-level flow control stopping all messages.

Dampening Switches

Suppose we design switches containing B buffers such that when there are k hotspots at a switch, we expect $B\alpha^k$ buffers not to be claimed by any of those hotspots (for some $\alpha < 1$). Such a switch design is called a *dampening switch*. The idea of a dampening switch is that as hotspots appear, each one is allowed to use fewer and fewer buffers. The first hotspots get to use a lot of buffers, but the switch can also handle a lot of hotspots. Since multiple hotspots can appear at once, a dampening switch cannot actually assign a given amount of hotspots to the nth hotspot that appears. Hence we define it in terms of the number or buffers not being claimed by a hotspot.

Dampening switches are appealing because we want to give a hotspot many buffers if there is only one hotspot to give better performance. But we want to be able to handle many hotspots. For example when switches near a processor go through brief periods of heavy traffic, we would like to allocate many buffers to a processor that appears hot. Suppose these switches accept, for example, $B/2$ of those messages as outstanding messages instead of declaring the processor as a hotspot after, for example, 3 of those messages. Then those messages may start clearing up before the traffic jam has a chance to cascade up the network to other switches farther away from the processor. These brief periods of traffic can occur randomly. For example if every processor sends a message to a randomly chosen processor, a standard balls-and-bins argument states that we expect that some processor to receive $\Theta(\log P/\log\log P)$ messages.

Counting Dampeners

The counting dampener method operates as follows. At each switch, we keep a sorted array of how many buffers are being used by each of the processors that have at least one outstanding message at the switch. Each element in the array consists of a processor number and the value by which the list is sorted. This value is referred to as the element's *value*) We call this list the *processor impact array*, PIA.

Then each time we receive (or transmit) a message from (to) our switch, we update the PIA. If every buffer is full, we stop all new messages from arriving. Otherwise, we find the largest k such that the first k elements in the PIA sum to at least $B(1 - \alpha^k)$. Note that k may be zero. We call this k *the hotspot counter*. We then adjust the flow control so that we block messages destined to all processors in the first k elements.

It turns out that one can maintain the PIA in $O(1)$ time per operation. Calculating the new value of k is also reasonably quick. The arrival or departure of a single message can result in substantial flow-control traffic, however.

Hashed Dampeners

The hashed dampener operates as follows. For each processor, we hash it to a random j-tuple of buffer numbers (that is, integers from 1 to B). We then allow each processor to use only the buffers named in the j-tuple. (We'll discuss how to choose j below.) If all such buffers are full, we block messages destined to that processor. Maintaining the data structure is straightforward, and it turns out that the flow control can be performed by blocking and unblocking $O(1)$ messages per message arrival or departure. As a result, the flow-control overhead can be kept small compared to the message traffic. It also turns out that the protocol, which performs $O(j)$ work per message, can be added to IEEE P802.1p priority-based flow control packet format with very little change. Note that any flow-control mechanism appears to require, in the worst case, $\Omega(j)$ probes into a table since it must look into the j possible buffer locations to find a free location.

To help choose j, the following result is relevant for hashed dampeners.

THEOREM 1. *When a hashed dampener has $(B/j)\ln B$ hotspots, we expect $O(1)$ of the buffers to be not in use.*

PROOF. It suffices to show that $\log_{B/(B-j)} B \approx (B/j)\ln B$.

$$\log_{B/(B-j)} B = \ln B / \ln(B/(B-j))$$
$$= \ln B / \ln \frac{\frac{B}{j}}{\frac{B}{j} - 1} \approx (B/j)\ln B.$$

$\square$

The analysis of this scheme is similar to analysis for Bloom filters. For example [10] provides a formula estimating the number of elements in a bloom filter of size B with j positions hashed to each element and a given number of bits set which can also be used to reach Theorem 1.

One Hotspot, $O(\log P)$ buffers

We can tolerate a single hotspot with $O(\log P)$ buffers per switch.

The idea is illustrated by this small example. Consider a machine containing 6 processors numbered 0 through 5 with switches containing 4 buffers each, named A, B, C, and D. We allow each processor to use only two switches, as shown in this table:

Processor	Allowed Buffers		
0	A	B	
1	A		C
2	A			D
3		B	C
4		B		D
5			C	D

Since $\binom{4}{2} = 6$ we can arrange that each processor has a distinct set of buffers attached to it. Now if any single processor stops receiving, all other processors still have at least one buffer they can use, so their messages continue to make progress.

The probability that a hot spot will block the network falls quickly as the number of buffers increase.

THEOREM 2. $O(\log(P/\epsilon))$ buffers yields less than ϵ probability of collision.

Proof sketch: The number of combinations is exponential in the number of buffers, and the probability of collision is less than P^2/C where C is the number of combinations.

Thus, even switches with $o(P)$ storage can provide a guarantee that a single hotspot will not stop messages from being delivered to any other processor, with high probability.

Many Hotspots with High Probability

It turns out that we can tolerate many hotspots if we have a few more buffers. For example, we can tolerate $\Theta(B/\log s)$ hotspots with any particular non-hotspot processor being blocked with probability $O(1/s)$. Or, assigning j buffers to each processor, we can tolerate $(B/j)(\ln(j) - t)$ hotspots with any particular coolspot processor being blocked with probability $1/e^{e^t}$.

Space Sharing

The trick of assigning restricting messages to particular buffers can also address space-sharing in an obliviously-routed butterfly network. In a butterfly network, we can use $O(\sqrt{P})$ buffers to get an interesting space-sharing isolation property. The problem is to divide a machine into disjoint sets of processors that work on different tasks. We want to avoid the messages from one partition from interfering with another. This kind of space sharing isolation was provided, for example, in the Connection Machine CM-5 [5] if the partitions of the machine employed disjoint subtrees of the fat-tree network. In contrast, we can provide a similar property with an arbitrary assignment of processors in a butterfly.

To illustrate how it works, we focus on a binary butterfly. A binary butterfly comprises $P \lg P$ two-input two-output switches. The switches are numbered with pairs (i, j) where $0 \le i < P$ and $0 < j < \lg P$, where switch (i, j) has outputs connected to the inputs of switch $(i, j+1)$ and $(i \oplus 2^j, j+1)$.

Observe that for messages traveling in the second half of the network, there are at most $\sqrt{P}$ different destinations to which a message can get. So we allocate $\sqrt{P}$ buffers in each node, and assign at least one buffer exclusively to each possible destination. In the first half of the network, there are at most $\sqrt{P}$ different sources that could have gotten to that node, so we assign buffers according to the source

Any message traveling within a partition is guaranteed not to use any buffer used by a message from another par-

tition, because in first half of the network, the message will employ buffers dedicated to the message's source, and in the second half, the message will employ buffers dedicated to the message's destination.

Cache Partitioning

In multithreaded programs one thread can sometimes grab all the cache lines in a shared cache, slowing down other threads. Dampening effectively change the buffer from a fully associative cache to a randomized j-way associative cache. By reducing the associativity, the behavior of the system is improved against processors that receive too many messages. To adapt this idea to solve the cache partitioning problem, we similarly restrict the associativity of the cache. (See [8] for a survey of cache partitioning.)

For caching, there is a clear advantage to allowing a large number of cache lines to be assigned to one thread. Therefore we might adjust the parameters so that, for example, a single uncontended thread can get half the cache.

Acknowledgments

Michael Bender observed that these ideas can be applied to cache partitioning.

This work was supported in part by NSF grants CCF-0937860, CCF-1162148, CNS-1017058, and CCF-1314547.

1. REFERENCES

[1] A. Bechtolsheim. Reinventing datacenter networking. In *HPTS*, Asilomar, Pacific Grove, CA, Sept. 2013.

[2] D. M. Dias and M. Kumar. Preventing congestion in multistage networks in the presence of hotspots. In *ICPP*, volume 1, pages 9–13, Aug. 1989.

[3] A. Gottlieb. An overview of the NYU Ultracomputer project. Ultracomputer Note 100, NYU, July 1986.

[4] M. Kumar and G. F. Pfister. The onset of hot spot contention. In *ICPP*, pages 28–34, 1986.

[5] C. E. Leiserson, Z. S. Abuhamdeh, D. C. Douglas, C. R. Feynman, M. N. Ganmukhi, J. V. Hill, W. D. Hillis, B. C. Kuszmaul, M. A. St. Pierre, D. S. Wells, M. C. Wong, S.-W. Yang, and R. Zak. The network architecture of the Connection Machine CM-5. *J. Parallel Distrib. Comput.*, 33(2):145–158, 1996.

[6] R. Merrit. Bechtolsheim brainstorms on next networking wave. *EE Times*, Oct. 17 2012.

[7] G. F. Pfister and V. A. Norton. "hot spot" contention and combining in multistage interconnection networks. *IEEE Trans. Comput.*, C-34(10):943–948, Oct. 1985.

[8] D. Sanchez and C. Kozyrakis. Scalable and efficient fine-grained cache partitioning with vantage. *IEEE Micro*, 32(3):26–37, May 2012.

[9] S. L. Scott and G. S. Sohi. The use of feedback in multiprocessors and its application to tree saturation control. *IEEE Trans. Parallel Distrib. Syst.*, 1(4):385–398, Oct. 1990.

[10] S. J. Swamidass and P. Baldi. Mathematical correction for fingerprint similarity measures to improve chemical retrieval. *J. Chem. Inf. Model.*, 47:952–965, 2007. http://www.igb.uci.edu/~pfbaldi/publications/journals/2007/ci600526a.pdf.

[11] Y. Tamir and G. L. Frazier. High-performance multi-queue buffers for VLSI communication switches. In *ISCA*, pages 343–354, Honolulu, HI, 1988.

[12] N.-F. Tzeng. Alleviating the impact of tree saturation on multistage interconnection network performance. *J. Parallel Distrib. Comput.*, 12(2):107–117, June 1991.

Brief Announcement: Queue Delegation Locking

David Klaftenegger
Dept. of Information Technology
Uppsala University, Sweden
david.klaftenegger@it.uu.se

Konstantinos Sagonas
Dept. of Information Technology
Uppsala University, Sweden
kostis@it.uu.se

Kjell Winblad
Dept. of Information Technology
Uppsala University, Sweden
kjell.winblad@it.uu.se

ABSTRACT

The scalability of parallel programs is often bounded by the performance of synchronization mechanisms used to protect critical sections. The performance of these mechanisms is in turn determined by their ability to use modern hardware efficiently and do useful work while or instead of waiting. This brief announcement sketches the idea and implementation of *queue delegation locking*, a synchronization mechanism that provides high throughput by allowing threads to efficiently delegate their critical sections to the thread currently holding the lock and by allowing threads that do not need a result from their critical section to continue executing immediately after delegating their work. Experiments show that queue delegation locking outperforms leading synchronization mechanisms due to the combination of its fast operation transfer with its ability to allow threads to continue doing useful work instead of waiting. Thanks to its simple building blocks, even its uncontended overhead is low, making queue delegation locking useful in a wide variety of applications.

Categories and Subject Descriptors

D.1.3 [**Programming Techniques**]: Concurrent Programming

Keywords

locking; multi-core; NUMA; synchronization

1. INTRODUCTION

Lock-based synchronization is a simple way to ensure that shared data structures are always in a consistent state. Threads synchronize on a lock, and only the lock holder can execute a critical section on the protected data. To be efficient, locking algorithms aim to minimize the time required to acquire and release locks when not contended and the lock handover time when locks are contended. In this work we focus on a locking approach that sends operations to the thread holding the lock instead of transferring the lock

SPAA'14, June 23–25, 2014, Prague, Czech Republic.
ACM 978-1-4503-2821-0/14/06.
http://dx.doi.org/10.1145/2612669.2612714.

between threads. This locking approach is called *delegation*, and the thread executing other threads' critical sections is called the *helper*. The main reason why delegation algorithms perform well is improved locality as the helper thread only seldomly needs to wait for memory transfers between caches in different cores or even NUMA nodes. In addition, *detached execution* allows threads to continue execution before the delegated critical section has been executed. However, in its original form [6] the detached execution algorithm has some overhead and severe starvation issues for the helper thread. Newer approaches [1, 2, 4] require threads to wait until their delegated sections are performed. By making the delegation itself faster they aim to further reduce the communication overhead. In comparison to these approaches, our locking mechanism, called *Queue Delegation (QD) locking*, allows efficient delegation while also permitting detached execution without starving the helper thread.

Main Ideas. The main idea of QD locking is simple. When a lock is contended, the threads do not wait for the lock to be released. Instead, they try to delegate their operation to the thread currently holding the lock. If successful, this thread becomes responsible for eventually executing the operation. The other threads can immediately continue their execution, possibly delegating more operations.

Delegated operations are placed in a *delegation queue*. As the queue preserves FIFO order, the correct order of operations is ensured. The linearization point is the successful enqueueing into the delegation queue. However, the enqueueing can fail when the lock holder is not accepting any more operations. This allows limiting the amount of work that the helper performs, and ensures that no operations are accepted when the lock is about to be released. If delegation fails the thread has to retry, until it succeeds to either take the lock itself or delegate its operation to a new lock holder.

The QD locking algorithm thus puts the burden of executing operations on the thread that succeeds in taking the lock. After performing its own operation, this thread must perform, in order, all operations it finds in the delegation queue. When it eventually finds no more operations in the delegation queue, it must make sure no further enqueue call succeeds before the lock is released.

All requirements for queue delegation locking are met by assembling two simple components: a *mutual exclusion lock* to determine which thread is executing operations, and a *queue* to delegate operations to the lock holder. We will describe these components in the next section. In the full paper [3] we also describe how to extend the basic algorithm

```
 1  void delegate(QDLock* l, Operation op) {
 2    while (true) {
 3      if (try_lock(&l->lock)) {
 4        open(&l->queue);
 5        execute(op);
 6        flush(&l->queue);
 7        unlock(&l->lock);
 8        return;
 9      } else if (enqueue(&l->queue, op)) return;
10      yield();
11    }
12  }
```

Figure 1: The **delegate** function

```
 1  void open(DelegationQueue* q) {
 2    q->counter = 0;
 3    q->closed = false;
 4  }
 5
 6  bool enqueue(DelegationQueue* q, Operation op) {
 7    if (q->closed) return CLOSED;
 8    int index = fetch_and_add(&q->counter, 1);
 9    if (index < ARRAY_SIZE) {
10      q->array[index] = op; /* atomic */
11      return SUCCESS;
12    } else return CLOSED;
13  }
14
15  void flush(DelegationQueue* q) {
16    int todo = 0;
17    bool open = true;
18    while (open) {
19      int done = todo;
20      todo = q->counter;
21      if (todo == done) { /* close queue */
22        todo = swap(&q->counter, ARRAY_SIZE);
23        open = false;
24        q->closed = true;
25      }
26      if (todo >= ARRAY_SIZE) { /* queue closed */
27        todo = ARRAY_SIZE;
28        open = false;
29        q->closed = true;
30      }
31      for (int index = done; index < todo; index++) {
32        while (q->array[index].fun_ptr == NULL); /* spin */
33        execute(q->array[index]);
34        q->array[index].fun_ptr = NULL; /* reset */
35      }
36    }
37  }
```

Figure 2: The delegation queue implementation

to allow parallel access to multiple readers efficiently, and hierarchical variants for NUMA systems.

2. IMPLEMENTATION

As mentioned, queue delegation locks are built from two components: a *mutual exclusion lock* and a *delegation queue*.

The mutual exclusion lock is used to determine whether the lock is free or taken. Its minimal interface consists of only two functions. The first is try_lock, which takes the lock if it is free and returns whether the lock has been taken. The second is unlock, which releases the lock.

The second component, the delegation queue, is required to store delegated operations. Semantically, it is a *tantrum queue* [5]. Calls to its enqueue operation are not guaranteed to succeed, but can return a *closed* value instead. This allows the QD lock to stop accepting more operations. The required interface for the delegation queue consists of only three functions: open, enqueue and flush. The first two are straightforward: open resets the queue from closed state to empty, and enqueue adds an element to the queue. The flush function is used instead of a dequeue operation: it dequeues all elements (performing their operation) and changes the queue's state to closed.

2.1 Queue Delegation Lock Implementation

We use the building blocks outlined above to assemble a QD lock as follows: The mutual exclusion lock determines in which way operations are accepted by the QD lock. When the mutual exclusion lock is free, it is taken, the delegation queue is opened, the operation is executed, the queue is flushed and finally the mutual exclusion lock is unlocked. However, when the mutual exclusion lock is already taken, the delegation queue is used to accept additional operations. The resulting QD lock therefore accepts operations even when the mutual exclusion lock is locked; threads only need to retry if the mutual exclusion lock is locked and the queue is closed.

The QD lock interface only consists of a delegate function which takes an operation as an argument; see Figure 1. It is guaranteed that the operation will be executed before any operations from subsequent calls to delegate are executed. The operation is semantically a self-contained *function object*, which means that it needs to store all required parameters from the local scope when delegated, similar to a *closure*. For returning values from operations, the QD lock uses the semantics of *futures*; i.e., the value is not returned immediately, but the operation can promise to provide the value at a specific location upon its execution. When the calling thread needs to read the return value, it has to wait until this value

is available. This can either be exposed to the application programmer or hidden by using a wrapper that immediately waits for the return value and returns the result.

2.2 Delegation Queue Implementation

The delegation queue can be efficiently implemented with a fixed-size buffer array and an index counter. The enqueue function tries to allocate a slot in the buffer array by incrementing the index counter with an atomic fetch_and_add operation. The queue is closed if the value of the index counter is greater than the index of the last slot in the array buffer. The flush function executes enqueued operations until the queue is closed and all operations have been processed. Pseudocode for the delegation queue is shown in Figure 2. Note that the closed flag in the pseudocode is just a performance optimization and is not needed for correctness.

2.3 Extensions

The basic QD locking algorithm can be extended in various ways, which we present in the full paper [3]. In particular, we describe a hierarchical variant (HQD), which targets NUMA systems as well as multi-reader QD (MR-QD) locks, which allow parallel access for readers as in traditional reader-writer locks. We also discuss how to adapt the algorithm to guarantee starvation freedom for all threads, and how to extend the interface to ease the porting process.

3. PERFORMANCE

Here we give a summary of a performance evaluation comparing QD locking with related synchronization algorithms. Refer to the full paper [3] for graphs and for more details.

3.1 Benchmark Descriptions

We measured the performance of different locking algorithms with a varying amount of threads and contention on a machine with four Intel(R) Xeon(R) E5-4650 CPUs (2.70GHz), eight cores each (i.e., a total of 64 hardware threads running on 32 cores), using three benchmarks. The first measures the throughput of random operations on a shared priority queue (`insert` and `extract_min`) implemented by protecting a sequential priority queue with the synchronization algorithms of Oyama *et al.* [6], with flat combining [2], with CC-Synch and H-Synch [1], and with QD lock and HQD lock. The second benchmark compares MR-QD locks with state of the art readers-writer locks. Finally, we applied MR-QD locks on the code of the Kyoto Cabinet in-memory database (version 1.2.76) to evaluate their performance on a code base that uses traditional locks.

3.2 Summary of the Results

The QD and HQD variants perform better than or similar to the best of the other synchronization mechanisms in all scenarios we tested. As clarified by experiments with variants of QD and HQD in the full paper [3], there are several reasons for this. First, QD locking allows a thread that performs a write only operation (`insert`) to continue execution directly after delegating the operation. Except for the QD variants, the Oyama *et al.* algorithm is the only locking scheme where threads can continue without waiting for delegated operations. However, that algorithm performs poorly compared to the QD variants because of the overheads it contains and its inability to take advantage of modern hardware. We also noticed that the helper thread is often starved in the scheme of Oyama *et al.* The positive effect of being able to continue without waiting for the issued operation becomes more apparent when the threads have more local work to do between the priority queue operations. Since continuing execution means the next priority operation is issued faster, there can be more helped operations per lock acquisition even under low contention. The high number of helped operations per lock acquisition is also the reason why QD locking performs better than HQD and H-Synch (the NUMA-aware variant of CC-Synch) with low contention levels even when the threads are running on different NUMA nodes. The node level contention is not large enough to fill the delegation queue while contention on a system level is high enough to fill it. Secondly, the helper thread can read and execute delegated operations extremely efficiently in the QD variants. Since a continuous array is used to store operations in the delegation queue, several operations can be read with only one cache miss which is not the case in the other delegation algorithms. Finally, we note that the atomic `fetch_and_add` instruction used to enqueue operations in the delegation queue is, unsurprisingly, better than simulating the `fetch_and_add` with a CAS loop, even though the CAS loop variant still performs well.

The results of the second benchmark show that traditional readers-writer locks can be outperformed by a QD lock with the MR extension on some workloads. Being able to delegate write operations without waiting for their actual execution plays very well with parallel read-only operations. Threads can continue and issue read operations directly after issuing a write operation so that read-only operations can bulk up and execute in parallel. Similar results are observed in the Kyoto Cabinet benchmark, which also shows that performance is dependent on both fast delegation and not having to wait for the execution of critical sections.

4. CONCLUDING REMARKS

We have sketched the idea and implementation of a novel synchronization mechanism called queue delegation locking, showing the essential building blocks only. A key advantage of QD locking is its ability to delegate operations without waiting for response, its simplicity and its small communication cost. Experiments show that QD locking can outperform current state-of-the-art synchronization algorithms such as that of Oyama *et al.*, flat combining, CC-Synch and H-Synch. Our results also suggest that multi-reader QD locks can be a more performant alternative to readers-writer locks for some use cases. For a more in-depth explanation of QD locking and its variants and for an extensive comparison with related work refer to the full paper [3].

Acknowledgments

This work has been supported in part by the European Union grant IST-2011-287510 "RELEASE: A High-Level Paradigm for Reliable Large-scale Server Software" and the Uppsala Programming for Multicore Architectures Research Center.

5. REFERENCES

[1] P. Fatourou and N. D. Kallimanis. Revisiting the combining synchronization technique. In *Proceedings of the 17th ACM SIGPLAN Symposium on Principles and Practice of Parallel Programming*, pages 257–266, New York, NY, USA, 2012. ACM.

[2] D. Hendler, I. Incze, N. Shavit, and M. Tzafrir. Flat combining and the synchronization-parallelism tradeoff. In *Proceedings of the 22nd ACM Symposium on Parallelism in Algorithms and Architectures*, pages 355–364, New York, NY, USA, 2010. ACM.

[3] D. Klaftenegger, K. Sagonas, and K. Winblad. Queue delegation locking, 2014. Preprint available from http://www.it.uu.se/research/group/languages/ software/qd_lock_lib.

[4] J.-P. Lozi, F. David, G. Thomas, J. Lawall, and G. Muller. Remote core locking: Migrating critical-section execution to improve the performance of multithreaded applications. In *Proceedings of the 2012 USENIX Annual Technical Conference*, pages 65–76, Berkeley, CA, USA, 2012. USENIX Association.

[5] A. Morrison and Y. Afek. Fast concurrent queues for x86 processors. In *Proceedings of the 18th ACM SIGPLAN Symposium on Principles and Practice of Parallel Programming*, pages 103–112, New York, NY, USA, 2013. ACM.

[6] Y. Oyama, K. Taura, and A. Yonezawa. Executing parallel programs with synchronization bottlenecks efficiently. In *Proceedings of the International Workshop on Parallel and Distributed Computing for Symbolic and Irregular Applications*, pages 182–204. World Scientific, 1999.

Brief Announcement: Fast Dual Ring Queues[*]

Joseph Izraelevitz   and   Michael L. Scott
Computer Science Department, University of Rochester
Rochester, NY 14627-0226, USA
{jhi1, scott}@cs.rochester.edu

ABSTRACT

In this paper, we introduce two new FIFO dual queues. Like all dual queues, they arrange for dequeue operations to block when the queue is empty, and to complete in the original order when data becomes available. Compared to alternatives in which dequeues on an empty queue return an error code and force the caller to retry, dual queues provide a valuable guarantee of fairness.

Our algorithms, based on the LCRQ of Morrison and Afek, outperform existing dual queues—notably the one in java.util.concurrent—by a factor of four to six. For both of our algorithms, we present extensions that guarantee lock freedom, albeit at some cost in performance.

1. INTRODUCTION

A container object (e.g., a queue) that supports insert (enqueue) and remove (dequeue) methods must address the question: what happens if the element one wants to remove is not present? The two obvious answers are to wait or to return an error code (or signal an exception). The latter option leads to spinning in applications that really need to wait (repeat until (x = try_dequeue()) != ⊥). The former option is problematic in nonblocking algorithms: how can a method be nonblocking if it sometimes blocks?

Dual data structures, introduced by Scherer and Scott [6], extend the notion of nonblocking progress to *partial* methods—those that must wait for a precondition to hold. Informally, a partial method on a nonblocking dual structure is redefined to be a total method that either performs the original operation (if the precondition holds) or else modifies the data structure in a way that makes the caller's interest in the precondition (its *request*) visible to subsequent operations. This convention allows the code of the structure to control the order in which stalled methods will complete when preconditions are satisfied. It also makes it easy to ensure that stalled threads impose no burden on active threads—in particular, that they induce no memory contention.

The original dual structures [5], used for task dispatch in the Java standard library, were based on the well-known M&S queue [3] and Treiber stack [7]. In the intervening years, significantly faster concurrent queues have been devised—notably the linked concurrent ring queue (LCRQ) of Morrison and Afek [4]. While the linked-list backbone of this queue is borrowed from the M&S queue, each list node is not an individual element but rather a fixed-length buffer dubbed a concurrent ring queue (CRQ). Most operations on an LCRQ are satisfied by an individual ring queue, which uses a hardware fetch_and_increment (FAI) instruction to eliminate the contention normally associated with compare_and_swap (CAS).

Unfortunately, like most nonblocking queues, the LCRQ "totalizes" dequeue by returning an error code when the queue is empty. Threads that call dequeue in a loop, waiting for it to succeed, reintroduce contention, and their requests, once data is available, may be satisfied in an arbitrary (i.e., unfair) order. In this vein, we introduce two dual versions of the LCRQ (detailed treatment can be found in a technical report [2]). In one version, all elements in a given CRQ are guaranteed to have the same "polarity"—they will all be data or all be requests ("antidata"). In the other version, a given CRQ may contain elements of both polarities. Within a single multicore processor, throughput scales with the number of cores. Once threads are spread across processors, throughput remains 4–6× higher than that of the M&S-based structure.

Notation: "Dual" structures take their name from their ability to hold either data or antidata. If any datum can be used to satisfy any request, a quiescent dual structure will always be empty, populated only with data, or populated only with antidata. Dualism implies that a thread calling the public enqueue method may either enqueue data or dequeue antidata "under the hood." Likewise, a thread calling the public dequeue method may either dequeue data or enqueue antidata. When discussing dual algorithms, we will thus refer to the *polarity* of both threads and the structure, with a *positive* polarity referring to data, and a *negative* polarity referring to antidata.

2. SINGLE POLARITY DUAL RING QUEUE

In our single polarity dual ring queue (SPDQ), each ring in the list has a single polarity—it can hold only data or only antidata. When the history of the queue moves from an excess of enqueues to an excess of dequeues, or vice versa, a new ring must be inserted in the list. This strategy has the advantage of requiring only modest changes to the underlying CRQ algorithm. Its disadvantage is that performance may be poor when the queue is near empty and "flips" frequently from one polarity to the other.

When the original LCRQ algorithm detects that a ring may be full, it *closes* the ring to prevent further insertions, and appends a new ring to the list. In the SPDQ, we introduce the notion of *sealing* an empty ring, to prevent further insertions, and we maintain the invariant that all non-sealed rings have the same polarity. Specifically, we ensure that the queue as a whole is always in one of three valid states: **uniform**—all rings have the same polarity; **twisted**—all rings except the head have the same polarity, and the

[*]This work was supported in part by NSF grants CCF-0963759, CCF-1116055, CNS-1116109, CNS-1319417, and CCF-1337224, and by support from the IBM Canada Centres for Advanced Study.

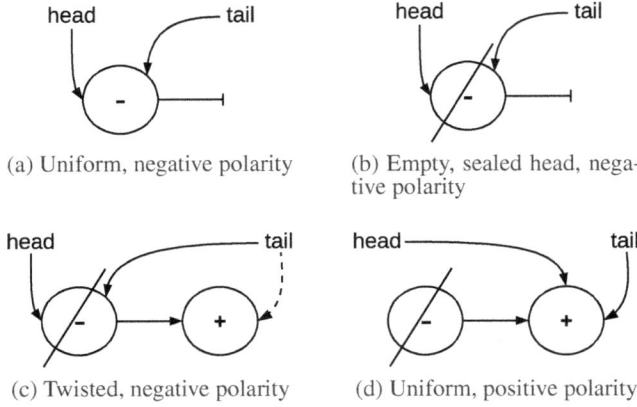

(a) Uniform, negative polarity

(b) Empty, sealed head, negative polarity

(c) Twisted, negative polarity

(d) Uniform, positive polarity

Figure 1: Flipping the polarity of the SPDQ

head is sealed (closed and empty); **empty**—only one ring exists, and it is sealed.

Unless an operation discovers otherwise, it assumes the queue is in the uniform state. Upon beginning an operation, a thread will check the polarity of the head ring, and from there extrapolate the polarity of the queue. If it subsequently discovers that the queue is twisted, it attempts to remove the head and retries. If it discovers that the queue is empty, it creates a new ring, enqueues itself in that ring, and appends it to the list, twisting the queue.

Public enqueue (positive) operations inherit lock-free progress from the LCRQ algorithm [4]. In the worst case, a FAI-ing enqueuer may chase an unbounded series of FAI-ing dequeuers around a ring, arriving at each slot too late to deposit its datum. Eventually, however, it "loses patience," creates a new ring buffer containing its datum, closes the current ring, and appends the new ring to the list. As in the M&S queue [3], the append can fail only if some other thread has appended a ring of its own, and the system will have made progress.

Because they may wait for data, public dequeue (negative) operations are more subtle. Scherer and Scott [6] model a partial operation on a dual structure in terms of a potentially unbounded sequence of nonblocking operations. The first operation linearizes the request for data of the calling thread, T. The last operation (the "successful follow-up") linearizes T's receipt of that data. In between, unsuccessful follow-up operations perform only local memory accesses, inducing no load on other threads. Finally, the total method (in our case, an enqueue) that satisfies T's pending request must ensure that no successful follow-up operation by another waiting thread can linearize in-between it (the satisfying operation) and an unsuccessful follow-up by T.

This final requirement is where the SPDQ as presented so far runs into trouble. A positive thread that encounters a negative queue must perform two key operations: remove the antidata from the queue and alert the waiting thread. Without additional care, an antidata slot will be removed from consideration by other threads the moment the corresponding enqueuer performs its FAI. Mixing will happen afterward, leaving a "preemption window" in which the enqueuer, if it stalls, can leave the dequeuer waiting indefinitely. In practice, such occurrences can be expected to be extremely rare, and indeed the SPDQ performs quite well, achieving roughly 85% of the throughput of the original LCRQ while guaranteeing FIFO service to pending requests (Sec. 5). In Section 4 we will describe a modification to the SPDQ that closes the preemption window, providing fully lock-free behavior (in the dual data structure sense) at essentially no additional performance cost.

3. MULTI POLARITY DUAL RING QUEUE

In contrast to the SPDQ, the multi polarity dual ring queue (MPDQ) incorporates the flipping functionality at the ring buffer level, and leaves the linked list structure of the LCRQ mostly unchanged.

In their original presentation of the CRQ [4], Morrison and Afek began by describing a hypothetical queue based on an infinite array. Similar intuition applies to the MPDQ. Since we are matching positive with negative operations, each thread, on arriving at a slot, must check if its partner has already arrived. If so, it mixes its data (antidata) with the antidata (data) of the corresponding operation. If not, it leaves its information in the slot (a negative thread also waits). As the program progresses, the data and antidata indices may repeatedly pass each other, flipping the polarity of the queue.

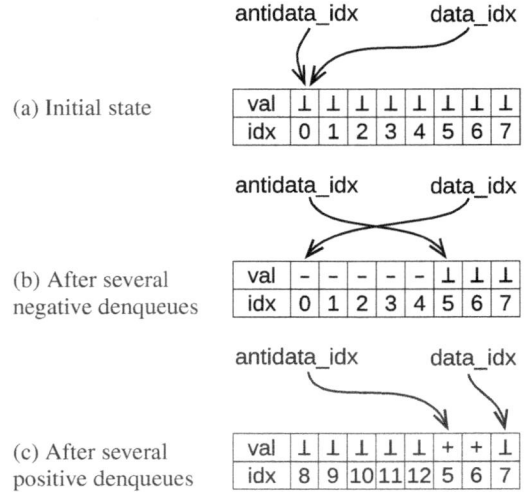

(a) Initial state

(b) After several negative denqueues

(c) After several positive denqueues

Figure 2: Flipping the polarity of the MPDQ

Like the SPDQ, the MPDQ as presented suffers from a preemption window in which a positive thread obtains an index, identifies its corresponding negative thread, but then stalls (e.g., due to preemption), leaving the negative thread inappropriately blocked and in a situation where no other thread can help it. The following section addresses this concern.

4. LOCK FREEDOM

The SPDQ and MPDQ, as presented so far, are eminently usable: they are significantly faster than the M&S-based dual queue of Scherer and Scott (rivaling the speed of the LCRQ), and provide fair, FIFO service to waiting threads. To make them fully nonblocking, however, we must ensure that once a positive thread has reserved its matching operation, the negative thread is able to continue after a bounded number of steps by non-blocked threads.

For both algorithms we can close the preemption window by treating FAI as a mere suggestion to positive threads. Before they enqueue, they must verify that all smaller indices have already been satisfied by searching backwards around the ring buffer. The changes are smaller in the SPDQ case and (as we shall see in Sec. 5) have almost no impact on performance. The changes are larger in the MPDQ case, with a larger performance impact.

As established in the original CRQ algorithm, only dequeue operations can change the index of a given ring slot, allowing it to be reused for a later element in the logical sequence of data flowing

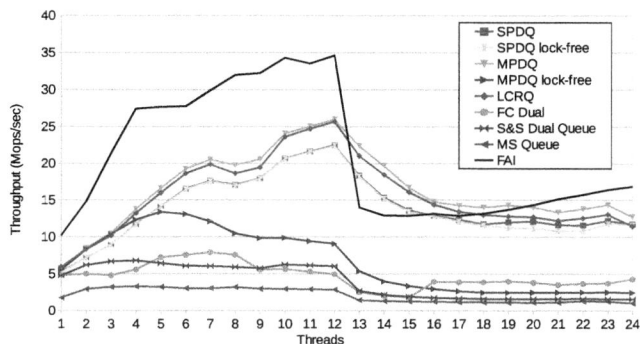

Figure 3: Performance on hot potato benchmark (second processor engaged at 13 cores)

through the queue. Thus, a discontinuity in indices (noticeable in Figure 2), indicates that a slot is ready and can be used to strictly order operations. In the SPDQ, since the preemption window only occurs when a positive thread dequeues from a negative ring, we can limit code changes to this single case. For the MPDQ, however, we must strictly order all positive operations. Since, at any point, the number of active threads is equal to the distance from the discontinuity to the head index, all threads will eventually succeed.

5. RESULTS

We evaluated our algorithms on a machine running Fedora Core 19 Linux on two six-core, two-way hyperthreaded Intel Xeon E5-2430 processors at 2.20GHz (i.e., with up to 24 hardware threads). Each core has private L1 and L2 caches; the last-level cache (15 MB) is shared by all cores of a given processor. As we increased the number of threads, we used all cores on a given processor first, and then all hyperthreads on that processor, before moving to the second processor. Code was written in C++ and compiled using g++ 4.8.2 at the -O3 optimization level.

To obtain as random an access pattern as possible without admitting deadlock, we developed a *hot potato* test in which one thread, at the start of the test, enqueues a special value, called the *hot potato*. For the duration of the test, all threads randomly decide to enqueue or dequeue. If a thread ever dequeues the *hot potato*, however, it waits a small amount of time ($1\mu s$) and then re-enqueues it. During the wait, the queue has an opportunity to flip back and forth between data and antidata. We run the test for several seconds and report performance as throughput. For every queue, we ran five tests and took the maximum run. No large deviations among tests were noted for any of the queues.

In addition to the **SPDQ** and **MPDQ** of Sections 2 and 3, we consider: **SPDQ lock-free** and **MPDQ lock-free**—the nonblocking variants described in Section 4; **S&S Dual Queue**—the algorithm of Scherer & Scott [6]; **M&S Queue** and **LCRQ**—the non-dual algorithms of Michael & Scott [3] and of Morrison & Afek [4], with an outer loop in which negative threads retry until they succeed; and **FC Dual**—a best-effort implementation of a flat-combining dual queue, using the methodology of Hendler et al. [1].

To obtain a sense of fundamental hardware limits, we also ran a test in which all threads contend on a FAI counter, performing updates as fast as they can.

As shown in Figure 3, our new algorithms have throughput significantly higher than any existing dual queue. Qualitatively, their scalability closely follows that of the LCRQ, across the full range of thread counts, while additionally providing fairness for dequeu-

ing threads. The SPDQ is perhaps 20% slower than the LCRQ on average, presumably because of the overhead of "flipping." The MPDQ is about 5% *faster* than the LCRQ on average, presumably because it avoids the empty check and the contention caused by retries in dequeuing threads.

All three algorithms (LCRQ, SPDQ, MPDQ) peak at 12 threads, where there is maximum parallelism without incurring chip-crossing overheads. The raw FAI test similarly scales well within a single chip. Under some conditions, the new dual queues may even outperform the single integer FAI test: depending on the state of the queue, active threads may spread their FAI operations over as many as three different integers (head, tail, and the head or tail of the next ring), distributing the bottleneck.

While the blocking versions of the SPDQ and MPDQ both outperform their lock-free variants, the performance hit is asymmetric. The lock-free SPDQ is almost imperceptibly slower than the blocking version. We expect this happens because the window closing code is only run rarely, when the queue's polarity is negative and many threads are waiting. The MPDQ takes a drastic hit in order to close the window: every positive thread must verify its order with respect to any other concurrent positive threads, adding several cache misses to the critical path of the hot potato test.

Overall, our algorithms outperform existing dual queues by a factor of 4–6× and scale much more aggressively. We encourage their consideration for thread pools and other applications that depend on fast inter-thread communication. We believe the basic, "almost nonblocking" versions should suffice in almost any "real world" application. Based on these tests, we recommend using the MPDQ in any application in which dequeuing threads need to wait for actual data. If one is unwilling to accept the possibility that a dequeuing thread may wait longer than necessary if its corresponding enqueuer is preempted at just the wrong point in time, the lock-free version of the SPDQ still provides dramatically better performance than the S&S dual queue.

6. REFERENCES

[1] D. Hendler, I. Incze, N. Shavit, and M. Tzafrir. Flat combining and the synchronization-parallelism tradeoff. In *Proc. of the 22nd ACM Symp. on Parallelism in Algorithms and Architectures (SPAA)*, Santorini, Greece, June 2010.

[2] J. Izraelevitz and M. L. Scott. Fast dual ring queues. Technical Report 990, Computer Science Dept., Univ. of Rochester, Jan. 2014.

[3] M. M. Michael and M. L. Scott. Simple, fast, and practical non-blocking and blocking concurrent queue algorithms. In *Proc. of the 15th ACM Symp. on Principles of Distributed Computing (PODC)*, Philadelphia, PA, May 1996.

[4] A. Morrison and Y. Afek. Fast concurrent queues for x86 processors. In *Proc. of the 18th ACM Symp. on Principles and Practice of Parallel Programming (PPoPP)*, Shenzhen, China, Feb. 2013.

[5] W. N. Scherer III, D. Lea, and M. L. Scott. Scalable synchronous queues. *Communications of the ACM*, 52(5):100–108, May 2009.

[6] W. N. Scherer III and M. L. Scott. Nonblocking concurrent data structures with condition synchronization. In *Proc. of the 18th Intl. Symp. on Distributed Computing (DISC)*, Amsterdam, The Netherlands, Oct. 2004.

[7] R. K. Treiber. Systems programming: Coping with parallelism. Technical Report RJ 5118, IBM Almaden Research Center, Apr. 1986.

Brief Announcement: Concurrent Data Structures for Efficient Streaming Aggregation

Daniel Cederman
Chalmers University of
Technology
cederman@chalmers.se

Vincenzo Gulisano
Chalmers University of
Technology
vinmas@chalmers.se

Yiannis Nikolakopoulos
Chalmers University of
Technology
ioaniko@chalmers.se

Marina Papatriantafilou
Chalmers University of
Technology
ptrianta@chalmers.se

Philippas Tsigas
Chalmers University of
Technology
tsigas@chalmers.se

ABSTRACT

We briefly describe our study on the problem of streaming multiway aggregation [5], where large data volumes are received from multiple input streams. Multiway aggregation is a fundamental computational component in data stream management systems, requiring low-latency and high-throughput solutions. We focus on the problem of designing concurrent data structures enabling for low-latency and high-throughput multiway aggregation; an issue that has been overlooked in the literature. We propose two new concurrent data structures and their lock-free linearizable implementations, supporting both order-sensitive and order-insensitive aggregate functions. Results from an extensive evaluation show significant improvement in the aggregation performance, in terms of both processing throughput and latency over the commonly-used techniques based on queues.

Categories and Subject Descriptors

E.1 [**Data Structures**]: Lists, stacks, and queues; H.2.4 [**Database Management**]: Systems—*Concurrency*; D.1.3 [**Programming Techniques**]: Concurrent Programming

Keywords

data streaming; data structures; lock-free synchronization

1. INTRODUCTION

Data streaming [13, 1, 6] emerged as an alternative to store-then-process computing. In data streaming, *continuous queries* (defined as directed acyclic graphs of interconnected operators) are executed by Stream Processing Engines (SPEs) that process incoming data in a real-time fashion, producing results on an on-going basis. As emphasized in [7], the low-latency and high-throughput requirements of the real-time complex processing of increasingly large data volumes makes parallelism a necessity. A good portion of the research has so far focused on leveraging the processing capacity of clusters of nodes and originally centralized SPEs [1] evolved rapidly to distributed [3] and parallel [8, 10] ones.

A data streaming application can be seen as a pipeline where data is continuously produced, processed and consumed. In a parallel environment the underlying data structures should provide the means for organizing the data so that the communication and the work imbalance between the concurrent threads of the computation are minimized while the pipeline parallelism is maximized. Although providing the appropriate data structures that best fit the needs of the application in a concurrent environment is a key research issue [11], providing the data structures that best fit data streaming applications has been overlooked. Existing SPEs such as [3, 8] still rely on basic data structures such as queues; similar is the case with work focusing on the improvement of SPEs' architectures [2] or continuous queries accessing the same stream of data [12].

Contributions. The shared access to the data by the collaborating threads defines new synchronization needs that can be integrated in the functionality provided by the shared data structures. By studying the use and limitations of existing aggregate designs and the data structures they use, we motivate the need for a new approach. We propose concurrent, linearizable and lock-free data structures (*T-Gate* and *W-Hive*) upon which we build enhanced multiway aggregate operators that outperform existing implementations in both order-sensitive and order-insensitive functions. We include indicative results from a study we conducted using two large datasets extracted from the SoundCloud[1] social media and from a smart grid metering network. For both datasets the enhanced aggregation resulted in large improvements, up to one order of magnitude, both in terms of processing throughput and latency. The full study is presented in the technical report [5].

1.1 Problem Description

A stream is defined as an unbounded sequence of tuples $t_0, t_1, \ldots$ sharing the same schema of attributes. Given a tuple t, attribute $t.ts$ represents its creation timestamp at the

---

[1] https://soundcloud.com/

data source. Following the data streaming literature (e.g., [3, 8]), we assume that each stream contains timestamp-sorted tuples. In the presence of multiple streams, tuples from different streams may arrive out of timestamp-order, posing a need to merge and synchronize them before processing. Data streaming *continuous queries* are defined as directed acyclic graphs. Nodes represent operators that consume and produce tuples, while edges specify how tuples flow among operators. Operators can be divided into *stateless* or *stateful*, depending on whether they keep any state while processing tuples. Due to the unbounded nature of streams, stateful operations are computed over a *sliding window*, defined by parameters *size* and *advance* (e.g., to group tuples received during periods of 5 minutes every 2 minutes, or the last 10 received tuples every 3 incoming tuples).

The multiway aggregate operator is defined by its window's *size* and *advance* parameters, by a function F applied to the tuples and by an optional *group-by* parameter K (a subset of the input tuple's attributes), which specifies if F is applied independently on tuples with different K value. We focus on deterministic functions, which can be *order-sensitive* (e.g., forward only the first received tuple) or *order-insensitive* (e.g., count the number of tuples) with respect to the processing order of the tuples that contribute to the same window. If the group-by parameter K is defined, the operator needs to keep separate windows not only for different time intervals, but also for different values of K. We define a *winset* as the set of windows covering the same time interval for different values of K.

In scenarios such as parallel-distributed SPEs [8, 4] and replica-based fault tolerant SPEs [3], it is desirable to provide deterministic processing of input tuples (i.e., to produce the same sequence of output tuples given the same sequences of input tuples). When dealing with multiple input streams, processing is not deterministic if tuples are simply processed in the order they are received (i.e., if the processing order depends on the input streams' inter-arrival times). To ensure deterministic processing, tuples from multiple input streams need to be *merged* into one sequence and *sorted* in timestamp order [8], an operation we refer to as *S-Merge*. A tuple is *ready* to be processed if at least one tuple with an equal or higher timestamp has been received at each input stream.

We consider systems of concurrent threads. Communication and information exchange relies on shared data and concurrent shared data structures provide common means for that. Concurrent shared data structures can be implemented in a *lock-free* way, i.e. guaranteeing that at least one of the threads operating on it is guaranteed to finish its operation in a bounded number of its own steps. The correctness of such implementations is commonly shown through *linearizability* [9], which guarantees that, given a history of concurrent operations, there exists a sequential ordering of them, consistent with their real-time ordering and with the sequential semantics of the data structure.

2. AGGREGATION'S PARALLELISM AND THE ROLE OF DATA STRUCTURES

Widely used SPEs such as Borealis [3] or StreamCloud [8] perform multiway aggregation by relying on per-input queues to store incoming tuples. Distinct threads insert and remove tuples from such queues and concurrent accesses are synchronized with the help of locks. Figure 1 presents this

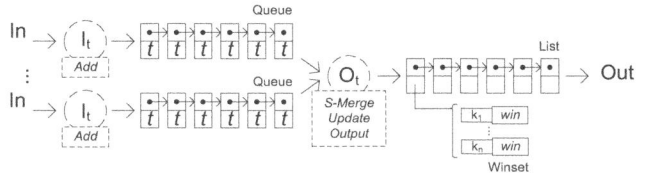

Figure 1: Baseline Multi-Queue based aggregate design.

design, which we refer to as Multi-Queue (MQ). The output thread O_t peeks the first tuple in each queue to determine which one is *ready* to be processed (input threads and output threads are denoted by I_t and O_t respectively). The same thread is also responsible for *updating* the windows a tuple contributes to, as well as producing and forwarding the *output* tuples when they are ready. Since O_t is the only thread in charge of updating windows, no synchronization mechanism is required to access the *winsets*, usually implemented as hash tables to easily support arbitrary numbers of windows and to locate them quickly given the tuple's group-by parameter K.

Parallelization challenges. In existing implementations, *S-Merge* usually relies on simple sorting techniques, whose cost is linear to the number of inputs. Examples include the *Input Merger* operator [8] or the *SUnion* operator [3]. For this reason, the first challenge relies on the parallelization of the *S-Merge* operation. To this end, extra inter-thread synchronization is needed to ensure *deterministic* processing. Another challenge is on the parallelization of the *Update* stage. Again, to guarantee deterministic processing, the result of a window should be outputted only after all its contributing tuples have been processed. For order-sensitive functions, *Update* cannot be invoked in parallel on tuples sharing the same K value or when no group-by parameter is defined. This restriction can be relaxed for order-insensitive functions, since the result of a window would not be affected by the order in which concurrent threads update it. In both cases, parallelism can be enhanced by a concurrent data structure that coordinates the access to the windows.

Utilizing concurrent data structures. We are looking for concurrent data structures that are capable of sorting input tuples at insertion time. In principle, tree-like data structures could provide concurrent logarithmic-time insertion operations. The need for extracting such tuples in timestamp order though, made us expect that a lock-free concurrent skip list [14] would be the right candidate due to its nodes' structure. Nevertheless, a skip list would not differentiate between tuples that are *ready* and tuples that are not. Because of that, checking whether a tuple is *ready* or not would still be penalized by a cost that is linear to the number of inputs as for the multi-queue implementations. Furthermore, it would provide unnecessary functionality (i.e., a more complex implementation) such as deletion of elements at arbitrary positions (only head elements need to be removed in our scenario). Similar considerations hold for a lock-free concurrent skip list that could potentially be used to maintain the operator's *winsets*.

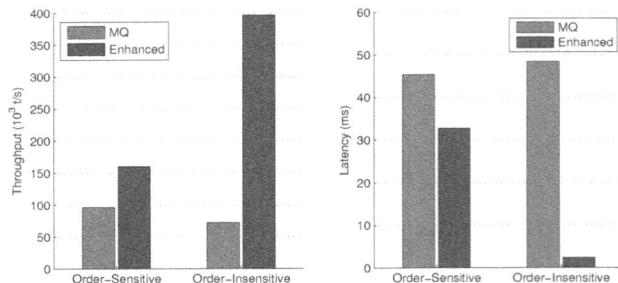

Figure 2: Throughput and latency for a fixed input rate.

New data structures and aggregate designs. We propose two concurrent, linearizable and lock-free data structures, T-Gate for managing tuples and W-Hive for managing *winsets*, which we use to build our enhanced multiway aggregate operators. T-Gate is used in a first step to efficiently store the incoming data in a concurrent manner and to offer proper synchronization on when the data will be accessed in order to provide a deterministic aggregate operator. In order to further parallelize the computation of the aggregate values with the use of multiple threads that produce output data, W-Hive takes care of synchronizing the output of the data according to the streaming model requirements (e.g. sorted). In another design we use only the W-Hive to focus on order insensitive aggregate functions (i.e. the processing order of tuples within a window does not affect the result - e.g.average - but still the order of characterizing tuples ready or inserting tuples in the windows is important for the determinism). Figure 2 shows how the respective enhanced aggregate designs perform against the baseline MQ implementation, for both the cases of order sensitive and insensitive functions, in terms of throughput and latency, for a fixed input rate of equal numbers of incoming streams.

3. CONCLUSIONS

We give an overview on how the parallelism of streaming multiway aggregation can be enhanced by leveraging application-tailored concurrent data structures. We propose new data structures for managing tuples and windows. Their operations and their lock-free implementations enable better interleaving and hence improve the balancing and the parallelism of the aggregate operator's processing stages. As shown in an extensive evaluation based on real-world datasets [5], our enhanced aggregate implementations outperform existing ones both in terms of throughput and latency, and are able to handle heavier streams, increasing the processing capacity up to one order of magnitude.

4. ACKNOWLEDGMENTS

The research leading to these results has been partially supported by the European Union Seventh Framework Programme (FP7/2007-2013) through the EXCESS Project (www.excess-project.eu) under grant agreement 611183, through the SysSec Project, under grant agreement 257007, through the FP7-SEC-285477-CRISALIS project, by the collaboration framework of Chalmers Energy Area of Advance and by the Chalmers Center for E-science.

5. REFERENCES

[1] D. J. Abadi, D. Carney, U. Çetintemel, M. Cherniack, C. Convey, S. Lee, M. Stonebraker, N. Tatbul, and S. Zdonik. Aurora: a new model and architecture for data stream management. *The International Journal on Very Large Data Bases*, 2003.

[2] S. Akram, M. Marazakis, and A. Bilas. Understanding and improving the cost of scaling distributed event processing. In *Proceedings of the 6th ACM International Conference on Distributed Event-Based Systems*, 2012.

[3] M. Balazinska, H. Balakrishnan, S. R. Madden, and M. Stonebraker. Fault-tolerance in the Borealis distributed stream processing system. *ACM Transactions on Database Systems (TODS)*, 2008.

[4] C. Balkesen, N. Tatbul, and M. T. Özsu. Adaptive input admission and management for parallel stream processing. In *Proceedings of the 7th ACM international conference on Distributed event-based systems*, DEBS '13, pages 15–26. ACM, 2013.

[5] D. Cederman, V. Gulisano, Y. Nikolakopoulos, M. Papatriantafilou, and P. Tsigas. Concurrent data structures for efficient streaming aggregation. Report, Chalmers University of Technology, 2013.

[6] A. Dobra, M. Garofalakis, J. Gehrke, and R. Rastogi. Processing complex aggregate queries over data streams. In *Proceedings of the 2002 ACM SIGMOD International Conference on Management of Data*, 2002.

[7] B. Gedik, R. R. Bordawekar, and S. Y. Philip. Celljoin: a parallel stream join operator for the cell processor. *The VLDB Journal*, 2009.

[8] V. Gulisano, R. Jimenez-Peris, M. Patino-Martinez, C. Soriente, and P. Valduriez. Streamcloud: An elastic and scalable data streaming system. *IEEE Transactions on Parallel and Distributed Systems*, 2012.

[9] M. P. Herlihy and J. M. Wing. Linearizability: a Correctness Condition for Concurrent Objects. *ACM Transactions on Programming Languages and Systems*, 1990.

[10] S. Loesing, M. Hentschel, T. Kraska, and D. Kossmann. Stormy: an elastic and highly available streaming service in the cloud. In *Proceedings of the 2012 Joint EDBT/ICDT Workshops*, 2012.

[11] M. M. Michael. The balancing act of choosing nonblocking features. *Commun. ACM*, 2013.

[12] A. L. Shenoda Guirguis, Panos K. Chrysanthis and M. A. Sharaf. Three-level processing of multiple aggregate continuous queries. *Proc. of the 28th IEEE International Conference on Data Engineering*, 2012.

[13] M. Stonebraker, U. Çetintemel, and S. Zdonik. The 8 requirements of real-time stream processing. *ACM SIGMOD Record*, 2005.

[14] H. Sundell and P. Tsigas. Fast and lock-free concurrent priority queues for multi-thread systems. *Journal of Parallel and Distributed Computing*, 2005.

Brief Announcement: Cache-Oblivious Scheduling of Streaming Applications

Kunal Agrawal
Washington Univ. in St. Louis
kunal@cse.wustl.edu

Jeremy T. Fineman
Georgetown University
jfineman@cs.georgetown.edu

ABSTRACT

This paper considers the problem of cache-obliviously scheduling streaming pipelines on uniprocessors with the goal of minimizing cache misses. Our recursive algorithm is not parameterized by cache size, yet it achieves the asymptotically minimum number of cache misses with constant factor memory augmentation.

Categories and Subject Descriptors

F.2 [**Analysis of Algorithms and Problem Complexity**]: General

Keywords

Cache-Oblivious Algorithms; Caching; Partitioning; Pipelines; Scheduling; Streaming; Synchronous Data Flow.

1. INTRODUCTION

As parallel processors such as multicores have become more prevalent, there has been an increasing interest in parallel programming paradigms such as *streaming*. Examples include academic projects like StreamIt [14] and StreamC/KernelC [8], community-based open-source projects like GNU Radio [7], and commercial products including Simulink® [11] and LabVIEW [10]. Streaming is used to express high-throughput applications such as audio and video processing, biological sequence or astrophysics data analysis, and financial modeling. In general a streaming application can be represented by a graph; in this paper, we restrict our attention to *streaming pipelines* — a chain topology commonly used in steaming applications.

Streaming Pipelines: A streaming pipeline consists of a sequence of n *computational modules*, $1, 2, ..., n$, and each module i has exactly one *incoming channel* (from the previous module $i - 1$) and one *outgoing channel* (to the subsequent module $i + 1$). The modules send data, in the form of *messages* or *data items* to each other via these channels. We assume that the incoming channel into module 1 (the first module) streams an infinite amount of data into the pipeline and the outgoing channel from module n streams it out.

Each module i has an associated state; we denote the size of this *state* by $s(i)$. In order to execute, or *fire* a module i, the entire state

SPAA'14, June 23–25, 2014, Prague, Czech Republic.
ACM 978-1-4503-2821-0/14/06.
http://dx.doi.org/10.1145/2612669.2612707.

of that module must be loaded into the cache. A standard (discrete) model is that when the module fires, it consumes $in(i)$ data items from its incoming channel, performs some computation, and then produces $out(i)$ data items on its outgoing channel, where $in(i)$ and $out(i)$ are static parameters of the module. This paper considers a slightly easier continuous model — when a module fires, it may consume any amount x of available data from its incoming channel, then produce $x \times in(i) / out(i)$ data on its outgoing channel. The key distinction in the continuous case is that it may produce a fractional amount of data, which alleviates any bottlenecks in the pipeline caused by integrality.

Cache-Efficient Scheduling: Cache efficiency is an important determinant of performance, and many cache-efficient algorithms have been studied (see [1, 4, 6] for a sample). In this paper, we adopt the ideal-cache model [6], which is an extension of a classic two-level memory model [1]. In this model, there is a fast cache of size M connected to slower storage, and each load (cache miss) moves a contiguous chunk of data, or *block*, of size B into cache.

Streaming applications exhibit two kinds of cache misses that can be controlled using intelligent scheduling. First, since modules access their state when they fire, it is advantageous to execute the same module many times once its state has been loaded. Second, it is advantageous to execute consecutive modules, say i and $i + 1$ in quick succession in order to keep the data produced by module i on its output channel in cache until module $i + 1$ consumes it. Since these heuristics are contradictory, we must balance concerns intelligently to design a good scheduling algorithm. While there has been extensive research, both theoretical and empirical, on scheduling streaming pipelines to optimize throughput and/or latency [9, 2, 5], most prior work on cache-efficiency has been empirical [13, 12].

In previous work [3], we show that if the size of the cache M is known in advance, then one can create a partitioned schedule that provides asymptotically optimal cache performance given constant factor cache augmentation. That is, if the optimal schedule, given a cache of size M, has X cache misses, then this partitioned schedule has $O(X)$ cache misses, given a cache of size $O(M)$. In the present paper, we extend a similar result to cache-oblivious [6] scheduling, albeit in a simpler continuous model. Specifically, without parameterizing by cache size M or block size B, we design a schedule that is asymptotically optimal in the number of cache misses given a constant-factor memory augmentation.

Assumptions and Definitions: We use the term "gain" to describe the amplification of messages along the pipeline. In particular, for an edge from module i to $i + 1$, the *gain* of the edge is defined as the number of messages produced along the edge for each input consumed by the first module in the pipeline. Therefore $gain(i) = \prod_{j=1}^{i} (out(j) / in(j))$.

In addition, we define some terms for a given partition of the pipeline from module i to module j, denoted by $\langle i,j \rangle$. The total size of the pipeline partition $\langle i,j \rangle$ is denoted by $total(i,j) = \sum_{k=i}^{j} s(k)$. Similarly, the largest module within the partition is $max(i,j) = \max_{k=i}^{j} s(k)$. Throughout the paper, we assume that the size of each module is at most $M/6$; that is, $max(1,n) \leq M/6$. Even the optimal algorithm requires that $max(1,n) \leq M$ to allow a module to be in cache when fired; we allow a factor of 6 augmentation over optimal.

2. CACHE-OBLIVIOUS PARTITIONING AND THE SCHEDULING ALGORITHM

This section describes the cache-oblivious scheduling algorithm for streaming pipelines. As with many cache-oblivious algorithms, this scheduling algorithm is recursive, meaning that contiguous sub-pipelines are scheduled recursively with buffers in between to accommodate messages. One of the challenges is controlling the amount of space used by buffers.

At the highest level, consider the entire pipeline $\langle 1,n \rangle$. Define $X = total(1,n)$ and $BASE = 6max(1,n)$. Here, $BASE$ specifies a base case for the recursion (even though M is unknown to the algorithm, the model assumes $M \geq 6max(1,n)$, as stated in Section 1). Without loss of generality, we assume the inputs to the entire pipeline arrive on a size-X input buffer B_1, and the output edge from the last module has an infinite-size buffer B_{n+1}.

Schedule: The scheduling is performed by recursively calling FIRE, specified in Figure 1. The call $\text{FIRE}(i,k,B_i,B_{k+1})$ corresponds to repeatedly executing the sub-pipeline $\langle i,k \rangle$ until (1) all of the inputs are removed from B_i, and (2) all buffers $B_i, \ldots, B_k$ are empty, i.e., all messages have moved to the output. The algorithm is carefully constructed so that B_{k+1} has enough capacity to store all outputs. The top-level call is $\text{FIRE}(1,n,B_1,B_{n+1})$, which may be repeated whenever X inputs become available to the pipeline.

The main idea of the algorithm is to recursively cut the pipeline into pieces that have nearly equal state, insert a buffer of size roughly their state between them, and then recursively schedule each of those pieces. For conciseness, this partitioning is specified in Figure 1, but it could be performed statically *a priori*.

The following lemma states that the preconditions and postconditions hold. The important feature here is that emptying internal buffers allows us to reclaim space (last line in Figure 1), and hence we can relate the (dynamically allocated) space used by the algorithm to the state in the subsequent lemma. This in turn leads to the corollary as long as the algorithm is careful about allocating space.

LEMMA 1. *Any recursive call made to* $\text{FIRE}(i,k,B_i,B_{k+1})$ *moves all x inputs from B_i to B_{k+1} without 1) overflowing the buffer B_{k+1} or 2) leaving any data in internal buffers.*

PROOF. To prove (2), assume inductively that the statement holds for lower levels in the recursion. (It trivially holds for the base case.) Observe that data moved to the middle buffer B_j is drained by inductive assumption in $\text{FIRE}(j,k,B_j,B_{k+1})$; hence all internal buffers are empty. The input buffer is also drained by construction.

For (1), induct starting from the top of the recursion, where it holds trivially since B_{n+1} has infinite size. It holds by construction for the next level of recursion as the number of times the first subpipeline fires is bounded by the size of B_j (i.e., case 1). □

LEMMA 2. *Let $t = total(i,k)$. During $\text{FIRE}(i,k,B_i,B_{k+1})$ the following are true: 1) At any point, the total recursively allocated buffer space that has not been freed is $\Theta(t)$, and 2) the input buffer B_i has size $\Theta(t)$.*

$\text{FIRE}(i,k,B_i,B_{k+1})$ //execute $\langle i,k \rangle = i, i+1, \ldots, k$
     // let x be the number of inputs on B_i
     // Precondition: B_{k+1} has capacity for all inputs on B_i, i.e.,
     //   i.e., at least $x\,gain(k)/gain(i-1)$
     // Postcondition: the input and all internal buffers are empty
1   let $t = total(i,k)$
2   **if** $t < BASE$
3   fire all modules in order until the input buffer is empty.
4   find the module j having minimum gain edge from $j-1$ to j
        such that $\min\{total(i,j-1), total(j,k)\} \geq t/3$
5   create buffers B_i' and B_j with size t
6   **if** $gain(j-1) \geq gain(i-1)$ //(case 1)
7   **repeat** $\lceil x*(gain(j-1)/gain(i-1))/t \rceil$ times
8   move $\frac{t}{gain(j-1)/gain(i-1)}$ items from B_i to B_i'
9             $\text{FIRE}(i,j-1,B_i',B_j)$
10   // there is t data is buffered at B_j
11            $\text{FIRE}(j,k,B_j,B_{k+1})$
12   **else** // $gain(j+1) < gain(i)$ (case 2)
13   **repeat** $\lceil x/t \rceil$ times
14   move t inputs from B_i to B_i'
15             $\text{FIRE}(i,j-1,B_i',B_j)$
16   // there is $< t$ data buffered at B_{j+1}
17            $\text{FIRE}(j,k,B_j,B_{k+1})$
18   deallocate or free buffers B_i' and B_{j+1}

Figure 1: Recursive pseudocode for the schedule.

PROOF. Since each partition has size at least $t/3$, the total state size of either subpipeline is at least $t/3$ and at most $2t/3$. Since each recursive call is given a buffer of size t, (2) holds by construction at each level of recursion. To prove (1), observe that every recursive call frees any space it allocates, and hence the outstanding space corresponds to the recurrence $S(t) \leq S(2t/3) + 2t$, where $2t$ is the space allocated to B_i' and B_j. This recurrence solves to $\Theta(t)$. □

COROLLARY 3. *For any partition $\langle i,k \rangle$ if total state satisfying $total(i,k) \leq M$, then $\text{FIRE}(i,k,B_i,B_{k+1})$ incurs at most $O(M/B)$ cache misses in addition to misses incurred writing the outputs to B_{k+1}.*

PROOF. By Lemma 2, then entire subcomputation with the exception of the output fits in $\Theta(M)$ space, and hence we need only load this state and buffer space once. □

Finally, we prove the main theorem, which bounds the cache cost with respect to gains of edges crossing the recursive partition.

THEOREM 4. *Let $P_1, P_2, \ldots, P_2$ be the maximal recursive sub-pipelines, passed to FIRE calls, such that $total(P_\ell) \leq M$. Let C be the set of edges crossing between these sub-pipelines. Then $\text{FIRE}(1,n,B_1,B_{n+1})$ incurs a total of $O((X/B)\sum_{(k,k+1)\in C} gain(k))$ cache misses, where X is the number of inputs processed per FIRE.*

PROOF. From Corollary 3, we know that each time P_ℓ is FIREd, the cost of firing it is $O(M/B)$ plus the cost of the outputs. (The cost of outputs trivially bounded by the sum of the gains.) The goal is thus to show that we can charge this $O(M/B)$ cost against the gain of an edge in C. In particular, let $\text{FIRE}(i,k,B_i,B_{k+1})$ be the nearest ancestor call (i.e., $P_\ell \subseteq \langle i,k \rangle$) such that the loop (case 1 or case 2) has more than 1 repetition (or the root if no such ancestor exists). Let $e \in \{(i-1,i),(j-1,j),(k,k+1)\} \subseteq C$ be the edge with maximum gain from among the input/middle/output edges. We will charge firing P_ℓ against e.

Note that by assumption, any sub-pipeline P_ℓ charged to e only fires once per iteration of the repeat loop (it could only be more than once if a nearer recursive call had multiple iterations). Thus, if there are q iterations, then there is at most $q \sum_{P_\ell \in \langle i,k \rangle} O(M/B) = O(q \cdot total(i,k))$ work charged to e. Moreover, there must be at least $\Omega(q \cdot total(i,k))$ data moving through edge e to cause $q \geq 1$ iterations (due to bounded buffer size in case 1 or 2). Thus, the cost charged per data on e is at most $O(1/B)$, or $O(X \, gain(e)/B)$ in total. Summing across all edges in C completes the proof. $\square$

We now argue that the cache-oblivious schedule shown in Figure 1 is asymptotically optimal given constant factor memory augmentation.

LEMMA 5. *If the optimal algorithm for scheduling pipelines has $\mathcal{M}$ memory and incurs Q cache misses, then the recursive schedule in Figure 1 incurs $O(Q)$ cache misses given $O(\mathcal{M})$ memory.*

PROOF. Our previous lower bound [3] argues the following: Consider any arbitrary partition of the pipeline into contiguous segments $S_1, S_2, \ldots, S_k$ such that each segment has total size at least $2\mathcal{M}$, where $\mathcal{M}$ is the memory afforded to the (optimal) algorithm. Define $gm_i = \min_{e \in S_i} gain(e)$ to be the smallest gain edge within segment S_i. On processing X inputs (for large enough X), the optimal algorithm incurs $\Omega((X/B) \sum_{i=1}^{k} gm_i)$ cache misses. In other words, the optimal algorithm has to "pay for" the minimum-gain edge of any segment with size $2\mathcal{M}$. While our previous statement of the lower bound [3] is with respect to the discrete model, the proof does not leverage discreteness, and hence the bound applies to the continuous model as well.

Our upper bound (Theorem 4) states that the cache-oblivious algorithm need only "pay for" edges crossing certain partitions. It remains only to show that these edges also contribute to the lower bound. Specifically, a size-$t > M$ segment is subdivided by splitting it at the minimum-gain edge in its middle size-$t/3$ subsegment (Figure 1, Line 4). As long as $t/3 > 2\mathcal{M}$, the optimal algorithm must also pay for this edge. Setting $\mathcal{M} = M/6$ implies that all of these crossing edges must also be paid for by the optimal algorithm with $\mathcal{M}$ memory. In conclusion, the number of cache misses incurred by the cache-oblivious scheduler is at most a constant factor more than the optimal algorithms cache misses if the cache-oblivious scheduler has constant factor more memory. $\square$

3. CONCLUSIONS

We have presented a cache-oblivious scheduling algorithm for streaming pipelines based on recursive partitioning of the pipeline. This algorithm is asymptotically optimal given constant factor memory augmentation under the continuous assumption — that is, when each module of the pipeline can consume and produce fractional items. Under the more realistic non-continuous assumption — when a module can only fire when it can consume integral number of items equal to its input rate — the problem of cache-oblivious scheduling remains open. In addition, the problem of cache-oblivious scheduling of streaming applications which can be described using directed acyclic graphs (instead of simple linear chains) also remains open.

Acknowledgements

This research was supported by NSF grants CCF-1218017, CCF-1150036, and CCF-1218188.

4. REFERENCES

[1] A. Aggarwal and J. S. Vitter. The input/output complexity of sorting and related problems. *Communications of the ACM*, 31(9):1116–1127, September 1988.

[2] K. Agrawal, A. Benoit, and Y. Robert. Mapping linear workflows with computation/communication overlap. In *Proceedings of the IEEE International Conference on Parallel and Distributed Systems (ICPADS)*, pages 195–202, Washington, DC, USA, 2008. IEEE Computer Society.

[3] K. Agrawal, J. T. Fineman, J. Krage, C. E. Leiserson, and S. Toledo. Cache-conscious scheduling of streaming applications. In *Proceedings of the ACM Symposium on Parallelism in Algorithms and Architectures (SPAA)*, pages 236–245, June 2012.

[4] M. A. Bender, E. Demaine, and M. Farach-Colton. Cache-oblivious B-trees. In *Proceedings of the 41st Annual Symposium on Foundations of Computer Science (FOCS)*, pages 399–409, 2000.

[5] S. M. Farhad, Y. Ko, B. Burgstaller, and B. Scholz. Orchestration by approximation mapping stream programs onto multicore architectures. *ACM SIGPLAN Notices*, 46:357–368, 2011.

[6] M. Frigo, C. E. Leiserson, H. Prokop, and S. Ramachandran. Cache-oblivious algorithms. *ACM Transactions on Algorithms*, January 2012.

[7] GNU Radio, 2001. Software, gnuradio.org.

[8] U. J. Kapasi, P. Mattson, W. J. Dally, J. D. Owens, and B. Towles. Stream scheduling. Concurrent VLSI Architecture Tech Report 122, Stanford University, Computer Systems Laboratory, March 2002.

[9] M. Karczmarek, W. Thies, and S. Amarasinghe. Phased scheduling of stream programs. *ACM SIGPLAN Notices*, 38(7):103–112, 2003.

[10] LabVIEW, 2011. Software, www.ni.com/labview.

[11] Mathworks. *Simulink User's Guide*, 2011. Release 2011b.

[12] A. Moonen, M. Bekooij, R. Van Den Berg, and J. Van Meerbergen. Cache aware mapping of streaming applications on a multiprocessor system-on-chip. In *Proceedings of the Conference on Design, Automation and Test in Europe (DATE)*, pages 300–305, 2008.

[13] J. Sermulins, W. Thies, R. Rabbah, and S. Amarasinghe. Cache aware optimization of stream programs. *ACM SIGPLAN Notices*, 40(7):115–126, 2005.

[14] W. Thies, M. Karczmarek, and S. P. Amarasinghe. Streamit: A language for streaming applications. In *Proceedings of the International Conference on Compiler Construction (CC)*, pages 179–196, London, UK, 2002. Springer-Verlag.

Brief Announcement : Persistent Unfairness Arising From Cache Residency Imbalance

Dave Dice
Oracle Labs
dave.dice@oracle.com

Virendra J. Marathe
Oracle Labs
virendra.marathe@oracle.com

Nir Shavit
MIT
shanir@csail.mit.edu

ABSTRACT

We describe a counter-intuitive performance phenomena relevant to concurrency research. On a modern multicore system with a shared last-level cache, a set of concurrently running identical threads that loop – each accessing the same quantity of distinct thread-private data – can suffer significant relative progress imbalance. If one thread, or a small subset of the threads, manages to transiently enjoy higher cache residency than the other threads, that thread will tend to iterate faster and keep more of its data resident, thus increasing the odds that it will continue to run faster. This emergent behavior tends to be stable over surprisingly long periods.

Categories and Subject Descriptors

D.1.3 [**Concurrent Programming**]: Parallel Programming

General Terms

Performance, experiments, algorithms

Keywords

Concurrency, threads, caches, multicore

1. INTRODUCTION

Multiple threads concurrently accessing a shared last-level cache (LLC) can encounter competition for cache residency and *destructive interference*. This behavior is well-known [2]. We observe, however, that such a group of homogeneous threads accessing private data regions can suffer from significant imbalance in their relative rates of progress. We found this behavior somewhat surprising and a possible confounding factor for experiments and benchmarks.

After analysis, we determined this unfairness occurs when a small subset of the threads manage to achieve relatively better LLC residency. Those threads then tend to run faster, which in turn supports their occupancy. This state can be stable over periods of minutes. When this form of residency-based unfairness is present, the progress rates of the threads tend to be bimodal : threads are either *fast* or *slow*. A thread's LLC miss rate and observed cycles-per-instruction (CPI) is inversely proportional to – and inversely correlated with – that thread's progress rate. The onset of the effect occurs when the sum of the private working sets of all the threads is near the capacity of the shared LLC. The stratification effect abates when the working set grows sufficiently larger than the cache capacity and most accesses miss in the LLC.

To further establish etiology and causation, we performed an experiment where we intentionally inserted a transient stall, and were able to transform a fast thread to a slow thread, as the stall caused the thread to lose LLC residency. Once disadvantaged, the thread remained slow.

We believe this new phenomena should be noted by designers and researchers and added to the set of existing concerns – such as false sharing, for example – taken into account when analyzing concurrent program behavior.

2. EVALUATION

Figure 1 depicts the magnitude of the phenomena on an Oracle SPARC T4-1 [6] system running Solaris 11 and an x86 system running Linux 3.11 on an Intel i7-4770 "haswell" processor. The T4-1 has 8 cores with 8 pipelines per core for a total of 64 logical thread contexts. The shared L3 LLC is 4MB with a non-most-recently-used (NMRU) replacement policy and is inclusive of the L1 and L2 caches. The i7-4770 has an 8MB LLC shared over 4 cores with 2 pipelines per core for a total of 8 logical thread contexts. Both systems are single-socket non-NUMA and have 64-byte LLC cache lines, and both have core-private L1 and L2 caches.

Each thread allocates a circular ring of intrusively linked nodes which form the thread-private data. Each node resides on its own cache line and is 64-bytes in length. The order of the nodes is randomized in order to reduce the influence of automatic hardware prefetch facilities. To reduce the influence of TLB pressure, each thread invokes mmap() to allocate a set of contiguous pages from which its set of nodes is in turn allocated via a simple "bump pointer". This gives the system the opportunity to provision the region underlying the nodes with large pages, and minimizes the number of pages underlying a given ring. This approach also ensures balanced placement of nodes over cache indices [1]. The number of elements in the ring – the circumference – is configurable via command line parameters.

We use a 60-second measurement interval during which each thread executes a top-level loop that repeatedly traverses its ring. At the end of the measurement interval the benchmark reports the number of traversals completed by each of the threads.

In our experiments we ran with 8 threads for all data points. Both the Linux and Solaris schedulers are work-conserving and all

SPAA'14, June 23–25, 2014, Prague, Czech Republic.
ACM 978-1-4503-2821-0/14/06.
http://dx.doi.org/10.1145/2612669.2612703.

8 threads ran for the entirety of the measurement interval. With just 8 ready threads, Solaris will place each thread on its own core in order to avoid contention for pipeline and L1/L2 resources. That is, Solaris balances the distribution of threads over core-level resources. On the Linux x86 platform, pairs of threads share a core.

On the X-axis we show the total size of all thread-private data expressed as a fraction of the LLC size. On the Y-axis we report the *spread* – the degree of unfairness as defined by the number of traversals completed by the fastest thread divided by the number of traversals completed by the slowest thread. We report the median spread from 7 runs. For our experiments *turbo boost* was disabled on the Intel processor and the clock rate was fixed at 3.4GHz for all cores.

In other experiments we replaced the per-thread rings with fetches from randomly selected locations in thread-private arrays. This variant exhibited similar unfairness.

In supplemental experiments we modified the loops executed by the threads to first acquire a contended central MCS lock [5], followed by by 10000 steps of a register-based random number generator [4]. No memory is accessed in the critical section. The thread then releases the lock and traverses its ring. No store instructions are executed, so there is no induced coherence traffic. We opted for a top-level loop with an MCS lock and critical section to illustrate that the problem manifests even under a fair FIFO lock. As configured, the lock is contended and threads typically wait for entry. Again, we observed similar levels of unfairness. It is commonly the case that a slow thread S might release the lock, passing ownership to some fast thread F, only to find that F completes the critical and non-critical sections more quickly than S can complete its non-critical section, so F races ahead and queues on the lock before S. F can erode S's residency faster than S can erode F's residency, so F maintains its relative advantage.

We note that being fast or slow seems to be happenstance from the perspective of the programmer, and is not to related to thread placement within the system topology or geography.

As can be seen in the graph, the onset of unfair progress rates starts near the LLC capacity, and the worst-case magnitude is over $5X$ for both platforms. Note that the onset occurs before the fraction reaches 1.0 because our caches are not ideal fully-associative. We believe the slightly different shapes exhibited by the T4-1 and the i7-4770 are due to differing cache architectures, the ability to leverage memory-level parallelism, and the depth of the speculation windows. Finally, notice that the i7-4770 exhibits minor unfairness when the LLC fraction is very low. We have 2 threads sharing the per-core L1 and L2 caches, and find the unfairness phenomena manifests at those levels of the cache hierarchy.

3. CONCLUSION

Cache behavior is taking an increasingly important role in multicore software design, and properly understanding cache sharing and eviction policies is often key to delivering good concurrent performance. We presented an interesting new cache phenomena whose effects should be noted by designers and researchers when analyzing concurrent program behavior.

We note that improved hardware cache replacement algorithms specifically designed for shared caches [3] may provide relief.

In the future we hope to explore techniques to better identify and respond to the phenomena. Experiments suggest that we may be able to moderate the behavior in software by periodically suspending randomly selected threads for a very brief period. This serves to disrupt and perturb the steady-state and provides statistical performance isolation over the long term by injection of randomized noise.

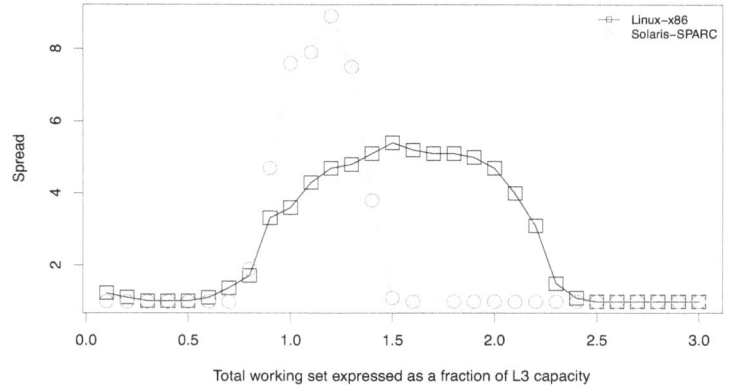

Figure 1: Fairness

Nir Shavit was supported in part by NSF grants CCF-1217921 and CCF-1301926, DoE ASCR grant ER26116/DE-SC0008923, and by grants from the Oracle and Intel corporations.

4. REFERENCES

[1] Y. Afek, D. Dice, and A. Morrison. Cache Index-aware Memory Allocation. In *Proceedings of the International Symposium on Memory Management*, ISMM '11, pages 55–64, New York, NY, USA, 2011. ACM.

[2] B. Brett, P. Kumar, M. Kim, and H. Kim. CHiP: A Profiler to Measure the Effect of Cache Contention on Scalability. In *Proceedings of the 2013 IEEE 27th International Symposium on Parallel and Distributed Processing Workshops and PhD Forum*, IPDPSW '13, pages 1565–1574, Washington, DC, USA, 2013. IEEE Computer Society.

[3] A. K. Katti and V. Ramachandran. Competitive Cache Replacement Strategies for Shared Cache Environments. In *Proceedings of the 2012 IEEE 26th International Parallel and Distributed Processing Symposium*, IPDPS '12, pages 215–226, Washington, DC, USA, 2012. IEEE Computer Society.

[4] G. Marsaglia. Xorshift RNGs. *Journal of Statistical Software*, 8(14):1–6, 7 2003.

[5] J. M. Mellor-Crummey and M. L. Scott. Algorithms for Scalable Synchronization on Shared-memory Multiprocessors. *ACM Trans. Comput. Syst.*, 9:21–65, February 1991.

[6] Oracle Corporation. Oracle's SPARC T4-1, SPARC T4-2, SPARC T4-4, and SPARC T4-1B Server Architecture, 2012.

Provably Good Scheduling for Parallel Programs that Use Data Structures through Implicit Batching

Kunal Agrawal
Washington Univ. in St. Louis
kunal@cse.wustl.edu

Jeremy T. Fineman
Georgetown University
jfineman@cs.georgetown.edu

Kefu Lu
Washington Univ. in St. Louis
kefu.lu@wustl.edu

Brendan Sheridan
Georgetown University
bss45@georgetown.edu

Jim Sukha
Intel Corporation
jim.sukha@intel.com

Robert Utterback
Washington Univ. in St. Louis
robert.utterback@wustl.edu

ABSTRACT

Although *concurrent data structures* are commonly used in practice on shared-memory machines, even the most efficient concurrent structures often lack performance theorems guaranteeing linear speedup for the enclosing parallel program. Moreover, efficient concurrent data structures are difficult to design. In contrast, *parallel batched data structures* do provide provable performance guarantees, since processing a batch in parallel is easier than dealing with the arbitrary asynchrony of concurrent accesses. They can limit programmability, however, since restructuring a parallel program to use batched data structure instead of a concurrent data structure can often be difficult or even infeasible.

This paper presents BATCHER, a scheduler that achieves the best of both worlds through the idea of *implicit batching*, and a corresponding general performance theorem. BATCHER takes as input (1) a dynamically multithreaded program that makes arbitrary parallel accesses to an abstract data type, and (2) an implementation of the abstract data type as a batched data structure that need not cope with concurrent accesses. BATCHER extends a randomized work-stealing scheduler and guarantees provably good performance to parallel algorithms that use these data structures. In particular, suppose a parallel algorithm has T_1 work, T_∞ span, and n data-structure operations. Let $W(n)$ be the total work of data-structure operations and let $s(n)$ be the span of a size-P batch. Then BATCHER executes the program in $O((T_1 + W(n) + ns(n))/P + s(n)T_\infty)$ expected time on P processors. For higher-cost data structures like search trees and large enough n, this bound becomes $((T_1 + n \lg n)/P + T_\infty \lg n)$, provably matching the work of a sequential search tree but with nearly linear speedup, even though the data structure is accessed concurrently. The BATCHER runtime bound also readily extends to data structures with amortized bounds.

Categories and Subject Descriptors

F.2.2 [**Analysis of Algorithms and Problem Complexity**]: Non-numerical Algorithms and Problems—*Sequencing and scheduling*; D.1.3 [**Programming Techniques**]: Concurrent Programming—*Parallel programming*; E.1 [**Data Structures**]: *Distributed data structures*

Keywords

Data structures, work stealing, scheduler, batched data structure, implicit batching

1. INTRODUCTION

A common approach when using data structures within parallel programs is to employ **concurrent data structures** — data structures that can cope with multiple simultaneous accesses. Not only is it challenging to design and analyze concurrent data structures, but the existing performance theorems do not often imply linear speedup for the enclosing program. The straightforward way to analyze a program that uses a concurrent data structure is to assume the worst-case latency for each access. For a limited set of concurrent data structures (see Section 6), the worst-case latency is low enough that this approach is effective. In more general cases, the worst-case latency is often linear in the number of processors in the system (or worse), e.g., for Braginsky and Petrank's lock-free B$^+$-tree [7].[1] If n data-structure accesses each keep a processor busy for $\Omega(P)$ timesteps, then the running time on P processors is at least $\Omega(nP/P) = \Omega(n)$. An $\Omega(n)$ bound means that accesses are essentially sequential — there is no significant speedup guarantee when running on P processors.

Concurrent data structures are in some sense overkill for use within a single parallel program because they are designed to cope with difficult access patterns. Since the data-structure accesses belong to the same enclosing program, they can, in principle, coordinate with each other. A key idea behind our work is to leverage a runtime scheduler and to handle this coordination.

The primary goal of this paper is to 1) describe a good scheduler for executing a broad class of parallel programs that make parallel

---

[1] The worst case occurs when all processors concurrently insert contiguous keys. The progress bound proven [7] is worse, since the data structure is designed to cope with processor failures. But even assuming no failures and simplifying the data structure, an $\Omega(P)$ worst-case bound still occurs when P processes attempt a compare-and-swap on the same node in the tree.

accesses to data structures, and 2) provide a corresponding general performance theorem for this scheduler. Our performance theorem exhibits an attractive modularity: the data structure may be analyzed in isolation of the program that uses it, and the parallel program may be analyzed without considering the specific implementation of the data structure. This modularity makes the theorem easy to apply while still achieving provably good speedup, e.g., for n parallel accesses to a search tree with large enough n, our scheduling theorem proves a completion time of $\Theta(n \lg n / P)$, which is asymptotically optimal and has linear speedup. We are unaware of any comparable aggregate bounds for concurrent search trees.

Runtime scheduling. This paper focuses on parallel programs expressed through *dynamic multithreading*[2] (see [11, Ch. 27]), which is common in many parallel languages and libraries, such as Cilk dialects [18, 26], Intel TBB [35], Microsoft Task Parallel Library [39] and subsets of OpenMP [30]. The programmer expresses algorithmic parallelism, through linguistic constructs such as "spawn" and "sync," "fork" and "join," or parallel loops. The programmer does not provide any mapping from subcomputations to processors. The program is typically scheduled using an efficient work-stealing scheduler (e.g., [6]) provided by the runtime system. A parallel program (without parallel data structure accesses) having T_1 **work** — the running time on 1 processor, and T_∞ **span** — the length of the critical path, can be executed in $O(T_1/P + T_\infty)$ (expected) time on P processors (or workers) using a work-stealing scheduler. This running time is asymptotically optimal and guarantees linear speedup to programs with sufficient parallelism.

This paper generalizes the above result by describing a scheduler and corresponding performance theorem for dynamic multithreaded programs that make parallel accesses to a data structure. This performance theorem implies that parallel programs (with sufficient parallelism) using efficient data-structure implementations can execute with linear speedup, even if the program's work is dominated by data-structure accesses.

Batched data structures. One way to programmatically coordinate data-structure accesses is to use only *batched data structures*, where the program invokes an entire set of data-structure operations synchronously, and the batched data structure performs these operations collectively in parallel. The main advantages of batched data structures are: (1) only one batch is active at a time, obviating the need for complicated concurrency control within the data structure, (2) parallelism may be used to accelerate individual batches, and (3) they are relatively easy to analyze; if a program generates a sequence of batches, we can simply add the running time of this sequence of batches to the running time of the program. For example, (batched) parallel priority queues [8, 12, 13, 36] have been utilized to prove efficient running time on parallel algorithms such as shortest paths and minimum spanning tree [8, 13, 32].

Getting provably good performance by replacing a concurrent data structure with a batched data structure can require drastic code restructuring, however, since the parallel program must explicitly group accesses into batches. In some cases, such a restructuring may not even be possible. For example, an on-the-fly race detector [29, 5, 34] updates a series-parallel-maintenance data structure on forks and joins while executing an input program. In this application, the data structure must be updated before the program flow continues past the calling point, so it seems impossible to reorganize the operations into batches by restructuring the algorithm.

Contributions

This paper shows we can achieve a modular analytic abstraction whereby the data structure $\mathcal{D}$ and the enclosing program C may be analyzed separated, then combined through a strong performance theorem guaranteeing good parallel running time. This result applies to the broad class of dynamically multithreaded computations. We achieve the runtime theorem through the novel technique of implicit batching coupled with an efficient runtime scheduler.

Implicit batching. This paper focuses on the novel technique of *implicit batching*, which achieves benefits of both concurrent and batched data structures. In implicit batching, the programmer provides two components: (1) a parallel program C containing parallel accesses to a abstract data type $\mathcal{D}$, and (2) a batched data-structure implementing the data structure $\mathcal{D}$. The scheduler dynamically and transparently organizes the program's parallel accesses to the data structure into batches, with at most one batch executing at a time.

Using implicit batching gives the benefits of batched data structures without restructuring the enclosing program C. The scheduler is responsible for grouping any concurrent accesses to the abstract data type $\mathcal{D}$ into batches and invoking the appropriate implementation of a batched operation. The data structure's batched operation may be implemented using dynamic multithreading (see Section 3 for examples). The data-structure's implementation need not cope with concurrency since at most one batch is executing at any time, and hence locks or atomic operations may be omitted. The scheduler handles all synchronization and communication between the parallel program C and the data structure $\mathcal{D}$.

Implicit batching closely resembles flat combining [21], where each concurrent access to a data-structure queues up in a list of operation records, and this list of records (i.e., a batch) is later executed sequentially. Implicit batching may be viewed as a generalization of flat combining in that it allows *parallel* implementations of batched operations, instead of only a sequential one allowed by flat combining. Due to sequential batches, flat combining does not guarantee provable speedup guarantees. However, flat combining has been shown to be more efficient in practice than some of the best concurrent data structures under certain loads. Viewing flat combining as a specific implementation of implicit batching, already shows the practical effectiveness of implicit batching — this paper focuses on obtaining a provably good runtime theorem.

Scheduler and performance theorem. Implicit batching poses its own challenges for performance analysis. For a parallel program using implicit batching, which sequence of batches should be analyzed? What overhead does the scheduler incur when creating batches? In general, the performance of a parallel program using implicit batching depends on the particular runtime scheduler used to execute the program.

To yield a performance theorem, we propose ***BATCHER***, a work-stealing scheduler designed for implicit batching. Given a dynamically multithreaded program C that makes parallel accesses to an ADT $\mathcal{D}$, and a batched implementation of $\mathcal{D}$, it yields the following bound, proven in Section 5:

THEOREM 1. *Consider a dynamically multithreaded program C having T_1 work and T_∞ span. Let n be the total number of data-structure operations (accesses to ADT $\mathcal{D}$), and m be the maximum number of data-structure operations along any sequential dependency chain. For the given implementation of $\mathcal{D}$, let $W(n)$ be the worst-case total work for n data-structure operations grouped arbitrarily into batches, and let $s(n)$ be the worst-case span of a parallel size-P batched operation.[3] Then the expected running time of*

---

[2]Dynamic multithreading is also sometimes called "fork-join" parallelism.

---

[3]We employ only binary forking, so $s(n) \geq \lg P$ implicitly.

85

this program on P processors using BATCHER[4] is at most

$$O\left(\frac{T_1}{P} + T_\infty + \frac{W(n) + ns(n)}{P} + ms(n)\right) .$$

An important feature about this bound is that T_1 and T_∞ are the work and span of the core program C, independent of the data structure implementation. Similarly, n and m count the data-structure calls in the program, and depend only on the program C, not the data structure implementation. Moreover, $s(n)$ and $W(n)$ are performance measures of the batched implementation $\mathcal{D}$ of the data structure, independent of the enclosing program. We are thus essentially adding the program's cost to the data structure's cost. This bound also applies when the analysis of the batched data structure is amortized, through a more general definition of $s(n)$ (see Section 2 for definitions). For many parallel batched data structures (see Section 3 for examples), this performance theorem implies nearly linear speedup.

The remainder of this paper is organized as follows. Section 2 presents the theoretical model we use to analyze parallel programs that make accesses to parallel data structures. Section 3 provides a high-level overview of BATCHER and applies the performance bound to example batched data structure. Section 4 presents the BATCHER scheduling algorithms, which is analyzed in Section 5; we built a prototype implementation of BATCHER and show preliminary experiments in Section 7. Section 6 discusses related work on using data structures in parallel.

2. DEFINITIONS AND ANALYTIC MODEL

Recall that a programmer provides two inputs to the BATCHER scheduler: (1) A parallel program C that makes parallel accesses to an abstract data type $\mathcal{D}$, and (2) a batched data structure that implements $\mathcal{D}$ and need only support one batch at a time. This section defines how the parallel program and the batched data structure are modeled.

Execution dag model. In the absence of data-structure operations, the execution of a dynamically multithreaded computation can be modeled as a directed acyclic graph (**dag**) that unfolds dynamically (see [11, Ch. 27]). In this execution dag, each node represents a unit-time sequential subcomputation, and each edge represents control-flow dependencies between nodes. A node that corresponds to a "fork" has two[5] outgoing edges, and a node corresponding to a "join" has two or more incoming edges.

A scheduler is responsible for choosing which nodes to execute on each processor during each timestep. The scheduler may only execute **ready nodes** — those unexecuted nodes whose predecessors have all been executed. The convenient feature about the computation dag is that it models the control-flow constraints within the program without capturing the specific choices made by the scheduler. The dag unfolds dynamically — only the immediate successors of executed nodes are revealed to the scheduler. This unfolding can also be nondeterministic. Hence the scheduler must make online decisions. All of our analyses are with respect to the *a posteriori* dag. The two key features of a dag are its **work**, which is the number of (unit-length) nodes in the dag, and its **span**, which is the length of the longest directed path through the dag.

---

[4]Just as in standard work-stealing results, our theoretical bounds assume that the only synchronization of the input algorithm occurs through "syncs" or "joins"; the algorithm or data structure code itself does not use explicit synchronization primitives, e.g., locks or compare-and-swaps.

[5]In general, forks may have arbitrary out-degree, but in this paper we pessimistically assume binary forking.

Extending the dag model to implicit batching. We first model the batched data structure that implements $\mathcal{D}$. An implementation of a batched operation is itself a parallel (sub)computation that may include forks and joins. We thus model the execution of each batch A by its own **batch dag** G_A. We use the terms **batch work**, denoted by w_A, and **batch span**, denoted by s_A, to refer to the work and span of the batch dag, respectively.

To analyze a batched data structure as a whole, we consider worst-case sequences of arbitrary batches, such that the total number of data structure operations across all batches is n, and each batch contains at most P data structure operations. We define the **data-structure work**, denoted by $W_P(n)$, to be the maximum total work of any such sequence of batches. We also define the **data-structure span**, denoted by $s_P(n)$, to be the worst-case span of any batch dag A in any such sequence subject to the the restrictions that $w_A/s_A = O(P)$, meaning that the batch has limited parallelism. In the case when the data structure's analysis is not amortized, the data-structure span may be stated more concisely as the worst-case span of any batch dag that represents a size-P batch, since all batches of the same size have the same span. For data structures with amortized analysis, however, batches with the same number of operations may have different spans — therefore, the batch span is defined in terms of the parallelism of the batch dag rather than the number of operations in the batch. Since P (the number of workers) is static throughout this paper, we use $W(n)$ and $s(n)$ as shorthands for $W_P(n)$ and $s_P(n)$. Note that whereas data-structure work corresponds to the total work of all batches that cumulatively contain n operations, the data-structure span corresponds to the span of a single batch with P operations. Thus far we have not considered a program that makes accesses to the data structure, we have only considered the data structure implementation. It should thus be clear that $W(n)$ and $s(n)$ are metrics of the data structure implementation itself.

We model the enclosing program C, which makes parallel calls to a data structure (these operations will be implicitly batched), as another kind of dag, called the **core dag** G. A core dag is just like a standard execution dag, except that it includes two kinds of nodes. Each data-structure operation (that is to be implicitly batched) is represented by a special **data-structure node**. All other non-data-structure nodes in the dag are called **core nodes**. Whereas all core nodes by definition take unit-time to execute on a processor, the data-structure nodes represent blocking calls that may take longer to complete. Our metrics for the core dag, however, avoid this issue — we define the **core work**, which we generally denote by T_1, to be the number of nodes in the core dag, and the **core span**, denoted by T_∞, to be the longest path through the core dag in terms of number of nodes. We also generally use n to refer to the number of data-structure nodes in the core dag, and m to denote the maximum number of data-structure nodes falling along any directed path through G. Although the core dag includes data-structure nodes whose "execution times" are not defined, the metrics T_1, T_∞, n, and m are functions of only the core program, not the implementation of batched operations.

No extra dependencies between data-structure nodes? It may be surprising that modeling the core dag and batch dags separately as described throughout this section can be sufficient for the analysis of any scheduler. A priori, one might expect execution-dependent "happens-before" relationships across all data-structure calls, particularly since the scheduler must group operations into batches. Moreover, one might be surprised that the "length" of data-structure nodes is not modeled anywhere. Nevertheless, in Section 5 we prove that this simple model is sufficient for the BATCHER scheduler, which is a key contribution of the paper.

3. IMPLICIT BATCHING IN BATCHER

This section overviews implicit batching in the context of the BATCHER scheduler with respect to the core and batch dags defined in Section 2. The specific algorithms employed by the scheduler itself are deferred to Section 4. This section also gives a simple example of a program using an implicitly batched data structure to provide concrete examples of applying the performance theorem.

Programming Interface. BATCHER provides distinct interfaces to the algorithm programmer, who writes a program C that makes parallel accesses to ADT $\mathcal{D}$; and the data-structure programmer, who provides the batched implementation of ADT $\mathcal{D}$. The runtime system stitches together these interfaces and does the scheduling. Figures 1 and 2 (discussed later in this section) show a simple example program making n parallel increments to a shared counter using this interface style.

To perform a data-structure operation, the program C makes a call into the runtime system, denoted by BATCHIFY here. As far as the algorithm programmer is concerned, BATCHIFY (corresponding to a data-structure node in the core dag) resembles a normal procedure call to access a *concurrent data structure*, and the control flow blocks at this point until the operation completes.

A BATCHER data structure, on the other hand, must provide an implementation of a parallel batched operation, which we denote by BOP. Since BOP is a batched implementation, it takes as input a set (i.e., an array) of operations to the ADT $\mathcal{D}$ to perform. Note that BOP is itself a dynamically multithreaded function that can use spawn/sync or parallel loops to generate parallelism. A single invocation of the BOP function corresponds to a single batch dag.

Batching. At a high level, calls to BATCHIFY correspond to data-structure nodes and BATCHER is responsible for implicitly batching these data structure operations and then executing these batches by calling BOP. When a worker p encounters a data-structure node u (i.e., p executes a call to BATCHIFY), p alerts the scheduler to the operation by creating an operation record op for that operation and placing it in a particular memory location reserved for this processor. Eventually, op will be part of some batch A and the scheduler will call BOP on A. Unlike core nodes, however, the data-structure node can logically block for longer than one time step and u's successor(s) in the dag do not become ready until after this call to BOP returns, that is, the operation corresponding to u is actually performed on the data structure as part of a batch. Thus from the perspective of the core program, a data-structure node u has the same semantics as a blocking access to a concurrent data structure.

Inherent to implicit batching is the idea that the batch the scheduler invokes only one batch at a time. Hence the data-structure implementation need not cope with concurrency, simplifying the data-structure design. The following invariant states this property for BATCHER.

INVARIANT 1. *At any time during a BATCHER execution, at most one batch is executing.*

There are many other choices that go into a scheduler for implicit batching. For BATCHER, we made specific choices guided by the goal of proving a performance theorem. Three of the main questions are what basic type of scheduler to use, how large batches should be, and when and how batches are launched. As far as the low-level details are concerned, we chose in favor of simplicity where possible. BATCHER is a distributed work-stealing scheduler. BATCHER also restricts batch sizes, as stated by the following invariant; this size cap ameliorates application of the main theorem as it simplifies the analysis of any specific data structure.

INVARIANT 2. *In a BATCHER execution, batches contain at most P data-structure nodes.*

Finally, whenever an operation record is created and no batch is currently in progress, BATCHER immediately launches a new batch; it does not wait for a certain number of operations to accrue; this decision is important for the theoretical analysis. Therefore, batches can contain as few as one operation. Launching a batch includes some (parallel) setup to gather all operation outstanding operation records, executing the provided (parallel) batched operation BOP thereby inducing a batch dag, and some (parallel) cleanup after completing. Since the setup/cleanup overhead is scheduler dependent, we account for the overhead separately, and the batch dag comprises only the steps of BOP.

Intuition behind the analysis. The analysis of BATCHER (Section 5) relies on specific features of the scheduling algorithm (Section 4). Nevertheless, we have already exposed one significant difficulty: since batches launch as soon as possible, some batches may contain just a single data-structure node. If this were true for every batch, then all operations would be sequentialized according to Invariant 1, and it would seem impossible to show good speedup. In addition, the batch setup and cleanup overhead is the same, regardless of batch size; therefore, having many small batches may incur significant overhead.

Fortunately, small batches fall into two cases, both being good. (1) Many data structure nodes accrue while a small batch is executing. These will be part of the next batch, meaning that the next batch will be large and make progress toward the batch work $W(n)$. (2) Not many data structure nodes are accruing. Then the core dag is not blocked on too many data-structure nodes, and progress is being made on the core work T_1. In both cases, the setup and cleanup overhead of the small batch can be amortized either against the work done in the next batch or the work done in the core dag.

Example and applying the performance bound

To understand the BATCHER performance bound (Theorem 1), let us turn to some specific examples. We are not developing new batched data structures here — the point is only to illustrate the power of batched data structures, and to see how to apply the bound.

As a simple example, consider a core program that makes n completely parallel increments to a shared counter, as given by Figure 1. This example is for illustration only, and is not intended to be very deep. This program has $\Theta(n)$ core work and $\Theta(\lg n)$ core span (with binary forking). The shared counter is an abstract data type that supports a single operation INCREMENT, which atomically adds a value (possibly negative) to the counter and returns its current value.

Concurrent counter. A trivial concurrent counter uses atomic primitives like fetch-and-add to INCREMENT. If the primitive is mutually exclusive (which is true for fetch-and-add on current hardware), then n INCREMENTs take $\Omega(n)$ time. The total running time of the program is thus $\Omega(n)$ regardless of the number of processors.

One could instead use a provably efficient concurrent counter, e.g., by using the more complicated combining funnels [37, 38]. Doing so would indeed yield a good overall running time, but these techniques are not applicable to more general data structures. As we shall see next, the implicitly batched counter achieves good asymptotic speedup with a trivial implementation.

Batched counter. Figure 2 shows a sample batched counter. Here, when the core program makes an INCREMENT call, it creates an operation record which is handed-off to the scheduler. The scheduler later runs the batch increment BOP on a set of increments. The main subroutine of the batched operation is "parallel prefix sums",

```
1  parallel_for i = 1 to n
2      do B[i] = INCREMENT(A[i])
```

Figure 1: A parallel loop that performs n parallel updates to a shared counter. Here, $A[1..n]$ is an array of values by which to increment (or decrement if negative) the counter, and $B[1..n]$ holds any return values from the INCREMENTs.

```
3  struct OpRecord {int value; int result;}
```

```
INCREMENT(int x)
4  OpRecord op
5  op.value = x
6  BATCHIFY(this, op) //ask the scheduler to batch op
7  return op.result
```

```
BOP(OpRecord D[1..size])
8  let v be the value of the counter
9  D[1]'s value field = v + D[1]'s value
10 perform parallel-prefix-sums on value fields of D[1..size],
                 storing sums into result fields of D[1..size]
   // now D[i]'s result = ∑_{k=1}^{i} D[k]'s value
11 set the counter to D[size]'s result
```

Figure 2: A batched-counter implementation. As we shall see in Section 4, line 6 _logically_ blocks, but the processor does not spin-wait. The BOP is called by the scheduler automatically.

which **in parallel** computes $\sum_{k=1}^{i} D[k]$ for every i. It is easy to prove that returning $\sum_{k=1}^{i} D[k]$ yields linearizable [25] counter operations. Prefix sums is a commonly used and powerful primitive in parallel algorithms, and hence we consider this 4-line implementation of BOP to be trivial. Adaptations of Ladner and Fischer's approach to prefix sums [28] to the fork-join model have $O(x)$ work and $(\lg x)$ span for x elements.

To analyze the execution of this program using BATCHER, we need only bound $W(n)$, the total work of arbitrarily batching n operations, and $s(n)$, the span of a batched operation that processes P operation records (performs P increment operations). Since the work of prefix sums is linear, we have $W(n) = \Theta(n)$. Since a size-P batch has $O(\lg P)$ span (dominated by prefix sums), we have $s(n) = O(\lg P)$. We thus get the bound $O(\frac{T_1 + n\lg P}{P} + m\lg P + T_\infty)$ for performing n INCREMENTs, with at most m along any path. The core dag of Figure 1 has $T_1 = O(n)$, $T_\infty = O(\lg n)$, $m = 1$, so we have a running time of $O(\frac{n\lg P}{P} + \lg n)$ for $n > P$. This nearly linear speedup is much better than for the trivial counter.

Applying BATCHER to a search tree. There exists an efficient batched 2-3 tree [33] in the PRAM model, and it is not too hard to adapt this algorithm to dynamic multithreading. The main challenge in a search tree is when all inserts occur in the same node of the tree, e.g., when inserting P identical keys. The main idea of this batched search tree is to first sort the new elements, then insert the middle element and recurse on each half of the remaining elements. This process allows for each of the new keys to be separated by existing keys without concurrency control. It is not obvious how to leverage the same idea in a concurrent search tree.

See [33] for details of the batched search tree. Suffice it to say that a size-x batch is dominated by two steps: 1) a parallel search for the location of each key in the tree, having $O(x\lg n)$ work and $O(\lg n + \lg x)$ span, and 2) a parallel sort of the x keys, having

$O(x\lg x)$ work. The data-structure span is thus $s(n) = O(\lg n + sort(P))$, where $sort(P) = O(\lg P\lg\lg P)$ [10] is the span of a parallel sort on P elements in the dynamic-multithreading model. The data-structure work $W(n)$ is maximized for n/P batches of size $x = P$, yielding $W(n) = O(n\lg n)$ data-structure work. Applying Theorem 1, we get a running time of $O(\frac{T_1 + W(n) + s(n)}{P} + ms(n) + T_\infty) = O(\frac{T_1 + n\lg n + n\lg P\lg\lg P}{P} + m\lg n + m\lg P\lg\lg P + T_\infty)$. For large enough n (specifically, $n = \Omega(P^{\lg\lg P})$), this reduces to $O(\frac{T_1 + n\lg n}{P} + m\lg n + T_\infty)$, which is asymptotically optimal in the comparison model and provides linear speedup for programs with sufficient parallelism. For instance, a program obtained by substituting the increment operation with an insert in Figure 1 would yield the running time of $O(n\lg n/P)$, implying linear speedup, even though the program only performs data structure accesses.

Amortized LIFO stack. We now briefly describe an example, namely a LIFO stack, which has amortized performance bounds. The data structure is an array that supports two operations: a PUSH that inserts an element at the end of the array, and a POP that removes and returns the last element. Such an array can be implemented using a standard table doubling [11] technique, whereby the underlying table is rebuilt (in parallel) whenever it becomes too full or too empty. To PUSH a batch of x elements into an n-element array, check if $n + x$ elements fit in the current array. If so, in parallel simply insert the ith batch element into the $(n + i)$th slot of the array. If not, first resize the array by allocating new space and copying all existing elements in parallel. POPs can be simultaneously supported by breaking the batch into a PUSH phase followed by a POP phase.

To analyze this data structure, the (amortized) work of a size-x batch is $\Theta(x)$, yielding $W(n) = \Theta(n)$ (worst case). The work of any individual batch, however, can be as high as $\Theta(n)$ when a table doubling occurs. More importantly, any batch A that has w_A batch work has batch span $s_A = O(\lg w_A)$. Hence any batch A that performs $w_A \geq P^2$ work has parallelism $w_A/s_A = \Omega(P^2/\lg P)$. We thus conclude that the data-structure span is $s(n) = O(\lg(P^2)) = O(\lg P)$. Plugging these bounds into Theorem 1, we get a total running time of $O(\frac{T_1 + n\lg P}{P} + m\lg P + T_\infty)$.

4. THE BATCHER SCHEDULER

This section presents the high-level design of the BATCHER scheduler, a variant of a distributed work-stealing scheduler. We use P to refer to the number of **workers**, or threads/cores, given to the scheduler. Since BATCHER is a distributed scheduler, there is no centralized scheduler thread and the operation of the scheduler can be described in terms of state-transition rules followed by each of the P workers. First, we describe the internal state that BATCHER maintains in order to implicitly batched data-structure operations and to coordinate between executing the core and batch dags. We then describe how batches are launched and how load-balancing is done using work-stealing.

BATCHER state. The BATCHER scheduler maintains three categories of shared state: (1) collections for tracking the implicitly batched data-structure operations, (2) status flags for synchronizing the scheduler, and (3) deques for each worker tracking execution-dag nodes (see Section 2) and used by work stealing. With the exception of one global flag, most of this state is distributed across workers, with each worker only managing specific updates according to the provided rules that define the scheduler.

To track active data-structure nodes, BATCHER maintains two arrays. When a worker encounters a data-structure node (executes a call to BATCHIFY(op)), instead of accessing the data-structure directly, an operation record op is created and placed in the **pending array** and the data-structure node is suspended. BATCHER guarantees that each worker has at most one suspended node / pending operation at any time; therefore this pending array may be maintained as a size-P array, with a dedicated slot for each of the P workers. BATCHER also maintains a **working set**, which is a densely packed array of all the operation records being processed as part of the currently executing batch.

To synchronize batch executions, BATCHER maintains a single global **active-batch** flag. In addition, each worker p has a local **work-status** flag (denoted $Status[p]$), which describes the status of p's current data-structure node. BATCHER guarantees that at any instant, each worker has at most one data-structure node u that it is trying to execute. For concreteness, think in terms of the following four states for worker status $Status[p]$:

- `pending`, if p has an operation record op for a suspended data structure node u in the pending array.
- `executing`, if p has an operation record op for a suspended data structure node u in the working set, i.e., a batch containing u is currently executing.
- `done`, if the batch A containing u has completed its computation, but p has not yet resumed the suspended node u.
- `free`, if p has no suspended data-structure node.

If $Status[p]$ is `pending`, `executing`, or `done`, we say p is **trapped** on operation u. Otherwise, we say p is **free**.

Finally, BATCHER maintains two deques of ready nodes on each worker: a **core deque** for ready nodes from the core dag, and a **batch deque** for ready nodes from a batch dag. In particular, the deques in BATCHER obey the following invariant:

INVARIANT 3. *Ready nodes belonging to the core dag G are always placed on some worker's core deque, whereas ready nodes that belong to some batch A's batch dag G_A are always placed on some worker's batch deque.*

Associated with these deques, each worker p also has an **assigned node** — the node that p is currently executing. At any instant, the assigned node of p may conceptually be associated with either the core deque or the batch deque, depending on the type of node being executed by that worker. Some workers may be executing core nodes while others are executing batch nodes.

Background: traditional work stealing. In a traditional work-stealing scheduler [6], each of P workers maintains a core deque of ready nodes, and at any time, a worker p has at most one assigned node u that the worker is currently executing. When u finishes, it may enable at most 2 nodes. If 1 or 2 node(s) are enabled, p assigns one to itself and places the other (if any) at the bottom of its deque. If none are enabled, then p removes the node at the bottom of its deque and assigns it to itself. If p's deque is empty, then p becomes a **thief**, randomly picks a **victim** worker and steals from the top of the victim's deque. If the victim's deque is not empty, then the steal attempt **succeeds**, otherwise it **fails**.

BATCHER algorithm. BATCHER uses a variant of work stealing, with some augmentations to support implicit batching. Free workers and trapped workers behave quite differently. Initially all workers are free, and all ready nodes belong to the core dag, and BATCHER behaves similarly to traditional work stealing. As data-structure nodes are encountered, however, the situation changes. The scheduling rules are outlined in Figure 3 and described below.

Free workers behave closest to traditional work stealing. A free worker is allowed to execute any node (core or batch), but it only steals if both of its deques are empty. Specifically, if either deque is nonempty, the worker executes a node off the nonempty deque, and

When p is free and both deques are empty:
      steal from random victim, using alternating-steal policy

When a data-structure node u is assigned to (free) worker p:
      insert operation record into $pending[p]$
      $Status[p] = $ `pending`
      suspend u
      // p is now trapped

When p is trapped and its batch deque is empty:
      if $Status[p] = $ `done`
        then $Status[p] = $ `free`
          resume executing the core deque from
               suspended data-structure node u
          // p is now free
        else **if** global batch flag = 0 and
            compare-and-swap(global batch flag, 0, 1)
          then run LAUNCHBATCH
          else steal from random victim's batch deque

Figure 3: Scheduler-state transition rules invoked by workers with empty deques. When the appropriate deque is not empty, the worker removes the bottom node from the deque and executes it.

any newly enabled nodes are placed on the same deque. BATCHER thus maintains the following invariant:

INVARIANT 4. *Workers that have `free` status in BATCHER can have at most one of their deques non-empty, i.e., they have nodes either on the batch deque or core deque, but not both.*

If both deques are empty, however, the free worker performs a steal attempt according to an **alternating-steal policy**: each worker's kth steal attempt (successful or not) is from a random victim's core deque if k is even, and from a random victim's batch deque if k is odd. The alternating-steal policy is important to achieve the performance bound in Section 5.

When a (free) worker p executes a data-structure node u, p first inserts the corresponding operation record op in its dedicated slot in the pending array, and then it changes its own status to `pending`. At this point, the p becomes trapped on u, and according to Invariant 4, it has an initially empty batch deque.

Unlike free workers, which are allowed to execute both core and batch work, trapped workers are only allowed to execute nodes from a batch deque. If a trapped worker p has a nonempty batch deque, it simply selects a node off the batch deque as in traditional work stealing. If it has an empty batch deque, however, it performs the following step. First, it checks whether its data-structure node u has finished, i.e., if $Status[p] = $ `done`. If so, it changes its own status to `free` and resumes from the suspended data-structure node on the core deque. Otherwise, it checks the global batch status flag and tries to set it using an atomic operation if no batch is executing. If successful in setting the flag, p "launches" a batch. If it is unsuccessful (someone else successfully set the flag and launched a batch) or if a batch is already executing (status flag was already 1) it simply tries to steal from a random victim's deque. BATCHER guarantees that if no batch is executing, then all workers have status either `pending`, `done` or `free`; therefore, only pending workers can succeed in launching a new batch.

LAUNCHBATCH()

1 **parallel_for** $i = 1$ to P
    do if $Status[i] = $ pending **then** $Status[i] = $ executing
2 compact all executing op records, moving them from
                          pending array to working set
    // using **parallel** prefix sums subroutine
3 execute BOP (the actual parallel batch) on records in working set
4 **parallel_for** $i = 1$ to P
    do if $Status[i] = $ executing **then** $Status[i] = $ done
        remove done op records from the working set.
5 reset global batch-status flag to 0

Figure 4: Pseudocode for launching a batch. This method executes as an ordinary task in a dynamic multithreaded computation, i.e., it may run using any number of workers between 1 to P workers, depending on how work-stealing occurs.

Launching a batch. Launching a batch corresponds to injecting the parallel task LAUNCHBATCH (see Figure 4), i.e., by inserting the root of the subdag induced by this code on a worker's batch deque. This process has five steps. First, the pending array is processed in parallel, changing the status of all pending workers to executing, thereby acknowledging the operation record. Second, the executing records are packed together in the working-set array, which can be performed in parallel using a parallel prefix sums computation. Third, the actual batched operation (BOP) is executed on the records in working set. Fourth, the pending array is again processed in parallel, changing the status of all executing workers to done. Finally, the batch-status flag is reset to 0. In practice, several of these steps can be merged, but we are not concerned about these low-level optimizations in this paper.

As mentioned above, launching a batch incurs some overhead, such as updating status fields and compacting the pending array into working-set, beyond the execution of the batched operation BOP itself. We refer to this overhead as the ***batch-setup overhead***. Note that this set-up procedure is itself a dynamic multithreaded program with $\Theta(P)$ work and $\Theta(\lg P)$ span, primarily due to the cost of the **parallel_for** and parallel prefix sums computations over P elements. This set-up work is performed in exactly the same way as the batched operation BOP is performed — that is, the nodes of this procedure are placed on batch deques and are executed in parallel (via work-stealing) by workers working on these deques. Note, however, that for the purposes of the dag metrics, the overhead is *not* counted as part of the batch work, batch span, or data-structure span defined in Section 2; this omission is by design since the overhead is a function of the scheduler, not the input program. This fact is one of the challenges in proving that BATCHER has a good running time, and it is exacerbated by the fact that the overhead is as high for a batch containing 1 operation as it is for a batch containing P operations. Nevertheless, we shall show (Section 5) that BATCHER is provably efficient.

Not trapped long. The following lemma shows that a worker is not trapped for very long by a particular operation (at most 2 batches).

LEMMA 2. *Once the operation record for a data-structure node u is put into the pending array, at most two batches execute before the node completes.*

PROOF. Consider an operation u whose status changes at time t to pending. Any batch finishing before time t does not delay u. Any batch A launched after time t observes u in the pending array, and incorporates it in A and completes it; this accounts for one

batch execution. According to Invariant 1, there can only be one batch that is launched before t and finishes after t, which accounts for the second batch. $\square$

Correctness of state changes. Each worker is responsible for changing its own state from done to free and free to pending. There is thus no risk of any races on these state changes. The changes from pending to executing and executing to done may be performed by an arbitrary worker, but these changes occur as part of the parallel computation LAUNCHBATCH. Since LAUNCHBATCH is itself race free and only one LAUNCHBATCH occurs at a time (protected by the global batch-status flag), these transitions are also safe.

5. ANALYSIS OF BATCHER

We now analyze the performance of BATCHER. We first provide some definitions and the statement of the completion time bounds. Then we use a potential function argument to prove these bounds.

Definitions and theorem statements. We will analyze the running time using the computation dag G and the set of batch dags that represent batches generated due to implicit batching performed by BATCHER. We will analyze the running time using an arbitrary parameter τ, which will be later related to the data-structure span $s(n)$. We define a few different types of batches. A batch A is τ-***wide*** if its batch work is more than $P\tau$. A batch is τ-***long*** if its batch span is more than τ. These definitions only count the work and span within the batched operations themselves, not the batch-setup overhead due to BATCHER. Since τ is implied, we often drop it and call batches wide or long. Finally, a batch is ***popular*** if it processes more than $P/4$ operation records; that is, it contains more than $P/4$ data structure nodes. A batch is ***big*** if it is either long, wide or popular, or if it occurs immediately before or after a long, wide or popular batch. All other batches are ***small***.

The above definitions are with respect to individual batches that arise during an execution. We next define a property of the data structure itself, analogous to data-structure work (Section 2).

DEFINITION 1. *Consider any sequence of parallel batched operations and a real value τ. The τ-**trimmed span of the sequence** of batches is the sum of the spans of the long batches in the sequence. The τ-**trimmed span of a data structure**, denoted by $S_\tau(n)$, is the worst-case τ-trimmed span for n data-structure nodes grouped arbitrarily into batches.*

We now state our main theorem, a bound on the total running time of a BATCHER computation, which is proven at the end of this section. The restriction that $\tau \geq \lg P$ arises from binary forking.

THEOREM 3. *Consider a computation with T_1 core work, T_∞ core span, and n data-structure nodes with at most m falling along any path through the dag. For any $\tau \geq \lg P$, let $S_\tau(n)$ and $W(n)$ denote the worst-case τ-trimmed span and total work of the data structure, respectively. Then BATCHER executes the program in $O\left(\frac{T_1 + W(n) + n\tau}{P} + T_\infty + S_\tau(n) + m\tau\right)$ expected time on P processors.*

This theorem holds for any $\tau \geq \lg P$; however, it does not provide intuition about which τ is best. There is a tradeoff: increasing τ increases $n\tau$ and $m\tau$, but decreasing τ increases $S_\tau(n)$ since more batches become long. As we shall see at the end of this section, setting $\tau = s(n)$, the data-structure span (defined in Section 2), yields Theorem 1 as a corollary since other terms dominate $S_\tau(n)$.

Intuition behind the analysis. As with previous work-stealing analyses, our analysis separately bounds the total number of processor steps devoted to various activities; in our case, these activities are core work, data-structure work, stealing (and failed steal attempts), and the batch-setup overhead. We then divide this total by P, since each processor performs one processor step per timestep, to get the completion time.

It is relatively straightforward to see that the number of processor steps devoted to core work is T_1 and the number of time steps devoted to data structure work is $W(n)$. The difficulty is in bounding the number of steal attempts and the batch set up overhead. To bound the number of steal attempts, we adopt a *potential function* argument similar to Arora et al.'s work-stealing analysis [2], henceforth referred to as ABP. In the ABP analysis, each ready node is assigned a potential that decreases geometrically with its distance from the start of the dag. For traditional work stealing, one can prove that most of the potential is in the ready nodes at the top of the deques, as these are the ones that occur earliest in the dag. Therefore, $\Theta(P)$ random steal attempts suffice to process all of these nodes on top of the deques, causing the potential to decrease significantly. Therefore, one can prove that $O(PT_\infty)$ steal attempts are sufficient to reduce the potential to 0 in expectation.

The ABP analysis does not directly apply to bounding the number of steal attempts by BATCHER for the following reason. When a data structure node u becomes ready and is assigned to worker p, p places the corresponding operation record in the pending array and u remains assigned (control flow does not go past u) until results from u are available. But u may contain most of the potential of the entire computation (particularly if p's deque is empty; in this case u has all of p's potential). Since u cannot be stolen, steals are no longer effective in reducing the potential of the computation until the batch containing u completes. To cope with this difficulty, we apply different progress arguments to big batches and small batches.

Bounding steal attempts during big batches: For big batches, we apply the ABP potential function to each batch's computation dag. Nodes in a batch dag are never "suspended" in the way data-structure nodes are, so the ABP argument applies nearly directly. We charge this case against the τ-trimmed span or the data-structure work. (As a technical detail, we must also show that P steal attempts overall equate to $\Omega(P)$ steal attempts from batch deques in order to complete the argument.)

Bounding other steal attempts: Unfortunately, small batches do not contribute to the τ-trimmed span, so the above approach does not apply.[6] Instead, we apply extra machinery to bound these steal attempts. The intuition is that if many steal attempts actually occur during a small batch, then the batch should complete quickly (i.e., within $O(\tau)$ timesteps). On the other hand, if few steal attempts occur then the workers are being productive anyway, since they are doing useful work (either core work or data-structure work) instead of stealing. To apply this intuition more formally within the ABP framework, we augment each data-structure node to comprise a chain of τ "dummy nodes," which captures these cases by appropriate potential decreases in the augmented dag.

Setup: dag augmentation and potential function. We create an augmented computation dag, the τ−*execution dag* $G(\tau)$, by adding a length $\Theta(\tau)$ chain of *dummy nodes* before each data-structure node in the computation dag. The work of this dag is $W_{G(\tau)} = T_1 + O(n\tau)$ and span is $S_{G(\tau)} = T_\infty + O(m\tau)$.

For the purpose of the analysis, we suppose the scheduler executes the augmented dag instead of the original dag. The scheduler

operates with one corresponding difference: when a worker encounters a data-structure node, this node remains assigned to the worker, but $\Theta(\tau)$ nodes of the dummy-node chain are placed at the bottom of its core deque. If a worker p steals from another worker p''s core deque and a dummy node is on the top of that deque, then p steals and immediately processes the dummy node. This steal is considered a successful steal attempt. When a worker returns from a batch, all the dummy nodes on the bottom of its deque disappear. Note that dummy nodes are only for accounting. Operationally, this runtime system is identical to the one described in Section 4, except the analysis now just counts some unsuccessful steals as successful steals. More precisely, whenever a dummy node is stolen from a victim's deque, the corresponding steal in the real execution is unsuccessful because the victim's deque was empty.

We now define the potentials using this augmented dag. Each node in G has **depth** $d(u)$ and **weight** $w(u) = S_G - d(u)$. Similarly, for a node u in the batch dag G_A, $d(u)$ is its depth in that dag, and its weight is $w(u) = s_A - d(u)$. The weights are always positive.

DEFINITION 2. *The **potential** Φ_u of a node u is $3^{2w(u)-1}$ if u is assigned, and $3^{2w(u)}$ if u is ready.*

The **core potential** of the computation is the sum of potentials of all (ready or assigned) nodes $u \in G$. The **batch potential** is the sum of the potentials of all $u \in G_A$ where A is the currently active batch (if one exists). The following structural lemmas follow in a straightforward manner from the arguments used throughout the ABP paper [2], so we state them without proof here. [7]

LEMMA 4. *The initial core potential is 3^{S_G} and it never increases during the computation.* □

LEMMA 5. *Let $\Phi(t)$ denote the potential of the core dag at time t. If no trapped worker's deque is empty, then after $2P$ subsequent steal attempts from core deques the core potential is at most $\Phi(t)/4$ with probability at least $1/4$.* □

LEMMA 6. *Suppose a computation (core or batch) has span S, and that every "round" decreases its potential by a constant factor with at least a constant probability. Then the computation completes after $O(S)$ rounds in expectation, and the total number of rounds is $O(S + \lg(1/\varepsilon))$ with probability at least $1 - \varepsilon$.* □

The following two lemmas extend Lemmas 4 and 5 to batch potentials. The proofs of these lemmas can also be derived from ABP proofs in a similar manner.

LEMMA 7. *The batch potential Φ_A increases from 0 to 3^{2s_A} when A becomes ready, and never increases thereafter.* □

LEMMA 8. *Let $\Phi_A(t)$ be the potential of batch A at time t. After $2P$ subsequent steal attempts from batch deques, the potential of A is at most $\Phi_A(t)/4$ with probability at least $1/4$.* □

Since different arguments are required for big and small batches, we partition steal attempts into three categories. A **big-batch steal attempt** is any steal attempt that occurs on a timestep during which a big batch is executing. A **trapped steal attempt** is a steal attempt made by a trapped worker (a worker whose status is not free) on a timestep when no big batch is active. A **free steal attempt** is a steal attempt by a free worker (a worker whose status is free) on

---

[6] Adding even P steal attempts for each of potentially n small batches would result in $\Omega(nP)$ steal attempts or $\Omega(n)$ running time, i.e., no parallelism.

[7] ABP does not explicitly capture these three lemmas as claims in their paper — some of their proof is captured by "Lemma 8" and "Theorem 9" of [2], but the rest falls to interproof dicussion within the paper .

91

a timestep when no big batch is active. We can now bound the different types of steal attempts and the batch-setup overhead.

Big-batch steal attempts. The big-batch steal attempts are bounded by the following lemma. The proof of this lemma is the most straightforward of the three cases.

LEMMA 9. *The expected number of big-batch steal attempts is* $O(n\tau + PS_\tau(n) + W(n))$.

PROOF. We first prove that if L is the set of big batches, the expected number of big batch steal attempts is $O(P\sum_{A\in L} s_A)$.

Consider a particular big batch A. When the first round starts, the potential of the batch is 3^{2s_A} (Lemma 7). Divide the steal attempts that occur while the batch is executing into rounds of $4P$ steal attempts, except for the last round, which may have fewer. While A is executing, at least half the steal attempts are from batch deques, since all the trapped steals are from batch deques, and half the free steals are from batch deques by the alternating steal policy. Therefore, in every round, at least $2P$ steal attempts are from batch deques. Applying Lemma 8, the potential of the batch decreases by a constant factor with probability $1/4$ during each round. Therefore, applying Lemma 6, we can conclude that there are expected $O(s_A)$ rounds while A is active.

We use linearity of expectation to add over all big batches. We first add over long, wide and popular batches. The total span of long batches is $S_\tau(n)$ by definition. There are at most $W(n)/P\tau$ wide batches, and at most n/P popular batches. If they are not also long, they have span less than τ. We triple the number to account for batches before and after long, wide or popular batches. Therefore, we can see that there are the number of rounds during big batches ar $O(S_\tau(n) + n\tau/P + W(n)/P)$. Since each round has at most $4P$ steal attempts, we get the desired bound. □

Free steal attempts. Here, each "round" consists of $4P$ consecutive free steal attempts (during which no big batch is active). Recall that when a worker becomes trapped, it places $\Theta(\tau)$ dummy nodes on the bottom of its core deque. We say that a round is ***bad*** if, at the beginning of the round, some trapped worker's core deque is empty (does not have any core nodes or dummy nodes). Otherwise, a round is ***good***. Note that bad rounds only occur while some batch is executing; otherwise no worker is trapped. We bound good and bad rounds separately.

Good rounds do not have the problem of too much potential being concentrated in a suspended data-structure node of a trapped worker. During a good round, there is more potential in the dummy nodes than the suspended data-structure node itself, and steal attempts reduce potential.

LEMMA 10. *The number of good rounds is $O(S_G)$ in expectation and $O(S_G + \lg(1/\varepsilon))$ with probability at least $1-\varepsilon$. Therefore, the number of free steal attempts in good rounds is $O(PS_G)$ in expectation and $O(PS_G + P\lg(1/\varepsilon))$ with probability at least $1-\varepsilon$.*

PROOF. During a good round, there are $4P$ total steal free steal attempts, and thus by the alternating steal policy, half of these ($2P$) are from core deques. Since no trapped worker's deque is empty when the round begins, we can apply Lemma 5 to conclude that each round decreases the core potential by a constant factor with a constant probability; being interrupted by a big batch only decreases the potential further. We can then apply Lemma 6 to conclude that there are $O(S_G)$ rounds show the requisite bound; multiplying by P gives the bound on the number of free steal attempts during good rounds. □

We can now bound the number of bad rounds using the following intuition. The number of bad rounds is small since small batches have small spans, chances are most small batches finish before any trapped worker runs out of dummy nodes.

LEMMA 11. *The total number of free steal attempts during bad rounds is $O(n\tau)$ in expectation.*

PROOF. A worker p places $\Theta(\tau) = b\tau$ dummy nodes, for constant b, on its core deque when it becomes trapped. There is a bad round if its core deque is stolen from at least $b\tau$ times before p becomes free again. There are two cases:

Case 1: worker p is trapped for $k\tau$ rounds, for some constant k; applying a Chernoff bounds, during $k\tau$ rounds, each core deque is stolen from $< k_1\tau + k_2\lg P$ times with probability $> (1 - 1/P^2)$ for appropriate settings of constants k_1 and k_2. If $\tau \geq \lg P$ and $b = k_1 + k_2$, then p's deque runs out of dummy nodes with probability $< 1/P^2$. Since there can be at most $k\tau$ bad rounds, we get the expected number of bad rounds $O(\tau/P)$.

Case 2: worker p is trapped for more than $k\tau$ rounds, for constant k. From Lemma 2, we know that p is trapped for at most 2 batches, say A_1 and A_2. Therefore, at least one of A_1 and A_2, say A_i, must be active for more than $k\tau/2$ rounds. We first bound the number of rounds during which A_i can be active, with high probability. If A_i is active throughout a round, then there are at least $2P$ steal attempts from batch deques during the round r (since half the free steal attempts hit batch deques) and Lemma 8 applies. If a batch starts or ends during r, its potential decreases by a constant factor trivially. We can then apply Lemma 6 to show that with probability at least $1 - \varepsilon$ the batch A_i is active for $O(s_{A_i} + \lg(1/\varepsilon)) = O(\tau + \lg(1/\varepsilon))$ rounds, since A_i is not long. (p is waiting for the small batch A_2; therefore, the preceding batch A_1 is also not long.) We know that $O(\tau + \lg 1/\varepsilon) < k_1\tau + k_2\lg 1/\varepsilon$ for some constants k_1 and k_2; we set $\varepsilon = 1/P^2$ and $k/2 = k_1 + 2k_2$. The probability that A_i is active for $k\tau/2$ rounds is at most $1/P^2$. There can be at most $P\tau$ bad rounds for A_i, since each round takes at least one timestep, and a small batch has at most $P\tau$ work. Therefore, the expected number is at most $O(\tau/P)$.

Adding over the n batches that can trap a worker, and over P workers, gives us $O(n\tau)$ in total. □

COROLLARY 12. *Ignoring the batch-setup overhead, the expected number of steps taken by free processors when no big batch is active is $O(T_1 + W(n) + n\tau + PS_G)$.*

PROOF. A free worker is either working (at most $T_1 + W(n)$ steps) or stealing (bounded by Lemmas 10 and 11). □

Trapped steal attempts and batch-setup overhead. We next analyze the steal attempts by trapped workers during small batches. The key idea is as follows. Recall that a worker is trapped by a batch A only if it has a pending data structure node whose operation record is being processed by A or will be processed by the succeeding batch A' (see Lemma 2). If more than $P/2$ workers are trapped on a A, then either A or A' must be popular, in which case A is called big. Therefore, at most $P/2$ workers a be trapped by a small batch.

LEMMA 13. *The expected number of processor steps taken due to batch-setup overhead and trapped steal attempts is $O(T_1 + W(n) + n\tau + PS_G + PS_\tau(n))$.*

PROOF. The batch-setup overhead is $O(P)$ per batch. After it launches, each batch executes for at least 1 timestep and only one batch executes at a time. For big batches, during this one timestep, the workers perform P steps of either work (bounded by $T_1 + W(n)$) or big batch steals (bounded by Lemma 9). We can amortize the batch-setup overhead against these P steps. For small batches, at least $P/2$ processors are free and again they perform either work or free steals (bounded by Corollary 12), and we can amortize the batch-setup overhead against this quantity. Adding these gives us the bound on batch-setup overhead.

Even if we pessimistically assume that trapped workers do nothing but steal during small batches, since at least half the workers are free, we can amortize these steals against the steps taken by free workers which either work or steal or perform batch setup steps. □

Overall running time. We can now bound the overall running time. We combine the bounds from Lemmas 9, 10 and 11, and substitute $S_G = T_\infty + m\tau$ and divide by P (since there are P workers performing these steps) to prove Theorem 3.

PROOF OF THEOREM 3. From Lemmas 9, 10, 11 and 13, we know that the expected number of big-batch steal attempts is $O(n\tau + PS_\tau(n) + W(n))$, free steal attempts is $O(PT_\infty + Pm\tau + n\tau)$, and trapped steal attempts is $O(T_1 + W(n) + n\tau + PS_G + PS_\tau(n))$. The total batch-setup overhead is $O(T_1 + W(n) + n\tau + PS_G + PS_\tau(n))$. Adding the total work and dividing by P gives the result. □

We can now set an appropriate value for τ to get the bound on BATCHER performance. This corollary is equivalent to Theorem 1.

COROLLARY 14. *BATCHER executes the program described in Theorem 3 in expected time* $O\left(\frac{T_1 + W(n) + ns(n)}{P} + ms(n) + T_\infty\right)$.

PROOF. We get this bound by setting τ to be equal to the data structure span $s(n)$. Recall that long batches are defined as batches with batch span longer than τ, and τ-trimmed span $S_\tau(n)$ is defined as the sum of the spans of all long batches. Recall, also, from the definition of the data-structure span $s(n)$ is defined as follows: For any sequence of batches comprising a total of n data structure nodes, such that no batch contains more than P data structure nodes, $s(n)$ is the worst case span of any batch individual A that also has parallelism limited by $w_A/s_A = O(P)$.

Since the program has a total of n data-structure nodes, and BATCHER only generates batches with at most P data structure nodes, the only batches with $s_A > s(n)$ are those where $w_A/s_A = \Omega(P)$. Now, say L is the set of long batches. For all $A \in L$, we have $w_A = \Omega(Ps_A)$, since all other batches have span smaller than $s(n)$, hence also smaller than τ, since $s(n) = \tau$. That is, the long batches are all batches with large parallelism. Therefore, $W(n) \geq \sum_{A \in L} w_A = \sum_{A \in L} \Omega(Ps_A)$. Since $S_\tau(n) = \sum_{A \in L} s_A$, we conclude that $W(n) = \Omega(PS_\tau(n))$, or $W(n)/P = \Omega(S_\tau(n))$. The bound follows from Theorem 3 as $W(n)/P$ dominates $S_\tau(n)$. □

6. RELATED WORK

BATCHER most closely resembles various software combining techniques, designed primarily to reduce concurrency overhead in concurrent data structures. In some combining techniques [15, 21, 31], each processor inserts a request in a shared queue and a single processor sequentially executes all outstanding requests later. These works provide empirical efficiency, but we are not aware of any theory bounding the running time of an algorithm using these combiners. BATCHER improves upon these techniques by operating on the "request queue" in parallel and by providing runtime theory. Other software-combining techniques include (static) combining trees [20] or (dynamic) combining funnels [38] which apply

directly to data structures with combinable operations like lock objects, counters, or stacks. These do have a provably $O(\lg P)$ overhead, but do not address more general structures

Several related mechanisms designed for dynamic multithreading have a grounding in theory. Reducers [17] in Cilk can be used to eliminate contention on some shared global variables, but are not designed to replace a generic concurrent data structure, since they create local views on each processor rather than maintain a single global view. It is also unclear how to analyze reducers that include highly variable amortized costs. Helper locks [1] provide a mechanism that allows blocked workers to help complete the critical section that is blocking them and is not specifically designed for data structures. Conceptually, one can use this mechanism to execute batches; however, directly applying the analysis of [1] leads to worse completion time bounds compared to using BATCHER.

Concurrent data structures themselves are widely studied [24]. Most theoretical work on concurrent data structures focuses on correctness and forward-progress guarantees like linearizability [25], lock freedom [23], or wait freedom [22]. While wait-free structures often include a worst-case performance bound, the bound may not be satisfying when applied in the context of an enclosing algorithm. For example, a universal wait-free construction of [9] has a worst-case cost that includes a factor of P, the number of processors, which implies serializing all data structure operations. Experimental studies of various concurrent B-tree data structures alone spans over 30 years of research [3, 4, 27, 7]. These results typically fall short of bounds on running time, with [4] being one exception assuming uniformly random accesses.

Several batched search trees exist, including 2-3 trees [33], weight-balanced B-trees [14], and red-black trees [16]. Moreover, some of these data structures [14, 16] exhibit good practical performance.

7. EXPERIMENTAL EVALUATION

We implemented a prototype of BATCHER within the Cilk-5 [19] runtime system. Our preliminary evaluation, presented here, is based around a skip-list data structure. Note that the primary contribution of this paper is the theory; these experiments are meant to be only proof of concept, not a comprehensive study. Nevertheless, the results indicate that implicit batching is a promising direction, at least for expensive data structures and large-enough batches. For the particular experiment here, BATCHER's performance on 1 processor is comparable to that of a sequential skip list, and hence the overhead is not prohibitive. In addition, BATCHER provides speedup when running on multiple processors.

We conducted experiments on a 2-socket machine with 8 cores per socket running Ubuntu 12.04. The processor was Intel Xeon E5-2687W. The machine has 64GB of RAM and 20MB of L3 cache per socket. For our experiments, we pinned the threads to a single socket on this machine.

BATCHER and skip-list implementations. We implemented the BATCHER scheduler by modifying the Cilk-5 runtime system, essentially as described in Section 4. The main difference between the theoretical and the practical design is within the LAUNCHBATCH operation (Figure 4). Because we are running on only 8 cores, we used a sequential implementation for the status changes status changes (lines 1 and 4) and the compaction (line 2).

Our batch insert (BOP) into the skip list has three steps. 1) build a new skip from a set of records, 2) perform searches for these nodes in the main skip list, and 3) splice the new list into the main list. Since the new list is small (batch size), we perform steps 1 and 3 sequentially, whereas the searches into the large main list in step 2 are performed in parallel. The core program is simply a parallel-for loop that inserts into the skip list in each iteration (e.g., as in Figure 1). Note that this is a bad case for BATCHER since all of the work happens within the data structure, and hence the overheads are tested.

Experimental scaling. In all our experiments, we first initialize the skip list with an initial size. We then timed the insertion of 100,000 additional elements into this skip list. To simulate bigger batches without the NUMA effects of going to multiple sockets, each BATCHIFY call creates 100 insertion records. We compared BATCHER with a sequential implementation where all 100,000 elements are inserted sequentially (without concurrency control).

Figure 5 shows the throughput of BATCHER and a sequential skip list with `initialSize` 20,000, 100,000, 1 million, 10 million and 100 million (e.g. BAT20000 shows BATCHER's with initial size 20,000). For initial size 20,000 and 100,000, SEQ performs better than BAT on a single processor. This is because inserts into small skip lists are so cheap that BATCHER's overheads begin to dominate. However, even on these small skip lists, BATCHER provides speedup, and outperforms the sequential skip list on multiple processors. For larger skip lists, the inserts get expensive enough that they dominate BATCHER's overhead, and BATCHER performs comparably with the sequential list even on 1 processor.

More interestingly, BATCHER's speedup increases as the skip list gets larger. At size 100 million, BATCHER provides a speedup of about $3\times$ on 6 processors, and $3.33\times$ on 8 workers.

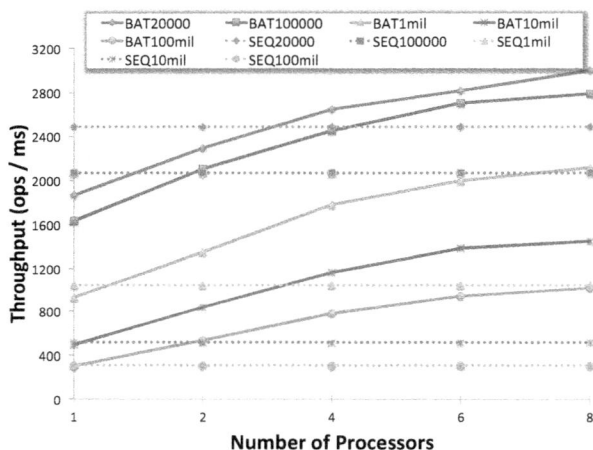

Figure 5: Throughput of BATCHER and sequential skip list insertion for various initial sizes of skip lists (higher is better).

Flat combining. We view flat combining [21] as a special case of implicit batching where batches execute sequentially. They show that flat combining significantly outperforms a good concurrent skip list, at least for certain workloads, validating the idea of implicit batching. On our experiments, flat combining and BATCHER perform similarly 1 processor. However, the performance of flat combining decreases with increasing cores (their experiments also show this). In contrast, the prototype BATCHER implementation shows speedup.

8. CONCLUSIONS AND FUTURE WORK

BATCHER scheduler is provably efficient, and preliminary experiments indicate that it could provide speedup in practice, especially when data structure operations are expensive enough to amortize the overheads. There are several open questions remaining. Is it possible to remove or reduce the $O(\lg P)$ overhead by using a more clever communication mechanism? What data struc-

tures are easily and efficiently expressible by this batch mechanism? Does BATCHER improve the performance of real parallel programs? Finally, although BATCHER is designed with work-stealing in mind, note that it may also be applicable to pthreaded programs that use data structures. A pthreaded program could run as normal, with data-structure calls replaced by BATCHER calls allowing work-stealing to operate over the data structure batches while static pthreading operates over the main program.

Acknowledgements

This research was supported by National Science Foundation grants CCF-1340571, CCF-1150036, CCF-1218017, CCF-1218188, and CCF-1314633.

9. REFERENCES

[1] K. Agrawal, C. E. Leiserson, and J. Sukha. Helper locks for fork-join parallel programming. In *Proceedings of the ACM SIGPLAN Symposium on Principles and Practice of Parallel Programming (PPoPP)*, pages 245–256, Jan. 2010.

[2] N. S. Arora, R. D. Blumofe, and C. G. Plaxton. Thread scheduling for multiprogrammed multiprocessors. In *Proceedings of the ACM Symposium on Parallel Algorithms and Architectures (SPAA)*, pages 119–129, 1998.

[3] R. Bayer and M. Schkolnick. Concurency of operations on B-trees. *Acta Informatica*, 9:1–21, 1977.

[4] M. A. Bender, J. T. Fineman, S. Gilbert, and B. C. Kuszmaul. Concurrent cache-oblivious B-trees. In *Proceedings of the ACM Symposium on Parallelism in Algorithms and Architectures (SPAA)*, pages 228–237, July 17–20 2005.

[5] M. A. Bender, J. T. Fineman, S. Gilbert, and C. E. Leiserson. On-the-fly maintenance of series-parallel relationships in fork-join multithreaded programs. In *Proceedings of the ACM Symposium on Parallelism in Algorithms and Architectures (SPAA)*, pages 133–144, June 27–30 2004.

[6] R. D. Blumofe and C. E. Leiserson. Scheduling multithreaded computations by work stealing. *Journal of the ACM*, 46(5):720–748, 1999.

[7] A. Braginsky and E. Petrank. A lock-free B+tree. In *Proceedings of the ACM Symposium on Parallelism in Algorithms and Architectures (SPAA)*, pages 58–67, 2012.

[8] G. S. Brodal, J. L. Träff, and C. D. Zaroliagis. A parallel priority queue with constant time operations. *Journal of Parallel and Distributed Computing*, pages 4–21, 1998.

[9] P. Chuong, F. Ellen, and V. Ramachandran. A universal construction for wait-free transaction friendly data structures. In *Proceedings of the ACM Symposium on Parallelism in Algorithms and Architectures (SPAA)*, pages 335–344, 2010.

[10] R. Cole and V. Ramachandran. Resource oblivious sorting on multicores. In *Proceedings of the International Colloquium on Automata, Languages, and Programming (ICALP)*, pages 226–237, 2010.

[11] T. H. Cormen, C. E. Leiserson, R. L. Rivest, and C. Stein. *Introduction to Algorithms*. The MIT Press, third edition, 2009.

[12] A. Crauser, K. Mehlhorn, U. Meyer, and P. Sanders. A parallelization of Dijkstra's shortest path algorithm. In *Proceedings of the International Symposium on Mathematical Foundations of Computer Science (MFCS)*, pages 722–731. Springer, 1998.

[13] J. R. Driscoll, H. N. Gabow, R. Shrairman, and R. E. Tarjan. Relaxed heaps: an alternative to Fibonacci heaps with

applications to parallel computation. *Communications of the ACM*, 31:1343–1354, 1988.

[14] S. Erb, M. Kobitzsch, and P. Sanders. Parallel bi-objective shortest paths using weight-balanced b-trees with bulk updates. In *Proceedings of the Symposium on Experimental Algorithms (SEA)*, 2014. to appear.

[15] P. Fatourou and N. D. Kallimanis. A highly-efficient wait-free universal construction. In *Proceedings of the ACM Symposium on Parallelism in Algorithms and Architectures (SPAA)*, pages 325–334, 2011.

[16] L. Frias and J. Singler. Parallelization of bulk operations for STL dictionaries. In *Euro-Par Workshops*, volume 4854 of *LNCS*, pages 49–58. Springer, 2007.

[17] M. Frigo, P. Halpern, C. E. Leiserson, and S. Lewin-Berlin. Reducers and other Cilk++ hyperobjects. In *Proceedings of the ACM Symposium on Parallelism in Algorithms and Architectures (SPAA)*, pages 79–90, Aug. 2009.

[18] M. Frigo, C. E. Leiserson, and K. H. Randall. The implementation of the Cilk-5 multithreaded language. In *Proceedings of the ACM SIGPLAN Conference on Programming Language Design and Implementation (PLDI)*, pages 212–223, 1998.

[19] M. Frigo, C. E. Leiserson, and K. H. Randall. The implementation of the Cilk-5 multithreaded language. In *Proceedings of the ACM SIGPLAN Conference on Programming Language Design and Implementation (PLDI)*, pages 212–223, 1998.

[20] J. R. Goodman, M. K. Vernon, and P. J. Woest. Efficient synchronization primitives for large-scale cache-coherent multiprocessors. In *International Conference on Architectural Support for Programming Languages and Operating Systems (ASPLOS)*, pages 64–75. ACM, 1989.

[21] D. Hendler, I. Incze, N. Shavit, and M. Tzafrir. Flat combining and the synchronization-parallelism tradeoff. In *Proceedings of the ACM Symposium on Parallelism in Algorithms and Architectures (SPAA)*, pages 355–364, 2010.

[22] M. Herlihy. Wait-free synchronization. *ACM Trans. Program. Lang. Syst.*, 13:124–149, January 1991.

[23] M. Herlihy. A methodology for implementing highly concurrent data objects. *ACM Transactions on Programming Languages and Systems*, 15:745–770, 1993.

[24] M. Herlihy and N. Shavit. *The Art of Multiprocessor Programming*. Morgan Kaufmann, 2008.

[25] M. P. Herlihy and J. M. Wing. Linearizability: a correctness condition for concurrent objects. *ACM Trans. Program. Lang. Syst.*, 12(3):463–492, July 1990.

[26] Intel Corporation. *Intel Cilk Plus Language Extension Specification, Version 1.1*, 2013. Document 324396-002US. Available from http://cilkplus.org/sites/default/files/open_specifications/Intel_Cilk_plus_lang_spec_2.htm.

[27] T. Johnson and D. Shasha. The performance of current B-tree algorithms. *ACM Trans. Database Syst.*, 18(1):51–101, 1993.

[28] R. E. Ladner and M. J. Fischer. Parallel prefix computation. *Journal of the ACM*, 27(4):831–838, Oct. 1980.

[29] J. Mellor-Crummey. On-the-fly detection of data races for programs with nested fork-join parallelism. In *Proceedings of Supercomputing*, pages 24–33, 1991.

[30] OpenMP Architecture Review Board. OpenMP specification and features. http://openmp.org/wp/, May 2008.

[31] Y. Oyama, K. Taura, and A. Yonezawa. Executing parallel programs with synchronization bottlenecks efficiently. In *Proceedings of the International Workshop on Parallel and Distributed Computing for Symbolic and Irregular Applications (PDSIA)*, pages 182–204, 1999.

[32] R. C. Paige and C. P. Kruskal. Parallel algorithms for shortest path problems. In *Int. Conference on Parallel Processing*, pages 14–20, 1985.

[33] W. J. Paul, U. Vishkin, and H. Wagener. Parallel dictionaries in 2-3 trees. In *Proceedings of the International Colloquium on Automata, Languages, and Programming (ICALP)*, pages 597–609, 1983.

[34] R. Raman, J. Zhao, V. Sarkar, M. Vechev, and E. Yahav. Scalable and precise dynamic datarace detection for structured parallelism. In *Proceedings of the ACM SIGPLAN Conference on Programming Language Design and Implementation (PLDI)*, pages 531–542, 2012.

[35] J. Reinders. *Intel Threading Building Blocks: Outfitting C++ for Multi-Core Processor Parallelism*. O'Reilly, 2007.

[36] P. Sanders. Randomized priority queues for fast parallel access. *Journal of Parallel Distributed Computing*, 49(1):86–97, 1998.

[37] N. Shavit and A. Zemach. Diffracting trees. *ACM Trans. Comput. Syst.*, 14(4):385–428, Nov. 1996.

[38] N. Shavit and A. Zemach. Combining funnels: a dynamic approach to software combining. *Journal of Parallel and Distributed Computing*, 60(11):1355–1387, 2000.

[39] The Task Parallel Library. http://msdn.microsoft.com/en-us/magazine/cc163340.aspx, Oct. 2007.

Phase-Concurrent Hash Tables for Determinism

Julian Shun
Carnegie Mellon University
jshun@cs.cmu.edu

Guy E. Blelloch
Carnegie Mellon University
guyb@cs.cmu.edu

ABSTRACT

We present a deterministic *phase-concurrent* hash table in which operations of the same type are allowed to proceed concurrently, but operations of different types are not. Phase-concurrency guarantees that all concurrent operations commute, giving a deterministic hash table state, guaranteeing that the state of the table at any quiescent point is independent of the ordering of operations. Furthermore, by restricting our hash table to be phase-concurrent, we show that we can support operations more efficiently than previous concurrent hash tables. Our hash table is based on linear probing, and relies on history-independence for determinism.

We experimentally compare our hash table on a modern 40-core machine to the best existing concurrent hash tables that we are aware of (hopscotch hashing and chained hashing) and show that we are 1.3–4.1 times faster on random integer keys when operations are restricted to be phase-concurrent. We also show that the cost of insertions and deletions for our deterministic hash table is only slightly more expensive than for a non-deterministic version that we implemented. Compared to standard sequential linear probing, we get up to 52 times speedup on 40 cores with dual hyperthreading. Furthermore, on 40 cores insertions are only about $1.3\times$ slower than random writes (scatter). We describe several applications which have deterministic solutions using our phase-concurrent hash table, and present experiments showing that using our phase-concurrent deterministic hash table is only slightly slower than using our non-deterministic one and faster than using previous concurrent hash tables, so the cost of determinism is small.

Categories and Subject Descriptors: D.1.3 [Programming Techniques]: Concurrent Programming—*Parallel Programming*

Keywords: Hash Table, Determinism, Applications

1. INTRODUCTION

Many researchers have argued the importance of deterministic results in developing and debugging parallel programs (see e.g. [32, 6, 8, 25, 3]). Two types of determinism are distinguished—external determinism and internal determinism. External determinism requires that the program produce the same output when given the

SPAA'14, June 23–25, 2014, Prague, Czech Republic.
Copyright 2014 ACM 978-1-4503-2821-0/14/06 ...$15.00
http://dx.doi.org/10.1145/2612669.2612687 .

same input, while internal determinism also requires certain intermediate steps of the program to be deterministic (up to some level of abstraction) [3]. In the context of concurrent access, a data structure is internally deterministic if even when operations are applied concurrently the final observable state depends uniquely on the set of operations applied, but not on their order. This property is equivalent to saying the operations commute with respect to the final observable state of the structure [36, 32]. Deterministic concurrent data structures are important for developing internally deterministic parallel algorithms—they allow for the structure to be updated concurrently while generating a deterministic result independent of the timing or scheduling of threads. Blelloch et al. show that internally deterministic algorithms using nested parallelism and commutative operations on shared state can be efficient, and their algorithms make heavy use concurrent data structures [3].

However, for certain data structures, the operations naturally do not commute. For example, in a hash table mixing insertions and deletions in time would inherently depend on ordering since inserting and deleting the same element do not commute, but insertions commute with each other and deletions commute with each other, independently of value. The same is true for searching mixed with either insertion or deletion. For a data structure in which certain operations commute but others do not, it is useful to group the operations into phases such that the concurrent operations within a phase commute. We define a data structure to be ***phase-concurrent*** if subsets of operations can proceed (safely) concurrently. If the operations within a phase also commute, then the data structure is deterministic. Note that phase-concurrency can have other uses besides determinism, such as giving more efficient data structures. It is the programmer's responsibility to separate concurrent operations into phases, with synchronization in between, which for most nested parallel programs is easy and natural to do.

In this paper, we focus on the hash table data structure. We describe a deterministic phase-concurrent hash table and prove its correctness. Our data structure builds upon a sequential history-independent hash table [4] and allows concurrent insertions, concurrent deletions, concurrent searches, and reporting the contents. It does not allow different types of operations to be mixed in time, because commutativity (and hence determinism) would be violated in general. We show that using one type of operation at a time is still very useful for many applications. The hash table uses open addressing with a prioritized variant of linear probing and guarantees that in a quiescent state (when there are no operations ongoing) the exact content of the array is independent of the ordering of previous updates. This allows, for example, quickly returning the contents of the hash table in a deterministic order simply by packing out the empty cells, which is useful in many applications. Returning the contents could be done deterministically by sorting, but this is more expensive. Our hash table can store key-value pairs either directly or via a pointer.

We present timings for insertions, deletions, finds, and returning the contents into an array on a 40-core machine. We compare these timings with the timings of several other implementations of concurrent and phase-concurrent hash tables, including the fastest concurrent open addressing [15] and closed addressing [20] hash tables that we could find, and two of our non-deterministic phase-concurrent implementations (based on linear probing and cuckoo hashing). We also compare the implementations to standard sequential linear probing, and to the sequential history-independent hash table. Our experiments show that our deterministic hash table significantly outperforms the existing concurrent (non-deterministic) versions on updates by a factor of 1.3–4.1. Furthermore, it gets up to a $52\times$ speedup over the (standard) non-deterministic sequential version on 40 cores with two-way hyper-threading. We compare insertions to simply writing into an array at random locations (a scatter). On 40 cores, and for a load factor of $1/3$, insertions into our table is only about $1.3\times$ the cost of random writes. This is because most insertions only involve a single cache miss, as does a random write, and that is the dominant cost.

Such a deterministic hash table is useful in many applications. For example, Delaunay refinement iteratively adds triangles to a triangulation until all triangles satisfy some criteria (see Section 5). "Bad triangles" which do not satisfy the criteria are broken up into smaller triangles, possibly creating new bad triangles. The result of Delaunay refinement depends on the order in which bad triangles are added. Blelloch et al. show that using a technique called *deterministic reservations* [3], triangles can be added in parallel in a deterministic order on each iteration. However, for the algorithm to be deterministic, the list of new bad triangles returned in each iteration must also be deterministic. Since each bad triangle does not know how many new bad triangles will be created, the most natural and efficient way to accomplish this is to add the bad triangles to a deterministic hash table and return the contents of the table at the end of each iteration. Without a hash table, one would either have to first mark the bad triangles and then look through all the triangles identifying the bad ones, which is inefficient, or use a fetch-and-add to a vector storing bad triangles (non-deterministic), leading to high contention, or possibly use a lock-free queue (non-deterministic), again leading to high contention. By using a deterministic hash table in conjunction with deterministic reservations, the order of the bad triangles is deterministic, giving a deterministic implementation of parallel Delaunay refinement.

We present six applications which use hash tables in a phase-concurrent manner, and show that our deterministic phase-concurrent hash table can be used both for efficiency and for determinism. For four of these applications—remove duplicates, Delaunay refinement, suffix trees and edge contraction—we believe the most natural and/or efficient way to write an implementation is to use a hash table. We show that for these applications, using our deterministic hash table is only slightly slower than using a non-deterministic one based on linear probing, and is faster than using cuckoo hashing or chained hashing (which are also non-deterministic). For two other applications—breadth-first search and spanning tree—we implement simpler implementations using hash tables, compared to array-based versions directly addressing memory. We show that the implementations using hash tables are not much slower than the array-based implementations, and again using our deterministic hash table is only slightly slower than using our non-deterministic linear probing hash table and faster than using the other hash tables.

Contributions. The contributions of this paper are as follows. First, we define the notion of phase-concurrency. Second, we show

that phase-concurrency can be applied to hash tables to obtain both determinism and efficiency. We prove correctness and termination of our deterministic phase-concurrent hash table. Third, we present a comprehensive experimental evaluation of our hash tables with the fastest existing parallel hash tables. We compare our deterministic and non-deterministic phase-concurrent linear probing hash tables, our phase-concurrent implementation of cuckoo hashing, hopscotch hashing, which is the fastest existing concurrent open addressing hash table as far as we know, and an optimized implementation of concurrent chained hashing. Finally, we describe several applications of our deterministic hash table, and present experimental results comparing the running times of using different hash tables in these applications.

2. RELATED WORK

A data structure is defined to be *history-independent* if its layout depends only on its current contents, and not the ordering of the operations that created it [13, 24]. For sequential data structures, history-independence is motivated by security concerns, and in particular ensures that examining a structure after its creation does not reveal anything about its history. In this paper, we extend a sequential history-independent hash table based on open addressing [4] to work phase-concurrently. Our motivation is to design a data structure which is deterministic independent of the order of updates. Although we are not concerned with exact memory layout, we want to be able to return the contents of the hash table very quickly and in an order that is independent of when the updates arrived. For a history-independent open addressing table, this can be done easily by packing the non-empty elements into a contiguous array, which just involves a parallel prefix sum and cache-block friendly writes.

Several concurrent hash tables have been developed over the years. There has been significant work on concurrent closed addressing hash tables using separate chaining [16, 9, 19, 23, 28, 12, 33, 20, 14]. It would not be hard to make one of these deterministic when reporting the contents of the buckets since each list could be sorted by a priority at that time. However, such hash tables are expensive relative to open address hashing because they involve more cache misses, and also because they need memory management to allocate and de-allocate the cells for the links. The fastest closed addressing hash we know of is Lea's `ConcurrentHashMap` from the Java Concurrency Package [20], and we compare with a C++ implementation of it, obtained from Herlihy et al. [15], in Section 6.

Martin and Davis [22], Purcell and Harris [27] and Gao et al. [11] describe lock-free hash tables with open addressing. For deletions, Gao et al.'s version marks the locations with a special "deleted" value, commonly known as tombstones, and insertions and finds simply skip over the tombstones (an insertion is not allowed to fill a tombstone). This means that the only way to remove deleted elements is to copy the whole hash table. All of these hash tables are non-deterministic and quite complex. In our experiments, we use an implementation of non-deterministic linear probing similar to that of Gao et al. (see Section 6).

Herlihy et al. [15] describe and implement an open addressing concurrent hash table called hopscotch hashing, which is based on cuckoo hashing [26] and linear probing. Their hash table guarantees that an element is within K locations of the location it hashed to (where K could be set to the machine word size), so that finds will touch few cache lines. To maintain this property, insertions which find an empty location more than K locations away from the location h that it hashed to will repeatedly displace elements closer to h until it finds an empty slot within K locations of h (or resizes if no empty slot is found). A deletion will recursively bring in elements later in the probe sequence to the empty slot created. Their hash table requires locks and its layout is non-deterministic even if only one type of operation is performed concurrently. Hopscotch hashing is the fastest concurrent hash table available as far as we know, and we use it for comparison in Section 6.

Kim and Kim [18] recently present several implementations of parallel hash tables, though we found our code and the hopscotch hashing code of [15] to be much faster. Van der Vegt and Laarman describe a concurrent hash table using a variant of linear probing called bidirectional linear probing [34, 35], however it requires a monotonic hash function, which may be too restrictive for many applications. Their hash table is non-deterministic and requires locks. Alcantara et al. describe a parallel hashing algorithm using GPUs [1], which involves a synchronized form of cuckoo hashing, and is non-deterministic because collisions are resolved non-deterministically. Concurrent cuckoo hashing has also been discussed by Fan et al. [10], and very recently by Li et al. [21]. The hash table of Fan et al. supports concurrent access by multiple readers and a single writer, but do not support concurrent writers. Li et al. extends this work by supporting concurrent writers as well.

Phase-concurrency has been previously explored in the work on room synchronizations by Blelloch et al. [2]. They describe phase-concurrent implementations of stacks and queues. However, they were concerned only about efficiency, and their data structures are not deterministic even within a single phase. We believe our hash table is the first deterministic phase-concurrent hash table.

3. PRELIMINARIES

We review the sequential history-independent hash table of Blelloch and Golovin [4]. The algorithm is similar to that of standard linear probing. It assumes a total order on the keys used as priorities. For insertion, the only difference is that if during the probe sequence a key currently in the location has lower priority than the key being inserted, then the two keys are swapped. An insertion probes the exact same number of elements as in standard linear probing. For finds, the only difference is that since the keys are ordered by priority, it means that a find for a key k can stop once it finds a location i with a lower priority key. This means that searching for keys not in the table can actually be faster than in standard linear probing. One common method for handling deletions in linear probing is to simply mark the location as "deleted" (a tombstone), and modify the insert and search accordingly. However, this would not be history-independent. Instead, for deletions in the history-independent hash table, the location where the key is deleted is filled with the next lower priority element in the probe sequence that hashed to or after that location (or the empty element if it is at the end of the probe sequence). This process is done recursively until the element that gets swapped in is the empty element.

Our code uses the atomic **compare-and-swap** (CAS) instruction. The instruction takes three arguments—a memory location (*loc*), an old value (*oldV*) and a new value (*newV*); if the value stored at *loc* is equal to *oldV* it atomically stores *newV* at *loc* and returns *true*, and otherwise it does not modify *loc* and returns *false*. We use $\&x$ to refer to the memory location of variable x.

We define phase-concurrency as follows:

DEFINITION 1 (PHASE-CONCURRENCY). *A data structure with operations O and operation subsets S is phase-concurrent if $\forall s \in S$, $s \subseteq O$ and all operations in s can proceed concurrently and are linearizable.*

4. DETERMINISTIC PHASE-CONCURRENT HASH TABLE

Our deterministic phase-concurrent hash table extends the sequential history-independent hash table to allow for concurrent inserts, concurrent deletes, and concurrent finds. The contents can also be extracted (referred to as the *elements* operation) easily by simply packing the non-empty cells. Using the notation of Definition 1, our hash table is phase-concurrent with:

- $O = \{$insert, delete, find, elements$\}$, and
- $S = \big\{ \{$insert$\}, \{$delete$\}, \{$find, elements$\} \big\}$

The code for insertion, deletion and find is shown in Figure 1, and assumes that the table is not full and that different keys have different priorities (total ordering). For simplicity, the code assumes there is no data associated with the key, although it could easily be modified for key-value pairs. Note that the code works for arbitrary key-value sizes as for structure sizes larger that what a compare-and-swap can operate on, a pointer (which fits in a word) to the structure can be stored in the hash table instead. The code assumes a hash function h that maps keys into the range $[0, \ldots, |M| - 1]$, and that the keys have a total priority ordering that can be compared with the function $<_p$. By convention, we assume that the empty element ($\perp$) has lower priority than all other elements. The code uses NEXTINDEX(i) and PREVINDEX(i) to increment and decrement the index modulo the table size. Note that both INSERT and DELETE do not have return values, so we only need to ensure that a set of inserts (or deletes) are commutative with respect to the resulting configuration of the table.

For a given element v, INSERT loops until it finds a location with $\perp$ (Line 3) or it finds that v is already in the hash table (Line 5), at which point it terminates. If during the insert, it finds a location that stores a lower priority value (Line 8), it attempts to replace the value there with v with a CAS, and if successful the lower priority key is temporarily removed from the table and INSERT is now responsible for inserting the replaced element later in the probe sequence, i.e. the replaced element is set to v (Line 9).

For a given element v, DELETE first finds v or an element after v in the probe sequence at location k (Lines 27–29) since v may either not be in the table or its position has been shifted back due to concurrent deletions. If v is not at location k, then DELETE decrements the location (Lines 30–32) until either v is found (Line 33) or the location becomes less than $h(v)$ (Line 30), in which case v is not in the table. After finding v, DELETE finds the replacement element for v by calling FINDREPLACEMENT (Line 34). FINDREPLACEMENT first increments the location until finding a replacement element that is either $\perp$ or a lower priority element that hashes after v (Lines 13–16). The resulting location will be one past the replacement element, so it is decremented on Line 17. Then because the replacement element could have shifted, it decrements the the location until finding the replacement element (Lines 18–23). DELETE then attempts to swap in the replacement element v' on Line 35, and if successful, and $v' \neq \perp$ (Line 36), there is now an additional copy of v' in the table so DELETE is responsible for deleting v' (Lines 37–39). Otherwise, if the CAS was unsuccessful, either v has already been deleted or used as a replacement element so possibly appears at some earlier location. DELETE decrements the location and continues looping (Line 41).

To FIND an element v, the algorithm starts at $h(v)$ and loops upward until finding either an empty location or a location with a key with equal or lower priority (Lines 43–45). Then it returns the result of the comparison of v with that key (Line 46). Since there is a total priority ordering on the keys, $M[i]$ will contain v if and only if v is in the table.

```
1    procedure INSERT(v)
2        i = h(v)
3        while (v ≠ ⊥)
4            c = M[i]
5            if (c = v) return
6            elseif (c >_p v) then
7                i = NEXTINDEX(i)
8            elseif (CAS(&M[i], c, v)) then
9                v = c
10               i = NEXTINDEX(i)

11   procedure FINDREPLACEMENT(i)
12       j = i
13       do
14           j = NEXTINDEX(j)
15           v = M[j]
16       while (v ≠ ⊥ and h(v) > i)
17       k = PREVINDEX(j)
18       while (k > i)
19           v' = M[k]
20           if (v' = ⊥ or h(v') ≤ i) then
21               v = v'
22               j = k
23           k = PREVINDEX(k)
24       return (j, v)

25   procedure DELETE(v)
26       i = h(v)
27       k = i
28       while (M[k] ≠ ⊥ and v <_p M[k])
29           k = NEXTINDEX(k)
30       while (k ≥ i)
31           if (v = ⊥ or v ≠_p M[k])
32               k = PREVINDEX(k)
33           else
34               (j, v') = FINDREPLACEMENT(k)
35               if (CAS(&M[k], v, v')) then
36                   if (v' ≠ ⊥) then
37                       v = v'
38                       k = j
39                       i = h(v)
40                   else return
41               else k = PREVINDEX(k)

42   procedure FIND(v)
43       i = h(v)
44       while (M[i] ≠ ⊥ and v <_p M[i])
45           i = NEXTINDEX(i)
46       return (M[i] = v)
```

Figure 1. Phase-concurrent deterministic hashing with linear probing.

Note that for INSERT, DELETE and FIND, it is crucial that the hash table is not full, otherwise the operations may not terminate. Throughout our discussion, we assume wraparound with modulo arithmetic. Since the table is not full, every cluster has a beginning, and when comparing the positions of two elements within a cluster, the "higher" position is the one further from the beginning of the cluster in the forward direction with wraparound. We want to show that when starting with an empty hash table, our phase-concurrent hash table maintains the following invariant:

DEFINITION 2 (ORDERING INVARIANT). *If a key v hashes to location i and is stored in location j in the hash table, then for all k, $i \leq k < j$ it must be that $M[k] \geq_p v$.*

As long as the keys are totally ordered by their priorities, the ordering invariant guarantees a unique representation for a given set of keys [4]. This invariant was shown to hold in the sequential history-independent hash table [4].

The concurrent versions of insert and delete work similarly to the sequential versions, but need to be careful about concurrent modifications. What we show is that the union of the keys being inserted

and the current content always equals the union of all initial keys and all insertions that started. A key property to make it work is that since only insertions are occurring, the priority of the keys at a given location can only increase. We note that this implementation should make clear that is not safe to run inserts concurrently with finds, since an unrelated key can be temporarily removed and invisible to a find.

The deletion routine is somewhat trickier. It allows for multiple copies of a key to appear in the table during deletions. In fact, with p concurrent threads it is possible that up to $p+1$ copies of a single key appear in the table at a given time. This might seem counterintuitive since we are deleting keys. Recall, however, that when a key v is deleted, a replacement v' needs to be found to fill its slot. When v' is copied into the slot occupied by v, there will temporarily be two copies of v', but the delete operation is now responsible for deleting one of them. The sequential code deletes the second copy, but in the concurrent version since there might be concurrent deletes aimed at the same key, the delete might end up deleting the version it copied into, another thread's copy, or it might end up not finding a copy and quitting. The important invariant is that for a value v the number of copies minus the number of outstanding deletes does not change (when a copy is made, the number of copies is increased but so is the number of outstanding deletes). A key property that makes deletions work is that since only deletions are occurring, the priority of the keys at a given location can only decrease, and hence a key can only move to locations with a lower index.

We now prove important properties of our hash table. We use M_v to indicate the set of (non-empty) values contained in the hash table, I_v to indicate the set of values in a collection of insertion operations I, and $|M|$ to indicate the size of the table.

THEOREM 1. *Starting with a table M that satisfies the ordering invariant and with no operations in progress, after any collection of concurrent insertions I complete (and none are in progress) with $|M_v \cup I_v| < |M|$, M will satisfy the following properties:*

- *M contains the union of the keys initially in the table and all values in I, and*
- *M satisfies the ordering invariant.*

Furthermore, all insertion operations are non-blocking and terminate in a finite number of steps.

PROOF. We assume all instructions are linearizable and consider the linearized sequential ordering of operations. We use *step* to refer to a position in this sequential ordering. At a given step, we use I_v to indicate the set of values for which an INSERT has started. Between when an INSERT starts and finishes, we say that it is *active* with some value. At its start, an INSERT(v) is active with the value v, but whenever it performs a successful CAS(&M[i], v, c) on Line 8, the INSERT becomes active with the value c on the next step (Line 9)—it is now responsible for inserting c instead of v. When it does a successful CAS(&M[i], v, ⊥) an INSERT is no longer active—it will terminate as soon as it gets to the next start of the while loop and do nothing to the shared state in the meantime. We also say that an INSERT is no longer active when it reads a value c on Line 4 that is equal to v—it will terminate on Line 5.

We use A_v to indicate the union of values of all INSERT's that are active. We use M_v to indicate the values contained in M on a given step, and M_s to be the initial values contained in M. We will prove that the following invariants are maintained on every step:

1. $M_v \cup A_v = M_s \cup I_v$, and
2. the table M satisfies the ordering invariant.

Since at the end $A_v = \emptyset$, these invariants imply properties 1 and 2 of the theorem.

Invariant 1 is true at the start since A_v and I_v are both empty and $M_s = M_v$ by definition. The invariant is maintained since (1) when an INSERT starts, its value is added to both A_v and I_v and therefore the invariant is unchanged, (2) when an INSERT terminates it reads a $M[i] = v$, so a v is removed from A_v but it exists in M_v so the union is unaffected, (3) every CAS with $c = \bot$ removes a v from A_v but inserts it into M_v, maintaining the union, and (4) every CAS with $c \neq \bot$ swaps an element in M_v with an element in A_v, again maintaining the union. In the code, whenever a CAS succeeds, c is placed in the location where v was (by the definition of CAS) and immediately afterward v is set to c (Line 9).

Invariant 2 is true at the start by assumption. The invariant is maintained since whenever a CAS$(\&M[i], v, c)$ succeeds it must be the case after the CAS that (1) all locations from $h(v)$ up to i have equal or higher priority than v, and (2) all keys that hash to or before i but appear after i have lower priority than v. These properties imply that the ordering invariant is maintained. The first case is true since the only time i is incremented for v is when $c = M[i]$ has a equal or higher priority (Lines 6–7) and since we only swap higher priority values with lower priority ones ($v >_p c$ for all CAS's), once a cell has an equal or larger priority than v, it always will. Also when we have a successful CAS, swap v and c, and increment i, it must be the case that all locations in the probe sequence for the new v and before the new i have priority higher than the new v. This is because it was true before the swap and the only thing changed by the swap was putting the old v into the table, which we know has a higher priority than the new v. The second case of invariant 2 is true since whenever we perform a CAS we are only increasing the priority of the value at that location.

The termination condition is true since when the hash table of size $|M|$ is not full, an INSERT can call NEXTINDEX at most $|M|$ times before finding an empty location. Therefore for p parallel INSERT's, there can be at most $p|M|$ calls to NEXTINDEX. Furthermore, any CAS failure of an INSERT is associated with a CAS success of another INSERT. A CAS success corresponds to either a call to NEXTINDEX (Line 7) or termination of the insertion. Therefore, for a set of p parallel INSERT's, there can be at most $p - 1$ CAS failures for any one CAS success and call to NEXTINDEX. So after $p^2|M|$ CAS attempts, all INSERT's have terminated. It is non-blocking because an INSERT can only fail on a CAS attempt if another INSERT succeeds and thus makes progress. $\square$

THEOREM 2. *Starting with a table M with $|M_v| < |M|$ that satisfies the ordering invariant and with no operations in progress, after any collection of concurrent deletes D complete (and none are in progress), the table will satisfy the following properties:*

- *M contains the difference of the keys initially in the table and all values in D, and*
- *M satisfies the ordering invariant.*

Furthermore, all delete operations are non-blocking and terminate in a finite number of steps.

PROOF. Similar to insertions, from when a DELETE starts until it ends, it is active with some value: initially it is active with the v it was called with and after a successful CAS$(\&M[k], v, v')$ for $v' \neq \bot$ it becomes active with v' (Lines 35–37). A DELETE finishes on CAS$(\&M[k], v, \bot)$ or when the condition of the while loop on Line 30 no longer holds (in this case, it finishes because v is not in the table).

During deletions, the table M can contain multiple copies of a key. The definition of the ordering invariant is still valid with multiple copies of a key, and for a fixed multiplicity the layout remains unique. Unlike insertions, to analyze deletions we need to keep track of multiplicities.

We use D_v to indicate the set of values in D, and M_s the initial contents of M. We use $A(v)$ to indicate the number of active DELETE's with value v, and $M(v)$ to indicate the number of copies of v in M. We will prove that the following invariants are maintained at every step:

1. $\forall v \in M_s$, if $v \in M_s \setminus D_v$ then $M(v) - A(v) = 1$, and otherwise $M(v) - A(v) < 1$,
2. the table M satisfies the ordering invariant allowing for repeated keys, and
3. on Line 30, the index k of a DELETE of v must point to or past the last copy of v ("rightmost" copy with respect to the cluster).

Since at the end $A(v) = 0$ for all v, these invariants prove the properties of the theorem.

Invariant 1 is true at the start since D_v is empty and $\forall v \in M_s$, $A(v) = 0$. To show that the invariant is maintained we consider all events that can change $M(v), A(v)$ or D_v. These are: (1) when a DELETE on v starts, then $A(v)$ is incremented making $M(v) - A(v)$ less than 1 (since it can be at most 1 before the start) and v is added to D_v so v is not in $M_s \setminus D_v$, (2) when a CAS$(\&M[k], v, \bot)$ succeeds, $A(v)$ and $M(v)$ are both decremented, therefore canceling out, (3) when a CAS$(\&M[k], v, v')$ for $v' \neq \bot$ succeeds, then by Lines 35–37, $A(v)$ and $M(v)$ are both decremented, canceling out, and $A(v')$ and $M(v')$ are both incremented, again canceling out, and (4) when a DELETE finishes due to the condition not holding on Line 30, the value v cannot be in the table because of invariant 3, so $A(v)$ is decremented, but $M(v) - A(v)$ is less than 1 both before and after since $M(v) = 0$.

Invariant 2 is true at the start by assumption. The only way it could become violated is if as a result of a CAS$(\&M[k], v, v')$, the value v' falls out of order with respect to values after location j (i.e. there is some key that hashes at or before j, is located after j, and has a higher priority than v'). This cannot happen since the replacement element found is the closest key to j that hashes after j and has lower priority than v. The loop in Lines 13–16 scans upward to find an element that hashes after v in the probe sequence, and the while loop at Lines 18–23 scans downward in case the desired replacement element was shifted down in the meantime by another thread. It is important that this loop runs backwards and is the reason that there are two redundant looking loops, one going up and one going back down.

Invariant 3 is true is since the initial find (Lines 27–29) locates an index of an element with priority lower that v, which must be past v, and FINDREPLACEMENT returns an index at or past the replacement v'. k is only decremented on a failed CAS, which in this case means that v can only be at an index lower than k.

To prove termination, we bound the number of index increments and decrements a single DELETE operation can perform while executing in parallel with other deletes. For a hash table of size $|M|$, the while loop on Lines 30–41 can execute at most $|M|$ times before i changes, and i will only increase since the replacement element must have a higher index than the deleted element. i can increase at most $|M|$ times before $v' = \bot$, so the number of calls to FINDREPLACEMENT is at most $|M|^2$. The number of decrements and assignments to k in the while loop on Lines 30–41 is at most $|M|$ per iteration of the while loop (for a total of $|M|^2$).

FINDREPLACEMENT contains a loop incrementing j, which eventually finishes because the condition on Line 16 will be true for a location containing $\perp$, and a loop decrementing j, which eventually finishes due to the condition on Line 18. So the total number of increments and decrements is at most $2|M|$ per call to FIND-REPLACEMENT. The initial find on Lines 27–29 involves at most $|M|$ increments. Therefore, a DELETE operation terminates after at most $|M| + |M|^2 + 2|M|^3$ increments/decrements, independent of the result of the CAS on Line 35. A collection of p DELETE's terminates in at most $p(|M| + |M|^2 + 2|M|^3)$ increments/decrements. Increments, decrements and all instructions in between are non-blocking and thus finish in a finite amount of time. Therefore, concurrent deletions are non-blocking. □

Combining. For a deterministic hash table that stores key-value pairs, if there are duplicate keys, we must decide how to combine the values of these keys deterministically. This can be done by passing a commutative combining function that is applied to the values of pairs with equal keys and updating the location (using a double-word CAS) with a pair containing the key with the combined values. Our experiments in Section 6 use min or $+$ as the combining function.

Resizing. Using well-known techniques it is relatively easy to extend our hash table with resizing [14]. Here we outline an approach for growing a table based on incrementally copying the old contents to a new table when the load factor in the table is too high. An IN-SERT can detect that a table is overfull when a probe sequence is too long. In particular, theoretically a probe sequence should not be longer than $k \log n$ with high probability for some constant k that depends on the allowable load factor. Once a process detects that the table is overfull, it allocates a new table of twice the size and (atomically) places a link to the new table accessible to all users. A lock can be used to avoid multiple processes allocating simultaneously. This would mean that an insertion will have to wait between when the lock is taken and the new table is available, but this should be a short time, and only on rare occasions.

Once the link is set, new INSERTs are placed in the new table. Furthermore, as long as the old table is not empty, every INSERT is responsible for copying at least two elements from the old table to the new one. The thread responsible for creating the new table allocates the elements to copy to other threads, and thereafter some form of work-stealing [5] is used to guarantee that a thread has elements to copy when there are still uncopied elements. As long as a constant number of keys are copied for every one that is inserted, the old table will be emptied before the new one is filled. This way only two tables are active at any time. There is an extra cost of indirection on every INSERT since the table has to be checked to find if it has been relocated. However, most of the time this pointer will be in a local cache in shared mode (loaded by any previous table access) and therefore the cost is very cheap. When there are two active tables, finds and deletes would look in both tables.

5. APPLICATIONS

In this section, we describe applications which use our deterministic hash table. For these applications, using a hash table is either the most natural and/or efficient way to implement an algorithm, or it simplifies the implementation compared to directly addressing the memory locations. Our hash table implementation contains a function ELEMENTS() which packs the contents of the table into an array and returns it. It is important that ELEMENTS() is deterministic to guarantee determinism for the algorithms that use it.

Delaunay refinement and breadth-first search use the WRITEMIN function for determinism, which takes two arguments–a memory location *loc* and a value *val* and stores *val* at *loc* if and only if *val* is less than the value at *loc*. It returns *true* if it updates the value at *loc* and *false* otherwise. WRITEMIN is implemented with a compare-and-swap [29].

Remove Duplicates. The ***remove duplicates*** problem takes as input a sequence of elements, a hash function on the elements and a comparison function, and returns a sequence in which duplicate elements are removed. This is a simple application which can be implemented using a hash table by simply inserting all of the elements into the table and returning the result of ELEMENTS(). For determinism, the sequence returned by ELEMENTS() should contain the elements in the same order every time, which is guaranteed by a deterministic hash table. This is an example of an application where the most natural and efficient implementation uses hashing (one could remove duplicates by sorting and removing consecutive equal-valued elements, but it would be less efficient).

Delaunay Refinement. A Delaunay triangulation of n points is a triangulation such that no point is contained in the circumcircle of any triangle in the triangulation. The ***Delaunay refinement*** problem takes as input a Delaunay triangulation and an angle α, and adds new points to the triangulation such that no triangle has an angle less than α. We refer to a triangle with an angle less than α as a ***bad triangle***.

Initially all of the bad triangles of the input triangulation are computed and stored into a hash table. On each iteration of Delaunay refinement, the contents of the hash table are obtained via a call to ELEMENTS() and the bad triangles mark (using a WRITEMIN with their index in the sequence) all of the triangles that would be affected if they were to be inserted. Bad triangles whose affected triangles all contain their mark are "active" and can proceed to modify the triangulation by adding their center point. This method guarantees there are no conflicts, as any triangle in the triangulation is affected by at most one active bad triangle. During each iteration of the refinement, new triangles with angles less than α are generated and they are inserted into the hash table as they are discovered. This process is repeated until either a specified number of new points are added or the triangulation contains no more bad triangles. For determinism, it is important that the call to ELEMENTS() is deterministic, as this makes the indices/priorities of the bad triangles, and hence the resulting triangulation deterministic.

This is an example of an application where using a hash table significantly simplifies the implementation. Prior to inserting a point, it is hard to efficiently determine how many new bad triangles it will create, and pre-allocate an array of the correct size to allow for storing the new bad triangles in parallel.

Suffix Tree. A ***suffix tree*** stores all suffixes of a string S in a trie where internal nodes with a single child are contracted. A suffix tree allows for efficient searches for patterns in S, and also has many other applications in string analysis and computational biology. To allow for expected constant time look-ups, a hash table is used to store the children of each internal node. Our phase-concurrent hash table allows for parallel insertions of nodes into a suffix tree and parallel searches on the suffix tree. This is an example of an application where hash tables are used for efficiency, and where the inserts and finds are naturally split into two phases.

Edge Contraction. The ***edge contraction*** problem takes as input a sequence of edges (possibly with weights) and a label array R, which specifies that vertex v should be relabeled with the value

$R[v]$. It returns a sequence of unique edges relabeled according to R. Edge contraction is used in recursive graph algorithms where certain vertices are merged into "supervertices" and the endpoints of edges need to be relabeled to the IDs of these supervertices. Duplicate edges are processed differently depending on the algorithm.

To implement edge contraction, we can insert the edges into a hash table using the two new vertex IDs as the key, and any data on the edge as the value. A commutative combining function can be supplied for combining data on duplicate edges. For example, we might keep the edge with minimum weight for a minimum spanning tree algorithm, or add the edge weights together for a graph partitioning algorithm [17]. To obtain the relabeled edges for the next iteration, we make a call to ELEMENTS(). To guarantee determinism in the algorithm, the hash table must be deterministic. This idea is used to remove duplicate edges on contraction in a recent connected components implementation [31].

Breadth-First Search. The ***breadth-first search*** (BFS) problem takes a graph G and a starting vertex r, and returns a breadth-first search tree rooted at r containing all nodes reachable from r. Vertices in each level of the BFS can be visited in parallel. A parallel algorithm stores the current level of the search in a ***Frontier*** array, and finds all unvisited neighbors of the Frontier array that belong to the next level in parallel. During this process, it also chooses a parent vertex for each unvisited neighbor in the next level. However, if multiple vertices on the frontier share an unvisited neighbor, one must decide which vertex becomes the parent of the neighbor. This can be done deterministically with the WRITEMIN function.

Another issue is how to generate the new Frontier array for the next level. One option is to have all parents copy all of its unvisited neighbors of the current Frontier array into a temporary array. To do this in parallel, one must first create an array large enough to contain all unvisited neighbors of all vertices in the Frontier array (since at this point we have not assigned parents yet), assign segments of the array to each vertex in Frontier, and have each vertex in Frontier copy unvisited neighbors that it is a parent of into the array. This array is then packed down with a prefix sums and assigned to Frontier.

An alternative solution is to use a concurrent hash table and insert unvisited neighbors into the table. Obtaining the next Frontier array simply involves a call to ELEMENTS(). With this method, duplicates are removed automatically, and the packing is hidden from the user. This leads to a much cleaner solution. If one wants to look at or store the frontiers or simply generate a level ordering of the vertices, then it is important that ELEMENTS() is deterministic. The pseudo-code for this algorithm is shown in Figure 2. This method gives a deterministic BFS tree. In Section 6 we show that using our deterministic phase-concurrent hash table does not slow down the code by much compared to the best previous deterministic BFS code [30], which uses memory directly as described in the first method above.

Spanning Forest. A ***spanning forest*** for an undirected graph G, is a subset of the edges that forms a forest (collection of trees) and spans all vertices in G. One way to implement a deterministic parallel spanning forest algorithm is to use the technique of *deterministic reservations* described by Blelloch et al. [3]. In this technique, the edges are assigned unique priorities at the beginning. Each iteration contains a reservation phase and a commit phase. The reservation phase involves the edges finding the components they connect (using a union-find data structure) and then reserving their components if they are different. The commit phase involves the edges checking if they made successful reservations on at least one

```
1: procedure BFS(G, r)                              ▷ r is the root
2:     Parents = {∞, . . . , ∞}        ▷ initialized to all ∞ (unvisited)
3:     Parents[r] = r
4:     Frontier = {r}
5:     while (Frontier ≠ {}) do
6:         Create hash table T
7:         parfor v ∈ Frontier do             ▷ loop over frontier vertices
8:             parfor ngh ∈ N(v) do              ▷ loop over neighbors
9:                 if (WRITEMIN(&Parents[ngh], v)) then
10:                    T.INSERT(ngh)
11:        Frontier = T.ELEMENTS()             ▷ get contents of T
12:        parfor v ∈ Frontier do
13:            Parents[v] = −Parents[v]      ▷ negative indicates visited
14:    return Parents
```

Figure 2. Hash Table-Based Breadth-First Search

component, and if so linking the components together. The unsuccessful edges connecting different components are kept for the next iteration and the process is repeated until no edges remain.

If the vertex IDs are integers from the range $[1, \ldots, n]$, then an array of size n can be used to store the reservations. However, if the IDs are much larger integers or strings, it may be more convenient to use a hash table to perform the reservations to avoid vertex relabeling. Determinism is maintained if the hash table is deterministic. For the reservation phase, edges insert into a hash table each of its vertices (as the key), with value equal to the edge priority. For a deterministic hash table, if duplicate vertices are inserted, the one with the value with the highest priority remains in the hash table. In the commit phase, each edge performs a hash table find on the vertex it inserted and if it contain the edge's priority value, then it proceeds with linking its two components together. We show in Section 6 that the implementation of spanning forest using a hash table is only slightly slower than the array-based version.

6. EXPERIMENTS

In this section, we analyze the performance of our concurrent deterministic history-independent hash table (***linearHash-D***) on its own, and also when used in the applications described in Section 5.

We compare it with two non-deterministic phase-concurrent hash tables that we implement, and with the best existing concurrent hash tables that we know of (hopscotchHash and chainedHash). ***linearHash-ND*** is a concurrent version of linear probing that we implement, which places values in the first empty location and hence depends on history (non-deterministic). It is based on the implementation of Gao et al. [11], except that for deletions it shifts elements back instead of using tombstones, and does not support resizing. We note that in linearHash-ND, insertions and finds can proceed concurrently (although we still separate them in our experiments), since inserted elements are not displaced. ***cuckooHash*** is a concurrent version of cuckoo hashing that we implement, which locks two locations for an element insertion, places the element in one of the locations, and recursively inserts any evicted elements. To prevent deadlocks, it acquires the locks in increasing order of location. It is non-deterministic because an element can be placed in either of its two locations based on the order of insertions. For key-value pairs, on encountering duplicate keys linearHash-D uses a priority function [29] on the values to deterministically decide which pair to keep, while the non-deterministic hash tables do not replace on duplicate keys.

hopscotchHash is a fully-concurrent open-addressing hash table by Herlihy et al. [15], which is based on a combination of linear probing and cuckoo hashing. It uses locks on segments of the hash table during insertions and deletions. We noticed that there is a time-stamp field in the code which is not needed if operations of different types are not performed concurrently. We modified the code accordingly and call this phase-concurrent version *hopscotchHash-PC*. *chainedHash* is a widely-used fully-concurrent closed-addressing hash table by Lea [20] which places elements in linked lists. It was originally implemented in Java, but we were able to obtain a C++ version from the authors of [15]. We also tried the chained hash map (`concurrent_hash_map`) implemented as part of Intel Threading Building Blocks, but found it to be slower than chainedHash. We implement the ELEMENTS() routine for both hopscotch hashing and chained hashing, as the implementations did not come with this routine. For hopscotch hashing, we simply pack out the empty locations. For chained hashing, we first count the number of elements per bucket by traversing the linked lists, compute each bucket's offset into an array using a parallel prefix sum, and then traverse the linked lists per bucket copying elements into the array (each bucket can proceed in parallel). The original implementation of chainedHash acquires a lock at the beginning of an insertion and deletion. This leads to high lock contention for distributions with many repeated keys. We optimized the chained hash table such that insertion only acquires a lock after an initial find operation does not find the key, and deletion only acquires a lock after an initial find operation successfully finds the key. This contention-reducing version is referred to as *chainedHash-CR*.

We also include timings for a serial implementation of the history-independent hash table using linear probing (*serialHash-HI*) and a serial implementation using standard linear probing (*serialHash-HD*).

For the applications, we compare their performance using the phase-concurrent hash tables that we implement and the chained hash table[1]. For breadth-first search and spanning tree we also compare with implementations that directly address memory and show that the additional cost of using hash tables is small.

We run our experiments on a 40-core (with hyper-threading) machine with 4×2.4GHz Intel 10-core E7-8870 Xeon processors (with a 1066MHz bus and 30MB L3 cache) and 256GB of main memory. We run all parallel experiments with two-way hyper-threading enabled, for a total of 80 threads. We compiled all of our code with g++ version 4.8.0 with the -O2 flag. The parallel codes were compiled with Cilk Plus, which is included in g++.

For our experiments, we use six input distributions from the Problem Based Benchmark Suite (PBBS) [30]. *randomSeq-int* is a sequence of n random integer keys in the range $[1, \ldots, n]$ drawn from a uniform distribution. *randomSeq-pairInt* is a sequence of n key-value pairs of random integers in the range $[1, \ldots, n]$ drawn from a uniform distribution. *trigramSeq* is a sequence of n string keys generated from trigram probabilities of English text (there are many duplicate keys in this input). *trigramSeq-pairInt* has the same keys as trigramSeq, but each key maintains a corresponding random integer value. For this input, the key-value pairs are stored as a pointer to a structure with a pointer to a string, and therefore involves an extra level of indirection. *exptSeq-int* is a sequence of n random integer keys drawn from an exponential distribution—this input is also used to test high collision rates in the hash table. *exptSeq-pairInt* contains keys from the same distribution, but with an additional integer value per key. For all distributions, we used $n = 10^8$. For the open addressing hash tables, we initialized a table of size 2^{28}.

Figures 3(a) and 3(b) compare the hash tables for several operations on randomSeq-int and trigramSeq-pairInt, respectively. For

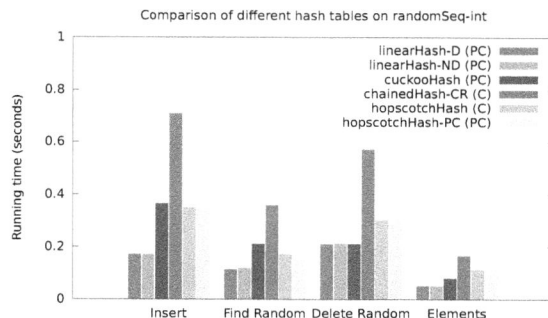

(a) Times (seconds) for 10^8 operations on randomSeq-int.

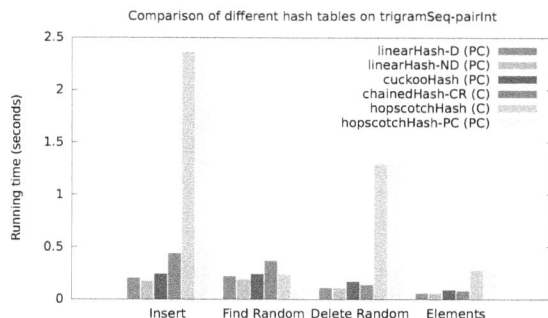

(b) Times (seconds) for 10^8 operations on trigramSeq-pairInt.

Figure 3. Times (seconds) for 10^8 operations for the hash tables on 40 cores (with hyper-threading). (PC) indicates a phase-concurrent implementation and (C) indicates a concurrent implementation.

Insert, we insert a random set of keys from the distribution starting from an empty table. For **Find Random** and **Delete Random** we first insert n elements (not included in the time) and then perform the operations for a random set of keys from the distribution. **Elements** is the time for returning the contents of the hash table in a packed array. Table 1 lists the parallel and serial running times (seconds) for insertions, finds, deletions and returning the elements for the various hash tables on different input sequences. For **Find** and **Delete** we first insert n elements (not included in the time) and then perform the operations either on the same keys (**Inserted**) or for a random set of keys from the distribution (**Random**).

As Figure 3 and Table 1 indicate, insertion, finds and deletions into the deterministic (history-independent) hash table are slightly more expensive than into the history-dependent linear probing version. This is due to the overhead of swapping and checking priorities. Elements just involves packing the contents of the hash table into a contiguous array, and since for a given input, the locations occupied in the hash table are the same in the linear probing tables, the times are roughly the same (within noise) between the two serial versions and the two parallel version. On a single thread, the serial versions are cheaper since they do not use a prefix sum.

Overall, linearHash-D and linearHash-ND are faster than cuckooHash, since cuckooHash involves more cache misses on average (it has to check two random locations). Elements is also slower for cuckooHash because each hash table entry includes a lock, which increases the memory footprint. For random integer keys, our linear probing hash tables are 2.3–4.1× faster than chainedHash and chainedHash-CR, as chained hashing incurs more cache misses. As expected, in parallel chainedHash performs very poorly under the sequences with many duplicates (trigramSeq, trigramSeq-pairInt, exptSeq and exptSeq-pairInt) due to high lock contention, while chainedHash-CR performs better.

---

[1]The source code for hopscotch hashing that we obtained online sometimes does not work correctly on our Intel machine (it was originally designed for a Sun UltraSPARC machine), so we do not use it in our applications.

(a)

Insert	randomSeq-int (1)	(40h)	randomSeq-pairInt (1)	(40h)	trigramSeq (1)	(40h)	trigramSeq-pairInt (1)	(40h)	exptSeq-int (1)	(40h)	exptSeq-pairInt (1)	(40h)
serialHash-HI	3.94	–	4.76	–	5.42	–	8.58	–	3.01	–	3.58	–
serialHash-HD	3.89	–	4.43	–	4.99	–	7.71	–	2.91	–	3.04	–
linearHash-D	4.53	0.171	5.45	0.216	5.53	0.115	8.66	0.204	3.08	0.119	3.71	0.141
linearHash-ND	4.52	0.17	4.77	0.213	5.02	0.108	8.2	0.174	2.96	0.109	3.12	0.119
cuckooHash	7.91	0.364	14.0	0.43	8.3	0.177	12.0	0.242	4.7	0.184	7.23	0.208
chainedHash	13.3	0.774	15.3	0.784	9.54	9.78	14.0	18.4	7.9	2.57	8.48	5.25
chainedHash-CR	14.4	0.708	16.8	0.71	9.1	0.324	13.7	0.438	7.19	0.35	7.56	0.401
hopscotchHash	9.19	0.349	9.21	0.363	7.04	1.54	9.63	2.36	6.15	1.97	6.0	2.02
hopscotchHash-PC	9.18	0.345	9.21	0.365	7.03	1.55	9.59	2.45	6.16	1.94	5.99	2.09

(b)

Find Random	randomSeq-int (1)	(40h)	randomSeq-pairInt (1)	(40h)	trigramSeq (1)	(40h)	trigramSeq-pairInt (1)	(40h)	exptSeq-int (1)	(40h)	exptSeq-pairInt (1)	(40h)
serialHash-HI	3.97	–	4.17	–	6.11	–	10.9	–	3.38	–	3.12	–
serialHash-HD	4.03	–	4.36	–	5.95	–	9.42	–	2.77	–	2.91	–
linearHash-D	4.23	0.114	4.19	0.149	6.17	0.12	10.6	0.219	3.16	0.069	3.11	0.07
linearHash-ND	4.02	0.119	4.35	0.144	5.89	0.117	10.1	0.19	2.79	0.067	2.91	0.078
cuckooHash	6.64	0.21	8.13	0.255	7.7	0.174	12.4	0.24	5.1	0.127	6.1	0.14
chainedHash	9.04	0.356	9.06	0.3	9.84	0.247	15.0	0.364	5.0	0.189	6.01	0.17
chainedHash-CR	9.06	0.359	9.05	0.301	9.74	0.245	15.0	0.365	5.9	0.188	5.99	0.168
hopscotchHash	5.2	0.173	5.02	0.169	6.8	0.167	10.2	0.236	3.51	0.094	3.49	0.091
hopscotchHash-PC	4.76	0.151	4.72	0.15	6.84	0.167	9.7	0.241	3.42	0.088	3.43	0.088

(c)

Find Inserted	randomSeq-int (1)	(40h)	randomSeq-pairInt (1)	(40h)	trigramSeq (1)	(40h)	trigramSeq-pairInt (1)	(40h)	exptSeq-int (1)	(40h)	exptSeq-pairInt (1)	(40h)
serialHash-HI	3.36	–	3.59	–	5.78	–	10.3	–	2.8	–	2.78	–
serialHash-HD	3.22	–	3.45	–	5.6	–	8.66	–	2.48	–	2.62	–
linearHash-D	3.36	0.109	3.6	0.142	5.73	0.114	9.94	0.204	2.6	0.067	2.6	0.068
linearHash-ND	3.22	0.106	3.44	0.125	5.5	0.11	9.55	0.195	2.48	0.064	2.61	0.073
cuckooHash	6.03	0.205	7.34	0.228	7.88	0.165	11.6	0.222	4.66	0.12	5.59	0.13
chainedHash	7.83	0.403	7.91	0.327	9.47	0.253	14.5	0.367	5.68	0.214	5.73	0.191
chainedHash-CR	7.87	0.406	7.89	0.327	9.36	0.249	14.5	0.366	5.69	0.213	5.7	0.188
hopscotchHash	4.67	0.168	4.67	0.166	6.44	0.157	9.31	0.22	3.22	0.09	3.22	0.09
hopscotchHash-PC	4.45	0.154	4.46	0.15	6.48	0.157	9.25	0.24	3.14	0.083	3.16	0.084

(d)

Delete Random	randomSeq-int (1)	(40h)	randomSeq-pairInt (1)	(40h)	trigramSeq (1)	(40h)	trigramSeq-pairInt (1)	(40h)	exptSeq-int (1)	(40h)	exptSeq-pairInt (1)	(40h)
serialHash-HI	4.89	–	5.8	–	3.69	–	4.17	–	2.82	–	3.13	–
serialHash-HD	4.87	–	5.85	–	3.09	–	3.77	–	2.83	–	3.14	–
linearHash-D	5.84	0.211	7.27	0.229	3.79	0.071	4.6	0.109	2.95	0.0968	3.7	0.099
linearHash-ND	5.9	0.213	7.43	0.235	3.85	0.071	4.64	0.109	3.02	0.0936	3.76	0.107
cuckooHash	6.16	0.21	7.16	0.266	5.57	0.15	8.01	0.166	4.25	0.109	4.69	0.142
chainedHash	16.2	0.63	16.4	0.597	4.79	2.38	6.02	2.7	7.16	2.79	7.28	7.01
chainedHash-CR	15.0	0.571	14.9	0.512	4.33	0.11	5.19	0.137	6.04	0.204	6.03	0.358
hopscotchHash	7.19	0.302	7.1	0.316	4.16	1.32	4.89	1.29	4.36	1.32	4.31	1.25
hopscotchHash-PC	7.07	0.301	7.06	0.32	4.15	1.33	4.95	1.34	4.36	1.31	4.28	1.24

(e)

Delete Inserted	randomSeq-int (1)	(40h)	randomSeq-pairInt (1)	(40h)	trigramSeq (1)	(40h)	trigramSeq-pairInt (1)	(40h)	exptSeq-int (1)	(40h)	exptSeq-pairInt (1)	(40h)
serialHash-HI	5.05	–	6.1	–	3.51	–	4.36	–	3.11	–	3.5	–
serialHash-HD	5.15	–	6.37	–	3.48	–	4.01	–	3.13	–	3.5	–
linearHash-D	6.13	0.24	7.98	0.264	3.73	0.068	4.59	0.102	3.33	0.115	4.18	0.126
linearHash-ND	6.36	0.242	8.38	0.269	3.8	0.07	4.34	0.102	3.35	0.11	4.23	0.119
cuckooHash	6.16	0.217	7.41	0.272	5.74	0.143	7.72	0.16	4.41	0.114	4.99	0.147
chainedHash	15.7	0.737	16.6	0.69	4.22	2.2	5.15	2.65	6.8	2.59	6.92	4.58
chainedHash-CR	14.9	0.714	14.9	0.624	3.77	0.126	4.62	0.153	5.64	0.372	5.65	0.45
hopscotchHash	7.2	0.33	7.8	0.343	3.96	1.32	4.89	1.28	4.69	1.38	4.54	1.29
hopscotchHash-PC	7.06	0.319	7.75	0.347	3.93	1.31	4.85	1.36	4.68	1.38	4.52	1.27

(f)

Elements	randomSeq-int (1)	(40h)	randomSeq-pairInt (1)	(40h)	trigramSeq (1)	(40h)	trigramSeq-pairInt (1)	(40h)	exptSeq-int (1)	(40h)	exptSeq-pairInt (1)	(40h)
serialHash-HI	0.974	–	1.1	–	0.758	–	0.753	–	0.603	–	0.821	–
serialHash-HD	0.986	–	1.08	–	0.759	–	0.761	–	0.554	–	0.814	–
linearHash-D	1.55	0.0511	2.25	0.0875	1.41	0.0575	1.43	0.056	1.05	0.0468	1.7	0.0514
linearHash-ND	1.55	0.0504	2.21	0.0857	1.42	0.0576	1.46	0.0554	1.06	0.0477	1.69	0.0794
cuckooHash	1.91	0.0791	2.54	0.115	2.45	0.0856	2.4	0.0866	1.64	0.0733	2.23	0.101
chainedHash	6.3	0.159	6.47	0.132	1.96	0.0782	1.97	0.0789	3.36	0.0934	3.38	0.0963
chainedHash-CR	6.33	0.165	6.44	0.131	1.97	0.0784	1.96	0.0785	3.38	0.091	3.37	0.0938
hopscotchHash	2.25	0.114	2.7	0.15	2.1	0.228	2.16	0.275	2.14	0.103	2.6	0.127
hopscotchHash-PC	2.26	0.112	2.73	0.147	2.09	0.229	2.16	0.274	2.14	0.1	2.61	0.128

Table 1. Times (seconds) for hash table operations with $n = 10^8$. (40h) indicates 40 cores with hyper-threading, and (1) indicates one thread.

Compared to hopscotch hashing, which is the fastest concurrent open addressing hash table that we are aware of, both of our phase-concurrent versions of linear probing are faster. For random integer keys, the deterministic version is about $2\times$ faster than hopscotch hashing for inserts, and $1.3\times$ faster for finds and deletes. For elements, we are also faster because we store less information per hash table entry. Hopscotch hashing does not get good speedup for insertions and deletions for the sequences with many repeats (i.e. the trigram and exponential sequences) due to lock contention. Compared to cuckooHash, on the lower-contention random integer sequence, hopscotch hashing is faster for finds and inserts but slower for deletes and elements (it stores more data).

Figures 4(a) and 4(b) show the speedup of linearHash-D relative to serialHash-HI on varying number of threads on randomSeq-int and trigramSeq-pairInt, respectively. We use a hash table of size

2^{28} and applied 10^8 operations of each type. We see that all of the operations get good speedup as we increase the number of threads.

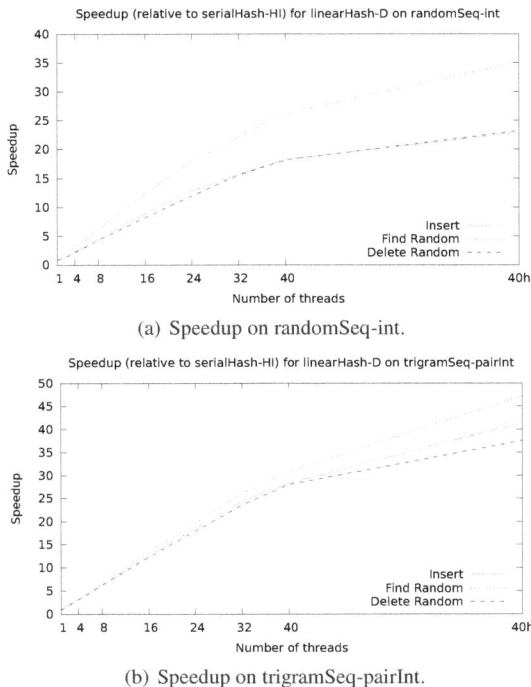

(a) Speedup on randomSeq-int.

(b) Speedup on trigramSeq-pairInt.

Figure 4. Speedup relative to serialHash-HI for linearHash-D versus number of threads. (40h) indicates 80 hyper-threads.

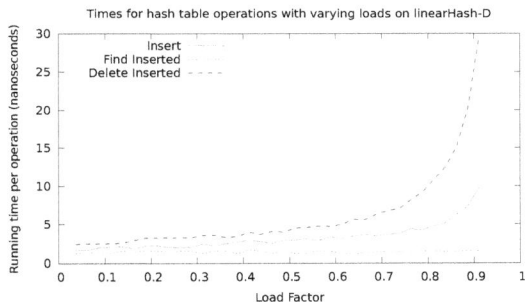

Figure 5. Times (nanoseconds) per operation with varying loads for linearHash-D on 40 cores (with hyper-threading). Values on the x-axis indicate the load factor (fraction of the table that is full).

Figure 5 shows the per operation running times on linearHash-D with varying loads. For this experiment, we used a hash table of size 2^{27}, and the table is first filled to the specified load before timing the operations. We note that inserts and deletes become more expensive as load increases, with a rapid increase as the load approaches 1.

We also compare the performance of hash table inserts to doing random writes (times for 10^8 writes are shown in Table 2). For a uniformly random sequence (randomSeq-int), parallel insertion into the deterministic hash table with a load of $1/3$ is $1.3\times$ slower than parallel random writes. We also compare with a conditional random write, which only writes to the location if it is empty, and the parallel running time is about the same as for random writes.

Very recently, Li et al. [21] describe a concurrent cuckoo hash table that achieves up to 40 million inserts per second for filling up a hash table to 95% load using 16 cores and integer key-value pairs, where the integers are 8 bytes each. On 16 cores, our linearHash-

Memory Operation	(1)	(40h)
Random write	1.62	0.129
Conditional random write	1.82	0.131
Hash table insertion	4.53	0.171

Table 2. Times (seconds) for 10^8 random writes (scatter)

ND performs 75 million inserts per second and linearHash-D performs 65 million inserts per second filling the table up to 95% load and using integer key-value pairs with 8-byte integers. As the performance of linear probing degrades significantly at high loads, for smaller loads we are faster than their hash table by a larger factor. However, the hash table of Li et al. is fully-concurrent, and optimizations can probably be made for a phase-concurrent setting.

Applications. For the applications, we compare implementations using different versions of the hash tables. For the open addressing hash tables, a larger table size decreases the load and usually leads to faster insertions, deletions and finds, but our algorithms require either returning the elements of the hash table or mapping over the elements, which takes time proportional to the size of the hash table. Due to this trade-off, we chose table sizes which gave the best overall performance per application. For chained hashing, we only present the times for chainedHash-CR, as we tried both chainedHash and chainedHash-CR and found that the timings were within 5% of each other as the inputs do not exhibit high contention. We did not use hopscotch hashing in our applications as the implementation we obtained did not always work correctly (see Footnote 2).

For remove duplicates, we use the same input distributions as in the previous experiments ($n = 10^8$), though we only report a subset of them due to space constraints. Removing duplicates involves a phase of insertions, which is more efficient with a larger table in open addressing, and a call to ELEMENTS(), which is more efficient with a smaller table in open addressing. We found that setting the table size to 2^{27} for the open addressing hash tables gave the best overall performance. The times for using linearHash-D, linearHash-ND, cuckooHash and chainedHash to remove duplicates are shown in Table 3. We see that our deterministic version of linear probing is 7–23% slower than our non-deterministic version on the key-value inputs with many duplicates because the deterministic version may perform a swap on duplicate keys. Both linear probing tables outperform the cuckoo and chained hash tables.

Remove Duplicates	randomSeq-int		trigramSeq-pairInt		exptSeq-int	
	(1)	(40h)	(1)	(40h)	(1)	(40h)
linearHash-D	6.36	0.212	10.4	0.242	3.72	0.139
linearHash-ND	6.33	0.212	9.64	0.213	3.63	0.116
cuckooHash	11.0	0.417	12.9	0.3	5.76	0.185
chainedHash-CR	19.9	1.32	15.6	0.586	9.67	0.541

Table 3. Times (seconds) for Remove Duplicates

For Delaunay refinement, we use as input the Delaunay triangulation of the 2D-cube and 2D-kuzmin geometry data from the PBBS [30], each of which contain 5 million points. The times for the hash table portion of one iteration of Delaunay refinement, which involves a call to ELEMENTS() and hash table insertions, are shown in Table 4. For the open addressing hash tables, we use a table size of twice the number of bad triangles rounded up to the nearest power of 2. LinearHash-D performs slightly slower than linearHash-ND, but allows for a deterministic implementation of Delaunay refinement. Both of our linear probing hash tables outperform the cuckoo hash table and chained hash tables for this application.

For suffix trees, we use three real-world texts (from http://people.unipmn.it/manzini/lightweight/corpus/): *etext99* (105 MB) and *rctail96* (115 MB) are taken from real English texts, and *sprot34.dat* (110 MB) is taken from a protein sequence. We measure the times for the portion of the code which

Delaunay Refinement	2DinCube		2Dkuzmin	
	(1)	(40h)	(1)	(40h)
linearHash-D	1.01	0.033	0.986	0.033
linearHash-ND	0.95	0.031	0.956	0.032
cuckooHash	1.62	0.051	1.56	0.054
chainedHash-CR	1.89	0.079	1.95	0.099

Table 4. Times (seconds) for Delaunay Refinement

inserts the nodes into the suffix tree (represented with a hash table), and also the times for searching one million random strings in the suffix tree (which uses hash table finds). For the searches, we use strings with lengths distributed uniformly between 1 and 50. Half of the search strings are random sub-strings of the text, which should all be found, and the other half are random strings, most of which will not be found. For the open addressing hash tables, we use a size of twice the number of nodes in the suffix tree rounded up to the nearest power of 2. The times are shown in Table 5. Again our deterministic linear probing hash table is only slightly slower than our non-deterministic one, and both of them outperform the cuckoo hash table and chained hash tables.

(a) Suffix Tree Insert (Size)	etext99 (105 MB)		rctial96 (115 MB)		sprot34.dat (110 MB)	
	(1)	(40h)	(1)	(40h)	(1)	(40h)
linearHash-D	4.84	0.12	4.96	0.117	4.77	0.115
linearHash-ND	4.6	0.114	4.74	0.112	4.57	0.109
cuckooHash	9.11	0.184	8.85	0.177	8.6	0.172
chainedHash-CR	7.72	0.256	7.65	0.238	7.39	0.235

(b) Suffix Tree Search	etext99		rctial96		sprot34.dat	
	(1)	(40h)	(1)	(40h)	(1)	(40h)
linearHash-D	1.08	0.023	0.728	0.015	0.803	0.017
linearHash-ND	1.07	0.023	0.713	0.015	0.787	0.017
cuckooHash	1.22	0.026	0.826	0.017	0.911	0.019
chainedHash-CR	1.35	0.03	0.91	0.02	1.01	0.023

Table 5. Times (seconds) for Suffix Tree operations

For edge contraction, breadth-first search and spanning forest, we use use three undirected graphs from PBBS. *3D-grid* is a grid graph in 3-dimensional space where every vertex has six edges, each connecting it to its 2 neighbors in each dimension. It has a total of 10^7 vertices and 3×10^7 edges. *random* is a random graph where every vertex has five edges to neighbors chosen randomly. It has a total of 10^7 vertices and 5×10^7 edges. The *rMat* graph [7] has a power-law degree distribution. It has a total of 2^{24} vertices and 5×10^7 edges.

We time one round of edge contraction when used as a part of a graph separator program. A maximal matching is first computed on the input graph to generate the vertex relabelings (not timed) and then edges with their relabeled endpoints are inserted into a hash table if the endpoints are different (timed). Duplicate edges between the same vertices after relabeling have their weights added together using a fetch-and-add. Since in linearHash-D, the edges may shift around during insertions, it requires using compare-and-swap on the entire edge. On the other hand, in linearHash-ND, once an element is inserted it no longer moves, so when encountering duplicate edges, it only needs to add the weight of the duplicate edge to the inserted edge and can use the faster `xadd` atomic hardware primitive to do this. The linear probing hash table sizes are set to $4/3$ times the number of edges, rounded up to the nearest power of 2. The times are shown in Table 6. Our deterministic version of linear probing is about 15% slower than the non-deterministic version, but guarantees a a deterministic ordering of the edges and hence a deterministic graph partition when used in a graph partitioning algorithm. Again, both of our linear probing hash tables outperform cuckoo hashing and chained hashing.

For each iteration of BFS, we use a hash table with size equal to the sum of the degrees of the frontier vertices rounded up to the nearest power of 2 for linear probing and twice that size for

Edge Contraction	3D-grid		random		rMat	
	(1)	(40h)	(1)	(40h)	(1)	(40h)
linearHash-D	6.03	0.154	10.9	0.265	10.8	0.272
linearHash-ND	5.4	0.136	9.09	0.229	9.18	0.235
cuckooHash	9.31	0.269	16.8	0.447	16.7	0.455
chainedHash-CR	11.6	0.55	20.1	0.907	20.0	0.917

Table 6. Times (seconds) for Edge Contraction

cuckoo hashing. Table 7 gives the running times for various BFS implementations where *serial* is the serial implementation, *array* is the implementation which uses a temporary array to compute new frontiers as described in Section 5. LinearHash-D is slightly slower than linearHash-ND, and both linear probing tables outperform cuckooHash and chainedHash-CR. In parallel, the deterministic hash table-based BFS is 16–35% slower than the array-based BFS. On a single thread, linearHash-D is faster on two of the inputs, however it does not get as good speedup. We observed that in parallel, the linear probing hash table-based BFS implementations spend 70-80% of the time performing hash table insertions, and sequentially they spend 80-90% of the time on insertions.

Breadth-First Search	3D-grid		random		rMat	
	(1)	(40h)	(1)	(40h)	(1)	(40h)
serial	2.3	–	2.89	–	3.33	–
array	3.57	0.271	4.89	0.169	6.81	0.225
linearHash-D	3.2	0.367	5.44	0.211	6.25	0.262
linearHash-ND	3.21	0.362	5.43	0.204	6.24	0.256
cuckooHash	4.56	0.454	7.3	0.292	9.1	0.373
chainedHash-CR	5.08	1.14	8.11	0.343	9.78	0.439

Table 7. Times (seconds) for Breadth-First Search

For spanning forest, we compare versions using hash tables with a serial version and an array-based version. For the versions using open addressing tables, we use a table of size twice the number of vertices rounded up to the nearest power of 2. The timings are shown in Table 8. LinearHash-D and linearHash-ND perform similarly, and they both outperform the cuckoo and chained hash tables. The deterministic hash table-based version is 14–26% slower than the array-based version, but avoids vertex relabeling when the vertex IDs are integers from a large range or are not integers.

Spanning Forest	3D-grid		random		rMat	
	(1)	(40h)	(1)	(40h)	(1)	(40h)
serial	1.42	–	1.87	–	2.35	–
array	3.54	0.186	4.68	0.226	6.13	0.289
linearHash-D	4.73	0.212	5.87	0.286	7.31	0.346
linearHash-ND	4.8	0.215	5.86	0.282	7.36	0.344
cuckooHash	5.86	0.251	7.08	0.341	9.08	0.387
chainedHash-CR	6.04	0.408	7.46	0.544	9.73	0.662

Table 8. Times (seconds) for Spanning Forest

For BFS and spanning forest, our experiments show that hash tables can replace directly addressing memory, while incurring only a small performance penalty.

7. CONCLUSION

We have described a phase-concurrent deterministic hash table based on linear probing and proved its correctness. We have shown experimentally that the performance of various operations on the deterministic hash table is competitive with those of a phase-concurrent history-dependent one based on linear probing, and achieves good speedup. Our deterministic hash table outperforms the best existing concurrent hash tables. We have described six applications which use phase-concurrent hash tables that we are aware of. We show that using our deterministic hash table within these applications gives performance that is competitive with or only slightly slower than using our non-deterministic linear probing hash table, and is faster than using the existing concurrent tables. Future work includes implementing automatic resizing in our hash table and exploring ways to automatically separate operations into phases efficiently, e.g. by using room synchronizations [2].

Acknowledgments

This work is supported by the National Science Foundation under grant number CCF-1314590, the Intel Labs Academic Research Office for the Parallel Algorithms for Non-Numeric Computing Program, the Intel Science and Technology Center for Cloud Computing (ISTC-CC) and a Facebook Graduate Fellowship. We thank Kristy Gardner and Phillip Gibbons for useful discussions.

References

[1] D. A. Alcantara, A. Sharf, F. Abbasinejad, S. Sengupta, M. Mitzenmacher, J. D. Owens, and N. Amenta. Real-time parallel hashing on the GPU. *ACM Trans. Graph.*, 28(5), 2009.

[2] G. E. Blelloch, P. Cheng, and P. B. Gibbons. Scalable room synchronizations. *Theory Comput. Syst.*, 36(5):397–430, 2003.

[3] G. E. Blelloch, J. T. Fineman, P. B. Gibbons, and J. Shun. Internally deterministic algorithms can be fast. In *Proceedings of Principles and Practice of Parallel Programming*, pages 181–192, 2012.

[4] G. E. Blelloch and D. Golovin. Strongly history-independent hashing with applications. In *IEEE Symposium on Foundations of Computer Science*, pages 272–282, 2007.

[5] R. D. Blumofe and C. E. Leiserson. Scheduling multithreaded computations by work stealing. *J. ACM*, 46(5):720–748, Sept. 1999.

[6] R. L. Bocchino, V. S. Adve, S. V. Adve, and M. Snir. Parallel programming must be deterministic by default. In *Usenix HotPar*, 2009.

[7] D. Chakrabarti, Y. Zhan, and C. Faloutsos. R-MAT: A recursive model for graph mining. In *SIAM International Conference on Data Mining*, pages 442–446, 2004.

[8] J. Devietti, B. Lucia, L. Ceze, and M. Oskin. DMP: Deterministic shared memory multiprocessing. In *Architectural Support for Programming Languages and Operating Systems*, pages 85–96, 2009.

[9] C. S. Ellis. Concurrency in linear hashing. *ACM Trans. Database Syst.*, 12(2):195–217, 1987.

[10] B. Fan, D. G. Andersen, and M. Kaminsky. MemC3: compact and concurrent memcache with dumber caching and smarter hashing. In *Proceedings of the 10th USENIX Conference on Networked Systems Design and Implementation*, pages 371–384, 2013.

[11] H. Gao, J. F. Groote, and W. H. Hesselink. Lock-free dynamic hash tables with open addressing. *Distributed Computing*, 18(1):21–42, 2005.

[12] M. Greenwald. Two-handed emulation: how to build non-blocking implementations of complex data-structures using DCAS. In *Principles of Distributed Computing*, pages 260–269, 2002.

[13] J. D. Hartline, E. S. Hong, A. E. Mohr, W. R. Pentney, and E. Rocke. Characterizing history independent data structures. *Algorithmica*, pages 57–74, 2005.

[14] M. Herlihy and N. Shavit. *The Art of Multiprocessor Programming*. Morgan Kaufmann, 2012.

[15] M. Herlihy, N. Shavit, and M. Tzafrir. Hopscotch hashing. In *International Symposium on Distributed Computing*, pages 350–364, 2008.

[16] M. Hsu and W.-P. Yang. Concurrent operations in extendible hashing. In *Proceedings of Very Large Data Bases*, pages 241–247, 1986.

[17] G. Karypis and V. Kumar. A fast and high quality multilevel scheme for partitioning irregular graphs. *SIAM J. Sci. Comput.*, 20(1):359–392, 1998.

[18] E. Kim and M.-S. Kim. Performance analysis of cache-conscious hashing techniques for multi-core CPUs. *International Journal of Control and Automation*, 6(2):121–134, Apr. 2013.

[19] V. Kumar. Concurrent operations on extendible hashing and its performance. *Commun. ACM*, 33(6):681–694, 1990.

[20] D. Lea. Hash table util.concurrent.concurrenthashmap in java.util.concurrent the Java Concurrency Package.

[21] X. Li, D. G. Anderson, M. Kaminsky, and M. J. Freedman. Algorithmic improvements for fast concurrent cuckoo hashing. In *EuroSys*, 2014.

[22] D. R. Martin and R. C. Davis. A scalable non-blocking concurrent hash table implementation with incremental rehashing. Unpublished manuscript, 1997.

[23] M. M. Michael. High performance dynamic lock-free hash tables and list-based sets. In *Symposium on Parallelism in Algorithms and Architectures*, pages 73–82, 2002.

[24] M. Naor and V. Teague. Anti-persistence: history independent data structures. In *Symposium on Theory of Computing*, pages 492–501, 2001.

[25] M. Olszewski, J. Ansel, and S. Amarasinghe. Kendo: Efficient deterministic multithreading in software. In *Architectural Support for Programming Languages and Operating Systems*, pages 97–108, 2009.

[26] R. Pagh and F. F. Rodler. Cuckoo hashing. *J. Algorithms*, 51(2):122–144, 2004.

[27] C. Purcell and T. Harris. Non-blocking hashtables with open addressing. In *International Symposium on Distributed Computing*, pages 108–121, 2005.

[28] O. Shalev and N. Shavit. Split-ordered lists: Lock-free extensible hash tables. *J. ACM*, 53(3):379–405, 2006.

[29] J. Shun, G. E. Blelloch, J. T. Fineman, and P. B. Gibbons. Reducing contention through priority updates. In *Symposium on Parallelism in Algorithms and Architectures*, pages 152–163, 2013.

[30] J. Shun, G. E. Blelloch, J. T. Fineman, P. B. Gibbons, A. Kyrola, H. V. Simhadri, and K. Tangwongsan. Brief announcement: the Problem Based Benchmark Suite. In *Symposium on Parallelism in Algorithms and Architectures*, pages 68–70, 2012.

[31] J. Shun, L. Dhulipala, and G. E. Blelloch. A simple and practical linear-work parallel algorithm for connectivity. In *Symposium on Parallelism in Algorithms and Architectures*, 2014.

[32] G. L. Steele Jr. Making asynchronous parallelism safe for the world. In *ACM POPL*, pages 218–231, 1990.

[33] J. Triplett, P. E. McKenney, and J. Walpole. Resizable, scalable, concurrent hash tables via relativistic programming. In *Proceedings of the USENIX Annual Technical Conference*, 2011.

[34] S. van der Vegt. A concurrent bidirectional linear probing algorithm. In *15th Twente Student Conference on Information Technology*, 2011.

[35] S. van der Vegt and A. Laarman. A parallel compact hash table. In *Proceedings of the 7th International Conference on Mathematical and Engineering Methods in Computer Science*, 2011.

[36] W. E. Weihl. Commutativity-based concurrency control for abstract data types. *IEEE Trans. Computers*, 37(12):1488–1505, 1988.

Scheduling Selfish Jobs
on Multidimensional Parallel Machines

Leah Epstein
Department of Mathematics.
University of Haifa, Haifa, Israel.
lea@math.haifa.ac.il

Elena Kleiman[*]
Faculty of Industrial Engineering and
Management. The Technion, Haifa, Israel.
elena.kleiman@gmail.com

ABSTRACT

We study the multidimensional vector scheduling problem with selfish jobs, both in non-cooperative and in cooperative versions. We show existence of assignments that are Nash, strong Nash, weakly and strictly Pareto optimal Nash equilibria in these settings. We improve upon the previous bounds on the price of anarchy for the non-cooperative case, and find tight bounds for every number of machines and dimension. For the cooperative case we provide tight bounds on the strong prices of anarchy and stability, as well as tight bounds on weakly and strictly Pareto optimal prices of anarchy and stability, for every number of machines and dimension.

Categories and Subject Descriptors

K.6.0 [**Management of Computing and information Systems**]: [General–Economics]; F.2.2 [**Nonnumerical Algorithms and Problems**]: [Sequencing and scheduling, Algorithmic Game Theory]

Keywords

Scheduling games, parallel machines, multidimensional scheduling, price of anarchy

1. INTRODUCTION

1.1 Motivation and framework

In this paper we study the d-dimensional vector scheduling problem, that is a generalization of the well-known job scheduling problem [20, 18], where each job has d distinct resource requirements, and each machine has d corresponding resources, in a game-theoretical setting. Such problems are often referred to as 'vector assignment' problems, as each job can be viewed as a d-dimensional vector, where each coordinate is associated with the corresponding requirement.

[*]Also affiliated with Department of Mathematics, ORT Braude College of Engineering, Karmiel, Israel.

This requirement can be available memory, disk space, CPU power, network bandwidth, or any other quality a computing unit may possess.[1]

Multidimensionality plays an important role in capturing incomparable characteristics of the jobs that are to be scheduled. For example, the memory requirements and the bandwidth requirements of a job in a distributed computer environment are incomparable. Multidimensionality also allows to differentiate between the costs that may be associated with each of these requirements.

Multidimensional assignment problems of the kind that we consider in this paper appear in practice. For example, the Google ROADEF/EURO challenge 2011-2012[2] involved a set of machines with several resources, such as RAM and CPU, running processes which consume those resources. However, so far these problems have received relatively little attention in the literature (see e.g. [19, 24, 10, 8]). With the rapidly growing popularity and importance of large-scale distributed computer environments such as the Internet, and more recently data centers implementing Cloud Computing [31, 3], it becomes crucial to address various issues that are often encountered in such settings. Problems concerning efficient resource allocation for better resource utilization, and multidimensional job scheduling and packing in particular, are being two of the most significant problems in Cloud Computing. This fact has rekindled the interest of researchers in these classical optimization problems that has been studied since the early 70's. A game-theoretic framework is a natural choice for the purpose of studying such problems, as the users of these systems act selfishly, and often even in an uncoordinated manner. The importance of studying scheduling and packing problems under a game-theoretical framework is by now very well established and widely acknowledged (see e.g. [26, 11, 28, 1, 17, 7, 14]). We attempt to add to this body of knowledge by considering the multidimensional variant.

1.2 The model

We now define the multidimensional job scheduling problem. There are n jobs $J = \{1, 2, \ldots, n\}$, each with $d \geq 2$ components, that are to be assigned to a set of m parallel machines $M = \{M_1, \ldots, M_m\}$ (also called machines $1, 2, \ldots, m$), each with $d \geq 2$ identical resources. The multi-

---

[1]In an accompanying paper [15], we consider also the d-dimensional vector packing problem, that can be seen as a scheduling problem where resources are limited on each component. Even though the motivations for both versions are related, the problems are of different flavors.
[2]http://challenge.roadef.org/2012/en/index.php

dimensional job scheduling game, or simply, vector scheduling game VS is characterized by a tuple

$$VS = \langle N, (\mathcal{M}_k)_{k \in N}, (c_k)_{k \in N} \rangle \,,$$

where N is the set of players. Each selfish player $k \in N$ controls a single job and selects the machine to which it will be assigned. We associate each player with the job it wishes to run, that is, $N = J$. The set of strategies $\mathcal{M}_k$ for each job $k \in N$ is the set M of all machines. i.e. $\mathcal{M}_k = M$. Each job must be assigned to one machine only. The outcome of the game is an assignment

$$\mathcal{A} = (\mathcal{A}_k)_{k \in N} \in \times_{k \in N} M_k$$

of jobs to the machines, where $\mathcal{A}_k$ for each $1 \leq k \leq n$ is the index of the machine that job k chooses to run on. Let $\mathcal{S}$ denote the set of all possible assignments.

Let the vector of a job $k \in \{1, 2, \dots, n\}$ be denoted by

$$p_k = (p_k^1, \dots, p_k^d) \,,$$

where $p_k^i \geq 0$, $1 \leq i \leq d$ and $\sum_{i=1}^{d} p_k^i > 0$. The value p_k^i is the size or processing time of job k for the ith component. Let $P^i = \sum_{k=1}^{n} p_k^i$ be the total processing time for the ith component. For a fixed schedule $\mathcal{A}$, we let L_ℓ^i denote the load of the ith component for machine M_ℓ. $L_\ell^i = \sum_{k: \mathcal{A}_k = M_\ell} p_k^i$. The load of machine M_ℓ is defined to be the maximum load in any dimension observed by machine M_ℓ in this assignment, that is $L_\ell(\mathcal{A}) = \max_{1 \leq i \leq d} L_\ell^i$.

The cost function of job $k \in N$ is denoted by $c_k : \mathcal{S} \to \mathbb{R}$. The cost c_k^i charged from job k for running on machine M_ℓ in a given assignment $\mathcal{A}$ is defined to be the load of machine M_ℓ, that is $c_k(\ell, \mathcal{A}_{-k}) = L_\ell(\mathcal{A})$, where $\mathcal{A}_{-k} \in \mathcal{S}_{-k}$; here $\mathcal{S}_{-k} = \times_{j \in N \setminus \{k\}} \mathcal{S}_j$ denotes the actions of all players except for player k. Each selfish job is interesting in reducing its cost by moving to a less loaded machine, if possible, which will result in better QoS. Similarly, for $K \subseteq N$ we denote by $\mathcal{A}_{-K} \in \mathcal{S}_{-K}$ the set of strategies of players outside of K in a strategy profile $\mathcal{A}$, when $\mathcal{S}_{-K} = \times_{j \in N \setminus K} \mathcal{S}_j$ is the action space of all players except for players in K. The social cost of an assignment $\mathcal{A}$ is defined as the maximum load on any dimension of a machine, over all the machines, also called makespan, and denoted by

$$SC(\mathcal{A}) = \max_{1 \leq k \leq n} c_k(\mathcal{A}) \,.$$

The maximum is taken over the players rather than the machines, but these are equivalent as for a non-empty set of players, an empty machine will not achieve the maximum, and the cost of a machine is equal to the cost of any job assigned to it. This kind of cost corresponds to a coordination mechanism called the *makespan coordination mechanism* or *makespan policy* [23], where each machine runs all its jobs using time sharing (with the purpose of fairness), and thus all of them are completed at the machine completion time.

Next, we provide definitions of Nash equilibria, weakly and strictly Pareto optimal Nash equilibria, and strong Nash equilibria in the vector scheduling game. We use the notation given above. A schedule $\mathcal{A}$ is a (pure) Nash equilibrium (NE) if no job in $\mathcal{A}$ has an incentive to unilaterally move to a different machine, given that all other jobs keep their positions unchanged. We measure the inefficiency of the equilibria by the prices of anarchy [26] and stability [2], which were established as prevalent measures. They are defined as the worst-case ratios between the social cost of the worst/best

Nash equilibrium to the social cost of an optimal solution, which is denoted by OPT, or by $OPT(G)$ for a given game G. The set of NE schedules for a game G is denoted by $NE(G)$. Formally:

Definition 1. (price of anarchy and stability) The price of anarchy (POA) of the vector scheduling game VS is defined by

$$PoA(VS) = \sup_{G \in VS} \sup_{\mathcal{A} \in NE(G)} \frac{SC(\mathcal{A})}{OPT(G)}.$$

If instead we consider the best Nash equilibrium of every instance, this leads to the definition of the price of stability (POS):

$$PoS(VS) = \sup_{G \in VS} \inf_{\mathcal{A} \in NE(G)} \frac{SC(\mathcal{A})}{OPT(G)}.$$

In what follows we sometimes use $\mathcal{A}$ to denote $SC(\mathcal{A})$. We let POA(m, d) denote the POA for m machines and dimension d, POA(d) denotes $\sup_m$ POA(m, d). We will use the lower bound $OPT(G) \geq \frac{P^i}{m}$ for $1 \leq i \leq d$. Let

$$p_{\max} = \max_{1 \leq j \leq n, 1 \leq i \leq d} p_j^i \,.$$

We will also use $OPT(G) \geq p_{\max}$.

Stronger concepts of stable solutions were defined in order to separate the effect of selfishness from that of lack of coordination. A strong equilibrium (an SNE) [4, 30, 22, 1, 17] is a solution concept where not only a single job cannot benefit from changing its strategy but no non-empty subset of jobs can form a coalition, where a coalition means that a subset of jobs change their strategies simultaneously, all gaining from the change. Obviously, by this definition, an SNE is an NE. The grand coalition is defined to be a coalition composed of the entire set of jobs. A solution is called *weakly Pareto optimal* if there is no alternative solution to which the grand coalition can deviate simultaneously and every job benefits from it. A solution is called *strictly Pareto optimal* if there is not alternative solution to which the grand coalition can deviate simultaneously, such that at least one job benefits from it, and no job has a larger cost as a result. The last two concepts are borrowed from welfare economics. The two requirements, that a solution is both (strictly or weakly) Pareto optimal and an NE results in two additional kinds of NE, Strictly Pareto optimal NE (SPNE) and Weakly Pareto optimal NE (WPNE) [12, 9, 13, 5]. By these definitions, every WPNE is an NE, every SPNE is a WPNE, and every SNE is a WPNE.

Strictly Pareto optimal solutions are of particular interest in economics, as stated in a textbook, in a chapter by Luc: "The concept of Pareto optimality originated in the economics equilibrium and welfare theories at the beginning of the past century. The main idea of this concept is that society is enjoying a maximum ophelimity when no one can be made better off without making someone else worse off" [27]. Even though these concepts are stronger than NE, still for many problems a solution which is an SNE, an SPNE, or a WPNE is not necessarily socially optimal. We define the strong prices of anarchy (SPOA) and stability (SPOS) [1], as well as the weakly Pareto optimal and strictly Pareto optimal prices of anarchy WPPOA and SPPOA and stability WPPOS and SPPOS, analogously to the standard prices of anarchy and stability, applying them each time for the respective worst/best cost solution concept.

By definition, it is clear that SPOA $\leq$ WPPOA $\leq$ POA. As any strictly Pareto optimal NE is also a weakly Pareto optimal NE, it must be the case that WPPOA $\geq$ SPPOA. However, we can show that in the vector scheduling game there is no immediate relation between the SPPOA and the SPOA as there are strong Nash equilibria that are not strictly Pareto optimal, while there are strictly Pareto optimal Nash equilibria that are not strong equilibria. We let SPOA(m, d) denote the SPOA for m machines and dimension d, SPOA(d) denotes $\sup_m$ SPOA(m, d). We use analogous notation for the other inefficiency measures.

1.3 Related work and our contribution

The one-dimensional case, i.e. $d = 1$ was extensively studied in [26, 11, 28, 1, 17, 5, 13]. In our overview of the known results we will limit our discussion only to results concerning the setting of pure strategies, as in our model. We discuss identical machines, related machines, and unrelated machines. The results of [16] show that in all three models the POS is 1. For m identical machines, the POA is exactly $\frac{2m}{m+1}$ [18, 29]. Andelman at el. [1] proved that for m identical machines the SPOA is also equal to $\frac{2m}{m+1}$, and showed that the SPOS is equal to 1. For related machines the POA is $\Theta(\frac{\log m}{\log \log m})$ [25, 11, 26], while the SPOA is of a smaller order of growth [17]. In the model of unrelated machines the POA is unbounded [6], which holds already for two machines, but the SPOA equals m [1, 17]. Weakly Pareto optimal Nash equilibria in one-dimensional job scheduling games was considered in [5] by Aumann and Dombb. In particular, they showed that any NE assignment is necessarily weakly Pareto optimal for identical machines and related machines. This result was generalized in [13] for strictly Pareto optimal schedules, and from these two results it follows that for identical machines and related machines, the SPPOA and the WPPOA are equal to the POA. For unrelated machines, it is shown in [13] that the SPPOA is equal to m, while the WPPOA is 2 for $m = 2$ and infinite for larger values of m. The papers [1, 5, 21] imply that the WPPOS and SPPOS are equal to 1 for all these machine models. The case $d = 1$ (not studied here) is therefore completely covered in previous work.

The multidimensional problem that we consider in this paper was studied recently by Ye and Chen in [32], where they call it 'server load balancing game', but they addressed it only in the non-cooperative setting. In that paper they claim to show the existence of pure Nash equilibria for this game, but in fact their proof is inaccurate, as discussed in Section 2. They have also considered the prices of anarchy and stability for the game, and provided non-tight lower and upper bounds of d and $d + 1 - d/m$ on the former, where m is the number of machines, and claimed to show tight bound of 1 on the latter, which we show is in fact correct, but their claim is based on a wrong assumption.

Here, we study the multidimensional vector scheduling game, both in the non-cooperative version and in the cooperative version. First, we show existence of assignments that are Nash, strong Nash, weakly and strictly Pareto optimal Nash equilibria in these settings. For the non-cooperative case we improve the bounds from [32] on the price of anarchy, and find tight bounds for every number of machines and dimension. We also show that the price of stability of the game is 1 that is, for any instance of the game, among the optimal schedules there is a schedule that is an NE. For the cooperative case we provide tight bounds on

the strong prices of anarchy and stability, as well as tight bounds on weak and strict Pareto optimal prices of anarchy and stability, for every number of machines and dimension. In particular, we show that POA$(d) = d + 1$, while SPOA$(d) =$ SPPOA$(d) =$ WPPOA$(d) = 2$. Moreover, POA(m, d) can be much smaller than $d + 1$ for multiple values of m and d, while the other measures are equal to 2 for all values of m and d except for $m = d = 2$. An interesting property of POA(m, d) is that for a fixed value of $d \geq 2$, this function (of m) is not monotone.

2. EXISTENCE OF EQUILIBRIA

We will show that the measures POA and POS for the vector scheduling game are well defined, by showing the existence of a schedule that is an NE for every instance of the game. The strong stability measures that we consider for the vector scheduling game are well defined only if for every instance of the game there exists a schedule that admits SNE and a schedule that admits SPNE (which will imply the existence of a WPNE). For this reason, we first study the existence of these concepts for this game.

Definition 2. A vector $(l_1, l_2, \ldots, l_m)$ is lexicographically larger than $(l'_1, l'_2, \ldots, l'_m)$, if for some $i \geq 1$, $l_i > l'_i$ and $l_k = l'_k$ for all $k < i$.

CLAIM 1. *For any instance of the vector scheduling game, there exists an assignment that is a WPNE, a SNE, and a SPNE. Moreover, for the vector scheduling game,* POS $=$ WPPOS $=$ SPPOS $=$ SPOS $= 1$.

PROOF. The proof uses elements that are related to the proof of [1] for the one-dimensional case, and to [21], where the lexicographic improvement property is studied. For a given game with n jobs, and a schedule $\mathcal{A}$, we define a cost vector of length n that is induced by $\mathcal{A}$. This vector consists of the costs of the jobs, where the components are sorted in non-increasing order. Consider a schedule $\mathcal{A}$ with the following properties. This schedule has a (lexicographically) minimal cost vector. In particular, it is socially optimal (since the first component is equal to the makespan, and thus the makespan of $\mathcal{A}$ is minimal over all schedules). Note that even though the problem studied in [1] is the one-dimensional variant of the problem that we study, we do not use machine load vectors for the proof (see the comment given after the proof).

First, we show that if a schedule $\mathcal{A}_2$ results from the schedule $\mathcal{A}_1$ by letting a job j move from machine ℓ to machine ℓ' while reducing its cost, then the cost vector of $\mathcal{A}_2$ is (lexicographically) smaller than that of $\mathcal{A}_1$. This will show that $\mathcal{A}$ is an NE, and that the POS is equal to 1 (and will be used later). Let x be the load of ℓ in $\mathcal{A}_1$, let x' be the load of ℓ in $\mathcal{A}_2$, and let y be the load of ℓ' in $\mathcal{A}_2$. We have $y < x$ and $x' \leq x$, since j benefits from moving, and ℓ has a subset of its jobs (in $\mathcal{A}_2$ compared to $\mathcal{A}_1$). The components of the two cost vectors that are strictly larger than x are exactly the same. The number of components equal to x in the second vector is smaller by at least 1 in the cost vector of $\mathcal{A}_2$ compared to that of $\mathcal{A}_1$. Thus, the second vector is smaller (lexicographically).

Next, we claim that $\mathcal{A}$ is strictly Pareto optimal (and thus weakly Pareto optimal). This will also show that SPPOS $=$ WPPOS $= 1$. Once again we consider schedules $\mathcal{A}_1$ and $\mathcal{A}_2$, this time $\mathcal{A}_2$ results from $\mathcal{A}_1$ by letting the grand coalition change their strategies. We claim that the resulting cost vector is smaller (lexicographically) than the one of $\mathcal{A}_1$. A component of value a of the vector of $\mathcal{A}_1$ that is smaller than the corresponding component in the cost vector of $\mathcal{A}_2$ would imply that some job increased its cost, since the number of jobs of cost at least a has increased. If the two vectors are identical, then we have that every job has exactly the same cost (since costs of jobs cannot increase), while by definition, at least one job has a smaller cost in $\mathcal{A}_2$.

Finally, we claim that $\mathcal{A}$ is an SNE (and thus weakly Pareto optimal), and SPOS $= 1$. Here we assume that $\mathcal{A}'$ results from $\mathcal{A}$ by letting a coalition of minimum cardinality deviate, such that all members of the coalition benefit from the deviation. As shown above, the coalition has at least two jobs. The set of machines that receives at least one new job at a deviation of the coalition is exactly the set that loses jobs. Indeed, let there be a machine ℓ that some job j moves to, but no job moves from. This would contradict the schedule $\mathcal{A}$ being an NE. Now, let there be a machine that some job moves from, but no job moves to. In this case, the deviating coalition could benefit from the deviation even without including this job, which contradicts the minimality of the chosen coalition. In the process of deviation, the loads of machines not participating in the coalition did not change. Sort the cost vector for $\mathcal{A}$ such that for every class of equal components, the components corresponding to jobs that belong to the coalition appear after the components of the jobs that do not belong to the coalition.

Let i be the first component of the vector for $\mathcal{A}$ that corresponds to a job of the coalition, and let b be its value. No job of the coalition has cost above b before or after the deviation. Thus, the prefixes of the cost vectors containing components strictly larger than b are equal, and moreover, these vectors are equal up to component $i - 1$. The jobs corresponding to the remaining components will have costs strictly below b in $\mathcal{A}'$. This is true for jobs of the coalition, as their costs before the deviation were at most b, and every job of the coalition reduces its cost. It is true for any job that does not belong to the coalition and no job migrated to its machine, since its cost did not change, and finally, it is true even for a job whose cost increased by some jobs moving to its machine, as the resulting cost of jobs assigned to such a machine in $\mathcal{A}'$ is below b. We find that the ith component of the (sorted) cost vectors is smaller in the cost vector of $\mathcal{A}'$ while components $1, \ldots, i - 1$ are equal in the cost vectors of $\mathcal{A}'$ and $\mathcal{A}$. This contradicts the choice of $\mathcal{A}$. $\square$

The proof given in [32] to show that an NE exists for every instance of the game is inaccurate. A machine load vector of a schedule is a vector of length m, where each component is the load of a machine (recall that for machine ℓ this is the maximum value L_ℓ^i over the components i), and the components of the load vector are sorted in non-increasing order. Consider the following example with $m = d = 2$, and the two jobs $(2, 0)$ and $(0, 1)$. The (lexicographically) minimal machine load vector is $(2, 0)$, and it results from assigning both jobs to one machine. This schedule is not an NE, as the second job would benefit from moving to the other machine. The load vector that results from this deviation is $(2, 1)$. Thus, the machine load vector can increase (lexicographically) when a job moves to another machine and reduces its cost, in contrary to what [32] claim in their proof. As for the cost vectors, the cost vector of the first schedule is $(2, 2)$, while the cost vector of the alternative schedule is $(2, 1)$.

3. NON-COOPERATIVE SETTINGS

In this section we provide a full analysis of POA(m, d).

PROPOSITION 1. *For any fixed $m \geq 2$, POA(m, d) is a monotonically non-decreasing function of d.*

PROOF. We show that any game with m machines and dimension d can be modified into a game with m machines and dimension $d + 1$. Given the jobs and machines, add a new $(d + 1)$th component to each vector, where for the jobs this component has value zero. The makespan of any schedule remains unchanged, and any schedule that was an NE remains an NE schedule. $\square$

THEOREM 1. *For every $m, d \geq 2$, let $j(m, d) = \lceil \frac{m-1}{d} \rceil$, $\tilde{j}(m, d) = \lceil \frac{m}{d} \rceil$, and $k(m, d) = \lfloor \frac{m-2}{j(m,d)+1} \rfloor + 1$. We have*

$$\text{POA}(m, d) = F(m, d) =$$

$$\max \left\{ \frac{m}{\tilde{j}(m, d)}, k(m, d), \frac{m \cdot (k(m, d) + 1)}{(j(m, d) + 1)k(m, d) + 1} \right\} .$$

Additionally, POA$(d) = d + 1$.

PROOF. Before we give the analysis of POA(m, d), we consider the properties of $F(m, d)$. First, we note that the values $j(m, d), \tilde{j}(m, d), k(m, d) \geq 1$ are integers as $m \geq 2$, and moreover $j(m, d) \leq m - 1$, $\tilde{j}(m, d) \leq m$, and $k(m, d) \leq \frac{m}{2} < m$. The motivation for defining these values comes from the games that provide lower bounds. These games always have one of two possible simple structures (see also the motivation for the lower bounds below). Informally, it can happen that one machine has large load in one component, and still jobs would not benefit from moving to other machines that have a different or the same heavily loaded component. It is possible that all jobs will not move due to one component of that alternative machine, or that different components play this role for different jobs. The first case is more difficult in the sense that in the second case the alternative machine has more than one heavily loaded component, yet both cases are considered. In the proof, we detect a component i that is heavily loaded on all machines on average. However, an optimal solution must schedule the same jobs, and thus there is a limit to how loaded it can actually be. We use weights to detect such a component, where a weight will be given to every pair of a machine and a component, except for the machine that determines the social cost of the considered NE schedule. We will assume (by contradiction) that the makespan exceeds $k(m, d)$, and thus in each case we will either prove that it does not exceed $F(m, d)$ either using the first term in its definition, or using the third term. We will start with finding upper bounds on loads of components, and later we use them to obtain a bound on P^i as a function of the makespan, where i is selected to be a component whose total weight (over all machines for which it is defined) is large.

Consider the first term. This term never exceeds d, since $\tilde{j}(m, d) \geq \frac{m}{d}$, so $\frac{m}{\tilde{j}(m,d)} \leq d$. We also have $\frac{m}{\tilde{j}(m,d)} \leq m$. Next, we show that the second term never exceeds d. We have $j(m, d) \geq \frac{m-1}{d}$, so

$$j(m, d) + 1 \geq \frac{m + d - 1}{d} ,$$

and

$$\frac{m - 2}{j(m, d) + 1} \leq \frac{d(m - 2)}{m + d - 1} < d ,$$

since $d > 1$. Thus, since $k(m,d)$ is an integer, $k(m,d) - 1 \leq d - 1$ holds. Finally, consider the third term. We will show that it never exceeds $\min\{m, d+1\}$. Since

$$k(m,d) + 1 < j(m,d)k(m,d) + k(m,d) + 1 \ ,$$

the third term never exceeds m. Next, we show that it never exceeds $d+1$. By the above, $k(m,d) + 1 \leq d+1$ holds, thus it is left to show

$$m \leq (j(m,d) + 1)k(m,d) + 1. \tag{1}$$

Assume by contradiction that $m \geq (j(m,d) + 1)k(m,d) + 2$ holds (recall the all variables are integral). Then, $\frac{m-2}{j(m,d)+1} \geq k(m,d)$. However, by definition, $k(m,d) > \frac{m-2}{j(m,d)+1}$, which is a contradiction.

The analysis of $F(m,d)$ implies that we will in particular prove $\text{POA}(d) \leq d+1$, which was already shown by [32]. In what follows, we will prove the stronger property $\text{POA}(d) = d+1$, that is, our lower bound of $F(m,d)$ will imply $\text{POA}(d) \geq d+1$.

We start with the upper bound. Let m, d be fixed. We use $j = j(m,d)$, $\tilde{j} = \tilde{j}(m,d)$, $k = k(m,d)$, and $F = F(m,d)$. Consider a schedule $\mathcal{A}$ that is an NE schedule for a game G. We let L be the makespan and assume without loss of generality (by scaling and renaming components and machines, if necessary) that L is achieved for the first component and the first machine (i.e., $L_1^1 = L$), and that $OPT(G) = 1$. Due to the assumption $OPT(G) = 1$, we have $p_j^i \leq 1$ for all i, j. We will now show an additional property of F, that $F \geq 2$ must hold. We have

$$\tilde{j} = \lceil m/d \rceil \leq \frac{m+d-1}{d} \ ,$$

giving (using the first term in the definition of F)

$$F \geq \frac{m}{\tilde{j}} = \frac{m}{\lceil m/d \rceil} \geq \frac{md}{m+d-1} \geq 2 \ ,$$

which is equivalent to $md \geq 2m + 2d - 2$ or alternatively to $(m-2)(d-2) \geq 2$. The last inequality holds for $m \geq 4$ and $d \geq 3$, and also for $m \geq 3$ and $d \geq 4$. We are left with the case $m = 2$ (and $d \geq 2 = m$), the case $m = 3$, with $d = 2, 3$, and the case $m \geq 4$, $d = 2$. In the case $m \leq d$,

$$\tilde{j} = \left\lceil \frac{m}{d} \right\rceil = 1 \ ,$$

and therefore (using the first term in the definition of F) $F \geq \frac{m}{\tilde{j}} = m \geq 2$. This covers, in particular, the case $m = 2$, as in this case $d \geq m$ must hold, and the case $m = 3$, $d = 3$. If $m = 3$ and $d = 2$, then we have $\tilde{j} = 2$, $j = 1$, $k = 1$, and therefore using the third term in the definition of F, $F \geq \frac{3 \cdot 2}{2 \cdot 1 + 1} = 2$. In the case $m \geq 4$ and $d = 2$: if m is even, then $\tilde{j} = \frac{m}{2}$, and the first term in F is equal to 2. The remaining case is odd m, $m \geq 5$, $d = 2$. We have $j = \frac{m-1}{2}$. As $k = \lfloor \frac{m-2}{(m+1)/2} \rfloor + 1$, we get $k = 2$ (since $m + 1 \leq 2m - 4 < 2m + 2$). The third term in the definition of F is $\frac{3m}{m+2} > 2$ for $m > 4$.

If $L \leq 2$, we get $\mathcal{A}/OPT(G) = L \leq 2 \leq F$. Thus, we will assume that $L > 2$. Let s denote the number of jobs assigned to the first machine in $\mathcal{A}$. Since $L > 2$, and no job component exceeds 1, we find $s \geq 3$. We will also use $L - 1 > \frac{L}{2}$ in the proof. Without loss of generality, we let the jobs assigned to the first machine in $\mathcal{A}$ be denoted by $1, 2, \ldots, s$. Since $\mathcal{A}$ is an NE, for every $1 \leq y \leq s$, every

machine $\ell > 1$ has a component i such that

$$L_\ell^i + p_y^i \geq L \ ,$$

in which case we say that component i of machine ℓ is *bad* for y. A component i of machine ℓ is called bad if it is bad for some $1 \leq y \leq s$. Every machine $2 \leq \ell \leq m$ must have a bad component for every y such that $1 \leq y \leq s$, and in particular, it has at least one bad component. A machine is called a *singleton* if it has a single bad component. We give every pair of machine $\ell > 1$ and component i a weight $w_{i,\ell}$ as follows. If i is not a bad component of ℓ, then $w_{i,\ell} = 0$. If ℓ is a singleton with the bad component i, then $w_{i,\ell} = 2$, and if ℓ is not a singleton, but i is a bad component of ℓ, then $w_{i,\ell} = 1$. We let the weight of component i be $W_i = \sum_{\ell=2}^m w_{i,\ell}$. The weight of machine ℓ is $\sum_{i=1}^d w_{i,\ell}$. Since every machine $2 \leq \ell \leq m$ has at least one bad component, and moreover, it is either a singleton or has at least two bad components, we have $\sum_{i=1}^d w_{i,\ell} \geq 2$, and the total weight satisfies

$$\sum_{i=1}^d W_i = \sum_{i=1}^d \sum_{\ell=2}^m w_{i,\ell} = \sum_{\ell=2}^m \sum_{i=1}^d w_{i,\ell} \geq (m-1) \cdot 2 = 2m - 2 \ .$$

Let $m = 1 + (j-1)d + \alpha$, where $1 \leq \alpha \leq d$ by the definition of j.

We find that since

$$2(m-1) = 2((j-1)d + \alpha) \geq 2jd - 2d + 2 \ ,$$

we either have that $W_1 \geq 2j$ holds, or that $W_i \geq 2j - 1$ holds for at least one $i > 1$ (or both), since W_i is integral, and the sum of weights is at least $2jd - 2d + 2$ as otherwise we find

$$\sum_{i=1}^d W_i \leq (2j-1) + (d-1)(2j-2) = 2jd - 2d + 1 \ .$$

Moreover, if $\alpha = d$, then $2(m-1) = 2jd$, and we either have $W_1 \geq 2j$, or $W_i \geq 2j + 1$ for some $i > 1$ (or both). Obviously, if $L \leq k$, then $L \leq F$ and we are done. Thus, in what follows we assume $L > k$ and therefore $s \geq \lceil L \rceil \geq k+1$.

In the next claim we find lower bounds on loads of bad components. These bounds will be used to bound each P^i for some $1 \leq i \leq d$.

CLAIM 2. *If machine $\ell \geq 2$ is a singleton with the bad component i, then $L_\ell^i \geq \frac{s-1}{s}L$. If i' is a bad component of machine $\ell' \geq 2$, then $L_{\ell'}^{i'} \geq L - 1$.*

PROOF. Since no component of ℓ is bad except for i, we have

$$L_\ell^i + p_y^i \geq L$$

for $1 \leq y \leq s$. Taking the sum for $1 \leq y \leq s$ gives $sL_\ell^i + L_1^i \geq sL$. Since $L_1^i \leq L$, we get $sL_\ell^i \geq (s-1)L$. The second claim follows from the property that

$$L_{\ell'}^{i'} + p_y^{i'} \geq L$$

holds for some y, and that $p_y^{i'} \leq 1$ for all i', y. $\square$

In the next three claims, we find upper bounds on L, first in the case that W_1 is large, and afterwards in the case that W_i is large, for some $2 \leq i \leq d$.

CLAIM 3. *We have*

$$P^1 \geq L(1 + \frac{W_1}{2} \cdot \frac{s-1}{s}) \ .$$

PROOF. Let σ be the number of singleton machines whose bad component is 1. There are $W_1 - 2\sigma$ additional machines for which component 1 is bad (but each such machine has at least one other bad component). The load of component 1 for the first machine is L, and by using the previous claim,

$$P^1 \geq L + \sigma \frac{s-1}{s} L + (W_1 - 2\sigma)(L - 1) \ .$$

Using

$$L - 1 \geq \frac{L}{2} \geq \frac{s-1}{s} \cdot \frac{L}{2} \ ,$$

we get

$$P^1 \geq L + (\frac{s-1}{s} L)(\sigma + W_1/2 - \sigma) \ ,$$

proving the claim. $\square$

CLAIM 4. *If $W_1 \geq 2j$, then $L \leq F$.*

PROOF. Using

$$P^1 \leq m \cdot OPT(G) = m \ ,$$

in combination with previous claim we get

$$L \leq \frac{m}{1 + \frac{s-1}{s} W_1/2} \leq \frac{m}{1 + \frac{k}{k+1} W_1/2} \ ,$$

since the maximum value is obtained for the smallest value of s (which is $k + 1$). Rewriting and using the assumption $W_1 \geq 2j$ and the third term in the definition of F, we get

$$L \leq \frac{m(k+1)}{k+1+kW_1/2} \leq \frac{m(k+1)}{k+1+kj} = \frac{m(k+1)}{(j+1)k+1} \leq F \ .$$

$\square$

CLAIM 5. *If $\alpha < d$ and $W_i \geq 2j-1$ holds for some $i > 1$, then $L \leq F$. If $\alpha = d$ and $W_i \geq 2j+1$ holds for some $i > 1$, then $L \leq F$.*

PROOF. In order to find a lower bound on P^i (which will allow us to find an upper bound for L), first we define a process of moving jobs from machine 1 to machines for which component i is bad. Let λ denote the number of singletons whose bad component is i. If there exists a machine ℓ that is not a singleton but its component i is bad, then there must exist at least one job of machine 1 that moving it to machine ℓ increases component i to at least L. This job is moved to machine ℓ. This step is not applied for further non-singleton machines even if multiple such machines exist, and in such a case it is only applied on one arbitrary singleton machine. If no non-singleton machine exists, this step is not applied (thus, this step is either applied once or not applied at all). Next, jobs are moved from machine 1 to the singletons with the bad component i one by one, increasing the component i of each such machine (that a job is moved to it) to at least L (so that each machine receives at most one job). The process stops when either no such singletons remain or all jobs were moved.

Consider the case that no singletons remain. Recall that λ is the original number of singletons. We bound P^i (that obviously did not change during the process). There are now λ machines, each of load at least L for component i (originally these machines were singletons, and some of this load was previously the load of component i of machine 1). If the first step was skipped, then since the weight of a singleton is 2 (and given the lower bound on the total weight of component i), $\lambda \geq j$ if $\alpha < d$ and $\lambda \geq j + 1$ if $\alpha = d$. Thus, $m \geq P^i \geq jL$ if $\alpha < d$ and $P^i \geq (j+1)L$ if $\alpha = d$. If $\alpha < d$, then $j = \tilde{j}$, and otherwise $\tilde{j} = j + 1$. We get $L \leq \frac{m}{\tilde{j}} \leq F$ in both cases, and $L \leq F$. If the first step were applied, machine ℓ also has load of at least L for component i, and then there are now $\lambda + 1$ machines of load L each (for component i), and additionally, there are at least $W_i - 2\lambda - 1$ other machines for which component i is bad, where the load of component i is at least $L - 1 \geq \frac{L}{2}$ for each such machine, resulting in a total of at least

$$L(\lambda + 1 + W_i/2 - \lambda - 1/2) = L \cdot (W_i + 1)/2$$

for component i. If $\alpha < d$, we find $P^i \geq Lj$, and if $\alpha = d$, we find $P^i \geq L(j + 1)$. As before, we get $L \leq F$.

Consider the case that at least one singleton remains. If there were only singletons originally, then $\lambda \geq j$, the load of component i for s singletons is at least L, and it is at least $\frac{s-1}{s} L$ for any other singleton, thus,

$$\begin{aligned} m &\geq P^i \geq sL + (j - s)\frac{s-1}{s}L \\ &= L(1 + j\frac{s-1}{s}) \geq L(1 + jk/(k+1)) \ , \end{aligned}$$

since the minimum value is obtained for the smallest value of s, and we find

$$L \leq \frac{m(k+1)}{(j+1)k+1} \leq F \ .$$

Otherwise, one non-singleton machine, that is bad for component i, and $s - 1$ former singletons now have loads of at least L for component i, and moreover, the remaining machines that are bad for component i have loads of at least $\frac{s-1}{s}L$ (for singletons), and of at least $L - 1 \geq \frac{L}{2}$ (otherwise). By the condition of this case, $\lambda \geq s$. We will prove $P^i \geq L(1 + j(s - 1)/s)$ as in the previous case. There are s machines with i-th components with loads of at least L, $\lambda - s + 1$ machines with load of at least $(s-1)L/s$ in the i-th component, and at least $W_i - 2\lambda - 1$ machines with load at least $\frac{L}{2}$ in the i-th component. The total is at least

$$L(s + (s-1)(\lambda - s + 1)/s + (W_i - 2\lambda - 1)/2) =$$

$$L(3/2 - \lambda/s - 1/s + W_i/2) \ .$$

We show

$$1/2 - \lambda/s - 1/s + W_i/2 \geq j(s-1)/s \ .$$

We have $\lambda \leq (W_i - 1)/2$ and $j \leq (W_i + 1)/2$. Thus

$$j(s-1)/s + (\lambda + 1)/s$$

$$\leq (W_i + 1)(s-1)/(2s) + (W_i + 1)/(2s) = (W_i + 1)/2 \ ,$$

as required. $\square$

This completes the proof of the upper bound as the condition of at least one of the two last claims must hold.

We note that none of the three terms (in the definition of F) is redundant. Let $d = 7$, and consider the following three values of m: $m_1 = 28$, $m_2 = 68$, and $m_3 = 69$. For $z =$

$1, 2, 3$, let $j_z = j(m_z, 7)$, $\tilde{j}_z = \tilde{j}(m_z, 7)$, $k_z = k(m_z, 7)$. We find $j_1 = \tilde{j}_1 = 4$ and $j_2 = \tilde{j}_2 = j_3 = \tilde{j}_3 = 10$. Additionally, $k_1 = 6$, $k_2 = k_3 = 7$. For m_1, we have $\frac{m_1}{j_1} = 7$, $k_1 = 6$, and

$$\frac{m_1 \cdot (k_1 + 1)}{(j_1 + 1)k_1 + 1} \approx 6.32 .$$

For m_2, we have $\frac{m_2}{j_2} = 6.8$, $k_2 = 7$, and

$$\frac{m_2 \cdot (k_2 + 1)}{(j_2 + 1)k_2 + 1} \approx 6.974 .$$

For m_3, we have $\frac{m_3}{j_3} = 6.9$, $k_2 = 7$, and

$$\frac{m_3 \cdot (k_3 + 1)}{(j_3 + 1)k_3 + 1} \approx 7.077 .$$

Thus, we find that for $z = 1, 2, 3$, the zth term (in the definition of F) is the dominant one for m_z.

Next, we prove lower bounds. Let $m, d \geq 2$. There are two types of worst case instances. The first type is similar to the one given in [32]. In such schedules for every machine, there is one component that is loaded heavily, while other components are not loaded at all. In the other kind of instances, introduced here, there is additionally one machine where all components are loaded heavily (more than other machines), and the difference in the load compared to other machines is exactly such that a job cannot benefit from migrating.

CLAIM 6. *We have*

$$\text{POA}(m, d) \geq \frac{m}{\tilde{j}(m, d)} .$$

PROOF. We provide a game G and an NE schedule $\mathcal{A}$ showing the lower bound. Such a game is obtained similarly to the example in [32]. Let $1 \leq \beta \leq d$ be such that $m = \kappa d + \beta$ for an integer $\kappa \geq 0$, i.e., $\kappa = \tilde{j}(m, d) - 1$. Let $\alpha = \frac{1}{(\kappa + 1)^2}$. For $1 \leq i \leq \beta$, there are $m(\kappa + 1)^2$ jobs whose ith component is equal to α and the other components are zeroes (these are jobs of kind i). For $\beta + 1 \leq i \leq d$, there are $m\kappa(\kappa + 1)$ jobs whose ith component is equal to α and the other components are zeroes (these are jobs of kind i). An alternative solution assigns at most $(\kappa + 1)^2$ jobs of each kind to every machine ($(\kappa + 1)^2$ jobs of each one of the first β types, and $\kappa(\kappa + 1)$ jobs of each of the next $d - \beta$ types), and has makespan 1. A solution $\mathcal{A}$ is defined as follows. For $1 \leq i \leq \beta$, there are $\kappa + 1$ machines with $m(\kappa + 1)$ jobs of kind i, and for $\beta + 1 \leq i \leq d$, there are κ machines with $m(\kappa + 1)$ jobs of kind i. The makespan is $\frac{m}{\kappa + 1}$, and it is left to show that this is an NE schedule. The last property holds since all machines have equal loads, so no job can benefit from migrating. $\square$

CLAIM 7. *We have*

$$\text{POA}(m, d) \geq \max\{k(m, d), \frac{m \cdot (k(m, d) + 1)}{(j(m, d) + 1)k(m, d) + 1}\} ,$$

and $\text{POA}(d) = d + 1$.

PROOF. We provide a game G and an NE schedule $\mathcal{A}$ showing the lower bound. Let $k = k(m, d)$, $j = j(m, d)$, and $\tilde{j} = \tilde{j}(m, d)$. Let $1 \leq \beta \leq d$ be such that $m = 1 + \kappa d + \beta$ for an integer $\kappa \geq 0$ (i.e., $\kappa = j - 1$).

We define a game G as follows. Let $0 < \alpha \leq 1$ be a rational number where $\alpha = \alpha_p / \alpha_q$ ($0 < \alpha_p \leq \alpha_q$ (to be fixed later), and both numbers are integral), and let $2 \leq s \leq m$ be an

integer. A set of *large* jobs consists of s jobs for which all d components are equal to α. Let

$$\theta = \frac{(s - 1)\alpha}{N} ,$$

where

$$N = \alpha_p(s - 1)$$

(so $\theta = 1/\alpha_q$). For $1 \leq i \leq d$, there are jobs for which only the ith component is positive, and it is equal to θ. For $1 \leq i \leq \beta$ there are $(\kappa + 1)N$ such jobs, and for $\beta + 1 \leq i \leq d$, there are κN such jobs. Consider a schedule $\mathcal{A}$ where the first machine receives all the first s jobs. Furthermore, for $1 \leq i \leq \beta$, there are $\kappa + 1$ machines such that each one receives N jobs whose ith component is positive, and for $\beta + 1 \leq i \leq d$, there are κ machines such that each one receives N jobs whose ith component is positive. By the numbers of jobs of each type, all jobs are scheduled. We show that this schedule is an NE. The load of the first machine is $s\alpha$, and the load of any other machine is $(s - 1)\alpha$. A job that moves from the first machine will increase the load of the machine that it moves to by α, since all the components of such a job are equal to α. A job that moves from another machine cannot benefit from moving as no machine has a smaller load.

An alternative solution has $m - s$ machines, each with at most α_q jobs of each type of the last d types, and s machines, each with one job of the first type, and at most $\alpha_q - \alpha_p$ jobs of each of the last d types. We may allocate space for a larger number of jobs than we actually have. The loads of the first $m - s$ machines are at most $\alpha_q \theta = 1$, and the loads of the remaining s machines are at most

$$\alpha + (\alpha_q - \alpha_p)\theta = \frac{\alpha_p + (\alpha_q - \alpha_p)}{\alpha_q} = 1 .$$

Since there are types for which the number of such jobs is smaller, we will assign only the existing jobs, and have $OPT(G) \leq 1$. We will show that for the choice of α that we use, all jobs can be assigned. We will use the properties that we allocated sufficient space for

$$(m - s)\alpha_q + s(\alpha_q - \alpha_p) = m\alpha_q - s\alpha_p$$

jobs for each one of the last d types, while the number of jobs of each type never exceeds

$$(\kappa + 1)\alpha_p(s - 1) .$$

We find $\mathcal{A} = s\alpha$ while $OPT(G) \leq 1$, giving a ratio of $s\alpha$.

We use two values of α. The first choice is $\alpha = 1$ (and thus $\alpha_q = \alpha_p = 1$), which allows us to prove $\text{POA}(m, d) \geq k$. If $k = 1$, then $\text{POA}(m, d) \geq k$ is obvious, and therefore we only consider the case $2 \leq k \leq m - 1$. In this case we set $s = k$, and showing that there is sufficient space for all jobs in the optimal solution is equivalent to showing $m - k \geq j(k - 1)$, or equivalently, $k \leq \frac{m + j}{j + 1}$. By definition,

$$k \leq \frac{m - 2}{j + 1} + 1 = \frac{m + j - 1}{j + 1} ,$$

as required. This proves $\text{POA}(m, d) \geq k(m, d)$.

The second choice for α is $\frac{m}{(j + 1)k + 1}$ (and thus $\alpha_q = (j + 1)k + 1$ and $\alpha_p = m$, and by (1), $k \leq d$, $m \leq (j + 1)k + 1$ holds and thus $\alpha \leq 1$). In this case we set $s = k + 1$, and have $2 \leq s \leq m$. Showing that there is sufficient space for

114

all jobs in the optimal solution is equivalent to showing

$$m((j+1)k+1) - m(k+1) \geq jkm ,$$

which holds with equality. This proves

$$\text{POA}(m,d) \geq \frac{m(k+1)}{(j+1)k+1} .$$

It is left to show $\text{POA}(d) \geq d+1$. Consider now the values of m for which $\beta = d$, and such that $\kappa \geq d-1$. We show that in this case, $k = d$. We already showed $k \leq d$, and it is sufficient to show

$$\frac{(\kappa+1)d-1}{\kappa+2} \geq d-1 .$$

The last expression is equivalent to $d \leq \kappa+1$. We find

$$\text{POA}(m,d) \geq \frac{((\kappa+1)d+1)(d+1)}{(\kappa+2)d+1} ,$$

which tends to $d+1$ for large values of m (and κ). $\square$

This proves the theorem. $\square$

Note that for $d = 1$, using the formula of the theorem still gives the correct bound of $\frac{2m}{m+1}$ (resulting from the third term). The following corollary summarizes several interesting special cases. In particular, it shows that $\text{POA}(m,d)$ is not a monotone function of m for any fixed $d \geq 2$.

COROLLARY 1. *If $m \leq d$, $\text{POA}(m,d) = m$. If $m = d+1$, then*

$$\text{POA}(m,d) = \frac{d}{2} + 1 = \frac{m}{2} + \frac{1}{2}$$

for even d and

$$\text{POA}(m,d) = \frac{(d+1)(d+3)}{2(d+2)} = \frac{m(m+2)}{2(m+1)} = \frac{m}{2} + \frac{m}{2(m+1)}$$

for odd d. If $d+2 \leq m \leq 2d$, then $\text{POA}(m,d) = m/2$. In the case $d = 2$, for odd m we have

$$\text{POA}(m,2) = \max\{2, \frac{3m}{m+2}\} ,$$

and for even m we have

$$\text{POA}(m,2) = \max\{2, \frac{3m}{m+3}\} .$$

The function $\text{POA}(m,d)$ is not monotone as a function of m for any fixed $d \geq 2$.

PROOF. Given a pair $m,d \geq 2$, let $j = j(m,d)$, $\tilde{j} = \tilde{j}(m,d)$, $k = k(m,d)$. Consider first the case $m \leq d$. We have $\tilde{j} = j = 1$ and $k = \lfloor \frac{m}{2} \rfloor$. The first term in the function F is equal to m, the second term is $k \leq \frac{m}{2} < m$, and the third term is $\frac{m(k+1)}{2k+1} < m$, since $k \geq 1$.

Consider the case $m = d+1$. In this case $j = 1$ and $\tilde{j} = 2$. If d is even, then $k = d/2$, and we have $m/\tilde{j} = \frac{d+1}{2}$. The third bound is $(d+1)(d/2+1)/(d+1) = d/2+1$. Thus, $\text{POA}(m,d) = d/2+1$ in this case. If d is odd, then $k = (d+1)/2$, and we still have $m/\tilde{j} = \frac{d+1}{2}$. The third bound is

$$(d+1)(d/2+3/2)/(d+2) = (d+1)(d+3)/(2(d+2)) .$$

Thus, $\text{POA}(m,d) = (d+1)(d+3)/(2(d+2))$ in this case.

Consider the case $d+2 \leq m \leq 2d$ (which is relevant for $m \geq 4$). In this case $j = \tilde{j} = 2$, and $k = \lfloor \frac{m-2}{3} \rfloor + 1 \leq \frac{m+1}{3}$.

We have $m/\tilde{j} = m/2 > \frac{m+1}{3}$ (where the last inequality holds for $m \geq 4$), and the last term in the definition of F is $m(k+1)/(3k+1) \leq m/2$ (which holds for any $k \geq 1$, a property that k always satisfies). Thus $\text{POA}(m,d) = m/2$ in this case.

Consider the case $d = 2$. By the above, $\text{POA}(m,2) = 2$ for $m = 2,3,4$. Thus, assume $m \geq 5$. Assume first that m is even. We have $\tilde{j} = j = \frac{m}{2}$, and $k = \lfloor \frac{m-2}{m/2+1} \rfloor + 1 = 2$ since $m+2 \leq 2(m-2) < 2(m+2)$ holds for $m \geq 6$. We get

$$F(m,d) = \min\{2, 2, \frac{3m}{m+3}\} = \frac{3m}{m+3} \geq 2 ,$$

since $m \geq 6$. Assume now that m is odd. We have $\tilde{j} = \frac{m+1}{2}$ and $j = \frac{m-1}{2}$, and $k = \lfloor \frac{m-2}{(m-1)/2+1} \rfloor + 1 = 2$ since $m+1 \leq 2(m-2) < 2(m+1)$ holds for $m \geq 5$. We get

$$F(m,d) = \min\{\frac{2m}{m+1}, 2, \frac{3m}{m+2}\} = \frac{3m}{m+2} > 2 ,$$

since $m \geq 5$.

For $d = 2$, the function is not monotone since the values $\text{POA}(m,2)$ for $m = 2,3,4,5,6,7,8$ are $2, 2, 2, 15/7, 2, 7/3$, and $24/11$, respectively. This behavior of the function continues for larger values of m; if $m \geq 6$ is even, then $F(m+1,2) > F(m,2)$ and $F(m+2,2) < F(m+1,2)$. For $d \geq 3$, we have $\text{POA}(d-1,d) = d-1$, $\text{POA}(d,d) = d > d-1$, and $\text{POA}(d+1,d) \leq \frac{d}{2}+1 < d$, showing that the function is not monotone. Similarly, we can show that the function is not monotone for larger values of m as well. Let $m = d^u$ for some integer $u \geq 3$, $m_1 = m-1$, $m_2 = m+1$, and $m_3 = m+2$. We find

$$j(m,d) = j(m_1,d) = j(m_2,d) = d^{u-1} ,$$

$$j(m_3,d) = d^{u-1} + 1,$$

$$\tilde{j}(m,d) = \tilde{j}(m_1,d) = d^{u-1} ,$$

$$\tilde{j}(m_2,d) = \tilde{j}(m_3,d) = d^{u-1} + 1 ,$$

$k(m,d) = k(m_1,d) = k(m_2,d) = d$, since $m_2 - 2 = d^u - 1 < d(d^{u-1}+1)$ and $m_1 - 2 \geq (d-1)(d^{u-1}+1)$ for $u \geq 2$, and

$$(d-1)(d^{u-1}+2) \leq m_3 - 2 = d^u < d(d^{u-1}+2) .$$

We find

$$F(m_1,d) = \min\{\frac{d^u-1}{d^{u-1}}, d, \frac{(d^u-1)(d+1)}{(d^{u-1}+1)d+1}\} .$$

The first two terms are no larger than d, and the last one is larger than d for $u \geq 3$. Thus,

$$F(m_1,d) = \frac{(d^u-1)(d+1)}{(d^{u-1}+1)d+1} .$$

We have

$$F(m,d) = \min\{\frac{d^u}{d^{u-1}}, d, \frac{d^u(d+1)}{(d^{u-1}+1)d+1}\} .$$

The first two terms are equal to d, and the last one is larger than d for $u \geq 3$. Thus,

$$F(m,d) = \frac{d^u(d+1)}{(d^{u-1}+1)d+1} .$$

Next,

$$F(m_2,d) = \min\{\frac{d^u+1}{d^{u-1}+1}, d, \frac{(d^u+1)(d+1)}{(d^{u-1}+1)d+1}\} .$$

The first two terms are at most d, and the last one is larger than d for $u \geq 3$. Thus,

$$F(m_2, d) = \frac{(d^u + 1)(d + 1)}{(d^{u-1} + 1)d + 1} .$$

Finally

$$F(m_3, d) = \min\left\{\frac{d^u + 2}{d^{u-1} + 1}, d, \frac{(d^u + 2)(d + 1)}{(d^{u-1} + 2)d + 1}\right\} .$$

The first two terms are at most d, and the last one is larger than d for $u \geq 3$. Thus,

$$F(m_3, d) = \frac{(d^u + 2)(d + 1)}{(d^{u-1} + 2)d + 1} .$$

We have $F(m_1, d) < F(m, d) < F(m_2, d)$, and $F(m_2, d) > F(m_3, d)$. $\square$

4. COOPERATIVE SETTINGS

In this section we study the stronger measures of stability.

THEOREM 2. *For any $m, d \geq 2$ such that $m + d \geq 5$,*

$$\text{WPPOA}(m, d) = \text{SPPOA}(m, d) = \text{SPOA}(m, d) = 2 .$$

Additionally,

$$\text{WPPOA}(2, 2) = \text{SPPOA}(2, 2) = \text{SPOA}(2, 2) = \frac{3}{2} .$$

PROOF. We will show lower bounds for the SPOA and SPPOA, and upper bounds for the WPPOA, since $\text{WPPOA}(m, d) \geq \max\{\text{SPPOA}(m, d), \text{SPOA}(m, d)\}$. Consider a schedule $\mathcal{A}$ for a game G that is a WPNE. That is, it is an NE, and there is no alternative schedule where every job decreases its cost. Assume $OPT(G) = 1$, let L be the makespan, and assume without loss of generality that $L_1^1 = L$. We claim that there exists a machine ℓ whose makespan is at most 1. If no such machine exists, then the cost of every job is strictly above 1, while an optimal schedule is such that no job has cost above 1, so this is an alternative schedule where every job has a smaller cost, contradicting the property that $\mathcal{A}$ is a WPNE. Consider a job j assigned to machine 1. There is a component i such that $L_\ell^i + p_j^i \geq L$. Since $OPT(G) = 1$, $p_j^i \leq 1$. By the choice of ℓ, $L_\ell^i \leq 1$, we find $L \leq L_\ell^i + p_j^i \leq 2$. Thus, $\text{WPPOA}(m, d) \leq 2$.

Consider the case $m = d = 2$, and assume by contradiction that $L > 1.5$. We have $L_1^1 + L_1^2 = P^1 \leq 2$, and since $L_1^1 = L > 1.5$, $L_1^2 < 0.5$. In this case ℓ as defined above satisfies $\ell \neq 1$, and therefore $\ell = 2$, and we have $L_2^2 \leq 1$. The first machine must have at least two jobs in $\mathcal{A}$ (since its load is strictly above 1). Let these jobs be denoted by $1, 2, \ldots, s$, where $s \geq 2$. For every $1 \leq j \leq s$, one of $L_2^1 + p_j^1 \geq L$ and $L_2^2 + p_j^2 \geq L$ must hold. However,

$$L_2^1 + p_j^1 < \frac{1}{2} + 1 = 1.5 < L ,$$

so $L_2^2 + p_j^2 \geq L$ must hold for $1 \leq j \leq s$. Taking the sum over $1 \leq j \leq s$, we have $s \cdot L_2^2 + L_1^2 \geq sL$. Since $L_1^2 + L_2^2 \leq 2$, we get $(s-1)L_2^2 + 2 \geq sL > 1.5s$, or alternatively,

$$L_2^2 > \frac{1.5s - 2}{s - 1} = 1.5 - \frac{1}{2s - 2} \geq 1 ,$$

a contradiction.

Now we proceed to show the lower bounds. We define three types of games G_1, G_2, G_3, and schedules $\mathcal{A}_1, \mathcal{A}_2$, and

$\mathcal{A}_3$, as follows. The game G_1 is defined for the case $m \geq 3$ and $d \geq 2$. There are $m+1$ jobs. The components $3, \ldots, d$ of all jobs are zeroes. The first two components of the first $m-1$ jobs are equal to $1-\varepsilon$, where $\varepsilon > 0$ is a small constant. There is one job for which the first two components are 0 and $1-\varepsilon$, respectively, and one job for which the first two components are 1 and 0, respectively. An optimal solution assigns the first $m-1$ jobs to different machines, and the remaining two jobs to the remaining machine. Thus, $OPT(G_1) = 1$. In the schedule $\mathcal{A}_1$, the first $m - 3$ jobs are assigned to the last $m - 3$ machines. Two additional jobs of the same size are assigned to the first machine, the last two jobs are assigned to the two remaining machines. The jobs that are assigned to dedicated machines cannot reduce their costs any further. A job that is assigned with another job can reduce its cost only if it will be assigned to a dedicated machine. Thus, the schedule is an SNE. The job of size $(0, 1 - \varepsilon, \ldots)$ would have a larger cost if it is combined with any other job. The job $(1, 0, \ldots)$ would have a larger cost if it is combined with any job except for the job of size $(0, 1 - \varepsilon, \ldots)$. Thus, the schedule is a SPNE. Since $\mathcal{A}_1 = 2(1 - \varepsilon)$, letting ε tend to zero shows that $\text{SPOA}(m, d) \geq 2$ and $\text{SPPOA}(m, d) \geq 2$.

The game G_2 is defined for the case $m = 2$ and $d \geq 3$. There are four jobs. The components $4, \ldots, d$ of all jobs are zeroes. The first job has size $(1 - \varepsilon, 1, 0, \ldots)$, the second job has size $(1 - \varepsilon, 0, 1, \ldots)$, the third job has size $(0, 1 - \varepsilon, 0, \ldots)$, and the fourth job has size $(0, 0, 1 - \varepsilon, \ldots)$. An optimal solution assigns the first and the fourth jobs to one machine, and the second and third jobs to the other machine. Thus, $OPT(G_2) = 1$. In the schedule $\mathcal{A}_2$, the first two jobs are assigned to the first machine, and the next two jobs are assigned to the second machine. The jobs that are assigned to the second machine cannot reduce their costs any further, and moreover, combining one of these jobs with a different job would increase its cost. Thus, there is no alternative schedule where they have costs that are not larger, and adding another job to these two jobs increases the cost of that job. Thus, the schedule is a SNE and a SPNE. Since $\mathcal{A}_2 = 2(1 - \varepsilon)$, letting ε tend to zero shows that $\text{SPOA}(2, d) \geq 2$ and $\text{SPPOA}(2, d) \geq 2$.

The game G_3 is defined for the case $m = 2$ and $d = 2$. There are four jobs. The first two jobs have sizes of $(3/4 - \varepsilon, 1/2 + \varepsilon)$, and the other two jobs have sizes of $(1/4 + \varepsilon, 1/2 - \varepsilon)$. An optimal solution assigns the first and the fourth jobs to one machine, and the second and third jobs to the other machine. Thus, $OPT(G_3) = 1$. In the schedule $\mathcal{A}_3$, the first two jobs are assigned to the first machine, and the next two jobs are assigned to the second machine. A job assigned to the second machine can reduce its cost only by being scheduled to a dedicated machine, and moreover, combining one of these jobs with a different job would increase its cost from $1 - 2\varepsilon$ to 1. Thus, there is no alternative schedule where they have costs that are not larger, and adding another job to these two jobs increases the cost of that job from $1.5 - 2\varepsilon$ to $1.5 - \varepsilon$. Thus, the schedule is a SNE and a SPNE. Since $\mathcal{A}_3 = 2(3/4 - \varepsilon)$, letting ε tend to zero shows that $\text{SPOA}(2, 2) \geq 1.5$ and $\text{SPPOA}(2, 2) \geq 1.5$. $\square$

5. CONCLUSION

In this paper we had considered several notions of equilibria for the vector scheduling game on parallel machines, both in cooperative and non-cooperative settings, and we measured their inefficiency. We showed that unlike the case

$d = 1$, for which the POA and SPOA are equal, for $d \geq 2$, the values POA(d) and SPOA(d) are very different. An interesting direction would be to consider various computational aspects of these notions.

6. REFERENCES

[1] N. Andelman, M. Feldman, and Y. Mansour. Strong price of anarchy. *Games and Economic Behavior*, 65(2):289–317, 2009.

[2] E. Anshelevich, A. Dasgupta, J. M. Kleinberg, É. Tardos, T. Wexler, and T. Roughgarden. The price of stability for network design with fair cost allocation. *SIAM Journal on Computing*, 38(4):1602–1623, 2008.

[3] M. Armbrust, A. Fox, R. Griffith, A. D. Joseph, R. Katz, A. Konwinski, G. Lee, D. Patterson, A. Rabkin, I. Stoica, and M. Zaharia. Above the clouds: A berkeley view of cloud computing. Technical report, University of California at Berkeley, Feb. 2009.

[4] R. J. Aumann. Acceptable points in general cooperative n-person games. In A. W. Tucker and R. D. Luce, editors, *Contributions to the Theory of Games IV, Annals of Mathematics Study 40*, pages 287–324. Princeton University Press, 1959.

[5] Y. Aumann and Y. Dombb. Pareto efficiency and approximate pareto efficiency in routing and load balancing games. In *Proc. of the 3rd International Symposium on Algorithmic Game Theory (SAGT2010)*, pages 66–77, 2010.

[6] B. Awerbuch, Y. Azar, Y. Richter, and D. Tsur. Tradeoffs in worst-case equilibria. *Theoretical Computer Science*, 361(2–3):200–209, 2006.

[7] V. Bilò. On the packing of selfish items. In *Proc. of the 20th International Parallel and Distributed Processing Symposium (IPDPS2006)*. IEEE, 2006.

[8] C. Chekuri and S. Khanna. On multidimensional packing problems. *SIAM J. Comput.*, 33(4):837–851, 2004.

[9] S. Chien and A. Sinclair. Strong and pareto price of anarchy in congestion games. In *Proc. of the 36th International Colloquium on Automata, Languages and Programming (ICALP2009)*, pages 279–291, 2009.

[10] J. Csirik, J. B. G. Frenk, M. Labbé, and S. Zhang. On the multidimensional vector bin packing. *Acta Cybern.*, 9(4):361–369, 1990.

[11] A. Czumaj and B. Vöcking. Tight bounds for worst-case equilibria. *ACM Transactions on Algorithms*, 3(1), 2007.

[12] P. Dubey. Inefficiency of Nash equilibria. *Mathematics of Operations Research*, 11(1):1–8, 1986.

[13] L. Epstein and E. Kleiman. On the quality and complexity of pareto equilibria in the job scheduling game. In *Proc. of the 10th International Conference on Autonomous Agents and Multiagent Systems (AAMAS2011)*, pages 525–532, 2011.

[14] L. Epstein and E. Kleiman. Selfish bin packing. *Algorithmica*, 60(2):368–394, 2011.

[15] L. Epstein and E. Kleiman. Vector packing with selfish items. *Work in progress*, 2013.

[16] E. Even-Dar, A. Kesselman, and Y. Mansour. Convergence time to Nash equilibrium in load balancing. *ACM Transactions on Algorithms*, 3(3):32, 2007.

[17] A. Fiat, H. Kaplan, M. Levy, and S. Olonetsky. Strong price of anarchy for machine load balancing. In *Proc. of the 34th International Colloquium on Automata, Languages and Programming (ICALP2007)*, pages 583–594, 2007.

[18] G. Finn and E. Horowitz. A linear time approximation algorithm for multiprocessor scheduling. *BIT Numerical Mathematics*, 19(3):312–320, 1979.

[19] M. R. Garey, R. L. Graham, and D. S. Johnson. Resource constrained scheduling as generalized bin packing. *J. Comb. Theory, Ser. A*, 21(3):257–298, 1976.

[20] R. L. Graham. Bounds on multiprocessing anomalies and related packing algorithms. In *Proceedings of the 1972 Spring Joint Computer Conference*, pages 205–217, 1972.

[21] T. Harks, M. Klimm, and R. H. Möhring. Strong equilibria in games with the lexicographical improvement property. *International Journal of Game Theory*, 42(2):461–482, 2013.

[22] R. Holzman and N. Law-Yone. Strong equilibrium in congestion games. *Games and Economic Behavior*, 21(1–2):85–101, 1997.

[23] N. Immorlica, L. E. Li, V. S. Mirrokni, and A. S. Schulz. Coordination mechanisms for selfish scheduling. *Theoretical Computer Science*, 410(17):1589–1598, 2009.

[24] L. T. Kou and G. Markowsky. Multidimensional bin packing algorithms. *IBM Journal of Research and Development*, 21(5):443–448, 1977.

[25] E. Koutsoupias, M. Mavronicolas, and P. G. Spirakis. Approximate equilibria and ball fusion. *Theory of Computing Systems*, 36(6):683–693, 2003.

[26] E. Koutsoupias and C. H. Papadimitriou. Worst-case equilibria. In *Proc. of the 16th Annual Symposium on Theoretical Aspects of Computer Science (STACS1999)*, pages 404–413, 1999.

[27] D. T. Luc. Pareto optimality. In A. Chinchuluun, P. M. Pardalos, A. Migdalas, and L. Pitsoulis, editors, *Pareto optimality, game theory and equilibria*, pages 481–515. Springer, 2008.

[28] M. Mavronicolas and P. G. Spirakis. The price of selfish routing. *Algorithmica*, 48(1):91–126, 2007.

[29] P. Schuurman and T. Vredeveld. Performance guarantees of local search for multiprocessor scheduling. *INFORMS Journal on Computing*, 19(1):52–63, 2007.

[30] M. Tennenholtz and O. Rozenfeld. Strong and correlated strong equilibria in monotone congestion games. In *Proc. of the 2nd International Workshop on Internet and Network Economics (WINE2006)*, pages 74–86, 2006.

[31] M. A. Vouk. Cloud computing - issues, research and implementations. *CIT*, 16(4):235–246, 2008.

[32] D. Ye and J. Chen. Non-cooperative games on multidimensional resource allocation. *Future Generation Comp. Syst.*, 29(6):1345–1352, 2013.

LP Rounding and Combinatorial Algorithms for Minimizing Active and Busy Time*

Jessica Chang
University of Maryland
College Park, MD, USA
jschang@umiacs.umd.edu

Samir Khuller
University of Maryland
College Park, MD, USA
samir@cs.umd.edu

Koyel Mukherjee[†]
Xerox Research Centre India
Bangalore, India
koyel.mukherjee@xerox.com

ABSTRACT

We consider fundamental scheduling problems motivated by energy issues. In this framework, we are given a set of jobs, each with release time, deadline and required processing length. The jobs need to be scheduled so that at most g jobs can be running on a machine at any given time. The duration for which a machine is active (i.e., "on") is referred to as its *active time*. The goal is to find a feasible schedule for all jobs, minimizing the total active time. When preemption is allowed at integer time points, we show that a minimal feasible schedule already yields a 3-approximation (and this bound is tight) and we further improve this to a 2-approximation via LP rounding. Our second contribution is for the non-preemptive version of this problem. However, since even asking if a feasible schedule on one machine exists is NP-hard, we allow for an unbounded number of virtual machines, each having capacity of g. This problem is known as the *busy time* problem in the literature and a 4-approximation is known for this problem. We develop a new combinatorial algorithm that is a 3-approximation. Furthermore, we consider the preemptive busy time problem, giving a simple and exact greedy algorithm when unbounded parallelism is allowed, that is, where g is unbounded. For arbitrary g, this yields an algorithm that is 2-approximate.

Categories and Subject Descriptors

F.2 [**Analysis of Algorithms and Problem Complexity**]: Nonnumerical Algorithms and Problems—*Sequencing and scheduling*; G.2 [**Discrete Mathematics**]: Combinatorics

Keywords

busy time; scheduling; packing

---

*This work has been supported by NSF Grants CCF-1217890 and CCF-0937865.

[†]This work was done while the author was a graduate student at the University of Maryland, College Park.

1. INTRODUCTION

Scheduling jobs on multiple parallel or batch machines has received extensive attention in the computer science and operations research communities for decades [5, 15, 9]. For the most part, these studies have focused primarily on "job-related" metrics such as minimizing makespan, total completion time, flow time, tardiness and maximizing throughput under various deadline constraints. Despite this rich history, some of the most environmentally (not to mention, financially) costly scheduling problems are those driven by a pressing need to reduce energy consumption and power costs, e.g., at data centers. Energy-aware algorithmic efforts notwithstanding [1, 2, 4], the need to understand algorithmic design for energy efficiency remains largely unaddressed, particularly by techniques and approaches of traditional scheduling objectives. Toward that end, our work is most concerned with minimization of the total time that a machine is on [6, 15, 11, 14, 17] to schedule a collection of jobs. This measure was recently introduced in an effort to understand energy-related problems in cloud computing contexts, and the busy and active time models cleanly capture many central issues in this space. Furthermore, it has connections to several key problems in optical network design, perhaps most notably in the minimization of the fiber costs of Optical Add Drop Multiplexers (OADMs) [11]. The application of busy time models to optical network design has been extensively outlined in the literature [11, 12, 13, 18].

With the widespread adoption of data centers and cloud computing, recent progress in virtualization has facilitated the consolidation of multiple virtual machines (VMs) into fewer hosts. As a consequence, many computers can be shut off, resulting in substantial power savings. Today, products such as Citrix XenServer and VMware Distributed Resource Scheduler (DRS) offer VM consolidation as a feature. In this sense, minimizing busy time is closely related to the basic problem of mapping VMs to physical hosts.

We first discuss the active time model [6]. In this model we have a collection $\mathcal{J}$ of n jobs that need to be scheduled on one machine. Each job j has release time r_j, deadline d_j and length p_j. We assume that time is slotted and that all job parameters are integral. The jobs need to be scheduled on a machine so that at most g jobs are running simultaneously. For a job j, we need to schedule p_j units in the window $[r_j, d_j)$ and at most one unit can be scheduled in any time slot. The goal is to minimize the *active time* of the machine, that is, the total duration for which the machine is on. If we are looking for a non-preemptive schedule, we can easily show that this problem is strongly NP-hard (even the feasibility question becomes NP-hard). In the special case that the jobs all have unit length, there is a fast algorithm [6, 15] that yields an optimal solution.

If we allow preemption at integer boundaries, the feasibility question is easily resolved by a network flow computation, as discussed by Chang and Khuller [7]. There is a node for every job and a node for every time slot. There is an edge from the source to each job node j with capacity p_j, and unit capacity edges from job node j to a slot node where j is feasible. Finally, all slot nodes are adjacent to the sink, with an edge capacitiy of g. Thus a flow of value $\sum_j p_j$ units corresponds to a feasible integral schedule for all the jobs.

Unfortunately, in such a construction, there is no control as to which slot nodes receive flow; to minimize active time suggests a shift from computing a maximum flow to computing a min-edge cost flow, where we only wish to send non-zero amount of flow through as few edges as possible that connect to the sink.

In this work, we first show that every minimal solution is a 3-approximation to this problem. We also show that this bound is tight. We then further improve the approximation ratio by considering a natural IP formulation and its LP relaxation to obtain a solution within twice the integer optimum (again this bound is tight). See Figure 1 for an example of an optimal solution, with preemption allowed at integral boundaries. This presents substantial progress on the problem left open earlier [6]. We also assume that the input is feasible as this can be easily verified by a simple network flow computation [7].

every input instance is feasible as we can simply create a virtual machine for each job.

A well-studied special case of this model is one in which each job j is "rigid", i.e., $d_j = p_j + r_j$, in which there is no question about when it must start. Jobs of this particular form are called *interval jobs*. Even in this case, the busy time problem is NP-hard for $g = 2$ [18]. We say the interval $[r_j, d_j)$ is the *span* of job j. The *span* of a job set $\mathcal{J}'$ is the union of the spans of jobs in $\mathcal{J}'$. Since the problem is NP-hard, we will be interested in approximation algorithms for this problem. What makes this special case particularly central is that one can convert an instance of the general busy time problem to an instance of interval jobs in polynomial time, by solving a dynamic program with unbounded g [14]. The dynamic program "fixes" the positions of the jobs to minimize their shadow, i.e., projection onto the time-axis. The span of the solution with g unbounded is the smallest possible span of any feasible solution to the original problem and can be used as a lower bound on the optimal solution. Then, one can adjust the release times and deadlines to artificially "fix" the position of each job to where it was scheduled in the solution for unbounded g. This creates an instance of interval jobs, on which we can then apply an approximation algorithm for the case of interval jobs. Figure 2 shows a collection of jobs and the corresponding packing that yields an optimal solution.

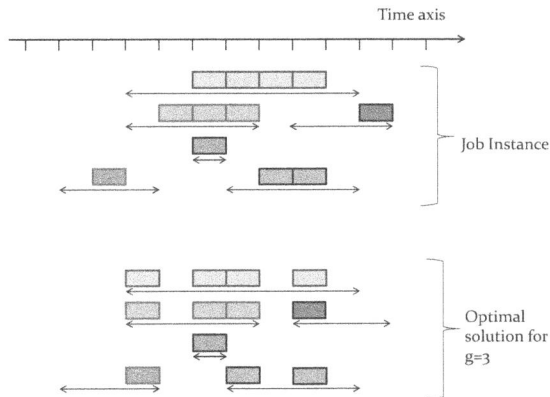

Figure 1: An optimal solution for the active time problem with integral preemption, for an instance of 6 jobs and $g = 3$.

We also consider a slight variant of the active time problem that has been considered previously in the literature [11, 14], and referred to as the *busy time* problem. The main variation from the active time problem is that an unbounded number of virtual machines is available, and we would like a non-preemptive schedule. We are given a collection $\mathcal{J}$ of n jobs that need to be scheduled on a set of identical machines. Each job j has release time r_j, deadline d_j and length p_j. The jobs need to be partitioned into groups (each group of jobs will be scheduled non-preemptively on a machine) so that at most g jobs are running simultaneously on a given machine. We say that a machine is *busy* at time t if there is at least one job running on the machine at t; otherwise the machine is *idle*. The time intervals during which a machine M is busy is called its *busy time* and we denote its length by *busy(M)*. The objective is to find a feasible schedule of all the jobs on the machines (partitioning jobs into groups) to minimize the cumulative busy time over all the machines. The schedule can potentially use an unbounded number of machines since each group is really a virtual machine, and thus

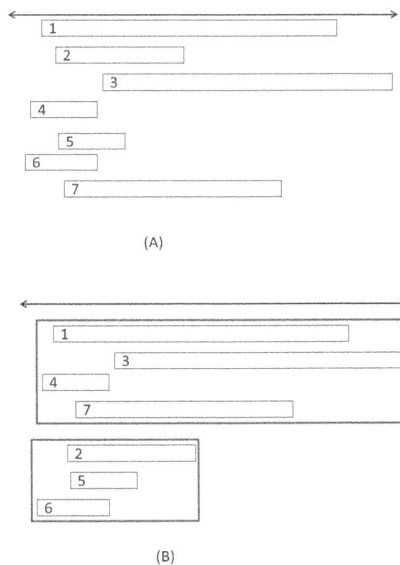

Figure 2: (A) Collection of interval jobs with unit demand, numbered arbitrarily. (B) Optimal packing of the jobs on two machines with $g = 3$ minimizing total busy time.

Busy time scheduling in this form was first studied by Flammini et al. [11]. They present a simple greedy algorithm FIRSTFIT for interval jobs and demonstrate that it always produces a solution of busy time at most 4 times that of the optimal solution. The algorithm considers jobs in non-increasing order by length, greedily packing each job in the first group in which it fits. In the same paper, they highlight an instance on which the cost of FIRSTFIT is three times that of the optimal solution. Closing this gap would be very interesting [1]. However, unknown to Flammini et al., earlier work by Alicherry and Bhatia [3] and Kumar and Rudra [16] already considered a problem in the context of wavelength assignment. One can show that their algorithms immediately yield two different 2-approximations for the the problem of minimizing the busy time for scheduling interval jobs.

Khandekar et al. [14] consider the generalization in which each job has an associated width or "demand" on its machine. For any set of jobs assigned to the same machine, the cumulative demand of the active ones can be at most g at any time. The authors apply FIRSTFIT principles to this problem to obtain a 5-approximation. The main idea involves partitioning jobs into those of "narrow" and "wide" demand. Each wide job is assigned to its own machine, while FIRSTFIT is applied to the set of narrow jobs. In addition, the authors give improved bounds for special cases of busy time scheduling with jobs of unit demand. When the interval jobs form a clique, they provide a PTAS. They also give an exact algorithm when the intervals of the jobs are laminar, i.e., two jobs' intervals intersect only if one interval is contained in the other. However, we note that for the case of unit width jobs, the same approach gives a 4-approximation for flexible jobs, by solving a dynamic program for unbounded g. With little effort [8] one can show via a similar extension that the methods of Kumar and Rudra [16] and Alicherry and Bhatia [3] also yield 4-approximations, and the bounds are tight. Details are in the full version of the paper [8]. We develop an improved algorithm with a bound of 3, using a completely different approach.

1.1 Our Results

In the active time problem, we are allowed preemption at integer time points and time is slotted. We show in Section 2 that any minimal feasible solution yields a 3-approximation. We then consider a natural IP formulation for this problem and show how its LP relaxation allows us to convert a fractional schedule to an integral one that is 2-approximate. We note that the integrality gap of 2 is tight. Earlier work [6] only addressed the special case where job lengths were unit, for which an optimal polynomial-time algorithm was given. Unfortunately, it is not clear how to extend that framework for the case of non-unit length jobs.

Since the busy time problem for interval jobs is NP-hard [18], the focus in this paper is on the development of a polynomial-time algorithm GREEDYTRACKING with a worst case approximation guarantee of 3. The central idea is to iteratively identify a set of jobs whose spans are disjoint; we will reference this set as a "track". Then, the set of jobs assigned to a particular machine is the union of g such tracks; we call the set of jobs assigned to the same machine a *bundle* of jobs. The *busy time* of a machine is the span of its bundle. The goal is to assign jobs to bundles so that at no time does a single bundle have more than g active jobs, and to do so in a way that minimizes the cumulative busy time. Intuitively, this approach is less myopic than FIRSTFIT, which schedules jobs one at a time.

We also give instances of interval jobs where GREEDYTRACKING yields a solution twice that of an optimum in the full version [8].

One important consequence of GREEDYTRACKING is an improved bound for the busy time problem on instances in which jobs may not be interval jobs. In the spirit of Khandekar et al. [14], we first solve the problem assuming unbounded machine capacity g to get a solution that minimizes the projection of the jobs onto the time-axis. We use this to map the original instance to one of interval jobs, forcing each job to start exactly as it did in the solution for unbounded capacity, over which we compute a solution via GREEDYTRACKING. We prove that in total, this approach has busy time within thrice that of the optimal solution, and the bound is tight. In addition, we explore the preemptive version of the problem, providing a greedy 2-approximation. However, we omit the discussion of this result from the extended abstract; details can be found in the full version of this paper [8].

2. ACTIVE TIME SCHEDULING OF PRE-EMPTIVE JOBS

Let us denote by T the length of the time window, spanning the union of the windows of the entire job instance. In other words, $T = |\bigcup_{j \in \mathcal{J}} [r_j, d_j)|$. We assume without loss of generality that the earliest release time of any job $j \in \mathcal{J}$ is 0 and the latest deadline of any job in $j \in \mathcal{J}$ is T. In this notation, let $\mathcal{T}$ denote the set of time slots $\{1, \ldots, T\}$.

DEFINITION 1. *A job j is live at slot t if $t \in [r_j, d_j)$.*

DEFINITION 2. *A slot is active or open if at least one job is scheduled in it. It is inactive or closed otherwise.*

DEFINITION 3. *An active slot is full if there are g jobs assigned to it, otherwise non-full.*

A feasible solution σ is specified by a set $\mathcal{A} \subseteq \mathcal{T}$ of active time slots and a mapping or assignment of jobs to time slots in $\mathcal{A}$, such that at most g jobs are scheduled in any slot in $\mathcal{A}$, at most one unit of any job j is scheduled in any time slot in $\mathcal{A}$ and every job j has been assigned to p_j active slots within its window $[r_j, d_j)$. Once $\mathcal{A}$ has been determined, a feasible integral assignment can be found via a max-flow computation [7].

The cost of a feasible solution σ is the number of active slots in it, i.e., $|\mathcal{A}|$. Let $\mathcal{A}_f$ denote the set of active slots that are full, and let $\mathcal{A}_n$ denote the set of active slots that are non-full. Then $|\mathcal{A}| = |\mathcal{A}_f| + |\mathcal{A}_n|$.

DEFINITION 4. *A minimal feasible solution is one in which no active slot can be made inactive, and still feasibly satisfy the entire job set.*

Given a feasible solution, one can easily find a minimal feasible solution as follows. Assume that all the slots are initially active. Now (in any order) make slots inactive, if one can feasibly do so (this might change the actual slots to which jobs are assigned at every iteration).

The cost $|\mathcal{A}_f|$ of the full slots can be charged to OPT. On the other hand, to bound the number of non-full active slots requires a concept specific to minimal feasible solutions.

DEFINITION 5. *A non-full-rigid job is one that is scheduled for one unit in every non-full slot in which it is live.*

LEMMA 1. *For a minimal feasible solution σ, there exists a solution σ' of the same cost in which each active non-full slot has at least one non-full-rigid job scheduled in it.*

[1]In an attempt to improve approximation guarantees, Flammini et al. [11] consider two special cases. The first case pertains to "proper intervals", where no job's interval is strictly contained in that of another. For instances of this type, they show that the greedy algorithm ordering jobs by release times is 2-approximate. The second special case involve instances whose corresponding interval graph is a clique - in other words, there exists a time t such that each interval $[r_j, d_j)$ contains it. In this case, a greedy algorithm also yields a 2-approximation. As with proper intervals, it is not obvious that minimizing busy time on clique instances is NP-hard. However, when the interval jobs are both proper *and* form a clique, a very simple dynamic program gives an optimal solution [17].

PROOF. Consider any non-full slot of a minimal feasible solution σ that does not have any non-full-rigid job scheduled in it. Move any job j in that slot to any other (non-full and active) slot that it may be scheduled in, and where it is not already scheduled. There must at least one such slot; otherwise j would be a non-full-rigid job. Continue this process for as long as possible. Note that in moving these jobs, we are not increasing the cost of the solution: we only move jobs to slots that are already active. If this process continues, eventually there will be no more jobs scheduled in this slot, we would have found a solution of smaller cost, violating our assumption of minimal feasibility. Thus, there must be at least one job j' scheduled in that slot that cannot be moved to any other active slot. This can only happen if all the slots in the window of j' are already assigned one unit of j', or are full or inactive, i.e., if j' is a non-full rigid job. Continue this process until each non-full slot has at least one non-full-rigid job scheduled. □

COROLLARY 1. *There exists a set of jobs $\mathcal{J}^*$ consisting of non-full-rigid jobs, such that at least one of these jobs is scheduled in every non-full slot of σ'.*

We say that such a set $\mathcal{J}^*$ covers the non-full slots.

LEMMA 2. *There exists a set $\mathcal{J}^*$ of non-full-rigid jobs covering all the non-full slots, such that no job window is completely contained within the window of another job. $\mathcal{J}^*$ is called a minimal set.*

PROOF. Let us consider a set $\mathcal{J}^*$ of non-full-rigid jobs that are covering all the non-full slots. Suppose it contains a pair of non-full-rigid jobs j and j', such that the $[r_j, d_j] \subseteq [r_{j'}, d_{j'}]$. One unit of j' must be scheduled in every non-full slot in the window of j'. However, this also includes the non-full slots in the window of j, hence we can discard j from $\mathcal{J}^*$ without any loss.

We repeat this with every pair of non-full-rigid jobs in $\mathcal{J}^*$, such that the window of one is contained within the window of another, till there exists no such pair. □

It can be proven that there exists a minimal set $\mathcal{J}^*$ such that at every time slot, at most two of the jobs in $\mathcal{J}^*$ are live. We charge the cost of the non-full slots to $\mathcal{J}^*$.

LEMMA 3. *There exists a minimal set $\mathcal{J}^*$ of non-full-rigid jobs such that at least one of these jobs is scheduled in every non-full slot, and at every time slot, at most two of the jobs in set $\mathcal{J}^*$ are live.*

PROOF. Consider the first time slot t where 3 or more jobs of $\mathcal{J}^*$ are live. Let these jobs be numbered according to their deadlines $(j_1, j_2, j_3, \ldots, j_\ell, \ell \geq 3)$. By definition, the deadline of all of these jobs must be $\geq t$ since they are all live at t. Moreover, they are all non-full-rigid, being a part of $\mathcal{J}^*$, which means they are scheduled one unit in every non-full active slot in their window. Since the set $\mathcal{J}^*$ is minimal, no job window is contained within another, hence none of the jobs $j_2, \ldots, j_\ell$ have release time earlier than that of j_1. Therefore, all non-full slots before the deadline of j_1 must be charging either j_1 or some other job with an earlier release time. Consequently, discarding any of the jobs $j_2, \ldots, j_\ell$ will not affect the charging of these slots.

Let t' be the first non-full active slot after the deadline of j_1. t' therefore needs to charge one of $j_2, j_3, \ldots, j_\ell$. Among these, all jobs which have a deadline earlier than t', can be discarded from $\mathcal{J}^*$, without any loss, since no non-full slot needs to charge it. Hence, let us assume that all of these jobs $j_2, j_3, \ldots, j_\ell$ are live at t'. However, all of them being non-full-rigid, and t' being non-full

and active, all of them must have one unit scheduled in t'. Therefore, if we discard all of the jobs $j_2, \ldots, j_{\ell-1}$ and keep j_ℓ alone, that would be enough since it can be charged all the non-full slots between t' and its deadline d_ℓ. Hence, after discarding these intermediate jobs from $\mathcal{J}^*$, there would be only two jobs j_1 and j_ℓ left which overlap at t.

Repeat this for the next slot t'' where 3 or more jobs of $\mathcal{J}^*$ are live, till there are no such time slots left. □

The cost of the non-full slots of the minimal feasible solution σ' is $|\mathcal{A}_n| \leq \sum_{j \in \mathcal{J}^*} p_j$.

THEOREM 1. *The cost of any minimal feasible solution is at most 3 times that of an optimal solution.*

PROOF. $\mathcal{J}^*$ can be partitioned into two job sets $\mathcal{J}_1$ and $\mathcal{J}_2$ such that the jobs in each set have windows disjoint from one another. Therefore the sum of the processing times of the jobs in each such partition is a lower bound on the cost of any optimal solution. Let us denote the cost of an optimal solution as OPT. Hence, the cost of the non-full slots is $|\mathcal{A}_n| \leq \sum_{j \in \mathcal{J}^*} p_j \leq \sum_{j \in \mathcal{J}_1} p_j + \sum_{j' \in \mathcal{J}_2} p_{j'} \leq 2OPT$. Furthermore, the full slots charge once to OPT, since they have a mass of g scheduled in them. This is also a lower bound on OPT. Thus, $|\mathcal{A}_f| \leq \frac{\sum_{j \in \mathcal{J}} p_j}{g} \leq OPT$ and in total the cost of any minimal feasible solution $cost(\sigma) = cost(\sigma') = |\mathcal{A}| = |\mathcal{A}_f| + |\mathcal{A}_n| \leq 3OPT$. This proves the theorem. □

The above bound is asymptotically tight (see Figure 3).

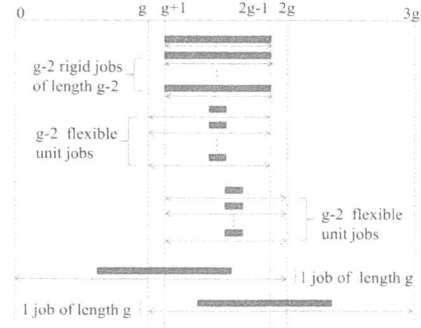

Figure 3: Instance where the minimal feasible solution is almost 3 times the optimal solution. The optimal solution keeps slots $g + 1$ and $2g$ open, assigning to them all of the flexible unit-length jobs. However, the minimal solution that forces slots $g + 1$ and $2g$ to inactive will necessarily schedule the two jobs of length g by themselves, thus incurring a total cost of $3g - 2$.

3. AN LP-ROUNDING 2-APPROXIMATION

In this section, we develop a 2-approximation for the active time problem via LP-rounding techniques. Recall that jobs may be non-unit in length and that preemption is permitted only at integral boundaries. In this section onwards, we will be using t to denote the slot $[t - 1, t)$ for ease of notation. Let $y_t \in \{0, 1\}$ denote the indicator variable for every time slot $t \in \mathcal{T}$. Let $x_{t,j} \in \{0, 1\}$

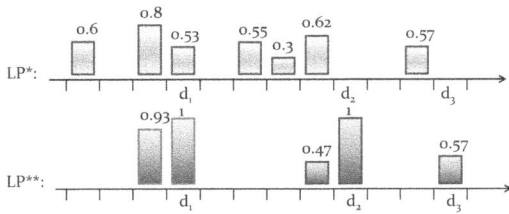

Figure 4: LP* is an optimal LP solution, and LP** is the right-shifted solution of the same cost.

denote the indicator variable for job $j \in \mathcal{J}$ and slot $t \in [r_j, d_j]$. The natural LP relaxation is as follows:

$$\min \sum_{t \in \mathcal{T}} y_t$$

$$x_{t,j} \leq y_t \qquad \forall\, j \in \mathcal{J}, t \in [r_j, d_j]$$

$$\sum_{j \in \mathcal{J}} x_{t,j} \leq g y_t \qquad \forall\, t \in \mathcal{T}$$

$$\sum_{t \in \mathcal{T}} x_{t,j} \geq p_j \qquad \forall\, j \in \mathcal{J}$$

$$x_{t,j}, y_t \geq 0 \qquad \forall\, t \in \mathcal{T}, j \in \mathcal{J}$$

Our approach computes an optimal fractional solution and rounds it to a feasible integral solution within twice the cost of the fractional one. Before we can round, we pre-process the fractional solution to get a certain structure without increasing the cost of the solution.

Let $\mathcal{D} = \{d_1, d_2, \ldots, d_\ell\}$ be the distinct deadlines of the instance, sorted in increasing order. The pre-processing step iteratively transforms the fractional solution to have a *right-shifted* structure: for deadline d_i, if any slot $t \in (d_{i-1}, d_i]$ is open to any extent, then every subsequent slot $t' \in (t, d_i]$ has the property that $y_{t'} = 1$. Informally, this structure is obtained by iteratively "pushing" all y_t values between d_{i-1} and d_i toward the right until it runs into d_i; details can be found in the full version of the paper [8].

See Figure 4 for an example of a right-shifted LP solution.

THEOREM 2. *There exists an optimal fractional solution that is right-shifted.*

Henceforth, we work with a right-shifted optimal LP solution.

Overview of Rounding

We iteratively process the deadlines of $\mathcal{D}$ in increasing order. We denote the set of jobs with deadline d_i as $\mathcal{J}_i$. At the end of iteration i, we have a set of integrally open slots $\mathcal{O}_i$. Let the cumulative y-value between consecutive deadlines be defined as $Y_i = \sum_{d_{i-1} < t \leq d_i} y_t$ ($d_0 = 0$). The rounding algorithm maintains the invariant that at the end of the ith iteration, the number of integrally open slots up to d_i is $|\mathcal{O}_i| \leq 2 \sum_{j \leq i} Y_j$. Furthermore, there exists a feasible fractional assignment of $\bigcup_{k \leq i} \mathcal{J}_k$ in $\mathcal{O}_i$. This will yield the 2-approximation by the end of the ℓth iteration. We refer to slots t with $y_t = 1$ as "fully open". Those with $\frac{1}{2} \leq y_t < 1$ are denoted as "half-open", and those with $0 < y_t < \frac{1}{2}$ are "barely open". Finally, slots with $y_t = 0$ are "closed".

Fully open slots do not charge anything extra to the LP solution. Half-open slots will be opened at a cost of at most 2, charging themselves. To open a barely open slot, we need to charge it to a fully open slot. We say that a barely open slot is "dependent" on the fully open slot that it charges. In this case, the y-value of the barely open slot is not charged at all. In other cases, we allow two

barely open slots on either side of a fully open slot to open up along with a fully open slot; this is permissible only when the sum of the y-values of the barely open slots and the fully open slot is at least $\frac{3}{2}$. We refer to such slots as a "trio". Note that in the case of a trio, we charge the y-value of the barely open slots.

The algorithm maintains the invariant that in each iteration, every barely open slot is either a dependent on a fully open slot or is part of a trio, and every fully open slot has at most one dependent or it is part of at most one trio. Half open slots charge themselves. This will ensure that we have charged the LP solution at most twice. Every time we open a barely open slot as a dependent, we make it a dependent on the earliest fully open slot that does not have a dependent and is not part of a trio.

Sometimes while processing a deadline d_i, the algorithm may choose to close a barely open slot $t \in (d_{i-1}, d_i]$. In such a case, it must also schedule elsewhere the job segments that were initially assigned to t. In particular, the algorithm accommodates jobs of later deadline by creating a *proxy* copy of the slot t and carrying it over to the next iteration. The y-value of this proxy slot is the y-value of the slot t we have just closed; note that we do not charge the y-value of t in this iteration, so the proxy slot may charge its y-value in the future.

Intuitively, proxy slots permit the algorithm to delay the scheduling of job segments, in the hope that the proxy slot can be merged with fractional slots of future iterations. Unlike methods for conventional scheduling problems, algorithms that minimize active time must favor delaying early jobs in the hopes that they can be batched with later jobs. The difficulty of the active time objective lies in balancing the tension between this bias and feasibility constraints: what should the algorithm do if it delays jobs only to discover later that the number of jobs needing to be scheduled (including those that were delayed) exceeds the time and resources available? To handle this, proxy slots maintain a pointer initialized to the actual slot from which it was derived; in this way, the proxy slot keeps track of a "safe" slot to which it can fall back in such cases of excess demand. As a proxy slot is propagated from one iteration to the next, it may update its y-value or the pointer to an actual slot.

If a proxy slot is passed to an iteration, the algorithm treats it as a regular fractionally open slot (though there may be no actual slot at that point). If this slot remains closed after the rounding, the proxy slot is propagated to the next iteration. If the algorithm determines that the proxy slot should be "opened", the actual slot to which the proxy slot points is opened. It is at this point that the cost of the proxy is charged to its y-value.

Thus, in each iteration i of the rounding algorithm, the y-value of any proxy slot (if it exists) is considered along with Y_i. In a single iteration, slots are opened from right to left, i.e., starting with d_i, then $d_i - 1$, and so forth. The algorithm first opens as many fully open slots as possible. If the remaining y-value is at least half, then the next slot (denote t'') is opened and charged to itself. If the remaining y-value is positive but less than half, the algorithm attempts to close t'' and find a feasible assignment of all jobs in $\bigcup_{j \leq i} \mathcal{J}_j$, using max-flow. If such an assignment exists, then t'' will remain closed and any remaining jobs that are not in $\mathcal{J}_i$ are passed on via a proxy slot. (Notice that there can exist at most one proxy slot at any time.) If such an assignment does not exist, then the algorithm is forced to open t'' as barely open. The cost of opening t'' will be charged to the earliest fully open slot that does not yet have a dependent; if no such fully open slot exists, then t'' forms a trio with the preceding fully open slot and its dependent. See Figure 5 for an example.

We will next argue that the algorithm will always be able to charge a barely open slot d_i that the rounding needs to open.

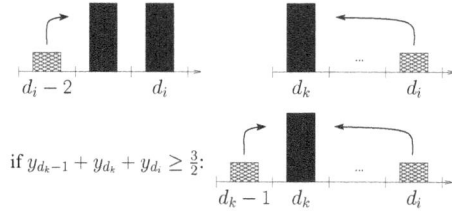

Figure 5: Three possible ways by which we can charge a barely open slot when max-flow cannot close it.

LEMMA 4. *If we need to open a barely open slot d_i in an iteration, then we will always find a fully open slot to charge it as a dependent or as a trio.*

In order to prove the above, let us first assume that it is not true, and we are in the situation where we could not close d_i which is barely open, and there are no fully open slots that we can charge it to. The rounding procedure (described in details in the full version [8]) ensures that this can only happen if the closest open slot to d_i is fully open. Since we could not charge d_i as a trio or as a dependent on any of the fully open earlier slots, all the fully open slots before d_i must have dependents.

The following lemma argues that if all the fully open slots before d_i have dependents, then the structure of the solution must have a specific form. There must be a deadline d_z, with the closest open slot before d_z being d_w (there may be no d_w if d_z is the first fully open deadline), such that either (1) there are at least $g + 1$ jobs in $\mathcal{J}_z$ with release time later than d_w; or (2) the sum of the number of rigid (unit) jobs with release time d_z and the length 2 jobs with release time at least d_w is at least $g + 1$. Let us call such a d_z a *stopping deadline*. In other words, any integral solution would have to open at least one slot in $d_w + 1, \ldots, d_z - 1$, along with d_z, since there are $g + 1$ job units to be scheduled between $d_w + 1$ and d_z. Between stopping deadline d_z and d_i, the fully open slots will be a subset of the set of deadlines, and for each deadline d_x that is fully open, the slot $d_x - 1$ is barely open and dependent on d_x. (Note that $d_x - 1$ can be another deadline itself). This structure is called an *alternating* structure.

LEMMA 5. *If the closest open slot to deadline d_i is fully open, and all the fully open slots before d_i have dependents, then without loss of generality, there is a stopping deadline d_z and between d_z and d_i, the structure of the solution must be alternating.*

PROOF. Let d_k be the closest open slot to d_i, and d_k is fully open. Given the structure of the solution that we start out with and the rounding process, this must be a deadline. All the fully open slots before d_i have dependents. Since no slot between d_k and d_i are open, the dependent on d_k has to be some earlier slot. Either it is a barely open slot t such that $d_{k-1} + 1 \leq t \leq d_k - 1$. Or it must be a proxy slot carried over from an earlier deadline than d_k. Only one barely open slot is opened in any iteration by the rounding process. Therefore, if we open a proxy slot in an iteration, then there can be no other local barely open slots open in this iteration. Any barely open slot is dependent on the earliest fully open slot without a dependent. If $Y_k \geq 2$, d_k would not have got charged in iteration k, and hence would have no dependents even at iteration i. Therefore, $Y_k < 2$ and only d_k is fully open in the slots after d_{k-1}.

If d_k is not charged by a proxy slot, then necessarily $d_k - 1$ is barely open. However, even if d_k is charged by a proxy slot, we show that any such proxy slot can be considered to be a local barely open slot without any loss of generality. Let us suppose

that the dependent on d_k is a proxy slot. In that case, the alternating structure may not hold when we open the actual slot for the proxy. That means, the actual slot must be occurring in at some t', $d_{j-1} \leq t' \leq d_j$, where $j < k$. No barely open or half open slots could have opened between j and k as otherwise it would have accounted for the proxy slot. If there is a fully open slot between d_j (inclusive of d_j) and d_k then the proxy can charge this slot as it must have been uncharged so far. Since the proxy is a dependent on d_k, d_k must be the first fully open slot from iteration j onwards. Moreover, all the jobs in $\bigcup_{x<k} \mathcal{J}_x$ do not need the proxy value for a feasible assignment. Hence, we can change the pointer of the proxy slot to $d_k - 1$ without any loss of generality and consider $d_k - 1$ as dependent on d_k. Note that $d_k - 1$ may also be equal to d_j. Therefore, even if d_k is charged by proxy slot, we can convert it to a local barely open slot $d_k - 1$.

Now, consider the rounding process in the iteration k. We must have first tried to close $d_k - 1$ and find a feasible assignment using max-flow. Clearly that must have failed. Also, no job in $\mathcal{J}$ with release time $> d_{k-1}$ can be of length > 1, because $Y_k < 2$. Therefore, one reason can be that there are $\geq g + 1$ unit jobs in $\mathcal{J}_k$ with release time $\geq d_{k-1}$. In that case, d_k is the stopping deadline, and we have the alternating structure trivially.

If that is not the case, then that necessarily means the closest earlier open slot, say d_p, was half-open or fully open. The closest open slot cannot be barely open in a feasible LP solution, otherwise max-flow would have been able to find a feasible assignment of the jobs in $\bigcup_{p \leq x \leq k} \mathcal{J}_k$ even after closing the barely open slot $d_k - 1$. If half-open, then clearly, $y_{d_p} + y_{d_k-1} > 1$, otherwise, an assignment could be found by max-flow. However, in this case, the rounding would have made d_p fully open, and charged the new $y_{d_k-1} = y_{d_p} + y_{d_k-1} - 1$ as a dependent to it, if no other fully open slots were available for charging. Therefore, the only possibility is that d_p is fully open, and has a dependent already. Then the same argument can be be repeated for d_p and $d_p - 1$. We repeat this argument for next closest open slot (which must be fully open with a dependent) till we come to a stopping deadline. We are guaranteed to find a stopping deadline because, if we ultimately come d_1, then that must also have a dependent $d_1 - 1$ (so no jobs in $\mathcal{J}_1$ can be of length > 1), and we know from our rounding rule for d_1, that $d_1 - 1$ is opened only when max flow failed, which implies there are $\geq g + 1$ unit jobs in $\mathcal{J}_1$. Hence, without loss we can convert our LP solution to the alternating form between d_i and the stopping deadline d_z. □

The following lemma shows that for any pair of intermediate deadlines, d_u and d_x in the alternating structure, there are $2g + 1$ units of jobs that need to be scheduled in the window $(d_u, d_x]$.

LEMMA 6. *Suppose d_z is the latest stopping deadline in the alternating structure going backwards from d_i. Then for every intermediate fully open deadline $d_x \notin \{d_z, d_i\}$, at least $2g + 1$ job units in $\mathcal{J}_u \cup \mathcal{J}_x$ must have release time at least d_u, where d_u is the latest open deadline before d_x.*

PROOF. We shall prove this by induction. Let the closest open slot before d_z be d_w. There are $\geq g + 1$ job units in d_z that need to be scheduled in slots $\{d_w + 1, \ldots, d_z\}$ due to release time constraints. This follows from the definition of a stopping deadline. Let the next fully open deadline after d_z in the alternating structure be d_a ($d_a > d_z$). Note that the total mass scheduled by the LP in $\{d_z - 1, d_z, d_a - 1, d_a\}$ is $\leq \frac{5g}{2}$, by the definition of the alternating structure. (The barely open slots could not form trio with each other.) We want to prove that there are $2g + 1$ job units in $\mathcal{J}_z \cup \mathcal{J}_a$ with release time at least d_z. Let us assume there are at most $2g$ units of jobs in $\mathcal{J}_z \cup \mathcal{J}_a$ with release time at least d_z, by way of contradiction. No job in $\mathcal{J}_a$ can be greater than or equal to

123

2 in length for a feasible LP solution since $Y_a < 2$. Let n_z denote the rigid jobs in $\mathcal{J}_x$ (those releasing at d_z), n'_z denote the flexible jobs in $\mathcal{J}_z$ which need to be assigned before d_w (if there is any d_w), $n_{a,2}$ denote the number of length 2 jobs in $\mathcal{J}_a$, $n_{a,1}$ denote the unit length jobs in $\mathcal{J}_a$ with release time d_a and $n'_{a,1}$ denote the unit length jobs in $\mathcal{J}_a$ with release time $\geq d_z$. We know that $n_z + 2n_{a,2} + n_{a,1} + n'_{a,1} \leq 2g$ by assumption, $n_z + n'_z \geq g+1$ by definition of d_z, and since d_z is the latest stopping deadline, $n_{a,1} + n_{a,2} \leq g$. Since max flow failed, the only possibility is that $n_z + n_{a,2} \geq g+1$. For LP feasibility, $n_z + \frac{n'_z}{2} + \frac{n_{a,2}}{2} \leq g$. However, $n_z + n'_z + n_z + n_{a,2} > 2g$. Hence we get a contradiction. Therefore, there must be $\geq 2g+1$ job units $\mathcal{J}_z \cup \mathcal{J}_a$ with release time $\geq d_z$.

For ease of notation, without loss of generality, assume that the deadlines are consecutive. Then, deadlines $\{d_z, d_{z+1}, \ldots, d_k\}$ are fully open (here, $d_a = d_{z+1}$). Now, assume by induction hypothesis, that the claim is true for all deadlines up to d_k in the alternating structure, and the next fully open slot is d_{k+1}. For any deadline d_p which is fully open in the alternating structure between d_z and d_{k+1}, let us denote by $n_{p,1}$ the unit length rigid jobs in $\mathcal{J}_p$, $n_{p,2}$ the length 2 jobs of release time $\geq d_{p-1}$, and $n'_{p,1}$ the unit length jobs of release time $\geq d_{p-1}$ in $\mathcal{J}_p$. By induction hypothesis, for any two adjacent open deadlines d_{p-1} and d_p, where $p \geq 2$, in the alternating structure, there are $\geq 2g+1$ job units in $\mathcal{J}_{p-1} \cup \mathcal{J}_p$ with release time $\geq d_{p-1}$, i.e., $n_{(p-1),1} + n_{p,1} + n'_{p,1} + 2n_{p,2} \geq 2g+1$. As in the base case, assume for contradiction, that there are $\leq 2g$ job units in $\mathcal{J}_k \cup \mathcal{J}_{k+1}$ with release time $\geq d_k$. Therefore, $n_{k,1} + n_{(k+1),1} + n'_{(k+1),1} + 2n_{(k+1),2} \leq 2g$. Since the latest stopping deadline $d_z < d_{k+1}$, it also holds that $n_{(k+1),1} + n_{(k+1),2} \leq g$. Therefore, for max-flow to fail, it must be that $n_{k,1} + n_{k+1,2} \geq g+1$. For LP feasibility, the $\sum_{z \leq p \leq k} n_{p,1} + \sum_{z \leq p \leq k} \frac{n'_{p,1}}{2} + \sum_{z \leq p \leq k} \frac{3n_{p,2}}{2} + \frac{n_{(k+1),2}}{2} \leq g(k-z+1)$. However, by the induction hypothesis, $2\sum_{z \leq p \leq k} n_{p,1} + \sum_{z \leq p \leq k} n'_{p,1} + 2\sum_{z \leq p \leq k} n_{p,2} + n_{(k+1),2} > 2g(k-z+1)$. Hence this case is also not possible. Therefore, max-flow can fail only if there are at least $2g+1$ job units (including flexible, unit length and non-unit length) in $\mathcal{J}_k \cup \mathcal{J}_{k+1}$ whose jobs are released by d_k.

Therefore, we have proved the claim by induction. $\square$

Proof of Lemma 4 continued:
Since we cannot charge d_i as a dependent or a trio, by arguments similar to those proving Lemma 6, it can be shown that there must be at least $g+1$ unit jobs with release time d_k in $\mathcal{J}_i \cup \mathcal{J}_k$.

Without loss of generality, we assume the deadlines are open in consecutive order. The alternating structure is over some set of deadlines $\{d_z, d_{z+1}, \ldots, d_i\}$. From Lemmas 5 and 6, the following hold: for d_z, we have that $n'_z + n_z \geq g+1$, where d_z is the stopping deadline, and n'_z denotes the number of length 2 jobs plus the flexible unit length jobs which must be scheduled before the closest earlier open deadline. For any $d_z < d_p < d_i$, $n_{p-1} + n_{p,1} + 2n_{p,2} + n'_{p,1} \geq 2g+1$, where $n_{p,1}$ denotes the number of unit length rigid jobs with release time d_p, $n_{p,2}$ denotes the number of length 2 jobs with release time at least d_{p-1} and $n'_{p,1}$ denotes the number of flexible unit length jobs with deadline at least d_{p-1}. Therefore, $\sum_{z \leq p \leq i} n'_{p,1} + 2\sum_{z \leq p \leq i} n_{p,1} + 2\sum_{z \leq p \leq i} n_{p,2} > 2(i-z)g$. However, for LP feasibility, jobs must be assigned to an extent of strictly less than $\frac{1}{2}$ in the barely open slots. Hence, $\sum_{z \leq p \leq i} \frac{n'_{p,1}}{2} + \sum_{z \leq p \leq i} \frac{3n_{p,2}}{2} + \sum_{z \leq p \leq i} n_{p,1} \leq (i-z)g$, which is a contradiction. Therefore we will always be able to charge a barely open slot which cannot be closed by max-flow assignment. $\square$

THEOREM 3. *There exists an algorithm whose active time is within twice the optimum, on non-unit length jobs that can be preempted on the integer time boundary.*

PROOF. From Lemma 4 and the rounding procedure, it follows that at the end of iteration i, the total number of integrally open slots $|\mathcal{O}_i| \leq 2\sum_{1 \leq k \leq i} Y_k$, and there exists a LP feasible fractional assignment of jobs in $\bigcup_{x \leq i} \mathcal{J}_x$ in $\mathcal{O}_i$. Hence the proof follows. An integral feasible assignment of all jobs can be found in the slots $\mathcal{O}_\ell$ via max-flow. $\square$

4. BUSY TIME: NOTATIONS AND PRELIMINARIES

DEFINITION 6. *Job j is an* interval job *means that its length p_j is equal to $d_j - r_j$.*

A job j is *active* on machine m at some time $t \in [r_j, d_j)$ if j is one of the jobs being processed by machine m at time t.

DEFINITION 7. *The length of a time interval $I = [a, b)$ is denoted $\ell(I) = b - a$, For a single contiguous interval, the length is the same as its span, and hence may be referred to interchangeably as the span of I, $|Sp(I)|$. For a set of intervals $\mathcal{I}$, the length of $\mathcal{I}$ is $\ell(\mathcal{I}) = \sum_{I \in \mathcal{I}} \ell(I)$. The span of $\mathcal{I}$ is $Sp(\mathcal{I}) = \bigcup_{I \in \mathcal{I}} I$.*

For the special case of interval jobs, we need to find a partition of the jobs into groups or bundles, such that in every bundle, there are at most g jobs active at any time t. We then schedule each bundle on a single machine. Let $\mathcal{B}_\kappa$ be the set of interval jobs assigned to bundle κ by some partitioning scheme. Then, the busy time of the machine on which the bundle κ will be scheduled is given by $|Sp(\mathcal{B}_\kappa)|$. Suppose we have partitioned all jobs into k feasible bundles (the feasibility respects the parallelism bound g as well as the release times and deadlines). Then the total cost of the solution is given by the cumulative busy time $\sum_{\kappa=1}^{k} |Sp(\mathcal{B}_\kappa)|$. The objective is to minimize this cost. We consider both the variants where g is unbounded and where $g < \infty$. For the *preemptive* version of the problem, the problem definition remains the same, the only difference being that the jobs can be processed preemptively across various machines.

To minimize busy time in the general case, the difficulty lies not just in finding a partition of jobs, but also in deciding when each job j should be scheduled. We study both the preemptive and non-preemptive versions of this problem.

We denote the cost of the optimal solution of an instance $\mathcal{J}$ by $OPT(\mathcal{J})$. We denote by $OPT_\infty(\mathcal{J})$ the cost of the optimal solution for the instance $\mathcal{J}$ when unbounded parallelism is allowed.

Without loss of generality, the busy time of a machine is contiguous. If it is not, we can break it up into disjoint periods of contiguous busy time, assigning each of them to different machines, without increasing the total busy time of the solution.

The following lower bounds on any optimal solution for a given instance $\mathcal{J}$ were introduced earlier ([3], [16]).

OBSERVATION 1. $OPT(\mathcal{J}) \geq \frac{\ell(\mathcal{J})}{g}$, where $g \geq 1$ and $\ell(\mathcal{J})$ denotes the sum of the processing lengths of the jobs in $\mathcal{J}$, interchangeably referred to as the mass of $\mathcal{J}$.

This holds because in any machine, we can have at most g jobs active simultaneously.

OBSERVATION 2. $OPT(\mathcal{J}) \geq OPT_\infty(\mathcal{J})$.

The above observation follows from the fact that if a lower cost solution exists for bounded g, then it is a feasible solution for unbounded g as well. If the jobs in $\mathcal{J}$ are interval jobs, then, $OPT_\infty(\mathcal{J})$ is equal to $|Sp(\mathcal{J})|$.

The following theorem follows from the works of Alicherry and Bhatia [3] and Kumar and Rudra [16].

THEOREM 4. *There exists a factor 2 approximation algorithm for the busy time problem on interval jobs. The approximation factor is tight.*

5. A 3-APPROXIMATION ALGORITHM FOR NON-PREEMPTIVE BUSY TIME

The busy time problem was studied by Khandekar et al. [14], who referred to it as the real-time scheduling problem. In fact, they gave a 5-approximation for a slight generalization, in which jobs can have arbitrary widths. (The generalized constraint is that at no point may the sum of widths of "live" jobs in a given bundle exceed g.) In the busy time problem as defined in this work, widths are all unit; under such assumptions, their analysis yields a 4-approximation. As a first step towards proving this, Khandekar et al. [14] show that if g is unbounded, then the problem is polynomial-time solvable via a dynamic program. Recall that an interval job j is defined to have the property $p_j = d_j - r_j$. The output of their dynamic program essentially converts a given busy time instance to one of interval jobs by fixing the start and end times of every job.

THEOREM 5. *[14] If g is unbounded, the real-time scheduling problem is polynomial-time solvable.*

By Theorem 5, the span of the output of the dynamic program is $OPT_\infty(\mathcal{J})$.

Once Khandekar et al. [14] obtain the modified interval instance, they apply the 5-approximation for non-unit width interval jobs to get the final bound. However, for jobs with unit width, their algorithm and analysis can be modified without loss to get a final bound of 4. Moreover, extending the algorithms of Alicherry and Bhatia [3] and Kumar and Rudra [16] to the busy time problem by converting a given instance to an interval instance (similar to the approach of Khandekar et al. [14]) also gives a 4-approximation[2].

In this section, we give a 3-approximation for the busy time problem, i.e., for unit width jobs, improving the existing 4-approximation. Analogous to Khandekar et al. [14], we first convert the instance $\mathcal{J}'$ to an instance $\mathcal{J}$ of interval jobs by temporarily removing the assumption that g is bounded, applying a dynamic program on $\mathcal{J}'$ and fixing the job windows according to the output of the dynamic program. Let $OPT_\infty(\mathcal{J}')$ denote the busy time of the output of the dynamic program. By Observation 2, we know that $OPT_\infty(\mathcal{J}') \leq OPT(\mathcal{J}')$.

Then, on the interval job instance $\mathcal{J}$, we will run our algorithm GREEDYTRACKING. For an interval job j, its window $[r_j, d_j)$ is denoted as the span $Sp(j)$ of j. For the remainder of the section, we assume that the input consists of interval jobs.

To describe GREEDYTRACKING requires the notion of a *track*.

DEFINITION 8. *A track of interval jobs is a set of interval jobs with disjoint spans.*

Given a feasible solution, one can think of each bundle $\mathcal{B}$ as the union of g individual tracks of jobs. The main idea behind the algorithm is to identify such tracks iteratively, bundling the first

---

[2]The bound of 4 for all these algorithms is tight [8].

g tracks into a single bundle, the second g tracks into the second bundle, etc. FIRSTFIT [11] suffers from the fact that it greedily considers jobs one-by-one; GREEDYTRACKING is less myopic in that it identifies sets of jobs, entire tracks at a time.

In the ith iteration, $i \geq 1$, the algorithm identifies a track $\mathcal{T}_i \subseteq \mathcal{J} \setminus \bigcup_{k=1}^{i-1} \mathcal{T}_k$ of maximum length $\ell(\mathcal{T}_i)$ and assigns it to bundle $\mathcal{B}_p$, where $p = \lceil \frac{i}{g} \rceil$. One can find such a track efficiently via weighted interval scheduling algorithms [10]. We consider the lengths of the interval jobs as their weights and find the maximum weight set of interval jobs with disjoint spans. If the final solution has κ bundles, the algorithm's total cost is $\sum_{i=1}^{\kappa} |Sp(\mathcal{B}_i)|$. The pseudocode for GREEDYTRACKING is provided in Algorithm 1.

Algorithm 1 GREEDYTRACKING. Inputs: $\mathcal{J}, g$.

1: $\mathcal{S} \leftarrow \mathcal{J}$, $i \leftarrow 1$.
2: **while** $\mathcal{S} \neq \emptyset$ **do**
3:     Compute the longest track $\mathcal{T}_i$ from $\mathcal{S}$ and assign it to bundle $\mathcal{B}_{\lceil \frac{i}{g} \rceil}$.
4:     $\mathcal{S} \leftarrow \mathcal{S} \setminus \mathcal{T}_i$, $i \leftarrow i + 1$.
5: **end while**
6: Return bundles $\{\mathcal{B}_p\}_{p=1}^{\lceil \frac{i-1}{g} \rceil}$

We next prove a key property of GREEDYTRACKING: the span of any track is at least half that of the remaining unscheduled jobs. In particular, the span of any bundle is at most twice that of the first track to be assigned to it.

LEMMA 7. *Let $\mathcal{T}_i$ be the ith track found by GREEDYTRACKING, for $i \geq 1$. Let $\mathcal{J}_i' \subseteq \mathcal{J}$ denote the set of unscheduled jobs $\mathcal{J} \setminus \bigcup_{k=1}^{i-1} \mathcal{T}_k$. Then $|Sp(\mathcal{J}_i')| \leq 2|Sp(\mathcal{T}_i)|$.*

PROOF. In order to prove this, we first prove the following. There exists two tracks $\mathcal{T}_1^*$ and $\mathcal{T}_2^*$, such that $\mathcal{T}_1^* \subseteq \mathcal{J}_i'$ and $\mathcal{T}_2^* \subseteq \mathcal{J}_i'$, $\mathcal{T}_1^* \cap \mathcal{T}_2^* = \emptyset$ and $Sp(\mathcal{T}_1^*) \cup Sp(\mathcal{T}_2^*) = Sp(\mathcal{J}_i')$. Let us assume, by way of contradiction, that the above is not true. In other words, for every pair of disjoint tracks from the set of yet unscheduled jobs $\mathcal{J}_i'$, the union of their spans does not cover $Sp(\mathcal{J}_i')$. Let $\mathcal{T}_1^*$ and $\mathcal{T}_2^*$ be two disjoint tracks from $\mathcal{J}_i'$, such that the union of their spans is maximum among all such tracks. By assumption, $|Sp(\mathcal{T}_1^* \cup \mathcal{T}_2^*)| < |Sp(\mathcal{J}_i')|$. This implies that there exists an interval $I \in Sp(\mathcal{J}_i')$, such that $I \notin Sp(\mathcal{T}_1^* \cup \mathcal{T}_2^*)$. Let I be $[t_I, t_I')$. Clearly, no job $j \in \mathcal{J}_i'$ has a window $\subseteq [t_I, t_I')$, by the maximality of $Sp(\mathcal{T}_1^* \cup \mathcal{T}_2^*)$. In fact, all jobs intersecting I, must intersect with some job in both $\mathcal{T}_1^*$ and $\mathcal{T}_2^*$, because of the same reason. In

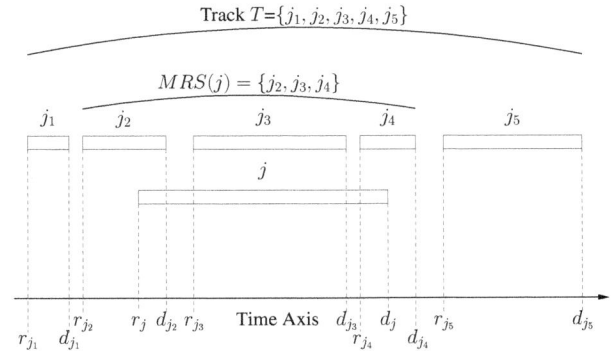

Figure 6: An example showing the minimum replaceable set of a job j, i.e., $MRS(j)$ with respect to a track T.

the following we prove that *no* such interval I can exist given our assumptions on $\mathcal{T}_1^*$ and $\mathcal{T}_2^*$.

Let us first define the notion of *minimum replaceable set*.

DEFINITION 9. *Consider track $\mathcal{T}$ and interval job j with window $[r_j, d_j)$. Let $j_f \in \mathcal{T}$ have the earliest deadline $d_{j_f} > r_j$ such that $r_{j_f} \leq r_j$. Let $j_\ell \in \mathcal{T}$ have the latest release time $r_{j_\ell} < d_j$, such that $d_{j_\ell} \geq d_j$. Then the set of jobs in $\mathcal{T}$ with windows in $[r_{j_f}, d_{j_\ell})$ is the minimum replaceable set $MRS(j, \mathcal{T})$ for j in $\mathcal{T}$, i.e., it is the set of jobs whose union has the minimum span, such that $\{\mathcal{T} \cup j\} \setminus MRS(j, \mathcal{T})$ is a valid track. If there exists no such job j_f (respectively, j_ℓ), then $MRS(j, \mathcal{T})$ consists of jobs in $[r_j, d_{j_\ell})$ (respectively, $[r_{j_f}, d_j)$). If neither j_f nor j_ℓ exists, then $MRS(j, \mathcal{T}) = \emptyset$. (See Figure 6 for an example.)*

CASE 1. *There exists a job j in $\mathcal{J}'_i \setminus \{\mathcal{T}_1^* \cup \mathcal{T}_2^*\}$, such that $r_j < t_I$ and $t_I < d_j < t'_I$.*

Consider $MRS(j, \mathcal{T}_1^*)$ and $MRS(j, \mathcal{T}_2^*)$. well as that in $MRS(j, \mathcal{T}_2^*)$ They cannot be empty, since otherwise, by adding j to the corresponding track, we could have increased $Sp(\mathcal{T}_1^* \cup \mathcal{T}_2^*)$. Let j_e be the job with the earliest release time r_e in $MRS(j, \mathcal{T}_1^*) \cup MRS(j, \mathcal{T}_2^*)$, and without loss of generality, suppose it belongs to $\mathcal{T}_1^*$. Replacing $MRS(j, \mathcal{T}_2^*)$ with j will increase $Sp(\mathcal{T}_1^* \cup \mathcal{T}_2^*)$: $Sp(MRS(j, \mathcal{T}_1^*) \cup MRS(j, \mathcal{T}_2^*)) < [r_e, t_I)$, but $Sp(j) \geq [d_e, t_I)$, so $Sp(MRS(j, \mathcal{T}_1^*) \cup j) > [r_e, t_I)$. See Figure 7 for an example. Hence, this case is not possible.

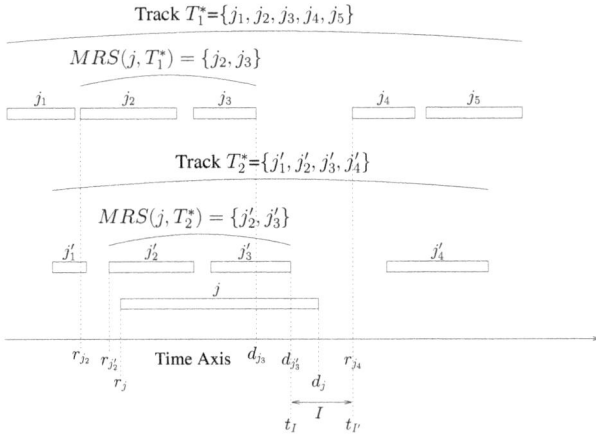

Figure 7: An example for Case 1 of Lemma 7. Replacing $MRS(j, \mathcal{T}_2^*)$ by j increases $Sp(\mathcal{T}_1^* \cup \mathcal{T}_2^*)$.

CASE 2. *There exists a job j in $\mathcal{J}'_i \setminus \{\mathcal{T}_1^* \cup \mathcal{T}_2^*\}$, such that $t_I < r_j < t'_I$ and $d_j > t'_I$.*

Consider $MRS(j, \mathcal{T}_1^*)$ and $MRS(j, \mathcal{T}_2^*)$. Without loss of generality, they cannot be empty sets as argued in Case 1. Let the job j_ℓ have the latest deadline d_ℓ in $MRS(j, \mathcal{T}_1^*) \cup MRS(j, \mathcal{T}_2^*)$. Without loss of generality, suppose j_ℓ belongs to $\mathcal{T}_1^*$. Then we can replace $MRS(j, \mathcal{T}_2^*)$ with j, thereby increasing $Sp(\mathcal{T}_1^* \cup \mathcal{T}_2^*)$. This is because, $Sp(MRS(j, \mathcal{T}_1^*) \cup MRS(j, \mathcal{T}_2^*)) \leq [t'_I, d_\ell)$, whereas $Sp(MRS(j, \mathcal{T}_1^*) \cup j) > [t'_I, d_\ell)$, since $Sp(j) > [t'_I, d_j)$.

Hence, this case is also not possible.

CASE 3. *There exists a job j, such that $[r_j, d_j) \supset [t_I, t'_I)$.*

Let the earliest release time (latest deadline, respectively) of any job in $MRS(j, \mathcal{T}_1^*) \cup MRS(j, \mathcal{T}_2^*)$ be r_e (d_e, respectively) and the corresponding job be j_e (j_ℓ, respectively). Without loss, these sets

are not empty. If j_e and j_ℓ belonged to the same track, say $\mathcal{T}_2^*$, we could have replaced $MRS(j, \mathcal{T}_2^*)$ with j in $\mathcal{T}_2^*$ and increased the union of the span of $\mathcal{T}_1^* \cup \mathcal{T}_2^*$: $Sp(j) \geq [d_e, r_\ell)$ and would include $I = [t_I, t'_I)$, whereas $Sp(MRS(j, \mathcal{T}_2^*) \setminus MRS(j, \mathcal{T}_1^*))$ would be at most $[d_e, r_\ell) \setminus [t_I, t'_I)$. Therefore, j_e and j_ℓ must belong to different tracks. Without loss of generality, let $j_e \in \mathcal{T}_1^*$ and $j_\ell \in \mathcal{T}_2^*$. Let us replace $MRS(j, \mathcal{T}_2^*)$ with j. Next, we put j_ℓ in $\mathcal{T}_1^*$ replacing $MRS(j_\ell, \mathcal{T}_1^*)$. Note that $d_e \leq t_I$, $r_\ell \geq t'_I$, and $t'_I - t_I > 0$ by our assumptions. Therefore, $j_e \notin MRS(j_\ell, \mathcal{T}_1^*)$. In fact, none of the jobs in $\mathcal{T}_1^*$ with release time $< t'_I$ are included in $MRS(j_\ell, \mathcal{T}_1^*)$, and hence none of them are discarded. Therefore, the loss of coverage by $\mathcal{T}_1^*$ after putting j_ℓ in place of $MRS(j_\ell, \mathcal{T}_1^*)$ is at most the interval $[t'_I, r_\ell)$. However, we have added j to $\mathcal{T}_2^*$, and not only does j span $[t_I, t'_I)$, but also the interval $[t'_I, r_\ell)$, since $d_j \geq r_\ell$ for j_ℓ to be originally a part of $MRS(j, \mathcal{T}_2^*)$. Hence, we would increase $Sp(\mathcal{T}_1^* \cup \mathcal{T}_2^*)$, which is a contradiction. Therefore, this case is also not possible.

Since no job window in $\mathcal{J}'_i$ can intersect I, there exists no such I in $Sp(\mathcal{J}'_i)$. Therefore, $Sp(\mathcal{T}_1^* \cup \mathcal{T}_2^*) = Sp(\mathcal{J}'_i)$. Furthermore, $|Sp(\mathcal{T}_1^* \cup \mathcal{T}_2^*)| \leq |Sp(\mathcal{T}_1^*)| + |Sp(\mathcal{T}_2^*)|$, in other words, the longer of $\mathcal{T}_1^*$ and $\mathcal{T}_2^*$ is $\geq \frac{|Sp(\mathcal{J}'_i)|}{2}$. Since, $\mathcal{T}_i$ is the longest track in $\mathcal{J}'_i$, therefore, $|Sp(\mathcal{J}'_i)| \leq 2|Sp(\mathcal{T}_i)|$. $\square$

We next prove that our algorithm generates a solution within 3 times the cost of an optimal solution via the following lemmas.

LEMMA 8. *For any $i > 1$, the span of bundle $\mathcal{B}_i$ can be bounded by the mass of the bundle $\mathcal{B}_{i-1}$ as follows: $|Sp(\mathcal{B}_i)| \leq 2\frac{\ell(\mathcal{B}_{i-1})}{g}$.*

PROOF. Let $\mathcal{T}_i^1$ denote the first track of the bundle $\mathcal{B}_i$. From Lemma 7, it follows that $|Sp(\mathcal{B}_i)| \leq 2|Sp(\mathcal{T}_i^1)|$. The jobs in $\mathcal{T}_i^1$ are disjoint by definition of a track, hence $|Sp(\mathcal{T}_i^1)| = \ell(\mathcal{T}_i^1)$, and $|Sp(\mathcal{B}_i)| \leq 2\ell(\mathcal{T}_i^1)$. Since $\mathcal{T}_i^1$ started the ith bundle, bundle $\mathcal{B}_{i-1}$ must already have had g tracks in it. Furthermore, the lengths of these tracks are longer than that of $\mathcal{T}_i^1$ since GREEDYTRACKING chooses tracks in non-increasing order of length. Therefore, $\ell(\mathcal{B}_{i-1}) = \sum_{p=1}^g \ell(\mathcal{T}_{i-1}^p) \geq g\ell(\mathcal{T}_i^1)$. And so we conclude that

$$|Sp(\mathcal{B}_i)| \leq 2\frac{\ell(\mathcal{B}_{i-1})}{g}$$

$\square$

LEMMA 9. *The total busy time of all the bundles except the first one is at most twice that of an optimal solution for the entire instance. Specifically, $\sum_{i>1} |Sp(\mathcal{B}_i)| \leq 2OPT(\mathcal{J}')$.*

PROOF. This proof follows from Lemma 8. For any $i > 1$, $|Sp(\mathcal{B}_i)| \leq 2\frac{\ell(\mathcal{B}_{i-1})}{g}$. Summing over all $i > 1$, we get the following: $\sum_{i>1} |Sp(\mathcal{B}_i)| \leq 2\frac{\sum_{i>1} \ell(\mathcal{B}_{i-1})}{g} = 2\frac{\sum_{i>1} \sum_{j \in \mathcal{B}_{i-1}} \ell(j)}{g}$. Therefore, $\sum_{i>1} |Sp(\mathcal{B}_i)| \leq 2\frac{\ell(\mathcal{J})}{g}$. Note that $\ell(\mathcal{J}) = \sum_{j \in \mathcal{J}'} p_j$, where $\mathcal{J}'$ is the original flexible interval job instance. This is true because the dynamic program converting a flexible instance to an interval instance, does not reduce the processing length of any job. Hence, from Observation 1, $OPT(\mathcal{J}') \geq \frac{\ell(\mathcal{J}')}{g}$. Therefore, $\sum_{i>1} |Sp(\mathcal{B}_i)| \leq 2OPT(\mathcal{J}')$. $\square$

THEOREM 6. *The cost of the algorithm is at most 3 times the cost of an optimal solution. Specifically, $\sum_i |Sp(\mathcal{B}_i)| \leq 3OPT(\mathcal{J})$.*

PROOF. From Lemma 9, $\sum_{i>1} |Sp(\mathcal{B}_i)| \leq 2OPT(\mathcal{J}')$. Furthermore, $|Sp(\mathcal{B}_1)| \leq OPT_\infty(\mathcal{J}')$. From Observation 2,

$$OPT_\infty(\mathcal{J}') \leq OPT(\mathcal{J}')$$

Therefore, $\sum_i |Sp(\mathcal{B}_i)| \leq 3OPT(\mathcal{J})$. $\square$

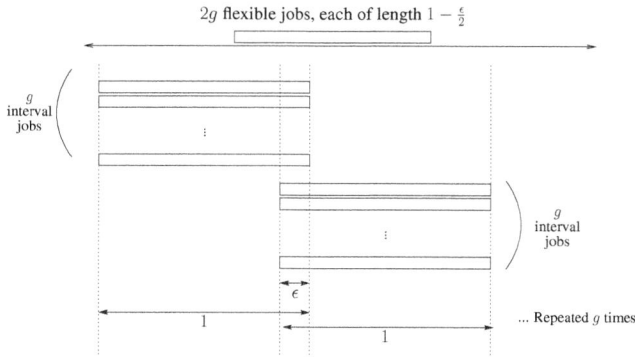

Figure 8: Construction for factor 3 for GREEDYTRACKING.

The bound for this algorithm is tight.

Figure 8 shows that the approximation factor of 3 achieved by GREEDYTRACKING is tight. In the instance shown, a small construction of $2g$ interval jobs is repeated g times. For each copy of the construction, there are g identical unit length interval jobs which overlap for ϵ amount with another g identical unit length interval jobs. The g copies are disjoint from one another, i.e., there is no overlap among the jobs of any two constructions. There are also $2g$ flexible jobs, whose windows span the windows of all g constructions. These jobs have length $1 - \frac{\epsilon}{2}$. An optimal packing would pack each set of g identical jobs of each copy in one bundle, and the flexible jobs in two bundles, yielding a total busy time of $2g + 2 - \epsilon$. However, since the dynamic program minimizing the span is oblivious to capacity, it may pack the flexible jobs 2 each with each of the g constructions, in a manner such that they intersect with all of the jobs of the construction. Hence, the flexible jobs cannot be considered in the same track as any unit interval job in the construction it is packed with. Due to the greedy nature of GREEDYTRACKING, the tracks selected would not consider the flexible jobs in the beginning, and the interval jobs may also get split up as in Figure 9, giving a total busy time of $4(1 - \epsilon)g + (2 - o(\epsilon))g = (6 - o(\epsilon))g$, hence it approaches a factor of 3 asymptotically.

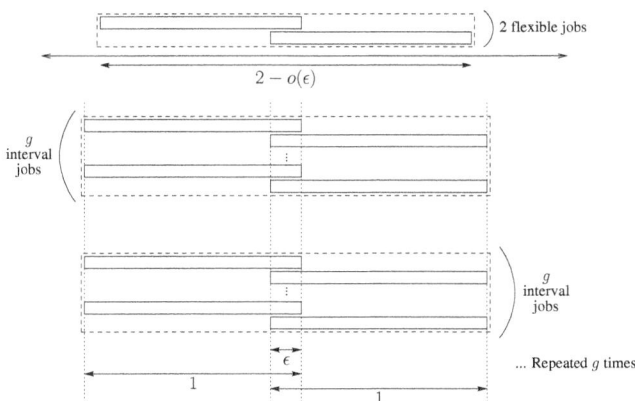

Figure 9: Possible packing produced by GREEDYTRACKING on the instance of Figure 8.

6. REFERENCES

[1] S. Albers. Algorithms for energy saving. *Efficient Algorithms*, 5760:173–186, 2009.

[2] S. Albers. Energy-efficient algorithms. *Communications of the ACM*, 53(5):86–96, 2010.

[3] M. Alicherry and R. Bhatia. Line system design and a generalized coloring problem. In *Proceedings of ESA*, pages 19–30, 2003.

[4] P. Baptiste. Scheduling unit tasks to minimize the number of idle periods: a polynomial time algorithm for offline dynamic power management. In *Proceedings of the 17th Annual ACM-SIAM SODA*, pages 364–367, 2006.

[5] P. Brucker. *Scheduling algorithms*. Springer, 2007.

[6] J. Chang, H. Gabow, and S. Khuller. A model for minimizing active processor time. In *Proceedings of ESA*, pages 289–300, 2012.

[7] J. Chang and S. Khuller. A min-edge cost framework for capacitated covering problems. In *Proceedings of the 15th Annual ALENEX*, pages 14–25, 2013.

[8] J. Chang, S. Khuller, and K. Mukherjee. LP rounding and combinatorial algorithms for minimizing active and busy time. http://www.cs.umd.edu/~samir/fv.pdf.

[9] A. Condotta, S. Knust, and N. V. Shakhlevich. Parallel batch scheduling of equal-length jobs with release and due dates. *Journal of Scheduling*, 13(5):463–477, 2010.

[10] T. H. Cormen, C. E. Leiserson, R. L. Rivest, and C. Stein. *Introduction to Algorithms*. MIT press, 2001.

[11] M. Flammini, G. Monaco, L. Moscardelli, H. Shachnai, M. Shalom, T. Tamir, and S. Zaks. Minimizing total busy time in parallel scheduling with application to optical networks. In *Proceedings of the IPDPS*, pages 1–12, 2009.

[12] M. Flammini, G. Monaco, L. Moscardelli, M. Shalom, and S. Zaks. Approximating the traffic grooming problem with respect to adms and oadms. In *Proceedings of Euro-Par*, pages 920–929, 2008.

[13] M. Flammini, L. Moscardelli, M. Shalom, and S. Zaks. Approximating the traffic grooming problem. In *Proceedings of ISAAC*, pages 915–924, 2005.

[14] R. Khandekar, B. Schieber, H. Shachnai, and T. Tamir. Minimizing busy time in multiple machine real-time scheduling. In *Proceedings of FSTTCS*, pages 169–180, 2010.

[15] F. Koehler and S. Khuller. Optimal batch schedules for parallel machines. In *Proceedings of WADS*, pages 475–486, 2013.

[16] V. Kumar and A. Rudra. Approximation algorithms for wavelength assignment. In *Proceedings of FSTTCS*, pages 152–163, 2005.

[17] G. B. Mertzios, M. Shalom, A. Voloshin, P. W. Wong, and S. Zaks. Optimizing busy time on parallel machines. In *IPDPS*, pages 238–248, 2012.

[18] P. Winkler and L. Zhang. Wavelength assignment and generalized interval graph coloring. In *Proceedings of the 14th Annual ACM-SIAM SODA*, pages 830 – 831, 2003.

Scheduling Shared Continuous Resources on Many-Cores

André Brinkmann*
Zentrum für Datenverarbeitung
Johannes Gutenberg–Universität Mainz
brinkmann@uni-mainz.de

Peter Kling†
Heinz Nixdorf Institute &
Computer Science Dept.
University of Paderborn
peter.kling@upb.de

Friedhelm Meyer auf der Heide†
Heinz Nixdorf Institute &
Computer Science Dept.
University of Paderborn
fmadh@upb.de

Lars Nagel*
Zentrum für Datenverarbeitung
Johannes Gutenberg–Universität Mainz
nagell@uni-mainz.de

Sören Riechers†
Heinz Nixdorf Institute &
Computer Science Dept.
University of Paderborn
soeren.riechers@upb.de

Tim Süß
Zentrum für Datenverarbeitung
Johannes Gutenberg–Universität Mainz
t.suess@uni-mainz.de

ABSTRACT

We consider the problem of scheduling a number of jobs on m identical processors sharing a continuously divisible resource. Each job j comes with a resource requirement $r_j \in [0,1]$. The job can be processed at full speed if granted its full resource requirement. If receiving only an x-portion of r_j, it is processed at an x-fraction of the full speed. Our goal is to find a resource assignment that minimizes the makespan (i.e., the latest completion time). Variants of such problems, relating the resource assignment of jobs to their *processing speeds*, have been studied under the term *discrete-continuous scheduling*. Known results are either very pessimistic or heuristic in nature.

In this paper, we suggest and analyze a slightly simplified model. It focuses on the assignment of shared continuous resources to the processors. The job assignment to processors and the ordering of the jobs have already been fixed. It is shown that, even for unit size jobs, finding an optimal solution is NP-hard if the number of processors is part of the input. Positive results for unit size jobs include an efficient optimal algorithm for 2 processors. Moreover, we prove that *balanced* schedules yield a $2 - 1/m$-approximation for a fixed number of processors. Such schedules are computed by our GREEDYBALANCE algorithm, for which the bound is tight.

Categories and Subject Descriptors

F.2.2 [**Analysis of Algorithms and Problem Complexity**]: Nonnumerical Algorithms and Problems—*sequencing and scheduling*

---

*Supported by the Federal Ministry of Education and Research (BMBF) under Grant 01IH13004 (Project "FAST").
†Supported by the German Research Foundation (DFG) within the Collaborative Research Center "On-The-Fly Computing" (SFB 901).

Keywords

scheduling; approximation algorithms; resources

1. INTRODUCTION

The processor scheduling problem considered in this paper is motivated by the observation that, in many cases, it is not a device's speed or energy consumption that limits the progress of a given computation but the fact that data cannot be provided at the necessary rate. In extreme cases, this may lead to situations where changing the available I/O rate (or bandwidth) by some factor x may directly affect the running time by (approximately) the same factor.

At first glance, this seems more a network issue than a problem of interest for processor scheduling. After all, bandwidth bottlenecks are typically imposed by the interconnection of devices (e.g., networks or data buses), and there is a huge body of literature concerned with such issues on the network layer. However, the analysis in this area typically concentrates on the *network's* performance. In contrast, our model focuses on how the distribution of the bandwidth shared by a fixed set of processing units can affect their *computational* performance. That is, given some information about the bandwidth requirement of a program (e.g., when does it need how much bandwidth to progress at full speed), the scheduler can speed up critical jobs by a suitable assignment of the available bandwidth to the different processors. Typical examples for such settings are many-core systems: They provide an immense computing power through the sheer number of processor cores. Yet, many (if not all) of the chip's cores share a single data bus to the outside world. If such a system has to process I/O-intensive tasks (as typical for scientific computing), the available bandwidth becomes the computational bottleneck, and the bandwidth distribution becomes the decisive scheduling factor. One can find similar effects, if at different scales, on many other levels. For example, consider virtual systems, where different virtual machines share a single, arbitrarily and dynamically divisible resource of a given host system.

A First Glimpse at the Model. From a more abstract point of view, the aforementioned bandwidth scheduling can be seen as a variant of resource constrained scheduling, the bandwidth being an example for the resource. Imagine a system consisting of several identical processors that run at a fixed speed and share a given resource. Assume that the resource is the system's performance bottleneck, in the sense that the running time of programs (tasks) depends directly (that is to say, linearly) on the share of the resource they are allowed to use. Each task provides information about its resource requirements by stating what share of the resource it needs at different phases of its processing to run at full speed. Thus, we can imagine a task i to consist of a number n_i of jobs that must be processed sequentially, one after another. Each job represents a phase of the task's processing where the resource requirement is constant. The length of the phase (i.e., the job's processing time) is minimal at full speed and increases by a factor of $1/x$ if only a portion $x \in [0, 1]$ of the requested resource share is provided. We use the term CRSHARING to refer to this problem of sharing continuous resources; see Section 3 for a more formal description.

We will see, especially in Section 2, that this type of resource assignment problem is comparatively complex. Most work considering similar problems seems to be of heuristic nature and analytical results are scarce (and, if surfaced, quite negative). Since we are interested in more analytical insights, we approach the problem by concentrating on the assignment of resources, removing the (classical) scheduling aspect almost completely. That is to say, we consider a scenario in which each processor has exactly one task, and each task consists of jobs of unit workload (but different resource requirements). Moreover, we assume discrete time steps, such that the scheduler can change the resource assignment only at the beginning of such a time step. As we will see, even this simple setting proves to be challenging.

Outline. Section 2 surveys the related work and describes our contribution in view of known results. A formal model description of the CRSHARING problem is provided in Section 3. Section 4 equips the reader with basic definitions and results and discusses a first, simple result for a round robin algorithm. Our main results are given in Sections 5 to 7, where we study the complexity and achievable approximation ratio for the CRSHARING problem. We conclude with a short outlook in Section 8.

2. RELATED WORK & CONTRIBUTION

The proposed CRSHARING problem is a classical resource constrained scheduling problem. In such settings, the scheduler does not only manage the computational resources (e.g., the assignment of jobs to processors) but also the allocation of one or more additional resources to the currently processed jobs. In our context (processor scheduling), the most obvious examples for such resources are probably bandwidth and memory. However, note that models similar to ours are also used in project planning or for manufacturing systems.

The following discussion focuses on results for so-called *discrete-continuous* models, in which the computational resource is discrete (e.g., several processors) and the additional resources are continuous (e.g., bandwidth allotted in a continuous manner to the available processors). For a more general overview of resource constrained scheduling, the interested reader is referred to [9, Chs. 23-24] and [1, Ch. 12].

Discrete-continuous Scheduling. The aforementioned notion of *discrete-continuous scheduling* traces back to several papers by Józefowska and Weglarz, first and foremost [4]. While most results in this area study scenarios where the amount of allocated resources influences the processing time or release dates of jobs (see [2] for a survey), Józefowska and Weglarz [4] consider the case where the amount of allocated resources influences the processing *speed* of jobs. More exactly, if the function $R_j := \mathbb{R}_{\geq 0} \to [0, 1]$ models the share of the resource that job j gets assigned at some time $t \in \mathbb{R}_{\geq 0}$, its workload is processed at a speed of $f_j(R_j(t))$. Here, f_j models how a job's processing speed is affected by the received resource amount and is assumed to be continuous and non-decreasing with $f_j(0) = 0$. Using this resource model, the authors consider the problem of scheduling n non-preemptable and independent jobs on m processors. They propose an analysis framework based on a mathematical programming formulation and demonstrate it for the objective of minimizing the schedule's makespan. For certain classes of f_j, this yields a simple analytical solution [4, 5]. This holds especially for convex functions f_j, which encourage the scheduler to assign the full resource to a single processor. Finding an optimal solution for more realistic cases (especially concave f_j) remains infeasible. The results in [4] initiated several research efforts in this area, including a transfer of the methodology to other scheduling variants (e.g., average flow time instead of makespan [3]) as well as several heuristic approaches to obtain practical solutions in the general case [6–8, 12]. A detailed and current survey about these results can be found in [13] (especially Section 7).

Our CRSHARING problem shares several characteristics with discrete-continuous scheduling problems. In particular, the jobs' resource requirements can be modeled via concave functions f_j of the form $f_j(R) = \min(R/r_j, 1)$, where the value r_j denotes the resource requirement of job j (cf. Section 3). That is, the speed used to process a job depends linearly on the share of the resource it receives, but is capped at one. Our model contains several other important differences, the most obvious being that the assignment of jobs to processors as well as the order of jobs on a given processor is fixed. This severely limits the possibilities of the scheduler, which can no longer try to distribute the jobs evenly among the available processors. Instead, it is compelled to use a sophisticated resource assignment in order to yield a schedule of low makespan. Still, this simplification allows us to focus on the inherent problem complexity of assigning the continuous resource such that the schedule's makespan is minimized, and to derive provably good algorithms. In contrast, most of the aforementioned results for the discrete-continuous setting are of heuristic nature and do not provide any provable quality guarantees with respect to the resulting schedules, and cases that can be analyzed analytically turn out to feature quite simple solution structures [4, 5].

Contribution. This paper introduces a new resource constrained scheduling model for multiple processors, where job processing speeds depend on the assigned share of a common resource. We concentrate on a variant with unit size jobs where the scheduler only has to manage the distribution of the resource among all processors. The objective is to minimize the total makespan (maximum completion time over all jobs). Even this simple variant turns out to be NP-hard in the number m of processors. For fixed $m = 2$, we show that the problem is solvable in time $O(n^2)$. While we do not determine the exact complexity for a constant number of three or more processors, we provide an approximation algorithm that achieves a worst-case approximation ratio of exactly $2 - 1/m$. Our approach uses a hypergraph representation that allows us to capture non-trivial structural properties. To the best of our knowledge, this is the first strong analytical result for this type of problem.

3. MODEL & NOTATION

We start by defining the model for the general version of the CRSHARING problem, for jobs of arbitrary sizes. Afterward, we discuss an interpretation of our model that eases the argumentation in the analysis part. Note that, while the model description considers jobs of arbitrary sizes, our analysis focuses on the case where all jobs are of unit size.

3.1 Formal Model Description

Consider a system of m identical fixed-speed processors sharing a common resource. At every time step $t \in \mathbb{N}$, the scheduler distributes the resource among the m processors. To this end, each processor i is assigned a share $R_i(t) \in [0,1]$ of the resource, which it is allowed to use in time step t. It is the responsibility of the scheduler to ensure that the resource is not overused. That is, it must guarantee that $\sum_{i=1}^{m} R_i(t) \leq 1$ holds for all $t \in \mathbb{N}$. For each processor i, there is a sequence of $n_i \in \mathbb{N}$ jobs that must be processed by the processor in the given order. We write (i,j) to refer to the j-th job on processor i. A processor is not allowed to process more than one job during any given time step. Each job (i,j) has a *processing volume* (size) $p_{ij} > 0$ and a *resource requirement* $r_{ij} \in [0,1]$. The resource requirement specifies what portion of the resource is needed to process one unit of processing volume in one time step. When a job is granted an x-portion of its resource requirement ($x \in [0,1]$), exactly x units of its processing volume are processed in that time step. There is no benefit in giving a job more than requested: its processing cannot be sped up by granting it, for example, twice its resource requirement.

A feasible schedule for a CRSHARING instance consists of m resource assignment functions $R_i: \mathbb{N} \to [0,1]$ that specify the resource's distribution among the processors for all time steps without overusing the resource. We measure a schedule's quality via its makespan (i.e., the time when all jobs are finished). Our goal is to find a feasible schedule having minimal makespan. To simplify notation, we will often identify a schedule S with its makespan (e.g., by writing S/OPT to denote the makespan of schedule S divided by the makespan of an optimal schedule OPT).

Alternative Model Interpretation. An alternative interpretation of our scheduling problem can be obtained by the following observation: Consider a job (i,j) whose processing is started at time step t_1. It receives a share $R_i(t_1) \in [0,1]$ of the resource. By the previous model definition, exactly $\min(R_i(t_1)/r_{ij}, 1)$ units of its processing volume are processed. Similarly, in the next time step $\min(R_i(t_1 + 1)/r_{ij}, 1)$ units of its processing volume are processed. Consequently, the job is finished at the minimal time step $t_2 \geq t_1$ with $\sum_{t=t_1}^{t_2} \min(R_i(t)/r_{ij}, 1) \geq p_{ij}$ or, equivalently if $r_{ij} > 0$, at the minimal time step $t_2 \geq t_1$ with

$$\sum_{t=t_1}^{t_2} \min(R_i(t), r_{ij}) \geq r_{ij} p_{ij} =: \tilde{p}_{ij}. \tag{1}$$

This observation allows us to get rid of the resource aspect by considering *variable speed* processors instead of fixed speed processors. The speed of such variable speed processors can be changed at runtime[1]. For our reinterpretation, think of a job (i,j) to have size $\tilde{p}_{ij}$ and of a processor i to be of variable speed. The value $R_i(t)$ denotes the speed processor i is set to during time step t. The scheduler is in control of these processor speeds, but it must ensure that the aggregated speed of all processors does never exceed one. Moreover, in addition to the system's speed limit, each job (i,j) is annotated with the maximum speed r_{ij} it can utilize. In this light, our CRSHARING problem becomes a speed scaling problem to minimize the makespan in which the scheduler is limited by both the system's maximum aggregated speed and a per-job speed limit. The unit size restriction for the CRSHARING problem translates into the restriction that job sizes $\tilde{p}_{ij}$ equal the corresponding resource requirements r_{ij}. In other words, all jobs must be processable in one time step if run at maximum speed.

During the analysis, it will sometimes be more convenient to think of our problem in the way described above. For example, since the total workload $\sum_{i=1}^{m} \sum_{j=1}^{n_i} \tilde{p}_{ij}$ is processed at a maximum speed of one in any time step, this view on the problem immediately yields a simple but useful observation:

OBSERVATION 1. *Any feasible schedule for our problem needs at least $\sum_{i=1}^{m} \sum_{j=1}^{n_i} r_{ij} p_{ij}$ time steps to finish a given set of jobs with resource requirements r_{ij} and sizes p_{ij}.*

At times, we will use the notion *remaining resource requirement* to denote the remnants of a job's initial workload $\tilde{p}_{ij}$.

Additional Notation & Notions. The following additional notions and notation will turn out to be helpful in the analysis and discussion. For a processor i with n_i jobs, we define $n_i(t)$ as the number of unfinished jobs at the start of time step t. In particular, we have $n_i(1) = n_i$. A processor i is said to be *active* at time step t if $n_i(t) > 0$. Similarly, we say that job (i,j) is *active* at time step t if $n_i - n_i(t) = j - 1$ (i.e., if processor i has finished exactly $j - 1$ jobs at the start of time step t). We use $M_j := \{ i \mid n_i \geq j \}$ to denote the set of all processors having at least j jobs to process. Finally, we define $n := \max_i n_i$ as the maximum number of jobs any processor has to process.

3.2 Graphical Representation

The remainder of this section introduces a hypergraph notation for CRSHARING schedules and unit size jobs.

Given a problem instance of CRSHARING with unit size jobs and a corresponding schedule S, we define a weighted hypergraph $H_S = (V, E)$ as follows: The nodes of H_S and their weights correspond to the jobs and their resource requirements, respectively. That is, the node set is given by $V = \{ (i,j) \mid i = 1, 2, \ldots, m \wedge j = 1, 2, \ldots, n_i \}$, and the weight of a node $(i,j) \in V$ is r_{ij}. The edges of H_S correspond to the schedule's time steps and contain the currently active jobs. More formally, the edge $e_t \subseteq V$ for time step t is defined as $e_t := \{ (i,j) \mid n_i(t) > 0 \wedge j = n_i - n_i(t) + 1 \}$. Thus, if we abuse S to also denote the makespan of schedule S, the edge set of H_S can be written as $E = \{ e_1, e_2, \ldots, e_S \}$. We call H_S the *scheduling graph* of S. See Figure 1a for an illustration.

---

[1] This is also known as *speed scaling* (cf. [14]).

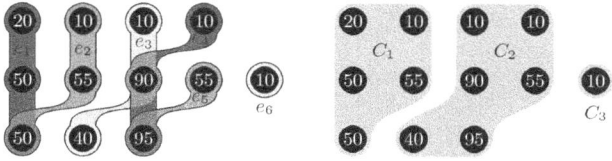

(a) Scheduling graph H_S trying to greedily finish as many jobs as possible.

(b) Connected components of the scheduling graph, ordered from left to right.

Figure 1: Hypergraph representation of a schedule for three processors. Resource requirements are given as node labels (in percent). Nodes are laid out such that each row corresponds to the job sequence of one processor (from left to right). Edges correspond to the schedule that prioritizes jobs in order of increasing remaining resource requirement.

Connected Components. In Section 4.1 and during the analysis in Section 7, we will see that the connected components formed by the edges of a scheduling graph H_S carry a lot of structural information about the schedule. To make use of this information, let us introduce some notation that allows us to directly argue via such components. We start with an observation that follows from the construction of H_S.

OBSERVATION 2. *Consider a connected component $C \subseteq V$ of H_S and two time steps $t_1 \leq t_2$ with $e_{t_1} \cup e_{t_2} \subseteq C$. Then, for all $t \in \{t_1, t_1 + 1, \ldots, t_2\}$ we have $e_t \subseteq C$.*

Let N denote the total number of connected components and let C_k denote the k-th connected component (for $k \in \{1, 2, \ldots, N\}$). Moreover, we use $\#_k$ to denote the number of edges of the k-th component. That is, we have $\#_k = |\{e_t \in E \mid e_t \subseteq C_k\}|$. Observation 2 implies that a component C_k consists of $\#_k$ consecutive time steps. This allows us to order the components such that, for any two components k, k' and edges $e_t \subseteq C_k, e_{t'} \subseteq C_{k'}$ with $t \leq t'$, we have $k \leq k'$. That is, we can think of the components being processed by the processors from left to right. See Figure 1b for an illustration.

The maximal size of an edge in the k-th component, which equals the size of its first edge, gives us a rough estimate for the amount of potential parallelism available during the corresponding time steps. Note that while the size of edges e_t is monotonously decreasing in t, a schedule that tries to balance the number of remaining jobs on each processor will decrease the edge size only at the end of a component (for all components but the last one). We will make use of this fact in the proof of Lemma 17. For now, let us honor its foreshadowed importance by the following definition:

DEFINITION 3 (COMPONENT CLASS). *For a component C_k, we define its class q_k as the size of its first edge. That is, $q_k := |e_t|$ with $t = \min\{t' \mid e_{t'} \subseteq C_k\}$.*

Besides being an upper bound on the size of a component's edges, q_k is also decreasing in k. Lemma 10 uses q_k to formulate an important relation between a component's size and the total number of its edges.

4. PRELIMINARIES

This section is intended to make the reader more comfortable with the introduced terms and notions and to equip her with the tools needed for the analysis in later sections. We start by discussing and proving some basic structural properties. Afterward, we analyze a simple round robin algorithm.

Note that in this and all following sections, we only consider problem instances in which all jobs are of unit size.

4.1 Structural Properties

Let us use the introduced notions and notation to point out some structural properties of schedules for the CRSHARING problem with unit size jobs. We start by defining two basic properties any reasonable schedule should have (and show in Lemma 6 that this is indeed the case).

DEFINITION 4 (NON-WASTING). *We say a schedule is non-wasting if it finishes all active jobs during every time step t with $\sum_{i=1}^m R_i(t) < 1$.*

DEFINITION 5 (PROGRESSIVE). *A schedule is progressive if, among all jobs that are assigned resources, at most one job is only partially processed during any time step t. More formally, we require for all $t \in \mathbb{N}$ that*

$$|\{i \mid n_i(t) = n_i(t+1) \wedge R_i(t) > 0\}| \leq 1. \quad (2)$$

LEMMA 6. *Given an arbitrary schedule S, we can transform it into a non-wasting and progressive schedule S' with $S' \leq S$ (S and S' denoting the corresponding makespans). Moreover, the resulting schedule S' finishes at least one job per time step.*

PROOF. Making a given schedule non-wasting is trivial because, given a time step t with $\sum_{i=1}^m R_i(t) < 1$ and an active job (i', j'), we can increase $R_{i'}(t)$ until either the job is finished or $\sum_{i=1}^m R_i(t) = 1$. In both cases, the schedule's makespan does not increase.

Given a non-wasting schedule S that is not progressive, consider two jobs (i_1, j_1) and (i_2, j_2) on different processors at a time step t such that $n_{i_1}(t) = n_{i_1}(t+1)$, $n_{i_2}(t) = n_{i_2}(t+1)$, and $R_{i_1}(t), R_{i_2}(t) > 0$. We will define the new schedule S' by providing two new resource assignment functions R'_{i_1} and R'_{i_2} that swap some of the resources assigned to jobs (i_1, j_1) and (i_2, j_2). To this end, let $t_1, t_2 > t$ be the time steps in which (i_1, j_1) and (i_2, j_2) are finished, respectively. Without loss of generality, assume $t_1 \leq t_2$. Let $R := \sum_{t'=t+1}^{t_1} R_{i_1}(t')$ denote the total resource assignment that job (i_1, j_1) receives after time step t. If $R \leq R_{i_2}(t)$, we define $R'_{i_1}(t) := R_{i_1}(t) + R$ and $R'_{i_2}(t) := R_{i_2}(t) - R$. This will finish job (i_1, j_1) at time step t, so that the resources formerly assigned to (i_1, j_1) after time step t can be freed. The inequality $t_1 \leq t_2$ implies that job (i_2, j_2) is active during the time steps $t + 1$ to t_1. Thus, we can set $R'_{i_1}(t') := 0$ and $R'_{i_2}(t') := R'_{i_2}(t') + R'_{i_1}(t')$ for all $t' \in \{t+1, t+2, \ldots, t_1\}$. For all remaining time steps t', we set $R'_{i_1}(t) := R_{i_1}(t)$ and $R'_{i_2}(t) := R_{i_2}(t)$. These changes result in a feasible schedule, do not increase the schedule's makespan, and do not waste any resources. Thus, by iterating this procedure we get a non-wasting and progressive schedule. □

Lemma 6 allows us to narrow our study to the subclass of non-wasting and progressive schedules, and from now on we will assume any schedule to have these properties (if not stated otherwise).

Intuitively, good schedules should try to balance the number of remaining jobs on each processor. This may provide the scheduler with more choices to prevent the underutilization of the resource later on (e.g., when only one processor with many jobs of low resource requirements remains). The better part of Section 7 serves the purpose of confirming this intuition. In the following, we formalize this balance property and, subsequently, work out further formal and concise properties of balanced schedules.

DEFINITION 7 (BALANCED). *We say a schedule is balanced if, whenever a processor i finishes a job at a time step t, any processor i' with $n_{i'}(t) > n_i(t)$ does also finish a job.*

PROPOSITION 8. *Every balanced schedule features the following properties:*

(a) *For all i_1, i_2 with $n_{i_1} \geq n_{i_2}$ and for all $t \in \mathbb{N}$, we have $n_{i_1}(t) \geq n_{i_2}(t) - 1$.*

(b) *For all i_1, i_2 with $n_{i_1} > n_{i_2}$ and for all $t \in \mathbb{N}$, we have $n_{i_1}(t) \leq n_{i_2}(t) + n_{i_1} - n_{i_2}$.*

PROOF. Both statements follow easily from the definition of balanced schedules. To see this, first note that both properties hold for $t = 1$, since $n_i(1) = n_i$ for all processors i. Moreover, at any time step t, the number $n_i(t)$ of remaining jobs cannot increase, and decreases by at most one during the current time step. Thus, it is sufficient to show that if one of the statements holds at some time step t with equality, it still holds at time step $t + 1$. For statement (a), $n_{i_1}(t) = n_{i_2}(t) - 1$ and the balance property imply that if i_1 finishes its job, then so must i_2. Thus, we have $n_{i_1}(t + 1) \geq n_{i_2}(t + 1) - 1$. The very same argument works for statement (b). $\square$

PROPOSITION 9. *Consider a balanced schedule and the set M_j of processors having at least j jobs. Let (i, j) be a job that is active at time step t and assume $n_i(t) > 1$ (i.e., it is not the last job on processor i). Then all processors $i' \in M_j$ are active at time step t.*

PROOF. Let $i' \in M_j$ be a processor with at least j jobs and consider the case $n_{i'} \geq n_i$. By Proposition 8(a), we have $n_{i'}(t) \geq n_i(t) - 1 > 0$, so processor i is active at time t. If $n_{i'} < n_i$, we can apply Proposition 8(b) and get

$$n_{i'}(t) \geq n_{i'} - (n_i - n_i(t)) = n_{i'} - (j - 1) \geq 1. \quad (3)$$

The equality uses the fact that job (i, j) is active at time step t, implying that the number $n_i - n_i(t)$ of jobs finished by processor i before time step t is exactly $j - 1$. The last inequality comes from $i' \in M_j$. $\square$

The final structural property of balanced schedules addresses, as indicated earlier, how a component's class allows us to relate its size (number of nodes) to the total number of its edges.

LEMMA 10. *Consider a non-wasting, progressive, and balanced schedule. The number of nodes and edges in a component are related via the following properties:*

(a) *The inequality $|C_k| \geq \#_k + q_k - 1$ holds for all $k \in \{1, 2, \ldots, N - 1\}$.*

(b) *The last component satisfies $|C_N| \geq \#_N$.*

PROOF. The second statement follows immediately from Lemma 6, which states that in each time step (i.e., for each edge) at least one job is finished.

For the first statement, fix a $k \in \{1, 2, \ldots, N - 1\}$ and consider the first edge e_t of the component C_k. By definition, this edge consists of q_k different nodes. We now show that

each of the remaining $\#_k - 1$ edges adds at least one new node to the component. So fix an edge $e_{t'} \subseteq C_k$ with $t' > t$ and consider the time step $t' - 1$. Since we know that at least one job is finished in every time step (Lemma 6) and that S is balanced, at least one of the processors having the maximal number of remaining jobs finishes its current job. More formally, there is some processor $i' = \arg\max_i n_i(t' - 1)$ that finishes its currently active job at time step $t' - 1$. Because of $k \neq N$, we also know that $n_{i'}(t' - 1) > 1$, such that there is a new active job for processor i' at time step t'. This yields the lemma's first statement. $\square$

4.2 Warm-up: Round Robin Approximation

Consider the following simple round robin algorithm for the CRSHARING problem (with unit size jobs): Given a problem instance where the maximal number of jobs on a processor is n, the algorithm operates in n phases. During phase j, it processes the j-th job on each processor, assigning the resource in an arbitrary way to any processors that have not yet finished their j-th job. Note that this algorithm may waste resources (although only between two phases) and is possibly non-progressive. Still, the following theorem shows that it results in schedules that are not too bad.

THEOREM 11. *The ROUNDROBIN algorithm for the CR-SHARING problem with unit job sizes has a worst-case approximation ratio of exactly 2.*

PROOF. We start with the upper bound on the approximation ratio. The ROUNDROBIN algorithm needs exactly $\left\lceil \sum_{i \in M_j} r_{ij} \right\rceil$ time steps to finish the j-th phase (cf. Section 3.1). Thus, the makespan of a ROUNDROBIN schedule can be bounded by

$$\sum_{j=1}^{n} \left\lceil \sum_{i \in M_j} r_{ij} \right\rceil \leq n + \sum_{j=1}^{n} \sum_{i \in M_j} r_{ij}. \quad (4)$$

Since any processor can finish at most one job per time step, even an optimal schedule has a makespan of at least n. Observation 1 yields another lower bound on the optimal makespan, namely $\sum_{j=1}^{n} \sum_{i \in M_j} r_{ij}$. Together, we get that ROUNDROBIN computes a 2-approximation.

For the lower bound on the approximation ratio, consider the following CRSHARING problem instance with unit size jobs on two processors: Let $n \in \mathbb{N}, \varepsilon := 1/n > 0$ and define the resource requirements for the first processor as $r_{1j} := j \cdot \varepsilon$ for $j \in \{1, 2, \ldots, n\}$. For the second processor, we define $r_{2j} := (1 + \varepsilon) - r_{1j}$. Note that each processor has to process n jobs. Figure 2 illustrates the instance as well as the resulting optimal and ROUNDROBIN schedules for $n = 100$. An optimal schedule, shown in Figure 2a, will waste no resource at all. In contrast, the ROUNDROBIN schedule, as indicated in Figure 2b, wastes a share of $1 - \varepsilon$ of the resource in every second time step. As a result, the ROUNDROBIN schedule needs $2n$ time steps, while an optimal schedule can finish the same workload in $n + 1$ time steps. Thus, for $n \to \infty$ we get an approximation ratio of 2. $\square$

5. PROBLEM COMPLEXITY

One of our first major results is the following theorem, showing that the CRSHARING problem is (even in the case of unit size jobs) NP-hard in the number of processors.

THEOREM 12. *CRSHARING with jobs of unit size is NP-hard if the number of processors is part of the input.*

(a) OPT schedule, wastes no resources and needs $n+1$ time steps.

(b) ROUNDROBIN, uses two time steps per phase and wastes 99% of the resource at the end of each phase.

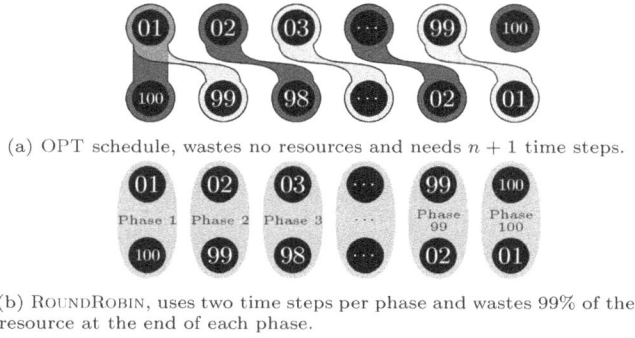

Figure 2: Worst-case example for ROUNDROBIN schedule. Node labels give the jobs' resource requirements in percent.

(a) Optimum for YES-instances.   (b) Optimum for NO-instances.

Figure 3: Problem instance and schedules used for the reduction from PARTITION to CRSHARING with unit size jobs.

PROOF. In the following, we prove the NP-hardness of the CRSHARING problem with unit size jobs via a reduction from the PARTITION problem. Our reduction transforms a PARTITION instance of n elements into a CRSHARING instance on n processors, each having three jobs to process.

Let $a_1, a_2, \ldots, a_n \in \mathbb{N}$ and $A \in \mathbb{N}$ with $\sum_{i=1}^{n} a_i = 2A$ be the input of the PARTITION instance (w.l.o.g., $A \geq 2$). For our transformation, let $\varepsilon \in (0, 1/n)$ and set $\delta := n\varepsilon < 1$. We define the first and last job on any processor i to have resource requirements $r_{i1} = r_{i3} = \tilde{a}_i := \frac{a_i}{A+\delta}$. The second job on any processor i has a resource requirement of $r_{i2} = \tilde{\varepsilon} := \frac{\varepsilon}{A+\delta}$. Note that no schedule can finish the first job of all tasks in only one time step as we have $\sum_{i=1}^{n} r_{i1} = \frac{2A}{A+\delta} > 1$ by construction. Now, with each task containing three jobs, any schedule needs at least four time steps to finish all jobs. To finish our reduction, we show that there is an optimal schedule with makespan 4 if and only if the given PARTITION instance is a YES-instance (i.e., if it can be partitioned into two sets that sum up to exactly A).

Assume we are given a YES-instance of PARTITION and let, w.l.o.g., the first k elements form one partition. The schedule shown in Figure 3a is feasible and has makespan 4. Now, assume we are given a NO-instance and an optimal schedule for the corresponding CRSHARING instance. W.l.o.g., exactly the first k processors finish their jobs in the first time step. This implies $\sum_{i=1}^{k} \tilde{a}_i \leq 1$, yielding the inequality $\sum_{i=1}^{k} a_i \leq A+\delta < A+1$. Since the given PARTITION instance is a NO-instance, we also have $\sum_{i=1}^{k} a_i \neq A$. Together this implies $\sum_{i=1}^{k} a_i \leq A-1$, which, in turn, yields $\sum_{i=k+1}^{n} a_i \geq A+1$. Since we have not yet finished the jobs $(k+1, 1), (k+2, 1), \ldots, (n, 1)$, we need at least two more time steps until we can start working on $(k+1, 3), (k+2, 3), \ldots, (n, 3)$. Their total resource requirement is at least

$$\sum_{i=k+1}^{n} \tilde{a}_i = \frac{\sum_{i=k+1}^{n} a_i}{A+\delta} \geq \frac{A+1}{A+\delta} > 1. \qquad (5)$$

Thus, after the first three time steps, we need at least two more time steps to finish the remaining jobs, yielding a makespan of at least 5. □

While Theorem 12 proves NP-hardness of our problem, it leaves at least two open questions concerning the problem's complexity for *constant* m: (1) Does it remain NP-hard for $m \geq 3$? (For $m = 2$, Section 6 gives an optimal polynomial–time algorithm.) (2) Is it even strongly NP-hard for $m \geq 3$? The latter question can be answered negatively. Assuming

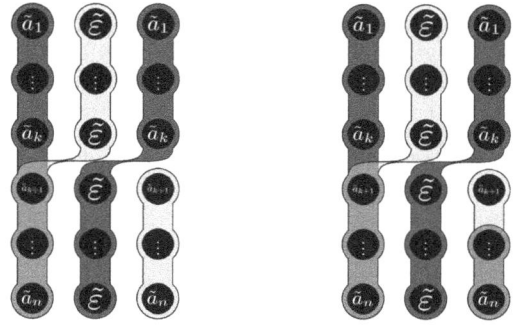

that the resource requirements are multiples of some $\rho \in \mathbb{R}$ (i.e., $r_{ij} \in \{ k \cdot \rho \mid k \in \{0, 1, \ldots, \lfloor 1/\rho \rfloor \} \}$), one can design a pseudo-polynomial time algorithm that runs roughly in time $O\big((n/\rho^2)^m\big)$. We leave the formal statement and proof for the full version of this paper. Also, note that we get the following lower bound from the proof of Theorem 12:

COROLLARY 13. *It is NP-hard to approximate* CRSHARING *with a factor better than* $5/4$.

6. ALGORITHM FOR TWO PROCESSORS

While the previous section proves NP-hardness in the number of processors, there is an efficient exact algorithm for two processors. Algorithm OPTRESASSIGNMENT traces out all reasonable scheduling decisions. To keep this approach feasible, we use Lemma 6 (implying the existence of an optimal schedule that finishes at least one job in each time step) and another structural property (see Lemma 14). These allow us to discard bad scheduling decisions early on.

Algorithm Description. OPTRESASSIGNMENT uses a dynamic programming approach. To this end, it maintains a two-dimensional array B of size $n_1 \times n_2$. Each entry holds a tuple $B[i_1, i_2] = (r, t)$, which states that there is a schedule that, at time step t, has finished all jobs $(1, j_1)$ with $j_1 < i_1$ and $(2, j_2)$ with $j_2 < i_2$, and for which the remaining resource requirements of $(1, i_1)$ and $(2, i_2)$ sum up to r. OPTRESASSIGNMENT fills B in $n_1 + n_2 - 1$ phases, one phase for each diagonal of B. It maintains the invariant that, from the start of phase ℓ on, all entries on the $(\ell-1)$-th diagonal (i.e., all $B[i_1, i_2]$ with $i_1 + i_2 = \ell$) are optimal. More exactly, such entries correspond to subschedules with minimal t (and, for this t, minimal r) reaching the jobs $(1, i_1)$ and $(2, i_2)$. See Algorithm 1 for the pseudocode. Note that, in our algorithm description, we compute only the makespan (and not a corresponding schedule) of an optimal solution. However, given the array B, one can easily trace back the final entry and derive an explicit schedule in linear time.

Correctness & Runtime. We start with an auxiliary lemma, which will be used later on to show that the diagonal-wise processing of B is correct.

LEMMA 14. *Consider two non-wasting, progressive schedules S and S' as well as a time step t such that $n_i(t) \leq n_i'(t)$ for $i \in \{1, 2\}$. Let $v_i(t)$ and $v_i'(t)$ be the remaining resource*

Algorithm 1 OptResAssignment

```
1:  // resource requirements are stored in A₁ and A₂
2:  // subschedules are stored in two-dimensional array B
3:  // extend A₁ as well as A₂ by an extra 0-entry
4:  n₁ = length(A₁); n₂ = length(A₂);
5:  initialize array B[1...n₁, 1...n₂] with null entries
6:  B[1,1] = (A₁[1] + A₂[1], 0)
7:  for ℓ = 2 ... n₁ + n₂ - 1 do
8:      for i₁ = max { 1, ℓ - n₂ } ... min { ℓ - 1, n₁ } do
9:          i₂ = ℓ - i₁
10:         (r, t) = B[i₁, i₂]
11:         if i₁ = n₁ then
12:             add(i₁, i₂ + 1, 0, A₂[i₂ + 1], t + 1)
13:         else if i₂ = n₂ then
14:             add(i₁ + 1, i₂, A₁[i₁ + 1], 0, t + 1)
15:         else if r ≤ 1 then
16:             add(i₁ + 1, i₂ + 1, A₁[i₁ + 1], A₂[i₂ + 1], t + 1)
17:             add(i₁, i₂ + 1, 0, A₂[i₂ + 1], t + 1)
18:             add(i₁ + 1, i₂, A₁[i₁ + 1], 0, t + 1)
19:         else
20:             add(i₁, i₂ + 1, A₁[i₁] + A₂[i₂] - 1, A₂[i₂ + 1], t + 1)
21:             add(i₁ + 1, i₂, A₁[i₁ + 1], A₁[i₁] + A₂[i₂] - 1, t + 1)
22: min = B[n₁, n₂]
23:
24: function add(i₁, i₂, v₁, v₂, t)
25:     r = v₁ + v₂
26:     (r_old, t_old) = B[i₁, i₂]
27:     if (r_old, t_old) = null ∨ t < t_old ∨ (t = t_old ∧ r < r_old) then
28:         B[i₁, i₂] = (r, t)
```

requirement of the job that is active at time t on processor $i \in \{1, 2\}$ in schedule S and S', respectively. If

(a) $n_1(t) < n_1'(t)$ or $n_2(t) < n_2'(t)$, or

(b) $n_1(t) = n_1'(t)$ and $n_2(t) = n_2'(t)$ and, w.l.o.g., $v_1(t) + v_2(t) \leq v_1'(t) + v_2'(t)$,

then we can transform S without changing the first $t - 1$ time steps such that $S \leq S'$.

PROOF. First observe that we already have $S \leq S'$ if one of the properties applies at the end of S. Thus, it suffices to show that the properties can be maintained from t to $t + 1$.

(a) Without loss of generality, assume $n_1(t) < n_1'(t)$. If S' finishes only one job, S can complete a job on the same processor and hence maintains the inequalities. If S' finishes both jobs, this yields $n_i'(t + 1) = n_i'(t) - 1$ for $i \in \{1, 2\}$. Thus, if S finishes a job on processor 2 and assigns the remaining bandwidth to the job on processor 1, this results in $n_1(t+1) = n_1(t) \leq n_1'(t+1)$ and $n_2(t+1) = n_2(t) - 1 \leq n_2'(t+1)$. If equality applies (otherwise (a) holds), then the same jobs are active at time $t + 1$ in S' and S, say j_1 and j_2. This yields $v_1(t+1) + v_2(t+1) \leq r_{1j_1} + r_{2j_2} = v_1'(t+1) + v_2'(t+1)$, therefore (b) applies.

(b) Now, suppose $v_1(t) + v_2(t) \leq v_1'(t) + v_2'(t)$. If S' finishes both jobs, S can do the same and (b) holds with equality. If S' only finishes one job (w.l.o.g., job $j - 1$ on processor 1), S can also finish that job. If $v_1(t) + v_2(t) \leq 1$, it also completes a second job and therefore (a) applies. On the other hand, if $v_1(t) + v_2(t) > 1$, this results in

$v_1(t+1) + v_2(t+1) = r_{1j} + (v_1(t) + v_2(t) - 1) \leq r_{1j} + (v_1'(t) + v_2'(t) - 1) = v_1'(t+1) + v_2'(t+1)$, thus case (b) applies. □

THEOREM 15. *Consider a* CRSharing *instance with unit size jobs and two processors. The following statements hold:*

(a) OptResAssignment *computes an optimal solution.*

(b) OptResAssignment *has running time* $O(n^2)$.

PROOF. The correctness of statement (b) is immediate, as OptResAssignment runs in $O(n)$ phases and each phase considers the $O(n)$ entries on the corresponding diagonal. It remains to prove the correctness of statement (a).

Remember the invariant from the algorithm description: At the beginning of phase ℓ, for each entry $B[i_1, i_2] = (r, t)$ on the $\ell - 1$-th diagonal the following holds: t is the earliest time at which all jobs preceding $(1, i_1)$ and $(2, i_2)$ can be finished and r is, for this t, the smallest possible sum of the remaining resource requirements of $(1, i_1)$ and $(2, i_2)$. If this invariant holds for phase $n_1 + n_2$, the correctness follows immediately (we use dummy jobs, so the last diagonal entry corresponds to all non-dummy jobs being fully processed). For the first phase, the invariant's correctness is obvious from the initialization, as there are no jobs preceding $(1, 1)$ and $(2, 1)$. Now assume the invariant holds for the first ℓ phases and consider an entry $B[i_1, i_2]$ processed in the $\ell + 1$-th phase. This entry corresponds to a subschedule that has processed all jobs preceding $(1, i_1)$ and $(2, i_2)$. Since each processor can finish at most one job in one time step, this subschedule must originate from one of the subschedules S_1, S_2, or S_3 that have finished all jobs preceding (i) $(1, i_1 - 1)$ and $(2, i_2)$, (ii) $(1, i_1)$ and $(2, i_2 - 1)$, and (iii) $(1, i_1 - 1)$ and $(2, i_2 - 1)$, respectively. By our induction hypothesis, the entries in $B[i_1 - 1, i_2]$, $B[i_1, i_2 - 1]$, and $B[i_1 - 1, i_2 - 1]$ correspond to the best possible such schedules. Since the algorithm uses these to compute $B[i_1, i_2]$ (lines 9-21) and the best of them is chosen as predecessor (line 27, correct by Lemma 14), the invariant is established for entry $B[i_1, i_2]$ (and, similarly, for all remaining entries on the same diagonal). □

One could try a similar approach to compute an optimal solution for more than two processors (in fact, the pseudopolynomial algorithm discussed at the end of Section 5 uses this idea). However, Lemma 14 does not extend to $m \geq 3$. Already in the case of three processors it seems hard to compare two subschedules S_1 and S_2 that have processed different (partial) workloads of jobs $(1, i_1)$, $(2, i_2)$, and $(3, i_3)$ (and fullly processed all predecessors).

An alternative implementation of the algorithm replaces the 2-dimensional array by a priority queue that orders intermediate schedules by their index sum $i_1 + i_2$. Although adding or retrieving such an entry has amortized costs of $O(\log(n))$, this implementation runs faster for most of the instances, as it only considers index pairs that actually point to a schedule and many index pairs are usually not used. Consider, for instance, pair $(1, 1)$. If $A_1[1] + A_2[1] \leq 1$, the algorithm will proceed with $(2, 2)$ and all entries $(1, i_2)$ and $(i_1, 1)$ with $i_1, i_2 > 1$ will never be used.

7. BALANCED SCHEDULES

This section builds up to our third major result, an approximation algorithm with a tight approximation ratio of

$2 - 1/m$, in Theorem 18. We start by providing two lower bounds for optimal schedules in terms of a given non-wasting and balanced schedule, respectively.

7.1 Lower Bounds for Optimal Schedules

The following lemma derives the first lower bound by exploiting the fact that, within a component, any non-wasting schedule always makes full use of the resource.

LEMMA 16. *Let* OPT *denote the minimal makespan of a given problem instance and consider the scheduling graph* H_S *of a non-wasting schedule* S. *Then* OPT *can be bounded by*

$$\text{OPT} \geq \sum_{k=1}^{N}(\#_k - 1). \quad (6)$$

PROOF. From Observation 1, we immediately get that $\text{OPT} \geq \sum_{i=1}^{m}\sum_{j=1}^{n_i} r_{ij}$. Consider a connected component C_k of our schedule containing the edges $t_1, t_1 + 1, \ldots, t_2$. Since S is non-wasting, $\sum_{i=1}^{m} R_i(t) = 1$ holds for all time steps $t \in \{t_1, t_1 + 1, \ldots, t_2 - 1\}$. If there were such a t with $\sum_{i=1}^{m} R_i(t) < 1$, the non-wasting property would imply that all active jobs are finished. But then the edge e_{t+1} would not be part of C_k, yielding a contradiction. For the last time step t_2 of C_k we have $\sum_{i=1}^{m} R_i(t_2) \geq 0$. Since S is feasible and, w.l.o.g., does not use more of the resource than necessary, it follows that $\sum_{t=1}^{S}\sum_{i=1}^{m} R_i(t) = \sum_{i=1}^{m}\sum_{j=1}^{n_i} r_{ij}$. Let $e^{(k)}$ denote the last edge of C_k. Then we get:

$$\text{OPT} \geq \sum_{i=1}^{m}\sum_{j=1}^{n_i} r_{ij} = \sum_{t=1}^{S}\sum_{i=1}^{m} R_i(t) = \sum_{k=1}^{N}\sum_{e_t \subseteq C_k}\sum_{(i,j)\in e_t} R_i(t)$$

$$\geq \sum_{k=1}^{N}\sum_{\substack{e_t \subseteq C_k \\ e_t \neq e^{(k)}}} 1 = \sum_{k=1}^{N}(\#_k - 1). \quad \square$$

The second lower bound centers around utilizing parallelism. In a problem instance where each processor has exactly n jobs, the maximum exploitable parallelism is m. On the other hand, in a schedule with components C_k of class q_k, the maximum parallelism that can be exploited in C_k is q_k. In a sense, the following lemma shows that, in the case of balanced schedules, this is not much worse than m.

LEMMA 17. *Let* OPT *be the minimal makespan of a given problem instance and* n *the maximum number of jobs any processor has to process. Given a balanced schedule* S *and its scheduling graph,* OPT *and* n *can be bounded by*

$$\text{OPT} \geq n \geq \sum_{k=1}^{N-1} \frac{|C_k|}{q_k} + \frac{|C_N|}{m}. \quad (7)$$

PROOF. Remember that M_j is the set of processors having at least j jobs to process. Since any schedule can process at most one job per processor in every time step, even an optimal schedule needs at least n time steps to finish all jobs. We can write n as $\sum_{(i,j)\in V} 1/|M_j|$, yielding

$$\text{OPT} \geq n = \sum_{(i,j)\in V} \frac{1}{|M_j|} = \sum_{k=1}^{N}\sum_{(i,j)\in C_k} \frac{1}{|M_j|}$$

$$\geq \sum_{k=1}^{N-1}\sum_{(i,j)\in C_k} \frac{1}{|M_j|} + \sum_{(i,j)\in C_N} \frac{1}{m}$$

$$= \sum_{k=1}^{N-1}\sum_{(i,j)\in C_k} \frac{1}{|M_j|} + \frac{|C_N|}{m}.$$

It remains to show that we have

$$\sum_{(i,j)\in C_k} \frac{1}{|M_j|} \geq \frac{|C_k|}{q_k} \quad (8)$$

for all but the last component. So fix $k \in \{1, 2, \ldots N-1\}$ and let $(i_0, j_0) \in C_k$ be a job of the k-th component with minimal j_0. Let t_0 be the first time step when (i_0, j_0) is active. The minimality of j_0 implies that e_{t_0} is the first edge of C_k and, thus, $q_k = |e_{t_0}|$. We distinguish two cases:

Case 1: $n_{i_0}(t_0) > 1$
By applying Proposition 9, we get that all processors $i \in M_{j_0}$ are active at time step t_0. This yields $|M_{j_0}| \leq |e_{t_0}| = q_k$. Moreover, for a job $(i,j) \in C_k$, the minimality of j_0 gives us $|M_{j_0}| \geq |M_j|$. Combining both inequalities implies $|M_j| \leq q_k$. Applying this to the first part of Equation (8) eventually yields the desired inequality.

Case 2: $n_{i_0}(t_0) = 1$
In this case, (i_0, j_0) is the last job on processor i_0 at time step t_0. However, for any job $(i,j) \in C_k \setminus e_{t_0}$ we have $n_i(t_0) > 1$. Given such a job, let (i, j') be the job processed on i at time step t_0. Note that we have $j' < j$ and, thus, $M_j \subseteq M_{j'}$. By applying Proposition 9, we get that all $i' \in M_{j'}$ are active at time step t_0. Together with $M_j \subseteq M_{j'}$, this yields $|M_j| \leq q_k$. Thus, to prove Equation (8), it only remains to show $\sum_{(i,j)\in e_{t_0}} 1/|M_j| \geq \sum_{(i,j)\in e_{t_0}} 1/q_k (= 1)$.

To this end, note that, since C_k is not the last component, there exists at least one job $(i_1, j_1) \in e_{t_0}$ with $n_{i_1}(t_0) > 1$. Let this job be such that j_1 is minimal. Once more, by applying Proposition 9 we get that all $i \in M_{j_1}$ are active at time step t_0. Consider a job $(i,j) \in e_{t_0}$ with $i \in M_{j_1}$. If it is the last job on i (i.e., if $n_i(t_0) = 1$), we have $j = n_i$. Together with the definition of M_{j_1} we get $j = n_i \geq j_1$, yielding $|M_j| \leq |M_{j_1}|$. Similarly, if it is not the last job on i (i.e., if $n_i(t_0) > 1$), the minimality of j_1 gives us $|M_j| \leq |M_{j_1}|$. This yields the desired inequality as follows:

$$\sum_{(i,j)\in e_{t_0}} \frac{1}{|M_j|} \geq \sum_{\substack{(i,j)\in e_{t_0} \\ i \in M_{j_1}}} \frac{1}{|M_j|} \geq \sum_{\substack{(i,j)\in e_{t_0} \\ i \in M_{j_1}}} \frac{1}{|M_{j_1}|} = 1. \quad \square$$

7.2 Deriving a $(2 - 1/m)$-Approximation

Finally, we have all the ingredients to prove our main result:

THEOREM 18. *Consider a* CRSHARING *instance with unit size jobs and a feasible schedule* S *for it that is non-wasting, progressive, and balanced. Then* S *is a* $2-1/m$-*approximation with respect to the optimal makespan.*

PROOF. In the following, let $\#_\varnothing := \sum_{k=1}^{N} \#_k/N$ denote the average number of edges in a component. Our proof uses two bounds on the approximation ratio. The first one follows easily from Lemma 16 and leads to a better approximation for instances with large $\#_\varnothing$. The second bound is much more involved and mainly based on Lemma 17. It yields a better approximation for instances with small $\#_\varnothing$. To get the first bound, we simply apply Lemma 16 and get

$$\frac{S}{\text{OPT}} \leq \frac{\sum_{k=1}^{N} \#_k}{\sum_{k=1}^{N}(\#_k - 1)} = \frac{\#_\varnothing}{\#_\varnothing - 1}. \quad (9)$$

Let us now consider the second bound, based on Lemma 17. Our goal is to show that the inequality

$$\frac{S}{\text{OPT}} \le \frac{m \cdot \#_\varnothing}{\#_\varnothing + m - 1} \qquad (10)$$

holds. Once this is proven, we can combine both bounds by realizing that the bound from Equation (9) is monotonously decreasing in $\#_\varnothing$ and the bound from Equation (10) is monotonously increasing in $\#_\varnothing$. Equalizing yields that their minimum's maximum is obtained at $\#_\varnothing = \frac{2m-1}{m-1}$, which results in an approximation ratio of $2 - 1/m$.

The rest of this proof is geared towards proving Equation (10). We distinguish two cases. The first case covers the easier part, where we have $\text{OPT} \ge n + 1$. That is, even an optimal solution cannot finish the jobs in n time steps. The second case, where we have $\text{OPT} = n$, turns out to be more difficult to prove. While we can apply a similar analysis, we have to take more care when bounding our algorithm's progress in the first two time steps.

Case 1: $\text{OPT} \ge n + 1$
Applying Lemma 17 to this case yields

$$\begin{aligned}
\frac{S}{\text{OPT}} &\le \frac{\sum_{k=1}^{N} \#_k}{\sum_{k=1}^{N-1} \frac{|C_k|}{q_k} + \frac{|C_N|}{m} + 1} \\
&\le \frac{N \cdot \#_\varnothing}{\sum_{k=1}^{N-1} \frac{\#_k + q_k - 1}{q_k} + \frac{\#_N + m - 1}{m}} \qquad (11) \\
&\le \frac{N \cdot \#_\varnothing}{\sum_{k=1}^{N} \frac{\#_k + m - 1}{m}} \le \frac{m \cdot \#_\varnothing}{\#_\varnothing + m - 1}
\end{aligned}$$

Case 2: $\text{OPT} = n$
If we apply the same analysis as in the first case, we will fall short of our desired approximation ratio. Surprisingly, it turns out to be sufficient to bound only the first two time steps more carefully. The idea of the following analysis is to consider the first two time steps of S and the remaining part of S separately. To this end, first note that we can assume, w.l.o.g., that $\#_1 > 1$ (i.e., the first two time steps belong to the same component). If this is not the case, our algorithm finishes all active jobs in the first time step and, thus, behaves optimally[2]. Consider the remaining jobs/workloads after the first two time steps. We can regard this as a subinstance of our original problem instance. Let S' denote the subschedule that results from restricting S to time steps $t \ge 3$. We use N', $\#'_k$, q'_k, and n' to refer to the corresponding properties of its scheduling graph $H_{S'}$. Note that we have $N' \ge N - 1$ (because of our assumption $\#_1 > 1$) as well as $N' \cdot \#'_\varnothing = N \cdot \#_\varnothing - 2$ (since exactly two time steps are missing in the subschedule). Moreover, we also have $n' = n - 2$. The inequality $n' \ge n - 2$ is obvious. For $n' \le n - 2$, note that OPT must finish the jobs in the set $\{(i, 1) \mid n_i(1) \ge n - 1\} \cup \{(i, 2) \mid n_i(1) \ge n\}$ during the first two time steps. Thus, the total resource requirement of these jobs is at most two. Since S is balanced, it will prioritize and, thus, finish these jobs in the first two time steps. Finally, we can bound our approximation ratio as follows (the first inequality applies Lemma 17 to S'):

$$\frac{S}{\text{OPT}} = \frac{N \cdot \#_\varnothing}{2 + n'} \le \frac{N \cdot \#_\varnothing}{2 + \sum_{k=1}^{N'-1} \frac{|C'_k|}{q'_k} + \frac{|C'_{N'}|}{m}}$$

---

[2]This reduces our analysis to a smaller problem instance.

$$\begin{aligned}
&\le \frac{N \cdot \#_\varnothing}{1 + \frac{1}{m} + \sum_{k=1}^{N'-1} \frac{\#'_k + q'_k - 1}{q'_k} + \frac{\#'_{N'}}{m} + \frac{m-1}{m}} \\
&\le \frac{N \cdot \#_\varnothing}{1 + \frac{1}{m} + \sum_{k=1}^{N'} \frac{\#'_k + m - 1}{m}} \\
&= \frac{N \cdot m \cdot \#_\varnothing}{m + 1 + N' \cdot \#'_\varnothing + N'(m - 1)} \\
&\le \frac{N \cdot m \cdot \#_\varnothing}{2 + (N \cdot \#_\varnothing - 2) + N(m - 1)} = \frac{m \cdot \#_\varnothing}{\#_\varnothing + m - 1}.
\end{aligned}$$

This proves that Equation 10 also holds in this case. $\square$

7.3 Tight Approximation Algorithm

So far, we analyzed the quality of balanced schedules in general, but did not yet provide a concrete example of a corresponding algorithm. One of the most natural greedy algorithms schedules jobs by prioritizing processors with a higher number of remaining jobs and, in the case of a tie, by prioritizing jobs with larger remaining resource requirements. We name this algorithm GREEDYBALANCE. In Section 7.2, we saw that balanced schedules and, as a consequence, the algorithm GREEDYBALANCE yield a $2 - 1/m$-approximation for the CRSHARING problem. Now, we show that this approximation ratio is tight for GREEDYBALANCE.

THEOREM 19. *The* GREEDYBALANCE *algorithm for the* CRSHARING *problem with jobs of unit size has a worst-case approximation ratio of exactly* $2 - 1/m$.

PROOF. Since GREEDYBALANCE computes only balanced schedules, the upper bound follows immediately from Theorem 18. For the lower bound, consider a family of problem instances defined as follows: We define blocks of $m \times m$ jobs with resource requirements as described below. For the first block, let $r_{i1} := 1 - i \cdot \varepsilon$ for $i \in \{1, 2, \ldots, m\}$, $r_{12} := 1 - \sum_{i=1}^{m}(1 - r_{i1}) + \varepsilon$, and $r_{i2} := \varepsilon$ for $i \in \{2, 3, \ldots, m\}$. Moreover, define $r_{ij} := \varepsilon$ for all $i \in \{1, 2, \ldots, m\}$ and $j \in \{3, 4, \ldots, m\}$. This finishes the first $m \times m$-block of jobs. Having constructed the l-th block, we construct the next block, starting with its first column $j := l \cdot m + 1$. We define $r_{ij} := 1 - (m - 1)\varepsilon$ for $i \in \{1, 2, \ldots, m - 1\}$ and $r_{mj} := 1 - \sum_{i'=1}^{m-1} r_{m-i', j-i'}$. For the second column of this block we set $r_{1,j+1} := 1 - \sum_{i=1}^{m}(1 - r_{ij}) + \varepsilon$, and $r_{i,j+1} := \varepsilon$ for $i \in \{2, 3, \ldots, m\}$. To finish the block, we set $r_{ij'} := \varepsilon$ for all $i \in \{1, 2, \ldots, m\}$ and $j' \in \{j + 2, j + 3, \ldots, j + m - 1\}$. We finish the construction once the next block would contain jobs with negative resource requirements. Note that by choosing ε small enough, we can make this construction arbitrarily long. See Figure 4 for an illustration of this construction and the schedules produced by GREEDYBALANCE and an optimal algorithm. Our construction is such that GREEDYBALANCE needs exactly $2m - 1$ time steps per block: By balancing the number of remaining jobs, it is forced to work m time steps on a block's first column (which contains a total resource requirement of roughly m) before it can finish the remaining $m - 1$ columns of a block. In contrast, the optimal algorithm ignores any balancing issues, which allows it to exploit that all diagonals have a total resource requirement of 1. $\square$

8. CONCLUSION & OUTLOOK

This paper introduced a new resource constrained scheduling problem where job processing speeds depend on the

(a) An optimal schedule.

(b) Schedule computed by GREEDYBALANCE.

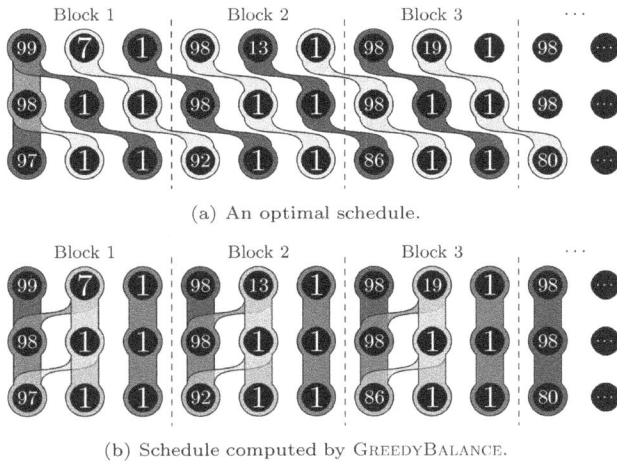

Figure 4: Construction and schedules used in the proof of Theorem 19 for $m = 3$ and $\varepsilon = 0.01$. Node labels show the corresponding job's resource requirement in percent (e.g., $r_{12} = 0.07$). Note that the optimal schedule needs (essentially) m time steps to finish a block, while S needs $2m - 1$ time steps per block.

share of the resource a job is assigned. Even for unit size jobs, this problem turned out to be NP-hard in the number of processors. However, we were able to derive an efficient optimal algorithm for two processors and an approximation algorithm with a worst-case approximation ratio of $2 - 1/m$ for m processors (both for unit size jobs). Still, the problem's complexity remains unsolved, as we were not yet able to prove or disprove weak NP-hardness if the number of processors is a constant larger or equal to 3. We did not give analytical results for jobs of arbitrary sizes, but we conjecture that almost all results should be transferable to this case. Our scheduling (hyper-)graphs can, with their current definition, not capture such problem instances, so that we cannot easily transfer the results from Section 7. And yet, intuition suggests that one should be able to extend our definitions and find similar properties for arbitrary job sizes.

Besides settling the problem's actual complexity and extending our results to jobs of arbitrary sizes, it seems worthwhile to extend the model to more realistic scenarios. What analytical results are possible if we re-introduce the classical scheduling aspect, where jobs of a task are not a priori fixed to a specific processor? It may also be possible to use our insights to get analytical results in special cases of discrete-continuous models as proposed by Józefowska and Weglarz [4]. Another interesting direction are models that consider energy as a continuously divisible resource. One might imagine a multiprocessor model in the spirit of the original speed scaling model by Yao et al. [14], but with a shared energy source (cf. [10, 11]).

References

[1] J. Błażewicz, K. H. Ecker, and E. Pesch. *Handbook on Scheduling: From Theory to Applications.* Springer, 2007.

[2] A. Janiak, W. Janiak, and M. Lichtenstein. Resource management in machine scheduling problems: A survey. *Decision Making in Manufacturing and Services*, 1(12):59–89, 2007.

[3] J. Józefowska and J. Weglarz. Discrete-continuous scheduling problems – mean completion time results. *European Journal of Operational Research*, 94(2): 302–309, 1996.

[4] J. Józefowska and J. Weglarz. On a methodology for discrete-continuous scheduling. *European Journal of Operational Research*, 107(2):338–353, 1998.

[5] J. Józefowska, M. Mika, R. Różycki, G. Waligóra, and J. Weglarz. Discrete-continuous scheduling to minimize the makespan for power processing rates of jobs. *Discrete Applied Mathematics*, 94(1):263–285, 1999.

[6] J. Józefowska, M. Mika, R. Różycki, G. Waligóra, and J. Weglarz. Solving the discrete-continuous project scheduling problem via its discretization. *Mathematical Methods of Operations Research*, 52(3): 489–499, 2000.

[7] J. Józefowska, M. Mika, R. Różycki, G. Waligóra, and J. Weglarz. A heuristic approach to allocating the continuous resource in discrete-continuous scheduling problems to minimize the makespan. *Journal of Scheduling*, 5(6):487–499, 2002.

[8] T. Kis. A branch-and-cut algorithm for scheduling of projects with variable-intensity activities. *Mathematical Programming*, 103(3):515–539, 2005.

[9] J. Y.-T. Leung. *Handbook of Scheduling: Algorithms, Models, and Performance Analysis.* Chapman & Hall/CRC, 2004.

[10] R. Różycki and J. Weglarz. Power-aware acheduling of preemptable jobs on identical parallel processors to minimize makespan. *Annals of Operations Research*, pages 1–18, 2011. ISSN 0254-5330. doi: 10.1007/s10479-011-0957-5.

[11] R. Różycki and J. Weglarz. Power-aware scheduling of preemptable jobs on identical parallel processors to meet deadlines. *European Journal of Operational Research*, 218(1):68–75, 2012. ISSN 0377-2217. doi: 10.1016/j.ejor.2011.10.017.

[12] G. Waligóra. Heuristic approaches to discrete-continuous project scheduling problems to minimize the makespan. *Computational Optimization and Applications*, 48(2):399–421, 2011.

[13] J. Weglarz, J. Józefowska, M. Mika, and G. Waligóra. Project scheduling with finite or infinite number of activity processing modes – a survey. *European Journal of Operational Research*, 208(3):177–205, 2011.

[14] F. F. Yao, A. J. Demers, and S. Shenker. A scheduling model for reduced cpu energy. In *Proceedings of the 36th Annual Symposium on Foundations of Computer Science (FOCS)*, pages 374–382, 1995.

A Note on Multiprocessor Speed Scaling with Precedence Constraints

Evripidis Bampis
Sorbonne Universités
UPMC Univ. Paris 06
UMR 7606, LIP6
F-75005, Paris, France
Evripidis.Bampis@lip6.fr

Dimitrios Letsios
Sorbonne Universités
UPMC Univ. Paris 06
UMR 7606, LIP6
F-75005, Paris, France
Dimitrios.Letsios@lip6.fr

Giorgio Lucarelli
Sorbonne Universités
UPMC Univ. Paris 06
UMR 7606, LIP6
F-75005, Paris, France
Giorgio.Lucarelli@lip6.fr

ABSTRACT

We consider the problem of scheduling a set of jobs, under precedence constraints, on a set of speed scalable parallel processors. The goal is to minimize the makespan of the schedule, i.e. the time at which the last job finishes its execution, without violating a given energy budget. This situation finds applications in computer devices whose lifetime depends on a limited battery efficiency. In order to handle the energy consumption we use the energy model introduced in [Yao et al., FOCS'95], which captures the intuitive idea that the higher is the processor's speed the higher is the energy consumption. We propose a $(2 - \frac{1}{m})$-approximation algorithm improving the best known poly-log(m)-approximation algorithm for the problem [Pruhs et al., TOCS 2008], where m is the number of the processors. We also extend the simple idea used for the above problem, in order to propose a generalized framework that finds applications to other scheduling problems in the speed scaling setting.

Categories and Subject Descriptors

F.2.2 [**Analysis of algorithms and problem complexity**]: Sequencing and scheduling

Keywords

Speed scaling; Scheduling; Approximation algorithms; Convex programming

1. INTRODUCTION

Due to the increasing use of computing devices and the need of more computing power in computer centers and of more autonomy in personal/mobile devices, the energy consumption in computer systems has become an important issue today. One standard way to handle the energy consumption is through the dynamic scaling of the voltage and the frequency of a processor, which is known as the *speed*

scaling mechanism. According to the cube-root rule for the CMOS devices, if a processor runs at speed s then the power needed is $P(s) = s^3$. However, recent experiments showed that the exponent is in practise smaller [10] (e.g., the exponent is equal to 1.11 for Intel PXA 270, 1.62 for Pentium M770 and 1.66 for a TCP offload engine). So, we can describe the power as $P(s) = s^\alpha$, where $\alpha > 1$ is a small constant that depends on the processor. The energy consumption is the power integrated over time. Intuitively, the speed scaling mechanism captures the idea that the higher is the processor's speed the higher is the energy consumption. The algorithmic study of the speed scaling mechanism is initiated by Yao et al. [11] in 1995. Since then, there is a series of works in the speed scaling setting (see the surveys [1, 2]).

A classical objective in scheduling is the minimization of the makespan, i.e., the time at which the last job finishes its execution. Unfortunately, makespan minimization and energy minimization are conflicting objectives. One of the ways to take into account the bicriteria nature of speed scaling problems is by adopting a budget approach where a fixed budget of energy is given and the only objective is the minimization of the makespan (see for example [3, 7]). This is a quite natural assumption in our setting where the energy of a battery may be assumed to be fixed.

In this context, Pruhs et al. considered in [7] the problem of scheduling a set of jobs on a set of speed scalable parallel processors subject to precedence constraints among the jobs. The goal is to minimize the makespan of the schedule without exceeding a given energy budget. The approach in [7] is based on *constant power schedules*, which are schedules that keep the total power of all processors constant over time. Based on this property and by performing a binary search to determine the value of the power, they transform the problem to the classical problem of minimizing the makespan for scheduling a set of jobs with precedence constraints on related parallel processors, in which each processor runs at a single predefined speed. Using the known $O(\log m)$-approximation algorithm for the latter problem presented in [4, 5], they give an approximation algorithm of ratio $O(\log^{1+2/\alpha} m)$ for the speed scaling problem with precedence constraints, where m is the number of the processors.

Note that, when the energy consumption is not taken into account, the speed scaling problem reduces to the classical makespan minimization scheduling problem on identical parallel processors with precedence constraints, in which all processors run at the same predefined constant speed which is NP-hard. Graham [6] proved that the simple list scheduling algorithm is a $(2 - \frac{1}{m})$-approximation algorithm for it. On the negative side, Svensson [9] showed that it is NP-hard to improve upon the approximation ratio obtained by Graham, assuming a new variant of the unique games conjecture.

A natural question arising here is whether it is possible to reduce the gap between the approximability of the scheduling problems on parallel processors with and without speed scaling. In this note, we propose a simple $(2 - \frac{1}{m})$-approximation algorithm for the speed scaling problem with precedence constraints, matching the approximation ratio for the classical setting. In fact, we even generalize the problem studied in [7] by taking into account that each job is available for execution after a given release date. For the more general problem, our algorithm becomes 2-approximate. Our approach is based on several ingredients of Graham's algorithm for the corresponding classical problem with precedence constraints and release dates. Initially, using the lower bounds for the optimal solution used by Graham, we give a convex programming relaxation for the speed scaling problem. By solving this convex program, we define a speed, and hence a processing time, for each job. As these processing times respect the energy budget, we transform our problem to the classical problem without speed scaling and we use the list scheduling algorithm to obtain a feasible schedule.

Interestingly, the idea of using the lower bounds used for the classical setting in order to obtain a convex programming relaxation for the speed scaling setting can be also applied in other speed scaling problems and directly pass the approximation ratios from the classical to the speed scaling environment. In this note, we propose a generalized framework and a characterization of such scheduling problems and we present applications of our method for shop scheduling environments in the speed scaling setting.

Organization of the Paper.

In Section 2 we present the $(2 - \frac{1}{m})$-approximation algorithm for the speed scaling problem with precedence constraints on multiprocessors, improving the best known polylog(m)-approximation algorithm for this problem [7]. Based on the approach that we used for this problem, we propose in Section 3 a general framework that can directly pass the approximation ratios from a classical problem (without caring about the energy consumption) to the corresponding speed scaling problem, and we present the ingredients needed for this transformation. Then, in Section 3.1 we give an application of our framework to a well-known problem in scheduling, namely the open shop problem. We conclude in Section 4.

2. PRECEDENCE CONSTRAINTS

In this section, we consider the makespan minimization problem of scheduling a set of jobs, with release dates and precedence constraints among them, on parallel speed scalable processors subject to a budget of energy and we present a 2-approximation algorithm. Henceforth, we denote this problem as PREC_S and the corresponding classical problem without speed scaling as PREC. In the case where there are no release dates, our algorithm is $(2 - \frac{1}{m})$-approximate.

Problem Statement and Notation.

In the PREC_S problem, we are given a set of jobs $\mathcal{J} = \{1, 2, \ldots, n\}$ which have to be scheduled on m speed scalable parallel processors. Each job $j \in \mathcal{J}$ is characterized by an amount of work w_j and a release date r_j. We do not allow preemptions of the jobs which means that, for a given job $j \in \mathcal{J}$, we must choose a single processor on which j will be executed without any interruption. There are precedence constraints among the jobs. Specifically, if the job j precedes the job j', then j' cannot start until j is completed. In this case, we call j a predecessor of j'. Our objective is to find a feasible schedule with minimum completion time (makespan) so that the energy consumption is not greater than a given energy budget E.

The precedence constraints are represented in the form of a directed acyclic graph $G = (V, A)$. The set of vertices V contains one vertex for each job and the arc (j, j') belongs to the set of arcs A if and only if the job j is constrained to precede the job j'. We denote by $\mathcal{C}$ the set of all the paths (or chains) in G. Note that these paths are not necessarily maximal. This means that there may exist paths that are completely included in other paths. For a path $c \in \mathcal{C}$, we denote by $\mathcal{J}(c)$ the set of jobs which appear in c and by $r(c)$ the release date of the first job in the path. Given the processing times of the jobs, the length of a path $c \in \mathcal{C}$ is the sum of the processing times of the jobs in c.

Algorithm's Ingredients.

Let us consider first the problem PREC in which the jobs have fixed processing times. That is, each job $j \in \mathcal{J}$ is characterized by a processing time p_j instead of an amount of work w_j. Next, we present two well-known lower bounds on the value C^* of any optimal solution for PREC and an approximation algorithm which is upper bounded by 2 times the maximum of these linear bounds.

In the best case, there is no idle period in the schedule and all the processors complete together. Therefore,

$$C^* \geq \frac{1}{m} \sum_{j \in \mathcal{J}} p_j$$

Because of the precedence constraints, for every $c \in \mathcal{C}$, we have that

$$C^* \geq r(c) + \sum_{j \in \mathcal{J}(c)} p_j$$

For PREC, Graham [6] proposed the well-known list scheduling algorithm which follows.

Algorithm 1

1: Every time that a processor i becomes available, schedule on i a released job for which all the predecessors have been completed.

THEOREM 1. [6] *Let C be the makespan of the schedule produced by Algorithm 1 for* PREC. *Then,*

$$C \leq 2 \cdot \max \left\{ \frac{1}{m} \sum_{j \in \mathcal{J}} p_j, \max_{c \in \mathcal{C}} \left\{ r(c) + \sum_{j \in \mathcal{J}(c)} p_j \right\} \right\}$$

The Algorithm.

Now, we turn back our attention to PREC_S. Note that, in an optimal schedule for this problem, each job $j \in \mathcal{J}$ is executed with a constant speed s_j due to the convexity of the speed-to-power function. Given this speed we can compute its processing time $p_j = \frac{w_j}{s_j}$ and its energy consumption $E_j = w_j s_j^{\alpha-1} = \frac{w_j^\alpha}{p_j^{\alpha-1}}$.

Based on this, we present a convex programming relaxation for PREC_S. We introduce a variable y for the makespan and a variable x_j for each job $j \in \mathcal{J}$ which corresponds to the processing time of j. The objective is to minimize y. Given the lower bounds that we described previously for PREC, we add two linear constraints that relate the processing times of the jobs with the makespan, as well as, a constraint which ensures that the energy budget is not exceeded. So, we obtain the following convex program, denoted as CP.

$$\min y$$

$$y \geq \frac{1}{m} \sum_{j \in \mathcal{J}} x_j \tag{1}$$

$$y \geq r(c) + \sum_{j \in \mathcal{J}(c)} x_j \qquad c \in \mathcal{C} \tag{2}$$

$$\sum_{j \in \mathcal{J}} \frac{w_j^\alpha}{x_j^{\alpha-1}} \leq E \tag{3}$$

$$x_j \geq 0 \qquad j \in \mathcal{J}$$

This convex program has an exponential number of constraints as the number of paths may be exponential to the size of the instance. However, we will consider for the moment that we can get an optimal solution of it, and we explain later how we can solve it in polynomial time through a transformation to another convex program of polynomial size. Based on CP, we propose the following algorithm for PREC_S.

Algorithm 2

1: Solve the convex program CP.
2: Let $\vec{x}_{CP}$ be the vector of the processing times of jobs obtained by CP.
3: Apply Algorithm 1 as if the jobs have processing times $\vec{x}_{CP}$ to create a feasible schedule for PREC_S.

THEOREM 2. *Algorithm 2 achieves an approximation ratio of 2 for* PREC_S.

PROOF. Consider an instance of PREC_S, and let SOL and OPT be the value of our algorithm's solution and of an optimal solution, respectively. Given a vector of processing times $\vec{x}$ which corresponds to a feasible solution of the convex program, we denote by $CP(\vec{x})$ the corresponding value of the convex program, i.e. the minimum possible value of y with respect to $\vec{x}$. Furthermore, let $\vec{x}_{CP}$ be the values of the variables in the optimal solution of the convex program produced by the Algorithm 2 and $\vec{x}_{OPT}$ be the processing times of the jobs in an optimal solution of the problem PREC_S. Clearly, $CP(\vec{x}_{CP})$ is the value of the optimal solution of the convex relaxation. We have that

$$SOL \leq \rho \cdot CP(\vec{x}_{CP}) \leq \rho \cdot CP(\vec{x}_{OPT}) \leq \rho \cdot OPT$$

The first inequality comes from the fact that $\rho = 2$ multiplied by the maximum of the lower bounds for PREC is an upper bound on the makespan of the schedule produced by Algorithm 1, i.e., Theorem 1. The second inequality holds because $\vec{x}_{CP}$ is an optimal solution of the convex relaxation and $\vec{x}_{OPT}$ corresponds to just a feasible one for CP. Finally, the third inequality is based on the fact that the convex program is a relaxation of the speed scaling problem. The theorem follows. $\square$

When the jobs have no release dates our result can be slightly improved and we obtain a $(2 - \frac{1}{m})$-approximation algorithm by using the same lower bounds. In this case, when the jobs have fixed processing times, Algorithm 1 is $(2 - \frac{1}{m})$-approximate w.r.t. these lower bounds.

COROLLARY 1. *Algorithm 2 achieves an approximation ratio of* $2 - \frac{1}{m}$ *for* PREC_S *when all jobs have the same release date.*

An Equivalent Polynomial Size Convex Program.

As mentioned before, CP has an exponential number of constraints. In order to deal with this, we propose an equivalent convex programming relaxation. Let y_j be a variable indicating the completion time of job $j \in \mathcal{J}$. We replace the constraints (2) of CP with the following constraints, and we obtain a new convex program CP'.

$$y_j \leq y \qquad j \in \mathcal{J} \tag{4}$$

$$r_j + x_j \leq y_j \qquad j \in \mathcal{J} \tag{5}$$

$$y_j + x_{j'} \leq y_{j'} \qquad (j, j') \in A \tag{6}$$

$$y_j \geq 0 \qquad j \in \mathcal{J}$$

Next, we prove that the two convex programs are equivalent. Hence, there exists a polynomial 2-approximation algorithm for PREC_S.

LEMMA 1. *The two convex programs are equivalent.*

PROOF. Assume that we are given a feasible solution $(\tilde{x}_j, \tilde{y})$ for CP. We will show that there exists a feasible solution for CP' of the same cost. The variables x_j and y have equal values in both solutions. So, the constraints (1) and (3) are satisfied. For a given job $j \in \mathcal{J}$, we denote by $\mathcal{C}(j)$ the set of paths that have the job j as a right extremity. We set the value of the variable y_j equal to $\tilde{y}_j = \max_{c \in \mathcal{C}(j)} \left\{ r(c) + \sum_{j' \in \mathcal{J}(c)} \tilde{x}_{j'} \right\}$. It remains to show that the constraints (4), (5) and (6) are satisfied. By considering the path $c \in \mathcal{C}(j)$ that contains only the job j on our definition of $\tilde{y}_j$, the constraints (5) are satisfied. Moreover, assume that $(j, j') \in A$. Based on our definition, let $\tilde{y}_j = r(c) + \sum_{j'' \in \mathcal{J}(c)} \tilde{x}_{j''}$, for some path c. Then, as $r(c) = r(c \cup \{j'\})$,

$$\tilde{y}_{j'} \geq r(c \cup \{j'\}) + \sum_{j'' \in \mathcal{J}(c \cup \{j'\})} \tilde{x}_{j''} = y_j + x_{j'}$$

and the constraints (6) are also satisfied. Given our definition of $\tilde{y}_j$ and the fact that the solution $(\tilde{x}_j, \tilde{y})$ satisfies the constraints (2), we conclude that the solution $(\tilde{x}_j, \tilde{y}_j, \tilde{y})$ satisfies the constraints (4) and it is indeed feasible for CP'.

To the other direction, assume that we have a feasible solution $(\tilde{x}_j, \tilde{y}_j, \tilde{y})$ for CP'. Then, we claim that the solution

$(\tilde{x}_j, \tilde{y})$ is feasible for CP. The constraints (1) and (3) are satisfied directly. Next, consider any path $c \in \mathcal{C}$ and assume that it contains the jobs $j^{(1)}, j^{(2)}, \ldots, j^{(k)}$ in this order. We have that

$$r(c) + \sum_{j \in \mathcal{J}(c)} \tilde{x}_j = r_{j^{(1)}} + \sum_{\ell=1}^{k-1} \tilde{x}_{j^{(\ell+1)}}$$

$$\leq r_{j^{(1)}} + \sum_{\ell=1}^{k-1} (\tilde{y}_{j^{(\ell+1)}} - \tilde{y}_{j^{(\ell)}}) \leq \tilde{y}_{j^{(k)}} \leq y$$

where the inequalities follow from the constraints (6), (5) and (4), respectively. $\square$

3. A GENERALIZED FRAMEWORK

In this section, we present a generalized method for obtaining approximation algorithms for speed scaling problems in which the objective function is the minimization of e.g. the makespan and there is a given budget of energy which must not be exceeded. The main assumption is that the energy consumption of any optimal schedule can be expressed as a convex function $E(\vec{x})$ of the vector of the processing times $\vec{x}$ of the jobs (or operations). This assumption is true if a processor satisfies the standard speed-to-power function $P(s) = s^{\alpha}$, where $\alpha > 1$ is a constant, because each job (or operation) is executed with a constant speed due to the convexity of $P(s)$.

Consider a classical makespan minimization problem Π in which the jobs have fixed processing times. We denote by Π_S the speed scaling variant of the problem where each job (or operation) has an amount of work instead of a fixed processing time, the processors' speed can be varied, the objective remains the same and we are given a budget of energy which must not be exceeded. In order to apply our method, we need the following ingredients.

- A set of ℓ linear bounds on Π's optimal solution of the form

$$C^* \geq f_k(\vec{p})$$

for $k = 1, 2, \ldots, \ell$, where $\vec{p}$ is the vector of processing times of the jobs and $f_k(\vec{p})$ is a linear function of $\vec{p}$.

- A ρ-approximation algorithm $\mathcal{A}$ for Π which always produces a solution such that $C \leq \rho \cdot \max_{k=1}^{\ell} f_k(\vec{p})$, where C is the value of the $\mathcal{A}$'s solution for Π.

Provided the above ingredients, we may obtain a ρ-approximation algorithm for the speed scaling problem Π_S by using the algorithm $\mathcal{A}$ as a black box. Let us describe in a general manner our approach.

Our first task consists in constructing a convex programming relaxation CP for Π_S by using the lower bounds of Π. We introduce a variable y for the makespan and a vector variable $\vec{x}$ which corresponds to the processing times of the jobs. The objective is to minimize y. We add linear constraints of the form $y \geq f_k(\vec{x})$, for $k = 1, 2, \ldots, \ell$, and a constraint which ensures that the budget of energy is not exceeded. So, we obtain the following convex program.

$$\begin{aligned} \min \ & y \\ & y \geq f_k(\vec{x}) && \forall 1 \leq k \leq \ell \\ & E(\vec{x}) \leq E \\ & \vec{x} \geq 0 \end{aligned}$$

Next, we propose the following algorithm for Π_S.

Algorithm 3

1: Solve the convex program CP.
2: Let $\vec{x}_{CP}$ the vector of the processing times obtained.
3: Apply the algorithm $\mathcal{A}$ as if the jobs have processing times $\vec{x}_{CP}$ to create a feasible schedule for Π_S.

The following theorem can be proved using the same arguments as for Theorem 2.

THEOREM 3. *Algorithm 3 achieves an approximation ratio of ρ for Π_S.*

3.1 An Example: Open Shop

In this section, we consider the speed scaling problem of minimizing the makespan in an open shop environment and we present a 2-approximation algorithm. We denote this problem as SHOP_S.

Problem Statement.

An instance of SHOP_S contains a set of n jobs $\mathcal{J} = \{1, 2, \ldots, n\}$ which have to be scheduled by a set of m parallel processors $\mathcal{P} = \{1, 2, \ldots, m\}$. The job $j \in \mathcal{J}$ consists of m operations $O_{1,j}, O_{2,j}, \ldots, O_{m,j}$ and the operation $O_{i,j}$, $i \in \mathcal{P}$, has to be entirely executed by the processor i. Every operation $O_{i,j}$, $i \in \mathcal{P}$ and $j \in \mathcal{J}$, is associated with an amount of work $w_{i,j} \geq 0$. The open shop constraint enforces that no pair of operations of the same job are executed at the same time. We do not allow preemptions of operations which means that each operation has to be executed without interruptions. Our objective is to find a feasible schedule with minimum completion time (makespan) whose energy consumption does not exceed a given budget E.

The study of the open shop problem is motivated by applications where each task is composed by operations that have to be executed on special purpose machines, for example machines for floating point operations or graphics operations, etc. The open shop constraint is implied by the fact that the operations of the same task have access to the same physical resources, and hence they cannot be executed at the same time.

Algorithm's Ingredients.

Let us consider the problem SHOP in which each operation $O_{i,j}$ has a fixed processing time $p_{i,j}$ instead of an amount of work $w_{i,j}$. We denote by C^* the makespan of an optimal solution for this problem. Next, we give a set of lower bounds for C^*.

Each processor completes when all the operations assigned to it are finished. Therefore, for every $i \in \mathcal{P}$, we have that

$$C^* \geq \sum_{j=1}^{n} p_{i,j}$$

Similarly, a job completes when all its operation are finished. Hence, because of the open shop constraint, for every $j \in \mathcal{J}$ it must hold that

$$C^* \geq \sum_{i=1}^{m} p_{i,j} \qquad \qquad ,$$

For SHOP, Racsmány[1] proposed the well-known list scheduling algorithm which follows.

Algorithm 4

1: Whenever a processor $i \in \mathcal{P}$ becomes available, schedule on i an operation $O_{i,j}$ of a job $j \in \mathcal{J}$ which is not processed by any other machine at the same time.

THEOREM 4. (Racsmány) *Let C be the makespan of the schedule produced by Algorithm 4 for* SHOP. *Then,*

$$C \leq 2 \cdot \max \left\{ \max_{i \in \mathcal{P}} \left\{ \sum_{j \in \mathcal{J}} p_{i,j} \right\}, \max_{j \in \mathcal{J}} \left\{ \sum_{i \in \mathcal{P}} p_{i,j} \right\} \right\}$$

Algorithm.

Let us now describe how we obtain a 2-approximation algorithm for SHOP$_S$. Initially, we give a convex programming relaxation CP for it. As we described in Section 3, we introduce a variable $x_{i,j}$ which corresponds to the processing time of the operation $O_{i,j}$ and a variable y that corresponds to the makespan. Then, we construct CP as follows.

$$\min y$$
$$y \geq \sum_{j=1}^{n} x_{i,j} \qquad i \in \mathcal{P}$$
$$y \geq \sum_{i=1}^{m} x_{i,j} \qquad j \in \mathcal{J}$$
$$\sum_{i=1}^{m} \sum_{j=1}^{n} \frac{w_{i,j}^{\alpha}}{x_{i,j}^{\alpha-1}} \leq E$$
$$x_{i,j} \geq 0 \qquad i \in \mathcal{P}, j \in \mathcal{J}$$

Provided the above convex program, we can apply Algorithm 3 in order to solve SHOP$_S$ by using Algorithm 4 as a black box. Then, Theorems 3 and 4 imply the following theorem.

THEOREM 5. *There exists a 2-approximation algorithm for* SHOP$_S$.

4. CONCLUSIONS

We have improved from poly-log(m) to $2 - \frac{1}{m}$ the approximation ratio for the multiprocessor speed scaling problem with precedence constraints where the objective is to minimize the makespan of the schedule subject to a given energy budget. In fact we have even generalized the problem by considering that jobs are subject to release dates. Our approach is much simpler than the previous one and it can be used to deal with other problems in the speed scaling setting, like the open shop problem as well as problems on other shop environments where similar linear lower bounds on the makespan are known for the classical setting. An interesting question is whether we can extend this approach to other scheduling problems and more specifically to other performance objectives, i.e., for the average completion time of the jobs. A positive answer to this question could give us

an insight to the difficulty that adds the consideration of the energy consumption in scheduling problems.

Finally, we note that our approach can be used not only for power functions of the form $P(s) = s^{\alpha}$, but for any convex speed-to-power function, as we just need the property of convexity.

Acknowledgements

We would like to thank Maxim Sviridenko for our helpful discussions.

Partially supported by the project ALGONOW, co-financed by the European Union (European Social Fund - ESF) and Greek national funds, through the Operational Program "Education and Lifelong Learning", under the program THALES. Partially supported by the project Mathematical Programming and Non-linear Combinatorial Optimization under the program PGMO.

5. REFERENCES

[1] S. Albers. Energy-efficient algorithms. *Communications of the ACM*, 53(5):86–96, 2010.

[2] S. Albers. Algorithms for dynamic speed scaling. In *STACS*, volume 9 of *LIPIcs*, pages 1–11. Schloss Dagstuhl - Leibniz-Zentrum fuer Informatik, 2011.

[3] D. P. Bunde. Power-aware scheduling for makespan and flow. In *SPAA*, pages 190–196. ACM, 2006.

[4] C. Chekuri and M. A. Bender. An efficient approximation algorithm for minimizing makespan on uniformly related machines. *Journal of Algorithms*, 41:212–224, 2001.

[5] F. A. Chudak and D. B. Shmoys. Approximation algorithms for precedence-constrained scheduling problems on parallel machines that run at different speeds. *Journal of Algorithms*, 30(2):323–343, 1999.

[6] R. Graham. Bounds for certain multiprocessor anomalies. *Bell System Technical Journal*, 45(9):1563–1581, 1966.

[7] K. Pruhs, R. van Stee, and P. Uthaisombut. Speed scaling of tasks with precedence constraints. *Theory of Computing Systems*, 43:67–80, 2008.

[8] D. B. Shmoys, C. Stein, and J. Wein. Improved approximation algorithms for shop scheduling problems. *SIAM Journal on Computing*, 23(3):617–632, 1994.

[9] O. Svensson. Conditional hardness of precedence constrained scheduling on identical machines. In *STOC*, pages 745–754, 2010.

[10] A. Wierman, L. L. H. Andrew, and A. Tang. Power-aware speed scaling in processor sharing systems. In *INFOCOM*, pages 2007–2015. IEEE, 2009.

[11] F. F. Yao, A. J. Demers, and S. Shenker. A scheduling model for reduced CPU energy. In *FOCS*, pages 374–382. IEEE Computer Society, 1995.

---
[1]Check [8] for more details.

A Simple and Practical Linear-Work Parallel Algorithm for Connectivity

Julian Shun
Carnegie Mellon University
jshun@cs.cmu.edu

Laxman Dhulipala
Carnegie Mellon University
ldhulipa@andrew.cmu.edu

Guy E. Blelloch
Carnegie Mellon University
guyb@cs.cmu.edu

ABSTRACT

Graph connectivity is a fundamental problem in computer science with many important applications. Sequentially, connectivity can be done in linear work easily using breadth-first search or depth-first search. There have been many parallel algorithms for connectivity, however the simpler parallel algorithms require super-linear work, and the linear-work polylogarithmic-depth parallel algorithms are very complicated and not amenable to implementation. In this work, we address this gap by describing a simple and practical expected linear-work, polylogarithmic depth parallel algorithm for graph connectivity.

Our algorithm is based on a recent parallel algorithm for generating low-diameter graph decompositions by Miller et al. [44], which uses parallel breadth-first searches. We discuss a (modest) variant of their decomposition algorithm which preserves the theoretical complexity while leading to simpler and faster implementations. We experimentally compare the connectivity algorithms using both the original decomposition algorithm and our modified decomposition algorithm. We also experimentally compare against the fastest existing parallel connectivity implementations (which are not theoretically linear-work and polylogarithmic-depth) and show that our implementations are competitive for various input graphs. In addition, we compare our implementations to sequential connectivity algorithms and show that on 40 cores we achieve good speedup relative to the sequential implementations for many input graphs. We discuss the various optimizations used in our implementations and present an extensive experimental analysis of the performance. Our algorithm is the first parallel connectivity algorithm that is both theoretically and practically efficient.

Categories and Subject Descriptors: F.2 [Analysis of Algorithms and Problem Complexity]: General

Keywords: Parallel Algorithms, Graph Connectivity, Experiments

1. INTRODUCTION

Finding the connected components of a graph is a fundamental problem in computer science that has been well-studied. The problem takes as input an undirected graph with n vertices and m edges,

SPAA'14, June 23–25, 2014, Prague, Czech Republic.
Copyright 2014 ACM 978-1-4503-2821-0/14/06 ...$15.00
http://dx.doi.org/10.1145/2612669.2612692 .

and assigns each vertex a label such that vertices in the same connected component have the same label, and vertices in different connected components have different labels. Graph connectivity has many important applications, such as in VLSI design and image analysis for computer vision.

Sequentially, connectivity can be easily implemented in linear work using breadth-first search (BFS) or depth-first search, or nearly linear work with union-find. On the other hand, computing connected components and spanning forests[1] in parallel has been a long studied problem [1, 2, 15, 16, 18, 26, 28, 30, 31, 33, 34, 36, 41, 45, 47, 49, 50, 52, 53, 60]. Some of the parallel algorithms developed are relatively simple, but require super-linear work. The algorithms of Shiloach and Vishkin [53] and Awerbuch and Shiloach [2] work by combining the vertices into trees such that at the end of the algorithm vertices in the same component will belong to the same tree. These algorithms guarantee that the number of trees decreases by a constant factor in each iteration, but do not guarantee that a constant fraction of the edges are removed, and thus require $O(m \log n)$ work. The random mate algorithms of Reif [52] and Phillips [50] work by contracting vertices in the same component together and guarantee that a constant fraction of the vertices decrease in expectation per iteration, but again do not guarantee that a constant fraction of the edges are removed. Therefore, these algorithms also require $O(m \log n)$ expected work and are not work-efficient.

Work-efficient polylogarithmic-depth parallel connectivity algorithms have been designed in theory [17, 19, 23, 24, 49, 51]. These algorithms are based on random edge sampling [19, 23, 24] or linear-work minimum spanning forest algorithms, which also involve sampling and filtering edges [17, 49, 51]. However, these algorithms are complicated and unlikely to be practical (there are no implementations of these algorithms available).

There has also been significant experimental work on parallel connectivity algorithms in the past. Hambrusch and TeWinkel [25] implement connected component algorithms on the Massively Parallel Processor (MPP). Greiner [22] implements and compares parallel connectivity algorithms using NESL [9]. Goddard et al. [21], Hsu et al. [29], Bader et al. [3, 4], Patwary et al. [48], Shun et al. [57], Slota et al. [58], and the Galois system [46] implement algorithms for shared-memory CPUs. Bus and Tvrdik [12], Krishnamurthy et al. [35], Bader and JaJa [5] and Caceres et al. [13] implement connected components algorithms for distributed-memory machines. There has been some recent work on designing connectivity algorithms for GPUs [27, 59, 6]. There have also been connectivity algorithms that require time proportional to the diameter of the graph in recent graph processing packages [32, 37, 38,

---

[1] A spanning forest algorithm can be used to compute connected components.

54]. None of the previous parallel algorithms implemented are theoretically work-efficient.

We note that a parallel BFS can be performed to visit the components of the graph one-by-one. While this approach is linear-work, the depth is proportional to the sum of the diameters of the connected components. Therefore this approach is not efficient as a general-purpose parallel connectivity algorithm, although it works well for low-diameter graphs with few connected components.

In this paper, we present a simple linear-work algorithm for connectivity requiring polylogarithmic depth, and experimentally show that it rivals the best existing parallel implementations for connectivity. Our algorithm is the first work-efficient parallel graph connectivity algorithm with an implementation, and furthermore the implementation also performs well in practice.

Our algorithm is based on a simple parallel algorithm for generating low-diameter decompositions of graphs by Miller et al. [44], which is an improvement of an algorithm by Blelloch et al. [10]. A low-diameter decomposition of a graph partitions the vertices, such that the diameter of each partition is small, and the number of edges between partitions is small [42]. Such decompositions have many uses in computer science, including in linear system solvers [10] and in metric embeddings [7]. The algorithm of Miller et al. partitions a graph such that the diameter of each partition is $O(\log n/\beta)$ and the number of edges between components is $O(\beta m)$ for $0 < \beta < 1$. It runs in linear work and $O(\log^2 n/\beta)$ depth with high probability[2]. Their algorithm is based on performing breadth-first searches from different starting vertices in parallel with start times drawn from an exponential distribution. Due to properties of the exponential distribution, the algorithm only needs to run the multiple breadth-first searches for at most $O(\log n/\beta)$ iterations before visiting all vertices.

We observe that this decomposition algorithm can be used to generate the connected components labeling of a graph. Our algorithm simply calls the decomposition algorithm recursively with β set to a constant fraction, and after each call contracts each partition into a single vertex, and relabels the vertices and edges between partitions. Since the number of edges decreases by a constant fraction in expectation in each recursive call, the algorithm terminates after $O(\log n)$ calls with high probability. Hence we obtain an algorithm for connected components labeling that runs in linear work and $O(\log^3 n)$ depth with high probability. An illustration of this algorithm is shown in Figure 1. Our implementation is based on parallel breadth-first searches and some simple parallel routines.

We also present a slight modification of the decomposition algorithm of Miller et al. which relaxes the relative ordering among vertices due to different breadth-first search start times. We show that this modification does not affect the asymptotic complexity of the decomposition algorithm, while leading to a simpler and faster implementation. We use this decomposition algorithm for connectivity and apply various optimizations to our implementations.

We experimentally compare our algorithm against the fastest existing parallel connectivity implementations (which are not theoretically linear-work and polylogarithmic-depth) [57, 48, 54, 58] on a variety of input graphs and show that our algorithm is competitive. On 40 cores, our parallel implementations achieve 18–39 times speedup over the same implementation run on a single thread, and achieve good speedups over the sequential implementations on many graphs. We show that on most graphs, the number of edges decreases by significantly more than predicted by the theoretical bounds due to duplicate edges between components. In addition,

---

[2]We use "with high probability" (w.h.p.) to mean probability at least $1 - 1/n^c$ for any constant $c > 0$.

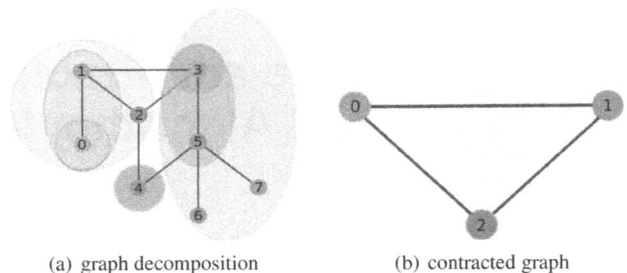

(a) graph decomposition   (b) contracted graph

Figure 1. Illustration of our decomposition-based connectivity algorithm. (a) At $t = 0$, vertex 0 starts a BFS (red ball), and at $t = 1$, vertices 3 (green ball) and 4 (blue ball) start BFS's. In this illustration, when there are ties (multiple BFS's visiting the same unvisited neighbor), the BFS center with the lowest ID wins. The balls represent the resulting partitions and the rings around the balls represent each level of the corresponding BFS. (b) Each ball is contracted into a single vertex, and the decomposition is applied recursively.

we study how the performance of our algorithms varies with different settings of β in the decomposition algorithms.

Contributions. The main contributions of this paper are as follows. Firstly, we describe a simple linear-work and polylogarithmic-depth parallel algorithm for connectivity. This is the first practical parallel connectivity algorithm with a linear-work guarantee. Secondly, we describe a (modest) variation of the parallel decomposition algorithm by Miller et al. that leads to a faster implementation and prove that it has the same theoretical guarantees as the original algorithm. Next, we present highly-optimized implementations of our algorithm. Finally, we present experimental results showing that our algorithm is competitive with the best previously available parallel implementations of graph connectivity.

2. NOTATION AND PRELIMINARIES

In this paper, we use the concurrent-read concurrent-write (CRCW) parallel random access machine model (PRAM). We state our results in the work-depth model, where **work** is equal to the number of operations required (equivalently, the product of the time and the number of processors) and **depth** is equal to the number of time steps required.

We use the atomic compare-and-swap and writeMin operations in our implementations. A **compare-and-swap** (CAS) is an atomic instruction that takes three arguments—a memory location (*loc*), an old value (*oldV*) and a new value (*newV*); if the value stored at *loc* is equal to *oldV* it atomically stores *newV* at *loc* and returns *true*, and otherwise it does not modify *loc* and returns *false*. A **writeMin** is an atomic instruction that takes three arguments—a memory location (*loc*), a value (*val*), and a comparison function $<$, and atomically updates the value at *loc* to be the minimum of the stored value and *val* according to $<$. It returns *true* if the value at *loc* was changed, and *false* otherwise. writeMin can be implemented with a loop, which reads the value at *loc* and applies a CAS if *val* is less than the value read according to $<$. The loop terminates when either a CAS is successful or when the read value is smaller than *val* according to $<$. The reader may refer to [56] for details.

A **connected component** in an undirected graph contains vertices such that any two vertices can reach one another through a path. The **connected components labeling** problem takes an undirected graph $G = (V, E)$, and returns a labeling L such that for two vertices u and v, $L(u) = L(v)$ if u and v belong in the same connected component, and $L(u) \neq L(v)$ otherwise.

144

A **breadth-first search (BFS)** algorithm takes an unweighted graph $G = (V, E)$ and a source vertex $r \in V$, and visits the vertices reachable from r in breadth-first order, i.e. for all reachable vertices $u, v \in V$, if $\text{dist}(r, u) < \text{dist}(r, v)$ then u will be visited before v, where $\text{dist}(x, y)$ is the length of the shortest path between x and y. A simple parallel algorithm processes each level of the BFS in parallel [11].

The **exponential distribution** with parameter λ is defined by the probability density function:

$$f(x, \lambda) = \begin{cases} \lambda e^{-\lambda x} & \text{if } x \geq 0 \\ 0 & \text{otherwise} \end{cases}$$

The mean of the exponential distribution is $1/\lambda$.

A (β, d)-**decomposition** $(0 < \beta < 1)$ of an undirected graph $G = (V, E)$ is a partition of V into subsets $V_1, \ldots, V_k$ such that (1) the shortest path between any two vertices in each V_i using only vertices in V_i is at most d, and (2) the number of edges $(u, v) \in E$ such that $u \in V_i$, $v \in V_j$, $i \neq j$ is at most βm.

Miller et al. present a parallel decomposition algorithm based on parallel BFS's [44], which we call DECOMP. They prove that for a value β, DECOMP generates a $(\beta, O(\frac{\log n}{\beta}))$ decomposition in $O(m)$ work and $O(\frac{\log^2 n}{\beta})$ depth with high probability on a CRCW PRAM. The algorithm works by assigning each vertex v a *shift value* δ_v drawn from an exponential distribution with parameter β (mean $1/\beta$). Miller et al. show that the maximum shift value is $O(\frac{\log n}{\beta})$ w.h.p. Each vertex v is then assigned to the partition S_u that minimizes the *shifted distance* $\text{dist}_{-\delta}(u, v) = \text{dist}(u, v) - \delta_u$. This can be implemented by performing multiple BFS's in parallel. Each iteration of the implementation explores one level of each BFS and at iteration t (starting with $t = 0$) breadth-first searches are started from the unvisited vertices v such that $\delta_v \in [t, t + 1)$. If multiple BFS's reach the same unvisited vertex w in the same time step, then w is assigned to the partition corresponding to the origin of the BFS with the smaller fractional portion of the shift value (equivalently, w is assigned to the partition whose origin has the smallest shifted distance to w). Since the maximum shift value is $O(\frac{\log n}{\beta})$, the algorithm terminates in $O(\frac{\log n}{\beta})$ iterations. Each iteration requires $O(\log n)$ depth for packing the frontiers of the BFS's, leading to an overall depth of $O(\frac{\log^2 n}{\beta})$ w.h.p. The BFS's are work-efficient, so the total work is $O(m)$.

3. LINEAR-WORK CONNECTIVITY

In this section, we describe our simple linear-work parallel algorithm for connectivity. As a subroutine, it uses the parallel decomposition algorithm DECOMP described in Section 2. By the definition of a decomposition, the number of inter-component edges remaining after a call to DECOMP starting with m edges is at most βm in expectation. We can contract each component into a single vertex and recurse on the remaining graph, whose edge count has decreased by at least a constant factor in expectation. This leads to a linear-work parallel connectivity algorithm, assuming the contraction and relabeling can be done efficiently.

The pseudo-code for our connected components algorithm (CC) is shown in Algorithm 1. The input to DECOMP is a graph $G(V, E)$ and a value β, and the output is a labeling L of the vertices in V, such that vertices in the same partition will have the same label. CONTRACT takes a graph $G(V, E)$ and a labeling L as input, and returns a new graph $G'(V', E')$ such that vertices with the same label in V according to L are contracted into a single vertex, forming the vertex set V', and the inter-component edges in E are relabeled

according to L and form the edge set E'. RELABELUP takes as input labelings L and L' and returns a new labeling L'' such that $L''[i] = L'[L[i]]$. RELABELUP is necessary because the original labels L must be updated with the labels L' returned by the recursive call to CC.

Algorithm 1 Parallel decomposition-based algorithm for connected components labeling

---
1:   β = some constant fraction in $(0, 1)$
2:   **procedure** CC($G(V, E)$)
3:      $L = \text{DECOMP}(G(V, E), \beta)$
4:            ▷ L contains the labels returned by DECOMP
5:      $G'(V', E') = \text{CONTRACT}(G(V, E), L)$
6:      **if** $|E'| = 0$ **then**
7:          **return** L
8:      **else**
9:          $L' = \text{CC}(G'(V', E'))$
10:        $L'' = \text{RELABELUP}(L, L')$
11:        **return** L''

THEOREM 1. *Algorithm 1 runs in $O(m)$ expected work and $O(\log^3 n)$ depth w.h.p. on a CRCW PRAM.*

PROOF. The algorithm sets β to a constant between 0 and 1. Since the number of edges decreases to at most βm in expectation after each recursive call, and the rate of reduction is independent across iterations, the total number of calls is $O(\log_{\frac{1}{\beta}} m)$ w.h.p. Each recursive call requires $O(\frac{\log^2 n}{\beta})$ depth w.h.p. and $O(m')$ work where m' is the number of remaining edges for DECOMP. Hence the total contribution of DECOMP to the depth of CC is $O(\log_{\frac{1}{\beta}} m \frac{\log^2 n}{\beta}) = O(\log^3 n)$ w.h.p. and the total contribution to the work of CC is upper bounded by $\sum_{i=0}^{\infty} \beta^i cm$ for some constant c, which is $O(m)$ in expectation.

We now discuss an implementation of DECOMP that allows us to do contraction and relabeling within the same complexity bounds. Recall that DECOMP performs multiple breadth-first searches in parallel, with each BFS corresponding to one of the components (partitions) of the graph. We can maintain all BFS's using a single frontier array, where vertices belonging to the same component are in consecutive positions in the frontier. In each iteration, vertices that need to start their own BFS are added to the end of this frontier array in parallel. We store all of the frontiers created throughout one call to DECOMP, and there are $O(\frac{\log n}{\beta})$ such frontiers w.h.p. Each individual BFS stores the starting and ending position of its component's vertices on each frontier, as well as the total number of edges for these vertices. Using this information, we can compute appropriate offsets into shared arrays for each component using prefix sums over all the $O(\frac{\log n}{\beta})$ frontiers for each BFS. For each iteration of CC, the work for computing offsets is $O(m')$ where m' is the number of edges at the beginning of the iteration, and the depth is $O(\frac{\log n'}{\beta})$.

As a vertex visits other vertices during the BFS's, if it encounters an edge to a vertex belonging to the same component (an intra-component edge), it will mark that edge as deleted (using some special value). These edges will be packed out at the end of DECOMP, which can be done in $O(m')$ total work and $O(\log m')$ depth, where m' is the number of edges at the beginning of the iteration. The rest of the edges will be inter-component edges and hence need to be kept for the next iteration. Each component will become a single vertex in the next iteration, with all of the edges of the component vertices merged. Since the vertices of each component are stored consecutively on the frontiers, we can create a new edge array and have the original vertices copy their edges in, guaranteeing that the resulting array will store each component's edges consecutively (we can compute each vertex's offset into this array with a prefix sum). We can remove duplicate edges within the complexity bounds of an iteration using parallel hashing [43, 20], although the number of edges decreases by a constant factor in expectation even if we do not remove duplicates.

To relabel the new vertices, we first compute the total number of components k and assign each original label with a new label in the range $[0, \ldots, k-1]$, which can be done using prefix sums. Singleton vertices are then removed, but their labels are kept. For the k' non-singleton vertices remaining, we relabel them to the range $[0, \ldots, k'-1]$ and recursively call CC. After the recursive call, the original labels are relabeled according to the result of CC. This can all be done using prefix sums in linear work in the number of remaining vertices and $O(\log n)$ depth per iteration.

We summarize the proof of this theorem. For a constant fraction β, there are $O(\log n)$ calls to DECOMP w.h.p., each of which does $O(\log n)$ iterations of BFS. Each iteration of BFS requires $O(\log n)$ depth for packing. The depth for contraction and relabeling is absorbed by the depth of DECOMP. This gives an overall depth of $O(\log^3 n)$ w.h.p. DECOMP, contraction and relabeling can be done work-efficiently, and each call to DECOMP decreases the number of edges by a constant fraction in expectation, leading to $O(m)$ expected work overall. □

We note that theoretically the depth of DECOMP could be improved to $O(\log n \log^* n)$ by using approximate compaction [20] (which is linear-work) for packing the frontiers of the BFS's. This would give us an algorithm with expected linear-work algorithm and $O(\log^2 n \log^* n)$ depth w.h.p.

We consider a slight variation of DECOMP which breaks ties arbitrarily among frontier vertices visiting the same unvisited neighbor in a given iteration of the BFS's. This modification simplifies our implementation and leads to improved performance as we discuss later in the paper. This variation is equivalent to rounding down all the δ_v values to the nearest integer and again assigning each vertex v to the partition S_u that minimizes $\text{dist}_{-\delta}(u, v) = \text{dist}(u, v) - \delta_u$, but breaking ties arbitrarily. We call this version **Decomp-Arb** and show that this modified version has the same theoretical guarantees (within a constant factor). In particular, we show that the number of inter-component edges in the decomposition is at most $2\beta m$ in expectation (the original bound was βm).

THEOREM 2. *Decomp-Arb generates a* $O(2\beta, O(\frac{\log n}{\beta}))$ *decomposition in* $O(m)$ *expected work and* $O(\frac{\log^2 n}{\beta})$ *depth w.h.p.*

PROOF. Since we are still picking values from an exponential distribution, the diameter of each component is $O(\frac{\log n}{\beta})$ w.h.p. as shown in [44]. Hence the depth of the algorithm is the same as the original algorithm, namely $O(\frac{\log^2 n}{\beta})$ w.h.p. The work is still $O(m)$ in expectation, since the BFS's are work-efficient. Hence we only need to show that the number of inter-component edges is at most $2\beta m$ in expectation.

As in [44], consider the midpoint w of an edge (u, v). Lemma 4.3 of [44] states that if u and v belong to different components, then $\text{dist}_{-\delta}(u', w)$ and $\text{dist}_{-\delta}(v', w)$ are within 1 of the minimum shifted distance to w. Decomp-Arb rounds all shifted distances down to the nearest integer. Hence when comparing two rounded shift distances, their difference is at most 1 if and only if the two original shift distances were within 2 of each other. In other words, suppose the two distances we are comparing are d_1 and d_2. Then $||d_2| - |d_1|| \le 1$ if and only if $|d_2 - d_1| < 2$. Hence we can

modify Lemma 4.3 of [44] to state that if u and v belong to different components, then $\text{dist}_{-\delta}(u', w)$ and $\text{dist}_{-\delta}(v', w)$ (using the original shift distances) are within 2 of the minimum shifted distance to w.

Lemma 4.4 of [44] uses properties of the exponential distribution to show that the probability that the smallest and second smallest shifted distance to w (corresponding to the first two BFS's that arrive at w) has a difference of less than c is at most βc. Here we have $c = 2$, so the probability that an edge is an inter-component edge is at most 2β. By linearity of expectations, the expected total number of inter-component edges is at most $2\beta m$. □

We can plug in Decomp-Arb into the proof of Theorem 1 and obtain a linear-work connectivity algorithm for $0 < \beta < 1/2$.

4. IMPLEMENTATION DETAILS

A naive implementation of Algorithm 1 would probably only require tens of lines of code. However to obtain the best performance in practice, an implementation must take into account constant factors, cache performance, and the synchronization primitives used. Therefore, in this section we describe our algorithmic engineering efforts to obtain a fast implementation of Algorithm 1. We describe three versions of DECOMP, referring to the original algorithm as Decomp-Min, the version which breaks ties arbitrarily as Decomp-Arb, and a variant of Decomp-Arb that we discuss later as Decomp-Arb-Hybrid.

We represent our graph using the adjacency array format, where we have an array of vertex offsets V into an array of edges E. The targets of the outgoing edges of vertex i are then stored in $E[V[i]], \ldots, E[V[i+1]] - 1$ (to deal with the edge case, we set $V[n] = m$). Our graph is undirected so each edge is stored in both directions. We also maintain an array D, where $D[i]$ stores the degree of the i'th vertex. Initially $D[i]$ is set to $V[i+1] - V[i]$.

As suggested in [44], in our implementations we simulate the assignment of values from the exponential distribution to vertices by generating a random permutation (in parallel), and in each round adding chunks of vertices starting from the beginning of the permutation as start centers for new BFS's, where the chunk size grows exponentially. If a vertex in a chunk has already been visited, then it is not added as a start center. Each vertex also draws a random integer from a large enough range to simulate the fractional part of its shift value (denoted by δ'_v for vertex v), used to break ties if multiple BFS's visit the same unvisited neighbor. We maintain the active frontier of the BFS's using a single array. New BFS centers are simply added to the end of this array in parallel. We note that parallel BFS can also be implemented using Cilk reducers [40] with similar performance.

Since we do not need to keep around the inter-component edges in recursive calls to CC, we pack out inter-component edges as we encounter them. Therefore as we explore vertices, we determine on-the-fly whether the incident edge to the explored vertex is an inter-component edge or an intra-component edge.

In contrast to the description in the proof of Theorem 1, in our implementations we do not store the frontiers of the BFS's and offsets of each BFS into the frontiers. Therefore the vertices of the same component will not be able to be accessed contiguously in memory. Instead, in the contraction phase we use an integer sort to collect all the vertices of the same component together. We found this to be more efficient than the method described in the proof of Theorem 1 because the amount of bookkeeping is reduced and the integer sort is only performed over the remaining inter-component edges, which is usually much fewer than the number of original edges. We use the linear-work and $O(m^\epsilon)$ depth ($0 < \epsilon < 1$) integer sort algorithm from the Problem Based Benchmark Suite [57].

Decomp-Min is split into two phases over the frontier vertices (pseudo-code shown in Algorithm 2). In our implementation, we use an array C to store both the component ID's of the vertices and to store the values that vertices write to resolve conflicts. In particular, the array C stores pairs (c_1, c_2) where for a vertex v, c_1 is used for markings from frontier vertices competing to visit v, and c_2 stores the component ID of vertex v. We will use $C_1[v]$ and $C_2[v]$ to refer to the first and second value of the pair $C[v]$, respectively. Decomp-Min uses the writeMin operation (described in Section 2) on integer pairs, where the comparison function (not shown in the pseudo-code) uses integer comparison on the first value of pair. Note that instead of keeping pairs in C we could keep two arrays, one to store the component IDs and the other to resolve conflicts, but this leads to an additional cache miss per vertex visit.

The entries of C are initialized to (∞, ∞) on Line 1. The ∞ in the second value of the pair indicates that the vertex has not yet been visited, and the first value of the pair is the identity value for the writeMin function. When a vertex v is added to the BFS on Lines 5–6 (i.e. it starts a new BFS), $C[v]$ is set to $(-1, v)$—the value -1 in $C_1[v]$ indicates that v has been visited, and the value v in $C_2[v]$ indicates that the component ID of v is its own vertex ID. In our implementation, inter-component edges are kept while intra-component edges are deleted on-the-fly. We overwrite the edge array E as we loop over the edges (Lines 17–18 and 21–22) using a counter k indicating the current position in the array (Line 11). In the first phase, frontier vertices mark unvisited neighbors with the writeMin primitive (Lines 14–16) with the fractional part of its BFS center's shift value, $\delta'_{C_2[v]}$ (the BFS center's ID is equal to $C_2[v]$, the component ID of v). We assume there are no ties as the numbers can be drawn from a large enough range to guarantee this w.h.p. Also, as long as for a neighbor w, $C_1[w] \neq -1$, this means the neighbor has not been visited in a *previous iteration*. In this case, we need to keep the edge (Lines 17–18) as we currently do not know whether it is an intra- or inter-component edge (this can only be determined once all other frontier vertices finish doing their writeMin's). Otherwise, the neighbor w has been visited in a previous iteration and we can determine the status of the edge to w—if w has component label different from v, it keeps the edge as it is an inter-component edge (Lines 20–22). It labels the endpoint of the edge with its new component ID (so that it does not have to be relabeled later) but sets the sign bit of the value (negates it and subtracts 1) to indicate that this edge need not be considered again in the second phase. Otherwise, the edge is an intra-component edge and is deleted. We set the degree of v to be the number of edges kept in this phase (Line 23).

In the second phase, the remaining edges incident on v are looped over and for edges which have a non-negative value (an edge whose status has not yet been determined from the first phase), we determine whether $\delta'_{C_2[v]}$ is stored on the neighbor w. If so, then v uses a compare-and-swap (CAS) to attempt to atomically set $C_1[w]$ to -1 (so that future writeMin's will not mark it again) and if successful adds w to the next frontier (Lines 30–31) and does not keep the edge (it is an intra-component edge). A CAS is required here since there could be multiple vertices from the same component exploring the same neighbor w (they all have the same $\delta'_{C_2[v]}$ value), and we want w to be added only once to the next frontier. If the condition on Line 30 does not hold, we check whether the component ID of w matches that of v, and if they differ, then the edge is an inter-component edge and we keep it (Lines 32–35). We set the sign bit of the value of its component ID and store it in E (Lines 34–35). If $C_2[w] = C_2[v]$, then (v, w) is an intra-component edge and we

do not keep it. If the edge has a negative value, then it was already processed in the first phase, and we just keep it (Lines 36–38). We set the degree of v to be the number of inter-component edges incident on v (Line 39). After the BFS's are finished, we unset the sign bit of the remaining (inter-component) edges, so that they can be properly processed during the relabeling phase after the call to DECOMP by the connected components algorithm.

Note that for high-degree vertices (e.g. degree greater than $k \log n$ for some constant k), the inner sequential for-loops over the neighbors of a vertex can be replaced with a parallel for-loop, marking the deleted edges with a special value and packing the edges with a parallel prefix sums after the for-loop.

Algorithm 2 Decomp-Min

1: $C = \{(\infty, \infty), \dots, (\infty, \infty)\}$
2: Frontier $= \{\}$
3: numVisited $= 0$
4: **while** (numVisited $< n$) **do**
5:      add to Frontier unvisited vertices v with $\delta_v <$ round $+ 1$
6:      and set $C[v] = (-1, v)$ ▷ new BFS centers
7:      numVisited $=$ numVisited $+$ size(Frontier)
8:      NextFrontier $= \{\}$
9:      **parfor** $v \in$ Frontier **do**
10:          start $= V[v]$ ▷ start index of edges in E
11:          $k = 0$
12:          **for** $i = 0$ to $D[v] - 1$ **do**
13:             $w = E[\text{start} + i]$
14:             **if** $C_1[w] \neq -1$ **then**
15:                **if** $C_1[w] > \delta'_{C_2[v]}$ **then**
16:                    writeMin($C[w], (\delta'_{C_2[v]}, C_2[v])$)
17:                $E[\text{start} + k] = w$
18:                $k = k + 1$
19:             **else**
20:                **if** $C_2[w] \neq C_2[v]$ **then**
21:                    $E[\text{start} + k] = -C_2[w] - 1$
22:                    $k = k + 1$
23:          $D[v] = k$
24:      **parfor** $v \in$ Frontier **do**
25:          start $= V[v]$ ▷ start index of edges in E
26:          $k = 0$
27:          **for** $i = 0$ to $D[v] - 1$ **do**
28:             $w = E[\text{start} + i]$
29:             **if** $w \geq 0$ **then**
30:                **if** $C_1[w] = \delta'_{C_2[v]}$ and CAS($C_1[w], \delta'_{C_2[v]}, -1$) **then**
31:                    add w to NextFrontier   ▷ v won on w
32:             **else**
33:                **if** $C_2[w] \neq C_2[v]$ **then**
34:                    $E[\text{start} + k] = -C_2[w] - 1$
35:                    $k = k + 1$
36:             **else**
37:                $E[\text{start} + k] = w$
38:                $k = k + 1$
39:          $D[v] = k$
40:      NextFrontier $=$ Frontier

Decomp-Min is split into two phases because we need all the vertices to apply the writeMin on their unvisited neighbors before we can determine a winner. Hence, a synchronization point is needed between the writeMin's and the checks to see if a vertex successfully visits a neighbor.

In contrast to Decomp-Min, Decomp-Arb only requires one phase over the edges of the frontier vertices and their outgoing edges (pseudo-code shown in Algorithm 3). Here C stores only a single integer value, indicating the component ID's of the vertices. Each entry is initialized to ∞ (Line 1) to indicate that the vertex has not yet been visited. The code of Decomp-Arb is similar to that of Decomp-Min, except that there is only a single phase over the edges of each frontier. Instead of using a writeMin as in Decomp-

Min, Decomp-Arb uses a CAS to mark an unvisited neighbor (Line 14) with the component ID of the frontier vertex. A vertex that successfully marks a neighbor can delete its edge to that neighbor since it is guaranteed to be an intra-component edge. That vertex is also responsible for adding the neighbor to the next frontier (Line 15). Otherwise, the vertex checks the component ID of its neighbor and if it differs from its own, it keeps the edge as an inter-component edge (Lines 17–19). It also marks the endpoint of the edge with its component ID so that it doesn't have to be relabeled later (Line 18). Note that although the pseudo-code shown does not make use of the fact that the degree is set to the number of inter-component edges on Line 20, we make use of it during the relabeling phase (not shown in the pseudo-code). Unlike in Decomp-Min, Decomp-Arb does not need to use the fractional part of the shift values (the δ'_v values) because an arbitrary BFS can mark an unvisited neighbor.

Decomp-Arb only requires a single phase over the edges of the frontier vertices because once a vertex w is visited by some vertex v and its component ID is set to the component ID of v, it can no longer be visited again by another vertex. At that point we know that the edge from v to w is an intra-component edge and can delete it, and any other neighbor of w with a different component ID than w that fails to mark w with the CAS has an inter-component edge to w which is kept.

Algorithm 3 Decomp-Arb

1: $C = \{\infty, \dots, \infty\}$
2: Frontier $= \{\}$
3: numVisited $= 0$
4: **while** (numVisited $< n$) **do**
5:     add to Frontier unvisited vertices v with $\delta_v <$ round $+ 1$
6:     and set $C[v] = v$ ▷ new BFS centers
7:     numVisited $=$ numVisited $+$ size(Frontier)
8:     NextFrontier $= \{\}$
9:     **parfor** $v \in$ Frontier **do**
10:        start $= V[v]$ ▷ start index of edges in E
11:        $k = 0$
12:        **for** $i = 0$ to $D[v] - 1$ **do**
13:            $w = E[\text{start} + i]$
14:            **if** $C[w] = \infty$ and $\text{CAS}(C[w], \infty, C[v])$ **then**
15:                add w to NextFrontier
16:            **else**
17:                **if** $C[w] \neq C[v]$ **then**   ▷ inter-component edge
18:                    $E[\text{start} + k] = C[w]$
19:                    $k = k + 1$
20:        $D[v] = k$
21:     NextFrontier $=$ Frontier

During the relabeling phase, we only need to relabel the source endpoint of each remaining edge, as the target endpoint was already relabeled during DECOMP. After relabeling, we use a parallel hash table [55] to remove duplicate edges between components. On the way back up from the recursive call to CC, we simply index into the labeling returned by CC with a parallel for-loop to relabel the original labels appropriately (corresponding to RELABELUP of Algorithm 1).

As we show experimentally in Section 5, Decomp-Arb performs better than Decomp-Min due to only requiring one pass over the edges of each frontier during the BFS's, and needing less bookkeeping overall.

We considered the *direction-optimizing* (hybrid) BFS idea first described by Beamer et al. [8] and later implemented for general graph traversal algorithms in Ligra [54]. In BFS, the idea is that when the frontier is large, it is cheaper to have all unvisited vertices read their incoming neighbors and once a vertex finds a neighbor on the frontier, it chooses it as its parent and quits (subsequent incoming edges to this vertex do not need to be examined). If a large

number of vertices' neighbors are on the frontier, then this possibly saves many edge traversals.

In contrast to a standard BFS, our connectivity algorithm requires all edges to be inspected, since we must decide whether the edge is an inter-component or an intra-component edge for the recursive call. Therefore, if we apply the optimization, we must introduce a post-processing step that inspects the edges determining whether or not they should be kept, so the total number of edges inspected is not reduced. We apply this optimization to Decomp-Arb, as it allows a vertex to select an arbitrary neighbor's component ID, and thus can exit the loop over the neighbors early. One modification is that edges that are relabeled on-the-fly during the write-based computation (e.g. Line 19 of Algorithm 3) must be marked that they have been relabeled, so that we do not process them again during the post-processing phase (we use the sign bit in the label for this purpose). Our experiments show that even though no edge traversals are saved, switching to the read-based computation when the frontier is large (the fraction of vertices on the frontier is greater than 20%) helps for some graphs, as the read-based computation is more cache-friendly, and does not require using an atomic operation, in contrast to the original Decomp-Arb which uses compare-and-swaps to resolve conflicts. We refer to the direction-optimizing version of Decomp-Arb as *Decomp-Arb-Hybrid*.

5. EXPERIMENTS

We compare our three implementations of the connectivity algorithm to the fastest available parallel connectivity algorithms that we are aware of [57, 48, 54, 58]. We refer to our algorithm using Decomp-Min as *decomp-min-CC*, Decomp-Arb as *decomp-arb-CC* and Decomp-Arb-Hybrid as *decomp-arb-hybrid-CC*. We also tried parallelizing over the edges for the high-degree vertices in our implementations (as discussed in Section 4), but due to the modest core count of our machine, we did not find a performance improvement. Patwary et al. [48] describe two parallel spanning forest implementations—a lock-based one and a verification-based one. We use their lock-based implementation (*parallel-SF-PRM*) since we found that the verification-based one sometimes fails to terminate. Furthermore, they found that their lock-based implementation usually outperforms their verification-based one. We also compare with the parallel spanning forest implementation in the Problem Based Benchmark Suite (PBBS) [57] (*parallel-SF-PBBS*). We note that these existing spanning forest-based parallel implementations are not theoretically work-efficient. As for connectivity based on BFS, we compare with the direction-optimizing BFS [8] available as part of Ligra [54], performed on each component of the graph. We refer to this implementation as *hybrid-BFS-CC*. This approach is work-efficient but the depth can be linear in the worst case. Very recently and independently of our work, Slota et al. [58] describe a connected components algorithm which combines direction-optimizing BFS with label propagation (*multistep-CC*). In label propagation, each vertex starts with a unique ID and in each iteration every vertex updates its ID to be the minimum of its own ID and all of its neighbors IDs; the label propagation terminates when no IDs change in an iteration. In the worst case, the algorithm of Slota et al. requires quadratic work and linear depth. We compare all of the parallel implementations to a simple sequential spanning forest-based connectivity algorithm using union-find (*serial-SF*) from the PBBS. The single-thread times for hybrid-BFS-CC and multistep-CC are sometimes better than serial-SF, and can also be used as a sequential baseline. For the spanning forest-based connectivity algorithms, we include in the timings a post-processing step that finds the ID of the root of the tree for each vertex (done in parallel for the parallel implementations).

We run our experiments on a 40-core (with hyper-threading) machine with 4×2.4GHz Intel 10-core E7-8870 Xeon processors (with a 1066MHz bus and 30MB L3 cache) and 256GB of main memory. We run all parallel experiments with two-way hyper-threading enabled, for a total of 80 hyper-threads. We compiled our code with `g++` version 4.8.0 with the `-O2` flag. The parallel codes use Cilk Plus [39] to express parallelism, which is supported by the `g++` compiler that we use. In particular, the parallel for-loops are written using the `cilk_for` construct. Divide-and-conquer parallelism, which is required by the parallel integer sort, is written using the `cilk_spawn` construct. When running in parallel, we use the command `numactl -i all` to evenly distribute the allocated memory among the processors.

We use a variety of synthetic graphs, the first three of which are taken from the PBBS [57], and a real-world graph. *random* is a random graph where every vertex has five edges to neighbors chosen randomly. The *rMat* graph [14] is a graph with a power-law degree distribution. *rMat2* uses the same generator as rMat, but with a higher edge-to-vertex ratio, giving a denser graph. *3D-grid* is a grid graph in 3-dimensional space where every vertex has six edges, each connecting it to its 2 neighbors in each dimension. *line* is a path of length $n - 1$ (i.e. each vertex has two neighbors except for the first and the last vertex in the path). This is a degenerate graph with diameter $n - 1$. *com-Orkut* is a social network graph downloaded from the Stanford Network Analysis Project (SNAP), available at `http://snap.stanford.edu`. For the synthetic graphs, the vertex labels are randomly assigned. The sizes of the graphs are shown in Table 1. For our decomposition-based algorithms we store an edge in each direction, so we use twice the number of edges than as noted in Table 1, while for the spanning forest-based algorithms, edges only need to be stored in one direction.

Input Graph	Num. Vertices	Num. Edges
random	10^8	5×10^8
rMat	2^{27}	5×10^8
rMat2	2^{20}	4.2×10^8
3D-grid	10^8	3×10^8
line	5×10^8	5×10^8
com-Orkut	3,072,627	117,185,083

Table 1. Input graphs

The serial and parallel running times of the implementations on the various inputs are summarized in Table 2. The times that we report are based on a median of three trials. We see that decomp-arb-CC and decomp-arb-hybrid-CC usually outperform decomp-min-CC (by up to 2.3 times). This is because (1) decomp-arb-CC and decomp-arb-hybrid-CC require only one pass over the edges of the frontier instead of two passes in decomp-min-CC and (2) the vertices store less data when computing the labeling. Decomp-arb-hybrid-CC is faster than decomp-arb-CC for most of the graphs, especially for the graphs whose frontier grows very large (e.g. about 2x faster for rMat2 and com-Orkut), as these graphs benefit more from the optimization of using a read-based computation for the large frontiers. For 3D-grid and line, the times are about the same for decomp-arb-CC and decomp-arb-hybrid-CC, since in decomp-arb-hybrid-CC the frontier never grows large enough to switch to the read-based computation. Among the two spanning forest-based parallel implementations, parallel-SF-PRM is faster than parallel-SF-PBBS in parallel. Compared to parallel-SF-PRM, decomp-arb-hybrid-CC is at most 70% slower in parallel, and faster sequentially. On 40 cores with hyper-threading, our parallel implementations achieve a self-relative speedup of between 18 and 39.

We observe that the implementations based on a single direction-optimizing BFS (hybrid-BFS-CC and multistep-CC) work well for dense graphs with low-diameter, such as random, rMat2 and com-

Orkut, outperforming the other implementations both sequentially and in parallel on these graphs. For the dense rMat2 graph, which requires only 5 levels of BFS to completely traverse, even the sequential times of these implementations are competitive with the parallel times of the other implementations. This is because the read-based optimization of direction-optimizing BFS significantly reduces the number of edges traversed. For graphs with many components (i.e. rMat with over 13 million components), hybrid-BFS-CC does poorly in parallel since it visits the components one-by-one, while multistep-CC does better because it uses parallel BFS to compute only one component, and then switches to label propagation to compute the rest. For the line graph, both implementations perform poorly and get no speedup due to the large diameter of the graph. Our fastest parallel implementation (decomp-arb-hybrid-CC) is faster than hybrid-BFS-CC and multistep-CC for the line graph, competitive for the rMat and 3D-grid graphs, and slower for the random, rMat2 and com-Orkut graphs. For graphs with only one component (random, rMat2, 3D-grid and line), multistep-CC and hybrid-BFS-CC both perform exactly one BFS, and the differences in running times are due to the choice of when to switch to the read-based computation, starting vertex of the BFS, and slight implementation differences. Note that on a single thread, multistep-CC outperforms serial-SF for four of the graphs, since the read-based optimization allows it to traverse many fewer edges for these graphs.

Compared to the best single-thread times among serial-SF, hybrid-BFS-CC and multistep-CC, on 40 cores our fastest implementation achieves up to a 13 times speedup. For the dense rMat2 graph, on 40 cores our parallel implementation is actually slower than hybrid-BFS-CC run on a single thread, but this is a special case on which the direction-optimizing BFS approach works particularly well.

Figure 2 shows the running time versus the number of threads for the different implementations on the input graphs. For the line graph, we do not plot hybrid-BFS-CC and multistep-CC as they perform very poorly and get no speedup. We see that our parallel implementations get good speedup, and except for rMat2 and com-Orkut, outperform the best sequential time with a modest number of threads. Our parallel implementations (decomp-arb-CC, decomp-arb-hybrid-CC and decomp-min-CC) perform reasonably well and are competitive with the other parallel implementations implementations, which are not theoretically linear-work and polylogarithmic-depth guarantee, for all graphs except rMat2 and com-Orkut, on which the direction-optimizing BFS implementations perform exceptionally well. While our parallel implementations do not achieve the fastest performance for any particular graph, due to their theoretical guarantees, they perform reasonable well across all inputs and do not suffer from poor performance on any "worst-case" inputs.

Figure 3 shows the 40-core running time of decomp-arb-CC, decomp-arb-hybrid-CC and decomp-min-CC as a function of the parameter β for several graphs. We see that the trends for the implementations are similar, and the β leading to the fastest running times is between 0.05 and 0.2. Figure 4 shows the number of edges remaining per iteration for decomp-arb-hybrid-CC as a function of β. As expected, the number of edges drops more quickly for smaller β, leading to fewer phases until reaching the base case. Furthermore, the upper bound of a 2β-fraction of edges being removed (or β-fraction for decomp-min-CC) per iteration does not account for the removal of duplicate edges between contracted components. For all our graphs except the line graph, there are (many) duplicate edges between components that are removed, leading to a much sharper decrease (up to an order of magnitude more than predicted by the upper bound) in the number of remaining edges per iteration.

Implementation	random		rMat		rMat2		3D-grid		line		com-Orkut	
	(1)	(40h)	(1)	(40h)	(1)	(40h)	(1)	(40h)	(1)	(40h)	(1)	(40h)
serial-SF	19.5	–	21.5	–	2.86*	–	17.5	–	68.6	–	0.82*	–
decomp-arb-CC	43.1	1.97	46.7	2.5	6.95	0.256	30.1	1.36	254	6.49	2.35	0.115
decomp-arb-hybrid-CC	38.7	1.89	39.8	2.22	4.11	0.116	30.6	1.39	247	6.5	1.22	0.058
decomp-min-CC	74.8	2.86	76.3	3.49	7.22	0.221	57.9	2.11	348	9.11	2.39	0.132
parallel-SF-PBBS	70.9	1.91	79.2	2.13	9.79	0.515	41.1	1.53	174	5.22	2.98	0.156
parallel-SF-PRM	48.8	1.64	42.2	1.3	4.51	0.1	30.3	1.33	313	4.02	1.25	0.04
hybrid-BFS-CC	28	1.3	25.9	13.3	0.111	0.009	22.1	1.51	304	304†	0.191	0.021
multistep-CC	9.74	1.29	15.9	2.06	0.23	0.05	27.0	1.22	343	343†	0.16	0.06

Table 2. Times (seconds) for connected components labeling. (40h) indicates 40 cores with hyper-threading. *We use the timing for the sequential spanning forest code from Patwary et al. [48] as we found it to be faster than the PBBS implementation. †We use the sequential time as the parallel time was higher due to overheads of parallel execution.

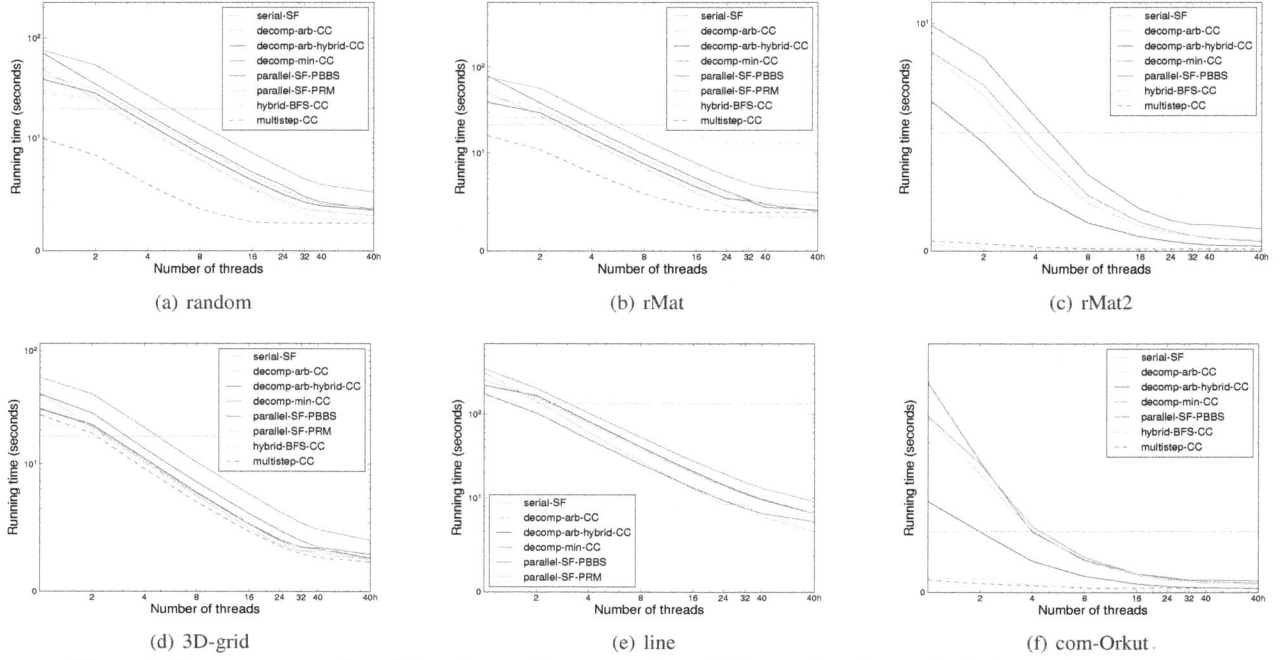

(a) random

(b) rMat

(c) rMat2

(d) 3D-grid

(e) line

(f) com-Orkut

Figure 2. Times versus number of threads on a 40-core machine with hyper-threading. (40h) indicates 80 hyper-threads.

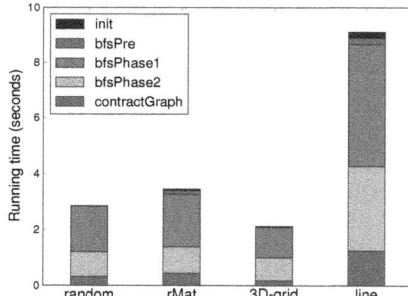

Figure 5. Breakdown of timings on 40 cores with hyper-threading for decomp-min-CC.

Figure 6. Breakdown of timings on 40 cores with hyper-threading for decomp-arb-CC.

Figure 5 shows the breakdown of the 40-core running time for decomp-min-CC on several graphs. In the figure, "init" refers to the time for generating random permutations and initializing arrays, "bfsPre" refers to adding new vertices to the BFS frontier and computing offsets into shared arrays for the frontier vertices, "bfsPhase1" refers to the first phase (Lines 9–23 of Algorithm 2), "bfsPhase2" refers to the second phase (Lines 24–39 of Algorithm 2), and "contractGraph" includes the time for removing duplicate edges, renumbering vertices and edges, creating the contracted graph for

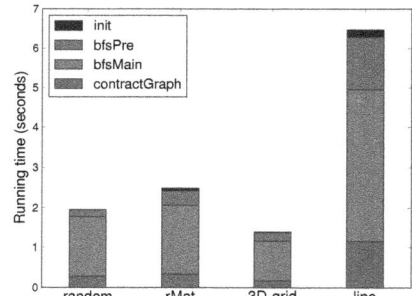

the recursive call, and relabeling after the recursive call. We see that 80–90% of the time is spent in the two BFS phases, with the first phase being the more expensive of the two.

Figure 6 shows the breakdown of the running time for decomp-arb-CC on 40 cores on several inputs. "bfsMain" refers to the single phase of the BFS iteration (Lines 9–20 of Algorithm 3), and the other sub-timings have the same meaning as in the previous paragraph. The majority of the time (55–75%) is spent in the main BFS phase. Compared to decomp-min-CC, the savings in running time

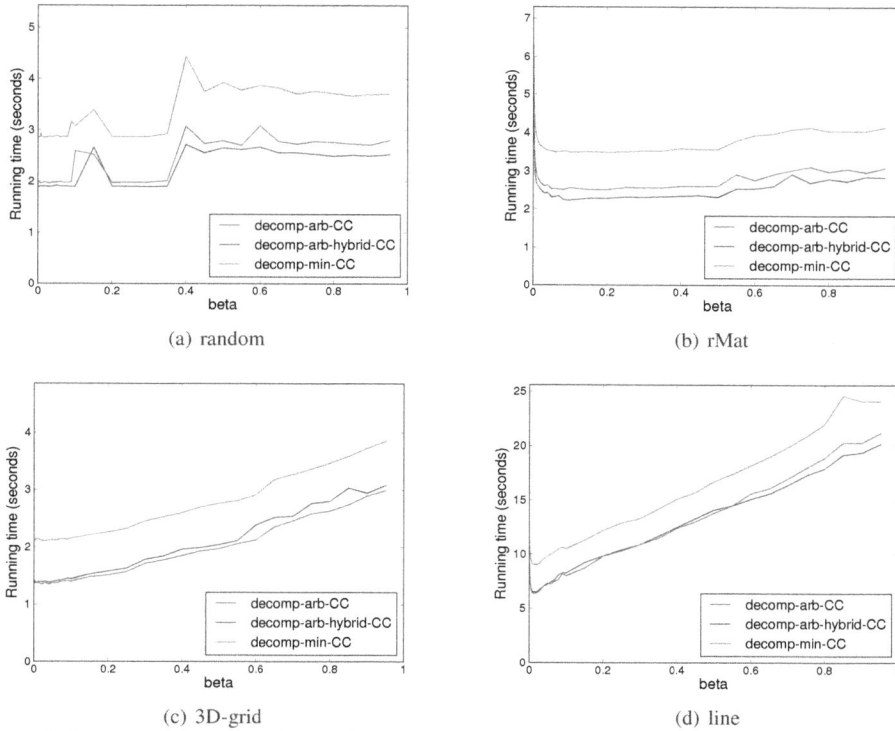

(a) random   (b) rMat

(c) 3D-grid   (d) line

Figure 3. Running time versus β on various input graphs on a 40-core machine using 80 hyper-threads.

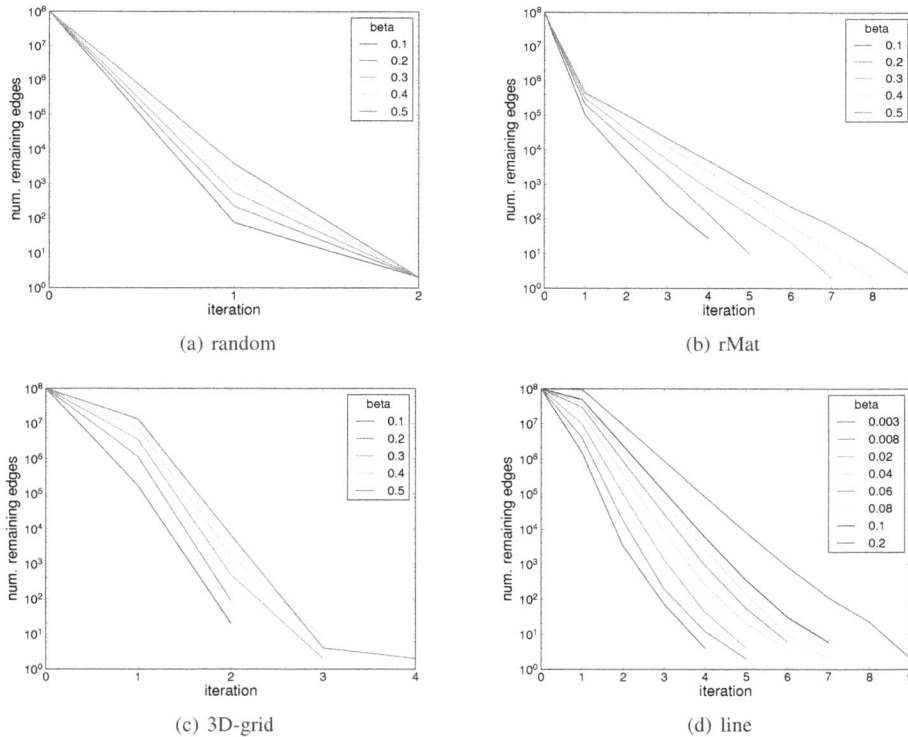

(a) random   (b) rMat

(c) 3D-grid   (d) line

Figure 4. Number of remaining edges per iteration versus β of decomp-arb-hybrid-CC on various graphs.

of decomp-arb-CC comes from this part of the computation due to requiring only one pass over the edges.

Figure 7 shows the breakdown of the 40-core running time for decomp-arb-hybrid-CC. "bfsSparse" refers to the time spent in the main phase of the BFS when performing the write-based compu-

tation for sparse frontiers, and "bfsDense" refers to the time spent in the main phase performing the read-based computation on the dense frontiers. As noted in Section 4, a post-processing step to filter out the intra-component edges is required, and "filterEdges" refers to this phase. We see that for 3D-grid and line, the frontier

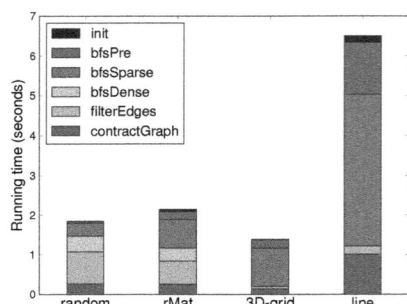

Figure 7. Breakdown of timings on 40 cores with hyper-threading for decomp-arb-hybrid-CC.

never becomes dense enough to switch to the read-based computation, hence all of the BFS time is captured by bfsSparse. On the other hand, random and rMat do have BFS frontiers that become dense enough where the read-based computation is invoked. Since they switch to the read-based computation, some edges do not get inspected and hence the filterEdges phase performs more work to filter out the intra-component edges. For random and rMat, about 40% of the time is spent in the main BFS phase.

Figure 8 shows the running time of decomp-arb-hybrid-CC on 80 hyper-threads as a function of graph size for random graphs with sizes from $m = 5 \times 10^7$ to 5×10^8, and $n = m/5$. The running time increases almost linearly as we increase the graph size.

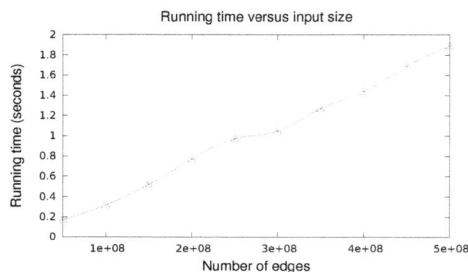

Figure 8. Running time of decomp-arb-hybrid-CC vs. problem size for random graphs on 40 cores with hyper-threading.

Besides PBBS and the implementations by Patwary et al., Bader and Cong describe a parallel spanning tree implementation based on parallel depth-first search [3]. However, Patwary et al. [48] show that their implementations are faster than Bader and Cong's implementation. Galois [46] also contains implementations of connected components based on union-find, but we found them to be slower than the implementation by Patwary et al, decomp-arb-hybrid-CC, and decomp-arb-CC for all of the input graphs. Several graph processing systems [54, 32, 37, 38] have connected components implementations based on label propagation, but the depth of the algorithm is proportional to the diameter of the graph and the algorithm is not work-efficient. As noted in [54], this algorithm usually does not perform as well as linear or near-linear work algorithms.

6. CONCLUSION

We have presented a simple linear-work parallel algorithm for finding the connected components of a graph. Our algorithm is the first practical work-efficient parallel algorithm with polylogarithmic depth for this problem. We present implementations of our algorithm and experimentally show that it is competitive with the fastest existing parallel algorithms for finding the connected components of a graph.

Acknowledgements. This work is supported by the National Science Foundation under grant number CCF-1314590, the Intel Labs Academic Research Office for the Parallel Algorithms for Non-Numeric Computing Program, the Intel Science and Technology Center for Cloud Computing (ISTC-CC) and a Facebook Graduate Fellowship. We thank Jeremy Fineman, Phillip Gibbons, Gary Miller and Shen Chen Xu for helpful discussions.

References

[1] A. Agrawal, L. Nekludova, and W. Lim. A parallel $O(\log N)$ algorithm for finding connected components in planar images. In *ICPP*, pages 783–786, 1987.

[2] B. Awerbuch and Y. Shiloach. New connectivity and MSF algorithms for Ultracomputer and PRAM. In *ICPP*, pages 177–187, 1983.

[3] D. A. Bader and G. Cong. A fast, parallel spanning tree algorithm for symmetric multiprocessors (SMPs). *Journal of Parallel and Distrib. Comput.*, 65(9):994–1006, 2005.

[4] D. A. Bader, G. Cong, and J. Feo. On the architectural requirements for efficient execution of graph algorithms. In *ICPP*, pages 547–556, 2005.

[5] D. A. Bader and J. JaJa. Parallel algorithms for image histogramming and connected components with an experimental study. *J. Parallel Distrib. Comput.*, 35(2):173–190, 1996.

[6] D. S. Banerjee and K. Kothapalli. Hybrid algorithms for list ranking and graph connected components. In *High Performance Computing*, pages 1–10, 2011.

[7] Y. Bartal. Graph decomposition lemmas and their role in metric embedding methods. In *ESA*, pages 89–97. 2004.

[8] S. Beamer, K. Asanović, and D. Patterson. Direction-optimizing breadth-first search. In *Supercomputing*, pages 12:1–12:10, 2012.

[9] G. E. Blelloch. NESL. In *Encyclopedia of Parallel Computing*, pages 1278–1283. 2011.

[10] G. E. Blelloch, A. Gupta, I. Koutis, G. L. Miller, R. Peng, and K. Tangwongsan. Near linear-work parallel SDD solvers, low-diameter decomposition, and low-stretch subgraphs. In *SPAA*, pages 13–22, 2011.

[11] G. E. Blelloch and B. M. Maggs. Parallel algorithms. In *The Computer Science and Engineering Handbook*, pages 277–315. 1997.

[12] L. Bus and P. Tvrdik. A parallel algorithm for connected components on distributed memory machines. In *Recent Advances in Parallel Virtual Machine and Message Passing Interface*, pages 280–287. 2001.

[13] E. Caceres, H. Mongelli, C. Nishibe, and S. W. Song. Experimental results of a coarse-grained parallel algorithm for spanning tree and connected components. In *High Performance Computing & Simulation*, pages 631–637, 2010.

[14] D. Chakrabarti, Y. Zhan, and C. Faloutsos. R-MAT: A recursive model for graph mining. In *SDM*, pages 442–446, 2004.

[15] F. Y. Chin, J. Lam, and I.-N. Chen. Efficient parallel algorithms for some graph problems. *Commun. ACM*, pages 659–665, 1982.

[16] K. Chong and T. Lam. Finding connected components in $O(\log n \log \log n)$ time on the EREW PRAM. *Journal of Algorithms*, 18(3):378–402, 1995.

[17] R. Cole, P. N. Klein, and R. E. Tarjan. Finding minimum spanning forests in logarithmic time and linear work using random sampling. In *SPAA*, pages 243–250, 1996.

[18] R. Cole and U. Vishkin. Approximate parallel scheduling. II. applications to logarithmic-time optimal parallel graph algorithms. *Information and Computation*, 92(1):1–47, 1991.

[19] H. Gazit. An optimal randomized parallel algorithm for finding connected components in a graph. *SIAM J. Comput.*, 20(6):1046–1067, Dec. 1991.

[20] J. Gil, Y. Matias, and U. Vishkin. Towards a theory of nearly constant time parallel algorithms. In *FOCS*, pages 698–710, 1991.

[21] S. Goddard, S. Kumar, and J. F. Prins. Connected components algorithms for mesh-connected parallel computers. In *Parallel Algorithms: 3rd DIMACS Implementation Challenge*, pages 43–58, 1995.

[22] J. Greiner. A comparison of parallel algorithms for connected components. In *SPAA*, pages 16–25, 1994.

[23] S. Halperin and U. Zwick. An optimal randomized logarithmic time connectivity algorithm for the EREW PRAM. *J. Comput. Syst. Sci.*, 53(3):395–416, 1996.

[24] S. Halperin and U. Zwick. Optimal randomized EREW PRAM algorithms for finding spanning forests. In *J. Algorithms*, pages 1740–1759, 2000.

[25] S. Hambrusch and L. TeWinkel. A study of connected component labeling algorithms on the MPP. In *Supercomputing*, pages 477–483, 1988.

[26] Y. Han and R. A. Wagner. An efficient and fast parallel-connected component algorithm. *J. ACM*, 37(3):626–642, July 1990.

[27] K. A. Hawick, A. Leist, and D. P. Playne. Parallel graph component labelling with GPUs and CUDA. *Parallel Comput.*, 36(12):655–678, Dec. 2010.

[28] D. S. Hirschberg, A. K. Chandra, and D. V. Sarwate. Computing connected components on parallel computers. *Commun. ACM*, 22(8):461–464, Aug. 1979.

[29] T.-S. Hsu, V. Ramachandran, and N. Dean. Parallel implementation of algorithms for finding connected components in graphs, 1997.

[30] K. Iwama and Y. Kambayashi. A simpler parallel algorithm for graph connectivity. *J. Algorithms*, 16(2):190–217, Mar. 1994.

[31] D. B. Johnson and P. Metaxas. Connected components in $O(\log^{3/2} n)$ parallel time for the CREW PRAM. *Journal of Computer and System Sciences*, 54(2):227–242, 1997.

[32] U. Kang, C. E. Tsourakakis, and C. Faloutsos. PEGASUS: mining peta-scale graphs. *Knowl. Inf. Syst.*, 27(2):303–325, 2011.

[33] D. R. Karger, N. Nisan, and M. Parnas. Fast connected components algorithms for the EREW PRAM. *SIAM J. Comput.*, 28(3):1021–1034, Feb. 1999.

[34] V. Koubek and J. Krsnakova. Parallel algorithms for connected components in a graph. In *Fundamentals of Computation Theory*, pages 208–217. 1985.

[35] A. Krishnamurthy, S. S. Lumetta, D. E. Culler, and K. Yelick. Connected components on distributed memory machines. In *Parallel Algorithms: 3rd DIMACS Implementation Challenge*, pages 1–21, 1994.

[36] C. Kruskal, L. Rudolph, and M. Snir. Efficient parallel algorithms for graph problems. *Algorithmica*, 5(1-4), 1990.

[37] A. Kyrola, G. E. Blelloch, and C. Guestrin. GraphChi: Large-scale graph computation on just a PC. In *Operating System Design and Implementation*, pages 31–46, 2012.

[38] A. Kyrola, J. Shun, and G. E. Blelloch. Beyond synchronous computation: New techniques for external memory graph algorithms. In *Symposium on Experimental Algorithms*, 2014.

[39] C. E. Leiserson. The Cilk++ concurrency platform. *The Journal of Supercomputing*, 51(3):244–257, 2010.

[40] C. E. Leiserson and T. B. Schardl. A work-efficient parallel breadth-first search algorithm (or how to cope with the nondeterminism of reducers). In *SPAA*, pages 303–314, 2010.

[41] W. Lim, A. Agrawal, and L. Nekludova. A fast parallel algorithm for labeling connected components in image arrays. In *Tech. Report NA86-2, Thinking Machines Corporation*, 1986.

[42] N. Linial and M. Saks. Low diameter graph decompositions. *Combinatorica*, 13(4):441–454, 1993.

[43] Y. Matias and U. Vishkin. On parallel hashing and integer sorting. *Journal of Algorithms*, 12(4):573–606, 1991.

[44] G. L. Miller, R. Peng, and S. C. Xu. Parallel graph decomposition using random shifts. In *SPAA*, pages 196–203, 2013.

[45] D. Nath and S. N. Maheshwari. Parallel algorithms for the connected components and minimal spanning tree problems. *Inf. Process. Lett.*, 14(1):7–11, 1982.

[46] D. Nguyen, A. Lenharth, and K. Pingali. A lightweight infrastructure for graph analytics. In *Symposium on Operating Systems Principles*, pages 456–471, 2013.

[47] N. Nisan, E. Szemeredi, and A. Wigderson. Undirected connectivity in $O(\log^{1.5} n)$ space. In *FOCS*, pages 24–29, 1992.

[48] M. Patwary, P. Refsnes, and F. Manne. Multi-core spanning forest algorithms using the disjoint-set data structure. In *IPDPS*, pages 827–835, 2012.

[49] S. Pettie and V. Ramachandran. A randomized time-work optimal parallel algorithm for finding a minimum spanning forest. *SIAM J. Comput.*, 31(6):1879–1895, 2002.

[50] C. A. Phillips. Parallel graph contraction. In *SPAA*, pages 148–157, 1989.

[51] C. K. Poon and V. Ramachandran. A randomized linear work EREW PRAM algorithm to find a minimum spanning forest. In *ISAAC*, pages 212–222, 1997.

[52] J. Reif. Optimal parallel algorithms for integer sorting and graph connectivity. *TR-08-85, Harvard University*, 1985.

[53] Y. Shiloach and U. Vishkin. An $O(\log n)$ parallel connectivity algorithm. *J. Algorithms*, 3(1):57–67, 1982.

[54] J. Shun and G. E. Blelloch. Ligra: A lightweight graph processing framework for shared memory. In *Principles and Practice of Parallel Programming*, pages 135–146, 2013.

[55] J. Shun and G. E. Blelloch. Phase-concurrent hash tables for determinism. In *SPAA*, 2014.

[56] J. Shun, G. E. Blelloch, J. T. Fineman, and P. B. Gibbons. Reducing contention through priority updates. In *SPAA*, pages 152–163, 2013.

[57] J. Shun, G. E. Blelloch, J. T. Fineman, P. B. Gibbons, A. Kyrola, H. V. Simhadri, and K. Tangwongsan. Brief announcement: the Problem Based Benchmark Suite. In *SPAA*, pages 68–70, 2012.

[58] G. M. Slota, S. Rajamanickam, and K. Madduri. BFS and coloring-based parallel algorithms for strongly connected components and related problems. In *IPDPS*, 2014.

[59] J. Soman, K. Kishore, and P. J. Narayanan. A fast GPU algorithm for graph connectivity. In *IPDPS*, pages 1–8, 2010.

[60] U. Vishkin. An optimal parallel connectivity algorithm. *Discrete Applied Mathematics*, 9(2):197–207, 1984.

Executing Dynamic Data-Graph Computations Deterministically Using Chromatic Scheduling

Tim Kaler   William Hasenplaugh   Tao B. Schardl   Charles E. Leiserson

MIT Computer Science and Artificial Intelligence Laboratory
32 Vassar Street
Cambridge, MA 02139

ABSTRACT

A *data-graph computation* — popularized by such programming systems as Galois, Pregel, GraphLab, PowerGraph, and GraphChi — is an algorithm that performs local updates on the vertices of a graph. During each round of a data-graph computation, an *update function* atomically modifies the data associated with a vertex as a function of the vertex's prior data and that of adjacent vertices. A *dynamic* data-graph computation updates only an active subset of the vertices during a round, and those updates determine the set of active vertices for the next round.

This paper introduces PRISM, a chromatic-scheduling algorithm for executing dynamic data-graph computations. PRISM uses a vertex-coloring of the graph to coordinate updates performed in a round, precluding the need for mutual-exclusion locks or other nondeterministic data synchronization. A *multibag* data structure is used by PRISM to maintain a dynamic set of active vertices as an unordered set partitioned by color. We analyze PRISM using work-span analysis. Let $G = (V, E)$ be a degree-Δ graph colored with χ colors, and suppose that $Q \subseteq V$ is the set of active vertices in a round. Define $size(Q) = |Q| + \sum_{v \in Q} \deg(v)$, which is proportional to the space required to store the vertices of Q using a sparse-graph layout. We show that a P-processor execution of PRISM performs updates in Q using $O(\chi(\lg(Q/\chi) + \lg\Delta) + \lg P)$ span and $\Theta(size(Q) + \chi + P)$ work. These theoretical guarantees are matched by good empirical performance. We modified GraphLab to incorporate PRISM and studied seven application benchmarks on a 12-core multicore machine. PRISM executes the benchmarks 1.2–2.1 times faster than GraphLab's nondeterministic lock-based scheduler while providing deterministic behavior.

This paper also presents PRISM-R, a variation of PRISM that executes dynamic data-graph computations deterministically even when updates modify global variables with associative operations. PRISM-R satisfies the same theoretical bounds as PRISM, but its implementation is more involved, incorporating a *multivector* data structure to maintain an ordered set of vertices partitioned by color.

This research was supported in part by the National Science Foundation under Grants CNS-1017058, CCF-1162148, and CCF-1314547 and in part by grants from Intel Corporation and Foxconn Technology Group. Tao B. Schardl was supported in part by an NSF Graduate Research Fellowship.

Categories and Subject Descriptors

D.1.3 [**Programming Techniques**]: Concurrent Programming; E.1 [**Data Structures**]: *distributed data structures, graphs and networks*; F.2.2 [**Analysis of Algorithms and Problem Complexity**]: Nonnumerical Algorithms and Problems—*graph algorithms, sequencing and scheduling*

Keywords

Data-graph computations; multicore; multithreading; parallel programming; chromatic scheduling; determinism; scheduling; work stealing

1. INTRODUCTION

Many systems from physics, artificial intelligence, and scientific computing can be represented naturally as a *data graph* — a graph with data associated with its vertices and edges. For example, some physical systems can be decomposed into a finite number of elements whose interactions induce a graph. Probabilistic graphical models in artificial intelligence can be used to represent the dependency structure of a set of random variables. Sparse matrices can be interpreted as graphs for scientific computing.

Intuitively, a data-graph computation is an algorithm that performs local updates on the vertices of a data graph. Several software systems have been implemented to support parallel data-graph computations, including Galois [63], Pregel [78], GraphLab [75, 76], PowerGraph [48], and GraphChi [64]. These systems often support "complex" data-graph computations, in which data can be associated with edges as well as vertices and updating a vertex v can modify any data associated with v, v's incident edges, and the vertices adjacent to v. For ease in discussing chromatic scheduling, however, we shall principally restrict ourselves to "simple" data-graph computations (which correspond to "edge-consistent" computations in GraphLab), although most of our results straightforwardly extend to more complex models. Indeed, six out of the seven GraphLab applications described in [74, 75] are simple data-graph computations.

Updates to vertices proceed in *rounds*, where each vertex can be updated at most once per round. In a *static* data-graph computation, the *activation set* Q_r of vertices updated in a round r — the set of *active* vertices — is determined *a priori*. Often, a static data-graph computation updates every vertex in each round. Static data-graph computations include Gibbs sampling [41, 42], iterative graph coloring [30], and n-body problems such as the fluidanimate PARSEC benchmark [10].

We shall be interested in *dynamic* data-graph computations, where the activation set changes round by round. Dynamic data-graph computations include the Google PageRank algorithm [21], loopy belief propagation [82, 87], coordinate descent [32], co-EM [84], alternating least-squares [54], singular-value decomposition [47], and matrix factorization [95].

We formalize the computational model as follows. Let $G = (V, E)$ be a data graph. Denote the **neighbors**, or **adjacent vertices**, of a vertex $v \in V$ by $\mathrm{Adj}[v] = \{u \in V : (u, v) \in E\}$. The **degree** of v is thus $\deg(v) = |\mathrm{Adj}[v]|$, and the **degree** of G is $\deg(G) = \max\{\deg(v) : v \in V\}$. A **(simple) dynamic data-graph computation** is a triple $\langle G, f, Q_0 \rangle$, where

- $G = (V, E)$ is a graph with data associated with each vertex $v \in V$;
- $f : V \rightarrow 2^{\mathrm{Adj}[v]}$ is an **update function**; and
- $Q_0 \subseteq V$ is the initial **activation set**.

The update $S = f(v)$ implicitly computes as a side effect a new value for the data associated with v as a function of the old data associated with v and v's neighbors. The update returns a set $S \subseteq \mathrm{Adj}[v]$ of vertices that must be updated later in the computation. During a round r of the dynamic data-graph computation, each vertex $v \in Q_r$ is updated at most once, that is, Q_r is a set, not a multiset. For example, an update $f(v)$ might activate a neighbor u only if the value of v changes significantly.

The advantage of dynamic over static data-graph computations is that they avoid performing many unnecessary updates. Studies in the literature [75, 76] show that dynamic execution can enhance the practical performance of many applications. We confirmed these findings by implementing static and dynamic versions of several data-graph computations. The results for a PageRank algorithm on a power-law graph of 1 million vertices and 10 million edges were typical. The static computation performed approximately 15 million updates, whereas the dynamic version performed less than half that number of updates.

A serial reference implementation

Before we address the issues involved in scheduling and executing dynamic data-graph computations in parallel, let us first hone our intuition with a serial algorithm for the problem. Figure 1 gives the pseudocode for SERIAL-DDGC. This algorithm schedules the updates of a data-graph computation by maintaining a FIFO queue Q of activated vertices that have yet to be updated. Sentinel values enqueued in Q on lines 4 and 9 demarcate the rounds of the computation such that the set of vertices in Q after the rth sentinel has been enqueued is the activation set Q_r for round r.

Given a data-graph $G = (V, E)$, an update function f, and an initial activation set Q_0, SERIAL-DDGC executes the data-graph computation $\langle G, f, Q_0 \rangle$ as follows. Lines 1–2 initialize Q to contain all vertices in Q_0. The **while** loop on lines 5–14 then repeatedly dequeues the next scheduled vertex $v \in Q$ on line 5 and executes the update $f(v)$ on line 11. Executing $f(v)$ produces a set S of activated vertices, and lines 12–14 check each vertex in S for membership in Q, enqueuing all vertices in S that are not already in Q.

We can analyze the time SERIAL-DDGC takes to execute one round r of the data-graph computation $\langle G, f, Q_0 \rangle$. Define the **size** of an activation set Q_r as

$$size(Q_r) = |Q_r| + \sum_{v \in Q_r} \deg(v) \, .$$

The size of Q_r is asymptotically the space needed to store all the vertices in Q_r and their incident edges using a standard sparse-graph representation, such as compressed-sparse-rows (CSR) format [93]. For example, if $Q_0 = V$, we have $size(Q_0) = |V| + 2|E|$ by the handshaking lemma [29, p. 1172–3]. Let us make the reasonable assumption that the time to execute $f(v)$ serially is proportional to $\deg(v)$. If we implement the queue as a dynamic (resiz-

```
SERIAL-DDGC(G, f, Q_0)
1   for v ∈ Q_0
2       ENQUEUE(Q, v)
3   r = 0
4   ENQUEUE(Q, NIL) // Sentinel NIL denotes the end of a round.
5   while Q ≠ {NIL}
6       v = DEQUEUE(Q)
7       if v == NIL
8           r += 1
9           ENQUEUE(Q, NIL)
10      else
11          S = f(v)
12          for u ∈ S
13              if u ∉ Q
14                  ENQUEUE(Q, u)
```

Figure 1: Pseudocode for a serial algorithm to execute a data-graph computation $\langle G, f, Q_0 \rangle$. SERIAL-DDGC takes as input a data graph G and an update function f. The computation maintains a FIFO queue Q of activated vertices that have yet to be updated and sentinel values NIL, each of which demarcates the end of a round. An update $S = f(v)$ returns the set $S \subseteq \mathrm{Adj}[v]$ of vertices activated by that update. Each vertex $u \in S$ is added to Q if it is not currently scheduled for a future update.

able) table [29, Section 17.4], then line 14 executes in $\Theta(1)$ amortized time. All other operations in the **for** loop on lines 12–14 take $\Theta(1)$ time, and thus all vertices activated by executing $f(v)$ are examined in $\Theta(\deg(v))$ time. The total time spent updating the vertices in Q_r is therefore $\Theta(Q_r + \sum_{v \in Q_r} \deg(v)) = \Theta(size(Q_r))$, which is **linear** time: time proportional to the storage requirements for the vertices in Q_r and their incident edges.

Parallelizing dynamic data-graph computations

The salient challenge in parallelizing data-graph computations is to deal effectively with races between updates, that is, logically parallel updates that read and write common data. A **determinacy race** [36] (also called a **general race** [83]) occurs when two logically parallel instructions access the same memory location and at least one of them writes to that location. Two updates in a data-graph computation **conflict** if executing them in parallel produces a determinacy race. A parallel scheduler must manage or avoid conflicting updates to execute a data-graph computation correctly and deterministically.

The standard approach to preventing races associates a mutual-exclusion lock with each vertex of the data graph to ensure that an update on a vertex v does not proceed until all locks on v and v's neighbors have been acquired. Although this locking strategy prevents races, it can incur substantial overhead from lock acquisition and contention, hurting application performance, especially when update functions are simple. Moreover, because runtime happenstance can determine the order in which two logically parallel updates acquire locks, the data-graph computation can act nondeterministically: different runs on the same inputs can produce different results. Without repeatability, parallel programming is arguably much harder [19, 67]. Nondeterminism confounds debugging.

A known alternative to using locks is **chromatic scheduling** [1, 9], which schedules a data-graph computation based on a coloring of the data-graph computation's **conflict graph** — a graph with an edge between two vertices if updating them in parallel would produce a race. For a simple data-graph computation, the conflict graph is simply the data graph itself. The idea behind chromatic scheduling is fairly simple. Chromatic scheduling begins by computing a **(vertex) coloring** of the conflict graph — an assignment of colors to the vertices such that no two adjacent vertices share the same color. Since no edge in the conflict graph connects two

Benchmark	$|V|$	$|E|$	χ	GraphLab	CILK+LOCKS	PRISM
PR/G	916,428	5,105,040	43	14.9	14.8	12.4
PR/L	4,847,570	68,475,400	333	217.1	227.9	172.3
ID/250	62,500	249,000	4	4.0	3.8	2.5
ID/1000	1,000,000	3,996,000	4	44.3	44.3	20.7
FBP/C1	87,831	265,204	2	13.7	7.4	7.6
FBP/C3	482,920	160,019	2	27.9	14.7	14.6
ALS/N	187,722	20,597,300	6	126.1	113.4	77.1

Figure 2: Comparison of dynamic data-graph schedulers on seven application benchmarks. All runtimes are in seconds and were calculated by taking the median 12-core execution time of 5 runs on an Intel Xeon X5650 with hyperthreading disabled. The runtime of PRISM includes the time used to color the input graph. PR/G and PR/L run a PageRank algorithm on the web-Google [72] and soc-LiveJournal [4] graphs, respectively. ID/250 and ID/1000 run an image denoise algorithm to remove Gaussian noise from 2D grayscale images of dimension 250 by 250 and 1000 by 1000. FBP/C1 and FBP/C3 perform belief propagation on a factor graph provided by the cora-1 and cora-3 datasets [79, 91]. ALS/N runs an alternating least squares algorithm on the NPIC-500 dataset [81].

vertices of the same color, updates on all vertices of a given color can execute in parallel without producing races. To execute a round of a data-graph computation, the set of activated vertices Q is partitioned into χ *color sets* — subsets of Q containing vertices of a single color. Updates are applied to vertices in Q by serially stepping through each color set and updating all vertices within a color set in parallel. The result of a data-graph computation executed using chromatic scheduling is equivalent to that of a slightly modified version of SERIAL-DDGC that starts each round (immediately before line 9 of Figure 1) by sorting the vertices within its queue by color.

Chromatic scheduling avoids both of the pitfalls of the locking strategy. First, since only nonadjacent vertices in the conflict graph are updated in parallel, no races can occur, and the necessity for locks and their associated performance overheads are precluded. Second, by establishing a fixed order for processing different colors, any two adjacent vertices are always processed in the same order, and the data-graph computation is executed deterministically. Although chromatic scheduling potentially loses parallelism because colors are processed serially, we shall see that this concern does not appear to be an issue in practice.

To date, chromatic scheduling has been applied to static data-graph computations, but not to dynamic data-graph computations. This paper addresses the question of how to perform chromatic scheduling efficiently when the activation set changes on the fly, necessitating a data structure for maintaining dynamic sets of vertices in parallel.

Contributions

This paper introduces PRISM, a chromatic-scheduling algorithm that executes dynamic data-graph computations in parallel efficiently in a deterministic fashion. PRISM employs a "multibag" data structure to manage an activation set as a list of color sets. The multibag achieves efficiency using "worker-local storage," which is memory locally associated with each "worker" thread executing the computation.

We analyze the performance of PRISM using work-span analysis [29, Ch. 27]. The *work* of a computation is intuitively the total number of instructions executed, and the *span* corresponds to the longest path of dependencies in the parallel program. We shall make the reasonable assumption that a single update $f(v)$ executes in $\Theta(\deg(v))$ work and $\Theta(\lg(\deg(v)))$ span.[1] Under this assumption, on a degree-Δ data graph G colored using χ colors, PRISM executes the updates on the vertices in the activation set

Q_r of a round r on P processors in $O(size(Q_r) + \chi + P)$ work and $O(\chi(\lg(Q_r/\chi) + \lg\Delta) + \lg P)$ span.

Surprisingly, the "price of determinism" incurred by using chromatic scheduling instead of the more common locking strategy appears to be negative for real-world applications. As Figure 2 indicates, on seven application benchmarks, PRISM executes 1.2–2.1 times faster than GraphLab's comparable, but nondeterministic, locking strategy. This performance gap is not due solely to superior engineering or load balancing. A similar performance overhead is observed in a comparably engineered lock-based scheduling algorithm, CILK+LOCKS. PRISM outperforms CILK+LOCKS on all but one benchmark and is on average (geometric mean) 1.18 times faster.

PRISM behaves deterministically as long as every update is *pure*: it modifies no data except for that associated with its target vertex. This assumption precludes the update function from modifying global variables to aggregate or collect values. To support this common use pattern, we describe an extension to PRISM, called PRISM-R, which executes dynamic data-graph computations deterministically even when updates modify global variables using associative operations. PRISM-R replaces each multibag PRISM uses with a "multivector," maintaining color sets whose contents are ordered deterministically. PRISM-R executes in the same theoretical bounds as PRISM, but its implementation is more involved.

Outline

The remainder of this paper is organized as follows. Section 2 reviews dynamic multithreading, the parallel programming model in which we describe and analyze our algorithms. Section 3 describes PRISM, the chromatic-scheduling algorithm for dynamic data-graph computations. Section 4 describes the multibag data structure PRISM uses to represent its color sets. Section 5 presents our theoretical analysis of PRISM. Section 6 describes a Cilk Plus [56] implementation of PRISM and presents empirical results measuring this implementation's performance on seven application benchmarks. Section 7 describes PRISM-R and its multivector data structure. Section 8 offers some concluding remarks.

2. BACKGROUND

We implemented the PRISM algorithm in Cilk Plus [56], a dynamic multithreading concurrency platform. This section provides background on the dag model of multithreading that embodies this and other similar concurrency platforms, including MIT Cilk [39], Cilk++ [70], Fortress [2], Habenero [6, 24], Hood [18], Java Fork/Join Framework [66], Task Parallel Library (TPL) [69], Threading Building Blocks (TBB) [88], and X10 [26]. We review

---

[1]Other assumptions about the work and span of an update can easily be made at the potential expense of complicating the analysis.

the Cilk model of multithreading, the notions of work and span, and the basic properties of the work-stealing runtime systems underlying these concurrency platforms. We briefly discuss worker-local storage, which PRISM's multibag data structure uses to achieve efficiency.

The Cilk model of multithreading

The Cilk model of multithreading [16, 17] is described in tutorial fashion in [29, Ch. 27]. The model views the executed computation resulting from running a parallel program as a **computation dag** in which each vertex denotes an instruction, and edges denote parallel control dependencies between instructions. To analyze the theoretical performance of a multithreaded program, such as PRISM, we assume that the program executes on an **ideal parallel computer**, where each instruction executes in unit time, the computer has ample bandwidth to shared memory, and concurrent reads and writes incur no overheads due to contention.

We shall assume that algorithms for the dag model are expressed using the Cilk-like primitives [29, Ch. 27] **spawn**, **sync**, and **parallel for**. The keyword **spawn** when preceding a function call F allows F to execute in parallel with its **continuation** — the statement immediately after the spawn of F. The complement of **spawn** is the keyword **sync**, which acts as a local barrier and prevents statements after the **sync** from executing until all earlier spawned functions return. These keywords can be used to implement other convenient parallel control constructs, such as the **parallel for** loop, which allows all of its iterations to operate logically in parallel. The work of a **parallel for** loop with n iterations is the total number of instructions in all executed iterations. The span is $\Theta(\lg n)$ plus the maximum span of any loop iteration. The $\Theta(\lg n)$ span term comes from the fact that the runtime system executes the loop iterations using parallel divide-and-conquer, and thus fans out the iterations as a balanced binary tree in the dag.

Work-span analysis

Given a multithreaded program whose execution is modeled as a dag A, we can bound the P-processor running time $T_P(A)$ of the program using **work-span analysis** [29, Ch. 27]. Recall that the work $T_1(A)$ is the number of instructions in A, and that the span $T_\infty(A)$ is the length of a longest path in A. Greedy schedulers [20, 35, 49] can execute a deterministic program with work T_1 and span T_∞ on P processors in time T_P satisfying

$$\max\{T_1/P, T_\infty\} \le T_p \le T_1/P + T_\infty , \qquad (1)$$

and a similar bound can be achieved by more practical "work-stealing" schedulers [16, 17]. The **speedup** of an algorithm on P processors is T_1/T_P, which Inequality (1) shows to be at most P in theory. The **parallelism** T_1/T_∞ is the greatest theoretical speedup possible for any number of processors.

Work-stealing runtime systems

Runtime systems underlying concurrency platforms that support the dag model of multithreading usually implement a **work stealing** scheduler [17, 23, 50], which operates as follows. When the runtime system starts up, it allocates as many operating-system threads, called **workers**, as there are processors. Each worker keeps a **ready queue** of tasks that can operate in parallel with the task it is currently executing. Whenever the execution of code generates parallel work, the worker puts the excess work into the queue. Whenever it needs work, it fetches work from its queue. When a worker's ready queue runs out of tasks, however, the worker becomes a **thief** and "steals" work from another **victim** worker's queue. If an application exhibits sufficient parallelism compared to the actual num-

```
PRISM(G, f, Q₀)
1   χ = COLOR-GRAPH(G)
2   r = 0
3   Q = Q₀
4   while Q ≠ ∅
5       𝒞 = MB-COLLECT(Q)
6       for C ∈ 𝒞
7           parallel for v ∈ C
8               active[v] = FALSE
9               S = f(v)
10              parallel for u ∈ S
11                  begin atomic
12                      if active[u] == FALSE
13                          active[u] = TRUE
14                          MB-INSERT(Q, u, color[u])
15                  end atomic
16      r = r + 1
```

Figure 3: Pseudocode for PRISM. The algorithm takes as input a data graph G, an update function f, and an initial activation set Q_0. COLOR-GRAPH colors a given graph and returns the number of colors it used. The procedures MB-COLLECT and MB-INSERT operate the multibag Q to maintain activation sets for PRISM. PRISM updates the value of r after each round of the data-graph computation.

ber of workers/processors, one can prove mathematically that the computation executes with linear speedup.

Worker-local storage

Worker-local storage refers to memory that is private to a particular worker thread in a parallel computation. In this paper, in a P-processor execution of a parallel program, a variable x implemented using worker-local storage is stored as an array of P copies of x. A worker accesses its local copy of x using a runtime-provided worker identifier to index the array of worker-local copies of x. The Cilk Plus runtime system, for example, provides the __cilkrts_get_worker_number() API call, which returns an integer identifying the current worker. PRISM assumes the existence of a runtime-provided GET-WORKER-ID function that executes in $\Theta(1)$ time and returns an integer from 0 to $P - 1$.

3. THE PRISM ALGORITHM

This section presents PRISM, a chromatic-scheduling algorithm for executing dynamic data-graph computations deterministically. We describe how PRISM differs from the serial algorithm in Section 1, including how it maintains activation sets that are partitioned by color using the multibag data structure.

Figure 3 shows the psuedocode for PRISM, which differs from the SERIAL-DDGC routine from Figure 1 in two main ways: the use of a multibag data structure to implement Q, and the call to COLOR-GRAPH on line 1 to color the data graph.

A **multibag** Q represents a list $\langle C_0, C_1, \ldots, C_{\chi-1} \rangle$ of χ bags (unordered multisets) and supports two operations:

- MB-INSERT(Q, v, k) inserts an element v into bag C_k in Q. A multibag supports parallel MB-INSERT operations.
- MB-COLLECT(Q) produces a collection $\mathcal{C}$ that represents a list of the nonempty bags in Q, emptying Q in the process.

PRISM stores a distinct color set in each bag of a multibag Q. Section 4 describes and analyzes the implementation of the multibag data structure.

PRISM calls COLOR-GRAPH on line 1 to color the given data graph $G = (V, E)$ and obtain the number χ of colors used. Although it is NP-complete to find either an **optimal** coloring of a graph [40] — a coloring that uses the smallest possible number of colors — or a $O(V^\varepsilon)$-approximation of the optimal col-

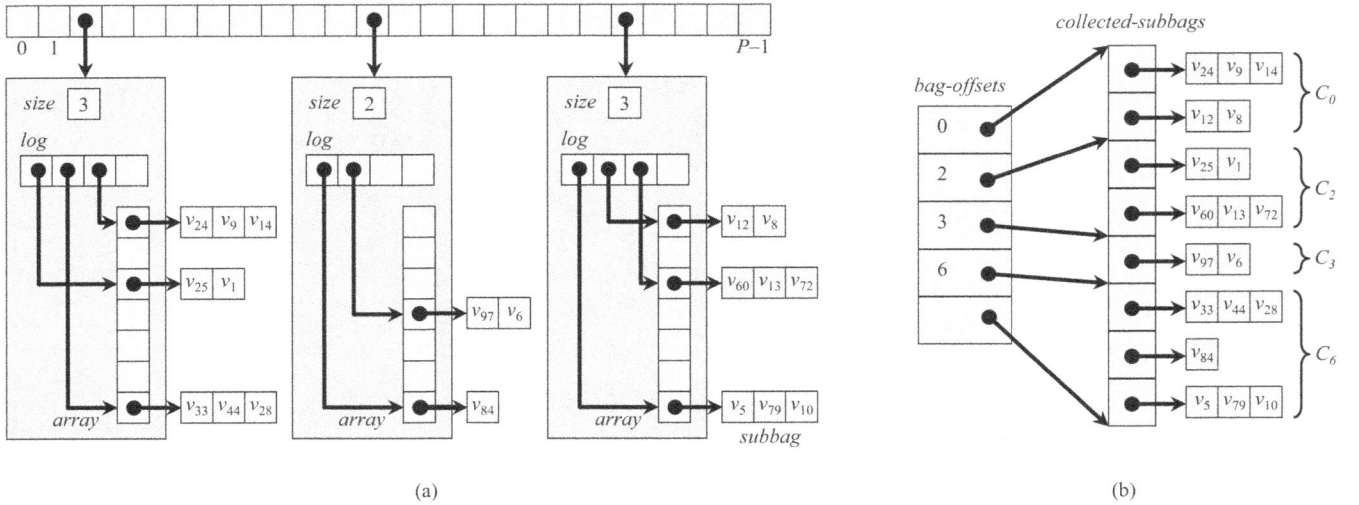

Figure 4: A multibag data structure. **(a)** A multibag containing 19 elements distributed across 4 distinct bags. The contents of each bag are partitioned across the corresponding subbags in 3 nonempty worker-local SPA's. **(b)** The output of MB-COLLECT when executed on the multibag in **(a)**. Sets of subbags in *collected-subbags* are labeled with the bag C_k that their union represents.

oring [77], as Section 6 discusses, an optimal coloring is not necessary for PRISM to perform well in practice, as long as the data graph is colored with sufficiently few colors. Many parallel coloring algorithms exist that satisfy the needs of PRISM (see, for example, [3, 5, 45, 46, 52, 59, 61, 62, 73, 94]). In fact, if the data-graph computation performs sufficiently many updates, a $\Theta(V + E)$-work greedy coloring algorithm, such as that introduced by Welsh and Powell [96], can suffice as well. Our program implementation of PRISM uses a multicore variant of the Jones and Plassmann algorithm [59] that produces a deterministic $(\Delta + 1)$-coloring of a degree-Δ graph $G = (V, E)$ in linear work and $O(\lg V + \lg \Delta \cdot \min\{\sqrt{E}, \Delta + \lg \Delta \lg V / \lg \lg V\})$ span [52].

Let us now see how PRISM uses chromatic scheduling to execute a dynamic data-graph computation $\langle G, f, Q_0 \rangle$. After line 1 colors G, line 3 initializes the multibag Q with the initial activation set Q_0, and then the **while** loop on lines 4–16 executes the rounds of the data-graph computation. At the start of each round, line 5 collects the nonempty bags $\mathscr{C}$ from Q, which correspond to the nonempty color sets for the round. Lines 6–15 iterate through the color sets $C \in \mathscr{C}$ sequentially, and the **parallel for** loop on lines 7–15 processes the vertices of each C in parallel. For each vertex $v \in C$, line 9 performs the update $S = f(v)$, which returns a set S of activated vertices, and lines 10–15 insert into Q the vertices in S that are not currently active.

To ensure that an activated vertex is not added to Q multiple times in a round, PRISM maintains an array *active* of Boolean flags, where entry *active*[v] indicates whether vertex v is currently active. Conceptually, flag *active*[v] indicates whether $v \in Q$ in the modified version of SERIAL-DDGC that is analogous to PRISM. To process a vertex v, line 8 of PRISM sets *active*[v] to FALSE, whereas SERIAL-DDGC removes v from Q. Lines 12 and 13 of PRISM set *active*[u] to TRUE only if *active*[u] was previously FALSE, whereas SERIAL-DDGC adds vertex u to Q only if $u \notin Q$. The **begin atomic** and **end atomic** statements on lines 11 and 15 ensure that *active*[u] is read and set atomically, thereby preventing a data race from adding vertex u to PRISM's multibag Q multiple times. Although alternative strategy exist to avoid this atomicity check, our empirical studies indicate that this limited use of atomics seems to work well in practice.

4. THE MULTIBAG DATA STRUCTURE

This section presents the multibag data structure employed by PRISM. The multibag uses worker-local sparse accumulators [44] and an efficient parallel collection operation. We describe how the MB-INSERT and MB-COLLECT operations are implemented, and we analyze them using work-span analysis [29, Ch. 27]. When used in a P-processor execution of a parallel program, a multibag Q of χ bags storing n elements supports MB-INSERT in $\Theta(1)$ worst-case time and MB-COLLECT in $O(n + \chi + P)$ work and $O(\lg n + \chi + \lg P)$ span.

A *sparse accumulator (SPA)* [44] implements an array that supports lazy initialization of its elements. A SPA T contains a sparsely populated array $T.array$ of elements and a log $T.log$, which is a list of indices of initialized elements in $T.array$. To implement multibags, we shall only need the ability to create a SPA, access an arbitrary SPA element, or delete all elements from a SPA. For simplicity, we shall assume that an uninitialized array element in a SPA has a value of NIL. When an array element $T.array[i]$ is modified for the first time, the index i is appended to $T.log$. An appropriately designed SPA T storing $n = |T.log|$ elements admits the following performance properties:

- Creating T takes $\Theta(1)$ work.
- Each element of T can be accessed in $\Theta(1)$ work.
- Reading all initialized elements of T takes $\Theta(n)$ work and $\Theta(\lg n)$ span.
- Emptying T takes $\Theta(1)$ work.

A multibag Q is an array of P worker-local SPA's, where P is the number of workers executing the program. We shall use p interchangeably to denote either a worker or that worker's unique identifier. Worker p's local SPA in Q is thus denoted by $Q[p]$. For a multibag Q of χ bags, each SPA $Q[p]$ contains an array $Q[p].array$ of size χ and a log $Q[p].log$. Figure 4(a) illustrates a multibag with $\chi = 7$ bags, 4 of which are nonempty. As Figure 4(a) shows, the worker-local SPA's in Q partition each bag $C_k \in Q$ into subbags $\{C_{k,0}, C_{k,1}, \ldots, C_{k,P-1}\}$, where $Q[p].array[k]$ stores subbag $C_{k,p}$.

Implementation of MB-INSERT and MB-COLLECT

The worker-local SPA's enable a multibag Q to support parallel MB-INSERT operations without creating races. Figure 5 shows

```
MB-INSERT(Q, v, k)
1   p = GET-WORKER-ID()
2   if Q[p].array[k] == NIL
3       APPEND(Q[p].log, k)
4       Q[p].array[k] = new subbag
5   APPEND(Q[p].array[k], v)
```

Figure 5: Pseudocode for the MB-INSERT multibag operation to insert an element v into bag C_k in multibag Q.

the pseudocode for MB-INSERT. When a worker p executes MB-INSERT(Q, v, k), it inserts element v into the subbag $C_{k,p}$ as follows. Line 1 calls GET-WORKER-ID to get worker p's identifier. Line 2 checks if subbag $C_{k,p}$ stored in $Q[p].array[k]$ is initialized, and if not, lines 3 and 4 initialize it. Line 5 inserts v into $Q[p].array[k]$.

Conceptually, the MB-COLLECT operation extracts the bags in Q to produce a compact representation of those bags that can be read efficiently. Figure 4(b) illustrates the compact representation of the elements of the multibag from Figure 4(a) that MB-COLLECT returns. This representation consists of a pair $\langle bag\text{-}offsets, collected\text{-}subbags \rangle$ of arrays that together resemble the representation of a graph in a CSR format. The *collected-subbags* array stores all of the subbags in Q sorted by their corresponding bag's index. The *bag-offsets* array stores indices in *collected-subbags* that denote the sets of subbags comprised by each bag. In particular, in this representation, the contents of bag C_k are stored in the subbags in *collected-subbags* between indices *bag-offsets*$[k]$ and *bag-offsets*$[k+1]$.

Figure 6 sketches how MB-COLLECT converts a multibag Q stored in worker-local SPA's into the representation illustrated in Figure 4(b). Steps 1 and 2 create an array *collected-subbags* of nonempty subbags from the worker-local SPA's in Q. Each subbag $C_{k,p}$ in *collected-subbags* is tagged with the integer index k of its corresponding bag $C_k \in Q$. Step 3 sorts *collected-subbags* by these index tags, and Step 4 creates the *bag-offsets* array. Step 5 removes all elements from Q, thereby emptying the multibag.

Analysis of multibags

We now analyze the work and span of the multibag's MB-INSERT and MB-COLLECT operations, starting with MB-INSERT.

LEMMA 1. *Executing* MB-INSERT *takes* $\Theta(1)$ *time in the worst case.*

PROOF. Consider each step of a call to MB-INSERT(Q, v, k). The GET-WORKER-ID procedure on line 1 obtains the executing worker's identifier p from the runtime system in $\Theta(1)$ time, and line 2 checks if the entry $Q[p].array[k]$ is empty in $\Theta(1)$ time. Suppose that $Q[p].log$ and each subbag in $Q[p].array$ are implemented as dynamic arrays that use a deamortized table-doubling scheme [22]. Lines 3–5 then take $\Theta(1)$ time each to append k to $Q[p].log$, create a new subbag in $Q[p].array[k]$, and append v to $Q[p].array[k]$. $\square$

The next lemma analyzes the work and span of MB-COLLECT.

LEMMA 2. *In a P-processor parallel program execution, a call to* MB-COLLECT(Q) *on a multibag Q of χ bags whose contents are distributed across m distinct subbags executes in* $O(m + \chi + P)$ *work and* $O(\lg m + \chi + \lg P)$ *span.*

PROOF. We analyze each step of MB-COLLECT in turn. We shall use a helper procedure PREFIX-SUM(A), which computes the all-prefix sums of an array A of n integers in $\Theta(n)$ work

```
MB-COLLECT(Q)
    1.  For each SPA Q[p], map each bag index k in Q[p].log to the pair
        ⟨k, Q[p].array[k]⟩.
    2.  Concatenate the arrays Q[p].log for all workers p ∈ {0, 1, ..., P−1}
        into a single array, collected-subbags.
    3.  Sort the entries of collected-subbags by their bag indices.
    4.  Create the array bag-offsets, where bag-offsets[k] stores the index of
        the first subbag in collected-subbags that contains elements of the
        kth bag.
    5.  For p = 0, 1, ..., P − 1, delete all elements from the SPA Q[p].
    6.  Return the pair ⟨bag-offsets, collected-subbags⟩.
```

Figure 6: Pseudocode for the MB-COLLECT multibag operation. Calling MB-COLLECT on a multibag Q produces a pair of arrays *collected-subbags*, which contains all nonempty subbags in Q sorted by their associated bag's index, and *bag-offsets*, which associates sets of subbags in Q with their corresponding bag.

and $\Theta(\lg n)$ span. (Blelloch [11] describes an appropriate implementation of PREFIX-SUM.) Step 1 replaces each entry in $Q[p].log$ in each worker-local SPA $Q[p]$ with the appropriate index-subbag pair $\langle k, C_{k,p} \rangle$ in parallel, which requires $\Theta(m + P)$ work and $\Theta(\lg m + \lg P)$ span. Step 2 gathers all index-subbag pairs into a single array. Suppose that each worker-local SPA $Q[p]$ is augmented with the size of $Q[p].log$, as Figure 4(a) illustrates. Executing PREFIX-SUM on these sizes and then copying the entries of $Q[p].log$ into *collected-subbags* in parallel therefore completes Step 2 in $\Theta(m + P)$ work and $\Theta(\lg m + \lg P)$ span. Step 3 can sort the *collected-subbags* array in $\Theta(m + \chi)$ work and $\Theta(\lg m + \chi)$ span using a variant of a parallel radix sort [15, 27, 98] as follows:

1. Divide *collected-subbags* into m/χ groups of size χ, and create an $(m/\chi) \times \chi$ matrix A, where entry A_{ij} stores the number of subbags with index j in group i. Constructing A can be done with $\Theta(m + \chi)$ work and $\Theta(\lg m + \chi)$ span by evaluating the groups in parallel and the subbags in each group serially.

2. Evaluate PREFIX-SUM on A^{T} (or, more precisely, the array formed by concatenating the columns of A in order) to produce a matrix B such that B_{ij} identifies which entries in the sorted version of *collected-subbags* will store the subbags with index j in group i. This PREFIX-SUM call takes $\Theta(m + \chi)$ work and $\Theta(\lg m + \lg \chi)$ span.

3. Create a temporary array T of size m, and in parallel over the groups of *collected-subbags*, serially move each subbag in the group to an appropriate index in T, as identified by B. Copying these subbags executes in $\Theta(m + \chi)$ work and $\Theta(\lg m + \chi)$ span.

4. Rename the temporary array T as *collected-subbags* in $\Theta(1)$ work and span.

Finally, Step 4 can scan *collected-subbags* for adjacent pairs of entries with different bag indices to compute *bag-offsets* in $\Theta(m)$ work and $\Theta(\lg m)$ span, and Step 5 can reset every SPA in Q in parallel using $\Theta(P)$ work and $\Theta(\lg P)$ span. Totaling the work and span of each step completes the proof. $\square$

Although different executions of a program can store the elements of Q in different numbers m of distinct subbags, notice that m is never more than the total number of elements in Q.

5. ANALYSIS OF PRISM

This section analyzes the performance of PRISM using work-span analysis [29, Ch. 27]. We derive bounds on the work and span of PRISM for any simple data-graph computation $\langle G, f, Q_0 \rangle$. Recall that we make the reasonable assumptions that a single update $f(v)$

Graph	$|V|$	$|E|$	χ	CILK+LOCKS	PRISM	Coloring
cage15	5,154,860	94,044,700	17	36.9	35.5	12%
soc-LiveJournal1	4,847,570	68,475,400	333	36.8	21.7	12%
randLocalDim25	1,000,000	49,992,400	36	26.7	14.4	18%
randLocalDim4	1,000,000	41,817,000	47	19.5	12.5	14%
rmat2Million	2,097,120	39,912,600	72	22.5	16.6	12%
powerGraph2Million	2,000,000	29,108,100	15	12.1	9.8	13%
3dgrid5m	5,000,210	15,000,600	6	10.3	10.3	7%
2dgrid5m	4,999,700	9,999,390	4	17.7	8.9	4%
web-Google	916,428	5,105,040	43	3.9	2.4	8%
web-BerkStan	685,231	7,600,600	200	3.9	2.4	8%
web-Stanford	281,904	2,312,500	62	1.9	0.9	11%
web-NotreDame	325,729	1,469,680	154	1.1	0.8	12%

Figure 7: Performance of PRISM versus CILK+LOCKS when executing $10 \cdot |V|$ updates of the PageRank [21] data-graph computation on a suite of six real-world graphs and six synthetic graphs. Column "*Graph*," identifies the input graph, and columns $|V|$ and $|E|$ specify the number of vertices and edges in the graph, respectively. Column χ gives the number of colors PRISM used to color the graph. Columns "CILK+LOCKS" and "PRISM" present 12-core running times in seconds for the respective schedulers. Each running time is the median of 5 runs. Column "*Coloring*" gives the percentage of PRISM's running time spent coloring the graph.

executes in $\Theta(\deg(v))$ work and $\Theta(\lg(\deg(v)))$ span, and that the update only activates vertices in $\mathrm{Adj}[v]$.

THEOREM 3. *Suppose that* PRISM *colors a degree-Δ data graph $G = (V, E)$ using χ colors, and then executes the data-graph computation $\langle G, f, Q_0 \rangle$. Then, on P processors,* PRISM *executes updates on all vertices in the activation set Q_r for a round r using $O(size(Q_r) + \chi + P)$ work and $O(\chi(\lg(Q_r/\chi) + \lg\Delta) + \lg P)$ span.*

PROOF. Let us first analyze the work and span of one iteration of lines 6–15 in PRISM, which perform the updates on the vertices belonging to one color set $C \in Q_r$. Consider a vertex $v \in C$. Lines 8 and 9 execute in $\Theta(\deg(v))$ work and $\Theta(\lg(\deg(v)))$ span. For each vertex u in the set S of vertices activated by the update $f(v)$, Lemma 1 implies that lines 11–15 execute in $\Theta(1)$ total work. The **parallel for** loop on lines 10–15 therefore executes in $\Theta(S)$ work and $\Theta(\lg S)$ span. Because $|S| \leq \deg(v)$, the **parallel for** loop on lines 7–15 thus executes in $\Theta(size(C))$ work and $\Theta(\lg C + \max_{v \in C} \lg(\deg(v))) = O(\lg C + \lg\Delta)$ span.

By processing each of the χ color sets belonging to Q_r, lines 6–15 therefore executes in $\Theta(size(Q_r) + \chi)$ work and $O(\chi(\lg(Q_r/\chi) + \lg\Delta))$ span. Lemma 2 implies that line 5 executes MB-COLLECT in $O(Q_r + \chi + P)$ work and $O(\lg Q_r + \chi + \lg P)$ span. The theorem follows, because $|Q_r| \leq size(Q_r)$. □

6. EMPIRICAL EVALUATION

This section describes our empirical evaluation of PRISM. We implemented PRISM in Cilk Plus [56] and compared its performance to that of three other schedulers for executing data-graph computations. This section presents three studies of PRISM's performance. The first study, which compared PRISM to a nondeterministic locking strategy, indicates that the overhead of managing multibags is less than the cost of a locking protocol. The second study, which compared PRISM to a chromatic scheduler for static data-graph computations, shows that the overhead of maintaining activation sets dynamically is only about 20% more than using static activation sets. This study suggests that it is worthwhile to use dynamic data-graph computations instead of static ones even if only modest amounts of work can be saved by avoiding unnecessary updates. The third study shows the performance of PRISM is relatively insensitive to the number of colors used to color the data graph, as long as there is sufficient parallelism.

Experimental setup

We implemented PRISM and the multibag data structure in Cilk Plus [56], compiling with the Intel C++ compiler, version 13.1.1. Our source code and data are available from http://supertech.csail.mit.edu. To implement the GET-COLOR procedure, the PRISM implementation used a deterministic multicore coloring algorithm [52], which was also coded in Cilk Plus. For comparison, we engineered three other schedulers for executing dynamic data-graph computations in parallel:

- CILK+LOCKS uses a locking scheme to avoid executing conflicting updates in parallel. The locking scheme associates a shared-exclusive lock with each vertex in the graph. Prior to executing an update $f(v)$, vertex v's lock is acquired exclusively, and a shared lock is acquired for each $u \in \mathrm{Adj}[v]$. A global ordering of locks is used to avoid deadlock.
- CHROMATIC treats the dynamic data-graph computation as a static one — it updates every vertex in every round — and it uses chromatic scheduling to avoid executing conflicting updates in parallel.
- ROUND-ROBIN treats the dynamic data-graph computation as a static one and uses the locking strategy to coordinate updates that conflict.

These schedulers were implemented within a modified multicore version of GraphLab. Specifically, we modified GraphLab's engine to replace GraphLab's explicit management of threads with the Cilk Plus runtime. Using the GraphLab framework, we tested these schedulers on existing GraphLab applications with little to no alteration of the application code.

The benchmarks were run on Intel Xeon X5650 machines, each with 12 2.67-GHz processing cores (hyperthreading disabled); 49 GB of DRAM; two 12-MB L3-caches, each shared among 6 cores; and private L2- and L1-caches of sizes 128 KB and 32 KB, respectively.

Overheads for locking and for chromatic scheduling

We compared the overheads associated with coordinating conflicting updates of a dynamic data-graph computation using locks versus using chromatic scheduling. We evaluated these overheads by comparing the 12-core execution times for PRISM and CILK+LOCKS to execute the PageRank [21] data-graph computation on a suite of graphs. We used PageRank for this study because of its relatively cheap update function, which updates a vertex v by first scanning v's incoming edges to aggregate the data from among

Benchmark	χ	# Updates	ROUND-ROBIN	CHROMATIC	PRISM
PR/L	333	48,475,700	19.2	11.4	17.8
FBP/C3	2	16,001,900	12.4	8.8	9.5
ID/1000	4	10,000,000	13.6	13.3	14.8
PR/G	43	9,164,280	2.4	1.0	2.0
FBP/C1	2	8,783,100	6.6	4.6	4.7
ALS/N	6	1,877,220	75.2	36.7	38.2
ID/250	4	625,000	0.8	0.9	1.0

Figure 8: Performance of three schedulers on the seven application benchmarks from Figure 2, modified so that all vertices are activated in every round. Column "# Updates" specifies the number of updates performed in the data-graph computation. Columns "ROUND-ROBIN," "CHROMATIC," and "PRISM," list the 12-core running times in seconds for the respective schedulers to execute each benchmark. Each running time is the median of 5 runs.

v's neighbors, and then scanning v's outgoing edges to activate v's neighbors.

We executed the PageRank application on a suite of six synthetic and six real-world graphs. The six real-world graphs came from the Stanford Large Network Dataset Collection (SNAP) [71], and the University of Florida Sparse Matrix Collection [31]. The six synthetic graphs were generated using the "randLocal," "powerLaw," "gridGraph," and "rMatGraph" generators included in the Problem Based Benchmark Suite [90].

We observed that PRISM often performed slightly fewer rounds of updates than CILK+LOCKS when both were allowed to run until convergence. Wishing to isolate scheduling overheads, we controlled this variation by limiting the total number of updates the two algorithms executed on a graph to 10 times the number of vertices. The accuracy requirements for the PageRank application were selected to ensure that neither scheduler completed the computation in fewer than $10 \cdot |V|$ updates.

Figure 7 presents our empirical results for this study. Figure 7 shows that over the 12 benchmark graphs, PRISM executed between 1.0 and 2.1 times faster than CILK+LOCKS on PageRank, exhibiting a geometric mean speedup factor of 1.5. From Figure 7, moreover, we see that, on average, 10.9% of PRISM's total running time is spent coloring the data graph. This statistic suggests that the cost PRISM incurs to color the data graph is approximately equal to the cost of executing $|V|$ updates. PRISM colors the data-graph once to execute the data-graph computation, however, meaning that its cost can be amortized over all of the updates in the data-graph computation. In contrast, the locking scheme that CILK+LOCKS implements incurs overhead for every update. Before updating a vertex v, CILK+LOCKS acquires each lock associated with v and every vertex $u \in \text{Adj}[v]$. For simple data-graph computations whose update functions perform relatively little work, this step can account for a significant fraction of the time to execute an update.

Dynamic-scheduling overhead

To investigate the overhead of using multibags to maintain activation sets, we compared the 12-core running times of PRISM, CHROMATIC, and ROUND-ROBIN on the seven benchmark applications from Figure 2. For this study, we modified the benchmarks slightly for each scheduler in order to provide a fair comparison. First, because PRISM typically executes fewer updates than a scheduler for static data-graph computations does, we modified the update functions PRISM used for each application so that every update on a vertex v always activates all vertices $u \in \text{Adj}[v]$. This modification guarantees that PRISM executes the same set of updates each round as a ROUND-ROBIN and CHROMATIC. Additionally, we modified the update functions used by ROUND-ROBIN and CHROMATIC to

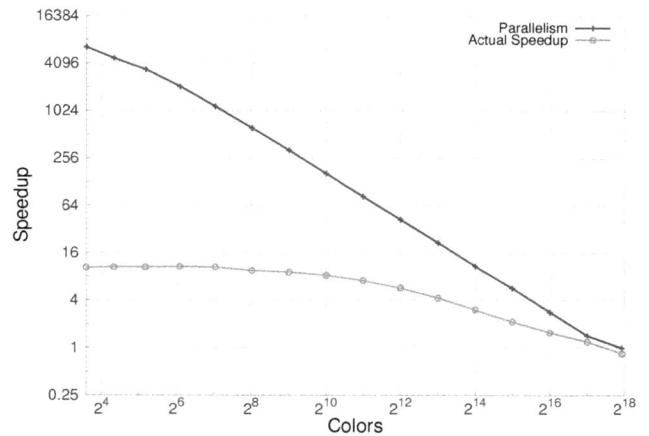

Figure 9: Scalability of PRISM on the image-denoise application as a function of χ, the number of colors used to color the data graph. The parallelism T_1/T_∞ is plotted together with the actual speedup T_1/T_{12} achieved on a 12-core execution. Parallelism values were measured using the Cilkview scalability analyzer [53], which measures the work and span of a Cilk program by counting instructions. Speedup on 12 cores was computed as the ratio of the 1-core and 12-core running times.

remove any work that would be unnecessary in a statically scheduled computation.

Figure 8 presents the results of these tests, which reveal the overhead PRISM incurs to maintain activation sets using a multibag. As Figure 8 shows, PRISM executed 1.0 to 2.0 times slower than CHROMATIC on the benchmarks with a geometric-mean slowdown of 1.2. PRISM nevertheless outperformed ROUND-ROBIN on all but the ID/250 and ID/1000 benchmarks due to ROUND-ROBIN's lock overhead. These results indicate that PRISM incurs relatively little overhead to maintain activation sets with multibags.

Scalability of PRISM

To study the parallel scalability of PRISM, we measured the parallelism T_1/T_∞ and the 12-core speedup T_1/T_{12} of PRISM executing the image-denoise application as we varied the number of colors used to color the application's data-graph. The image-denoise application performs belief propagation to remove Gaussian noise added to a gray-scale image. The data graph for the image-denoise application is a 2D grid in which each vertex represents a pixel, and there is an edge between any two adjacent pixels. PRISM typically colors this data-graph with just 4 colors. To perform this study, we artificially increased χ by repeatedly taking a random nonempty subset of the largest set of vertices with the same color and assigning those vertices a new color. Using this technique, we ran the image-denoise application on a 500-by-500 pixel input image for values of χ between 4 and 250,000 — the last data point corresponding to a coloring that assigns all pixels distinct colors.

Figure 9 plots the results of these tests. As Figure 9 shows, although the parallelism of PRISM is inversely proportional to χ, PRISM's speedup on 12 cores is relatively insensitive to χ, as long as the parallelism is greater than 120. This result harmonizes with the rule of thumb that a program with parallelism above 10 times the number of workers ought to achieve near perfect linear speedup [28].

7. THE PRISM-R ALGORITHM

This section introduces PRISM-R, a chromatic-scheduling algorithm that executes a dynamic data-graph computation determinis-

```
FLATTEN(L,A,i)
1   A[i] = L
2   if L.left ≠ NIL
3       spawn FLATTEN(L.left,A,i − L.right.size − 1)
4   if L.right ≠ NIL
5       FLATTEN(L.right,A,i − 1)
6   sync
```

Figure 10: Pseudocode for the FLATTEN operation for a log tree. FLATTEN performs a post-order parallel traversal of a log tree to place its nodes into a contiguous array.

```
IDENTITY()
1   L = new log tree node
2   L.sublog = new vector
3   L.size = 1
4   L.left = NIL
5   L.right = NIL
6   return L
```

```
REDUCE(L_l,L_r)
1   L = IDENTITY()
2   L.size = L_l.size + L_r.size + 1
3   L.left = L_l
4   L.right = L_r
5   return L
```

Figure 11: Pseudocode for the IDENTITY and REDUCE log-tree reducer operations.

tically even when updates modify global variables using associative operations. The multivector data structure, which is a theoretical improvement to the multibag, is used by PRISM-R to maintain activation sets that are partitioned by color and ordered deterministically. We describe an extension of the model of simple data-graph computations that permits an update function to perform associative operations on global variables using a parallel reduction mechanism. In this extended model, PRISM-R executes dynamic data-graph computations deterministically while achieving the same work and span bounds as PRISM.

Data-graph computations that modify global variables

Several frameworks for executing data-graph computations allow updates to modify global variables in limited ways. Pregel aggregators [78], and GraphLab's sync mechanism [75], for example, both support data-graph computations in which an update can modify a global variable in a restricted manner. These mechanisms coordinate parallel modifications to a global variable using *parallel reductions* [12,25,57,58,60,65,80,88], that is, they coordinate these modifications by applying them to local *views* (copies) of the variable and then *reducing* (combining) those copies together using a binary *reduction operator*.

A *reducer (hyperobject)* [38,68] is a general parallel reduction mechanism provided by Cilk Plus and other dialects of Cilk. A reducer is defined on an arbitrary data type T, called a *view type*, by defining an IDENTITY operator and a binary REDUCE operator for views of type T. The IDENTITY operator creates a new view of the reducer. The binary REDUCE operator defines the reducer's reduction operator. A reducer is a particularly general reduction mechanism because it guarantees that, if its REDUCE operator is associative, then the final result in the global variable is deterministic: every parallel execution of the program produces the same result. Other parallel reduction mechanisms, including Pregel aggregators and GraphLab's sync mechanism, provide this guarantee only if the reduction operator is also commutative.

Although PRISM is implemented in Cilk Plus, PRISM does not produce a deterministic result if the updates modify global variables using a noncommutative reducer. The reason is that the order in which a multibag stores the vertices of an activation set depends on how the computation is scheduled. As a result, the order in which lines 7–15 of PRISM evaluate the vertices in a color set C can differ depending on scheduling. Therefore, if two updates on vertices in C modify the same reducer, then the relative order of these modifications can differ between runs of PRISM, even if a single worker happens to execute both updates.

PRISM-R extends PRISM to support data-graph computations that use reducers. Before presenting PRISM-R, we first describe the multivector data structure that is used by PRISM-R to maintain deterministically ordered color sets.

The multivector data structure

A *multivector* represents a list of χ *vectors* (ordered multisets). It supports two operations — MV-INSERT and MV-COLLECT — which are analogous to the multibag operations MB-INSERT and MB-COLLECT, respectively. We now sketch the design of the multivector data structure.

The multivector relies on properties of a work-stealing runtime system. Consider a parallel program modeled by a computation dag A in the Cilk model of multithreading. The *serial execution order* $R(A)$ of the program lists the vertices of A according to a depth-first traversal of A. A work-stealing scheduler partitions $R(A)$ into a sequence $R(A) = \langle t_0, t_1, \ldots, t_{M-1} \rangle$, where each *trace* $t_i \in R(A)$ is a contiguous subsequence of $R(A)$ executed by exactly one worker. A multivector represents each vector as a sequence of *trace-local subvectors* — subvectors that are modified within exactly one trace. The ordering properties of traces imply that concatenating a vector's trace-local subvectors in order produces a vector whose elements appear in the serial execution order. The multivector data structure assumes that a worker can query the runtime system to determine when it starts executing a new trace.

A multivector stores its nonempty trace-local subvectors in a *log tree*, which represents an ordered multiset of elements and supports $\Theta(1)$-work append operations. A log tree is a binary tree in which each node L stores a dynamic array $L.sublog$. The ordered multiset that a log tree represents corresponds to a concatenation of the tree's dynamic arrays in a post-order tree traversal. Each log-tree node L is augmented with the size of its subtree $L.size$ counting the number of log-tree nodes in the subtree rooted at L. Using this augmentation, the operation FLATTEN($L,A,L.size-1$) described in Figure 10 flattens a log tree rooted at L of n nodes and height h into a contiguous array A using $\Theta(n)$ work and $\Theta(h)$ span.

To handle parallel MV-INSERT operations, a multivector employs a *log-tree reducer*, that is, a Cilk Plus reducer whose view type is a log tree. Figure 11 presents the pseudocode for the IDENTITY and REDUCE operations for the log-tree reducer. Notice that the log-tree reducer's REDUCE operation is logically associative, that is, for any three log-tree reducer views a, b, and c, the views produced by REDUCE(REDUCE(a,b),c) and REDUCE(a,REDUCE(b,c)) represent the same ordered multiset.

To maintain trace-local subvectors, a multivector Q consists of an array of P worker-local SPA's, where P is the number of processors executing the computation, and a log-tree reducer. The SPA $Q[p]$ for worker p stores the trace-local subvectors that worker p appended since the start of its current trace. The log-tree reducer $Q.log\text{-}reducer$ stores all nonempty subvectors created.

Figure 12 sketches the MV-INSERT(Q,v,k) operation to insert element v into the vector $C_k \in Q$. MV-INSERT differs from MB-INSERT in two ways. First, when a new subvector is created and added to a SPA, lines 6–7 additionally append that subvector to $Q.log\text{-}reducer$, thereby maintaining the log-tree reducer. Second, lines 2–3 reset the contents of the SPA $Q[p]$ after worker p begins

```
MV-INSERT(Q, v, k)
1   p = GET-WORKER-ID()
2   if worker p began a new trace since last insert
3       reset Q[p]
4   if Q[p].array[k] == NIL
5       Q[p].array[k] = new subvector
6       L = GET-LOCAL-VIEW(Q.log-reducer)
7       APPEND(L.sublog, Q[p].array[k])
8   APPEND(Q[p].array[k], v)
```

Figure 12: Pseudocode for the MV-INSERT multivector operation to insert an element v into vector C_k in multivector Q.

executing a new trace, thereby ensuring that $Q[p]$ stores only trace-local subvectors.

Figure 13 sketches the MV-COLLECT operation, which returns a pair $\langle subvector\text{-}offsets, collected\text{-}subvectors \rangle$ analogous to the return value of MB-COLLECT. MV-COLLECT differs from MB-COLLECT primarily in that Step 1, which replaces Steps 1 and 2 in MB-COLLECT, flattens the log tree underlying $Q.log\text{-}reducer$ to produce the unsorted array $collected\text{-}subvectors$. MV-COLLECT also requires that $collected\text{-}subvectors$ be sorted using a stable sort on Step 2. The integer sort described in the proof of Lemma 2 for MB-COLLECT is a stable sort suitable for this purpose.

Analysis of multivector operations

We now analyze the work and span of the MV-INSERT and MV-COLLECT operations, starting with MV-INSERT.

LEMMA 4. *Executing* MV-INSERT *takes* $\Theta(1)$ *time in the worst case.*

PROOF. Resetting the SPA $Q[p]$ on line 3 can be done in $\Theta(1)$ worst-case time with an appropriate SPA implementation, and appending a new subvector to a log tree takes $\Theta(1)$ time. The theorem thus follows from the analysis of MB-INSERT in Lemma 1. □

Lemma 5 bounds the work and span of MV-COLLECT.

LEMMA 5. *Consider a computation A with span $T_\infty(A)$, and suppose that the contents of a multivector Q of χ vectors are distributed across m subvectors. Then a call to MV-COLLECT(Q) incurs $\Theta(m + \chi)$ work and $\Theta(\lg m + \chi + T_\infty(A))$ span.*

PROOF. Flattening the log-tree reducer in Step 1 is accomplished in two steps. First, the FLATTEN operation writes the nodes of the log tree to a contiguous array. FLATTEN has span proportional to the depth of the log tree, which is bounded by $O(T_\infty(A))$, since at most $O(T_\infty(A))$ reduction operations can occur along any path in A and REDUCE for log trees executes in $\Theta(1)$ work [38]. Second, using a parallel-prefix sum computation, the log entries associated with each node in the log tree can be packed into a contiguous array, incurring $\Theta(m)$ work and $\Theta(\lg m)$ span. Step 1 thus incurs $\Theta(m)$ work and $O(\lg m + T_\infty(A))$ span. The remaining steps of MV-COLLECT, which are analogous to those of MB-COLLECT and analyzed in Lemma 2, execute in $\Theta(\chi + \lg m)$ span. □

Deduplication

In addition to using a multivector in place of a multibag, PRISM-R differs from PRISM in how it ensures that the activation set for a given round contains each vertex at most once. Recall that PRISM uses atomic operations in lines 11–15 to determine whether to insert an activated vertex into its multibag. Although it is inconsequential in PRISM which update of a neighbor of a vertex caused

```
MV-COLLECT(Q)
1. Flatten the log-reducer tree so that all subvectors in the log appear in
   a contiguous array, collected-subvectors.
2. Sort the subvectors in collected-subvectors by their vector indices
   using a stable sort.
3. Create the array vector-offsets, where vector-offsets[k] stores the in-
   dex of the first subvector in collected-subvectors that contains ele-
   ments of the vector $C_k \in Q$.
4. Reset Q.log-reducer and for p = 0, 1, ..., P − 1, reset Q[p].
5. Return the pair ⟨vector-offsets, collected-subvectors⟩.
```

Figure 13: Pseudocode for the MV-COLLECT multivector operation. Calling MV-COLLECT on a multivector Q produces a pair $\langle vector\text{-}offsets, collected\text{-}subvectors \rangle$ of arrays, where $collected\text{-}subvectors$ contains all nonempty subvectors in Q sorted by their associated vector's color, and $vector\text{-}offsets$ associates sets of subvectors in Q with their corresponding vector.

the vertex to be added to the multibag, in PRISM-R, color sets must be ordered in a deterministic manner. To meet this requirement, PRISM-R assigns each vertex v a priority $priority[v]$, stores vertex-priority pairs in its multivector, (rather than just vertices), and replaces the Boolean array $active$ in PRISM with a comparable array that stores priorities. For each vertex $u \in \text{Adj}[v]$ activated by update $f(v)$, the vertex-priority pair $\langle u, priority[v] \rangle$ is inserted into the multivector, and a priority-write operation [89] is performed to set $active[u] = \max\{active[u], priority[v]\}$ atomically. After executing MV-COLLECT in a round, PRISM-R performs a deduplication step, iterating over the vertex-priority pairs in parallel and deleting any pair $\langle v, p \rangle$ for which $p \neq active[v]$.

Analysis of PRISM-R

The next theorem shows that PRISM-R achieves the same theoretical bounds as PRISM.

THEOREM 6. *Let G be a degree-Δ data graph. Suppose that PRISM-R colors G using χ colors. Then PRISM-R executes updates on all vertices in the activation set Q_r for a round r of a simple data-graph computation $\langle G, f, Q_0 \rangle$ in $O(size(Q_r) + \chi)$ work and $O(\chi(\lg(Q_r/\chi) + \lg \Delta))$ span.*

PROOF. PRISM-R can perform a priority write to its $active$ array with $\Theta(1)$ work, and it can remove duplicates from the output of MV-COLLECT in $O(size(Q_r))$ work and $O(\lg(size(Q_r))) = O(\lg Q_r + \lg \Delta)$ span. The theorem follows by applying Lemmas 4 and 5 appropriately to the analysis of PRISM in Theorem 3. □

8. CONCLUSION

Researchers over multiple decades have advocated that the difficulty of parallel programming can be greatly reduced by using some form of deterministic parallelism [7, 8, 13, 19, 33, 34, 36, 37, 43, 51, 55, 85, 86, 92, 97]. With a deterministic parallel program, the programmer observes no logical concurrency, that is, no nondeterminacy in the behavior of the program due to the relative and nondeterministic timing of communicating processes such as occurs when one process arrives at a lock before another. The semantics of a deterministic parallel program are therefore serial, and reasoning about such a program's correctness, at least in theory, is no harder than reasoning about the correctness of a serial program. Testing, debugging, and formal verification is simplified, because there is no need to consider all possible relative timings (interleavings) of operations on shared mutable state.

The behavior of PRISM corresponds to a variant of SERIAL-DDGC that sorts the activated vertices in its queue by color at the start of each round. Whether PRISM executes a given data graph on 1 processor or many, it always behaves the same. With PRISM-R, this property holds even when the update function can perform reductions. Lock-based schedulers do not produce such a strong guarantee of determinism. Although updates in a round executed by a lock-based scheduler appear to execute according to some linear order, this order is nondeterministic due to races on the acquisition of locks.

Blelloch, Fineman, Gibbons, and Shun [14] argue that deterministic programs can be fast compared with nondeterministic programs, and they document many examples where the overhead for converting a nondeterministic program into a deterministic one is small. They even document a few cases where this "price of determinism" is *slightly* negative. To their list, we add the execution of dynamic data-graph computations as having a price of determinism which is *significantly* negative. We conjecture that research will uncover many more parallel applications that admit to efficient deterministic solutions.

9. ACKNOWLEDGMENTS

Thanks to Guy Blelloch of Carnegie Mellon University for sharing utility functions from his Problem Based Benchmark Suite [90]. Thanks to Aydın Buluç of Lawrence Berkeley Laboratory for helping us in our search for collections of large sparse graphs. Thanks to Uzi Vishkin of University of Maryland for helping us track down early work on parallel sorting. Thanks to Fredrik Kjolstad, Angelina Lee, and Justin Zhang of MIT CSAIL and Guy Blelloch, Julian Shun, and Harsha Vardhan Simhadri of Carnegie Mellon University for providing helpful discussions.

10. REFERENCES

[1] L. Adams and J. Ortega. A multi-color SOR method for parallel computation. In *ICPP*, 1982.

[2] E. Allen, D. Chase, J. Hallett, V. Luchangco, J.-W. Maessen, S. Ryu, G. L. Steele Jr., and S. Tobin-Hochstadt. *The Fortress Language Specification Version 1.0*. Sun Microsystems, Inc., 2008.

[3] N. Alon, L. Babai, and A. Itai. A fast and simple randomized parallel algorithm for the maximal independent set problem. *J. Algorithms*, 1986.

[4] L. Backstrom, D. Huttenlocher, J. Kleinberg, and X. Lan. Group formation in large social networks: membership, growth, and evolution. In *ACM SIGKDD*, 2006.

[5] L. Barenboim and M. Elkin. Distributed $(\Delta+1)$-coloring in linear (in Δ) time. In *STOC*, 2009.

[6] R. Barik, Z. Budimlic, V. Cavè, S. Chatterjee, Y. Guo, D. Peixotto, R. Raman, J. Shirako, Y. Taşırlar, Y. Yan, et al. The Habanero multicore software research project. In *OOPSLA*, 2009.

[7] T. Bergan, O. Anderson, J. Devietti, L. Ceze, and D. Grossman. CoreDet: A compiler and runtime system for deterministic multithreaded execution. In *ASPLOS*, 2010.

[8] E. D. Berger, T. Yang, T. Liu, and G. Novark. Grace: Safe multithreaded programming for C/C++. In *OOPSLA*, 2009.

[9] D. P. Bertsekas and J. N. Tsitsiklis. *Parallel and Distributed Computation: Numerical Methods*. Prentice-Hall, Inc., 1989.

[10] C. Bienia, S. Kumar, J. P. Singh, and K. Li. The PARSEC benchmark suite: Characterization and architectural implications. In *PACT*, 2008.

[11] G. E. Blelloch. Prefix sums and their applications. Technical Report CMU-CS-90-190, School of Computer Science, Carnegie Mellon University, 1990.

[12] G. E. Blelloch. NESL: A nested data-parallel language. Technical Report CS-92-103, Carnegie Mellon University, Pittsburgh, PA, 1992.

[13] G. E. Blelloch. Programming parallel algorithms. *CACM*, 1996.

[14] G. E. Blelloch, J. T. Fineman, P. B. Gibbons, and J. Shun. Internally deterministic parallel algorithms can be fast. In *Proceedings of Principles and Practice of Parallel Programming*, pp. 181–192, 2012.

[15] G. E. Blelloch, C. E. Leiserson, B. M. Maggs, C. G. Plaxton, S. J. Smith, and M. Zagha. A comparison of sorting algorithms for the Connection Machine CM-2. In *SPAA*, 1991.

[16] R. D. Blumofe and C. E. Leiserson. Space-efficient scheduling of multithreaded computations. *SICOMP*, 1998.

[17] R. D. Blumofe and C. E. Leiserson. Scheduling multithreaded computations by work stealing. *JACM*, 1999.

[18] R. D. Blumofe and D. Papadopoulos. Hood: A user-level threads library for multiprogrammed multiprocessors. Technical Report, University of Texas at Austin, 1999.

[19] R. L. Bocchino, Jr., V. S. Adve, S. V. Adve, and M. Snir. Parallel programming must be deterministic by default. In *First USENIX Conference on Hot Topics in Parallelism*, 2009.

[20] R. P. Brent. The parallel evaluation of general arithmetic expressions. *JACM*, 1974.

[21] S. Brin and L. Page. The anatomy of a large-scale hypertextual Web search engine. *Comput. Netw. ISDN Syst.*, 1998.

[22] A. Brodnik, S. Carlsson, E. Demaine, J. Ian Munro, and R. Sedgewick. Resizable arrays in optimal time and space. In *Algorithms and Data Structures*, volume 1663 of *LNCS*. Springer Berlin Heidelberg, 1999.

[23] F. W. Burton and M. R. Sleep. Executing functional programs on a virtual tree of processors. In *ICFP*, 1981.

[24] V. Cavé, J. Zhao, J. Shirako, and V. Sarkar. Habanero-Java: the new adventures of old x10. In *PPPJ*. ACM, 2011.

[25] B. L. Chamberlain, S.-E. Choi, E. C. Lewis, C. Lin, L. Snyder, and W. D. Weathersby. ZPL: A machine independent programming language for parallel computers. *IEEE TSE*, 2000.

[26] P. Charles, C. Grothoff, V. Saraswat, C. Donawa, A. Kielstra, K. Ebcioglu, C. von Praun, and V. Sarkar. X10: An object-oriented approach to non-uniform cluster computing. In *OOPSLA*, 2005.

[27] R. Cole and U. Vishkin. Deterministic coin tossing and accelerating cascades: micro and macro techniques for designing parallel algorithms. In *STOC*, 1986.

[28] T. H. Cormen, C. E. Leiserson, R. L. Rivest, and C. Stein. *Introduction to Algorithms*. The MIT Press and McGraw-Hill, second edition, 2001.

[29] T. H. Cormen, C. E. Leiserson, R. L. Rivest, and C. Stein. *Introduction to Algorithms*. The MIT Press, third edition, 2009.

[30] J. C. Culberson. Iterated greedy graph coloring and the difficulty landscape. Technical report, University of Alberta, 1992.

[31] T. A. Davis and Y. Hu. The University of Florida sparse matrix collection. *ACM TOMS*, 2011.

[32] J. E. Dennis Jr. and T. Steihaug. On the successive projections approach to least-squares problems. *SIAM J. Numer. Anal.*, 1986.

[33] J. Devietti, B. Lucia, L. Ceze, and M. Oskin. DMP: Deterministic shared memory multiprocessing. In *ASPLOS*, 2009.

[34] J. Devietti, J. Nelson, T. Bergan, L. Ceze, and D. Grossman. RCDC: A relaxed consistency deterministic computer. In *ASPLOS*, 2011.

[35] D. L. Eager, J. Zahorjan, and E. D. Lazowska. Speedup versus efficiency in parallel systems. *IEEETC*, 1989.

[36] M. Feng and C. E. Leiserson. Efficient detection of determinacy races in Cilk programs. In *SPAA*, 1997.

[37] M. Feng and C. E. Leiserson. Efficient detection of determinacy races in Cilk programs. *Theory of Computing Systems*, 32(3):301–326, 1999.

[38] M. Frigo, P. Halpern, C. E. Leiserson, and S. Lewin-Berlin. Reducers and other Cilk++ hyperobjects. In *SPAA*, 2009.

[39] M. Frigo, C. E. Leiserson, and K. H. Randall. The implementation of the Cilk-5 multithreaded language. In *PLDI*, 1998.

[40] M. Garey, D. Johnson, and L. Stockmeyer. Some simplified NP-complete graph problems. *Theoretical Computer Science*, 1976.

[41] A. E. Gelfand and A. F. M. Smith. Sampling-based approaches to calculating marginal densities. *Journal of the American Statistical Association*, 1990.

[42] S. Geman and D. Geman. Stochastic relaxation, Gibbs distributions, and the Bayesian restoration of images. *PAMI*, 1984.

[43] P. B. Gibbons. A more practical PRAM model. In *SPAA*, 1989.

[44] J. R. Gilbert, C. Moler, and R. Schreiber. Sparse matrices in MATLAB: Design and implementation. *SIAM J. Matrix Anal. Appl*, 1992.

[45] A. V. Goldberg, S. A. Plotkin, and G. E. Shannon. Parallel symmetry-breaking in sparse graphs. In *SIAM J. Disc. Math*, 1987.

[46] M. Goldberg and T. Spencer. A new parallel algorithm for the maximal independent set problem. *SIAM Journal on Computing*, 1989.

[47] G. H. Golub and W. Kahan. Calculating the singular values and pseudo-inverse of a matrix. *J. SIAM Numer. Anal.*, 1965.

[48] J. E. Gonzalez, Y. Low, H. Gu, D. Bickson, and C. Guestrin. PowerGraph: distributed graph-parallel computation on natural graphs. In *OSDI*, 2012.

[49] R. L. Graham. Bounds for certain multiprocessing anomalies. *The Bell System Technical Journal*, 1966.

[50] R. H. Halstead, Jr. Implementation of Multilisp: Lisp on a multiprocessor. In *Lisp and Functional Programming*, 1984.

[51] R. H. Halstead, Jr. Multilisp: A language for concurrent symbolic computation. *ACM TOPLAS*, 1985.

[52] W. Hasenplaugh, T. Kaler, T. B. Schardl, and C. E. Leiserson. Ordering heuristics for parallel graph coloring. In *SPAA*, 2014.

[53] Y. He, C. E. Leiserson, and W. M. Leiserson. The Cilkview scalability analyzer. In *SPAA*, 2010.

[54] F. L. Hitchcock. The expression of a tensor or a polyadic as a sum of products. *Journal of Mathematical Physics*, 1927.

[55] D. R. Hower, P. Dudnik, M. D. Hill, and D. A. Wood. Calvin: Deterministic or not? Free will to choose. In *HPCA*, 2011.

[56] Intel Corporation. *Intel Cilk Plus Language Specification*, 2010. Available from http://software.intel.com/sites/products/cilk-plus/cilk_plus_language_specification.pdf.

[57] Intel Corporation. *Intel(R) Threading Building Blocks*, 2012. Available from http://software.intel.com/sites/products/documentation/doclib/tbb_sa/help/index.htm.

[58] K. E. Iverson. *A Programming Language*. John Wiley & Sons, 1962.

[59] M. T. Jones and P. E. Plassmann. A parallel graph coloring heuristic. *SIAM Journal on Scientific Computing*, 1993.

[60] C. H. Koelbel, D. B. Loveman, R. S. Schreiber, G. L. Steele Jr., and M. E. Zosel. *The High Performance Fortran Handbook*. The MIT Press, 1994.

[61] F. Kuhn. Weak graph colorings: distributed algorithms and applications. In *SPAA*, 2009.

[62] F. Kuhn and R. Wattenhofer. On the complexity of distributed graph coloring. In *PODC*, 2006.

[63] M. Kulkarni, M. Burtscher, C. Cascaval, and K. Pingali. Lonestar: A suite of parallel irregular programs. In *ISPASS*, 2009.

[64] A. Kyrola, G. Blelloch, and C. Guestrin. GraphChi: large-scale graph computation on just a PC. In *OSDI*. USENIX, 2012.

[65] C. Lasser and S. M. Omohundro. *The Essential *Lisp Manual, Release 1, Revision 3*. Thinking Machines Technical Report 86.15, Cambridge, MA, 1986.

[66] D. Lea. A Java fork/join framework. In *Conference on Java Grande*, 2000.

[67] E. A. Lee. The problem with threads. *IEEE Computer*, 2006.

[68] I.-T. A. Lee, A. Shafi, and C. E. Leiserson. Memory-mapping support for reducer hyperobjects. In *SPAA*, 2012.

[69] D. Leijen and J. Hall. Optimize managed code for multi-core machines. *MSDN Magazine*, 2007. Available from http://msdn.microsoft.com/magazine/.

[70] C. E. Leiserson. The Cilk++ concurrency platform. *Journal of Supercomputing*, 2010.

[71] J. Leskovec. SNAP: Stanford network analysis platform. Available from http://snap.stanford.edu/data/index.html, 2013.

[72] J. Leskovec, K. J. Lang, A. Dasgupta, and M. W. Mahoney. Community structure in large networks: Natural cluster sizes and the absence of large well-defined clusters. *CoRR*, 2008.

[73] N. Linial. Locality in distributed graph algorithms. *SIAM J. Comput.*, 1992.

[74] Y. Low, D. Bickson, J. Gonzalez, C. Guestrin, A. Kyrola, and J. M. Hellerstein. Distributed GraphLab: a framework for machine learning and data mining in the cloud. *Proceedings of the VLDB Endowment*, pp. 716–727, 2012.

[75] Y. Low, J. Gonzalez, A. Kyrola, D. Bickson, C. Guestrin, and J. M. Hellerstein. GraphLab: A new parallel framework for machine learning. In *UAI*, 2010.

[76] Y. Low, J. Gonzalez, A. Kyrola, D. Bickson, C. Guestrin, and J. M. Hellerstein. Distributed GraphLab: a framework for machine learning and data mining in the cloud. In *PVLDB*, 2012.

[77] C. Lund and M. Yannakakis. On the hardness of approximating minimization problems. *JACM*, 1994.

[78] G. Malewicz, M. H. Austern, A. J. Bik, J. C. Dehnert, I. Horn, N. Leiser, and G. Czajkowski. Pregel: a system for large-scale graph processing. In *SIGMOD*, 2010.

[79] A. McCallum. Cora data set. Available from http://people.cs.umass.edu/~mccallum/data.html.

[80] D. McCrady. Avoiding contention using combinable objects. Microsoft Developer Network blog post, Sept. 2008.

[81] T. Mitchell. NPIC500 data set. Available from http://www.cs.cmu.edu/~tom/10709_fall09/NPIC500.pdf, 2009.

[82] K. P. Murphy, Y. Weiss, and M. I. Jordan. Loopy belief propagation for approximate inference: An empirical study. In *UAI*, 1999.

[83] R. H. B. Netzer and B. P. Miller. What are race conditions? *ACM Letters on Programming Languages and Systems*, 1992.

[84] K. Nigam and R. Ghani. Analyzing the effectiveness and applicability of co-training. In *CIKM*, 2000.

[85] M. Olszewski, J. Ansel, and S. Amarasinghe. Kendo: efficient deterministic multithreading in software. In *ASPLOS*, 2009.

[86] S. S. Patil. Closure properties of interconnections of determinate systems. In J. B. Dennis, editor, *Record of the Project MAC Conference on Concurrent Systems and Parallel Computation*. ACM, 1970.

[87] J. Pearl. *Probabilistic Reasoning in Intelligent Systems: Networks of Plausible Inference*. Morgan Kaufmann, 1988.

[88] J. Reinders. *Intel Threading Building Blocks: Outfitting C++ for Multi-core Processor Parallelism*. O'Reilly Media, Inc., 2007.

[89] J. Shun, G. E. Blelloch, J. T. Fineman, and P. B. Gibbons. Reducing contention through priority updates. In *SPAA*, 2013.

[90] J. Shun, G. E. Blelloch, J. T. Fineman, P. B. Gibbons, A. Kyrola, H. V. Simhadri, and K. Tangwongsan. Brief announcement: the Problem Based Benchmark Suite. In *SPAA*, 2012.

[91] P. Singla and P. Domingos. Entity resolution with markov logic. In *ICDM*, 2006.

[92] G. L. Steele Jr. Making asynchronous parallelism safe for the world. In *POPL*, 1990.

[93] J. Stoer, R. Bulirsch, R. H. Bartels, W. Gautschi, and C. Witzgall. *Introduction to Numerical Analysis*. Springer, New York, 2002.

[94] M. Szegedy and S. Vishwanathan. Locality based graph coloring. In *STOC*, 1993.

[95] A. M. Turing. Rounding-off errors in matrix processes. *The Quarterly Journal of Mechanics and Applied Mathematics*, 1948.

[96] D. J. A. Welsh and M. B. Powell. An upper bound for the chromatic number of a graph and its application to timetabling problems. *The Computer Journal*, 1967.

[97] J. Yu and S. Narayanasamy. A case for an interleaving constrained shared-memory multi-processor. In *ISCA*, 2009.

[98] M. Zagha and G. E. Blelloch. Radix sort for vector multiprocessors. In *Supercomputing*, 1991.

Ordering Heuristics for Parallel Graph Coloring

William Hasenplaugh   Tim Kaler   Tao B. Schardl   Charles E. Leiserson

MIT Computer Science and Artificial Intelligence Laboratory
32 Vassar Street
Cambridge, MA 02139

ABSTRACT

This paper introduces the largest-log-degree-first (LLF) and smallest-log-degree-last (SLL) ordering heuristics for parallel greedy graph-coloring algorithms, which are inspired by the largest-degree-first (LF) and smallest-degree-last (SL) serial heuristics, respectively. We show that although LF and SL, in practice, generate colorings with relatively small numbers of colors, they are vulnerable to adversarial inputs for which any parallelization yields a poor parallel speedup. In contrast, LLF and SLL allow for provably good speedups on arbitrary inputs while, in practice, producing colorings of competitive quality to their serial analogs.

We applied LLF and SLL to the parallel greedy coloring algorithm introduced by Jones and Plassmann, referred to here as JP. Jones and Plassman analyze the variant of JP that processes the vertices of a graph in a random order, and show that on an $O(1)$-degree graph $G = (V, E)$, this JP-R variant has an expected parallel running time of $O(\lg V / \lg \lg V)$ in a PRAM model. We improve this bound to show, using work-span analysis, that JP-R, augmented to handle arbitrary-degree graphs, colors a graph $G = (V, E)$ with degree Δ using $\Theta(V + E)$ work and $O(\lg V + \lg \Delta \cdot \min\{\sqrt{E}, \Delta + \lg \Delta \lg V / \lg \lg V\})$ expected span. We prove that JP-LLF and JP-SLL— JP using the LLF and SLL heuristics, respectively — execute with the same asymptotic work as JP-R and only logarithmically more span while producing higher-quality colorings than JP-R in practice.

We engineered an efficient implementation of JP for modern shared-memory multicore computers and evaluated its performance on a machine with 12 Intel Core-i7 (Nehalem) processor cores. Our implementation of JP-LLF achieves a geometric-mean speedup of 7.83 on eight real-world graphs and a geometric-mean speedup of 8.08 on ten synthetic graphs, while our implementation using SLL achieves a geometric-mean speedup of 5.36 on these real-world graphs and a geometric-mean speedup of 7.02 on these synthetic graphs. Furthermore, on one processor, JP-LLF is slightly faster than a well-engineered serial greedy algorithm using LF, and likewise, JP-SLL is slightly faster than the greedy algorithm using SL.

This research was supported in part by the National Science Foundation under Grants CNS-1017058, CCF-1162148, and CCF-1314547 and in part by grants from Intel Corporation and Foxconn Technology Group. Tao B. Schardl was supported in part by an NSF Graduate Research Fellowship.

Categories and Subject Descriptors

D.1.3 [**Programming Techniques**]: Concurrent Programming— *parallel programming*; E.1 [**Data Structures**]: *graphs and networks*; F.2.2 [**Analysis of Algorithms and Problem Complexity**]: Nonnumerical Algorithms and Problems—*graph algorithms*; G.2.2 [**Discrete Mathematics**]: Graph Theory—*graph labeling*

Keywords

Parallel algorithms; graph coloring; ordering heuristics; Cilk

1. INTRODUCTION

Graph coloring is a heavily studied problem with many real-world applications, including the scheduling of conflicting jobs [4, 25, 44, 51], register allocation [13, 15, 16], high-dimensional nearest-neighbor search [6], and sparse-matrix computation [19, 36, 48], to name just a few. Formally, a *(vertex)-coloring* of an undirected graph $G = (V, E)$ is an assignment of a *color v.color* to each vertex $v \in V$ such that for every edge $(u, v) \in E$, we have $u.color \neq v.color$, that is, no two adjacent vertices have the same color. The *graph-coloring problem* is the problem of determining a coloring which uses as few colors as possible.

We were motivated to work on graph coloring in the context of "chromatic scheduling" [1, 7, 37] of parallel "data-graph computations." A *data graph* is a graph with data associated with its vertices and edges. A *data-graph computation* is an algorithm implemented as a sequence of "updates" on the vertices of a data graph $G = (V, E)$, where *updating* a vertex $v \in V$ involves computing a new value associated with v as a function of v's old value and the values associated with the *neighbors* of v: the set of vertices adjacent to v in G, denoted $v.adj = \{u \in V : (v, u) \in E\}$. To ensure atomicity of each update, rather than using mutual-exclusion locks or other nondeterministic means of data synchronization, chromatic scheduling first colors the vertices of G and then sequences through the colors, scheduling all vertices of the same color in parallel. The time to perform a data-graph computation thus depends both on how long it takes to color G and on the number of colors produced by the graph-coloring algorithm: more colors means less parallelism. Although the coloring can be performed offline for some data-graph computations, for other computations the coloring must be produced online, and one must accept a trade-off between coloring *quality* — number of colors — and the time to produce the coloring.

Although the problem of finding an *optimal* coloring of a graph — a coloring using the fewest colors possible — is in NP-complete [26], heuristic "greedy" algorithms work reasonably well in practice. Welsh and Powell [51] introduced the original *greedy* coloring algorithm, which iterates over the vertices and assigns each vertex the smallest color not assigned to a neighbor. For a graph $G = (V, E)$, define the **degree** of a vertex $v \in V$ by $\deg(v) = |v.adj|$, the number of neighbors of v, and let the **degree** of G be $\Delta = \max_{v \in V}\{\deg(v)\}$. Welsh and Powell show that the greedy algorithm colors a graph G with degree Δ using at most $\Delta + 1$ colors.

Ordering heuristics

In practice, however, greedy coloring algorithms tend to produce much better colorings than the $\Delta + 1$ bound implies, and moreover, the order in which a greedy coloring algorithm colors the vertices affects the quality of the coloring.[1] To reduce the number of colors a greedy coloring algorithm uses, practitioners therefore employ **ordering heuristics** to determine the order in which the algorithm colors the vertices [2, 11, 35, 45].

The literature includes many studies of ordering heuristics and how they affect running time and coloring quality. Here are six of the more popular heuristics:

FF The **first-fit** ordering heuristic [42, 51] colors vertices in the order they appear in the input graph representation.

R The **random** ordering heuristic [35] colors vertices in a uniformly random order.

LF The **largest-degree-first** ordering heuristic [51] colors vertices in order of decreasing degree.

ID The **incidence-degree** ordering heuristic [19] iteratively colors an uncolored vertex with the largest number of colored neighbors.

SL The **smallest-degree-last** ordering heuristic [2, 45] colors the vertices in the order induced by first removing all the lowest-degree vertices from the graph, then recursively coloring the resulting graph, and finally coloring the removed vertices.

SD The **saturation-degree** ordering heuristic [11] iteratively colors an uncolored vertex whose colored neighbors use the largest number of distinct colors.

The experimental results overviewed in the Appendix (Section 12) indicate that we have listed these heuristics in rough order of coloring quality from worst to best, confirming the findings of Gebremedhin and Manne [27], who also rank the relative quality of R, LF, ID, and SD in this order.

Although an ordering heuristic can be viewed as producing a permutation of the vertices of a graph $G = (V, E)$, we shall find it convenient to think of an ordering heuristic H as producing an injective (1-to-1) **priority function** $\rho : V \to \mathbb{R}$.[2] We shall use the notation $\rho \in H$ to mean that the ordering heuristic H produces a priority function ρ.

Figure 1 gives the pseudocode for GREEDY, a greedy coloring algorithm. GREEDY takes a vertex-weighted graph $G = (V, E, \rho)$ as input, where $\rho : V \to \mathbb{R}$ is a priority function produced by some ordering heuristic. Each step of GREEDY simply selects the uncol-

---

[1] In fact, for any graph $G = (V, E)$, some ordering of V causes a greedy algorithm to color G optimally, although finding such an ordering is NP-hard [46].

[2] If the rule for an ordering heuristic allows for ties in the priority function (the priority function is not injective), we shall assume that ties are broken randomly. Formally, suppose that an ordering heuristic H produces a priority function ρ_H which may contain ties. We extend ρ_H to a priority function ρ that maps each vertex $v \in V$ to an ordered pair $\langle \rho_H(v), \rho_R(v) \rangle$, where the priority function ρ_R is produced by the random ordering heuristic R. To determine which of two vertices $u, v \in V$ has higher priority, we compare the ordered pairs $\rho(u)$ and $\rho(v)$ lexicographically. Notwithstanding this subtlety, we shall still adopt the simplifying convenience of viewing the priority function as mapping vertices to real numbers. In fact, the range of the priority function can be any linearly ordered set.

GREEDY(G)

```
1   let G = (V, E, ρ)
2   for v ∈ V in order of decreasing ρ(v)
3       C = {1, 2, ..., deg(v) + 1}
4       for u ∈ v.adj such that ρ(u) > ρ(v)
5           C = C − {u.color}
6       v.color = min C
```

Figure 1: Pseudocode for a serial greedy graph-coloring algorithm. Given a vertex-weighted graph $G = (V, E, \rho)$, where the priority of a vertex $v \in V$ is given by $\rho(v)$, GREEDY colors each vertex $v \in V$ in decreasing order according to $\rho(v)$.

JP(G)

```
7    let G = (V, E, ρ)
8    parallel for v ∈ V
9        v.pred = {u ∈ V : (u, v) ∈ E and ρ(u) > ρ(v)}
10       v.succ = {u ∈ V : (u, v) ∈ E and ρ(u) < ρ(v)}
11       v.counter = |v.pred|
12   parallel for v ∈ V
13       if v.pred == ∅
14           JP-COLOR(v)
```

JP-COLOR(v)

```
15   v.color = GET-COLOR(v)
16   parallel for u ∈ v.succ
17       if JOIN(u.counter) == 0
18           JP-COLOR(u)
```

GET-COLOR(v)

```
19   C = {1, 2, ..., |v.pred| + 1}
20   parallel for u ∈ v.pred
21       C = C − {u.color}
22   return min C
```

Figure 2: The Jones-Plassmann parallel coloring algorithm. JP uses a recursive helper function JP-COLOR to process a vertex once all of its predecessors have been colored. JP-COLOR uses the helper routine GET-COLOR to find the smallest color available to color a vertex v.

ored vertex with the highest priority according to ρ and colors it with the smallest available color. Generally, for a coloring algorithm A and ordering heuristic H, let A-H denote the coloring algorithm A that runs on vertex-weighted graphs whose priority functions are produced by H. In this way, we separate the behavior of the coloring algorithm from that of the ordering heuristic.

GREEDY, using any of these six ordering heuristics, can be made to run in $\Theta(V + E)$ time theoretically. Although some of these ordering heuristics involve more bookkeeping than others, achieving these theoretical bounds for GREEDY-FF, GREEDY-R, GREEDY-LF, GREEDY-ID, and GREEDY-SL is straightforward [29, 45]. Despite conjectures to the contrary [19, 29], GREEDY-SD can also be made to run in $\Theta(V + E)$ time, as we shall show in Section 8.

In practice, to produce a better quality coloring tends to cost more in running time. That is, the six heuristics, which are listed in increasing order of coloring quality, are also listed in increasing order of running time. The only exception is GREEDY-ID, which is dominated by GREEDY-SL in both coloring quality and runtime. The experiments discussed in the Appendix (Section 12) summarize our empirical findings for serial greedy coloring.

Parallel greedy coloring

There is a historical tension between coloring quality and the parallel scalability of greedy graph coloring. While the traditional ordering heuristics FF, LF, ID, and SL are efficient using GREEDY, it can be shown that any parallelization of them requires worst-case span of $\Omega(V)$ for a general graph $G = (V, E)$. Of the various attempts to parallelize greedy coloring [18, 22, 43], the algorithm first proposed by Jones and Plassmann [35] extends the greedy algorithm in a straightforward manner, uses work linear in size of the graph, and is deterministic given a random seed. Jones and Plassmann's original paper demonstrates good parallel performance for

$O(1)$-degree graphs using the random ordering heuristic R. Unfortunately, in practice, R tends to produce colorings of relatively poor quality relative to the other traditional ordering heuristics. But the other traditional ordering heuristics are all vulnerable to adversarial graph inputs which cause JP to operate in $\Omega(V)$ time and thus exhibit poor parallel scalability. Consequently, there is need for new ordering heuristics for JP that can achieve both good coloring quality and guaranteed fast parallel performance.

Figure 2 gives the pseudocode for JP, which colors a given graph $G = (V, E, \rho)$ in the order specified by the priority function ρ. The algorithm begins in lines 9 and 10 by partitioning the neighbors of each vertex into **predecessors** — vertices with larger priorities — and **successors** — vertices with smaller priorities. JP uses the recursive JP-COLOR helper function to color a vertex $v \in V$ once all vertices in $v.pred$ have been colored. Initially, lines 12–14 in JP scan the vertices of V to find every vertex that has no predecessors and colors each one using JP-COLOR. Within a call to JP-COLOR(v), line 15 calls GET-COLOR to assign a color to v, and the loop on lines 16–18 broadcasts in parallel to all of v's successors the fact that v is colored. For each successor $u \in v.succ$, line 17 tests whether all of u's predecessors have already been colored, and if so, line 18 recursively calls JP-COLOR on u.

Jones and Plassmann analyze the performance of JP-R for $O(1)$-degree graphs. Although they do not discuss using the naive FF ordering heuristic, it is apparent that there exist adversarial input orderings for which their algorithm would fail to scale. For example, if the graph $G = (V, E)$ is simply a chain of vertices and the input order of V corresponds to their in order in the chain, JP-FF exhibits no parallelism. Jones and Plassmann show that a random ordering produced by R, however, allows the algorithm to run in $O(\lg V / \lg \lg V)$ expected time on this chain graph — and on any $O(1)$-degree graph, for that matter. Section 3 of this paper extends their analysis of JP-R to arbitrary-degree graphs.

Although JP-R scales well in theory, as well as in practice, when it comes to coloring quality, R is one of the weaker ordering heuristics, as we have noted. Of the other heuristics, JP-LF and JP-SL suffer from the same problem as FF, namely, it is possible to construct adversarial graphs that cause them to scale poorly, which we explore in Section 4. The ID heuristic tends to produce worse colorings than SL, and since GREEDY-ID also runs more slowly than GREEDY-SL, we have dropped ID from consideration. Moreover, because of our motivation to use the coloring algorithm for online chromatic scheduling, where the performance of the coloring algorithm cannot be sacrificed for marginal improvements in the quality of coloring, we also have dropped the SD heuristic. Since SD produces the best-quality colorings of the six ordering heuristics, however, we see parallelizing it as an interesting opportunity for future research.

Consequently, this paper focuses on alternatives to the LF and SL ordering heuristics that provide comparable coloring quality while exhibiting the same resilience to adversarial graphs that R shows compared with FF. Specifically, we introduce two new randomized ordering heuristics — "largest log-degree first" (LLF) and "smallest log-degree last" (SLL) — which resemble LF and SL, respectively, but which scale provably well when used with JP. We demonstrate that JP-LLF and JP-SLL provide good parallel scalability in theory and practice and are resilient to adversarial graphs.

Figure 3 summarizes our empirical findings. The data suggest that the LLF and SLL ordering heuristics produce colorings that are nearly as good as LF and SL, respectively. With respect to performance, our implementations of JP-LLF and JP-SLL actually operate slightly faster on 1 processor than our highly tuned im-

H	H'	$\dfrac{C_{H'}}{C_H}$	$\dfrac{\text{GREEDY-}H}{\text{JP-}H'_1}$	$\dfrac{\text{JP-}H'_1}{\text{JP-}H'_{12}}$
FF	R	1.011	0.417	7.039
LF	LLF	1.021	1.058	7.980
SL	SLL	1.037	1.092	6.082

Figure 3: Summary of ordering-heuristic behavior on a suite of 8 real-world graphs and 10 synthetic graphs when run on a machine with 12 Intel Xeon X5650 processor cores. Column H lists three serial heuristics traditionally used for GREEDY, and column H' lists parallel heuristics for JP, of which LLF and SLL are introduced in this paper. Column "$C_{H'}/C_H$" shows the geometric mean of the ratio of the number of colors the parallel heuristic uses compared to the serial heuristic. Column "GREEDY-H/JP-H'_1" shows the geometric mean of the ratio of serial running times of GREEDY with the serial heuristic versus JP with the analogous parallel heuristic when run on 1 processor. Column "JP-H'_1/JP-H'_{12}" shows the geometric mean of the speedup of each parallel heuristic going from 1 processor to 12.

plementations of GREEDY-LF and GREEDY-SL, respectively, and they scale comparably to JP-R.

Outline

The remainder of this paper is organized as follows. Section 2 reviews the asynchronous parallel greedy coloring algorithm first proposed by Jones and Plassmann [35]. We show how JP can be extended to handle arbitrary-degree graphs and arbitrary priority functions. Using work-span analysis [21, Ch. 27], we show that JP colors a Δ-degree graph $G = (V, E, \rho)$ in $\Theta(V + E)$ work and $O(L \lg \Delta + \lg V)$ span, where L is the length of the longest path in G along which the priority function ρ decreases. Section 3 analyzes the performance of JP-R, showing that it operates using linear work and $O(\lg V + \lg \Delta \cdot \min\{\sqrt{E}, \Delta + \lg \Delta \lg V / \lg \lg V\})$ span. Section 4 shows that there exist "adversarial" graphs for which JP-LF and JP-SL exhibit limited parallel speedup. Section 5 analyzes the LLF and SLL ordering heuristics. We show that, given a Δ-degree graph G, JP-LLF colors $G = (V, E, \rho)$ using $\Theta(V + E)$ work and $O(\lg V + \lg \Delta (\min\{\Delta, \sqrt{E}\} + \lg^2 \Delta \lg V / \lg \lg V))$ expected span, while JP-SLL colors $G = (V, E, \rho)$ using same work and an additive $\Theta(\lg \Delta \lg V)$ additional span. Section 6 evaluates the performance of JP-LLF and JP-SLL on a suite of 8 real-world and 10 synthetic benchmark graphs. Section 7 discusses the software engineering techniques used in our implementation of JP-R, JP-LLF, and JP-SLL. Section 8 introduces an algorithm for computing the SD ordering heuristic using $\Theta(V + E)$ work. Section 9 discusses related work, and Section 10 offers some concluding remarks. The Appendix (Section 12) presents some experimental results for serial ordering heuristics.

2. THE JONES-PLASSMANN ALGORITHM

This section reviews JP, the parallel greedy coloring algorithm introduced by Jones and Plassmann [35], whose pseudocode is given in Figure 2. We first review the dag model of dynamic multithreading and work-span analysis [21, Ch. 27]. Then we describe how JP can be modified from Jones and Plassmann's original algorithm to handle arbitrary-degree graphs and arbitrary priority functions. We analyze JP with an arbitrary priority function ρ and show that on a Δ-degree graph $G = (V, E, \rho)$, JP runs in $\Theta(V + E)$ work and $O(L \lg \Delta + \lg V)$ span, where L is the longest path in the "priority dag" of G induced by ρ.

The dag model of dynamic multithreading

We shall analyze the parallel performance of JP using the dag model of dynamic multithreading introduced by Blumofe and Leiserson [9, 10] and described in tutorial fashion in [21, Ch. 27]. The dag model views the executed computation resulting from running a parallel algorithm as a **computation dag** A, in which each vertex denotes an instruction, and edges denote parallel control dependencies between instructions. Although the model encompasses other parallel control constructs, for our purposes, we need only understand that the execution of a **parallel for** loop can be modeled as a balanced binary tree of vertices in the dag, where the leaves of the tree denote the initial instructions of the loop iterations.

To analyze the performance of a dynamic multithreading program theoretically, we assume that the program executes on an *ideal parallel computer*: each instruction executes in unit time, the computer has ample memory bandwidth, and the computer supports concurrent writes and read-modify-write instructions [33] without incurring overheads due to contention.

Given a dynamic multithreading program whose execution is modeled as a dag A, we can bound the parallel running time $T_P(A)$ of the computation as follows. The *work* $T_1(A)$ is the number of strands in the computation dag A. The *span* $T_\infty(A)$ is the length of the longest path in A. A deterministic algorithm with work T_1 and span T_∞ can always be executed on P processors in time T_P satisfying $\max\{T_1/P, T_\infty\} \le T_P \le T_1/P + T_\infty$ [9,10,12,24,32]. The *speedup* of an algorithm on P processors is T_1/T_P, which is at most P in theory, since $T_P \ge T_\infty$. The *parallelism* T_1/T_∞ is the greatest theoretical speedup possible for any number P of processors.

Analysis of JP

To analyze the performance of JP, it is convenient to think of the algorithm as coloring the vertices in the partial order of a "priority dag," similar to the priority dag described by Blelloch *et al.* [8]. Specifically, on a vertex-weighted graph $G = (V, E, \rho)$, the priority function ρ induces a *priority dag* $G_\rho = (V, E_\rho)$, where $E_\rho = \{(u, v) \in V \times V : (u, v) \in E \text{ and } \rho(u) > \rho(v)\}$. Notice that G_ρ is a dag, because ρ is an injective function and thus induces a total order on the vertices V. We shall bound the span of JP running on a graph G in terms of the *depth* of G_ρ, that is, the length of the longest path through G_ρ. We analyze JP in two steps.

First, we bound the work and span of calls during the execution of JP to the helper routine GET-COLOR(v), which returns the minimum color not assigned to any vertex $u \in v.pred$.

LEMMA 1. *The helper routine* GET-COLOR, *shown in Figure 2, can be implemented so that during the execution of* JP *on a graph* $G = (V, E, \rho)$, *a call to* GET-COLOR(v) *for a vertex* $v \in V$ *costs* $\Theta(k)$ *work and* $\Theta(\lg k)$ *span, where* $k = |v.pred|$.

PROOF. Implement the set C in GET-COLOR as an array whose ith entry initially stores the value i. The ith element from this array can be removed by setting the ith element to ∞. With this implementation, lines 20–21 execute in $\Theta(k)$ work and $\Theta(\lg k)$ span. The min operation on line 22 can be implemented as a parallel minimum reduction in the same bounds. □

Second, we show that JP colors a graph $G = (V, E, \rho)$ using work $\Theta(V + E)$ and span linear in the depth of the priority dag G_ρ.

THEOREM 2. *Given a Δ-degree graph* $G = (V, E, \rho)$ *for some priority function* ρ, *let* G_ρ *be the priority dag induced on* G *by* ρ, *and let* L *be the depth of* G_ρ. *Then* JP(G) *runs in* $\Theta(V + E)$ *work and* $O(L \lg \Delta + \lg V)$ *span.*

PROOF. Let us first bound the work and span of JP-COLOR excluding any recursive calls. For a single call to JP-COLOR on a vertex $v \in V$, Lemma 1 shows that line 15 takes $\Theta(\deg(v))$ work and $\Theta(\lg(\deg(v)))$ span. The JOIN operation on line 17 can be implemented as an atomic decrement-and-fetch operation [33] on the specified counter. Hence, excluding the recursive call, the loop on lines 16–18 performs $\Theta(\deg(v))$ work and $\Theta(\lg(\deg(v)))$ span to decrement the counters of all successors of v.

Because JP-COLOR is called once per vertex, the total work that JP spends in calls to JP-COLOR is $\Theta(V + E)$. Furthermore, the span of JP-COLOR is the length of any path of vertices in G_ρ, which is at most L, times $\Theta(\lg \Delta)$. Finally, the loop on lines 8–11 executes in $\Theta(V + E)$ work and $\Theta(\lg V + \lg \Delta)$ span, and the parallel loop on lines 12–14, excluding the call to JP-COLOR, executes in $\Theta(V + E)$ work and $\Theta(\lg V)$ span. □

3. JP WITH RANDOM ORDERING

This section bounds the depth of a priority dag G_ρ induced on a Δ-degree graph $G = (V, E, \rho)$ by a random priority function ρ in R. We show that the expected depth of G_ρ is $O(\min\{\sqrt{E}, \Delta + \lg \Delta \lg V / \lg \lg V\})$. Combined with Theorem 2, this bound implies that the expected span of JP-R is $O(\lg V + \lg \Delta \cdot \min\{\sqrt{E}, \Delta + \lg \Delta \lg V / \lg \lg V\})$. This bound extends Jones and Plassmann's $O(\lg V / \lg \lg V)$ bound for the depth of G_ρ when $\Delta = \Theta(1)$ [35].

To bound the depth of a priority dag G_ρ induced on a graph G by $\rho \in R$, let us start by bounding the number of length-k paths in G_ρ. Each path in G_ρ corresponds to a unique *simple* path in G, that is, a path in which each vertex in G appears at most once. The following lemma bounds the number of length-k simple paths in G.

LEMMA 3. *The number of length-k simple paths in any Δ-degree graph* $G = (V, E)$ *is at most* $|V| \cdot \min\{\Delta^{k-1}, (2|E|/(k-1))^{k-1}\}$.

PROOF. Consider selecting a length-k simple path $p = \langle v_1, \ldots, v_k \rangle$ in G. There are $|V|$ choices for v_1, and for all $i \in \{1, \ldots, k-1\}$, given a choice of $\langle v_1, \ldots, v_i \rangle$, there are at most $\deg(v_i)$ choices for v_{i+1}. Hence there are at most $J = |V| \cdot \prod_{i=1}^{k-1} \deg(v_i)$ simple paths in G of length k. Let $V_k \subseteq V$ denote some set of $k-1$ vertices in V, and let $\delta = \max_{V_{k-1}} \{\sum_{v \in V_{k-1}} \deg(v)/(k-1)\}$ be the maximum average degree of any such set. Then we have $J \le |V| \cdot \delta^{k-1}$.

The proof follows from two upper bounds on δ. First, because $\deg(v) \le \Delta$ for all $v \in V$, we have $\delta \le \Delta$. Second, for all $V_{k-1} \subseteq V$, we have $\sum_{v \in V_{k-1}} \deg(v) \le \sum_{v \in V} \deg(v) = 2|E|$ by the handshaking lemma [21, p. 1172–3], and thus $\delta \le 2|E|/(k-1)$. □

Intuitively, the bound on the expected depth of G_ρ follows by arguing that although the number of simple length-k paths in a graph G might be exponential in k, for sufficiently large k, the probability is tiny that any such path is a path in G_ρ. To formalize this argument, we make use of the following technical lemma.

LEMMA 4. *Define the function* $g(\alpha, \beta)$ *for* $\alpha, \beta > 1$ *as*

$$g(\alpha, \beta) = e^2 \frac{\ln \alpha}{\ln \beta} \ln \left(e \frac{\beta \ln \alpha}{\alpha \ln \beta} \right).$$

Then for all $\beta \ge e^2$, $\alpha \ge 2$, *and* $\beta \ge \alpha$, *we have* $g(\alpha, \beta) \ge 1$.

PROOF. We consider the cases when $\alpha \ge e^2$ and when $\alpha < e^2$ separately.

When $\alpha > e^2$, the partial derivative of $g(\alpha, \beta)$ with respect to β is

$$\frac{\partial g(\alpha, \beta)}{\partial \beta} = e^2 \frac{\ln \alpha}{\beta \ln^2 \beta} \ln \left(\frac{\alpha}{e^2} \frac{\ln \beta}{\ln \alpha} \right)$$
$$\ge 0,$$

since $\alpha \ln \beta / e^2 \ln \alpha \ge 1$ when $\alpha \ge e^2$ and $\beta \ge \alpha$. Thus, $g(\alpha, \beta)$ is a nondecreasing function in its second argument when $\alpha \ge e^2$ and $\beta \ge \alpha$. Since we have

$$g(\alpha, \alpha) = e^2 (\ln \alpha / \ln \alpha) \ln(e(\alpha \ln \alpha)/(\alpha \ln \alpha))$$
$$\ge 1,$$

it follows that $g(\alpha,\beta) \geq 1$ for $\alpha \geq e^2$ and $\beta \geq \alpha$.

When $e^2 > \alpha \geq 2$, we make use of the fact that $2\beta/e\ln\beta > \sqrt{\beta}$ for all $\beta > e^2$:

$$
\begin{aligned}
g(\alpha,\beta) &\geq (e^2\ln 2/\ln\beta)\ln(2\beta/(e\ln\beta)) \\
&\geq (e^2\ln 2/\ln\beta)\ln\left(\sqrt{\beta}\right) \\
&\geq (e^2\ln 2\ln\beta)/(2\ln\beta) \\
&\geq 1 . \quad \square
\end{aligned}
$$

The following theorem applies Lemmas 3 and 4 to establish the bound on the depth of G_ρ.

THEOREM 5. *Let* $G = (V,E)$ *be a* Δ-*degree graph, let* $n = |V|$ *and* $m = |E|$, *and let* G_ρ *be a priority dag induced on* G *by a random priority function* $\rho \in R$. *For any constant* $\varepsilon > 0$ *and sufficiently large* n, *with probability at most* $n^{-\varepsilon}$, *there exists a directed path of length* $e^2 \cdot \min\{\Delta, \sqrt{m}\} + (1+\varepsilon)\min\{e^2\ln\Delta\ln n/\ln\ln n, \ln n\}$ *in* G_ρ.

PROOF. Let $p = \langle v_1,\ldots,v_k \rangle$ be a length-k simple path in G. Because ρ is a random priority function, ρ induces each possible permutation among $\{v_1,\ldots,v_k\}$ with equal probability. If p is a directed path in G_ρ, then we must have that $\rho(v_1) < \rho(v_2) < \cdots < \rho(v_k)$. Hence, p is a length-k path in G_ρ with probability at most $1/k!$. If J is the number of length-k simple paths in G, then by the union bound, the probability that a length-k directed path exists in G_ρ is at most $J/k!$, which is at most $J(e/k)^k$ by Stirling's approximation [21, p. 57].

We consider cases when $\Delta < \ln n$ and $\Delta \geq \ln n$ separately. First, suppose that $\Delta < \ln n$. By Lemma 3, the number of length-k simple paths in G is at most $n\Delta^{k-1} \leq n\Delta^k$. By the union bound, the probability that a length-k path exists in G_ρ is at most $n(e\Delta/k)^k$. We assume, without loss of generality, that $\Delta > 2$, since the theorem holds for $O(1)$-degree graphs as a result of [35].

For $\Delta \geq 2$, observe that, by Lemma 4, the function $g(\alpha,\beta) = e^2(\ln\alpha/\ln\beta)\ln(\beta\ln\alpha/\alpha\ln\beta)$ is at least 1 for all $\alpha \geq 2$ and $\beta \geq e^2$. Letting $\alpha = \Delta$, $\beta = \ln n$, and $k = e^2(\Delta + (1+\varepsilon)\ln\Delta\ln n/\ln\ln n)$, we conclude that

$$
\begin{aligned}
n(e\Delta/k)^k &= n \cdot \exp(-k\ln(k/e\Delta)) \\
&\leq n \cdot \exp\left(-e^2(1+\varepsilon)\ln n\frac{\ln\Delta}{\ln\ln n}\ln\left(e\frac{\ln n\ln\Delta}{\Delta\ln\ln n}\right)\right) \\
&= n \cdot \exp(-(1+\varepsilon)(\ln n)\cdot g(\Delta,\ln n)) \\
&\leq n e^{-(1+\varepsilon)\ln n} \\
&= n^{-\varepsilon} .
\end{aligned}
$$

Next, given $\Delta \geq \ln n$, consider the cases when $\Delta < \sqrt{m}$ and $\Delta \geq \sqrt{m}$, separately. When $\Delta < \sqrt{m}$, letting $k = e^2\Delta + (1+\varepsilon)\ln n$, the theorem follows from the facts that $k \geq (1+\varepsilon)\ln n$ and $k \geq e^2\Delta$. When $\Delta \geq \sqrt{m}$, let $k = e^2\sqrt{m} + (1+\varepsilon)\ln n$. By Lemma 3, the number of length-k simple paths is at most $n(2m/(k-1))^{k-1} \leq n(4m/k)^k$, and thus the probability that a length-k path exists in G_ρ is at most $n(4em/k^2)^k$. The theorem follows from the facts that $k \geq (1+\varepsilon)\ln n$ and $k^2 \geq e^4 m$. $\square$

COROLLARY 6. *Given a graph* $G = (V,E,\rho)$, *where* $\rho \in R$ *is a random priority function, the expected depth of the priority dag* G_ρ *is* $O(\min\{\sqrt{E}, \Delta + \lg\Delta\lg V/\lg\lg V\})$, *and thus* JP-R *colors all vertices of* G *with* $O(\lg V + \lg\Delta \cdot \min\{\sqrt{E}, \Delta + \lg\Delta\lg V/\lg\lg V\})$ *expected span.*

PROOF. Theorems 2 and 5 imply the corollary. $\square$

4. THE LF AND SL HEURISTICS

This section shows that the largest-first (LF) and smallest-last (SL) ordering heuristics can inhibit parallel speedup when used by JP. We examine a "clique-chain" graph and show that JP-LF incurs $\Omega(\Delta^2)$ span to color a Δ-degree clique-chain graph $G = (V,E)$, whereas JP-R colors G incurring only $O(\Delta\lg\Delta + \lg^2\Delta\lg V/\lg\lg V)$ expected span. We formally review the SL ordering heuristic and observe that this formulation of SL means that JP-SL requires $\Omega(V)$ span to color a path graph $G = (V,E)$.

The LF ordering heuristic

The LF ordering heuristic colors the vertices of a graph $G = (V,E,\rho)$ for some ρ in LF in order of decreasing degree. Formally, $\rho \in$ LF is defined for a vertex $v \in V$ as $\rho(v) = \langle \deg(V), \rho_R(v) \rangle$, where ρ_R is randomly chosen from R.

Although LF has been used in parallel greedy graph-coloring algorithms in the past [2, 29], Figure 4 illustrates a Δ-degree "clique-chain" graph $G = (V,E)$ for which JP-LF incurs $\Omega(\Delta^2)$ span to color, but JP-R colors with only $O(\Delta\lg\Delta + \lg^2\Delta\lg V/\lg\lg V)$ expected span. Conceptually, the ***clique-chain*** graph comprises a set of cliques of increasing size that are connected in a "chain" such that JP-LF is forced to color these cliques sequentially from largest to smallest. Figure 4 illustrates a Δ-degree clique-chain graph $G = (V,E)$, where 3 evenly divides Δ. This clique-chain graph contains a sequence of cliques $\mathcal{K} = \{K_1, K_4, \ldots, K_{\Delta-2}\}$ of increasing size, each pair of which is separated by two additional vertices forming a linear chain. Specifically, for $r \in \{1,4,\ldots,\Delta-2\}$, each vertex $u \in K_r$ is connected to each vertex $u \in K_{r+3}$ by a path $\langle u, x_{r+1}, x_{r+2}, v \rangle$ for distinct vertices $x_{r+1}, x_{r+2} \in V$. Additional vertices, shown above the chain in Figure 4, ensure that the degree of each vertex in K_r is $r+2$, and the degrees of the vertices x_{r+1} and x_{r+2} are $r+3$ and $r+4$, respectively. Clique-chain graphs of other degrees are structured similarly.

THEOREM 7. *For any* $\Delta > 0$, *there exists a* Δ-*degree graph* $G = (V,E)$ *such that* JP-LF *colors* G *in* $\Omega(\Delta^2)$ *span and* JP-R *colors* G *in* $O(\Delta\lg\Delta + \lg^2\Delta\lg V/\lg\lg V)$ *expected span.*

PROOF. Assume without loss of generality that 3 evenly divides Δ and that G is a clique-chain graph. The span of JP-R follows from Corollary 6. Because JP-LF trivially requires $\Omega(1)$ span to process each vertex in G, the span of JP-LF on G can be bounded by showing that the length of the longest path p in the priority dag G_ρ induced on G by any priority function ρ in LF is $\Delta^2/6 + \Delta/2 + 2$. Because LF assigns higher priority to higher-degree vertices, p starts at some vertex in $K_{\Delta-2}$, which has degree Δ, and passes through the $\Delta - 2$ vertices in $K_{\Delta-2}$ followed by $x_{\Delta-3}$ and $x_{\Delta-4}$.[3] The remainder of p is a longest path through the clique-chain graph G' of degree $\Delta - 3$ in the remaining graph $G - K_{\Delta-2} - \{x_{\Delta-3}, x_{\Delta-4}\}$, which has a longest path p' of length $|p'| = (\Delta-3)^2/6 + (\Delta-3)/2 + 2$ by induction. The length of p is thus $\Delta + |p'| = \Delta^2/6 + \Delta/2 + 2$. $\square$

The SL ordering heuristic

We focus on the formulation of the SL ordering heuristic due to Allwright *et al.* [2], because our experiments indicate that it gives colorings using fewer colors than other formulations [45].

Given a graph $G = (V,E)$, the SL ordering heuristic produces a priority function ρ via an iterative algorithm that assigns priorities to the vertices V in rounds to induce an ordering on V. For $i \geq 0$, let $G_i = (V_i, E_i)$ denote the subgraph of G remaining at the start of round i, and let δ_i denote an upper bound on the

---

[3]Notice that it does not matter how ties are broken in the priority function.

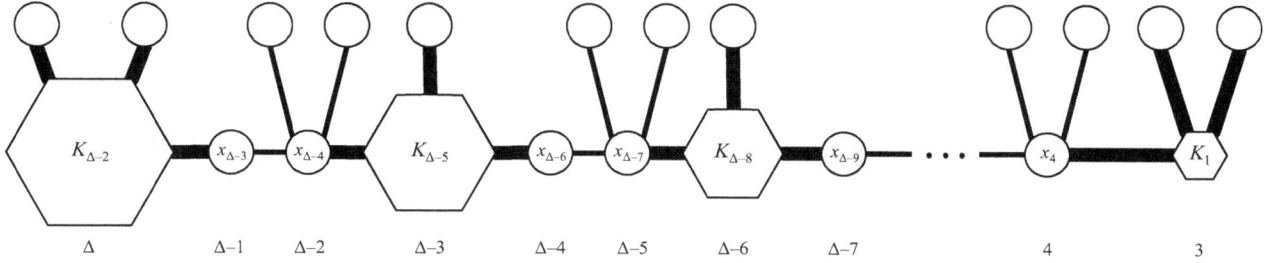

Figure 4: A Δ-degree clique-chain graph G, which Theorem 7 shows is adversarial for JP-LF. This graph contains $\Theta(\Delta^2)$ vertices arranged as a chain of cliques. Each hexagon labeled K_r represents a clique of r vertices, and circles represent individual vertices. A thick edge between an individual vertex and a clique indicates that the vertex is connected to every vertex within the clique. A label below an individual vertex indicates the degree of the associated vertex, and a label below a clique indicates the degree of every vertex within that clique.

smallest degree of any vertex $v \in V_i$. Assume that $\delta_0 = 1$. At the start of round i, remove all vertices $v \in V_i$ such that $\deg(v) \leq \max\{\delta_{i-1}, \min_{v \in V_i}\{\deg(v)\}\}$. For a vertex v removed in round i, a priority function $\rho \in \text{SL}$ is defined as $\rho(v) = \langle i, \rho_\text{R}(v)\rangle$ where $\rho_\text{R} \in \text{R}$ is a random priority function.

The following theorem shows that there exist graphs for which JP-SL incurs a large span, whereas JP-R incurs only a small span.

THEOREM 8. *There exists a class of graphs such that for any $G = (V, E, \rho)$ in the class and for any priority function $\rho \in \text{SL}$, JP-SL incurs $\Omega(V)$ span and JP-R incurs $O(\lg V / \lg\lg V)$ span.*

PROOF. Consider the algorithm to compute the priority function ρ for all vertices in a path graph G. By induction over the rounds, the graph G_i at the start of round i is a path with $|V| - 2i + 2$ vertices, and in round i the 2 vertices at the endpoints of G_i will be removed. Hence $\lceil |V|/2 \rceil$ rounds are required to assign priorities for all vertices in G. A similar argument shows that the resulting priority dag G_ρ contains a path of length $|V|/2$ along which the priorities strictly decrease. JP-SL trivially incurs $\Omega(1)$ span through each vertex in the longest path in G_ρ. Since there are $\Theta(V)$ total vertices along the path and by Corollary 6 with $\Delta = \Theta(1)$, the theorem follows. □

We shall see in Section 5 that it is possible to achieve coloring quality comparable to LF and SL, but with guaranteed parallel performance comparable to JP-R.

5. LOG ORDERING HEURISTICS

This section describes the largest-log-degree-first (LLF) and smallest-log-degree-last (SLL) ordering heuristics. Given a Δ-degree graph G, we show that the expected depth of the priority dag G_ρ induced on G by a priority function $\rho \in \text{LLF}$ is $O(\min\{\Delta, \sqrt{E}\} + \lg^2 \Delta \lg V / \lg\lg V)$. The same bound applies to the depth of a priority dag G_ρ induced on a graph G by a priority function $\rho \in \text{SLL}$, though $O(\lg\Delta\lg V)$ additional span is required to calculate ρ using the method given in Figure 5. Combined with Theorem 2, these bounds imply that the expected span of JP-LLF is $O(\lg V + \lg\Delta(\min\{\Delta, \sqrt{E}\} + \lg^2\Delta\lg V / \lg\lg V))$ and the expected span of JP-SLL is $O(\lg\Delta\lg V + \lg\Delta(\min\{\Delta, \sqrt{E}\} + \lg^2\Delta\lg V / \lg\lg V))$.

The LLF ordering heuristic

The **LLF *ordering heuristic*** orders the vertices in decreasing order by the logarithm of their degree. More precisely, given a graph $G = (V, E, \rho)$ for some $\rho \in \text{LLF}$, the priority of each $v \in V$ is equal to $\rho(v) = \langle \lceil \lg(\deg(v)) \rceil, \rho_\text{R}(v)\rangle$, where $\rho_\text{R} \in \text{R}$ is a random priority

function and $\lg x$ denotes $\log_2 x$. [4] For a given graph G, the following theorem bounds the depth of the priority dag G_ρ induced by $\rho \in \text{LLF}$.

THEOREM 9. *Let $G = (V, E)$ be a Δ-degree graph, and let G_ρ be the priority dag induced on G by a priority function $\rho \in \text{LLF}$. The expected length of the longest directed path in G_ρ is $O(\min\{\Delta, \sqrt{E}\} + \lg^2\Delta\lg V / \lg\lg V)$.*

PROOF. Consider a length-k path $p = \langle v_1, \ldots, v_k \rangle$ in G_ρ. Let $G(\ell) \subseteq G_\rho$ be the subdag of G_ρ induced by those vertices $v \in V$ for which $\rho(v) = \lceil \lg(\deg(v)) \rceil = \ell$. Suppose that $v_i \in G(\ell)$ for some $v_i \in p$. Since $\lceil \lg(\deg(v_{i-1})) \rceil \geq \lceil \lg(\deg(v_i)) \rceil$ for all $i > 1$, we have $v_{i-1} \in G(\ell')$ for some $\ell' \geq \ell$. We can therefore decompose p into a sequence of paths $p = \langle p_{\lceil\lg\Delta\rceil}, \ldots, p_0 \rangle$ such that each subpath $p_\ell \in p$ is a path through $G(\ell)$. By definition of LLF, the subdag $G(\ell)$ is a dag induced on a graph with degree 2^ℓ by a random priority function.

By Corollary 6, the expected length of p_ℓ is $O(2^\ell + \ell \lg V / \lg\lg V)$. Linearity of expectation therefore implies that

$$\text{E}[|p|] = \sum_{\ell=0}^{\lceil\lg\Delta\rceil} O\left(2^\ell + \ell \lg V / \lg\lg V\right)$$
$$= O\left(\Delta + \lg^2\Delta\lg V / \lg\lg V\right).$$

To establish the $\sqrt{E}$ bound, observe that at most $E/2^\ell$ vertices have degree at least 2^ℓ. Consequently, for $\ell > \lg\sqrt{E}$, the depth of $G(\ell)$ can be at most $E/2^\ell$. Hence we have

$$\text{E}[|p|] \leq \sum_{\ell=0}^{\lceil\lg\sqrt{E}\rceil} O\left(2^\ell\right) + \sum_{\ell=\lceil\lg\sqrt{E}\rceil}^{\infty} E/2^\ell$$
$$+ \sum_{\ell=0}^{\lceil\lg\Delta\rceil} O(\ell\lg V / \lg\lg V)$$
$$= O\left(\sqrt{E} + \lg^2\Delta\lg V / \lg\lg V\right). \quad \square$$

COROLLARY 10. *Given a graph $G = (V, E, \rho)$ for some $\rho \in \text{LLF}$, JP-LLF colors all vertices in G with expected span $O(\lg V + \lg\Delta(\min\{\sqrt{E}, \Delta\} + \lg^2\Delta\lg V / \lg\lg V))$.* □

---

[4] The theoretical results in this section assume only that the base b of the logarithm is a constant. In practice, however, it is possible that the choice of b could have impact on the coloring quality or runtime of JP-LLF. We studied this trade-off and found that there is only a minor dependence on b. In general, the coloring quality and runtime of JP-LLF smoothly transitions from the behavior of JP-LF for small b and the behavior of JP-R for large b, sweeping out a Pareto-efficient frontier of reasonable choices. We chose $b = 2$ for our experiments, because $\log_2 x$ can be calculated conveniently by native instructions on modern architectures.

SLL-ASSIGN-PRIORITIES(G, r)

```
23   let G = (V, E)
24   i = 1
25   U = V
26   let Δ be the degree of G
27   let ρ_R ∈ R be a random priority function
28   for d = 0 to lg Δ
29       for j = 1 to r
30           Q = {u ∈ U : |u.adj ∩ U| ≤ 2^d}
31           parallel for v ∈ Q
32               ρ(v) = ⟨i, ρ_R(v)⟩
33           U = U − Q
34           i = i + 1
35   return ρ
```

Figure 5: Pseudocode for SLL-ASSIGN-PRIORITIES, which computes a priority function $\rho \in$ SLL for the input graph. The input parameter r denotes the maximum number of times SLL-ASSIGN-PRIORITIES is permitted to remove vertices of at most a particular degree 2^d on lines 29–34.

PROOF. The corollary follows from Theorem 2. □

The SLL ordering heuristic

To understand the **SLL *ordering heuristic***, it is convenient to consider in isolation how to compute its priority function. The pseudocode in Figure 5 for SLL-ASSIGN-PRIORITIES describes algorithmically how to perform this computation on a given graph $G = (V, E)$. As Figure 5 shows, a priority function $\rho \in$ SLL can be computed by iteratively removing low-degree vertices from G in rounds. The priority of a vertex $v \in V$ is the round number in which v is removed, with ties broken randomly. As with SL, SLL colors the vertices of G in the reverse order in which they are removed, but SLL-ASSIGN-PRIORITIES determines when to remove a vertex using a degree bound that grows exponentially. SLL-ASSIGN-PRIORITIES considers each degree bound for a maximum of r rounds. Effectively, a vertex is removed from G based on the logarithm of its degree in the remaining graph.

We can formalize the behavior of SLL as follows. Given a graph G, let $G_i = (V_i, E_i)$ denote the subgraph of G remaining at the start of round i. As Figure 5 shows, for each $d \in \{0, 1, \ldots, \lg \Delta\}$, SLL-ASSIGN-PRIORITIES executes r rounds in which it removes vertices $v \in V_i$ such that $\deg(v) \leq 2^d$ in G_i.[5]

For a given graph G, the following theorem bounds the depth of the priority dag G_ρ induced by a priority function $\rho \in$ SLL.

THEOREM 11. *Let $G = (V, E)$ be a Δ-degree graph, and let G_ρ be the priority dag induced on G by a random priority function $\rho \in$ SLL. The expected length of the longest directed path in G_ρ is $O(\min\{\Delta, \sqrt{E}\} + \lg^2 \Delta \lg V / \lg \lg V)$.*

PROOF. We begin with an argument similar to the proof of Theorem 9. Let $p = \langle v_1, \ldots, v_k \rangle$ be a length-k path in G_ρ, and let $G(\ell) \subseteq G_\rho$ be the subdag of G_ρ induced by those vertices $v \in V$, where $\rho(v) = \ell$. Since lines 29–34 of SLL-ASSIGN-PRIORITIES remove vertices with degree at most 2^d exactly r times for each $d \in [0, \ldots, \lg \Delta]$, we have that $\lfloor \rho(v) / r \rfloor = d$, and thus the degree of $G(\ell)$ is at most $2^{\lfloor \ell / r \rfloor}$. Suppose that $v_i \in G(\ell)$ for some $v_i \in p$. Since $\rho(v_{i-1}) \leq \rho(v_i)$ for all $i > 1$, we have $v_{i-1} \in G(\ell')$ for some $\ell' \geq \ell$. We can therefore decompose p into a sequence of paths

---

[5] As with LLF, the degree cutoff 2^d on line 30 of Figure 5 could be b^d for an arbitrary constant base b with no harm to the theoretical results. We explored the choice of base empirically, but found that there was only a minor dependence on b. Generally, JP-SLL smoothly transitions from the behavior of JP-SL for small b to the behavior of JP-R and for large b. We therefore chose $b = 2$ for our experiments because of its implementation simplicity.

$p = \langle p_{\lceil r \lg \Delta \rceil}, \ldots, p_0 \rangle$ where each $p_\ell \in p$ is a path in $G(\ell)$. By definition of SLL, the subdag $G(\ell)$ is a dag induced on a subgraph with degree at most $2^{\lfloor \ell / r \rfloor}$ by a random priority function.

By Corollary 6, the expected length of p_ℓ is $O(2^{\lfloor \ell / r \rfloor} + \lfloor \ell / r \rfloor \lg V / \lg \lg V)$. Linearity of expectation therefore implies that

$$E[|p|] = \sum_{\ell=0}^{\lceil r \lg \Delta \rceil} O\left(2^{\lfloor \ell / r \rfloor} + \lfloor \ell / r \rfloor \lg V / \lg \lg V\right)$$
$$= O\left(\Delta + \lg^2 \Delta \lg V / \lg \lg V\right).$$

Next, because at most $E / 2^{\lfloor \ell / r \rfloor}$ vertices can have degree at least $2^{\lfloor \ell / r \rfloor}$, we have for $\ell > r \lg \sqrt{E}$ that the longest path through the subdag $G(\ell)$ is no longer than $E / 2^{\lfloor \ell / r \rfloor}$. We thus conclude that

$$E[|p|] \leq \sum_{\ell=0}^{\lceil r \lg \sqrt{E} \rceil} O\left(2^{\lfloor \ell / r \rfloor}\right) + \sum_{\ell=\lceil r \lg \sqrt{E} \rceil}^{\infty} E / 2^{\lfloor \ell / r \rfloor}$$
$$+ \sum_{\ell=0}^{\lceil r \lg \Delta \rceil} O(\lfloor \ell / r \rfloor \lg V / \lg \lg V)$$
$$= O\left(\sqrt{E} + \lg^2 \Delta \lg V / \lg \lg V\right). \quad \square$$

COROLLARY 12. *Given a graph $G = (V, E, \rho)$ for some $\rho \in$ SLL, JP-SLL colors all vertices in G with expected span $O(\lg \Delta \lg V + \lg \Delta (\min\{\sqrt{E}, \Delta\} + \lg^2 \Delta \lg V / \lg \lg V))$.*

PROOF. The procedure SLL-ASSIGN-PRIORITIES calls the parallel loop on line 31 $O(\lg \Delta)$ times, each of which has expected span $O(\lg V)$. The proof then follows from Theorems 2 and 11. □

6. EMPIRICAL EVALUATION

This section evaluates the LLF and SLL ordering heuristics empirically using a suite of eight real-world and ten synthetic graphs. We describe the experimental setup used to evaluate JP-R, JP-LLF, and JP-SLL, and we compare their performance with GREEDY-FF, GREEDY-LF, and GREEDY-SL. We compare the ordering heuristics in terms of the quality of the colorings they produce and their execution times. We conclude that LLF and SLL produce colorings with quality comparable to LF and SL, respectively, and that JP-LLF and JP-SLL scale well. We also show that the engineering quality of our implementations appears to be competitive with COLPACK [28], a publicly available graph-coloring library. Our source code and data are available from http://supertech.csail.mit.edu.

Experimental setup

To evaluate the ordering heuristics, we implemented JP using Intel Cilk Plus [34] and engineered it to use the parallel ordering heuristics R, LLF, and SLL. To compare these parallel codes against their serial counterparts, we implemented GREEDY in C to use the FF, LF, or SL ordering heuristics. In order to empirically evaluate the potential parallel performance of the serial ordering heuristics, we also engineered JP to use FF, LF, or SL. We evaluated our implementations on a dual-socket Intel Xeon X5650 with a total of 12 processor cores operating at 2.67-GHz (hyperthreading disabled); 49 GB of DRAM; 2 12-MB L3-caches, each shared between 6 cores; and private L2- and L1-caches with 128 KB and 32 KB, respectively. Each measurement was taken as the median of 7 independent trials, and the averages of those measurements reported in Figure 7 were taken across 5 independent random seeds.

			GREEDY	JP						JP			
Graph	H	C_H	T_S	T_1	T_{12}	T_S/T_1	T_1/T_{12}	H'	$C_{H'}$	T_1	T_{12}	T_S/T_1	T_1/T_{12}
com-orkut	FF	175	2.23	4.16	0.817	0.54	5.09	R	132	4.44	0.817	0.50	5.43
$\|E\| = 117.2M$	LF	87	3.54	6.43	1.067	0.55	6.02	LLF	98	5.74	0.846	0.62	6.79
$\|E\|/\|V\| = 38.1$ $\Delta = 33{,}313$	SL	83	10.59	12.94	8.264	0.82	1.57	SLL	84	9.90	1.865	1.07	5.31
soc-LiveJournal1	FF	352	0.89	1.69	0.275	0.52	6.15	R	330	2.08	0.231	0.43	8.98
$\|E\| = 42.9M$	LF	323	2.34	2.89	0.365	0.81	7.91	LLF	326	2.23	0.286	1.05	7.80
$\|E\|/\|V\| = 8.8$ $\Delta = 20{,}333$	SL	322	4.69	4.76	2.799	0.98	1.70	SLL	327	4.03	0.704	1.16	5.73
europe-osm	FF	5	1.32	∞	∞	∞	∞	R	5	4.04	0.391	0.33	10.34
$\|E\| = 36.0M$	LF	4	17.15	5.16	0.587	3.33	8.79	LLF	4	4.93	0.473	3.48	10.41
$\|E\|/\|V\| = 0.7$ $\Delta = 9$	SL	3	19.87	∞	∞	∞	∞	SLL	3	7.28	1.232	2.73	5.91
cit-Patents	FF	17	0.50	0.99	0.152	0.50	6.47	R	21	1.08	0.163	0.46	6.67
$\|E\| = 16.5M$	LF	14	2.00	1.52	0.211	1.31	7.22	LLF	14	1.46	0.160	1.37	9.11
$\|E\|/\|V\| = 2.7$ $\Delta = 793$	SL	13	3.21	3.05	1.579	1.05	1.93	SLL	14	2.90	0.519	1.11	5.58
as-skitter	FF	103	0.24	0.55	0.109	0.45	5.00	R	81	0.58	0.114	0.42	5.07
$\|E\| = 11.1M$	LF	71	2.43	0.69	0.133	3.51	5.21	LLF	72	0.63	0.106	3.84	5.99
$\|E\|/\|V\| = 1.0$ $\Delta = 35{,}455$	SL	70	2.79	1.19	0.733	2.35	1.62	SLL	71	1.04	0.269	2.67	3.88
wiki-Talk	FF	102	0.09	0.23	0.046	0.38	4.99	R	85	0.28	0.053	0.31	5.28
$\|E\| = 4.7M$	LF	72	0.49	0.37	0.073	1.30	5.12	LLF	70	0.34	0.050	1.43	6.78
$\|E\|/\|V\| = 1.9$ $\Delta = 100{,}029$	SL	56	0.61	0.57	0.293	1.08	1.93	SLL	62	0.55	0.124	1.12	4.43
web-Google	FF	44	0.09	0.20	0.036	0.47	5.62	R	44	0.21	0.029	0.44	7.44
$\|E\| = 4.3M$	LF	45	0.25	0.29	0.042	0.88	6.85	LLF	44	0.27	0.030	0.94	8.92
$\|E\|/\|V\| = 4.7$ $\Delta = 6{,}332$	SL	44	0.47	0.53	0.278	0.89	1.92	SLL	44	0.50	0.093	0.94	5.44
com-youtube	FF	57	0.06	0.16	0.027	0.39	6.07	R	46	0.18	0.026	0.36	6.86
$\|E\| = 3.0M$	LF	32	0.25	0.24	0.040	1.03	6.12	LLF	33	0.22	0.028	1.11	7.97
$\|E\|/\|V\| = 2.6$ $\Delta = 28{,}754$	SL	28	0.35	0.36	0.181	0.98	1.99	SLL	28	0.35	0.073	1.01	4.75
constant1M-50	FF	33	0.90	1.70	0.230	0.53	7.40	R	32	1.93	0.255	0.47	7.55
$\|E\| = 50.0M$	LF	32	1.16	2.96	0.386	0.39	7.68	LLF	32	2.70	0.323	0.43	8.35
$\|E\|/\|V\| = 50.0$ $\Delta = 100$	SL	34	2.96	5.09	2.023	0.58	2.52	SLL	32	4.63	0.610	0.64	7.59
constant500K-100	FF	52	0.74	1.26	0.286	0.59	4.42	R	52	1.50	0.190	0.49	7.89
$\|E\| = 50.0M$	LF	52	0.84	2.55	0.444	0.33	5.73	LLF	52	2.01	0.273	0.42	7.34
$\|E\|/\|V\| = 99.9$ $\Delta = 200$	SL	53	1.97	3.50	1.435	0.56	2.44	SLL	52	3.33	0.498	0.59	6.69
graph500-5M	FF	220	1.83	2.86	0.560	0.64	5.11	R	220	2.99	0.558	0.61	5.35
$\|E\| = 49.1M$	LF	159	3.69	3.99	0.649	0.92	6.15	LLF	160	3.74	0.542	0.99	6.89
$\|E\|/\|V\| = 5.9$ $\Delta = 121{,}495$	SL	158	8.43	9.45	5.576	0.89	1.69	SLL	162	7.63	1.056	1.10	7.23
graph500-2M	FF	206	0.52	0.98	0.208	0.53	4.72	R	208	1.01	0.212	0.51	4.77
$\|E\| = 19.2M$	LF	153	0.98	1.34	0.221	0.73	6.06	LLF	154	1.24	0.151	0.79	8.19
$\|E\|/\|V\| = 9.2$ $\Delta = 70{,}718$	SL	153	2.22	2.72	1.559	0.81	1.75	SLL	156	2.25	0.324	0.99	6.94
rMat-ER-2M	FF	12	0.47	1.11	0.169	0.42	6.60	R	12	1.25	0.149	0.37	8.40
$\|E\| = 20.0M$	LF	11	1.07	1.72	0.204	0.62	8.45	LLF	12	1.63	0.198	0.66	8.25
$\|E\|/\|V\| = 9.5$ $\Delta = 44$	SL	11	2.22	3.07	1.362	0.72	2.25	SLL	11	3.13	0.506	0.71	6.18
rMat-G-2M	FF	27	0.48	0.88	0.130	0.55	6.74	R	27	0.91	0.144	0.53	6.33
$\|E\| = 20.0M$	LF	15	1.18	1.42	0.200	0.83	7.09	LLF	17	1.34	0.204	0.88	6.54
$\|E\|/\|V\| = 9.5$ $\Delta = 938$	SL	15	2.59	3.09	1.712	0.84	1.81	SLL	15	2.75	0.432	0.94	6.36
rMat-B-2M	FF	105	0.50	0.84	0.151	0.60	5.53	R	105	0.86	0.149	0.58	5.78
$\|E\| = 19.8M$	LF	67	1.00	1.28	0.191	0.79	6.68	LLF	68	1.18	0.149	0.85	7.94
$\|E\|/\|V\| = 9.4$ $\Delta = 14{,}868$	SL	67	2.41	2.84	1.691	0.85	1.68	SLL	68	2.38	0.376	1.01	6.31
big3dgrid	FF	4	0.41	1.68	0.173	0.24	9.69	R	7	1.66	0.178	0.25	9.31
$\|E\| = 29.8M$	LF	7	4.07	1.53	0.198	2.66	7.72	LLF	7	1.89	0.216	2.15	8.76
$\|E\|/\|V\| = 3.0$ $\Delta = 6$	SL	7	4.77	2.60	1.074	1.83	2.42	SLL	7	2.63	0.307	1.81	8.57
clique-chain-400	FF	399	0.05	0.09	0.224	0.51	0.40	R	399	0.09	0.012	0.50	7.77
$\|E\| = 3.6M$	LF	399	0.05	∞	∞	∞	∞	LLF	399	0.12	0.015	0.41	7.70
$\|E\|/\|V\| = 132.4$ $\Delta = 400$	SL	399	0.08	0.14	0.265	0.55	0.54	SLL	399	0.16	0.024	0.47	6.70
path-10M	FF	2	0.18	∞	∞	∞	∞	R	3	0.85	0.074	0.21	11.54
$\|E\| = 10.0M$	LF	3	2.49	0.76	0.092	3.26	8.27	LLF	3	0.98	0.083	2.54	11.87
$\|E\|/\|V\| = 1.0$ $\Delta = 2$	SL	2	2.58	∞	∞	∞	∞	SLL	3	1.36	0.169	1.90	8.04

Figure 7: Performance measurements for a set of real-world graphs taken from Stanford's SNAP project [40] are included above the center line. Five classes of synthetically generated graph are included below the center line: constant degree, rMat, 3D grid, clique chain and path. The column heading H denotes that the priority function used for the experiment in a particular row was produced by the ordering heuristic listed in the column. The average number of colors used by the corresponding ordering heuristic and graph is C_H. The time in seconds of GREEDY, JP with 1 worker and with 12 workers is given by T_S, T_1 and T_{12}, respectively, where a value of ∞ indicates that the program crashed due to excessive stack usage. Details of the experimental setup and graph suite can be found in Section 6.

Graph	$|V|$	a	b	c	d
graph500-5M	5M	0.57	0.19	0.19	0.05
graph500-2M	2M	0.57	0.19	0.19	0.05
rMat-ER-2M	2M	0.25	0.25	0.25	0.25
rMat-G-2M	2M	0.45	0.15	0.15	0.25
rMat-B-2M	2M	0.55	0.15	0.15	0.15

Figure 6: Parameters for the generation of rMat graphs [17], where $a + b + c + d = 1$ and $b = c$, when the desired graph is undirected. An rMat graph is built by adding $|E|$ edges independently at random using the following rule: Let k be the number of 1's in a binary representation of i. As each edge is added, the probability that the ith vertex v_i is selected as an endpoint is $(a+c)^k(b+d)^{\lg n-k}$.

These implementations were run on a suite of eight real-world graphs and ten synthetic graphs. The real-world graphs came from the Large Network Dataset Collection provided by Stanford's SNAP project [40]. The synthetic graphs consist of the adversarial graphs described in Section 4 and a set of graphs from three classes: constant degree, 3D grid, and "recursive matrix" (rMat) [14, 17]. The adversarial graphs — clique-chain-400 and path-10M — are described in Figure 4 with $\Delta = 400$ and Theorem 8 with $|V| = 10,000,000$, respectively. The constant-degree graphs — constant1M-50 and constant500K-100 — have 1M and 500K vertices and constant degrees of 100 and 200, respectively. These graphs were generated such that every pair of vertices is equally likely to be connected and every vertex has the same degree. The graph big3dgrid is a 3-dimensional grid on 10M vertices. The rMat graphs were generated using the parameters in Figure 6.

Coloring quality of R, LLF, and SLL

Figure 7 presents the coloring quality of the three parallel ordering heuristics R, LLF, and SLL alongside that of their serial counterparts FF, LF, and SL.

The number of colors used by LLF was comparable to that used by LF on the vast majority of the 18 graphs. Indeed, LLF produced colorings that were within 2 colors of LF on all synthetic graphs and all but 2 real-world graphs: com-orkut and soc-LiveJournal. Similarly, SLL produced colorings that were within 3 colors of SL for all synthetic graphs and all but 2 real-world graphs: soc-LiveJournal and wiki-Talk.

The soc-LiveJournal graph appears to benefit little from the ordering heuristics we considered. Every heuristic uses more than 300 colors, and the biggest difference between the number of colors used by any heuristic is less than 10.

The wiki-Talk and com-orkut graphs appear to benefit from ordering heuristics and illustrate what we believe is a coarse hierarchy of coloring quality in which FF < R < LLF < LF < SLL < SL. On com-orkut, LLF produced a coloring of size 98, which was better than the 175 and 132 colors used by FF and R, respectively, but not as good as the 87 colors used by LF. In contrast, SLL nearly matched the superior coloring quality of SL, producing a coloring of size 84. On wiki-Talk, SLL produced a coloring of size 62, which was better than LF, LLF, R, and FF by a margin of between 8 to 40 colors, but not as good as SL, which used only 56 colors. These trends appear to exist, in general, for most of the graphs in the suite.

Scalability of JP-R, JP-LLF, and JP-SLL

The parallel performance of JP was measured by computing the speedup it achieved on 12 cores and by comparing the 1-core runtimes of JP to an optimized serial implementation of GREEDY. These results are summarized in Figure 7.

Overall, JP-LLF obtains a geometric-mean speedup — the ratio of the runtime on 1 core to the runtime on 12 cores — of 7.83 on the eight real-world graphs and 8.08 on the ten synthetic graphs.

Similarly, JP-SLL obtains a geometric-mean speedup of 5.36 and 7.02 on the real-world and synthetic graphs, respectively.

Figure 7 also includes scalability data for JP-FF, JP-LF, and JP-SL. Historically, JP-LF has been used with mixed success in practical parallel settings [2, 29, 35, 49]. Despite the fact that it offers little in terms of theoretical parallel performance guarantees, we have measured its parallel performance for our graph suite, and indeed JP-LF scales reasonably well: $\text{JP-LF}_1/\text{JP-LF}_{12} = 6.8$ as compared to $\text{JP-LLF}_1/\text{JP-LLF}_{12} = 8.0$ in geometric mean, not including clique-chain-400, which is omitted since JP-LF crashes due to excessive stack usage on clique-chain-400. The omission of clique-chain-400 highlights the dangers of using algorithms without good performance guarantees: it is difficult to know if the algorithm will behave badly given any particular input. In this respect, JP-FF is particularly vulnerable to adversarial inputs, as we can see by the fact that it crashes on europe-osm, which is not even intentionally adversarial. We also see this vulnerability with JP-SL, as well as generally poor scalability on the entire suite.

To measure the overheads introduced by using a parallel algorithm, the runtime T_1 of JP on 1 core was compared with the runtime T_S of an optimized implementation of GREEDY. This comparison was performed for each of the three parallel ordering heuristics we considered: R, LLF, and SLL. The serial runtime of GREEDY using FF is 2.5 times faster than JP-R on 1 core for the eight real-world graphs and 2.3 times faster on the ten synthetic graphs. We conjecture that GREEDY gains its advantage due to the spatial-locality advantage that results from processing the vertices in the linear order they appear in the graph representation. JP-LLF and JP-SLL on 1 core, however, are actually faster than GREEDY with LF and SL by 43.3% and 19% on the eight real-world graphs and 6% and 3% on the whole suite, respectively.

In order to validate that our implementation of GREEDY is a credible baseline, we compared it with a publicly available graph-coloring library, COLPACK [28], developed by Gebremedhin et al. and found that the two implementations appeared to achieve similar performance. For example, using the SL ordering heuristic, GREEDY is 19% faster than COLPACK in geometric-mean across the graph suite, though GREEDY is slower on 5 of the 16 graphs and as much 2.22 times slower for as-skitter.

7. IMPLEMENTATION TECHNIQUES

This section describes the techniques we employed to implement JP and GREEDY for the evaluation in Section 6. We describe three techniques — join-trees [23], bit-vectors, and software prefetching — that improve the practical performance of JP. Where applicable, these same techniques were used to optimize the implementation of GREEDY. Overall, applying these techniques yielded a speedup of between 1.6 and 2.9 for JP and a speedup of between 1.2 and 1.6 for GREEDY on the rMat-G-2M, rMat-B-2M, web-Google, and as-skitter graphs used in Section 6.

Join trees for reducing memory contention

Although the theoretical analysis of JP in Section 2 does not concern itself with contention, the implementation of JP works to mitigate overheads due to contention. The pseudocode for JP in Figure 2 shows that each vertex u in the graph has an associated counter $u.counter$. Line 17 of JP-COLOR executes a JOIN operation on $u.counter$. Although Section 2 describes how JOIN can treat $u.counter$ as a join counter [20] and update $u.counter$ using an atomic decrement and fetch operation, the cache-coherence protocol [47] on the machine serializes such atomic operations, giving rise to potential memory contention. In particular, memory con-

```
GREEDY-SD(G)
36    let G = (V, E)
37    for v ∈ V
38        v.adjColors = ∅
39        v.adjUncolored = v.adj
40        PUSHORADDKEY(v, Q[0][|v.adjUncolored|])
41    s = 0
42    while s ≥ 0
43        v = POPORDELKEY(Q[s][max KEYS(Q[s])])
44        v.color = min({1, 2, . . . , |v.adjUncolored| + 1} − v.adjColors)
45        for u ∈ v.adjUncolored
46            REMOVEORDELKEY(u, Q[|u.adjColors|][|u.adjUncolored|])
47            u.adjColors = u.adjColors ∪ {v.color}
48            u.adjUncolored = u.adjUncolored − {v}
49            PUSHORADDKEY(u, Q[|u.adjColors|][|u.adjUncolored|])
50            s = max{s, |u.adjColors|}
51        while s ≥ 0 and Q[s] == ∅
52            s = s − 1
```

Figure 8: The GREEDY-SD algorithm computes a coloring for the input graph $G = (V, E)$ using the SD heuristic. Each uncolored vertex $v \in V$ maintains a set *v.adjColors* of colors used by its neighbors and a set *v.adjUncolored* of uncolored neighbors of v. The PUSHORADDKEY method adds a specified key, if necessary, and then adds an element to that key's associated set. The POPORDELKEY and REMOVEORDELKEY methods remove an element from a specified key's associated set, deleting that key if the set becomes empty. The variable s maintains the maximum saturation degree of G.

tention may harm the practical performance of JP on graphs with large-degree vertices.

Our implementation of JP mitigates overheads due to contention by replacing each join counter *u.counter* with a join tree having $\Theta(|u.pred|)$ leaves. In particular, each join tree was sized such that an average of 64 predecessors of u map to each leaf through a hash function that maps predecessors to random leaves. We found that the join tree reduces T_1 for JP by a factor of 1.15 and reduces T_{12} for JP by between 1.1 and 1.3.

Bit vectors for assigning colors

To color vertices more efficiently, the implementation of JP uses vertex-local bit vectors to store information about the availability of low-numbered colors. Because JP assigns to each vertex the lowest-numbered available color, vertices tend to be colored with low-numbered colors. To take advantage of this observation, we store a 64-bit word per vertex u to track the colors in the range $\{1, 2, . . . , 64\}$ that have already been assigned to a neighbor of u. The bit vector on *u.vec* is computed as a "self-timed" OR reduction that occurs during updates on u's join tree. Effectively, as each predecessor v of u executes JOIN on u's join tree, if *v.color* is in $\{1, 2, . . . , 64\}$, then v OR's the word $2^{v.color-1}$ into *u.vec*. When GET-COLOR(u) subsequently executes, GET-COLOR first scans for the lowest unset bit in *u.vec* to find the minimum color in $\{1, 2, . . . , 64\}$ not assigned to a neighbor of u. Only when no such color is available does GET-COLOR(u) scan its predecessors to assign a color to u.

We discovered that a large fraction of vertices in a graph can be colored efficiently using this practical optimization. We found that this optimization improved T_{12} for JP by a factor of 1.4 to 2.2, and a similar optimization sped up the implementation of GREEDY by a factor of 1.2 to 1.6.

Software prefetching

We used software prefetching to improve the latency of memory accesses in JP. In particular, JP uses software prefetching to mitigate the latency of the indirect memory access encountered when accessing the join trees of the successors of a vertex v on line 16 of

JP-COLOR in Figure 2. This optimization improves T_{12} for JP by a factor of 1.2 to 1.5.

Interestingly, our implementation of GREEDY did not appear to benefit from using software prefetching in a similar context, specifically, to access the predecessors of a vertex on line 4 of GREEDY in Figure 1. We suspect that because GREEDY only reads the predecessors of a vertex on this line and does not write them, the processor hardware is able to generate many such reads in parallel, thereby mitigating the latency penalty introduced by cache misses.

8. THE SD HEURISTIC

Our experiments with serial heuristics detailed in the Appendix (Section 12) indicate that the SD heuristic tends to provide colorings with higher quality than the other heuristics we have considered, confirming similar findings by Gebremedhin and Manne [27]. Although we leave the problem of devising a good parallel algorithm for SD as an open question, we were able to devise a linear-time serial algorithm for the problem, despite conjectures in the literature [19, 29] that superlinear time is required. This section briefly describes our linear-time serial algorithm for SD.

Figure 8 gives pseudocode for the GREEDY-SD algorithm, which implements the SD heuristic. Rather than trying to define a priority function for SD, the figure gives the coloring algorithm GREEDY-SD itself, since the calculation of such a priority function would color the graph as a byproduct. At any moment during the execution of the algorithm, the **saturation degree** of a vertex v as the number $|v.adjColors|$ of distinct colors of v's neighbors, and the **effective degree** of v as $|v.adjUncolored|$, its degree in the as yet uncolored graph.

The main loop of GREEDY-SD (lines 42–52) first removes a vertex v of maximum saturation degree from Q (line 43) and colors it (line 44). It then updates each uncolored neighbor $u \in v.adjUncolored$ of v (lines 45–50) in three steps. First, it removes u from Q (line 46). Next, it updates the set *u.adjUncolored* of u's **effective neighbors** — u's uncolored neighbors in G — and the set *u.adjColors* of colors used by u's neighbors (lines 47–48). Finally, it enqueues u in Q based on u's updated information (lines 49–50).

The crux of GREEDY-SD lies in the operation of the queue data structure Q, which is organized as an array of **saturation tables**, each of which supports the three methods PUSHORADDKEY, POPORDELKEY, and REMOVEORDELKEY described in the caption of Figure 8. A saturation table can support these operations in $\Theta(1)$ time and allow its keys K to be read in $\Theta(K)$ time. At the start of each main loop iteration, entry $Q[i]$ stores the uncolored vertices in the graph with saturation degree i in a saturation table. The PUSHORADDKEY, POPORDELKEY, and REMOVE-ORDELKEY methods maintain the invariant that, for each table $Q[i]$, each key $j \in$ KEYS($Q[i]$) is associated with a nonempty set of vertices, such that each vertex $v \in Q[i][j]$ has saturation degree i and effective degree j.

THEOREM 13. GREEDY-SD *colors a graph* $G = (V, E)$ *according to the* SD *ordering heuristic in* $\Theta(V + E)$ *time.*

PROOF. PUSHORADDKEY, POPORDELKEY, and REMOVE-ORDELKEY operate in $\Theta(1)$ time, and a given saturation table's key set K can be read in $\Theta(K)$ time. Line 43 can thus find a vertex v with maximum saturation degree s in $\Theta(|$KEYS($Q[s]$)$|)$ time. Line 44 can color v in $\Theta(\deg(v))$ time, and lines 50–52 maintain s in $\Theta(s)$ time. Because $s + |$KEYS($Q[s]$)$| \leq \deg(v)$, lines 42–52 evaluate v in $\Theta(\deg(v))$ time. The handshaking lemma [21, p. 1172–3] implies the theorem, because each vertex in V is evaluated once. □

Graph	C							T_S						
	FF	R	LF	ID	SL	SD	Spark	FF	R	LF	ID	SL	SD	Spark
com-orkut	175	132	87	86	83	76	▮▮▪▪▪	2.23	3.39	3.54	44.13	10.59	46.60	▪▪▮▪▮
soc-LiveJournal1	352	330	323	325	322	326	▮▮▮▮▮	0.89	2.05	2.34	17.93	4.69	19.75	▪▪▮▮▮
europe-osm	5	5	4	4	3	3	▮▮▮▮▮	1.32	13.36	17.15	48.59	19.87	52.73	▪▪▮▮▮
cit-Patents	17	21	14	14	13	12	▮▮▮▮▪	0.50	1.62	2.00	9.82	3.21	10.08	▪▪▮▮▮
as-skitter	103	81	71	72	70	70	▮▮▮▮▮	0.24	1.70	2.43	9.41	2.79	9.94	▪▪▮▮▮
wiki-Talk	102	85	72	57	56	51	▮▮▮▪▪	0.09	0.35	0.49	2.79	0.61	2.90	▪▪▮▮▮
web-Google	44	44	45	45	44	44	▮▮▮▮▮	0.09	0.22	0.25	1.68	0.47	1.77	▪▪▮▮▮
com-youtube	57	46	32	28	28	26	▮▮▮▪▪	0.06	0.19	0.25	1.50	0.35	1.55	▪▪▮▮▮
constant1M-50	33	32	32	34	34	26	▮▮▮▮▮	0.90	1.13	1.16	16.07	2.96	17.23	▪▪▮▪▮
constant500K-100	52	52	52	55	53	44	▮▮▮▮▮	0.74	0.88	0.84	14.20	1.97	15.51	▪▪▮▪▮
graph500-5M	220	220	159	157	158	147	▮▮▮▮▮	1.83	3.14	3.69	25.19	8.43	35.29	▪▪▮▮▮
graph500-2M	206	208	153	152	153	141	▮▮▮▮▮	0.52	0.77	0.98	8.09	2.22	11.68	▪▪▮▮▮
rMat-ER-2M	12	12	11	11	11	8	▮▮▮▮▮	0.47	0.93	1.07	10.10	2.22	9.13	▪▪▮▮▮
rMat-G-2M	27	27	15	15	15	11	▮▮▮▪▪	0.48	0.92	1.18	9.17	2.59	9.07	▪▪▮▮▮
rMat-B-2M	105	105	67	67	67	59	▮▮▮▮▮	0.50	0.83	1.00	8.44	2.41	8.64	▪▪▮▮▮
big3dgrid	4	7	7	4	7	5	▪▮▮▮▮	0.41	3.34	4.07	13.61	4.77	15.30	▪▪▮▮▮
clique-chain-400	399	399	399	399	399	399	▮▮▮▮▮	0.05	0.05	0.05	0.81	0.08	2.06	▪▪▪▪▮
path-10M	2	3	3	2	2	2	▮▮▮▮▮	0.18	1.95	2.49	7.34	2.58	7.96	▪▪▮▮▮

Figure 9: Performance measurements for six serial ordering heuristics used by GREEDY, where measurements for real-world graphs appear above the center line and those for synthetic graphs appear below. The columns under the heading C present the average number of colors obtained by each ordering heuristic. The columns under the heading T_S present the average serial running time for each heuristic. The "*Spark*" columns under the C and T_S headings contain bar graphs that pictorially represent the coloring quality and serial running time, respectively, for each of the ordering heuristics. The height of the bar for the coloring quality C_H of ordering heuristic H is proportional to C_H. The bar heights are similar for T_S except that the log of times are used. Section 6 details the experimental setup and graph suite used.

9. RELATED WORK

Parallel coloring algorithms have been explored extensively in the distributed computing domain [3,5,30,31,35,38,39,41]. These algorithms are evaluated in the message-passing model, where nodes are allowed unlimited local computation and exchange messages through a sequence of synchronized rounds. Kuhn [38] and Barenboim and Elkin [5] independently developed $O(\Delta + \lg^* n)$-round message passing algorithms to compute a deterministic greedy coloring.

Several greedy coloring algorithms have been described in synchronous PRAM models. Goldberg *et al.* [30] describe an algorithm for finding a greedy coloring of $O(1)$-degree graphs in $O(\lg n)$ time in the EREW PRAM model using a linear number of processors. They observe that their technique can be applied recursively to color Δ-degree graphs in $O(\Delta \lg \Delta \lg n)$ time. Their strategy incurs $\Omega(\lg \Delta (V + E))$ (superlinear) work, however.

Catalyurek *et al.* [14] present the algorithm ITERATIVE, which first speculatively colors a graph G and then fixes coloring conflicts, that is, corrects the coloring where two adjacent vertices are assigned the same color. The process of fixing conflicting colors can introduce new conflicts, though the authors observe empirically that comparatively few iterations suffice to find a valid coloring. We ran ITERATIVE on our test system and found that JP-LLF uses 13% fewer colors and takes 19% less time in geometric mean of number of colors and relative time, respectively, over all graphs in our test suite. Furthermore, we found that JP-SLL uses 17% fewer colors, but executes in twice the time of ITERATIVE. We do not know the extent to which the optimizations enjoyed by our algorithms could be adopted by speculative-coloring algorithms, however, and so it is likely too soon to draw conclusions about comparisons between the strategies.

10. CONCLUSION

Because of the importance of graph coloring, considerable effort has been invested over the years to develop ordering heuristics for serial graph-coloring algorithms. For the traditional "serial" LF and SL ordering heuristics, we have developed "parallel" analogs — the LLF and SLL heuristics, respectively — which approximate the traditional orderings, generating colorings of comparable quality while offering provable guarantees on parallel scalability. The correspondence between serial ordering heuristics and their parallel analogs is fairly direct for LF and LLF. LLF colors any two vertices whose degrees differ by more than a factor of 2 in the same order as LF. In this sense, LLF can be viewed as a simple coarsening of the vertex ordering used by LF. Although SLL is inspired by SL, and both heuristics tend to color vertices of smaller degree later, the correspondence between SL and SLL is not as straightforward. We relied on empirical results to determine the degree to which SLL captures the salient properties of SL.

We had hoped that the coarsening strategy LLF and SLL embody would generalize to the other serial ordering heuristics, and we are disappointed that we have not yet been able to devise parallel analogs for the other ordering heuristics, and in particular, for SD. Because the SD heuristic appears to produce better colorings in practice than all of the other serial ordering heuristics, SD appears to capture an important phenomenon that the others miss.

The problem with applying the coarsening strategy to SD stems from the way that SD is defined. Because SD determines the order to color vertices while serially coloring the graph itself, it seems difficult to parallelize, and it is not clear how SD might correspond to a possible parallel analog. Thus, it remains an intriguing open question as to whether a parallel ordering heuristic exists that captures the same "insights" as SD while offering provable guarantees on scalability.

11. ACKNOWLEDGMENTS

Thanks to Guy Blelloch of Carnegie Mellon University for sharing utility functions from his Problem Based Benchmark Suite with us [50]. Thanks to Aydın Buluç of Lawrence Berkeley Laboratory for helping us in our search for collections of large sparse graphs. Thanks to Mahantesh Halappanavar of Pacific Northwest National Laboratory for providing us with the code for ITERATIVE [14]. Thanks to Assefaw Gebremedhin for input regarding the publicly available graph-coloring library COLPACK [28]. Thanks to Jack Dennis of MIT CSAIL for helping us track down early work on parallel sorting and join counters. Thanks to Jeremy Fineman for helpful discussions on the amortized analysis of SD. Thanks to Angelina Lee and Justin Zhang of MIT CSAIL and Julian Shun and Harsha Vardhan Simhadri of Carnegie Mellon University for several helpful discussions.

12. APPENDIX: PERFORMANCE OF SERIAL ORDERING HEURISTICS

Figure 9 summarizes our empirical evaluation of GREEDY run on our suite of real-world and synthetic graphs using the six ordering heuristics from Section 1. The measurements were taken using the same machine and methodology as was used for Figure 7. As Figure 9 shows, we found that, in order, FF, R, LF, SL, and SD generally produce better colorings at the cost of greater running times. ID was outperformed in both time and quality by SL. The figure indicates that LF tends to produce better colorings than FF and R at some performance cost, and SL produces better colorings than LF at additional cost. We found that SD produces the best colorings overall, at the cost of a 4.5 geometric-mean slowdown versus SL.

13. REFERENCES

[1] L. Adams and J. Ortega. A multi-color SOR method for parallel computation. In *ICPP*, 1982.

[2] J. R. Allwright, R. Bordawekar, P. D. Coddington, K. Dincer, and C. L. Martin. A comparison of parallel graph coloring algorithms. Technical report, Northeast Parallel Architecture Center, Syracuse University, 1995.

[3] N. Alon, L. Babai, and A. Itai. A fast and simple randomized parallel algorithm for the maximal independent set problem. *J. Algorithms*, 1986.

[4] E. M. Arkin and E. B. Silverberg. Scheduling jobs with fixed start and end times. *Discrete Applied Mathematics*, 1987.

[5] L. Barenboim and M. Elkin. Distributed $(\Delta + 1)$-coloring in linear (in Δ) time. In *ACM STOC*, 2009.

[6] S. Berchtold, C. Böhm, B. Braunmüller, D. A. Keim, and H.-P. Kriegel. Fast parallel similarity search in multimedia databases. In *ACM SIGMOD Int. Conf. on Management of Data*, 1997.

[7] D. P. Bertsekas and J. N. Tsitsiklis. *Parallel and Distributed Computation: Numerical Methods*. Prentice-Hall, 1989.

[8] G. E. Blelloch, J. T. Fineman, and J. Shun. Greedy sequential maximal independent set and matching are parallel on average. In *ACM SPAA*, 2012.

[9] R. D. Blumofe and C. E. Leiserson. Space-efficient scheduling of multithreaded computations. *SICOMP*, 1998.

[10] R. D. Blumofe and C. E. Leiserson. Scheduling multithreaded computations by work stealing. *JACM*, 1999.

[11] D. Brélaz. New methods to color the vertices of a graph. *CACM*, 1979.

[12] R. P. Brent. The parallel evaluation of general arithmetic expressions. *JACM*, 1974.

[13] P. Briggs. *Register allocation via graph coloring*. PhD thesis, Rice University, 1992.

[14] Ü. V. Çatalyürek, J. Feo, A. H. Gebremedhin, M. Halappanavar, and A. Pothen. Graph coloring algorithms for muti-core and massively multithreaded architectures. *CoRR*, 2012.

[15] G. J. Chaitin. Register allocation & spilling via graph coloring. In *ACM SIGPLAN Notices*, 1982.

[16] G. J. Chaitin, M. A. Auslander, A. K. Chandra, J. Cocke, M. E. Hopkins, and P. W. Markstein. Register allocation via coloring. *Computer Languages*, 1981.

[17] D. Chakrabarti, Y. Zhan, and C. Faloutsos. R-MAT: A recursive model for graph mining. In *SDM*. SIAM, 2004.

[18] R. Cole and U. Vishkin. Deterministic coin tossing with applications to optimal parallel list ranking. *Inf. Control*, 1986.

[19] T. Coleman and J. Moré. Estimation of sparse Jacobian matrices and graph coloring problems. *SIAM J. Numer. Anal.*, 1983.

[20] M. E. Conway. A multiprocessor system design. In *AFIPS*, 1963.

[21] T. H. Cormen, C. E. Leiserson, R. L. Rivest, and C. Stein. *Introduction to Algorithms*. The MIT Press, third edition, 2009.

[22] K. Diks. A fast parallel algorithm for six-colouring of planar graphs. In *Mathematical Foundations of Computer Science*. 1986.

[23] C. Dwork, M. Herlihy, and O. Waarts. Contention in shared memory algorithms. In *STOC*, 1993.

[24] D. L. Eager, J. Zahorjan, and E. D. Lazowska. Speedup versus efficiency in parallel systems. *IEEE Trans. Comput.*, 1989.

[25] M. Fischetti, S. Martello, and P. Toth. The fixed job schedule problem with spread-time constraints. *Operations Research*, 1987.

[26] M. Garey, D. Johnson, and L. Stockmeyer. Some simplified NP-complete graph problems. *Theoretical Computer Science*, 1976.

[27] A. H. Gebremedhin and F. Manne. Scalable parallel graph coloring algorithms. *Concurrency: Practice and Experience*, 2000.

[28] A. H. Gebremedhin, D. Nguyen, M. M. A. Patwary, and A. Pothen. ColPack: Software for graph coloring and related problems in scientific computing. *ACM Trans. on Mathematical Software*, 2013.

[29] R. K. Gjertsen Jr., M. T. Jones, and P. E. Plassmann. Parallel heuristics for improved, balanced graph colorings. *JPDC*, 1996.

[30] A. V. Goldberg, S. A. Plotkin, and G. E. Shannon. Parallel symmetry-breaking in sparse graphs. In *SIAM J. Disc. Math*, 1987.

[31] M. Goldberg and T. Spencer. A new parallel algorithm for the maximal independent set problem. *SICOMP*, 1989.

[32] R. L. Graham. Bounds for certain multiprocessing anomalies. *The Bell System Technical Journal*, 1966.

[33] M. Herlihy and N. Shavit. *The Art of Multiprocessor Programming*. Morgan Kaufmann Publishers Inc., 2008.

[34] Intel. Intel Cilk Plus. Available from http://software.intel.com, 2013.

[35] M. T. Jones and P. E. Plassmann. A parallel graph coloring heuristic. *SIAM Journal on Scientific Computing*, 1993.

[36] M. T. Jones and P. E. Plassmann. Scalable iterative solution of sparse linear systems. *Parallel Computing*, 1994.

[37] T. Kaler, W. Hasenplaugh, T. B. Schardl, and C. E. Leiserson. Executing dynamic data-graph computations deterministically using chromatic scheduling. In *SPAA*, 2014.

[38] F. Kuhn. Weak graph colorings: distributed algorithms and applications. In *ACM SPAA*, 2009.

[39] F. Kuhn and R. Wattenhofer. On the complexity of distributed graph coloring. In *PODC*, 2006.

[40] J. Leskovec. SNAP: Stanford Network Analysis Platform. Available from http://snap.stanford.edu/data/index.html, 2013.

[41] N. Linial. Locality in distributed graph algorithms. *SICOMP*, 1992.

[42] L. Lovász, M. Saks, and W. T. Trotter. An on-line graph coloring algorithm with sublinear performance ratio. *Discrete Math.*, 1989.

[43] M. Luby. A simple parallel algorithm for the maximal independent set problem. *SIAM J. Comput.*, 1986.

[44] D. Marx. Graph colouring problems and their applications in scheduling. *John von Neumann Ph.D. Students Conf.*, 2004.

[45] D. W. Matula and L. L. Beck. Smallest-last ordering and clustering and graph coloring algorithms. *JACM*, 1983.

[46] J. Mitchem. On various algorithms for estimating the chromatic number of a graph. *The Computer Journal*, 1976.

[47] M. S. Papamarcos and J. H. Patel. A low-overhead coherence solution for multiprocessors with private cache memories. In *ISCA*, 1984.

[48] Y. Saad. *SPARSKIT: A basic toolkit for sparse matrix computations*. Research Institute for Advanced Computer Science, NASA Ames Research Center, 1990.

[49] A. Sariyuce, E. Saule, and U. Catalyurek. Improving graph coloring on distributed-memory parallel computers. In *HiPC*, 2011.

[50] J. Shun, G. E. Blelloch, J. T. Fineman, P. B. Gibbons, A. Kyrola, H. V. Simhadri, and K. Tangwongsan. Brief announcement: the Problem Based Benchmark Suite. In *SPAA*, 2012.

[51] D. J. A. Welsh and M. B. Powell. An upper bound for the chromatic number of a graph and its application to timetabling problems. *The Computer Journal*, 1967.

The PCL Theorem.
Transactions cannot be Parallel, Consistent and Live

Victor Bushkov
EPFL, IC, LPD
victor.bushkov@epfl.ch

Dmytro Dziuma
FORTH-ICS
ddziuma@ics.forth.gr

Panagiota Fatourou [*]
University of Crete &
FORTH-ICS
faturu@csd.uoc.gr

Rachid Guerraoui
EPFL, IC, LPD
rachid.guerraoui@epfl.ch

ABSTRACT

We show that it is impossible to design a transactional memory system which ensures **parallelism**, i.e. transactions do not need to synchronize unless they access the same application objects, while ensuring very little **consistency**, i.e. a consistency condition, called *weak adaptive consistency*, introduced here and which is weaker than snapshot isolation, processor consistency, and any other consistency condition stronger than them (such as opacity, serializability, causal serializability, etc.), and very little **liveness**, i.e. that transactions eventually commit if they run solo.

Categories and Subject Descriptors

D.1.3 [**Programming Techniques**]: Concurrent Programming

Keywords

transactional memory; disjoint-access-parallelism; snapshot isolation; processor consistency; weak adaptive consistency; obstruction-freedom; lower bounds; universal constructions

1. INTRODUCTION

The paradigm of *transactions* [20, 26, 35] is appealing for its simplicity but implementing it efficiently is challenging. Ideally a transactional system should not introduce any contention between transactions beyond that inherently due to the actual code of the transactions. In other words, if two transactions access disjoint sets of data items, then none of these transactions should delay the other one, i.e., these transactions should not *contend* on any base object. This requirement has been called *strict disjoint-access-parallelism* [2,

---

[*]Currently with École Polytechnique Fédérale de Lausanne (EPFL), Switzerland, as an EcoCloud visiting professor.

SPAA '14 Prague, Czech Republic
Copyright 2014 ACM 978-1-4503-2821-0/14/06 ...$15.00.
http://dx.doi.org/10.1145/2612669.2612690.

22]. *Base objects* are low-level objects, which typically provide atomic *primitives* like *read/write, load linked/store conditional, compare-and-swap*, used to implement transactional systems. Two transactions *contend* on some base object if both access that object during their executions and one of them performs a *non-trivial* operation on that object, i.e. an operation which updates its state.

Strict disjoint access parallelism can be ensured by blocking transactional memory (TM) systems; indeed, TL [14], a lock-based TM algorithm, ensures strict disjoint-access-parallelism and strict serializability [30]. It was shown in [21] that a strictly disjoint-access-parallel TM algorithm cannot ensure both obstruction-freedom (i.e. a weak non-blocking liveness condition) and serializability (i.e. a consistency condition weaker than strict serializability). Specifically, *obstruction-freedom* [25] ensures that a transaction is aborted only if step contention is encountered during the course of its execution. *Serializability* [30] ensures that, in any execution, all committed transactions (and some that have not completed yet) execute like in a legal sequential execution.

In this paper, we study the following question: can we ensure strict disjoint-access-parallelism and obstruction freedom if we weaken safety? In other words, is serializability indeed a major factor against strong parallelism? We focus on a new weak consistency condition that we introduce in this paper, called *weak adaptive consistency*. Weak adaptive consistency is weaker than (a weak variant of) snapshot isolation [10] and processor consistency [19]. Thus, it is weaker than serializability, causal serializability and all other consistency conditions that are stronger than processor consistency (or snapshot isolation or even the union of both). Our PCL theorem states that even with weak safety and weak liveness, the described task is still impossible: specifically, it is not possible to implement a transactional memory system which ensures strict disjoint-access-parallelism (Parallelism), weak adaptive consistency (Consistency), and obstruction-freedom (Liveness).

Weak adaptive consistency weakens snapshot isolation in two ways: (1) each process is allowed to have its own sequential view and (2) it is possible to partition the transactions of an execution in such a way that each set of transactions in the partition satisfies either snapshot isolation or processor consistency. *Snapshot isolation* [10] requires that transactions should be executed as if every read operation observes a consistent snapshot of the memory that was taken when the transaction started. To make our result stronger, in our definition of snapshot isolation, we do not require the extra constraint (met in the literature [10, 16, 33] for snapshot isolation) that from two concurrent transactions writing to the same data item, only one can commit, and we do not impose any restriction on the value that a *read* on some data item x by a transaction T may return if T has written x before invoking this read. *Processor consistency* [19, 3] allows each process to have its own sequential view which should respect the process-order of writes, additionally it requires writes to the same data item appear in the same order in all sequential views. Processor consistency is stronger than *PRAM consistency* [28, 3], which does not require writes to the same data item to appear in the same order in all sequential views, but weaker than *causal serializability* [32], which requires each sequential view to respect a relation on transactions, called *causality relation*.

The proof of our impossibility result is based on indistinguishability arguments. The main difficulty comes from the fact that the read operations of a transaction do not have to be serialized at the same point as its write operations. Basically, snapshot isolation and especially weak adaptive consistency allow more executions to be correct and it is much harder to construct an execution which violates it. We end up constructing two legal executions where a transaction must read the same values for data items. We then prove that in one of these two executions this is not the case.

This paper is structured as follows. Section 2 gives an overview of the related work. Section 3 gives a system model and all necessary definitions. Section 4 gives the PCL theorem and its proof. Section 5 presents concluding remarks.

2. RELATED WORK

The notion of disjoint-access-parallelism appears in the literature [2, 8, 15, 22, 27, 31] in many flavors. Disjoint-access-parallelism was first introduced in [27] through the notion of conflicting transactions. Later variants [2, 8, 15] employed the concept of a conflict graph. A *conflict graph* is a graph whose nodes represent transactions (or operations) performed in an execution interval α (i.e. the execution interval of those transactions overlap with α) and an edge exists between two nodes if the corresponding transactions (operations) access the same data item in α (i.e they *conflict* in α). In most of these definitions, *disjoint-access-parallelism* requires any two transactions to contend on a base object only if there is a path in the conflict graph of the minimal execution interval that contains the execution intervals of both transactions such that every two consecutive transactions in the path conflict. In [2, 5, 6, 27], additional constraints are placed on the length of the path in the conflict graph, resulting in what is known as *d-local contention property*, where d is an upper bound on the length of the path. In [27], where disjoint-access-parallelism originally appeared, an additional constraint on the step complexity of each operation was provided in the definition. Stronger versions of disjoint-access-parallelism usually result in more parallelism and therefore they are highly desirable when designing TM implementations. Weaker versions of disjoint-access-parallelism may result in less parallelism but are easier to implement.

Attiya *et al.* [8] proved that no disjoint-access-parallel TM implementation can support wait-free and *invisible* read-only transactions. A *read-only* transaction does not perform writes on data items; an *invisible* transaction does not perform non-trivial operations on base objects when reading data items. The variant of disjoint-access-parallelism considered in [8] stipulates that processes executing two transactions concurrently contend on a base object only if there is a path between the two transactions in the conflict graph. Although our impossibility does not hold for this variant of disjoint-access-parallel, our impossibility result considers a much weaker liveness property and holds even for TM algorithms where read-only transactions are visible.

Recent work [12] proved that, if the TM algorithm does not have access to the code of each transaction, a property similar to *wait-freedom*, called *local progress*, cannot be ensured by any TM algorithm. In [15], it was proved that *wait-freedom* cannot be achieved even if this restriction is abandoned (given that each time a transaction aborts, it restarts its execution), if the TM algorithm ensures strict serializability and a weak version of disjoint-access-parallelism, called *feeble disjoint-access-parallelism*. Thus, one must consider weaker consistency or progress properties as we do here.

Pelerman *et al.* [31] proved that no disjoint-access-parallel TM algorithm can be strictly serializable and MV-permissive. The impossibility result holds under the assumptions that the TM algorithm does not have access to the code of transactions and the code for reading and writing data items terminates within a finite number of steps. Pelerman *et al.* [31] considered the same variant of disjoint-access-parallelism as in [8]. A TM implementation satisfies *MV-permissiveness* if a transaction aborts only if it is a write transaction that conflicts with another write transaction. This impossibility result can be beaten [7] if the stated assumptions do not hold. Our impossibility result holds if the TM ensures just weak snapshot isolation, even if it is MV-permissive.

Several software TM implementations [35, 14, 17, 29, 36, 25] are disjoint-access-parallel: TL [14] ensures strict disjoint-access-parallelism but is blocking since it uses locks; the rest satisfy weaker forms of disjoint-access-parallelism [8]. Among them OSTM [17] is lock-free. The TM in [35] is also lock-free but it has been designed for *static* transactions that access a pre-determined set of memory locations. Aparently, our impossibility result does not contradict these implementations because all of them, except TL, ensure weaker variants of disjoint-access-parallelism and some of them weaker progress as well. Also, our impossibility result does not contradict TL since TL uses locks and consequently does not ensure obstruction-freedom. Linearizable *universal constructions* [23, 24], which ensure some form of disjoint-access-parallelism, are presented in [1, 9, 15, 37]. Barnes [9] implementation is lock-free. The universal construction in [15] ensures wait-freedom when applied to objects that have a bound on the number of data items accessed by each operation they support, and lock-freedom in other cases. Disjoint-access-parallel wait-free universal constructions when each operation accesses a fixed number of predetermined memory locations are provided in [2, 37].

Snapshot isolation was originally introduced as an isolation level for database transactions [10, 16] to increase throughput for long read-only transactions. In TM computing, snapshot isolation has been studied in [4, 13, 33, 34]. An STM algorithm, called SI-STM, which ensures snapshot isolation is presented in [33]. SI-STM employs a global clock mechanism and therefore, it is not disjoint-access-parallel. In [13], static analysis techniques are presented to detect, at compile time, consistency anomalies that may arise when the TM algorithm satisfies snapshot isolation or other safety properties. Snapshot isolation on TM for message-passing systems has been studied in [4].

Our definition of snapshot isolation is weaker than that defined for database transactions [10] for the following reasons. First, we do not put any constraint on the value returned by any read that occurs after a write to the same data item in the same transaction. Second, we do not place the "first committer wins" rule, i.e. we abandon the requirement to abort one out of two concurrent transactions that are writing to the same data item. By introducing these constraints, we would make our impossibility result weaker.

3. PRELIMINARIES

System. We consider an *asynchronous system* with n processes which communicate by accessing shared base objects. A *base object* provides atomic *primitives* to access or modify its state. The system may support various types of base objects like read/write registers, CAS, etc. A primitive that does not change the state of an object is called *trivial* (otherwise it is called *non-trivial*).

Transactions. *Transactional memory* (TM) employs *transactions* to execute pieces of sequential code in a concurrent environment. Each piece of code contains accesses to pieces of data, called *data items*, that may be accessed by several processes when the code is executed concurrently; so TM should synchronize these accesses. To achieve this, a TM algorithm usually provides a shared representation for each data item by using base objects. A transaction may either *commit*, in which case all its updates become visible to other transactions, or *abort* and then its updates are discarded.

A TM algorithm provides implementations for the routines $x.read()$, which returns a value for x if the operation was successful or A_T if the transaction has to abort, and $x.write(v)$, which writes value v to data item x and returns ok if the write was successful or A_T if the transaction has to abort. In addition, a TM algorithm provides implementations for the routines $begin_T$, which is called when a transaction T starts and returns ok, $commit_T$, which is called when T tries to commit and returns either C_T (commit) or A_T (abort), and $abort_T$, which aborts T and returns A_T. Each time a transaction calls one of these routines we say that it *invokes* an *operation*; when the execution of the routine completes, a *response* is returned.

Executions and configurations. A *configuration* is a vector with components comprising the state of each process and the state of each base object. In an *initial configuration*, processes and base objects are in initial states. A *step* of a process consists of a single primitive on a single base object, the response to that primitive, and zero or more local operations that are performed after the access and which may cause the internal state of the process to change; each step is executed atomically. Invocations and responses performed by transactions are considered as steps. An *execution* α is a sequence of steps. An execution is *legal* starting from a configuration C if the sequence of steps performed by each process follows the algorithm for that process (starting from its state in C) and, for each base object, the responses to the operations performed on the object are in accordance with its specification (and the state of the object at configuration C). We use $\alpha \cdot \beta$ to denote the execution α immediately followed by the execution β and say that α is a *prefix* of

$\alpha \cdot \beta$. An execution is *solo* if every step is performed by the same process. Two executions α_1 and α_2 starting from configurations C_1 and C_2, respectively, are *indistinguishable* to some process p, if the state of p is the same in C_1 and C_2, and the sequence of steps performed by p (and thus also the responses p receives) are the same during both executions.

Fix an execution α in which a transaction T is executed. Transaction T *completes* in α, if α contains C_T or A_T. Transaction T *accesses* x in α, if α contains either $x.write()$ or $x.read()$. The *execution interval* of a completed transaction T in α is the subsequence of consecutive steps of α starting with the first step executed by any of the operations invoked by T and ending with the last such step. The *execution interval* of a transaction T that does not complete in α is the suffix of α starting with the first step executed by any of the operations invoked by T. The *active execution interval* of any transaction (completed or not) T in α is the subsequence of consecutive steps of α starting with the first step executed by any of the operations invoked by T and ending with the last such step. A TM algorithm is *obstruction-free* if a transaction T can be aborted only when other processes take steps during the execution interval of T.

Histories. A *history* H is a sequence of invocations and responses performed by transactions. Given an execution α, we denote by H_α the sequence of invocations and responses performed by the transactions in α. We denote by $H|T$ the longest subsequence of H consisting only of invocations and responses of a transaction T. Transaction T is in history H if $H|T$ is not empty. History H is *well-formed* if for every transaction T in H the following holds for $H|T$: (i) $H|T$ is a sequence of alternating invocations and responses starting with $begin_T \cdot ok$, (ii) each read invocation is followed either by a value or by A_T, (iii) each write invocation is followed by either an ok response or A_T, (iv) each invocation of $commit_T$ is followed by C_T or A_T, (v) each invocation of $abort_T$ is followed by A_T, (vi) no invocation follows after C_T or A_T. Herein, we consider only well-formed histories. We say that T commits (aborts) in H if $H|T$ ends with C_T (A_T). If T does not commit or abort in H, then T is *live* in H. If $H|T$ ends with an invocation of $commit_T$, then T is *commit-pending*. Transaction T_1 precedes transaction T_2 in execution α (denoted $T_1 <_\alpha T_2$), if T_1 is not live in H_α and A_{T_1} or C_{T_1} precedes $begin_{T_2}$ in H_α. If $T_1 \not<_\alpha T_2$ and $T_2 \not<_\alpha T_1$, then T_1 and T_2 are *concurrent* in α.

A history H is *sequential* if no two transactions are concurrent in H. H is *complete* if it does not contain any live transactions. Transaction T is *legal* in a *sequential history* H, if for every $x.read()$ by T which returns some value v the following holds: (i) if T executes an $x.write()$ before $x.read()$, then v is the argument of the last such $x.write()$ invocation in T; otherwise, (ii) if there is an invocation of $x.write()$ by some committed transaction that precedes T, then v is the argument of the last such $x.write()$ in H; otherwise (iii) v is the initial value of x. A complete sequential history H is *legal* if each transaction is legal in H.

Disjoint-access-parallelism. For proving the impossibility result presented in Section 4, we consider a collection of simple static transactions. Hence, to simplify the definitions in this paragraph, we assume that transactions are static and predefined[1], i.e. we assume that the data items on which T invokes *read* and *write* (in any execution con-

---

[1] Apparently, this assumption makes the impossibility result proved in Section 4 stronger.

taining T) are the same and can be derived by inspecting T's code; we call the set of these data items the *data set* $D(T)$ of T. Note that the set of data items accessed by T in a specific execution might be a proper subset of $D(T)$ if T is not committed in this execution. For example, consider a transaction T whose code implies that T accesses data items x and y and let α be an execution in which transaction T invokes $x.read()$ and gets A_T as a response; then, $D(T) = \{x, y\}$ but T accesses only data item x in α.

We say that two transactions T_1 and T_2 conflict, if $D(T_1) \cap D(T_2) \neq \emptyset$. We say that two executions *contend* on a base object o if they both contain a primitive operation on o and one of these primitive operations is non-trivial. Denote by $\alpha|T$ the subsequence of α consisting of all steps executed by T. A TM implementation $\mathcal{I}$ is *strict disjoint-access-parallel*, if in each execution α of $\mathcal{I}$, and for every two transactions T_1 and T_2 executed in α, $\alpha|T_1$ and $\alpha|T_2$ contend on some base object, only if T_1 and T_2 conflict.

Consistency. A read operation $x.read()$ by some transaction T is *global* if T has not invoked $x.write()$ before invoking $x.read()$. Let T be a committed or commit-pending transaction executed by a process p_i in a history H. Let $T|read_g$ be the longest subsequence of $H|T$ consisting only of global read invocations and their corresponding responses and $T|write$ be the longest subsequence of $H|T$ consisting only of write invocations and their corresponding responses. Let λ denote the empty history. Then we define transactions T_{gr} and T_w (both executed by p_i) in the following way:

- (1) $T_{gr} = T|read_g \cdot commit_{T_{gr}} \cdot C_{T_{gr}}$ if $T|read \neq \lambda$, and $T_{gr} = \lambda$ otherwise, and

- (2) $T_w = T|write \cdot commit_{T_w} \cdot C_{T_w}$ if $T|write \neq \lambda$, and $T_w = \lambda$ otherwise.

DEFINITION 3.1 (SNAPSHOT ISOLATION). *An execution α satisfies* snapshot isolation, *if (i) there exists a set $com(\alpha)$ consisting of all committed and some of the commit-pending transactions in α and (ii) it is possible to insert (in α) a global read serialization point $*_{T,gr}$ and a write serialization point $*_{T,w}$, for each of transactions $T \in com(\alpha)$, so that if σ_α is the sequence defined by these serialization points, the following holds:*

1. *$*_{T,gr}$ precedes $*_{T,w}$ in σ_α,*

2. *both $*_{T,gr}$ and $*_{T,w}$ are inserted within the active execution interval of T,*

3. *if H_{σ_α} is the history we get by replacing each $*_{T,gr}$ with T_{gr} and each $*_{T,w}$ with T_w in σ_α, then H_{σ_α} is legal.*

An STM implementation I satisfies snapshot isolation, if each of the executions produced by I satisfies snapshot isolation.

Since we require neither consistency for local reads nor aborting two concurrent transactions writing to the same data item, our definition of snapshot isolation is weaker than standard definitions of snapshot isolation for databases [10]. This makes our impossibility result stronger.

To strengthen our impossibility result even more, we prove it for a much weaker consistency property, called *weak adaptive consistency* which allows (i) each process to have its own sequential view and (ii) to switch between snapshot isolation and processor consistency (defined below) during the course

of an execution; specifically, the transactions of the execution can be partitioned into groups so that either snapshot isolation or processor consistency is ensured for the transactions of each group. Processor consistency is a safety property which allows each process to have its own sequential view but requires that writes to the same data item occur in the same order in each sequential view.

DEFINITION 3.2 (PROCESSOR CONSISTENCY). *An execution α is* processor consistent *if (i) there exists a set $com(\alpha)$ consisting of all committed and some of the commit-pending transactions in α and (ii) for each process p_i, it is possible to insert (in α) a serialization point $*_T$, for each transaction $T \in com(\alpha)$, so that if σ_α^i is the sequence defined by these serialization points, the following holds:*

1. *$\forall T_1, T_2 \in com(\alpha)$:*

   (a) *if T_1 and T_2 are executed by the same process and $T_1 <_\alpha T_2$, then $*_{T_1}$ precedes $*_{T_2}$ in σ_α^i,*

   (b) *if T_1 and T_2 write to the same data item and $*_{T_1}$ precedes $*_{T_2}$ in σ_α^i, then $\forall j \in \{1, \ldots, n\}$, $*_{T_1}$ precedes $*_{T_2}$ in σ_α^j,*

2. *if $H_{\sigma_\alpha^i}$ is the history we get by replacing each $*_T$ in σ_α^i with $H|T$, if T commits in α, or with $H|T \cdot C_T$, if T is commit-pending in α, then every transaction executed by p_i is legal in $H_{\sigma_\alpha^i}$.*

Let T_l and T_r be two transactions in an execution α such that either T_l and T_r are the same or the invocation of $begin_{T_l}$ precedes the invocation of $begin_{T_r}$. A *consistency group* $G(T_l, T_r)$ of α is a set of transactions from α such that: (1) T_l and T_r belong to $G(T_l, T_r)$, and (2) a transaction T_k belongs to $G(T_l, T_r)$ if the invocation of $begin_{T_k}$ occurs in α between the invocation of $begin_{T_l}$ and the invocation of $begin_{T_r}$. In other words, a consistency group $G(T_l, T_r)$ of α is a set containing the transactions that start their execution between the beginning of T_l and the beginning of T_r (inclusive). An *active execution interval* of $G(T_l, T_r)$ is the longest execution interval of α which includes all steps in α from the first step of T_l to the last step of any transaction from $G(T_l, T_r)$. A consistency group $G(T_l, T_r)$ *precedes* a consistency group $G(T_l', T_r')$ in α, if the last step of any transaction from $G(T_l, T_r)$ precedes the first step of T_l' in α.

A *consistency partition* $P(\alpha)$ of an execution α is a sequence $G(T_{l,1}, T_{r,1}), G(T_{l,2}, T_{r,2}), \ldots G(T_{l,n}, T_{r,n})$ of consistency groups such that:

1. $T_{l,1}$ is the transaction which invokes the first *begin* in α and $T_{r,n}$ is the transaction which invokes the last *begin* in α,

2. $\forall k \in \{1, \ldots, n\}$, either $T_{l,k} = T_{r,k}$ or $begin_{T_{l,k}}$ precedes $begin_{T_{r,k}}$ in α,

3. $\forall k \in \{1, \ldots, n-1\}$, $begin_{T_{r,k}}$ precedes $begin_{T_{l,k+1}}$ in α, and there is no transaction that invokes *begin* between $begin_{T_{r,k}}$ and $begin_{T_{l,k+1}}$ in α.

DEFINITION 3.3 (WEAK ADAPTIVE CONSISTENCY). *An execution α satisfies* weak adaptive consistency *if it is possible to do all of the following: (i) choose a consistency partition $P(\alpha)$, (ii) partition all groups in $P(\alpha)$ into two disjoint sets of groups: a set $SI(P(\alpha))$ of snapshot isolation groups and a set $PC(P(\alpha))$ of processor consistency groups, (iii) choose a set $com(\alpha)$ consisting of all committed and some of* the commit-pending transactions in α, and (iv) for each process p_i insert (in α) a global read serialization point $*_{T,gr}$ and a write serialization point $*_{T,w}$, for each transaction $T \in com(\alpha)$, so that if σ_α^i is the sequence defined by these serialization points, the following holds:

1. $*_{T,gr}$ precedes $*_{T,w}$ in σ_α^i,

2. $\forall T_1, T_2 \in com(\alpha)$, if T_1 and T_2 write to the same data item and $*_{T_1,w}$ precedes $*_{T_2,w}$ in σ_α^i, then $\forall j \in \{1, \ldots, n\}$, $*_{T_1,w}$ precedes $*_{T_2,w}$ in σ_α^j,

3. for each group $G(T_{l,k}, T_{r,k}) \in SI(P(\alpha))$ the following holds: $\forall T_m \in G(T_{l,k}, T_{r,k}) \cap com(\alpha)$, both $*_{T_m,gr}$ and $*_{T_m,w}$ are inserted within the active execution interval of T_m,

4. for each group $G(T_{l,k}, T_{r,k}) \in PC(P(\alpha))$ the following holds: $\forall T_m \in G(T_{l,k}, T_{r,k}) \cap com(\alpha)$, no other serialization point is inserted between $*_{T_m,gr}$ and $*_{T_m,w}$ and both $*_{T_m,gr}$ and $*_{T_m,w}$ are inserted within the active execution interval of $G(T_{l,k}, T_{r,k})$,

5. if $H_{\sigma_\alpha^i}$ is the history we get by replacing each $*_{T,gr}$ with T_{gr} and each $*_{T,w}$ with T_w in σ_α^i, then every transaction executed by p_i is legal in $H_{\sigma_\alpha^i}$.

Consider an execution α that satisfies weak adaptive consistency, let σ_α^i be the sequence of serialization points for process p_i. For simplicity, we use the following notation: $*_{T,l_1} <_i *_{T',l_2}$, where $T, T' \in com(\alpha)$ and $l_1, l_2 \in \{gr, w\}$, to identify that $*_{T,l_1}$ precedes $*_{T',l_2}$ in σ_α^i. We remark that items 3 and 4 of Definition 3.3 imply that the global read and write serialization points of any transaction $T \in com(\alpha)$ are placed within the active execution interval of the consistency group to which T belongs.

An STM implementation I satisfies weak adaptive consistency, if each of the executions produced by I satisfies weak adaptive consistency. Weak adaptive consistency is weaker than processor consistency, and consequently is weaker than causal serializability, serializability, opacity and any other property stronger than processor consistency. This is so because if an execution α satisfies processor consistency, then there exists a consistency partition $P(\alpha) = G(T_l, T_r)$ consisting only of one processor consistency group such that the active execution interval of $G(T_l, T_r)$ is exactly α, and therefore, serialization points of transactions from $G(T_l, T_r)$ can be inserted anywhere in α. Weak adaptive consistency is weaker than snapshot isolation because in the definition of snapshot isolation there is only one sequential view σ_α, and condition 2 of the above definition trivially holds for the case of a single sequential view σ_α. In fact, weak adaptive consistency is even weaker than the union of snapshot isolation and processor consistency.

4. THE PCL THEOREM

In this section we show that it is impossible to implement a TM which ensures weak adaptive consistency, obstruction-freedom, and strict disjoint-access-parallelism. The main idea behind the proof is the following. We design two legal executions $\alpha = \alpha_1 \cdot \alpha_2 \cdot s_1 \cdot s_2 \cdot \alpha_7$ and $\alpha' = \alpha_1 \cdot \alpha_2 \cdot s_2 \cdot s_1 \cdot \alpha_7'$, where α_1 and α_2 are parts of solo executions of some transactions T_1 (executed by process p_1) and T_2 (executed by process p_2), respectively, s_1 and s_2 are single steps by T_1 and T_2, respectively, and α_7 and α_7' are solo executions of T_7 (executed by process p_7) until it commits. We prove that

s_1 and s_2 are steps accessing different base objects, so α_7 is indistinguishable from α_7' to process p_7. We also prove that there exists a data item in T_7's read set for which T_7 reads a different value in α_7 from the value read for the same data item in α_7', which is a contradiction.

THEOREM 4.1 (THE PCL THEOREM). *There is no TM implementation which is strict disjoint-access-parallel and satisfies weak adaptive consistency and obstruction-freedom.*

PROOF. Assume, by contradiction, that there exists an obstruction-free implementation I which is strict disjoint-access-parallel and satisfies weak adaptive consistency.

We use the following notation: we denote by b_k, c_k, d_k data items written by transaction T_k and by $e_{k,m}$ data items written by both transactions T_k and T_m. Consider the following transactions (the initial value of every data item is considered to be 0):

- T_1, executed by process p_1, which reads data items b_3 and b_7, and writes the value 1 to data items a, b_1, c_1, d_1, $e_{1,3}$,

- T_2, executed by process p_2, which reads data items b_5 and b_7, and writes the value 2 to data items a, b_2, c_2, d_2, $e_{2,5}$, $e_{2,7}$,

- T_3, executed by process p_3, which reads data items b_1 and b_4, and writes the value 1 to data items b_3, c_3, $e_{1,3}$, $e_{3,4}$,

- T_4, executed by process p_4, which reads data items d_2 and c_3, and writes the value 1 to data items b_4, $e_{3,4}$,

- T_5, executed by process p_5, which reads data items b_2 and b_6, and writes the value 1 to data items b_5, c_5, $e_{2,5}$, $e_{5,6}$,

- T_6, executed by process p_6, which reads data items d_1 and c_5, and writes the value 1 to data items b_6, $e_{5,6}$,

- T_7, executed by process p_7, which reads data items a, c_1, and c_2, and writes the value 1 to data items b_7, $e_{2,7}$.

Definition of α_1 and s_1: Let transaction T_1 be executed solo from the initial configuration C_0. Because p_1 runs solo and I is obstruction-free, T_1 eventually commits. In the resulting execution, T_1 reads the value 0 for data items b_3 and b_7 because I satisfies weak adaptive consistency and there is no transaction that writes to these data items in this execution. Let C' be the configuration resulting from the execution of the last step of T_1.

If T_3 is executed solo from the initial configuration C_0, then in the resulting execution, T_3 reads 0 for b_1 (since I satisfies weak adaptive consistency and no transaction writes to b_1 in this execution).

Consider now the execution δ_1 where transaction T_3 is executed solo from C' until it commits. We prove that T_3 reads the value 1 for data item b_1 in δ_1. Since I satisfies weak adaptive consistency, there exists a consistency partition $P(\delta_1)$ which satisfies the conditions of Definition 3.3. We consider the following cases:

- Assume first that $P(\delta_1) = G(T_1, T_3)$ and $SI(P(\delta_1)) = \{G(T_1, T_3)\}$. Since $G(T_1, T_3)$ is a snapshot isolation group, then $*_{T_1,w}$ must be placed within the active execution interval of T_1 and $*_{T_3,gr}$ must be placed within

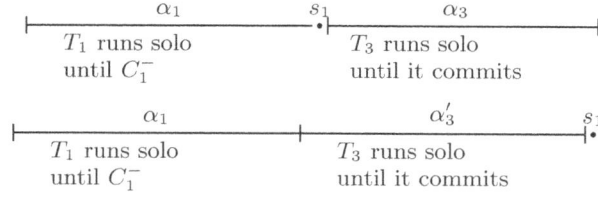

Figure 1: Executions α_1, α_3, α_3', and step s_1.

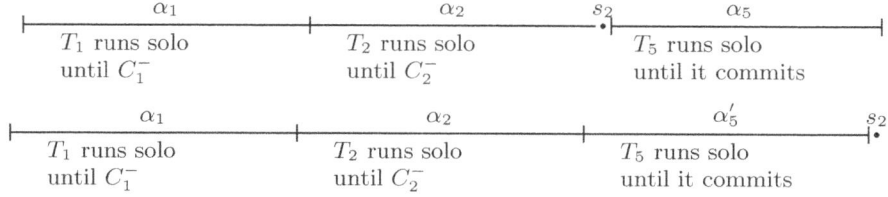

Figure 2: Executions α_1, α_2, α_5, α_5', and step s_2.

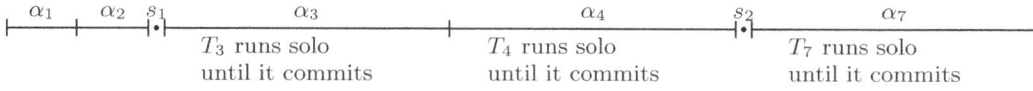

Figure 3: Execution β.

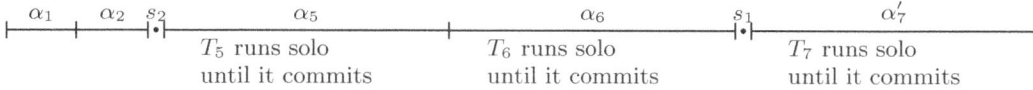

Figure 4: Execution β'.

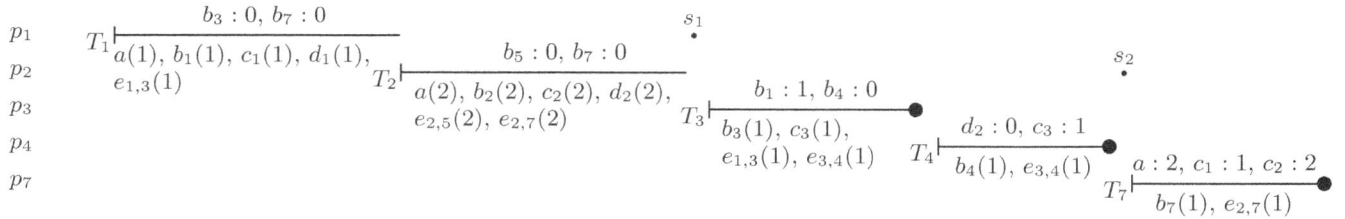

Figure 5: Values read by transactions in execution β. Where $x : v$ denotes a read from x which returns value v, $x(v)$ denotes a write to x which writes value v, and $\bullet$ denotes a commit event.

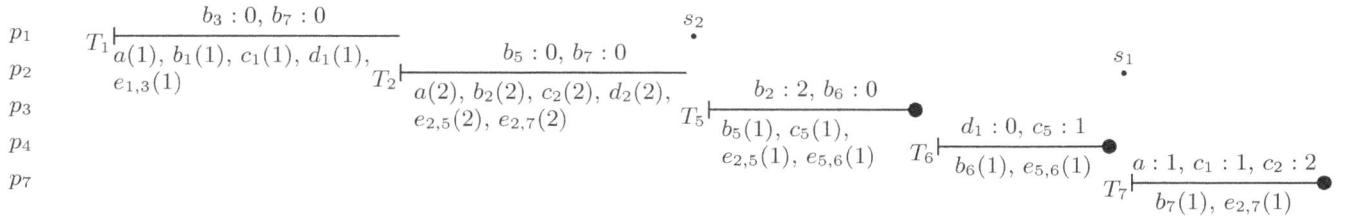

Figure 6: Values read by transactions in execution β'.

183

the active execution interval of T_3[2]. Since $T_1 <_{\delta_1} T_3$, then $*_{T_1,w} <_3 *_{T_3,gr}$. It follows that T_3 must observe the update performed on data item b_1 by T_1, and consequently T_3 must read 1 for b_1.

- Assume that $P(\delta_1) = G(T_1, T_3)$ and $PC(P(\delta_1)) = \{G(T_1, T_3)\}$. Because T_1 reads 0 for b_3 in δ_1, it follows that $*_{T_1,gr} <_1 *_{T_3,w}$. Since $G(T_1, T_3)$ is a processor consistency group, no serialization point is inserted between $*_{T_1,gr}$ and $*_{T_1,w}$. Thus, $*_{T_1,w} <_1 *_{T_3,w}$. Because T_1 and T_3 write to the same data item $e_{1,3}$, it follows that $*_{T_1,w} <_3 *_{T_3,w}$. Since no serialization point is inserted between $*_{T_3,gr}$ and $*_{T_3,w}$, it follows that $*_{T_1,w} <_3 *_{T_3,gr}$, so T_3 must read 1 for b_1.

- Assume now that $P(\delta_1) = G(T_1, T_1), G(T_3, T_3)$. Because $T_1 <_{\delta_1} T_3$, it follows that $G(T_1, T_1)$ precedes $G(T_3, T_3)$ in δ_1. Since $*_{T_1,w}$ should be placed within the execution interval of $G(T_1, T_1)$ and $*_{T_3,gr}$ should be placed within the execution interval of $G(T_3, T_3)$, $*_{T_1,w} <_3 *_{T_3,gr}$. Hence, T_3 must read 1 for b_1.

Since in the solo execution of T_3 from C_0, T_3 reads 0 for b_1, whereas in the solo execution of T_3 from C', T_3 reads 1 for b_1, it follows that there exists some step s_1 in the solo execution of T_1 from C_0, resulting in a configuration C_1, such that: (I) if α'_3 is the solo execution of T_3 from configuration C_1^- (where C_1^- is the configuration just before s_1), then, in α'_3, T_3 reads 0 for b_1; and (II) if α_3 is the solo execution of T_3 from configuration C_1, then in α_3, T_3 reads 1 for b_1. (If there are more than one steps with this property, let s_1 be the first of them.)

Denote by α_1 the solo execution of T_1 from C_0 until C_1^- is reached (Figure 1). Note that T_3 reads 0 for b_4 in α_3 since there is no transaction in $\alpha_1 \cdot s_1 \cdot \alpha_3$ which writes to b_4.

Claim 1: *Transaction T_1 invokes $commit_{T_1}$ in α_1.*

Proof: Assume, by contradiction, that T_1 does not invoke $commit_{T_1}$ in α_1. We argue that the execution $\alpha_1 \cdot s_1 \cdot \alpha_3$ does not satisfy weak adaptive consistency. This is so because, by definition of s_1, T_3 reads 1 for b_1 in this execution but T_1 is not yet commit-pending and therefore we cannot assign a write serialization point to T_1 in this execution. $\square$

Claim 2: *Step s_1 applies a non-trivial operation op on some base object o_1 for which the following holds: T_3 reads o_1 in α_3 and α'_3.*

Proof: If op is a trivial operation on o_1 or T_3 does not read o_1 in α_3 (or in α'_3), then α_3 and α'_3 are indistinguishable to p_3. This is a contradiction, since by the definition of s_1, T_3 reads a different value for b_1 in these two executions. $\square$

Definition of α_2 and s_2: Using a similar reasoning as above, we can show that in an execution where T_2 is executed solo from C_1^- until it commits, there is a step s_2, resulting in a configuration C_2, such that:

1. if α'_5 is the solo execution of T_5 from configuration C_2^-, where C_2^- is the configuration just before the execution of s_2, then T_5 reads 0 for b_2 in α'_5;

2. if α_5 is the solo execution of T_5 from configuration C_2, then T_5 reads 2 for b_2 and 0 for b_6 in α_5,

3. if α_2 is the solo execution of T_2 from C_1^- until C_2^- is reached (Figure 2), then T_2 invokes $commit_{T_2}$ in α_2,

4. T_2 reads the value 0 for data items b_5 and b_7 in α_2,

5. s_2 applies a non-trivial operation on some base object o_2 which is read in α_5 and α'_5.

Claim 3: $o_1 \neq o_2$

Proof: Assume that $o_1 = o_2$. Consider an execution $\alpha_1 \cdot \alpha_2 \cdot s'_1 \cdot \gamma_3$, where s'_1 is a single step by p_1 and γ_3 is a solo execution of T_3 by p_3 until T_3 commits. We argue that $s'_1 = s_1$ and γ_3 is indistinguishable from α_3 to p_3. Obviously, since s'_1 is the step that p_1 is poised to perform after α_1, s_1 and s'_1 access the same base object, namely object o_1. Thus, if s_1 and s'_1 are different, they differ in their response.

Since T_3 and T_2 do not conflict, strict disjoint-access-parallelism implies that α_2 does not contain any non-trivial operation on base objects read in γ_3. Thus, the prefix of α_3 until the point that o_1 is first accessed is also a prefix of γ_3. Therefore, T_3 reads o_1 in γ_3 (as it does in α_3).

Because γ_3 reads o_1, and T_3 and T_2 do not conflict, strict disjoint-access-parallelism implies that α_2 does not contain a non-trivial operation on $o_1 = o_2$. It follows that $s_1 = s'_1$. This and the fact that T_3 and T_2 do not conflict imply that γ_3 is indistinguishable from α_3 to p_3. So, execution $\alpha_1 \cdot \alpha_2 \cdot s_1 \cdot \alpha_3$ is legal.

Since p_2 is poised to execute a step which applies a non-trivial operation on $o_2 = o_1$ after $\alpha_1 \cdot \alpha_2 \cdot s_1 \cdot \alpha_3$ and o_1 is read in α_3, it follows that in execution $\alpha_1 \cdot \alpha_2 \cdot s_1 \cdot \alpha_3 \cdot s'_2$, where s'_2 is a single step by p_2, strict disjoint-access-parallelism is violated. This is a contradiction. Thus, $o_1 \neq o_2$. $\square$

Consider executions $\alpha = \alpha_1 \cdot \alpha_2 \cdot s_1 \cdot s_2 \cdot \alpha_7$ and $\alpha' = \alpha_1 \cdot \alpha_2 \cdot s_2 \cdot s_1 \cdot \alpha'_7$, where α_7 and α'_7 are solo executions of T_7 until T_7 commits. Since steps s_1 and s_2 access different base objects, α_7 is indistinguishable from α'_7 to process p_7.

Consider an execution $\alpha_1 \cdot \alpha_2 \cdot s_1 \cdot \alpha_3 \cdot \alpha_4 \cdot s''_2$, where α_4 is the solo execution of T_4 until it commits. We first argue that $s''_2 = s_2$.

Recall that $\alpha_1 \cdot \alpha_2 \cdot s_1 \cdot \alpha_3$ is legal, so $\alpha_1 \cdot \alpha_2 \cdot s_1 \cdot \alpha_3 \cdot \alpha_4$ is legal. Notice that s''_2, like s_2, accesses base object o_2. It remains to argue that the response of s''_2 is the same as that of s_2. Recall that α_3 does not contain a non-trivial operation on o_2. It remains to argue that the same is true for α_4.

Consider the execution $\delta_2 = \alpha_1 \cdot \alpha_2 \cdot s_1 \cdot \alpha_3 \cdot \alpha_4 \cdot \alpha'_5$. Recall that α'_5 is the solo execution of T_5 from configuration C_2^-. Since T_5 does not conflict with T_1, T_3, and T_4, strict disjoint-access-parallelism implies that $\alpha_1 \cdot \alpha_2 \cdot s_1 \cdot \alpha_3 \cdot \alpha_4 \cdot \alpha'_5$ is legal. Since α'_5 reads o_2 and T_5 does not conflict with T_4, strict disjoint-access-parallelism implies that α_4 does not contain a non-trivial operation on o_2. It follows that $s''_2 = s_2$.

Let $\beta = \alpha_1 \cdot \alpha_2 \cdot s_1 \cdot \alpha_3 \cdot \alpha_4 \cdot s_2 \cdot \alpha_7$ (see Figure 3). We first argue that β is legal. This is so because T_7 does not conflict neither with T_3 nor with T_4, so α_7 does not access any base object modified in α_3 or α_4.

We now argue that T_7 reads 2 for data items a and c_2, and 1 for data item c_1 in α_7.

Claim 4: *T_7 reads the value 2 for data items a and c_2, and the value 1 for data item c_1 in α_7.*

Proof: *We first prove that transaction T_4 reads 0 for d_2 in α_4.* Recall that $\delta_2 = \alpha_1 \cdot \alpha_2 \cdot s_1 \cdot \alpha_3 \cdot \alpha_4 \cdot \alpha'_5$ is legal. Since I satisfies weak adaptive consistency, there exists a consistency partition $P(\delta_2)$ and a set $com(\delta_2)$ of committed and commit-pending transactions from δ_2 which satisfy the conditions of Definition 3.3. We argue that $T_2 \notin com(\delta_2)$.

---
[2] For simplicity, throughout the proof, we use the term *execution interval* instead of *active execution interval*, whenever it is clear from the context.

Assume, by contradiction, that $T_2 \in com(\delta_2)$. We consider the following cases.

- Assume first that $P(\delta_2)$ includes $G(T_i, T_5)$ for some $i \in \{3, 4, 5\}$. Since the execution intervals of T_2 and T_1 precede the execution intervals of T_3, T_4, and T_5, and the execution intervals of T_3, T_4, and T_5 do not overlap in δ_2, it follows that the execution interval of the consistency group containing T_2 in $P(\delta_2)$ precedes the execution interval of $G(T_i, T_5)$. Thus, $*_{T_2,w} <_5 *_{T_5,gr}$. This contradicts the fact that T_5 reads 0 for b_2 in α'_5.

- Assume that $P(\delta_2)$ includes $G(T_i, T_5)$ for some $i \in \{1, 2\}$ and $G(T_i, T_5) \in SI(P(\delta_2))$. Since $G(T_i, T_5)$ is a snapshot isolation group and the execution interval of T_2 precedes the execution interval of T_5 in δ_2, it follows that $*_{T_2,w} <_5 *_{T_5,gr}$. This contradicts the fact that T_5 reads 0 for b_2 in α'_5.

- Assume that $P(\delta_2)$ includes $G(T_i, T_5)$ for some $i \in \{1, 2\}$ and $G(T_i, T_5) \in PC(P(\delta_2))$. Because T_2 reads 0 for b_5 in α_2, it follows that $*_{T_2,gr} <_2 *_{T_5,w}$. Since no point is inserted between $*_{T_2,gr}$ and $*_{T_2,w}$, it follows that $*_{T_2,w} <_2 *_{T_5,w}$. Because T_2 and T_5 write to the same data item $e_{2,5}$, it follows that $*_{T_2,w} <_5 *_{T_5,w}$. Since no point is inserted between $*_{T_5,gr}$ and $*_{T_5,w}$, it follows that $*_{T_2,w} <_5 *_{T_5,gr}$. This contradicts the fact that T_5 reads 0 for b_2 in α'_5.

Hence, $T_2 \notin com(\delta_2)$, and consequently T_4 reads 0 for d_2 in α_4.

We next argue that T_4 reads 1 for c_3 in α_4. Since $\delta_3 = \alpha_1 \cdot \alpha_2 \cdot s_1 \cdot \alpha_3 \cdot \alpha_4$ is legal and I satisfies weak adaptive consistency, there exists a consistency partition $P(\delta_3)$ and a set $com(\delta_3)$ of committed and commit-pending transactions from δ_3 which satisfy the conditions of Definition 3.3. We consider the following cases:

- Assume first that $P(\delta_3)$ includes $G(T_4, T_4)$. Since the execution interval of any consistency group containing transaction T_3 precedes the execution interval of $G(T_4, T_4)$, it follows that $*_{T_3,w} <_4 *_{T_4,gr}$.

- Assume now that $P(\delta_3)$ includes $G(T_i, T_4)$ for some $i \in \{1, 2, 3\}$ and that $G(T_i, T_4) \in SI(P(\delta_3))$. Since $T_3 <_{\delta_3} T_4$, it follows that $*_{T_3,w} <_4 *_{T_4,gr}$.

- Assume now that $P(\delta_3)$ includes $G(T_i, T_4)$ for some $i \in \{1, 2, 3\}$ and that $G(T_i, T_4) \in PC(P(\delta_3))$. Since T_3 reads 0 for b_4 in α_3, it follows that $*_{T_3,gr} <_3 *_{T_4,w}$. Since no point is inserted between $*_{T_3,gr}$ and $*_{T_3,w}$, it follows that $*_{T_3,w} <_3 *_{T_4,w}$. Because T_3 and T_4 write to the same data item $e_{3,4}$, it follows that $*_{T_3,w} <_4 *_{T_4,w}$. Since no point is inserted between $*_{T_4,gr}$ and $*_{T_4,w}$, it follows that $*_{T_3,w} <_4 *_{T_4,gr}$.

We conclude that (in all cases) $*_{T_3,w} <_4 *_{T_4,gr}$. Thus, T_4 reads 1 for c_3 in α_4.

We now prove that T_7 reads 2 for c_2 in α_7. Notice that $\alpha_1 \cdot \alpha_2 \cdot s_1 \cdot s_2 \cdot \alpha_5$ is legal. This is so because s_1 and s_2 are steps on different base objects and T_5 does not conflict with T_1, so it does not access o_1 in α_5. We argue that $\delta_4 = \alpha_1 \cdot \alpha_2 \cdot s_1 \cdot s_2 \cdot \alpha_5 \cdot \alpha_7$ is also legal. This is so because $\alpha_1 \cdot \alpha_2 \cdot s_1 \cdot s_2 \cdot \alpha_5$ and $\alpha_1 \cdot \alpha_2 \cdot s_1 \cdot s_2 \cdot \alpha_7$ are legal and T_7 does not conflict with T_5.

Since I satisfies weak adaptive consistency, there exists a consistency partition $P(\delta_4)$ and a set $com(\delta_4)$ of committed and commit-pending transactions from δ_4 which satisfy the conditions of Definition 3.3. Since T_5 reads 2 for b_2 in α_5, it follows that $T_2 \in com(\delta_4)$ and $*_{T_2,w} <_5 *_{T_5,gr}$. We consider the following cases.

- Assume first that $P(\delta_4)$ includes $G(T_i, T_7)$ for some $i \in \{5, 7\}$. Since the execution intervals of T_1 and T_2 do not overlap with the execution intervals of T_5 and T_7 in δ_4, it follows that the execution interval of the consistency group of $P(\delta_4)$ that contains transaction T_2 precedes the execution interval of $G(T_i, T_7)$. Therefore, $*_{T_2,w} <_7 *_{T_7,gr}$, and consequently T_7 must read 2 for c_2 in α_7.

- Assume now that $P(\delta_4)$ includes $G(T_i, T_7)$, for some $i \in \{1, 2\}$ and that $G(T_i, T_7) \in SI(P(\delta_4))$. Since the execution interval of T_2 precedes the execution interval of T_7 and $T_2, T_7 \in G(T_i, T_7)$, which is a snapshot isolation group, it follows that $*_{T_2,w} <_7 *_{T_7,gr}$. Thus, T_7 must read 2 for c_2 in α_7.

- Assume now that $P(\delta_4)$ includes $G(T_i, T_7)$, for some $i \in \{1, 2\}$ and that $G(T_i, T_7) \in PC(P(\delta_4))$. Because T_2 reads 0 for b_7 in α_2, it follows that $*_{T_2,gr} <_2 *_{T_7,w}$. Since no point is inserted between $*_{T_2,gr}$ and $*_{T_2,w}$, it follows that $*_{T_2,w} <_2 *_{T_7,w}$. Because T_2 and T_7 write to the same data item $e_{2,7}$, it follows that $*_{T_2,w} <_7 *_{T_7,w}$. Since no point is inserted between $*_{T_7,gr}$ and $*_{T_7,w}$, it follows that $*_{T_2,w} <_7 *_{T_7,gr}$. Thus, T_7 must read 2 for c_2 in α_7.

Since T_3 reads 1 for b_1 in β, it follows that $*_{T_1,w} <_3 *_{T_3,gr} <_3 *_{T_3,w}$. Because T_1 and T_3 write to the same data item $e_{1,3}$, it follows that $*_{T_1,w} <_4 *_{T_3,w}$. Since T_4 reads 0 for d_2 and 1 for c_3, it follows that $*_{T_3,w} <_4 *_{T_4,gr} <_4 *_{T_2,w}$. Thus, $*_{T_1,w} <_4 *_{T_2,w}$. Because T_1 and T_2 write to the same data item a, it follows that $*_{T_1,w} <_7 *_{T_2,w}$. Since T_7 reads 2 for c_2, it follows that $*_{T_2,w} <_7 *_{T_7,gr}$. Thus, $*_{T_1,w} <_7 *_{T_2,w} <_7 *_{T_7,gr}$, and consequently, it follows that T_7 reads 2 for a and 1 for c_1 in α_7 (see Figure 5). $\square$

Consider now execution $\alpha_1 \cdot \alpha_2 \cdot s_2 \cdot \alpha_5 \cdot \alpha_6 \cdot s''_1$, where α_6 is the solo execution of T_6 until it commits. We first argue that $s''_1 = s_1$.

Recall that $\alpha_1 \cdot \alpha_2 \cdot s_2 \cdot \alpha_5$ is legal, so $\alpha_1 \cdot \alpha_2 \cdot s_2 \cdot \alpha_5 \cdot \alpha_6$ is legal. Notice that s''_1, like s_1, accesses base object o_1. It remains to argue that the response of s''_1 is the same as that of s_1. Recall that α_5 does not contain a non-trivial operation on o_1. It remains to argue that the same is true for α_6.

Consider an execution $\delta_5 = \alpha_1 \cdot \alpha_2 \cdot s_2 \cdot \alpha_5 \cdot \alpha_6 \cdot \alpha'_3$. Since T_3 does not conflict with T_2, T_5, and T_6, strict disjoint-access-parallelism implies that $\alpha_1 \cdot \alpha_2 \cdot s_2 \cdot \alpha_5 \cdot \alpha_6 \cdot \alpha'_3$ is legal. Recall that α'_3 reads o_1. Since T_3 does not conflict with T_6, strict disjoint-access-parallelism implies that α_6 does not contain a non-trivial operation on o_1. It follows that $s''_1 = s_1$.

Let $\beta' = \alpha_1 \cdot \alpha_2 \cdot s_2 \cdot \alpha_5 \cdot \alpha_6 \cdot s_1 \cdot \alpha'_7$ (see Figure 4). We first argue that β' is legal. This is so because T_7 does not conflict neither with T_5 nor with T_6, so α'_7 does not access any base object modified in α_5 or α_6.

Claim 5: *T_7 reads 1 for a in α'_7.*

Proof: *We first prove that transaction T_6 reads 0 for d_1 in α_6.* Recall that $\delta_5 = \alpha_1 \cdot \alpha_2 \cdot s_2 \cdot \alpha_5 \cdot \alpha_6 \cdot \alpha'_3$ is legal. Since I satisfies weak adaptive consistency, there exists a consistency partition $P(\delta_5)$ and a set $com(\delta_5)$ of committed and commit-pending transactions from δ_5 which satisfy the conditions of Definition 3.3. We argue that $T_1 \notin com(\delta_5)$.

Assume, by contradiction, that $T_1 \in com(\delta_5)$. We consider the following cases.

- Assume first that $P(\delta_5)$ includes $G(T_i, T_3)$ for some $i \in \{2, 3, 5, 6\}$. Since the execution interval of T_1 precedes the execution intervals of T_2, T_3, T_6 and T_5, and the executions intervals of T_2, T_3, T_6 and T_5 do not overlap in δ_5, it follows that the execution interval of the consistency group containing T_1 precedes the execution interval of $G(T_i, T_3)$ in δ_5. Thus, $*_{T_1,w} <_3 *_{T_3,gr}$. This contradicts the fact that T_3 reads 0 for b_1 in α'_3.

- Assume now that $P(\delta_5) = G(T_1, T_3)$ and that it holds that $SI(P(\delta_5)) = \{G(T_1, T_3)\}$. Since the execution interval of T_1 precedes the execution interval of T_3 in δ_5, it follows that $*_{T_1,w} <_3 *_{T_3,gr}$. This contradicts the fact that T_3 reads 0 for b_1 in α'_3.

- Assume now that $P(\delta_5) = G(T_1, T_3)$ and that it holds that $PC(P(\delta_5)) = \{G(T_1, T_3)\}$. Because T_1 reads 0 for b_3 in α_1, it follows that $*_{T_1,gr} <_1 *_{T_3,w}$. Since no point is inserted between $*_{T_1,gr}$ and $*_{T_1,w}$, it follows that $*_{T_1,w} <_1 *_{T_3,w}$. Because T_1 and T_3 write to the same data item $e_{1,3}$, it follows that $*_{T_1,w} <_3 *_{T_3,w}$. Since no point is inserted between $*_{T_3,gr}$ and $*_{T_3,w}$, it follows that $*_{T_1,w} <_3 *_{T_3,gr}$. This contradicts the fact that T_3 reads 0 for b_1 in α'_3.

Hence, $T_1 \notin com(\delta_5)$, and consequently T_6 reads 0 for d_1 in α_6.

We next argue that T_6 reads 1 for c_5 in α_6. Since $\delta_6 = \alpha_1 \cdot \alpha_2 \cdot s_2 \cdot \alpha_5 \cdot \alpha_6$ is legal and I satisfies weak adaptive consistency, there exists a consistency partition $P(\delta_6)$ and a set $com(\delta_6)$ of committed and commit-pending transactions from δ_6 which satisfy the conditions of Definition 3.3. We consider the following cases:

- Assume first that $P(\delta_6)$ includes $G(T_6, T_6)$. Since the execution interval of any consistency group containing transaction T_5 must precede the execution interval of $G(T_6, T_6)$, it follows that $*_{T_5,w} <_6 *_{T_6,gr}$.

- Assume now that $P(\delta_6)$ includes $G(T_i, T_6)$ for some $i \in \{1, 2, 5\}$ and that $G(T_i, T_6) \in SI(P(\delta_6))$. Since $T_5 <_{\delta_6} T_6$, it follows that $*_{T_5,w} <_6 *_{T_6,gr}$.

- Assume now that $P(\delta_6)$ includes $G(T_i, T_6)$ for some $i \in \{1, 2, 5\}$ and that $G(T_i, T_6) \in PC(P(\delta_6))$. Since T_5 reads 0 for b_6 in α_5, it follows that $*_{T_5,gr} <_5 *_{T_6,w}$. Since no point is inserted between $*_{T_5,gr}$ and $*_{T_5,w}$, it follows that $*_{T_5,w} <_5 *_{T_6,w}$. Because T_5 and T_6 write to the same data item $e_{5,6}$, it follows that $*_{T_5,w} <_6 *_{T_6,w}$. Since no point is inserted between $*_{T_6,gr}$ and $*_{T_6,w}$, it follows that $*_{T_5,w} <_6 *_{T_6,gr}$.

We conclude that (in all cases) $*_{T_5,w} <_6 *_{T_6,gr}$. Thus, T_6 reads 1 for c_5 in α_6.

Because α'_7 and α_7 are indistinguishable to p_7, it follows that T_7 reads the same values in α'_7 and α_7. Since T_5 reads 2 for b_2 in β', it follows that $*_{T_2,w} <_5 *_{T_5,gr} <_5 *_{T_5,w}$. Because T_2 and T_5 write to the same data item $e_{2,5}$, it follows that $*_{T_2,w} <_6 *_{T_5,w}$. Since T_6 reads 0 for d_1 and 1 for c_5, it follows that $*_{T_5,w} <_6 *_{T_6,gr} <_6 *_{T_1,w}$. Thus, $*_{T_2,w} <_6 *_{T_1,w}$. Because T_1 and T_2 write to the same data item a, it follows that $*_{T_2,w} <_7 *_{T_1,w}$. Since T_7 reads 1 for c_1, it follows that $*_{T_1,w} <_7 *_{T_7,gr}$. Thus, $*_{T_2,w} <_7 *_{T_1,w} <_7 *_{T_7,gr}$ in β', and consequently, it follows that T_7 reads 1 for a in β' (see Figure 6) and in α'_7. $\square$

Claim 4 states that T_7 reads 2 for data item a in α_7, and Claim 5 states that T_7 reads 1 for data item a in α'_7. Since α_7 is indistinguishable from α'_7 to process p_7 this is a contradiction. $\square$

5. DISCUSSION

We proved the PCL theorem: in transactional systems it is impossible to ensure strict disjoint-access-parallelism (Parallelism), weak adaptive consistency (Consistency), and obstruction-freedom (Liveness). To circumvent the impossibility result it is sufficient to weaken just one of the three requirements. Weakening obstruction-freedom to a blocking liveness property makes it possible to ensure strict disjoint-access-parallelism and strong consistency (e.g. strict serializability) by using locks; these are the properties ensured by TL [14]. Likewise, weakening consistency makes it possible to ensure strict disjoint-access-parallelism and strong liveness. For example, allowing writes to the same data item to be viewed differently, as in PRAM consistency [28], makes it possible to trivially ensure strict disjoint-access-parallelism and wait-freedom, the strongest liveness property, without any synchronization between processes. In [11], we design a simple variant of DSTM [25], which satisfies snapshot isolation, obstruction-freedom, and the following weakening of strict disjoint-access-parallelism: two write operations on different data items contend on the same base object only if there is a chain of transactions starting with the transaction that performs one of these write operations and ending with the transaction that performs the other, such that every two consecutive transactions in the chain *conflict*. The PCL theorem shows that the distance between strict disjoint-access-parallelism and its non-strict forms draws a sharp line in the design of transactional systems.

Our theorem might at first glance look close to the CAP theorem [18] which states that it is impossible to ensure *consistency*, *availability*, and *partition* in a distributed system and weakening at least one of these requirements circumvents the impossibility result. In fact, they are different results. While consistency can be viewed as a safety property, and availability can be viewed as a liveness property, partition is not analogous to disjoint-access-parallelism. Specifically, partition tolerance ensures that the system tolerates arbitrary network partitions. Disjoint-access-parallelism on the other hand, does not ensure tolerance against failures but imposes that logical components of a system (transactions or operations) do not contend at low level (i.e. on base objects) if they do not conflict at high level (i.e. do not access the same data items).

Our definition of snapshot isolation is incomparable to strict serializability [30] and opacity [22]. This is because strict serializability and opacity are defined in terms of execution intervals whereas our definition of snapshot isolation is based on *active* execution intervals. The same holds for previous definitions of snapshot isolation, both in the database world [10], and in TM computing [4, 33]. We can easily remedy this problem by defining snapshot isolation in terms of execution intervals. Indeed, we did so in [11] and we were able to prove [11] that no TM implementation satisfies that version of snapshot isolation, obstruction-freedom, and strict disjoint-access-parallel. This impossibility result [11] also holds if a primitive accesses up to k base objects in one atomic step.

6. ACKNOWLEDGEMENTS

This work has been supported by the European Commission under the 7th Framework Program through the Trans-Form (FP7-MC-ITN-238639) project and by the ARISTEIA Action of the Operational Programme Education and Life-long Learning which is co-funded by the European Social Fund (ESF) and National Resources through the GreenVM project.

7. REFERENCES

[1] Y. Afek, D. Dauber, and D. Touitou. Wait-free made fast. In *Proceedings of ACM STOC '95*.

[2] Y. Afek, M. Merritt, G. Taubenfeld, and D. Touitou. Disentangling multi-object operations (extended abstract). In *Proceedings of ACM PODC '97*.

[3] M. Ahamad, R. A. Bazzi, R. John, P. Kohli, and G. Neiger. The power of processor consistency. In *Proceedings of ACM SPAA '93*.

[4] M. S. Ardekani, P. Sutra, and M. Shapiro. The impossibility of ensuring snapshot isolation in genuine replicated stms. In *WTTM'11*.

[5] H. Attiya and E. Dagan. Universal operations: unary versus binary. In *Proceedings of ACM PODC '96*.

[6] H. Attiya and E. Hillel. Built-in coloring for highly-concurrent doubly-linked lists. In *Proceedings of ACM DISC'06*.

[7] H. Attiya and E. Hillel. Single-version stms can be multi-version permissive. In *Proceedings of ICDCN'11*. Springer-Verlag.

[8] H. Attiya, E. Hillel, and A. Milani. Inherent limitations on disjoint-access parallel implementations of transactional memory. In *Proceedings of ACM SPAA '09*.

[9] G. Barnes. A method for implementing lock-free shared-data structures. In *Proceedings of ACM SPAA '93*.

[10] H. Berenson, P. Bernstein, J. Gray, J. Melton, E. O'Neil, and P. O'Neil. A critique of ansi sql isolation levels. *ACM SIGMOD Rec.*, 24(2):1–10, 1995.

[11] V. Bushkov, D. Dziuma, P. Fatourou, and R. Guerraoui. Snapshot isolation does not scale either. Technical Report TR-437, FORTH-ICS, 2013.

[12] V. Bushkov, R. Guerraoui, and M. Kapałka. On the liveness of transactional memory. In *Proceedings of ACM PODC '12*.

[13] R. J. Dias, J. Seco, and J. M. Lourenço. Snapshot isolation anomalies detection in software transactional memory. In *Proceedings of InForum 2010*.

[14] D. Dice and N. Shavit. What really makes transactions faster? In *Proceedings of ACM TRANSACT'06*.

[15] F. Ellen, P. Fatourou, E. Kosmas, A. Milani, and C. Travers. Universal constructions that ensure disjoint-access parallelism and wait-freedom. In *Proceedings of ACM PODC '12*.

[16] A. Fekete, D. Liarokapis, E. O'Neil, P. O'Neil, and D. Shasha. Making snapshot isolation serializable. *ACM Trans. Database Syst.*, 30(2), 2005.

[17] K. Fraser and T. Harris. Concurrent programming without locks. *ACM Trans. Comput. Syst.*, 25(2), 2007.

[18] S. Gilbert and N. Lynch. Brewer's conjecture and the feasibility of consistent, available, partition-tolerant web services. *ACM SIGACT News*, 33(2), 2002.

[19] J. R. Goodman. Cache consistency and sequential consistency. Technical report, Technical Report 61, IEEE Scalable Coherent Interface Working Group, 1989.

[20] J. Gray. A transaction model. In *Proceedings of ICALP '80*. Springer-Verlag.

[21] R. Guerraoui and M. Kapalka. On obstruction-free transactions. In *Proceedings of ACM SPAA '08*.

[22] R. Guerraoui and M. Kapalka. On the correctness of transactional memory. In *Proceedings of ACM PPoPP '08*.

[23] M. Herlihy. A methodology for implementing highly concurrent data structures. *ACM SIGPLAN Not.*, 25(3), 1990.

[24] M. Herlihy. Wait-free synchronization. *ACM Trans. Program. Lang. Syst.*, 13(1), 1991.

[25] M. Herlihy, V. Luchangco, M. Moir, and W. N. Scherer, III. Software transactional memory for dynamic-sized data structures. In *Proceedings of ACM PODC'03*.

[26] M. Herlihy and J. E. B. Moss. Transactional memory: Architectural support for lock-free data structures. *SIGARCH Comput. Archit. News*, 21(2), 1993.

[27] A. Israeli and L. Rappoport. Disjoint-access-parallel implementations of strong shared memory primitives. In *Proceedings of ACM PODC '94*.

[28] R. J. Lipton and J. S. Sandberg. Pram: A scalable shared memory. Technical Report CS-TR-180-88, Princeton University, 1988.

[29] V. J. Marathe, W. N. Scherer, and M. L. Scott. Adaptive software transactional memory. In *Proceedings of DISC'05*. Springer-Verlag.

[30] C. H. Papadimitriou. The serializability of concurrent database updates. *J. ACM*, 26(4), 1979.

[31] D. Perelman, R. Fan, and I. Keidar. On maintaining multiple versions in stm. In *Proceedings of ACM PODC '10*.

[32] M. Raynal, G. Thia-Kime, and M. Ahamad. From serializable to causal transactions for collaborative applications. In *Proceedings of EUROMICRO '97*.

[33] T. Riegel, C. Fetzer, and P. Felber. Snapshot isolation for software transactional memory. In *Proceedings of ACM TRANSACT'06*.

[34] M. Saeida Ardekani, P. Sutra, M. Shapiro, and N. Preguiça. On the scalability of snapshot isolation. In *Euro-Par Parallel Processing*. Springer Berlin Heidelberg, 2013.

[35] N. Shavit and D. Touitou. Software transactional memory. In *Proceedings of ACM PODC '95*.

[36] F. Tabba, M. Moir, J. R. Goodman, A. W. Hay, and C. Wang. Nztm: nonblocking zero-indirection transactional memory. In *Proceedings of ACM SPAA '09*.

[37] J. Turek, D. Shasha, and S. Prakash. Locking without blocking: making lock based concurrent data structure algorithms nonblocking. In *Proceedings of ACM PODS '92*.

Adaptive Integration of Hardware and Software Lock Elision Techniques

Dave Dice
Oracle Labs
dave.dice@oracle.com

Alex Kogan
Oracle Labs
alex.kogan@oracle.com

Yossi Lev
Oracle Labs
yossi.lev@oracle.com

Timothy Merrifield
University of Illinois at Chicago
tmerri4@uic.edu

Mark Moir
Oracle Labs
mark.moir@oracle.com

ABSTRACT

Transactional Lock Elision (TLE) and optimistic software execution can both improve scalability of lock-based programs. The former uses hardware transactional memory (HTM) without requiring code changes; the latter involves modest code changes but does not require special hardware support. Numerous factors affect the choice of technique, including: critical section code, calling context, workload characteristics, and hardware support for synchronization.

The ALE library integrates these techniques, and collects detailed, fine-grained performance data, enabling policies that decide between them at runtime for each critical section execution. We describe an adaptive policy and present experiments on three platforms, two of which support HTM, showing that—without tuning for specific platforms or workload—the adaptive policy is competitive with and often significantly better than hand-tuned static policies.

Categories and Subject Descriptors

D.1.3 [**Programming Techniques**]: Concurrent Programming; E.1 [**Data Structures**]

Keywords

Lock elision; transactional memory; sequence locks

1. INTRODUCTION

Effectiveness of techniques for improving concurrent programs' scalability depends on factors such as the workload, hardware platform, and synchronization support. Some techniques that are well-suited to some use cases are ineffective—sometimes even harmful—for others; some techniques depend on hardware support not available on all systems, and others use software techniques that are difficult or impossible to apply in some cases. Selecting (combinations of) techniques and tuning them for a particular context is often

SPAA'14, June 23–25, 2014, Prague, Czech Republic.
Copyright 2014 ACM 978-1-4503-2821-0/14/06 ...$15.00.
http://dx.doi.org/10.1145/2612669.2612696.

impractical because these choices depend on numerous factors including the workload, which may change over time, even for a given application on a given platform.

Adaptive Lock Elision (ALE) provides pragmatic support for improving scalability of legacy lock-based applications. *Lock elision* techniques can improve scalability without using finer-grained locking or non-blocking synchronization, both of which significantly complicate applications and may harm performance for some platforms and workloads.

Transactional Lock Elision (TLE) [3, 11] allows critical sections protected by the same lock to execute concurrently, exploiting hardware transactional memory (HTM) to detect conflicts between them and retry if necessary. Optimistic software techniques behave similarly, but use software techniques (e.g., *seqlocks* [1]) to detect conflicts. The required changes to critical sections can be achieved via compiler support in some cases [13], but are manual in this paper.

Our ALE library can execute a given critical section in one of three *modes*: HTM (i.e., TLE), SWOpt (i.e., software optimistic execution), and Lock (i.e., acquiring the lock). Integrating these techniques enables the choice of mode for a given critical section to be made heuristically at runtime.

The library collects statistics and profiling information that provide guidance for programmers about which modes should be enabled for which critical sections, and furthermore are used by pluggable *policies* that determine at runtime how to execute each critical section. This approach is preferable to programmers determining execution modes in advance, as the choices can be made based on factors such as the platform, workload, and calling context.

Section 3 describes in detail a HashMap implemented using the proposed approach, which enables all three execution modes, and uses the ALE library to decide between them at runtime. Section 4 describes the implementation of the library and two simple policies: a static one based on fixed parameters, and an adaptive one that chooses execution modes and retry parameters based on observed runtime behavior.

Section 5 describes experiments on three platforms, two of which support HTM. (Experiments on additional platforms are not shown due to lack of space.) We use a simple HashMap microbenchmark, as well as a more complex Kyoto Cabinet [8] benchmark that demonstrates use of ALE with a readers-writer lock and nesting. Experiments with simple static policies demonstrate the importance of choosing execution modes based on observed runtime behavior. Our adaptive policy is almost always competitive with the best static policy, without tuning for the platform and workload.

2. BACKGROUND

In the *Transactional Lock Elision* (TLE) technique [3, 11], critical sections are executed atomically using HTM, while confirming that the lock is not held. If no data conflicts between two critical sections occur, then they can execute in parallel, even if using the same lock. If hardware transactions fail often (e.g., due to conflicts or HTM limitations), performance can degrade. Reasons for transactions failing and the best retry strategy both depend on numerous factors, including the HTM implementation, the workload, etc.

With *optimistic execution*, critical sections can be executed concurrently provided they do not conflict; if a critical section experiences a conflict, no harm is done, and it can be retried. (The lock can be acquired if this occurs repeatedly.) In this paper, conflict detection is achieved using a variant on sequence locks (seqlocks). A *seqlock* [1, 9] is a lock that has an associated sequence number that is initially zero and is incremented on each acquire and release. Data protected by a seqlock can be read without acquiring the lock, provided the sequence has the same even value—implying that the lock is never held—during reading.

Optimistic execution and TLE can both be viewed as forms of lock elision. For both techniques, operations may be attempted concurrently, and may fail and need to be retried depending on a number of factors, including aspects of the workload that may change over time. Despite these similarities, different situations favor different techniques. Optimistic execution can be highly scalable in read-heavy workloads but less effective with more frequent mutating operations. TLE can greatly improve scalability even in the face of frequent mutating operations, but depends on HTM and its effectiveness for the given workload.

Together, TLE and optimistic execution can benefit a wide variety of workloads. However, they do not interoperate effectively if combined naively: mutating operations can succeed concurrently using TLE, but incrementing the sequence number as required for optimistic software execution causes concurrent operations using TLE to conflict with each other, defeating TLE's benefit. We demonstrate that these conflicts can be reduced, and even eliminated in some cases, significantly improving performance and scalability.

We combine TLE and optimistic execution so that either technique can be used effectively, and the choice of which one to use can be made dynamically, depending on the availability and behavior of each option for the current platform and workload. Thus, we show that programmers can get the "best of both worlds" of TLE and optimistic execution.

The idea of dynamically selecting between multiple integrated synchronization techniques is not new. For example, Lim's reactive locking algorithm [10] can switch between fast and scalable alternatives for locking depending on the workload. It can adapt differently for different locks, but it does not support concurrent use of different techniques for different critical sections for the same lock, and does not exploit techniques such as TLE or optimistic execution.

Another example is Adaptive Transactional Memory [12], which is similar in spirit, using profiling and machine learning techniques to adapt between a number of software TM (STM) implementations. Our approach applies to an established lock-based programming model that does not require new compiler and language support, and is thus more pragmatic and more immediately practical.

Other work (e.g., [5, 7, 14]) explores adapting TLE retry

parameters, but we are not aware of previous attempts to integrate it with software optimistic execution. Furthermore, to our knowledge, ALE provides more detailed and finer-grained reporting and adaptation than prior efforts.

3. USING THE ALE LIBRARY

Next, we describe the use of the ALE library with a simple HashMap example. The HashMap supports three operations. An Insert operation inserts a new key-value pair if the key is not already present and overwrites the value associated with the key otherwise; a Remove operation removes the specified key if it is present and has no effect otherwise; and a Get operation copies the value associated with the specified key to a specified memory area and returns true if the key is present, or returns false otherwise.

In the base implementation, the HashMap is protected by a single lock, tblLock, and every operation is executed in a single critical section that holds this lock. In Section 3.1, we describe how to integrate this implementation with ALE, and how to enable the use of HTM mode with it. In Section 3.2, we explain how to add a SWOpt execution alternative.

3.1 Basic use of ALE

Integrating a lock with ALE is achieved by macros via two simple changes. The first, in the same scope as the lock's declaration, associates a label with the lock and causes metadata to be declared for the lock. The second, in the same scope as the lock initialization code, causes the library to initialize this metadata. The type and name of the metadata are transparent to the programmer: All communication with the library for a given lock uses the lock's label.

Next, the BEGIN_CS and END_CS macros are used to replace locking and unlocking code for each critical section to be enabled for ALE (see example in Section 3.2).

The library can now collect statistics and profiling information for these critical sections. Even without using the HTM or SWOpt modes, ALE's reports provide valuable insights to guide optimization efforts. This is particularly useful in larger and more complex examples. Enabling HTM mode for ALE-integrated critical sections is as simple as using appropriate compilation flags for the application and library.

3.2 Adding a simple optimistic alternative

Enabling HTM mode is simple because changes are required only at critical section boundaries, not to the critical section code itself. Adding a SWOpt alternative is more complicated. In particular, a critical section executed in SWOpt mode can be executed concurrently with other critical sections protected by the same lock, and these may cause it to observe inconsistent data (if they execute in HTM or Lock mode).

The programmer must ensure that the SWOpt path can detect such interference in order to retry in this case, and that unsuccessful attempts have no harmful side effects. The HashMap example illustrates one simple way to achieve this.

A critical section is prepared for SWOpt execution by using a variant of the BEGIN_CS macro and by adding SWOpt support code to the critical section that is executed only if the GET_EXEC_MODE macro (provided by the library) indicates that the critical section is running in SWOpt mode.

Programmers using ALE to integrate a SWOpt path into a critical section must follow some simple rules:

- Interference with the SWOpt path should be caused only

by concurrent execution of a critical section protected by the same lock, while executed not in SWOpt mode.

- Such executions must provide the means for the SWOpt path to detect any (potential) interference they cause.

- Critical sections executed in SWOpt mode must avoid any harmful side effects due to such interference. When interference is detected, the SWOpt execution can be explicitly retried (if desired), after notifying the library of the failed attempt.

Many possibilities exist for constructing SWOpt paths. We have enhanced the simple seqlock-based approach described earlier to overcome several disadvantages. First, as discussed in Section 2, the simple seqlock-based approach loses the benefit of HTM mode. Even if HTM is not available, the entire critical section is executed between the two increments of the sequence number when the lock is acquired, preventing successful execution of any SWOpt path associated with the same lock for this entire interval. This is unnecessary if conflicting actions rarely occur, or occur during only a small fraction of the critical section's execution. It is thus better to explicitly identify code regions that may perform conflicting actions than to conservatively assume that any part of the critical section may do so.

To illustrate these ideas with our simple HashMap implementation, we first add to the HashMap class a version number field tblVer, initialized to zero. We also add BeginConflictingAction and EndConflictingAction methods, both of which simply increment tblVer, and a GetVer method, which returns the value of tblVer, first waiting until it is even if a boolean argument indicates this is required. (Concurrency could be improved by using multiple version numbers, say one for each HashMap bucket. We have not yet experimented with this option.)

The first two methods are used to bracket part(s) of critical section code that may interfere with concurrent SWOpt execution of a critical section protected by the same lock. The GetVer method is used both for reading the version number at the beginning of a SWOpt execution of a critical section (first waiting until tblVer is even), and for checking whether the version number has since changed.

The obvious first SWOpt candidate is Get, as concurrent executions of it do not interfere with each other. Conflicting actions can be performed only by concurrent Insert or Remove operations. A Remove operation that explicitly identifies its conflicting region might look like this:

```
1  BEGIN_CS(&LockAPI, &tblLock, md_tblLock);
2  < search a node containing a given key>
3  if ( < node is found > ) {
4      BeginConflictingAction();
5      unlink( < node > );
6      EndConflictingAction();
7  }
8  END_CS(&LockAPI, &tblLock, md_tblLock);
```

(Here, md_tblLock is the label associated with tblLock, and LockAPI is a structure that identifies methods used to acquire and release this lock, as well as an is_locked method that is used to check and monitor a lock when an associated critical section is executed in HTM mode. This approach enables the ALE library to be used with any type of lock). Note that Remove conflicts with concurrent SWOpt executions only briefly and only if it actually removes a node.

```
1  template <bool SWOptMode>
2  int32_t HashMap::GetImp(const& key_t key,
3              uint32_t hashedKey, value_t& retVal) {
4      if (SWOptMode) v = GetVer(true);
5      idx = hashedKey % this->numBuckets;
6      Bucket* barr = this->buckets;
7      if (SWOptMode && (v != GetVer(false))) return -1;
8      BucketNode* bP = barr[idx].firstNodeP;
9      if (SWOptMode && (v != GetVer(false))) return -1;
10     while (bP && !keyEqual(bP->key, key)) {
11         bP = bP->next;
12         if (SWOptMode && (v != GetVer(false))) return -1;
13     }
14     if (bp != NULL) {
15         retVal = bp->val;
16         if (SWOptMode && (v != GetVer(false))) return -1;
17         return 1;
18     }
19     return 0;
20 }
```

Figure 1: Auxiliary method used by the Get method.

To integrate a SWOpt path into the Get method, we begin by creating a utility method GetImp, shown in Figure 1, which factors out the main functionality of the Get method.

We use a boolean template argument SWOptMode to create two versions of the GetImp method—one for SWOpt mode and one for other modes—that differ only as shown in orange.

The main difference between the two versions is validation when executing in SWOpt mode; in the absence of compiler support for this purpose, the programmer adds this validation manually. The general rule of thumb is to validate before using any value that was read since the last validation. However, some validations can be omitted if the use of the value cannot cause any error even if it is invalid. (In some systems, optimistically reading could cause an error if the data has already been deallocated, and the page in which it resides has been returned to the operating system and removed from the address space. This issue does not apply in many cases, including the commercial applications motivating our work, because the application does not deallocate memory during its lifetime, or the operating system does not deallocate freed pages. In some other contexts, the issue may be addressed by using non-faulting loads.)

The Get method itself is implemented as a simple wrapper method that begins a critical section (using a variant of the BEGIN_CS macro that specifies that a SWOpt path exists), and uses GET_EXEC_MODE to determine whether it is in SWOpt mode and should call GetImp<true>, or otherwise call GetImp<fasle>. Because GetImp<true> may return -1, indicating that it did not complete successfully due to a conflict, the Get method is executed inside a loop that only terminates when an execution completes successfully.

3.3 Advanced usage and optimizations

Identifying conflicting regions allows SWOpt executions of critical sections using the same lock to detect interference. The COULD_SWOPT_BE_RUNNING library macro returns a (possibly conservative) indication of whether such executions exist. This allows executions in HTM mode to elide the conflict indication when no SWOpt path is running, thus avoiding unnecessary aborts due to modifications of tblver.

Next, as mentioned above, some operations cause conflicts in some cases, but not in others. This suggests that it might sometimes be profitable to allow a critical section to be executed in SWOpt mode only in some cases, as determined at runtime. We describe two ways this can be achieved.

One approach is to use the "self abort" idiom: a critical section executes in SWOpt mode, and if a conflicting region is encountered, retries the critical section, indicating that the SWOpt path should *not* be used. Self abort is simple and convenient, but provides less benefit as conflicting operations become more common. We address this case next.

While *searching* for the specified key, Insert and Remove do not interfere with SWOpt paths. Therefore, we can provide a SWOpt path for the first parts of these methods too. However, when they perform an action that interferes with other SWOpt executions, this cannot be done in SWOpt mode, so a nested critical section that has no SWOpt path must be used to perform such actions. (The ALE library's support for nesting is described in Section 4.1.) Some care is required due to the possibility of the SWOpt execution being invalidated before or during the lock acquisition by the nested critical section. Therefore, the nested critical section must first check if a conflict has occurred, and if so, the critical section should be ended without performing the conflicting action, and the whole operation should be retried (after reporting the SWOpt failure to the library).

While additional code can be executed in the outer SWOpt critical section *after* the short critical section is completed, in general code that might be invalidated by concurrent operations should be avoided: the effects of the short critical section may already be seen by other threads, so retrying in SWOpt mode after this point is generally undesirable.

3.4 Statistics and profiling information

The ALE library collects statistics and profiling information for policies to use when choosing execution modes. Reports based on this information are useful in their own right. Even without using HTM or SWOpt modes, these reports provide insights into application behavior on a given platform or workload. These insights provide guidance about which critical sections might benefit from a SWOpt path, for example. The reports have also been invaluable in understanding and improving behavior of adaptive policies.

Different executions of a given source-level critical section may use different locks, and may be executed in different "contexts" (see below). These factors can affect the best choice of execution mode. The library therefore collects statistics and profiling information at the granularity of <lock, context> pairs.

Each critical section integrated with the ALE library (using a library macro such as BEGIN_CS) defines a *scope*. A thread's *context* is an initially-empty sequence of scopes. When a thread begins execution of a critical section, its scope is added to the thread's context; when the critical section is completed, the scope is removed.

As described so far, a thread's context is determined by the ALE-enabled critical sections within which it is executing. However, programmers can explicitly create additional scopes, allowing the library to collect statistics and profiling information at even finer granularity.

The importance of this ability is shown by the C++ "scoped locking" idiom. A scoped lock is a class that encapsulates a lock, and whose constructor and destructor are responsible for acquiring and releasing the lock, respectively. Enabling critical sections introduced in this way for ALE involves using the BEGIN_CS and END_CS macros (or variants thereof) in the constructor and destructor. Thus, there is only a single critical section at the source level, implying a single set of statistics for all acquisitions of each lock used this way, so policies cannot specialize behavior for (effectively) different critical sections. This issue can be addressed by declaring additional scopes explicitly, as follows:

```
1 void foo() {
2   ...
3   BEGIN_SCOPE("foo.CS1");
4   {
5     ScopedLock(&myLock);
6     // CS body
7   }
8   END_SCOPE();
9 }
```

Here, the BEGIN_SCOPE macro introduces a new scope, with label "foo.CS1". The result is that the critical section that begins in the constructor of ScopedLock will execute in different contexts depending on where the constructor is called from, allowing the library to distinguish the different cases.

For a given <lock, context> pair, the library may record: how often a critical section was executed using this lock in this context; how many times each mode (HTM, SWOpt, or Lock) was attempted/successful; how much time was spent in each mode, etc.

Another way to use different contexts for the same critical section allows for cases in which it is expected that different execution modes may be best for different cases, as in:

```
1  if (<condition>)
2    BEGIN_CS_NAMED(&LockAPI, &tblLock,
3          md_tblLock, "condition is true");
4  else
5    BEGIN_CS_NAMED(&LockAPI, &tblLock,
6          md_tblLock, "condition is false");
7  {
8    <CS body>
9  }
10 END_CS(&LockAPI, &tblLock, md_tblLock)
```

This results in associating a different scope, and thus a separate context and statistics, with each call to BEGIN_CS_NAMED, allowing the library to adapt differently depending on whether the condition holds. The label provided to BEGIN_CS_NAMED describes the scope, improving readability of reports.

4. LIBRARY IMPLEMENTATION

The ALE library separates common, policy-independent functionality from a pluggable policy. The policy-independent code provides two interfaces: one for programs that use the library (e.g., via the ALE macros described in Section 3), and one for policy code, which the library uses to determine the mode for each critical section execution attempt.

Each ALE-enabled lock has associated metadata, which is allocated and initialized once. In addition, the library associates *granule* metadata with each <lock,context> pair with which a critical section is executed, which is used to record information and statistics about these executions. The lock and granule metadata may be used by the policy code when determining the mode for an execution attempt, and their structure may be policy-dependent. The library's API, however, abstracts away any dependency on the policy by providing the macros for defining lock labels and scope IDs that uniquely identify the associated metadata.

Each time a critical section is attempted, the library invokes the policy to determine the mode in which it should be executed (HTM, SWOpt, or Lock), and executes appropriate critical section preamble code accordingly. For Lock mode, it acquires the lock. For HTM mode, it first waits for the lock to be free, then begins a hardware transaction, and then checks that the lock is not held, aborting the transaction and retrying (possibly in a different mode) if the lock is held, and returning to user code to execute the critical section otherwise. For SWOpt execution, the library returns to user code without acquiring the lock. The library keeps track of the execution mode, which can be obtained via the GET_EXEC_MODE macro (see example in Section 3.2). We also note that using the is_locked function provided by the lock's API, the library estimates whether a hardware transaction has been aborted due to a concurrent lock acquisition by another thread. To reduce the chance for a cascade effect, the library accounts for such aborts in a much lighter way than for others.

4.1 Nesting

Nesting of ALE-enabled critical sections may be motivated by performance, as in Section 3.3, and is also likely to arise as a natural consequence of modularity. In this section, we describe the ALE library's support for nesting.

ALE-enabled critical sections must be properly nested: a lock released at the end of or within an ALE-enabled critical section must be the most recently acquired lock that has not since been released. This requirement is an outcome of our design choice, whereby per-thread stacks of *frames* are used to record information associated with the critical section executed at each nesting level, including the lock accessed and its associated metadata, the relevant granule, and information about the current mode and execution attempt.

For each critical section execution, a frame is pushed onto the thread's stack before the first attempt, and removed after successful completion. (For reasons explained below, no frame is pushed for a critical section that is nested within another that is executing in HTM mode.)

If a critical section is not nested within another ALE-enabled critical section, then the eligible modes for executing the critical section are determined by the availability of HTM and of a SWOpt path (unless the programmer explicitly prohibits one or both). For a *nested* critical section attempt, the library further restricts the choice of modes in some cases.

First, if a critical section (nested or not) is executed using HTM, all critical sections nested within it are also executed using the same hardware transaction, while checking that their associated locks are not held. (If a nested critical section does not allow HTM mode, the hardware transaction is aborted.) This is because committing a transaction for an enclosing critical section in order to begin a nested critical section in another mode would likely violate the atomicity of the enclosing critical section. To minimize the duration of hardware transactions, and to reduce the amount of data written within them, a frame is pushed onto the stack only for the outermost critical section executed in HTM mode.

Next, if a thread already holds the lock accessed by a nested critical section, a SWOpt path is not used even if available. This is because there would be no benefit to doing so, and allowing this case would complicate the library. In this case, HTM mode may be chosen but, to avoid an unnecessary abort, the library does not check whether the lock is held.

Finally, SWOpt mode is not eligible if the thread is already executing in SWOpt mode for a critical section associated with a *different* lock. We believe that using the library correctly in this way would be too difficult and error prone. This does not imply that programmers cannot nest SWOpt-capable critical sections, only that the library will not choose SWOpt mode for the nested critical section in this case.

4.2 Policies

Below we describe two policies we have implemented. These policies use parameters X (respectively, Y) for the number of attempts to use in HTM (respectively, SWOpt) mode before switching to the next mode in the chosen progression. The *static* policy uses fixed parameters, while the *adaptive* one "learns" parameters based on observed behavior.

Static policy.

The static policy uses fixed values of X and Y for all critical section executions. It makes up to X attempts using HTM (if available). If unsuccessful it then makes up to Y attempts using the SWOpt path (if available). It resorts to acquiring the lock if these attempts are also unsuccessful.

Adaptive policy.

The adaptive policy is more flexible and more dynamic than the static policy, as it may choose a different number of attempts in each mode for each granule (a combination of a lock and a context), and it chooses these values based on a learning mechanism that takes into account the statistics collected by the library for the granule. This allows the policy to recognize, for example, that the fastest execution of one critical section in a given context is likely to be achieved by using HTM, while SWOpt is preferable for another, and determine the number of attempts to be used for each such context. Finally, adaptive policies can exploit ALE's fine-grained statistics to improve performance by controlling concurrency; one example is described next.

Grouping mechanism. Recall that a SWOpt path is caused to retry only if a critical section protected by the same lock executes a conflicting region (implying that the latter is executed in either HTM or Lock mode). Thus, if such critical section executions for that lock are temporarily prevented from executing, then all SWOpt paths for critical sections associated with the same lock can execute in parallel without interference. Therefore, we employ a *grouping mechanism* that attempts to run executions of SWOpt paths associated with the same lock concurrently, while delaying the execution of critical sections that may conflict with them.

In most cases, this approach is sufficient to guarantee that any critical section for which a SWOpt path is available can always complete without acquiring the lock. However, this is not guaranteed in some complex nesting cases. Thus, the Adaptive policy still sets Y to a large value to ensure that (rare) livelocks do not persist indefinitely. However, in our experience so far, grouping is effective enough that SWOpt mode always succeeds with much fewer than Y attempts.

The grouping mechanism uses a scalable non-zero indicator (SNZI) [6] to track whether any threads executing SWOpt are retrying. If so, executions that potentially conflict with `SWOpt` executions wait for the SNZI to indicate that all such `SWOpt` executions have completed. Though we have not yet done so, concurrency could be increased by respecting the SNZI probabilistically, which would still ensure that potentially conflicting executions will *eventually* defer to concurrent `SWOpt` executions. Grouping can improve performance significantly when `SWOpt` executions retry multiple times.

Learning mechanism. Each lock goes through one learning phase for each mode progression (`Lock`, `SWOpt+Lock`, `HTM+Lock`, `HTM+SWOpt+Lock`). Phase transitions for lock L occur when some context of L completes a certain number of executions. (We do not wait for this to occur for *all* contexts of L as some contexts may be used infrequently.) In each learning phase, statistics including the average time of successful and failed attempts in each mode are collected for each granule, and these are used to choose relevant X and Y parameters for the granule, as described below.

To choose X parameters, phases for combinations that include `HTM` mode comprise three sub-phases. In the first sub-phase, we start with X set to a large number, and then adjust its value to the maximal number of attempts so far required to complete executions of the critical section using `HTM`, plus a small constant. In the second sub-phase, using the value learned in the first, we create a histogram of the number of attempts required to succeed in `HTM` mode, and count the number of executions that did not complete using `HTM`. Using the histogram and the timing statistics, we estimate the expected execution time of the critical section for each possible number of `HTM` attempts, as explained below, and set the X parameter for use in the third (performance measurement) sub-phase to the number of attempts that yields the lowest estimate.

To estimate the expected execution time for a given number of `HTM` attempts, we must estimate the time to execute the critical section if `HTM` is unsuccessful. We use as an upper bound the time measured during learning when `HTM` was not attempted (i.e., in `Lock` or `SWOpt+Lock` learning phase), and as a lower bound the time taken after failing the maximum number of `HTM` attempts. For each number of `HTM` attempts, we interpolate between these bounds, i.e., we assume that the non-`HTM` execution time grows linearly from the lower bound to the upper bound as we reduce the number of `HTM` attempts from the maximum to zero. While this simple model ignores many practical factors, we have had good success with it (see Section 5).

Having measured execution times for each mode progression for each lock, we could choose for each granule the mode progression that yielded the lowest average execution time for that granule. However, as different granules associated with the same lock may choose different mode progressions, this may result in a combination of mode progressions that has not been measured. This may or may not result in performance that is better than any of the measured mode progressions, because interactions between concurrent use of different mode progressions for different granules may help performance or hurt it. For example, executing one granule with the `HTM+Lock` progression concurrently with another granule using `SWOpt+Lock` may result in many conflicts between `HTM` and `SWOpt` executions that never occurred during the learning phases. Conversely, some mixtures of mode progressions can interact beneficially, such as when some lock

acquisitions make it easier for `SWOpt` executions to run without interference.

For this reason, we run one more "custom" measurement phase for each lock, based on the per-granule choices, and only use these local choices if they yield a lower average execution time than was measured during the learning phases; otherwise we choose for all granules of that lock the mode progression that achieved the lowest average execution time during the learning phases.

Finally, we note that the custom phase still does not necessarily find the configuration that maximizes the throughput for critical sections under a particular lock because the per-granule mode progression choices and the X values used are based on measurements taken when all granules used the same mode progression. Evaluating all possible configurations is impractical (exponential in the number of contexts). Nonetheless, finding more sophisticated learning mechanisms is part of our future work.

4.3 Statistics counters

Historical summary information recorded by the library includes counts of events, such as number of attempts and successes using a given method, and timing information, such as average lock acquisition time. We use two approaches to avoid excessive overhead and contention that naive methods for synchronizing this information would entail.

For time intervals, we measure the time period of interest for approximately 3% of events, and use CAS to update summary variables. Exponential backoff is employed to mitigate any remaining contention, which is typically low due to the sampling. While this approach is simple and reasonably effective, it does not provide a reliable level of accuracy until many hundreds of events have been measured.

For counting events, a higher level of accuracy, especially after a relatively smaller number of events, is desirable. For this purpose, we use a statistical counter algorithm (the BFP algorithm in [4]), which gradually reduces the probability of updating shared data, while maintaining high accuracy even after relatively small numbers of events. This algorithm supports counters that are incremented only by one, and thus cannot be used to record time-based statistics.

5. INITIAL EXPERIENCE WITH ALE

We have experimented with `ALE` using a HashMap microbenchmark and the `wicked` benchmark of the Kyoto Cabinet [8] on four platforms, including two that support best-effort HTM: Rock [5], a 1-socket 16-core SPARC system, and Haswell [14], a 1-socket hyper-threaded 4-core x86 system. Below, we present some of our experiments on these systems, and a 2-socket, 128-thread SPARC T2+ (T2-2).

In all figures, `Instrumented` denotes a version that is integrated with `ALE`, so that statistics and profiling information is available, but only the lock is used to execute critical sections. `Uninstrumented` denotes a baseline implementation that is not integrated with `ALE`. Other versions are named by the policy, the techniques used—`HTM`, `SWOpt`, or both (denoted as `All`)—and relevant parameters, if any. For example, `Static-All-10:10` is the static policy that tries with HTM up to 10 times and then with `SWOpt` up to 10 times. Irrelevant parameters are omitted. For example, `Static-HTMLock-2` denotes a version in which `SWOpt` is disabled and the static policy attempts HTM at most twice. For readability in figures, we abbreviate `HTMLock` as `HL` and `SWOPTLock` as

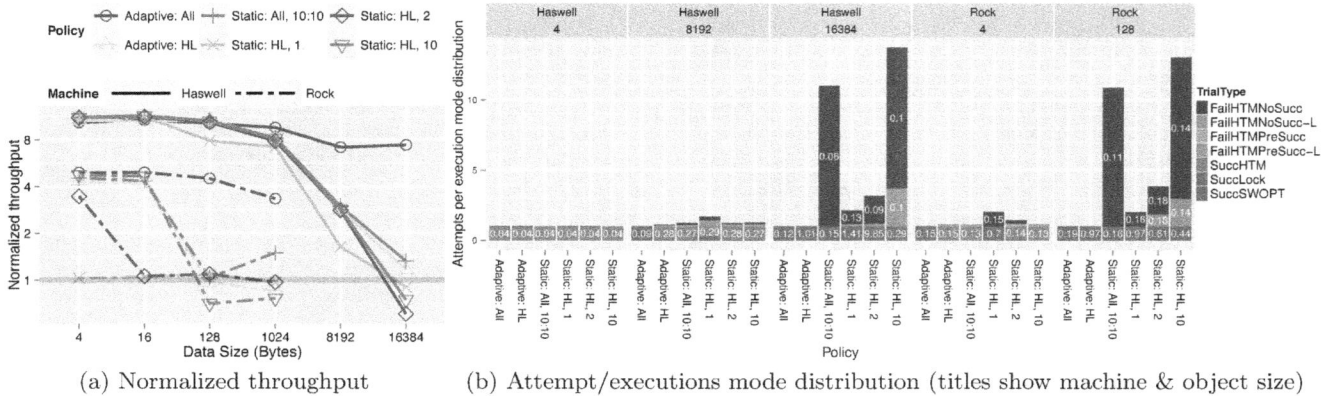

(a) Normalized throughput   (b) Attempt/executions mode distribution (titles show machine & object size)

Figure 2: Evaluating policies on Haswell and Rock with `Get`-only HashMap workload, 4 threads, and different object sizes.

SL, and use more readable notation such as "`Static: HL, 2`" for `Static-HTMLock-2`. Each data point is the median over five runs. Most results exhibit negligible variance.

5.1 HashMap microbenchmark

In this microbenchmark, each of a fixed number of buckets (1,024 in our experiments) holds an unsorted list of key-value pairs whose keys hash to that bucket. `Insert`, `Remove` and `Get` operations are supported; `Get` copies the return value into a caller-provided memory location. In these experiments, only `Get` uses a `SWOpt` path. The table is protected by a single `pthread_mutex_t` lock.

Figure 2(a) shows a `Get`-only workload on the two HTM systems using HashMaps for various object sizes, chosen to reflect the systems' different capabilities in terms of how much data can be written in transactions. To focus on this difference, a small key range of 16 is used and the table is initially full, so the key sought by every `Get` operation is always present. Results are shown for 4-thread runs, and are normalized to `Instrumented` for a meaningful comparison between experiments with different object sizes. Note that we use log-scale for y-axis and discrete values for x-axis.

Focusing first on the `HTMLock` cases (i.e., those that do not use the `SWOpt` path), for "large" objects (which cannot be copied in a hardware transaction), the static policies all perform worse than the `Instrumented` (Lock-only) configuration because time spent on failed `HTM` attempts is wasted. On the other hand, for "small" objects, HTM can copy the objects, so throughput is improved if `HTM` mode is retried enough to succeed. Due to the different capabilities of the two platforms, objects that are "large" for Rock can be "small" for Haswell. Furthermore, the poor performance with one and two `HTM` trials on Rock clearly shows that the best choice for the number of trials is architecture-dependent, and thus the best policy choices depend on both the platform and the workload. Thus, while no static policy suffices for all cases, the adaptive policy achieves competitive performance with all static policies in all cases.

Adding `SWOpt` mode improves the performance for both the static and the adaptive polices; however, it has a much bigger impact with the adaptive policy, which avoids the failed `HTM` attempts prior to using `SWOpt`.

Figure 2(b) uses data collected by the library to shed more light on the results in Figure 2(a). The height of the bars in the figure shows, for each <policy, machine, object size>

combination, the average number of attempts for each successful execution. Each bar breaks down these attempts by category, indicating their mode, whether they were successful, what happened subsequently, and for HTM failures, whether we conjecture that the failure is due to the lock being held (indicated by the "-L" suffix of the label). For example, `FailHTMNoSucc` represents attempts in `HTM` mode that failed in critical section executions that were not eventually completed in `HTM` mode, while `FailHTMPreSucc` represents failures in `HTM` mode for critical sections that eventually succeeded in `HTM` mode. Finally, the numbers presented in some of the categories' bars indicate the average *time* of a trial in that category, relative to the average time it took to execute the operation in the `Instrumented` (Lock-only) version.

The figure confirms that, on both machines, for "large" objects, the static policies pay a significant overhead for wasted `FailHTMNoSucc` and `FailHTMNoSucc-L` attempts, even when `SWOpt` is enabled. Still, when comparing `Static-All-10:10` and `Static-HL-10`, we can clearly see that the successful attempt in `SWOpt` is up to three times faster than that in `Lock` mode. The failed trials in `HTM` are also faster when `SWOpt` is enabled, because they do not need to wait for the lock to be free prior to starting a hardware transaction. Indeed, the static policy with `SWOpt` achieved the best results among all static polices in this experiment. The adaptive policy, on the other hand, does not make any attempts in `HTM`, which explains why it outperforms all static policies.

We also see that the adaptive policy chooses to use `SWOpt` even for 4B objects on Rock, while on Haswell it uses `HTM` for this case, and only uses `SWOpt` for larger objects. This choice is due to the *relatively* higher overhead of validation when the object is small, and the fact that on Haswell we almost always succeed using `HTM` on the first attempt with 4B objects. This is not the case on Rock, as demonstrated by the bar for the static policy with one attempt in `HTM`.

Another interesting phenomenon with large objects is how additional failed attempts in `HTM` reduce the contention on the lock, and thus the time it takes to execute the last trial of an execution. The figure shows that `SuccLock` trials take less time with `Static-HL-10` than with versions like `Instrumented` and `Adaptive-HL` that acquire the lock immediately. On the other hand, there are some cases where adding only a few failed attempts in `HTM` makes the average attempt using the lock significantly worse, like in the case for `Static-HL-2` on Haswell. We looked into this case using

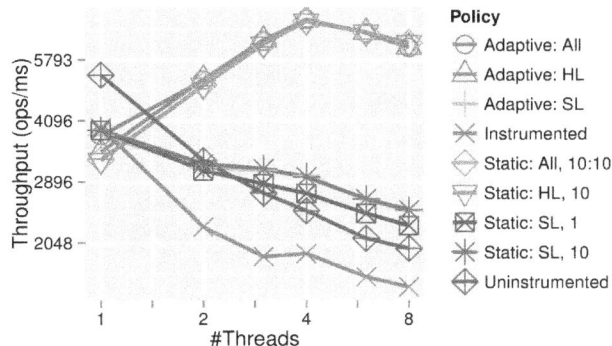

Figure 3: Mixed workload on Haswell (log-log scale)

additional stats (not shown) and noticed that, in these cases, there was always unfairness between the threads, where one thread acquired the lock much more frequently (and without contention), while the others were delayed for a long time. The number of factors and tradeoffs involved clearly makes it impractical to tune static policies manually for different platforms and workloads. This highlights the importance of adaptive policies that can make these decisions based on observed behavior.

These `Get`-only experiments may suggest that `SWOpt` alone is sufficient and `HTM` is not needed. However, the advantages of `HTM` over `SWOpt` are clearly demonstrated in the next experiment. Figure 3 shows results with a mixed workload (60% `Get`, 20% `Insert`, 20% `Remove`) on Haswell, for a HashMap with a key range of 4,096 and 1,024 buckets. The HashMap is initially half full, so there are about two pairs per bucket on average throughout the experiment. The object size is 1,024B, so `Get` can succeed in `HTM`.

First, `Instrumented` achieves 26% less throughput relative to `Uninstrumented` in single-threaded experiments. The gap reduces to less than 20% at 8 threads, as the instrumentation cost introduced by `ALE` is hidden by lock contention. However, all other `ALE`-enabled versions outperform `Uninstrumented` for two or more threads, demonstrating that the scalability and analytic benefits gained from using `ALE` far outweigh the cost of instrumentation.

Because the `Insert` and `Remove` methods acquire the lock, the `SWOpt` path for `Get` encounters significantly more interference in this case. Therefore, while `SWOpt` improves performance relative to `Uninstrumented`, it still exhibits negative scalability. Configurations with `HTM` fare significantly better for two or more threads by exploiting `HTM`'s ability to execute multiple `Insert` and/or `Remove` operations in parallel.

The `Adaptive-All` version performs comparably with or better than other configurations (except `Uninstrumented` at one thread). Data collected by `ALE` reveals that the adaptive policy sometimes avoids `HTM`, and uses `SWOpt` or `Lock` for `Get`. This allows `Adaptive-All` to outperform `Static-All-10:10` at small thread counts.

5.2 Kyoto Cache Benchmark

The CacheDB variant of the Kyoto Cabinet (KC) library implements an in-memory database containing records in a hash table [8]. We used the `wicked` benchmark provided with the KC library, modified to keep the key range and the total number of operations independent of the number of threads, for easier scalability evaluation. The benchmark applies a random series of database operations.

We first used `ALE` solely to collect statistics, without using any optimistic techniques. The statistics revealed that the most common method is `accept` and that contention between read acquisitions of a `pthread_rwlock_t` readers-writer (RW) lock [2] in this method caused *negative* scalability, even at low thread counts. (Using `ALE` with the RW-lock is achieved by using different `LockAPI` structures to express acquisitions for reading and writing.)

The statistics also revealed that one of two methods (in the original benchmark) that begins a database transaction has a performance bug. Only one percent of the benchmark's operations try to begin a transaction, and only half of these use the buggy method. We changed the benchmark to use the non-buggy method for all begin transaction operations.

The purpose of the RW-lock is to allow some operations— such as beginning and ending a database transaction—to gain exclusive database access; these operations acquire the RW-lock for writing, and all other database access operations acquire it for reading.

The `accept` method searches by key for a hash table entry and, if found, applies a caller-provided operation on it. The hash table has 16 *slots*, each comprising a number of *buckets*, implemented as search trees. A key is first hashed to identify the slot where its bucket resides, and then hashed again to identify its bucket in that slot.

Each slot has an associated `pthread_mutex_t` slot lock. The `accept` method acquires the slot lock for the slot containing the specified key; the critical section that acquires this lock is nested within another one that acquires the RW-lock in read mode, as discussed above.

Providing a `SWOpt` path for `accept`'s read acquisition of the RW-lock is more interesting than the simple cases discussed so far, because of the critical section nested within it that acquires one of the slot locks. For space reasons, below we sketch only the most important aspects of our fairly detailed exploration of using `ALE` to improve KC performance.

When no entry associated with the specified key is present, the `accept` method does not modify shared state other than the RW-lock and the relevant slot lock. These actions do not conflict with other operations, and therefore it is straightforward to provide a `SWOpt` path in which the outer critical section (which acquires the RW-lock) is executed in `SWOpt` mode, and the nested critical section (which acquires a slot lock) has no `SWOpt` path. (Some care is required after acquiring the slot lock, because another thread may acquire the RW-lock in write mode and expect that no other thread is holding any slot lock. Thus, for example, `SWOpt` execution must be validated while traversing the entries in a bucket (even though the slot lock is held by the traversing thread) because of a potential conflict with an operation that holds the RW-lock in write mode and may modify entries in the bucket without acquiring the slot lock.)

The case in which the key *is* present is less straightforward. The simplest option is to use the self abort idiom described earlier: in this case, the `SWOpt` attempt is abandoned, and the critical section is retried, acquiring the RW-lock. This approach, denoted as `nomutate`, still avoids acquiring the RW-lock when the specified key is not found.

A better solution is to instead acquire the RW-lock in read mode, and then validate the `SWOpt` execution to detect interference that may have occurred during the acquisition. If validation succeeds, it is as if the RW-lock were acquired as normal in the first place. However, reversing the order of

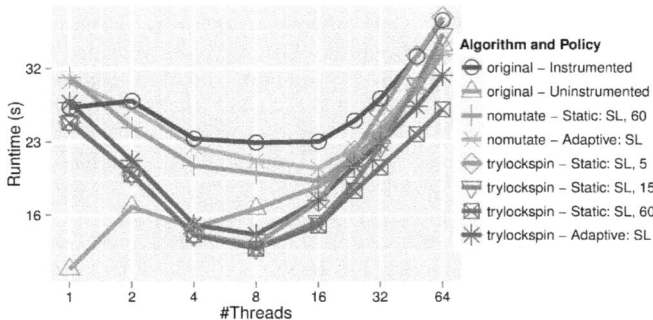

Figure 4: Execution time for KC (log-log scale) on T2-2

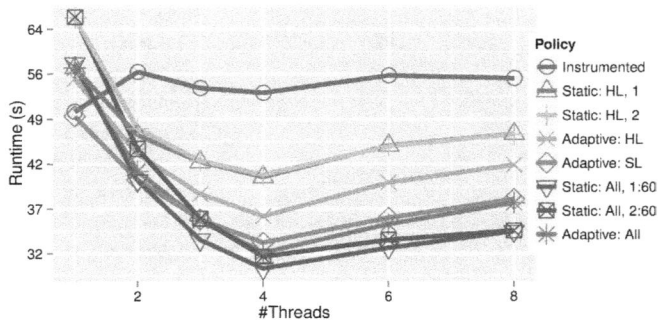

Figure 5: Execution time for KC on Haswell

acquiring the RW-lock and the slot lock introduced a potential deadlock. We therefore use `pthread_rwlock_tryrdlock` to *attempt* to acquire the RW-lock in read mode. If the attempt succeeds, all the locks that are required to complete the operation are held, and the `SWOpt` execution is validated one last time before completing the operation.

If the attempt to acquire the RW-lock for read fails, we could use the self-abort idiom as before, and retry the critical section after acquiring the RW-lock. However, because of the recent failure to acquire the RW-lock, it is likely that a thread has acquired or is waiting to acquire it for write and will be granted the lock first. We therefore implemented an optimization that performs a bounded wait for the version number to be modified and then retries, using another `SWOpt` attempt, avoiding additional contention on the RW-lock. To avoid starvation, the library will eventually acquire the RW-lock, but with the adaptive policy and the grouping mechanism this never happens in practice. We denote this algorithm as `trylockspin`.

Figure 4 presents results on T2-2, clearly showing that both of our algorithms, `nomutate` and `trylockspin`, outperform the version without `SWOpt` (`Instrumented`), and scale up to 16 and 8 threads, respectively. The figure also shows that `trylockspin` performs better than `nomutate`. Next we compare `trylockspin` with the adaptive policy to three variants of the static policy, which perform 5, 15, and 60 attempts in `SWOpt`, respectively. These choices reflect the manual tuning required to find that the best performing static policy for this algorithm is achieved with 60 trials in `SWOpt`. The adaptive policy, on the other hand, is generally competitive with this variant and does not require any manual tuning.

None of the solutions scale beyond 16 threads. The statistics showed high contention on the RW-lock due to *write* acquisitions, which in turn imposed a significant delay on the `SWOpt` attempts that do find the key, as these have to succeed in their attempt to acquire the RW-lock for reading in order to complete; we note that the `pthread_rwlock_t` implementation prevents readers from acquiring the lock not only when a writer is holding the lock, but also when a writer is waiting for the lock. Thus, a `SWOpt` execution has to wait for all the pending writers to complete their operations before it can succeed; this results in both additional `SWOpt` attempts as well as in longer waiting for the version number to change when a `SWOpt` attempt fails.

Next, we explore the use of `HTM` on Haswell to optimize `accept`. We first evaluate what can be achieved without requiring the code changes to implement a `SWOpt` path.

The simplest approach is to enable `HTM` mode for both the inner and outer critical sections, and fall back to the lock when `HTM` fails; our nesting mechanism allows both critical sections to be executed within a hardware transaction, checking that neither lock is held. We tested this approach by using the `HTMLock` configuration with both the adaptive policy, as well as with two static policies that use one and two attempts in `HTM` mode, respectively. The results are presented in Figure 5, with a log-scale y axis.

Focusing on the `HTMLock` results, we see that the static policy with a single trial in `HTM` outperforms the one with two trials in `HTM` with only one thread, but the two behave similarly at higher thread counts. The adaptive policy delivers better performance than both static variants for `HTMLock`, at all thread counts. This was also true with more `HTM` attempts with the static policy (not shown). The reason for that is because the static policy uses the same number of `HTM` attempts for both the internal and external critical sections. So, for example, with a single thread, because the external critical section has very little code that is executed outside of the internal critical section, it does not make sense to try the internal critical section with `HTM` given that the external already failed in `HTM`; still, the static policies attempt the internal critical section once or twice before acquiring the slot lock. The statistics showed that about 20% of `accept` executions failed to commit using `HTM`, even when running single threaded, and regardless of the number of trials. For static policies it means a total overhead of two or four failed hardware transactions for 20% of the executions. The adaptive policy, on the other hand, chooses to execute the internal critical section using the `Lock` method, and thus saves the failed `HTM` attempts for these 20% of the executions. Furthermore, the statistics showed that the remaining 80% of executions that do succeed on `HTM`, require just one attempt when the number of threads is low, and at least three attempts, on average, at higher thread counts. Indeed, the adaptive policy sets the limit on the number of `HTM` attempts to one when run single-threaded, and to five when run with eight threads.

We note that, in general, our learning mechanism is not sophisticated enough to take nesting into account; in particular, the learning of the internal critical section is done concurrently with that of the external critical section, and thus learning of the internal critical section is not limited to executions where the external critical section failed executing in `HTM`. However, for the `HTMLock` case, because we have only two learning phases (`LockOnly` and `HTMLock`), the policy was able to choose the right combination.

Despite the good results with the `HTMLock` configuration, the `SWOptLock` configuration achieves even better results (cf.

Figure 5). The statistics of the `nomutate` variant on T2-2, showed that 42% of the executions did not find the object they were seeking, and hence succeeded using `SWOpt`. The implication for the `trylockspin` algorithm is that in 42% of the cases the RW-lock is not acquired, and hence only the cost of a single acquisition of a slot lock is paid, while the remaining 58% of the cases incur an additional acquisition attempt of the RW-lock, which is usually successful when the number of threads is low. With `HTMLock` a relatively large hardware transaction is executed (and fails in 20% of the cases) and two lock acquisitions are needed: one of the RW-lock and the other of the slot lock.

These results led us to explore the case in which we enable both `HTM` and `SWOpt` for the external critical section, and only `HTM` for the internal critical section. The results are shown by the `{Static,Adaptive}:All` curves in Figure 5.

As the figure shows, except for the single thread case, the adaptive policy that uses both `HTM` and `SWOpt` matches or outperforms the adaptive policy that uses only `SWOpt`. The reason is that using `HTM` for the external critical section reduces the number of acquisition trials for the RW-Lock, which reduces contention at higher thread counts. In this case, however, both static policies outperform the adaptive policy at high thread counts. Based on the statistics, this is primarily because our learning mechanism is not sophisticated enough to deal with nesting. We hope to address this issue in future work.

These results reinforce two important conclusions from our work. First, the combination of software and hardware lock elision techniques achieves considerably better results than when only one of the techniques is available. Second, adaptive policies can perform comparably with the best static policy, without manual tuning.

6. CONCLUDING REMARKS

The `ALE` library integrates transactional lock elision using hardware transactional memory and optimistic execution of operations in software, so that either technique can be used to improve performance and scalability. Decisions regarding whether, when and which technique to use can be made by a pluggable policy, which can collect various profiling information and statistics, and can use this information to guide its decisions. This allows the choice of mechanism to be made at runtime based on the platform, availability of hardware features, and workload characteristics.

Using the library with a simple adaptive policy, we have achieved significant improvements in performance and scalability for a HashMap microbenchmark across a range of platforms and workload parameters, even though different techniques are better for different circumstances. This demonstrates the potential of our approach and establishes a foundation on which to explore more sophisticated policies, for example that can adapt to workloads that change over time.

We have further explored the use of our library in a real example. This effort again showed that we could achieve significant improvements using the adaptive policy, which is highly competitive with hand-tuned static policies, none of which is effective for all cases. Furthermore, the library has proved valuable simply for analyzing an application's behavior, and assessing which locks and critical sections are likely to be most profitable to optimize. Our work also revealed additional challenges that arise when using such techniques in realistic code bases, leading us to develop more sophis-

ticated support for nesting, for example. In ongoing work, we are applying these techniques to a wider range of benchmarks and applications, and continuing to improve on our adaptive policy.

Acknowledgments: We are grateful to Tim Harris and Victor Luchangco for feedback on early drafts.

7. REFERENCES

[1] Corbet. Driver porting: mutual exclusion with seqlocks, February 2003. `lwn.net/Articles/22818/`.

[2] P. J. Courtois, F. Heymans, and D. L. Parnas. Concurrent control with "readers" and "writers". *Commun. ACM*, 14(10):667–668, 1971.

[3] Dave Dice, Maurice Herlihy, Doug Lea, Yossi Lev, Victor Luchangco, Wayne Mesard, Mark Moir, Kevin Moore, and Dan Nussbaum. Applications of the adaptive transactional memory test platform. In *Workshop on Trans. Computing (Transact)*, 2008.

[4] Dave Dice, Yossi Lev, and Mark Moir. Scalable statistics counters. In *Proc. ACM SPAA*, 2013.

[5] Dave Dice, Yossi Lev, Mark Moir, Dan Nussbaum, and Marek Olszewski. Early experience with a commercial hardware transactional memory implementation. Technical Report TR-2009-180, Sun Microsystems Laboratories, 2009.

[6] Faith Ellen, Yossi Lev, Victor Luchangco, and Mark Moir. SNZI: scalable nonzero indicators. In *Proc. ACM PODC*, pages 13–22, 2007.

[7] Tomas Karnagel, Roman Dementiev, Ravi Rajwar, Konrad Lai, Thomas Legler, Benjamin Schlegel, and Wolfgang Lehner. Improving in-memory database index performance with Intel TSX. In *Proc. IEEE HPCA*, 2014.

[8] FAL Labs. Kyoto Cabinet: A straightforward implementation of DBM. `http://fallabs.com/kyotocabinet`.

[9] Christoph Lameter. Effective synchronization on Linux/NUMA systems. In *Gelato Conference*, 2005. `www.lameter.com/gelato2005.pdf`.

[10] Beng-Hong Lim and Anant Agarwal. Reactive synchronization algorithms for multiprocessors. In *Proc. ASPLOS*, pages 25–35, 1994.

[11] Ravi Rajwar and James R. Goodman. Speculative lock elision: Enabling highly concurrent multithreaded execution. In *Proc. IEEE/ACM Micro*, pages 294–305, 2001.

[12] Qingping Wang, Sameer Kulkarni, John Cavazos, and Michael Spear. Towards applying machine learning to adaptive transactional memory. In *Workshop on Trans. Computing (Transact)*, 2011.

[13] Lingxiang Xiang and Michael L. Scott. Compiler aided manual speculation for high performance concurrent data structures. In *Proc. ACM PPOPP*, pages 47–56, 2013.

[14] Richard M. Yoo, Christopher J. Hughes, Konrad Lai, and Ravi Rajwar. Performance evaluation of Intel® transactional synchronization extensions for high-performance computing. In *Proc. SC*, 2013.

Transaction-Friendly Condition Variables*

Chao Wang
Lehigh University
chw412@lehigh.edu

Yujie Liu
Lehigh University
lyj@lehigh.edu

Michael Spear
Lehigh University
spear@cse.lehigh.edu

ABSTRACT

Recent microprocessors and compilers have added support for transactional memory (TM). While state-of-the-art TM systems allow the replacement of lock-based critical sections with scalable, optimistic transactions, there is not yet an acceptable mechanism for supporting the use of condition variables in transactions.

We introduce a new implementation of condition variables, which uses transactions internally, which can be used from within both transactions and lock-based critical sections, and which is compatible with existing C/C++ interfaces for condition synchronization. By moving most of the mechanism for condition synchronization into user-space, our condition variables have low overhead and permit flexible interfaces that can avoid some of the pitfalls of traditional condition variables. Performance evaluation on an unmodified PARSEC benchmark suite shows equivalent performance to lock-based code, and our transactional condition variables also make it possible to replace all locks in PARSEC with transactions.

Categories and Subject Descriptors

D.1.3 [**Programming Techniques**]: Concurrent Programming—*Parallel Programming*

Keywords

Transactional Memory, Semaphore, Condition Synchronization

1 Introduction

The current Draft C++ TM Specification [1] is particularly well-suited to transactionalizing legacy code: one need only replace lock-based critical sections with lexically scoped transactions, and then annotate functions that are called by the transaction. This effort is sufficient for simple critical sections (even those performing I/O), but fails when there is condition synchronization. Both Ruan et al. [17] and Skyrme and Rodriguez [19] observed this problem

*This work was supported in part by the National Science Foundation under grants CNS-1016828, CCF-1218530, and CAREER-1253362.

in the course of their efforts to transactionalize memcached and luaproc, respectively.

In C++, a condition variable must be associated with a named mutex. A thread must hold the mutex to WAIT on the condition variable, and the act of waiting effectively completes one critical section. The thread can then be put to sleep and another thread may safely acquire the mutex and modify shared state. If its modifications satisfy a programmer-specified predicate, it must NOTIFY the condition variable. The waiting thread can then be woken, at which point it attempts to acquire the mutex to execute the continuation of its critical section.

In existing concurrent programs, the act of breaking atomicity at the point of a thread's WAIT does not compromise correctness: the programmer is responsible for checking and restoring invariants when the thread resumes execution. Thus a straightforward translation of the synchronizing critical section to a pair of transactions is not, itself, a concern. The problem is that a waiting thread must release the lock and put itself to sleep in a single atomic operation; if the sleep is delayed until after the lock is released, then it is possible for an intervening NOTIFY to "miss" the waiting thread.

Traditionally this problem is solved by implementing the locking and waiting mechanisms within the operating system (OS). In this manner, the OS is able to mark the thread as waiting, release the lock, and schedule another thread in a way that appears atomic with respect to all other threads. A common practice in this case is to relax the guarantees made by the OS: in Mesa, a NOTIFY could accidentally wake more than one thread [4], and in the POSIX specification, a WAIT can return without being paired with a NOTIFY. It should be noted that modern code accepts these relaxations, and employs a few simple patterns (i.e., calling WAIT within a `while` loop) to overcome any potential spurious wake-ups.

In this paper, we present a novel implementation of condition variables that is compatible with both locks and TM. Our work is inspired by prior work by Dudnik and Swift [6], which discusses an extension to the Solaris OS that supports condition variables within a research hardware TM prototype, and AtomCaml [16], which was the first to consider splitting WAIT operations within transactions. The key innovation in our work is that each condition variable is implemented as a transactional queue of per-thread counting semaphores. This design avoids several pitfalls identified by Birrell [3], and makes it possible to implement condition variables portably, without OS modification. The result is *simpler* and *more flexible* than traditional condition variables, does not have a noticeable impact on performance, and is agnostic to the TM implementation (i.e., it is compatible with both hardware and software transactions). Furthermore, our implementation is immune to the spurious wake-ups that can occur when condition variables are implemented within the OS.

Algorithm 1: The CondVar Specification

shared states
   Q : Set<Thread>   // waiting threads; initially $\emptyset$

// p refers to the thread that performs the operation

procedure WAITSTEP1()
   $Q \leftarrow Q \cup \{p\}$

function WAITSTEP2() : Boolean
   return $p \in Q$

procedure NOTIFYONE()
   if $\exists\, x \in Q$ **then** $Q \leftarrow Q \setminus \{x\}$

procedure NOTIFYALL()
   $Q \leftarrow \emptyset$

The remainder of this paper is organized as follows. Section 2 presents our condition variable algorithm. Section 3 discusses our implementation in C++, and Section 4 discusses implementation challenges for a transactionalizing compiler and runtime system. In Section 5, we evaluate our algorithm using both lock-based and transactionalized versions of the PARSEC [2] benchmark suite. In Section 6, we review related work, with a focus on programming models. Section 7 discusses future work and concludes.

2 Specification and Algorithm

Unlike linearizable concurrent data structures, a condition variable does not naively admit a sequential specification: an invocation of the WAIT method cannot produce a response without it paring with an intervening operation (a NOTIFY) by another thread. Nonetheless, we require a specification of the behavior of condition variables before we can describe an algorithm that can be proven correct. To that end, we begin by presenting an abstract specification modeled after that proposed by Birrell et al. [4], and the sequential specification of a lower-level CondVar object. Using this specification, we introduce a generic algorithm and prove that it is both correct and immune to spurious wake-ups. We then discuss other desirable properties of the algorithm.

2.1 Conventional Specification

In order for a condition variable to be useful, a programmer must be able to reason about the order in which WAIT and NOTIFY operations are performed. Traditionally, this is accomplished by coupling the use of condition variables with mutual exclusion locks.

Birrell et al. [4] proposed a semantics that is widely adopted by many implementations of condition variables. In Birrell's specification, the abstract states of a condition variable object consist of a set Q of waiting threads (initially empty) and a mutual exclusion lock L. The object supports three operations specified as follows:

- A WAIT operation must be invoked within a critical section where L is held by the invoking thread p. The operation consists of two *separate* atomic steps: the first step adds p to Q and releases L atomically; in the second step, the thread is suspended until reaching a state where $p \notin Q$ and L is not acquired, at which point it acquires L and returns.
- A NOTIFY operation atomically removes some non-empty proper subset of threads from Q if Q is not empty.
- A NOTIFYALL operation atomically makes Q empty.

2.2 A Common Specification

Our aim is to produce a specification of condition variables that is compatible with both locks and transactions. To this end, we need to eliminate the notion of locks from the specification. We also notice that in Birrell's specification, NOTIFY can be simply implemented as a NOTIFYALL, and thus, we replace the former operation with a NOTIFYONE operation to allow removing exactly one thread from the set of waiting threads.

We introduce *atomic sequences* as the foundation of our common specification. An atomic sequence $\langle S \rangle$ is a dynamic sequence of instructions S executed by some thread p, which are enclosed by special beginning and ending instructions. The sequence of instructions S in $\langle S \rangle$ is executed atomically if there is no occurrence of a WAIT operation in S. Atomic sequences are flat-nested, that is, a nested atomic sequence $\langle S_0 \,;\, \langle S_1 \rangle \,;\, S_2 \rangle$ is semantically equivalent to $\langle S_0 \,;\, S_1 \,;\, S_2 \rangle$.

A WAIT operation can appear only in an atomic sequence. An atomic sequence $\langle S; \text{WAIT}; C \rangle$, where S is the preceding sequence before the first occurrence of WAIT and C is the continuation sequence after the WAIT operation, is semantically equivalent to the following sequence:

$$\langle S \,;\, Q \leftarrow Q \cup \{p\} \rangle \,;\, \langle \textbf{assert } p \notin Q \rangle \,;\, \langle C \rangle$$

A NOTIFYONE or NOTIFYALL operation can appear either in an atomic sequence or not. In either case, a NOTIFYONE is equivalent to $\langle \textbf{if } \exists x \in Q \textbf{ then } Q \leftarrow Q \setminus \{x\} \rangle$, and a NOTIFYALL is equivalent to $\langle Q \leftarrow \emptyset \rangle$.

We extract the interface of a CondVar object from the above specification. The interface consists of four operations listed in Algorithm 1: WAITSTEP1, WAITSTEP2, NOTIFYONE, and NOTIFYALL. Intuitively, a WAIT operation (Step1 and Step2) adds the caller thread to the waiting set and suspends the caller. A NOTIFYONE wakes a thread that has performed WAITSTEP1 on the same CondVar but has not yet been woken, and NOTIFYALL wakes all threads that have performed a WAITSTEP1 on a CondVar but have not yet been woken.

We define the set of *legal* histories by imposing constraints on the set of all sequential histories permitted by the CondVar object in Algorithm 1.

DEFINITION 1. *A sequential history of a CondVar object is legal if it satisfies the following:*
(1) *For every thread, a* WAITSTEP1 *operation is immediately followed by a* WAITSTEP2 *in the thread's history.*
(2) *Every* WAITSTEP2 *operation returns false.*

2.3 A Generic Implementation

Let us now consider an implementation of condition variables that satisfies this specification. We represent each condition variable as a set of thread identifiers, and additionally require per-thread flags. The set stores the identities of all threads waiting on a particular CondVar; the flags are a convenience mechanism that provides a means for decoupling set operations from the instructions that allow waiting threads to continue.

In this algorithm, a thread performs WAITSTEP1 by setting its flag and then inserting its unique identifier into a particular CondVar's set. To wake a thread, should there be one waiting, a thread uses NOTIFYONE to remove one entry from the set, and then clears the corresponding thread's flag. The NOTIFYALL method is similar to NOTIFYONE, except it wakes all threads that are sleeping on the CondVar.

We now prove a few properties of this generic implementation. For the proofs, we assume that each line in the code listing is exe-

Algorithm 2: A Generic CondVar Implementation

shared states

Q : Set<Thread>   // waiting threads; initially $\emptyset$
$spin_p$: Boolean   // per-thread flag; initially **false**

procedure WAITSTEP1()

1    $spin_p \leftarrow$ **true**
2    $Q \leftarrow Q \cup \{p\}$

function WAITSTEP2() : Boolean

3   **while true do if** $\neg spin_p$ **then return false**

procedure NOTIFYONE()

   // remove from Q an arbitrary element x if exists
4   **if** $\exists\, x \in Q$ **then** $\{Q \leftarrow Q \setminus \{x\}; e \leftarrow$ **true**$\}$ **else** $e \leftarrow$ **false**
   // clear $spin_x$ if some x is removed from Q by last step
5   **if** e **then** $spin_x \leftarrow$ **false**

procedure NOTIFYALL()

   // move all elements from Q to Q'
6    $\langle Q' \leftarrow Q\,;\ Q \leftarrow \emptyset \rangle$
   // remove some x from Q' and clear $spin_x$
7   **while** $\exists x \in Q'$ **do** $\{Q' \leftarrow Q' \setminus \{x\}; spin_x \leftarrow$ **false**$\}$

Algorithm 3: Data Types and Variables

type QueueNode

sem : sem_t   // reference to a semaphore
$next$: QueueNode   // next entry in queue

thread local variables

my_node : QueueNode   // reference to a queue node

shared variables

$head$: QueueNode   // reference to head of queue
$tail$: QueueNode   // reference to tail of queue

Algorithm 4: The Wait algorithm, using continuation passing

procedure WAIT($Sync, Cont$)

1    $my\_node.next \leftarrow$ **nil**
   // Insert thread's semaphore into CondVar's queue
2   BEGINTRANSACTION ()
3   **if** $tail =$ **nil and** $head =$ **nil then**
4      $head \leftarrow tail \leftarrow my\_node$
5   **else**
6      $tail.next \leftarrow my\_node$
7      $tail \leftarrow my\_node$
8   ENDTRANSACTION()
   // Break atomicity by completing enclosing sync block
9   ENDSYNCBLOCK($Sync$)
   // Wait for a notify
10   SEMWAIT($my\_node.sem$)
   // Execute continuation using same sync mechanism
11   BEGINSYNCBLOCK($Sync$)
12   EXECUTE($Cont$)
13   ENDSYNCBLOCK($Sync$)

---

cuted as an atomic step. Note that for the while-loops at lines 3 and 7, "executing as an atomic step" means executing one iteration of the loop as an atomic step, including the evaluation of the condition and at most one execution of the loop body. We use the notation $p@k$ to denote that thread p is about to execute the step at line k.

The main obligation of the proof is to show that there exists a refinement mapping from the generic implementation to the CondVar specification. The following invariants capture the basic properties of the algorithm, which can be proved together (as one conjunction) by induction over reachable states.

LEMMA 2. *The following statements hold as invariants:*
(1) $p@1 \implies \neg spin_p$
(2) $p@2 \implies spin_p$
(3) $p \in Q \implies p@3 \land spin_p$
(4) $p@5 \land e \implies x@3 \land spin_x$
(5) $p@7 \land x \in Q' \implies x@3 \land spin_x$

THEOREM 3. *The generic CondVar implementation is linearizable.*

PROOF. We define the linearization point of each operation as follows:

- A WAITSTEP1 linearizes at line 2.
- A WAITSTEP2 linearizes at line 3 where it reads $spin_p$ is false.
- A NOTIFYONE linearizes at line 4.
- A NOTIFYALL linearizes at line 6.

A refinement mapping function simply takes set Q of the generic CondVar implementation as the abstract set Q in the specification. It is easy to see that every WAITSTEP1, NOTIFYONE and NOTIFYALL operations linearizes at its linearization point, by adding or removing threads from the set. When a WAITSTEP2 operation by thread p linearizes, by Lemma 2, we have $p \notin Q$, and hence, the operation always returns a correct response. □

3 Design and Implementation

We now present a complete implementation of condition variables that is compatible with both locks and transactions. The implementation satisfies the specification from Algorithm 2.

3.1 Data Structures

A practical condition variable implementation must ensure threads yield the CPU when they are waiting for a notification, and that they wake quickly in response to NOTIFY (i.e., calling yield in a loop is insufficient; the thread must be explicitly woken up). Typically, this is achieved by implementing condition variables as OS objects. In contrast we represent each condition variable as a queue in user-space, with the per-thread $spin_p$ flags implemented as binary semaphores. The queue stores references to individual threads' semaphores. By initializing the semaphores to 0, we can remove line 1 from Algorithm 2 and implement line 3 as as SEMWAIT(sem_p). The instances of $spin_x \leftarrow false$ on lines 5 and 7 can each be replaced with SEMPOST(sem_x). Algorithm 3 presents the data structures for this implementation.

3.2 Algorithm Description

In the interest of generality, we assume a continuation-passing style of execution. The call to WAIT thus takes two parameters: an abstract description of the synchronization context, and the continuation to execute after the thread resumes execution. As we discuss later in this section, our implementation can be adapted to other styles with little effort. Algorithm 4 presents an implementation of WAIT using this interface, and Algorithm 5 presents NOTIFYONE.

Algorithm 5: The NotifyOne algorithm

procedure NOTIFYONE()
1   BEGINTRANSACTION ()
    // If queue not empty, dequeue head element
2     $sn \leftarrow head$
3   **if** $sn = $ **nil then**
4   **return**
5   **if** $head = tail$ **then**
6       $head \leftarrow tail \leftarrow$ **nil**
7   **else**
8       $head \leftarrow head.next$
    // Wake the thread when exiting from outermost txn
9   REGISTERHANDLER ($\{$SEMPOST($sn.sem$)$\}$)
10   ENDTRANSACTION ()

We expect WAIT to be called from an active synchronization context. That is, *Sync* should refer to a mutual exclusion lock that is held by the caller, or a transaction that is being executed by the caller. (We defer discussion of nested critical sections until Section 4). The thread uses a transaction to enqueue its unique node into the CondVar's queue. The use of transactions provides generality and safety: since both WAIT and NOTIFYONE use transactions to access the queue, both methods can be called from any combination of lock-based code, transactional code, and even unsynchronized code, without risking data races on the queue. Strictly speaking, if the CondVar methods are always called from the same type of synchronization context (locks or transactions), this inner transaction is not necessary.

Once the thread has enqueued its semaphore, it then completes its caller's synchronization block, by either releasing the lock or committing the transaction. At this point, we know that descheduling of the caller cannot lead to deadlock: it does not hold resources that are required by another thread. Thus it is safe for the thread to wait on its semaphore. Once the semaphore is signaled, the thread will awake, and execute the continuation (*Cont*) in a synchronized manner, in keeping with the synchronization description present in *Sync*. In comparison to Algorithm 2, we see that the only changes are (a) introducing a synchronization context, and (b) replacing spin-waiting on per-thread flags with the use of per-thread semaphores. Note, too, that by explicitly ending one synchronization context and then instantiating another, we can be sure that there is no active hardware or software transaction at the time of the call to SEMWAIT(*sem*). Without this guarantee, hardware transactions would abort, due to the system call.

The behavior of NOTIFYONE is simple: using a transaction, the caller removes exactly one element from a nonempty queue, and schedules a signal operation on that element's semaphore. As with WAIT, the use of a transaction ensures race freedom even in the case of naked notifies (i.e., when NOTIFYONE is called from an unsynchronized context). One subtlety is that we use an "onCommit" handler to schedule the semaphore signal to occur when the transaction commits. When NOTIFYONE is called while a lock is held, or from an unsynchronized context, the signal will happen immediately after line 9 completes. However, if NOTIFYONE is called from a transaction, then a waiting thread will not be woken until the notifier's outermost transaction commits. From the perspective of Mesa-style semantics, there is no harm in this approach; the wake-up operation can delay. By delaying the operation, we can be sure that (a) there is no wake-up caused by a transaction that ultimately does not commit, and (b) there is no attempt to call SEMPOST(*sem*) from an active hardware transactional context. As

with WAIT, such a call would cause the hardware transaction to abort and restart in software mode. Note, too, that the current GCC TM implementation maintains the necessary data structures to allow a hardware transaction to store onCommit handlers and run them after transaction commit.

3.3 Supporting NotifyAll

Adding NOTIFYALL support is relatively straightforward. We need only dequeue all elements from the CondVar's queue, and then schedule each element's semaphore to be signaled. An implementation appears in Algorithm 6.

Algorithm 6: The NotifyAll algorithm

procedure NOTIFYALL()
1   BEGINTRANSACTION ()
    // If queue not empty, dequeue all elements
2     $sn \leftarrow head$
3   **if** $sn = $ **nil then**
4   **return**
5     $head \leftarrow tail \leftarrow$ **nil**
    // Wake all threads when exiting from outermost txn
6   **while** $sn \neq$ **nil do**
7   REGISTERHANDLER ($\{$SEMPOST($sn.sem$)$\}$)
8       $sn \leftarrow sn.next$
9   ENDTRANSACTION ()

The principal burden of this algorithm is to ensure that accesses to a queue node's *next* pointer do not race with nontransactional accesses on line 1 of WAIT. Note that there is a form of privatization taking place: once a thread's node is removed from the queue, there should be no references to the node from any thread other than the node's owner; otherwise, the unsynchronized write on line 1 of WAIT would not be correct.

NOTIFYALL guarantees that all accesses to *next* fields are performed within a transaction. In order for these elements to be accessible to the thread, the element owner must have committed a transaction on line 8 of WAIT, and there cannot have been an intervening NOTIFYONE or NOTIFYALL that removed that thread's node from the queue. Thus it is impossible for the waiting thread to have reached line 11 of WAIT, and no race is possible.

3.4 Algorithm Properties

Our implementation provides the following properties and guarantees to programmers:

Yielding The history of monitors extends back to a time when uniprocessors were prevalent. Even with multicore CPUs, multiprogramming and oversubscription of threads necessitate support for descheduling a waiting thread, and running another thread on the same CPU. Any practical implementation of condition variables must ensure that upon reaching line 3 of Algorithm 2, the calling thread is put to sleep, and also that the delay between when NOTIFYONE is called, and when the corresponding thread wakes, is minimal. Clearly, our generic algorithm fails in this regard, as it uses a busy wait loop. Even replacing the busy wait with a call to *sched_yield* would not suffice, as it would not guarantee quick wake-up after a notification. However, our use of semaphores addresses this requirement.

Deterministic Wake-Up Semantics In Hoare's work [9], the set associated with a condition variable is explicitly stated to be a queue. Furthermore, a NOTIFYONE operation (there was no NOTIFYALL) was required to be performed while holding a lock, and immediately transferred the lock to the thread at the head of the queue. Mesa, on the other hand, delayed NOTIFY until the notifier reached the end of the critical section. This delay, and the absence of an explicit hand-off of the lock, allowed for higher performance at the cost of weaker semantics: when thread a notified thread b, there was no mechanism to prevent some other thread c from entering the monitor after a completed but before b resumed. This property is shared by our implementation: When a NOTIFYONE pairs with a WAIT operation, attempts to enter critical sections or run irrevocable transactions in other threads can cause the appearance of an unbounded delay after line 10 of WAIT.

On the other hand, the use of a generic set, rather than a queue, matches the C++11 and pthread specifications. Thus it is possible that NOTIFYONE may wake any waiting thread, without regard for which thread began waiting first. Scherer and Scott argued that both stack (LIFO) and queue (FIFO) semantics are sometimes advantageous [18], particularly with respect to caching. Our relaxed (i.e., Mesa) semantics for condition variables, coupled with the user-space implementation, allow for arbitrary thread selection policies, with FIFO as the default. Indeed, since the set is in user-space, it is possible to provide a NOTIFYBEST operation, which traverses the set and selects the best thread to wake (possibly using priority, or an additional parameter provided to the WAIT operation to describe the predicate upon which each thread is waiting).

Spurious Wake-Ups Our specification does not allow spurious wake-ups. That is, a call to WAIT cannot return unless it matches with exactly one notifying operation. This is not expensive in our algorithm, because the act of putting a thread to sleep need not be atomic with the linearization of its upper half, and thus we do not require custom OS support.

In contrast, both the C++11 and pthread specifications allow for a call to WAIT to return even in the absence of a subsequent NOTIFYONE or NOTIFYALL. This relaxation of the specification appears to be a consequence of how operating systems implement condition variables, and in particular how they respond to interrupts that arrive while a call to WAIT is in the midst of transitioning between user-space and kernel execution. In these systems, it must be assumed that *any* call to WAIT may simply return, without a matching NOTIFYONE or NOTIFYALL. Thus even in programs whose logic prevents oblivious wake-ups (see below), WAIT should be called from a loop in order to detect spurious wake-ups. In contrast, our specification does not allow such spurious returns from the WAIT method.

Oblivious Wake-Ups The addition of NOTIFYALL to monitors arose from a common usage pattern in which several threads wait on different predicates, but use the same condition variable. Since traditional condition variables maintain the set of waiting threads in the operating system, it is not possible for NOTIFYONE to know which thread to wake. Consequently, a NOTIFYONE might wake the "wrong" thread, which then must call NOTIFYONE before putting itself back to sleep. The solution, NOTIFYALL, wakes all threads sleeping on a condition variable. When more than one thread is sleeping, we refer to these as "oblivious" wake-ups, since they wake up all of a CondVar's waiting threads, regardless of whether the predicates upon which they depend have been satisfied.

The possibility of spurious wake-ups necessitates that all threads double-check program data upon return from WAIT, so allowing oblivious wakeups for legacy condition variables imposes no added burden on the programmer in the general case. Given the absence of spurious wake-ups, our implementation only requires double-checking after a WAIT for specific patterns. For example, such checks are not required for single-producer/single-consumer patterns. Note that detecting oblivious wakeups may require the continuation to recursively call WAIT if the caller's desired predicate does not hold.

4 Implementation and Usage

Up to this point, we have avoided details related to the synchronization contexts within which our CondVar objects may be accessed. Clearly the use of transactions to protect shared data suffices to allow the WAIT, NOTIFYONE, and NOTIFYALL methods to be called from any context. In practice, however, undesirable orderings between waiting threads and notifying threads require that WAIT only be called in conjunction with synchronization mechanisms, such as lock-based critical sections and transactions.

4.1 Lock-Based Critical Sections

When the synchronization context (*Sync* in Algorithm 4) represents a single lock, there are two manners in which our CondVars can be used in place of traditional condition variables. In the first case, if WAIT is the last instruction within a critical section, then the implementation will observe a null continuation. In this case, we can elide lines 11–13 of the WAIT algorithm: the thread adds itself to the set, calls ENDSYNCBLOCK() to release its lock, and then calls SEMWAIT(). Upon wakeup, the thread need not re-acquire the lock, run an empty continuation, and release the lock. For uses that fit this pattern, this optimization avoids a lock acquire/release pair, decreasing latency and reducing contention on the lock.

In legacy code, rather than create explicit continuations, an alternative is to remove lines 12–13 from Algorithm 4, and remove the *Cont* parameter. With this interface, the behavior of our CondVar, when called from a lock-based critical section, is indistinguishable from pthread or C++11 condition variables: the caller executes the continuation upon returning from the call to WAIT, and does so using the same synchronization mechanism (the same lock) as was in use at the time of the call to WAIT.

This situation can be generalized to a nested monitor environment, in which several locks are held. If *Sync* stores references to all locks held at the time of the call to WAIT, then all locks can be released (in any order) on line 9, and then can be re-acquired (presumably in order from outermost to innermost [24]) on line 11, after which the function returns. As with the single-lock setting, the use of a continuation is not required.

4.2 Software Transactional Contexts

The main benefit of a continuation-based API is for calls to WAIT from a software transaction. This is due to the way that stack variables are managed within a transactional context.

To illustrate the subtleties of using a non-continuation-based interface with software transactions, consider the code in Algorithm 7. In this code, a thread initializes function-local variable `outer` on line 1, then begins a transaction. The transaction uses `outer`, along with transaction-local variable `inner` to create the parameters to MAYINVOKEWAIT. The MAYINVOKEWAIT function potentially calls WAIT. Upon return, both `outer` and `inner` are used within the continuation to compute the final value of `outer`, which is then used outside of the transaction.

In the absence of condition variables, BEGINTRANSACTION creates a new lexical scope, which is closed by ENDTRANSACTION. The compiler uses a lightweight instrumentation to checkpoint any stack variables that are both live-in and live-out to the transaction, and which are modified by the transaction. In our example, `outer`

Algorithm 7: An example illustrating the subtleties of mid-transaction calls to *cond_wait*.

```
   procedure EXAMPLE(param)
1    stackvar outer ← F1(param)
2    BEGINTRANSACTION ()
3      txnvar inner ← F1(outer)
4      outer ← F1(outer)
5      inner ← F2(outer, inner)
6      MAYINVOKEWAIT(outer, inner)
7      outer ← F1(outer)
8      inner ← F1(inner) // Abort happens here
9      outer ← F2(outer, inner)
10   ENDTRANSACTION ()
11   F1(outer)
```

is subject to this checkpointing. Since line 7 is dominated by line 4, `outer` need only be checkpointed once, on line 4.

Committing a transaction early (Algorithm 4, line 9) does not create a substantial burden on the STM: If the STM uses undo logging, then the commit discards its checkpoint; no updates to memory are performed. If the STM uses redo logging, the commit must write-back its updates to shared memory. If the address of `inner` had been passed to F2(), in which case aliasing might result in updates to `inner` appearing in the redo log, then ENDTRANSACTION must update `inner`. If the STM assumed lexically scoped transactions, such an update would be to an invalid stack frame, and would be skipped. With early commits, the stack frame storing `inner` is valid at the time of the early commit. Thus we require a small modification to the ENDTRANSACTION function for redo-log STM systems, so that WAIT can end a transaction via ENDSYNCBLOCK() (line 9). Since the continuation is scheduled in a lexically scoped transaction (lines 11-13), there are no further concerns.

Now suppose that the continuation style is replaced with a more traditional approach. Lines 12-13 of Algorithm 4 would be removed, so that after waking, the thread would begin a transactional context and return. The first concern is somewhat esoteric: if the stack frame for WAIT is on a different virtual page than the stack frame for EXAMPLE, then after WAIT returns, the OS must not invalidate that page, or else an abort on lines 7-9 of example would result in an attempt to restore a stack frame on an invalid page. To the best of our knowledge, modern operating systems do not reclaim stack pages in this manner.

The greater challenge is that if an abort occurs on line 9, after `inner` and `outer` have been modified, then when the transaction restarts (on line 11 of WAIT), the variables must be restored to their state at the time of the call to MAYINVOKEWAIT. This requires two new forms of stack checkpointing.

First, observe that if the compiler is unaware of the possibility of WAIT causing an early commit, then the compiler will not checkpoint `inner`: it is local to the transaction. Thus the implicit BEGINTRANSACTION on line 11 of WAIT must create a checkpoint of the stack frames between it and the outermost transaction involved in the *Sync* context. This requires a small change to BEGINTRANSACTION in the common case: it must store the address of the bottom of its stack frame. Then, when line 11 of WAIT calls BEGINTRANSACTION, it must also copy all stack contents between the stored address and the currently active stack frame. Upon an abort, these contents can be restored, thereby resetting `inner` to its value at the time of the call to MAYINVOKEWAIT().

The second technique is to checkpoint variables, like `outer`, that are neither shared nor transaction-local. With our above modifications to BEGINTRANSACTION, line 2 of Algorithm 7 may or may not believe that `outer` is within its stack frame (the outcome is dependent on the compiler optimization level). However, if `outer` is modified within the transaction and before the call to MAYINVOKEWAIT, then there will be a checkpoint record in the transaction's undo log. Within WAIT, an ad-hoc checkpoint must be created at some point between lines 9 and 11: Before resetting the undo log of the transaction that began on line 2 of EXAMPLE(), we must traverse the undo log to find any address a that is (a) on the caller's stack, (b) not transaction-local, and (c) not shared.[1] Every such address is dereferenced so that the address and its current value can be stored in the ad-hoc checkpoint. If the transaction then aborts (e.g., on line 9 of EXAMPLE), then the transaction can restore the ad-hoc checkpoint before resuming, so that, e.g., `outer` will hold the value that was set on line 4.

4.3 Other Considerations

The complexity of the above mechanism is offset by a number of special cases in which it is not needed. First and foremost, we observe that hardware transactions need not be lexically scoped [10, 11]. Thus when *Sync* is a hardware transaction, the checkpoints are not required. Similarly, if it is known that the code between WAIT and the ultimate commit of the outer transaction does not include self-abort, then it is possible to run the continuation irrevocably [22, 23], in which case checkpointing is not necessary, and rollback is not possible. Of course, for long-running continuations, such an approach could greatly impede scalability.

Second, we observe that as with lock-based critical sections, empty continuations avoid this complexity. If lines 7-8 of EXAMPLE were no-ops, then instead of checkpointing and starting a new transaction, line 11 of WAIT could set a flag. WAIT would then return, and the call to ENDTRANSACTION on line 9 of EXAMPLE would immediately return if the flag was set. Another approach when the continuation is empty is to remove line 9 of WAIT, schedule line 10 via REGISTERHANDLER, and then return. In this setting, the empty continuation implies that control flow will return directly to the ENDTRANSACTION in EXAMPLE, which will commit and call its handlers; this, in turn, will call SEMWAIT().

Lastly, we note that unlike lock-based critical sections, transactions are likely to be nested, such that the *Sync* context may represent the flat nesting of several transactions. In STM, this is typically represented by a counter, and thus when WAIT begins a new transactional context on line 11, it must set the counter appropriately. In hardware TM, it may be necessary to call the hardware transaction begin function repeatedly, in order to re-create the appropriate nesting level. Depending on the implementation, this might require a small extension to the software runtime for hardware transactions, to track the nesting depth.

5 Evaluation

In this section, we evaluate the performance of our implementation of transaction-safe condition variables. We seek to answer two questions, one quantitative and the other qualitative:

- What is the overhead of these condition variables, versus pthread condition variables, in lock-based code?
- What anomalies arise when using these condition variables from transactions?

---

[1] Verifying this last property is not difficult for most STM algorithms, given the metadata they keep about locations they have read and written.

5.1 Experimental Platforms

We performed experiments using two machines. "Westmere" indicates a 6-core/12-thread Intel Xeon X5650 CPU running at 2.67GHz; "Haswell" indicates a 4-core/8-thread Intel Core i7-4770 CPU running at 3.40GHz. Both machines ran Ubuntu 13.04 with kernel version 3.8.0. All benchmarks were compiled using an experimental version of GCC, version 4.9.0. The compiler was configured to use its ml_wt software TM algorithm on Westmere, and to use its HTM algorithm on Haswell. All code was compiled at -O3 optimization level, and experiments are the average of five trials. Variance was uniformly low.

5.2 Benchmarks

We evaluated the performance of our condition variable library using eight benchmarks from the PARSEC benchmark suite [2]: facesim, ferret, fluidanimate, streamcluster, bodytrack, x264, raytrace and dedup. Of the 16 benchmarks in PARSEC, three are "network" versions of other benchmarks within PARSEC, and five benchmarks (blackscholes, freqmine, swaptions, vips and canneal) do not use condition variables. We evaluate the remaining eight benchmarks, which are expected to be representative of the general conditional synchronization patterns that are used widely in current shared-memory multi-threaded programs:

- **facesim** computes the animation of an input modeled face by simulating its underlying physics. It uses condition variables to implement a dynamic and load-balanced task queue that is shared by a group of working threads. The main program adds tasks to each task queue and waits for the completion of these tasks by the working threads.
- **ferret** is a benchmark for content-based similarity search. To process input data (i.e., images), ferret uses a pipeline that contains 6 stages, each stage containing a thread pool and a job queue. From the perspective of condition synchronization, this benchmark represents a pipelined multi-producer, multi-consumer problem.
- **fluidanimate** simulates incompressible fluid for interactive animation. Condition synchronization is only used to implement a barrier, in place of `pthread_barrier`.
- **streamcluster** solves an online clustering problem. It uses condition variables to implement a barrier, and also employs condition variables to allow a master thread to distribute work in a master/slaves pattern.
- **bodytrack** is a computer vision application that can track the 3-D pose of a human body through a series of images. Condition variables are used to implement three synchronization facilities: a barrier, a multi-threaded synchronization queue, and a persistent thread pool.
- **x264** is an H.264/AVC video encoder in which each thread encodes one frame at a time and all threads work in parallel. The use of condition variables in x264 is to coordinate the threads in the encoding process and threads waiting for reference frames.
- **raytrace** is a renderer that generates animated 3D scenes. Multiple threads use a multi-threaded task queue, which employs condition variables.
- **dedup** compresses data streams via a 5-stage pipeline, where each stage employs a queue. Condition variables are used in two settings: the per-stage queues, and a coordination mechanism between worker threads and the (serial) output thread.

Of these benchmarks, fluidanimate, streamcluster and bodytrack use condition variables in place of pthread barriers. Strictly speaking, these uses are not necessary. We measure the condition variable-based barrier nonetheless. All benchmarks except facesim and flu-

Benchmark	Total Transactions	CondVar Transactions	Refactored Continuations
facesim	9	2	0
ferret	3	2	2
fluidanimate	9	2 (2)	2 (2)
streamcluster	7	3 (2)	2 (2)
bodytrack	9	2 (1)	2 (1)
x264	4	1	0
raytrace	14	4 (1)	0
dedup	10	3	3
TOTAL	65	19 (6)	11 (5)

Table 1: Synchronization characteristics of PARSEC source code. Numbers in parenthesis indicate calls to `cond_wait` used in the barrier implementation.

idanimate can run with any number of threads. facesim can only run with a number of threads designated by its input file, while fluidanimate can only run with a power-of-2 number of threads. All benchmarks were tested with their largest available inputs: for facesim, we use input "sim_dev", for others, we use input "native".

5.3 Software Systems Compared

We compare three alternatives. Parsec+pthreadCondVar, the baseline, uses pthread locks to protect critical sections in PARSEC, and pthread condition variables for condition synchronization. Second, we evaluate our transaction-friendly condition variables in a setting where PARSEC still uses pthread locks (Parsec+TMCondVar). This implementation uses transactions internally to protect the condition variables' internal queues, and thus is compatible with code that calls CondVar methods from lock-based, transactional, or unsynchronized contexts. By comparing Parsec+TMCondVar to Parsec+pthreadCondVar, we can determine whether our mechanism offers competitive performance for lock-based code relative to the current state-of-the-art, and thus implicitly whether the use of transactions in the implementation creates unacceptable overheads. Note that on the "Westmere" machine, the internal implementation uses software transactions, but on "Haswell" the internal implementation employs hardware TM.

Our third comparison point, TMParsec+TMCondVar, replaces all locks in the eight PARSEC benchmarks with transactions, and uses our transaction-friendly implementation of condition variables. To ensure a consistent interface, we opted not to use the continuation passing style, and instead to use manual refactoring to split transactions at the point of a WAIT (see Section 4). Table 1 shows that this effort required refactoring of very few critical sections.

5.4 Performance

Figures 1 and 2 show the performance of PARSEC benchmarks on the Westmere and Haswell machines. Figure 3 presents the geometric mean speedup of each software system, versus the baseline (pthread) implementation of condition variables.

Cost of Transaction-Friendly Condition Variables Comparing Parsec+pthreadCondVar to Parsec+TMCondVar reveals the overheads that come from using semaphores and transactions to implement condition variables, instead of an OS mechanism. On both Westmere (software TM) and Haswell (hardware TM), the cost of our implementation is negligible: at times, our mechanism outperforms pthread condition variables by a small margin, and otherwise it is outperformed by a similarly small margin. Since all transactions are small (fewer than 10 locations), neither artificial conflicts (STM) or artificial fallbacks to a single lock (HTM) occur.

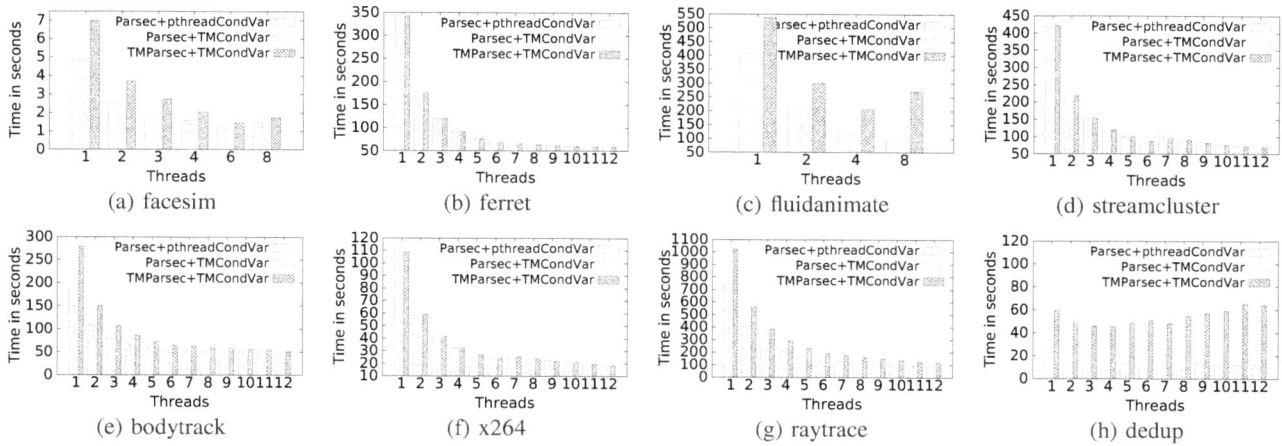

Figure 1: Westmere performance

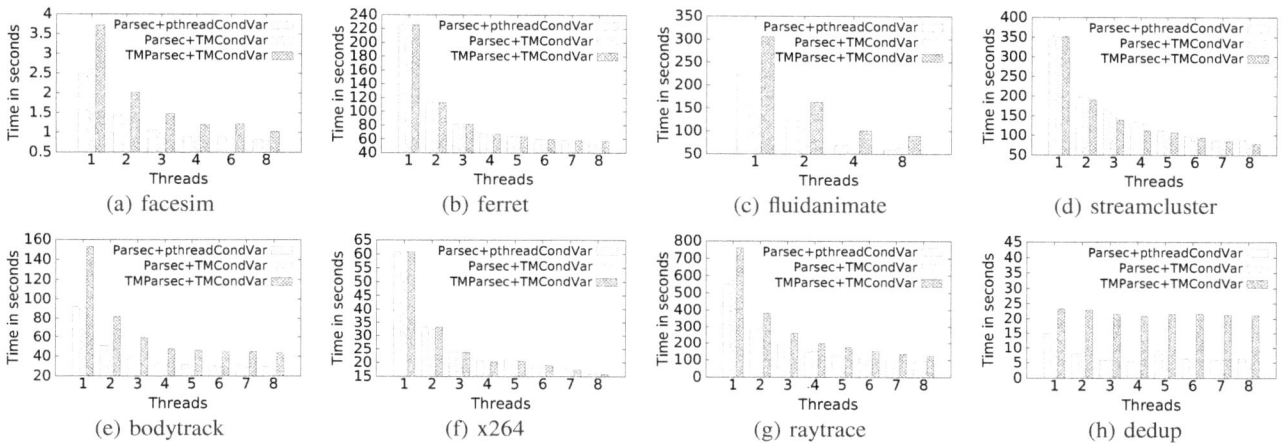

Figure 2: Haswell performance

Transactionalized PARSEC TMParsec+TMCondVar represents the first time that these PARSEC benchmarks have been transactionalized on a real-world system, since no prior work has provided support for condition variables. The benchmark performance roughly falls into three categories. First, on streamcluster, ferret, and x264, performance is roughly equivalent to baseline when all locks are replaced with transactions. Second, in facesim, fluidanimate, bodytrack, and raytrace, performance shows the same tendencies as for lock-based code, but with higher overhead. This should not be a surprise: naive transactionalization should not be expected to outperform carefully-tuned lock-based code, especially for large or conflicting transactions. We leave as future work investigation into the exact causes of these slowdowns, and remedies.

The final benchmark, dedup, exhibits virtually no scaling. In dedup, there is a critical section that performs I/O within a relaxed transaction. These relaxed transactions cannot run in parallel with any other transactions, and thus during I/O, there is no concurrency. While this situation has long been expected by the research community, dedup provides a concrete data point.

Summary Figure 3 summarizes these results: our transaction-friendly condition variables impose negligible performance degradation across all benchmarks, on both machines. The best case

speedup, on bodytrack, reaches 120% on the Westmere system, and 110% on the Haswell system. While there is clearly more work to be done before TM performs as well as locks for PARSEC, the road ahead should be much clearer now that it is possible to transactionalize these 8 benchmarks. Regarding the TMParsec+TMCondVar bars, we encourage the reader to treat the results as qualitative: at long last, condition variables can be supported when transactionalizing legacy code, and for many condition synchronization patterns, such integration is seamless and does not impair performance. These benchmarks still may require tuning to perform well when using transactions, but such an effort is outside of the scope of this paper.

6 Related Work

Research into condition synchronization mechanisms for transactions covers a wide spectrum. On one side, there are efforts, like ours, to improve the implementation of condition variables and/or provide transaction-safe condition variables. On the other side of the spectrum are efforts to craft new alternative condition synchronization mechanisms, which bear little resemblance to traditional monitors and condition variables. While our work is the first to explore condition synchronization in a manner that is compatible with both commodity hardware TM and the C++ TM specification,

(a) Westmere

(b) Haswell

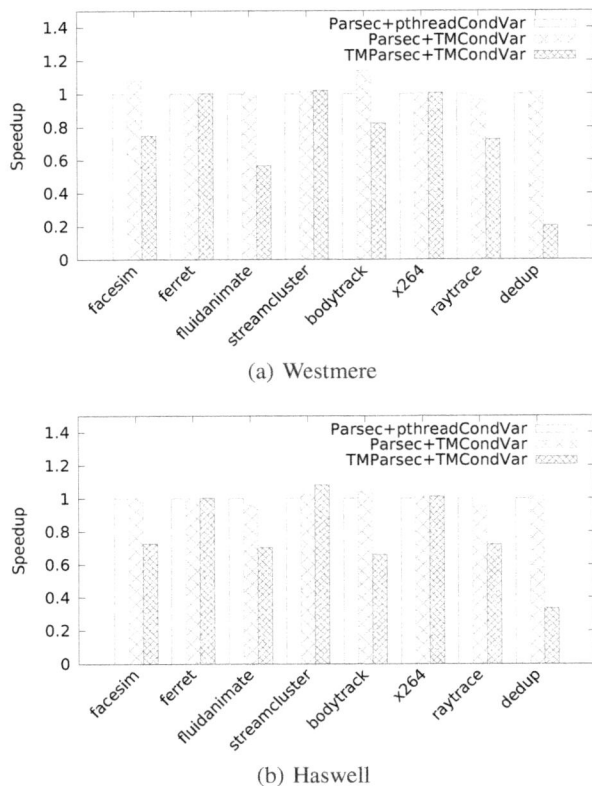

Figure 3: Geometric mean speedup versus baseline

its relationship with prior work is complex. We highlight salient foundational and related work below.

Our work to replace condition variables with semaphores bears a similarity to efforts undertaken by Birrell [3]. That work attempted to create condition variables for a general-purpose operating system (Win32) using only semaphores. A key consideration was whether it would be possible to implement each condition variable with a constant number of semaphores. Many corner cases arose, which ultimately led to the creation of first-class condition variables in later versions of Win32 operating systems. Birrell's work preceded widespread language-level support for thread-local variables, and thus did not consider the alternative we propose, of using per-thread semaphores instead of per-condition-variable semaphores.

In another closely related project, Dudnik and Swift [6] explored the hardware and OS mechanisms required to make transactions compatible with the Solaris OS's implementation of condition variables. Their work considered a robust hardware TM that had internal support for onCommit handlers, and emphasized compatibility with a legacy implementation of condition variables. As a result, the main considerations dealt with supporting system calls from within a hardware transaction, and making OS mechanisms compatible with transactional synchronization. In contrast, our work moves all but the most bare-bones scheduler interaction into user-space, and does so in a manner that is agnostic to the TM implementation and OS. Our work thus generalizes and simplifies this earliest effort at transaction-safe condition variables.

Smaragdakis et al. proposed punctuated transactions as a means of handling I/O and condition synchronization [20]. A punctuating action commits one transaction; user code can then run non-

transactionally, after which the continuation executes in a transaction. The continuation must contain programmer-supplied code to verify or restore any invariants that were violated during the period between the two "halves" of the transaction. This model has largely been ignored by the TM community for its complexity; however, the notion of restoring invariants upon resumption of a continuation is precisely the model used for monitor-based synchronization. Our implementation of WAIT can thus be thought of as a specialization of punctuated transactions, in which the only code between the punctuated halves is a SEMWAIT(sem). It should be straightforward to generalize our implementation to support other forms of punctuation, in a manner that is compatible with both hardware and software transactions.

Harris and Fraser [7], and later the X10 group [5], suggested a Conditional Critical Regions style of synchronization. In this model, the read-only prefix of a transaction determines if a predicate holds, and if not, the transaction aborts and retries. When the predicate holds, the continuation runs in the same context as the predicate test, as a single atomic transaction. To optimize this model, a transaction may make visible the locations it read to compute the predicate, so that it can yield the CPU. The transaction is woken by another thread, after that thread's transaction changes any of the locations upon which the sleeping thread's predicate depends. Harris et al. later extended this approach to a "retry" construct [8], in which transactions can, at any time, determine that a predicate does not hold. At such a point, the transaction may "retry", which rolls back the transaction's effects, makes the transaction's read set visible, and then yields the CPU until some other transaction commits a write to a location that the sleeping transaction had tried to read. Spear et al. [21] later showed that it is possible to manage retry-based read and write set tracking in a manner that is orthogonal to the underlying TM implementation. However, no existing hardware TM systems support "retry": software instrumentation is currently required.

Luchangco and Marathe [15] and Lesani and Palsberg [12] proposed mechanisms for synchronizing transactions via group commit. In these proposals, which can be extended to more closely resemble condition variables [14], an object mediates dependencies between transactions, and certain interactions (such as one transaction waiting and another signaling) create a requirement for the transactions to commit or abort atomically with each other. As with retry, this mechanism is not compatible with hardware TM: since current hardware TM proposals implement one-phase commit, they cannot ensure that two transactions commit or abort together [13]. As a result, coordinating transactions must execute in software on modern commodity hardware TM.

7 Conclusions and Future Work

This work introduces an implementation of the legacy interface for condition variables that is compatible with transactions. We make it possible, for the first time, to replace locks with transactions in existing software, even when those locks are used for both mutual exclusion and condition synchronization. In experiments on the PARSEC benchmark suite, we showed that the overhead of our mechanism relative to pthread condition variables is negligible, and that the ability to make condition synchronization compatible with transactions allows the discovery of performance anomalies when transactionalizing highly-tuned lock-based code.

Despite this improvement to the state-of-the-art, there is much work that remains, particularly with regard to programming models. In our work, we focus on lock-based code, and thus we do not need to concern ourselves with the use of the "transaction_cancel" construct. Suppose, however, that following the return of a WAIT, the continuation attempts to cancel itself. In this case, it is not clear what should happen: should the outer scope be canceled, in which case a NOTIFYONE might be lost? Should only the continuation be canceled? Real-world uses of both cancellation and transactional condition synchronization are needed before a preferred approach can be known. Indeed, the best approach might be to use a mechanism like *retry* instead. In that case, a significant challenge will be to allow uninstrumented hardware transactions to run concurrently with a retrying transaction, and to be able to call retry themselves.

Despite these challenges, we are confident that our work will enable more widespread use of transactions. In particular, our effort to make condition variables compatible with hardware TM and the C++ specification ensures that programmers can transactionalize more legacy code, and write new transactional code that uses familiar programming idioms.

Acknowledgments

We thank Victor Luchangco and Michael Scott for many helpful suggestions during the conduct of this research.

8 References

[1] A.-R. Adl-Tabatabai, T. Shpeisman, and J. Gottschlich. Draft Specification of Transactional Language Constructs for C++, Feb. 2012. Version 1.1, http://justingottschlich.com/tm-specification-for-c-v-1-1/.

[2] C. Bienia, S. Kumar, J. P. Singh, and K. Li. The PARSEC Benchmark Suite: Characterization and Architectural Implications. In *Proceedings of the 17th International Conference on Parallel Architectures and Compilation Techniques*, Oct. 2008.

[3] A. Birrell. Implementing Condition Variables with Semaphores. In *Computer Systems*, Monographs in Computer Science, pages 29–37. Springer New York, 2004.

[4] A. Birrell, J. Guttag, J. Horning, and R. Levin. Synchronization Primitives for a Multiprocessor: A Formal Specification. In *Proceedings of the 11th ACM Symposium on Operating Systems Principles*, Austin, TX, Nov. 1987.

[5] P. Charles, C. Donawa, K. Ebcioglu, C. Grothoff, A. Kielstra, C. von Praun, V. Saraswat, and V. Sarkar. X10: An Object-Oriented Approach to Non-Uniform Cluster Computing. In *Proceedings of the 20th ACM Conference on Object-Oriented Programming, Systems, Languages, and Applications*, San Diego, CA, Oct. 2005.

[6] P. Dudnik and M. M. Swift. Condition Variables and Transactional Memory: Problem or Opportunity? In *Proceedings of the 4th ACM SIGPLAN Workshop on Transactional Computing*, Raleigh, NC, Feb. 2009.

[7] T. Harris and K. Fraser. Language Support for Lightweight Transactions. In *Proceedings of the 18th ACM Conference on Object-Oriented Programming, Systems, Languages, and Applications*, Oct. 2003.

[8] T. Harris, S. Marlow, S. Peyton Jones, and M. Herlihy. Composable Memory Transactions. In *Proceedings of the 10th ACM Symposium on Principles and Practice of Parallel Programming*, Chicago, IL, June 2005.

[9] C. A. R. Hoare. Monitors: An Operating System Structuring Concept. *Communications of the ACM*, 17(10):549–557, 1974.

[10] Intel Corp. *Intel Architecture Instruction Set Extensions Programming Reference*, 319433-012a edition, Feb. 2012.

[11] C. Jacobi, T. Slegel, and D. Greiner. Transactional Memory Architecture and Implementation for IBM System Z. In *Proceedings of the 45th International Symposium On Microarchitecture*, Vancouver, BC, Canada, Dec. 2012.

[12] M. Lesani and J. Palsberg. Communicating Memory Transactions. In *Proceedings of the 16th ACM Symposium on Principles and Practice of Parallel Programming*, San Antonio, TX, Feb. 2011.

[13] Y. Liu, S. Diestelhorst, and M. Spear. Delegation and Nesting in Best Effort Hardware Transactional Memory. In *Proceedings of the 24th ACM Symposium on Parallelism in Algorithms and Architectures*, Pittsburgh, PA, June 2012.

[14] V. Luchangco and V. Marathe. Revisiting Condition Variables and Transactions. In *Proceedings of the 6th ACM SIGPLAN Workshop on Transactional Computing*, San Jose, CA, June 2011.

[15] V. Luchangco and V. Marathe. Transaction Communicators: Enabling Cooperation Among Concurrent Transactions. In *Proceedings of the 16th ACM Symposium on Principles and Practice of Parallel Programming*, San Antonio, TX, Feb. 2011.

[16] M. Ringenburg and D. Grossman. AtomCaml: First-Class Atomicity via Rollback. In *Proceedings of the 10th ACM International Conference on Functional Programming*, Tallinn, Estonia, Sept. 2005.

[17] W. Ruan, T. Vyas, Y. Liu, and M. Spear. Transactionalizing Legacy Code: An Experience Report Using GCC and Memcached. In *Proceedings of the 19th International Conference on Architectural Support for Programming Languages and Operating Systems*, Salt Lake City, UT, Mar. 2014.

[18] W. Scherer and M. Scott. Nonblocking Concurrent Data Structures with Condition Synchronization. In *Proceedings of the 18th International Symposium on Distributed Computing*, Amsterdam, The Netherlands, Oct. 2004.

[19] A. Skyrme and N. Rodriguez. From Locks to Transactional Memory: Lessons Learned from Porting a Real-world Application. In *Proceedings of the 8th ACM SIGPLAN Workshop on Transactional Computing*, Houston, TX, Mar. 2013.

[20] Y. Smaragdakis, A. Kay, R. Behrends, and M. Young. Transactions with Isolation and Cooperation. In *Proceedings of the 22nd ACM Conference on Object Oriented Programming, Systems, Languages, and Applications*, Montreal, Quebec, Canada, Oct. 2007.

[21] M. Spear, L. Dalessandro, V. J. Marathe, and M. L. Scott. A Comprehensive Strategy for Contention Management in Software Transactional Memory. In *Proceedings of the 14th ACM Symposium on Principles and Practice of Parallel Programming*, Raleigh, NC, Feb. 2009.

[22] M. Spear, M. Silverman, L. Dalessandro, M. M. Michael, and M. L. Scott. Implementing and Exploiting Inevitability in Software Transactional Memory. In *Proceedings of the 37th International Conference on Parallel Processing*, Portland, OR, Sept. 2008.

[23] A. Welc, B. Saha, and A.-R. Adl-Tabatabai. Irrevocable Transactions and their Applications. In *Proceedings of the 20th ACM Symposium on Parallelism in Algorithms and Architectures*, Munich, Germany, June 2008.

[24] H. Wettstein. The Problem of Nested Monitor Calls Revisited. *SIGOPS Operating Systems Review*, 12(1):19–23, Jan. 1978.

Brief Announcement: Fairness-Efficiency Tradeoffs in Tiered Storage Allocation

Peter Varman
Rice University
Houston, TX 77005
pjv@rice.edu

Hui Wang
Rice University
Houston, TX 77005
hw5@rice.edu

ABSTRACT

The paper examines the problem of fair bandwidth allocation in heterogeneous storage systems in the framework of multi-resource allocation. We first extend the Bottleneck Aware Allocation model recently proposed by the authors to directly compute the maximum allocation satisfying local fairness, envy freedom and sharing incentive. Next, we broaden the solution space to all allocations that satisfy envy freedom and sharing incentive even if they do not satisfy local fairness. We present an efficient algorithm to maximize the system utilization in the more general model.

Categories and Subject Descriptors

D.4.2 [**Operating Systems**]: Storage Management—*secondary storage, Allocation/deallocation strategies, Storage hierarchies*; K.6 [**Management of Computing and Information Systems**]: Installation Management—*Pricing and resource allocation*

Keywords

Multiple Resource Allocation; Hybrid Storage; QoS; Fair Allocation; Envy Free; Scheduling

1. INTRODUCTION

Multi-tiered storage has fundamentally changed the problem of QoS scheduling in storage systems [6]. It is no longer enough to treat the storage system as a block box with a certain IOPS (IO operations per second) capacity to be divided among the clients. Instead, the system needs to be managed as a heterogeneous system with multiple devices, and managed in the framework of fair multi-resource allocation (see [3, 2, 4, 5, 6]).

There is an unavoidable tension between fairness and resource utilization in allocating heterogeneous resources. Fair division of multiple resources in computer systems was addressed in a fundamental paper by Ghodsi et al [3], who advocated the Dominant Resource Fairness (DRF) model.

SPAA'14, June 23–25, 2014, Prague, Czech Republic.
ACM 978-1-4503-2821-0/14/06.
http://dx.doi.org/10.1145/2612669.2612709 .

DRF and others [2, 4, 5] define fairness as equalizing the usage of each client's dominant resource – the resource most heavily used (as a fraction of its capacity) by the client. A theoretical framework called Bottleneck-based fairness [1] proves constructively the existence of an allocation giving each client its entitlement on some system-wide *global bottleneck* resource. While these models significantly advance issues of fairness, they largely ignore their effect on system utilization. In [6] we proposed a model called Bottleneck Aware Allocation (BAA) based on the notion of *local bottleneck sets*. Clients in the same set receive allocations in proportion to their entitlements; the algorithm adjusts allocation ratios across sets to maximize system utilization. The "goodness" of all these solutions rests on the provable fairness properties of the allocation: Envy Freedom (EF), Sharing Incentive (SI) and Pareto Optimality (PO). EF means no client can increase its throughput by swapping its allocation with any other client, SI requires every client to get at least as much throughput as it would from an equal partitioning of each resource, and PO implies no client can increase its throughput without reducing that of some other client.

In this paper, we propose a simple model to trade efficiency and fairness. Unlike previous approaches we do not define any fairness ratio (dominant shares or entitlements) between the clients. Instead, we look at the fairness *outcomes* (EF, SI, PO) of the previously proposed models, and use these as primary *constraints* to our optimization problem. Subject to these requirements we find an allocation that maximizes utilization. Our solution is guaranteed to satisfy the *fairness properties* obtained by DRF and BAA, but with higher utilization.

2. MODEL

The system consists of two types of devices: solid-state disks (SSDs) and hard disks (HDs). The *capacity* of a device is its maximum throughput (IOPS). The capacities of the SSD and HD are denoted by C_s and C_d IOPS respectively. There are n clients in the system. Each client is continuously backlogged with I/O requests. The fraction of client i's requests that are directed to the HD is referred to as its *HD access ratio* and is denoted by d_i; similarly the fraction of requests to the SSD is called its *SSD access ratio* and is denoted by s_i; $d_i + s_i = 1$. Let $\delta_i = s_i/d_i$ and $\delta^b = C_s/C_d$.

A client i is said to *bottlenecked* on the HD if $\delta_i \leq \delta^b$; else it is bottlenecked on the SSD. Let $\mathcal{D}$ and $\mathcal{S}$ denote the sets of clients that are bottlenecked on the HD and SSD respectively. $\mathcal{D}$ and $\mathcal{S}$ are referred to as *local bottleneck sets*. Define client i's *entitlement*, E_i, to to be the throughput it would receive if the capacity of each device was equally partitioned among all the clients.

Example 1: Suppose $C_d = 100$ IOPS and $C_s = 500$ IOPS and there are two clients with SSD access ratios $s_1 = 1/5$ and $s_2 = 9/10$. Hence, $\delta^b = 5$, $\delta_1 = 1/4$ and $\delta_2 = 9$. Client 1 is bottlenecked on the HD and client 2 is bottlenecked on the SSD. To calculate the entitlements, we act as if each client is given a virtual HD of 50 IOPS capacity and a virtual SSD of 250 IOPS capacity. Since client 1 is HD bottlenecked it will use all 50 IOPS from the HD and $50\delta_1 = 12.5$ IOPS from the SSD for a total throughput of 62.5 IOPS, which is its entitlement. Client 2 is SSD bottlenecked and it will use all 250 IOPS from the SDD and $250/\delta_2 = 27.7$ IOPS from the HD, for an entitlement of 277.7 IOPS.

An *allocation* assigns each client i a throughput A_i made up of Δ_i IOPS from the HD and Γ_i from the SSD. $A_i = \Delta_i + \Gamma_i$, $\Delta_i = A_i d_i$ and $\Gamma_i = A_i s_i$. We are interested in feasible allocations which satisfy the capacity constraints: $\sum_i \Delta_i \leq C_d$ and $\sum_i \Gamma_i \leq C_s$. The system throughput is $\sum_i A_i$, which may be less than the capacity $C_s + C_d$.

An allocation is *locally fair* (LF) if the throughputs of clients in the *same bottleneck set* are in proportion to their entitlements. That is, for every pair of clients i, j where both belong to $\mathcal{D}$ or both belong to $\mathcal{S}$, $A_i/A_j = E_i/E_j$. An allocation is *envy free* (EF) if no client envies any other client. Client i envies j if and only if $\Delta_j > \Delta_i$ and $\Sigma_j > \Sigma_i$. In an envy-free allocation no client can increase its throughput by swapping its assignment with another client. An allocation is said to be *sharing incentivized* (SI) if every client gets a throughput at least equal to its entitlement.

BAA [6] finds an allocation that maximizes system throughput and is LF, EF and SI. DRF [3] allocations satisfy these properties but do not generally maximize throughput. The relaxation of BAA described in Section 3.2 finds an allocation that is EF and SI (but not necessarily LF) which maximizes system throughput. This can result in better system utilization without violating fairness of EF and SI.

3. RESULTS

We make two contributions in the paper. We improve the BAA model proposed in [6] by providing a simple direct method (Algorithm 1) for finding the BAA allocation that maximizes system throughput. In [6] the problem was formulated as a less compact LP optimization. In Section 3.2 we describe an algorithm to find the maximal allocation by relaxing the requirement of local fairness.

3.1 BAA Allocations

In this section we consider allocations that are LF, EF, and SI. For clients $i, j \in \mathcal{D}$, $E_i = (C_d/n)/d_i$ and $E_j = (C_d/n)/d_j$. By definition of local fairness, $A_i/A_j = E_i/E_j$. Hence, $A_i d_i = A_j d_j$. Define constant γ_d where $A_i d_i = \gamma_d$ for all $i \in \mathcal{D}$. Similarly define γ_s where $A_j s_j = \gamma_s$ for all $j \in \mathcal{S}$. Finally, define a quantity $Q = 1/\delta^b \times (\gamma_s/\gamma_d)$.

LEMMA 1. *Consider the situation where both $\mathcal{D}$ and $\mathcal{S}$ have at least one client. Consider allocations that are LF, EF, and SI. For full utilization of both devices, we require that* $Q = \frac{\sum_{i \in D}(1 - \delta_i/\delta^b)}{\sum_{j \in S}(1 - \delta^b/\delta_j)}$.

PROOF. (Sketch) For $i \in \mathcal{D}$: $\Delta_i = A_i d_i = \gamma_d$ and $\Gamma_i = A_i s_i = \gamma_d \delta_i$. Similarly, for $j \in \mathcal{S}$: $\Gamma_j = A_j s_j = \gamma_s$ and

$\Delta_j = A_j d_j = \gamma_s/\delta_j$. The total throughput from the HD is $\sum_{k=1}^{n} \Delta_i = \sum_{i \in D} \gamma_d + \sum_{j \in S} \gamma_s/\delta_j$. The total throughput from the SSD is $\sum_{k=1}^{n} \Gamma_i = \sum_{i \in D} \gamma_d \delta_i + \sum_{j \in S} \gamma_s$. For full utilization, we require the total throughput from the HD (SSD) to equal C_d (respectively, C_s). Hence: $\sum_{k=1}^{n} \Delta_k/C_d = 1 = \sum_{k=1}^{n} \Gamma_i/C_s$. Recalling the definitions of δ^b and Q and rearranging the result follows. $\square$

LEMMA 2. *If an allocation is locally fair and envy free then* $\alpha \leq Q \leq \beta$, *where* $\alpha = max\{\delta_i/\delta^b : i \in D\}$ *and* $\beta = min\{\delta_j/\delta^b : j \in S\}$. *Furthermore, the allocation is also SI.*

PROOF. See [6]. $\square$

The details of the allocation are described in Algorithm 1, and illustrated with an example. Theorem 1 summarizes the main result.

Algorithm 1: Bottleneck-Aware Allocation
Step 1. Compute Q, α and β defined in Lemmas 1 and 2 respectively.
Step 2. If $Q < \alpha$, then choose $Q = \alpha$; else if $Q > \beta$ choose $Q = \beta$.
Step 3. Compute $\nu^1 = \gamma_d(\lvert D \rvert + Q\delta^b \sum_{j \in S} 1/\delta_j)$ and $\nu^2 = \gamma_d(\sum_{i \in D} \delta_i + Q\delta^b \lvert S \rvert)$, the throughputs of the HD and SSD respectively. Set $\gamma_d = min\{C_d/\nu^1, C_s/\nu^2\}$ and $\gamma_s = Q\delta^b\gamma_d$. Calculate all A_i using γ_d and γ_s.

THEOREM 1. *Algorithm 1 computes the allocations that maximizes system utilization and satisfies local fairness, envy freedom, and sharing incentive.*

Example 2: Let $C_d = 100$ and $C_S = 200$ IOPS, so $\delta^b = 2$. There are 6 clients, $\mathcal{A}, \mathcal{B}, \mathcal{C}, \mathcal{P}, \mathcal{Q}, \mathcal{R}$ with HD access ratios 0.1, 0.2, 0, 3, 0.7, 0.8, 0.85 respectively. $\mathcal{D} = \{\mathcal{A}, \mathcal{B}, \mathcal{C}\}$ and $\mathcal{S} = \{\mathcal{P}, \mathcal{Q}, \mathcal{R}\}$. The value of Q computed from Lemma 1 equals 2.01. From Lemma 2, $\alpha = 0.21$ and $\beta = 1.17$. Table 3.1 shows the allocations using $Q = 2.01$ (columns 2-4) and that computed by Algorithm 1 with $Q = \beta = 1.17$ (columns 5-7).

For $Q = 2.01$, we use the full capacity of both devices as expected. Also $\mathcal{A}, \mathcal{B}, \mathcal{C}$ have equal HD allocations (15.5), and $\mathcal{P}, \mathcal{Q}, \mathcal{R}$ have equal SSD allocations (62.6), satisfying LF. However, since $Q > \beta$ the allocation *does not satisfy* EF. Specifically, $\mathcal{A}, \mathcal{B}$ and $\mathcal{C}$ all envy both $\mathcal{P}$ and $\mathcal{Q}$, since they can increase their throughput by swapping allocations with either $\mathcal{P}$ or $\mathcal{Q}$. To satisfy EF, Q is reduced to β as required by Step 2 of Algorithm 1. The last three columns of Table 3.1 shows the allocations for this value of Q. Only 155.9 of the SSD capacity of 200 IOPS is utilized but the allocations are all envy free.

3.2 Relaxing Local Fairness

What if the allocation of Algorithm 1 does not achieve full system utilization? That is Q was set to either α or β to meet EF requirements at the cost of system throughput. Can we find another allocation that is still EF and SI but with higher utilization by relaxing the requirements of local fairness?

i	A_i	Δ_i	Γ_i	A_i	Δ_i	Γ_i
A	17.2	15.5	1.7	22.2	20.0	2.2
B	19.4	15.5	3.9	25.0	20.0	5.0
C	22.1	15.5	6.6	28.6	20.0	8.6
P	89.4	26.8	62.6	66.7	20.0	46.7
Q	78.3	15.7	62.6	58.4	11.7	46.7
R	73.6	11.0	62.6	55.0	8.3	46.7
Sum	300.0	100.0	200.0	255.9	100.0	155.9

Table 3.1: $\mathcal{D} = \{\mathcal{A}, \mathcal{B}, \mathcal{C}\}$, $\mathcal{S} = \{\mathcal{P}, \mathcal{Q}, \mathcal{R}\}$, $\alpha = 0.21, \beta = 1.17$. **Allocations for** $Q = 2.01$ **are shown in columns** $2 - 4$ **and those for** $Q = 1.17$ **in columns** $5 - 7$.

Order the clients in non-decreasing order of s_i, so that $s_1 \leq s_2 \cdots \leq s_n$. Let $\mathcal{D} = \{1, \cdots r\}$ and $\mathcal{S} = \{r + 1, \cdots n\}$. Assume that both sets are not empty. The allocation made by Algorithm 1 satisfies the following property. First, $\Delta_1 = \Delta_2 = \cdots = \Delta_r$ and $\Gamma_{r+1} = \Gamma_{r+2} = \cdots = \Gamma_n$, due to the local fairness requirement. In addition, if only the HD is fully utilized then $\Delta_r = \Delta_{r+1}$; else if only the SSD is fully utilized then $\Gamma_r = \Gamma_{r+1}$. This follows since the allocation made by Algorithm 1 is EF and also maximizes the throughput. In Example 2, $\Delta_A = \Delta_B = \Delta_C = 20.0$ and $\Gamma_P = \Gamma_Q = \Gamma_R = 46.7$. Further, the HD is fully utilized while the SSD is not. Notice that $\Delta_P = \Delta_C$ as expected.

In the rest of this section we assume that Algorithm 1 set Q to be β so the HD is fully utilized but the SSD is not. A symmetrical argument holds when Q is set to α and the SSD is fully utilized. Algorithm 2 iteratively relaxes the local fairness requirements of clients in $\mathcal{S}$, one client at time. The algorithm successively tries to increase the SSD allocation Γ_i of clients in $\mathcal{S}$ in the order n down to $r + 1$. Due to EF requirements, Γ_i can be increased as long as Δ_i does not exceed Δ_{i-1}. Function $FindSysBottleneck(i)$ uses Equations (1) and (2) to identify which of the HD or SSD is the system bottleneck, when $\Delta_i = \Delta_{i+1} \cdots = \Delta_n$ and $\Delta_r = \Delta_{r+1}$.

$$\Delta_1 \left(\sum_{k=1}^{r} \delta_k + \delta_{r+1}(i - r - 1) + (\delta_{r+1}/\delta_i) \sum_{k=i}^{n} \delta_k \right) \leq C_s \quad (1)$$
$$\Delta_1 \left(r + \delta_{r+1} \sum_{k=r+1}^{i-1} 1/\delta_k + (\delta_{r+1}/\delta_i)(n - i + 1) \right) \leq C_d \quad (2)$$

Suppose the loop exits with loop index $i = i^*$. If $i^* = r$ then the maximum throughput is obtained by setting $\Delta_j = C_d/n$ for all clients j. If $i^* > r$, then we can revert to the allocation of the previous iteration where $i = i^* + 1$, which is EF and still has HD as the system bottleneck. In this case we have $\Delta_1 = \Delta_2 \cdots = \Delta_r = \Delta_{r+1}, \Gamma_{r+1} = \Gamma_{r+2} \cdots = \Gamma_{i^*+1}$, and $\Delta_{i^*+1} = \Delta_{i^*+2} \cdots = \Delta_n$. The capacity of iteration $i^* + 1$ is an approximation to the maximum capacity. To find the exact maximum we replace the condition $\Delta_r = \Delta_{r+1}$ with the weaker EF requirement $\Delta_{r+1} \leq \Delta_r = \Delta_1$, and set up an LP with just two variables Δ_1 and Δ_{r+1}. We maximize the total throughput subject to the two device capacity constraints, and the additional EF constraint $\Delta_{r+1} \leq \Delta_1$. Solving this 2-variable 3-constraint LP gives the maximum allocation.

Table 3.2 (columns $2-4$) shows the allocations starting from that for $Q = \beta$ in Table 3.1, after the first iteration of Algorithm 2. With $\Delta_Q = \Delta_R$, SSD throughput increases to 169.3. The next iteration with $\Delta_R = \Delta_Q = \Delta_P$ fails as equation (2) is violated. The allocation of the previous iteration (169.5 IOPS) is an approximate solution. For the maximum solution, we relax the $\Delta_C = \Delta_P$ constraint, and

Algorithm 2: Relax SSD Local Fairness

```
RelaxSSDLF ()
begin
    for (i = n-1; i > r; i = i-1)
    begin
        SysBottleneck = FindSysBottleneck(i);
        begin
            if SysBottlneck is SSD then
                break;
        end
    end
    Allocate(i);
end
```

i	A_i	Δ_i	Γ_i	A_i	Δ_i	Γ_i
A	21.4	19.3	2.1	19.8	17.8	2.0
B	24.1	19.3	4.8	22.2	17.8	4.4
C	27.6	19.3	8.3	23.4	17.8	7.6
P	64.4	19.3	45.1	51.7	15.5	36.2
Q	56.5	11.4	45.1	77.5	15.5	62.0
R	75.3	11.4	63.9	103.3	15.5	87.8
Sum	269.3	100.0	169.3	300.0	100.0	200.0

Table 3.2: Allocations after 1 iteration (columns $2 - 4$) and the maximum allocation (columns $5 - 7$)

.

solve a 2-variable (Δ_A and Δ_P) LP problem. Columns $5 - 7$ of Table 3.2 shows the allocation that achieves full utilization of both devices.

4. REFERENCES

[1] D. Dolev, D. G. Feitelson, J. Y. Halpern, R. Kupferman, and N. Linial. No justified complaints: On fair sharing of multiple resources. In *Proceedings of the 3rd Innovations in Theoretical Computer Science Conference*, ITCS '12, pages 68–75, New York, NY, USA, 2012. ACM.

[2] A. Ghodsi, V. Sekar, M. Zaharia, and I. Stoica. Multi-resource fair queueing for packet processing. In *Proc, of the ACM SIGCOMM 2012*, pages 1–12, New York, NY, USA, 2012. ACM.

[3] A. Ghodsi, M. Zaharia, B. Hindman, A. Konwinski, S. Shenker, and I. Stoica. Dominant resource fairness: fair allocation of multiple resource types. In *Proc. 8th USENIX NSDI*, pages 24–24, Berkeley, CA, USA, 2011. USENIX Association.

[4] D. C. Parkes, A. D. Procaccia, and N. Shah. Beyond dominant resource fairness: Extensions, limitations, and indivisibilities. In *Proceedings of the 13th ACM Conference on Electronic Commerce*, EC '12, pages 808–825, New York, NY, USA, 2012. ACM.

[5] A. D. Procaccia. Cake cutting: Not just child's play. *Communications of the ACM*, 56(7):78–87, 2013.

[6] H. Wang and P. Varman. Balancing fairness and efficiency in tiered storage systems with bottleneck-aware allocation. In *Proc. 12th Usenix FAST*. USENIX Association, 2014.

Brief Announcement: Deadline-Aware Scheduling of Big-Data Processing Jobs

Peter Bodík
Microsoft Research
Redmond, WA
peterb@microsoft.com

Ishai Menache
Microsoft Research
Redmond, WA
ishai@microsoft.com

Joseph (Seffi) Naor[*]
CS Department, Technion
Haifa, Israel
naor@cs.technion.ac.il

Jonathan Yaniv
CS Department, Technion
Haifa, Israel
jyaniv@cs.technion.ac.il

ABSTRACT

This paper presents a novel algorithm for scheduling big data jobs on large compute clusters. In our model, each job is represented by a DAG consisting of several stages linked by precedence constraints. The resource allocation per stage is *malleable*, in the sense that the processing time of a stage depends on the resources allocated to it (the dependency can be arbitrary in general). The goal of the scheduler is to maximize the total value of completed jobs, where the value for each job depends on its completion time. We design an algorithm for the problem which guarantees an expected constant approximation factor when the cluster capacity is sufficiently high. To the best of our knowledge, this is the first constant-factor approximation algorithm for the problem. The algorithm is based on formulating the problem as a linear program and then rounding an optimal (fractional) solution into a feasible (integral) schedule using randomized rounding.

Keywords

Scheduling algorithms; big data; deadline-aware scheduling

1. INTRODUCTION

Background and Motivation. Big data processing is increasingly receiving more attention today, as many companies process huge amounts of data to gain valuable insight into data patterns and behavior that previously were not observable. Frameworks such as MapReduce [3] or Cosmos [2] run on tens of thousands of machines and schedule jobs that process terabytes or even petabytes of data. These jobs are often used for business critical decisions and have strict deadlines associated with them. For example, outputs of some jobs are used by business analysts; delaying job completion would significantly lower their productivity. In other cases,

a job computes the charges to customers in cloud computing settings, and delays in sending the bill might have serious business consequences. If the output of a job is used by external customers, missing a deadline often results in actual financial penalty.

In practice, production jobs vary significantly in many aspects. First, they vary in *urgency*: some jobs cannot suffer delays, whereas other jobs have looser time constraints and can be pushed back. Second, they vary in *utility*: some jobs are more important than others, and as a result users have higher value assessments for their jobs meeting predefined deadlines. Finally, they vary in *structure*. Big data jobs typically have complex internal structure which makes their scheduling challenging. Jobs are composed of computation *stages*, where each stage represents a logical operation on the data, such as extraction of raw data, filtering of data, or aggregation of certain columns. The number of stages varies between jobs; for example, MapReduce jobs have only two stages, while several large production jobs in Cosmos can have up to hundreds of stages. Stages are linked by input-output dependencies that induce precedence constraints between stages. These constraints form a directed acyclic graph (DAG) structure that must be preserved when scheduling the job.

However, currently used schedulers in production typically do not support hard or soft deadlines. In most cases, a user simply submits a job with a certain resource requirement which is not necessarily matched with a concrete desired completion time. The purpose of this paper is to design a deadline-aware scheduler with provable performance guarantees for executing complex job structures on large computation clusters.

The question is, up to what level of granularity should jobs be broken into? Stages themselves typically consist of numerous vertices (also known as subtasks or worker nodes) that also induce a DAG structure. In principle, one can think of a scheduler that bypasses the stage hierarchy, treating each job as a large DAG of vertices and assigning vertices to compute slots. While a vertex-level scheduler could lead in principle to efficient allocations, it might not scale to multiple big-data jobs having millions of vertices each, which are fairly common. Consequently, allocating resources at stage-level becomes an appealing scalable alternative. On the other extreme, allocating resources at the job level would significantly reduce the scale of the problem, but might lead to very inefficient schedules. For example, different stages in a job require different level of parallelism and process different amounts of data (up to five or more orders of magnitude) and should thus be treated differently by the scheduler. Rather than allocating a fixed amount of resources

[*]Work supported in part by the Technion-Microsoft Electronic Commerce Research Center, and by ISF grant 954/11.

SPAA'14, June 23–25, 2014, Prague, Czech Republic.
ACM 978-1-4503-2821-0/14/06.
http://dx.doi.org/10.1145/2612669.2612702.

to the entire job, a stage-level scheduler can assign a different number of resources for each stage, based on the number of vertices, the amount of data to be processed within the stage, etc. Towards this end, stages are treated as *malleable* tasks, i.e., tasks that can be allocated different amounts of resources, such that increasing the number of allocated slots can reduce the stage processing time.

In this paper, we consider the problem of scheduling a set of big-data jobs on a cluster with C identical computing resources (e.g., a server or a core within a server). We summarize below the main aspects of our model.

1. Jobs consist of stages that are DAG-structured: A directed dependency edge between two stages symbolizes a precedence constraint, that is, a stage cannot be processed before its dependencies have been completed.

2. Allocations are malleable, assuming arbitrary speedups: Each stage can be allocated different amounts of resources. For example, the user may specify per stage low and high thresholds on the required amount of resources. The number of resources per stage is fixed during the execution of the stage. As mentioned, we assume that speedups can be arbitrary, i.e., the relation between the number of allocated resources and stage processing time can arbitrary. Our allocation model also enables the processing time to depend not only on the number of resources dedicated to processing the stage, but also on the specific time during which the stage started its processing. For example, the processing time can increase during times when the cluster is known to be congested.

3. Value gained by job completion depends on completion time: Each job j is associated with a value function $v_j(t)$ which represents the value gained by completing job j at a time t. The value functions can be arbitrary. Note that our model generalizes the single deadline scenario[1], as it allows for several "soft" deadlines when delayed completion time is still somewhat valuable to the user. The objective of the scheduler is to find a feasible assignment maximizing the total value extracted from fully completed jobs.

4. Jobs are known in advance (offline allocation model): In practice, deadline-bound jobs tend to be *recurring*, i.e., they are scheduled periodically, e.g., on an hourly or daily basis. One can thus use the execution statistics from past instances of these jobs to produce per-stage response curves which can serve as input to the scheduler. For example, [4] describes a method for estimating the duration of a stage with n vertices, by forming empirical distributions for each vertex which rely on past executions of the stage, and then estimating the stage duration via Monte Carlo simulations, where vertex latencies are drawn from the per vertex distributions.

Related Work. Scheduling problems of DAG-structured jobs have been widely studied in the parallel processing literature (see [9] for a survey). More related to our work, papers on scheduling DAG jobs with malleable tasks focus mainly on global system objectives such as makespan minimization (see [5, 8] and references therein). Recently, a deadline-aware scheduler for malleable tasks has been proposed [4], however the paper only proposed heuristics for the single job case. To the best of our knowledge, the objective of maximizing aggregate (completion-time) values has not been considered in the literature.

The value maximization objective has been previously considered by [6, 7, 10, 11, 1]; however, these papers treated each job as a single entity, while abstracting away inner stage dependencies and stage malleability. Such simplifications might result in inefficient resource allocation, especially for jobs with heterogenous stage profiles.

---

[1] A single strict deadline d_j can be modeled by setting $v_j(t)$ to some constant for $t \leq d_j$ and 0 otherwise.

2. PROBLEM STATEMENT

System. The system consists of a computing cluster containing C identical compute units (we use the terms compute units, resources, servers interchangeably). We assume that the timeline is divided into a discrete set of slots $1, 2, \ldots, T$ and that all of the servers are available throughout each time slot. The cluster receives a set of job processing requests. We consider the offline allocation model, in which all jobs are fully known in advance, and the goal is to schedule the jobs on the C servers during the time slots $1, 2, \ldots, T$.

Jobs. Each job j submitted to the system is described by a directed acyclic graph $G_j = (V_j, E_j)$. Nodes of the graph represent stages of the job, while edges represent the dependencies between stages. For clarity, we use the term "node" instead of "stage" to maintain consistency with graph notation. Each job j consists of n_j nodes, denoted $V_j = \{1, 2, \ldots, n_j\}$. We assume that the nodes in G_j are topologically ordered, such that $(v, v') \in E_j$ implies $v < v'$. An edge $(v, v') \in E_j$ in the graph symbolizes a precedence constraint between nodes, meaning, node v' cannot begin its execution before node v has been completed. We define the *width* ω_j of a directed acyclic graph G_j as the largest number of nodes in G_j that can be simultaneously processed without violating precedence constraints. Denote by $n = \max_j\{n_j\}$ and $\omega = \max_j\{\omega_j\}$ the largest graph size and graph width of the input jobs.

Each job is associated with a value function $v_j(t)$ that specifies the value gained by fully completing job j at any time t. The completion time of a job is defined as the latest completion time of all its nodes. The value functions are given explicitly to the scheduler, which attempts to maximize the total gained value.

Node Allocations. Allocations of resources to nodes are shaped as rectangles. A rectangle A describes an allocation of resources to a node during a time slot interval $[s(A), e(A)]$, where $s(A)$ and $e(A)$ are the processing start and end times, respectively. The height of the rectangle $k(A)$ represents the number of resources allocated to the node. A tuple $(k(A), s(A), e(A))$ is termed a *node allocation* and is denoted by A. For a time slot t, we shorten the notation of $t \in [s(A), e(A)]$ to simply $t \in A$.

Each job j specifies a set $\mathcal{A}_{j,v}$ of feasible node allocations per node[2] $v \in V_j$. To allocate node v, the system must choose exactly one node allocation from $\mathcal{A}_{j,v}$. We note that we make no additional assumptions on the relation between the number of allocated resources and the node processing time, though in practice the processing time typically decreases in the number of allocated resources. We denote by $k = \max\{k(A) \mid j, v, A \in \mathcal{A}_{j,v}\}$ the largest number of resources that may be allocated to a node.

3. DAG SCHEDULING

We present the first offline approximation algorithm for scheduling DAG-structured jobs with malleable stages to maximize the total value of completed jobs. The algorithm guarantees an expected constant approximation factor when $C = \Omega(\omega k \log n)$. The approximation algorithm is based on a randomized rounding technique, where a relaxed fractional formulation of the problem is optimally solved and then rounded to a feasible schedule of the DAG-structured jobs via randomized methods. The algorithm consists of four steps, each summarized next.

---

[2] Each set $\mathcal{A}_{j,v}$ is specified by the job owner and is part of the input to the problem. We note that the set $\mathcal{A}_{j,v}$ need not necessarily include all possible node allocations; in practice it may include only a small subset of "attractive" allocation options as perceived by the job owner.

Step 1: Linear Program. We first solve a relaxed formulating of the DAG scheduling problem as a linear program. We define a variable $x(A) \in [0,1]$ for each node allocation $A \in \mathcal{A}_{j,v}$ of job j and node $v \in V_j$, denoting the fractional allocation of A.

$$\max \quad \sum_j \sum_{A \in \mathcal{A}_{j,n_j}} v_j(e(A)) \cdot x(A)$$

$$\text{s.t.} \quad \sum_{A \in \mathcal{A}_{j,v}} x(A) \leq 1 \qquad \forall j, v$$

$$\sum_{\substack{j,v}} \sum_{\substack{A \in \mathcal{A}_{j,v}: \\ t \in A}} k(A) \cdot x(A) \leq C \qquad \forall t$$

$$\sum_{\substack{A \in \mathcal{A}_{j,v}: \\ e(A) < t}} x(A) \geq \sum_{\substack{A' \in \mathcal{A}_{j,v'}: \\ s(A') \leq t}} x(A') \qquad \forall j, (v,v') \in E_j, t$$

$$x(A) \geq 0 \qquad \forall j, v, A \in \mathcal{A}_{j,v}$$

The first two set of constraints are standard demand and capacity constraints, and the final set of constraints are the *precedence constraints* of the linear program. We define the value of a fractional solution x as the value of the objective function obtained by x.

Rounding a fractional solution x can be very difficult due to the inherit structure of x. Specifically, the support of x may contain two node allocations that cannot coexist in a feasible schedule, since their existence violates a dependency constraint; see Fig. 1 for an example. To overcome this difficulty, we first extract meaningful job allocations from x (see step 3 for definition) and then round the job allocations (step 4). Before decomposing x, we apply a preliminary correcting step called balancing (step 2).

Step 2: Balancing. The balancing step is a preliminary step used to simplify the decomposition of a fractional solution x, as described in step 3. For a fractional solution x, job j and node $v \in V_j$, we define $x_{j,v} = \sum_{A \in \mathcal{N}_{j,v}} x(A)$ as the total completed fraction of node v according to x.

DEFINITION 1. *A fractional solution x is called* balanced *if $x_{j,v} = x_{j,v'}$ for every job j and nodes $v, v' \in V_j$.*

LEMMA 3.1. *Every fractional solution x can be balanced in polynomial time without changing the value of x.*

Step 3: Decomposing a Balanced Solution. We decompose x^* into *job allocations*, which are eventually used to construct the rounded solution. A decomposition can be viewed as an alternate representation of a fractional solution in which node allocations in x are grouped into job allocations; see Fig. 1 for an example.

DEFINITION 2. *A job allocation of a job j is a set of node allocations $J = \{A_1, A_2, \ldots, A_{n_j}\}$, one allocation $A_v \in \mathcal{A}_{j,v}$ per node $v \in V_j$, which satisfies allocation precedence constraints. Formally, for every dependency edge $(v,v') \in E_j$ and corresponding node allocations $A_v, A_{v'} \in J$, we have $e(A_v) < s(A_{v'})$.*

DEFINITION 3. *A decomposition of a balanced fractional solution x is a tuple $(\mathcal{S}, y)$. The decomposition consists of a set $\mathcal{S}$ of job allocations and a mapping $y : \mathcal{S} \to [0,1]$ that satisfies for every job j, node $v \in V_j$ and node allocation $A \in \mathcal{A}_{j,v}$:*

$$x(A) = \sum_{J \in \mathcal{S}: A \in J} y(J). \qquad (1)$$

LEMMA 3.2. *A decomposition $(\mathcal{S}, y)$ of a balanced fractional solution x can be generated in polynomial time.*

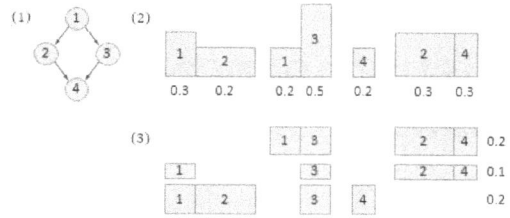

Figure 1: The figure shows an example of a job j and its fractional allocation. (1) DAG structure of job j; (2) fractional solution x (only job j shown); (3) weighted decomposition of x.

Step 4: Randomized Rounding. Our algorithm decomposes an optimal fractional solution x^* and randomly selects job allocations from the decomposition. We note that randomly generating a feasible solution, while obtaining an expected high value, is non-trivial and requires several algorithmic insights.

THEOREM 3.3. *The DAG scheduling problem admits a randomized approximation algorithm that obtains an expected approximation ratio of $\alpha(\lambda)$ for every $\lambda > 0$, where:*

$$\alpha(\lambda) \triangleq \frac{1}{\lambda} \cdot e^{-\frac{1}{\lambda}} \cdot \left[1 - e^{-\frac{\left(1 - \frac{1}{\lambda}\right)C - k}{2\omega k} \cdot \ln\left(\lambda \cdot \left(1 - \frac{k}{C}\right)\right)} \right]^n.$$

4. REFERENCES

[1] A. Bar-Noy, R. Bar-Yehuda, A. Freund, J. Naor, and B. Schieber. A unified approach to approximating resource allocation and scheduling. *Journal of the ACM (JACM)*, 48:1069–1090, 2001.

[2] R. Chaiken, B. Jenkins, P. Larson, B. Ramsey, D. Shakib, S. Weaver, and J. Zhou. SCOPE: Easy and Efficient Parallel Processing of Massive Datasets. In *VLDB*, 2008.

[3] J. Dean and S. Ghemawat. Mapreduce: simplified data processing on large clusters. In *OSDI*, 2004.

[4] A. Ferguson, P. Bodik, S. Kandula, E. Boutin, and R. Fonseca. Jockey: guaranteed job latency in data parallel clusters. In *ECCS*, pages 99–112. ACM, 2012.

[5] E. Günther, F. G. König, and N. Megow. Scheduling and packing malleable and parallel tasks with precedence constraints of bounded width. *J Combinatorial Optimization*, 27:164–181, 2012.

[6] N. Jain, I. Menache, J. Naor, and J. Yaniv. A truthful mechanism for value-based scheduling in cloud computing. In *SAGT*, pages 178–189, 2011.

[7] N. Jain, I. Menache, J. Naor, and J. Yaniv. Near-optimal scheduling mechanisms for deadline-sensitive jobs in large computing clusters. In *SPAA*, pages 255–266, 2012.

[8] K. Jansen and H. Zhang. Scheduling malleable tasks with precedence constraints. *Journal of Computer and System Sciences*, 78(1):245–259, 2012.

[9] Y.-K. Kwok and I. Ahmad. Static scheduling algorithms for allocating directed task graphs to multiprocessors. *ACM Computing Surveys (CSUR)*, 31(4):406–471, 1999.

[10] B. Lucier, I. Menache, J. Naor, and J. Yaniv. Efficient online scheduling for deadline-sensitive jobs: extended abstract. In *SPAA*, pages 305–314, 2013.

[11] C. A. Phillips, R. N. Uma, and J. Wein. Off-line admission control for general scheduling problems. In *SODA*, pages 879–888, 2000.

Brief Announcement: Parallelization of Asynchronous Variational Integrators for Shared Memory Architectures *

M. Amber Hassaan
Dept. of Electrical and
Computer Engineering
m.a.hassaan@utexas.edu

Donald Nguyen
Dept. of Computer Science
ddn@cs.utexas.edu

Keshav Pingali
Dept. of Computer Science
pingali@cs.utexas.edu

The University of Texas at Austin, Austin, TX, USA.

ABSTRACT

Asynchronous variational integrators (AVIs) are used in computational mechanics and graphics to solve complex contact mechanics problems. The parallelization of AVI is a difficult problem because it is not possible to build a dependence graph for AVI either at compile-time or at runtime. However, we show that if the dependence graph for AVI can be updated incrementally as the computation is performed, it is possible to parallelize AVI in a systematic way. Using this approach, we are able to obtain speedups of up to 20 on 24 cores for relatively small AVI problems.

Categories and Subject Descriptors

D.1.3 [**Concurrent Programming**]: Parallel Programming

Keywords

asynchronous variational integrators; dependence graph; scheduling

1. ASYNCHRONOUS VARIATIONAL INTEGRATORS

Asynchronous Variational Integration (AVI) [4] is an algorithm for solving time-dependent partial differential equations (PDEs) using a finite-element method that is irregular both in space and time. The domain of the PDE is discretized by a mesh of triangles. In conventional finite-elements, time is advanced across the entire mesh at a uniform rate, so the method is irregular in space but regular in time. For obvious reasons, this is called a *synchronous* approach to time advancement. In many problems, there is some high frequency phenomenon in some parts of the domain whereas other parts of the domain change at a relatively slow rate. In the synchronous approach, the global time-step is dictated by the need to capture the high-frequency phenomenon, so even the

---

*The work presented in this paper has been supported by NSF grants CCF 1337281, CCF 1218568, ACI 1216701, and CNS 1064956. Donald Nguyen was supported by a DOE Sandia Fellowship.

SPAA'14, June 23–25, 2014, Prague, Czech Republic.
ACM 978-1-4503-2821-0/14/06.
http://dx.doi.org/10.1145/2612669.2612713 .

---

parts of the domain that are relatively quiescent may be updated frequently. AVI seeks to eliminate this inefficiency by permitting different parts of the domain to advance at different rates, an approach that is sometimes called an *asynchronous* approach to advancing time.

```
1  Mesh mesh;
2  PriorityQueue<Triangle> pq;
3  // pq ordered by timestamp
4  pq.addAll(mesh.allTriangles());
5
6  while(!pq.emtpy()){
7      Triangle tri = pq.popMin();
8      for(Vertex v: mesh.vertices(tri)){
9          v.values = AVI-update(v,tri);
10     }
11     tri.timeStamp += tri.timeStep;
12     if(tri.timeStamp < EndTime)
13         pq.add(tri);
14 }
```

Figure 1: Pseudo-code for serial AVI algorithm

The parallelization of AVI codes is challenging because of the asynchronous way in which time advances in the domain. Pseudocode for an abstract AVI problem is shown in Figure 1. To understand the pseudocode, consider the triangular mesh shown in Figure 3. The nodes of the mesh contain fields with values for properties such as position, velocity, *etc*. Each iteration of the loop in the pseudocode processes one triangle; when a triangle is processed, the values at its nodes are read, and new values are written to those fields.

To ensure that causality is respected, the pseudocode performs triangle updates in increasing time order. Conceptually, each triangle has a time-stamp and a time-step. The time-stamp indicates when that triangle must be processed next; after it is processed, its time-stamp is updated by the time-step for that triangle. At any point during the execution, there is at most one pending update for each triangle. To ensure that updates are scheduled in increasing time order, the pseudocode maintains a priority-queue that is initialized with all the triangles in the mesh. The priority-queue is sorted in increasing time-stamp order. In each iteration of the `while` loop, the triangle with earliest time-stamp is removed from the priority queue, updated, and added back to the priority-queue for future update. This process continues until the time-stamp exceeds the simulation end time. The procedure `AVI-update` performs the integration step on the triangle, by first gathering the existing values of fields at the vertices of the triangle in the mesh, and then computing new values for them. The time-stamp of the triangle is updated by its time-step and the triangle is added back to the priority-queue.

2. PARALLELISM IN AVI

It is not clear from Figure 1 what the opportunities for exploiting parallelism in AVI are. However, if a triangle has the lowest time-stamp among the triangles that surround it in the mesh, then it can be updated regardless of the priority-queue order. The only true dependences among triangles are due to sharing of vertex data. This observation about triangles at *local minima* has been used by Huang *et al.*, and, Kale *et al.*, to parallelize AVI [2, 3].Therefore, the priority-queue order of Figure 1 is too restrictive for most inputs.

Using the insight that triangles at local-minima can be updated in parallel, regardless of the global priority order, we can parallelize the while loop of Figure 1. Each loop iteration is a task. However, we need a structure that captures the dependences among tasks due sharing of vertices among triangles, and allows us to identify the triangles at local minima. Notice that we cannot build a static dependence graph for this loop, because the dependences among triangles (tasks) are input dependent. Furthermore, even if we build a dependence graph after reading the mesh, we cannot use it to schedule tasks, because in AVI, tasks create new tasks (*i.e.*, the next update for the triangle). The number of updates is equal to the number of times the triangle is added to the priority-queue, which is again input dependent and can only be known after the execution (unless the time-step is known).

3. AVI PARALLELIZATION

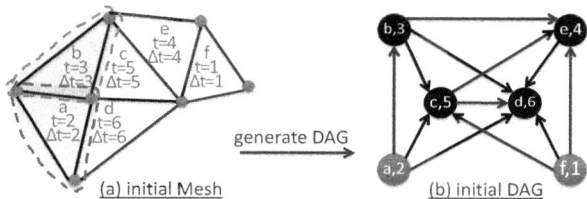

Figure 2: Generating a dependence DAG from input

While we cannot build a static DAG for the loop in Figure 1, we can build dependence graph $G = (V, E)$, for a specific state of the mesh in AVI, at runtime. V has a node for every triangle, since there is at most one pending update for a triangle at any point during the execution. Since dependences are due to sharing of vertices between triangles, we create an edge in E between all pairs of triangles that share a vertex in the mesh. The edges are directed from lower time-stamp to higher time-stamp in G, in order to maintain time-monotonicity of vertex updates. Since time-stamp order is a total order, G is a DAG[1]. A DAG has one or more *source* nodes, which are nodes with no incoming edges. The sources in a dependence DAG correspond to tasks that are ready to execute. Figure 2 shows the dependence DAG for a simple AVI mesh. The shaded regions in the mesh show the vertex data that would be read and written to, when updating triangles a and b. Tasks for triangles a, and f are sources in this DAG.

We can pick sources from the dependence DAG for some specific state of AVI and schedule them for execution. However, the state of the DAG after executing and removing a source, does not correspond to the state of the mesh. Figure 4(b) shows the state of the DAG for our simple input, after the task for triangle a has been removed from the DAG and executed. But we also must create a new task for next update for a, *i.e.*, $(a, 4)$. Figure 4(b), therefore,

---

[1]if time-stamps of two adjacent triangles are equal, we break the tie using their unique IDs

does not correspond to the state of the mesh after updating triangle a, which is shown in Figure 3(b). In summary, we cannot use a dependence DAG for AVI in the manner static dependence graphs have been used classically, where we know the set of tasks and their dependences before execution, and once the graph is built, we simply remove sources from the graph and execute them. In case of AVI, we can either rebuild the DAG (from scratch) from the new state of the mesh, or, we can fix the DAG by adding a node for the next update to a triangle, after we remove a task for execution. This incremental fixing of the DAG is more efficient than rebuilding the DAG from scratch. Notice that the new task is for the same triangle that was update by the source task, *e.g.*, triangle a in Figure 4(c). Therfore, the new node in the DAG has the same neighbors as the removed task, however, since the timestamp of triangle a was incremented, we must update the direction of the edges of the new task $(a, 4)$. Notice that in Figure 4(c), the node $(a, 4)$ is no longer a source, while node $(b, 3)$ has become a source. By scanning the neighbors of the new node in the DAG, we can find if any of them have become a source, or if the new node is a source, either of which can be scheduled next.

3.1 Implementation Details

Figure 4 shows an example of how a DAG can be used for scheduling of tasks in AVI, by repeatedly adding the task (for next triangular update) to the DAG after a task has executed. Notice that in AVI, the new task has same neighbors in the DAG as the source task it replaces. Therefore, it may be more efficient to implement the DAG-update as follows: i) update the timestamp of the source task after execution, ii) compare the new time-stamp against the neighbors of this task and flip the edges if necessary. For correctness, the new direction on the edges must be consistent with the time-stamp order. As a further optimization, the flipping of the edges can be performed implicitly using flag variables. One implementation of the DAG uses an undirected graph, where edge directions are maintained using a counter on each node that maintains its in-degree. A node is a source in the DAG if its in-degree is 0. Similarly, flipping a edge means incrementing the counter on the source of the node, while decrementing it on the destination of the node. This optimization has been used by Huang *et al.* [2].

We implemented this parallelization strategy using Galois framework, which provides parallel programming extensions to C++ [1]. We use the `foreach` loop provided by Galois, which iterates over the worklist of sources. Threads process iterations of this loop in parallel, each of which executes one source and performs the updates to the dependence DAG. New sources are added to the worklist by scanning the neighbors of the source that is processed. Since the structure of the DAG is an undirected graph, which does not change during execution, it does not need to be protected for concurrent accesses. The in-degree counter can be implemented using an atomic integer from C++ STL.

4. EXPERIMENTAL RESULTS

We show the performance of our parallel implementation of AVI compared to a serial implementation. The serial implementation is based on a *priority-queue* from the C++ standard template library. We used two inputs, small and large. The inputs are listed in Figure 5. For each input, we also show the size of the dependence DAG.

We used a 24-core Xeon E7540 server for our experiments. The cores are organized as 4 packages (6 cores per package), running at 2 GHz. Each package has an 18 MB L3 cache. The system has 128 MB of RAM, and runs Scientific Linux 6.3. We compiled our

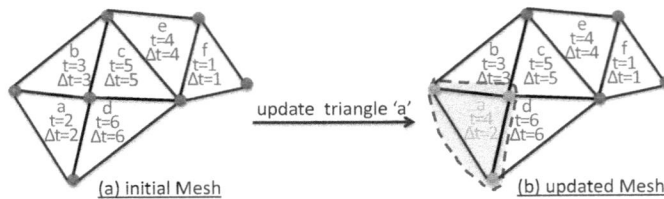

Figure 3: Showing the changes to state when a triangle is updated

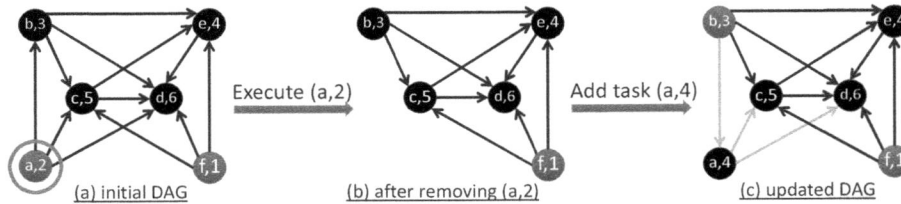

Figure 4: Updating the DAG, when a task is processed and a new task for same triangle is created

	Input Stats		DAG Stats		Serial	Parallel	
	Triangles	Vertices	$|V|$	$|E|$		T=1	T=24
Small	41k	21k	41k	253k	61	72	2.9
Large	166k	84k	166k	999k	110	149	5.3

Figure 5: Inputs and running times (in seconds) for serial and parallel implementation

code with GCC 4.7 (-O3 optimization level). We also take advantage of 2MB huge pages supported by this system.

Figure 5 shows running times (in seconds) of our serial and parallel code. Our parallel implementation achieves a best-case speedup of 21X and 20.75X on the small and large inputs respectively. Figure 6 plots the speedup against serial for up to 24 threads. The plot shows that our parallel implementation scales well with the number of threads.

5. CONCLUSION

We have shown how AVI can be parallelized by incrementally updating a DAG, which captures the changing dependences in the application. To improve the performance of DAG construction, an edge-flipping rule which allows a DAG for one state to be constructed from the DAG of the previous state can be used. Comparison with a sequential implementation shows that our approach leads to good parallel performance. We leave to future work whether this approach can be generalized to other applications.

6. REFERENCES

[1] http://iss.ices.utexas.edu/?p=projects/galois.

[2] Jen-Chih Huang, Xiangmin Jiao, Richard M. Fujimoto, and Hongyuan Zha. Dag-guided parallel asynchronous variational integrators with super-elements. In *Proceedings of the 2007 summer computer simulation conference*, SCSC, pages 691–697, San Diego, CA, USA, 2007. Society for Computer Simulation International.

[3] Kedar G. Kale and Adrian J. Lew. Parallel asynchronous variational integrators. *International Journal for Numerical Methods in Engineering*, 70(3):291–321, 2007.

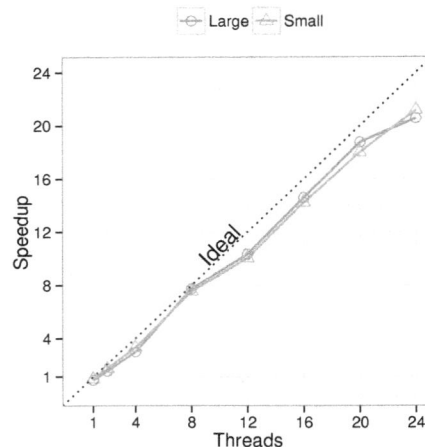

Figure 6: Speedup against serial implementation

[4] A. Lew, J. E. Marsden, M. Ortiz, and M. West. Asynchronous variational integrators. *ARCHIVE FOR RATIONAL MECHANICS AND ANALYSIS*, 2003.

Brief Annoucement: A Distributed Minimum Cut Approximation Scheme [*]

Hsin-Hao Su
University of Michigan
Ann Arbor, MI 48109
hsinhao@umich.edu

ABSTRACT

In this paper, we study the problem of approximating the minimum cut in a distributed message-passing model, the CONGEST model. The minimum cut problem has been well-studied in the context of centralized algorithms. However, there were no known non-trivial algorithms in the distributed model until the recent work of Ghaffari and Kuhn. They gave randomized algorithms for finding cuts of size $O(\epsilon^{-1}\lambda)$ and $(2+\epsilon)\lambda$ in $O(D) + \tilde{O}(n^{1/2+\epsilon})$ rounds and $\tilde{O}(D + \sqrt{n})$ rounds respectively, where λ is the size of the minimum cut. This matches the lower bound they provided up to a polylogarithmic factor. Yet, no scheme that achieves $(1+\epsilon)$-approximation ratio is known. We give a distributed randomized algorithm that finds a cut of size $(1 + \epsilon)\lambda$ in $\tilde{O}(D + \sqrt{n})$ time, which is optimal up to polylogarithmic factors.

Categories and Subject Descriptors

F.2.2 [**Analysis of Algorithms and Problem Complexity**]: Nonnumerical Algorithms and Problems—*computations on discrete structures*; G.2.2 [**Discrete Mathematics**]: Graph Theory—*graph algorithms, network problems*

Keywords

distributed approximation; CONGEST model; minimum cut

1. INTRODUCTION

The minimum cut problem is a fundamental problem in graph algorithms and network design. Given a weighted undirected graph $G = (V, E)$, a cut $C = (S, V \setminus S)$ where

$\emptyset \subset S \subset V$, is a partition of vertices into two non-empty sets. The weight of a cut, $w(C)$, is defined to be the sum of the edge weights crossing C. The minimum cut problem is to find a cut with the minimum weight. The exact version of the problem as well as the approximate version have been studied for many years [5, 9, 7, 12, 11, 3, 14, 8] in the context of centralized models of computation, resulting in nearly linear time algorithms [8, 11, 7].

Elkin [2] and Das Sarma et al. [1] addressed the problem in the distributed, synchronous message-passing model. The problem has trivial time complexity of $\Theta(D)$ (unweighted diameter) in the LOCAL model, where the message size is unlimited. Ghaffari and Kuhn [4] recently developed approximation algorithms for this problem in the CONGEST model where each message is bounded by $\Theta(\log n)$ bits. They assume that the edges of G have integer weights from $\{1, \dots, n^{\Theta(1)}\}$ and treat G as an unweighted multigraph, where an edge e with weight $w(e)$ is converted to $w(e)$ parellel edges, while still only $\Theta(\log n)$ bits can be sent over these parallel edges together in each round. Let λ be the value of the minimum cut, they give an algorithm that finds a cut of size at most $O(\epsilon^{-1}\lambda)$ with high probability[1] in $O(D) + O(n^{1/2+\epsilon} \log^3 n \log \log n \log^* n)$ time. Moreover, they gave an algorithm that finds a cut of size at most $(2+\epsilon)\lambda$ w.h.p. in $O((D+\sqrt{n}\log^* n)\log^2 n \log\log n \frac{1}{\epsilon^5})$ time. Das Sarma et al. [1] showed that α-approximating the minimum cut requires $\tilde{\Omega}(D + \sqrt{n})$ rounds for weighted graphs for any $\alpha \geq 1$. Ghaffari and Kuhn extended their lower bound for unweighted multigraphs (which is equivalent to the setting where one is allowed to send messages of size $w \cdot \Theta(\log n)$ over an edge of weight w in weighted graphs). For unweighted simple graphs, they also gave a lower bound of $\tilde{\Omega}(D+\sqrt{n/\alpha})$. Therefore, the upper bound and lower bound provided by Ghaffari and Kuhn match up to a polylogarithmic factor.

However, still no approximation algorithms exist for any approximation factor less than 2. In this paper, we give a simple algorithm that finds a minimum cut of size at most $(1+\epsilon)\lambda$ w.h.p. in $\tilde{O}(D + \sqrt{n})$ time. In particular, our algorithm runs in $O((\log^{11} n/\epsilon^{17})(D + \sqrt{n}\log^* n))$ rounds.

Our approach uses the semi-duality between minimum cuts and tree packings as in [8, 16]. Karger [8] showed that if we greedily pack enough trees, then for any minimum cut, there is a tree crossing the cut at most twice. However, it is technically not easy to utilize this fact to find minimum cuts in the distributed model. Instead, we use a lemma by

[*]This work is supported by NSF grants CCF-0746673, CCF-1217338, and CNS-1318294 and a grant from the US-Israel Binational Science Foundation. This work was done while visiting MADALGO at Aarhus University. A detailed version of the paper is available at arXiv.org [15].

SPAA'14, June 23–25, 2014, Prague, Czech Republic.
ACM 978-1-4503-2821-0/14/06.
http://dx.doi.org/10.1145/2612669.2612706.

[1] *With high probability* (w.h.p.) means with probability $1 - 1/n^c$, for a fixed constant c.

Thorup [16], which shows that if we pack more trees then there is at least one minimum cut that is crossed by a tree exactly once. We take some ingredients from Ghaffari and Kuhn's algorithm and Thurimella's algorithm [17] for identifying biconnected components to devise a procedure that is able to simultaneously test the values of the $n-1$ cuts induced by deleting one of the $n-1$ edges in a tree. Note that the number of trees we have to pack is polynomial in the value of the minimum cut. Thus, we will first use the sampling lemma of Karger [6] to obtain a sampled graph that scales the value of the minimum cut down to $O(\log n/\epsilon^2)$. Then we only have to pack polylogarithmic number of trees. Finally, we combine the resampling procedure, the tree packing, and the procedure for testing tree-induced-cuts to find an approximate minimum cut.

Very recently, Nanongkai [13] independently gave a $(1+\epsilon)$-approximation algorithm that runs in $\tilde{O}(\sqrt{n}+D)$ time. His algorithm also uses Thorup's tree packing lemma. However, the way he computes the cuts that are crossed once by the trees is by Karger's dynamic programming approach [8], which is very different from ours.

2. DISTRIBUTED MINIMUM CUT APPROXIMATION

Let G be a connected graph with integer weights from $\{1,\ldots,W\}$, where $W = n^{\Theta(1)}$. We will treat G as a multigraph with uniform edge weights. Let λ be the weight of the minimum cut of G. We show how to find such an approximate minimum cut whose weight is at most $(1+\epsilon)\lambda$.

An edge e is a *bridge* if there does not exist a cycle in G passing through e (or equivalently, deleting e breaks G into two connected components). Given two graph A and B with the same vertex set, $A + B$ is the multigraph obtained by including edges in A and edges in B.

A *tree packing* $\mathcal{T}$ is a multiset of spanning trees. The *load* of an edge e with respect to $\mathcal{T}$ is the number of trees in $\mathcal{T}$ containing e. Given a tree T, we say a cut is *induced* by T if such a cut is obtained by deleting an edge $e \in T$. We will denote this cut by $C(T,e)$. A tree packing $\mathcal{T} = \{T_1,\ldots,T_k\}$ is *greedy* if each T_i is a minimum spanning tree with respect to the loads induced by $\{T_1,\ldots,T_{i-1}\}$. Let $\epsilon' = \Theta(\epsilon)$ such that $(1+\epsilon')^3/(1-\epsilon') = 1+\epsilon$.

LEMMA 2.1 (THORUP [16]). *A greedy tree packing with $96(\lambda+1)^7 \log^3 m$ trees contains a tree crossing some min-cut only once.*

We describe our algorithm in Algorithm 1. The subroutine $\text{Test}(T,\kappa)$ returns a cut whose weight is at most $(1+\epsilon')\kappa$ w.h.p. if there exists a cut in G induced by T with weight at most κ.

We show that w.h.p. the algorithm will output a cut C with $w(C) \le (1+\epsilon)\lambda$. In particular, consider the iteration i where $\lambda \in [X_i, X_{i+1}]$. Let λ' denote the value of the minimum cut in the sampled graph H_i. If $i = 0$, then it is clear that $\lambda' = \lambda \le X_1 = 20\ln n/\epsilon'^2$. If $i > 0$, since we sampled with probability $1/2^i = 20\ln n/(\epsilon'^2 X_{i+1}) = 10\ln n/(\epsilon'^2 X_i) \ge 10\ln n/(\epsilon'^2\lambda)$, we know that w.h.p. for any cut C [6, Corollary 2.4],

$$(1-\epsilon') \cdot w_G(C)/2^i \le w_{H_i}(C) \le (1+\epsilon') \cdot w_G(C)/2^i.$$

Therefore, $\lambda' \le (1+\epsilon')\lambda/2^i \le (1+\epsilon')20\ln n/\epsilon'^2$. If we pack $96(\lambda'+1)^7 \log^3 m$ trees in $\mathcal{T}$, then by Lemma 2.1 there

---

```
1:  X_0 ← 1
2:  i ← 0
3:  repeat
4:      X_{i+1} ← 2^i · 20 ln n/ε'^2
5:      (We are assuming λ ∈ [X_i, X_{i+1}] in this iteration)
6:      Let H_i be the subgraph sampled with probability p = 1/2^i on each edge of G.
7:      Find a greedy tree packing T with 96((1 + ε')20 ln n/ε'^2 + 1)^7 ln^3 m trees in H_i
8:      γ ← X_i
9:      repeat
10:         for each T ∈ T do
11:             Call Test(T, (1 + ε')γ).
12:             If Test(T, (1 + ε')γ) returns a cut C, output C and terminate.
13:         end for
14:         γ ← (1 + ε')γ
15:     until γ > (1+ε')/(1-ε') · X_{i+1}
16:     i ← i + 1
17: until X_{i+1} > nW
```

Algorithm 1: $(1+\epsilon)$-approximate minimum cut

exists a tree crossing some minimum cut C^* of H_i only once. Notice that for any other cut C',

$$w_G(C^*) \le 2^i \cdot \frac{w_{H_i}(C^*)}{1-\epsilon'} = 2^i \cdot \frac{\lambda'}{1-\epsilon'}$$
$$\le 2^i \cdot \frac{w_{H_i}(C')}{1-\epsilon'} \le \frac{1+\epsilon'}{1-\epsilon'} \cdot w_G(C')$$

Therefore, one of the cuts induced by some $T \in \mathcal{T}$ is an $(1+\epsilon')/(1-\epsilon')$ approximate minimum cut. Denote this cut by C', so $w(C') \in [X_i, ((1+\epsilon')/(1-\epsilon')) \cdot X_{i+1}]$. Therefore in the i'th iteration, there exists γ in the loop (Line 9–Line 15) such that $w(C') \in [\gamma, (1+\epsilon')\gamma]$. So w.h.p. we will output a cut with weight at most $(1+\epsilon')^2\gamma \le (1+\epsilon')^2 w(C') \le (1+\epsilon')^3/(1-\epsilon')w(C^*) = (1+\epsilon)w(C^*)$.

2.1 Distributed Implementation

We have shown the correctness of this algorithm. It remains to show how to implement it in $\tilde{O}(D+\sqrt{n})$ distributed rounds, and in particular, to implement the tree packing (Line 7) and $\text{Test}(T,\kappa)$ in Algorithm 1. To pack k trees, it is straightforward to apply k MST computations on the graph where the edge weights are equal to the number of trees including it. This can be done in $O(k(D+\sqrt{n}\log^* n))$ rounds [10].

Given a partition $\mathcal{P}$ of G into components, Ghaffari and Kuhn [4] devised a testing procedure to test if there is a cut induced by a component in $\mathcal{P}$ that has weight less than κ in $\tilde{O}(D+\sqrt{n})$ rounds. Given a spanning tree T, we describe in Algorithm 2 how to test the $n-1$ cuts induced by T also in $\tilde{O}(D+\sqrt{n})$ rounds.

LEMMA 2.2. *If T induces a cut $C(T,e)$ with weight at most κ, then $\text{Test}(T,\kappa)$ returns a cut w.h.p. Moreover, any cut returned by the algorithm has weight at most $(1+\epsilon')\kappa$ w.h.p.*

PROOF. Consider a cut $C(T,e)$. First observe that G_i contains an edge crossing $C(T,e)$ if and only if e is not a bridge in the multigraph $G_i + T$. Therefore, $\text{E}[Y_{e,i}] = 1 - (1 - (1 - 2^{-1/\kappa}))^{w(C(T,e))} = 1 - 2^{-w(C(T,e))/\kappa}$.

218

1: **for** $i \leftarrow 1 \ldots k = \Theta(\frac{\log n}{\epsilon^2})$ **do**
2:      Let G_i be the subgraph obtained by sampling each edge of G independently with probability $1 - 2^{-1/\kappa}$.
3:      For each edge $e \in T$, determine if e is a **bridge** in $G_i + T$.
4:      Let $Y_{e,i} = \begin{cases} 1 & \text{if } e \text{ is not a bridge in } G_i + T. \\ 0 & \text{otherwise.} \end{cases}$
5: **end for**
6: If there is $e \in T$ such that $\sum_{i=1}^{k} Y_{e,i} \leq k/2 + \epsilon' k/8$, then return the cut $C(T, e)$

Algorithm 2: $\text{Test}(T, \kappa)$. $\text{Test}(T, \kappa)$ returns a cut whose weight is at most $(1 + \epsilon')\kappa$ w.h.p. if there exists a cut in G induced by T with weight at most κ. Note that the sample probability $1 - 2^{-1/\kappa} = \Theta(1/\kappa)$.

If $w(C(T, e)) \leq \kappa$, then $\mathrm{E}[Y_{e,i}] \leq 1/2$ and $\mathrm{E}[\sum_i Y_{e,i}] \leq k/2$. By Hoeffding's inequality, $\Pr(\sum_i Y_{e,i} > k/2 + \epsilon' k/8) \leq \Pr(\sum_i Y_{e,i} > \mathrm{E}[\sum_i Y_{e,i}] + \epsilon' k/8) \leq e^{-\frac{2(\epsilon' k/8)^2}{k}} = e^{-\epsilon'^2 k/32} = 1/\text{poly}(n)$. By taking the union bound over the $n - 1$ cuts induced by T, we conclude that w.h.p. the algorithm will return a cut if there is a cut whose weight is at most κ.

On the other hand if $w(C(T, e)) > (1 + \epsilon')\kappa$, then $\mathrm{E}[Y_{e,i}] = 1 - 2^{-1-\epsilon'} \geq 1/2 + \epsilon'/4$ when $\epsilon' \leq 1$, since $2^{-\epsilon'} \leq 1 - \epsilon'/2$ when $\epsilon' \leq 1$. So $\mathrm{E}[\sum_i Y_{e,i}] \geq k/2 + \epsilon' k/4$. By Hoeffding's inequality, $\Pr(\sum_i Y_{e,i} \leq k/2 + \epsilon' k/8) \leq \Pr(\sum_i Y_{e,i} \leq \mathrm{E}[\sum_i Y_{e,i}] - \epsilon' k/8) \leq e^{-\frac{2(\epsilon' k/8)^2}{k}} = e^{-\epsilon'^2 k/32} = 1/\text{poly}(n)$. By taking the union bound over the $n-1$ cuts induced by T, we conclude the cut returned by the algorithm has weight at most $(1 + \epsilon')\kappa$ w.h.p. $\square$

Given a subgraph G_i of G, it remains to show how to determine what edges of T are bridges in the subgraph $T + G_i$ in $\tilde{O}(D + \sqrt{n})$ rounds. Thurimella [17] gave an algorithm for computing the biconnected components of the underlying graph in $\tilde{O}(D + \sqrt{n})$ rounds. With simple modifications, it can be applied to compute which edges of T are bridges in the *subgraph G_i* of the underlying graph G. Note that even if we have the algorithm for computing the bridges of T in $G + T$, it is not clear whether we can directly simulate it to compute the bridges of T in $G_i + T$, for we want the running time to depend on the diameter of G rather than that of G_i. We describe the algorithm and the necessary changes in [15].

2.2 Running Time

Now we analyze the running time of Algorithm 1. The outerloop runs for $O(\log n)$ iterations. Therefore, the tree packing, Line 7, is executed $O(\log n)$ times, each taking $O(\log^{10} n/\epsilon^{14}(D + \sqrt{n} \log^* n))$ rounds.

Let $k = O(\log(nW))$ be the largest index such that $X_k \leq nW$. The total number of iterations that the innerloop runs is at most

$$\sum_{i=0}^{k} \log_{1+\epsilon'} \left(\frac{1 + \epsilon'}{1 - \epsilon'} \cdot \frac{X_{i+1}}{X_i} \right) = O(k) + \sum_{i=0}^{k} \log_{1+\epsilon'} \frac{X_{i+1}}{X_i}$$

$$= O(k) + \log_{1+\epsilon'}(X_{k+1}) = O(\log n/\epsilon)$$

Therefore, $\text{Test}(T, \kappa)$ is invoked at most $O((\log n/\epsilon) \cdot (\log^{10} n/\epsilon^{14}))$ times, each taking $O((\log n/\epsilon^2)(D + \sqrt{n} \log^* n))$ rounds.

Therefore, the total running time is $O((\log^{12} n/\epsilon^{17}) \cdot (D + \sqrt{n} \log^* n)) = \tilde{O}(D + \sqrt{n})$.

REMARK 2.3. *The total iterations of the outerloop and innerloop in Algorithm 1 can be reduced to $O(1)$ and $O(1/\epsilon)$ by first approximating λ within constant factor by Ghaffari and Kuhn's algorithm. Then, we can reduce our running time to $O((\log^{11} n/\epsilon^{17})(D + \sqrt{n} \log^* n))$.*

3. REFERENCES

[1] A. Das Sarma, S. Holzer, L. Kor, A. Korman, D. Nanongkai, G. Pandurangan, D. Peleg, and R. Wattenhofer. Distributed verification and hardness of distributed approximation. *SIAM Journal on Computing*, 41(5):1235–1265, 2012.

[2] M Elkin. Distributed approximation: A survey. *SIGACT News*, 35(4):40–57, 2004.

[3] H. N. Gabow. A matroid approach to finding edge connectivity and packing arborescences. *Journal of Computer and System Sciences*, 50(2):259 – 273, 1995.

[4] M. Ghaffari and F. Kuhn. Distributed minimum cut approximation. In *Proc. 27th Symposium on Distributed Computing (DISC)*, pages 1–15. 2013.

[5] D. R. Karger. Global min-cuts in RNC, and other ramifications of a simple min-out algorithm. In *Proc. 4th Annual ACM-SIAM Symposium on Discrete Algorithms (SODA)*, pages 21–30, 1993.

[6] D. R. Karger. Random sampling in cut, flow, and network design problems. In *Proce. 26th ACM Symposium on Theory of Computing (STOC)*, pages 648–657, 1994.

[7] D. R. Karger. Using randomized sparsification to approximate minimum cuts. In *Proc. 5th Annual ACM-SIAM Symposium on Discrete Algorithms (SODA)*, pages 424–432, 1994.

[8] D. R. Karger. Minimum cuts in near-linear time. *J. ACM*, 47(1):46–76, January 2000.

[9] D. R. Karger and C. Stein. An $\tilde{O}(n^2)$ algorithm for minimum cuts. In *Proc. 25th ACM Symposium on Theory of Computing (STOC)*, pages 757–765, 1993.

[10] S. Kutten and D. Peleg. Fast distributed construction of k-dominating sets and applications. In *Proc. 14th ACM Symposium on Principles of Distributed Computing (PODC)*, pages 238–251, 1995.

[11] D. W. Matula. A linear time $2 + \epsilon$ approximation algorithm for edge connectivity. In *Proc. 4th Annual ACM-SIAM Symposium on Discrete Algorithms (SODA)*, pages 500–504, 1993.

[12] H. Nagamochi and T. Ibaraki. Computing edge-connectivity in multigraphs and capacitated graphs. *SIAM J. Discret. Math.*, 5(1):54–66, 1992.

[13] D. Nanongkai. Brief announcement: Almost-tight approximation distributed algorithm for minimum cut. *CoRR*, abs/1403.6188, 2014.

[14] M. Stoer and F. Wagner. A simple min-cut algorithm. *J. ACM*, 44(4):585–591, 1997.

[15] H.-H. Su. A distributed minimum cut approximation scheme. *CoRR*, abs/1401.5316, 2014.

[16] M. Thorup. Fully-dynamic min-cut. *Combinatorica*, 27(1):91–127, 2007.

[17] R. Thurimella. Sub-linear distributed algorithms for sparse certificates and biconnected components. *Journal of Algorithms*, 23(1):160 – 179, 1997.

Brief Announcement:
Amoebot—A New Model for Programmable Matter

Zahra Derakhshandeh
Arizona State University
zderakhs@asu.edu

Shlomi Dolev
Ben-Gurion University
dolev@cs.bgu.ac.il

Robert Gmyr
University of Paderborn
gmyr@mail.upb.de

Andréa W. Richa
Arizona State University
aricha@asu.edu

Christian Scheideler
University of Paderborn
scheideler@mail.upb.de

Thim Strothmann
University of Paderborn
thim@mail.upb.de

ABSTRACT

The term *programmable matter* refers to matter which has the ability to change its physical properties (shape, density, moduli, conductivity, optical properties, etc.) in a programmable fashion, based upon user input or autonomous sensing. This has many applications like smart materials, autonomous monitoring and repair, and minimal invasive surgery, so there is a high relevance of this topic to industry and society in general. While programmable matter has just been science fiction more than two decades ago, a large amount of research activities can now be seen in this field in the recent years. Often programmable matter is envisioned, as a very large number of small locally interacting computational *particles*. We propose the Amoebot model, a new model which builds upon this vision of programmable matter. Inspired by the behavior of amoeba, the Amoebot model offers a versatile framework to model self-organizing particles and facilitates rigorous algorithmic research in the area of programmable matter.

Categories and Subject Descriptors

F.m [**Theory of Computation**]: Miscellaneous

Keywords

programmable matter; self-organization; nano-computing; mobile robots

1. INTRODUCTION

Recent advances in microfabrication and cellular engineering foreshadow that in the next few decades it might be possible to assemble simple information processing units at almost no cost. Myriads of these small-scale units could be combined to powerful systems capable of solving intricate tasks. This vision of building cheap microscopic processing units is supported by the progress made in manufacturing

SPAA'14, June 23–25, 2014, Prague, Czech Republic.
ACM 978-1-4503-2821-0/14/06.
http://dx.doi.org/10.1145/2612669.2612712.

microelectronic mechanical components, such that one can anticipate integrating logic circuits, microsensors, actuators, and communications devices on the same chip. Also, there has been intriguing progress in understanding the biochemical mechanisms of individual cells such as the mechanisms behind cell signaling and cell movement. Moreover, recent results have demonstrated that, in principle, biological cells can be turned into finite automata or even pushdown automata. Therefore, one can imagine to tailor-make biological cells to operate as sensors and actuators, as programmable delivery devices, and as chemical factories for the assembly of nano-scale structures.

One can envision producing vast quantities of microscopic computing elements to form *programmable matter* [8]. Programmable matter refers to matter which has the ability to change its physical properties (shape, density, moduli, conductivity, optical properties, etc.) in a programmable fashion, based upon user input or autonomous sensing. This has many applications like smart materials, autonomous monitoring and repair, and minimal invasive surgery, so there is a high relevance of this topic to industry and society in general. While programmable matter has just been science fiction more than two decades ago, a large amount of research activities can now be seen in this field in the recent years. These activities include research on passive systems like DNA computing [4, 7, 10] as well as active systems like swarm robotics [5, 6] and modular robotic systems [2, 3, 9]. Most related to our research is the recently proposed *nubot* model [11].

We propose *Amoebot*, a new amoeba-inspired model for programmable matter. In our model, the programmable matter consists of particles that can bond to neighboring particles and use these bonds to form connected structures. Particles only have local information and have modest computational power. The particles achieve locomotion by expanding and contracting, which resembles the behavior of amoeba [1].

2. MODEL

Consider the *equilateral triangular graph*, see Figure 1. A *particle* occupies either a single node or a pair of adjacent nodes in this graph, and every node can be occupied by at most one particle. Two particles occupying adjacent nodes are defined to be *connected*.

Every particle has a *state* from a finite set Q. Connected particles can communicate via the edges connecting them in

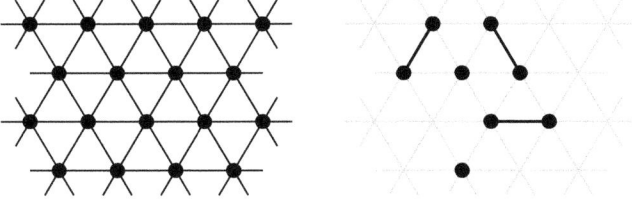

Figure 1: The left half of the figure depicts a section of the infinite equilateral triangular graph. Nodes are shown as black circles. The right half shows five particles on the graph. When depicting particles we draw the graph as a gray mesh without nodes. A particle occupying a single node is depicted as a black circle, and a particle occupying two nodes is depicted as two black circles connected by an edge.

Figure 2: The three parts of the figure show a moving particle together with the labels seen by the particle. On the left, the particle occupies only a single node. The particle then expands in the direction of the edge labeled 4 resulting in the particle occupying two nodes as depicted in the middle. Since the expansion changes the number of edges leaving the particle, the edges have to be relabeled. The direction of the edge labeled 0 remains constant. Because of the restriction for the label 0 mentioned in the text, this uniquely defines the edge that will receive the label 0 after the expansion. Next the particle contracts out of one of the nodes it currently occupies towards the direction of the edge labeled 6 resulting in the particle occupying only a single node as depicted on the right. Again, the edges leaving the particle are relabeled.

the following way. A particle p holds a *flag* from a finite alphabet Σ for each edge that leaves p (i.e., all edges incident in a node occupied by p except the edge between the occupied nodes if p occupies two nodes). A particle occupying the node on the other side of such an edge can read this flag. This communication process can be used in both directions over an edge. In order to allow a particle p to address the edges leaving it, the edges are labeled from the local perspective of p. This labeling starts with 0 at an edge leading to a node that is only adjacent to one of the nodes occupied by p and increases counter-clockwise around the particle. The restriction for label 0 will be used below to uniquely define which edge is labeled 0 when a particle moves.

Particles move through *expansion* and *contraction*: If a particle occupies one node, it can expand into an unoccupied adjacent node to occupy two nodes. If a particle occupies two nodes, it can contract out of one of these nodes to occupy only a single node. During these movements, the direction of the edge labeled 0 remains constant, even though the edge itself might change. Figure 2 shows an example of the movement of a particle. Besides executing expansions and contractions in isolation, we allow pairs of connected particles to combine these primitives to perform a coordinated movement: One particle can contract out of a certain node at the same time as another particle expands into that node. We call this movement a *handover*, see Figure 3. The particles involved in a handover are defined to remain connected during its execution.

Computationally, particles resemble finite state machines. A particle acts according to a *transition function*

$$\delta : Q \times \Sigma^{10} \ \to \ \mathcal{P}(Q \times \Sigma^{10} \times M).$$

For a particle p the function takes the current state of p and the flags p can read via its leaving edges as arguments. Here, the i-th coordinate of the tuple Σ^{10} represents the flag read via the edge labeled i when numbering the coordinates of the tuple starting at 0. If for a label i there is no edge with that label or if the respective edge leads to a node that is not occupied, the coordinate of the tuple is defined to be ε. The value $\varepsilon \in \Sigma$ is reserved for this purpose and cannot be set as a flag by a particle. The transition function maps to a set of *turns*. A turn is a tuple specifying a combination of a state to assume, flags to set, and a movement to execute.

Figure 3: Two particles performing a handover.

The set of movements is defined as

$$
\begin{aligned}
M = \ & \{\text{idle}\} \cup \\
& \{\text{expand}_i \mid i \in [0,9]\} \cup \\
& \{\text{contract}_i \mid i \in [0,9]\} \cup \\
& \{\text{handoverContract}_i \mid i \in [0,9]\}.
\end{aligned}
$$

The movement *idle* means that p does not move, and *expand$_i$* and *contract$_i$* are defined as mentioned above. The index i specifies the edge that defines the direction along which the movement should take place, as shown in the example in Figure 2. The movement *handoverContract$_i$* specifies a contraction that can only be executed as part of a handover. Summarizing, a transition function specifies a set of turns a particle would like to perform based on the locally available information.

A system of particles progresses by executing atomic *actions*. An action is either the execution of an isolated turn for a single particle or the execution of a turn for each of two particles resulting in a handover between those particles. Note that if a movement is not executable, the respective action is not enabled: For example, a particle occupying two nodes cannot expand although it might specify this movement in a turn. As another example, a particle cannot expand into an occupied node except as part of a handover. Finally, an action consisting of an isolated turn involving the movement $handoverContract_i$ is never enabled as this movement can only be performed as part of a handover. The transition function is applied for each particle to determine the set of enabled actions in the system. From this set, a single action is arbitrarily chosen and executed. The process of evaluating the transition function and executing an action continues indefinitely.

3. DISCUSSION

The general Amoebot model as described in the previous section can take various specific forms depending on how systems of particles are initialized, what information particles keep track of in their state, and what information they share over their leaving edges. For example, the model does not specify how the labeling of the edges leaving a particle is initially set up. Always assigning the label 0 to an edge pointing upwards for every particle results in a full-compass model, while assigning this label differently for each particle results in a no-compass model where particles only share their sense of orientation. As an example for the influence of communication, in the no-compass variant of the model two particles can compare the relative rotation of the direction of their respective edges with label 0 by communicating, but this is by no means mandatory. As a final example, the particles can be set up to know whether they occupy one or two nodes, they can keep track of this information during the progression of the system, and they can communicate this information over their leaving edges, but again none of this is mandatory.

While the model allows for many variations, it also has fixed core features. Some of these features represent our idea on how programmable matter consisting of discrete particles would work: The particles have constant memory (in particular, they have no identifiers) and modest computational power. Particles act asynchronously and make their decision based on local information. Finally, particles can only move themselves and not other particles because of limited physical strength. However, the most striking feature of the Amoebot model, namely the use of expansion and contraction as locomotion primitives together with handovers as their combination, is motivated by the problems we want to investigate using the model: We want to study problems in which all particles in a system have to form a *single connected component* at all times. An example of why our type of locomotion is favorable in this context is that it allows arbitrarily long chains of (initially contracted) particles to move along a common trajectory without losing connectivity. All particles of such a chain simply expand and contract in alternation. The first particle in the chain determines the trajectory by deciding the direction of its expansion, the expansion of the remaining particles is always in direction of their predecessor in the chain. Furthermore, a contraction is always in the same direction in the grid as the previous expansion and all contractions are handover-contractions except the contractions of the last particle in the chain.

4. RESEARCH CHALLENGES

We would like to use the Amoebot model to investigate various problems in which the system of particles has to form a *single connected component* at all times. As an example, the class of *coating problems* might be considered. Here, the surface of an object is to be coated as uniformly as possible by the particles of a system. A second example is the class of *shape formation problems* in which a system has to arrange to form a specific shape. Finally, in *bridging problems* particles have to bridge gaps in given structures. We see the coating problems as an algorithmic primitive for solving other problems. For example, the formation of a shape can be achieved by creating an initially small instance of that shape which is then iteratively coated to form increasingly large instances until the number of particles in the system is exhausted.

Also, variants of the model might be of interest. Firstly, in a physical realization particles may become faulty and a system may not be well-initialized. For a system to handle such occurrences it may be necessary to allow particles to detect other faulty particles and to cope with them. Such a model would require self-stabilizing algorithms. Secondly, the model may be extended from two to three dimensions For more information, including preliminary results on coating problems and more related work please see http://amoebot.cs.upb.de.

5. REFERENCES

[1] R. Ananthakrishnan and A. Ehrlicher. The forces behind cell movement. *International Journal of Biological Sciences*, 3(5):303–317, 2007.

[2] Z. Butler, S. Murata, and D. Rus. Distributed replication algorithms for self-reconfiguring modular robots. In *Distributed Autonomous Robotic Systems 5*, pages 37–48. Springer, 2002.

[3] Z. J. Butler, K. Kotay, D. Rus, and K. Tomita. Generic decentralized control for lattice-based self-reconfigurable robots. *International Journal of Robotics Research*, 23(9):919–937, 2004.

[4] K. C. Cheung, E. D. Demaine, J. R. Bachrach, and S. Griffith. Programmable assembly with universally foldable strings (moteins). *IEEE Transactions on Robotics*, 27(4):718–729, 2011.

[5] S. Kernbach, editor. *Handbook of Collective Robotics – Fundamentals and Challanges*. Pan Stanford Publishing, 2012.

[6] J. McLurkin. *Analysis and Implementation of Distributed Algorithms for Multi-Robot Systems*. PhD thesis, Massachusetts Institute of Technology, 2008.

[7] R. Nagpal, A. Kondacs, and C. Chang. Programming methodology for biologically-inspired self-assembling systems. Technical report, AAAI Spring Symposium on Computational Synthesis, 2003.

[8] T. Toffoli and N. Margolus. Programmable matter: concepts and realization. *Physica D: Nonlinear Phenomena*, 47(1):263–272, 1991.

[9] J. E. Walter, J. L. Welch, and N. M. Amato. Distributed reconfiguration of metamorphic robot chains. *Distributed Computing*, 17(2):171–189, 2004.

[10] E. Winfree, F. Liu, L. A. Wenzler, and N. C. Seeman. Design and self-assembly of two-dimensional dna crystals. *Nature*, 394(6693):539–544, 1998.

[11] D. Woods, H.-L. Chen, S. Goodfriend, N. Dabby, E. Winfree, and P. Yin. Active self-assembly of algorithmic shapes and patterns in polylogarithmic time. In *ITCS*, pages 353–354, 2013.

Brief Announcement: Faster 3-Periodic Merging Networks

Marek Piotrów

Institute of Computer Science, University of Wrocław, 50-383 Wrocław, Poland

Marek.Piotrow@ii.uni.wroc.pl

ABSTRACT

We consider the problem of merging two sorted sequences on a comparator network that is used repeatedly, that is, if the output is not sorted, the network is applied again using the output as input. The challenging task is to construct such networks of small depth (called a period in this context). The first constructions of merging networks with a constant period were described by Kutyłowski et al. They gave 3-periodic network that merges two sorted sequences of N numbers in time $12 \log N$ and a similar network of period 4 that works in $5.67 \log N$. We present a new family of 3-periodic merging networks with merging time upper-bounded by $6 \log N$. The construction can be easily generalized to larger constant periods with decreasing running time, for example, to 4-periodic ones that work in time upper-bounded by $4 \log N$.

Categories and Subject Descriptors

F.2.2 [**Analysis of Algorithms and Problem Complexity**]: Non-numerical Algorithms and Problems—*Sorting and searching*

Keywords

parallel merging; oblivious merging; merging network; comparator

1. INTRODUCTION

Comparator networks are probably the simplest parallel model that is used to solve such tasks as sorting, merging or selecting [6]. Each network represents a data-oblivious algorithm, which can be easily implemented in hardware. Moreover, sorting networks can be applied in secure, multi-party computation (SMC) protocols. They are also strongly connected with switching networks [9]. The most famous constructions of sorting networks are Odd-Even and Bitonic networks of depth $\frac{1}{2} \log^2 N$ due to Batcher [2] and AKS networks of depth $O(\log N)$ due to Ajtai, Komlos and Szemeredi [1]. The long-standing disability to decrease a large constant hidden behind the asymptotically optimal complexity of AKS networks to a practical value has resulted in studying easier, sorting-related problems, whose optimal networks have small constants.

A comparator network consists of a set of N registers, each of which can contain an item from a totally ordered set, and a sequence of comparator stages. Each stage is a set of comparators that connect disjoint pairs of registers and, therefore, can work in parallel (a comparator is a simple device that takes a contents of two registers and performs a compare-exchange operation on them: the minimum is put into the first register and the maximum into the second one). Stages are run one after another in synchronous manner, hence we can consider the number of stages as the running time. The size of a network is defined to be the total number of comparators in all its stages.

A network A consisting of stages $S_1, S_2, \ldots, S_d$ is called p-periodic if $p < d$ and for each i, $1 \le i \le d - p$, stages S_i and S_{i+p} are identical. A periodic network is easy to implement, especially in hardware, because one can use the first p stages in a cycle: if the output of p-th stage is not correct (sorted, for example), the sequence of p stages is run again. In pure oblivious context, such computations are stopped after a predefined number of passes. We can also define a p-periodic network just by giving the total number of stages and a description of its first p stages. A challenging task is to construct a family of small-periodic networks for sorting-related problems with the running time equal to, or not much greater than that of non-periodic networks.

Dowd et al. [5] gave the construction of $\log N$-periodic sorting networks of N registers with running time of $\log^2 N$. Bender and Williamson introduced a large class of such networks [3]. Kutyłowski et al. [8] introduced a general method to convert a non-periodic sorting network into a 5-periodic one, but the running time increases by a factor of $O(\log N)$ during the conversion. For simpler problems such as merging or correction there are constant-periodic networks that solve the corresponding problem in asymptotically optimal logarithmic time [7, 10, 11]. In particular, Kutyłowski, Loryś and Oesterdikhoff [7] gave 3-periodic network that merges two sorted sequences of N numbers in time $12 \log N$ and a similar network of period 4 that works in $5.67 \log N$. They sketched also a construction of merging networks with periods larger than 4 and running time decreasing asymptotically to $2.25 \log N$. Note that 2-periodic merging networks require linear time.

In this paper, we introduce a new family of constant-periodic merging networks that are based on the Canfield and Williamson $O(\log N)$-periodic sorter [4] and are constructed by a certain periodification technique. Our 3-periodic merging networks work in time upper-bounded by $6 \log N$ and 4-periodic ones - in time upper-bounded by $4 \log N$. The construction can be easily generalized to larger constant periods with decreasing running time.

The advantage of constant-periodic networks is that they have pretty simple patterns of communication links, that is, each node (register) of such a network can only be connected to a constant number of other nodes. Such patterns are easier to implement, for example, in hardware. Moreover, a node uses these links in a sim-

SPAA'14, June 23–25, 2014, Prague, Czech Republic.
ACM 978-1-4503-2821-0/14/06.
http://dx.doi.org/10.1145/2612669.2612700.

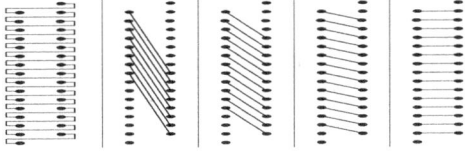

Figure 1: The CW_5 5-pass 5-periodic sorter. Registers and comparators are represented by dots and edges, respectively. Stages are separated by vertical lines.

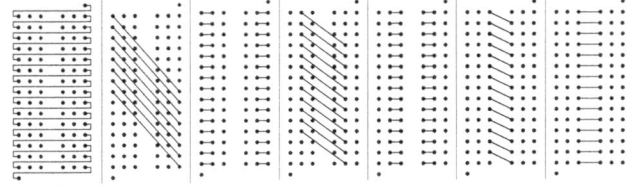

Figure 2: P_5 as an implementation of CW_5. Stages with short horizontal comparators are inserted between stages with long comparators.

ple periodic manner and this can save control login and simplify timing considerations. We can also easily implement an early stopping property with k-periodic networks: if none of the comparators exchanged values in the last k stages, we could stop the computation.

The paper is organized as follows. In Section 2 we introduce a new periodification scheme, define our new family of 3-periodic merging networks and give the main theorem. Section 3 contains a sketch of its proof, where we order the set of registers into a matrix and analyze the behavior of our network by tracing the numbers of ones in its columns.

2. PERIODIC MERGING NETWORKS

Our merging networks are based on the Canfield and Williamson [4] ($\log N$)-periodic sorters. In the following proposition we recall the definition of the networks and their merging/sorting properties (see also Fig. 1). Recall that $[i : j]$ denotes a comparator connecting registers i and j.

PROPOSITION 1. *[4] Let $S_1 = \{[2i : 2i+1] | 0 \leq i < 2^{k-1}\}$ and let $S_{j+1} = \{[2i+1 : 2i + 2^{k-j}] | 0 \leq i < 2^{k-1} - 2^{k-j-1} - 1\}$ for $j = 1, \ldots, k-1$ and $k \geq 1$. Let $CW_k = S_1, \ldots, S_k$ be a network of $N_k = 2^k$ registers numbered $0, \ldots, N_k - 1$. Then (i) if two sorted sequences of length 2^{k-1} are given in registers with odd and even indices, respectively, then CW_k is a merging network; (ii) CW_k is a k-pass periodic sorting network.*

We would like to implement a version of this network as a 3-periodic comparator network. We begin with the definition of a intermediate construction P_k which structure is similar to the structure of CW_k. Then we transform it to 3-periodic network M_k. Observe that in any N-register merging network we must have all short comparators $[i : i+1]$, $0 \leq i < N-1$, and consecutive short comparators $[i-1 : i]$ and $[i : i+1]$ must be in different stages. The idea is to replace each register i in CW_k (except the first and the last ones) with a sequence of $k-2$ consecutive registers, move the endpoints of long comparators one register further or closer depending on the parity of i and insert between each pair of stages containing long comparators a stage with short comparators joining the endpoints of those long ones. The result is depicted in Fig. 2. In this way, we obtain a network in which each register is used in at most three consecutive stages. Therefore the network P_k can be packed into the first 3 stages and used periodically to get the desired 3-periodic merging network.

Let $rgs(\{[i_1 : j_1], \ldots, [i_r : j_r]\})$ denotes the set $\{i_1, j_1, \ldots, i_r, j_r\}$. For an N-register network $A = S_1, S_2, \ldots, S_d$, where $S_1, S_2, \ldots, S_d$ denote stages, and for an integer $j \in \{1, \ldots, N\}$, let: $fst(j, A) = \min\{1 \leq i \leq d | j \in rgs(S_i)\}$, $lst(j, A) = \max\{1 \leq i \leq d | j \in rgs(S_i)\}$ and $delay(A) = \max_{1 \leq j \leq N}\{lst(j, A) - fst(j, A) + 1\}$.

Let us define formally the new family of merging networks. For each $k \geq 3$ we would like to transform the network CW_k into a new network P_k.

Definition 1. Let $n_k = 2^{k-1} - 1$ be one less than the half of the number of registers in CW_k and $b_k = 2(k-2)$. The number of registers of P_k is defined to be $N_k = n_k \cdot b_k + 2$. The stages of $P_k = S_{k,1} \cup \{[0 : 1], [N_k - 2 : N_k - 1]\}, S_{k,2}, \ldots, S_{k,2k-3}$ are defined by the following equations, where $j = 1, \ldots, \frac{b_k}{2}$:

$$S_{k,1} = \{[b_k i : b_k i + 1] : i = 1, \ldots, n_k - 1\}$$

$$S_{k,2j} = \Big\{[b_k i + j : b_k(i + 2^{k-j-1} - 1) + (b_k - j + 1)] :$$
$$i = 0, \ldots, n_k - 2^{k-j-1}\Big\}$$

$$S_{k,2j+1} = \{[b_k i + j : b_k i + j + 1],$$
$$[b_k i + (b_k - j) : b_k i + (b_k - j + 1)] : i = 0, \ldots, n_k - 1\}$$

The network P_5 is depicted in Figure 2.

FACT 1. $delay(P_k) = 3$ for $k \geq 3$. $\square$

Let $A = S_1, S_2, \ldots, S_d$ and $A' = S'_1, S'_2, \ldots, S'_{d'}$ be N-input comparator networks such that for each i, $1 \leq i \leq \min(d, d')$, $rgs(S_i) \cap rgs(S'_i) = \emptyset$. Then $A \cup A'$ is defined to be a network with stages $(S_1 \cup S'_1), (S_2 \cup S'_2), \ldots, (S_{\max(d,d')} \cup S'_{\max(d,d')})$, where empty stages are added at the end of the network of smaller depth.

For any comparator network $A = S_1, \ldots, S_d$ and $D = delay(A)$, let us define a network $B = T_1, \ldots, T_D$ to be a *compact form* of A, where $T_q = \bigcup \{S_{q+pD} : 0 \leq p \leq (d-q)/D\}$, $1 \leq q \leq D$. Observe that B is correctly defined due to the delay of A. Moreover, $depth(B) = delay(B) = delay(A)$.

Definition 2. For $k \geq 3$ let M_k denote the compact form of P_k with the first and the last registers deleted. That is, the network $M_k = T_1^k, T_2^k, T_3^k$ is using the set of registers numbered $\{1, 2, \ldots, N_k\}$, where $N_k = (2^{k-1} - 1) \cdot 2(k-2)$, and for $j = 1, 2, 3$ the stage T_j^k is defined as $\bigcup \{S_{k,j+3i} : 0 \leq i \leq \frac{2k-j-3}{3}\}$.

It is not necessary to delete the first and the last registers of P_k but this simplifies our quite complicated proofs. The network M_5 is given in Fig. 3. The following is the main theorem of the paper.

THEOREM 1. *There exists a family of 3-periodic comparator networks M_k, $k \geq 3$, such that each M_k is a $2k - 5$-pass merger of two sorted sequences given in odd and even registers, respectively. The running time of M_k is $6k - 15 \leq 6 \log N_k$, where $N_k = (2^k - 2)(k - 2)$ is the number of registers in M_k.*

In a similar way, we can convert CW_k into a 4-periodic merging network. Assume that k is even. We replace each register (except the first and the last ones) with a sequence of $(k-2)/2$ consecutive registers, move the endpoints of long comparators in such a way that exactly two long comparators start or end at each new register and insert after each pair of stages containing long comparators a stage with short comparators joining the endpoints of those long comparators. The detailed description will be given in the full version of the paper.

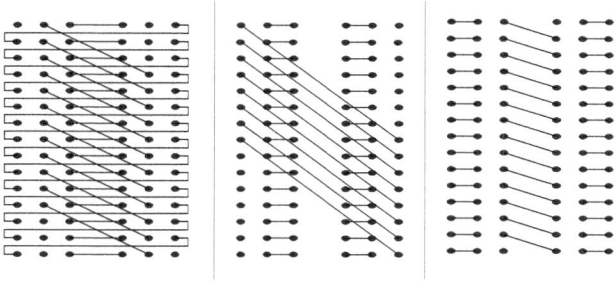

Figure 3: The M_5 network that is 3-periodic.

3. SKETCH OF PROOF OF THEOREM 1

The proof is based on the general observation that M_k merges $k-2$ pairs of sorted subsequences, one after another, in pipeline fashion. The well-known Zero-One Principle states that any comparator network that sorts (merges) 0-1 input sequences correctly sorts (merges) also arbitrary input sequences [6]. It follows that we can analyze computations of the network M_k, $k \geq 3$, by describing each state of registers as a 0-1 sequence $\bar{x} = (x_1, \ldots, x_{N_k})$, where x_i represents the content of register i. If $\bar{x}$ is an input sequence for $2k-5$ passes of M_k, then by $\bar{x}^{(i)}$ we denote the content of registers after i passes of M_k, $i = 0, \ldots, 2k-5$, that is, $\bar{x}^{(0)} = \bar{x}$ and $\bar{x}^{(i+1)} = M_k(\bar{x}^{(i)})$. Since M_k consists of three stages T_1^k, T_2^k and T_3^k, we extend the notation to describe the output of each stage: $\bar{x}^{(i,0)} = \bar{x}^{(i)}$ and $\bar{x}^{(i,j)} = T_j^k(\bar{x}^{(i,j-1)})$, for $j = 1, 2, 3$.

Now let us fix some technical notations and definitions. A 0-1 sequence can be represented as a word over $\Sigma = \{0, 1\}$. A non-decreasing (also called *sorted*) 0-1 sequence has a form of 0^*1^* and can be equivalently represented by the number of ones (or zeros) in it. For any $x \in \Sigma^*$ let $ones(x)$ denote the number of 1 in x. If $x \in \Sigma^n$ then x_i, $1 \leq i \leq n$, denotes the i-th letter of x. Generally, for $A = \{i_1, \ldots, i_m\}, 1 \leq i_1 < \ldots < i_m \leq n$, let x_A denotes the word $x_{i_1} \ldots x_{i_m}$. We say that a sequence $\bar{x} = (x_1, \ldots, x_{N_k})$ is *2-sorted* if both $(x_1, x_3, \ldots, x_{N_k-1})$ and $(x_2, x_4, \ldots, x_{N_k})$ are sorted.

For any $k \geq 3$ let $n_k = 2^{k-1} - 1$, $b_k = 2(k-2)$ (thus $N_k = n_k \cdot b_k$). The set of registers $Reg_k = \{1, \ldots, N_k\}$ can be analyzed as an $n_k \times b_k$ matrix with $C_j^k = \{j + ib_k : 0 \leq i < n_k\}$, $j = 1, \ldots, b_k$, as columns. A content of all registers in the matrix, that is $x \in \Sigma^{N_k}$, can be equivalently represented by the sequence of contents of registers in $C_1, C_2, \ldots, C_{b_k}$, that is $(x_{C_1}, \ldots, x_{C_{b_k}})$.

LEMMA 1. *If the initial content of registers is a 2-sorted 0-1 sequence x then after each stage of multi-pass computation of $M_k = T_1^k, T_2^k, T_3^k$ the content of each column C_j, $j = 1, \ldots, b_k$, is sorted, that is, each $(x^{(p,i)})_{C_j}$ is of the form 0^*1^*, $p = 0, \ldots$, $i = 1, 2, 3$.*

From now on, instead of looking at 0-1 sequences with sorted columns, we can analyze the computations of M_k on sequences of integers $\bar{c} = (c_1, \ldots, c_{b_k})$, where c_t, $t = 1, \ldots, b_k$, denote the number of ones in a sorted column C_t. We say that $\bar{c}$ is *flat* if $c_1 \leq c_2 \leq \ldots, c_{b_k/2} \leq c_1 + 1$. We say that a sequence $\bar{c}$ is *2-flat* if subsequences $(c_1, c_3, \ldots, c_{b_k-1})$ and $(c_2, c_4, \ldots, c_{b_k})$ are flat. Stages T_1^k, T_2^k and T_3^k can be represented by the following sets of mappings, where dec_i^k, mov_i^k and cyc^k represent transformations of 0-1 sequences defined by sets S_j, $j = 1, \ldots, 2k-3$.

Definition 3. Let $k \geq 3$. Let Q_1^k, Q_2^k and Q_3^k denote the following sets of functions. $Q_1^k = \{cyc^k\} \cup \{dec_{3i-1}^k\}_{i=1}^{\lfloor \frac{k-1}{3} \rfloor} \cup \{mov_{3i}^k\}_{i=1}^{\lfloor \frac{k-2}{3} \rfloor}$, $Q_2^k = \{dec_{3i-2}^k\}_{i=1}^{\lfloor \frac{k}{3} \rfloor} \cup \{mov_{3i-1}^k\}_{i=1}^{\lfloor \frac{k-1}{3} \rfloor}$ and $Q_3^k = \{dec_{3i}^k\}_{i=1}^{\lfloor \frac{k-2}{3} \rfloor} \cup$

$\{mov_{3i-2}^k\}_{i=1}^{\lfloor \frac{k}{3} \rfloor}$, where $b_k = 2(k-2)$, $h_i = 2^{k-i-1} - 1$, $1 \leq i \leq k-2$, and the functions dec_i^k, mov_i^k and cyc^k over sequences of b_k reals are defined with a helper function $mm_{i,j,h}^k$ with $i \neq j$ and $h \in \mathbb{R}$. Let $\bar{c} = (c_1, \ldots, c_{b_k})$ and $t \in \{1, \ldots, b_k\}$.

$$(mm_{i,j,h}^k(\bar{c}))_t = \begin{cases} \min(c_i, c_j + h) & \text{if } t = i \\ \max(c_i - h, c_j) & \text{if } t = j \\ c_t & \text{otherwise} \end{cases}$$

Then $dec_i^k = mm_{i,b_k-i+1,h_i}^k$, $cyc^k = mm_{b_k,1,1}^k$ and $mov_i^k = mm_{i,i+1,0}^k \circ mm_{b_k-i,b_k-i+1,0}^k$.

Now we are ready to reduce the proof of Theorem 1 to the proof of following lemma.

LEMMA 2. *Let $k \geq 3$. If for each 2-flat sequence $\bar{c} = (c_1, \ldots, c_{b_k})$ of integers from $[0, 2^{k-1} - 1]$ the result of application $(Q_3^k \circ Q_2^k \circ Q_1^k)^{2k-5}$ to $(\bar{c})$ is a flat sequence, then M_k is a $2k-5$-pass merger of two sorted sequences given in odd and even registers, respectively.*

Due to Lemma 2 one can only analyze the results of periodic application of the functions Q_1^k, Q_2^k and Q_3^k to a sequence of integers representing the numbers of ones in each register column. We know also that an initial sequence is 2-flat.

THEOREM 2. *Let $k \geq 3$ and let $\bar{c} = (c_1, \ldots, c_{b_k})$ be a 2-flat sequence of integers from $[0, 2^{k-1} - 1]$. Let $f = f_{6k-15} \circ f_{6k-14} \circ \ldots \circ f_1$, where $f_i = Q_{((i-1) \bmod 3)+1}^k$, $i = 1, \ldots, 6k-15$. Then $f(\bar{c})$ is a flat sequence.*

Theorem 1 follows directly from Theorem 2 and Lemma 2. To prove Theorem 2 we firstly analyze (so called) balanced columns.

4. REFERENCES

[1] M. Ajtai, J. Komlós and E. Szemerédi. Sorting in c log n parallel steps. *Combinatorica*, 3(1):1–9, 1983.

[2] K. E. Batcher. Sorting networks and their applications. *Proc. AFIPS 1968 SJCC*, Vol. 32, AFIPS Press, pages 307–314.

[3] E. A. Bender and S. G. Williamson. Periodic sorting using minimum delay, recursively constructed merging networks. *The Electronic Journal of Combinatorics* 5(1):1–21, 1998.

[4] E. R. Canfield and S. G. Williamson. A sequential sorting network analogous to the Batcher merge. *Linear and Multilinear Algebra*, 29(1):43–51, 1991.

[5] M. Dowd, Y. Perl, M. Saks and L. Rudolph. The periodic balanced sorting network. *J. ACM*, 36(4):738–757, 1989.

[6] D.E. Knuth. *The Art of Computer Programming Vol. 3, 2nd edition* Addison Wesley, Reading, MA, 1975.

[7] M. Kutyłowski, K. Loryś and B. Oesterdiekhoff. Periodic merging networks. *Theory of Computing Systems*, 31(5):551–578, 1998.

[8] M. Kutyłowski, K. Loryś, B. Oesterdiekhoff and R. Wanka. Periodification scheme: Constructing sorting networks with constant period. *J. ACM*, 47(5):944-967, 2000.

[9] F.T. Leighton. *Introduction to Parallel Algorithms and Architectures: Arrays, Trees and Hypercubes*. Morgan Kaufmann Publishers Inc., San Francisco, CA, USA, 1992.

[10] B. Oesterdiekhoff. Periodic comparator networks. *Theor. Comput. Sci.*, 245(2):175-202, 2000.

[11] M. Piotrów. Periodic, random-fault-tolerant correction networks. In *Proceedings of the Thirteenth Annual ACM Symposium on Parallel Algorithms and Architectures*, SPAA '01, pages 298–305, New York, USA, 2001. ACM.

Automatic Complexity Analysis of Explicitly Parallel Programs

Torsten Hoefler
ETH Zurich
Zurich, Switzerland
htor@inf.ethz.ch

Grzegorz Kwasniewski
ETH Zurich
Zurich, Switzerland
grzegorz.kwasniewski@inf.ethz.ch

ABSTRACT

The doubling of cores every two years requires programmers to expose maximum parallelism. Applications that are developed on today's machines will often be required to run on many more cores. Thus, it is necessary to understand how much parallelism codes can expose. The work and depth model provides a convenient mental framework to assess the required work and the maximum parallelism of algorithms and their parallel efficiency. We propose an automatic analysis to extract work and depth from a source-code. We do this by statically counting the number of loop iterations depending on the set of input parameters. The resulting expression can be used to assess work and depth with regards to the program inputs. Our method supports the large class of practically relevant loops with affine update functions and generates additional parameters for other expressions. We demonstrate how this method can be used to determine work and depth of several real-world applications. Our technique enables us to prove if the theoretically maximum parallelism is exposed in a practical implementation of a problem. This will be most important for future-proof software development.

Categories and Subject Descriptors

F.2 [**Analysis of Algorithms and Problem Complexity**]: general

General Terms

Theory

Keywords

Loop iterations; Polyhedral model; Work and depth analysis

1. INTRODUCTION

Parallelism in today's computers is still growing exponentially, currently doubling approximately every two years.

This implies that programmers need to expose exponentially growing parallelism to exploit the full potential of the architecture. Parallel programming is generally hard and practical implementations may not always expose enough parallelism to be considered future-proof. This is exaggerated by continuous application development and the fact that applications are developed on systems with significantly lower core counts than their production environment. Thus, it is increasingly important that programmers understand bounds on the scalability of their implementation.

Parallel codes are manifold and numerous programming frameworks exist to implement parallel versions of sequential codes. We define the class of *explicitly parallel* codes as applications that statically divide their workload into several pieces which are processed in parallel. Explicitly parallel codes are the the most prevalent programming style in large-scale parallelism using the Pthreads, OpenMP, the Message Passing Interface (MPI), Partitioned Global Address Space (PGAS), or Compute Unified Device Architecture (CUDA) APIs. Many high-level parallel frameworks (e.g., [18]) and domain-specific languages (e.g., [16]) compile to such explicitly parallel languages.

The work and depth model is a simple and effective model for parallel computation. It models computations as vertices and data dependencies as edges of a directed acyclic graph (DAG). The total number of vertices in the graph is the *total work* W and the length of a longest path is called the *depth* D (sometimes also called span). We will now describe more properties of the model and possible analyses.

1.1 Work and depth and parallel efficiency

In practice, analyses are often not used to predict exact running times of an implementation on a particular architecture. Instead, they often determine how the running time behaves with regards to the input size. The work and depth model links sequential running time and parallelism elegantly. The work W is proportional to the time T_1 required to compute the problem on a single core. The depth D is the longest sequential chain and thus proportional to a lower bound to the time T_∞ required to compute the problem with an infinite number of cores.

Work and depth models are often used to develop parallel algorithms (e.g., [33]) or to describe their properties (e.g., in textbooks [22, 23]). Those algorithms are then often adapted in practical settings. We propose to use the same model, somewhat in the inverse direction, to analyze existing applications for bounds on their scalability and available parallelism. Our results can also be used to prove an implementation asymptotically optimal with regards to its parallel efficiency if bounds on work and depth of the problem are known. In our analysis we use the assumption from [13] that all operations are performed in unit time and the time required for accessing data, storing results, etc., is ignored.

Brent's lemma [13] bounds running times on p cores with $\frac{W}{p} \leq T_p \leq \frac{W}{p} + D$. D measures the sequential parts of the calculation and is equivalent to time t needed to perform an operation with sufficient number of processes, W is equivalent to the number of operations q in Brent's notation and $B = \frac{D}{W}$ is a lower bound of the sequential fraction that limits the returns from adding more cores. Applying Amdahl's law [2] shows that the speedup is limited to $S_p = \frac{T_1}{T_p} \leq \frac{1}{B + \frac{1-B}{p}}$. If we consider the parallel efficiency $E_p = \frac{S_p}{p}$, then we can bound the maximally achievable efficiency using the work and depth model as $E_p = \frac{T_1}{pT_p} \leq \frac{1}{1 + B(p-1)}$. We observe that for fixed B, $\lim_{P \to \infty} E_p = 0$ such that every fixed-size computation can only utilize a limited number of cores *efficiently*, i.e., $E_p \geq 1 - \epsilon$.

This observation allows us to define *available parallelism* and good scaling in terms of ϵ as the maximum number of processes p for which T_p may decrease. Bounds on work and depth for certain problems also allow us to differentiate between a problem that is hard to parallelize (e.g., depth first search (DFS)) and a suboptimal parallelization; we can also define the *distance* of a given parallel code to a *parallelism-optimal* solution.

Work and depth are typically functions of the input size. In structured programming [17], loops and recursion are the only techniques to increase the work depending on program input parameters. Here, we focus on loops only and we assume that each program can be abstracted as a set of loops that determine the number of executions for each statement. We model each statement as a work item that takes unit time. To simplify the explanation further, we also assume that there is only one statement in each loop (since all statements will have identical iteration counts). Now, the problem of determining the work is equivalent to determine the loop iteration counts for each statement. The depth is relative to a special parameter p that represents the number of processes. We now discuss a simple motivating example:

Example I: Parallel sorting skeleton.

Assume the following loop is executed by $p > 0$ processes[1] (p equally divides n, $n>0$ and n is a power of 2):

```
for(x=0; x<n/p; x++)
  for(y=1; y<n; y*=2) S1;
```

All variables that are not changed in the loop but influence the iteration counts are called *parameters*. The parameter n represents size of the input problem. S1 is an arbitrary computation statement that models one work item. We now analyze work and depth for this explicitly parallel loop.

For any loop, the elements that determine the number of iterations can be split into three classes:

1. Initial assignment: x=0, y=1
2. Loop guards: x<n/p, y<n
3. Loop updates: x++, y*=2

---

[1] We use typewriter font to denote source code variables

The number of iterations of statement S1 in this loop (depending on the parameters n and p) can be counted as

$$N(\mathtt{n}, \mathtt{p}) = T_p = \mathtt{n}/\mathtt{p} \cdot \log_2(\mathtt{n}).$$

From $N(\mathtt{n}, \mathtt{p})$, we can determine that the total work and depth is

$$W(\mathtt{n}) = N(\mathtt{n}, 1) = T_1 = \mathtt{n} \cdot \log_2(\mathtt{n})$$

$$D(\mathtt{n}) = N(\mathtt{n}, \infty) = T_\infty = \log_2(\mathtt{n}).$$

The parallelization is work-conserving and the parallel efficiency $E_p = 1$. If this loop implements parallel sorting, then our analysis shows that it is asymptotically optimal in work and depth [25], and thus exposes maximum parallelism. In this paper, we will show how to perform this analysis automatically.

Example II: Parallel reductions.

Our second example illustrates a common problem in parallel shared memory codes: reductions. Programmers often employ inefficient algorithms because efficient tree-based schemes are significantly harder to implement. A sequential reduction would be implemented as follows (addition operations on the variable sum are performed atomically):

```
sum=0;   for(i=0; i<n; i++) sum=sum+a[i];
```

A simple parallelization (assuming n > p) would be

```
for(i=id*n/p; i<min((id+1)*n/p,n); i++)
    s[id]+=a[i];
for(i=0; i<p; i++) sum=sum+s[i];
```

where id is the thread number and s is an array of size p for keeping the partial sums of each thread. The total number of iterations of the most loaded process is $N(\mathtt{n}, \mathtt{p}) = T_p = \lceil \mathtt{n}/\mathtt{p} \rceil + \mathtt{p}$ and the efficiency $E_p = (n+1)/(\mathtt{p} \lceil \mathtt{n}/\mathtt{p} \rceil + \mathtt{p}^2)$. This implementation is not work-efficient because the lower bound is $T_p = \Omega(\mathtt{n}/\mathtt{p} + \log_2(\mathtt{p}))$ and the efficiency decreases with $\mathtt{p}^2$. The lower bound can be achieved if we combine partial results of the sum in a tree structure

```
for(i=id*n/p; i<min((id+1)*n/p,n); i++)
    s[id]+=a[i];
for(i=1; i<p; i*=2) combine_partial_sums(s);
```

with the iteration count of the most loaded process $N(\mathtt{n}, \mathtt{p}) = T_p = \lceil \mathtt{n}/\mathtt{p} \rceil + \lceil \log_2(\mathtt{p}) \rceil$. The work of this solution is $W(\mathtt{n}) = T_1 = \mathtt{n}$ and the depth $D(\mathtt{n}) = T_\infty = \infty$ because the parallelization is not work-conserving (more work is created as threads are added). The parallel efficiency is $E_p = \mathtt{n}/(\mathtt{p} \lceil \mathtt{n}/\mathtt{p} \rceil + \mathtt{p} \lceil \log_2(\mathtt{p}) \rceil)$ which decreases slowly because $\log_2(\mathtt{p})$ work is added per process. From E_p, we can derive that the available parallelism is $\mathtt{n}$.

This example shows that it is crucial to catch loop behavior in the analysis of parallel programs. Different implementations solving the same problem may have different work and depth, some of which resulting in limited scalability. Experiments at small scale may not expose those limitations as the constants are often rather small. However, our analysis enables us to find those issues early during the development. The main contributions of this work are:

- We develop a mechanism to symbolically bound the number of iterations in program loops depending on the input parameters and the number of processes.

- We show how to interpret the iteration counts in terms of work and depth. This allows the user to determine the parallel efficiency of a given code.

- We briefly outline how our method can be implemented in a compiler or code analysis tool.

- We demonstrate the applicability of our method and analyze a set of real-world applications for their parallel work and depth and efficiencies.

2. PROBLEM DESCRIPTION

Counting numbers of loop iterations of arbitrary codes is impossible because even termination of arbitrary loop nests cannot be decided [34]. In our work, we focus on the class of loops where all loop update functions and loop guards are affine functions of *iteration variables*, i.e., variables that change during loop execution. It was shown in previous works that a subset of this class covers many important codes in parallel computing [9].

Our method is strictly more powerful than other iteration counting approaches (e.g., [6]) that require that loop update functions are valid expressions in Presburger arithmetic (which supports only addition and subtraction of symbolic values and constants). We refer the reader to Section 8 for a more detailed differentiation. In this paper we focus on the extraction of work and depth for affine loop nests. To do so, we need to find the number of iterations of the program as a function of the number of processes.

Affine loop. Let $x \in \mathbb{Z}^m$ be an integer-valued *iteration variable vector* and x_0 its *initial assignment* right before entering the loop. We call a loop *affine* if we can present it in the form[2]:

```
x ← x₀                  // Initial assignment
while(cᵀx < g)          // Loop guard
    x ← Ax + b          // Loop update
```

Listing 1: Affine Loop

The *loop guard* $c^T x < g$ is determined by the constant vector $c \in \mathbb{R}^m$ and bounded by a scalar constant g. The loop update function $Ax + b$, consisting of a real matrix $A \in \mathbb{R}^{m \times m}$ and a constant vector $b \in \mathbb{R}^m$, determines how the iteration variables are updated during each iteration. Each constant may represent a symbolic loop parameter.

Perfectly Nested Loops. We extend our definition to a program consisting of r nested affine loops:

1. Each *loop guard* $c_k^T x < g_k$ at level k is an affine predicate of the iteration variables from levels $1 \ldots k$.

2. Each loop body at levels $1 \ldots r - 1$ consists of three elements:

   (a) initial assignment - $A_k x + b_k$
   (b) nested loop(s)
   (c) loop update - $U_k x + v_k$

We require well-structured programs [17]: For a loop at level k, the initial assignment, loop guard and loop update may only use variables defined at the same or higher levels $1 \ldots k$. Iteration variables of any parent loop at level $1 \ldots k - 1$ may not be changed in nested loops at levels $k \ldots r$. Such loops can thus be expressed in the general form

---

[2]We use an arrow ($\leftarrow$) symbol to denote an assignment in math notation

```
while(c₁ᵀx < g₁) {
    x ← A₁x + b₁
    while(c₂ᵀx < g₂) {
        ...
        x ← A_{k-1}x + b_{k-1}
        while(c_kᵀx < g_k) {
            x ← A_kx + b_k
            while(c_{k+1}ᵀx < g_{k+1}) {...}
            x ← U_kx + v_k }
        x ← U_{k-1}x + v_{k-1}}
    ...
    x ← U₁x + v₁}
```

where $A_k, U_k \in \mathbb{R}^{m \times m}$, $b_k, v_k, c_k \in \mathbb{R}^m$, $g_k \in \mathbb{R}$ and $k = 1 \ldots r$. Furthermore, $\forall i < k, i \neq j : A_{k,i,j} = U_{k,i,j} = 0$, $\forall i < k, i = j : A_{k,i,j} = U_{k,i,j} = 1$ and $\forall i > k : g_{k,i} = 0$.

Note that even though all the assignments and loop guards are affine, the number of iterations of such a nested loop may not be affine. For example the following affine loop will iterate $\lceil \log_2(n) \rceil$ times:

```
x=1;
while(x<n) x=2*x;
```

Perfectly nested loops are rare and loops often contain multiple loops at the same level. We now outline how our scheme also supports multipath loops.

Multipath Loops are loops that may contain multiple nested loops in one parent loop body. The example in Listing 2 shows such a loop: Inside the outer loop body we have two inner loops. How multiple loops are combined to fit the model description is covered in Section 4.5.

```
x=1;
while(x<n/p+1) {
    y=x;
    while(y<m) {S1; y=2*y;}
    z=x;
    while(z<m) {S2; z=z+x;}
    x=2*x;}
```

Listing 2: Complex Multipath Loop Nest

It is time-consuming and error-prone for humans to derive work and depth of complex loops like the one shown in Listing 2. Our algorithm computes work and depth for each statement automatically. For example, the number of executions N of the statement S2 is bounded by

$$2\mathtt{m}\left(1 - \left\lceil \frac{\mathtt{n}}{\mathtt{p}} + 1 \right\rceil^{-1}\right) - \log_2\left(\left\lceil \frac{\mathtt{n}}{\mathtt{p}} + 1 \right\rceil\right) \leq N \leq \mathtt{m}\left(2 - \left\lceil \frac{\mathtt{n}}{\mathtt{p}} + 1 \right\rceil^{-1}\right).$$

This bounds the work W on a single process

$$2\mathtt{m}\left(1 - (\mathtt{n}+1)^{-1}\right) - \log_2(\mathtt{n}+1) \leq W \leq \mathtt{m}\left(2 - (\mathtt{n}+1)^{-1}\right)$$

and the depth D

$$0 \leq D \leq \mathtt{m}.$$

3. SKETCH OF THE ALGORITHM

We first introduce the concept of a closed-form *affine representation*. The affine representation of a single affine loop consists of two elements:

1. A single affine statement, which represents the value of the vector x after i iterations of the loop

$$x(i) = L(i) \cdot x_0 + p(i), \text{ and}$$

2. the *counting function* $n(x_0)$ that states how many times the loop will iterate before the loop guard $c^T x(i) < g$ is violated.

The variable i represents the current iteration step. We will refer to i as the *iteration counter*; x_0 is the value of the vector x before entering the loop.

We now provide an intuitive sketch of our algorithm: Given r perfectly nested affine loops, starting from the inner loop, we replace each loop with its affine representation. For r nested loops the result is

$$x(i_1, \ldots, i_r) = A_{final}(i_1, \ldots, i_r) x_0 + b_{final}(i_1, \ldots, i_r) \quad (1)$$

where $i_k = 0 \ldots n_k(x_{0,k})$, matrix A_{final} and vector b_{final} are the compositions of all L_k and p_k, $k = 1 \ldots r$.

The function $n_k(x_{0,k})$ represents the number of iterations in the kth loop with the starting conditions $x_{0,k}$. The starting conditions depend on iteration counters of all the loops at higher levels, i.e., $x_{0,k} = \phi_k(i_1, \ldots, i_{k-1})$.

Number of iterations. We can compute the total number of iterations of the innermost loop using the counting function of each loop:

$$N = \sum_{i_1=0}^{n_1(x_{0,1})} \sum_{i_2=0}^{n_2(x_{0,2})} \cdots \sum_{i_{r-1}=0}^{n_{r-1}(x_{0,r-1})} n_r(x_{0,r}). \quad (2)$$

To solve Equation (2), we need to compute:

1. the affine representations for all the loops together with their counting functions $n_k(x_{0,k})$,

2. the starting conditions for all loops as functions of iteration counters $x_{0,k} = \phi_k(i_1, \ldots, i_{k-1})$, and

3. all the sums in Equation (2).

Work and depth analysis. The number of processes in explicitly parallel programs is always available as a special variable which we call p. In parallelized codes, p is used in loop guards or loop update functions to divide the work into p pieces. Our algorithm determines the number of iterations as a function of all program parameters. We can then define the work of a program as $W = N|_{p=1}$ and depth $D = N|_{p \to \infty}$. Parallel efficiency and exposed parallelism can be computed as described in Section 1.1.

4. ALGORITHM DESCRIPTION

We now describe all the steps and approximations needed to solve Equation (2) which determines the final loop count.

4.1 Affine representation of nested loops

We now explain how we transform a perfectly nested loop into a single affine statement. This statement can then be combined with the initial assignments and the original loop update function of the parent loop into a new loop update function that represents the whole loop nest.

Each loop update statement $x \leftarrow Ax + b$ is a recursive formula for the value of the vector x in the current step, given the value in the previous step. The closed form of that

formula for vector x after i iterations and with the starting value x_0 can be written as

$$\hat{x}(i, x_0) = A^i \cdot x_0 + \sum_{j=0}^{i-1} A^j b. \quad (3)$$

Using $x(i, x_0)$, we compute the number of iterations d after which the loop guard is not satisfied

$$n(x_0) = \left\lceil \underset{d}{\operatorname{argmin}}(c^T \cdot x(d, x_0) \geq g) \right\rceil. \quad (4)$$

Equation (4) defines the *counting function* $n(x_0)$. Let $L = A^i$ and $p = \sum_{j=0}^{i-1} A^j b$ from Equation (3). After we have obtained the closed affine form of a loop at level $k+1$, we can transform the loop nest at level k to

```
while(c_k^T x < g_k) {
    x ← A_k x + b_k     // Initial assignment (x_{0,k+1})
    x ← L_k x + p_k     // Nested loop (aff. rep.)
    x ← U_k x + v_k}    // Loop update
```

where $x = L_k x + p_k$ is the closed-form representation of the $(k+1)$st loop. Furthermore, the three affine statements can be combined to one

$$x \leftarrow U_k(L_k(A_k x + b_k) + p_k) + v_k. \quad (5)$$

We can then use it to form the affine representation of the parent loop. Applying this procedure recursively for all k loop nests will produce the final affine representation $x = A_{final} x_0 + b_{final}$ that expresses the whole loop nest (cf. Equation (1)).

Example of an affine representation.

The following example illustrates how to transform a loop into its affine representation. Consider the following loop

```
y=y_0;  z=z_0;
while(y<z) {y+=2; z--;}
```

that we can write in matrix form as

$$x_0 = \begin{pmatrix} y_0 \\ z_0 \end{pmatrix}, \quad x(i+1) = \begin{pmatrix} 1 & 0 \\ 0 & 1 \end{pmatrix} x(i) + \begin{pmatrix} 2 \\ -1 \end{pmatrix}, \quad c = \begin{pmatrix} 1 \\ -1 \end{pmatrix}$$

and $g = 0$. Using Equation (3), we get the *affine representation* of that loop

$$x(d, x_0) = \begin{pmatrix} 1 & 0 \\ 0 & 1 \end{pmatrix} x_0 + \begin{pmatrix} 2d \\ -d \end{pmatrix}.$$

Equation (4) results in

$$\left\lceil \underset{d}{\operatorname{argmin}} \left(\begin{pmatrix} 1 & -1 \end{pmatrix} \cdot \left(\begin{pmatrix} 1 & 0 \\ 0 & 1 \end{pmatrix} x_0 + \begin{pmatrix} 2d \\ -d \end{pmatrix} \right) \geq 0 \right) \right\rceil,$$

that can be simplified to $\lceil \operatorname{argmin}_d(z_0 - y_0 \leq 3d) \rceil$. A symbolic solver (e.g., MuPAD[10]) will determine the solution for $\lceil d = (z_0 - y_0)/3 \rceil$, which leads to the counting function $n(x_0) = \lceil (y_0 - y_0)/3 \rceil$.

4.2 Starting conditions

The starting conditions $x_{0,k+1}$ for a loop at level $k+1$ are determined by the value of the vector x before entering the loop. For each loop, at depths $k = 1, \ldots, r$, let $\hat{x}_k$ denote the corresponding function defined in equation (3), giving the i_kth *initial assignment* at level k, for $i_k = 1, \ldots, n_k(x_{0,k})$,

$$x_{0,k+1} = A_k \cdot \hat{x}_k(i_k, x_{0,k}) + b_k. \quad (6)$$

We can now count the starting conditions recursively until we reach the top level, where $x_{0,1} = x_0$. In general, the starting condition at level k are compositions of affine representations and initial assignments of all the loops from level $1 \ldots k-1$, treating all iteration variables $i_1, i_2, \ldots, i_{k-1}$ as parameters.

Example for the starting condition.

We now show a small example to illustrate the computation of the starting conditions for inner loops. Given the two nested loops

```
y=y_0; z=z_0;
while(y<m) {
  z=y;
  while(z<m) {z++;}
  y*=2;}
```

Listing 3: Nested Loop

The affine representation for the inner loop with iterator i_2 and starting conditions $x_{0,2}(i_1)$ depending on the outer loop

$$x(i_2) = \begin{pmatrix} 1 & 0 \\ 0 & 1 \end{pmatrix} x_{0,2}(i_1) + \begin{pmatrix} 0 \\ i_2 \end{pmatrix}, \ n_2 = \mathtt{m} - \begin{pmatrix} 0 & 1 \end{pmatrix} \cdot x_{0,2}(i_1),$$

and for the outer loop with iterator i_1 and starting conditions x_0

$$x(i_1) = \begin{pmatrix} 2^{i_1} & 0 \\ \frac{2^{i_1}}{2} & 0 \end{pmatrix} x_0 + \begin{pmatrix} 0 \\ i_2 \end{pmatrix}, \ n_1 = \left\lceil \log_2\left(\frac{\mathtt{m}}{(1 \ 0) \cdot x_0}\right) \right\rceil.$$

The initial assignment for the outer loop is

$$A_1 = \begin{pmatrix} 1 & 0 \\ 1 & 0 \end{pmatrix}; \quad b_1 = \begin{pmatrix} 0 \\ 0 \end{pmatrix}; \quad x_0 = \begin{pmatrix} \mathtt{y_0} \\ \mathtt{z_0} \end{pmatrix}.$$

Starting conditions for the inner loop using Equation (6) are

$$x_{0,2}(i_1) = A_1 x(i_1) + b_1 = \begin{pmatrix} 2^{i_1} & 0 \\ 2^{i_1} & 0 \end{pmatrix} x_0 = \begin{pmatrix} 2^{i_1} \mathtt{y_0} \\ 2^{i_1} \mathtt{y_0} \end{pmatrix}.$$

Using Equation (2) leads to the exact number of iterations.

4.3 Counting the number of iterations

All counting functions and starting conditions can be combined into a final symbolic iteration count. First, we compute all r starting conditions $x_{0,1}, x_{0,2}, \ldots, x_{0,r}$ in the form $x_{0,1} = x_0$, $x_{0,2} = f_2(i_1, x_0)$, $\ldots$, $x_{0,r} = f_r(i_1, i_2, \ldots, i_{r-1}, x_0)$. Then, we compute all counting functions in the form $n_1(x_{0,1}), n_2(x_{0,2}), \ldots, n_r(x_{0,r})$. This enables us to calculate the sums of Equation (2) and solve for the final loop iteration count and derive work and depth from this. We use a symbolic solver to simplify and solve the equations.

In some cases, it is not possible to symbolically determine the exact solution from Equation (2). We differentiate two cases:

1. The counting function contains a ceiling, e.g.,
$$\sum_{i=1}^{\lceil \frac{n}{2} \rceil} i = \begin{cases} \frac{(n+2)n}{8} & \text{if } n \text{ is even} \\ \frac{(n+3)(n+1)}{8} & \text{if } n \text{ is odd} \end{cases}$$

2. The symbolic solver cannot find a closed form, e.g.,
$\sum_{i=1}^{n} i \cdot \log_2(i)$.

In both cases, we derive lower and upper bounds of the respective sum.

Bounded Sum Approximation (BSA) Algorithm. We now show our BSA algorithm that tightly approximates lower and upper bounds of Equation (2) in the two cases where the exact solution cannot be determined.

Obtaining bounds in the first case is simple. For a function $\lceil f(n) \rceil$, we determine the upper bound as $f(n) + 1$ and the lower bound as $f(n)$.

For the second case, with no symbolic solution for a sum, we approximate the sum with an integral [28]. For a non-decreasing function $f_1(i)$

$$\int_0^{n+1} f_1(x-1) \, \mathrm{d}x \le \sum_{i=0}^{n} f_1(i) \le \int_0^{n+1} f_1(x) \, \mathrm{d}x,$$

and for a non-increasing function $f_2(i)$

$$\int_0^{n+1} f_2(x-1) \, \mathrm{d}x \ge \sum_{i=0}^{n} f_2(i) \ge \int_0^{n+1} f_2(x) \, \mathrm{d}x.$$

If $f(i)$ is not monotonic in the interval $[0, n]$, then we split it into smaller intervals in which $f(i)$ is monotonic. For this, we compute the first $\frac{df}{di}$ and second $\frac{d^2 f}{di^2}$ derivatives symbolically. Then we apply the approximation in each segment and combine them to get the proper upper and lower bounds.

While solving Equation (2) we need to carry the lower and upper bounds forward recursively. In the branch of the lower bounds, we only consider lower bounds of parent loops and similarly in the upper bound branch. We may require case differentiations if some counting functions are not monotonic. However, we rarely observed non monotonic counting functions in practice.

Example for bounded sum approximation.

Assume the following nested loop:

```
k=1; l=2;
while(k>0) {
  m = k;
  while(m<s) m++;
  k = k+1;
  l--;}
```

We see that $\mathtt{k_{0,1}} = \mathtt{k_0} = 1$ and $\mathtt{l_{0,1}} = \mathtt{l_0} = 2$. The counting function for the inner loop is

$$n_2 = \mathtt{s} - \mathtt{k_{0,2}}$$

and for the outer loop

$$n_1 = \left\lceil \mathtt{l_{0,1}} + \frac{\sqrt{4\mathtt{l_{0,1}}^2 + 4\mathtt{l_{0,1}} + 8\mathtt{k_{0,1}} + 1} + 1}{2} \right\rceil = 6.$$

The starting conditions for the inner loop are

$$\mathtt{k_{0,2}} = \mathtt{k_{0,1}} + i_1 \cdot \mathtt{l_{0,1}} - \frac{i_1 \cdot (i_1 - 1)}{2} = -\frac{1}{2} i_1^2 + \frac{5}{2} i_1 + 1.$$

The number of iterations of the loop nest, according to Equation 2 is

$$N = \sum_{i_1=0}^{n_1} n_2 = \sum_{i_1=0}^{n_1} (\mathtt{s} + \frac{1}{2} i_1^2 - \frac{5}{2} i_1 - 1)$$

We now approximate this sum with an integral. Analyzing the first and second derivative of n_2 shows that within

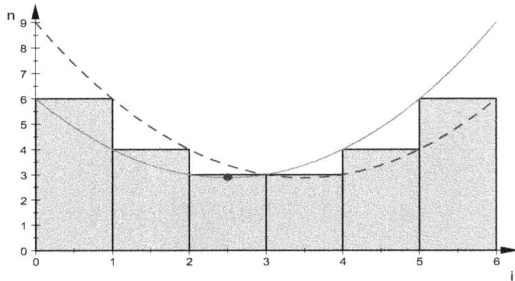

Figure 1: **Series approximation.** Bars represent the series $n_2(i)$, the red line shows the function $n_2(k)$ and the dashed green line shows the function $n_2(k-1)$. The function $n_2(k)$ over-approximates the series in the interval $[0,2]$ and under-approximates it in the interval $[3,6]$; the dot shows the saddle point.

the interval $(0,n_1)$ the function is decreasing in $(0,2.5)$ and increasing in $(2.5,n_1)$. The sum can then be bounded from above by

$$U = \int_0^2 n_2(i_1-1)\,\mathrm{d}i_1 + n_2(2) + \int_3^{n_1} n_2(i_1)\,\mathrm{d}i_1 = 6s - \frac{47}{12}$$

and from below by

$$L = \int_0^2 n_2(i_1)\,\mathrm{d}i_1 + n_2(2) + \int_3^{n_1} n_2(i_1-1)\,\mathrm{d}i_1 = 6s - \frac{161}{12}.$$

Figure 1 illustrates the example.

4.4 Correctness of the algorithm

All the steps of the algorithm except the sum approximation are proper algebraic transformations. If no approximation is needed then the algorithm produces the exact number of iterations. For example for the loops in Listing 3 the total number of iterations of the inner loop is exactly

$$N = \mathtt{y}_0 - 2^{\left\lceil \log_2\left(\frac{\mathtt{m}}{\mathtt{y}_0}\right)\right\rceil}\mathtt{y}_0 + \mathtt{m}\left\lceil \log_2\left(\frac{\mathtt{m}}{\mathtt{y}_0}\right)\right\rceil.$$

If approximation is required, then we need to prove that we obtain proper upper and lower bounds and that this property propagates further through the algorithm.

Lemma 4.1. *The Bounded Sum Approximation algorithm gives valid lower and upper bounds for Equation (2).*

Proof. Ceiling upper and lower bound for type 1 approximations are correct by the definition of the ceiling function. Let us consider type 2 sum approximations.

First we need to prove that the upper and lower bounds for a series $f(n)$, where $n = 0, \ldots, k$, found by the algorithm are correct. Let's denote

$$U_{[a,b]}(x) = \begin{cases} f(x), & \text{if } \forall x \in [a,b]: \frac{df}{dx} \geq 0 \\ f(x-1), & \text{if } \forall x \in [a,b]: \frac{df}{dx} \leq 0 \end{cases}$$

$$L_{[a,b]}(x) = \begin{cases} f(x-1), & \text{if } \forall x \in [a,b]: \frac{df}{dx} \geq 0 \\ f(x), & \text{if } \forall x \in [a,b]: \frac{df}{dx} \leq 0 \end{cases}$$

as upper and lower bounds of the monotonic series f in the interval $[a,b]$, as stated in Section 4.3.

Let $c \in [0,k]$ be the only saddle point of function $f(x)$. Intervals with multiple saddle points can be split to smaller intervals where each contains a single saddle point. Then, U and L will change from $f(x-1)$ to $f(x)$ or from $f(x)$

to $f(x-1)$ at that point c. The upper bound $U_{[0,\lfloor c\rfloor]} = U_{[0,c]} \neq U_{[c,k]} = U_{[\lceil c\rceil,k]}$ does not change in the intervals $[0,\lfloor c\rfloor]$ and $[\lceil c\rceil,k]$. We can then bound the value of $f(\lfloor c\rfloor)$ with $U_{[0,c]}(\lfloor c\rfloor)$. Thus,

$$\int_0^{\lfloor c\rfloor} U_{[0,c]}(x)\,\mathrm{d}x \geq \sum_{i=0}^{\lfloor c\rfloor} f(i), \int_{\lceil c\rceil}^k U_{[c,k]}(x)\,\mathrm{d}x \geq \sum_{i=\lceil c\rceil}^k f(i)$$

$$U_{[a,c]}(\lfloor c\rfloor) \geq f(\lfloor c\rfloor).$$

From this follows that the upper bound of the non-monotonic sum of series $\sum_{i=0}^k f(i)$, with saddle point c, can be expressed as:

$$U = \int_0^{\lfloor c\rfloor} U_{[0,c]}(x)\,\mathrm{d}x + U_{[0,c]}(c) + \int_{\lceil c\rceil}^k U_{[c,n]}(x)\,\mathrm{d}x \geq \sum_{i=0}^k f(i).$$

The lower bounds discussion follows a similar reasoning.

We now prove propagation of this property through consecutive sums in Equation 2: Let f_k be the kth sum from Equation 2, and U_k and L_k upper and lower bounds of f_k. We then can present it as

$$\sum_{i_k=0}^{n_k} n_{k+1}(i_1, \ldots, i_{k-1}, x_0) = f_k(i_1 \ldots, i_k, x_0)$$

and bound it with

$$L_k(i_1 \ldots, i_{k-1}, x_0) \leq f_k(i_1, \ldots, i_{k-1}, x_0) \leq U_k(i_1, \ldots, i_{k-1}, x_0).$$

The next sum at level $k-1$ will be

$$\sum_{i_{k-1}=0}^{n_{k-1}} f_k(i_1, \ldots, i_{k-1}, x_0)$$

Upper and lower bounds are not changed by summing, such that

$$\sum_{i_{k-1}=0}^{n_{k-1}} f_k(i_1, \ldots, i_{k-1}, x_0) \geq \sum_{i_{k-1}=0}^{n_{k-1}} L_k(i_1, \ldots, i_{k-1}, x_0)$$

and

$$\sum_{i_{k-1}=0}^{n_{k-1}} f_k(i_1, \ldots, i_{k-1}, x_0) \leq \sum_{i_{k-1}=0}^{n_{k-1}} U_k(i_1, \ldots, i_{k-1}, x_0)$$

implies $L_1(x_0) \leq f_1(x_0) = N \leq U_1(x_0)$. $\qquad \square$

4.5 Multipath loops

We formalize a loop containing multiple statements as

```
while(c_k^T x < g_k) {
    x ← A_{k,1}x + b_{k,1}
    x ← A_{k,2}x + b_{k,2}
    ...
    x ← A_{k,m}x + b_{k,m}}
```

where each of the statements $x \leftarrow A_{k,i}x + b_{k,i}$ may be a simple assignment or an affine representation of a loop. We compose them in the same way as we did in Equation (5), forming a single affine statement.

Starting conditions. We compute the starting conditions for each loop by generalizing Equation (6). For multipath loops the starting condition for a loop represented by its affine representation $x \leftarrow A_{k,i}x + b_{k,i}$ is the composition of all the affine statements that precede it:

$$x_{0,k+1,i} = A_{k,i-1}(\ldots(A_{k,1}\cdot\hat{x}_k(i_k, x_{0,k-1})+b_{k,1})\ldots)+b_{k,i-1}$$

For illustration consider the following example loop:

```
while(c_k^T x < g_k) {
    x ← A_{k,1}x + b_{k,1}
    x ← A_{k,2}x + b_{k,2}
    x ← A_{k,3}x + b_{k,3}
    x ← A_{k,4}x + b_{k,4}
    x ← A_{k,5}x + b_{k,5}}
```

Assume that in the example above, $x \leftarrow A_{k,2}x + b_{k,2}$, $x \leftarrow A_{k,3}x + b_{k,3}$ and $x \leftarrow A_{k,4}x + b_{k,4}$ are affine representations of three nested loops. Then, the starting condition for the third loop $x \leftarrow A_{k,4}x + b_{k,4}$ is

$$x_{0,k+1,4} = A_{k,3}(A_{k,2}(A_{k,1} \cdot \hat{x}_k(i_k, x_{0,k-1}) + b_{k,1}) + b_{k,2}) + b_{k,3}.$$

Counting the number of iterations. We solve Equation (2) using the appropriate counting function $n_r(x_{0,r})$ for each loop. The series of sums is formed according to the hierarchy of loops starting at the innermost loop.

5. PRACTICAL CONSIDERATIONS

We now briefly outline how the developed method can be used to assess work and depth of real applications. This paper is focusing on the fundamental techniques, yet, we want to provide a coarse view of how we apply our method in practical settings.

The whole mechanism can be implemented in a source-code analysis tool or a compiler. We use the Low Level Virtual Machine (LLVM [26]) and will outline the implementation. LLVM's internal program representation uses Single Static Assignment (SSA), which makes it simple to determine loops (identified by back-edges), loop guards (identified by conditional branches with back-edges), and all dependent variables.

From this information, we create initial assignments, loop guards, and loop updates for each loop and apply the procedure described in Section 4. While the vast majority of loops in practical programs are affine, some loops may depend on more complex conditions and thus do not fit our framework. However, one of the main strengths of our method is that we can still compute the number of iterations of loop nests containing non-affine functions as we will describe in the following section.

5.1 Extensions for non-affine loops

If a loop guard is not an affine function of iteration variables and constant parameters then we may not be able to determine the exact number of iterations statically. Examples are loops with iteration counts determined by unknown functions or complex sources like arrays that keep dynamic data. This is often the case in applications that iterate until a complex convergence criterion is reached, e.g., conjugate gradient methods. If the loop exit conditions cannot be represented as affine statements, then the whole block is treated as a symbolic value u (*undefined*).

A strength of our method is that it still solves the remaining affine loop nests symbolically as u is simply treated as a parameter that propagates while solving Equation 2. In addition to just treating non-affine loops as new symbolic parameters, our tool enables the user to annotate such loops with affine upper and lower bound functions.

We demonstrate the technique with a loop that we found during one of our case studies. The following Fortran code is extracted from the NAS CG benchmark.

```
do j=1,lastrow-firstrow+1
    sum = 0.d0
    do k=rowstr(j),rowstr(j+1)-1
        sum = sum + a(k)*p(colidx(k))
    enddo
    w(j) = sum
enddo
```

Our tool traces the expression `lastrow-firstrow+1` back to the program parameter $\text{row\_size} = \frac{na}{nprows}$ or $\text{row\_size} = \frac{na}{nprows} + 1$, depending on the process id. This reflects the fact that `nprows` may not divide `na`, where `na` is the problem size. However, the value of `rowstr(j)` cannot be determined statically because it represents the location of the first nonzero value in row j of one of the program arrays. Our algorithm then represents the previous loop nest as:

```
j=1;
while(j<=row_size) {u; j++;}
```

u is treated as a loop with the fixed number of iterations $u = $`rowstr(j+1)-rowstr(j)`. The total number of iterations of this code fragment for the most busy process is represented as

$$N = \left\lceil \frac{na}{nprows} \right\rceil u.$$

It is possible to provide the user with information about the exact code fragment that is the origin of u. Users can then determine upper and lower bounds for each unknown parameter.

6. CASE STUDIES

In this section we present our results from analyzing several benchmarks. We compute work and depth of several parallel programs to demonstrate the insight we gained into the bounds on parallel efficiency of those practical codes. Our analysis allows us to make statements about parallel efficiency without studying the problem or implementation.

We analyzed major loops of the NAS parallel benchmarks version 3.2 [3] and the Mantevo micro applications version 2.0 [5]. We only present an interesting subset in our case studies due to space constraints.

In all the cases presented, no approximation was needed, so presented results give exact number of iterations (with respect to the introduced constants). If not stated otherwise, in the following benchmarks m represents the problem scale, n is a program parameter to NAS specifying the number of iterations to perform, and p denotes number of processes. In some cases processes are arranged into multiple dimensions. In those cases, $p_1, p_2, \ldots, p_k$ represents number of processes in corresponding dimensions and $p = \prod_{i=1}^{k} p_i$. We also assume that the decomposition is square, i.e., $p_1 \approx p_2 \approx \cdots \approx p_k$. For easier work-depth analysis, presented results are simplified by replacing constant terms with auxiliary constants c_i. We use constants instead of asymptotic notation to retain lower-order terms.

6.1 NAS Parallel Benchmarks: EP

The NAS EP benchmark represents a typical Monte Carlo simulation and thus performs nearly no communication. Our analysis found that only one out of seven loops could not be resolved due to a conditional `goto` statement, resulting in a single u. The work of EP is

$$N = \left\lceil \frac{2^{m-16} \cdot (u + 2^{16})}{p} \right\rceil.$$

The following listing shows the non-affine loop that determines u after removing all statements that do not influence the iteration count:

```
u:    do i=1,100
        ik =kk/2
        if (ik .eq. 0) goto 130
        kk=ik
      continue
```

A programmer can easily determine that $u \leq 100$, which is negligible compared to 2^{16}. Thus, we can approximate the work using one thread $W = T_1 \approx 2^m$ and depth $D = T_\infty \approx 1$. This shows that the the parallelization is work-optimal and the efficiency

$$E_p \approx \frac{2^m}{p \left\lceil \frac{2^m}{p} \right\rceil}.$$

This means that $E_p \approx 1$ if $p \lesssim 2^m$ and $E_p \approx 2^m/p$ if $p \gtrsim 2^m$. We conclude that the maximum available parallelism in EP is 2^m, because N cannot further decrease for $p \gtrsim 2^m$. This does not mean that the code will efficiently execute with 2^m tasks, however, it specifies an upper bound to the speedup. This is an expected result since the code is considered "embarrassingly parallel".

6.2 NAS Parallel Benchmarks: CG

The NAS CG program represents a typical conjugate gradient solver. Our tool found that only 2 out of 23 analyzed loops were not affine (cf. Section 5.1). The two undefined loops had identical guards, resulting in a single parameter u that can be bounded as $0 \leq u \leq m$. This allows us to bound the number of iterations

$$N \lesssim n \left(g \left\lceil \frac{m}{p} \right\rceil + (6 + 5g) \sqrt{\left\lceil \frac{m}{p} \right\rceil} + (3g + 4) \log_2(\sqrt{p}) \right)$$

where g is the program parameter `cgitmax`. We can approximate work on one thread $W = T_1 \lesssim (g\, m + \sqrt{m}(5g + 6))n$. However, CG is not work optimal as the parallel work is monotonically growing. This causes the depth to be $D = T_\infty = \infty$. If we treat the problem size m as constant, then CG's parallel efficiency is

$$E_p = c_1 \left(c_2\, p \log_2(\sqrt{p}) + c_3 \left\lceil \frac{m}{p} \right\rceil + c_4 \sqrt{\left\lceil \frac{m}{p} \right\rceil} \right)^{-1}.$$

This means that the work per process increases with $\log_2(\sqrt{p})$ due to a parallel reduction among $\sqrt{p}$ processes. The available parallelism is m.

6.3 NAS Parallel Benchmarks: IS

The NAS IS program represents a parallel bucket sort algorithm. In each iteration, all processes perform their local sorting and exchange information. The communication overhead is expected to grow with the number of processes. A total of 5 out of 15 analyzed loops were not affine. Those five loops fall in two classes: the first class iterates over maximum and minimum key

value represented as u_1=`max_key_val-min_key_val+1`; the second class iterates over the buckets after redistribution and is represented as u_2=`bucket_distrib_ptr2[k] - bucket_distrib_ptr1[k]`. Both loop iteration counts depend on the structure of the input and the distribution and can thus not easily be bounded tightly. The total number of iterations of IS is

$$N = n \left(3(b + t) + 2 \left\lceil \frac{m}{p} \right\rceil + p + 2 \cdot u_1 + 2 \cdot u_2 \right)$$

where b is the number of buckets, t is the size of the test array, and m is the number of keys to be sorted. The total work on one thread is

$$W = T_1 = n(3(b + t) + 2m + 2u_1 + 2u_2 + 1).$$

The depth $D = \infty$ because the parallelization is not work efficient which is due to the necessary inter-process communications. The parallel efficiency of IS is $E_p = c_1 / \left(p^2 + c_2\, p + c_3\, p \left\lceil \frac{m}{p} \right\rceil \right)$, which drops quickly with the number of processes used. The reason is that each process may need to communicate with each other process. The available parallelism is also m in this case.

6.4 Mantevo Benchmarks: CoMD

The Mantevo CoMD benchmark represents a classical molecular dynamics simulation. Eight out of 18 analyzed loops contain non-affine statements. The code distributes atoms to processes. The first class updates atoms in the partitions and u_1 represents the number of iterations of those loops.

```
u₁:  while(i<boxes->nAtoms[iBox]) {
        int jBox=getBox(atoms->r[iOff+i]);
        if (jBox!=iBox) moveAtom(i,iBox,jBox);
        else ++i;}
```

The second class u_2=`qsort(nAtoms[iBox])` is limited by the data sizes to be sorted. The number of iterations of the CoMD Benchmark is

$$N = n \left(g(B + 3) \left\lceil \frac{m}{p} \right\rceil + g\, T \left(\left\lceil \frac{m}{p} \right\rceil u_1 + u_2 \right) + \left\lceil \frac{m}{p\, B} \right\rceil + 2 \right)$$

where B is the fixed amount of atoms in each box, g is the `print rate` program parameter, and T is the total number of boxes:

$$T = 2 \left(\frac{\sqrt[3]{m}}{p_1} + 2 \right) \left(\frac{\sqrt[3]{m}}{p_2} + \frac{\sqrt[3]{m}}{p_3} + 2 \right) + \frac{\sqrt[3]{m^2}}{p_2\, p_3} + \frac{m}{p_1\, p_2\, p_3}.$$

If we bound $u_1 < B^2$ and $u_2 < B \log_2(B)$, then we can approximate work and depth: $W \lesssim c_1\, m + c_2\, m^{2/3} + c_3\, m^{1/3} + c_4$, and $D \lesssim n(c_5 + c_6\, B(\log_2(B)))$. The implementation is work-optimal and the efficiency $E_p \lesssim c_7 / (p + c_8)$ is decreasing with number of processors, which is the result of sequential parts of the program that cannot be parallelized. The available parallelism is m.

Scalability Analysis.

We were able to determine bounds for work, depth, parallel efficiency, and available parallelism for several real-world applications. We see that the available parallelism in all investigated applications scales linearly with the input problem size. While this suggests good scaling, we show that for CG and IS communication overheads increase the work with the number of processes. For example, for IS, this overhead grows linearly with the number of used processes.

We were able to perform those analyses by pure code introspection which was guided by our tool without requiring knowledge of the implemented methods or algorithms. If the solved problem is known, then one could even proof optimality in terms of parallel efficiency or available parallelism. However, this is outside the scope of this paper.

7. DISCUSSION

We now discuss the limitations of our approach and briefly outline potential additional use-cases.

Limitations.

Since our analysis only counts loop iterations and does not account for the exact costs of each loop, we can only provide bounds on the expected execution time on a parallel system. However, those bounds are always asymptotically correct. Since we limit ourselves to the work and depth model, we cannot account for communication or synchronization overheads in real codes. Yet, the bounds we provide are useful to determine the relative behavior of work and depth and allow us to reason about exposed parallelism and parallel efficiency just like the work and depth model.

Extending the Models.

While outside the scope of this paper, it is simple to extend our work and depth models to account for system parameters such as memory or network latency and bandwidth. Blelloch [12] discusses further options.

Model-based Mapping to Heterogeneous Systems.

Having a model for the work and depth of each loop in a program can be useful when the program is to be mapped to future heterogeneous architectures. Those systems will most likely contain Latency Compute Units (LCU, cf. today's CPU cores) and Throughput Compute Unites (TCU, cf. today's accelerators such as GPUs or Xeon Phi). A compiler would need to determine the target architecture for each loop statically. It could use the generated work/depth models to assign code pieces with low parallelism (small W/D) to LCUs and code pieces with larger parallelism (large W/D) to TCUs.

8. RELATED WORK

Counting loop iterations and assessing scalability of parallel codes are important research problems. Rodriguez-Carbonell and Kapur [31] find polynomial loop invariants using an algebraic approach. Sharma et al. [32] use a data driven approach to iteratively guess the correct polynomial loop invariant and then check its correctness, and Matringe et al. [30] generate loop invariants also for non-linear differential systems. Loop invariants can be used to bound loop iteration counts but the resulting bounds are often not tight.

Multiple research groups use the polyhedral model (PM) to determine the exact number of loop iterations [1, 8, 37]. In this case, the number of iterations can be approximated by counting integer points in that polyhedron using a polynomial-time algorithm [6]. The PM is widely used, not only in loop analysis [9]. However, it has a serious limitation - it requires that the loop update function can be expressed in Presburger arithmetic and thus cannot deal with non-

constant updates such as $x = 2 * x$. To the best of our knowledge, no previous work handled such cases properly. Methods like the one proposed by Blanc et al. [11] require explicitly that loops cannot include such statements.

Other works utilize dynamic approaches to extrapolate program performance and assess scalability in practical settings. Barnes et al. [4] use regression to linear and logarithmic functions to predict scalability of nearly linear-scaling HPC applications. Calotoiu et al. [14] select a scaling model from a set of predefined candidate functions and fit the parameters with regression. Other works, such as [20, 27] use multi-layer neural networks or statistical techniques to predict scalability.

More complex performance prediction frameworks consider the effect of communication [15, 29] and extrapolate single-node runs [36]. Partial execution [35] can improve those techniques. Other studies provide advice for modeling the general performance [21] and scalability [19] of parallel applications. In addition, many application-specific studies exist but cannot be generalized [7, 24].

We extend previous work significantly in two directions: first, we show a technique that can tightly bound the numbers of iterations of arbitrary affine loop nests and second, we show how this method can be used to assess work and depth of parallel applications.

9. CONCLUSIONS

We show a method to symbolically count loop iterations of practical codes in terms of their input sizes. Our method provides either an exact solution or tight upper and lower bounds using bounded sum approximation. It is applicable to affine and non-affine loops. While it can bound all affine loops accurately, it handles non-affine loop counts as a symbolic constant and allows the user to provide lower and upper bounds.

We show how to derive parallel work and depth from the loop count models. Using the work and depth model we approximate bounds on the parallel efficiency of those codes. This technique allows us to specify upper bounds to scalability of practical parallel codes. In general, our method allows a developer to quickly check how an explicitly parallel code scales with the numbers of processes and input sizes.

We are applying a standard algorithmic analysis technique (measuring work and depth) to real source codes. Our developed techniques pave the way to quickly and automatically assess program scalability and will thus quickly become an important tool for future parallel application development and analysis.

Acknowledgments

We thank the anonymous reviewers for outstandingly helpful comments to improve the quality of the paper.

References

[1] C. Alias, A. Darte, P. Feautrier, and L. Gonnord. Multi-dimensional rankings, program termination, and complexity bounds of flowchart programs. In *Static Analysis*, volume 6337 of *Lecture Notes in Computer Science*, pages 117–133. 2011.

[2] G. M. Amdahl. Validity of the single processor approach to achieving large scale computing capabilities. In *Proc. of the April 18-20, 1967, Spring Joint Computer Conference*, AFIPS '67 (Spring), pages 483–485, 1967.

[3] D. H. Bailey et al. The NAS Parallel Benchmarks: Summary and Preliminary Results. In *Proc. of 1991 ACM/IEEE Supercomputing*, pages 158–165, 1991.

[4] B. J. Barnes, B. Rountree, D. K. Lowenthal, J. Reeves, B. de Supinski, and M. Schulz. A regression-based approach to scalability prediction. In *Proc. of the 22nd Intl. Conf. on Super.*, ICS '08, pages 368–377, 2008.

[5] R. F. Barrett, M. A. Heroux, P. T. Lin, C. T. Vaughan, and A. B. Williams. Poster: Mini-applications: Vehicles for co-design. In *Proc. of the 2011 ACM/IEEE Supercomputing Companion*, SC '11, pages 1–2, 2011.

[6] A. I. Barvinok. A polynomial time algorithm for counting integral points in polyhedra when the dimension is fixed. *Math. Oper. Res.*, 19(4):769–779, Nov. 1994.

[7] G. Bauer, S. Gottlieb, and T. Hoefler. Performance Modeling and Comparative Analysis of the MILC Lattice QCD Application su3 rmd. In *Proc. of the 2012 12th IEEE/ACM Intl. Symposium on Cluster, Cloud and Grid Computing*, pages 652–659, May 2012.

[8] A. M. Ben-Amram and S. Genaim. On the linear ranking problem for integer linear-constraint loops. *SIGPLAN Not.*, 48(1):51–62, Jan. 2013.

[9] M.-W. Benabderrahmane, L.-N. Pouchet, A. Cohen, and C. Bastoul. The Polyhedral Model Is More Widely Applicable Than You Think. In R. Gupta, editor, *Compiler Construction*, volume 6011 of *LNCS*, pages 283–303. 2010.

[10] L. Bernardin. A review of symbolic solvers. *SIGSAM Bull.*, 30(1):9–20, Mar. 1996.

[11] R. Blanc, T. Henzinger, T. Hottelier, and L. Kovacs. ABC: Algebraic Bound Computation for Loops. In E. Clarke and A. Voronkov, editors, *Logic for Programming, Artificial Intelligence, and Reasoning*, volume 6355 of *LNCS*, pages 103–118. 2010.

[12] G. E. Blelloch. Programming parallel algorithms. *Commun. ACM*, 39(3):85–97, Mar. 1996.

[13] R. P. Brent. The parallel evaluation of general arithmetic expressions. *J. ACM*, 21(2):201–206, Apr. 1974.

[14] A. Calotoiu, T. Hoefler, M. Poke, and F. Wolf. Using automated performance modeling to find scalability bugs in complex codes. In *Proc. of 2013 ACM/IEEE Supercomputing*, SC '13, pages 45:1–45:12, 2013.

[15] L. Carrington, A. Snavely, and N. Wolter. A performance prediction framework for scientific applications. *Future Gener. Comput. Syst.*, 22(3):336–346, Feb. 2006.

[16] Z. DeVito et al. Liszt: A Domain Specific Language for Building Portable Mesh-based PDE Solvers. In *Proc. of 2011 ACM/IEEE Supercomputing*, SC '11, pages 9:1–9:12, 2011.

[17] E. W. Dijkstra. Structured programming. chapter Notes on Structured Programming, pages 1–82. 1972.

[18] T. Goodale, G. Allen, G. Lanfermann, J. Massó, T. Radke, E. Seidel, and J. Shalf. The cactus framework and toolkit: Design and applications. In *High Performance Computing for Computational Science*, pages 197–227. 2003.

[19] T. Hoefler, W. Gropp, M. Snir, and W. Kramer. Performance Modeling for Systematic Performance Tuning. In *Proc. of the 2011 ACM/IEEE Supercomputing*, Nov. 2011.

[20] E. Ipek, B. R. de Supinski, M. Schulz, and S. A. McKee. An approach to performance prediction for parallel applications. In *Proc. of the 11th Intl.*

[21] R. Jain. *The Art Of Computer Systems Performance Analysis: Techniques for Experimental Design, Measurement, Simulation, and Modeling.* 2008.

[22] J. JáJá. *An Introduction to Parallel Algorithms.* 1992.

[23] R. M. Karp and V. Ramachandran. Handbook of Theoretical Computer Science (Vol. A). chapter Parallel Algorithms for Shared-memory Machines, pages 869–941. 1990.

[24] D. J. Kerbyson et al. Predictive performance and scalability modeling of a large-scale application. In *Proc. of the 2001 ACM/IEEE conference on Supercomputing*, pages 37–37. ACM, 2001.

[25] D. E. Knuth. *Sorting and Searching, The Art of Computer Programming, Volume 3: (2Nd Ed.).* 1998.

[26] C. Lattner and V. Adve. LLVM: A Compilation Framework for Lifelong Program Analysis & Transformation. In *Proc. of the Intl. Symposium on Code Generation and Optimization: Feedback-directed and Runtime Optimization*, CGO '04, 2004.

[27] B. C. Lee, D. M. Brooks, B. R. de Supinski, M. Schulz, K. Singh, and S. A. McKee. Methods of inference and learning for performance modeling of parallel applications. In *Proc. of the 12th ACM SIGPLAN Symp. on Principles and Practice of Parallel Programming*, PPoPP '07, pages 249–258, 2007.

[28] C. E. Leiserson, R. L. Rivest, C. Stein, and T. H. Cormen. *Introduction to Algorithms.* 2001.

[29] G. Marin and J. Mellor-Crummey. Cross-architecture performance predictions for scientific applications using parameterized models. In *Proc. of the Joint Int'l Conf. on Measurement and Modeling of Computer Systems*, SIGMETRICS '04, pages 2–13, 2004.

[30] N. Matringe, A. Moura, and R. Rebiha. Generating invariants for non-linear hybrid systems by linear algebraic methods. In *Static Analysis*, volume 6337 of *LNCS*, pages 373–389. 2011.

[31] E. Rodríguez-Carbonell and D. Kapur. Automatic generation of polynomial loop invariants: Algebraic foundations. In *Proc. of 2004 Intl. Symp. on Symb. and Alg. Comp.*, ISSAC '04, pages 266–273, 2004.

[32] R. Sharma, S. Gupta, B. Hariharan, A. Aiken, P. Liang, and A. Nori. A data driven approach for algebraic loop invariants. In M. Felleisen and P. Gardner, editors, *Progr. Languages and Systems*, volume 7792 of *LNCS*, pages 574–592. 2013.

[33] Y. Shiloach and U. Vishkin. An $O(n^2 \log n)$ Parallel Max-flow Algorithm. *J. Alg.*, 3(2):128–146, Feb. 1982.

[34] A. M. Turing. On Computable Numbers, with an Application to the Entscheidungsproblem. *Proc. London Math. Soc.*, 2(42):230–265, 1936.

[35] L. T. Yang, X. Ma, and F. Mueller. Cross-platform performance prediction of parallel applications using partial execution. In *Proc. of the 2005 ACM/IEEE Conference on Supercomputing*, SC '05, 2005.

[36] J. Zhai, W. Chen, and W. Zheng. Phantom: Predicting performance of parallel applications on large-scale parallel machines using a single node. In *Proc. of the 15th ACM Symp. on Princ. and Prac. of Par. Progr.*, PPoPP '10, pages 305–314, 2010.

[37] F. Zuleger, S. Gulwani, M. Sinn, and H. Veith. Bound analysis of imperative programs with the size-change abstraction. In E. Yahav, editor, *Static Analysis*, volume 6887 of *Lecture Notes in Computer Science*, pages 280–297. 2011.

Parallel Streaming Frequency-Based Aggregates

Kanat Tangwongsan*
Computer Science Program
Mahidol University
International College
kanat.tan@mahidol.ac.th

Srikanta Tirthapura
Dept. of Electrical and
Computer Engineering
Iowa State University
snt@iastate.edu

Kun-Lung Wu
IBM T.J. Watson Research
Center, Yorktown Heights
klwu@us.ibm.com

ABSTRACT

We present efficient parallel streaming algorithms for fundamental frequency-based aggregates in both the sliding window and the infinite window settings. In the sliding window setting, we give a parallel algorithm for maintaining a space-bounded block counter (SBBC). Using SBBC, we derive algorithms for basic counting, frequency estimation, and heavy hitters that perform no more work than their best sequential counterparts. In the infinite window setting, we present algorithms for frequency estimation, heavy hitters, and count-min sketch. For both the infinite window and sliding window settings, our parallel algorithms process a "minibatch" of items using linear work and polylog parallel depth. We also prove a lower bound showing that the work of the parallel algorithm is optimal in the case of heavy hitters and frequency estimation. To our knowledge, these are the first parallel algorithms for these problems that are provably work efficient and have low depth.

Categories and Subject Descriptors

H.1.0 [**Information Systems**]: Models and Principles—*General*; F.2.0 [**Theory of Computation**]: Analysis of Algorithms and Problem Complexity—*General*

Keywords

parallel streaming; stream processing; heavy hitter; basic counting

1. INTRODUCTION

Today's applications need to monitor massive volumes of data and derive insights from it in real-time. In such applications, it is natural to employ parallel computing to improve processing throughput. However, parallel stream monitoring needs fundamentally new algorithms, and there does not seem to have been much work in this direction so far. In this work, we consider the design and analysis of parallel algorithms for processing a high-velocity data stream on a shared-memory machine (e.g., a multicore machine).

Following the paradigm used by streaming systems such as Apache Spark [ZDL+13], we assume the model of a *discretized stream*. The

---

*Corresponding author.

system receives data from one or more sources and divides the resulting stream into "minibatches". The streaming algorithm processes a minibatch, potentially using parallel processing, and updates its state. After processing one minibatch, the system moves onto the next minibatch. This model of processing elements has the following advantages: (1) Each minibatch can potentially be processed in parallel without a sequential bottleneck, whether in data ingestion or in processing, and (2) the view of a user of the system is simple. Queries can be answered on data received until, and including the most recent mini-batch that was processed.

While there is a long line of research on sequential streaming algorithms for a variety of problems, and empirical and experimental work on parallel streaming algorithms, basic questions on algorithms for parallel stream processing remain open. This work initiates a systematic study of parallel streaming algorithms for fundamental aggregates, with a rigorous analysis of both the algorithms' cost and accuracy guarantees.

To process a stream in parallel, one approach is to use *independent per-processor data structures* (see Figure 1). Suppose there are p processors; the stream S is partitioned into sub-streams $S_1, S_2, \ldots, S_p$, one per processor. Each processor i processes S_i and maintains a data structure D_i local to processor i. The different data structures $D_i, i = 1 \ldots p$ are merged together periodically, or whenever a query is posed. For this approach to work, the data structures should be *mergeable* (see, e.g., [ACH+13]). Even if mergeable data structures exist for a given aggregate, there are inherent shortcomings of the independent data structure approach in our context. In particular, the approach does not take advantage of available shared memory, and the merging step can be a sequential bottleneck. See Section 5.4 for further discussion of the independent data structure approach for heavy hitter identification.

We take a different approach to processing a stream in parallel. Instead of a per-processor data structure, we use a *single shared data structure* (see Figure 1) that the processors update cooperatively update in parallel . Updates and queries can be interleaved, and our algorithms require no locking. This approach has the following advantages when compared with the independent data structure approach: (1) the *total workspace is smaller* than the independent data structure approach. For instance, in the case of approximate heavy hitter identification, a shared data structure takes the same total memory as a sequential algorithm such as [MG82], while the independent data structure approach requires memory p times larger. (2) There is no need for a further merge step to combine different data structures. This eliminates a sequential bottleneck, and allows polylogarithmic depth parallel algorithms.

1.1 Our Contributions

We present efficient parallel algorithms for estimating fundamental frequency based aggregates on a stream in the infinite window

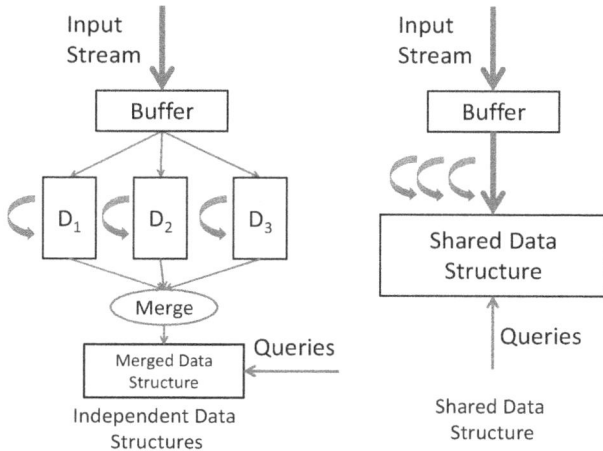

Figure 1: Two approaches to parallel streaming algorithms for a shared memory multiprocessor.

and the sliding window models. In the *infinite window* model, the aggregate is desired over the entire stream from the start, whereas in *sliding window* model, the aggregate is desired only over the most recent elements of the stream. We consider the count-based sliding window, defined as the n most recent elements in the stream. We assume that n is much larger than the size of a minibatch, and that it is undesirable to store the entire window in the main memory.

Our algorithms operate in the work-depth model assuming an underlying CRCW machine. As is standard, *work* is the total operation count of an algorithm, and *depth*, traditionally known as "parallel time", is the longest chain of dependencies within a parallel computation. Throughout, we measure space in terms of words, unless stated otherwise.

We derive algorithms for the following problems:

—*Basic Counting*: On a stream of bits, maintain the number of 1s within a count-based sliding window of size n. Though easy in the model of infinite window, this aggregate is non-trivial in the sliding window model, and is a fundamental problem; the work of Datar et al. [DGIM02] show how to reduce other aggregates on a sliding window, such as approximate histograms, hash tables, and ℓ_p norms of vectors to basic counting on a bit stream.

—*Sum*: This is a generalization of basic counting. On a stream of non-negative integers, maintain the sum of the elements within a sliding window. The maintenance of the mean of non-negative integers can be reduced to the sum.

—*Frequency Estimation*: Approximately track the frequency of items either within an infinite window or a sliding window.

—*Heavy Hitters*: Continuously track ϕ-heavy hitters in a stream. This is a fundamental problem in stream monitoring, and has received widespread attention due to its importance in monitoring applications, including network monitoring [EV03, CH10]. We consider tracking heavy hitters in both the infinite window and sliding window settings.

—*Count-Min Sketch* [CM05]: While not an aggregate in itself, this data structure is a useful summary of frequency-based properties of a stream, and can be used for answering a variety of queries on the input stream, including point and range queries, quantiles, and heavy hitters.

Except for count-min sketch, our algorithms provides a notion

of deterministic guarantee, namely an *ε-approximation*, where the estimate has worst-case relative error at most ε. However, our algorithms are randomized; hence, we state their work and depth bounds in expectation.

Our algorithms are work efficient; i.e., they perform no more work, up to constant factors, than their most efficient sequential counterparts. They also have low depth, which is polylogarithmic in the input size and in the workspace, for almost all cases. Their memory requirements are also of the same order as their sequential counterparts [1]. To our knowledge, these are the first parallel streaming algorithms that simultaneously have all these properties. Previous work on parallel and distributed streaming algorithms have mostly focused on the case of independent data structures and are unable to achieve a parallel depth that is smaller than the size of the data structure. In the case of frequency estimation and heavy hitters, we are able to, for the first time, break the barrier of $\Omega(1/\varepsilon)$ for the parallel depth.

At a high level, the difference between the infinite window case and the sliding-window case can be seen as keeping a regular counter versus keeping a counter that slides with the window. We design a synopsis data structure, called a *space-bounded block counter*, that maintains an approximate count of the number of 1s in a sliding window via deterministic sampling, while supporting parallel ingestion of a sequence of bits, which we use internally to process a minibatch. We use the parallel space-bounded block counter as a building block in algorithms for basic counting and sum over a sliding window, and in frequency estimation and heavy hitters.

1.2 Related Work

There have been several related works on parallel and distributed processing of a data stream, but they have usually not considered the (theoretical) efficiency of parallel algorithms for the problem.

Work on the distributed streaming model, both one-shot processing [GT01, GT04], as well as continuous monitoring [Cor13, CMYZ12, TW11, ABC09], considers computation of aggregates over the union of multiple distributed streams that are observed by different processors. A significant difference between distributed stream processing and parallel stream processing is that in the distributed case, there are physically different input streams that are observed and processed by geographically different processors. But in the parallel case, the stream is processed by multiple processors only to improve the throughput. In the distributed streams model, the focus is on minimizing the communication between processors, while in the shared-memory parallel case, the focus is more on the processing efficiency.

Das et al. [DAAE09] consider tracking frequent elements in a stream using a shared memory multicore machine. Their work uses shared data structures among multiple threads, and supports our approach of using shared data structures as opposed to independent per-processor data structures. However, unlike our work, they do not provide theoretical guarantees about the parallel performance of their algorithms. In particular, they do not have an analysis of the cost of their parallel algorithm. Cafaro and Tempesta [CT11] present a parallel algorithm for maintaining frequent elements in a stream; this algorithm uses the independent data structure approach, and employs a sequential merge step, so the depth of the algorithm is at least $\Omega(\frac{1}{\varepsilon^2})$, while our algorithm for infinite window has a depth that is polylogarithmic in $\frac{1}{\varepsilon}$. Other works on parallel streaming algorithms for frequent items includes [ZSZ+13], and our work differs in providing provable guarantees on the cost.

---

[1] The exception is that our algorithm for the Sum is a factor of $\log R$ worse in work and memory than the best sequential algorithm.

Sequential streaming algorithms for basic counting on a sliding window were first studied by [DGIM02], and there has been much follow up work since then, including [GT04, LT06a, XTB08, BO10]. We do not attempt a detailed survey of the prior sequential algorithms in this area, but to our knowledge, there has been no work on parallel algorithms with a provable guarantee on both performance and accuracy. There are many sequential streaming algorithms for finding frequent elements, including counter-based algorithms such as the Misra-Gries algorithm [MG82], Lossy Counting [MM02], and Space-Saving [MAE06], and sketch-based algorithms, such as Count-Sketch [CCFC02] and Count-Min sketch [CM05]. Frequent elements over sliding windows has been considered in [LT06b, HLT10].

2. PRELIMINARIES AND NOTATION

Throughout the paper, let $[n]$ denote the set $\{1, \ldots, n\}$ and denote by $[\alpha, \beta]$ the interval $\{x \in \mathbb{R} \mid \alpha \leq x \leq \beta\}$. A sequence is written as $\langle x_1, x_2, \ldots, x_{|X|} \rangle$, and for a sequence X, the i-th element is denoted by X_i or $X[i]$. We say that an event happens with high probability (**whp**) if it happens with probability at least $1 - n^{-\Omega(1)}$.

A *stream* S is an infinite sequence of elements $e_1 e_2 e_3 \ldots$, where e_i belongs to a universe $\mathcal{U}$. When we want to emphasize the universe, we say that S is a $\mathcal{U}$-stream. A *stream segment* is a finite sequence of consecutive elements of a stream. For example, a minibatch is a stream segment. In many cases, we are only interested in prefixes of the infinite stream. Define $S_t = e_1 e_2 \ldots e_t$. On this stream, a *window* of size n, denoted by $\mathcal{W}_n(S_t)$, is the segment of S_t consisting of the latest n entries, i.e., $e_{t-n+1}, \ldots, e_t$.

Often in this paper, we deal with $\{0, 1\}$-streams, which we also refer to as *binary streams*. A *compacted stream segment* (CSS) is an encoding of a segment of a binary stream where only the positions of the 1 bits and the length of the segment itself are recorded. In particular, for a binary stream segment T, the CSS of T, denoted by $\text{CSS}(T)$ is an ordered pair (ℓ, s), where ℓ is the length of the segment, and s is a sequence of length $\|T\|_0$, where s_i stores the position of the i-th 1 in the segment T. Here, the 0-th norm $\|\cdot\|_0$ denotes the number of non-zero entries in a stream segment. Given a binary stream, it is easy to construct its CSS using standard techniques [JáJ92]:

Lemma 2.1 *The CSS of a binary stream segment T can be computed in $O(n)$ work and $O(\log n)$ depth, where n is the length of the segment T.*

We will also rely on the following result:

Theorem 2.2 (Parallel Integer Sort [RR89]) *There is an algorithm* intSort *that takes a sequence of integer keys $a_1, a_2, \ldots, a_n$, each a number between 0 and $c \cdot n$, where $c = O(1)$, and produces a sorted sequence in $O(n)$ work and* polylog(n) *depth.*

Linear-Work Histogram: Common to many of our algorithms is a routine for determining the frequencies of the elements in a stream segment, a problem which we call histogram construction. The following theorem shows how to do this for a stream segment of length μ in $O(\mu)$ work and $O(\text{polylog}(\mu))$ depth.

Theorem 2.3 *There is an algorithm* buildHist *that takes a sequence $a_1 a_2 \ldots a_\mu$, $a_i \in \mathcal{U}$ and produces a sequence $\langle (\text{elt} = \cdot, \text{freq} = \cdot) \rangle$ of distinct elements and their frequencies, reported in any order. Further, the algorithm takes $O(\mu)$ work and $O(\text{polylog}(\mu))$ depth.*

PROOF. Let $h : \mathcal{U} \to \{1, \ldots, R\}$, where $R = O(\mu)$, be a hash function. It suffices to use, for example, a $O(\log \mu)$-wise independent family. The algorithm proceeds as follows: First, it hashes each

a_i using the hash function $h(\cdot)$ and buckets elements with the same hash values together. This can be accomplished using intSort in $O(\mu)$ work and depth as the range of the hash function is $R = O(n)$.

Suppose the nonempty buckets are $B_1, \ldots, B_t$, where B_i contains the elements which hash to value i. We know that all elements of the same key are in the same bucket and we will process each of these buckets in parallel. That is, we call collectBin(B_i) for each i, in parallel, and concatenate their results together.

def collectBin(B):
(1) If B is empty, return an empty sequence.
(2) Pick an arbitrary element $e \in B$.
(3) Let n_e be the number of times e occurs in B.
(4) Let B' be B without any occurrences of e
(5) **return** collectBin(B') ++ $\langle \text{elt} = e, \text{freq} = n_e \rangle$.

Correctness of this algorithm is straightforward and its performance depends essentially on how many distinct elements fall into the same bucket. More specifically, each pass through Steps 2–4 requires at most $O(|B_i|)$ work and $O(\log |B_i|) \leq O(\log \mu)$ depth. Hence, in terms of work, the total cost across all buckets is at most

$$ W \leq \sum_{e:\text{ unique elts}} r_e n_e, $$

where n_e is the number of occurrences of item e and r_e is the number of unique elements in the bucket that e hashes to. We conclude that $\mathbf{E}[W]$ is $O(\mu)$ because $\mathbf{E}[r_e] \leq \mu/R = O(1)$ and $\sum_e n_e = \mu$. As for depth, the overall depth is $D \leq \max_i \{r_i \log \mu\}$, where r_i is the number of unique elements in B_i. Since $r_i \leq O(\log \mu)$ **whp**, by balls-and-bins analysis, we have $D \leq O(\log^2 \mu)$ **whp**. This concludes the proof. $\square$

3. SPACE-BOUNDED BLOCK COUNTER

In this section, we describe a data structure for maintaining an approximate count of the number of 1s (i.e., 1-bits) in a sliding window. This data structure is an important building block of the algorithms presented later in this paper.

In a nutshell, for a parameter λ that controls the accuracy-vs.-space tradeoff, the data structure consumes roughly m/λ space and gives an additive-error guarantee of λ, where m is the number of 1s in the sliding window. We achieve this tradeoff by devising a parallel variant of the deterministic sampling scheme of Lee and Ting [LT06b, LT06a]. In addition, this data structure has a means to limit the total space consumption to a preset limit σ.

3.1 γ-Snapshots

We begin by reviewing an elegant deterministic-sampling synopsis due to Lee and Ting [LT06b, LT06a] that forms the basis of our parallel counter data structure. Let $S_t = \langle b_1, b_2, \ldots, b_t \rangle$ be a stream and let ω_i be the position of the i-th 1 in the stream. In γ-snapshots, the stream is subdivided into equal-sized blocks with γ elements each. That is, $b_1, \ldots, b_\gamma$ is block $\mathbf{B}_1$. Then, $b_{\gamma+1}, \ldots, b_{2\gamma}$ is block $\mathbf{B}_2$. In general, the range $b_{(k-1)\gamma-1}, \ldots, b_{k\gamma}$ is block $\mathbf{B}_k$. We write $\beta(i)$ for the block number which b_i belongs to.

To build a snapshot, the scheme specifies deterministically which of these blocks are sampled We provide a slightly different view from [LT06b] although it is equivalent to the original definition:

Definition 3.1 (γ-Snapshot) *Let n be the sliding-window size. A γ-snapshot for the stream $S_t = \langle b_1, b_2, \ldots, b_t \rangle$, denoted by $\text{SS}_{\gamma,n}(S_t)$, is an ordered pair (Q, ℓ) where*
(1) $Q = \{\beta(\omega_{\gamma i}) : \text{block } \mathbf{B}_{\beta(\omega_{\gamma i})} \text{ overlaps with or falls in the window } b_{t-n+1}, \ldots, b_t\}$; and

sequence id: 1 2 3 | 4 5 6 | 7 8 9 | ¹0 1 2 | 3 4 5 | 6 7 8 | 9 ²0 1 | 2 3

in window

bit stream: 0 1 1 [1] 1 1 [1] 1 1 0 [1] 0 0 0 0 0 1 1 1 1 [1] 1 0

block id: ① ② ③ ④ ⑤ ⑥ ⑦

☐ = locations of 1s that are multiple of γ

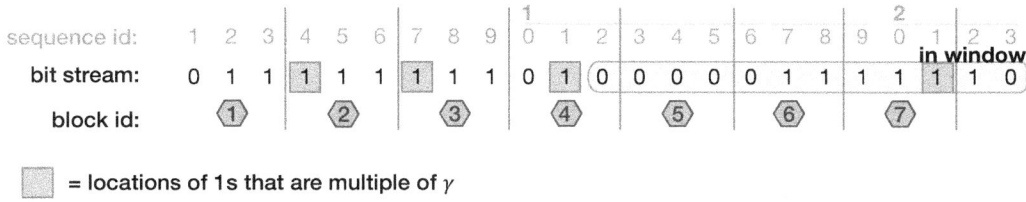

Figure 2: An illustration of γ-snapshot for a window of size 12 and $\gamma = 3$, showing the 1 bits located at multiple of $\gamma = 3$ indices. This results in $(Q = \{4, 7\}, \ell = 1)$.

(2) if $p^* = \max\{\omega_{\gamma i} : \omega_{\gamma i} \leqslant t\}$, then ℓ is the number of 1s in the window after p^* (i.e., how many 1s in $b_{\max(p^*+1, t-n+1)}, \ldots, b_t$).

Figure 2 shows γ-snapshot in action, showing the 1 bits located at multiple of $\gamma = 3$ indices, the block ids, and the resulting snapshot.

As Lee and Ting [LT06b] show, a γ-snapshot has the following guarantees:

Lemma 3.2 ([LT06b]) Let $SS_{\gamma,n}(S_t) = (Q, \ell)$. Then,

$$\mathrm{val}(SS_{\gamma,n}(S_t)) \overset{\mathrm{def}}{=} \gamma |Q| + \ell$$

satisfies

$$m \leqslant \mathrm{val}(SS_{\gamma,n}(S_t)) \leqslant m + 2\gamma,$$

where m the true number of 1s in the window $\mathcal{W}_n(S_t) = b_{t-n+1}, \ldots, b_t$. Furthermore, $\ell < \gamma$ and $|Q| \leqslant O(m/\gamma)$.

We represent a snapshot $SS_{\gamma,n}(S_t) = (Q, \ell)$ as a sequence listing the elements of Q and the number ℓ. In this representation, $\mathrm{val}(SS_{\gamma,n}(S_t))$ takes $O(1)$ work to evaluate because val only needs to know the size of Q and the value of ℓ. Furthermore, shrinking the window is easy in this representation: given a snapshot for a size-n window, we can easily construct a snapshot for a smaller-sized window n', simply by filtering out samples that are "too old" for n'. We have the following:

Lemma 3.3 There is an algorithm $\mathtt{shrink}(r)$ that takes as input a γ-snapshot $SS_{\gamma,n}(S_t) = (Q, \ell)$ and produces a γ-snapshot $SS_{\gamma,n-r}(S_t)$ in $O(|Q|)$ work and $O(\log |Q|)$ depth.

3.2 Maintaining Space-Bounded Counter

We present the design and analysis of a parallel space-bounded block counter, a data structure that maintains internally a γ-snapshot while taking advantage of parallelism to support its operations. We describe an interface and the corresponding guarantees in the following theorem:

Theorem 3.4 Let $\sigma, \lambda > 0$ be parameters and n be the window size. There is a data structure (σ, λ)-space bounded block counter, or a (σ, λ)-SBBC(n), supporting operations

- $\mathtt{new}()$ – create a new instance
- $\mathtt{advance}(T)$ – incorporate a minibatch encoded as a CSS into the data structure
- $\mathtt{query}()$ – retrieve a γ-snapshot for the window. Specifically, the return value of $\mathtt{query}$ satisfies
  - If it returns OVERFLOWED, then $m \geqslant \sigma \cdot \lambda$;
  - Otherwise, it returns $SS_{\lambda/2,n}(S_t)$.
- $\mathtt{decrement}(r)$ – changes the latest r 1s to 0, effectively decrementing the counter by r (valid when the counter is not "overflowed" and the counter value is positive)

where m is the actual number of 1s in the window. Furthermore, the space consumption is at most $O(\min\{\sigma, m/\lambda\})$. The operation

$\mathtt{advance}$ takes $O(\min\{\sigma, m/\lambda\} + |T|/\lambda)$ work; and $\mathtt{decrement}$ takes $O(m/\lambda)$ work. The other operations take constant work. Every operation has at most polylog depth (polylog in the size of the data structure and the input).

For a SBBC Γ, let the value of Γ be defined as $\mathrm{val}(\Gamma.\mathtt{query}())$ or undefined when the counter "overflows." Then, as a direct consequence of Theorem 3.4, we have the following corollary:

Corollary 3.5 If $\hat{m}$ is the value of a counter, then $m \leqslant \hat{m} \leqslant m + \lambda$, where m is the actual number of 1s in $\mathcal{W}_n(S_t)$.

We prove this theorem by providing an implementation. An instance of (σ, λ)-SBBC(n) maintains a $\frac{\lambda}{2}$-snapshot and certain demarcation information. It is kept as a tuple $(t, r, SS = SS_{\lambda/2,r}(S_t))$. The main component of this tuple is the $\frac{\lambda}{2}$-snapshot SS. But we need the other two components track the coverage of the snapshot. Specifically, the numbers t and r indicate that the snapshot SS is $SS_{\lambda/2,r}(S_t)$—i.e., representing the window $\mathcal{W}_r(S_t) = \{b_{t-r+1}, \ldots, b_t\}$.

Importantly, even though we instruct the data structure to track a window of size n, it is possible that due to the capacity limit σ, the snapshot cannot cover the whole size-n window; it has been truncated to a smaller window size, indicated by r.

As such, the operation $\mathtt{new}$ is straightforward. The operation $\mathtt{query}$ returns OVERFLOWED if $r < n$ or otherwise, returns SS. The operation $\mathtt{decrement}(r)$ updates the snapshot SS as follows: Suppose the snapshot is (Q, ℓ). If $r < \ell$, update SS to $(Q, \ell - r)$. Otherwise, update SS to (Q', ℓ'), where Q' drops the latest (i.e., the largest) $\lceil \frac{r-\ell}{\lambda} \rceil$ elements from Q and $\ell' = \lambda \cdot \lceil \frac{r-\ell}{\lambda} \rceil - r$.

We devote the rest of this section to $\mathtt{advance}$ and analyzing the data structure's properties. Before we describe an implementation of $\mathtt{advance}$, notice that in the definition of γ-snapshot, we are only interested in the positions of every γ-th one (i.e., $\omega_1, \omega_\gamma, \omega_{2\gamma}, \ldots$). Therefore, if the snapshot maintained is (Q, ℓ), then the next 1 that would be of interest (be a multiple of γ) is the $(\frac{\lambda}{2} - \ell)$-th 1 in the stream segment being added. We implement $\mathtt{advance}(T)$, where $T = (T_\ell, T_s)$ is the new stream segment encoded as CSS, by first extending (Q, ℓ) to a snapshot for a window of size $r + T_\ell$ then shrinking it back to a window of size n or smaller (depending on the size limit σ).

Hence, to implement $\mathtt{advance}(T)$, we will look at $T_s[\frac{i \cdot \lambda}{2} - \ell]$ for $i = 1, 2, \ldots$. Then, We use $\beta(\cdot)$ to compute the block id's and append these to Q, adjusting ℓ accordingly. Subsequently, we use $\mathtt{shrink}$ to make the window size n or some smaller r if the number of entries still is at least $2\sigma + 1$.

Work and Depth Analysis: Clearly, both $\mathtt{new}$ and $\mathtt{query}$ take constant work and depth. The operation $\mathtt{decrement}$ can be implemented by going over the sequence Q of length at most $O(m/\lambda)$, so the work is $O(m/\lambda)$ and the depth is $\log(m/\lambda)$. Moreover, the operation $\mathtt{advance}$ looks at every $\lambda/2$-th element of T to determine the block id's to append to Q, taking $O(T_\ell/\lambda)$ work. Note that the sequence Q before shrinking has length at most $\Lambda = \min\{\sigma, m/\lambda\} + T_\ell/\lambda$, so shrinking takes at most $O(\Lambda)$ work. All these operations require at most $O(\log(T_\ell + \min\{\sigma, m/\lambda\}))$ depth.

Finally, we show that if query returns OVERFLOWED, the actual number of 1s in the window $\mathcal{W}_n(\mathcal{S}_t)$ is at least $\sigma \cdot \lambda$. In the advance operation, the snapshot is trimmed to a window size smaller than n if the sequence Q for the window of size n has at least $2\sigma + 1$ elements. By Lemma 3.2, we know that $m \geqslant \gamma(2\sigma + 1) - 2\gamma = \lambda \cdot \sigma$.

4. BASIC COUNTING AND SUM

As the first application of SBBC, we consider basic counting, which asks for a space-efficient data structure to estimate, at any moment, the number of 1s in either a sliding window of interest, or the stream observed thus far. While trivial in the case of infinite window, the problem is more involved in the case of sliding windows, and has been extensively studied with many applications. We present a parallel streaming algorithm for basic counting on a sliding window. For a sliding window of size n, this problem seeks an approximation with relative error at most ε to the number of 1s in the sliding window $\mathcal{W}_n(\mathcal{S}_t)$. More specifically, we prove the following theorem:

Theorem 4.1 *Let $\varepsilon > 0$ and n be a fixed window-size. There is a parallel data structure for basic counting on a sliding window with a relative error at most ε requiring $S = O(\varepsilon^{-1} \log n)$ space such that incorporating a minibatch of length μ takes $O(S + \mu)$ work and $O(\mathrm{polylog}(S, \mu))$ depth.*

This means that if the minibatch is at least $\Omega(S)$ long, which is likely, the average per-element update cost is $O(1)$.

To prove this theorem, we will rely on the space-bounded block counters from Section 3; however, such a counter provides an additive guarantee whereas the basic counting problem seeks a relative guarantee. We need a bit more work because these types of guarantees behave differently for different ranges of values: an SBBC precise enough to ε-estimate a small count of 1s would consume too much space than we can afford, and a small-footprint SBBC sufficient to ε-estimate a large count of 1s would be too coarse for tracking a small count of 1s.

For this, we keep $O(\log n)$ different counters to cover the whole range of possible values (an integer between 0 and n) using a geometric scale, an idea also used in prior algorithms. Further, we set an upper bound on how much space each counter can consume. This not only controls the total space consumption but also serves to provide a coarse lower bound on the number of 1s in the window (by determining which counters have exceeded the space quota). Then, to incorporate a minibatch, we advance all the SBCCs simultaneously. To answer a query for the count, we simply look for the most precise SBBC that has not overflowed and return its estimate. We formalize this idea as follows:

PROOF OF THEOREM 4.1. Fix $\varepsilon > 0$ and $n > 0$. Further, let $k = \min\{i \mid \varepsilon n/2^i < 1\}$. Following Lee and Ting [LT06a], we maintain $k + 1$ SBBCs $\Gamma_0, \Gamma_1, \ldots, \Gamma_k$ such that Γ_i is a (σ_i, λ_i)-SBBC(n), where $\sigma_i = 2/\varepsilon$ and $\lambda_i = \varepsilon n/2^i$. Hence, it follows directly from Theorem 3.4 that the total space requirement is $k \cdot \frac{2}{\varepsilon} = O(\varepsilon^{-1} \log n)$. Next, we consider the cost of handling a minibatch and the accuracy of our estimate.

When a minibatch T, $|T| = \mu$, arrives, we incorporate it by calling advance(T) on all k SBBCs in parallel. Because by Theorem 3.4, the depth of advance is polylogarithmic, the depth of incorporating a minibatch remains polylogarithmic. Furthermore, since the work

of advance on Γ_i is $O(\sigma_i + \mu/\lambda_i)$, the total work across k SBCCs is

$$\sum_{i=0}^{k} \left(\frac{2}{\varepsilon} + \frac{\mu}{(n/2^i) \cdot \varepsilon} \right) \leqslant O(\varepsilon^{-1} \log n + \mu) = O(S + \mu),$$

where we note that $\sum_{i=0}^{k} \frac{1}{(n/2^i) \cdot \varepsilon} \leqslant \sum_{j \geqslant 0} 1/2^j \leqslant 2$.

To analyze the accuracy of the estimate, we first derive a lower bound on the number of 1s in the sliding window. Let i^* be the largest (i.e., the finest) index i where Γ_i does not return OVERFLOWED. We note that this i^* exists because the number of 1s in the window is at most n which never "overflows" Γ_0 as $\sigma_0 \lambda_0 = 2n > n$. Then, Γ_{i^*+1} returns OVERFLOWED and by the property of query (Theorem 3.4), the number of 1s in the window m satisfies $m \geqslant \sigma_{i^*+1} \lambda_{i^*+1} = \frac{2}{\varepsilon} \cdot \frac{\varepsilon n}{2^{i^*+1}} = n/2^{i^*}$.

In addition, querying Γ_{i^*} returns a snapshot SS where

$$m \leqslant \mathrm{val}(\mathrm{SS}) \leqslant m + \lambda_{i^*} \leqslant m + \frac{\varepsilon n}{2^{i^*}}$$

by Corollary 3.5. But $m \geqslant n/2^{i^*}$, so $m \leqslant \mathrm{val}(\mathrm{SS}) \leqslant m + \varepsilon m = (1 + \varepsilon)m$, which concludes the proof. $\square$

4.1 Sum

We discuss a direct application of the basic counting data structure. Given a stream S of non-negative integers (i.e., $b_i \in \{0, 1, \ldots R\}$), the *sum problem* is to maintain the sum of the most recent n items in the stream. This problem has been considered in the past [DGIM02, GT04], for which an algorithm for the single stream case is known: Gibbons and Tirthapura [GT04] present an ε-approximation to the sum using space $O(\varepsilon^{-1} \log n)$ words and constant processing time per item [2].

For incoming value $x, 0 \leqslant x \leqslant R$, let x^i denote the i-th least significant bit in the binary representation of x, i.e. x^0 is the least significant bit, x^1 is the bit to the left of x^0, and so on. We maintain multiple basic counting data structures (Theorem 4.1), D^i for $i = 0, \ldots, \log R$, where D^i counts the number of 1s among the x^is for all x within the sliding window. A minibatch $B = s_1, s_2, \ldots, s_\mu$ of length μ is processed as follows. In parallel, we compute the binary sequences $B^1, B^2, \ldots, B^{\log R}$, where $B^i = \langle s_1^i, s_2^i, \ldots, s_\mu^i \rangle$. For $i = 1, \ldots, \log R$, in parallel, sequence B^i is inserted into basic counter D^i. Since we are able to estimate the total number of 1-bits in each bit position i to an ε-relative error using counter D^i, we are able to estimate the sum also to within an ε-relative error, by computing the weighted sum of the basic counts of the different data structures, where the count from D_i is assigned a weight of 2^i.

The total depth of this algorithm is of the same order as the depth of the basic counter, since the only additional operations are to extract the bit s_j^i from element s_j, which can be done in $O(1)$ time, and to finally add the results of all data structures D^is, which can be done in parallel in $O(\log \log R)$ depth. The total work of the above algorithm is $O(\log R)$ times the work of the basic counter, and the total workspace used is also $O(\log R)$ times the workspace of the parallel basic counter.

Theorem 4.2 *Let $\varepsilon > 0$ be given and n be a fixed window-size. There is a parallel data structure for continuously maintaining the sum of non-negative integers chosen from $\{0, \ldots, R\}$ on a sliding window with relative error at most ε requiring $S = O(\varepsilon^{-1} \log n \log R)$ space such that incorporating a minibatch of length μ takes $O((S + \mu) \log R)$ work and $O(\mathrm{polylog}(S, \mu))$ depth.*

---

[2] The space bound assumes that $\log n = \Theta(\log R)$

5. FREQUENCY ESTIMATION AND HEAVY HITTERS

We now consider two related problems, *frequency estimation*, and *heavy hitters*. Suppose the input is a stream of elements, where each element is an item identifier. Let N denote the number of elements, and f_e the number of occurrences of item e in the stream so far. Given a parameter $\varepsilon, 0 < \varepsilon < 1$, the frequency estimation task is to maintain for every item e, an estimate $\hat{f}_e$ such that $f_e - \varepsilon N \leqslant \hat{f}_e \leqslant f_e$.

In the related problem of identifying heavy hitters from a stream, there are two parameters $\phi, 0 < \phi < 1$, a threshold for frequency, and $\varepsilon, 0 < \varepsilon < \phi$, a threshold for error, and the task is to output all elements e such that $f_e \geqslant \phi N$, and output no element e such that $f_e \leqslant (\phi - \varepsilon)N$. If a streaming algorithm can solve frequency estimation, then it can solve heavy hitter identification—the algorithm can simply output every element e such that $\hat{f}_e \geqslant (\phi - \varepsilon)N$, and it will satisfy the conditions required for heavy hitter identification. In the remainder of this section, we focus on frequency estimation; all our results are applicable to heavy hitter identification.

5.1 Misra-Gries Summary

We begin by reviewing an algorithm for frequency estimation commonly known as the Misra-Gries (MG) algorithm [MG82], though it has been rediscovered at least twice [DLOM02, KSP03] since Misra and Gries proposed it in 1982. For a parameter $\varepsilon > 0$ that controls the space consumption and accuracy, the MG algorithm maintains a summary, which we will refer to as a MG summary, where up to $S = \lceil 1/\varepsilon \rceil$ items along with their counters are maintained. When a stream element e arrives, MG performs the steps in Algorithm 1 to update the summary.

Algorithm 1: Sequential Misra-Gries
---
def update(e):
if e is an item in the summary **then**
    ⌊ Increment the counter for e
else
    if the summary contains less than S items **then**
        ⌊ Add e to the summary with a count of 1
    else
        ⌊ Decrement all counters maintained by 1 and remove all counters that reach 0.

From this description, the space requirement of a MG summary is $O(1/\varepsilon)$ because it never keeps more than S items and counters. Let C_e be the value of the counter for item e (it is 0 if item e is not maintained in the summary). Further, let f_e be the true frequency of item e in the stream. It was shown that C_e is a good estimate for f_e; we reproduce a proof of this lemma as the reasoning here will form the basis for the analysis of our parallel algorithms.

Lemma 5.1 ([MG82, DLOM02, KSP03]) *For any item $e \in \mathcal{U}$, the estimate satisfies $f_e - \varepsilon m \leqslant C_e \leqslant f_e$, where m is the length of the stream observed so far.*

PROOF. Recall that we set $S = \lceil 1/\varepsilon \rceil$. We will focus on showing that $f_e - m/S \leqslant C_e$ as the relation $C_e \leqslant f_e$ follows directly from the description.

To prove this, we establish a bound on the number of times the counter for an element e can possibly be decremented. If this number is τ, we have that $C_e \geqslant f_e - \tau$. We give a bound on τ by considering that every time a counter is decremented, a total of at least S counters, corresponding to unique items, are decremented. Viewed differently, when update(e) decrements counters, it (virtually) deletes S unique items from the stream: e itself and each of

the S items maintained in the summary. Because there have been m items in the stream so far, we know that $S\tau \leqslant m$. Hence, we have $\tau \leqslant m/S$, proving that $C_e \geqslant f_e - m/S \geqslant f_e - \varepsilon m$. □

5.2 Parallel Infinite Window

We describe a parallel streaming algorithm for frequency estimation based on the Misra-Gries algorithm. We prove the following theorem:

Theorem 5.2 *Let $\varepsilon > 0$. There is a parallel algorithm for frequency estimation requiring $O(\varepsilon^{-1})$ space such that incorporating any minibatch of size μ takes $O(\varepsilon^{-1} + \mu)$ work and $O(\mathrm{polylog}(\varepsilon^{-1}, \mu))$ depth and for any item e, it can provide an estimate $\hat{f}_e \in [f_e - \varepsilon m, f_e]$, where f_e is the true frequency of e in the stream and $m = \sum_e f_e$ is the length of the stream thus far.*

Set $S = \lceil 1/\varepsilon \rceil$. Like in the sequential setting, our parallel algorithm keeps a selected set of S elements and their corresponding frequency estimates. This is kept as a sequence $\langle (e_i, \hat{f}_i) \rangle_{i=1}^{S}$, where $\hat{f}_i$ is the frequency estimate of the element e_i. To process a minibatch, we show how to augment a MG summary with the minibatch in a way that results in a new MG summary. At the heart of our algorithm is a parallel routine MGaugment that takes as input a MG summary and a histogram of frequencies in the minibatch, and outputs a MG summary of the combined data.

Conceptually, MGaugment combines together the corresponding counters from input MG summary and the histogram. This, however, can lead to more than S counters in the result. The algorithm then systematically decrements certain counters so that at most S of them remain. To meet the accuracy guarantees, we make sure that each time a counter is decremented, at least S unique counters are decremented together, though this has to be performed implicitly to achieve the parallelism we intended for. We formalize this idea as follows:

Lemma 5.3 *Let $F = \langle (e_i, \hat{f}_i) \rangle_{i=1}^{S}$ be a MG summary and $H = \langle (e_i', f_i') \rangle_{i=1}^{p}$ be a histogram. There is an algorithm MGaugment that takes F and H, and produces a MG summary of size S combining together F and H in $O(S + p)$ work and $O(\log(S + p))$ depth. Moreover, the resulting summary still satisfies $C_e \in [f_e - \varepsilon m, f_e]$.*

PROOF. We first form a sequence $H' = \langle \mathtt{elt} = \cdot, \mathtt{freq} = \cdot \rangle$, adding up the corresponding frequencies–i.e., f_i from F and f_i' from H. This step can be accomplished in $O(S + p)$ work and $O(\log^2(S + p))$ depth using, for example, a hash table of size $O(S + p)$.

Then, we find an integer φ such that *at most* S items in H' have $\mathtt{freq} \geqslant \varphi$. Although H' is arbitrarily ordered, computing φ can be done in $O(|H'|)$ work and $O(\log^2 |H'|)$ depth using a variant of quick select, which can find any element of a given rank. Following that, the algorithm subtracts φ from all the frequencies in H' and returns as its output the frequencies that remain positive.

By definition of φ, it is easy to see that the output is a summary with at most S items. We will now show that it has the promised accuracy guarantees. To do this, we start by observing that our process—subtracting φ from all frequencies and retaining only the positive ones—has the same net effect as performing φ batches ($i = 1, \ldots, \varphi$) of decrementing where the i-th batch decrements precisely the counters for all items whose $\mathtt{freq} \geqslant i$.

Now since $i \leqslant \varphi$, we know that each batch decrements at least S unique counters. Therefore, using the reasoning in Lemma 5.1, we know that the frequency in the output summary is at most m/S smaller than the true frequency. Since C_e is clearly at most f_e, we conclude that $f_e \geqslant C_e \geqslant f_e - m/S \geqslant f_e - \varepsilon m$, completing the proof. □

Using this lemma, we can derive an algorithm for Theorem 5.2 by first running `buildHist` (Theorem 2.3) on the minibatch and feeding the result to `MGaugment`. For a minibatch of length μ, `buildHist` takes $O(\mu)$ work and polylog depth, so the total depth remains polylog and the total work to process this minibatch is $O(\mu + S + p) \leq O(\mu + S)$ because the number of distinct elements in a minibatch is at most the size of the minibatch—i.e., $p \leq \mu$. This proves Theorem 5.2.

5.3 Parallel Sliding Window

We now turn to the sliding window case, beginning with a basic parallel algorithm that meets neither the space nor work bound. Following that, we improve upon the basic algorithm to achieve the promised bounds. The main result for the sliding window case is as follows:

Theorem 5.4 *Let $\varepsilon > 0$. Let $n \geq 1$ be the sliding-window size. There is a parallel algorithm for sliding-window frequency estimation requiring $O(\varepsilon^{-1})$ space such that incorporating any minibatch of size μ takes $O(\varepsilon^{-1} + \mu)$ work and $O(\varepsilon^{-1} + \text{polylog}(\mu))$ depth and for any item e, it can provide an estimate $\hat{f}_e \in [f_e - \varepsilon n, f_e]$, where f_e is the true frequency of e in the sliding window.*

5.3.1 The Basic Parallel Algorithm

We present a basic algorithm for the sliding-window case, which is a direct application of SBBC. Let $\varepsilon > 0$ be given. We set $S = \lceil 1/\varepsilon \rceil$. The algorithm is very simple: it keeps an SBBC for every item. Let Γ_e be the $(\infty, n/S)$-SBBC(n) for item e. Let $\mathcal{B}$ be a collection of SBBCs that the algorithm maintains. Then, we can support operations for incorporating a minibatch and querying for a frequency estimate as follows.

To query for item e's frequency, we return the estimate from Γ_e if $\Gamma_e \in \mathcal{B}$; otherwise, we return 0. To process a minibatch T, $\mu = |T|$, we perform the following steps:

(1) For each item e present in T or $\mathcal{B}$, create a CSS $\chi^{(e)}$ for the binary sequence $\langle \mathbf{1}_{\{T_j = e\}} : j = 1, \ldots, |T| \rangle$.

(2) For each item e present in T or $\mathcal{B}$, create Γ_e if it does not already exist in $\mathcal{B}$ and then call `advance` with $\chi^{(e)}$.

Step 1 can be implemented in $O(\mu \log \mu)$ work and $O(\log \mu)$ depth by first marking each element of T with its position and then using a parallel sort routine to gather identical items together. Then, Step 2 performs at most $O(\sum_e \lceil \frac{n_e}{n/S} + n'_e \rceil) = O(S + \mu) = O(\varepsilon^{-1} + \mu)$ work, where n_e is the true frequency of e in the sliding window before adding T and n'_e is the frequency of e in T. Hence, the cost of processing a minibatch T is $O(\varepsilon^{-1} + \mu \log \mu)$ work and $O(\text{polylog}(\varepsilon^{-1}, \mu))$ depth.

We provide an estimate for an item e by reporting

$$\hat{f}_e = \text{val}(\Gamma_e.\text{query}()) - n/S.$$

As a direct consequence of Theorem 3.4, we know that for any item e, our estimate $\hat{f}_e$ satisfies $f_e - n/S \leq \hat{f}_e \leq f_e$, where f_e is the true frequency in the window after adding T. This implies $f_e - \varepsilon n \leq \hat{f}_e \leq f_e$, as promised. Moreover, the SBBCs combined require $O(|\mathcal{B}|) + \sum_e O(\frac{f_e}{n/S}) = O(|\mathcal{B}| + \varepsilon^{-1})$ space, where we have used the fact that $\sum_e f_e = n$.

We summarize the guarantees of the basic algorithm in the following theorem:

Theorem 5.5 *Let $\varepsilon > 0$. Let $n \geq 1$ be the sliding-window size. There is a parallel algorithm for sliding-window frequency estimation such that incorporating any minibatch of size μ takes*

$O(\varepsilon^{-1} + \mu \log \mu)$ *work and* $O(\text{polylog}(\varepsilon^{-1}, \mu))$ *depth and for any item e, it can provide an estimate $\hat{f}_e \in [f_e - \varepsilon n, f_e]$, where f_e is the true frequency of e in the sliding window. Further, this algorithm requires $O(|\mathcal{B}| + \varepsilon^{-1})$ space, where $\mathcal{B}$ is the collection of SBBCs it keeps.*

We note that $\mathcal{B}$ may be as large as $\Omega(n)$, much larger than that of the best sequential algorithm for this problem, which uses only $O(\varepsilon^{-1})$ space.

5.3.2 First Improvement: Space

The basic parallel algorithm has two significant drawbacks: First, as already noted, it can consume more space than the best sequential algorithm, especially when there are many unique items. Second, it performs more work than the best sequential counterpart (not work efficient). In this section, we improve upon the space requirement and in the section that follows, we will improve on the work bound.

Like in the sequential case (e.g., [LT06b]), the basic idea is to track the frequencies of a selected few items approximately. To ensure that the estimate is accurate, we use the `decrement` operation of SBBCs to mimic the decrement actions in the Misra-Gries algorithm, where the counters whose count drops to zero are discarded. In essence, our algorithm is a parallelization of Lee and Ting's algorithm [LT06b].

We assume without loss of generality (WLOG) that *the minibatch is smaller than the window size n*. Otherwise, we could throw away the state and start over by looking at the most recent n items in the minibatch, resetting any error accumulated.

Let $\varepsilon > 0$. Fix $S = 8/\varepsilon$ and $\lambda = \varepsilon n/4$. Our updated algorithm keeps track of (∞, λ)-SBBC(n) counters, similar to the basic algorithm (but with less error), but we will make sure that the collection $\mathcal{B}$ never grows larger than S. We accomplish this by adding a pruning step after Step 2 of the basic algorithm. The new step decrements a number of counters so that at most S of them remain positive. We arrive at the algorithm presented in Algorithm 2.

Algorithm 2: A space-efficient algorithm for windowed frequency estimation.

---

1. For each item e present in T or $\mathcal{B}$, create a CSS $\chi^{(e)}$ for the binary sequence $\langle \mathbf{1}_{\{T_j = e\}} : j = 1, \ldots, |T| \rangle$.

2. For each item e present in T or $\mathcal{B}$, create Γ_e if it does not already exist in $\mathcal{B}$ and then call `advance` with $\chi^{(e)}$.

3. Prune $\mathcal{B}$ by

   (a) Compute a value φ such that *at most S* counters in $\mathcal{B}$ have values[3] at least φ.

   (b) For each $\Gamma_e \in \mathcal{B}$ whose value is at least φ, **in parallel**, call $\Gamma_e.\text{decrement}(\varphi)$, dropping a counter if its value goes to 0. All the other counters will just be deleted.

We analyze the updated algorithm:

Claim 5.6 *The space-efficient version requires $O(\varepsilon^{-1})$ space. Furthermore, processing a length-μ minibatch takes $O(\varepsilon^{-1} + \mu \log \mu)$ work and $O(\text{polylog}(\varepsilon^{-1}, \mu))$ depth.*

PROOF. After this pruning step, the size of $\mathcal{B}$ is clearly at most S, so the space consumption of the updated algorithm is $O(|\mathcal{B}|) + \sum_e O(\frac{f_e}{\lambda}) = O(\varepsilon^{-1})$ space, where, again, f_e is the frequency of e in the window after adding T and $\sum f_e = n$. Furthermore, let $\mathcal{B}'$ be

---

[3]Remember that the value of a counter Γ is $\text{val}(\Gamma.\text{query}())$.

the collection $\mathcal{B}$ before pruning, so the work in Step 3 is

$$|\mathcal{B}'| + \sum_{e:\Gamma_e \in \mathcal{B}} \frac{f_e}{\lambda} \leqslant |\mathcal{B}'| + O(\varepsilon^{-1}) = O(\mu + \varepsilon^{-1})$$

by Theorem 3.4; the depth is polylog in μ and ε^{-1}. The work and depth of Steps 1 and 2 are unchanged: $O(\varepsilon^{-1} + \mu \log \mu)$ work and $O(\text{polylog}(\varepsilon^{-1}, \mu))$ depth, concluding the proof. $\square$

It remains to show that the estimate is still accurate:

Claim 5.7 *The space-efficient version provides estimates such that for any item e, our estimate $\tilde{f}_e \in [f_e - \varepsilon n, f_e]$, where f_e is the true frequency of e in the window.*

PROOF. If we maintained all the counters (without decrementing or discarding), we would look up the counter Γ_e and returns an estimate $\hat{f}_e = \text{val}(\Gamma_e.\text{query}()) - \lambda$ satisfying $f_e - \lambda \leqslant \hat{f} \leqslant f_e$.

The space efficient algorithm, however, decremented and removed several counters. To analyze this portion of error, we follow the line of reasoning of Lemma 5.1. Note that our decrement process can be conceptually broken down into φ batches, where each batch decrements at least S counters by exactly 1 (cf. Lemma 5.3).

Suppose the last item in the minibatch is b_t. We consider the counters' states *right before* the minibatch containing item b_{t-n+1} arrived. Let Ψ_0 be the total number of 1's these counters maintained (i.e., Ψ_0 is the sum of all $\text{val}(\Gamma_e.\text{query}())$ at that point). Furthermore, let Ψ_1 be the number of 1's added to counters created or advanced after that point. We establish that $\Psi_0 \leqslant (\sum_e f_e') + S \cdot \lambda \leqslant 3n$ because there can be at most S counters (due to pruning). Also, we know that $\Psi_1 \leqslant 2n$ because there are n elements between b_{t-n+1} and b_t and the minibatch containing b_{t-n+1} itself has size at most n, as we had assumed WLOG. Hence, we can upper bound the error due to counter decrementing for any element e as $(\Psi_0 + \Psi_1)/S \leqslant 5n/S = \frac{5}{8}\varepsilon n < \frac{3}{4}\varepsilon n$. Hence, the total error is at most $\frac{3}{4}\varepsilon n + \lambda = \varepsilon n$. $\square$

Therefore, with the space improvement, we have:

Theorem 5.8 *Let $\varepsilon > 0$. Let $n \geqslant 1$ be the sliding-window size. There is a parallel algorithm for sliding-window frequency estimation such that incorporating any minibatch of size μ takes $O(\varepsilon^{-1} + \mu \log \mu)$ work and $O(\text{polylog}(\varepsilon^{-1}, \mu))$ depth and for any item e, it can provide an estimate $\hat{f}_e \in [f_e - \varepsilon n, f_e]$, where f_e is the true frequency of e in the sliding window. Further, this algorithm requires $O(\varepsilon^{-1})$ space.*

5.3.3 Second Improvement: Work

With the space improvement, the space bound now matches that of the best sequential algorithm. We now turn to the work aspect. The previous algorithm (Algorithm 2) would have been work efficient if we had been able to construct all CSSs $\chi^{(e)}$ in linear work in parallel. We, however, do not know how to accomplish that. Instead, we observe that if we can predict which counters will survive after the pruning step, we will not have to construct sequences for counters that will be thrown away in the end. Building on this idea, we devise an algorithm for determining which counters will be kept. Then, we give a linear-work parallel algorithm that constructs CSS $\chi^{(e)}$ for the items that will be kept, though this latter algorithm has depth $O(\varepsilon^{-1})$, which is linear in the number of counters to be kept.

Predicting Survivors: We describe predict, an algorithm for computing the set K of items that will be retained after the pruning step, as well as the pruning "cut off" φ. Before we give the description, keep in mind that we have assumed WLOG that each minibatch is smaller than the window size n. First, we construct a histogram H for the minibatch; this requires at most $O(n)$ work and polylog depth. Then, we read off the values of the existing SBBCs

after "shrinking" the window to evict elements too old for the new window (using val(shrink(Γ.query))). It is easy to see that adding the corresponding counts together gives us the counts if we were to perform Steps 1–2 in the previous algorithm.

With these counts calculated, we can easily compute the cutoff φ in Step (3a) of the previous algorithm (see Lemma 5.3 for an algorithm). Using φ, we know how much the surviving counters must be decremented by and which counters will be retained.

All these can be performed in $O(1/\varepsilon + \mu)$ work: buildHist takes linear work; the work performed by shrink across all counters is $\sum_{e:\Gamma_e \in \mathcal{B}} f_e/\lambda = O(1/\varepsilon)$; and computing φ takes at most $O(1/\varepsilon + \mu)$ work. Further, all these operations have polylog($\mu, 1/\varepsilon$) depth.

Constructing Selected Sequences: Given a set K of items that we will retain after processing the minibatch, we describe an algorithm to construct the CSS $\chi^{(e)}$ for all $e \in K$ simultaneously:

Lemma 5.9 *There is an algorithm $\text{sift}(T, K)$ that takes a stream segment $T = \langle a_1, a_2, \ldots, a_{|T|} \rangle$ and an index set K, and produces $|K|$ sequences $\{\chi^{(\kappa)}\}_{\kappa \in K}$ such that $\chi_i^{(\kappa)}$ is the CSS representing the binary sequence $\langle \mathbf{1}_{\{a_j = e\}} : j = 1, \ldots, |T| \rangle$. Moreover, sift runs in $O(|T| + |K|)$ work and $O(|K| + \log(|K| + |T|))$ depth.*

PROOF. We describe an algorithm consisting of two steps: First, it produces a subsequence s' of T containing only elements that are in K, where each element of s' is tagged with its original position in T. For $i = 1, \ldots, |s'|$, let p_i denote the position of the element s_i' in T. This can be accomplished in $O(|T|)$ work and $O(\log |T|)$ depth using standard techniques [JáJ92]. Then, we derive the sequences for CSS $\chi^{(\kappa)}$'s as follows.

Let us observe that given the sequences s' and p, we can easily derive the sequences $\{\chi^{(\kappa)}\}_{\kappa \in K}$ in $O(|s'|)$ work and $O(|s'|)$ depth using sequential radix sort, which is stable. To parallelize this process, we divide s' (and p) into $|s'|/|K|$ equal-sized pieces (each is $|K|$ long) and run the sequential algorithm on these pieces *in parallel*. Each of these pieces requires $O(|K|)$ work and $O(|K|)$ depth, resulting in $O(\frac{|s'|}{|K|} \cdot |K|) = O(|s'|)$ work and $O(|K|)$ depth for the all pieces combined. At this point, each piece has been converted into $|K|$ sequences, one for each $\kappa \in K$. To generate the final output, we concatenate sequences of the same κ together, preserving order. For each κ, while the depth is bounded by $O(\log |s'|)$, the work is $O(|s'|/|K| + \ell_\kappa)$, where ℓ_κ is the length of the final sequence $\chi^{(\kappa)}$. The $|s'|/|K|$ term is due to a prefix-sum operation to determine the position in the output, and the ℓ_κ reflects the cost to write a sequence of that length. Since there are $|K|$ values of κ, we have that the work for concatenation is $O(|K|\frac{|s'|}{|K|} + \sum_{\kappa \in K} \ell_\kappa) = O(|s'| + |K|) \leqslant O(|s| + |K|)$, which concludes the proof. $\square$

Using the output from the routine predict for predicting survivors (i.e., K and φ), we call $\text{sift}(T, K)$ to generate $\chi^{(e)}$ for all $e \in K$. Following that, we update the counters by calling advance with $\chi^{(e)}$ (we create it if it did not exist) and subsequently calling decrement with φ for all $e \in K$. Finally, we delete all existing counters that do not exist in K.

Because this algorithm simulates the effects of the previous algorithm, the space bound and accuracy guarantees follow from the previous analysis. It remains to analyze the work and depth of this algorithm. We have shown that predict takes $O(1/\varepsilon + \mu)$ work and polylog($1/\varepsilon, \mu$) depth. Also, the set K has size at most $O(1/\varepsilon)$. So then, $\text{sift}(T, K)$ takes $O(\mu + 1/\varepsilon)$ work and $O(1/\varepsilon + \log(\mu))$ depth. Finally, the combined work performed by advance and decrement is at most $O(1/\varepsilon)$, as analyzed before. This proves Theorem 5.4.

5.3.4 Lower Bound

We show a lower bound on the work required to identify all heavy hitters from a stream in the infinite window case, proving work optimality of our algorithm.

Lemma 5.10 *On a stream of total length N, any deterministic algorithm that outputs all items with frequency ϕN or greater, and no item with frequency less than $(\phi - \epsilon)N$ must have work $\Omega(N)$.*

PROOF. We argue that every deterministic algorithm that has the above property must examine $\Omega(N)$ elements of the stream. We prove this using contradiction; suppose there was a deterministic algorithm $\mathcal{A}$ with the above property that examined less than $(1 - \phi)N$ stream elements.

Consider an input I_1 where the algorithm output the set S_1. We construct another input I_2 as follows. Let y be an item that does not belong to S_1; such an element y must exist since the algorithm cannot output all elements as a part of S_1, and every element that is output must have a minimum frequency. I_2 is identical to I_1, except that in every position of I_1 that was not examined by $\mathcal{A}$, I_2 contains y. The frequency of y in I_2 is at least ϕn, and hence y must be output by $\mathcal{A}$ upon observing input I_2. However, the behavior of $\mathcal{A}$ on input I_2 must be identical to its behavior on input I_1, since every input element examined by $\mathcal{A}$ is identical in both cases. Hence, $\mathcal{A}$ will not output y on input I_2, which contradicts the assumption that $\mathcal{A}$ correctly outputs all items with a frequency ϕn or greater. Hence, the algorithm $\mathcal{A}$ must examine at least $(1 - \phi)N$ elements of the input, and this takes $\Omega(N)$ time. $\square$

Note that the above lower bound does not hold for randomized algorithms which allow a (small) probability of not satisfying the requirements of heavy hitter identification. Indeed, there are algorithms for identifying heavy hitters by examining only a random sample whose size is much smaller than the length of the stream [MM02, EV03].

We also note that the same argument in Lemma 5.10, of the algorithm needing to examine a majority of the input, also applies to frequency estimation; hence, the linear lower bound on work also applies to frequency estimation. The following corollary follows by observing that if $\mu = \Omega(1/\epsilon)$, then Theorem 5.2 gives a $O(\mu)$ work bound:

Corollary 5.11 *Our parallel algorithm for frequency estimation and heavy hitter identification for infinite window (Theorem 5.2) is work-optimal if the batch size μ is $\Omega(\frac{1}{\epsilon})$.*

5.4 Comparison with Independent Data Structure Approach

We compare our algorithm for frequency estimation and heavy hitters with a parallel algorithm based on the independent data structure approach. As described in [ACH⁺13], there is a mergeable data structure for approximate heavy hitter identification that takes space $O(1/\epsilon)$ per processor. Suppose there are p processors; the input stream $\mathcal{S}$ is partitioned into sub-streams $\mathcal{S}_1, \mathcal{S}_2, \ldots, \mathcal{S}_p$, one per processor. Processor i processes $\mathcal{S}_i$ and maintains a local data structure D_i. Since the D_is are mergeable, it is possible to construct the data structure D for $\mathcal{S}$ given only $D_1, D_2, \ldots, D_p$, without access to the individual streams $\mathcal{S}_1, \mathcal{S}_2, \ldots$. Hence, the algorithm can simply send all the D_is to a single processor who merges them to construct D, which can be used to answer queries about frequency estimation and heavy hitters on $\mathcal{S}$.

The total memory taken by the parallel algorithm across all processors is $O(p/\epsilon)$. Note that this is a factor of p worse than the sequential algorithm, as well as p times worse that our parallel algorithm.

Further, merging two data structures D_i and D_j from processors i and j is a sequential operation, and the time taken to merge all p summaries at query time can be $O(p/\epsilon)$, if done at a single processor. Even if merging is done by organizing the processors into a log p-deep hierarchy, the depth of this parallel algorithm is $\Omega(\epsilon^{-1} \log p)$. With the approach of independent data structures, it seems hard to overcome this bottleneck, and achieve work-optimality and depth that is polylog in ϵ^{-1}.

6. COUNT-MIN SKETCH

In this section, we describe another application of the techniques developed so far in this paper. We devise a parallel version of the Count-Min (CM) sketch [CM05]. In the sequential setting, CM sketch has proved to be a versatile summary for frequency-based properties of a stream that can be used for answering a variety of queries on the input stream, including point and range queries, quantiles, and heavy hitters, among others.

Unlike the other algorithms considered in this work, the CM sketch gives a notion of probabilistic guarantee, namely an (ϵ, δ)-approximation, where the quantity being reported has relatively error at most ϵ with probability at least $1 - \delta$.

For $\epsilon, \delta > 0$, the CM sketch algorithm maintains a 2-d array A with $d = \lceil \ln(1/\delta) \rceil$ rows and $w = \lceil e/\epsilon \rceil$ columns, together with d hash functions $h_1, h_2, \ldots, h_d$ chosen from a family of pair-wise independent hash functions. The array A is initially all 0. The sequential CM algorithm answers a query about an item e by reporting

$$a_e = \min \{A[i, h_i(e)] \mid i = 1, \ldots, d\}.$$

Moreover, when an element e shows up in the stream, it updates A by going through $i = 1, \ldots, d$, adding 1 to $A[i, h_i(e)]$. As Cormode and Muthukrishnan show, this gives the guarantee that with probability at least $1 - \delta$, $a_e \leqslant f_e + \epsilon m$, where f_e is the true frequency of item e and m is the length of the stream so far.

A Parallel Implementation: Instead of updating A each time a new stream element shows up, we observe that if the same item e shows up k times, they will all be hashed to the same locations and the count at that location will be incremented by k. Like before, we work in minibatches. When a minibatch T arrives, we use the `buildHist` algorithm to compute a histogram of frequencies $H = \langle (\text{elt} = \cdot, \text{freq} = \cdot) \rangle$. For each $(\text{elt}, \text{freq}) \in H$, we increment $A[i, h_e(\text{elt})]$ by `freq` for $i = 1, \ldots, d$ simultaneously in parallel.

Simultaneously incrementing these counters, however, requires some care since some of the locations may be shared by different items. To increment them in parallel, we gather for each row, the frequencies that hash to the same column. This can be done in $O(\mu + w)$ work and polylog(max $\{\mu, w\}$) depth using parallel integer sort [RR89], where we note that the hash values are $\{1, \ldots, w\}$. Hence, processing a minibatch of size μ takes $O(\mu + (\mu + w)d)$ work and $O(\text{polylog}(\mu, w))$ depth—or if we assume $\mu = \Omega(w)$, then we have $O(\log(1/\delta))$ work per item on average.

To answer a query about e, we report $a_e = \min\{A[i, h_i(e)] \mid i = 1, \ldots, d\}$ as before, but we compute min in parallel using a reduce operation (which for length-p data has $O(p)$ work and $O(\log p)$ depth in the length of the data. Hence, a query costs $O(d) = O(\ln(1/\delta))$ work and $O(\log \log(1/\delta))$ depth.

We summarize the results as follows:

Theorem 6.1 *There is a data structure for maintaining the count-min sketch in space $O(\epsilon^{-1} \log(1/\delta))$ such that incorporating a minibatch of size μ takes $O(\log(\frac{1}{\delta}) \max\{\mu, \frac{1}{\epsilon}\})$ work and $O(\text{polylog}(\mu, \frac{1}{\epsilon}))$ depth, and a query about any element takes $O(\log(1/\delta))$ work and $O(\log \log(1/\delta))$ depth.*

7. CONCLUSION

We have presented parallel algorithms for maintaining frequency-based aggregates on a high-velocity stream. The aggregates considered include heavy hitters, basic counting, frequency estimation, sum, and the count-min sketch. These algorithms perform linear-work (i.e., constant work per element on average) and have low depth. These are the first parallel algorithms for the problems that are provably work-optimal and low-depth.

Acknowledgments

This research was in part sponsored by the U.S. Defense Advanced Research Projects Agency (DARPA) under the Social Media in Strategic Communication (SMISC) program, Agreement Number W911NF-12-C-0028. Tirthapura was partially supported by the National Science Foundation, through grant numbers 0834743 and 0831903. The views and conclusions contained in this document are those of the author(s) and should not be interpreted as representing the official policies, either expressed or implied, of the U.S. Defense Advanced Research Projects Agency, National Science Foundation, or the U.S. Government. The U.S. Government is authorized to reproduce and distribute reprints for Government purposes notwithstanding any copyright notation hereon.

References

[ABC09]   Chrisil Arackaparambil, Joshua Brody, and Amit Chakrabarti. Functional monitoring without monotonicity. In *ICALP '09*, pages 95–106, 2009.

[ACH⁺13] Pankaj K. Agarwal, Graham Cormode, Zengfeng Huang, Jeff M. Phillips, Zhewei Wei, and Ke Yi. Mergeable summaries. *ACM Trans. Database Syst.*, 38(4), 2013.

[BO10]   Vladimir Braverman and Rafail Ostrovsky. Effective computations on sliding windows. *SIAM J. Comput.*, 39(6):2113–2131, 2010.

[CCFC02] Moses Charikar, Kevin Chen, and Martin Farach-Colton. Finding frequent items in data streams. In *ICALP*, pages 693–703, 2002.

[CH10]   Graham Cormode and Marios Hadjieleftheriou. Methods for finding frequent items in data streams. *VLDB J.*, 19(1):3–20, 2010.

[CM05]   Graham Cormode and S. Muthukrishnan. An improved data stream summary: the count-min sketch and its applications. *J. Algorithms*, 55(1):58–75, 2005.

[CMYZ12] Graham Cormode, S. Muthukrishnan, Ke Yi, and Qin Zhang. Continuous sampling from distributed streams. *J. ACM*, 59(2), 2012.

[Cor13]   Graham Cormode. The continuous distributed monitoring model. *SIGMOD Record*, 42(1):5–14, 2013.

[CT11]   Massimo Cafaro and Piergiulio Tempesta. Finding frequent items in parallel. *Concurrency and Computation: Practice and Experience*, 23(15):1774–1788, 2011.

[DAAE09] Sudipto Das, Shyam Antony, Divyakant Agrawal, and Amr El Abbadi. Thread cooperation in multicore architectures for frequency counting over multiple data streams. *PVLDB*, 2(1):217–228, 2009.

[DGIM02] Mayur Datar, Aristides Gionis, Piotr Indyk, and Rajeev Motwani. Maintaining stream statistics over sliding windows. *SIAM J. Comput.*, 31(6), 2002.

[DLOM02] Erik D. Demaine, Alejandro López-Ortiz, and J. Ian Munro. Frequency estimation of internet packet streams with limited space. In *ESA*, pages 348–360, 2002.

[EV03]   Cristian Estan and George Varghese. New directions in traffic measurement and accounting: Focusing on the elephants, ignoring the mice. *ACM Trans. Comput. Syst.*, 21(3):270–313, 2003.

[GT01]   P. Gibbons and S. Tirthapura. Estimating simple functions on the union of data streams. In *SPAA'01*, pages 281–291, 2001.

[GT04]   P. Gibbons and S. Tirthapura. Distributed streams algorithms for sliding windows. *Theory of Computing Systems*, 37:457–478, 2004.

[HLT10]   Regant Y. S. Hung, Lap-Kei Lee, and Hing-Fung Ting. Finding frequent items over sliding windows with constant update time. *Inf. Process. Lett.*, 110(7):257–260, 2010.

[JáJ92]   Joseph JáJá. *An Introduction to Parallel Algorithms*. Addison-Wesley, 1992.

[KSP03]   Richard M. Karp, Scott Shenker, and Christos H. Papadimitriou. A simple algorithm for finding frequent elements in streams and bags. *ACM Trans. Database Syst.*, 28:51–55, 2003.

[LT06a]   Lap-Kei Lee and H. F. Ting. Maintaining significant stream statistics over sliding windows. In *SODA*, pages 724–732, 2006.

[LT06b]   Lap-Kei Lee and H. F. Ting. A simpler and more efficient deterministic scheme for finding frequent items over sliding windows. In *PODS'06*, pages 290–297, 2006.

[MAE06]   Ahmed Metwally, Divyakant Agrawal, and Amr El Abbadi. An integrated efficient solution for computing frequent and top-*k* elements in data streams. *ACM Trans. Database Syst.*, 31(3):1095–1133, 2006.

[MG82]   Jayadev Misra and David Gries. Finding repeated elements. *Sci. Comput. Program.*, 2(2):143–152, 1982.

[MM02]   Gurmeet Singh Manku and Rajeev Motwani. Approximate frequency counts over data streams. In *VLDB*, pages 346–357, 2002.

[RR89]   Sanguthevar Rajasekaran and John H. Reif. Optimal and sublogarithmic time randomized parallel sorting algorithms. *SIAM J. Comput.*, 18(3):594–607, 1989.

[TW11]   Srikanta Tirthapura and David P. Woodruff. Optimal random sampling from distributed streams revisited. In *Proc. International Symposium on Distributed Computing (DISC)*, pages 283–297, 2011.

[XTB08]   B. Xu, S. Tirthapura, and C. Busch. Sketching asynchronous data streams over sliding windows. *Distributed Computing*, 20(5):359–374, 2008.

[ZDL⁺13] M. Zaharia, T. Das, H. Li, T. Hunter, S. Shenker, and I. Stoica. Discretized streams: Fault-tolerant streaming computation at scale. In *Proc. ACM Symposium on Operating Systems Principles (SOSP)*, pages 423–438, 2013.

[ZSZ⁺13] Yu Zhang, Yue Sun, Jianzhong Zhang, Jingdong Xu, and Ying Wu. An efficient framework for parallel and continuous frequent item monitoring. *Concurrency and Computation: Practice and Experience*, 2013.

A Universal Approach to Data Center Network Design

Bruce Maggs

Department of Computer Science, Duke University
Durham, North Carolina, USA

Abstract

This talk proposes an approach to the design of large-scale general-purpose data center networks based on the notions of volume and area universality introduced by Leiserson in the 1980's in the context of VLSI design. In particular, we suggest that the principle goal of the network designer should be to build a single network that is provably competitive, for any application, with any network that can be built for the same amount of money. We illustrate our approach by walking through the design of a hierarchical data center network using the various networking components available today commercially.

Joint work with Aditya Akella, Theo Benson, Bala Chandrasekaran, Cheng Huang, and David Maltz.

Categories and Subject Descriptors

B.4.3 Interconnections (Subsystems); C.2.1 Network Architecture and Design; F.2.2 Nonnumerical Algorithms and Problems -- Routing and layout

Short Bio

Bruce Maggs received the S.B., S.M., and Ph.D. degrees in computer science from the Massachusetts Institute of Technology in 1985, 1986, and 1989, respectively. His advisor was Charles Leiserson. After spending one year as a Postdoctoral Associate at MIT, he worked as a Research Scientist at NEC Research Institute in Princeton from 1990 to 1993. In 1994, he moved to Carnegie Mellon, where he stayed until joining Duke University in 2009 as a Professor in the Department of Computer Science. While on a two-year leave-of-absence from Carnegie Mellon, Maggs helped to launch Akamai Technologies, serving as its Vice President for Research and Development, before returning to Carnegie Mellon. He retains a part-time role at Akamai as Vice President for Research.

SPAA'14, June 23–25, 2014, Prague, Czech Republic.
ACM 978-1-4503-2821-0/14/06.
http://dx.doi.org/10.1145/2612669.2612729

Simple Dynamics for Plurality Consensus*

Luca Becchetti
"Sapienza" Università di Roma
becchett@dis.uniroma1.it

Andrea Clementi
Università "Tor Vergata" di Roma
clementi@mat.uniroma2.it

Emanuele Natale
"Sapienza" Università di Roma
natale@di.uniroma1.it

Francesco Pasquale
"Sapienza" Università di Roma
pasquale@di.uniroma1.it

Riccardo Silvestri
"Sapienza" Università di Roma
silvestri@di.uniroma1.it

Luca Trevisan
Stanford University
trevisan@stanford.edu

ABSTRACT

We study a *Plurality Consensus* process in which each of n anonymous agents of a communication network supports an initial opinion (a color chosen from a finite set $[k]$) and, at every time step, he can revise his color according to a random sample of neighbors. The goal (of the agents) is to let the process converge to the *stable* configuration where all nodes support the *plurality color*. It is assumed that the initial color configuration has a sufficiently large *bias* s, that is, the number of nodes supporting the plurality color exceeds the number of nodes supporting any other color by an additive value s.

We consider a basic model in which the network is a clique and the update rule (called here the *3-majority dynamics*) of the process is that each agent looks at the colors of three random neighbors and then applies the majority rule (breaking ties uniformly at random).

We prove a tight bound on the convergence time which grows as $\Theta(k \log n)$ for a wide range of parameters k and n. This *linear-in-k* dependence implies an exponential time-gap between the plurality consensus process and the *median* process studied in [7].

A natural question is whether looking at more (than three) random neighbors can significantly speed up the process. We provide a negative answer to this question: in particular, we show that samples of polylogarithmic size can speed up the process by a polylogarithmic factor only.

Categories and Subject Descriptors

F.2 [**Theory of Computation**]: Analysis of Algorithms and Problem Complexity

---

*Partially supported by Italian MIUR-PRIN 2010-11 Project *ARS TechnoMedia* and the EU FET Project *MULTIPLEX* 317532.

Keywords

Plurality Consensus; Parallel Randomized Algorithms; Markov Chains.

1. INTRODUCTION

We consider a communication network in which each of n anonymous nodes supports an initial opinion (a color chosen from a finite set $[k]$). In the *Plurality Consensus* problem, it is assumed that the initial color configuration has a sufficiently large *bias* s towards a fixed color $m \in [k]$ - that is, the number c_m of nodes supporting the plurality color (in short, the *initial plurality size*) exceeds the number c_j of nodes supporting any other color j by an additive value s - and the goal is to design an efficient fully-distributed protocol that lets the network converge to the *plurality consensus*, i.e., to the monochromatic configuration in which all nodes support the plurality color.

Reaching plurality consensus in a distributed system is a fundamental problem arising from several areas such as Distributed Computing [7, 16], Communication Networks [17], and Social Networks [6, 15, 14]. Inspired by some recent works analyzing simple updating-rules (called *dynamics*) for this problem [1, 7], we study a discrete-time, synchronous process in which, at every time step, each of the n anonymous nodes revises his color according to a (small) random sample of neighbors. We consider one of the simplest models, in which the network is a clique, and the updating rule, called here 3-*majority dynamics*, is that each node samples at random three neighbors, and picks the majority color among them (breaking ties uniformly at random). Let us remark that looking at less than three random neighbors would yield a coloring process that may converge to a *minority* color with constant probability even for $k = 2$ and large initial bias (i.e. $s = \Theta(n)$).

In [7], a tight analysis of a 3-neighbor dynamics for the *median* problem on the clique has been presented: the goal here is to converge to a stable configuration where all nodes support a value which is a "good" approximation of the *median* of the initial color configuration. It turns out that, in the binary case (i.e $k = 2$), the median problem is equivalent to the majority consensus one and the 3-input dynamics for the median is equivalent to the 3-majority dynamics: as a result, they obtain, for any bias $s \geqslant c\sqrt{n \log n}$ for some constant $c > 0$, an optimal bound $\Theta(\log n)$ on the convergence time of the 3-majority dynamics for the binary case of the problem considered in this paper.

However, for any $k \geqslant 3$, it is easy to see that the two problems above are different from each other (the median may be very different from the plurality) and, thus, the two dynamics are different from each other as well. Moreover, the analysis in [7] - strongly based on the properties of the median function - cannot be adapted to bound the convergence time of the 3-majority dynamics. The role of parameter $k = k(n)$ in the convergence time of this dynamics is currently unknown and, more generally, the existence of efficient dynamics reaching plurality consensus for $k \geqslant 3$ is left as an important open issue in [2, 7, 1].

Our contribution. We present a new analysis of the 3-majority dynamics in the general case (i.e. for any $k \in [n]$). Our analysis shows that, with high probability (in short, $w.h.p.$[1]), the process converges to plurality consensus within time $\mathcal{O}\left(\min\{k, (n/\log n)^{1/3}\} \log n\right)$, provided that the initial bias is $s \geqslant c\sqrt{\min\{2k, (n/\log n)^{1/3}\} n \log n}$, for some constant $c > 0$.

Our proof technique is accurate enough to get another interesting form of the above upper bound that does not depend on k. Indeed, when the initial plurality size c_m is larger than $n/\lambda(n)$ for any function $\lambda(n)$ such that $3 \leqslant \lambda(n) < \sqrt{n}$ and $s \geqslant \sqrt{\lambda(n) n \log n}$, then the process converges in time $\mathcal{O}(\lambda(n) \log n)$ w.h.p., no matter how large k is. Hence, when $c_m \geqslant n/\text{polylog}(n)$ and $s \geqslant \sqrt{n}\,\text{polylog}(n)$, the convergence time is polylogaritmic.

We then show that our upper bound is tight for a wide range of the input parameters. When $k \leqslant (n/\log n)^{1/4}$, we in fact prove a lower bound $\Omega(k \log n)$ on the convergence time of the 3-majority dynamics starting from some configurations with bias $s \leqslant (n/k)^{1-\epsilon}$, for an arbitrarily small constant $\epsilon > 0$. Observe that this range largely includes the initial bias required by our upper bound when $k \leqslant (n/\log n)^{1/4}$. So, the *linear-in-k* dependence of the convergence time cannot be removed for a wide range of the parameter k.

Our analysis also provides a clear picture of the 3-majority dynamic process. Informally speaking, the larger the initial value of c_m is (w.r.t. n), the smaller the required initial bias s and the faster the convergence time are. On the other hand, our lower-bound argument shows, as a by-product, that the initial plurality size c_m needs $\Omega(k \log n)$ rounds just to increase from $n/k + o(n/k)$ to $2n/k$.

We then prove a general negative result: in the considered distributed model, there is no dynamics with at most 3 inputs (but the majority one) that w.h.p. converges to plurality consensus starting from any initial bias s such that $s = o(n)$. In other words, not only there is no hope to find a 3-input dynamics faster than $k \log n$ but the 3-majority dynamics is the only one getting the plurality consensus, no matter in how much time. Rather interestingly, by comparing the $\mathcal{O}(\log n)$ bound for the median [7] to our negative results for the plurality on the same distributed model, we get an exponential time-gap between the the task of computing the median and that of computing the plurality (this happens for instance when $k = n^a$, for any constant $0 < a < 1/4$).

A natural question arising from our results is whether a (slightly) larger random sample of neighbors might lead to a significant speed-up of the convergence time to plurality consensus. We provide a negative answer to this question. We consider the generalization of the 3-majority dynamics, the h-plurality one, where every node, at every time step, updates his color according to the plurality of the colors supported by h random neighbors. We prove a lower bound $\Omega\left(k/h^2\right)$ on the convergence time of the h-plurality dynamics, for integers k and h such that $k/h = \mathcal{O}\left(n^{1/4-\epsilon}\right)$, where ϵ is an arbitrarily-small positive constant. We emphasize that scalable and efficient protocols must yield low communication complexity and small node congestion at every time step. These properties are guaranteed by the h-plurality dynamics only when h is small, say $h = \mathcal{O}(\text{polylog}(n))$: in this case, our lower bound says that the resulting speed up is only polylogarithmic with respect to the 3-majority dynamics.

One motivation for adopting dynamics in reaching (*simple*) consensus[2] (such as the median dynamics shown in [7]) lies in their provably-good *self-stabilizing* properties against *dynamic adversary corruptions*: it turns out that the 3-majority dynamics has good self-stabilizing properties for the *plurality consensus* problem. More formally, a T-bounded adversary knows the state of every node at the end of each round and, based on this knowledge, he can corrupt the color of up to T nodes in an arbitrary way, just before the next round starts. In this case, the goal is to achieve an almost-stable phase where all but at most $\mathcal{O}(T)$ nodes agree on the plurality value. This "almost-stability" phase must have $\text{poly}(n)$ length, with high probability. Our analysis implicitly shows that the 3-majority dynamics guarantees the self-stabilization property for plurality consensus for any k and for $T = o(s/k)$ if the initial bias is $s \geqslant c\sqrt{\min\{2k, (n/\log n)^{1/3}\} n \log n}$, for some constant $c > 0$.

Related works. The plurality consensus problem arises in several applications such as distributed database management where data redundancy or replication and majority rules are used to manage the presence of unknown faulty processors [7, 16]. The objective here is to converge to the version of the data supported by the majority of the initial distributed copies (it is reasonable that a sufficiently large majority of the nodes are not faulty and thus have the correct data). Another application comes from the task of distributed item ranking where every node initially has ranked some item and the goal is to agree on the rank of the item based on the initial majority opinion [17]. Further applications of majority updating rules in networks can be found in [10, 16].

The results most related to our contribution are those in [7] which have been already discussed above. Several variants of the binary majority consensus have been studied in different distributed models [2, 15]. As for the *population model*, where there is only one random node-pair interaction per round (so the dynamics are strictly sequential), the binary case on the clique has been analyzed in [2] and their generalization to multivalued case ($k \geqslant 3$) does not converge to plurality even starting from large bias $s = \Theta(n)$. The polling rule (a somewhat sequential-interaction version of the 1-majority dynamics) has been extensively studied on

---

[2]In the (simple) consensus problem the goal is to reach any stable monochromatic configuration (any color is accepted) starting from any initial configuration.

several classes of graphs (see [16]). More expensive and complex protocols have been considered in order to speed up the process. For instance, in [11], a protocol for the sequential-interaction model is presented that requires $\Theta(\log n)$ memory per node and converges in time $\mathcal{O}(n^7)$. Other protocols for the sequential-interaction model have been analyzed in [5, 12] (with no time bound). In [1, 3, 8, 17], the polling rule (with 1 more auxiliary state) on the continuous-time population model is proved to converge in $\mathcal{O}(n \log n)$ expected time only for $k = \Theta(1)$ and $s = \Theta(n)$: even assuming such strong restrictions, the bound does not hold in "high probability" and, moreover, their analysis, based on real-valued differential-equations, do not work for the discrete-time parallel model considered in this paper. Protocols for specific network topologies and some "social-based" communities have been studied in [1, 8, 14, 17].

Roadmap of the paper. Section 2 formalizes the basic concepts and gives some preliminary results. Section 3 is devoted to the proofs of the upper bounds on the convergence time of the 3-majority dynamics. In Section 4, the lower bounds for the studied dynamics are described. Section 5 discusses some interesting open questions such as the tightness of the initial bias. In the Appendix A, we recall some standard results (such as Chernoff-Bernstein's inequalities) and provide a useful probabilistic result on Markov chains (we have not found its explicit proof in the literature). Due to lack of space, several proofs are omitted. They can be found in the full-version of the paper [4].

2. PRELIMINARIES

A *k-color distribution* (for short *k-cd*) is any k-tuple $\bar{c} = (c_1, \ldots, c_k)$ such that c_js are non negative integers and $\sum_{j=1,\ldots,k} c_j = n$. A color m is said to be a *plurality color* of $\bar{c}$ if $c_m \geqslant c_j$ for every other color $j \in [k] \setminus \{m\}$. We say that $\bar{c}$ is *s-biased* if a color m exists such that $c_m \geqslant c_j + s$ for every other color $j \in [k] \setminus \{m\}$.

The 3-majority protocol works as follows:

> *At every time step, every node picks three nodes uniformly at random (including itself and with repetitions) and recolors itself according to the majority of the colors it sees. If it sees three different colors, it chooses the first one.*

Clearly, in the case of three different colors, choosing the second or the third one would not make any difference. The same holds even if the choice would be uniformly at random among the three colors.

For any time step t and for any $j \in [k]$, let $C_{j,t}$ be the r.v. counting the number of nodes colored j at time step t and let $C_t = (C_{1,t}, \ldots, C_{k,t})$ denote the random variable indicating the k-cd at time t of the execution of the 3-majority protocol.

For every $j \in [k]$ let $\mu_j(\bar{c})$ be the expected number of nodes with color j at the next step when the current k-cd is $\bar{c}$, i.e. $\mu_j(\bar{c}) = \mathbb{E}[C_{j,t+1} \mid C_t = \bar{c}]$. The proof of the next lemma is a straightforward computation.

LEMMA 2.1 (NEXT EXPECTED COLORING). *For any k-cd $\bar{c}$ and for every $j \in [k]$, it holds that*

$$\mu_j(\bar{c}) = c_j \left[1 + \frac{1}{n^2} \left(nc_j - \sum_{h \in [k]} c_h^2 \right) \right]$$

3. UPPER BOUNDS FOR 3-MAJORITY

In this section, we show an upper bound on the convergence time of the 3-majority dynamics that holds with high probability. To this aim, we need to consider the following r.v.s For a k-cd $\bar{c}$, we define

$$m(\bar{c}) = \max_{h \in [k]} c_h$$

$$M(\bar{c}) = \{ j \in [k] \mid c_j = m(\bar{c}) \}$$

$$s(\bar{c}) = \begin{cases} m(\bar{c}) - \max_{h \in [k] - M(\bar{c})} c_h & \text{if } |M(\bar{c})| = 1 \\ 0 & \text{otherwise} \end{cases}$$

$$\alpha(\bar{c}) = \frac{(n - m(\bar{c}))s(\bar{c})}{n^2}$$

$$\gamma(\bar{c}) = \frac{n \cdot m(\bar{c}) - \sum_{h \in [k]} c_h^2}{n^2} - \alpha(\bar{c})$$

The next lemma gives some useful inequalities relating the above quantities.

LEMMA 3.1. *For any k-cd $\bar{c}$, the followings hold*

a) $0 \leqslant s(\bar{c}) \leqslant m(\bar{c}) - \frac{n - m(\bar{c})}{k-1}$

b) $0 \leqslant \alpha(\bar{c}) \leqslant \min\{\frac{s(\bar{c})}{n}, \frac{1}{4}\}$

c) $0 \leqslant \gamma(\bar{c}) \leqslant \frac{1}{8}$

The above lemma allows us to give a new expression for $\mu_j(\bar{c})$ that will be useful in the proofs of Lemmas 3.3 and 3.4.

LEMMA 3.2. *Let $\bar{c}$ be any k-cd. Let m be any color in $M(\bar{c})$ and let $\ell \in [k] - \{m\}$ be such that $c_\ell = \max_{h \in [k] - \{m\}} c_h$.*

a) $\mu_m(\bar{c}) = c_m(1 + \gamma(\bar{c}) + \alpha(\bar{c}))$

b) $\forall j \in [k] - M(\bar{c}) \quad \mu_j(\bar{c}) = c_j \left(1 + \gamma(\bar{c}) + \alpha(\bar{c}) - \frac{m(\bar{c}) - c_j}{n} \right)$

c) $\mu_\ell(\bar{c}) = c_\ell \left(1 + \gamma(\bar{c}) + \alpha(\bar{c}) - \frac{s(\bar{c})}{n} \right)$

We now evaluate the increasing rate of the bias of a k-cd during a generic step of the 3-majority dynamics.

LEMMA 3.3 (INCREASING RATE OF THE BIAS). *Let $\bar{c}$ be any k-cd such that $M(\bar{c}) = \{m\}$ for some $m \in [k]$. Then it holds that, for any $j \in [k] - m$,*

$$\mathbf{P}\left(C_{m,t+1} - C_{j,t+1} \leqslant s(\bar{c}) \left(1 + \gamma(\bar{c}) + \frac{c_m \alpha(\bar{c})}{2s(\bar{c})} \right) \,\middle|\, C_t = \bar{c} \right)$$

$$\leqslant \exp\left(-\frac{c_m \alpha(\bar{c})^2}{25} \right) \quad (1)$$

This is the key-lemma to get our upper bound on the convergence time so, before giving its proof, let us provide a rough but useful evaluation of Eq. 1 for a fixed setting of parameters k and s, i.e., $k = n^{1/4}$ and $s = c\sqrt{n^{3/4} \log n}$, for some constant $c > 0$. Consider the "initial phase" of the coloring process where c_m is still $\Theta(n/k) = \Theta(n^{3/4})$ and s is still $o(c_m)$. Then, by replacing the values of $\alpha(\bar{c})$ and $\gamma(\bar{c})$ in Eq. 1 (and doing some simple calculations), we get that the bias s increases by a factor $1 + \Theta(1/k)$ w.h.p. This is exactly what we need to get the upper bound $\mathcal{O}(k \log n)$ on the convergence time. The bound in Eq. 1 has a more complex, general shape since it must work for the whole process and it must lead to our stronger bound $\mathcal{O}\left(\min\{k, (n/\log n)^{1/3}\} \log n \right)$.

PROOF. (of Lemma 3.3)
In the sequel we tacitly assume that all probabilities, expected values and random variables are conditioned to "$C_t = \bar{c}$". For any fixed color $j \in [k] - \{m\}$, we consider the the random variable

$$Z = C_{m,t+1} - C_{j,t+1}$$

It holds that

$$\mathbb{E}[Z] = \mu_m(\bar{c}) - \mu_j(\bar{c})$$
$$= c_m(1 + \gamma(\bar{c}) + \alpha(\bar{c})) - c_j \left(1 + \gamma(\bar{c}) + \alpha(\bar{c}) - \frac{m(\bar{c}) - c_j}{n} \right)$$
$$\text{(from Lemma 3.2)}$$
$$= (c_m - c_j)(1 + \gamma(\bar{c})) + c_m\alpha(\bar{c}) + c_j \left(\frac{m(\bar{c}) - c_j}{n} - \alpha(\bar{c}) \right)$$
$$= (c_m - c_j)(1 + \gamma(\bar{c})) + c_m\alpha(\bar{c}) + c_j \left(\frac{m(\bar{c}) - c_j}{n} - \alpha(\bar{c}) \right)$$
$$\geqslant (c_m - c_j)(1 + \gamma(\bar{c})) + c_m\alpha(\bar{c}) + c_j \left(\frac{s(\bar{c})}{n} - \alpha(\bar{c}) \right)$$
$$\text{(since } m(\bar{c}) - c_j \geqslant s(\bar{c}))$$
$$\geqslant (c_m - c_j)(1 + \gamma(\bar{c})) + c_m\alpha(\bar{c})$$
$$\text{(since } \tfrac{s(\bar{c})}{n} \geqslant \alpha(\bar{c}) \text{ by Lemma 3.1)}$$
$$\geqslant s(\bar{c}) \left(1 + \gamma(\bar{c}) + \frac{c_m\alpha(\bar{c})}{s(\bar{c})} \right) \qquad (2)$$
$$\text{(since } c_m - c_j \geqslant s(\bar{c}))$$

We now introduce, for any $i \in [n]$, the random variable
$$Z_i = \begin{cases} 1 & \text{if node } i \text{ gets color } m \text{ at time } t+1 \\ -1 & \text{if node } i \text{ gets color } j \text{ at time } t+1 \\ 0 & \text{otherwise} \end{cases}$$

Clearly, the Z_i's are independent and it holds that

$$Z = \sum_{i \in [n]} Z_i$$

In order to apply the Bernstein's Inequality (Lemma A.3) to $-Z$, we firstly observe that

$$-Z_i - \mathbb{E}[-Z_i] \leqslant 2,$$

so we can choose $b = 2$. As for the variance σ^2 of $-Z$, we have that

$$\sigma^2 = \mathbf{Var}[-Z] = \sum_{i \in [n]} \mathbf{Var}[-Z_i]$$
$$= \sum_{i \in [n]} \left(\mathbb{E}[(-Z_i)^2] - \mathbb{E}[-Z_i]^2 \right) = \sum_{i \in [n]} \left(\mathbb{E}[Z_i^2] - \mathbb{E}[Z_i]^2 \right)$$
$$\leqslant \sum_{i \in [n]} \mathbb{E}[Z_i^2] = \sum_{i \in [n]} \left(\mathbf{P}(Z_i = 1) + \mathbf{P}(Z_i = -1) \right)$$
$$= \mu_m(\bar{c}) + \mu_j(\bar{c})$$
$$\leqslant 2\mu_m(\bar{c}) \qquad \text{(since } \mu_j(\bar{c}) \leqslant \mu_m(\bar{c}) \text{ by Lemma 3.2)}$$
$$= 2c_m(1 + \gamma(\bar{c}) + \alpha(\bar{c}))$$
$$\leqslant 2c_m(1 + \tfrac{1}{8} + \tfrac{1}{4}) \qquad \text{(from Lemma 3.1)}$$
$$\leqslant 3c_m \qquad (3)$$

For the sake of convenience, let us define

$$P = \mathbf{P}\left(Z < s(\bar{c})\left(1 + \gamma(\bar{c}) + \frac{c_m\alpha(\bar{c})}{2s(\bar{c})}\right)\right)$$

Now we conclude the proof by applying the Bernstein's Inequality

$$P = \mathbf{P}\left(-Z > -s(\bar{c})\left(1 + \gamma(\bar{c}) + \frac{c_m\alpha(\bar{c})}{s(\bar{c})}\right) + \frac{c_m\alpha(\bar{c})}{2} \right)$$
$$\leqslant \mathbf{P}\left(-Z > \mathbb{E}[-Z] + \frac{c_m\alpha(\bar{c})}{2} \right)$$
$$\text{(since } \mathbb{E}[-Z] \leqslant -s(\bar{c})\left(1 + \gamma(\bar{c}) + \frac{c_m\alpha(\bar{c})}{s(\bar{c})}\right) \text{ by Ineq. 2)}$$
$$\leqslant \exp\left(-\frac{\left(\frac{c_m\alpha(\bar{c})}{2}\right)^2}{2\sigma^2 + (4/3)\frac{c_m\alpha(\bar{c})}{2}} \right)$$
$$\text{(from Lemma A.3 with } b = 2 \text{ and } \lambda = \frac{c_m\alpha(\bar{c})}{2})$$
$$\leqslant \exp\left(-\frac{c_m^2\alpha(\bar{c})^2}{24c_m + (8/3)c_m\alpha(\bar{c})} \right) \qquad \text{(from Ineq. 3)}$$
$$\leqslant \exp\left(-\frac{c_m\alpha(\bar{c})^2}{25} \right) \qquad \text{(since } \alpha(\bar{c}) \leqslant 1/4 \text{ by Lemma 3.1)}$$

$\square$

The next lemma derives from Lemmas 3.1 and 3.2.

LEMMA 3.4. *Let* $\bar{c}$ *be any* k-cd *such that* $M(\bar{c}) = \{m\}$ *for some* $m \in [k]$. *It holds that*

$$\mathbf{P}\left(C_{m,t+1} \leqslant c_m\left(1 + \gamma(\bar{c}) + \frac{\alpha(\bar{c})}{2}\right) \,\Big|\, C_t = \bar{c} \right) \leqslant \exp\left(-\frac{c_m\alpha(\bar{c})^2}{11} \right)$$

PROOF. Let

$$P_m = \mathbf{P}\left(C_{m,t+1} \leqslant c_m\left(1 + \gamma(\bar{c}) + \frac{\alpha(\bar{c})}{2}\right) \,\Big|\, C_t = \bar{c} \right)$$

and let

$$\delta_m = \frac{\alpha(\bar{c})}{2(1 + \gamma(\bar{c}) + \alpha(\bar{c}))}$$

From Lemma 3.1, $\gamma, \alpha \geqslant 0$, and thus $0 < \delta_m < 1$. Thanks to the Chernoff bound we have that

$$P_m = \mathbf{P}\left(C_{m,t+1} \leqslant (1 - \delta_m)\mu_m \,|\, C_t = \bar{c} \right) \qquad \text{(from Lemma 3.2)}$$
$$\leqslant \exp\left(-\frac{\delta_m^2\mu_m}{2} \right) \qquad \text{(by the Chernoff bound)}$$
$$= \exp\left(-\frac{1}{2}\left(\frac{\alpha(\bar{c})}{2(1 + \gamma(\bar{c}) + \alpha(\bar{c}))} \right)^2 c_m(1 + \gamma(\bar{c}) + \alpha(\bar{c})) \right)$$
$$= \exp\left(-\frac{c_m\alpha(\bar{c})^2}{8(1 + \gamma(\bar{c}) + \alpha(\bar{c}))} \right)$$
$$\leqslant \exp\left(-\frac{c_m\alpha(\bar{c})^2}{11} \right)$$
$$\text{(since } \gamma(\bar{c}) + \alpha(\bar{c}) \leqslant 3/8 \text{ by Lemma 3.1)}$$

$\square$

We now use Lemmas 3.3 and 3.4 in order to get some bounds on the increasing rate of the bias: they will lead to a bound on convergence time that does not depend on k.

LEMMA 3.5 (LARGE PLURALITY AND LARGE BIAS). *Let* $\bar{c}$ *be any* k-cd *such that* $M(\bar{c}) = \{m\}$ *for some* $m \in [k]$. *For any value* λ *with* $0 < \lambda \leqslant 2/3$, *if* $\lambda n \leqslant c_m \leqslant (2/3)n$ *and* $s(\bar{c}) \geqslant 22\sqrt{(1/\lambda)n \log n}$, *then, for every* $j \in [k] - \{m\}$,

$$\mathbf{P}\left(C_{m,t+1} - C_{j,t+1} \leqslant s(\bar{c})\left(1 + \frac{\lambda}{6}\right) \,\Big|\, C_t = \bar{c} \right) \leqslant \frac{1}{n^2}$$

and

$$\mathbf{P}\left(C_{m,t+1} \leqslant c_m \mid C_t = \bar{c} \right) \ \leqslant \ \frac{1}{n^2}$$

PROOF. From Lemma 3.3 we have that

$$\mathbf{P}\left(C_{m,t+1} - C_{j,t+1} \leqslant s(\bar{c})\left(1 + \gamma(\bar{c}) + \frac{c_m \alpha(\bar{c})}{2s(\bar{c})} \right) \ \middle| \ C_t = \bar{c} \right)$$

$$\leqslant \exp\left(-\frac{c_m \alpha(\bar{c})^2}{25} \right) \quad (4)$$

It holds that

$$\frac{c_m \alpha(\bar{c})}{2s(\bar{c})} = \frac{c_m(n - c_m)}{2n^2} \geqslant \frac{\lambda n(n/3)}{2n^2} \geqslant \frac{\lambda}{6} \quad (5)$$

As regards the exponent of the probability bound of Ineq. 4 we get

$$\frac{c_m \alpha(\bar{c})^2}{25} = \frac{c_m(n - c_m)^2 s(\bar{c})^2}{25 n^4}$$

$$\geqslant \frac{c_m s(\bar{c})^2}{225 n^2} \quad \text{(since } c_m \leqslant (2/3)n\text{)}$$

$$\geqslant \frac{\lambda n 484(1/\lambda) n \log n}{225 n^2}$$

(by the hypothesis bounds on c_m and $s(\bar{c})$)

$$\geqslant 2 \log n \quad (6)$$

By combining Ineq.s 4, 5, and 6 we obtain the first probability bound. As for the second bound, from Lemma 3.4 it holds that

$$\mathbf{P}\left(C_{m,t+1} \leqslant c_m \mid C_t = \bar{c} \right)$$

$$\leqslant \mathbf{P}\left(C_{m,t+1} \leqslant c_m\left(1 + \gamma(\bar{c}) + \frac{\alpha(\bar{c})}{2} \right) \ \middle| \ C_t = \bar{c} \right)$$

$$\leqslant \exp\left(-\frac{c_m \alpha(\bar{c})^2}{11} \right)$$

and, from Ineq. 6,

$$\frac{c_m \alpha(\bar{c})^2}{11} \geqslant \frac{c_m \alpha(\bar{c})^2}{25} \geqslant 2 \log n$$

$\square$

For any $m \in [k]$, let $\overline{C}_{m,t} = n - C_{m,t}$ denote the random variable counting the number of nodes with colors different from m at time t. For any k-cd $\bar{c}$ and for any $m \in [k]$, we also consider its expected value $\overline{\mu}_m(\bar{c}) = \mathbb{E}\left[\overline{C}_{m,t+1} \ \middle| \ C_t = \bar{c} \right]$, and provide the following bounds

LEMMA 3.6. *For any k-cd $\bar{c}$ and for any $m \in M(\bar{c})$, it holds that*

$$(n - c_m)\left(1 - \frac{c_m^2}{n^2} \right) \ \leqslant \ \overline{\mu}_m(\bar{c}) \ \leqslant \ (n - c_m)\left(1 - \frac{s(\bar{c})c_m}{n^2} \right)$$

We now use the above bounds to show that, when the bias of a k-cd is at least $n/3$, then the number of nodes that do not have the plurality color decreases at an exponential rate.

LEMMA 3.7 (VERY-LARGE PLURALITY). *Let $\bar{c}$ be any k-cd such that $s(\bar{c}) \geqslant n/3$ for some $m \in [k]$. If $n - c_m \geqslant \sqrt[4]{n} \log n$, then*

$$\mathbf{P}\left(\overline{C}_{m,t+1} \geqslant \frac{17}{18}(n - c_m) \ \middle| \ C_t = \bar{c} \right) \leqslant \frac{1}{n^2}$$

If $n - c_m < \sqrt[4]{n} \log n$, then

$$\mathbf{P}\left(\overline{C}_{m,t+1} > 0 \ \middle| \ C_t = \bar{c} \right) \leqslant \frac{1}{\sqrt[5]{n}}$$

$$\mathbf{P}\left(\overline{C}_{m,t+1} \geqslant \sqrt[4]{n} \log n \ \middle| \ C_t = \bar{c} \right) \leqslant \frac{1}{n^2}$$

We now exploit Lemmas 3.5 and 3.7 in order to prove the main result of this section.

THEOREM 3.8 (THE GENERAL UPPER BOUND). *Let λ be any value such that $3 \leqslant \lambda < \sqrt{n}$. If $\bar{c}$ is a k-cd such that, for some $m \in [k]$, $M(\bar{c}) = \{m\}$, $c_m \geqslant n/\lambda$, and $s(\bar{c}) \geqslant 22\sqrt{\lambda n \log n}$, then the 3-majority protocol converges to color m in $\mathcal{O}(\lambda \log n)$ time w.h.p.*

PROOF. For the sake of convenience, let

$$\Lambda = 22\sqrt{\lambda n \log n}$$

Notice that $\Lambda \leqslant 22 n^{3/4}\sqrt{\log n}$. In order to make use of Lemma A.4 (see the appendix), we consider the Markov chain determined by the 3-majority protocol. The states of the Markov chain are all the possible assignments of the k colors to the n nodes. For any assignment $\mathbf{a}$, let $\bar{c}(\mathbf{a})$ denote the k-cd determined by $\mathbf{a}$ and let $c_j(\mathbf{a})$ denote any its component. Let X_t be the random variable that is the state at time t given that X_0 is a state whose k-cd is $\bar{c}$. Define

$$T_1 = \left\lfloor 1 + \frac{\log \frac{n}{3\Lambda}}{\log\left(1 + \frac{1}{6\lambda} \right)} \right\rfloor$$

$$T_2 = \left\lfloor 1 + \frac{3}{2\log(18/17)} \log \frac{n^{3/4}}{\log n} \right\rfloor$$

For any $i = 1, \ldots, T_1$, let

$A_i =$

$$\left\{ \mathbf{a} \ \middle| \ c_m(\mathbf{a}) > \frac{2}{3}n \ \vee \right.$$

$$\left. \left(M(\bar{c}(\mathbf{a})) = \{m\} \wedge c_m(\mathbf{a}) \geqslant \frac{n}{\lambda} \wedge s(\bar{c}(\mathbf{a})) \geqslant \Lambda\left(1 + \frac{1}{6\lambda} \right)^{i-1} \right) \right\}$$

Observe that $X_0 \in A_1$ and $A_1 \supseteq A_2 \supseteq \cdots \supseteq A_{T_1}$. For any $i = 1, \ldots, T_2$, let

$A_{T_1 + i} =$

$$\left\{ \mathbf{a} \ \middle| \ M(\bar{c}(\mathbf{a})) = \{m\} \wedge s(\bar{c}(\mathbf{a})) \geqslant \frac{n}{3} \wedge n - c_m(\mathbf{a}) \leqslant \frac{2n}{3}\left(\frac{17}{18} \right)^{i-1} \right\}$$

and let

$A_{T_1 + T_2 + 1} =$

$$\left\{ \mathbf{a} \ \middle| \ M(\bar{c}(\mathbf{a})) = \{m\} \wedge s(\bar{c}(\mathbf{a})) \geqslant \frac{n}{3} \wedge n - c_m(\mathbf{a}) < \sqrt[4]{n} \log n \right\}$$

$$A_{T_1 + T_2 + 2} = \{ \mathbf{a} \mid c_m(\mathbf{a}) = n \}$$

It is easy to verify that $A_{T_1} \supseteq A_{T_1 + 1} \supseteq A_{T_1 + 2} \supseteq \cdots \supseteq A_{T_1 + T_2} \supseteq A_{T_1 + T_2 + 1} \supseteq A_{T_1 + T_2 + 2}$. Thus it holds that $A_1 \supseteq \cdots \supseteq A_{T_1 + T_2 + 2}$. Taking into account that $c_m(\mathbf{a}) > (2/3)n$ implies $s(\bar{c}(\mathbf{a})) \geqslant n/3$, from Lemma 3.5 we have that, for any $i = 1, \ldots, T_1$,

$$\mathbf{P}\left(X_t \in A_i \mid X_{t-1} \in A_i \right) \geqslant 1 - \frac{1}{n^2} \quad \text{and}$$

$$\mathbf{P}\left(X_t \in A_{i+1} \mid X_{t-1} \in A_i \right) \geqslant 1 - \frac{1}{n^2}$$

From Lemma 3.7 we get, for any $i = T_1 + 1, \ldots, T_1 + T_2$

$$\mathbf{P}\left(X_t \in A_i \mid X_{t-1} \in A_i\right) \geqslant 1 - \frac{1}{n^2} \quad \text{and}$$

$$\mathbf{P}\left(X_t \in A_{i+1} \mid X_{t-1} \in A_i\right) \geqslant 1 - \frac{1}{n^2}$$

moreover

$$\mathbf{P}\left(X_t \in A_{T_1+T_2+1} \mid X_{t-1} \in A_{T_1+T_2+1}\right) \geqslant 1 - \frac{1}{n^2} \quad \text{and}$$

$$\mathbf{P}\left(X_t \in A_{T_1+T_2+2} \mid X_{t-1} \in A_{T_1+T_2+1}\right) \geqslant 1 - \frac{1}{\sqrt[5]{n}}$$

Hence, by applying Lemma A.4 with $\epsilon = 1/n^2$ and $\nu = 1/\sqrt[5]{n}$ with $\ell = 10$, we obtain

$$\mathbf{P}\left(X_{10T} \in A_T \mid X_0 \in A_1\right) \geqslant 1 - T\left(\frac{10}{n^2} + \left(\frac{1}{\sqrt[5]{n}}\right)^{10}\right)$$

$$= 1 - \frac{11T}{n^2}$$

It easy to see that $T < n/11$. Thus in time $10T$ the 3-majority protocol converges to color m w.h.p. Now we bound T in a more precise way. It holds that

$$T = T_1 + T_2 + 2$$

$$\leqslant 4 + \frac{\log \frac{n}{3\Lambda}}{\log\left(1 + \frac{1}{6\lambda}\right)} + \frac{3}{2\log(18/17)}\log\frac{n^{3/4}}{\log n}$$

$$\leqslant 4 + 27\log n + \frac{\log \frac{n}{66\sqrt{\Lambda n \log n}}}{\log\left(1 + \frac{1}{6\lambda}\right)}$$

$$\leqslant 28\log n + \frac{\log\left(\frac{1}{66}\sqrt{\frac{n}{\lambda \log n}}\right)}{\frac{1/(6\lambda)}{1+1/(6\lambda)}} \quad \text{(since } \log(1+x) \geqslant \frac{x}{1+x})$$

$$\leqslant 26\log n + 7\lambda\log(n/\lambda)$$

$$\leqslant 10\,\lambda\log n$$

$\square$

OBSERVATION 3.9. *Let us consider a dynamic adversary (see the Introduction) that can change the color of up to T nodes at the beginning of each time step and assume $T = o(\lambda \cdot s)$. Then, Theorem 3.8 still holds since the impact of such a T-bounded adversary is negligible in the growth of the bias s (this can be easily seen in the proof of Lemma 3.5). For instance, when $k \leqslant 2\sqrt[3]{\frac{n}{\log n}}$, then the tolerance of the 3-majority dynamics is $T = o(s/k)$.*

The next three corollaries of Theorem 3.8 address three relevant special cases. Corollary 3.10 is obtained by setting $\lambda = \min\left\{2k, \sqrt[3]{\frac{n}{\log n}}\right\}$ and it provides a bound which does not assume any condition on c_m.

COROLLARY 3.10. *If $\overline{c}$ is a k-cd such that, for some $m \in [k]$, $M(\overline{c}) = \{m\}$ and*

$$s(\overline{c}) \geqslant 22\sqrt{\min\left\{2k, \sqrt[3]{\frac{n}{\log n}}\right\} n \log n}$$

then, the 3-majority protocol converges to color m in $\mathcal{O}\left(\min\left\{2k, \sqrt[3]{\frac{n}{\log n}}\right\}\log n\right)$ time w.h.p.

Corollaries 3.11 and 3.12 are obtained by setting $\lambda = \text{poly}\log(n)$ and $\lambda = \Theta(1)$, respectively. They require some lower bounds on c_m.

COROLLARY 3.11. *If $\overline{c}$ is a k-cd such that, for some $m \in [k]$, $M(\overline{c}) = \{m\}$, $c_m \geqslant n/\log^\ell n$, and $s(\overline{c}) \geqslant 22\sqrt{n\log^{\ell+1} n}$, then the 3-majority protocol converges to color m in $\mathcal{O}(\log^{\ell+1} n)$ time w.h.p.*

COROLLARY 3.12. *If $\overline{c}$ is a k-cd such that, for some $m \in [k]$, $M(\overline{c}) = \{m\}$, $c_m \geqslant n/\beta$, and $s(\overline{c}) \geqslant 22\sqrt{\beta n \log n}$, for some constant $\beta \geqslant 3$, then the 3-majority protocol converges to color m in $\mathcal{O}(\log n)$ time w.h.p.*

4. LOWER BOUNDS

This section is organized in 3 subsections: in the first one, we prove a lower bound on the convergence time of the 3-majority dynamics; in the second subsection, we show that 3-majority is essentially the only 3-input dynamics that converges to plurality consensus; finally, in the third subsection, we provide a lower bound on the convergence time of the h-plurality dynamics for $h > 3$.

4.1 Lower bound for 3-majority

In this section we show that if the 3-majority dynamics starts from a sufficiently balanced configuration (i.e., at the beginning there are $n/k \pm o(n/k)$ nodes of every color) then it will take $\Omega(k\log n)$ steps w.h.p. to reach one of the absorbing configurations where all nodes have the same color. In what follows, all events and random variables thus concern the Markovian process yielded by the 3-majority dynamics.

In the next lemma we show that if there are at most $n/k+b$ nodes of a specific color, where b is smaller than n/k, then at the next time step there are at most $n/k + (1 + 3/k)b$ nodes of that color w.h.p.

LEMMA 4.1. *Let the number of colors k be such that $k \leqslant (n/\log n)^{1/4}$, let b be any number with $k\sqrt{n\log n} \leqslant b \leqslant n/k$, and let $\{X_t\}$ be the sequence of random variables where X_t is the number of a specific color at time t. If $X_t = n/k + a$ for some $a \leqslant b$ then $X_{t+1} \leqslant n/k + (1 + 3/k)b$ w.h.p.; more precisely, for any $a \leqslant b$ it holds that*

$$\mathbf{P}\left(X_{t+1} \geqslant \frac{n}{k} + \left(1 + \frac{3}{k}\right)b \;\middle|\; X_t = \frac{n}{k} + a\right) \leqslant \frac{1}{n^2}$$

PROOF. For a color h and time step t, let $C_{h,t}$ be the random variable indicating the number of nodes with color h, let $C_t = (C_{1,t}, \ldots, C_{k,t})$ be the random variable indicating the *coloring* at time t. For any coloring $\overline{c} = (c_1, \ldots, c_k)$ with $\sum_{h=1}^k c_h = n$ and any color $h \in [k]$, the expected value of the number of nodes colored h at time $t+1$ given $C_t = \overline{c}$ is (see Lemma 2.1)

$$\mathbf{E}[C_{h,t+1} \mid C_t = \overline{c}] = c_{h,t}\left(1 + \frac{c_{h,t}}{n} - \frac{1}{n^2}\sum_{j=1}^k c_j^2\right)$$

Observe that, since $\sum_{j=1}^k c_j = n$, from Jensen inequality (see Lemma A.2) it follows that $(1/n^2)\sum_{j=1}^k c_j^2 \geqslant 1/k$. Hence, if X_t is the random variable counting the number of nodes of one specific color, then we can give an upper bound on the expectation of X_{t+1} that depends only on X_t and not on the whole coloring at time t, namely

$$\mathbf{E}\left[X_{t+1} \mid X_t\right] \leqslant X_t\left(1+\frac{X_t}{n}-\frac{1}{k}\right)$$

If we condition on the number of nodes of that specific color being of the form $n/k + a$ for some $a \leqslant b$ we get

$$
\begin{aligned}
\mathbf{E}\left[X_{t+1} \mid X_t = n/k + a\right] &\leqslant \left(\frac{n}{k}+a\right)\left(1+\frac{n/k+a}{n}-\frac{1}{k}\right) \\
&= \frac{n}{k}+\left(1+\frac{1}{k}\right)a+\frac{a^2}{n} \\
&\leqslant \frac{n}{k}+\left(1+\frac{1}{k}\right)b+\frac{b^2}{n} \\
&\leqslant \frac{n}{k}+\left(1+\frac{2}{k}\right)b
\end{aligned}
$$

where in the last two inequalities we used that $a \leqslant b$ and $b \leqslant n/k$.[3] Since X_t can be written as a sum of n independent Bernoulli random variables, from Chernoff bound (see Lemma A.1) we thus get that for every $a \leqslant b$ it holds that

$$
\begin{aligned}
\mathbf{P}\left(X_{t+1} \geqslant \frac{n}{k}+\left(1+\frac{3}{k}\right)b \mid X_t = n/k + a\right) &\leqslant e^{-2(b/k)^2/n} \\
&\leqslant \frac{1}{n^2}
\end{aligned}
$$

where in the last inequality we used that $b \geqslant k\sqrt{n\log n}$. $\quad\square$

Let us say that a coloring $\bar{c} = (c_1, \ldots, c_k) \in \{0, 1, \ldots, n\}^k$ with $\sum_{h=1}^{k} c_h = n$ is *monochromatic* if there is an $h \in [k]$ such that $c_h = n$. In the next theorem we show that if we start from a sufficiently *balanced* coloring, then the 3-majority protocol takes $\Omega(k \log n)$ time steps w.h.p. to reach a monochromatic coloring.

THEOREM 4.2. *Let C_t be the random variable indicating the coloring at time t according to the 3-majority protocol and let $\tau = \inf\{t \in \mathbb{N} : C_t \text{ is monochromatic}\}$ be the random variable indicating the first time step such that C_t is monochromatic. If the initial number of colors is $k \leqslant (n/\log n)^{1/4}$ and the initial coloring is $C_0 = (c_1, \ldots, c_k)$ with $\max\{c_h : h = 1, \ldots, k\} \leqslant \frac{n}{k} + \left(\frac{n}{k}\right)^{1-\varepsilon}$ then $\tau = \Omega(k \log n)$ w.h.p.*

A full-detailed proof is given in the full-version [4], we here provide its main argument.

Idea of the proof. For a color $h \in [k]$ let us denote the difference $C_{h,t} - n/k$ as the *positive unbalance*. In Lemma 4.1 we proved that, as long as the positive unbalance of a color is smaller than n/k, this will increase by a factor smaller than $(1 + 3/k)$ at every time step (w.h.p.). Hence, if a color starts with a positive unbalance smaller than $(n/k)^{1-\varepsilon}$, then it will take $\Omega(k \log n)$ time steps to reach an unbalance of n/k w.h.p. By union bounding on all the colors, we can get the stated lower bound. $\quad\square$

It may be worth noticing that what we actually prove in Theorem 4.2 is that $\Omega(k \log n)$ time steps are required in order to go from a configuration where the majority color has at most $n/k + (n/k)^{1-\varepsilon}$ nodes to a configuration where it has $2n/k$ colors.

---
[3]Notice that the inequality holds in particular for negative a as well

4.2 A negative result for 3-input dynamics

In order to prove that dynamics that differ from the majority ones do not solve plurality consensus, we first give some formal definitions of the dynamics we are considering.

DEFINITION 4.3 ($\mathcal{D}_h(k)$ PROTOCOLS). *An h-dynamics is a synchronous protocol where at each time step every node picks h random neighbors (including itself and with repetition) and recolors itself according to some deterministic rule that depends only on the colors it sees. Let $\mathcal{D}_h(k)$ be the class of h-dynamics and observe that a dynamics $\mathcal{P} \in \mathcal{D}_h$ can be specified by a function*

$$f : [k]^h \to [k]$$

such that $f(x_1, \ldots, x_h) \in \{x_1, \ldots, x_h\}$. Where $f(x_1, \ldots, x_h)$ is the color chosen by a node that sees the (ordered) sequence $(x_1, \ldots, x_h)$ of colors.

In the class $\mathcal{D}_3(k)$, there is a subset $\mathcal{M}^3$ of equivalent protocols called 3-majority dynamics having two key-properties described below: the clear-majority and the uniform one.

DEFINITION 4.4 (CLEAR-MAJORITY PROPERTY). *Let $(x_1, x_2, x_3) \in [k]^3$ be a triple of colors. We say that (x_1, x_2, x_3) has a clear majority if at least two of the three entries have the same value. A dynamics $\mathcal{P} \in \mathcal{D}_3(k)$ has the clear-majority property if whenever its f sees a clear majority it returns the majority color.*

Given any 3-input dynamics function $f(x_1, x_2, x_3)$, for any triple of distinct colors $r, g, b \in [k]$, let $\Pi(r, g, b)$ be the subset of permutations of the colors r, g, b and define the following "counters":

$$
\begin{aligned}
\delta_r &= |\{(z_1, z_2, z_3) \in \Pi(r, g, b), \ s.t. \ f(z_1, z_2, z_3) = r\}| \\
\delta_g &= |\{(z_1, z_2, z_3) \in \Pi(r, g, b), \ s.t. \ f(z_1, z_2, z_3) = g\}| \\
\delta_b &= |\{(z_1, z_2, z_3) \in \Pi(r, g, b), \ s.t. \ f(z_1, z_2, z_3) = b\}|
\end{aligned}
$$

Observe that for any 3-inputs dynamics it must hold $\delta_g + \delta_r + \delta_b = 6$.

DEFINITION 4.5 (UNIFORM PROPERTY). *A dynamics $\mathcal{P} \in \mathcal{D}_3(k)$ has the uniform property if, for any triple of distinct colors $r, g, b \in [k]$, it holds that $\delta_r = \delta_g = \delta_b \ (= 2)$.*

Informally speaking, the clear-majority and the uniform properties provide a clean characterization of those dynamics that are good solvers for plurality consensus. This fact is formalized in the next definitions and in the final theorem.

DEFINITION 4.6 (3-MAJORITY DYNAMICS). *A protocol $\mathcal{P} \in \mathcal{D}_3(k)$ belongs to the class $\mathcal{M}^3 \subset \mathcal{D}_3(k)$ of 3-majority dynamics if its function $f(x_1, x_2, x_3)$ has the clear-majority and the uniform properties.*

DEFINITION 4.7 ((s, ε)-PLURALITY CONSENSUS SOLVER). *We say that a protocol $\mathcal{P}$ is an (s, ε)-solver (for the plurality consensus problem) if for every initial s-biased coloring $\bar{c}$, when running $\mathcal{P}$, with probability at least $1 - \varepsilon$ there is a time step t by which all nodes gets the plurality color of c.*

Let us observe that, by definition of h-dynamics, any monochromatic configuration is an absorbing state of the relative Markovian process. Moreover, the smaller s and ε the better an (s, ε)-solver is; in other words, if a dynamics is an (s, ε)-solver then it is also an (s', ε')-solver for every $s' \geqslant s$ and $\varepsilon' \geqslant \varepsilon$. In Section 3, we showed that any dynamics in $\mathcal{M}^3$ is a $\left(\Theta(\sqrt{\min\{2k, (n/\log n)^{1/3}\}} n \log n), \Theta(1/n) \right)$-solver in $\mathcal{D}_3$. We can now state the main result of this section.

THEOREM 4.8 (PROPERTIES FOR GOOD SOLVERS). *(a) If a protocol $\mathcal{P}$ is an $(n/4, 1/4)$-solver in $\mathcal{D}_3$ then its f must have the clear-majority property.*

(b) A constant $\eta > 0$ exists such that, if $\mathcal{P}$ is an $(\eta \cdot n, 1/4)$-solver, then its f must have the uniform property.

The above theorem also provides the clear reason why some dynamics can solve consensus but cannot solve plurality consensus in the non-binary case. A relevant example is the *median* dynamics studied in [7]: it has the clear-majority property but not the uniform one.

For readability sake, we split the proof of the above theorem in two technical lemmas: in the first one, we show the first claim about clear majority while in the second lemma we show the second claim about the uniform property.

LEMMA 4.9 (CLEAR MAJORITY). *If a protocol $\mathcal{P} \in \mathcal{D}_3$ is an $(n/4, 1/4)$-solver, then it chooses the majority color every time there is a triple with a clear majority.*

PROOF. For every triple of colors $(x_1, x_2, x_3) \in [k]^3$ that has a clear majority, let us define $\delta(x_1, x_2, x_3)$ to be 1 if protocol $\mathcal{P}$ behaves like the majority protocol over triple (x_1, x_2, x_3) and 0 otherwise. Consider an initial configuration with only two colors, say red (r) and blue (b), with c_r red nodes and $c_b = n - c_r$ blue nodes. Let us define Δ_r and Δ_b as follows

$$\Delta_r = \delta(r, r, b) + \delta(r, b, r) + \delta(b, r, r)$$
$$\Delta_b = \delta(b, b, r) + \delta(b, r, b) + \delta(r, b, b)$$

We can write the probability that a node chooses color red as

$$
\begin{aligned}
p(r) &= \left(\frac{c_r}{n}\right)^3 + \left(\frac{c_r}{n}\right)^2 \frac{c_b}{n} \cdot \Delta_r + \left(\frac{c_b}{n}\right)^2 \frac{c_r}{n} (3 - \Delta_b) \\
&= \frac{c_r}{n^3} \left(c_r^2 + c_b (c_r \Delta_r - c_b \Delta_b) + 3 c_b^2 \right)
\end{aligned} \tag{7}
$$

Observe that for a majority protocol we have that $\Delta_r = \Delta_b = 3$. In what follows we show that if this is not the case then there are configurations where the majority color does not increase in expectation. We distinguish two cases, case $\Delta_r \neq \Delta_b$ and case $\Delta_r = \Delta_b$.

Case $\Delta_r \neq \Delta_b$: Suppose w.l.o.g. that $\Delta_r < \Delta_b$, and observe that since they have integer values it means $\Delta_r \leqslant \Delta_b - 1$. Now we show that, if we start from a coloring where the red color has the majority of nodes, the number of red nodes decreases in expectation. By using $\Delta_r \leqslant \Delta_b - 1$ in (7) we get

$$p(r) \leqslant \frac{c_r}{n^3} \left(c_r^2 + c_b(c_r - c_b)\Delta_b - c_r c_b + 3 c_b^2 \right) \tag{8}$$

If the majority of nodes is red then $c_r - c_b$ is positive, and since Δ_b can be at most 3 from (8) we get

$$p(r) \leqslant \frac{c_r}{n^3} \left(c_r^2 + 2 c_r c_b \right) \tag{9}$$

Finally, if we put $c_r = n/2 + s$ and $c_b = n/2 - s$, for some positive s, in (9), we get that

$$p(r) \leqslant \frac{c_r}{n^3} \left(\frac{3}{4} n^2 + (n - s)s \right) \leqslant \frac{c_r}{n} \tag{10}$$

Case $\Delta_r = \Delta_b$: When $\Delta_r = \Delta_b$, observe that if the protocol is not a majority protocol then it must be $\Delta_r = \Delta_b \leqslant 2$. Hence, if we start again from a configuration where $c_r \geqslant c_b$, from (7) we get that

$$p(r) \leqslant \frac{c_r}{n^3} \left(c_r^2 + 2 c_b(c_r - c_b) + 3 c_b^2 \right) = \frac{c_r}{n} \tag{11}$$

In both cases, for any protocol $\mathcal{P}$ that does not behave like a majority protocol on triples with a clear majority, if we name X_t the random variable indicating the number of red nodes at time t, from (10) and (11) we get that $\mathbf{E}\left[X_{t+1} \mid X_t\right] \leqslant X_t$, hence X_t is a supermartingale. Now let τ be the random variable indicating the first time the chain hits one of the two absorbing states, i.e.

$$\tau = \inf\{t \in \mathbb{N} : X_t \in \{0, n\}\}$$

Since $\mathbf{P}\left(\tau < \infty\right) = 1$ and all X_t's have values bounded between 0 and n, from the martingale stopping theorem[4] we get that $\mathbf{E}\left[X_\tau\right] \leqslant \mathbf{E}\left[X_0\right]$. If we start from a configuration that is $n/4$-unbalanced in favor of the red color, we have that $X_0 = n/2 + n/8$, and if we call ε is the probability that the process ends up with all blue nodes we have that $\mathbf{E}\left[X_\tau\right] = (1 - \varepsilon)n$. Hence it must be $(1 - \varepsilon)n \leqslant n/2 + n/8$ and the probability to end up with all blue nodes is $\varepsilon \geqslant 5/8 > 1/4$. Thus the protocol is not a $(n/4, 1/4)$-solver. $\square$

LEMMA 4.10 (UNIFORM PROPERTY). *A constant $\eta > 0$ exists such that, if $\mathcal{P}$ is an $(\eta n, 1/4)$-solver, then its f must have the uniform property.*

PROOF. Thanks to the previous lemma, we can assume that f has the clear-majority property but a triple (r, g, b) exists such that $\delta_r < \max\{\delta_g, \delta_b\}$. Let us start the process with the following initial configuration having only the above 3 colors and then show that the process w.h.p. will not converge to the plurality color r.

$$\bar{c} = (c_r, c_g, c_b),$$
$$\text{where } c_r = \frac{n}{3} + s, \ c_g = n/3, \ c_b = \frac{n}{3} - s$$
$$\text{with } s = \Theta(\sqrt{n \log n})$$

We consider the "hardest" case where $\delta_r = 1$: the case $\delta_r = 0$ is simpler since in this case, no matter how the other $\delta's$ are distributed, it is easy to see that the r.v. c_r will decrease exponentially to 0 starting from the above configuration.

- **Case $\delta_r = 1$, $\delta_g = 3$, and $\delta_b = 2$** (and color-symmetric cases). Starting from the above initial configuration, we can compute the probability $p(r) = \mathbf{P}\left(X_v = r \mid C = \bar{c}\right)$ that a node gets the color r.

$$
\begin{aligned}
p(r) &= \left(\frac{c_r}{n}\right)^3 + 3 \left(\frac{c_r}{n}\right)^2 \frac{n - c_r}{n} + \frac{c_r c_g c_b}{n^3} \\
&= \frac{n + 3s}{3n^3} \left(\left(\frac{n}{3} + s\right)^2 + 3 \left(\frac{n}{3} + s\right) \left(\frac{2}{3} n - s\right) + \left(\frac{n}{3}\right) \left(\frac{n}{3} - s\right) \right)
\end{aligned}
$$

After some easy calculations, we get

$$p(r) = \frac{8}{27} \left(1 + O\left(\frac{s}{n}\right) \right)$$

As for $p(g)$, by similar calculations, we obtain the following bound

---

[4]See e.g. Chapter 17 in [13] for a summary of martingales and related results

254

$$p(g) = \frac{10}{27}\left(1 - O\left(\frac{s^2}{n^2}\right)\right)$$

From the above two equations, we get the following bounds on the expectation of the r.v.'s X^r and X^g counting the nodes colored with r and g, respectively (at the next time step).

$$\mathbb{E}\left[X^r \mid C = \bar{c}\right] \leqslant \frac{8}{27}\,n + O(s) \quad\text{and}$$

$$\mathbb{E}\left[X^g \mid C = \bar{c}\right] \geqslant \frac{10}{27}\,n - O\left(\frac{s^2}{n}\right)$$

By a standard application of Chernoff's Bound, we can prove that, if $s \leqslant \eta n$ for a sufficiently small $\eta > 0$, the initial value c_r will w.h.p. decreases by a constant factor, going much below the new plurality c_g. Then, by applying iteratively the above reasoning we get that the process will not converge to r, w.h.p.

- **Case** $\delta_r = 1$, $\delta_g = 4$, **and** $\delta_b = 1$ (and color-symmetric cases). In this case it is even simpler to show that w.h.p., starting from the same initial configuration considered in the previous case, the process will not converge to color r. $\square$

4.3 A lower bound for h-plurality

In Subsection 4.1, we have shown that the 3-majority protocol takes $\Theta(k \log n)$ time steps w.h.p. to converge in the worst case. A natural question is whether by using the h-plurality protocol, with h slightly larger than 3, it is possible to significantly speed-up the process. We prove that this is not the case.

Let us consider a set of n nodes, each node colored with one out of k colors. The h-plurality protocol works as follows:

> At every time step, every node picks h nodes uniformly at random (including itself and with repetitions) and recolors itself according to the plurality of the colors it sees (breaking ties u.a.r.)

Let $j \in [k]$ be an arbitrary color, in the next lemma we prove that, if the number of j-colored nodes is smaller than $2n/k$ and if $k/h = \mathcal{O}(n^{(1-\varepsilon)/4})$, then the probability that the number of j-nodes increases by a factor $(1 + \Theta(h^2/k))$ is exponentially small.

LEMMA 4.11. *Let $j \in [k]$ be a color and let X_t be the random variable counting the number of j-colored nodes at time t. If $k/h = \mathcal{O}(n^{(1-\varepsilon)/4})$, then for every $(n/k) \leqslant a \leqslant 2(n/k)$ it holds that*

$$\mathbf{P}\left(X_{t+1} \geqslant \left(1 + \frac{h^2}{k}\right)a \mid X_t = a\right) \leqslant e^{-\Theta(n^\varepsilon)}$$

PROOF. Consider a specific node, say $u \in [n]$, let N_j be the number of j-colored nodes picked by u during the sampling stage of the t-th time step and let Y be the indicator random variable of the event that node u chooses color j at time step $t+1$. We give an upper bound on the probability of the event $Y = 1$ by conditioning it on $N_j = 1$ and $N_j \geqslant 2$ (observe that if $N_j = 0$ node u cannot choose j as its color at the next time step)

$$\mathbf{P}\left(Y_u = 1\right) \leqslant \mathbf{P}\left(Y_u = 1 \mid N_j = 1\right)\mathbf{P}\left(N_j = 1\right) + \mathbf{P}\left(N_j \geqslant 2\right) \tag{12}$$

Now observe that

- $\mathbf{P}\left(Y_u = 1 \mid N_j(u) = 1\right) \leqslant 1/h$ since it is exactly $1/h$ if all other sampled nodes have distinct colors and it is 0 otherwise;

- $\mathbf{P}\left(N_j = 1\right) \leqslant h\frac{a}{n}$ since it can be bounded by the probability that at least one of the h samples gives color j;

- $\mathbf{P}\left(N_j \geqslant 2\right) \leqslant \binom{h}{2}\frac{a^2}{n^2}$ since it is the probability that a pair of sampled nodes exist with the same color j.

Hence, in (12) we have that

$$\mathbf{P}\left(Y = 1\right) \leqslant \frac{a}{n} + \frac{h^2}{2}\cdot\frac{a^2}{n^2}$$

Thus, for the expected number of j-colored nodes at the next time step we get

$$\mathbf{E}\left[X_{t+1} \mid X_t = a\right] \leqslant a + \frac{h^2}{2n}a^2 = a\left(1 + \frac{h^2}{2n}a\right) \leqslant a\left(1 + \frac{h^2}{k}\right)$$

where in the last inequality we used the hypothesis $a \leqslant 2(n/k)$. Since X_{t+1} is a sum of n independent Bernoulli random variables, from Chernoff bound (Lemma A.1 with $\lambda = ah^2/k$) we finally get

$$\mathbf{P}\left(X_{t+1} \geqslant a\left(1 + 2\frac{h^2}{k}\right) \mid X_t = a\right) \leqslant \exp\left(-\frac{2(ah^2/k)^2}{n}\right)$$
$$\leqslant \exp\left(-\Omega(n^\varepsilon)\right)$$

where in the last inequality we used $a \geqslant n/k$ and $k/h = \mathcal{O}(n^{(1-\varepsilon)/4})$. $\square$

By adopting a similar argument to that used for proving Theorem 4.2, we can get a lower bound $\Omega(k/h^2)$ on the completion time of the h-plurality.

THEOREM 4.12. *Let $\mathbf{C}_t$ be the random variable indicating the coloring at time t according to the h-plurality protocol and let $\tau = \inf\{t \in \mathbb{N} : \mathbf{C}_t \text{ is monochromatic}\}$. If the initial coloring is $\mathbf{C}_0 = (c_1, \dots, c_k)$ with $\max\{c_j : j = 1, \dots, k\} \leqslant \frac{3}{2}\cdot\frac{n}{k}$ then $\tau = \Omega(k/h^2)$ w.h.p.*

PROOF. Since in the initial coloring the plurality color has $a \leqslant (3/2)(n/k)$ nodes, from Lemma 4.11 it follows that the number of nodes supporting the plurality color increases at a rate smaller than $(1 + 2h^2/k)$ with probability exponentially close to 1. This easily implies a recursive relation of the form $X_{t+1} \leqslant (1 + 2h^2/k)X_t$ which, in turn, gives

$$X_t \leqslant \left(1 + 2h^2/k\right)^t X_0 \leqslant \left(1 + 2h^2/k\right)^t \frac{3}{2}\cdot\frac{n}{k}$$

We thus have that

$$(3/2)\left(1 + \frac{2h^2}{k}\right)^t \leqslant 2 \quad\text{for}\quad t \leqslant \frac{k}{h^2}\log(4/3)$$

$\square$

5. OPEN QUESTIONS

A general open question on the plurality consensus problem is whether an *efficient* dynamics exists that achieves plurality consensus in polylogarithmic time for any function $k = k(n)$. By *efficient* dynamics for our adopted model, we mean any dynamics that requires small (i.e. $\mathcal{O}(\log n)$) memory, small random samples, and small message size.

A more specific question about our simple distributed model is to explore the case in which the initial bias s is smaller than the lower bound assumed in our analysis (i.e. $s \geqslant c\sqrt{\min\{2k, (n/\log n)^{1/3}\} n \log n}$). Notice that when k is polylogarithmic, we required a bias which is only a polylogarithmic factor larger than the standard deviation $\Omega(\sqrt{n})$: the latter is a lower bound for the initial bias to converge (w.h.p.) to the plurality color. As for larger k, we cannot derive any stronger bound on the required bias, however, in the full-version of the paper [4], we show that there are initial configurations with bias $s = \mathcal{O}(\sqrt{kn})$ for which the initial bias *decreases* in a single round with constant probability. This result implies that, when the initial bias s is "slightly" smaller than "ours", the process may be *non-monotone* w.r.t. the bias function $s(t)$. On the contrary, the fact that $s(t)$ is an increasing function played a key-role in the proof of our upper bound. So, under such a weaker assumption, if any upper bound similar to ours might be proved then a much more complex argument (departing from ours) seems to be necessary.

In this work, we were mainly interested in deriving sufficient conditions under which the h-plurality dynamics converges in polylogarithmic time. A further interesting open question is to derive conditions on the parameters k, s, and h under which this dynamics converges very fast, i.e., in sublogarithmic time.

6. REFERENCES

[1] M. A. Abdullah and M. Draief. Majority consensus on random graphs of a given degree sequence. *arXiv:1209.5025*, 2012.

[2] D. Angluin, J. Aspnes, and D. Eisenstat. A simple population protocol for fast robust approximate majority. In *Proc. of 21st DISC*, volume 4731 of *LNCS*, pages 20–32. Springer, 2007.

[3] A. Babaee and M. Draief. Distributed multivalued consensus. In *Computer and Information Sciences III*, pages 271–279. Springer, 2013.

[4] L. Becchetti, A. Clementi, E. Natale, F. Pasquale, R. Silvestri, and L. Trevisan. Simple dynamics for plurality consensus. *arXiv:1310.2858*, 2013.

[5] F. Bénézit, P. Thiran, and M. Vetterli. Interval consensus: from quantized gossip to voting. In *Proc. of ICASSP*, pages 3661–3664. IEEE, 2009.

[6] A. Clementi, M. Di Ianni, G. Gambosi, E. Natale, and R. Silvestri. Distributed community detection in dynamic graphs. In *SIROCCO*. Springer, 2013.

[7] B. Doerr, L. A. Goldberg, L. Minder, T. Sauerwald, and C. Scheideler. Stabilizing consensus with the power of two choices. In *Proc. of 23rd SPAA*, pages 149–158. ACM, 2011.

[8] M. Draief and M. Vojnovic. Convergence speed of binary interval consensus. *SIAM J. on Control and Optimization*, 50(3):1087–1109, 2012.

[9] D. P. Dubhashi and A. Panconesi. *Concentration of measure for the analysis of randomized algorithms*. Cambridge University Press, 2009.

[10] D. Easley and J. Kleinberg. *Networks, Crowds, and Markets*. Cambridge University Press, 2010.

[11] M. Kearns and J. Tan. Biased voting and the democratic primary problem. In *Proc. of 4th WINE*, volume 5385 of *LNCS*, pages 639–652. Springer, 2008.

[12] M. W. S. Land and R. K. Belew. No two-state ca for density classification exists. *Phys. Rev. Letters*, 74(25):5148–5150, 1995.

[13] D. Levin, Y. Peres, and E. L. Wilmer. *Markov Chains and Mixing Times*. AMS, 2008.

[14] E. Mossel, J. Neeman, and O. Tamuz. Majority dynamics and aggregation of information in social networks. *Autonomous Agents and Multi-Agent Systems*, 28(3):408–429, 2014.

[15] E. Mossel and G. Schoenebeck. Reaching consensus on social networks. In *Proc. of ICS*, pages 214–229. Tsinghua University Press, 2010.

[16] D. Peleg. Local majorities, coalitions and monopolies in graphs: a review. *Theor. Comput. Sci.*, 282(2), 2002.

[17] E. Perron, D. Vasudevan, and M. Vojnovic. Using three states for binary consensus on complete graphs. In *Proc. of INFOCOM*, pages 2527–2535. IEEE, 2009.

APPENDIX

A. USEFUL BOUNDS

LEMMA A.1 (CHERNOFF BOUNDS). *Let* $X = \sum_{i=1}^{n} X_i$ *where* X_i's *are independent Bernoulli random variables and let* $\mu = \mathbf{E}[X]$. *Then,*

1. *For any* $0 < \delta \leqslant 4$, $\mathbf{P}(X > (1+\delta)\mu) < e^{-\frac{\delta^2 \mu}{4}}$;

2. *For any* $\delta \geqslant 4$, $\mathbf{P}(X > (1+\delta)\mu) < e^{-\delta\mu}$;

3. *For any* $\lambda > 0$, $\mathbf{P}(X \geqslant \mu + \lambda) \leqslant e^{-2\lambda^2/n}$.

LEMMA A.2 (JENSEN INEQUALITY). *Let* $\phi : \mathbb{R} \to \mathbb{R}$ *be a convex function and* $x_1, \ldots x_k \in \mathbb{R}$ *be* k *real numbers, then*

$$\phi\left(\frac{1}{k}\sum_{i=1}^{k} x_i\right) \leqslant \frac{1}{k}\sum_{i=1}^{k}\phi(x_i)$$

LEMMA A.3 (BERNSTEIN INEQUALITY [9]). *Let the random variables* $X_1, \ldots, X_n$ *be independent with* $X_i - \mathbb{E}[X_i] \leqslant b$ *for each* $i \in [n]$. *Let* $X = \sum_i X_i$ *and let* $\sigma^2 = \sum_i \sigma_i^2$ *be the variance of* X. *Then, for any* $\lambda > 0$,

$$\mathbf{P}(X > \mathbb{E}[X] + \lambda) \leqslant \exp\left(-\frac{\lambda^2}{2\sigma^2(1 + b\lambda/3\sigma^2)}\right)$$

We now provide a useful result on finite Markov chains. The proof is given in the full-version [4].

LEMMA A.4. *Let* $\{X_t\}_t$ *be a finite-state Markov chain with state space* S. *If* $A_1, \ldots, A_T$ *are such that* $S \supseteq A_1 \supseteq A_2 \supseteq \cdots \supseteq A_T$ *and, for any* $i = 1, \ldots, T$, $\mathbf{P}(X_t \in A_i \mid X_{t-1} \in A_i) \geqslant 1 - \epsilon$ *and for* $i < T$, $\mathbf{P}(X_t \in A_{i+1} \mid X_{t-1} \in A_i) \geqslant 1 - \nu$ *where* $0 \leqslant \epsilon \leqslant \nu < 1$, *then, for any integer* $\ell \geqslant 1$ *it holds that*

$$\mathbf{P}(X_{\ell T} \in A_T \mid X_0 \in A_1) \geqslant 1 - T(\ell\epsilon + \nu^\ell)$$

(Near) Optimal Resource-Competitive Broadcast with Jamming

[Extended Abstract]

Seth Gilbert*
Dept. of Computer Science
National Univ. of Singapore
Singapore
seth.gilbert@comp.nus.edu.sg

Valerie King
Dept. of Computer Science
University of Victoria
Victoria, BC, Canada
val@cs.uvic.ca

Seth Pettie †
Dept. of Electrical Engineering
and Computer Science
University of Michigan
Ann Arbor, MI, USA
pettie@umich.edu

Ely Porat
Dept. of Computer Science
Bar-Ilan University
Ramat Gan, Israel
porately@cs.biu.ac.il

Jared Saia‡
Dept. of Computer Science
University of New Mexico
Albuquerque, NM, USA
saia@cs.unm.edu

Maxwell Young‡
Dept. of Computing
Drexel University
Philadelphia, PA, USA
myoung@cs.drexel.edu

ABSTRACT

We consider the problem of broadcasting a message from a sender to $n \geq 1$ receivers in a time-slotted, single-hop, wireless network with a single communication channel. Sending and listening dominate the energy usage of small wireless devices and this is abstracted as a unit cost per time slot. A jamming adversary exists who can disrupt the channel at unit cost per time slot, and aims to prevent the transmission of the message. Let T be the number of slots jammed by the adversary. Our goal is to design algorithms whose cost is *resource-competitive*, that is, whose per-device cost is a function, preferably $o(T)$, of the adversary's cost. Devices must work with limited knowledge. The values n, T, and the adversary's jamming strategy are unknown.

For 1-to-1 communication, we provide an algorithm with an expected cost of $O(\sqrt{T \ln(1/\epsilon)} + \ln(1/\epsilon))$, which succeeds with probability at least $1 - \epsilon$ for any tunable parameter $\epsilon > 0$. For 1-to-n broadcast, we provide a very different algorithm that succeeds with high probability and yields an expected cost per device of $O(\sqrt{T/n} \log^4 T + \log^6 n)$. Therefore, the bigger the system, the better advantage achieved over the adversary!

We complement our upper bounds with *tight or nearly tight lower bounds*. We prove that any 1-to-1 communication algorithm with
constant probability of success has expected cost $\Omega(\sqrt{T})$. For 1-to-n broadcast we show that some node has cost $\Omega(\sqrt{T/n})$. Finally, we consider a more powerful adversary that can spoof messages from the receiver, rather than just jam the channel. We prove that any 1-to-1 communication algorithm in this model has expected cost $\Omega(T^{\varphi-1})$, where $\varphi = \frac{1+\sqrt{5}}{2}$ is the golden ratio. This matches an earlier upper bound of King, Saia, and Young.

Categories and Subject Descriptors

C.2.1 [**Computer Communications Networks**]: Network Architecture and Design—*Wireless communication*; F.2.2 [**Analysis of Algorithms and Problem Complexity**]: Nonnumerical Algorithms and Problems—*Routing and layout*

Keywords

Distributed algorithms; theory; resource competitive; attack resistance; jamming; wireless sensor networks

1. INTRODUCTION

The nature of the wireless medium allows malicious devices to threaten the availability of a network by disrupting communication. Such *jamming attacks* have been demonstrated empirically [4, 7] and they challenge the security of sensor networks, future wireless technologies such as the Michigan Micro-Mote [24], SPECK-NET [38], and amorphous computing [1, 12].

Wireless devices (*nodes*) are typically battery-powered and once this energy supply is exhausted, replacement may be impossible. How can energy-starved devices defend themselves against a powerful jamming adversary? Gilbert et al. [20] formalized a model of *resource-competitiveness* to deal with problems of this nature. Both the nodes *and* the adversary possess a common resource (energy, in this case) and the goal is to design algorithms whose resource consumption grows asymptotically slower than that of the adversary's. The model is summarized below.

1.1 Resource-Competitiveness

An implicit assumption in many models is that malicious (bad) nodes incur zero cost for attacking. However, this premise is false since attacking requires the expenditure of network resources such

*This research is supported in part by the Agency for Science, Technology and Research (A*STAR), Singapore, under SERC Grant 1224104049.

†This research is supported by NSF grants CCF-1217338 and CNS-1318294 and a grant from the US-Israel Binational Science Foundation. Part of this work was performed at the MADALGO center at Aarhus University, supported by the Danish National Research Foundation grant no. DNRF84.

‡This research is supported by NSF grant CNS-1318294.

as bandwidth, computation, or energy. In wireless networks populated by battery-powered devices, an algorithm's performance can be measured by the relative energy costs inflicted upon both the good and bad nodes. If the costs to the latter are disproportionately high, then sustained attacks are not feasible since the bad nodes will rapidly deplete their onboard energy supply; the bad nodes are effectively *bankrupted*.

We now formally define what it means for a distributed algorithm $\mathcal{A}$ to be *resource competitive*; this was recently proposed in [20]. Assume a system of n nodes where node v is classified as either *good*, if its actions are prescribed by $\mathcal{A}$, or *bad* if otherwise. Define G as the set of good nodes and F as the set of bad nodes. We assume that the bad nodes may collude and coordinate their attacks; to this end, we assume they are controlled by a single adversary.

Let $\mathcal{C}(i)$ denote the energy expenditure incurred by node i over an execution of algorithm $\mathcal{A}$. If node i is good, then $\mathcal{C}(i)$ is node i's cost for executing the actions prescribed by $\mathcal{A}$. Otherwise, node i is bad and $\mathcal{C}(i)$ is node i's cost for pursuing an arbitrary strategy. Let $T = \sum_{j \in F} \mathcal{C}(j)$ be the total cost to the adversary. That is, T is what the adversary spends in trying to disrupt the network, and we assume that T is *unknown* to the good nodes. Let ρ be a function of T, and possibly other parameters like n; call this the *cost function*. Let τ be a function of any variables except T; call this the *efficiency function*. Algorithm $\mathcal{A}$ is *resource competitive* if it guarantees $\max_{i \in G} \{\mathcal{C}(i)\} = O(\rho + \tau)$.

The cost function ρ intuitively captures the relative performance between good nodes and the adversary when $T > 0$. Clearly, *a small ρ is desirable* and, in many cases, we can achieve a function ρ that is *asymptotically* smaller than T (i.e. $o(T)$). However, when $T = 0$, the efficiency function τ captures the unavoidable cost to attain a goal even in the absence of attack. Efficiency in the absence of an attack is important since an algorithm that is costly even when $T = 0$ is undesirable; therefore, τ should also be small (i.e. $O(1)$ or, for large systems of n nodes, $O(\text{polylog } n)$). It is useful to make this separation between the cases $T > 0$ and $T = 0$ explicit via defining these two functions.

1.2 Network Model

Time is divided into discrete *slots* and a node incurs a cost of 1 for sending or listening per slot. If not sending/listening, a node is assumed to be in the energy-efficient sleep state, which has zero cost. This aligns with the operational costs of current devices, which are dominated by transceiver (*radio*) usage [31].

The adversary represents all bad nodes (who may collude and coordinate their attacks if they wish) and pursues an arbitrary jamming strategy. Her energy budget is finite but *unknown* to the (good) nodes. The adversary is *adaptive*: she knows the actions of all nodes in previous time slots and uses this information to inform future attacks. While we consider malicious attacks, in practice the adversary may also represent an abstraction for noise due to collisions, fading effects, or other non-malicious interference.

An *ℓ-uniform adversary* may partition n nodes into at most $1 \leq \ell \leq n$ sets, each of which experiences a different jamming schedule (see [34]). For 1-to-1 communication, we consider a powerful 2-uniform adversary and assume that both devices can be authenticated, i.e., the adversary cannot spoof messages from either device. For 1-to-n communication, we consider a 1-uniform adversary and only assume that the message m can be authenticated. This is a partially-authenticated model where only a *single public key* (the original sender's key) is known. For more on authentication in practice, see [22, 39]. Therefore, the adversary cannot modify m without this being detected and ignored, and we omit further discussion of this in our analysis. Critically, authentication does not imply the existence of shared secrets between nodes.

When two or more messages are sent in the same slot, a message collision occurs and a good node who is listening receives only noise. In practice, noise is detected via *clear channel assessment (CCA)* [33]. When a node hears noise, it cannot tell whether this noise is the result of jamming or due to legitimate messages colliding. A slot is *clear* if it contains neither noise nor any message.

The adversary is assumed to know our protocols except for any random bits generated in the current slot. We adopt the standard assumption that each node can generate independent random bits. The use of randomness in wireless sensor networks is common in the literature (for example [6, 26, 34–36]) and underlies the analysis of frequency hopping spread-spectrum techniques (see [25, 28]) and standard backoff protocols (see [8] and references therein). In practice, the research community has developed functionality along these lines in [17, 37]. Furthermore, without any randomness, an adversary can easily force a cost of $T + 1$ since sending and listening will be deterministic.

1.3 Main Results

We address fundamental communication problems and provide algorithms that are optimally or near optimally resource competitive. Our algorithms are randomized and each has some small probability of failure. We say an event holds *with high probability* (or w.h.p.) if its probability is at least $1 - \frac{1}{\max\{n^c, T^c\}}$ for some tunable constant $c > 0$. Throughout, n is unknown to the good nodes. Let T be the number of slots the adversary jams (this is also unknown to the good nodes). Our results are as follows.

THEOREM 1. *Assume a 2-uniform adaptive adversary. Let $\epsilon > 0$ be a (small) tunable parameter and assume that both Alice (the sender of m) and Bob (the receiver) can be authenticated. There exists an algorithm for 1-to-1 communication with the following guarantees.*

- *Bob receives m with probability at least $1 - \epsilon$.*

- *Alice and Bob incur an expected cost of $O(\sqrt{T \ln(1/\epsilon)} + \ln(1/\epsilon))$.*

- *Alice and Bob terminate within an expected $O(T)$ slots, which is asymptotically optimal.*

Therefore, when Bob can be authenticated, we improve on the (Las Vegas) algorithm of [23] with expected cost $O(T^{\varphi-1} + 1) = O(T^{0.62} + 1)$, where φ is the golden ratio. By combining both algorithms one can achieve expected cost $O(\min\{\sqrt{T \log(1/\epsilon)} + \log(1/\epsilon), T^{\varphi-1} + 1\})$, that is, one with no dependence on ϵ when $T = 0$. We show that Theorem 1 is asymptotically optimal for constant error rate ϵ.

THEOREM 2. *Consider any 1-to-1 communication algorithm in which Alice sends a message to Bob with probability $1 - \epsilon$ for any constant $\epsilon > 0$. Let A and B be Alice's and Bob's costs, respectively. A 1-uniform adaptive adversary can force $\mathrm{E}(A) \cdot \mathrm{E}(B) > (1 - O(\epsilon))T$. In particular, $\max\{\mathrm{E}(A), \mathrm{E}(B)\} = \Omega(\sqrt{T})$.*

A natural problem is to communicate a message m from a source node to all n nodes in the system. While a cost of roughly $O(\sqrt{T})$ (in expectation) can be obtained via an extension of Theorem 1, we achieve a much more powerful result.

THEOREM 3. *Assume a 1-uniform adaptive adversary and assume m can be authenticated. There exists an algorithm for 1-to-n communication with the following guarantees:*

- *The cost to each node is $O\left(\sqrt{\frac{T}{n}} \cdot \log^4 T + \log^6 n\right)$ w.h.p.*

- *All nodes terminate in $O(T + n\log^2 n)$ time slots, w.h.p. This latency is optimal as a function of T.*

Therefore, the expected resource costs incurred by good nodes decrease as n grows! Define a *fair* algorithm to be one where all nodes have the same expected cost. To within a polylogarithmic factor, the cost function in Theorem 3 is asymptotically optimal.

THEOREM 4. *Assume a 1-uniform adaptive adversary. Any fair algorithm that achieves 1-to-n communication with constant probability of failure imposes a cost of $\Omega(\sqrt{T/n})$ per node.*

Theorem 1 holds when messages from Alice and Bob can be authenticated, and Theorem 3 holds when only m can be authenticated. We prove that giving the adversary the power to spoof messages from Bob actually changes the asymptotic complexity of 1-1 communication. The bound in Theorem 5 matches an algorithm of King, Saia, and Young [23].

THEOREM 5. *Consider a 1-to-1 communication protocol such that Alice sends a message to Bob with constant probability of failure, given a 2-uniform adaptive adversary who can spoof messages from Bob. In any such protocol, the expected cost to either Alice or Bob is $\Omega(T^{\varphi-1})$ where $\varphi = \frac{1+\sqrt{5}}{2}$ is the golden ratio.*

1.4 Related Work

King et al. [23] provide a Las Vegas resource-competitive algorithm for 1-to-1 communication with an expected cost of $O(T^{\varphi-1} + 1) = O(T^{0.62} + 1)$ where $\varphi = \frac{\sqrt{5}+1}{2}$ is the golden ratio. The accompanying 1-to-n broadcast algorithm in [23] requires that $\log n$ is *known* and a cost of roughly $T^{\varphi-1} \log n$; therefore, the performance of this algorithm *worsens as n increases*. Gilbert and Young [21] give a Monte Carlo 1-to-n partial broadcast algorithm with a better cost ratio. However, the result critically depends on knowing n (not just $\log n$) and still allows the adversary to prevent a small, but constant, fraction of the nodes from receiving the broadcast. Our results address these previous shortcomings by obtaining a cost ratio that improves as n increases without having any information about n, and informing all nodes with high probability.

Much of the work on mitigating jamming attacks focuses on heuristics [3, 5, 10, 13, 25, 28, 32, 40]. We only summarize those with worst-case guarantees. Gilbert et al. [19] derive bounds on the duration for which communication can be disrupted between two devices using deterministic protocols. Pelc and Peleg [30] examine an adversary who jams randomly. Koo et al. [9] address a jamming adversary whose energy budget is known. An interesting series of results by Awerbuch et al. [6] and Richa et al. [34–36] address an adversary whose jamming is bounded within any sufficiently large time window; Dams et al. [11] employs distributed-learning algorithms to overcome this same type of windowed-jamming adversary. Alistarh et al. [2] demonstrate non-cryptographic authentication given a jamming adversary. Ogierman et al. [29] study medium access with adversarial jamming under the signal-to-interference-plus-noise ratio (SINR) model. In the case of multiple channels, Dolev et al. [14, 15] and Gilbert et al. [18], and Emek and Wattenhofer [16] examine communication problems when the adversary cannot jam all channels simultaneously, while Meier et al. [26] examine the problem of node discovery.

These previous results provide valuable solutions to challenging attack models, however, many also require nodes to incur significant costs, either due to sending or listening, relative to the adversary, and this aspect may pose problems in the energy-constrained

wireless networks (a few of these results are incomparable given certain model assumption). By taking a resource-competitive approach, we can show that whatever costs are incurred by the nodes are exceeded (asymptotically) by the costs to the adversary.

1.5 Outline

In Sections 2 and 3, we present resource-competitive algorithms for 1-to-1 and 1-to-n broadcast and in Section 4 we give tight or nearly tight lower bounds for these problems.

2. 1-TO-1 COMMUNICATION

Figure 1 provides the pseudocode for 1-to-1 BROADCAST with the canonical players Alice and Bob as sender and receiver, respectively. Let $\epsilon > 0$ be a tunable parameter set prior to execution. The algorithm proceeds in epochs indexed by $i \geq 11 + \lg \ln(8/\epsilon)$, each consisting of a send phase and a nack (negative acknowledgement) phase, each lasting 2^i time slots.[1] We will classify each phase based on the fraction of slots jammed by the adversary.

DEFINITION 1. (*q*-**Blocking**) *The adversary q-blocks a phase if it jams at least a q fraction of the slots, for $0 \leq q \leq 1$. A repetition that is not q-blocked is q-unblocked.*

The rationale for the send phase is clear. According to a birthday paradox argument, if Alice sends in $\Theta(\sqrt{2^i \ln(1/\epsilon)})$ random slots and Bob listens in $\Theta(\sqrt{2^i \ln(1/\epsilon)})$ random slots, then, in the absence of jamming, Alice will transmit m to Bob with probability $1 - \epsilon$ and Bob will halt. To stop transmission of m the adversary must jam Bob for at least a constant fraction of the slots. However, because the adversary is 2-uniform Alice cannot tell if Bob was jammed and therefore does not know if m was transmitted. If Bob has yet to receive m, he sends a nack message back to Alice using the same protocol, which, in the absence of jamming, Alice will correctly receive with probability $1 - \epsilon$. If Alice does not receive a nack (and was not heavily jammed) she assumes Bob received m and already halted; therefore she halts as well. How does Bob know to halt in the event that Alice prematurely halted? If, in a subsequent epoch, Bob hears little jamming and yet does not receive m, he assumes Alice has halted prematurely and halts. In a similar fashion Alice will halt in the nack phase only if she hears little jamming and does not receive a nack.

Adaptive adversaries are difficult to reason about because their choices can be subtly informed by nodes' past behavior. Lemma 1 allows us to focus on a restricted class of adversarial strategies.

LEMMA 1. *Without loss of generality, in any phase all of the un-jammed slots precede all the jammed slots.*

PROOF. Within one phase of epoch i, the behavior of nodes in each slot (whether they send or listen) is independent of their past behavior. The adversary can gain no information from the nodes by jamming, nor can it influence their future behavior by jamming. Thus, an adversary that chooses to jam slot k after leaving slots 1 through $k - 1$ unjammed is equivalent to an adversary that leaves slot k unjammed as well but commits to jamming the last time slot 2^i. In this way all jamming can, without loss of generality, be postponed to a contiguous interval at the end of the phase. □

Lemma 1 shows that we can assume the adversary observes the behavior of all nodes up until a certain point and then *jams for the remainder of the phase*, independent of the nodes' behavior. The point at which such jamming begins is clearly a choice that needs to be made online.

---

[1] We use $\lg x$ to refer to $\log_2 x$.

1-to-1 BROADCAST for epoch $i \geq 11 + \lg \ln(8/\epsilon)$

- Send Phase — For each of the 2^i slots, do:
  - With probability $\sqrt{\frac{\ln(8/\epsilon)}{2^{i-1}}}$, Alice sends m.
  - With probability $\sqrt{\frac{\ln(8/\epsilon)}{2^{i-1}}}$, Bob listens.

- If Bob receives m or hears less than $\frac{\sqrt{2^{i-1}\ln(8/\epsilon)}}{4}$ noisy slots without hearing m, he terminates.

- Nack Phase — For each of the 2^i slots, do:
  - With probability $\sqrt{\frac{\ln(8/\epsilon)}{2^{i-1}}}$, Bob sends nack.
  - With probability $\sqrt{\frac{\ln(8/\epsilon)}{2^{i-1}}}$, Alice listens.

- If Alice hears less than $\frac{\sqrt{2^{i-1}\ln(8/\epsilon)}}{4}$ noisy slots without hearing a nack, she terminates.

Figure 1: Pseudocode for epoch i of 1-to-1 BROADCAST.

PROOF. (Theorem 1) The 1-to-1 BROADCAST algorithm can fail in several ways: Alice or Bob can exceed their energy budgets, as a function of the adversaries cost T; Alice can halt prematurely, before Bob receives m; and Bob can halt prematurely, falsely thinking that Alice has already halted prematurely. We first show that with probability $1 - o(\epsilon)$, Alice's and Bob's costs never exceed twice their expectations, then address halting. Let $i = s + \lg \ln(8/\epsilon)$ be the epoch index, where $s \geq 11$, and let $p_i = \sqrt{\ln(8/\epsilon)/2^{i-1}}$ be the sending/listening probability in epoch i.

Costs: Let X be the actual cost of Alice (or Bob) in epoch i. By linearity of expectation $E(X) \leq p_i(2 \cdot 2^i) = \sqrt{\ln(8/\epsilon)/2^{i-1}} \cdot 2^{i+1} = \sqrt{2^{i+3}\ln(8/\epsilon)}$. By a Chernoff bound the probability that X exceeds twice its expectation is less than $\exp(-E(X)/3)$. The probability that Alice's cost in *any* epoch exceeds twice its expectation is at most $\sum_{i \geq 11 + \lg\ln(8/\epsilon)} \exp\left(-\sqrt{2^{i+3}\ln(8/\epsilon)}/3\right) < \sum_{s \geq 11}(\epsilon/8)^{2^{(s+3)/2}/3} = o(\epsilon)$.

Note that the expected cost to Alice and Bob in phases $11 + \lg\ln(8/\epsilon)$ through i is $O(\sqrt{2^i\ln(1/\epsilon)} + \ln(1/\epsilon))$. If the adversary jams $T = \Omega(2^i)$ slots in phase i then Alice and Bob have spent $O(\sqrt{T\ln(1/\epsilon)} + \ln(1/\epsilon))$, that is, neither will exceed their energy budget through epoch i. For Alice or Bob to exceed their energy budget the adversary must, at the very least, get one or both parties to continue to epoch $i+1$ while jamming $o(2^i)$ slots. By Lemma 1, we can assume the adversary jams a suffix of the 2^i slots, though the moment when she begins jamming can be chosen adaptively, by observing the behavior of Alice and Bob.

Send Phase — Alice is still running: We need to prove two claims. First, any adversarial strategy that stops Alice from transmitting m to Bob with probability $1 - O(\epsilon)$ must jam $\Omega(2^i)$ slots. Second, if the adversary does, in fact, jam $\Omega(2^i)$ slots Bob will not halt (correctly) and proceed to epoch $i + 1$, with high probability. For the first claim, the probability that Alice fails to transmit the message to Bob in the first unjammed $2^i/2$ slots is $(1 - p_i^2)^{2^{i-1}} = \epsilon/8$. Thus, any adversarial strategy that stops the transmission of m with probability greater than $\epsilon/8$ must be committed to jamming at least half the slots. Turning to the second claim, if the adversary decides to jam the last $2^i/2$ slots, the expected number of jammed slots heard by Bob is at least $\sqrt{2^{i-1}\ln(8/\epsilon)}$ and the probability he hears less than $\sqrt{2^{i-1}\ln(8/\epsilon)}/4$ (possibly halting prematurely) is, by a Chernoff bound, less than $\exp(-(3/4)^2\sqrt{2^{i-1}\ln(8/\epsilon)}/2) < (\epsilon/8)^{2^{(s-5)/2}} < \epsilon/8$.

Send Phase — Alice has halted prematurely: It is no longer possible for the message m to be sent so the correct behavior is for Bob to halt. To prevent this the adversary must cause Bob to hear a large number of jammed slots. If the adversary jams less than $2^i/16$ slots then the expected number heard by Bob is less than $\sqrt{2^{i-1}\ln(8/\epsilon)}/8$ and, by a Chernoff bound, the probability that Bob hears less than $\sqrt{2^{i-1}\ln(8/\epsilon)}/4$ is $\exp(-\sqrt{2^{i-1}\ln(8/\epsilon)}/24) = (\epsilon/8)^{2^{(s-1)/2}/24} < \epsilon/8$.

Nack Phase: The analysis of the nack phase is identical. If Bob is still running, the adversary cannot stop Alice from receiving a nack with probability greater than $\epsilon/8$ without jamming $2^i/2$ slots. If the adversary does jam Alice for least $2^i/2$ slots then Alice will hear a sufficient number to continue to epoch $i+1$, with probability $1 - (\epsilon/8)^{2^{(s-5)/2}}$. Finally, if Bob has halted (after receiving m or prematurely), then Alice will halt with probability at least $1 - \epsilon/8$ unless the adversary jams $2^i/16$ slots.

To sum up, if the adversary wants to prevent Bob from receiving m, or prevent Alice from receiving a nack, or prevent the the second party to halt after the first has halted, it must $(1/16)$-block one of the phases. If the adversary does not $(1/16)$-block one of the phases, the probability of any type of failure in this epoch is at most $2(\epsilon/8 + (\epsilon/8)^{2^{(s-5)/2}} + (\epsilon/8)^{2^{(s-1)/2}/24}) < \epsilon/2$, where $s = i - \lg\ln(8/\epsilon) \geq 11$. So long as epoch i is the *last* epoch that is at least $(1/16)$-blocked by the adversary, the expected cost to Alice or Bob after epoch i is at most $\sum_{j \geq i+1} E(\text{cost in epoch } j) \cdot \Pr(\text{still running in epoch } j)$, which is $\sum_{j \geq i+1} p_j 2^{j+1} \cdot (\epsilon/2)^{j-(i+1)} = O(\sqrt{2^i\ln(1/\epsilon)}) = O(\sqrt{T\ln(1/\epsilon)})$. A similar calculation gives the total latency as $O(2^i) = O(T)$ which is asymptotically optimal since the adversary can always force T latency. □

3. 1-TO-n COMMUNICATION

The pseudocode for *epoch i* of 1-to-n BROADCAST is provided in Figure 2. Each epoch consists of $b\,i^2$ *repetitions* each consisting of 2^i slots. The *status t_u* of node u is initially informed if u is the sender and uninformed otherwise. The variable S_u is reset to 16 at the beginning of each epoch and is non-decreasing throughout the epoch. The parameters $b > 0$ and $d > 0$ are sufficiently large constants and the *first* epoch i is some sufficiently large constant.

While the pseudocode is simple, the design decisions and mechanisms that lead to correctness are intricate. We take some time to provide a discussion of these decisions now.

3.1 A Tour of the Algorithm

The variable S_u controls the probability that u is sending or listening in a given slot. We want S_u to be sufficiently high so that the message is quickly disseminated, but not so high that u expends too much energy. The right bound for an epoch-i repetition, for $i > \log n$, is about $\sqrt{2^i/n}$.[2] However, we do not assume u knows n, even approximately, so it cannot jump straight to the ideal S_u value. We implicitly determine an estimate of n by the following strategy. In each slot of a repetition every u sends with probability $S_u/2^i$; if u is informed, then it sends the message and if it is uninformed then it sends noise. The purpose of sending noise is to let all nodes gauge how large n is relative to 2^i (assuming no

---

[2] We want the number of informed nodes to increase geometrically in each repetition. An n-party version of the birthday paradox shows this is possible if each informed node sends in $\Theta(\sqrt{2^i/n})$ random slots and uninformed nodes listen in $\Theta(\sqrt{2^i/n})$ random slots. However, as we will show, the required analysis is far more involved than a birthday paradox argument.

1-to-n BROADCAST for epoch i with node u

- $S_u \leftarrow 16$
- Repeat $b \cdot i^2$ times:
  - For each of the 2^i slots:
    - If $t_u \in \{\texttt{informed},\ \texttt{helper}\}$, then send m with probability $\frac{S_u}{2^i}$
    - If $t_u = \texttt{uninformed}$, then send noise with probability $\frac{S_u}{2^i}$
    - Listen with probability $\frac{S_u di^3}{2^i}$
  - Let C_u be the number of clear slots heard and $C'_u = \max\{0, C_u - \frac{1}{2}S_u di^3\}$
    - $S_u \leftarrow S_u \cdot 2^{C'_u/(S_u di^4)}$
  - Execute at most one of the following Cases (in order):
    1. If $S_u > 360 \cdot 2^{i/2}$, then terminate
    2. $t_u = \texttt{uninformed}$: If m is heard, then $t_u \leftarrow \texttt{informed}$
    3. $t_u = \texttt{informed}$: If m is heard more than $\frac{di^3}{200}$ times, then $t_u \leftarrow \texttt{helper}$ and $n_u \leftarrow \frac{2^i}{(S_u)^2}$
    4. $t_u = \texttt{helper}$: If $S_u \geq 360\sqrt{\frac{2^i}{n_u}}$, then terminate

Figure 2: Pseudocode for epoch i of 1-to-n BROADCAST

jamming). If a node u hears a sufficient number of clear slots it increases S_u. Note that u expects to listen in $S_u di^3$ slots; if all are clear then S_u will increase by a roughly $2^{1/(2i)}$ factor at the end of the repetition, which is quite small. There are two reasons we need the $\{S_u\}$-values to increase slowly. First, we need to spend about $\log n < i$ repetitions when $S_u \approx \sqrt{2^i/n}$ in order to quickly disseminate the message, so it is important that we do not increase S_u too aggressively and overshoot the ideal value. Second, in order for all nodes to have roughly the same cost, it is important that S_u/S_w be bounded for any two nodes u and w. By increasing S_u and S_w tentatively, we can bound the divergence S_u/S_w over all bi^2 repetitions. (Of course, the adversary can artificially keep S_u low by jamming a large fraction of the slots. To push the nodes into epoch $i \gg \log n$ it will need to jam about $T = \Omega(i^2 2^i)$ slots.)

It is clearly a bad idea for nodes to halt as soon as they receive the message. In order to distribute the costs effectively, $\texttt{informed}$ nodes must stay around to help further disseminate the message. The question is *how long* should they keep running and under what circumstances? A natural halting criterion is *stop when u has heard the message a sufficient number of times*, say poly(i). By a Chernoff bound, a node u that halts can deduce that all nodes have heard the message at least once, w.h.p. This idea does not lead naturally to an algorithm with cost $\tilde{O}(\sqrt{T/n})$. The adversary can jam at a rate that will cause roughly half the nodes to hear messages beyond the halting threshold, leaving the other half to continue running the protocol. To get the remaining nodes to hear the message a sufficient number of times they must up their sending rates (the $\{S_u\}$ values) by a constant factor. The adversary can jam at a rate to cause half the nodes to halt again, necessitating the remaining nodes to up their sending rates, and so on. The last node running will therefore spend about $\tilde{O}(\sqrt{T/n} + \sqrt{T/(n/2)} + \sqrt{T/(n/4)} + \cdots) = \tilde{O}(\sqrt{T})$. That is, an algorithm employing this strategy does not benefit from having a large number of nodes.

Our solution is somewhat counterintuitive. When a node u hears the message a sufficient number of times in one repetition in epoch j ($dj^3/200$) it becomes a $\texttt{helper}$ and, assuming S_u is about the ideal value $\sqrt{2^j/n}$, estimates n by $n_u = 2^j/(S_u)^2$. It continues to act exactly like an $\texttt{informed}$ node, except that when S_u climbs to $360\sqrt{2^i/n_u}$, in a subsequent epoch $i \geq j$, it halts. We prove that when S_u reaches this threshold, all other nodes have $\texttt{helper}$ status w.h.p. An important feature of this approach is that once $\texttt{helper}$ nodes begin halting, the ability of other nodes to halt is not affected. Note that it is hearing *silence* that causes S_u

to grow from 16 to $360\sqrt{2^i/n_u}$ in one epoch, and silence is *free*. To prevent $\texttt{helpers}$ from halting the adversary is forced to jam a constant fraction of the slots.

There is one last issue related to halting. With some tiny but non-zero probability, all but one node will become a $\texttt{helper}$ and halt. The remaining node will never become a $\texttt{helper}$, and therefore never reach the halting condition described above, i.e., its expected cost would be *infinite*. Therefore, we need an alternative halting condition (Case 1 in the pseudocode) to force these exceptionally unlucky nodes to halt and preserve our cost function of $\tilde{O}(\sqrt{T/n})$.

3.2 Preliminaries

Before we begin our main analysis, we state some technical lemmas regarding the version of Chernoff bounds used here. We also prove some preliminary results that are used later on.

Standard Chernoff Bounds: We review well-established Chernoff bounds that we employ in this work:

THEOREM 6. *([27]) Let $X_1, \ldots, X_n$ be independent trials such that $\Pr(X_i) = p$ and let $X = \sum_{i=1}^n X_i$. For any $\delta > 0$,*

$$\Pr(X > (1+\delta)\,\mathrm{E}[X]) \leq \left[\frac{e^\delta}{(1+\delta)^{(1+\delta)}}\right]^{\mathrm{E}[X]}$$

$$\Pr(X < (1-\delta)\,\mathrm{E}[X]) \leq \left[\frac{e^{-\delta}}{(1-\delta)^{(1-\delta)}}\right]^{\mathrm{E}[X]}.$$

We only use the following corollaries of Theorem 6.

COROLLARY 1. *([27]) Let $X_1, \ldots, X_n$ be independent trials such that $\Pr(X_i) = p$ and let $X = \sum_{i=1}^n X_i$. For any δ, where $0 < \delta < 1$,*

$$\Pr(X > (1+\delta)\,\mathrm{E}[X]) \leq e^{-\delta^2 \mathrm{E}[X]/3}$$
$$\Pr(X < (1-\delta)\,\mathrm{E}[X]) \leq e^{-\delta^2 \mathrm{E}[X]/2}$$

Furthermore: $\Pr(|X - \mathrm{E}[X]| > \sqrt{3\,\mathrm{E}[X]\ln(1/\epsilon)}) < 2\epsilon$

The last bound of Corollary 1 is obtained from the first two by setting $\delta = \sqrt{3\ln(1/\epsilon)/\mathrm{E}[X]}$, if $\delta < 1$, and from Theorem 6 if $\delta \geq 1$. In our application we normally set $\epsilon < 1/\text{poly}(n)$. The following inequality is well known:

FACT 1. $1 - y \geq e^{-2y}$ *for any* $0 \leq y \leq 1/2$.

Useful Properties of Our Algorithm: Let A be the set of all non-terminated nodes that currently know m at some point in epoch i. Let V be the set of all nodes that have not terminated. Define $S_A = \sum_{u \in A} \frac{S_u}{2^i}$ and $S_V = \sum_{u \in V} \frac{S_u}{2^i}$. Define p_m to be the probability that exactly one node sends m while all others stay silent, and let p_c be the probability that an unjammed slot is clear. We have the following bounds on p_m and p_c.

LEMMA 2. *Throughout 1-to-n* BROADCAST, $S_A \cdot e^{-2S_V} \leq p_m \leq e S_A \cdot e^{-S_V}$ *and* $e^{-2S_V} \leq p_c \leq e^{-S_V}$.

PROOF. The probability that some node $u \in A$ transmits m while $V - \{u\}$ stay silent is $\sum_{u \in A} \left(\frac{S_u}{2^i} \cdot \prod_{v \in V - \{u\}} (1 - \frac{S_v}{2^i}) \right)$. By Fact 1 this is at least $\sum_{u \in A} \frac{S_u}{2^i} \cdot e^{-2S_V} = S_A e^{-2S_V}$ and at most $\sum_{u \in A} \frac{S_u}{2^i} \cdot e^{-(S_V - S_u/2^i)} < e S_A e^{-S_V}$. The probability of an unjammed slot being clear is $p_c = \prod_{v \in V} (1 - \frac{S_v}{2^i})$, which is at most e^{-S_V} and at least e^{-2S_V}, by Fact 1. $\square$

We establish properties about S_u and t_u that later allow us to make guarantees about epochs $i > \lg n$.

LEMMA 3. *With high probability, every node u has $S_u = 16$ for all epochs $i \leq \lg n$.*

PROOF. The probability that a slot is clear is at most $p_c < e^{-S_V} = e^{-\sum_v S_v/2^i} \leq e^{-16n/2^i}$. When $i \leq \frac{1}{2} \lg n$ $p_c < e^{-16\sqrt{n}}$ and the probability that there are *any* clear slots is superpolynomially small. For any $i \leq \lg n$ we have $p_c \leq e^{-16}$. The expected number of clear slots heard by u is at most $S_u di^3/e^{16}$ but it must hear at least $S_u di^3/2$ to increase S_u. By a Chernoff bound this happens with probability $\exp(-\Omega(i^3)) = \exp(-\Omega(\lg^3 n))$. $\square$

LEMMA 4. *In epochs $i \leq \lg n$, w.h.p. no node becomes a* helper *or terminates, i.e., each node is either* uninformed *or* informed.

PROOF. By Lemma 3, when $i \leq \lg n$, $S_u = 16$ for all u. The probability m is successfully sent in a slot is $p_m \leq e S_A \cdot e^{-S_V}$ by Lemma 2, which is at most $e|A|(16/2^i)e^{-16n/2^i} \leq 16e^{-15}$. A node u will hear less than $(16e^{-15}) \cdot S_u di^3 = (16)^2 e^{-15} di^3$ transmissions of m in expectation but must hear $di^3/200$ to become a helper. By a Chernoff bound, w.h.p. this does not happen. $\square$

3.3 Informing All Nodes

In this section, we analyze how nodes adjust their sending and listening probabilities, and the rate at which m is disseminated. We begin by addressing the divergence between $\{S_u\}$ values.

LEMMA 5. *Consider any epoch $i > \lg n$. With probability $1 - \exp(-\Omega(i))$, we have $S_u/S_v \leq 2$ throughout the epoch, for any two nodes u and v.*

PROOF. We begin with an informal argument. Suppose that in one repetition a $q \leq 1$ fraction of the slots are clear. We expect u to hear $C_u = q di^3 S_u$ clear slots, so $C'_u = \max\{0, (q-1/2)\} \cdot di^3 S_u$. Then, S_u updates to $S_u \cdot 2^{\frac{C'_u}{S_u di^4}} = S_u \cdot 2^{\frac{\max\{0,(q-1/2)\}}{i}}$. However, C_u may not be close to its expectation, due to both random chance *and* the adversary's choice of when to begin jamming. We will show that for all u, regardless of the adversary's choice, $C_u = q di^3 S_u \pm O(\sqrt{S_u di^4})$ with probability $1 - \exp(-\Omega(i))$. That is, S_u will drift from its ideal value by a factor of $2^{O(1/\sqrt{S_u di^4})}$. Over bi^2 repetitions the total drift of S_u will be bounded by $\sqrt{2}$, hence S_u/S_v will be bounded by 2.

Fix a repetition j in epoch i, a node u, and a specific time slot when the adversary begins jamming; by Lemma 1 we can assume

the adversary jams for an interval at the end of the repetition. Let q be the actual fraction of clear slots and C_u be the number observed by u. By linearity of expectation we have $E[C_u] = q di^3 S_u \leq di^3 S_u$. Fix a constant c and let $R_u = \sqrt{c \cdot di^4 S_u}$, i.e., R_u is at least as large as $\sqrt{E[C_u] \cdot ci}$ since $q \leq 1$. By a Chernoff bound the probability that $|E[C_u] - C_u| > R_u$ is less than $2e^{-ci/3}$. By the union bound it follows that for each repetition j (bi^2 values), node u (n values), and each jamming time (2^i values) both C_u and C'_u are within $\sqrt{c \cdot di^4 S_u}$ of their expectations with probability $1 - bi^2 n 2^{i+1} e^{-ci/3} > 1 - e^{-(c/3 - O(1))i}$, since $i > \lg n$.

At the end of repetition j, node u sets $S_u = S_u \cdot 2^{C'_u/(di^4 S_u)}$, which w.h.p. is $S_u \cdot 2^{(E[C'_u] \pm R_u)/di^4 S_u} = S_u \cdot 2^{\max\{0,(q-1/2)\}/i}$. $2^{\pm\sqrt{c/(di^4 S_u)}}$, where q is common to all nodes u in repetition j. Note that since $S_u \geq 16$, the error factor is never more than $2^{\pm\sqrt{c/(16di^4)}}$. Over bi^2 repetitions the accumulated error factor is, with high probability, at most $2^{\pm\sqrt{c/(16di^4)}bi^2} = 2^{\pm\sqrt{cb^2/(16d)}}$. For $d > 4cb^2/16$ sufficiently large the error factor is between $1/\sqrt{2}$ and $\sqrt{2}$ and S_u/S_v bounded by 2, for any u and v. $\square$

Lemma 5 makes a claim about all epochs greater than $\log n$ whereas several lemmas stated later are concerned with epochs beyond $\log n + 8$. We are not concerned about whether m is quickly disseminated in those 8 epochs, so long as other properties relating to correctness are maintained. For example, Lemma 6 states that we never simultaneously have both uninformed and helper nodes, w.h.p.

LEMMA 6. *In a repetition of epoch $i > \lg n$, if any node becomes a* helper *node then no nodes remain* uninformed, *with probability $1 - \exp(-\Omega(i^3))$, regardless of the adversary's jamming strategy.*

PROOF. Recall that p_m is the probability that any given unjammed time slot contains a message. Suppose, for the purpose of analysis, that the adversary commits to leaving a q fraction of the slots unjammed. The expected number of messages heard by u is $L_u = q p_m S_u di^3$. If $L_u < di^3/400$ then by a Chernoff bound the probability that u hears $2 \cdot L_u$ messages (meeting the threshold to become a helper) is $\exp(-\Omega(i^3))$. If $L_u \geq di^3/400$ the probability that u hears zero messages (and stays uninformed) is $\exp(-\Omega(i^3))$ for d large enough, also by a Chernoff bound. By Lemma 5, S_u and S_w differ by a factor of at most 2, so the analysis above applies equally well to all nodes. By a union bound over all n nodes and all 2^i jamming fractions q, the probability that one helper node and one uninformed node exist after the repetition is $n \cdot 2^i \cdot \exp(-\Omega(i^3)) = \exp(-\Omega(i^3))$. $\square$

LEMMA 7. *Call a repetition in epoch i successful if each node u increases S_u by a factor at least $2^{1/(10i)}$. Consider a repetition in epoch $i \geq \lg n + 8$ where $S_V < \sqrt{\frac{n}{2^i}}$. The probability that the adversary can prevent the repetition from being successful without $\frac{1}{10}$-blocking it is $\exp(-\Omega(i^3))$.*

PROOF. By Lemma 1 the adversary can be assumed to jam an interval of slots at the end of the repetition. The adversary wants to prevent nodes from hearing clear slots, so his best strategy is to jam the maximum $2^i/10$ slots allowed in an unblocked repetition, leaving $9 \cdot 2^i/10$ unjammed. By Lemma 2, the expected number of clear slots witnessed by u is at least $p_c \cdot \frac{9}{10} S_u di^3 \geq e^{-2S_V} \cdot \frac{9}{10} \cdot S_u di^3 \geq \frac{9 \cdot S_u di^3}{10 \cdot e^{1/8}} > 0.79 \cdot S_u di^3$. (The lower bound on i and upper bound on S_V implies $2S_V \leq 1/8$.) By a Chernoff bound the probability that u witnesses less than $0.6 S_u di^3$ clear slots is $\exp(-\Omega(i^3))$. If $C_u \geq 0.6 S_u di^3$ then $C'_u \geq 0.1 S_u di^3$ and S_u is increased by a $2^{1/(10i)}$ factor. By a union bound over all $n < 2^i$ nodes, the probability that each u grows S_u by this factor is $1 - \exp(-\Omega(i^3))$. $\square$

262

LEMMA 8. *Consider any epoch $i \geq \lg n + 8$ and threshold $h > 0$. If $S_V \leq h$ before one repetition and $S_V \geq 4h$ later in the epoch then at least $3i$ of the intervening repetitions were $\frac{1}{2}$-unblocked, with probability $1 - \exp(-\Omega(i))$.*

PROOF. The proof the Lemma 5 shows that the divergence in S_u-values from their expectations (due to random chance and any adversarial jamming strategy) is by a factor between $\frac{1}{\sqrt{2}}$ and $\sqrt{2}$ over the entire epoch, with probability $1 - \exp(-\Omega(i))$. That is, of the factor 4 increase in S_V (from h to $4h$), at most $\sqrt{2}$ is due to the samples $\{C_u\}$ deviating from their expectations. We can therefore assume without loss of generality that C_u always matches its expectation and analyze the number of $\frac{1}{2}$-unblocked repetitions that cause S_V to grow by a $2\sqrt{2}$ factor.

If the adversary q'-blocks a repetition then the fraction q of clear slots must be at most $1 - q'$. If $q \leq 1/2$ then S_u (and S_V) does not increase. If $q > 1/2$ (implying the repetition is $\frac{1}{2}$-unblocked) then S_u (and S_V) increases by a $2^{(q-1/2)/i} \leq 2^{1/(2i)}$ factor, since $q \leq 1$. Thus, to achieve a $2\sqrt{2} = 2^{3/2}$ factor increase in S_V we need $(3/2)/(1/(2i)) = 3i$ repetitions that are $\frac{1}{2}$-unblocked. $\square$

To summarize, Lemmas 7 and 8 imply that after approximately $10\,i \lg(\sqrt{2^i/n}) < 5\,i^2 \frac{1}{10}$-unblocked repetitions, w.h.p. $S_V \geq \sqrt{\frac{n}{2^i}}$. If, later in the epoch, $S_V > 4\sqrt{\frac{n}{2^i}}$ then we have witnessed $3i$ or more $\frac{1}{2}$-unblocked repetitions. We set $b \geq 10$ so there are ample repetitions for S_V to grow sufficiently large. We will now prove that in those $3i$ $\frac{1}{2}$-unblocked repetitions, all nodes will become `informed` and attain `helper` status.

LEMMA 9. *Consider an epoch $i \geq \lg n + 8$ before any nodes have achieved `helper` status. With probability $1 - \exp(-\Omega(i))$ the adversary cannot prevent S_V from exceeding $4\sqrt{n/2^i}$ and cannot prevent all nodes from attaining `helper` status, without $\frac{1}{10}$-blocking a constant fraction of the repetitions.*

PROOF. By Lemma 7 the adversary cannot prevent S_V from growing to $\sqrt{\frac{n}{2^i}}$ without $\frac{1}{10}$-blocking a constant fraction of the repetitions. Moreover, it cannot prevent S_V from then growing to $4\sqrt{\frac{n}{2^i}}$ without $\frac{1}{2}$-blocking a constant fraction of the remaining repetitions. By Lemma 8 there are at least $3i$ $\frac{1}{2}$-unblocked repetitions while $\sqrt{\frac{n}{2^i}} \leq S_V \leq 4\sqrt{\frac{n}{2^i}}$.

To prevent dissemination of m, the adversary's optimum strategy is to jam as much as possible; namely, $2^i/2 - 1$ slots in a $\frac{1}{2}$-unblocked repetition, and all 2^i slots in a $\frac{1}{2}$-blocked repetition. By Lemma 1, we can assume that the adversary commits to jamming an interval of slots at the end of a repetition. We allow the adversary to decide whether to $\frac{1}{2}$-block the repetition *after* all nodes have committed to which slots they will send and listen. If they can accomplish a task in the first $2^i/2$ slots, then to stop them the adversary is forced to $\frac{1}{2}$-block the repetition. Therefore, we analyze the probability of accomplishing a task within $2^i/2$ slots.

So long as $S_V \leq 4\sqrt{\frac{n}{2^i}}$ we will have $S_V \leq 1/4$ since $i \geq \lg n + 8$. Recall that A is the set of `informed` nodes at the beginning of some repetition, and $S_A = \sum_{u \in A} S_u/2^i$. The probability that an unjammed slot contains m is p_m, which is at least $S_A/e^{2S_V} \geq S_A/e^{1/2}$. By Lemma 5, if $S_V \geq \sqrt{\frac{n}{2^i}}$ then for every node u, $S_u \geq \frac{1}{2}\sqrt{\frac{2^i}{n}}$. Therefore, $p_m \geq S_A/e^{1/2} \geq \frac{|A|}{e^{1/2}2\sqrt{2^i n}}$.

Let X_m be the number of slots containing m and I_m be the number of nodes that hear m. We will show that conditioned on X_m being a constant fraction of its expectation, I_m will be at least a constant fraction of its expectation (about $i^3|A|$) with probability $1 - \exp(-\Omega(i^3))$. When $|A|$ is very small, however, the probability that X_m is too small may not be completely negligible.

By linearity of expectation we have $\mathrm{E}[X_m] \geq p_m \cdot \frac{1}{2}2^i \geq \frac{|A|\sqrt{2^i}}{4e^{1/2}\sqrt{n}} \geq \frac{|A|\cdot\sqrt{2^i}}{6.6\sqrt{n}}$. By a Chernoff bound, the probability that X_m is less than $\mathrm{E}[X_m]/3$ is at most $\exp(-(2/3)^2\,\mathrm{E}[X_m]/2) = \exp(-(2/9)\,\mathrm{E}[X_m])$. Call a repetition good if this holds and bad otherwise. We will proceed under the assumption that the repetition is good, i.e., $X_m \geq \mathrm{E}[X_m]/3 > \frac{|A|\cdot\sqrt{2^i}}{19.8\sqrt{n}}$. The probability that a node u hears m in this repetition is at least $1 - \left(1 - \frac{di^3 S_u}{2^i}\right)^{X_m}$

$$\geq 1 - e^{-\frac{di^3 S_u}{2^i} \cdot \frac{|A|\cdot\sqrt{2^i}}{19.8\sqrt{n}}} \quad \text{By the lower bound on } X_m$$

$$\geq 1 - e^{-\frac{di^3}{2\sqrt{2^i \cdot n}} \cdot \frac{|A|\cdot\sqrt{2^i}}{19.8\sqrt{n}}} \quad \text{By the lower bound on } S_u$$

$$\geq \begin{cases} \frac{di^3|A|}{79.2n} & \text{If the exponent is} \geq -1 \text{ and Fact 1} \\ 1 - 1/e & \text{Otherwise} \end{cases}$$

If we are in the second case in the last inequality then $\mathrm{E}[I_m] \geq n(1 - 1/e)$ by linearity of expectation and, by a Chernoff bound, I_m is at least $n/4$ with probability $1 - \exp(-\Omega(n))$. If we are in the first case then $\mathrm{E}[I_m] \geq di^3|A|/79.2$ and $I_m \geq i^3|A|$ with probability $1 - \exp(-\Omega(i^3))$, again by a Chernoff bound assuming that $d > 79.2$. Thus, after $\lg(n/4)/\lg(i^3)$ good repetitions, the number of `informed`/`helper` nodes will be at least $n/4$ with high probability. We need to bound the number of bad repetitions, where $X_m < \mathrm{E}[X_m]/3$, and show that when $|A| \geq n/4$, all nodes become helpers with high probability. The second claim is easy to establish. If $|A| \geq n/4$ then the expected number of messages heard by a node u is at least $X_m \cdot di^3 S_u/2^i \geq di^3|A|/39.6n > di^3/160$. The probability that u hears at least $di^3/200$ messages (exceeding the threshold to become a `helper`) is, by a Chernoff bound, $1 - \exp(-\Omega(i^3))$.

By this analysis, the probability of a bad repetition is $\Pr[X < \frac{\mathrm{E}[X_m]}{3}] < \exp(-(\frac{2}{9})\,\mathrm{E}[X_m]) < \exp(-(\frac{2}{9})\frac{|A|\cdot\sqrt{2^i}}{6.6\sqrt{n}})$, which is $\exp(-\Omega(i^3))$ for $|A| \geq i^3$. However, for all $|A| \geq 1$, it is at most $\exp(-(\frac{2}{9}) \cdot \frac{16}{6.6}) < 0.59$ since $\sqrt{2^i/n} \geq 16$. From the adversary's perspective, there is no need to block bad repetitions, only good ones. Moreover, after the first $\frac{1}{2}$-unblocked good repetition $|A|$ will be i^3 and we only need $\lg(n/4)/\lg(i^3)$ more repetitions for all nodes to attain `helper` status, with probability $1 - \exp(-\Omega(i^3))$. By Lemma 8 there is room for $3i$ $\frac{1}{2}$-unblocked repetitions until $S_V \geq 4\sqrt{n/2^i}$. With probability $1 - \exp(-\Omega(i))$, we do not have $3i - \frac{\lg(n/4)}{\lg(i^3)}$ bad repetitions before the first good one. $\square$

3.4 Terminating the Algorithm

In this section, we show that w.h.p. all `helper` nodes terminate and derive the cost and efficiency functions.

LEMMA 10. *If node u assumes `helper` status in epoch $i > \lg n$, then w.h.p. $S_u \geq \frac{2^{i/2}}{45 \cdot \sqrt{n}}$.*

PROOF. Let u be an `informed` node that changes its status to `helper`. Can $S_u < \frac{2^{i/2}}{45\sqrt{n}}$ when u receives enough messages to assume `helper` status? If so, then by Lemma 5 we know that each other node w has $S_w \leq 2 \cdot \frac{2^{i/2}}{45\sqrt{n}}$ which implies that $S_V < \frac{1}{2^i}(n \cdot \frac{2 \cdot 2^{i/2}}{45\sqrt{n}}) \leq \frac{2 \cdot \sqrt{n}}{45 \cdot 2^{i/2}}$. Then, the expected number of messages that u hears is then at most $p_m \cdot S_u\,di^3 \leq \frac{eS_A S_u di^3}{e^{S_V}} \leq eS_A S_u\,di^3 \leq eS_V S_u\,di^3 < e \cdot \frac{1}{2^i} \cdot (n \cdot \frac{2 \cdot 2^{i/2}}{45\sqrt{n}})(\frac{2^{i/2}}{45\sqrt{n}})di^3 < \frac{di^3}{370}$. By Chernoff bounds and a union bound, it follows that w.h.p. u would not receive more than $\frac{di^3}{200}$ messages and therefore would not change its status to `helper`. $\square$

LEMMA 11. *Consider an epoch $i > \lg n$. If $S_u \geq \frac{360 \cdot 2^{i/2}}{\sqrt{n_u}}$, then w.h.p. all nodes have* `helper` *status.*

PROOF. $S_u = \frac{2^{j/2}}{\sqrt{n_u}}$ when u changes its status to `helper` in some epoch j. By Lemma 10, $S_u \geq \frac{2^{j/2}}{45\sqrt{n}}$ and so it follows that $\sqrt{n_u} \leq 45\sqrt{n}$. In some epoch $i \geq j$, by assumption $S_u \geq \frac{360 \cdot 2^{i/2}}{\sqrt{n_u}} \geq \frac{8 \cdot 2^{i/2}}{\sqrt{n}}$. By Lemma 5, this implies that $S_V > \frac{4\sqrt{n}}{2^{i/2}}$. By Lemma 9, this implies that all nodes have already set their status to `helper`. $\square$

LEMMA 12. *Consider an epoch $i > \lg n$ and let u have status* `helper`. *W.h.p. the adversary cannot prevent S_u from exceeding $\frac{360 \cdot 2^{i/2}}{\sqrt{n_u}}$ without $\frac{1}{10}$-blocking a constant fraction of the repetitions in the epoch.*

PROOF. By Lemma 1, the adversary's jammed slots can be allocated to the end of the repetition. The expected number of clear slots that a node u hears in a repetition where the adversary is not blocking is at least $\frac{9 p_c S_u di^3}{10} \geq \frac{9 p_c S_u di^3}{10 e^{2 S_V}} \geq 0.12 S_u di^3$. By Chernoff bounds and a union bound, the probablity that any node u hears less than $0.1 S_u di^3$ clear slots is $e^{-\Omega(i)}$. S_u increases by at least a $2^{0.1/i}$ factor in each such repetition, and over at least $bi^2 - 1$ such repetitions, S_u will increase to $2^{0.1 \, bi} \geq 2^i$ since $b \geq 10$. Therefore, w.h.p. S_u will exceed $\frac{360 \cdot 2^{i/2}}{\sqrt{n_u}}$ in this epoch. $\square$

To summarize, Lemma 11 implies that a `helper` node u can safely terminate when $S_u \geq \frac{360 \cdot 2^{i/2}}{\sqrt{n_u}}$ because w.h.p., all remaining nodes will also have their status set to `helper`. Lemma 12 guarantees w.h.p. that $S_u \geq \frac{360 \cdot 2^{i/2}}{\sqrt{n_u}}$ will be achieved for every `helper` node. We can now prove the main claims of Theorem 3.

PROOF. First, we analyze the cost of the algorithm when the adversary never $\frac{1}{10}$-blocks a constant fraction of the repetitions in an epoch. For epochs $i \leq \lg n$, Lemma 3 guarantees w.h.p. that $S_u = 16$ so in these epochs the expected cost per node is $O(i^5) = O(\log^5 n)$ (a cost of $O(i^3)$ per repetition for $O(i^2)$ repetitions) regardless of the adversary's behavior. Furthermore, in epochs $i \leq \lg n$ Lemma 4 guarantees that w.h.p. all nodes have status `uninformed` or `informed`. Given this property, Lemma 9 shows that w.h.p. all nodes assume `helper` status by the end of epoch $i = 8 + \lg n$ at the latest. By Lemmas 11 and 12, w.h.p. all `helper` nodes terminate in the next epoch at the latest. At this point, Lemmas 9 implies w.h.p. $S_V \leq \frac{4\sqrt{n}}{2^{i/2}}$ and so, by Lemma 5, w.h.p that each node u has $S_u = O(\sqrt{2^i/n}) = O(1)$. The total cost is therefore $O(\lg^6 n)$ since we have a cost of $O(\lg^5 n)$ per epoch for $\lg n + O(1)$ epochs.

Now consider the case where the adversary does $1/10$-block a constant fraction of the repetitions in some epoch; let ℓ be the last such epoch. The cost to the adversary is $T = \Omega(2^\ell \ell^2)$. The expected cost to a node u, as a function of its final S_u value, is $O(S_u d \ell^5) = O(\sqrt{\frac{2^\ell}{n}} \ell^5) = O(\sqrt{\frac{T/\ell^2}{n}} \ell^5) = O(\sqrt{T/n} \lg^4 T)$.

We now turn to the latency. If the adversary never $1/10$-blocks a constant fraction of the repetitions in an epoch, the algorithm will terminate in epoch $\ell \leq \lg n + 8$ with high probability. The latency will be $O(\ell^2 2^\ell) = O(n \log^2 n)$. Let ℓ be the last epoch that the adversary $1/10$-blocks a constant fraction of the repetitions. With high probability all nodes will halt in epoch $\ell + 1$, so the latency will be $O(\ell^2 2^\ell) = O(T)$ which is asymptotically optimal in T given that the adversary can force at least T latency by jamming.

All events analyzed so far hold with high probability, yet a node u may be unlucky and never achieve `informed` or `helper` status before all other nodes have become helpers and halted. Without

an alternative halting criterion the expected cost per node would be infinite. Under normal circumstances a node u will become `informed`, then become a `helper` in some epoch j, setting $n_u = 2^j/(S_u)^2$, then halt in an epoch $i \geq j$ when $S_u \geq 360\sqrt{2^i/n_u}$, which is at most $360 \cdot 2^{i/2}$. If any node u finds that $S_u > 360 \cdot 2^{i/2}$, it knows that some correctness/efficiency property has already been violated and can therefore halt. Moreover, to keep u from detecting such a violation, the adversary is forced to $1/10$-block most repetitions in an epoch. $\square$

4. LOWER BOUNDS

We present lower bounds for the 1-to-1 and 1-to-n communication problems. Throughout, we abuse terminology somewhat by referring to T as the adversary's *budget* which may be a fixed upper bound on what the adversary actually spends (perhaps the budget is dictated by the amount of energy supplied by the adversary's battery). However, an adversary who has a fixed budget (known or unknown to the nodes) is certainly no stronger than our original adversary, and thus the lower bounds we derive will also hold against our original adversary. Our lower bounds are also strong in that Theorems 2 and 4 assume only a (weak) 1-uniform adaptive adversary that can jam but not send any meaningful messages. Theorem 5 shows that the 1-to-1 communication problem is very sensitive to the power of the adversary. In particular, it is provably more expensive to perform 1-to-1 communication against a 2-uniform adversary that can broadcast messages indistinguishable from Bob's. In [23], the authors give a 1-to-1 communication algorithm in this model with cost $O(T^{\varphi-1})$, where $\varphi = \frac{1+\sqrt{5}}{2}$. Theorem 5 shows that this is asymptotically optimal.

Theorem 2. *Consider a 1-to-1 communication protocol in which Alice sends a message to Bob with probability $1 - \epsilon$ for any constant $\epsilon > 0$. Let A and B be Alice and Bob's empirical costs, and T be the budget of an adaptive, 1-uniform adversary. The adversary can force $\mathrm{E}(A)\,\mathrm{E}(B) > (1 - O(\epsilon))T$. In particular, $\max\{E(A), E(B)\} = \Omega(\sqrt{T})$.*

PROOF. In general, Alice and Bob do not know the adversary's budget T, nor do they know the behavior of the other party. However, for the lower bound proof we assume that T is common knowledge, and that after each time slot both Alice and Bob know the action taken by the other. In particular, when Alice sends and Bob listens, both parties know the message is sent and can halt immediately. These assumptions only make our lower bound stronger.

The adversary commits to the following strategy. Let a_i and b_i be the probability of sending/listening chosen by Alice and Bob just before the ith time slot. The adversary jams if and only if it has not already jammed T slots and $a_i b_i > 1/T$. Alice and Bob can clearly pursue one of two strategies: (i) force the adversary to exhaust her budget in the first T slots by setting $(a_i)_{i \leq T}$ and $(b_i)_{i \leq T}$ sufficiently high, then send the message in the next round by setting $a_{T+1} = b_{T+1} = 1$. Alternatively, they can (ii) choose (a_i) and (b_i) sufficiently low such that the adversary never jams. Furthermore, no mixture of strategies (i) and (ii) can have a strictly lower expected cost than pursuing the best of (i) and (ii). We analyze strategy (ii) then note that the analysis extends to strategy (i).

The rest of the proof is organized as follows. We show that (I) rather than charging 1 unit for sending/listening and 0 for sleeping, it suffices to consider a fractional cost model, (II) without loss of generality, Alice and Bob choose the infinite vectors (a_i) and (b_i) obliviously, (III) it is advantageous to always maximize $a_i b_i$ and to set all coordinates of (a_i) equal and all coordinates of (b_i) equal.

(I) In slot i Alice chooses to send/listen with probability a_i. Rather than charge her 1 if she does, in fact, send/listen we charge her a_i regardless. By linearity of expectation, the expected cost to Alice and Bob in this fractional model is exactly their cost in the 0/1 cost model. We now need to argue that all non-oblivious algorithms can be made oblivious in the fractional model without increasing their expected costs.

(II) In general an adaptive algorithm for (Alice,Bob) is an infinite decision tree. A node at depth i is labeled with a pair (a_i, b_i) where $a_i b_i \leq 1/T$; it has four children labeled with the empirical behavior of Alice and Bob in the ith time step, i.e., whether they send/listen or sleep. One child is a leaf (Alice sends, Bob listens, and the algorithm halts) whereas the other three children are identified with behaviors at round $i + 1$. Since, by (I), Alice's/Bob's cost for the ith round are *independent of the empirical behavior* of Alice/Bob, if they do not terminate after round i they are free to follow *any* of the other three children. Without loss of generality, we can assume they commit to taking the *best* child; the one minimizing $\mathrm{E}(A)\,\mathrm{E}(B)$. In this way all branching can be eliminated without degrading expected costs. In other words, Alice and Bob can be assumed to commit to vectors (a_i) and (b_i) in advance.

(III) Suppose that Bob commits to (b_i). We first show that without loss of generality, Alice's best response is to choose (a_i) such that each $a_i = 0$ or a_i is maximum, that is, such that $a_i b_i = 1/T$. Consider some vector (a_i) that violates the claim, where $0 < a_1 < 1/(b_1 T)$. Let z be the expected cost to Alice in all slots $i \geq 2$, conditioned on not halting after slot 1. Her expected cost over all slots $i \geq 1$ is $a_1 + (1 - a_1 b_1)z = z + a_1(1 - b_1 z)$, which can always be minimized by setting $a_1 = 0$ (if $b_1 z \leq 1$) or $a_1 = 1/(b_1 T)$ (if $b_1 z \geq 1$). The same argument applies to Bob as well. We can clearly ignore any slots in which $a_i = b_i = 0$, so without loss of generality $a_i b_i = 1/T$, for all i. Since Alice and Bob need only succeed with some constant probability we can assume that they halt (unsuccessfully) after some fixed step $t = \Omega(T)$. The probability of failure is $(1 - 1/T)^t < e^{-t/T}$. Define $\hat{a} = (\prod_{i \leq t} a_i)^{1/t}$ and $\hat{b} = (\prod_{i \leq t} b_i)^{1/t}$ to be the geometric means of their probability vectors. Since $(\hat{a}, \hat{a}, \cdots)$ and $(\hat{b}, \hat{b}, \ldots)$ are also valid vectors (that is, they do not induce the adversary to jam any slots) since $\hat{a} \cdot \hat{b} = (\prod_{i \leq t} a_i b_i)^{1/t} = (1/T^t)^{1/t} = 1/T$. Let $p_i = (1 - 1/T)^{i-1}$ be the probability that the algorithm is still running at time step i. Then:

$$
\begin{aligned}
\mathrm{E}(A) \cdot \mathrm{E}(B) &= \left(\sum_{i \leq t} a_i p_i\right) \cdot \left(\sum_{i \leq t} b_i p_i\right) \\
&= \sum_{i,j \leq t} a_i b_j \left(1 - \frac{1}{T}\right)^{i+j-2} \\
&\geq \sum_{i,j \leq t} \hat{a}\hat{b} \left(1 - \frac{1}{T}\right)^{i+j-2}
\end{aligned}
$$

since the geometric mean < arithmetic mean

$$
\begin{aligned}
&= \hat{a}\hat{b}((1 - O(\exp(-t/T)))T)^2 \\
&= \Omega(T) \qquad \text{since } \hat{a}\hat{b} = 1/T
\end{aligned}
$$

The $O(\exp(-t/T))$ reflects the fact that the sums are truncated at t. Thus, the limit of $\mathrm{E}(A)\,\mathrm{E}(B)$ is exactly T as the probability of failure goes to zero.

Suppose Alice and Bob pursue strategy (i) and exhaust the adversary's budget. By the same argument $a_i b_i$ should be infinitesimally larger than $1/T$ to trigger the adversary to jam. Furthermore, $\mathrm{E}(A)\,\mathrm{E}(B)$ is optimized when all a_i (and all b_i) are equal, which implies that $\sum_{i \leq T} a_i > T^{1-\delta}$ and $\sum_{i \leq T} b_i > T^{\delta}$, for some $\delta > 0$. Finally, since our argument makes no assumption on the

k-uniformity of the adversary, we assume the weakest adversary (to obtain the strongest lower bound) which is 1-uniform. □

Theorem 4. *Assume a 1-uniform adaptive adversary. Any fair algorithm that achieves 1-to-n communication with probability at least $1/2$ imposes an expected cost per node of $\Omega(\sqrt{T/n})$.*

PROOF. Assume a *fair* algorithm $\mathcal{A}$ (Section 1.3) that achieves 1-to-n broadcast with constant probability at least $\epsilon > 0$ and has an expected cost $g(T)$ for the sender and each receiver. We now design a new algorithm $\mathcal{A}'$ for two players, Alice and Bob, as follows. Bob will simulate those actions taken by the n receivers under $\mathcal{A}$. We must be careful as Bob cannot send and listen simultaneously. This is not an issue for communications between just the n receivers, all of which are simulated by Bob. However, we must address communication between the sender and any of the n receivers. We allocate a pair of slots in $\mathcal{A}'$ for each slot in $\mathcal{A}$. If there was (a probability of) both sending and listening in a slot by receivers under $\mathcal{A}$, then Bob sends in the first slot and listens in the second slot of the corresponding pair. Alice will simulate actions taken by the sender, duplicating the action in each pair of slots.

By construction, $\mathcal{A}'$ solves the 1-to-n broadcast with probability at least that of $\mathcal{A}$; thus, $\mathcal{A}'$ succeeds with probability $\geq 1/2$. Let $E(A)$ denote Alice's expected cost under $\mathcal{A}'$ and note that $E(A) \leq 2 \cdot g(T)$. Let $E(B)$ denote Bob's expected cost under $\mathcal{A}'$ and note that $E(B) \leq n \cdot g(T)$. By Theorem 3, $E(A) \cdot E(B) = \Omega(T)$. Since $E(A) \cdot E(B) \leq 2 \cdot n \cdot g(T)^2$, we must have $g(T) = \Omega(\sqrt{T/n})$. □

Theorem 5. *Consider a 1-to-1 communications protocol such that Alice sends a message to Bob with constant probability of failure, given a 2-uniform adaptive adversary that can spoof messages from Bob. In any such protocol, the expected cost to either Alice or Bob is $\Omega(T^{\varphi-1})$ where $\varphi = \frac{1+\sqrt{5}}{2}$.*

PROOF. The adversary announces a budget of $\tilde{T}$ and that it will jam Bob (but not Alice, which is possible due to 2-uniformity) if and only if $a_i b_i > 1/\tilde{T}$ and it has not already jammed $\tilde{T}$ slots. It then chooses to either (i) commit to this strategy or (ii) take the place of Bob and *simulate* Bob in scenario (i). In other words, in scenario (ii) the adversary *is* Bob, there is no jamming whatsoever, and there is no correctness criterion for Alice, only a resource-competitive criterion. In scenario (i) the adversary's cost is at most $T = \tilde{T}$ whereas in scenario (ii) its cost is $T = B$, the actual cost incurred by simulating Bob's side of the protocol. Note that since Alice cannot detect when Bob is being jammed, she cannot distinguish scenarios (i) and (ii). Suppose the expected costs incurred by Alice and a (non-adversary) Bob are $O(T^\alpha)$, where $\alpha < 1$. According to Theorem 2, $\mathrm{E}(A) \cdot \mathrm{E}(B) = \Omega(\tilde{T})$. Let $\delta > 0$ be such that $\mathrm{E}(A) = \Omega(\tilde{T}^{1-\delta})$ and $\mathrm{E}(B) = \Omega(\tilde{T}^{\delta})$. In scenario (ii) (where $T = B$), Alice's expected cost is $\Omega(\tilde{T}^{1-\delta}) = \Omega(T^{(1-\delta)/\delta})$, hence $(1-\delta)/\delta \leq \alpha$. Note that since $\alpha < 1$, it must be that $\delta > 1/2$. In scenario (i) (where $T = \tilde{T}$) Bob's expected cost is $\Omega(T^\delta)$, hence $\delta \leq \alpha$. Since $(1 - \delta)/\delta$ is decreasing in δ, $\max\{(1-\delta)/\delta, \delta\}$ is minimized when $\delta = \frac{1-\delta}{\delta} = \frac{-1+\sqrt{5}}{2} = \varphi - 1$. In other words, either Bob's cost is $\Omega(T^\alpha)$ in scenario (i) or Alice's cost is $\Omega(T^\alpha)$ in scenario (ii), where $\alpha = \varphi - 1 > 0.618$. □

5. REFERENCES

[1] Robobees. http://robobees.seas.harvard.edu.

[2] Dan Alistarh, Seth Gilbert, Rachid Guerraoui, Zarko Milosevic, and Calvin Newport. Securing Your Every Bit: Reliable Broadcast in Byzantine Wireless Networks. In *Proceedings of the Symposium on Parallelism in Algorithms and Architectures (SPAA)*, pages 50–59, 2010.

[3] Ghada Alnifie and Robert Simon. A Multi-Channel Defense Against Jamming Attacks in Wireless Sensor Networks. In *Proceedings of the*

3rd ACM Workshop on QoS and Security for Wireless and Mobile Networks, pages 95–104, 2007.

[4] Nils Aschenbruck, Elmar Gerhards-Padilla, and Peter Martini. Simulative Evaluation of Adaptive Jamming Detection in Wireless Multi-hop Networks. In *International Conference on Distributed Computing Systems Workshops*, pages 213–220, 2010.

[5] Farhana Ashraf, Yih-Chun Hu, and Robin Kravets. Demo: Bankrupting the Jammer. In *Proceedings of the 9th International Conference on Mobile Systems, Applications, and Services (MobiSys)*, 2011.

[6] Baruch Awerbuch, Andrea Richa, and Christian Scheideler. A Jamming-Resistant MAC Protocol for Single-Hop Wireless Networks. In *Proceedings of the 27th ACM Symposium on Principles of Distributed Computing (PODC)*, pages 45–54, 2008.

[7] Emrah Bayraktaroglu, Christopher King, Xin Liu, Guevara Noubir, Rajmohan Rajaraman, and Bishal Thapa. On the Performance of IEEE 802.11 Under Jamming. In *INFOCOM*, pages 1265–1273, 2008.

[8] Michael A. Bender, Martin Farach-Colton, Simai He, Bradley C. Kuszmaul, and Charles E. Leiserson. Adversarial Contention Resolution for Simple Channels. In *Proceedings of the Seventeenth Annual ACM Symposium on Parallelism in Algorithms and Architectures (SPAA)*, pages 325–332, 2005.

[9] Vartika Bhandhari, Jonathan Katz, Chiu-Yuen Koo, and Nitin Vaidya. Reliable Broadcast in Radio Networks: The Bounded Collision Case. In *Proceedings of the ACM Symposium on Principles of Distributed Computing (PODC)*, pages 258 – 264, 2006.

[10] Timothy Brown, Jesse James, and Amita Sethi. Jamming and Sensing of Encrypted Wireless Ad Hoc Networks. In *Proceedings of the 7th ACM International Symposium on Mobile Ad Hoc Networking and Computing*, pages 120–130, 2006.

[11] Johannes Dams, Martin Hoefer, and Thomas Kesselheim. Jamming-Resistant Learning in Wireless Networks. http://arxiv.org/abs/1307.5290, 2013.

[12] Christian Decker, Albert Krohn, Michael Beigl, and Tobias Zimmer. The Particle Computer System. In *Proceedings of the 4th International Symposium on Information Processing in Sensor Networks (IPSN)*, pages 443–448, 2005.

[13] Jing Deng, Richard Han, and Shivakant Mishra. Defending Against Path-Based DoS Attacks in Wireless Sensor Networks. In *Proceedings of the 3rd ACM Workshop on Security of Ad Hoc and Sensor Networks*, pages 89–96, 2005.

[14] Shlomi Dolev, Seth Gilbert, Rachid Guerraoui, and Calvin Newport. Gossiping in a Multi-channel Radio Network: An Oblivious Approach to Coping with Malicious Interference. In *Proceedings of the International Symposium on Distributed Computing (DISC)*, pages 208–222, 2007.

[15] Shlomi Dolev, Seth Gilbert, Rachid Guerraoui, and Calvin Newport. Secure Communication over Radio Channels. In *Proceedings of the Symposium on Principles of Distributed Computing (PODC)*, pages 105–114, 2008.

[16] Yuval Emek and Roger Wattenhofer. Frequency Hopping against a Powerful Adversary. In *Proceedings of the 27th International Symposium Distributed Computing (DISC)*, pages 329–343, 2013.

[17] Aurélien Francillon and Claude Castelluccia. TinyRNG: A Cryptographic Random Number Generator for Wireless Sensors Network Nodes. In *Proceedings of the 5th International Symposium on In Modeling and Optimization in Mobile, Ad Hoc and Wireless Networks and Workshops (WiOpt)*, pages 1–7, 2007.

[18] Seth Gilbert, Rachid Guerraoui, Dariusz Kowalski, and Calvin Newport. Interference-Resilient Information Exchange. In *INFOCOM*, pages 2249–2257, 2009.

[19] Seth Gilbert, Rachid Guerraoui, and Calvin C. Newport. Of Malicious Motes and Suspicious Sensors: On the Efficiency of Malicious Interference in Wireless Networks. In *International Conference On Principles Of Distributed Systems (OPODIS)*, pages 215–229, 2006.

[20] Seth Gilbert, Valerie King, Jared Saia, and Maxwell Young. Resource-Competitive Analysis: A New Perspective on Attack-Resistant Distributed Computing. In *Proceedings of the 8th ACM International Workshop on Foundations of Mobile Computing (FOMC)*, 2012.

[21] Seth Gilbert and Maxwell Young. Making Evildoers Pay: Resource-Competitive Broadcast in Sensor Networks. In *Proceedings of the 31th Symposium on Principles of Distributed Computing (PODC)*, pages 145–154, 2012.

[22] Chris Karlof, Naveen Sastry, and David Wagner. TinySec: A Link Layer Security Architecture for Wireless Sensor Networks. In *Proceedings of the 2nd International Conference on Embedded Networked Sensor Systems*, pages 162–175, 2004.

[23] Valerie King, Jared Saia, and Maxwell Young. Conflict on a Communication Channel. In *Proceedings of the 30th Symposium on Principles of Distributed Computing (PODC)*, pages 277–286, 2011.

[24] Yoonmyung Lee, Gyouho Kim, Suyoung Bang, Yejoong Kim, Inhee Lee, Prababl Dutta, Dennis Sylvester, and David Blaauw. A Modular $1mm^3$ Die-Stacked Sensing Platform with Optical Communication and Multi-Modal Energy Harvesting. In *2012 IEEE International Solid-State Circuits Conference Digest of Technical Papers (ISSCC)*, pages 402–404, 2012.

[25] Xin Liu, Guevara Noubir, Ravi Sundaram, and San Tan. SPREAD: Foiling Smart Jammers Using Multi-Layer Agility. In *INFOCOM*, pages 2536–2540, 2007.

[26] Dominic Meier, Yvonne Anne Pignolet, Stefan Schmid, and Roger Wattenhofer. Speed Dating Despite Jammers. In *Proceedings of the International Conference on Distributed Computing in Sensor Systems (DCOSS)*, pages 1–14, 2009.

[27] Rajeev Motwani and Prbhakar Raghavan. *Randomized Algorithms*. Cambridge University Press, 1995.

[28] Vishnu Navda, Aniruddha Bohra, Samrat Ganguly, and Dan Rubenstein. Using Channel Hopping to Increase 802.11 Resilience to Jamming Attacks. In *INFOCOM*, pages 2526–2530, 2007.

[29] Adrian Ogierman, Andrea Richa, Christian Scheideler, Stefan Schmid, and Jin Zhang. Competitive MAC under Adversarial SINR. http://arxiv.org/abs/1307.7231, 2013.

[30] Andrzej Pelc and David Peleg. Feasibility and Complexity of Broadcasting with Random Transmission Failures. In *Proceedings of the ACM Symposium on Principles of Distributed Computing (PODC)*, pages 334–341, 2005.

[31] Joseph Polastre, Robert Szewczyk, and David Culler. Telos: Enabling Ultra-Low Power Wireless Research. In *IPSN*, 2005.

[32] Christina Pöpper, Mario Strasser, and Srdjan Čapkun. Jamming-Resistant Broadcast Communication Without Shared Keys. In *Proceedings of the 18th USENIX Security Symposium*, 2009.

[33] Iyappan Ramachandran and Sumt Roy. Clear Channel Assessment in Energy-Constrained Wideband Wireless Networks. *IEEE Wireless Communications*, 14(3):70–78, 2007.

[34] Andrea Richa, Christian Scheideler, Stefan Schmid, and Jin Zhang. A Jamming-Resistant MAC Protocol for Multi-Hop Wireless Networks. In *Proceedings of the International Symposium on Distributed Computing (DISC)*, pages 179–193, 2010.

[35] Andrea Richa, Christian Scheideler, Stefan Schmid, and Jin Zhang. Competitive and Fair Medium Access Despite Reactive Jamming. In *Proceedings of the 31st International Conference on Distributed Computing Systems (ICDCS)*, pages 507–516, 2011.

[36] Andrea Richa, Christian Scheideler, Stefan Schmid, and Jin Zhang. Competitive and Fair Throughput for Co-Existing Networks Under Adversarial Interference. In *Proceedings of the 31st ACM Symposium on Principles of Distributed Computing (PODC)*, pages 291–300, 2012.

[37] Deva Seetharam and Sokwoo Rhee. An Efficient Pseudorandom Number Generator for Low-Power Sensor Networks. In *29th Annual IEEE International Conference on Local Computer Networks*, pages 560–562, 2004.

[38] SPECKNET. http://www.specknet.org/.

[39] R. Watro, D. Kong, S. Cuti, C. Gariner, C. Lynn, and P. Kruus. TinyPK: Securing Sensor Networks with Public Key Technology . In *SASN*, pages 59–64, 2004.

[40] Wenyuan Xu, Ke Ma, Wade Trappe, and Yanyong Zhang. Jamming Sensor Networks: Attack and Defense Strategies. IEEE *Networks*, 20(3):41–47, 2006.

Ephemeral Networks with Random Availability of Links: Diameter and Connectivity*

Eleni C. Akrida
Department of Computer Science
University of Liverpool, UK
eleni.akrida@liverpool.ac.uk

George B. Mertzios
School of Engineering and Computing Sciences
Durham University, UK
george.mertzios@durham.ac.uk

Leszek Gąsieniec
Department of Computer Science
University of Liverpool, UK
l.a.gasieniec@liverpool.ac.uk

Paul G. Spirakis
Department of Computer Science
University of Liverpool, UK
p.spirakis@liverpool.ac.uk

ABSTRACT

In this work we consider temporal networks, the links of which are available only at random times (*randomly available temporal networks*). Our networks are *ephemeral*: their links appear sporadically, only at certain times, within a given maximum time (*lifetime* of the net). More specifically, our temporal networks notion concerns networks, whose edges (arcs) are assigned one or more random discrete-time labels drawn from a set of natural numbers. The labels of an edge indicate the discrete moments in time at which the edge is available. In such networks, information (e.g., messages) have to follow *temporal paths*, i.e., paths, the edges of which are assigned a strictly increasing sequence of labels. We first examine a very hostile network: a clique, each edge of which is known to be available *only one random time* in the time period $\{1, 2, \ldots, n\}$ (n is the number of vertices). How fast can a vertex send a message to all other vertices in such a network? To answer this, we define the notion of the Temporal Diameter for the random temporal clique and prove that it is $\Theta(\log n)$ with high probability and in expectation. In fact, we show that information dissemination is very fast with high probability even in this hostile network with regard to availability. This result is similar to the results for the random phone-call model. Our model, though, is weaker. Our availability assumptions are different and randomness is provided only by the input. We show here that the temporal diameter of the clique is crucially affected by the clique's lifetime, a, e.g., when a is asymptotically larger than the number of vertices, n, then the temporal diameter must be $\Omega(\frac{a}{n} \log n)$. We, then, consider the least number, r, of *random points in time* at which an edge is available, in order to guarantee at least a temporal path between any pair of vertices of the network (notice that the clique is the only network for which just one instance of availability per edge, even non-random, suffices for this). We show that r is $\Omega(\log n)$ even for some networks of diameter 2. Finally, we compare this cost to an (optimal) deterministic allocation of labels of availability that guarantees a temporal path between any pair of vertices. For this reason, we introduce the notion of the *Price of Randomness* and we show an upper bound for general networks.

Categories and Subject Descriptors

G.2.2 [**Discrete Mathematics**]: Graph Theory—*graph labelling, network problems, path and circuit problems*; G.3 [**Probability and Statistics**]: survival analysis

General Terms

Theory

Keywords

Temporal networks, random input, diameter, availability.

1. INTRODUCTION

A temporal network is a network that changes with time. Many networks of today have links that are not always available. In this work, embarking from the foundational work of Kempe et al. [19] and from the sequel [21], we consider time to be discrete, that is, we consider networks in which the links are available *only at certain moments in time*, e.g., days or hours. Such networks can be described via an underlying graph $G = (V, E)$ (*the links of which can become available*) and an assignment L assigning a set of discrete labels to each edge (arc) of G.

We consider here both the single-label-per-edge model of [19] and the multi-labelled one, which allows links to be available at multiple times (i.e., more than one label per edge). These labels are drawn from the natural numbers (in fact from a set of discrete times $S = \{1, 2, \ldots, a\}$) and indicate the discrete moments in time at which the corresponding connection is available. Usually, we take $a = |V(G)|$ (a

*Supported in part by (i) the School of EEE and CS of the Univeristy of Liverpool, (ii) the FET EU IP Project MULTIPLEX under contract No. 317532, and (iii) the EPSRC Grant EP/K022660/1.

normalized case). Note that such networks are *ephemeral*: No link is available at any time after time (day) a. We call a the *lifetime* of the network.

In many (worst case) situations, availability of links comes at a cost. Available links may correspond, e.g., to connections in physical systems requiring high energy. They may also correspond to very rare moments in time, in which the link of a hostile network is "unguarded" and, thus, one can pass a message at that time without putting the message in danger.

A temporal path (or journey) in such a network is a path on the edges (arcs) of which one can find *strictly increasing* labels. The time label used on the last edge of a temporal path would then indicate the time at which a message would arrive at the last vertex of the path.

Imagine a very hostile *clique-network* G, the links of which are all usually guarded. Whenever a link is guarded it is impossible to pass a message through it. We may pass a message to a neighbour (in G) only when the link to this neighbour is unguarded (i.e., available). Now, let us assume that each link will become available only at a *random time* in S. Let us look at the case where $S = \{1, 2, \ldots, n\}$ (where $n = |V(G)|$). After time n, no link of the clique is ever available! Such a random time indicates a break in the security of the link. How fast can we pass a message (starting from a vertex s) to all the other vertices in the clique? Certainly, one possibility is to wait (for each destination t) for the link (s, t) to become available. But this may mean a passing time equal to $\frac{n}{2}$ in expectation. Can we spread a message faster? In this paper, we show that for the temporal clique with a single random moment of availability per link, one can still pass the message to all vertices in time $\Theta(\log n)$ with high probability. That is, a seemingly very hostile clique (each link of which is unguarded only for one random moment) is, in fact, not so secure with respect to fast dissemination of enemy information.

Note that the clique is the only graph G which achieves *temporal reachability* of all vertices, even when each edge (link) of it is only available at one time, chosen from the set $\{1, 2, \ldots, n\}$.

One now may wish to pay for greater (more) availability of links. In fact, given a graph G, one may wish to find the minimum total number of labels, over all edges, (OPT) that guarantee a temporal path between any $s, t \in V(G)$. But, there are cases in which this OPT quantity is not even approximable in P unless $P = NP$ [21]. Instead, you may bargain locally (per link) to "buy" a *number of random times for which the link is available*. We assume here that we are given a complicated network. Each node has no information about the network topology, but knows the number of vertices, n, and the diameter, d, of the net. We assume that *global coordination over availability of all edges is impossible*. (Otherwise, an assignment of *the same* d consecutive labels per edge would guarantee all-pairs reachability. But this requires global coordination.) However, we allow adjacent vertices to agree on a number, $r(n)$, of *random available times for the edge joining them*. This is a local operation that uses local, random availability to replace the lack of global knowledge and global coordination. What is the least r to guarantee a temporal path between any pair of vertices in G, with high probability? In this paper, we show that r is lower bounded by $\Omega(\log n)$ *even for some graphs of diameter 2*. We then estimate sufficient values of r to guarantee

temporal paths between all node-pairs (with high probability) for any graph G. In this paper, we write that an event holds "with high probability" when there exists a constant $c \geq 1$ such that the probability of the event is at least $1 - \frac{1}{n^c}$, where n is the number of vertices.

In this work we, thus, initiate the study of "random" ephemeral temporal networks. We define notions like the *temporal diameter* (to capture fast dissemination of information) and the *Price of Randomness*, PoR (to capture the cost to pay per link in order to guarantee temporal reachability of all node-pairs by local random available times with high probability). Intuitively, PoR is the ratio $\frac{mr}{OPT}$, where r random times of availability for each and every link are able to guarantee all-pairs temporal reachability with high probability. We believe that our work will motivate further research on both temporal networks and random temporal networks.

1.1 Relation to the Random Phone-Call Model

The first logarithmic time results for probabilistic information dissemination were obtained in the classical Random Phone-Call model defined in [9]. In [9], the authors present a push algorithm that uses $\Theta(\log n)$ time and $\Theta(n \log n)$ message transmissions. For complete graphs of size n, Frieze and Grimmett [15] presented an algorithm that broadcasts in time $\log_2 n + \ln n + o(\log n)$ with a probability of $1 - o(1)$. Later, Pittel [27] showed that (with probability $1 - o(1)$) it is possible to broadcast a message in time $\log_2 n + \ln n + f(n)$, where $f(n)$ can be any slow growing function.

Karp et al. [17] presented a push and pull algorithm which reduces the total number of transmissions to $O(n \log \log n)$, with probability $1 - n^{-1}$, and showed that this result is asymptotically optimal. For sparser graphs it is not possible to stay within $O(n \log \log n)$ message transmissions together with a broadcast time of $O(\log n)$ in this phone-call model, not even for random graphs [11]. However, if each node is allowed to remember a small number of neighbors to which it has communicated in some previous steps, then the number of message transmissions can be reduced to $O(n \log \log n)$, with probability $1 - n^{-1}$ [3, 12].

The network model adopted in this paper resembles the Random Phone-Call model to some extent, however, it is essentially different. The dependence of the temporal diameter (of the hostile clique) on its lifetime, for example, cannot be captured by the random phone-call model. The model described here is, in fact, considerably weaker. In the phone-call model, each node, at each step, can communicate with a random neighbour (in fact, a node may do this at several times). In our model, each link is given a (single) random moment of existence, by the input. A node can send via this link only at that moment. That is, randomness is not a part of our algorithmic techniques and can not be used at arbitrary time steps.

1.2 Other related work

In this section we provide a short survey of papers with studies on networks labelled by time units or segments.
Labelled Graphs. Labelled graphs have been widely used both in Computer Science and in Mathematics, e.g., [25].
Single-labelled and multi-labelled Temporal Networks. The model of temporal networks that we consider in this work is a direct extension of the single-labelled model

studied in [19] as well as the multi-labelled model studied in [21]. The prior results of [19, 21] do not consider randomness at all, and therefore are different in nature to this work. The initial paper [19] considers the case of one (non-random) label per edge and examines shortest journey algorithms. The second paper [21] extends this (non-random) model to many labels per edge and mainly examines the number of labels needed to guarantee several graph properties with certainty.

Continuous Availabilities (Intervals). Some authors have assumed the availability of an edge for a whole time-interval $[t_1, t_2]$ or multiple such time-intervals and not just for discrete moments as we assume here. Although this is a clearly natural assumption, we design and develop techniques for the discrete case which are quite different from those needed in the continuous case [6, 14].

Dynamic Distributed Networks. In recent years, there is a growing interest in distributed computing systems that are inherently dynamic [1, 2, 4, 7, 8, 10, 20, 22–24, 26, 28].

Distance labelling. A distance labelling of a graph G is an assignment of unique labels to vertices of G so that the distance between any two vertices can be inferred from their labels alone [16, 18].

2. PRELIMINARIES

In this section we first define *temporal networks* (cf. Definition 1) by assigning a set $L_e \subseteq \mathbb{N}$ of *time-labels* to every edge e of a (di)graph $\widetilde{G} = (V, E)$.

DEFINITION 1. *Let $\widetilde{G} = (V, E)$ be a (di)graph. A temporal network on $\widetilde{G}$ is a triplet $G = (\widetilde{G}, L)$ (also denoted as $G = (V, E, L)$), where $L = \{L_e \subseteq \mathbb{N} : e \in E\}$ is an assignment of labels on the edges of $\widetilde{G}$.*

When for every edge e, $L_e \subseteq \{1, 2, \ldots, a\}$, for some $a \in \mathbb{N}$, the network is called *ephemeral* and a is called the *lifetime* of the network.

The values assigned to each edge of the graph are called time labels of the edge and indicate the times at which we can cross it (from one end to the other in arbitrary direction, if the edge is undirected, or from its start to its end, if the edge is directed).

In the context of this paper, we mainly study *random temporal networks*, in which the labels assigned to the edges are chosen at random from a set of available time labels. More specifically, the *model* that we consider is that of random temporal networks, an instance of the labels of each edge of which is given in advance to the algorithm, so that the traveller can see all adjacent edges to all vertices at every moment in time.

2.1 Further Definitions

We can now talk about temporal edges (or time edges) that are considered to be triplets (u, v, l), where u, v are the ends of an edge in the temporal network and $l \in L_{\{u,v\}}$ is a time label of this edge. That is, if an edge $e = \{u, v\}$ has more than one time labels, e.g., has a set of three time labels, $L_e = \{l_1, l_2, l_3\}$, then this edge has three corresponding time edges, (u, v, l_1), (u, v, l_2) and (u, v, l_3).

DEFINITION 2. *A temporal path or journey j from a vertex u to a vertex v ((u, v)-journey) is a sequence of time edges (u, u_1, l_1), (u_1, u_2, l_2), ..., (u_{k-1}, v, l_k), such that $l_i <$*

l_{i+1}, *for each $1 \le i \le k - 1$. We call the last time label of journey j, l_k, arrival time of the journey.*

DEFINITION 3. *A (u, v)-journey j in a temporal network is called foremost journey if its arrival time is the minimum arrival time of all (u, v)-journeys' arrival times, under the labels assigned to the graph's edges. We call this arrival time temporal distance of target vertex v from source vertex u and we denote $\delta(u, v)$.*

Now, consider any ephemeral temporal network $G = (V, E, L)$. Let every edge receive exactly one time label, chosen randomly, independently from one another from a set $L_0 = \{1, 2, \ldots, a\}$, where $a \in \mathbb{N}$, with the probability of an edge label to be i, $\forall i \in L_0$, equal to $\frac{1}{a}$ (**UNI-CASE**).

DEFINITION 4. *A temporal network that satisfies UNI-CASE is called Uniform Random Temporal Network (U-RTN).*

In the special case, where the largest label, a, that can be assigned to the edges of a graph is equal to the number of its vertices, the formed network is called *Normalized Uniform Random Temporal Network (Normalized U-RTN).*

Note.

There could be prospective study of cases in which each edge of a graph may receive several time labels, selected randomly and independently of one another from the set $L_0 = \{1, 2, \ldots, a\}$, where $a \in \mathbb{N}$, with the selection following a distribution F (*F-**CASE***). In such cases, the networks under consideration would be called *F-Random Temporal Networks (F-RTN)* respectively.

In the following section, we focus on the study of uniform random temporal networks, where the underlying graph is complete (clique). Under this scope, we define a statistical property of the uniform random temporal clique, namely its temporal diameter.

DEFINITION 5. *Consider an instance (G, L) of a uniform random temporal clique, G. The Temporal Diameter of G, denoted by TD, is the expected value of the maximum temporal distance over all pairs of vertices in G:*

$$TD(G) = E\left(max_{s,t \in V(G)} \delta(s, t)\right)$$

3. THE TEMPORAL DIAMETER OF THE NORMALIZED UNIFORM RANDOM TEMPORAL CLIQUE

Let $G = K_n$ be a directed clique[1] of n vertices and let us consider its normalized U-version. That is, every edge $e \in E(K_n)$ is given a single availability label, l_e, and those labels are chosen randomly and independently from one another from the set $L_0 = \{1, 2, \ldots, n\}$, with the probability that the label of a particular edge equals i being equal to $\frac{1}{n}$, $\forall i \in L_0$.

We give an algorithmic construction (Algorithm 1) which can, with high probability, find a journey with small expected arrival time from any given source vertex s to any given target vertex t in the directed normalized uniform random temporal clique, K_n.

---

[1] for every pair of vertices $u, v \in K_n$, there exist both the directed edges $\{u, v\}$ and $\{v, u\}$

REMARK 1. *It is easy to see that the same result holds for the undirected uniform random temporal clique. In this case, an edge e of the clique with a random label l corresponds to two directed edges e' and e'' of the directed clique and the analysis is not significantly affected.*

Algorithm 1 The directed normalized U-RT clique Expansion Process algorithm

---

Input: An instance of a directed normalized uniform random temporal clique of n vertices, K_n

1: $d = \Theta(\log n)$; {the exact value of d and of the constants c_1, c_2 below will be determined by the analysis}
2: $\Gamma_1(s) = \{v \in V : l_{\{s,v\}} \in (0, c_1 \log n]\}$;
3: **for** $i = 2, \ldots, d+1$ **do**
4: $\quad \Gamma_i(s) = \{v \in V : l_{\{w,v\}} \in (c_1 \log n + (i-2)c_2, c_1 \log n + (i-1)c_2]$ for some $w \in \Gamma_{i-1}(s)\}$;
5: $\Gamma'_1(t) = \{v \in V : l_{\{v,t\}} \in (2c_1 \log n + 2dc_2, 3c_1 \log n + 2dc_2]\}$;
6: **for** $i = 2, \ldots, d+1$ **do**
7: $\quad \Gamma'_i(t) = \{v \in V : l_{\{v,w\}} \in (2c_1 \log n + (2d - i + 1)c_2, 2c_1 \log n + (2d - i + 2)c_2]$ for some $w \in \Gamma'_{i-1}(s)\}$;
8: **if** $\exists u \in \Gamma_{d+1}(s), v \in \Gamma'_{d+1}(t)$ such that $l_{\{u,v\}} \in (c_1 \log n + dc_2, 2c_1 \log n + dc_2]$ **then**
9: $\quad$ Follow the directed path from s to u, the directed edge (u, v) and the directed path from v to t;
10: $\quad$ **return** success;
11: **else**
12: $\quad$ **return** failure;

Analysis of the Expansion Process Algorithm.

Next, we analyze the Expansion Process algorithm and we prove that it succeeds with high probability, thus giving a short, $O(\log n)$, journey from s to t.

Note. In the following analysis, we reveal each arc's random label only once, when examined (*delayed revelation of random values*). Thus, we are consistent with the fact that the input is a specific instance (with all random labels drawn).

Denote by p_1 the probability that an outgoing edge of s has a label in the desired interval, i.e., $(0, c_1 \log n]$. p_1 is also the probability that an outgoing edge of some vertex in $\Gamma_{d+1}(s)$ to $\Gamma'_{d+1}(t)$ has label in the desired interval, i.e., $(c_1 \log n + dc_2, 2c_1 \log n + dc_2]$. Finally, p_1 is also the probability that an incoming edge of t has a label in the desired interval, i.e., $(2c_1 \log n + 2dc_2, 3c_1 \log n + 2dc_2]$. It is:

$$p_1 = \frac{c_1 \log n}{n}$$

Denote by p_2 the probability that a vertex $v \in \Gamma_i(s)$ (or a $v \in \Gamma'_i(t)$), $i = 1, 2, \ldots, d$, has an outgoing edge (or incoming edge, respectively) with label that falls in the desired interval, i.e., $(c_1 \log n + (i-1)c_2, c_1 \log n + ic_2]$ (or $(2c_1 \log n + (2d-1)c_2, 2c_1 \log n + (2d-i+1)c_2]$, respectively). It is:

$$p_2 = \frac{c_2}{n}$$

Also, denote by Δ_i, Δ^* and Δ'_i, $i = 1, 2, \ldots, d+1$ the desired intervals in each case, namely:

$$
\begin{aligned}
\Delta_1 &= (0, c_1 \log n] \\
\Delta_2 &= (c_1 \log n, c_1 \log n + c_2] \\
\Delta_3 &= (c_1 \log n + c_2, c_1 \log n + 2c_2] \\
&\cdots \\
\Delta_{d+1} &= (c_1 \log n + (d-1)c_2, c_1 \log n + dc_2] \\
\Delta^* &= (c_1 \log n + dc_2, 2c_1 \log n + dc_2] \\
\Delta'_{d+1} &= (2c_1 \log n + dc_2, 2c_1 \log n + (d+1)c_2] \\
&\cdots \\
\Delta'_2 &= (2c_1 \log n + (2d-1)c_2, 2c_1 \log n + 2dc_2] \\
\Delta'_1 &= (2c_1 \log n + 2dc_2, 3c_1 \log n + 2dc_2]
\end{aligned}
$$

Note. If there exists at least one edge with label in the corresponding Δ_i, Δ^* or Δ'_i, $i = 1, 2, \ldots, d+1$ at each step of the expansion, then the time needed to reach t starting from s is at most $3c_1 \log n + 2dc_2$.

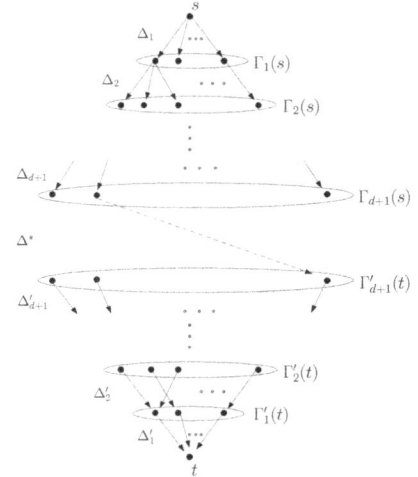

Figure 1: The Expansion Process.

Figure 1 illustrates how the expansion process from s to t works. That is, starting from s, we find the set $\Gamma_1(s)$ of vertices to which there is an edge from s with label within Δ_1, then the set $\Gamma_2(s)$ of vertices to which there is an edge from a vertex in $\Gamma_1(s)$ with label within Δ_2, etc. We show that, with high probability, there is a journey from s to t through vertices in the consecutive Γ_is.

3.1 The first step of the expansion process

The first step of the expansion process aims in establishing with high probability a number of $\Theta(\log n)$ neighbours of s, so that the edge from s to each one of them is in Δ_1. Note that the probability of a label on an edge $(s, u), u \in V$ being in Δ_1 is exactly $p_1 = \frac{c_1 \log n}{n}$, because of the uniform selection of labels.

Let $\mathcal{E}_1$ be the event that $\frac{1}{2}E(|\Gamma_1(s)|) \leq |\Gamma_1(s)| \leq \frac{3}{2}E(|\Gamma_1(s)|)$. Note that:

$$E(|\Gamma_1(s)|) = (n-1)p_1 = (n-1)\frac{c_1 \log n}{n}$$

By the Chernoff bound on the Binomial $B(N, p_1)$, where $N = n - 1$, $\forall \beta \in (0, 1)$, it holds:

$$Pr(\#successes \in (1 \pm \beta)Np_1) \geq 1 - e^{-\frac{\beta^2}{2}Np_1}$$

Now, use $\beta = \frac{1}{2}$. We get:

$$
\begin{aligned}
Pr(\#successes \in (\frac{1}{2}, \frac{3}{2})Np_1) &\geq 1 - e^{-\frac{1}{8}Np_1} \\
&\geq 1 - e^{-\frac{1}{8}(c_1 \log n - \frac{c_1 \log n}{n})} \\
&\geq 1 - e^{-\frac{1}{8}(c_1 - 1)\log n} \\
&\geq 1 - \frac{1}{n^{\frac{c_1 - 1}{8}}}
\end{aligned}
$$

We now choose $c_1 \geq 33$, and thus $\frac{c_1 - 1}{8} \geq 4$. So we have established the following:

LEMMA 1. *It holds that:*

$$Pr(\mathcal{E}_1) = Pr\left(|\Gamma_1(s)| \in (\frac{1}{2}, \frac{3}{2})(c_1 \log n(1 - \frac{1}{n}))\right) \geq 1 - \frac{1}{n^4}$$

3.2 The expansion process until reaching $\Theta(\sqrt{n})$ vertices

We now show that given:

- $|\Gamma_1(s)| = \Theta(\log n)$, and

- the probability of an edge having a label in a particular interval $\Delta_i, i = 2, \ldots, d+1$ is exactly $p_2 = \frac{|\Delta_i|}{n} = \frac{c_2}{n}$

the vertices reachable from s via temporal paths grow (almost) geometrically.

In particular, let us now condition on the event that $\frac{1}{8}c_1 \log n \leq |\Gamma_i(s)| \leq \lambda\sqrt{n}$, for some fixed $\lambda > 0$. To find the set $\Gamma_{i+1}(s)$, we consider the vertices which are *not* in all the $\Gamma_j(s)$, $j = 1, 2, \ldots, i$ (and the fact that we look for directed edges), i.e.,

$$n_i = n - |\bigcup_{j=1}^{i} \Gamma_j(s)|$$

The probability that a vertex u (out of the n_i vertices) belongs to $\Gamma_{i+1}(s)$ is exactly the probability that the label of some $(v, u) \in E, v \in \Gamma_i(s)$, is in the interval Δ_{i+1}, i.e., equal to:

$$
\begin{aligned}
q &= 1 - Pr(u \notin \Gamma_{i+1}(s)) \\
&= 1 - (1 - p_2)^{|\Gamma_i(s)|} \\
&= 1 - (1 - \frac{c_2}{n})^{|\Gamma_i(s)|}
\end{aligned}
$$

We need the following fact:

FACT 1. *It holds that* $(1 - \frac{c_2}{n})^{|\Gamma_i(s)|} \leq 1 - \frac{c_2|\Gamma_i(s)|}{2n}$

PROOF. Let $p = \frac{c_2}{n}$ and $k = |\Gamma_i(s)|$. We know that:

$$(1 - p)^k \leq 1 - kp + \binom{k}{2}p^2 \tag{1}$$

We will show that:

$$-kp + \binom{k}{2}p^2 \leq -\frac{kp}{2}$$

and, thus, by relation 1 it holds that:

$$(1 - p)^k \leq 1 - \frac{kp}{2}$$

Indeed, we have:

$$
\begin{aligned}
-kp + \binom{k}{2}p^2 &\leq -\frac{kp}{2} \Leftrightarrow \\
\frac{k(k-1)}{2}p &\leq \frac{k}{2} \Leftrightarrow \\
(k-1)p &\leq 1 \Leftrightarrow \\
(|\Gamma_i(s)| - 1)c_2 &\leq n
\end{aligned}
$$

The latter holds for n sufficiently large. $\square$

Thus, we have:

$$
\begin{aligned}
q &\geq 1 - (1 - \frac{c_2|\Gamma_i(s)|}{2n}) \\
&= \frac{c_2|\Gamma_i(s)|}{2n} \\
&\geq \frac{c_1 c_2 \log n}{16n} = q'
\end{aligned}
$$

The random variable $|\Gamma_{i+1}(s)|$ follows the Binomial distribution $B(n_i, q)$ and dominates $B(n_i, q')$. Therefore, by the Chernoff bound (with $\beta = \frac{1}{2}$), we have:

$$Pr\left(|\Gamma_{i+1}(s)| \in (\frac{1}{2}n_i q, \frac{3}{2}n_i q)\right) \geq 1 - e^{-\frac{1}{8}n_i q'} \tag{2}$$

But, $n_i \geq n - (\lambda\sqrt{n})d \geq \frac{n}{2}$. So, relation 2 becomes:

$$
\begin{aligned}
Pr\left(|\Gamma_{i+1}(s)| \in (\frac{1}{2}n_i q, \frac{3}{2}n_i q)\right) &\geq 1 - e^{-\frac{1}{16}n\frac{c_1 c_2 \log n}{16n}} \\
&\geq 1 - e^{-\frac{1}{256}c_1 c_2 \log n} \\
&\geq 1 - \frac{1}{n^{\frac{c_1 c_2}{256}}}
\end{aligned}
$$

We will select c_2 so that $\frac{c_1 c_2}{256} \geq 4$. So, with probability at least $1 - \frac{1}{n^4}$, it is:

$$
\begin{aligned}
\frac{3}{2}n_i q &\geq |\Gamma_{i+1}(s)| \geq \frac{1}{2}n_i q \Rightarrow \\
\frac{3}{2}n_i \frac{c_2|\Gamma_i(s)|}{2n} &\geq |\Gamma_{i+1}(s)| \geq \frac{1}{2}n_i \frac{c_2|\Gamma_i(s)|}{2n} \Rightarrow \\
\frac{3}{4}c_2|\Gamma_i(s)| &\geq |\Gamma_{i+1}(s)| \geq \frac{1}{8}c_2|\Gamma_i(s)|
\end{aligned}
$$

We have proved that the event

$$\mathcal{E}_i = \text{``}|\Gamma_{i+1}(s)| \text{ is at most } \frac{3}{4}c_2|\Gamma_i(s)| \text{ and at least } \frac{1}{8}c_2|\Gamma_i(s)|\text{''}$$

holds with probability at least $1 - \frac{1}{n^4}$, provided that $\frac{1}{8}c_1 \log n \leq \Gamma_i(s) \leq \lambda\sqrt{n}$.

Thus, by conditioning on the event $\mathcal{E} = \bigcap_{i=1}^{d} \mathcal{E}_i$, we have that:

$$|\Gamma_{d+1}(s)| \geq \frac{1}{8}(\frac{c_2}{8})^d c_1 \log n$$

and also

$$|\Gamma_{d+1}(s)| \leq \frac{1}{8}(\frac{3c_2}{4})^d c_1 \log n$$

Choose d so that:

$$\frac{1}{8}(\frac{3c_2}{4})^d c_1 \log n \leq \lambda' \sqrt{n}, \text{ for some constant } \lambda' > 0$$

$$\Rightarrow d \leq \frac{\log \frac{8\lambda' \sqrt{n}}{c_1 \log n}}{\log \frac{3c_2}{4}}$$

and also:

$$\frac{1}{8}(\frac{c_2}{8})^d c_1 \log n > \sqrt{n}$$

$$\Rightarrow d > \frac{\log \frac{8\sqrt{n}}{c_1 \log n}}{\log \frac{c_2}{8}}$$

The probability that one or more of the events $\mathcal{E}_1, \mathcal{E}_2, \ldots, \mathcal{E}_d$ fail is (by the union bound) at most:

$$d\frac{1}{n^4} \leq c' \log n \frac{1}{n^4} \leq \frac{1}{n^3}, \text{ for some } c' > 0$$

Thus, we have shown the following:

THEOREM 1. *With probability at least $1 - \frac{1}{n^3}$, the expansion process out of s arrives at $\Theta(\sqrt{n})$ vertices with temporal paths of length $d + 1 = \Theta(\log n)$, consistently labelled in the intervals Δ_i, $i = 1, 2, \ldots, d + 1$, in time at most $c_1 \log n + dc_2 = \Theta(\log n)$.*

3.3 The reverse expansion process (out of t)

Consider the edges reaching t *reversed* and consider the process that labels them in Δ'_1. Let $\Gamma'_1(t)$ be the vertices derived in this way, i.e., reaching t with an edge labelled in Δ'_1. Continue the reverse expansion process until we reach $\Theta(\sqrt{n})$ vertices. By symmetry and independence, we get exactly the same result as in Theorem 1:

THEOREM 2. *The expansion process out of t arrives at $\Theta(\sqrt{n})$ vertices with temporal paths (reverse direction) of length $d + 1 = \Theta(\log n)$, consistently labelled in the intervals Δ'_i, $i = 1, 2, \ldots, d + 1$. Thus, it arrives to each of these vertices in time at most $c_1 \log n + dc_2 = \Theta(\log n)$ with probability at least $1 - \frac{1}{n^3}$.*

3.4 The matching argument

The probability that both $|\Gamma_{d+1}(s)|$ and $|\Gamma'_{d+1}(t)|$ are of size at least $\lambda' \sqrt{n}$, $\lambda' > 0$ is at least $1 - 2\frac{1}{n^3}$. Note that we just need one edge $(v_1, v_2), v_1 \in \Gamma_{d+1}(s), v_2 \in \Gamma'_{d+1}(t)$ with label in the interval Δ^* in order to demonstrate the existence of a temporal path of largest label at most $\Theta(\log n)$ from s to t. Note also that for a *given edge* $(v_1, v_2), v_1 \in \Gamma_{d+1}(s), v_2 \in \Gamma'_{d+1}(t)$, its label is in Δ^* with probability exactly:

$$p_1 = \frac{|\Delta^*|}{n} = \frac{c_1 \log n}{n}$$

Thus, the probability of the event $A = $ "existence of such an edge" is:

$$p = 1 - \left(1 - \frac{c_1 \log n}{n}\right)^{|\Gamma_{d+1}(s)| \cdot |\Gamma'_{d+1}(t)|}$$

and due to Theorems 1 and 2, it is:

$$
\begin{aligned}
p &\geq 1 - \left(1 - \frac{c_1 \log n}{n}\right)^{(\lambda')^2 n} \\
&\geq 1 - e^{-(\lambda')^2 c_1 \log n} \\
&= 1 - \frac{1}{n^{(\lambda')^2 c_1}}
\end{aligned}
$$

We can choose c_1 through the analysis so that we have:

$$p \geq 1 - \frac{1}{n^3}$$

The probability of any of the events of Theorems 1 and 2 or event A failing is at most $3\frac{1}{n^3}$. Thus,

THEOREM 3. *In the directed normalized uniform random temporal clique, given any vertices s, t, we can go from s to t via a temporal path of length at most $\gamma \log n$, for some constant $\gamma > 1$, with probability at least $1 - \frac{3}{n^3}$.*

But, then we get our main theorem, as follows:

THEOREM 4. *The Temporal Diameter of the directed normalized uniform random temporal clique is (with high probability) at most $\gamma \log n$, for some constant $\gamma > 1$.*

PROOF. The probability that there exists a pair of vertices $s, t \in V$ so that Theorem 3 fails is less than $n^2 \frac{3}{n^3} = \frac{3}{n}$ (by the union bound). So, with probability at least $1 - \frac{3}{n}$, it holds that:

$$max_{s,t \in V}\{\text{temporal distance of } t \text{ from } s\} \leq \gamma \log n$$

Thus,

$$TD \leq \gamma \log n, \text{ with probability at least } 1 - \frac{3}{n}$$

and

$$TD > \gamma \log n \text{ (but still } \leq n\text{), with probability at most } \frac{3}{n}$$

Therefore,

$$
\begin{aligned}
TD &\leq (1 - \frac{3}{n})\gamma \log n + \frac{3}{n}n \\
&\leq \gamma \log n - \frac{3 \log n}{n} + 3
\end{aligned}
$$

$\square$

Remark.

One can easily see that the latter is a *threshold* and that the Temporal Diameter of the directed normalized uniform random temporal clique cannot be any less than $\Omega(\log n)$. Assume the event E_1, where the temporal diameter of the directed normalized uniform random temporal clique G is $TD(G) = o(\log n)$, i.e.,

$$\exists \alpha(n) \xrightarrow[n \to +\infty]{} +\infty : TD(G) \leq \frac{\log n}{\alpha(n)}$$

Conditional on E_1, the label in every edge of G realizing the diameter is within the interval $(0, \frac{\log n}{\alpha(n)})$. Then, the probability of an edge e "existing" at some moment within the interval $(0, n)$ is:

$$\frac{l_e}{n} \leq \frac{\log n}{n\alpha(n)} = p$$

The temporal connectivity of G is dominated by the probability that $G_{n,p}$ is connected. But when $p = o(\frac{\log n}{n})$, then $G_{n,p}$ will almost surely be disconnected [5].

3.5 Spreading a message in the directed uniform random temporal clique

Let us consider again the very hostile clique network G of n vertices in which each edge is available only one random time in the time period $\{1, 2, \ldots, n\}$, and let us consider the case where a vertex s wishes to propagate a message to all other vertices. How fast can this message from s be disseminated to the whole network? Consider the following protocol:

$\forall u \in V(G)$, if u has the message from s, then:
when an arc out of u becomes available, send the message through that arc;

The expansion process described in Algorithm 1 is a construction that demonstrates a temporal path with $O(\log n)$ arrival time from any vertex of the directed uniform random temporal clique to any other vertex with high probability. The above protocol merely exploits Algorithm 1. Thus, it will achieve the dissemination of the message from a specific vertex s to all other vertices of the directed uniform random temporal clique network in *logarithmic time*, $O(\log n)$.

3.6 Temporal Diameter and lifetime - A lower bound

It is easy to see that the following theorem holds:

THEOREM 5. *Let G be the uniform random temporal clique network of n vertices and of lifetime a, i.e., each edge is available exactly one random time within the time period $\{1, 2, \ldots, a\}$, for some $a \in \mathbb{N}$. If a is asymptotically larger than n, then the temporal diameter must be $\Omega(\frac{a}{n} \log n)$.*

PROOF. Assume that the temporal diameter was $k < \frac{a}{n} \log n$. Now, consider (only) the arcs with labels up to k. Since the probability distribution of the labels on the edges of G is uniform, this edge-induced subgraph is the Erdös-Rényi random graph $G_{n,p}$ [5,13], where $p = \frac{k}{a} < \frac{\log n}{n}$. However, it is well known that for such p, $G_{n,p}$ is disconnected with high probability. Therefore, with high probability, the maximum label in a temporal path between at least one pair of vertices is at least $k + 1$, i.e. $\Omega(\frac{a}{n} \log n)$. □

The dependence of the Temporal Diameter on the lifetime is a phenomenon that is not captured by static models (such as the random phone-call model).

4. GUARANTEEING TEMPORAL REACHABILITY WITH HIGH PROBABILITY: GRAPHS OF SMALL DIAMETER

4.1 Definitions

Note that the clique is the only graph for which temporal reachability is guaranteed even with 1 random label per edge (drawn from any distribution). This is the case, because one can always follow the edge (s, t) from any s to any t at the time given by the label. For other networks, one may hope that temporal reachability can be guaranteed (whp) with a number of *random* labels per edge.

In the following, we consider selection of labels from the set $\{1, 2, \ldots, n\}$ for a graph $G = (V, E)$ with $|V| = n$ (nor-

malized case). We focus on *independent* and *uniformly random* selection of labels (available times) for each edge.

Let $G = (V, E)$ be a (di)graph and L be an assignment of time labels on the edges of G. Consider the property $T_{reach} = $ "$\forall u, v \in V$, $\exists (u, v)$-path in $G \Leftrightarrow \exists (u, v)$-journey in (G, L)".

DEFINITION 6. *An assignment L of temporal labels to the edges of a graph G preserves the reachability of G if (G, L) has the property T_{reach}.*

DEFINITION 7. *Let $G = (V, E)$ be a connected (di)graph with $|V| = n$. A random experiment E which assigns $r(n)$ independent random labels to every edge of G strongly guarantees temporal reachability with high probability, if the probability of the property T_{reach} (in the experiment E) is at least $1 - \frac{1}{n^a}$, for some $a \geq 1$.*

DEFINITION 8. *Let $G = (V, E)$ be a connected (di)graph with $|V| = n$ and $E = m$. Let $r(n)$ be the smallest number of random labels per edge which, when assigned to the edges of G, strongly guarantees temporal reachability with high probability. Let, also, $OPT = \sum_{e \in E} |L_e|$ be the total number of labels assigned to the edges of G in the optimal[2] (deterministic) assignment which preserves the reachability of G. The Price of Randomness for G is:*

$$PoR(G) = m \frac{r(n)}{OPT}$$

Note that, for some cases, it has been shown that OPT is hard to approximate (there exists no $PTAS$) unless $P = NP$ [21].

4.2 The Price of Randomness can be high

We show here that $PoR(G)$ is *not bounded by any constant* even for graphs G of *diameter* 2.

THEOREM 6. *There is a graph $G = (V, E)$ of n vertices and diameter 2 for which:*

$$PoR(G) = \Theta(\log n)$$

PROOF. Let us consider the *star* graph G_n of n vertices, that is the complete bipartite graph $K_{1,n-1}$: a tree with one internal node and $n - 1$ leaves. Note that $OPT = 2m$, since there exists an assignment of 2 labels per edge (e.g., labels 1, 2 for every edge) which preserves the reachability of G_n, and obviously any assignment of 1 label per edge does not. We will show that $PoR(G_n) = \Theta(\log n)$.

(a) First, we establish that $r(n) = \Theta(\log n)$ random labels per edge are enough to strongly guarantee temporal reachability whp. Let us use $r(n) = \rho \log n$ ($\rho > 8$) random labels per edge. Denote by c the center vertex of G_n. Now consider two fixed leafs, u_1, u_2, of G_n.

Each of the edges $e_1 = \{u_1, c\}$ and $e_2 = \{c, u_2\}$ is assigned $r(n)$ random labels. Let us denote by s_1, s_2 the sets of labels assigned to e_1 and e_2 respectively. We call *2-split* (u_1, u_2)-journey any (u_1, u_2)-journey, where the first temporal edge has a label within the interval $(0, \frac{n}{2})$ and the second temporal edge has a label within the interval $(\frac{n}{2}, n)$ (see Figure 2).

---

[2] By optimal assignment, we mean the assignment with the least total number of labels.

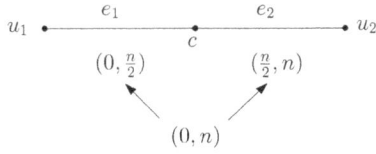

Figure 2: 2-split journey in a star graph.

The probability that an element of s_1 falls within the interval $(0, \frac{n}{2})$ is $\frac{1}{2}$. So, the probability that no element of s_1 falls within this interval is:

$$
\begin{aligned}
Pr(\text{all labels of } e_1 \geq \frac{n}{2}) &= \left(1 - \frac{1}{2}\right)^{\rho \log n} \\
&\leq e^{-\frac{\rho \log n}{2}} \\
&= \frac{1}{n^{\frac{\rho}{2}}}
\end{aligned}
$$

Similarly, the probability that an element of s_2 falls within the interval $(\frac{n}{2}, n)$ is $\frac{1}{2}$. So, the probability that no element of s_2 falls within this interval is:

$$
\begin{aligned}
Pr(\text{all labels of } e_2 \leq \frac{n}{2}) &= \left(1 - \frac{1}{2}\right)^{\rho \log n} \\
&\leq \frac{1}{n^{\frac{\rho}{2}}}
\end{aligned}
$$

Hence, the probability that we can find a label $l_1 \in s_1$ and a label $l_2 \in s_2$ such that $l_1 \in (0, \frac{n}{2})$ and $l_2 \in (\frac{n}{2}, n)$, i.e., the probability that there exists a *2-split* (u_1, u_2)-journey, is:

$$
\begin{aligned}
&Pr(\exists 2\text{-}split(u_1, u_2) - journey) \\
&= Pr(\exists l_1 \in s_1, l_2 \in s_2 : l_1 \in (0, \frac{n}{2}) \,\&\, l_2 \in (\frac{n}{2}, n)) \\
&= Pr(\exists l_1 \in s_1 : l_1 \in (0, \frac{n}{2})) \\
&\quad \cdot Pr(\exists l_2 \in s_2 : l_2 \in (\frac{n}{2}, n)) \\
&= (1 - Pr(\text{all labels of } e_1 \geq \frac{n}{2})) \\
&\quad \cdot (1 - Pr(\text{all labels of } e_2 \leq \frac{n}{2})) \\
&\geq (1 - \frac{1}{n^{\frac{\rho}{2}}})^2 \geq 1 - \frac{2}{n^{\frac{\rho}{2}}}
\end{aligned}
$$

Therefore, it is almost sure that we can find a *2-split* (u_1, u_2)-journey in (G, L). Now, the probability that there exists a pair of vertices $s, t \in V(G)$ such that there is no *2-split* (s, t)-journey in (G, L) is:

$$
\begin{aligned}
&Pr(\exists s, t \in V(G) : \nexists 2\text{-}split(s, t) - journey) \\
&\leq \sum_{s, t \in V(G)} Pr(\nexists 2\text{-}split(s, t) - journey) \\
&\leq n(n-1)\frac{2}{n^{\frac{\rho}{2}}} \\
&< \frac{2}{n^2}, \text{ for } \rho > 8
\end{aligned}
$$

We conclude that almost surely $r(n) = \rho \log n$, $\rho > 8$, random labels per edge[3] suffice for an assignment

---

[3] the labels are selected uniformly at random from the set $L_0 = \{1, 2, \ldots, n\}$ and the edges receive their labels independently of one another

to strongly guarantee temporal reachability with high probability in the star graph G_n.

(b) Surprisingly, we now show that, for the assignment to strongly guarantee temporal reachability whp, $r(n)$ has to be $\Omega(\log n)$. Suppose that, through an assignment L, each edge of G_n now receives $k = \frac{\log n}{\beta(n)}$ random labels (from the set $\{1, 2, \ldots, n\}$), where $\beta(n) \to +\infty$ as $n \to +\infty$. Consider two fixed leafs $u_1, u_2 \in V(G)$ and let $e_1 = \{u_1, c\}, e_2 = \{c, u_2\}$ and E_{u_1, u_2} be the following event:

> *There exists no (u_1, u_2)-journey in (G_n, L)*
> $\equiv \exists a \in \{2, 3, \ldots, n-2\} :$ *all of e_1's labels fall within (a, n) and all of e_2's labels within $(0, a)$*

Given a specific $a \in \{2, 3, \ldots, n-2\}$, the probability that all of e_1's labels fall within (a, n) *and* all of e_2's labels fall within $(0, a)$ is:

$$
\begin{aligned}
&Pr(\text{all of } e_1\text{'s labels fall within } (a, n) \\
&\quad \text{and all of } e_2\text{'s labels fall within } (0, a)) \\
&= (1 - \frac{a}{n})^k (\frac{a}{n})^k
\end{aligned}
$$

Now, the probability that event E_{u_1, u_2} occurs is at least as large as the probability that all of e_1's labels fall within (a, n) *and* all of e_2's labels fall within $(0, a)$, for a specific $a \in \{2, 3, \ldots, n-2\}$, e.g., for $a = \frac{n}{2}$. So:

$$
\begin{aligned}
Pr(E_{u_1, u_2}) &\geq Pr(e_1\text{'s labels fall within } (\frac{n}{2}, n) \text{ and} \\
&\quad\quad e_2\text{'s labels fall within } (0, \frac{n}{2})) \\
&= (\frac{1}{2})^k (\frac{1}{2})^k = (\frac{1}{2})^{2k} = \frac{1}{2^{2k}}
\end{aligned}
$$

The probability that no a, such that all of e_1's labels fall within (a, n) *and* all of e_2's labels fall within $(0, a)$, exists is:

$$
Pr(\neg E_{u_1, u_2}) = 1 - Pr(E_{u_1, u_2}) \leq 1 - \frac{1}{2^{2k}}
$$

Note that also $Pr(E_{u_2, u_1}) \geq \frac{1}{2^{2k}}$ (by symmetry).

In the star graph G_n, we can group the leafs in $\lfloor \frac{n-1}{2} \rfloor = n'$ disjoint pairs $\{u_1, u_2\}, \{u_3, u_4\}, \ldots, \{u_{n'-1}, u_{n'}\}$ defining the paths $(start, center, end)$ $P_1 = (u_1, c, u_2), P_2 = (u_3, c, u_4), \ldots, P_{n'} = (u_{n'-1}, c, u_{n'})$. These paths receive *independent labels* since no edges of P_i overlap with any edge of P_j, $i, j = 1, 2, \ldots, n'$, $i \neq j$. So:

$$
\begin{aligned}
Pr(\neg E \text{ holds for all these pairs}) &\leq (1 - \frac{1}{2^{2k}})^{n'} \\
&\leq e^{-\frac{n'}{2^{2k}}}
\end{aligned}
$$

i.e.,

$$
Pr(\text{there are temporal paths between each } (u_i, u_j),
$$
$$
i = 1, 3, \ldots, j = 2, 4, \ldots) \leq e^{-\frac{n'}{2^{2k}}}
$$

Since $k = \frac{\log n}{\beta(n)}$, we get:

$$\frac{n'}{2^{2k}} = \frac{\lfloor \frac{n-1}{2} \rfloor}{2^{\frac{2\log n}{\beta n}}} = \lfloor \frac{n-1}{2} \rfloor \left(4^{-\log n}\right)^{\frac{1}{\beta(n)}}$$

$$= \lfloor \frac{n-1}{2} \rfloor \left(\frac{1}{n^2}\right)^{\frac{1}{\beta(n)}}$$

So:

$$\frac{n'}{2^{2k}} \geq \frac{n}{3}\left(\frac{1}{n^2}\right)^{\frac{1}{\beta(n)}} > \log n \qquad (3)$$

Relation (3) holds, since:

$$\frac{n}{3}\left(\frac{1}{n^2}\right)^{\frac{1}{\beta(n)}} > \log n \Leftrightarrow \left(\frac{3\log n}{n}\right)^{\beta(n)} < \frac{1}{n^2}$$

But:

$$\left(\frac{3\log n}{n}\right)^{\beta(n)} < \left(\frac{1}{\sqrt{n}}\right)^{\beta(n)} = \left(\frac{1}{n}\right)^{\frac{\beta(n)}{2}} < \frac{1}{n^2},$$

because $\frac{\beta(n)}{2} > 2$. So, by relation (3), we have:

$$-\frac{n'}{2^{2k}} < -\log n \Rightarrow e^{-\frac{n'}{2^{2k}}} < e^{-\log n} = \frac{1}{n}$$

$$\Rightarrow Pr(\exists \text{temporal paths } P_i, \forall i = 1,2,\ldots,n') \leq \frac{1}{n}$$

Thus, it must be:

$$r(n) > \frac{\log n}{\beta(n)}, \text{ for every such } \beta(n) \to +\infty$$

i.e.,

$$PoR(G) > \frac{\log n}{2\beta(n)}, \text{ for all } \beta(n) \to +\infty$$

$$\Rightarrow PoR(G) \geq c\log n - o(n), \text{ for some } c > 0$$

By parts (a) and (b) we obtain that $PoR(G) = \Theta(\log n)$, for the star graph G_n. $\square$

5. THE PRICE OF RANDOMNESS IN GENERAL GRAPHS

Let $G = (V, E)$ be an arbitrary connected graph of $|V| = n$ vertices. Let the set of available times (labels) be $S = \{1, 2, \ldots, q\}$. Let $d(G) = diam(G)$ be the diameter of G. Clearly, for an assignment L to preserve the reachability of G, there must be a label in (G, L) at least equal to G's diameter, since otherwise a path in G realizing the diameter cannot be made a journey. So, $q \geq d(G)$.

For each edge e of G, consider a structure $s(e)$ being a sequence of boxes $B_1(e), B_2(e), \ldots, B_{d(G)}(e)$ (see Figure 3).

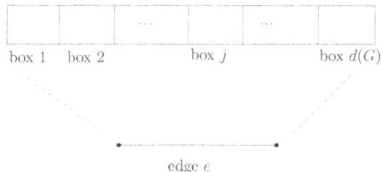

Figure 3: Structure $s(e)$.

Let each Box_i of e be assigned to a corresponding range (sequence) $L_i(e)$ of labels, each of size (#labels) equal to

$\lambda = \frac{q}{d(G)}$, so that:

$$\forall i = 1, 2, \ldots, d(G),$$
$$Box_i \text{ corresponds to } L_i(e) = \{(i-1)\lambda + 1, \ldots, i\lambda\}$$

CLAIM 1. *If $\forall e \in E(G), \forall Box_i(e)$ we put in $Box_i(e)$ one of the labels of $L_i(e)$, then temporal reachability is guaranteed in G.*

PROOF. For any s, t, any shortest path p from s to t will be of length $|p| \leq d(G)$. Any edge e may be at any "place" in p (first, second, ..., even last) or not belong to p at all. The journey from s to t is the path $p = \left(e_{p_1} = \{s, u_1\}, e_{p_2} = \{u_1, u_2\}, \ldots, e_{p_{last}} = \{u_{|p|-1}, t\}\right)$ with the label per edge e_{p_i} in the $(Box_{p_i}(e_{p_i}))$. $\square$

Note now that when we assign a random label in edge e (drawn uniformly, independently from L), the probability that this label falls in $Box_i(e)$ is exactly $\frac{\lambda}{q}$. For r random labels assigned to e, the probability that none of them falls is $Box_i(e)$ is $\left(1 - \frac{\lambda}{q}\right)^r$. Thus, the probability of the event:

$$A(e) = \text{"there exists a box of } e \text{ without a label"}$$

is at most $d(G)\left(1 - \frac{\lambda}{q}\right)^r$.

Clearly,

$$\left(1 - \frac{\lambda}{q}\right)^r \leq e^{-\frac{\lambda r}{q}}$$

and since $d(G) \leq n$, it is enough to have $\frac{\lambda r}{q} > 2\log n$ to get $d(G)\left(1 - \frac{\lambda}{q}\right)^r < n\frac{1}{n^2} = \frac{1}{n}$. But,

$$\frac{\lambda r}{q} > 2\log n \Leftrightarrow r > 2d(G)\log n$$

So, we have shown the following.

THEOREM 7. *If we assign any $r > 2d(G)\log n$ random labels at each edge of G, then temporal reachability is guaranteed with high probability. So,*

$$r(n) \leq 2d(G)\log n + \varepsilon, \text{ for some } \varepsilon > 0.$$

Since $OPT \geq n-1$ (at least $n-1$ edges must be labelled in order to have a labelled spanning tree), we get the following.

THEOREM 8. *For every connected graph G, it holds that:*

$$PoR(G) \leq (2d(G)\log n + \varepsilon)\frac{m}{n-1}, \text{ for some } \varepsilon > 0.$$

Note. The upper bound on the PoR for general graphs can be improved slightly by the *Coupon Collector theorem.*

6. CONCLUSIONS AND FURTHER RESEARCH

In this work, we initiated research on networks with *sparse random* availability of links. The subject of designing the availability of a net (by combining random availabilities and optimal local availabilities) is a subject of our current research.

7. REFERENCES

[1] D. Angluin, J. Aspnes, Z. Diamadi, M. Fischer, and R. Peralta. Computation in networks of passively mobile finite-state sensors. *Distributed Computing*, pages 235–253, 2006.

[2] C. Avin, M. Koucký, and Z. Lotker. How to explore a fast-changing world (cover time of a simple random walk on evolving graphs). In *Proceedings of the 35th International Colloquium on Automata, Languages and Programming (ICALP)*, pages 121–132, 2008.

[3] P. Berenbrink, R. Elsässer, and T. Friedetzky. Efficient randomised broadcasting in random regular networks with applications in peer-to-peer systems. In *Proceedings of the 27th ACM Symposium on Principles of Distributed Computing (PODC)*, pages 155–164, 2008.

[4] B. Bollobás. *Modern Graph Theory*. Springer, 1998.

[5] B. Bollobás. *Random Graphs, 2nd Edition*. Cambridge University Press, 2001.

[6] B.-M. Bui-Xuan, A. Ferreira, and A. Jarry. Computing shortest, fastest, and foremost journeys in dynamic networks. *International Journal of Foundations of Computer Science*, 14(2):267–285, 2003.

[7] A. Casteigts, P. Flocchini, W. Quattrociocchi, and N. Santoro. Time-varying graphs and dynamic networks. *International Journal of Parallel, Emergent and Distributed Systems (IJPEDS)*, 27(5):387–408, 2012.

[8] A. E. F. Clementi, C. Macci, A. Monti, F. Pasquale, and R. Silvestri. Flooding time of edge-markovian evolving graphs. *SIAM Journal on Discrete Mathematics (SIDMA)*, 24(4):1694–1712, 2010.

[9] A. J. Demers, D. H. Greene, C. Hauser, W. Irish, J. Larson, S. Shenker, H. E. Sturgis, D. C. Swinehart, and D. B. Terry. Epidemic algorithms for replicated database maintenance. In *Proceedings of the 6th ACM Symposium on Principles of Distributed Computing (PODC)*, pages 1–12, 1987.

[10] C. Dutta, G. Pandurangan, R. Rajaraman, Z. Sun, and E. Viola. On the complexity of information spreading in dynamic networks. In *Proceedings of the 24th Annual ACM-SIAM Symposium on Discrete Algorithms (SODA)*, pages 717–736, 2013.

[11] R. Elsässer. On the communication complexity of randomized broadcasting in random-like graphs. In *Proceedings of the 18th ACM Symposium on Parallel Algorithms and Architectures (SPAA)*, pages 148–157, 2006.

[12] R. Elsässer and T. Sauerwald. The power of memory in randomized broadcasting. In *Proceedings of the 19th Annual ACM-SIAM Symposium on Discrete Algorithms (SODA)*, pages 218–227, 2008.

[13] P. Erdös and A. Rényi. On random graphs, i. *Publicationes Mathematicae Debrecen*, 6:290–297, 1959.

[14] L. Fleischer and É. Tardos. Efficient continuous-time dynamic network flow algorithms. *Operations Research Letters*, 23(3-5):71–80, 1998.

[15] A. Frieze and G. Grimmett. The shortest-path problem for graphs with random arc-lengths. *Discrete Applied Mathematics*, 10(1):57–77, 1985.

[16] C. Gavoille, D. Peleg, S. Perennes, and R. Raz. Distance labeling in graphs. In *Proceedings of the 12th Annual ACM-SIAM Symposium on Discrete Algorithms (SODA)*, pages 210–219, 2001.

[17] R. M. Karp, C. Schindelhauer, S. Shenker, and B. Vöcking. Randomized rumor spreading. In *Proceedings of the 41st Annual Symposium on Foundations of Computer Science (FOCS)*, pages 565–574, 2000.

[18] M. Katz, N. A. Katz, A. Korman, and D. Peleg. Labeling schemes for flow and connectivity. *SIAM Journal on Computing*, 34(1):23–40, 2004.

[19] D. Kempe, J. M. Kleinberg, and A. Kumar. Connectivity and inference problems for temporal networks. In *Proceedings of the 32nd annual ACM symposium on Theory of computing (STOC)*, pages 504–513, 2000.

[20] F. Kuhn, N. A. Lynch, and R. Oshman. Distributed computation in dynamic networks. In *Proceedings of the 42nd Annual ACM Symposium on Theory of Computing (STOC)*, pages 513–522, 2010.

[21] G. B. Mertzios, O. Michail, I. Chatzigiannakis, and P. G. Spirakis. Temporal network optimization subject to connectivity constraints. In *Proceedings of the 40th International Colloquium on Automata, Languages and Programming (ICALP), Part II*, pages 657–668, 2013.

[22] O. Michail, I. Chatzigiannakis, and P. G. Spirakis. Mediated population protocols. *Theoretical Computer Science*, 412(22):2434–2450, 2011.

[23] O. Michail, I. Chatzigiannakis, and P. G. Spirakis. *New Models for Population Protocols*. Synthesis Lectures on Distributed Computing Theory. Morgan & Claypool Publishers, 2011.

[24] O. Michail, I. Chatzigiannakis, and P. G. Spirakis. Causality, influence, and computation in possibly disconnected synchronous dynamic networks. In *OPODIS*, pages 269–283, 2012.

[25] M. Molloy and B. Reed. *Graph colouring and the probabilistic method*, volume 23 of *Algorithms and Combinatorics*. Springer, 2002.

[26] R. O'Dell and R. Wattenhofer. Information dissemination in highly dynamic graphs. In *Proceedings of the 2005 joint workshop on Foundations of Mobile Computing (DIALM-POMC)*, pages 104–110, 2005.

[27] B. Pittel. Linear probing: The probable largest search time grows logarithmically with the number of records. *J. Algorithms*, 8(2):236–249, 1987.

[28] C. Scheideler. Models and techniques for communication in dynamic networks. In *Proceedings of the 19th Annual Symposium on Theoretical Aspects of Computer Science (STACS)*, 2002.

Locality-based Network Creation Games

Davide Bilò
Dipartimento di Scienze
Umanistiche e Sociali
Università di Sassari, Italy
davide.bilo@uniss.it

Luciano Gualà
Dipartimento di Ingegneria
dell'Impresa
Università di Roma "Tor
Vergata", Italy
guala@mat.uniroma2.it

Stefano Leucci
Dipartimento di Ingegneria e
Scienze dell'Informazione e
Matematica
Università degli Studi
dell'Aquila, Italy
stefano.leucci@univaq.it

Guido Proietti
Dipartimento di Ingegneria e
Scienze dell'Informazione e
Matematica
Università degli Studi
dell'Aquila, Italy
guido.proietti@univaq.it

ABSTRACT

Network creation games have been extensively studied, both from economists and computer scientists, due to their versatility in modeling individual-based community formation processes, which in turn are the theoretical counterpart of several economics, social, and computational applications on the Internet. However, the generally adopted assumption is that players have a *common and complete* information about the ongoing network, which is quite unrealistic in practice. In this paper, we consider a more compelling scenario in which players have only limited information about the network they are embedded in. More precisely, we explore the game theoretic and computational implications of assuming that players have a view of the network restricted to their *k-neighborhood*, which is one of the most qualified *local-knowledge models* used in distributed computing. To this respect, we define a suitable equilibrium concept and we provide a comprehensive set of upper and lower bounds to the price of anarchy for the entire range of values of k.

Categories and Subject Descriptors

G.2.2 [**Discrete Mathematics**]: Graph Theory—*network problems*

Keywords

Game Theory, Network Creation Games, Price of Anarchy, Local Knowledge

1. INTRODUCTION

In a *network creation game* (NCG), we are given n players (identified as the nodes of a graph) which attempt to settle an undirected interconnection network. This is realized by letting each player connecting herself *directly* to a subset of players, through the activation of the corresponding set of incident links. These links can then be freely used by everyone, and so a player remains connected to non-adjacent players *indirectly*, i.e., by following a *shortest path* in the currently active network. In such a decentralized process, a player has then to strategically balance the sum of two costs: the *building cost*, which is given by the sum of the costs she incurs in activating her links, and the *routing cost*, which is a function of the length of the shortest paths towards the other players.

Due to their generality, it is in clear evidence that NCGs can model very different practical situations. Just to mention an example, NCGs are fit to model the decentralized construction of *communication* networks, in which the constituting components (e.g., routers and links) are activated and maintained by different owners, as in the Internet. In the very first formulation of the game [12], the building and routing costs are defined as follows. Concerning the building cost, each activated link (i, j) has a cost c_{ij} (resp., c_{ji}) for player i (resp., j), and the formation of a link requires the consent of both players involved (since each of the parties pays the corresponding activating cost), while link severance can be done unilaterally. On the other hand, the routing cost is given by the sum of distances to all the other players. Later on, Fabrikant *et al.* [9] developed a simplified version of this model, which is also the most popular one in the field of *Algorithmic Game Theory* (AGT), namely that in which the activation of each link has a fixed cost $\alpha > 0$, and this is incurred by the activating player only, without the consent of the adjacent player. Besides this simplification, the merit of such a paper was that of emphasizing how the social utility for a (very large) system as a whole is affected by the selfish behavior of the players, which was instead downplayed by the economists, that were more focused on system stability issues. This new perspective inspired then a sequel of papers in the AGT community, as detailed in the following.

Previous work on NCGs.

More formally, the form of a NCG as provided in [9], which we call SumNCG, is as follows: we are given a set of n players, say V, where the strategy space of player $u \in V$ is the power set $2^{V \setminus \{u\}}$. Given a combination of strategies $\sigma = (\sigma_u)_{u \in V}$, let $G(\sigma)$ denote the underlying undirected graph whose node set is V, and whose edge set is $E(\sigma) = \{(u,v) : u \in V \wedge v \in \sigma_u\}$. Then, the *cost* incurred by player u in σ is

$$C_u(\sigma) = \alpha \cdot |\sigma_u| + \sum_{v \in V} d_{G(\sigma)}(u,v) \qquad (1)$$

where $d_{G(\sigma)}(u,v)$ is the distance between u and v in $G(\sigma)$. When a player takes an action (i.e., activates a subset of incident edges), she aims to keep this cost as low as possible. Under the assumption of a complete knowledge of $G(\sigma)$, we therefore have that a player u is fully aware that after switching from strategy σ_u to strategy σ'_u, the network will transit to $G(\sigma_{-u}, \sigma'_u)$. Thus, a *Nash Equilibrium*[1] (NE) for the game is a strategy profile $\bar{\sigma}$ such that for every player u and every strategy profile σ_u, we have that $C_u(\bar{\sigma}) \leq C_u(\bar{\sigma}_{-u}, \sigma_u)$. If we characterize the space of NE in terms of the *Price of Anarchy* (PoA), then it has been shown this is constant for all values of α except for $n^{1-\varepsilon} \leq \alpha < 65\,n$, for any $\varepsilon \geq 1/\log n$ (see [17, 18]). Moreover, very recently, in [10] it was proven that for all constant non-integral $\alpha \geq 2$, the PoA is bounded by $1 + o(1)$.

A first natural variant of SumNCG was introduced in [6], where the authors redefined the player cost function as follows:

$$C_u(\sigma) = \alpha \cdot |\sigma_u| + \max\{d_{G(\sigma)}(u,v) : v \in V\}. \qquad (2)$$

This variant, named MaxNCG, received further attention in [18], where the authors improved the PoA of the game on the whole range of values of α, obtaining in this case that the PoA is constant for all values of α except for $129 > \alpha = \omega(1/\sqrt{n})$.

Besides these two basic models, many variations on the theme have been defined. They range from limiting the modification a player can do on her current strategy (see [1, 16, 19]) by budgeting either the number of edges a player can activate or her eccentricity (see [14, 8, 4]), and finally by constraining the set of activable links to a host graph (see [3, 7]). Generally speaking, in all the above models the obtained bounds on the PoA are asymptotically worse than those we get in the two basic models.

Criticisms to the standard model.

Observe that while the general assumption that players have a *common and complete* information about the ongoing network is feasible for small-size instances of the game, this becomes unrealistic for large-size networks. This is rather problematic, since the asymptotic analysis which guides the AGT literature requires instead a growing size of the input. Moreover, quite paradoxically, the full-knowledge assumption is not simplifying at all: it makes computationally un-

feasible for a player to select a best-response strategy, or even to check whether she is actually in a NE!

Very recently, the same observation leads Ballester Pla *et al.* to consider in [2] a more compelling scenario for the related class of *network* (or *graphical*) *games*. In a graphical game, players are embedded in a network, and the cost of a player depends on her action and that of her neighbors, and thus is correlated to the entire network. However, the authors assume that players have a complete knowledge of the network structure up to a given radius k, and use this information to make up a belief about the rest of the network. For this model, they provide a closed formula to compute a *Bayes-Nash equilibrium* for the game, and show an interesting relationship with a scenario in which players have a *bounded rationality* (i.e., they take a step by only exploring a subset of the strategy space).

Another work which constrains the available strategies of the players according to a concept of locality is [11]. In this work the author studies the non-coordinated process of matching formation where each player can (potentially) match with any other player having distance at most k in a graph which depends on the current state of the game.

Our model.

In this paper we concentrate on SumNCG and MaxNCG, but we deviate from the standard full-knowledge model, and we explore the theoretical implications on the two games induced by the assumption that players have a partial view of the network. More precisely, we consider the players to have only knowledge of their *k-neighborhood* (as in [2]), i.e., each player knows k and the entire network up to the nodes at distance at most k from herself, and they do not even know the size n of the network (in distributed computing terminology, the system is *uniform*).[2]

Despite of this partial knowledge of the network structure, the players keep on using the entire network, and so their cost function is still given by Eqs. (1) and (2), respectively. However, such a cost must now be revised as *incurred* by the players – as a consequence of using the network – rather than being explicitly known. On the other hand, consistently with the model, the strategy space of a player is now restricted to selecting a subset of nodes in her *k-neighborhood*. So, it is in the best interest of a player to reduce an unknown *global* cost, but with the limitation of only knowing and modifying *local* portion of the network. This ambitious task must be modeled through a coherent definition of the players' rational behavior, as we explain in the following. Actually, a player has a partial (defective) view of the network, and thus before taking a step, she has to evaluate whether such a choice is convenient in *every* realizable network which is compatible with her current view. More formally, let $\mathcal{G}$ denote the set of realizable networks according to u's view, and let $C_u(\sigma, G)$ denote what her cost would be if the actual network was $G \in \mathcal{G}$. Then, let

$$\Delta(\sigma_u, \sigma'_u) = \max_{G \in \mathcal{G}}\{C_u((\sigma_{-u}, \sigma'_u), G) - C_u(\sigma, G)\} \qquad (3)$$

denote the worst possible cost difference player u would have in switching from σ_u to σ'_u. For our model, we define the following suitable equilibrium concept (weaker than NE), that we call *Local Knowledge Equilibrium* (LKE), and is defined

---

[1] In this paper, we only focus on *pure*-strategy Nash equilibria.

[2] According to the spirit of the game, we assume that in our model the players initially sit on a connected network.

as a strategy profile $\bar{\sigma}$ such that for every player u and every strategy profile σ_u, we have that $\Delta(\bar{\sigma}_u, \sigma_u) \geq 0$.

As the set $\mathcal{G}$ used in (3) can be infinite, it might appear that a player is not even able to determine if a strategy is convenient. In Section 2 we will show that, in contrast with the intuition, this is not the case. In particular, for MAXNCG we will show that the worst case scenario for a player is the one in which the network coincides with her view. Therefore the player only needs to take into account her view when evaluating a new strategy. This also means that, in our model, a player behaves exactly as in the full-knowledge game played on the graph induced by her k-neighborhood, as if she does not care about the portion of the network she cannot see. Besides that, we point out another remarkable property of our model: differently from the standard model, we have that the computational hardness of establishing an improving strategy is now depending not on the size of the entire network, but only on the size of her k-neighborhood. Therefore, although in principle this one could be $\Theta(n)$ already for small values of k, we believe that in the practice the situation may be quite different, as the size of the known network is expected to be constant (or at least very small) compared to n.

Regarding SUMNCG it is easy to see that, in a worst-case scenario, every improving strategy for a player cannot increase the distance of any vertex x at distance exactly k in her view. Indeed, as the rest of the network is unknown to the player, it might be the case that a large number of nodes is appended to x (hence their distance increases as well). Moreover, for every other strategy, we show that the worst case network coincides with the player's view. In conclusion, the above discussion shows that the player can choose and evaluate her strategies as in the classical SUMNCG, with the exception of the strategies that increase the distances of the nodes at distance k, which are forbidden.

Our results.

Having this solution concept in mind, we characterize the space of equilibria with respect to the social optimum through the study of upper and lower bounds to the PoA. We remark that, as the set of LKEs is broader than the set of NEs, the PoA in our model can only be worse than the PoA in the full-knowledge model.

First, we consider MAXNCG and we give three lower bounds to the PoA which are based on different constructions each holding in different ranges of k and α. One of these is based on a dense graph, while the other two will have an high social cost due to their large diameter. In this latter case, the difficulty of the construction relies on the fact that, when α is small, we need to guarantee that no player can decrease her cost by buying new edges. We deal with this issue by carefully exploiting the defective views of the players. We provide a non-trivial construction where every player is not aware that buying a small number of edge would reduce her cost.

We also provide an upper bound to the PoA by considering both the density and the diameter of an equilibrium graph. In order to prove this bound, we take inspiration from techniques successfully used, for example, in [1, 6] which allow to (lower) bound the number of nodes within a certain distance from a player. However these techniques cannot be directly applied to our model since they require additional work to cope with the concept of locality.

The bounds to the PoA that arise from the various combinations of these results are discussed in detail in Section 3.3 and they are essentially tight for many ranges of α and k. Here we just outline some prominent implications of our results. For example, for constant values of k (regardless of α) we are able to exhibit stable graphs having diameter $\Omega(n)$. This immediately implies that the PoA is $\Omega(\frac{n}{1+\alpha})$ which is fairly bad. However, one might expect the PoA to decrease for large values of α. This is not the case as we can show a tight lower bound of $\Omega(n^{\frac{1}{\Theta(k)}})$. This is in sharp contrast with the classical full-knowledge version of the game where the PoA is constant as soon as $\alpha \geq 129$. On the other hand, when k increases the PoA decreases, although this happens quite slowly. Indeed, even when $k = O(2^{\sqrt{\log n}})$ and $\alpha = O(\log n)$ the PoA is still $\Omega(n^{1-\epsilon})$ for every $\epsilon > 0$. On the bright side, as soon as $k = \Omega(n^\epsilon)$ for any $\epsilon > 0$ we have that, in every LKE, each player has a complete knowledge of the network and so the PoA coincides with the PoA of the full-knowledge game and hence is mostly constant.

Finally, we consider the sum version of the game and we provide some preliminary results. We show that some of the lower bound schemes used for MAXNCG can be extended to SUMNCG as well. In particular, for $\alpha \leq n$ the set of LKEs coincides with the set of NEs as soon as $k \geq c \cdot \sqrt{\alpha}$ for a suitable constant c, while a strong lower bound of $\Omega\left(\frac{n}{k}\right)$ to the PoA holds if $k \leq c' \cdot \sqrt[3]{\alpha}$ for a suitable constant c'. Observe that the latter lower bound is at least $\Omega(n^{\frac{2}{3}})$.

The paper is organized as follows: in Section 2 we characterize the player's behavior and we provide some quick remarks on the complexity of computing a best-response strategy and on the convergence issues of the iterated version of the game, while in Section 3 we focus on the main results of this paper, namely the study of the PoA for MAXNCG. Finally, Section 4 is about SUMNCG.

2. PRELIMINARY REMARKS

We start by showing that, despite the defective knowledge of the network, a player is able to evaluate whether a strategy is convenient in a worst-case scenario. In particular, when a player u changes her strategy from σ_u to σ'_u, she needs to evaluate $\Delta(\sigma_u, \sigma'_u)$ by figuring out a network $G \in \mathcal{G}$ maximizing (3). In the following propositions we will characterize this worst-case network for both MAXNCG and SUMNCG.

Let H be the view of u in $G(\sigma)$, i.e. the subgraph of $G(\sigma)$ induced by the k-neighborhood of u and let $G \in \mathcal{G}$ be a generic realizable network w.r.t. H. Let $G' = G \setminus (\{u\} \times \sigma_u) \cup (\{u\} \times \sigma'_u)$ be the network G after the strategy change. In a similar manner, let $H' = H \setminus (\{u\} \times \sigma_u) \cup (\{u\} \times \sigma'_u)$ be the old view of u modified according to the strategy change. Notice that H' might not coincide with the view of u in G'.

PROPOSITION 1. *In* MAXNCG, *the worst case network maximizing* (3) *coincides with* H.

PROOF. Consider a generic network G. In switching from σ_u to σ'_u the player u is paying an additional cost of:

$$\alpha(|\sigma'_u| - |\sigma_u|) + \max_v d_{G'}(u, v) - \max_v d_G(u, v). \quad (4)$$

Let y be the vertex maximizing $\max_v d_{G'}(u, v)$. If $d_G(u, y) < k$ then y belongs to both H and thus to H' as well, therefore the formula (4) can be upper-bounded by $\alpha(|\sigma'_u -$

$|\sigma_u|) + \max_{v \in V(H')} d_{H'}(u,v) - \max_{v \in V(G)} d_G(u,v)$ which is attained when $G = H$ (hence $G' = H'$) since any graph in $\mathcal{G}$ is a supergraph of H. Otherwise, let x be the unique vertex in a shortest path π from u to y in G such that $d_G(u,x) = k$. Notice that the subpath of π between x and y also lies in G', hence $d_{G'}(x,y) \leq d_G(x,y)$. We can rewrite (4) as follows: $\alpha(|\sigma'_u| - |\sigma_u|) + d_{G'}(u,y) - \max_v d_G(u,v) \leq \alpha(|\sigma'_u| - |\sigma_u|) + d_{G'}(u,x) + d_{G'}(x,y) - d_G(u,y) \leq \alpha(|\sigma'_u| - |\sigma_u|) + d_{H'}(u,x) + d_G(x,y) - d_G(u,x) - d_G(x,y) = \alpha(|\sigma'_u| - |\sigma_u|) + d_{H'}(u,x) - k \leq \alpha(|\sigma'_u| - |\sigma_u|) + \max_{v \in V(H')} d_{H'}(u,v) - \max_{v \in V(H)} d_H(u,v)$. $\square$

Notice that, according to the above discussion, the players do not even need to know the value of k in order to play the game. Regarding SumNCG, let us define as F the set a vertices at distance exactly k from u in H.

PROPOSITION 2. *In* SumNCG, *every strategy that increases the distance of some vertex of F in H' is not convenient for u. For every other strategy of u, the worst case network maximizing (3) coincides with H.*

PROOF. Consider a generic network G. When u switches from σ_u to σ'_u she pays an additional cost of:

$$\alpha(|\sigma'_u| - |\sigma_u|) + \sum_v d_{G'}(u,v) - \sum_v d_G(u,v). \quad (5)$$

We first notice that if there exists a vertex y such that $d_G(u,y) = d_H(u,y) = k$ and $d_{H'}(u,y) > k$ then u is not improving in the worst case scenario. Indeed we can make (5) positive by letting G be equal to the graph H where a large number η of nodes has been appended to y, as (5) becomes at least $\alpha(|\sigma'_u| - |\sigma_u|) + \sum_{v \in H} d_{G'}(u,v) - \sum_{v \in H} d_G(u,v) + \eta$. Therefore, we restrict to strategies σ'_u where if $d_H(u,y) = k$ then $d_{H'}(u,y) \leq k$. Call P the set of vertices x such that $d_G(u,x) < k$, the formula (5) becomes: $\alpha(|\sigma'_u| - |\sigma_u|) + \sum_{v \in P} \left(d_{G'}(u,v) - d_G(u,v) \right) + \sum_{v \notin P} \left(d_{G'}(u,v) - d_G(u,v) \right) \leq \alpha(|\sigma'_u| - |\sigma_u|) + \sum_{v \in P} \left(d_{H'}(u,v) - d_H(u,v) \right) + \sum_{v \notin P} \left(d_{G'}(u,v) - d_G(u,v) \right) \leq \alpha(|\sigma'_u| - |\sigma_u|) + \sum_{v \in P} \left(d_{H'}(u,v) - d_H(u,v) \right)$, since for every $v \notin P$ we have $d_{G'}(u,v) \leq d_G(u,v)$. This upper bound to (5) is attained when $G = H$. $\square$

We now provide some quick remarks on the complexity of computing a best response strategy and on convergence issues. We start by noticing that the NP-hardness reductions which are known in the full-knowledge model for finding a best response in SumNCG and MaxNCG also hold in our game for $k \geq 2$ once we assume that a player owns the entire set of edges towards all the other players.

Now, let us consider the iterated version of the game.[3] A natural question is whether an improving-response or best-response dynamic always converges to an equilibrium state.

Unfortunately, a negative answer to this question follows from the divergence results presented in [13] on the full-knowledge model for SumNCG and MaxNCG since they are based on an instance having (small) constant diameter. This immediately implies the existence of a cycling best response dynamic for both games as soon as $k \geq c$ for a constant c.

---

[3]We assume that the players other than being *myopic* are also *oblivious*, namely at each time they only argue about the current view, without taking care of previous views.

3. RESULTS FOR MaxNCG

For the sake of exposition, we first analyze MaxNCG, and we then consider SumNCG. Also, for technical convenience, we will assume $\alpha > 1$ although our constructions can also be extended to the case $\alpha \leq 1$. We recall that in the full-knowledge version of the game the spanning star is the social optimum and has a cost of $\Theta(\alpha n + n)$.

3.1 Lower bounds for MaxNCG

We present three lower bounds to the PoA based on three graphs with high social cost which are in equilibrium for different ranges of α and k. The first is a cycle. We have the following.

LEMMA 1. *If $k \geq 1$ and $\alpha \geq k - 1$ then $PoA = \Omega(\frac{n}{1+\alpha})$.*

PROOF. Consider a cycle on $n \geq 2k + 2$ vertices where each player owns exactly one edge. The view of each player u is a path of length $2k$ with u as the center vertex. In order to decrease her eccentricity u has to buy at least one edge. This will decrease the usage cost of u by at most $k - 1$ and increase the building cost of u by at least α. Then, $PoA = \Omega\left(\frac{\alpha n + n^2}{\alpha n + n}\right) = \Omega\left(\frac{n}{1+\alpha}\right)$. $\square$

Next lower bound is based on a dense graph of large girth.

LEMMA 2. *For each $2 \leq k = o(\log n)$ and $\alpha \geq 1$ the PoA is $\Omega(n^{\frac{1}{2k-2}})$.*

PROOF. For each even integer $g \geq 6$ and prime power q there exists a q-regular graph of girth at least g with n vertices and $\Omega(n^{1+\frac{1}{g-4}})$ edges [15].

We choose $g = 2k + 2$ and construct such a graph. The view of each player u is a tree of height k with $q(q-1)^{i-1}$ vertices on level i. Moreover the player u owns at most q edges.

In order to reduce her usage cost by i, player u must buy at least $q(q-1)^i - q$ additional edges. If we choose $q \geq 3$ then the increase in the building cost will exceed the decrease in the usage cost. Hence, we have that the PoA is at least $\Omega(\frac{\alpha n^{1+\frac{1}{g-4}}}{(1+\alpha)n}) = \Omega(n^{\frac{1}{2k-2}})$.

It can be shown that the previous construction holds for $k = o(\log n)$. $\square$

The last lower bound is based on a sparse graph with large diameter. The construction is non-trivial and it is a generalization of the graph shown in [1]. Although the precise definition is critical, we now give some intuition on how the graph is built. Roughly speaking, the original graph resembles a 2-dimensional square grid that was rotated by $45°$ and had the vertices on the opposite sides identified in order to form a toroidal shape. This graph has several useful properties: it is vertex-transitive and the diameter is about the length of a "side" of the grid. Moreover if the value of k is small, each player u is not aware of the toroidal shape as she only sees a "square" subgraph. This subgraph has 4 vertices at distance k from u whose pairwise distance are $2k$. This fact can be used to show that, actually, this graph is stable for small values of α and k, e.g. $\alpha = k = 1$. Unfortunately this is no longer true for larger values of k since, for example, the addition of 4 edges suffices to reduce the eccentricity of $\Omega(k)$. Moreover if α is large, a player has convenience in removing an edge as this results in a constant increase in

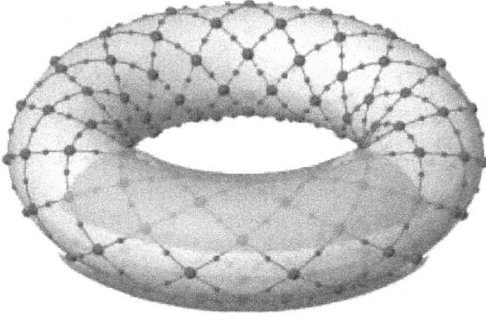

Figure 1: Graph with $d = 2$ dimensions of sizes $\delta_1 = 15$ and $\delta_2 = 5$ and $\ell = 2$. Intersection vertices have a bigger size than non-intersection vertices. In this example the view of the intersection vertex (k^*, k^*) for $k = 4$ is in red. Notice that the vertex (k^*, k^*) lies on an invisible portion of the torus.

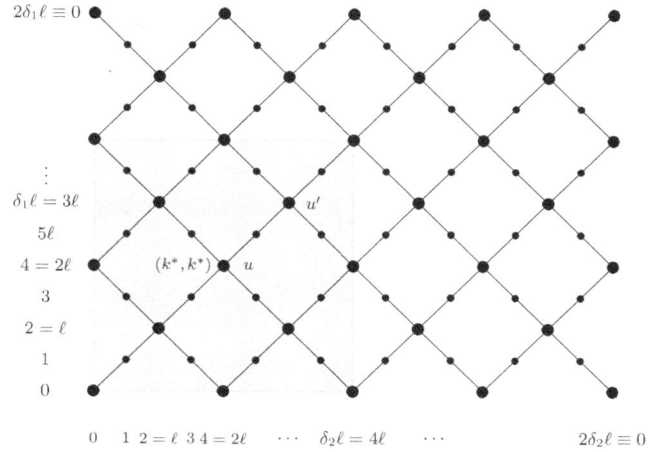

Figure 2: Graph with $d = 2$ dimensions of sizes $\delta_1 = 3$ and $\delta_2 = 4$ and $\ell = 2$. Intersection vertices have a bigger size than non-intersection vertices. The vertices on the first row (resp. column) coincide with the corresponding vertices on last row (resp. column). In this example the view of the intersection vertex (k^*, k^*) for $k = 4$ is highlighted in gray.

her eccentricity. To deal with these issues we generalize this construction in three ways. First, we increase the number of dimensions from 2 to a parameter d so that the graph now resembles a rotated d-dimensional cube grid where each face has been identified with the opposite one. For each vertex u we are now able to find 2^d other vertices that are at a distance of k from u and whose pairwise distances are at least $2k$. Second, in order to get a graph with large diameter, we no longer restrict the dimensions to be equal to each other. Intuitively, instead of starting with a d-dimensional "cube", we start with a d-dimensional hyper-rectangle. Finally, we "stretch" the graph by replacing each edge with a path of length $1 \leq \ell = \Theta(\alpha)$ between its endpoints. This causes the addition of $\ell - 1$ new vertices per edge. We call these new vertices "non-intersection vertices" to distinguish them from the already existing "intersection vertices". Non-intersection vertices will buy all the links of the graph and we will show that they cannot remove edges as this would result in an increase of at least $\Omega(\ell)$ in their eccentricity.

We now give the details of the construction, which will depend on $\ell \geq 1$, $d \geq 2$, and $\delta_1, \ldots, \delta_d \geq 1$, where δ_i is the "length" of the i-th dimension. Vertices will be named after their coordinates and we will interpret the i-th coordinate modulo $2\delta_i$, that is $2\delta_i \equiv 0$.

The graph is built by starting from an empty graph and proceeding in the following way: add the set of *intersection vertices*, each of these vertices is a d-tuple $(\ell \cdot a_1, \ell \cdot a_2, \ldots, \ell \cdot a_d)$ such that $a_1 \equiv a_2 \equiv \cdots \equiv a_d \pmod 2$ where each a_i with $1 \leq i \leq d$ is an integer between 0 and $2\delta_i - 1$. Then, connect each intersection vertex $(x_1, \ldots, x_d)$ to 2^d other vertices, using a path of length ℓ (so if $\ell = 1$ we only need to add edges). More precisely, we connect such a vertex to $(x_1 \pm \ell, x_2 \pm \ell, \ldots, x_d \pm \ell)$ for every possible choice of the $\pm$ signs. We label the $\ell - 1$ non-intersection vertices on the paths by varying the coordinates of the endpoints according to the choice of $\pm$ signs, that is we traverse the path from one endpoint to another and label each non-intersection vertex by adding or subtracting 1 from the coordinates of the previous vertex. In the following, for convenience, when we choose a vertex, we will assume that the i-th coordinate is between 0 and $2\delta_i - 1$.

We will consider graphs where $\delta_1 = \cdots = \delta_{d-1} = \lceil \frac{k}{\ell} \rceil + 1$ and $\delta_d \geq \lceil \frac{k}{\ell} \rceil + 1$. Let $k^* = \ell(\delta_1 - 1)$, u be the vertex $(k^*, \ldots, k^*)$ and u' be the vertex $(k^* + \ell, \ldots, k^* + \ell)$.

Two examples of this construction, with different parameters, are shown in Figure 1 and in Figure 2.

The following result is not hard to prove:

LEMMA 3. *Let $x = (x_1, \ldots, x_d)$ and $y = (y_1, \ldots, y_d)$ be two vertices. We have $d(x, y) \geq \max_{1 \leq i \leq d} \min\{|x_i - y_i|, 2\delta_i \ell - |x_i - y_i|\}$. If at least one of x and y is an intersection vertex, then the previous inequality is strict.*

COROLLARY 1. *The diameter of the graph is at least $\ell \cdot \delta_d$.*

PROOF. By Lemma 3 the distance between the vertex $(0, \ldots, 0)$ and any vertex whose last coordinate is $\ell \delta_d$ is at least $\ell \delta_d$. □

We also consider an "open" version of the previous graph, that is built in an similar way except that we do not treat the coordinates in a modular fashion: a_i is now between 1 and δ_i and we connect intersection vertices (with paths) only when all their coordinates differ by exactly ℓ. It is not hard to see that the view of each player is isomorphic to a subgraph of this "open" graph, and that Lemma 3 becomes:

LEMMA 4. *Let $x = (x_1, \ldots, x_d)$ and $y = (y_1, \ldots, y_d)$ be two vertices in the "open" graph. We have $d(x, y) \geq \max_{1 \leq i \leq d} |x_i - y_i|$. If at least one of x and y is an intersection vertex, then the previous inequality is strict.*

We now prove a general lemma that will be very useful in the following proofs:

LEMMA 5. *Let H be a graph, $u \in V(H)$ and $L = \{v_1, \ldots, v_{|L|}\} \subseteq V(H) \setminus \{u\}$. If $d_H(u, v_i) \geq h$ for every $1 \leq i \leq |L|$ and $d_H(v_i, v_j) \geq 2h - 2$ for every $1 \leq i, j \leq |L|$ with $i \neq j$, and F is a set of edges such that: (i) each edge in F has u as an endpoint, and (ii) $d_{H+F}(u, v_i) < h$ for every $1 \leq i \leq |L|$, then it holds $|F| \geq |L|$.*

PROOF. Every shortest path from u to a vertex $v \in L$ in $H + F$ must use exactly one edge $(u, y) \in F$ and $d_H(v, y) \leq h - 2$ must hold.

For every other vertex $v' \in L \setminus \{u\}$, the shortest path between u and v' in $H + F$ cannot use the edge (u, y), otherwise we would have:

$$d_{H+F}(u, v') = 1 + d_H(y, v') = 1 + d_H(y, v') + d_H(y, v)$$
$$- d_H(y, v) \geq d_H(v', v) - d_H(y, v) \geq 2h - 2 - (h - 2) \geq h.$$

This implies that F must contain at least one edge for each vertex of L. $\square$

We now define the ownership of the edges. Consider the path $\langle u = x_0, x_1, \ldots, x_{\ell-1}, x_\ell = u' \rangle$ from u to u'. For $i = 1, \ldots, \ell - 1$, vertex x_i buys the edge towards x_{i-1}, and $x_{\ell-1}$ also buys the edge towards u'. The ownership of the edges of the other paths are defined symmetrically. Observe that the intersection vertices buy no edges.

Given an intersection vertex $v = (x_1, x_2, \ldots, x_d)$ we define $\mathcal{F}^h(v)$ as the set of vertices reachable by traversing an edge incident to v and then proceeding in the same direction for a total of h steps, i.e., $\mathcal{F}^h(v) = \{(x_1 \pm h, x_2 \pm h, \ldots, x_d \pm h)\}$, for every possible choice of $\pm$ signs. If $h \leq k$ then $|\mathcal{F}^h(v)| = 2^d$ and, by Lemma 3, the distance between v and any of those vertices is exactly h.

The following lemmas are instrumental to prove the lower bound to the PoA for MaxNCG as they will provide sufficient conditions for intersection and non-intersection vertices to be in equilibrium.

LEMMA 6. If $d \geq \log \frac{k-1}{\alpha}$ then the intersection vertices are in equilibrium.

PROOF. By symmetry, let us consider only the intersection vertex u. As u has not bought any edge, she can modify her strategy only by buying new edges. Every vertex in the set $\mathcal{F}^k(u)$ is at distance k from u, moreover, by Lemma 4, any two distinct vertices in $\mathcal{F}^k(u)$ have a distance of at least $2k$ in the view of u.

By Lemma 5, u needs to buy at least 2^d edges in order to reduce her eccentricity. If she does so, she saves at most $k - 1$ on the usage cost while paying at least $\alpha 2^d$, but we have $\alpha 2^d \geq k - 1$. $\square$

LEMMA 7. If $k \geq \ell$, for every non-intersection vertex v, there is a set L of 2^d vertices at distance k from v and at distance at least $2k - \ell$ between each other in the view of v.

PROOF. By symmetry, let $v = (k^* + \ell - z, \ldots, k^* + \ell - z)$ with $1 < z \leq \lfloor \frac{\ell}{2} \rfloor$. The nearest intersecting vertex from v is u'. Let $L' = \mathcal{F}^{k-z}(u') \setminus \{(k^* + \ell - (k-z), \ldots, k^* + \ell - (k-z))\}$. Any pair of vertices in L' differs by at least one coordinate and, by Lemma 4, is at distance at least $2k - 2z \geq 2k - \ell$ in the view of v.

Let v' be a vertex of L', the shortest path from v to v' must contain either u or u'. By Lemma 4, if it contains u then we have: $d(v, v') = d(v, u) + d(u, v') \geq \ell - z + \ell + k - z = 2\ell + k - 2z \geq k$, otherwise it contains u' and we have: $d(v, v') = d(v, u') + d(u', v') \geq z + k - z = k$. Therefore $d(u', v') \geq k$.

Now consider the vertex $y = (k^* + \ell - z - k, \ldots, k^* + \ell - z - k)$. We have that $y \notin L'$ and, by Lemma 4, $d(v, y) \geq k$ and $d(y, v') \geq 2k$.

The claim follows as we can define $L = L' \cup \{y\}$. $\square$

LEMMA 8. If $\frac{\alpha+1}{2} \leq \ell \leq \alpha + 2$ and $d \geq \log(\frac{k-1}{\alpha} + 2)$, then every non-intersection vertex v is in equilibrium w.r.t. all the strategies that increase the number of bought edges.

PROOF. Notice that each non-intersection vertex has bought at most 2 edges and consider a strategy that increases the number of bought edges.

If $k \leq \ell - 1$ then the building cost increases by at least α while the usage cost decreases at most by $k - 1$, but we have $\alpha \geq \ell - 2 \geq k - 1$.

Otherwise $k \geq \ell$ and, by Lemma 7, there exists a set of at least 2^d vertices at distance at least $k \geq k - \frac{\ell}{2}$ from v and $2k - \ell$ between each other. By Lemma 5, v needs to have at least 2^d incident edges in order to reduce her eccentricity by at least $\frac{\ell}{2}$.

If, in the new strategy, v has less than 2^d incident edges then the building cost increases by at least α and the usage cost decreases by at most $\frac{\ell}{2} - 1$, but we have $\alpha \geq \frac{\ell}{2} - 1$.

If, in the new strategy, v has at least 2^d incident edges, then the building cost increases by at least $\alpha(2^d - 2)$ and the eccentricity decreases by at most $k - 1$, but we have $\alpha(2^d - 2) \geq k - 1$. $\square$

LEMMA 9. If $\ell \geq \alpha$, every non-intersection vertex v is in equilibrium w.r.t. all the strategies that decrease the number of bought edges.

PROOF. By symmetry, let $v = (k^* + z, \ldots, k^* + z)$ with $1 \leq z < \ell$. The vertex v can decrease the number of bought edges by at most 1, thus saving α on the building cost.

Let G' be the view of v where the edges incident to the vertex v have been removed, $x = (k^* + z + k, \ldots, k^* + z + k)$ and $x' = (k^* + z - k, \ldots, k^* + z - k)$. If x and x' are not connected in G', then v cannot decrease the number of bought edges.

Otherwise let π be a shortest path between x and x' in G'. Let $y = (k^* + z + h, \ldots, k^* + z + h)$ be the first vertex in π such that the following vertex in π is different from $(k^* + i, \ldots, k^* + i)$ for all values of $i \in \mathbb{Z}$. Notice that y must be an intersection vertex and let y' be the first intersection vertex following y in π. At least one of the coordinates of y' must be $k^* + z + h + \ell$.

We have $d_{G'}(v, x) = d_{G'}(v, x') = +\infty$ and, by Lemma 4:

$$d_{G'}(x, x') \geq d_{G'}(x, y) + d_{G'}(y, y') + d_{G'}(y', x')$$
$$\geq k - h + \ell + k + h + \ell \geq 2k + 2\ell.$$

By Lemma 5, u needs at least 2 incident edges for her eccentricity to be under $k + \ell$. If v decreases the number of bought edges then v has at most 1 incident edge and her usage cost increases by at least ℓ, but we have $\alpha \leq \ell$. $\square$

LEMMA 10. If $\alpha \leq \ell \leq \alpha + 2$, $k \geq \ell$, and $d \geq \log(\frac{k-1}{\alpha} + 2)$, then every non-intersection vertex v is in equilibrium.

PROOF. By Lemma 8 and Lemma 9 v is in equilibrium w.r.t. all the strategies that either increase or decrease the number of bought edges.

We now show that v is also in equilibrium w.r.t. the strategies that do not change the number of bought edges. As the building cost of v remains the same, v must save on her usage cost in order to change her strategy.

We will show that v cannot decrease her usage even when she buys the new edges in addition to the ones already bought.

If v owns only one edge then let, by symmetry, $v = (k^* + z, \ldots, k^* + z)$ with $1 \leq z < \ell$ and let the bought edge be towards $(k^* + z + 1, \ldots, k^* + z + 1)$. The vertices $(k^* + z + k, \ldots, k^* + z + k)$ and $(k^* + z - k, \ldots, k^* + z - k)$ are at distance k from v and $2k$ between each other. By Lemma 5, v needs at least 2 new incident edges to decrease her eccentricity under k, but she can only add one.

If v owns two edges then, by symmetry, let $v = (k^* + \ell - 1, \ldots, k^* + \ell - 1)$ so she has an edge towards u'.

The vertices in $\mathcal{F}^{k-1}(u') \setminus (k + \ell - k + 1, \ldots, k + \ell - k + 1)$ are at distance k from v and $2k - 2$ between each other, in the view of v. By Lemma 5, v needs at least $2^d - 1 \geq 3$ new incident edges in order to decrease her eccentricity under k, but she can only add two. $\square$

We are now ready to prove the following:

THEOREM 1. *If $1 < \alpha \leq k \leq 2^{\sqrt{\log n} - 3}$, then the PoA of* MAXNCG *is* $\Omega\left(\dfrac{n}{\alpha \cdot 2^{(\log \frac{k}{\ell} + 3) \log \frac{k}{\ell}}}\right)$.

PROOF. Fix $\ell = \lceil \alpha \rceil$ and notice that $k \geq \ell \geq 2$ holds as k must be an integer. Fix $d = \left\lceil \log\left(\frac{k}{\ell} + 2\right) \right\rceil$, this implies $d \geq 2$. We will use the following inequalities: $\log\left(\frac{k}{\ell}\right) \leq d \leq \log\left(\frac{k}{\ell}\right) + 3$. Finally, as already said, we set $\delta_1, \ldots, \delta_{d-1}$ to $\left\lceil \frac{k}{\ell} \right\rceil + 1$.

In order to be $\delta_d \geq \delta_1$ it suffices for k to be at most $2^{\sqrt{\log n} - 3}$, as shown by the following calculations.

The number of intersection vertices of the graph is $N = 2 \prod_{i=1}^{d} \delta_i = 2(\lceil \frac{k}{\ell} \rceil + 1)^{d-1} \delta_d$ while the total number of vertices is: $n = N + 2^{d-1} N(\ell - 1) = N(2^{d-1}(\ell - 1) + 1)$ therefore $N = \frac{n}{2^{d-1}(\ell-1)+1} \geq \frac{n}{2^{d-1}\ell}$.

$$\delta_d \geq \delta_1 \iff \frac{N}{2(\lceil \frac{k}{\ell} \rceil + 1)^{d-1}} \geq \left\lceil \frac{k}{\ell} \right\rceil + 1$$

$$\impliedby \frac{n}{2^d \ell} \geq \left(\left\lceil \frac{k}{\ell} \right\rceil + 1\right)^d \impliedby k \leq \frac{n^{\frac{1}{d}}}{2} \ell^{1 - \frac{1}{d}} - 2\ell$$

$$\impliedby 6k \leq n^{\frac{1}{d}} \iff d \log 6k \leq \log n$$

$$\impliedby (\log k + 3)^2 \leq \log n \impliedby k \leq 2^{\sqrt{\log n} - 3}.$$

By Corollary 1, the diameter of the graph is at least:

$$\ell \, \delta_d = \Omega\left(\frac{N\ell^d}{2k^{d-1}}\right) = \Omega\left(\frac{n\ell^{d-1}}{2^d k^{d-1}}\right) = \Omega\left(\frac{n\ell^d}{k^d}\right)$$

$$= \Omega\left(\frac{n}{(\frac{k}{\ell})^d}\right) = \Omega\left(\frac{n}{2^{d \log \frac{k}{\ell}}}\right) = \Omega\left(\frac{n}{2^{(\log \frac{k}{\ell} + 3) \log \frac{k}{\ell}}}\right).$$

By Lemma 6 and Proposition 10 the graph is in equilibrium. As every vertex in the graph owns at most 2 edges, the total number of edges is at most $2n$ and the PoA is:

$$\Omega\left(\frac{\alpha n + n\ell\delta_d}{\alpha n}\right) = \Omega\left(\frac{\ell\delta_d}{\alpha}\right) = \Omega\left(\frac{n}{\alpha \cdot 2^{(\log \frac{k}{\alpha} + 3) \log \frac{k}{\alpha}}}\right). \quad \square$$

3.2 Upper bounds for MAXNCG

Given a graph H, we denote by $\beta_{H,h}(v)$ the *ball* of radius h centered at node v in H, namely the set of vertices whose distance from v in H is at most h. When the graph H is clear from the context we will drop the corresponding subscript. The following lemma shows a relation between k and the number of nodes that a player sees in an equilibrium graph G. A similar result is shown in [6] for the original game.

LEMMA 11. *Let G be an equilibrium graph whose radius is greater than or equal to $k/2$ and let $N = |\beta_{G,k}(u)|$ be the number of nodes that u sees in G. If $\alpha \leq k - 1$ we have that $k = O(\min\{\sqrt[3]{N\alpha^2}, \alpha\, 4^{\sqrt{\log N}}\})$.*

PROOF. First, we need to prove that $k = O(\sqrt{N\alpha})$, we do so by showing that $N = \Omega(k^2/\alpha)$. For every $1 \leq i \leq k/2$, let L_i be the vertices of $\beta_{G,k}(u)$ whose distance from u is equal to i. We show that $|L_i| = \Omega(i/\alpha)$. If u bought the edges towards all the vertices in L_i she would decrease her eccentricity by at least $k - \max\{k - i, i\} = k - k + i = i$ and increase her building cost by $\alpha|L_i|$. As G is an equilibrium graph, we have that $\alpha|L_i| \geq i$, i.e., $|L_i| \geq i/\alpha$. Therefore, $N \geq \sum_{i=1}^{\lfloor k/2 \rfloor} |L_i| \geq \sum_{i=1}^{\lfloor k/2 \rfloor} i/\alpha = \Omega(k^2/\alpha)$.

Now we prove that $k = O(\sqrt[3]{N\alpha^2})$ by showing that $N = \Omega(k^3/\alpha^2)$. Let $h = \lfloor k/8 \rfloor - 1$ and let $\bar{h} = k - 2h = k - 2\lfloor k/8 \rfloor + 2$. By the choice of h and $\bar{h}$, every path of length less than or equal to $2h$ between two vertices of $\beta_{G,\bar{h}}(u)$ is entirely contained in $\beta_{G,k}(u)$. We select a subset of vertices in $\beta_{G,\bar{h}}(u)$ as *center points* by the following greedy algorithm. First, we unmark all vertices in $\beta_{G,\bar{h}}(u)$. Then we repeatedly select an unmarked vertex x in $\beta_{G,\bar{h}}(u)$ as center point, and mark all unmarked vertices in $\beta_{G,\bar{h}}(u)$ whose distances in the graph induced by $\beta_{G,k}(u)$ are at most $2h$ from x.

Suppose that we select l vertices $x_1, x_2, \ldots, x_l$ as center points. By construction, every vertex in $\beta_{G,k}(u)$ has distance of at most $4h$ to some center point. If player u bought the l edges towards the l vertices $x_1, x_2, \ldots, x_l$, she would decrease her eccentricity w.r.t. all the vertices in $\beta_{G,k}(u)$ by at least $k - (4h + 1) \geq k - 4\lfloor k/8 \rfloor + 3 > k/2$ and increase her building cost by αl. Because G is an equilibrium graph, we have $\alpha l \geq k/2$ and thus $l \geq k/(2\alpha)$. By the choice of h and $\bar{h}$, the distance in G between any pair of center points is greater than or equal to $2h + 1$ and furthermore, $\beta_{G,h}(x_i) \subseteq \beta_{G,k}(u)$ for every $i = 1, \ldots, l$. As a consequence, the balls of radius h centered at the center points are pairwise disjoint and thus

$$N = |\beta_{G,k}(u)| \geq \sum_{i=1}^{l} |\beta_{G,h}(x_i)| = l \cdot \Omega(k^2/\alpha) = \Omega(k^3/\alpha^2).$$

Finally we prove that $k = O\left(\alpha\, 4^{\sqrt{\log N}}\right)$ by showing that $N = \Omega\left(2^{\log_4^2(k/\alpha)}\right)$ for every value of $\alpha \leq k - 1$. First, we prove the following useful claim:

CLAIM 1. *Let $i < k/5$ and let $\bar{N} = \min_{v \in V} |\beta_{G,i}(v)|$. Either there exists a vertex having eccentricity strictly less than $5i$ or $|\beta_{G,4i+1}(v)| \geq (\bar{N}i)/\alpha$ for every vertex v.*

PROOF. If there is a vertex having eccentricity strictly less than $5i$, then the claim is obvious. Otherwise, for every vertex v, we have that the eccentricity of v is greater than or equal to $5i$. Let S be the set of vertices whose distance from u is $3i + 1$. By the choice of i, every path of length less than or equal to $2i$ between pair of vertices in $\beta_{G,3i+1}(u)$ is entirely contained in $\beta_{G,k}(u)$. We select a subset of S, called *center points*, by the following greedy algorithm. First we unmark all vertices in S. Then we select an unmarked vertex $x \in S$ as a center point, mark all unmarked vertices in S whose distance from x is less than or equal to $2i$, and assign these vertices to x.

Suppose that we select l vertices $x_1, x_2, \ldots, x_l$ as center points. We prove that $l \geq i/\alpha$. If player u bought the l edges towards the vertices $x_1, x_2, \ldots, x_l$, she would decrease her eccentricity w.r.t. all the vertices in $\beta_{G,k}(u)$, by at least $k - \max\{k - i, 3i + 1\} = k - (k - i) = i$. Because u has not bought these edges, we must have $l\alpha \geq i$.

According to the greedy algorithm, the distance between any pair of center points is greater than or equal to $2i + 1$; hence the balls of radius i centered at the vertices x_j are pairwise disjoint. Therefore,

$$\left| \bigcup_{j=1}^{l} \beta_{G,i}(x_j) \right| = \sum_{j=1}^{l} |\beta_{G,i}(x_j)| \geq l\bar{N} \geq (\bar{N}i)\alpha.$$

For every $j = 1, \ldots, l$, we have $d(u, x_j) = 3k+1$, so $\beta_{G,i}(x_j) \subseteq \beta_{G,4i+1}(u)$. Therefore, $|\beta_{G,4i+1}(u)| \geq (\bar{N}i)/\alpha$. $\square$

Let $\bar{N}_i = \min_{v \in V} |\beta_{G,i}(v)|$. Because G is a connected equilibrium and $\lceil \alpha \rceil \leq k$, $\bar{N}_{\lceil \alpha \rceil} \geq \lceil \alpha \rceil$. By Lemma 1, for every $i < k/5$, either there exists a vertex having eccentricity strictly less than $5i$ or $\bar{N}_{4i+1} \geq \bar{N}_i$. Define the numbers $a_0, a_1, \ldots$ using the recurrence relation $a_i = 4a_{i-1} + 1$ with $a_0 = \lfloor \alpha \rfloor$. By induction, $a_i \geq \alpha 4^i$. If the radius of G is strictly less than k, then let j be the least number such that the radius of G is less than or equal to $5a_j$; otherwise, let j be the least number such that $a_j \geq k/5$. As the radius of G is greater than or equal to $k/2$, we have that $a_j = \Theta(k)$. By definition of j, $\bar{N}_{a_{i+1}} \geq (a_i \bar{N}_{a_i})/\alpha \geq 4^i \bar{N}_{a_i}$, for every $i < j$. From these inequalities we derive that $\bar{N}_{a_j} \geq 4^{\sum_{i=0}^{j-1} i}$. But $\bar{N}_{a_j} \leq N$, so $\sum_{i=1}^{j-1} i = j(j-1)/2 \leq \log_4 N$. This inequality implies that $j \leq 1 + \sqrt{2 \log_4 N} = 1 + \sqrt{\log N}$. Solving the recurrence relation, $a_j = O(\alpha 4^j) = O(\alpha 4^{\sqrt{\log N}})$. As $a_j = \Theta(k)$, $k = O(\alpha 4^{\sqrt{\log N}})$. $\square$

From this, it immediately follows:

COROLLARY 2. *If* $\alpha \leq k - 1$ *and* $k > c \cdot \min\{n, \sqrt[3]{n\alpha^2}, \alpha 4^{\sqrt{\log n}}\}$, *for a suitable constant* c, *then in every equilibrium graph each player sees the whole graph, thus the set of LKEs coincides with the set of NEs.*

Now, we provide an upper bound to the diameter of an equilibrium graph.

LEMMA 12. *Let* G *be an equilibrium graph of diameter* d. *If* $|\beta_{G,k}(v)| \geq \gamma$ *for every vertex* v, *then* $d \leq \frac{3kn}{\gamma}$.

PROOF. Let $\pi = (x_0, \ldots, x_d)$ be a diametral path of G. We select a set of vertices C such that the k-neighborhoods of the vertices of C are pairwise disjoint and cover all the nodes of π. We must have $|C|\gamma \leq n$ which implies that $|C| \leq \frac{n}{\gamma}$, and thus the diameter of G is at most $|C|(2k+1) = \frac{(2k+1)n}{\gamma} \leq \frac{3kn}{\gamma}$. $\square$

LEMMA 13. *If* $\alpha \leq k - 1$ *the diameter of an equilibrium graph* G *is* $O\left(\frac{kn}{2^{\log_4^2 \frac{k}{\alpha}}}\right)$.

PROOF. Consider a generic vertex v and let $N = |\beta_{G,k}(v)|$. From Lemma 11, we have that $k = O(\min\{\sqrt[3]{N\alpha^2}, \alpha 4^{\sqrt{\log N}}\})$ which implies that $N = \Omega(\max\{\frac{k^3}{\alpha^2}, 2^{\log_4^2 \frac{k}{\alpha}}\})$. Now, using Lemma 12, we have that the diameter of G must be $O\left(\min\{\frac{n\alpha^2}{k^2}, \frac{kn}{2^{\log_4^2 \frac{k}{\alpha}}}\}\right)$. $\square$

We now derive an upper bound to the density of an equilibrium graph. We argue on the girth of the graph in a way similar to [6].

LEMMA 14. *The number of the edges of an equilibrium graph* G *is* $O(n^{1+\frac{2}{\min\{\alpha, 2k\}}})$.

PROOF. Let g be the girth of G. We first show that $g \geq 2 + \min\{\alpha, 2k\}$ and then the claim follows from the fact that a graph with girth g' must have at most $O(n^{1+\frac{2}{g'-2}})$ edges [5]. Assume by contradiction that there is a cycle C of length strictly less than $2 + \min\{\alpha, 2k\}$. Then consider a player u that owns an edge of the cycle. Since u can see the cycle, she can remove the edge. The deletion would increase the distance to any other node by at most $|C| - 2$ while u would save $\alpha > |C| - 2$, and hence G cannot be an equilibrium. $\square$

We can now prove the following:

THEOREM 2. *The PoA of* MAXNCG *is* $O\left(n^{\frac{2}{\min\{\alpha, 2k\}}} + \frac{n}{1+\alpha}\right)$ *if* $\alpha \geq k - 1$ *and* $O\left(n^{\frac{2}{\alpha}} + \min\{\frac{n\alpha}{k^2}, \frac{nk}{\alpha \cdot 2^{\frac{1}{4} \log_2^2 \frac{k}{\alpha}}}\}\right)$ *if* $\alpha \leq k - 1$.

PROOF. If $\alpha \geq k-1$ then the claim follows from Lemma 14 and from the fact that the diameter of an equilibrium graph is at most $n - 1$. Otherwise $\alpha \leq k - 1$ and the claim immediately follows from Lemma 14 and Lemma 13. $\square$

3.3 Putting all together

Here we summarize our lower and upper bounds to the PoA for MAXNCG by showing how they combine depending on the values of α and k.

First, recall that whenever the view of the players is sufficiently large, then in every LKE, players actually have a *full knowledge* of the network, and so LKEs coincides with NEs (hence the PoA is the same as in the full knowledge version of the game) as shown in Corollary 2. The corresponding region is shown in gray in Figure 3. Concerning our three lower bounds, the first one of $\Omega\left(\frac{n}{1+\alpha}\right)$ holds for $\alpha \geq k - 1$, i.e. in the regions numbered ②, ③ and ⑥ in Figure 3. For $1 < \alpha \leq k$ and $k \leq 2^{\sqrt{\log n}-3}$ we provided a strong lower bound of $\Omega(\frac{n}{\alpha^2 2^{\Theta(\log^2 \frac{k}{\alpha})}})$ (regions ①, ④, ⑤ in Figure 3). Notice that when $k = \Theta(\alpha)$ this lower bound boils down to $\Omega(\frac{n}{\alpha})$ which is tight. Unfortunately, if $\alpha > k$, the previous lower bound is no longer valid, instead we provided a third lower bound of $\Omega(n^{\frac{1}{\Theta(k)}})$ holding for $k = o(\log n)$ (regions ①, ②, ③ in Figure 3).

Turning to the upper bounds to the PoA, in Theorem 2, we proved them by considering both the density and the diameter of an equilibrium graph. We showed that the number of edges can be at most $O(n^{1+\frac{2}{\min\{\alpha, 2k\}}})$. Regarding the diameter, since for $\alpha \geq k - 1$ it can be shown to be $\Omega(n)$, we considered the case $\alpha \leq k - 1$ where we gave an upper bound of $O(\min\{\frac{n\alpha}{k^2}, \frac{nk}{2^{\Theta(\log^2 \frac{k}{\alpha})}}\})$. Notice that this upper bound is a minimum of two terms. Intuitively, the first one is better when k is not too big w.r.t. α, e.g. when $k = O(\alpha \operatorname{polylog}(\alpha))$. The corresponding region lies between the dashed gray curve and the line of equation $\alpha = k - 1$ shown in Figure 3.

The bounds to the PoA that arise from the various combinations of these results are summarized in Figure 3. Notice that the bounds for the regions under the line $k = \alpha + 1$ are essentially tight.

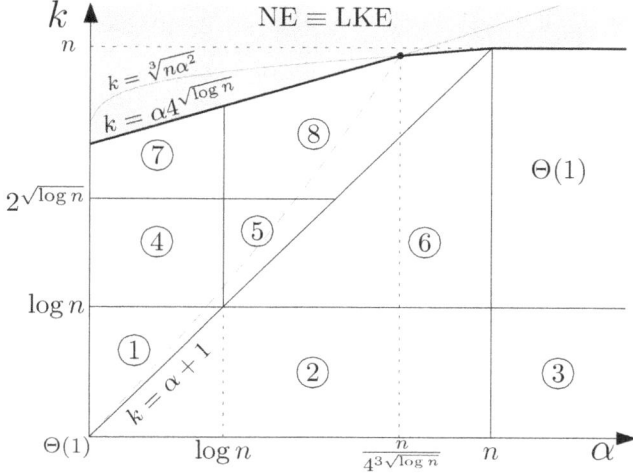

#	Lower Bound	Upper Bound
①	$\Omega\left(\max\{\frac{n}{\alpha 2^{\Theta(\log^2 \frac{k}{\alpha})}}, n^{\frac{1}{\Theta(k)}}\}\right)$	$O\left(n^{\frac{2}{\alpha}} + \min\{\frac{n\alpha}{k^2}, \frac{nk}{\alpha 2^{\Theta(\log^2 \frac{k}{\alpha})}}\}\right)$
②	$\Theta\left(\max\{\frac{n}{1+\alpha}, n^{\frac{1}{\Theta(k)}}\}\right)$	
③	$\Theta\left(n^{\frac{1}{\Theta(k)}}\right)$	
④	$\Omega\left(\frac{n}{\alpha 2^{\Theta(\log^2 \frac{k}{\alpha})}}\right)$	$O\left(n^{\frac{2}{\alpha}} + \min\{\frac{n\alpha}{k^2}, \frac{nk}{\alpha 2^{\Theta(\log^2 \frac{k}{\alpha})}}\}\right)$
⑤	$\Omega\left(\frac{n}{\alpha 2^{\Theta(\log^2 \frac{k}{\alpha})}}\right)$	$O\left(\min\{\frac{n\alpha}{k^2}, \frac{nk}{\alpha 2^{\Theta(\log^2 \frac{k}{\alpha})}}\}\right)$
⑥	$\Theta\left(\frac{n}{1+\alpha}\right)$	
⑦	$O\left(n^{\frac{2}{\alpha}} + \frac{nk}{\alpha 2^{\Theta(\log^2 \frac{k}{\alpha})}}\right)$	
⑧	$O\left(\min\{\frac{n\alpha}{k^2}, \frac{nk}{\alpha 2^{\Theta(\log^2 \frac{k}{\alpha})}}\}\right)$	

Figure 3: Lower and upper bounds to the PoA for MaxNCG. The partition in regions comes up by the combination of the various bounds that we give in Section 3. Notice that the gray region is the set of pairs (α, k) such that, in every LKE, players actually have a full knowledge of the network, and so LKEs coincides with NEs.

4. RESULTS FOR SumNCG

Here we give some preliminary results for SumNCG. Recall that in the full-knowledge version of the game the spanning star is the social optimum and has a cost of $\Theta(\alpha n + n^2)$. We start with a quite strong lower bound to the PoA.

Consider a graph similar to the one shown in Figure 2, whose construction has been described in Section 3.1. In particular, we build such a graph using the following parameters: $d = 2$, $\ell = 2$, $\delta_1 = \lceil \frac{k}{2} \rceil + 1$ and $\delta_2 \geq \delta_1$ which will be specified later. We know that $N = 2\delta_1\delta_2$ and that $n = 6\delta_1\delta_2$. We want $\delta_2 \geq \delta_1 \iff \frac{n}{6\delta_1} \geq \delta_1 \iff \delta_1 \leq \sqrt{\frac{n}{6}} \impliedby k \leq \sqrt{\frac{2n}{3}} - 4$. We have the following:

LEMMA 15. *For $\alpha \geq 2k^3$, the previous graph is an equilibrium.*

PROOF. First notice that each vertex v sees at most $4k^2$ other vertices. As $\alpha \geq 4k^3$ and v can reduce the distance to each vertex by at most $(k-1)$, v cannot increase the number of bought edges.

Suppose that the player v changes her strategy from σ_v to σ'_v, let L be the set of vertices that are at distance k from v. Consider the view of v before the strategy changes, where the edges of σ_v have been removed and replaced with the edges of σ'_v. Each vertex of L must be at distance at most k from v in this new graph. Otherwise, suppose the existence of a vertex $x \in L$ that is at distance at least $k+1$ in this new graph. When v computes $\Delta(\sigma_v, \sigma'_v)$ it will also consider the case where a certain number of (new) vertices η are adjacent to x, therefore her usage will be at least $k\eta$ which, for a suitable value of η, is greater than the cost of v in σ.

Let $v = (k^* + 1, k^* + 1)$ and consider the set of vertices $L = \left(\mathcal{F}^{k-1}(u) \cup \mathcal{F}^{k-1}(u')\right) \setminus \{(k^* + 3 - k, k^* + 3 - k), (k^* + k - 1, k^* + k - 1)\}$.

It is easy to see that all the vertices in L are at distance k from v and that every vertex x in the view of v, that is not a neighbor of v, has at most 2 vertices of L that are at distance at most $k-1$. Finally, every vertex x in the view of v has at least one vertex of L at a distance at least k.

This suffices to conclude that every vertex v is currently playing a best response and, therefore, the graph is in equilibrium. □

Using the above lemma we can prove the following:

THEOREM 3. *Let $\alpha \geq 4k^3$. For any $k \leq \sqrt{\frac{2n}{3}} - 4$, the PoA for SumNCG is $\Omega(n/k)$ if $\alpha \leq n$, and $\Omega(1 + \frac{n^2}{k\alpha})$ otherwise.*

PROOF. By the above lemma, the graph is in equilibrium and has diameter $\Omega(\delta_2) = \Omega(\frac{n}{k})$. Moreover it is easy to see that each vertex has $\Omega(n)$ vertices at distance $\Omega(\frac{n}{k})$. Since the graph has $\Theta(n)$ edges, we have that the cost of the graph is $\Omega(\alpha n + n^2/k)$ while the social optimum is a star with cost $O(\alpha n + n^2)$. The claim follows. □

The following theorem provides a lower bound for a different range of values of the parameters α and k.

THEOREM 4. *If $\alpha \geq kn$ and $k \geq 2$, the PoA for SumNCG is $\Omega(n^{\frac{1}{2k-2}})$.*

PROOF. We use the same construction of Lemma 2. Remind that the view of each vertex v is a tree of height k with $q(q-1)^{i-1}$ vertices on level i. Therefore v has to buy at least q edges. Moreover if she buys exactly q edges, then she cannot improve her cost as her neighbors are the medians of the corresponding subtrees.

As $\alpha \geq kn$, v cannot improve her cost by increasing the number of bought edges. The claim follows. □

Finally, we have:

THEOREM 5. *If $k > 1 + 2\sqrt{\alpha}$, then in every equilibrium graph each player sees the whole graph, thus the set of LKEs coincides with the set of NEs.*

PROOF. Let G be an equilibrium with diameter at least k (otherwise the claim is trivially true) and let u and v be two vertices such that $d_G(u,v) = k$. By buying the edge (u,v), the player u could decrease the cost needed to reach the last $\lfloor \frac{k}{2} \rfloor$ vertices along the shortest path between u and v by at least $\frac{k^2}{4} - \frac{2}{4}$. As G is an equilibrium we must have $\frac{k^2}{4} - \frac{2}{4} \leq \alpha$ which implies $k \leq 2\sqrt{\alpha} + 1$. □

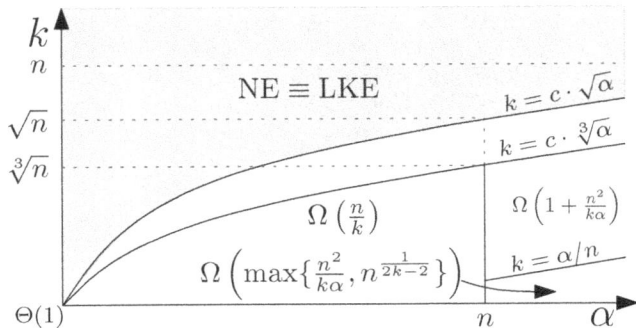

Figure 4: Lower bounds to the PoA for SumNCG. The behavior of the PoA in the region between the two curves is open. Notice that the gray region is the set of pairs (α, k) such that, in every LKE, players actually have a full knowledge of the network, and so LKEs coincide with NEs.

The previous results are summarized in Figure 4. Notice that it remains open to establish a lower bound to the PoA for values of k between $\Theta(\sqrt[3]{\alpha})$ and $\Theta(\sqrt{\alpha})$. Moreover we plan in the future to study the corresponding upper bounds.

5. ACKNOWLEDGMENTS

This work was partially supported by the Research Grant PRIN 2010 "ARS TechnoMedia", funded by the Italian Ministry of Education, University, and Research.

6. REFERENCES

[1] N. Alon, E.D. Demaine, M. Hajiaghayi, and T. Leighton, Basic network creation games, in *SIAM Journal on Discrete Mathematics 27*, 656-668, 2013.

[2] P.C. Ballester Pla, G. Ponti, and M.J. van der Leij, Bounded rationality and incomplete information in network games, presented at the *24th Annual Congress of the European Economic Association and 63rd Econometric Society European Meeting (EEC/ESEM'09)*, 2009.

[3] D. Bilò, L. Gualà, S. Leucci, and G. Proietti, The max-distance network creation game on general host graphs, in *Proceedings of the 8th International Workshop on Internet and Network Economics (WINE'12)*, LNCS 7695, Springer, 393–406, 2012.

[4] D. Bilò, L. Gualà, and G. Proietti, Bounded-distance network creation games, in *Proceedings of the 8th International Workshop on Internet and Network Economics (WINE'12)*, LNCS 7695, Springer, 72–85, 2012.

[5] B. Bollobás, *Extremal graph theory*, Academic Press, New York, 1978.

[6] E.D. Demaine, M. Hajiaghayi, H. Mahini, and M. Zadimoghaddam, The price of anarchy in network creation games, in *ACM Transactions on Algorithms 8(2)*, 2012.

[7] E.D. Demaine, M. Hajiaghayi, H. Mahini, and M. Zadimoghaddam, The price of anarchy in cooperative network creation games, in *Proceedings of the 26th International Symposium on Theoretical Aspects of Computer Science (STACS'09)*, Leibniz International Proceedings in Informatics 3, 301–312, 2009.

[8] S. Ehsani, M. Fazli, A. Mehrabian, S.S. Sadeghabad, M. Saghafian, S. Shokatfadaee, and M. Safari, On a bounded budget network creation game, in *Proceedings of the 23rd ACM Symposium on Parallelism in Algorithms and Architectures (SPAA'11)*, ACM Press, 207–214, 2011.

[9] A. Fabrikant, A. Luthra, E. Maneva, C.H. Papadimitriou, and S. Shenker, On a network creation game, in *Proceedings of the 22nd Symposium on Principles of Distributed Computing (PODC'03)*, ACM Press, 347–351, 2003.

[10] R. Graham, L. Hamilton, A. Levavi, and P.-S. Loh, Anarchy is free in network creation, in *Proceedings of the 10th International Workshop on Algorithms and Models for the Web Graph (WAW'13)*, LNCS 8305, Springer, 220–231, 2013.

[11] M. Hoefer, Local matching dynamics in social networks, *Information and Computation* 222, 20–35, 2013.

[12] M.O. Jackson and A. Wolinsky, A strategic model of social and economic networks, *Journal of Economic Theory* 71(1), 44–74, 1996.

[13] B. Kawald and P. Lenzner, On dynamics in selfish network creation, in *Proceedings of the 25th ACM Symposium on Parallelism in Algorithms and Architectures (SPAA'13)*, ACM Press, 83–92, 2013.

[14] N. Laoutaris, L.J. Poplawski, R. Rajaraman, R. Sundaram, and S.-H. Teng, Bounded budget connection (BBC) games or how to make friends and influence people, on a budget, in *Proceedings of the 27th ACM Symposium on Principles of Distributed Computing (PODC'08)*, ACM Press, 165–174, 2008.

[15] F. Lazebnik, V.A. Ustimenko, and A.J. Woldar, A new series of dense graphs of high girth, in bull. AMS (New Series) 32, 1, 73–79, 1995.

[16] P. Lenzner, in Greedy Selfish Network Creation, in *Proceedings of the 8th International Workshop on Internet and Network Economics (WINE'12)*, LNCS 7695, Springer, 142–155, 2012.

[17] A. Mamageishvili, M. Mihalák, D. Müller, Tree Nash Equilibria in the Network Creation Game, in *Proceedings of the 10th International Workshop on Algorithms and Models for the Web Graph (WAW'13)*, LNCS 8305, Springer, 118–129, 2013.

[18] M. Mihal'ák and J.C. Schlegel, The price of anarchy in network creation games is (mostly) constant, in *Proceedings of the 3rd International Symposium on Algorithmic Game Theory (SAGT'10)*, LNCS 6386, Springer, 276–287, 2010.

[19] M. Mihal'ák and J.C. Schlegel, Asymmetric swap-equilibrium: a unifying equilibrium concept for network creation games, in *Proceedings of the 37th International Symposium on Mathematical Foundations of Computer Science (MFCS'12)*, LNCS 7464, Springer, 693–704, 2012.

Finding Approximate Partitions and Splitters in External Memory[*]

Xiaocheng Hu[†] Yufei Tao[†] Yi Yang[‡] Shuigeng Zhou[‡]

[†]Chinese University of Hong Kong
{xchu, taoyf}@cse.cuhk.edu.hk

[‡]Fudan University
{yyang1, sgzhou}@fudan.edu.cn

ABSTRACT

This paper studies two fundamental problems both of which are defined on a set S of elements drawn from an ordered domain. In the first problem—called *approximate K-partitioning*—we want to divide S into K disjoint partitions $P_1, ..., P_K$ such that (i) every element in P_i is smaller than all the elements in P_j for any i, j satisfying $1 \le i < j \le K$, and (ii) the size of each P_i ($1 \le i \le K$) falls in a given range $[a, b]$. In the second problem—called *approximate K-splitters*—we want to find $K - 1$ elements $s_1, ..., s_{K-1}$ from S, such that the size of $S \cap (s_i, s_{i-1}]$ falls in a given range $[a, b]$ (define dummy $s_0 = -\infty$ and $s_K = \infty$). We present I/O-efficient comparison-based algorithms for solving these problems, and establish their optimality by proving matching lower bounds. Our results reveal that the two problems are separated in terms of I/O complexity when K is small, but have the same hardness when K is large.

Categories and Subject Descriptors

F.2.2 [**Analysis of algorithms and problem complexity**]: Nonnumerical Algorithms and Problems

Keywords

Approximate partitioning, approximate splitters, external memory, lower bound

1. INTRODUCTION

Let S be a set of N elements drawn from an ordered domain. Given two elements e_1, e_2, we use the natural notations $e_1 < e_2$ and $e_1 > e_2$ to indicate that e_1 is before and after e_2 in their domain, respectively. Furthermore, in the former (latter) case, we say that e_1 is *smaller* (*larger*) than

[*]Xiaocheng Hu and Yufei Tao were supported in part by projects GRF 4165/11, 4164/12, and 4168/13 from HKRGC. Yi Yang and Shuigeng Zhou were supported in part by the Research Innovation Program of Shanghai Municipal Education Commission under grant No. 13ZZ003.

e_2. Also, by $[e_1, e_2]$, we refer to the set of elements e in the underlying domain such that $e_1 \le e \le e_2$. Notations $(e_1, e_2]$ and $[e_1, e_2)$ are defined analogously (i.e., exclusive at e_1 and e_2, respectively). Denote by $-\infty$ and ∞ two special elements that are smaller and larger than all the elements in S, respectively.

We study two problems defined on S. In the first problem—called *approximate K-partitioning*—we are given (i) an integer K of which N is a multiple and (ii) an integer interval $[a, b]$, and want to divide S into K disjoint partitions $P_1, ..., P_K$ such that both of the following hold:

- Every element in P_i is smaller than all the elements in P_j for any i, j satisfying $1 \le i < j \le K$.

- $a \le |P_i| \le b$ for all $i \in [1, K]$.

The algorithm is required to output $P_1, ..., P_K$ in a linked list, where the elements of P_1 precede those of P_2, followed by those of P_3, and so on. The relative positions of the elements in the *same* partition are not important.

In the second problem—called *approximate K-splitters*—it is not necessary to actually perform the partitioning; instead, the goal is to indicate *where to*. Formally, we are given the same parameters as in approximate K-partitioning, but want to find $K - 1$ elements $s_1, ..., s_{K-1}$ from S called *splitters* with the property below:

- Suppose $s_1 < ... < s_{K-1}$, and let $s_0 = -\infty$ and $s_K = \infty$. Then, $a \le |S \cap (s_{i-1}, s_i]| \le b$ for every $i \in [1, K]$.

An algorithm can output the splitters in any order.

Motivation. Both the above problems are frequently encountered in manipulating ordered elements. Partitioning naturally arises, for example, in distributing S onto a number K of machines for parallel processing. Achieving a perfectly balanced load (where each machine is responsible for N/K elements) is a special instance of approximate K-partitioning with $a = b = N/K$. As we will see, interestingly, the cost of partitioning can be reduced if one is satisfied with a roughly balanced distribution where each machine is allocated at least a but at most b elements (with $a \ne b$). Splitters, on the other hand, have been very useful in building statistical profiles of S. For example, the bucket boundaries of an *equi-depth* histogram of K buckets (also known as a $(1/K)$-*quantile*) correspond to the output of the approximate K-splitters problem with $a = b = N/K$. If one can accept a *nearly equi-depth* histogram where each bucket covers at least a but at most b elements, then the bucket boundaries can be found in less—sometimes even sublinear—time, as we will show in this paper.

Math Conventions and Computation Model. We are interested in solving the two problems in the *external memory* (EM) model [1]. In this model, a machine is equipped with memory of size M words, and a disk that has been formatted into *blocks* of size B words. It holds that $M \geq 2B$. An I/O operation either reads a block of data from the disk to memory, or writes B words in memory to a disk block. The cost of an algorithm is measured by the number of I/Os performed. CPU calculation is free. All the algorithms discussed in this paper are comparison based, and adhere to the *indivisibility assumption* that each data element is always stored as a whole.

We define $\lg_x y = \max\{1, \log_x y\}$. The base x equals 2 if omitted. *Linear cost* refers to $O(N/B)$ when the problem at hand has an input size of N.

1.1 Parameter Ranges and Companion Problems

It is easy to see that the parameters a, b and K must satisfy the conditions

$$a \leq N/K \text{ and } b \geq N/K;$$

otherwise, the approximate K-partitioning and K-splitters problems both have no solution.

Let us quickly get rid of the case $K = N$. In such a scenario, approximate K-partitioning degenerates into *sorting*, while for approximate K-splitters an algorithm can simply return the input S directly. Henceforth, we will consider $K \leq N/2$.

When $a = 0$, the approximate K-partitioning/splitters problem is said to be *left-grounded*. Similarly, when $b = N$, the problem is *right-grounded*. When $a \neq 0$ and $b \neq N$, the problem is said to be *two-sided*.

The problems we study are closely related to two other important problems:

- *Multi-Partition*: Besides S, we are given $K-1$ integers $\sigma_1, ..., \sigma_{K-1}$, and need to partition S into $P_1, ..., P_K$ such that (i) $|P_i| = \sigma_i$ for each $i \in [1, K-1]$, and (ii) all elements in P_i are smaller than those in P_j for any i, j satisfying $1 \leq i < j \leq K$.

- *Multi-Selection*: Besides S, we are given K ranks[1] $r_1, ..., r_K$, and need to report K elements $e_1, ..., e_K$ in S such that e_i $(1 \leq i \leq K)$ has rank r_i in S.

1.2 Previous Results

It is clear that all the above problems can be trivially solved by sorting in $O(\frac{N}{B} \lg_{M/B} \frac{N}{B})$ I/Os. The interesting question is when it is possible to do better.

The multi-partition problem is already well understood. Aggarwal and Vitter [1] gave an algorithm that performs $O(\frac{N}{B} \lg_{M/B} K)$ I/Os, which is optimal (we suspect that the optimality may be folklore, but we are not aware of a published proof of the lower bound; thus, we give one in the appendix—see the proof of Lemma 5).

Multi-selection can be also be solved in $O(\frac{N}{B} \lg_{M/B} K)$ I/Os by first doing a multi-partition, and then returning the

---

[1] We follow the convention that, in an ordered set, the element with rank i is the i-th smallest in the set.

largest element of each partition. In internal memory, the problem requires $\Theta(N \lg K)$ comparisons [7]. Combining the internal-memory lower bound with a general result of Arge, Knudsen and Larsen [2] gives a lower bound $\Omega(\frac{N}{B} \lg_{M/B} \frac{K}{B})$ in EM. Therefore, the aforementioned approach (by resorting to multi-partition) is not optimal when K is small. It remains open to close this gap.

A multi-partition algorithm can be directly applied to solve the approximate K-partitioning problem: simply divide S into K partitions of equal size. Therefore, regardless of a and b, approximate K-partitioning can always be settled in $O(\frac{N}{B} \lg_{M/B} K)$ I/Os. This further implies that the same bound holds on the approximate K-splitters problem (first do approximate K-partitioning and then return each partition's max element).

Recently, Hu et al. [6] studied a special instance of the approximate K-splitters problem, where $K = M$, $a = c_1 N/M$, and $b = c_2 N/M$, with c_1 and c_2 being some constant. They gave an algorithm solving the problem in $O(N/B)$ I/Os. Unfortunately, their algorithm does not extend to the case where $K > M$, and/or arbitrary a and b.

1.3 Our Main Results

In this work, we present matching upper and lower bounds for both the approximate K-partitioning and splitters problems.

Lower Bounds. Concerning approximate K-splitters, our first result is:

THEOREM 1. *For any* $a \in [2, N/K]$, *any comparison-based algorithm solving the right-grounded approximate K-splitters problem must perform* $\Omega((1 + \frac{aK}{B}) \lg_{M/B} \frac{K}{B})$ *I/Os in the worst case.*

Note that when $a = o(N/(K \lg_{M/B} \frac{K}{B}))$, the lower bound is sublinear (as we will see, this bound is tight)! This is interesting because all the existing lower bound machineries [1, 2, 5] in EM are inherently designed to prove bounds at least linear, while our argument circumvents this obstacle.

Our second result on approximate K-splitters is:

THEOREM 2. *For any* $b \in [N/K, N/2]$, *any comparison-based algorithm solving the left-grounded approximate K-splitters problem must perform* $\Omega(\frac{N}{B} \lg_{M/B} \frac{N}{bB})$ *I/Os in the worst case.*

As a corollary, for any $a \in [2, N/K]$ and any $b \in [N/K, N/2]$, any algorithm solving the two-sided approximate K-splitters problem must incur

$$\Omega\left(\max\left\{\left(1 + \frac{aK}{B}\right) \lg_{M/B} \frac{K}{B}, \frac{N}{B} \lg_{M/B} \frac{N}{bB}\right\}\right)$$

I/Os in the worst case.

Concerning approximate K-partitioning, we prove:

THEOREM 3. *If* $\lg N \leq B \lg \frac{M}{B}$, *any comparison-based algorithm solving the approximate K-partitioning problem must perform* $\Omega(\frac{N}{B} \lg_{M/B} \min\{\frac{N}{b}, \frac{N}{B}\})$ *I/Os in the worst case.*

Interestingly, our proof of the above theorem does not use combinatorial arguments, but is instead derived from an elegant reduction from multi-partition to left-grounded approximate K-partitioning.

		Lower bound	Upper bound	Remarks
K-splitters	right	$\Theta((1+\frac{aK}{B})\lg_{M/B}\frac{K}{B})$		Thm 1, 5
	left	$\Theta(\frac{N}{B}\lg_{M/B}\frac{N}{bB})$		Thm 2, 5
	2-sided	$\Theta\left((1+\frac{aK}{B})\lg_{M/B}\frac{K}{B}+\frac{N}{B}\lg_{M/B}\frac{N}{bB}\right)$		Thm 1, 2, 5
K-partitioning	right	$\Omega(N/B)$	$O(\frac{N}{B}+\frac{aK}{B}\lg_{M/B}\min\{K,\frac{aK}{B}\})$	Sec 3, Thm 6
	left	$\Theta(\frac{N}{B}\lg_{M/B}\min\left\{\frac{N}{b},\frac{N}{B}\right\})$		Thm 3, 6
	2-sided	$\Omega(\frac{N}{B}\lg_{M/B}\min\left\{\frac{N}{b},\frac{N}{B}\right\})$	$O(\frac{aK}{B}\lg_{M/B}\min\{K,\frac{aK}{B}\}+\frac{N}{B}\lg_{M/B}\min\{\frac{N}{b},\frac{N}{B}\})$	Sec 3, Thm 3, 6

Table 1: Summary of our results

Upper Bounds. In terms of algorithms, our main contribution is an optimal solution to multi-selection:

THEOREM 4. *There is an algorithm that solves the multi-selection problem in $O(\frac{N}{B}\lg_{M/B}\frac{K}{B})$ I/Os.*

This finally closes the gap between the upper and lower bounds on this problem. Equipped with this new weapon, we present algorithms for both the approximate K-splitters and approximate K-partitioning problems with optimal performance (except for a single case of approximate K-partitioning where the value of aK is close to N). Table 1 summarizes these results.

The establishment of Theorem 4 has another implication. As mentioned earlier, there is a lower bound of $\Omega(\frac{N}{B}\lg_{M/B}K)$ on the multi-partition problem. Hence, Theorem 4 formally separates multi-selection from multi-partition in terms of I/O-complexity. Notice that the separation occurs only for small K, whereas for large K, the two problems have the same hardness. This phenomenon is interesting because in internal memory the two problems have exactly the same complexity: both demand $\Theta(N\lg K)$ comparisons.

2. LOWER BOUNDS: APPROXIMATE K-SPLITTERS

In this section, we establish our lower bounds for the approximate K-splitters problem. As before, let $s_1,...,s_{K-1}$ in ascending order be the splitters returned by an algorithm. Define dummy $s_0=-\infty$ and $s_K=\infty$. Given a pair of consecutive splitters s_{i-1} and s_i ($1\le i\le K$), we say that they *induce* a partition P on the dataset $\mathcal{S}$ where $P=\mathcal{S}\cap(s_{i-1},s_i]$. Recall that $|P|$ must fall between a and b.

2.1 Right-Grounded

This subsection serves as a proof for Theorem 1 (i.e., $b=N$). Let us first discuss the simple case $K<\alpha M$—where α is a constant to be determined later—under which the target lower bound is $\Omega(1+\frac{aK}{B})$. Consider an algorithm that sees $N_0\in[0,N]$ elements $\mathcal{S}$ during its execution. In the K partitions induced by the returned splitters, there must exist a partition P containing at most N_0/K seen elements. Since all the other $N-N_0$ elements have not been seen, they can have any possible ranks in $\mathcal{S}$, so it is possible that none of them is in P, i.e., $|P|\le N_0/K$. By problem definition, $|P|\ge a$, which gives $N_0/K\ge a$. Hence, $N_0\ge aK$, which means the algorithm must spend $\Omega(1+\frac{N_0}{B})=\Omega(1+\frac{aK}{B})$ I/Os.

The rest of the subsection assumes $K\ge\alpha M$, where our target lower bound becomes $\Omega(\frac{aK}{B}\lg_{M/B}\frac{K}{B})$. We define a

family Π_{hard} of hard permutations of $\mathcal{S}$ as follows. First recall that $\mathcal{S}$ is initially stored in N/B input blocks, each with B elements. For each $i\in[1,B]$, let $\mathcal{S}_i$ be the set consisting of the i-th element of every input block. Then, Π_{hard} consists of all those permutations where for any i,j satisfying $1\le i<j\le B$, every element in $\mathcal{S}_i$ is smaller than all elements in $\mathcal{S}_j$. Clearly, $|\Pi_{hard}|=((N/B)!)^B$.

Consider an algorithm that solves the problem in H I/Os. Let Π be the set of permutations in Π_{hard} that are consistent with all the comparisons performed by the algorithm. A standard argument (see appendix) shows that:

LEMMA 1. $|\Pi|\ge((N/B)!)^B/\binom{M}{B}^H$.

Next, we will derive an upper bound on $|\Pi|$ (which will then yield a lower bound on H together with Lemma 1). For this purpose, we will analyze $|\Pi|$ by resorting to order theory. Let us first define some general concepts concerning partial orders. Let $\prec$ be a partial order defined on some domain. Consider a set X of elements from this domain, and π a permutation of X. We say that π is *consistent* with $\prec$ if, for any $x,y\in X$ such that $x\prec y$, x precedes y in π. Let $CP(\prec,X)$ be the set of permutations of X consistent with $\prec$.

Now we are ready to proceed with our analysis on $|\Pi|$. First, define a partial order $\prec_\star$ over $\mathcal{S}$ as follows: given two elements $x,y\in\mathcal{S}$, $x\prec_\star y$ if and only if x precedes y in *all* the permutations in Π. We prove the following intuitive fact in the appendix:

FACT 1. $\Pi=CP(\prec_\star,\mathcal{S})$.

Let x,y be two different elements in $\mathcal{S}$. If either $x\prec_\star y$ or $y\prec_\star x$ holds, we say that they are *comparable*; otherwise, they are *incomparable*. We observe:

FACT 2. *For any i,j satisfying $1\le i<j\le K-1$, s_i and s_j are comparable.*

PROOF. Suppose that s_i and s_j are incomparable. Then we can find a permutation $\pi\in CP(\prec_\star,\mathcal{S})$ in which s_i precedes s_j without any element between them. By Fact 1, $\pi\in\Pi$, so the algorithm has to be correct on π. However, the partition induced on π between s_i and s_j has only one element s_j, contradicting the requirement that each partition has size at least $a\ge 2$ (as is a condition of Theorem 1). □

By Fact 2, we have that $s_1\prec_\star...\prec_\star s_{K-1}$. For each $i\in[2,K-1]$, define $T_i=\{x\in\mathcal{S}\mid s_{i-1}\prec_\star x\prec_\star s_i\}$. Also define $T_1=\{x\in\mathcal{S}\mid x\prec_\star s_1\}$ and $T_K=\{x\in\mathcal{S}\mid s_{K-1}\prec_\star x\}$.

FACT 3. $|T_i|\ge a-1$ for each $i\in[1,K-1]$, and $|T_K|\ge a$.

PROOF. For any $i \in [2, K-1]$, there exists a permutation $\pi \in \mathrm{CP}(\prec_\star, \mathcal{S}) = \Pi$ in which only elements in T_i are between s_{i-1} and s_i. Therefore, the partition induced on π between the two splitters is exactly $T_i \cup \{s_i\}$, implying that $|T_i| \geq a-1$. $|T_1| \geq a-1$ and $|T_K| \geq a$ can be proved similarly. $\square$

We also need the following basic facts from order theory:

FACT 4. *Let $\prec$ be a partial order over a finite set X. If X can be divided into disjoint partitions X_1 and X_2, such that $x \prec y$ holds for any $x \in X_1$ and $y \in X_2$, then $|\mathrm{CP}(\prec, X)| = |\mathrm{CP}(\prec, X_1)| \cdot |\mathrm{CP}(\prec, X_2)|$.*

FACT 5. *Let $\prec$ be a partial order over a finite set X. For any subset $Y \subseteq X$, it holds that $|\mathrm{CP}(\prec, X)| \leq |\mathrm{CP}(\prec, Y)| \cdot |\mathrm{CP}(\prec, X \setminus Y)| \cdot \binom{|X|}{|Y|}$.*

Now we are ready to give an upper bound of $|\Pi| = |\mathrm{CP}(\prec_\star, \mathcal{S})|$, as promised earlier:

LEMMA 2.
$$\lg |\mathrm{CP}(\prec_\star, \mathcal{S})| \leq B \lg((N/B)!) - aK \lg(K/B) + O(K \lg a)$$

PROOF. In this proof, we abbreviate $\mathrm{CP}(\prec_\star, X)$ into $\mathrm{CP}(X)$ for any $X \subseteq \mathcal{S}$. Recall that the elements in $\mathcal{S}$ come from B disjoint sets $\mathcal{S}_1, ..., \mathcal{S}_B$, where each $\mathcal{S}_i$ ($1 \leq i \leq B$) takes the i-th element of every input block. In any permutation $\pi \in \Pi$, for any $x \in \mathcal{S}_i$ and $y \in \mathcal{S}_j$ ($1 \leq i < j \leq B$), we have that x precedes y in π because $\Pi \subseteq \Pi_{hard}$. Therefore, $x \prec_\star y$ by the definition of $\prec_\star$.

For each $i \in [1, K-1]$, let A_i be a set consisting of s_i and $a-1$ arbitrary elements from T_i. Also let A_K be a set consisting of a arbitrary elements in T_k. By Fact 3, $A_1, ..., A_K$ exist. By definition, for any $x \in A_i$ and $y \in A_j$ ($1 \leq i < j \leq K$), we have that $x \prec y$. Let $A = A_1 \cup ... \cup A_K$. Therefore,

$$|\mathrm{CP}(\mathcal{S})|$$
$$= \prod_{i=1}^{B} |\mathrm{CP}(\mathcal{S}_i)| \quad \text{(by Fact 4)}$$
$$\leq \prod_{i=1}^{B} \left(\binom{|\mathcal{S}_i|}{|\mathcal{S}_i \setminus A|} \cdot |\mathrm{CP}(\mathcal{S}_i \setminus A)| \cdot |\mathrm{CP}(\mathcal{S}_i \cap A)| \right)$$
$$\text{(by Fact 5)}$$
$$= \prod_{i=1}^{B} \left(\binom{|\mathcal{S}_i|}{|\mathcal{S}_i \setminus A|} \cdot |\mathrm{CP}(\mathcal{S}_i \setminus A)| \cdot \prod_{j=1}^{K} |\mathrm{CP}(\mathcal{S}_i \cap A_j)| \right)$$
$$\text{(by Fact 4)}$$
$$\leq \prod_{i=1}^{B} \left(\binom{|\mathcal{S}_i|}{|\mathcal{S}_i \setminus A|} \cdot |\mathcal{S}_i \setminus A|! \cdot \prod_{j=1}^{K} |\mathcal{S}_i \cap A_j|! \right). \quad (1)$$

Then the lemma follows from simplification of (1), which can be found in the appendix. $\square$

Let β be the hidden constant in the term $O(K \lg a)$ in 2. Now we fix $\alpha = 2^{2\beta}$. Lemmas 1 and 2 give

$$B \lg((N/B)!) - H \lg \binom{M}{B}$$
$$\leq B \lg((N/B)!) - aK \lg(K/B) + \beta K \lg a.$$

Hence:

$$H \lg \binom{M}{B} \geq aK \lg(K/B) - \beta K \lg a$$
$$\Rightarrow H \cdot B \lg \frac{M}{B} = \Omega\left(aK \lg(K/B) - \beta K \lg a \right)$$
$$\Rightarrow H = \Omega((aK/B) \lg_{M/B}(K/B))$$

as needed, where the last step used the fact that $a \lg(K/B) \geq a \lg(\alpha M/B) \geq 2a\beta$.

2.2 Left-Grounded

This subsection will prove Theorem 2 (i.e., $a = 0$). Let us first start with the simple case $N/b < \alpha M$—where α is a constant to be determined later—under which our target lower bound becomes $\Omega(N/B)$. Consider an algorithm that sees $N_0 \in [0, N]$ elements in $\mathcal{S}$ during its execution. Then, we can construct a permutation, such that all the $N - N_0$ unseen elements are in the same partition induced by the splitters. By problem definition, $N - N_0 \leq b$, which together with the condition $b \leq N/2$ (of Theorem 2) implies that $N_0 \geq N/2$. Hence, the algorithm must perform $\Omega(N/B)$ I/Os.

The rest of the subsection assumes that $N/b \geq \alpha M$. Let Π_{hard} and H be defined in the same way as in Section 2.1. Lemma 1 still holds, giving a lower bound on $|\Pi|$.

To prove an upper bound on $|\Pi|$, we consider the same partial order $\prec_\star$ defined in Section 2.1. As before, given elements $x, y \in \mathcal{S}$, they are *comparable* if either $x \prec_\star y$ or $y \prec_\star x$ holds; otherwise, they are *incomparable*. Fact 1 still holds.

Define $T_i = \mathcal{S}_i \setminus \{s_1, ..., s_{K-1}\}$ for each $i \in [1, B]$, i.e., T_i is the set of non-splitter elements in $\mathcal{S}_i$. Let $T = T_1 \cup ... \cup T_B$, i.e., T is the set of all the non-splitter elements. Note that $|T| \geq N/2$ because $K \leq N/2$.

FACT 6. *For any $i \in [1, B]$, let A be a subset of T_i, such that all the elements in A are pairwise incomparable. Then $|A| \leq b$.*

PROOF. Since the elements in A are pairwise incomparable, there exists a permutation $\pi \in \mathrm{CP}(\prec_\star, \mathcal{S}) = \Pi$, such that all the elements of A appear consecutively in π. Furthermore, $A \subseteq T_i$ implies that A does not contain any splitter. Therefore, there exists a partition induced on π by the splitters which contains all the elements in A. The size of the partition must be at most b, so $|A| \leq b$. $\square$

In the appendix, we prove a general lemma in order theory:

LEMMA 3. *Consider a partial order $\prec$ over a finite set X of n elements. Any set of pairwise incomparable elements from X has size at most w. Then, $\lg |\mathrm{CP}(\prec, X)| \leq n \lg w + O(\lg n)$.*

Combining Fact 6 and Lemma 3, we know that, for each $i \in [1, B]$:

$$\lg |\mathrm{CP}(\prec_\star, T_i)| \leq |T_i| \lg b + O(\lg |T_i|). \quad (2)$$

Now we show an upper bound on $|\mathrm{CP}(\prec_\star, \mathcal{S})|$:

LEMMA 4.
$$\lg |\mathrm{CP}(\prec_\star, \mathcal{S})| \leq B \lg((N/B)!) - |T| \lg(|T|/(bB)) + O(|T|)$$

PROOF. In this proof, we abbreviate $CP(\prec_\star, X)$ into $CP(X)$ for any $X \subseteq \mathcal{S}$. Recall that for any $1 \le i < j \le B$, $x \in \mathcal{S}_i$ and $y \in \mathcal{S}_j$, it holds that $x \prec_\star y$. Therefore,

$$
\begin{aligned}
&|CP(\mathcal{S})| \\
=\ & \prod_{i=1}^{B} |CP(\mathcal{S}_i)| \quad \text{(by Fact 4)} \\
\le\ & \prod_{i=1}^{B} \binom{|\mathcal{S}_i|}{|T_i|} \cdot |CP(\mathcal{S}_i \setminus T_i)| \cdot |CP(T_i)| \quad \text{(by Fact 5)} \\
\le\ & \prod_{i=1}^{B} \binom{|\mathcal{S}_i|}{|T_i|} \cdot |\mathcal{S}_i \setminus T_i|! \cdot |CP(T_i)|. \quad (3)
\end{aligned}
$$

Then the lemma follows from combining and simplifying (2) and (3). See appendix for details. $\square$

Let β be the hidden constant in the term $O(|T|)$ in Lemma 4. Now we set constant α to be $2^{2\beta}$. From Lemmas 1 and 4, we have

$$
\begin{aligned}
& B \lg((N/B)!) - H \lg \binom{M}{B} \\
\le\ & B \lg((N/B)!) - |T| \lg(|T|/(bB)) + \beta|T|.
\end{aligned}
$$

Therefore,

$$
\begin{aligned}
H \lg \binom{M}{B} &\ge\ |T| \lg(|T|/(bB)) - \beta|T| \\
\Rightarrow H \cdot B \lg(M/B) &=\ \Omega(|T| \lg(|T|/(bB)) - \beta|T|) \\
\Rightarrow H &=\ \Omega((N/B) \lg_{M/B}(N/(bB)))
\end{aligned}
$$

as needed, where the last step used the fact that $\lg \frac{|T|}{bB} \ge \lg \frac{N}{2bB} \ge \lg \frac{\alpha M}{2B} \ge 2\beta$.

3. LOWER BOUNDS: APPROXIMATE K-PARTITIONING

In this section, we will prove the lower bound in Theorem 3 for the approximate K-partitioning problem. Recall that the goal is to divide the dataset $\mathcal{S}$ into K partitions by respecting the ordering, such that the size of each partition falls in $[a, b]$. As in Section 2, we will discuss the left- and right-grounded versions of the problem separately. Theorem 3 will then follow from our results for these versions.

Right-Grounded. When $b = N$, any algorithm must see all the elements at least once, as long as $a \ge 1$ and $K \ge 2$. To understand this, suppose that the algorithm terminates without seeing all elements. Consider an arbitrary seen element e and an arbitrary unseen element e'. Regardless of whether the algorithm puts e, e' in the same partition, the adversary can always manipulate the value of e' to call the algorithm wrong. Therefore, any algorithm must perform $\Omega(N/B)$ I/Os.

Left-Grounded. Now we will prove a lower bound for the case where $a = 0$. For this purpose, let us define the *precise K-partitioning problem* as the special instance of the multi-partition problem with $\sigma_1 = ... = \sigma_{K-1} = N/K$. We will first present a reduction from precise K-partitioning to left-grounded approximate K-partitioning. Then, we will prove a lower bound for the former problem.

Our reduction works as follows. Suppose that there is an algorithm solving the left-grounded problem in $F(N, K, b)$ I/Os (recall that $b \ge N/K$ needs to hold). The same argument we gave for the right-grounded case implies that $F(N, K, b) = \Omega(N/B)$ when $b < N$ and $K \ge 2$. Assuming that N is a multiple of b, we can perform precise (N/b)-partitioning as follows:

1. Solve an approximate K-partitioning problem to divide $\mathcal{S}$ into partitions $P_1, ..., P_K$ (in this order), where each partition has size at most b.

2. Let R be an initially empty set. We process $P_1, ..., P_K$ in turn. At P_i ($i \in [1, K]$), we first append the entire P_i to R. If $|R| > b$, divide R into disjoint partitions R_1 and R_2 such that every element in R_1 is smaller than all elements in R_2, and $|R_1| = b$. Then R_1 is returned as the next partition in the precise (N/b)-partitioning, and R_2 replaces R as we proceed to process P_{i+1}.

The first step requires $F(N, K, b)$ I/Os, while the second step requires $O(N/B)$ I/Os in total. Therefore, we can solve the precise (N/b)-partitioning in $F(N, K, b) + O(N/B) = O(F(N, K, b))$ I/Os. However, in the appendix, we prove:

LEMMA 5. *If $K \ge 2$ and $\lg N \le B \lg \frac{M}{B}$, a comparison-based algorithm solving the precise K-partitioning problem must perform $\Omega(\frac{N}{B} \lg_{M/B} \min\{K, \frac{N}{B}\})$ I/Os in the worst case.*

The lemma then implies

$$ F(N, K, b) = \Omega((N/B) \lg_{M/B} \min\{N/b, N/B\}). $$

Note that K has no effect on the lower bound. We thus complete the proof of Theorem 3.

4. MULTI-SELECTION

This section develops a new algorithm for the multi-selection problem. Towards this purpose, we will first solve a relevant problem called *L-intermixed selection* in Section 4.1, and then leverage our solution to attack multi-selection in Section 4.2.

4.1 *L*-Intermixed Selection

Set $m = cM$ for some sufficiently small constant c. Given an integer $L \in [1, m]$, the *L-intermixed selection* is defined as follows. The input consists of:

- A set $\mathcal{D}$ with each element being a pair $e = (k_e, g_e)$, where k_e is drawn from an ordered domain, and g_e is an integer in $[1, L]$. We refer to k_e (g_e) as the *key* (*group id*) of e. For each $i \in [1, L]$, denote by $\mathcal{D}_i$ the set of elements in $\mathcal{D}$ with group id i. Each of $\mathcal{D}_1, ..., \mathcal{D}_L$ is called a *group*.

- L integers $t_1, ..., t_L$, where $1 \le t_i \le |\mathcal{D}_i|$ for each $i \in [1, L]$.

The objective is to report, for each $i \in [1, L]$, the element e_i with the t_i-th smallest key in $\mathcal{D}_i$. Intuitively, we want to solve L instances of rank selection, but the L datasets are intermixed.

Algorithm. Whenever we compare two elements e and e' from the same group, we are comparing their keys k_e and $k_{e'}$.

Similarly, when we say e is the median of a subset S of some group, we mean that e has the median key in S. If $|\mathcal{D}| \le M/3$, the problem can be solved trivially by loading $\mathcal{D}$ and $t_1, ..., t_L$ entirely into memory. The subsequent discussion assumes $|\mathcal{D}| > M/3$.

Our algorithm can be thought of as concurrently running L threads of the "median-of-medians" selection algorithm [3]. However, doing so naively would demand a block of memory dedicated to each thread. This is an issue because it will allow us to do only $O(M/B)$ threads at a time, whereas $L = \Omega(M)$. Next we show how to overcome the obstacle by using only $O(1)$ words of memory for each thread.

In the first step, by scanning $\mathcal{D}$ only once, we can divide each group arbitrarily into *subgroups* of size at most 5, and collect the median of each subgroup into a set Σ. To do so, maintain L sets $S_1, ..., S_L$ in memory, which are initially empty. For each element $e = (k_e, g_e)$ in $\mathcal{D}$, we first insert e into S_{g_e}. If $|S_{g_e}| = 5$, then S_{g_e} makes a subgroup, so we add the median of S_{g_e} to Σ, and then clear the contents of S_{g_e}. After all elements have been scanned, if any S_i ($1 \le i \le L$) is non-empty, then S_i is the last subgroup of $\mathcal{D}_i$; its median is added to Σ.

Now Σ consists of the medians of all the subgroups. For each $i \in [1, L]$, denote by Σ_i the set of elements with group id i in Σ. By recursion, we can find the medians of $\Sigma_1, ..., \Sigma_L$, denoted as $\mu_1, ..., \mu_L$, respectively. With another scan of $\mathcal{D}$, we can obtain the rank θ_i of μ_i in $\mathcal{D}_i$ for each $i \in [1, L]$.

In the last step, we construct another (smaller) instance of L-intermixed selection, with $\mathcal{D}' = \mathcal{D}'_1 \cup ... \cup \mathcal{D}'_L$ and $t'_1, ..., t'_L$ as the input. For each $i \in [1, L]$, if $t_i \le \theta_i$, then $\mathcal{D}'_i = \mathcal{D}_i \cap (-\infty, \mu_i]$ and $t'_i = t_i$; otherwise, $\mathcal{D}'_i = \mathcal{D}_i \cap (\mu_i, \infty)$ and $t'_i = t_i - \theta_i$. Clearly, by solving this instance, we also solve the original L-intermixed selection problem. To create the instance, we keep in memory $t_1, ..., t_L, \mu_1, ..., \mu_L, \theta_1, ..., \theta_L$. Then, $t'_1, ..., t'_L$ can be computed in memory. $\mathcal{D}'$ can be generated with another scan of $\mathcal{D}$ in $O(|\mathcal{D}|/B)$ I/Os as follows. For each element $e \in \mathcal{D}$, let $i \in [1, L]$ be its group id (i.e., $g_e = i$). By comparing e with μ_i and t_i with θ_i, we know whether $e \in \mathcal{D}'_i$; if so, add e to $\mathcal{D}'_i$.

Analysis. We now prove the efficiency of our algorithm:

LEMMA 6. *The above algorithm solves the L-intermixed selection problem in $O(|\mathcal{D}|/B)$ I/Os.*

PROOF. Let $F(\mathcal{D})$ be the cost of our algorithm on dataset $\mathcal{D}$. When $|\mathcal{D}| \le M/3$, the algorithm simply solves the problem in memory. When $|\mathcal{D}| > M/3$, the algorithm recurses on Σ and $\mathcal{D}'$, respectively, and scans $\mathcal{D}$ for a constant number of times. Therefore,

$$F(\mathcal{D}) = \begin{cases} O(|\mathcal{D}|/B), & \text{if } |\mathcal{D}| \le M/3 \\ O(|\mathcal{D}|/B) + F(\Sigma) + F(\mathcal{D}'), & \text{if } |\mathcal{D}| > M/3 \end{cases}.$$

Clearly, $|\Sigma| = \sum_{i=1}^{L} \lceil |\mathcal{D}_i|/5 \rceil \le |\mathcal{D}|/5 + L$. By the analysis in [3], we can show that $|\mathcal{D}'_i| \le \frac{7}{10}|\mathcal{D}_i| + 3$ for each $i \in [1, L]$. Hence, $|\mathcal{D}'| \le \frac{7}{10}|\mathcal{D}| + 3L$. So we have

$$|\Sigma| + |\mathcal{D}'| \le \frac{9}{10}|\mathcal{D}| + 4L \le \frac{9}{10}|\mathcal{D}| + 4cM \le \left(\frac{9}{10} + 12c\right)|\mathcal{D}|,$$

where the last inequality follows from $|\mathcal{D}| > M/3$. By setting c sufficiently small, $|\Sigma| + |\mathcal{D}'|$ is at most $\frac{19}{20}|\mathcal{D}|$. Then by standard analysis, the recursion is solved as $F(\mathcal{D}) = O(|\mathcal{D}|/B)$. □

4.2 Solving Multi-Selection

Recall that in the multi-selection problem, we need to find elements $e_1, ..., e_K$ from $\mathcal{S}$, such that each e_i ($1 \le i \le K$) has rank r_i in $\mathcal{S}$. Let m be as defined in Section 4.1. We first show that the in the *base case* where $K \le m$, the problem can be solved in linear I/Os. After that, we solve the *general case* where $K > m$ by decomposing it into base cases.

Base Case $K \le m$. As mentioned in Section 1.3, Hu et al. [6] has solved the special case $K = M, a = c_1 N/M$ and $b = c_2 N/M$ of approximate K-splitters in linear I/Os for some constants c_1 and c_2. Let $s_1 < ... < s_{M-1}$ be the splitters returned by their algorithm on $\mathcal{S}$. Define $P_i = \mathcal{S} \cap (s_{i-1}, s_i]$ for each $i \in [1, M]$ (define dummy $s_0 = -\infty$ and $s_M = \infty$). Note that $|P_i| = \Theta(N/M)$.

Consider the following instance of the K-intermixed selection problem. For each $i \in [1, K]$, let P_j ($1 \le j \le M$) be the partition such that e_i is in P_j. Define group $\mathcal{D}_i = \{(e, i) \mid e \in P_j\}$, and rank $t_i = r_i - (|P_1| + ... + |P_{j-1}|)$. Then, $\mathcal{D} = \mathcal{D}_1 \cup ... \cup \mathcal{D}_K$. The output of this instance is exactly the set of elements $e_1, ..., e_K$ we want for the original multi-selection problem. The instance can be solved in $O(|\mathcal{D}|/B)$ I/Os by Lemma 6, which is $O(N/B)$ because each group has size $\Theta(N/M)$ and there are $K < M$ groups.

It suffices to show that the instance can be constructed in $O(N/B)$ I/Os. To do so, we first obtain $|P_1|, ..., |P_M|$ with one scan of $\mathcal{S}$, while keeping $s_1, ..., s_{M-1}$ memory resident. After this, $t_1, ..., t_K$ can be calculated in memory. We scan $\mathcal{S}$ one more time to construct $\mathcal{D}$ as follows. For each element $e \in \mathcal{S}$, by comparing it with the splitters, we get the partition id $j \in [1, M]$ such that $e \in P_j$. Then, by from the ranks $r_1, ..., r_K$ and the partition sizes $|P_1|, ..., |P_M|$, we can find (in memory) those group ids $i \in [1, K]$ such that $\mathcal{D}_i$ should contain pair (e, i): specifically, find every i that $|P_1| + ... + |P_{j-1}| < r_i \le |P_1| + ... + |P_j|$. Once such an i is found, insert pair (e, i) into $\mathcal{D}$. In this manner, we generate $\mathcal{D}$ in $O(N/B)$ I/Os.

General Case: $K > m$. Set $g = \lceil K/m \rceil$. Perform multi-partition (using an algorithm of [1], which is reviewed in Section 1.2) to divide $\mathcal{S}$ at ranks $r_m, r_{2m}, ..., r_{(g-1)m}$ into g partitions $P_1, ..., P_g$. Now for each $i \in [1, g-1]$, the elements of ranks $r_{(i-1)m+1}, ..., r_{im}$ must be in P_i, and the elements of ranks $r_{(g-1)m+1}, ..., r_K$ must be in P_g. Since at most m elements need to be selected from each partition, it suffices to solve a base case on each of them.

Generating the partitions takes $O((N/B) \lg_{M/B} g) = O((N/B) \lg_{M/B}(K/B))$ I/Os, while solving all the base cases requires altogether $O(\sum_{i=1}^{g} |P_i|/B) = O(N/B)$ I/Os. We thus have completed the proof of Theorem 4.

5. ALGORITHMS FOR APPROXIMATE K-SPLITTERS AND K-PARTITIONING

This section presents algorithms for the approximate K-splitters and K-partitioning problems.

5.1 Approximate K-Splitters

Right-Grounded. Take a set $\mathcal{S}'$ of aK arbitrary elements in $\mathcal{S}$ in $O(1 + aK/B)$ I/Os. Then, simply return the $\frac{1}{K}$-quantile of $\mathcal{S}'$ as the splitters $s_1, ..., s_{K-1}$, namely, s_i ($1 \le i \le K-1$) has rank ia in $\mathcal{S}'$. The cost is $O((1+\frac{aK}{B}) \lg_{M/B} \frac{K}{B})$ by Theorem 4.

Left-Grounded. Set $K' = \lceil N/b \rceil$. Pick splitters $s_1, ..., s_{K'-1}$ from $\mathcal{S}$ such that s_i ($1 \le i \le K'-1$) has rank ib in $\mathcal{S}$. This demands $O(\frac{N}{B} \lg_{M/B} \frac{K'}{B}) = O(\frac{N}{B} \lg_{M/B} \frac{N}{bB})$ I/Os by Theorem 4. After that, if $K' < K$, we select $s_{K'}, ..., s_{K-1}$ as $K - K'$ arbitrary distinct elements in $\mathcal{S} \setminus \{s_1, ..., s_{K'-1}\}$. The total cost is $O(\frac{N}{B} \lg_{M/B} \frac{N}{bB})$.

Two-Sided. We first get rid of the scenario where $a \ge N/2K$ or $b \le 2N/K$. In this case, we simply return the $\frac{1}{K}$-quantile of $\mathcal{S}$ as the splitters (namely, splitter s_i has rank iN/K in $\mathcal{S}$, where $1 \le i \le K - 1$). The cost is $O(\frac{N}{B} \lg_{M/B} \frac{K}{B}) = O(\max\{\frac{aK}{B} \lg_{M/B} \frac{K}{B}, \frac{N}{B} \lg_{M/B} \frac{N}{B}\})$.

Henceforth, we assume $a < N/2K$ and $b > 2N/K$. Set $K' = \lfloor \frac{bK-N}{b-a} \rfloor$. It is easy to verify that $K' \in [1, K-1]$. Our algorithm partitions $\mathcal{S}$ into $\mathcal{S}_{low}$ and $\mathcal{S}_{high}$, such that $\mathcal{S}_{low}$ consists of the aK' smallest elements of $\mathcal{S}$, and $\mathcal{S}_{high}$ the remaining ones. After that, we determine the splitters $s_1, ..., s_{K-1}$ of $\mathcal{S}$ as follows:

- $s_{K'}$ is the largest element of $\mathcal{S}_{low}$;

- $s_1, ..., s_{K'-1}$ constitute the $\frac{1}{K'}$-quantile of $\mathcal{S}_{low}$;

- $s_{K'+1}, ..., s_{K-1}$ constitute the $\frac{1}{K-K'}$-quantile of $\mathcal{S}_{high}$.

To see the correctness of our algorithm, consider the K partitions induced by $s_1, ..., s_{K-1}$. Among them, we get K' even partitions of $\mathcal{S}_{low}$, and $K - K'$ even partitions of $\mathcal{S}_{high}$. Since $|\mathcal{S}_{low}| = aK'$, each of the partitions from $\mathcal{S}_{low}$ has exactly a elements. To show that the partitions from $\mathcal{S}_{high}$ have legal sizes, it suffices to prove that $|\mathcal{S}_{high}| = N - aK'$ is in the range $[a(K - K'), b(K - K')]$. This is true by our choice of K' and the facts that $a < N/2K$ and $b > 2N/K$.

It takes $O(N/B)$ I/Os to obtain $\mathcal{S}_{low}$, $\mathcal{S}_{high}$ and $s_{K'}$. By Theorem 4, it takes $O((|\mathcal{S}_{low}|/B) \lg_{M/B}(K'/B))$ I/Os to get $s_1, ..., s_{K'-1}$ from $\mathcal{S}_{low}$, and $O((|\mathcal{S}_{high}|/B) \lg_{M/B}(K - K')/B)$ I/Os to get $s_{K'+1}, ..., s_{K-1}$ from $\mathcal{S}_{high}$. As $K - K' = \Theta(\frac{N-aK}{b-a}) = \Theta(N/b)$, $|\mathcal{S}_{low}| = aK' < aK$, and $|\mathcal{S}_{high}| < N$, we know that the total cost is bounded by $O(\frac{aK}{B} \lg_{M/B} \frac{K}{B} + \frac{N}{B} \lg_{M/B} \frac{N}{bB})$.

THEOREM 5. *For the approximate K-splitters problem, there is an algorithm that solves*

- *the right-grounded version in $O((1 + \frac{aK}{B}) \lg_{M/B} \frac{K}{B})$ I/Os;*

- *the left-grounded version in $O(\frac{N}{B} \lg_{M/B} \frac{N}{bB})$ I/Os;*

- *the two-sided version in $O(\frac{aK}{B} \lg_{M/B} \frac{K}{B} + \frac{N}{B} \lg_{M/B} \frac{N}{bB})$ I/Os.*

The cost for all three versions is optimal according to the lower bounds in Theorems 1 and 2.

5.2 Approximate K-Partitioning

Right-Grounded. Take the set $\mathcal{S}'$ of the $a(K-1)$ smallest elements of $\mathcal{S}$ in $O(N/B)$ I/Os. Then, divide $\mathcal{S}'$ into $K - 1$ partitions of size a using the multi-partition algorithm of [1] in $O((1 + \frac{aK}{B}) \lg_{M/B} \min\{K, \frac{aK}{B}\})$ I/Os. Simply treat $\mathcal{S} \setminus \mathcal{S}'$ as the K-th partition (whose size is $N - a(K-1) \ge a$).

Left-Grounded. Let $K' = \lceil N/b \rceil$. Perform multi-partition to divide $\mathcal{S}$ into K' partitions of size at most b. If $K' <$

K, simply add $K - K'$ empty partitions. The total cost is $O(\frac{N}{B} \lg_{M/B} \min\{\frac{N}{b}, \frac{N}{B}\})$.

Two-Sided. The algorithm is analogous to our two-sided approximate K-splitters algorithm, by simply replacing multi-selection with multi-partition. More specifically, we generate $\mathcal{S}_{low}$ and $\mathcal{S}_{high}$ using the same K'. Then, we divide $\mathcal{S}_{low}$ into K' partitions of the same size, and $\mathcal{S}_{high}$ into $K - K'$ partitions of the same size, both respecting the ordering. The total cost is $O(\frac{aK}{B} \lg_{M/B} \min\{K, \frac{aK}{B}\} + \frac{N}{B} \lg_{M/B} \min\{\frac{N}{b}, \frac{N}{B}\})$.

THEOREM 6. *For the approximate K-partitioning problem, there is an algorithm that solves*

- *the right-grounded version in $O(\frac{N}{B} + \frac{aK}{B} \lg_{M/B} \min\{K, \frac{aK}{B}\})$ I/Os;*

- *the left-grounded version in $O(\frac{N}{B} \lg_{M/B} \min\{\frac{N}{b}, \frac{N}{B}\})$ I/Os;*

- *the two-sided version in $O(\frac{aK}{B} \lg_{M/B} \min\{K, \frac{aK}{B}\} + \frac{N}{B} \lg_{M/B} \min\{\frac{N}{b}, \frac{N}{B}\})$ I/Os.*

The cost for all three versions is optimal according to the discussion in Section 3. In particular, we have matching upper and lower bounds whenever $\log N < B \log(M/B)$ (which is the condition of Theorem 3) and $a \le N/(K \lg_{M/B} K)$.

6. REFERENCES

[1] Alok Aggarwal and Jeffrey Scott Vitter. The input/output complexity of sorting and related problems. *Communications of the ACM (CACM)*, 31(9):1116–1127, 1988.

[2] Lars Arge, Mikael Knudsen, and Kirsten Larsen. A general lower bound on the I/O-complexity of comparison-based algorithms. In *Algorithms and Data Structures Workshop (WADS)*, pages 83–94, 1993.

[3] Manuel Blum, Robert W. Floyd, Vaughan R. Pratt, Ronald L. Rivest, and Robert Endre Tarjan. Time bounds for selection. *Journal of Computer and System Sciences (JCSS)*, 7(4):448–461, 1973.

[4] Robert P. Dilworth. A decomposition theorem for partially ordered sets. *The Annals of Mathematics*, 51(1):161–166, 1950.

[5] Jeff Erickson. Lower bounds for external algebraic decision trees. In *Proceedings of the Annual ACM-SIAM Symposium on Discrete Algorithms (SODA)*, pages 755–761, 2005.

[6] Xiaocheng Hu, Cheng Sheng, Yufei Tao, Yi Yang, and Shuigeng Zhou. Output-sensitive skyline algorithms in external memory. In *Proceedings of the Annual ACM-SIAM Symposium on Discrete Algorithms (SODA)*, pages 887–900, 2013.

[7] Kanela Kaligosi, Kurt Mehlhorn, J. Ian Munro, and Peter Sanders. Towards optimal multiple selection. In *International Colloquium on Automata, Languages and Programming (ICALP)*, pages 103–114, 2005.

APPENDIX

Proof of Lemma 1

In our context, the algorithm only needs to focus on the permutations in Π_{hard}. Therefore, prior to reading a block, the algorithm must have already known the ordering of the elements there, regardless of whether the block had been written by the algorithm before. Thus, the algorithm can be described with a decision tree with fanout at most $\binom{M}{B}$. The lemma follows from the fact that $|\Pi_{hard}| = ((N/B)!)^B$.

Proof of Fact 1

We first show $\Pi \subseteq \mathrm{CP}(\prec_\star, \mathcal{S})$. Suppose that there is a permutation $\pi \in \Pi$ but $\pi \notin \mathrm{CP}(\prec_\star, \mathcal{S})$. This means that there exist elements x, y such that $x \prec_\star y$ but y precedes x in π. This is a contradiction by the definition of $\prec_\star$.

Next we show $\mathrm{CP}(\prec_\star, \mathcal{S}) \subseteq \Pi$. Suppose that there is a permutation $\pi \in \mathrm{CP}(\prec_\star, \mathcal{S})$ but $\pi \notin \Pi$. There must be elements x, y such that x precedes y in π, but the algorithm can infer $y < x$ from the comparisons it has performed. But $y < x$ implies that $y \prec_\star x$, which contradicts the assumption that $\pi \in \mathrm{CP}(\prec_\star, \mathcal{S})$.

Simplification of (1)

For each $i \in [1, B]$ and $j \in [1, K]$, let $a_{ij} = |\mathcal{S}_i \cap A_j|$. Also let $a_i = |\mathcal{S}_i \cap A| = \sum_{j=1}^K a_{ij}$ for each $i \in [1, B]$. By plugging in $|\mathcal{S}_1| = \ldots = |\mathcal{S}_B| = N/B$, we have

$$
\begin{aligned}
|\mathrm{CP}(\mathcal{S})| &\leq (1) \\
&= \left(\prod_{i=1}^B \binom{N/B}{a_i} \cdot (N/B - a_i)! \right) \cdot \left(\prod_{j=1}^K \prod_{i=1}^B a_{ij} \right)! \\
&\leq \left(\prod_{i=1}^B \frac{(N/B)!}{a_i!} \right) \cdot \left(\prod_{j=1}^K \left(\sum_{i=1}^B a_{ij} \right)! \right)
\end{aligned}
$$

(in general, $x! y! \leq (x+y)!$)

$$
= ((N/B)!)^B \cdot (a!)^K / \prod_{i=1}^B a_i!
$$

(for each $j \in [1, K]$, $\sum_{i=1}^B a_{ij} = |A_j| = a$).

This leads to:

$$
\begin{aligned}
&\lg |\mathrm{CP}(\mathcal{S})| \\
&\leq B \lg((N/B)!) + K \lg(a!) - \sum_{i=1}^B \lg(a_i!) \\
&\leq B \lg((N/B)!) + aK \lg a - \sum_{i=1}^B a_i \lg a_i + O(K \lg a)
\end{aligned}
$$

(by Stirling's formula)

$$
\begin{aligned}
&\leq B \lg((N/B)!) + aK \lg a \\
&\quad - \left(\sum_{i=1}^B a_i \right) \lg \left(\frac{1}{B} \cdot \sum_{i=1}^B a_i \right) + O(K \lg a)
\end{aligned}
$$

(by convexity of function $x \lg x$)

$$
\leq B \lg((N/B)!) + aK \lg a - aK \lg(aK/B) + O(K \lg a)
$$

(by $\sum_{i=1}^B a_i = |A| = aK$)

$$
= B \lg((N/B)!) - aK \lg(K/B) + O(K \lg a).
$$

Proof of Lemma 3

We will need:

THEOREM 7 (DILWORTH'S THEOREM [4]). *Let X be a set of n elements, and $\prec$ a partial order over X. If X contains at most w pairwise incomparable elements, then X can be divided into w disjoint partitions $X_1, ..., X_w$, such that elements in each X_i ($1 \leq i \leq w$) are pairwise comparable.*

In the sequel, we abbreviate $\mathrm{CP}(\prec_\star, X)$ into $\mathrm{CP}(X)$ for any $X \subseteq \mathcal{S}$. Let $X_1, ..., X_w$ be as defined in the above theorem, and $n_i = |X_i|$ ($1 \leq i \leq n$). By Fact 5,

$$
|\mathrm{CP}(X)| \leq \frac{n!}{\prod_{i=1}^w n_i!} \cdot \prod_{i=1}^w |\mathrm{CP}(X_i)|.
$$

For each $i \in [1, w]$, since the elements in X_i are pairwise comparable, there is only one permutation of X_i that is consistent with $\prec$. Therefore, $|\mathrm{CP}(X_i)| = 1$. Hence,

$$
|\mathrm{CP}(X)| \leq \frac{n!}{\prod_{i=1}^w n_i!}.
$$

Taking logarithms at both sides gives

$$
\begin{aligned}
&\lg |\mathrm{CP}(X)| \\
&\leq \lg(n!) - \sum_{i=1}^w \lg(n_i!) \\
&\leq n \lg n - \sum_{i=1}^w n_i \lg n_i + O(\lg n)
\end{aligned}
$$

(by Stirling's formula)

$$
\leq n \lg n - n \lg(n/w) + O(\lg n)
$$

(by convexity of function $x \lg x$)

$$
= n \lg w + O(\lg n).
$$

Simplification of (3)

By substitution of $|\mathcal{S}_1| = \ldots = |\mathcal{S}_B| = N/B$, we have

$$
\begin{aligned}
|\mathrm{CP}(\mathcal{S})| \leq (3) &\leq \prod_{i=1}^B \binom{N/B}{|T_i|} \cdot (N/B - |T_i|)! \cdot |\mathrm{CP}(T_i)| \\
&= \prod_{i=1}^B (N/B)! \cdot |\mathrm{CP}(T_i)| / |T_i|!.
\end{aligned}
$$

Taking logarithms at both sides gives

$$
\begin{aligned}
&\lg |\mathrm{CP}(\mathcal{S})| \\
&\leq B \lg((N/B)!) - \sum_{i=1}^B (\lg(|T_i|!) - \lg |\mathrm{CP}(T_i)|) \\
&\leq B \lg((N/B)!) - \sum_{i=1}^B (\lg(|T_i|!) - |T_i| \lg b - O(\lg |T_i|))
\end{aligned}
$$

(by (2))

$$
\leq B \lg((N/B)!) - \sum_{i=1}^B (|T_i| \lg |T_i| - |T_i| \lg b - O(|T_i|))
$$

(by Stirling's formula)

$$
\leq B \lg((N/B)!) - (|T| \lg(|T|/B) - |T| \lg b - O(|T|))
$$

(by convexity of function $x \lg x$)

$$
= B \lg((N/B)!) - |T| \lg(|T|/(bB)) + O(|T|).
$$

Proof of Lemma 5

For $K \geq 2$, any algorithm must spend $\Omega(N/B)$ I/Os reading the entire dataset (by our right-grounded argument in Section 3). Hence, the lemma holds for $K \leq 16M/B$, in which case our target lower bound is $\Omega(N/B)$.

Let us also get rid of another simple case $K > N/B$. Under this condition, we can sort $\mathcal{S}$ by (i) running a precise K-partitioning algorithm on $\mathcal{S}$, and (ii) sorting the elements inside each partition. Since the size of each partition is $N/K \leq B$, step (ii) takes only $O(N/B)$ I/Os; and the running time of the algorithm is dominated by step (i). Consequently, the time for precise K-partitioning cannot be smaller than the lower bound $\Omega(\frac{N}{B} \lg_{M/B} \frac{N}{B})$ of sorting.

The rest of the proof focuses on $K \in [16M/B, N/B]$, where our target lower bound becomes $\Omega(\frac{N}{B} \lg_{M/B} K)$. We also assume that the algorithm uses at most $N \lg N$ blocks (otherwise, the algorithm has already written more blocks than the target lower bound). We consider the memory $\mathcal{M}$ as a multiset of size M, and the i-th block $\mathcal{B}_i$ as a multiset of size B for each $i \in [1, N \lg N]$. Each element in $\mathcal{M}$ or $\mathcal{B}_i$ is either an element of $\mathcal{S}$ or *nil*.

At any moment during the execution of an algorithm, the *machine state* can be represented as a sequence $\mathcal{M}, \mathcal{B}_1, ..., \mathcal{B}_{N \lg N}$. For each $t \geq 0$, let MS(t) be the set of all the possible machine states that can be generated by the algorithm after t I/Os. Using a standard argument (see [1]), we know:

LEMMA 7. *For any* $t \geq 0$, $|\mathrm{MS}(t)| \leq (2N \lg N \cdot \binom{M}{B})^t$.

Let H be the worst-case I/O cost of the algorithm. By Lemma 7, during the execution of the algorithm, at most $|\mathrm{MS}(H)| \leq (2N \lg N \cdot \binom{M}{B})^H$ machine states can be gener-

ated. The following lemma shows that, the algorithm has to be able to generate a large number of machine states in order to ensure its correctness.

LEMMA 8. $|\mathrm{MS}(H)| \geq \frac{N!}{(N/K)!^K}$.

PROOF. Let $P_1, ..., P_K$ be the partitions output by the algorithm. Set $g = \lceil N/KB \rceil$, i.e., g is the minimum number of blocks required to store a partition. We can safely assume that, when the algorithm finishes, $P_1, ..., P_K$ are stored on the disk as follows: for each $i \in [1, K]$, blocks $\mathcal{B}_{(i-1)g+1}, ..., \mathcal{B}_{ig}$ store all and only the elements of P_i (any algorithm can be slightly modified to satisfy this assumption by spending additional $O(N/B)$ I/Os). Therefore, whenever the output partitions are different, the algorithm's final machine state is also different. There are $N!/(N/K)!^K$ different ways to divide $\mathcal{S}$ into K partitions of size N/K. This completes the proof. $\square$

By combining Lemmas 7 and 8, we have

$$\left(2N \lg N \cdot \binom{M}{B} \right)^H \geq \frac{N!}{(N/K)!^K}.$$

Taking logarithms at both sides and then applying Stirling's formula yield

$$H \left(\lg N + B \lg \frac{M}{B} \right) = \Omega(N \lg K),$$

When $\lg N \leq B \lg \frac{M}{B}$, it follows that

$$H = \Omega \left(\frac{N}{B} \lg_{M/B} K \right).$$

On Characterizing the Data Movement Complexity of Computational DAGs for Parallel Execution

Venmugil Elango
The Ohio State University
elango.4@osu.edu

Fabrice Rastello
Inria
Fabrice.Rastello@inria.fr

Louis-Noël Pouchet
Univ. of California–Los Angeles
pouchet@cs.ucla.edu

J. Ramanujam
Louisiana State University
ram@cct.lsu.edu

P. Sadayappan
The Ohio State University
saday@cse.ohio-state.edu

ABSTRACT

Technology trends are making the cost of data movement increasingly dominant, both in terms of energy and time, over the cost of performing arithmetic operations in computer systems. The fundamental ratio of aggregate data movement bandwidth to the total computational power (also referred to the *machine balance parameter*) in parallel computer systems is decreasing. It is therefore of considerable importance to characterize the inherent data movement requirements of parallel algorithms, so that the minimal architectural balance parameters required to support it on future systems can be well understood.

In this paper, we develop an extension of the well-known red-blue pebble game to develop lower bounds on the data movement complexity for the parallel execution of computational directed acyclic graphs (CDAGs) on parallel systems. We model multi-node multi-core parallel systems, with the total physical memory distributed across the nodes (that are connected through some interconnection network) and in a multi-level shared cache hierarchy for processors within a node. We also develop new techniques for lower bound characterization of non-homogeneous CDAGs. We demonstrate the use of the methodology by analyzing the CDAGs of several numerical algorithms, to develop lower bounds on data movement for their parallel execution.

Categories and Subject Descriptors

F.2 [**Analysis of Algorithms and Problem Complexity**]: General; B.4.4 [**Hardware**]: Input/Output and Data Communications—*Performance Analysis and Design Aids*; D.2.8 [**Software**]: Metrics—*Complexity measures*

Keywords

I/O complexity, Red-blue pebble game, Parallel data movement complexity, Lower bounds

1. INTRODUCTION

Recent technology trends have resulted in much greater rates of improvement in computational processing rates of processors than the bandwidths for data movement across nodes or between the memory/cache hierarchies within nodes in a parallel system. This mismatch between maximum computational rate and peak memory bandwidth means that data movement and communication costs of an algorithm will be increasingly dominant determinants of performance. Although hardware techniques for data prefetching and overlapping of computation with communication can alleviate the impact of memory access latency on performance, the mismatch between maximum computational rate and peak memory bandwidth is much more fundamental; *the only solution is to limit the total rate of data movement between components of a parallel system to rates that can be sustained by the interconnects at different components and levels of a parallel computer system.*

It is therefore of considerable importance to develop techniques to characterize lower bounds on the data movement complexity of parallel algorithms. We address this problem in this paper. We formalize the problem by developing a parallel extension of the red-blue pebble game model introduced by Hong and Kung in their seminal work [16] on characterizing the data access complexity (called *I/O complexity* by them) for sequential execution of computational directed acyclic graphs (CDAGs). Our extended pebble game abstracts data movement in scalable parallel computers today, that consist of multiple nodes interconnected by a high-bandwidth interconnection network, with each node containing a number of cores that share a hierarchy of caches and the node's physical main memory.

In contrast to some other prior efforts that have modeled lower bounds for data movement in parallel computations, we focus on relating data movement lower bounds to the critical architectural balance parameter of the ratio of peak data movement bandwidth (in GBytes/sec) to peak computational throughput (in GFLOPs) at different levels of a parallel system. We develop techniques for deriving lower bounds for data movement for CDAGs under the parallel red-blue pebble game, and use these techniques to analyze a number of numerical algorithms. Interesting insights are provided on architectural bottlenecks that limit the performance of the algorithms.

This paper makes several contributions:
- It develops an extension of the red-blue pebble game that effectively models essential characteristics of scalable parallel computers with multi-level parallelism; (i) multiple nodes

with local physical memory that are interconnected via a high-speed interconnection network like Infiniband or a custom interconnect (e.g., IBM BlueGene system [17], or Cray XE6 [10]), and (ii) many cores at each node, that share a hierarchy of caches and the node's physical main memory.

- It develops a lower bound analysis methodology that is effective for analyzing non-homogeneous CDAGs using a decomposition approach.
- It develops new parallel lower-bounds analysis for a number of numerical algorithms.
- It presents insights into implications on different architectural parameters in order to achieve scalable parallel execution of the analyzed algorithms.

2. BACKGROUND: THE RED-BLUE PEBBLE GAME

2.1 Computational Model

The model of computation we use is a computational directed acyclic graph (CDAG), where computational operations are represented as graph vertices and the flow of values between operations is captured by graph edges. Two important characteristics of this abstract form of representing a computation are that (1) there is no specification of a particular order of execution of the operations: the CDAG abstracts the schedule of operations by only specifying partial ordering constraints as edges in the graph; and (2) there is no association of memory locations with the source operands or the result of any operation. We use the notation of Bilardi & Peserico [5] to formally describe CDAGs. We begin with the model of CDAG used by Hong & Kung.

DEFINITION 1 (CDAG-HK).
A computational directed acyclic graph (CDAG) is a 4-tuple $C = (I, V, E, O)$ of finite sets such that: (1) $I \subset V$ is the input set and all its vertices have no incoming edges; (2) $E \subseteq V \times V$ is the set of edges; (3) $G = (V, E)$ is a directed acyclic graph; (4) $V \setminus I$ is called the operation set and all its vertices have one or more incoming edges; (5) $O \subseteq V$ is called the output set.

2.2 The Red-Blue Pebble Game

Hong & Kung used this computational model in their seminal work [16]. minimal number of I/O operations needed while optimally playing the The *Red-Blue pebble game*. game uses two kinds of pebbles: a fixed number of red pebbles that represent small fast local memory (could represent cache, registers, etc.), and an arbitrarily large number of blue pebbles that represent the large slow main memory. Starting with blue pebbles on all inputs nodes in the CDAG, the game involves the generation of a sequence of steps to finally produce blue pebbles on all outputs. A game is defined as follows.

DEFINITION 2 (RED-BLUE PEBBLE GAME [16]).
Given a CDAG $C = (I, V, E, O)$ such that any vertex with no incoming (resp. outgoing) edge is an element of I (resp. O), S red pebbles and arbitrary number of blue pebbles, with a blue pebble on each input vertex, a complete calculation is any sequence of steps using the following rules that results in a final state with blue pebbles on all output vertices:

R1 (Input) A red pebble may be placed on any vertex that has a blue pebble (load from slow to fast memory),

R2 (Output) A blue pebble may be placed on any vertex that has a red pebble (store from fast to slow memory),

R3 (Compute) If all immediate predecessors of a vertex of $V \setminus I$ have red pebbles, a red pebble may be placed on that vertex (execution or "firing" of operation),

R4 (Delete) A red pebble may be removed from any vertex (reuse storage).

The number of I/O operations for any complete calculation is the total number of moves using rules R1 or R2, i.e., the total number of data movements between the fast and slow memories. The inherent I/O complexity of a CDAG is the smallest number of such I/O operations that can be achieved, among all possible complete calculations on that CDAG. An *optimal* calculation is a complete calculation achieving the minimal number of I/O operations.

2.3 S-partitioning for Lower Bounds on I/O Complexity

This red-blue pebble game provides an operational definition for the I/O complexity problem. However, it is not practically feasible to generate all possible complete calculations for large CDAGs. Hong & Kung developed a novel approach for deriving I/O lower bounds for CDAGs by relating the red-blue pebble game to a graph partitioning problem defined as follows.

DEFINITION 3 (S-PARTITIONING OF CDAG [16]).
Given a CDAG C, an S-partitioning of C is a collection of h subsets of V such that:
P1 $\forall i \neq j, V_i \cap V_j = \emptyset$, and $\bigcup_{i=1}^{h} V_i = V$
P2 there is no cyclic dependence between subsets
P3 $\forall i, \exists D \in Dom(V_i)$ such that $|D| \leq S$
P4 $\forall i, |Min(V_i)| \leq S$
where a dominator set of V_i, $D \in Dom(V_i)$ is a set of vertices such that any path from I to a vertex in V_i contains some vertex in D; the minimum set of V_i, $Min(V_i)$ is the set of vertices in V_i that have all its successors outside of V_i; and $|Set|$ is the cardinality of the set Set.

Corresponding to any complete calculation on that CDAG using S red pebbles, Hong & Kung showed a construction for a 2S-partition of a CDAG, with a tight relationship between the number of vertex sets h in the 2S-partition and the number of I/O moves q in the complete calculation, as follows.

THEOREM 1 (PEBBLE GAME, I/O AND 2S-PARTITION [16]).
Any complete calculation of the red-blue pebble game on a CDAG using at most S red pebbles is associated with a 2S-partition of the CDAG such that $S \times h \geq q \geq S \times (h-1)$, where q is the number of I/O moves in the complete calculation and h is the number of subsets in the 2S-partition.

The tight association from the above theorem between any complete calculation and a corresponding 2S-partition provides the following key lemma that served as the basis for Hong & Kung's approach to deriving lower bounds on the I/O complexity of CDAGs.

LEMMA 1 (LOWER BOUND ON I/O [16]). *Let H(2S) be the minimal number of vertex sets for any valid 2S-partition of a given CDAG (such that any vertex with no incoming – resp. outgoing – edge is an element of I – resp. O). Then the minimal number, Q, of I/O operations for any complete calculation of the CDAG is bounded by: $Q \geq S \times (H(2S) - 1)$*

This key lemma has been useful in proving I/O lower bounds for several CDAGs [16] by reasoning about the maximal number of vertices that could belong to any vertex-set in a valid 2S-partition.

3. ENABLING BOUNDS FOR COMPOSITE CDAGS: THE RBW PEBBLE GAME

Application codes are typically constructed from a number of sub-computations using the fundamental composition mechanisms of sequencing, iteration and recursion. For instance, the conjugate gradient method, described in Sec. 5.2, consists of sequence of sparse matrix-vector product, vector dot-product and SAXPY operations, for every iteration. Applying the I/O lower bounding techniques directly on the CDAG of such composite application codes can produce very weak lower bounds. For instance, consider the following code segment.

```
1   Inputs: p, q, r, s: Vectors of size N
2   Output: sum: Scalar
3   A = p × q^T
4   B = r × s^T
5   C = AB
6   sum = ∑_{i=1}^{N} ∑_{j=1}^{N} C_{ij}
```

The computational complexity of this computation can be simply obtained by adding together the computational costs of the constituent steps, i.e., $N^2 + N^2 + 2N^3 + N^2$ arithmetic operations. In contrast, the data movement complexity for this computation cannot so simply be obtained by adding together the data movement lower bounds for the individual steps. Let us consider data movement costs in a two-level memory hierarchy with unbounded main memory and a limited number of words (S) in fast storage – this might represent the number of registers in the processor, or scratchpad memory or cache memory. It is known [16, 18, 3] that an asymptotic lower bound on data movement between (arbitrarily large) slow memory and fast memory for matrix multiplication of $N \times N$ matrices is $N^3/2\sqrt{2S}$. An outer-product of two vectors of size N requires $2N$ input operations from slow memory and output of the N^2 results back to slow memory, i.e., total I/O of $2N + N^2$, independent of the fast memory capacity S. Similarly, the last step has a data movement complexity of $N^2 + 1$ I/O operations between slow and fast memory. But a lower bound on the data movement complexity of the total computation cannot be obtained by simply adding together contributions for the steps. It is not even possible to assert that the maximum among them is a valid lower bound on the data movement complexity of the total computation. The reason is that data from a previous step could possibly be passed to a later step in fast storage without having to be stored in main memory. With $4N + 4$ fast memory locations, it is feasible to perform the above computation with a total of only $4N + 1$ I/O operations, $4N$ to bring in the four input vectors into fast memory, and repeatedly recompute elements of A and B to contribute to an element of C, and when ready, accumulate it into sum. The I/O complexity of the composite multi-step computation is thus lower than that of the matrix multiply step contained in it. This motivates us to split the CDAG based on individual sub-computations, determine the lower bound for each sub-CDAG separately, and finally compose the result to obtain the I/O lower bound of the whole computation. However, using the original red/blue pebble game model of Hong & Kung, as elaborated below, it is not feasible to analyze the I/O complexity of sub-computations and simply combine them by addition.

The Hong & Kung red/blue pebble game model places blue pebbles on all CDAG vertices without predecessors, since such vertices are considered to hold inputs to the computation, and therefore assumed to start off in slow memory. Similarly, all vertices without successors are considered to be outputs of the computation, and must have blue pebbles at the end of the game. If the vertices of a CDAG corresponding to a composite application are disjointly par-

titioned into sub-DAGs, the analysis of each sub-DAG under the Hong & Kung red/blue pebble game model will require the initial placement of blue pebbles on all predecessor-free vertices in the sub-DAG, and final placement of blue pebbles on all successor-free vertices in the sub-DAG. The optimal calculation for each sub-DAG will require at least one load (R1) operation for each input and a store (R2) operation for each output. But in playing the red/blue pebble game on the full composite CDAG, clearly it may be possible to pass values in a red pebble between vertices in different sub-DAGs, so that the I/O complexity is less than the sum of the I/O costs for the optimal calculations for each sub-DAG. In fact, it is not even possible to assert that the maximum among the I/O lower bounds for sub-DAGs of a CDAG is a valid lower bound for the composite CDAG.

In order to enable such decomposition, a modified game called the Red-Blue-White pebble game [14] was defined, with the following changes to the Hong & Kung pebble game model (the Red-Blue-White pebble game is formally defined in Sec. 3.1):

1. **Flexible input/output vertex labeling:** Unlike the Hong & Kung model, where all vertices without predecessors must be input vertices, and all vertices without successors must be output vertices, the RBW model allows flexibility in indicating which vertices are labeled as inputs and outputs. In the modified variant of the pebble game, predecessor-free vertices that are not designated as input vertices do not have an initial blue pebble placed on them. However, such vertices are allowed to fire using rule R3 at any time, since they do not have any predecessor nodes without red pebbles. Vertices without successors that are not labeled as output vertices do not require placement of a blue pebble at the end of the game. However, all compute vertices (i.e., vertices in the operation set) in the CDAG are required to have fired for any complete calculation.

2. **Prohibition of multiple evaluations of compute vertices:** The RBW game disallows recomputation of values on the CDAG, i.e., each non-input vertex is only allowed to evaluate once using rule R3. Several other efforts [3, 4, 5, 26, 19, 22, 23, 25, 9, 18, 20, 21] have also imposed such a restriction on the pebble game model. While such a model is indeed more restrictive than the original Hong & Kung model, the restriction in the model enables the development of techniques to form tighter lower bounds [14].

3.1 The Red-Blue-White Pebble Game

DEFINITION 4 (RED-BLUE-WHITE (RBW) PEBBLE GAME). *Given a CDAG $C = (I, V, E, O)$, S red pebbles and arbitrary number of blue and white pebbles, with a blue pebble on each input vertex, a complete calculation is any sequence of steps using the following rules that results in a final state with white pebbles on all vertices and blue pebbles on all output vertices:*

R1 (Input) A red pebble may be placed on any vertex that has a blue pebble; a white pebble is also placed along with the red pebble, unless the vertex already has a white pebble on it.

R2 (Output) A blue pebble may be placed on any vertex that has a red pebble.

R3 (Compute) If a vertex v does not have a white pebble and all its immediate predecessors have red pebbles on them, a red pebble along with a white pebble may be placed on v.

R4 (Delete) A red pebble may be removed from any vertex (reuse storage).

In the modified rules for the RBW game, all vertices are required to have a white pebble at the end of the game, thereby ensuring that the entire CDAG is evaluated. Non-input vertices without predecessors do not have an initial blue pebble on them, but they are allowed to fire using rule R3 at any time – since they have no predecessors, the condition in rule R3 is trivially satisfied. But if all successors of such a node cannot be fired while maintaining a red pebble, "spilling" and reloading using R2 and R1 is forced because the vertex cannot be fired again using R3.

Definition 3 is adapted to this new game so that Theorem 1 and thus Lemma 1 can hold for the RBW pebble game.

DEFINITION 5 (*S*-PARTITIONING OF CDAG – RBW GAME). *Given a CDAG C, an S-partitioning of C is a collection of h subsets of $V \setminus I$ such that:*

P1 $\forall i \neq j$, $V_i \cap V_j = \emptyset$, and $\bigcup_{i=1}^{h} V_i = V \setminus I$
P2 *there is no cyclic dependence between subsets*
P3 $\forall i$, $|In(V_i)| \leq S$
P4 $\forall i$, $|Out(V_i)| \leq S$

where the input set of V_i, $In(V_i)$ is the set of vertices of $V \setminus V_i$ that have at least one successor in V_i; the output set of V_i, $Out(V_i)$ is the set of vertices of V_i also part of the output set O or that have at least one successor outside of V_i.

The proof of Theorem 1 under the RBW pebble game is provided in [14].

For (sub-)graphs without input/output sets, the application of S-partitioning will however lead to a trivial partition with all vertices in a single set (e.g., $h = 1$). A careful tagging of vertices as virtual input/output nodes will be required for better I/O complexity estimates, as described below.

3.2 Decomposition

Definition 4 allows the partitioning of a CDAG C into sub-CDAGs $C_1, C_2, \ldots, C_p$, to compute lower bounds on the I/O complexity of each sub-CDAG $IO(C_1), IO(C_2), \ldots, IO(C_p)$ independently and simply add them to bound the I/O complexity of C. This is stated in the following decomposition theorem, whose proof may be found in [14].

THEOREM 2 (DECOMPOSITION).
Let $C = (I, V, E, O)$ be a CDAG. Let $V_1, V_2, \ldots, V_p$ be an arbitrary (not necessarily acyclic) disjoint partitioning of V ($i \neq j \Rightarrow V_i \cap V_j = \emptyset$ and $\bigcup_{i=1}^{p} V_i = V$) and $C_1, C_2, \ldots, C_p$ be the induced partitioning of C ($I_i = I \cap V_i$, $E_i = E \cap V_i \times V_i$, $O_i = O \cap V_i$). Then $\sum_{i=1}^{p} IO(C_i) \leq IO(C)$. In particular, if LB_i is a lower bound on the I/O cost of C_i, then $\sum_{i=1}^{p} LB_i$ is a lower bound on the I/O cost of C.

We state the following corollary and theorem, which are useful in practice for deriving tighter lower bounds. The complete proofs can be found in [14].

COROLLARY 1 (INPUT/OUTPUT DELETION). *Let C and C' be two CDAGs: $C' = (I \cup dI, V \cup dI \cup dO, E', O \cup dO)$, $C = (I, V, E' \cap V \times V, O)$. Then $IO(C')$ can be bounded below by $IO(C)$ as follows:*

$$IO(C) + |dI| + |dO| \leq IO(C') \tag{1}$$

There are cases where separating input/output vertices leads to very weak lower bounds. This happens when input vertices have high fan out such as for matrix-multiplication: if we consider the CDAG for matrix-multiplication and remove all input and output vertices, we get a set of independent chains that can each be computed with no more than 2 red pebbles. To overcome this problem, the following theorem allows us to compare the I/O of two CDAGs: a CDAG $C' = (I', V, E, O')$ and another $C = (I, V, E, O)$

built from C' by just transforming some vertices without predecessors into input vertices, and some others into output nodes so that $I' \subset I$ and $O' \subset O$. In contrast to the prior development above, instead of adding/removing input/output vertices, here we do not change the vertices of a CDAG but instead only change the labeling (tag) of some vertices as inputs/outputs in the CDAG. So the CDAG remains the same, but some input/output vertices are relabeled as standard computational vertices, or vice-versa.

THEOREM 3 (INPUT/OUTPUT (UN)TAGGING – RBW).
Let C and C' be two CDAGs of the same DAG $G = (V, E)$: $C = (I, V, E, O)$, $C' = (I \cup dI, V, E, O \cup dO)$. Then, $IO(C)$ can be bounded below by $IO(C')$ as follows (tagging):

$$IO(C') - |dI| - |dO| \leq IO(C) \tag{2}$$

Reciprocally, $IO(C')$ can be bounded below by $IO(C)$ as follows (untagging):

$$IO(C) \leq IO(C') \tag{3}$$

Some algorithms will benefit from decomposing their CDAGs into non-disjoint vertex sets. For instance, when we have computations that are surrounded by an outer time loop, a common technique to derive their lower bound is to decompose the CDAG, where vertices computed during each outer loop iteration are placed in separate sub-CDAGs. In such cases, when the vertices, V', computed in iteration t are used as inputs for iteration $t + 1$, by placing V' in the sub-DAGs corresponding to both iterations t and $t + 1$, we could obtain a lower bound that is tighter by at least a constant factor.

Before we state the non-disjoint decomposition theorem, we introduce needed definitions here. Given a DAG $G = (V, E)$ and some vertex $x \in V$, the ancestor set, $Anc(x)$ is the set of vertices from which there is a non-empty directed path to x in G ($x \notin Anc(x)$); the descendant set, $Desc(x)$ is the set of vertices to which there is a non-empty directed path from x in G ($x \notin Desc(x)$). For some $V_i \subset V$, $InSet(V_i)$ is the set of vertices of V_i, that have atleast one predecessor outside V_i.

THEOREM 4 (NON-DISJOINT DECOMPOSITION).
Let $C = (I, V, E, O)$ be a CDAG and $x \in V$ be some vertex. Let $V_2 = Desc(x)$ and $C_2 = (I_2, V_2, E_2, O_2)$ be the induced sub-graph ($I_2 = I \cap V_2$, $E_2 = E \cap V_2 \times V_2$, $O_2 = O \cap V_2$). Let $V_a = V \setminus Desc(x)$. The sub-graph $C_1 = (I_1 = I \cap V_1, V_1, E_1, O_1 = O \cap V_1)$ is built as follows: (1) start with vertices $V_1 = V_a \cup InSet(Desc(x))$ and edges $E_1 = E \cap V_a \times V_a$; (2) Add an edge from x to each vertex in $InSet(Desc(x))$, i.e., $\forall d \in InSet(Desc(x)), E_1 = E_1 \cup x \times d$. Then, $IO(C_1, S + 1) + IO(C_2, S) \leq IO(C, S)$, where, $IO(C, S)$ represents the I/O cost for computing C with S red pebbles.

PROOF. Consider a complete calculation $\mathcal{P}$ of C with S red pebbles. We let Q_{L1} be the number of R1 transitions (loads) in C associated to the vertices of $V \setminus [Desc(x) + x]$. We let Q_{S1} be the number of R2 transitions (stores) in C associated to the vertices of $V \setminus Desc(x)$. We let Q_2 be the number of R1 and R2 transitions (loads/stores) in C associated to a vertex in $Desc(x)$. We have that $IO(C, S) >= Q_{L1} + Q_{S1} + Q_2$. The idea of the proof is to show that $Q_{L1} + Q_{S1} >= IO(C_1, S + 1)$ and that $Q_2 >= IO(C_2, S)$.

Let us first prove that $Q_{L1} + Q_{S1} >= IO(C_1, S + 1)$. We consider the restriction of $\mathcal{P}$ to V_1. This is not a complete calculation for C_1 yet, as the predecessors of the vertices in $InSet(Desc(x))$ need not be the same in C_1 as in C. We have one additional red pebble that we can dedicate to stay on x. Hence, all the R1 (load) and R4 (delete) transitions associated to vertex x, after the execution of x in $\mathcal{P}$, can be removed. This gives a complete calculation for C_1 as follows:

- As the sub-graph induced by V_a is a sub-graph of C, all transitions associated to vertices of $V \setminus [\mathsf{Desc}(x) + x]$ plus the transition R3 (compute) of x are valid (this part of the complete calculation from $\mathcal{P}$ has been unchanged).
- For the vertices in $\mathsf{InSet}(\mathsf{Desc}(x))$, the only transitions are R3/R2 (compute/ store) and is valid as all the associated transitions of its predecessors in V_a are unchanged (apart from x which holds a red pebble as soon as it is computed). The cost of this complete calculation (with $S + 1$ red pebbles) for C_1 is $Q_{L1} + Q_{S1}$.

This proves the inequality.

Let us now prove that $Q_2 >= IO(C_2, S)$. We consider the restriction of C to the vertex of $C_2 = \mathsf{Desc}(x)$. This is a complete calculation for C_2 of cost Q_2 which proves the second inequality. $\square$

3.3 Min-Cut for I/O Complexity Lower Bound

In [14], we developed an alternative lower bounding approach. It was motivated from the observation that the Hong & Kung 2S-partitioning approach does not account for the internal structure of a CDAG, but essentially focuses only on the boundaries of the partitions. In contrast, the min-cut based approach captures internal space requirements using the abstraction of wavefronts. This section describes the approach.

Definitions: We first present needed definitions. Given a graph $G = (V, E)$, a cut is defined as any partition of the set of vertices V into two parts $\mathcal{S}$ and $\mathcal{T} = V - \mathcal{S}$. An $s - t$ cut is defined with respect to two distinguished vertices s and t and is any $(\mathcal{S}, \mathcal{T})$ cut satisfying the requirement that $s \in \mathcal{S}$ and $t \in \mathcal{T}$. Each cut defines a set of cut edges (the cut-set), i.e., the set of edges (u, v) where $u \in \mathcal{S}$ and $v \in \mathcal{T}$. The capacity of a cut is defined as the sum of the weights of the cut edges. The minimum cut problem (or min-cut) is one of finding a cut that minimizes the capacity of the cut. We define vertex u as a cut vertex with respect to an $(\mathcal{S}, \mathcal{T})$ cut, as a vertex $u \in \mathcal{S}$ that has a cut edge incident on it. A related problem of interest for this paper is the *vertex min-cut* problem which is one of finding a cut that minimizes the number of cut vertices.

We consider a convex cut $(\mathcal{S}_x, \mathcal{T}_x)$ associated to x as follows: $\mathcal{S}_x$ includes $x \cup \mathsf{Anc}(x)$; $\mathcal{T}_x$ includes $\mathsf{Desc}(x)$; in addition, $\mathcal{S}_x$ and $\mathcal{T}_x$ must be constructed such that there is no edge from $\mathcal{T}_x$ to $\mathcal{S}_x$. With this, the sets $\mathcal{S}_x$ and $\mathcal{T}_x$ partition the graph G into two convex partitions. We define the wavefront induced by $(\mathcal{S}_x, \mathcal{T}_x)$ to be the set of vertices in $\mathcal{S}_x$ that have at least one outgoing edge to a vertex in $\mathcal{T}_x$.

Schedule Wavefront: Consider a complete calculation $\mathcal{P}$ that corresponds to some scheduling (i.e., execution) of the vertices of the graph $G = (V, E)$ that follows the rules R1–R4 of the Red-Blue-White pebble game (see Definition 4 in Sec. 3.1). We view this complete calculation $\mathcal{P}$ as a string that has recorded all the transitions (applications of pebble game rules). Given $\mathcal{P}$, we define the *wavefront* $W_{\mathcal{P}}(x)$ induced by some vertex $x \in V$ at the point when x has just fired (i.e., a white pebble has just been placed on x) as the union of x and the set of vertices $u \in V$ that have already fired and that have an outgoing edge to a vertex $v \in V$ that have not fired yet. Viewing $\mathcal{P}$ as a string, $W_{\mathcal{P}}(x)$ is the set of vertices x and those white-pebbled vertices to the left of x in the string associated with $\mathcal{P}$ that have an outgoing edge in G to not-white-pebbled vertices that occur to the right of x in $\mathcal{P}$. With respect to a complete calculation $\mathcal{P}$, the set $W_{\mathcal{P}}(x)$ defines the memory requirements at the time-stamp just after x has fired.

Correspondence with Graph Min-cut Note that there is a close correspondence between the wavefront $W_{\mathcal{P}}(x)$ induced by some vertex $x \in V$ and the $(\mathcal{S}_x, \mathcal{T}_x)$ partition of the graph G. For a valid convex partition $(\mathcal{S}_x, \mathcal{T}_x)$ of G, we can construct a complete calculation $\mathcal{P}$ in which at the time-stamp when x has just fired, the subset of vertices of V that are white pebbled exactly corresponds to $\mathcal{S}_x$; the set of fired (white-pebbled) nodes that have a successor that is not white-pebbled constitute a wavefront $W_{\mathcal{P}}(x)$ associated with x. Similarly, given wavefront $W_{\mathcal{P}}(x)$ associated with x in a pebble game instance $\mathcal{P}$, we can construct a valid $(\mathcal{S}_x, \mathcal{T}_x)$ convex partition by placing all white pebbled vertices in $\mathcal{S}_x$ and all the non-white-pebbled vertices in $\mathcal{T}_x$.

A minimum cardinality wavefront induced by x, denoted $W_G^{\min}(x)$ is a vertex min-cut that results in an $(\mathcal{S}_x, \mathcal{T}_x)$ partition of G defined above. We define $w_G^{\max}$ as the maximum value over the size of all possible minimum cardinality wavefronts associated with vertices, i.e., define $w_G^{\max} = \max_{x \in V} \left(\left| W_G^{\min}(x) \right| \right)$.

LEMMA 2. *Let $C = (\emptyset, V, E, O)$ be a CDAG with no inputs. For any $x \in V$,* $$2 \left(\left| W_G^{min}(x) \right| - S \right) \leq IO(C).$$ *In particular,* $$2 \left(w_G^{max} - S \right) \leq IO(C).$$

4. PARALLEL I/O LOWER BOUNDS

In this section, we develop an approach to model data movement complexity for parallel execution. We describe our abstraction of a parallel computer, define a pebble game adapted for characterizing lower bounds for parallel computation, and then present the methodology for developing parallel lower bounds.

4.1 Parallel Machine Model

Our abstraction of a parallel computer is shown in Fig. 1. The model seeks to capture the essential characteristics of large-scale parallel systems, which exhibit multi-level parallelism and a hierarchical storage structure. The parallel computer has a set of N_{nodes} multi-core nodes connected by an interconnection network. Each node has a number of cores and a hierarchy of storage elements: a set of private registers (at level 1) for each core, a private L1 cache per core (at level 2), and a hierarchy of zero or more additional levels of cache (through level L-1), and a shared main memory (at level L). The total number of storage entities at level l is denoted N_l, and the capacity of each entity at level l is S_l words. The hierarchical structure means that each storage entity at level l is connected to a unique storage entity at level l+1, and an integral multiple (usually a power of 2) of entities at level l-1. The total number of main memory modules N_L equals the number of nodes N_{nodes} in the system.

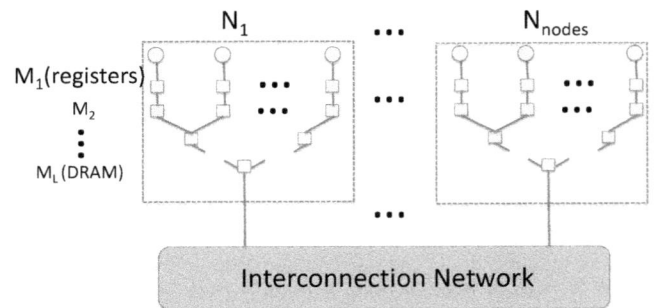

Figure 1: Model of parallel system

4.2 P-RBW: The Parallel Red-Blue-White Pebble Game

In this sub-section, we present the framework for developing lower bounds on the data movement complexity for parallel execution. In particular, we consider two types of data movement:

1. *Movement across the levels of the storage hierarchy within a node*, called **vertical data movement**;
2. *Movement between nodes*, called **horizontal data movement**.

The model used here may be viewed as an extension of the Multiprocessor Memory Hierarchy Game (MMHG) game proposed by Savage and Zubair [24], which modeled "vertical" data movement in a shared storage hierarchy but not the "horizontal" movement of data between the memories of nodes in the parallel system. Thus, whereas Savage's model assumes a common shared level of memory that can be directly accessed by all processors, we model a collection of shared-memory multiprocessor nodes coupled by an interconnection network. As demonstrated later in Sec. **??**, this distinction allows better modeling of fundamental data movement constraints of parallel algorithms on intra-node memory bandwidth (between off-chip main memory and on-chip cache(s) on a node) versus interconnection network bandwidth (e.g., Gigabit Ethernet of Infiniband used to connect nodes in a scalable parallel system).

With the Parallel RBW (P-RBW) game, a different set of red pebbles is associated with each storage entity in the parallel system – we can consider there to be different shades of red, one per distinct storage entity. Associated with the storage entities at a level l in the hierarchy, we have N_l distinct shades of red pebbles, each associated with one of the N_l distinct storage entities in the system at that level. The rules of the P-RBW are stated below, and encode the constraints on movement of data in the parallel computer: i) vertical data movement can occur between physically connected entities in the storage hierarchy (Rules R4 and R5), and ii) data can be moved via the interconnection network between the memories of any pair of nodes (Rule R3).

DEFINITION 6 (PARALLEL RBW (P-RBW) PEBBLE GAME).
Let $C = (I, V, E, O)$ be a CDAG. Given for each level $1 \leq l \leq L$, $N_l \times S_l$ number of red pebbles of different shades $R_l^1, R_l^2, \cdots, R_l^{N_l}$, respectively, and unlimited blue and white pebbles, with a blue pebble on each input vertex, a complete calculation is any sequence of steps using the following rules that results in a final state with white pebbles on all vertices and blue pebbles on all output vertices:

R1 (Input) *A level-L pebble, R_L^i can be placed on any vertex that has a blue pebble; a white pebble is also placed along with the shade of red pebble, unless the vertex already has a white pebble on it.*

R2 (Output) *A blue pebble can be placed on any vertex that has a level-L pebble on it.*

R3 (Remote get) *A level-L pebble, R_L^i can be placed on any vertex that has another level-L shade pebble R_L^j.*

R4 (Move up) *For $1 \leq l < L$, a level-l red pebble, R_l^i can be placed on any vertex that has a level-$(l+1)$ pebble R_{l+1}^j where R_l^i is in a cache that is a child of the cache that holds R_{l+1}^j.*

R5 (Move down) *For $1 < l \leq L$, a level-l red pebble, R_l^j can be placed on any vertex that has a level-$(l-1)$ pebble R_{l-1}^i where R_{l-1}^i is in a cache that is a child of the cache that holds R_l^j.*

R6 (Compute) *If a vertex v does not have a white pebble and all its immediate predecessors have level-1 red pebbles of shade p on them, then a level-1 red pebble R_1^p along with a white peb-*

ble may be placed on v; here p is the index of the processor that computes vertex v.

R7 (Delete) *Any shade of red pebble may be removed from any vertex (reuse storage).*

4.3 I/O Lower Bound for Vertical Data Movement

The hierarchical memory can enforce either the inclusion or exclusion policy. In case of inclusive hierarchical memory, when a copy of a value is present at a level-l, it is also maintained at all the levels $l + 1$ and higher. These values may or may not be consistent with the values held at the lower levels. The exclusive cache, on the other hand, does not guarantee that a value present in the cache at level-l will be available at the higher levels. The following result is derived for the inclusive case. But, they also hold true for the exclusive case, where the difference lies only in the number of red pebbles that we consider in the corresponding two-level pebble game.

THEOREM 5 (VERTICAL I/O COST).
Let $C = (I, V, E, O)$ be a CDAG. Consider any complete calculation on C using the rules of P-RBW pebble game; for this complete calculation, consider the level-l storage j with the maximum number of R4/R5 transitions with its children at level-$(l-1)$. Then, the corresponding amount of data movement between the level-l storage j and its children is at least $IO_1(C, S_{l-1} \times N_{l-1})/N_l$, where $IO_1(C, S)$ is the I/O lower bound of C for a single processor with fast memory of size S.

PROOF. Consider a complete calculation of C using the rules of P-RBW game that minimizes the overall amount of I/O between levels $k < l$ and level l storage. This amount of I/O will be bounded by $IO_1(C, S_{l-1} \times N_{l-1})$. Consider one of the N_l caches with the maximum amount of I/O. It will be bounded by $IO_1(C, S_{l-1} \times N_{l-1})/N_l$. □

It is possible to obtain tighter results for the cases that use S-partitioning techinque to derive the vertical I/O lower bounds. The following theorem extends the S-partitioning techinque to the vertical case.

THEOREM 6 (S-PARTITIONING BASED VERTICAL I/O COST).
Let $C = (I, V, E, O)$ be a CDAG. Consider any complete calculation on C using the rules of P-RBW game; for this complete calculation, consider the level-l storage j whose group of processors P_l^j perform the maximum number of R6 (compute) transitions. Then, the corresponding amount of data movement between the level-l storage j and its children is at least $\left(\frac{|V|}{U(C, 2S_{l-1}) \times N_l} - \frac{N_{l-1}}{N_l} \right) \times S_{l-1} \approx \frac{|V| \times S_{l-1}}{U(C, 2S_{l-1}) \times N_l}$, where, $|V|$ is the total number of vertices in C, $U(C, 2S)$ is the largest vertex-set in any 2S-partition of C.

PROOF. Consider a complete calculation that minimizes the overall amount of I/O between levels $k < l$ and level-l storage. Consider the group of P/N_l processors that do the maximum computation. They do at least $|V|/N_l$ amount of work. Let us consider the partition of those P/N_l processors into N_{l-1}/N_l sets of P/N_{l-1} processors that share the same level-$(l-1)$ storage unit. Each set of processors (that we denote by P_{l-1}^i, $0 < i \leq N_{l-1}/N_l$) does at least $\alpha^i \times \frac{|V|}{N_l}$ amount of work where $\sum_i \alpha^i = 1$. We let V^i be the subset of vertices of C fired by P_{l-1}^i.

Let us denote S_{l-1} by S to simplify the notations. The goal is to show that each P_{l-1}^i performs at least $\left\lfloor |V^i|/U(C, 2S) - 1 \right\rfloor \times S$

I/O to its level-l storage, where, $U(C,2S)$ is the largest 2S-partition (RBW pebble game) of CDAG C. Consider a complete calculation of C with RBW game with S red pebbles. Consider the partitioning of the complete calculation $\mathcal{P}$ into $\mathcal{P}_1, \cdots, \mathcal{P}_h$ used in the proof of Theorem 1 for RBW. We let V_j^i be the set of vertices of V^i fired in $\mathcal{P}_j$ ($\bigcup_{j=1}^h V_j^i = V^i$; $\forall_{j \neq j'} V_j^i \cap V_{j'}^i = \emptyset$). With the usual reasoning we can prove that $|\mathsf{In}(V_j^i)| \leq 2S$ and $|\mathsf{Out}(V_j^i)| \leq 2S$, i.e., each V_j^i is a 2S-partition of C. Thus for each j, $|V_j^i| \leq U(C,2S)$. Now from a complete calculation for P-RBW game, we can build a complete calculation for RBW game. By construction, each V_j^i is associated to at least S I/O to level-l storage in the complete calculation for the P-RBW game. Thus the total amount of I/O for P_{l-1}^i is at least

$$\left[|V^i| / |V_j^i| - 1 \right] \times S \geq \left[|V^i| / U(C,2S) - 1 \right] \times S. \text{ Finally,}$$

$$\sum_{i=1}^{N_{l-1}/N_l} \left(\frac{|V^i|}{U(C,2S_{l-1})} - 1 \right) \times S_{l-1} = \sum_{i=1}^{N_{l-1}/N_l} \left(\frac{\alpha_i \times (|V|/N_l)}{U(C,2S_{l-1})} - 1 \right) \times S_{l-1}$$

$$= \left(\frac{|V|}{U(C,2S_{l-1}) \times N_l} - \frac{N_{l-1}}{N_l} \right) \times S_{l-1} \approx \frac{|V| \times S_{l-1}}{U(C,2S_{l-1}) \times N_l}. \quad \square$$

4.4 I/O Lower Bound for Horizontal Data Movement

The following theorem extends the S-partitioning technique to the horizontal case.

THEOREM 7 (S-PARTITIONING BASED HORIZONTAL I/O COST). *Let $C = (I, V, E, O)$ be a CDAG. Consider any complete calculation on C using the rules of P-RBW game; for this complete calculation, consider the level-L storage i whose group of processors P_L^i perform the maximum number of R6 (compute) transitions. The corresponding amount of remote get transitions are at least $\left(\frac{|V|}{U(C,2S_L) \times N_L} - 1 \right) \times S_L$, where, $|V|$ is the total number of vertices in C, $U(C,2S)$ is the largest vertex-set in any 2S-partition of C.*

PROOF. We let V^i be the subset of vertices of C fired by the set of processors P_L^i. Let us denote S_L by S for simplicity. Consider a complete calculation $\mathcal{P}$ on C using RBW game with S red pebbles. Consider the partitioning of this complete calculation into $\mathcal{P}_1, \cdots, \mathcal{P}_h$ used in the proof of Theorem 1 for RBW. We let V_j^i be the set of vertices of V^i fired in $\mathcal{P}_j$ ($\bigcup_{j=1}^h V_j^i = V^i$; $\forall_{j \neq j'} V_j^i \cap V_{j'}^i = \emptyset$). With the usual reasoning we can prove that $\left| \mathsf{In}(V_j^i) \right| \leq 2S$ and $\left| \mathsf{Out}(V_j^i) \right| \leq 2S$, i.e., each V_j^i is a 2S-partition of C. Thus for each j, $|V_j^i| \leq U(C,2S)$. Now from a complete calculation for P-RBW game, we can build a complete calculation for RBW game. By construction, each V_j^i is associated to at least S I/O operations in the complete calculation for the P-RBW game. Thus the total amount of I/O for P_L^i is at least $\left[|V^i| / |V_j^i| - 1 \right] \times S \geq \left[|V^i| / U(C,2S) - 1 \right] \times S$.

Since the group P_L^i performs maximum number of computations, $|V^i| \geq |V|/N_L$. Hence, the total amount of remote get of processors P_L^i is at least $\left(\frac{|V|}{U(C,2S_L) \times N_L} - 1 \right) \times S_L$. $\square$

5. ILLUSTRATION OF USE

Lower and upper bound analysis of algorithms can help us identify whether an algorithm is bandwidth bound at different levels of the memory hierarchy. Lower bound results can be related to architectural parameters. Consider a multi-node/multi-core system with P processors. Let N_l be the total storage capacity (in data elements) available at level l. Consider a memory unit at level l, M_l^i, that incurs the maximum communication. M_l^i, is shared by the processor

set P_l^i, such that $|P_l^i| = P/N_l$. Let $\mathcal{B}_l^i$ denote the total available memory bandwidth between M_l^i and all its children at level $l-1$.

Let $C = (I, V, E, O)$ be the CDAG of the algorithm being analyzed and $C_l^i \subset C$ be the sub-CDAG executed by the processors P_l^i. The time taken for execution of C is given by $T \geq \max(T_l^i, T_{comp})$, where, T_l^i denotes the communication time at M_l^i and T_{comp} denotes the computation time for C. For the algorithm to be not bound by memory bandwidth at level l,

$$T_l^i \leq T_{comp} \qquad (4)$$

Let IO_l^i denote the amount of data transferred between M_l^i and all its children at level $l-1$ for the execution of C_l^i. Then,

$$T_l^i = \frac{IO_l^i}{\mathcal{B}_l^i} \geq \frac{LB_l^i}{\mathcal{B}_l^i} \qquad (5)$$

where, LB_l^i denotes the lower bound on the amount of data transfer at memory unit M_l^i for any valid execution of C_l^i. The computation time of C is given by (F below indicates processor performance in floating-point arithmetic operations per second per core)

$$T_{comp} = \frac{W}{P} \times \frac{1}{F} \qquad (6)$$

where, W is the total number of arithmetic operations. From Equations (4), (5) and (6), we have,

$$\frac{LB_l^i}{\mathcal{B}_l^i} \leq \frac{W}{P} \times \frac{1}{F} \quad \text{or} \quad \frac{LB_l^i}{W} \leq \frac{\mathcal{B}_l^i}{P} \times \frac{1}{F}$$

As $P = |P_l^i| \times N_l$,

$$\frac{LB_l^i \times N_l}{W} \quad \leq \quad \frac{\mathcal{B}_l^i}{|P_l^i| \times F} \qquad (7)$$

The term at the right-hand side of Equation (7) is the machine balance value for the machine at level-l. Any algorithm that fails to satisfy the Equation (7), will be invariably bandwidth bound at level-l.

Through similar argument, given that UB_l^i is the upper bound on the minimum amount of data transfer required by the algorithm at memory unit M_l^i, we can show that if the algorithm is bandwidth bound, then it definitely satisfies the condition,

$$\frac{UB_l^i \times N_l}{W} \geq \frac{\mathcal{B}_l^i}{|P_l^i| \times F} \qquad (8)$$

Hence, if an algorithm fails to satisfy Equation (8), we can safely conclude that there is at least one execution order of C that is not constrained by the memory bandwidth at level l.

In particular, we are interested in understanding the memory bandwidth requirements (1) between the main memory and last level cache (LLC) within each node, and, (2) between different nodes, for various algorithms. For simplicity, we assume that the LLC is shared by all the cores within a node, which is common in practice.

Considering the particular case of data movement between LLC and the main memory, Equation (7) becomes,

$$\frac{LB_{vert} \times N_{nodes}}{W} \leq \frac{\mathcal{B}_{vert}}{N_{cores} \times F} \qquad (9)$$

where, LB_{vert} is the vertical data movement lower bound, $\mathcal{B}_{vert}$ is the total bandwidth between DRAM and LLC, N_{nodes} represents the number of nodes in the system, and N_{cores} represents the number of cores within each node. Similarly, considering the inter-node communication, Equation (8) becomes,

$$\frac{UB_{horiz} \times N_{nodes}}{W} \geq \frac{\mathcal{B}_{horiz}}{N_{cores} \times F} \tag{10}$$

where, UB_{horiz} and $\mathcal{B}_{horiz}$ represent the upper bound on the horizontal data movement cost and inter-processor communication bandwidth, respectively.

Specifications for some of the computing systems are shown in table 1.

Table 1: Specifications of various computing systems

Machine	N_{nodes}	Mem. (GB)	LLC (MB)	Vertical balance (words / FLOP)	Horiz. balance (words / FLOP)
IBM BG/Q	2048	16	32	0.052	0.006
Cray XT5	9408	16	6	0.0256	0.005

5.1 Example: Solving the Heat Equation

Many compiute intensive applications involve the numerical solution of partial differential equations (PDEs). As an example, consider the heat flow on a long thin bar of unit length, of uniform material and insulated, so that heat can enter and exit only at the boundaries (Fig. 2(a)). Let $u(x,t)$ represent the temperature at position $0 \leq x \leq 1$, and time $t \geq 0$. The objective is to determine the change in temperature over time ($u(x,t)$). The governing *heat equation* that describes this distribution of heat is given by the PDE:

$$\frac{du(x,t)}{dt} = \alpha \times \frac{d^2 u(x,t)}{dx^2}$$

where, α is the thermal diffusivity of the bar. (For mathematical treatment, it is sufficient to consider $\alpha = 1$).

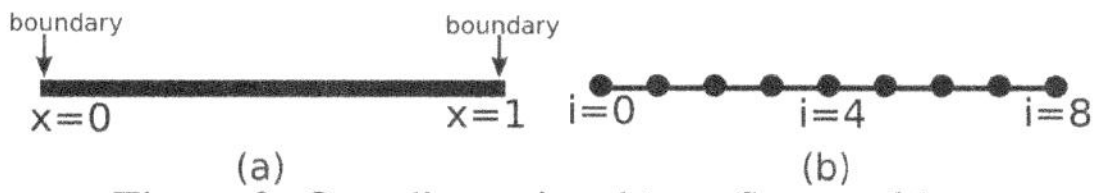

Figure 2: One-dimensional heat flow problem

Since the problem is continuous, to numerically solve the heat equation, it needs to be *discretized* (through *finite difference* approximation) to reduce it to a finite problem. In the discretized problem, the values of $u(x,t)$ are only computed at discrete points at regular intervals of the bar, called the *computational grid* or *mesh*. The state variables at these grid points are given by $u(x(i),t(m))$, where $x(i) = i \times h$, $0 \leq i \leq n+1 = 1/h$ and $t(m) = m \times k$; h and k are the *grid spacing* and *timestep*, respectively. Fig. 2(b) shows an example grid obtained by discretizing the one-dimensional bar.

The governing equation, after discretization, yields the following equation at grid point i and timestamp $m+1$.

$$\frac{-a}{2} \times U(i-1,m+1) + (1+a) \times U(i,m+1) - \frac{a}{2} \times U(i+1,m+1) =$$

$$\frac{a}{2} \times U(i-1,m) + (1-a) \times U(i,m) + \frac{a}{2} \times U(i+1,m)$$

where, $U(p,q) = u(x(p),t(q))$ and $a = k/h^2$. Hence, the solution to the problem involves solving a linear system of $n-1$ equations at each timestamp till convergence. Each timestamp $m+1$ is dependant on values of the previous timestamp m.

This linear system can be represented in tridiagonal matrix form as follows:

$$\begin{pmatrix} 1+a & -\frac{a}{2} & & & & \\ -\frac{a}{2} & 1+a & -\frac{a}{2} & & & \\ & -\frac{a}{2} & 1+a & -\frac{a}{2} & & \\ & & \ddots & \ddots & \ddots & \\ & & & -\frac{a}{2} & 1+a & -\frac{a}{2} \\ & & & & -\frac{a}{2} & 1+a \end{pmatrix} \times \begin{pmatrix} U(1,m+1) \\ U(2,m+1) \\ U(3,m+1) \\ \vdots \\ U(n-1,m+1) \\ U(n,m+1) \end{pmatrix} = \begin{pmatrix} b(1,m) \\ b(2,m) \\ b(3,m) \\ \vdots \\ b(n-1,m) \\ b(n,m) \end{pmatrix} \tag{11}$$

where, $b(i,m)$ represents the right-hand side of the i-th equation at timestamp $m+1$. Solving this linear system of the form $\mathbf{Ax} = \mathbf{b}$ for vector $\mathbf{x}$ provides the solution to the original problem. In general, for a d-dimensional problem, the coefficient matrix is of size n^d-by-n^d, while the vectors are of size n^d. In practice, the elements of the matrix are not explicitly stored. Instead, their values are directly embedded in the program as constants thus eliminating the space requirement and the associated I/O cost for the matrix.

Many iterative methods have been developed to efficiently solve such large linear systems of equations. The following section derives the vertical and horizontal data movement bounds for some of these iterative linear system solvers using the results from Sections 3 and 4 and compares it against the machine balance values.

5.2 Conjugate Gradient (CG)

The Conjugate Gradient method [15] is suitable for solving symmetric positive-definite linear systems. CG maintains 3 vectors at each timestep - the approximate solution $\mathbf{x}$, its residual $\mathbf{r} = \mathbf{Ax} - \mathbf{b}$, and a search direction $\mathbf{p}$. At each step, $\mathbf{x}$ is improved by searching for a better solution in the direction $\mathbf{p}$.

Each iteration of CG involves one sparse matrix-vector product, three vector updates, and three vector dot-products. The complete pseudocode is shown in Fig. 3.

```
1   x is the initial guess
2   p ← r ← b − Ax
3   do
4       v ← Ap                      //SpMV
5       b ← (r.r)                   //Dot−prod
6       a ← b/(p.v)                 //Dot−prod
7       x ← x + ap                  //AXPY
8       r ← r − av                  //AXPY
9       g ← (r.r)/b                 //Dot−prod
10      p ← r + gp                  //AXPY
11  until ((r.r) is small)
```

Figure 3: Conjugate Gradient method

5.2.1 Vertical data movement cost

In this sub-section, we provide the lower bound for the amount of data movement between different levels of hierarchy for CG.

THEOREM 8 (MIN-CUT BASED I/O LOWER BOUND FOR CG). *For a d-dimensional grid of size n^d, the minimum I/O cost to solve the linear system using CG, Q, satisfies $Q \geq 6n^d T/P$, when $n^d \gg S$; where, T represents the number of outer loop iterations, and P is the number of processors.*

PROOF. Let C be the CDAG for CG. Consider the vertex υ_x, corresponding to computation of the scalar a at line 6. The $2n^d$ predecessor vertices of υ_x, corresponding to elements of vectors $\mathbf{p}$ and $\mathbf{v}$, have disjoint paths to the $\mathsf{Desc}(\upsilon_x)$ (due to computations in lines 7 and 8, respectively). This gives us a wavefront of size $\left|W_G^{min}(\upsilon_x)\right| = 2n^d$. Similarly, considering the vertex, υ_y, corresponding to the computation of scalar g, at line 9, we obtain a wavefront of size $\left|W_G^{min}(v_y)\right| = n^d$, due to the disjoint paths from the predecessors $\mathbf{r}$ to $\mathsf{Desc}(x)$ (due to the computation at line 10).

Recursively applying Theorem 4 on the complete CDAG C, provides us T sub-CDAGs, $C_1, C_2, \ldots, C_T$, corresponding to each outer loop iteration. (Vertices corresponding to the elements of vector $\mathbf{p}$ computed at line 10 are shared between neighboring sub-CDAGs). Further, non-disjointly sub-dividing each of these sub-CDAGs, C_i, into $C_{i_{|x}} and C_{i_{|y}}$ (vertices corresponding to the computation of vector $\mathbf{r}$ from line 8 are shared between $C_{i_{|x}} and C_{i_{|y}}$), to decompose the effects of wavefronts $W_G^{min}(v_x)$ and $W_G^{min}(v_y)$, we obtain a lower bound of,

$$\begin{aligned} Q &\geq T \times (2(2n^d - S)) + T \times (2(n^d - S)) \\ &= T \times (2(3n^d - 2S)) \end{aligned}$$

which tends to $6n^d T$ when $n^d \gg S$. Finally, application of Theorem 5 provides a lower bound of $6n^d T/P$ for the parallel case. $\square$

5.2.2 *Horizontal data movement cost*

Consider the block partitioning of the input grid among the processors, with block size along each dimension $B = n/N_{nodes}^{1/d}$. Each processor holds the input data corresponding to its local grid points and computes the data needed by those grid points. Computation of the sparse matrix-vector product, at line 4 in Fig. 3, requires send and receive of values at the ghost cells of size $(B+2)^d - B^d$ at each timestep with the neighboring processors. If Q is the minimum I/O cost for executing CG, then,

$$\begin{aligned} Q &\leq 2 \times ((B+2)^d - B^d) \times T \\ &= 2 \times (B^d + \binom{d}{1}B^{d-1}2^1 + \binom{d}{2}B^{d-2}2^2 \\ &\quad + \cdots + \binom{d}{d-1}B^1 2^{d-1} + \binom{d}{d}B^0 2^d - B^d) \times T \\ &= O(4dB^{d-1}T) \end{aligned}$$

5.2.3 *Analysis*

Equations (9) and (10) provided us conditions to determine the vertical and horizontal memory constraints of the algorithms. We will use them to show that the running time of CG is mainly constrained by the vertical data movement. We consider a three-dimensional problem ($d = 3$) for the analysis.

Operation count: The vector dot-product at line 6 requires $2n^d$ operations. The computation of $(\mathbf{r}.\mathbf{r})$, at lines 9, 11 and 5, requires a single vector dot-product of operation count $2n^d$. The vector update operations at lines 7, 8 and 10 have operation count of $2n^d$ each. The SpMV operation at line 4 is a stencil computation that requires $2.(2d+1).n^d$ operations. This provides a total operation count of $24n^3 T$ for a three-dimensional problem.

The vertical I/O lower bound per node, $LB_{vert} = 6n^3 T/N_{nodes}$. Hence,

$$\frac{LB_{vert} \times N_{nodes}}{W} = \frac{\left(6n^3 T/N_{nodes}\right) \times N_{nodes}}{24n^3 T} = \frac{6}{24} = 0.25$$

This value is higher than the vertical machine balance value of various machine (refer table 1), leaving Equation (9) unsatisfied. This shows that CG will be unavoidably bandwidth bound along the vertical direction for the problems that cannot fit into the cache. The only way to improve the performance would be to increase the main memory bandwidth.

On the other hand, let us consider the horizontal data movement cost.

$$\begin{aligned} \frac{UB_{horiz} \times N_{nodes}}{W} &= \frac{12B^2 T \times N_{nodes}}{24n^3 T} \\ &= \frac{12\left(n/N_{nodes}^{(1/3)}\right)^2 N_{nodes}}{24n^3} = \frac{N_{nodes}^{(1/3)}}{2n} \end{aligned}$$

This value is much lower than the horizontal machine balance values of various machines for the problem size typically encountered in practice, indicating that it is the intra-node memory bandwidth that is much more of a fundamental bottleneck than inter-node communication for CG.

5.3 Jacobi Method

Jacobi's method involves stencil computation, starting with an initial guess for the unknown vector $\mathbf{x}$ and iteratively replacing the current approximate solution at each grid point by a weighted average of its nearest neighbors on the grid. Hence, the information at one grid point can only propagate to its adjacent grid points in one iteration. Thus, it takes at least n steps to propogate the information throughout the grid and reach to the solution.

5.3.1 *Vertical data movement cost*

In this section, we derive the I/O lower bound for Jacobi computation on a d-dimensional grid. We provide the proof for a 2D-grid below, which can be generalized to a grid of d-dimensions as shown later.

THEOREM 9 (I/O LOWER BOUND FOR JACOBI).
For the two-dimensional 5-points Jacobi computation of size $n \times n$ with $T - 1$ time steps, the minimum I/O cost, Q, satisfies $Q \geq \frac{N^2 T}{4P\sqrt{2S}}$, where P is the number of processors.

PROOF. The CDAG for the Jacobi computation has the property that all inputs can reach all outputs through vertex-disjoint paths. These vertex-disjoint paths will be called *lines*, for simplicity. Let $F(d)$ denote a monotonically increasing function such that for any two vertices u and v on the same line that are at least distance d apart, $F(d)$ has the following properties: (1) none of these $F(d)$ vertices belong to the same line; (2) Each of these vertices belongs to a path connecting u and v. In [16, Theorem 5.1], Hong & Kung showed that for any CDAG C that satisfies the above mentioned properties, its largest vertex-set in any $2S$-partition of C, $U(C, 2S) = 2.(F^{-1}(2S) + 1)$, and the serial I/O lower bound, Q_s can be bounded by $Q_s \geq L/(2.(F^{-1}(2S) + 1))$, where L is the total number of vertices on the lines. From the structure of CDAG for 2D-Jacobi computation, it can be seen that $F^{-1}(2S) = 2\sqrt{2S} - 1$. Hence, $U(C, 2S) = 4\sqrt{2S}$, and from Theorem 6, the parallel I/O cost, $Q \geq n^2 T/(4P\sqrt{2S})$. $\square$

With the similar reasoning, the I/O lower bound can be extended to higher dimensions, leading to the I/O cost of $Q \geq n^d T/(4P(2S)^{1/d})$, for a d-dimensional grid. The well-known tiled Jacobi implementation (of tile size S) with scheduling for wavefront parallelism has an I/O cost of $Q \leq (4d+2)n^d T/(PS^{1/d})$. Hence, the parallel I/O lower bound derived above is asymptotically tight.

5.3.2 *Horizontal data movement cost*

The well-known distributed memory tiled Jacobi implementation incurs data communication cost at the boundaries due to the exchange of ghost cell values, similar to the Conjuagte Gradient method. Hence, the upper bound on the horizontal data movement cost for the Jacobi method, $Q = O(4dB^{d-1}T)$, where, $B = n/N_{nodes}^{1/d}$ is the block size along each dimension.

5.3.3 Analysis

We consider a three-dimensional problem ($d = 3$) for the analysis in this section. The operation count for a three-dimensional 7-point Jacobi method is $7n^3T$. The vertical I/O lower bound per node, $LB_{vert} = n^3T/(4(2S)^{1/3}N_{nodes})$. Hence,

$$\frac{LB_{vert} \times N_{nodes}}{W} = \frac{\left(n^3T/4.(2S)^{1/3}.N_{nodes}\right) \times N_{nodes}}{7n^3T} = \frac{1}{35.3 \times S^{1/3}}$$

For an LLC of size $S = 6$ MB (i.e., 0.75 MWords), $LB_{vert} = 3 \times 10^{-4}$ words/FLOP. This value falls below the vertical machine balance parameter of various architectures (refer Table 1). Now, considering the vertical I/O upper bound per node, $UB_{vert} = 14n^dT/(S^{1/d}N_{nodes})$.

$$\frac{UB_{vert} \times N_{nodes}}{W} = \frac{\left(14n^3T/S^{1/3}.N_{nodes}\right) \times N_{nodes}}{7n^3T} = \frac{2}{S^{1/3}}$$

For $S = 0.75$ MWords, $UB_{vert} = 0.022$ words/FLOP. This value falls sightly below the vertical machine balance parameters shown in Table 1, showing that the Jacobi method need not be necessarily bandwidth bound along the vertical direction, as opposed to CG.

Similarly, for the horizontal case,

$$\frac{UB_{horiz} \times N_{nodes}}{W} = \frac{12B^2T \times N_{nodes}}{7n^3T} = \frac{1.714 \times N_{nodes}^{(1/3)}}{n}$$

As in the case of CG, this value is much lower than the horizontal machine balance values of different machines for the common problem sizes, indicating that the horizontal data movement is not a bottleneck.

This shows that even though Jacobi method might require more iterations to converge, its lower ratio of I/O cost to the computational cost along both vertical and horizontal directions might make methods similar to it a more attractive alternative to CG for solving large sparse systems of linear equations on future machines that have more skewed machine balance parameters than current systems.

6. RELATED WORK

Hong & Kung provided the first characterization of the I/O complexity problem using the red/blue pebble game and the equivalence to $2S$-partitioning of CDAGs [16]. Their $2S$-partitioning approach uses dominators of incoming edges to partitions but does not account for the internal structure of partitions. In this paper, in addition to using the $2S$-partitioning technique, we also use an alternate lower bound approach that models the internal structure of CDAGs, and uses graph mincut as the basis. In addition, Hong & Kung's original model does not lend itself easily to development of effective lower bounds for a CDAG from bounds for component sub-graphs. With a change of the pebble game model to the RBW game, we were able to use CDAG decomposition to develop tight composite lower bounds for inhomogeneous CDAGs.

Several works followed Hong & Kung's work on I/O complexity in deriving lower bounds on data accesses [2, 1, 18, 6, 5, 22, 23, 19, 20, 28, 13, 3, 4, 8, 27, 25]. Aggarwal et al. provided several lower bounds for sorting algorithms [2]. Savage [22, 23] developed the notion of S-span to derive Hong-Kung style lower bounds and that model has been used in several works [19, 20, 25]. Irony et al. [18] provided a new proof of the Hong-Kung result on I/O complexity of matrix multiplication and developed lower bounds on commu-

nication for sequential and parallel matrix multiplication. More recently, Demmel et al. have developed lower bounds as well as optimal algorithms for several linear algebra computations including QR and LU decomposition and all-pairs shortest paths problem [3, 4, 13, 27]. Bilardi et al. [6, 5] develop the notion of access complexity and relate it to space complexity. Bilardi and Preparata [7] developed the notion of the closed-dichotomy size of a DAG G that is used to provide a lower bound on the data access complexity in those cases where recomputation is not allowed. Our notion of schedule wavefronts is similar to the closed-dichotomy size in their work. Extending the scope of the Hong & Kung model to more complex memory hierarchies has been the subject of some research. Savage provided an extension together with results for some classes of computations that were considered by Hong & Kung, providing optimal lower bounds for I/O with memory hierarchies [22]. Valiant proposed a hierarchical computational model [28] that offers the possibility to reason in an arbitrarily complex parameterized memory hierarchy model.

Unlike Hong & Kung's original model, several models have been proposed that do not allow recomputation of values (also referred to as "no repebbling") [3, 4, 5, 26, 19, 22, 23, 25, 9, 18, 20, 21]. Savage [22] develops results for FFT using no repebbling. Bilardi and Peserico [5] explore the possibility of coding a given algorithm so that it is efficiently portable across machines with different hierarchical memory systems, without the use of recomputation. Ballard et al. [3, 4] assume no recomputation is allowed in deriving lower bounds for linear algebra computations. Ranjan et al. [19] develop better bounds than Hong & Kung for FFT using a specialized technique adapted for FFT-style computations on memory hierarchies. Ranjan et al. [20] derive lower bounds for pebbling r-pyramids under the assumption that there is no recomputation. Recently, Ranjan et al. [21] developed a technique for binomial graphs. Very recent work from U.C. Berkeley [8] has developed a very novel approach to developing parametric I/O lower bounds applicable/effective for a class of nested loop computations but is either inapplicable or produces weak lower bounds for other computations (e.g., stencil computations, FFT, etc.).

The P-RBW game developed in this paper extends the parallel model for shared-memory architectures by Savage and Zubair [24] to also include the distributed-memory parallelism present in all scalable parallel architectures. The works of Irony et al. [18] and Ballard et al. [3] model communication across nodes of a distributed-memory system. Bilardi and Preperata [7] develop lower bound results for communication in a distributed-memory model specialized for multi-dimensional mesh topologies. Our model in this paper differs from the above efforts in defining a new integrated pebble game to model both horizontal communication across nodes in a parallel machine, as well as vertical data movement through a multi-level shared cache hierarchy within a multi-core node.

Czechowski et al. [11, 12] consider the relationship between the ratio of an algorithm's data movement cost to arithmetic work and the machine balance ratio of memory bandwidth to peak performance. Our analysis of algorithms in this paper involves a very similar theme as theirs, but we develop new lower bounds analyses. Further, we compare and contrast data movement demands for horizontal across-node communication versus vertical within-node data movement and observe that the latter is often the more constraining factor.

7. CONCLUSION

Characterizing the parallel data movement complexity of a program is a cornerstone problem, that is particularly important with current and emerging power-constrained architectures where the data transfer cost will be the dominant energy and performance bottleneck. In this paper, we have presented an extension to the Hong and Kung red-blue pebble game model to enable development of lower bounds on data movement for parallel execution of CDAGs. The model distinguishes horizontal data movement between nodes of a distributed-memory parallel system from vertical data movement within the multi-level memory/cache hierarchy within a multi-core node. The utility of the model and the developed lower bounding techniques was demonstrated by analysis of several numerical algorithms and the garnering of interesting insights on the relative significance of horizontal versus vertical data movement for different algorithms.

Acknowledgments.

This work is supported in part by the U.S. National Science Foundation through awards 0811457, 0904549, 0926127, 0926687, and 0926688, by the U.S. Department of Energy through award DE-SC0008844, and by the U.S. Army through contract W911NF-10-1-000.

8. REFERENCES

[1] A. Aggarwal, B. Alpern, A. K. Chandra, and M. Snir. A model for hierarchical memory. In *19th STOC*, pages 305–314, 1987.

[2] A. Aggarwal and J. S. Vitter. The input/output complexity of sorting and related problems. *Commun. ACM*, 31:1116–1127, 1988.

[3] G. Ballard, J. Demmel, O. Holtz, and O. Schwartz. Minimizing communication in numerical linear algebra. *SIAM J. Matrix Analysis Applications*, 32(3):866–901, 2011.

[4] G. Ballard, J. Demmel, O. Holtz, and O. Schwartz. Graph expansion and communication costs of fast matrix multiplication. *J. ACM*, 59(6):32, 2012.

[5] G. Bilardi and E. Peserico. A characterization of temporal locality and its portability across memory hierarchies. *Automata, Languages and Programming*, pages 128–139, 2001.

[6] G. Bilardi, A. Pietracaprina, and P. D'Alberto. On the space and access complexity of computation dags. In *Graph-Theoretic Concepts in Computer Science*, volume 1928 of *LNCS*, pages 81–92. 2000.

[7] G. Bilardi and F. P. Preparata. Processor - Time Tradeoffs under Bounded-Speed Message Propagation: Part II, Lower Bounds. *Theory Comput. Syst.*, 32(5):531–559, 1999.

[8] M. Christ, J. Demmel, N. Knight, T. Scanlon, and K. Yelick. Communication lower bounds and optimal algorithms for programs that reference arrays - part 1. EECS Technical Report EECS–2013-61, UC Berkeley, May 2013.

[9] S. A. Cook. An observation on time-storage trade off. *J. Comput. Syst. Sci.*, 9(3):308–316, 1974.

[10] Cray XE6. http://www.cray.com/Products/Computing/XE.aspx.

[11] K. Czechowski, C. Battaglino, C. McClanahan, A. Chandramowlishwaran, and R. Vuduc. Balance principles for algorithm-architecture co-design. In *Proceedings of the 3rd USENIX Conference on Hot Topic in Parallelism*, HotPar'11, pages 9–9, 2011.

[12] K. Czechowski and R. Vuduc. A theoretical framework for algorithm-architecture co-design. In *Proceedings of the 2013 IEEE 27th International Symposium on Parallel and Distributed Processing*, IPDPS '13, pages 791–802, 2013.

[13] J. Demmel, L. Grigori, M. Hoemmen, and J. Langou. Communication-optimal parallel and sequential QR and LU factorizations. *SIAM J. Scientific Computing*, 34(1), 2012.

[14] V. Elango, F. Rastello, L.-N. Pouchet, J. Ramanujam, and P. Sadayappan. Data access complexity: The red/blue pebble game revisited. Technical Report OSU-CISRC-7/13-TR16, Ohio State University, September 2013.

[15] M. R. Hestenes and E. Stiefel. Methods of conjugate gradients for solving linear systems, 1952.

[16] J.-W. Hong and H. T. Kung. I/O complexity: The red-blue pebble game. In *Proc. of the 13th annual ACM sympo. on Theory of computing (STOC'81)*, pages 326–333. ACM, 1981.

[17] IBM Blue Gene team. The ibm blue gene project. *IBM Journal of Research and Development*, 57(1/2):0:1–0:6, 2013.

[18] D. Irony, S. Toledo, and A. Tiskin. Communication lower bounds for distributed-memory matrix multiplication. *J. Parallel Distrib. Comput.*, 64(9):1017–1026, 2004.

[19] D. Ranjan, J. Savage, and M. Zubair. Strong I/O lower bounds for binomial and FFT computation graphs. In *Computing and Combinatorics*, volume 6842 of *LNCS*, pages 134–145. Springer, 2011.

[20] D. Ranjan, J. E. Savage, and M. Zubair. Upper and lower I/O bounds for pebbling r-pyramids. *J. Discrete Algorithms*, 14:2–12, 2012.

[21] D. Ranjan and M. Zubair. Vertex isoperimetric parameter of a computation graph. *Int. J. Found. Comput. Sci.*, 23(4):941–, 2012.

[22] J. Savage. Extending the Hong-Kung model to memory hierarchies. In *Computing and Combinatorics*, volume 959 of *LNCS*, pages 270–281. 1995.

[23] J. E. Savage. *Models of computation - exploring the power of computing*. Addison-Wesley, 1998.

[24] J. E. Savage and M. Zubair. A unified model for multicore architectures. In *Proceedings of the 1st international forum on Next-generation multicore/manycore technologies*, page 9. ACM, 2008.

[25] J. E. Savage and M. Zubair. Cache-optimal algorithms for option pricing. *ACM Trans. Math. Softw.*, 37(1), 2010.

[26] M. Scquizzato and F. Silvestri. Communication lower bounds for distributed-memory computations. *CoRR*, abs/1307.1805, 2013.

[27] E. Solomonik, A. Buluç, and J. Demmel. Minimizing communication in all-pairs shortest paths. In *IPDPS*, 2013.

[28] L. G. Valiant. A bridging model for multi-core computing. *J. Comput. Syst. Sci.*, 77:154–166, Jan. 2011.

Tradeoffs between Synchronization, Communication, and Computation in Parallel Linear Algebra Computations

Edgar Solomonik
UC Berkeley
EECS Department
solomon@cs.berkeley.edu

Erin Carson
UC Berkeley
EECS Department
carson@cs.berkeley.edu

Nicholas Knight
UC Berkeley
EECS Department
knight@cs.berkeley.edu

James Demmel
UC Berkeley
EECS Department
Mathematics Department
demmel@cs.berkeley.edu

ABSTRACT

This paper derives tradeoffs between three basic costs of a parallel algorithm: synchronization, data movement, and computational cost. These tradeoffs are lower bounds on the execution time of the algorithm which are independent of the number of processors, but dependent on the problem size. Therefore, they provide lower bounds on the parallel execution time of any algorithm computed by a system composed of any number of homogeneous components, each with associated computational, communication, and synchronization payloads. We employ a theoretical model counts the amount of work and data movement as a maximum of any execution path during the parallel computation. By considering this metric, rather than the total communication volume over the whole machine, we obtain new insights into the characteristics of parallel schedules for algorithms with non-trivial dependency structures. We also present reductions from BSP and LogP algorithms to our execution model, extending our lower bounds to these two models of parallel computation. We first develop our results for general dependency graphs and hypergraphs based on their expansion properties, then we apply the theorem to a number of specific algorithms in numerical linear algebra, namely triangular substitution, Gaussian elimination, and Krylov subspace methods. Our lower bound for LU factorization demonstrates the optimality of Tiskin's LU algorithm [26] answering an open question posed in his paper, as well as of the 2.5D LU [21] algorithm which has analogous costs. We treat the computations in a general manner by noting that the computations share a similar dependency hypergraph structure and analyzing the communication requirements of lattice hypergraph structures.

1. INTRODUCTION

We model a parallel machine as a network of processors which communicate via asynchronous point-to-point messages and col-

lective (though not necessarily global) synchronizations. This model has three basic architectural parameters, α – network latency (time) for a synchronization between two or more processors β – time to inject a word of data into (or extract it from) the network, γ – time to perform a floating point operation on local data, which are associated with three algorithmic costs, S – number of synchronizations (network latency cost), W – number of words of data moved (bandwidth cost / communication cost), F – number of local floating point operations performed (computational cost).

We describe our execution schedule model and show how S, W, and F are measured in any schedule in Section 3. Each quantity is accumulated along some path of dependent executions in the schedule. The sequence of executions done locally by any processor corresponds to one such path in the schedule, so our costs are at least as large as those incurred by any single processor during the execution of the schedule. The parallel execution time of the schedule is closely proportional to these three quantities, namely,

$$\max(\alpha \cdot S, \beta \cdot W, \gamma \cdot F) \leq \text{execution time} \leq \alpha \cdot S + \beta \cdot W + \gamma \cdot F.$$

Since our analysis will be asymptotic, we do not consider overlap between communication and computation and are able to measure the three quantities separately. Our model is similar to the LogP [8] and BSP [27] models.

Our theoretical analysis also precludes recomputation within a parallelization of an algorithm, as we associate an algorithm with a set of vertices, each of which is a computation, and assign them to unique processors. However, a parallel algorithm which employs recomputation has a different dependency graph structure, to which our analysis may subsequently be applied. While there are many existing parallel algorithms for the applications we explore that employ recomputation, to the best of our knowledge none of them perform less communication than the recomputation-excluding lower bounds we present.

We reason about parallel algorithms by considering the dependency graphs of certain computations. We will first derive theoretical machinery for obtaining lower bounds on dependency graphs with certain expansion parameters and then show how this result yields lower bounds on S, W, F for several algorithms in numerical linear algebra with common dependency structures. Most of our lower bounds apply to computations which have $\Omega(n^d)$ vertices, with a d-dimensional lattice dependency structure, and take the form

$$F \cdot S^{d-1} = \Omega\left(n^d\right), \quad W \cdot S^{d-2} = \Omega\left(n^{d-1}\right).$$

These bounds indicate that a growing amount of local computation, communication, and synchronization must be done to solve a larger global problem. Thus, the bounds are important because they highlight a scalability bottleneck dependent only on local processor/network speed and independent of the number of processors involved in the computation.

In particular, we show that: (1) for solving a dense n-by-n triangular system by substitution (TRSV),

$$F_{\text{TR}} \cdot S_{\text{TR}} = \Omega\left(n^2\right),$$

(2) for Gaussian elimination (GE) of a dense n-by-n matrix,

$$F_{\text{GE}} \cdot S_{\text{GE}}^2 = \Omega\left(n^3\right), \qquad W_{\text{GE}} \cdot S_{\text{GE}} = \Omega\left(n^2\right),$$

(3) for computing an s-step Krylov subspace basis with a $(2m+1)^d$-point stencil (defined in Section 6.3),

$$F_{\text{Kr}} \cdot S_{\text{Kr}}^d = \Omega\left(m^d \cdot s^{d+1}\right), \qquad W_{\text{Kr}} \cdot S_{\text{Kr}}^{d-1} = \Omega\left(m^d \cdot s^d\right).$$

The lower bounds which we derive in this paper establish the communication optimality of the parallel algorithms for LU factorization given by Tiskin [17] and Solomonik and Demmel [21]. The parallel schedules for LU and QR in these papers are parameterized and exhibit a trade-off between synchronization and communication bandwidth cost. Our paper answers an open question posed by Tiskin in [26], showing that it is not possible to achieve an optimal bandwidth cost for LU factorization without an associated increase in synchronization cost (within the limits of our assumptions).

In [21], a lower bound proof was given which demonstrated this trade-off for LU factorization. However, the proof argument in [21] did not consider the possibility of overlap between the communication necessary to factorize each block, and therefore was incorrect. This paper extends the idea of this tradeoff to a more general theoretical context, and presents a fixed and strengthened proof in this new framework. We show that Gaussian elimination is just one of many numerical algorithms whose dependency structure necessitates the tradeoff. In particular, we conjecture that our results extend to other dense matrix factorizations such as QR and graph algorithms with similar dependence structures, as well as some dynamic programming algorithms.

2. PREVIOUS WORK

Theoretical lower bounds on communication volume and synchronization can be parameterized by the local/fast memory size M. Most previous work has considered the total sequential or parallel communication volume Q, which corresponds to the amount of data movement across the network (by all processors), or through the memory hierarchy. Hong and Kung [15] introduced sequential communication volume lower bounds for computations including n-by-n matrix multiplication, $Q_{\text{MM}} = \Omega(n^3/\sqrt{M})$, the n-point FFT, $Q_{\text{FFT}} = \Omega(n \log(n)/\log(M))$, and the d-dimensional diamond DAG (a Cartesian product of line graphs of length n), $Q_{\text{dmd}} = \Omega(n^d/M^{1/(d-1)})$. Irony et al. [14] extended this approach to distributed-memory matrix multiplication on p processors, obtaining the bound $W_{\text{MM}} = \Omega(n^3/(p\sqrt{M}))$. Aggarwal et al. [1] proved a version of the memory-independent lower bound $W_{\text{MM}} = \Omega(n^3/p^{2/3})$, and Ballard et al. [2] explored the relationship between these memory-dependent and memory-independent lower bounds. Ballard et al. [3] extended the results for matrix multiplication to Gaussian elimination of n-by-n matrices and many other matrix algorithms with similar structure, finding

$$W_{\text{GE}} = \Omega\left(\frac{n^3}{p\sqrt{\min(M, n^2/p^{2/3})}}\right).$$

Bender et al. [5] extended the sequential communication lower bounds introduced in [15] to sparse matrix vector multiplication. This lower bound is relevant to our analysis of Krylov subspace methods, which essentially perform repeated sparse matrix vector multiplications. However, [5] used a sequential memory hierarchy model and established bounds in terms of memory size and track (cacheline) size, while we focus on interprocessor communication.

Papadimitriou and Ullman [18] demonstrated tradeoffs for the 2-dimensional diamond DAG (a slight variant of that considered in [15]). They proved that the amount of computational work F_{dmd} along some execution path (in their terminology, execution time) is related to the communication volume Q_{dmd} and synchronization cost S_{dmd} as

$$F_{\text{dmd}} \cdot Q_{\text{dmd}} = \Omega\left(n^3\right) \text{ and } F_{\text{dmd}} \cdot S_{\text{dmd}} = \Omega\left(n^2\right).$$

These tradeoffs imply that in order to decrease the amount of computation done along the critical path of execution, more communication and synchronization must be performed. For instance, if an algorithm has 'execution time' cost of $F_{\text{dmd}} = \Omega(nb)$, it requires $S_{\text{dmd}} = \Omega(n/b)$ synchronizations and a communication volume of $Q_{\text{dmd}} = \Omega(n^2/b)$. The tradeoff on $F_{\text{dmd}} \cdot S_{\text{dmd}}$ is a special case of the d-dimensional bubble latency lower bound tradeoff we derive in the next section, with $d = 2$. These diamond DAG tradeoffs were also demonstrated by Tiskin [24].

Bampis et al. [4] considered finding the optimal schedule (and number of processors) for computing d-dimensional grid graphs, similar in structure to those we consider in Section 6. Their work was motivated by [18] and took into account dependency graph structure and communication, modeling the cost of sending a word between processors as equal to the cost of a computation. Tradeoffs in parallel schedules have also been studied in the context of data locality on mesh network topologies by Bilardi et al [6].

We will introduce lower bounds that relate synchronization to computation and data movement along dependency paths. Our work is most similar to the approach in [18]; however, we attain bounds on W (the parallel communication volume along some dependency path), rather than Q (the total communication volume). Our theory obtains tradeoff lower bounds for a more general set of dependency graphs which allows us to develop lower bounds for a wider set of computations.

3. THEORETICAL MODEL

We first introduce a couple of notational conventions which we will employ throughout this and later sections: sets are defined as uppercase letters (S, V); vectors are defined as lowercase boldface letters ($\mathbf{v}$) and the ith element of $\mathbf{v}$ is indexed as v_i; accordingly, matrices and tensors are defined as uppercase boldface letters ($\mathbf{A}, \mathbf{T}$), with elements A_{ij}, T_{ijk}.

The **dependency graph** of a program is a directed acyclic graph (DAG) $G = (V, E)$. The vertices $V = I \cup Z \cup O$ correspond to either input values I (the vertices with indegree-0), or the results of (distinct) operations, in which case they are either temporary (or intermediate) values Z, or outputs O (including all vertices of outdegree-0). There is an edge $(u, v) \in E \subset V \times (Z \cup O)$ for each operand u of the operation computing v. These edges represent data dependencies, and impose limits on the parallelism available within the computation. For instance, if the dependency graph $G = (V, E)$ is a line graph with $V = \{v_1, \ldots, v_n\}$ and $E = \{(v_1, v_2), \ldots, (v_{n-1}, v_n)\}$, the computation is entirely sequential, and a lower bound on the execution time is the time it takes a single processor to compute $F = n - 1$ operations. Using graph expansion and hypergraph analysis, we will derive lower bounds for computation and communication for dependency graphs with certain properties. In the following subsections, we develop a formal model of a parallel schedule in detail and show that our construction generalizes the BSP and the LogP models. While some of the model formalism is used in the proof of our main result in Section 4.2, the details of the model are not critical to the proof and are not at all referenced in the analysis applications in Section 6.

3.1 Parallel execution model

A **parallelization** of an algorithm corresponds to a coloring of its dependency graph $G = (V, E)$, i.e., a partition of the vertices into p disjoint sets $V = \bigcup_{i=1}^{p} C_i$, where processor i for $i \in \{1, \ldots, p\}$ computes $C_i \cap (Z \cup O)$. We require that in any parallel execution among p processors, at least two processors compute $\lfloor |Z \cup O|/p \rfloor$ elements; this assumption is necessary to avoid the case of a single processor computing the whole problem sequentially (without parallel communication). Any vertex v of color i ($v \in C_i$) must be communicated to a different processor j if there is an edge from v to a vertex in C_j, though there need not necessarily be a message going directly between processor i and j, as the data can move through intermediate processors. We define each processor's **communicated set** as

$$T_i = \{u : (u, w) \in [(C_i \times (V \setminus C_i)) \cup ((V \setminus C_i) \times C_i)] \cap E\}.$$

We note that each T_i is a vertex separator in G between $C_i \setminus T_i$ and $V \setminus (C_i \cup T_i)$.

We define a **(parallel) schedule** of an algorithm with dependency graph $G = (V, E)$ as a DAG $\bar{G} = (\bar{V}, \bar{E})$, which consists of a set of p edge-disjoint paths, Π, each $\pi \in \Pi$ corresponding to the tasks executed by a certain processor. In our notation, functions that have domain $\bar{V}$ will have hats and functions that have domain $\bar{E}$ will have tildes. Each vertex $v \in \bar{V}$ corresponds to a unique type within the following types of tasks:

$v \in \bar{V}_{\text{comp}}$, the computation of $\hat{f}(v) \subset V$,

$v \in \bar{V}_{\text{sync}}$, a synchronization point,

$v \in \bar{V}_{\text{send}}$, the sending of a message $\hat{s}(v) \subset V$

$v \in \bar{V}_{\text{recv}}$, the reception of a message $\hat{r}(v) \subset V$

We assign a unique color (processor number) i using function $\tilde{c}$ to the edges along each path π, so that for every edge $e \in (\pi \times \pi) \cap \hat{E}$, $\tilde{c}(e) = i$. Each vertex $u \in \bar{V}_{\text{comp}} \cup \bar{V}_{\text{send}} \cup \bar{V}_{\text{recv}}$ should be adjacent to at most one incoming edge e_i and at most one outgoing edge e_o. We assign u the same color $\hat{c}(u) = \tilde{c}(e_i) = \tilde{c}(e_o)$ as the processor which executes it (the single path that goes through it). Each vertex $v \in \bar{V}_{\text{sync}}$ corresponds to a synchronization of k processors and should have k incoming as well as k outgoing edges. With every edge $e \in \bar{E}$, we associate the data kept by processor $\tilde{c}(e)$ in memory as $\tilde{m}(e) \subset V$, the data kept in the send buffer as a collection of sets $\tilde{s}(e) = \{W_1, W_2, \ldots\}$ where each $W_i \subset V$ denotes the contents of a sent point-to-point message posted at some node u with $\hat{s}(u) = W_i$, and the data kept in the receive buffer as a collection of sets $\tilde{r}(e) = \{W_1', W_2', \ldots\}$ where each $W_i' \subset V$ denotes the contents of a point-to-point message received at node v with $\hat{r}(v) = W_i'$. The schedule has p indegree-0 vertices, corresponding to startup tasks $\bar{I} \subset \bar{V}_{\text{comp}}$, i.e., 'no-op' computations which we assume have no cost. The single outgoing edge of each startup task is assigned a disjoint part of the input data, so that $\bigcup_{e \in (\bar{I} \times \bar{V}) \cap \bar{E}} \tilde{m}(e) = I$.

In our model, each message is point-to-point in the sense that it has a single originating and destination processor. However, multiple messages may be transferred via the same synchronization

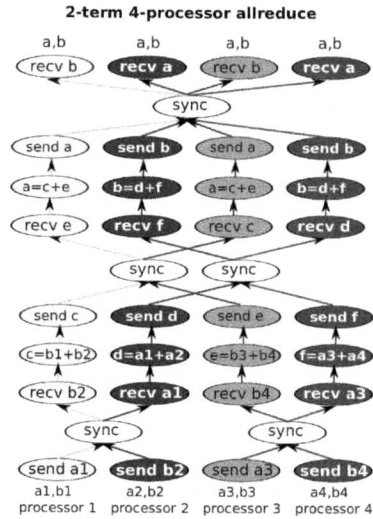

2-term 4-processor allreduce

Figure 1: Depiction of a sample 4-processor execution schedule in our model for an all-reduction, which computes $a = \sum_i a_i$ and $b = \sum_i b_i$.

vertex. We say the schedule $\bar{G}$ is **point-to-point** if each synchronization vertex has no more than two paths going through it. Each message is sent asynchronously, but a synchronization is required before the communicated data may change control. We illustrate an example schedule, which demonstrates the messaging behavior within our model in Figure 1.

We enforce the validity of the schedule via the following constraints. For every task v executed by processor i, with incoming edge e_{in} and outgoing edge e_{out}, if $v \in \bar{V}_{\text{comp}} \setminus \bar{I}$,

1. $(\forall f \in \hat{f}(v))(\forall (g, f) \in E), g \in \hat{f}(v)$ or $g \in \tilde{m}(e_{\text{in}})$, and

2. $\tilde{m}(e_{\text{out}}) \subset \hat{f}(v) \cup \tilde{m}(e_{\text{in}})$;

if $v \in \bar{V}_{\text{send}}$,

1. $\exists w \in \bar{V}_{\text{recv}}$ with $\hat{s}(v) = \hat{r}(w)$ and a path from v to w in $\bar{G}$,

2. $\hat{s}(v) \subset \tilde{m}(e_{\text{in}})$ and $\tilde{s}(e_{\text{out}}) = \tilde{s}(e_{\text{in}}) \cup \{\hat{s}(v)\}$, and

3. $\tilde{m}(e_{\text{out}}) \subset \tilde{m}(e_{\text{in}})$;

or, if $v \in \bar{V}_{\text{recv}}$,

1. $\hat{r}(v) \in \tilde{r}(e_{\text{in}})$ and $\tilde{r}(e_{\text{out}}) = \tilde{r}(e_{\text{in}}) \setminus \{\hat{r}(v)\}$, and

2. $\tilde{m}(e_{\text{out}}) \subset \tilde{m}(e_{\text{in}}) \cup \hat{r}(v)$.

At a synchronization task $u \in \bar{V}_{\text{sync}}$, data may be exchanged.

1. If processor i posted a send $v_i \in \bar{V}_{\text{send}}$ and processor j posted the matching receive $v_j \in \bar{V}_{\text{recv}}$, i.e., $\hat{s}(v_i) = \hat{r}(v_j)$, and if there exist paths $\pi_i = \{v_i, \ldots, w_i, u\}$ and $\pi_j = \{u, w_j, \ldots, v_j\}$ in $\bar{G}$, they may exchange the message during task u by moving the data $\hat{s}(v_i)$ from $\tilde{s}((w_i, u))$ to $\tilde{r}((u, w_j))$.

2. $\bigcup_{(v,u) \in \bar{E}} \tilde{s}((v, u)) \setminus \bigcup_{(u,w) \in \bar{E}} \tilde{s}((u, w)) = \bigcup_{(u,w) \in \bar{E}} \tilde{r}((u, w)) \setminus \bigcup_{(v,u) \in \bar{E}} \tilde{r}((v, u))$.

3. $\tilde{c}((v, u)) = \tilde{c}((u, w)) \Rightarrow \tilde{m}((v, u)) = \tilde{m}((u, w))$.

309

The runtime of the schedule,

$$T(\bar{G}) = \max_{\pi \in \Pi} \sum_{v \in \pi} \hat{t}(v),$$

is maximum total weight of any path in the schedule, where each vertex is weighted according to its task's cost,

$$\hat{t}(v) = \begin{cases} \gamma \cdot |\hat{f}(v)| & v \in \bar{V}_{\mathrm{comp}} \\ \alpha & v \in \bar{V}_{\mathrm{sync}} \\ \beta \cdot |\hat{s}(v)| & v \in \bar{V}_{\mathrm{send}} \\ \beta \cdot |\hat{r}(v)| & v \in \bar{V}_{\mathrm{recv}} \end{cases}.$$

The runtime T is by construction at least the cost incurred by any individual processor, since each processor's workload is a path through the schedule. (Note that our construction allows us to ignore idle time, since a processor can only be idle at a message node if there exists a costlier path to that node.)

3.2 Relation to existing models

Our theoretical model is closest to, and can efficiently simulate, the LogP model [8], which differs from our model most notably with its three hardware parameters,

L, interprocessor latency cost incurred on network,

o, messaging overhead incurred by sending and receiving processes,

g, inverse bandwidth (per byte cost) of a message.

Both models are asynchronous and measure the cost of an algorithm along the longest execution path in a given schedule, so a close relationship is expected. Since our model only has a single latency parameter α, while the LogP model considers overhead o, injection rate g, and interprocessor latency L, we will consider the special case where $L = o$, i.e., the sequential overhead of sending a message is equivalent to the network latency of message delivery.

THEOREM 3.1. *If there exists a LogP algorithm for computation G with cost $L \cdot s + g \cdot b$, there exists a point-to-point parallel schedule $\bar{G}$ with synchronization cost $O(\alpha \cdot s)$ and bandwidth cost $O(\beta \cdot b)$.*

PROOF. Consider the given LogP algorithm for G, which encodes a timeline of LogP actions for each processor. We now construct an equivalent schedule $\bar{G} = (\bar{V}, \bar{E})$. Consider the kth (LogP) action of the ith processor, which is either a local computation, a sent message, or a received message. For each computation, add a vertex to $\bar{V}_{\mathrm{comp}} \subset \bar{V}$. If the kth action of the ith processor is a send of dataset U which is received as the lth action of processor j, add nodes v_1, s, and v_2 to $\bar{V}$ where

- $v_1 \subset \bar{V}_{\mathrm{send}}$, $\hat{s}(v_1) = U$, $\hat{c}(v_1) = i$, and v_1 succeeds the $(k-1)$th action of processor i and precedes s,

- $s \subset \bar{V}_{\mathrm{sync}}$ and s has an incoming edge from v_1 as well as from the $(l-1)$th action of processor j, and outgoing edges to v_2 and the $(k+1)$th action of processor i,

- $v_2 \subset \bar{V}_{\mathrm{recv}}$, $\hat{r}(v_2) = U$, and v_2 is of color j with an incoming edge from s.

Since each synchronization node has two paths through it, $\bar{G}$ is a point-to-point schedule. A runtime bound on the LogP algorithm provides us with a bound on the cost of any path in $\bar{G}$, since any path in the LogP algorithm exists in $\bar{G}$ and vice versa. Every adjacent pair of actions on this path will be done consecutively on a single processor or the path will follow some message of size

m. In the former case, the cost of the LogP message on the path is $o + g \cdot m$, while the cost of this portion of the path in $\bar{G}$ is $\alpha + \beta \cdot m$. In the latter case, the cost of the LogP message is $o \cdot 2 + L + g \cdot m$, while a path in $\bar{G}$ which goes from the sending to the receiving node will incur cost $\alpha + \beta \cdot 2m$. Since we limit our analysis to $L = o$, this means each LogP message cost of $O(L + g \cdot m)$ translates to a cost of $O(\alpha + \beta \cdot m)$ in the constructed schedule. $\square$

Our theoretical model is also a generalization of the BSP model [27]. We show a reduction from any BSP algorithm to an algorithm in our model by adding a global synchronization vertex for every BSP timestep, which follows the local computations and sends posted at each timestep and precedes the receives of these sends at the beginning of the next BSP timestep.

THEOREM 3.2. *Given a BSP algorithm for computation G with t synchronizations and b words communicated, there exists a parallel schedule $\bar{G}$ with synchronization cost $O(\alpha \cdot t)$ and bandwidth cost $O(\beta \cdot b)$.*

PROOF. We construct $\bar{G} = (\bar{V}, \bar{E})$ from the BSP schedule by adding a single synchronization vertex to $\bar{V}_{\mathrm{sync}}$ for each (BSP) timestep and connecting all processors' execution paths to this vertex. So, for the jth of the t timesteps, we define a global synchronization vertex s_j, as well as vertices $F_{1j}, \ldots, F_{pj}$ in $\bar{V}_{\mathrm{comp}}$ corresponding to the local computation done by each processor during that timestep. For the kth message sent by processor i during timestep j, we add a vertex S_{ijk} to $\bar{V}_{\mathrm{send}}$ and for the lth message received by processor i, we add a vertex R_{ijl} to $\bar{V}_{\mathrm{recv}}$. The execution path of processor i will then take the form

$$\pi_i = \{ \ldots, F_{ij}, S_{ij1}, S_{ij2}, \ldots, s_j, R_{ij1}, R_{ij2}, \ldots, F_{i,j+1}, \ldots \}.$$

The communication cost of $\bar{G}$ constructed in this way will be at least $\alpha \cdot t + \beta \cdot b$ but no more than $\alpha \cdot t + \beta \cdot 2b$, since for every timestep, the cost of $\bar{G}$ includes not only all paths which correspond to tasks performed (sequentially) on each processor, but also paths which count the sends of one processor and the receives of the next, so the bandwidth cost of some messages may be double-counted (vs. BSP), hence the $\beta \cdot 2b$ upper bound. $\square$

4. GENERAL LOWER BOUND THEOREM VIA BUBBLE EXPANSION

In this section, we introduce the concept of dependency bubbles and their expansion. Bubbles represent sets of interdependent computations, and their expansion allows us to analyze the cost of computation and communication for any parallelization and communication schedule. We will show that if a dependency graph has a path along which bubbles expand as some function of the length of the path, any parallelization of this dependency graph must sacrifice synchronization or incur higher computational and data volume costs, which scale with the total size and cross-section size (minimum cut size) of the bubbles, respectively.

4.1 Bubble expansion

Given a directed graph $G = (V, E)$, we say $v_n \in V$ **depends on** $v_1 \in V$ if and only if there is a path $\mathcal{P} \subset V$ connecting v_1 to v_n, i.e., $\mathcal{P} = \{v_1, \ldots, v_n\}$ such that $\{(v_1, v_2), \ldots, (v_{n-1}, v_n)\} \subset E$. We denote a sequence of (not necessarily adjacent) vertices $\{w_1, \ldots, w_n\}$ a **dependency path**, if for $i \in \{1, \ldots, n-1\}$, w_{i+1} depends on w_i. Any subsequence of a dependency path is again a dependency path, called simply a **subpath**, which context will disambiguate from its usual definition.

The (**dependency**) **bubble** around a dependency path $\mathcal{P}$ connecting v_1 to v_n is a subgraph $\zeta(G, \mathcal{P}) = (V_\zeta, E_\zeta)$ where $V_\zeta \subset V$,

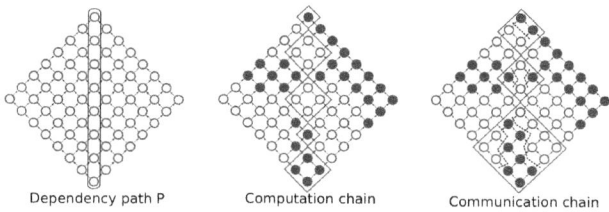

Figure 2: Illustration of the construction in the proof of Theorem 4.1 in the case of a diamond DAG (e.g., [18]), depicting a dependency path, and communication and computation chains about that path, for a 2-processor parallelization.

each vertex $u \in V_\zeta$ lies on a dependency path $\{v_1, \ldots, u, \ldots, v_n\}$ in G, and $E_\zeta = (V_\zeta \times V_\zeta) \cap E$. (If G is a dependency graph, this bubble corresponds to all vertices which must be computed between the start and end of the path.) Equivalently, the bubble may be defined as the union of all paths between v_1 and v_n.

4.2 Lower bounds based on bubble expansion

A $\frac{1}{q}$-**balanced vertex separator** $Q \subset V$ of a directed graph $G = (V, E)$ splits $V \setminus Q = V_1 \cup V_2$ so that $\min(|V_1|, |V_2|) \geq \lfloor |V|/q \rfloor$ and $E \subset (V_1 \times V_1) \cup (V_2 \times V_2) \cup (Q \times V) \cup (V \times Q)$. We denote the minimum size $|Q|$ of a $\frac{1}{q}$-balanced separator Q of G as $\chi_q(G)$. If $\zeta(G, \mathcal{P})$ is the bubble around dependency path $\mathcal{P}$, we say $\chi_q(\zeta(G, \mathcal{P}))$ is its **cross-section expansion**.

We call a directed graph G a (ϵ, σ)-**path-expander** if there exists a dependency path $\mathcal{P}$ in G and a positive integer constant $k \ll |\mathcal{P}|$ such that every subpath $\mathcal{R} \subset \mathcal{P}$ of length $|\mathcal{R}| \geq k$ has bubble $\zeta(G, \mathcal{R}) = (V_\zeta, E_\zeta)$ with cross-section expansion $\chi_q(\zeta(G, \mathcal{R})) = \Omega(\epsilon(|\mathcal{R}|))$ for all real numbers $2 \leq q \ll |\mathcal{P}|$, and bubble size $|V_\zeta| = \Theta(\sigma(|\mathcal{R}|))$, for the given real-valued functions ϵ, σ which for all real numbers $b \geq k$ are positive and increasing with $1 \leq \epsilon(b+1) - \epsilon(b) \leq c_\epsilon \epsilon(b)$ and $1 \leq \sigma(b+1) - \sigma(b) \leq c_\sigma \sigma(b)$ for some positive real constants $c_\epsilon, c_\sigma \ll |\mathcal{P}|$.

THEOREM 4.1 (GENERAL BUBBLE LOWER BOUNDS). *Suppose a dependency graph G is a (ϵ, σ)-path-expander about dependency path $\mathcal{P}$. Then, for any schedule of G corresponding to a parallelization (of G) in which no processor computes more than half of the vertices of $\zeta(G, \mathcal{P})$, there exists an integer $b \in [k, |\mathcal{P}|]$ such that the computation (F), bandwidth (W), and latency (S) costs incurred are*

$$F = \Omega\left(\sigma(b) \cdot |\mathcal{P}|/b\right), \quad W = \Omega\left(\epsilon(b) \cdot |\mathcal{P}|/b\right), \quad S = \Omega\left(|\mathcal{P}|/b\right).$$

PROOF. We consider any possible parallelization, which implies a coloring of the vertices of $G = (V, E)$, $V = \bigcup_{i=1}^p C_i$, and show that any schedule $\bar{G} = (\bar{V}, \bar{E})$, as defined in Section 3, incurs the desired computation, bandwidth, and latency costs. Our proof technique works by defining a chain of bubbles within G in a way that allows us to accumulate the costs along the chain.

The tradeoff between work and synchronization, $F = \Omega(\sigma(b) \cdot |\mathcal{P}|/b)$ and $S = \Omega(|\mathcal{P}|/b)$, can be derived by considering a computation chain: a sequence of monochrome bubbles along $\mathcal{P}$, each corresponding to a set of computations performed sequentially by some processor (see computation chain in Figure 2). However, to obtain the bandwidth lower bound, we must instead show that there exists a sequence of bubbles in which some processor computes a constant fraction of each bubble; we then sum the bandwidth costs incurred by each bubble in the sequence. We show a communication chain (a sequence of multicolored bubbles) for a diamond DAG in Figure 2.

By hypothesis, there exists $k \ll |\mathcal{P}|$ such that every subpath $\mathcal{R} \subset \mathcal{P}$ of length $|\mathcal{R}| \geq k$ induces a bubble $\zeta(G, \mathcal{R}) = (V_\zeta, E_\zeta)$ of size $|V_\zeta| = \Theta(\sigma(|\mathcal{R}|))$. The Θ-notation implies that there exists a positive finite constant $d \ll |\mathcal{P}|$ such that for all $|\mathcal{R}| \geq k$,

$$\sigma(|\mathcal{R}|)/d \leq |V_\zeta| \leq d \cdot \sigma(|\mathcal{R}|).$$

We also fix the constant

$$q = \max\left\{d^2(c_\sigma + 1) + 1, d \cdot \sigma(k)\right\};$$

note that $2 \leq q \ll |\mathcal{P}|$, since $d \geq 1$ and $k, d, c_\sigma, \sigma(k) \ll |\mathcal{P}|$.

We define the bubbles via the following procedure, which partitions the dependency path $\mathcal{P}$ into subpaths by iteratively removing leading subpaths. In this manner, assume we have defined subpaths $\mathcal{R}_j$ for $j \in \{1, \ldots, i-1\}$. Let the tail (remaining trailing subpath) of the original dependency path be

$$\mathcal{T}_i = \mathcal{P} \setminus \bigcup_{j=1}^{i-1} \mathcal{R}_j = \left\{t_1, \ldots, t_{|\mathcal{T}_i|}\right\}.$$

Our procedure defines the next leading subpath of length r, $\mathcal{R}_i = \{t_1, \ldots, t_r\}, k \leq r \leq |\mathcal{T}_i|$, with bubble $\zeta(G, \mathcal{R}_i) = (V_i, E_i)$. Suppose processor l computes t_1. The procedure picks the shortest leading subpath of $\mathcal{T}_i$ of length $r \geq k$ which satisfies the following two conditions, and terminates if no such path can be defined.

Condition 1: The subset of the bubble that processor l computes, $C_l \cap V_i$, is of size $|C_l \cap V_i| \geq \lfloor |V_i|/q \rfloor$

Condition 2: The subset of the bubble that processor l does not compute, $V_i \setminus C_l$, is also of size $|V_i \setminus C_l| \geq \lfloor |V_i|/q \rfloor$

Let c be the number of subpaths the procedure outputs and $\mathcal{T} = \mathcal{P} \setminus \bigcup_{j=1}^c \mathcal{R}_j = \{t_1, \ldots, t_{|\mathcal{T}|}\}$ be the tail remaining at the end of the procedure. We consider the two cases, $|\mathcal{T}| = \Omega(|\mathcal{P}|)$ and $\sum_j |\mathcal{R}_j| = \Omega(|\mathcal{P}|)$, at least one of which must hold. We show that in either case, the theorem is true for some value of b.

If $|\mathcal{T}| = \Omega(|\mathcal{P}|)$ (the tail is long), we show that Condition 1 must be satisfied for any leading subpath of $\mathcal{T}$. Our proof works by induction on the length of the leading subpath $k \leq r \leq |\mathcal{T}|$, with the subpath given by $\mathcal{K}_r = \{t_1, \ldots, t_r\}$. We define the bubble about $\mathcal{K}_r$ as $\zeta(G, \mathcal{K}_r) = (V_r, E_r)$. When $r = k$, Condition 1 is satisfied because $|V_r|/q \leq d \cdot \sigma(k)/q \leq 1$ and processor l computes at least one element, t_1.

For $r > k$, we have

$$|V_r| \leq d \cdot \sigma(r) \leq d(c_\sigma + 1) \cdot \sigma(r-1) \leq (q-1)/d \cdot \sigma(r-1).$$

Further, by induction, Condition 1 was satisfied for $\mathcal{K}_{r-1}$ which implies Condition 2 was not satisfied for $\mathcal{K}_{r-1}$ (otherwise the procedure would have terminated with a subpath of length $r-1$). Now, using bounds on bubble growth we that since Condition 2 was not satisfied for $\mathcal{K}_{r-1}$, Condition 1 has to be satisfied for the subsequent bubble, $\mathcal{K}_r$,

$$\begin{aligned}
|C_l \cap V_r| &\geq |C_l \cap V_{r-1}| \geq |V_{r-1}| - \lfloor |V_{r-1}|/q \rfloor \\
&\geq (q-1)/q \cdot |V_{r-1}| \geq (q-1)/(dq) \cdot \sigma(r-1) \\
&\geq 1/q \cdot |V_r| \geq \lfloor |V_r|/q \rfloor,
\end{aligned}$$

so Condition 1 holds for $\mathcal{K}_r$ for $r \in \{k, \ldots, |\mathcal{T}|\}$. Further, since the tail is long, $|\mathcal{T}| = \Omega(|\mathcal{P}|)$, due to Condition 1, processor l must compute $F \geq \lfloor |V_{\zeta(G, \mathcal{T})}|/q \rfloor = \Omega(\sigma(|\mathcal{T}|))$ vertices. Since, by assumption, no processor can compute more than half of the vertices of $\zeta(G, \mathcal{P})$, we claim there exists a subpath $\mathcal{Q}$ of $\mathcal{P}$, $\mathcal{T} \subset \mathcal{Q} \subset \mathcal{P}$, where processor l computes $\lfloor |V_{\zeta(G, \mathcal{Q})}|/q \rfloor$ vertices and does not compute $\lfloor |V_{\zeta(G, \mathcal{Q})}|/q \rfloor$ vertices. The subpath $\mathcal{Q}$ may always be found to satisfy these two conditions simultaneously, since we can grow $\mathcal{Q}$ backward from $\mathcal{T}$ until Condition 2 is satisfied, i.e., processor l does not compute at least $\lfloor |V_{\zeta(G,\mathcal{Q})}|/q \rfloor$ vertices, and we will not violate the first condition that $|C_l \cap V_{\zeta(G,\mathcal{Q})}| \geq \lfloor |V_{\zeta(G,\mathcal{Q})}|/q \rfloor$, which holds for $\mathcal{Q} = \mathcal{T}$, due to bounds on growth of $|V_{\zeta(G,\mathcal{Q})}|$. The proof of this assertion is the same as the inductive proof above which showed that Condition 1 holds on $\mathcal{K}_r$. So, the size of processor l's communicated set is at least the size of a $\frac{1}{q}$-balanced vertex separator of $\zeta(G, \mathcal{Q})$, showing that $W = \Omega(\epsilon(|\mathcal{Q}|)) = \Omega(\epsilon(|\mathcal{T}|))$. Since these costs are incurred along a path in the schedule consisting of the work and communication done only by processor l, the bounds hold for $b = |\mathcal{T}|$; note that $\Omega(|\mathcal{P}|/|\mathcal{T}|) = \Omega(1)$, because $|\mathcal{T}| = \Omega(|\mathcal{P}|)$.

In the second case, $\sum_j |\mathcal{R}_j| = \Omega(|\mathcal{P}|)$, the procedure generates subpaths with a total size proportional to the size of $\mathcal{P}$. For each $i \in \{1, \ldots, c\}$, consider

- the task $u \in \bar{V}$ during which processor l computed the first vertex t_1 on the path $\mathcal{R}_i$, i.e., $t_1 \in F(u)$;

- the task $v \in \bar{V}$ during which processor l computed its last vertex within the ith bubble, so $\hat{f}(v) \cap V_i \cap C_l \neq \emptyset$.

- the task $w \in \bar{V}$ during which the last vertex on the subpath $\mathcal{R}_i$, t_r, was computed, i.e., $t_r \subset F(w)$.

Since t_r depends on all other vertices in V_i, there will be an execution path $\pi_i = \{u, \ldots, v, \ldots w\} \subset \bar{V}$ in the schedule $\bar{G}$. Since $F(u)$ contains the first vertex of $\mathcal{R}_i$, all communication necessary to satisfy the dependencies of processor l (dependencies of $V_i \cap C_l$) within bubble V_i must be incurred along π_i. This communicated set is given by

$$\hat{T}_{il} = \{u : (u, w) \in [(C_l \times (V_i \setminus C_l)) \cup ((V_i \setminus C_l) \times C_l)] \cap E_i\},$$

which is a separator of $\zeta(G, \mathcal{R}_i)$ and is $\frac{1}{q}$-balanced due to Conditions 1 and 2 in the definition of $\mathcal{R}_i$. We use the lower bound on the minimum separator of a bubble to obtain a lower bound on the size of the communicated set for processor l in the ith bubble,

$$|\hat{T}_{il}| \geq \chi_q(\zeta(G, \mathcal{R}_i)) = \Omega(\epsilon(|\mathcal{R}_i|)),$$

where we are able to bound the cross-section expansion of $\zeta(G, \mathcal{R}_i)$, since $|\mathcal{R}_i| \geq k$. There exists a dependency path between the last element of $\mathcal{R}_i$ and the first of $\mathcal{R}_{i+1}$ since they are subpaths of $\mathcal{P}$, so every bubble $\zeta(G, \mathcal{R}_i)$ must be computed entirely before any members of $\zeta(G, \mathcal{R}_{i+1})$ are computed. Therefore, there is an execution path π_{critical} in the schedule $\bar{G}$ which contains $\pi_i \subset \pi_{\text{critical}}$ as a subpath for every $i \in \{1, \ldots, c\}$. The execution cost of $\bar{G}$ is bounded below by the cost of π_{critical},

$$T(\bar{G}) \geq \sum_{v \in \pi_{\text{critical}}} \hat{t}(v) = \alpha \cdot S + \beta \cdot W + \gamma \cdot F,$$

which we can bound below component-wise,

$$F = \sum_{v \in \pi_{\text{critical}} \cap \bar{V}_{\text{comp}}} |\hat{f}(v)| \geq \sum_{i=1}^{c} \frac{1}{q} |\zeta(G, \mathcal{R}_i)| = \Omega\left(\sum_{i=1}^{c} \sigma(|\mathcal{R}_i|)\right),$$

$$W = \sum_{v \in \pi_{\text{critical}} \cap \bar{V}_{\text{send}}} |\hat{s}(v)| + \sum_{v \in \pi_{\text{critical}} \cap \bar{V}_{\text{recv}}} |\hat{r}(v)| \geq \sum_{i=1}^{c} \chi_q(\zeta(G, \mathcal{R}_i))$$

$$= \Omega\left(\sum_{i=1}^{c} \epsilon(|\mathcal{R}_i|)\right).$$

Further, since each bubble contains vertices computed by multiple processes, between the first and last vertex on the subpath forming

each bubble, each π_i must go through at least one synchronization vertex, therefore, we also have a lower bound on latency cost,

$$S \geq \sum_{v \in \pi_{\text{critical}} \cap V_{\text{sync}}} 1 \geq c.$$

Because $|\mathcal{R}_i| \geq k$, $\sigma(b+1) - \sigma(b) \geq 1$ and $\epsilon(b+1) - \epsilon(b) \geq 1$ for all $b \geq k$, and the sum of all the lengths of the subpaths is bounded, $\sum_i |\mathcal{R}_i| \leq |\mathcal{P}|$, the above lower bounds for F and W are minimized when all values $|\mathcal{R}_i|$ are equal[1]. Thus, we can replace $|\mathcal{R}_i|$ for each i by $b = \lfloor \sum_j |\mathcal{R}_j|/c \rfloor = \Theta(|\mathcal{P}|/c)$, simplifying the bounds to obtain the conclusion. $\square$

COROLLARY 4.2 (*d-DIMENSIONAL BUBBLE LOWER BOUNDS*). *Suppose there exists a dependency path $\mathcal{P}$ in a dependency graph G and integers $2 \leq d \ll k \ll |\mathcal{P}|$ such that every subpath $\mathcal{R} \subset \mathcal{P}$ of length $|\mathcal{R}| \geq k$ has bubble $\zeta(G, \mathcal{R}) = (V_\zeta, E_\zeta)$ with cross-section expansion $\chi_q(\zeta(G, \mathcal{R})) = \Omega(|\mathcal{R}|^{d-1})$ for all real numbers $2 \leq q \ll |\mathcal{P}|$, and has bubble size $|V_\zeta| = \Theta(|\mathcal{R}|^d)$. Then, the computation (F), bandwidth (W), and latency (S) costs incurred by any schedule of G corresponding to a parallelization (of G) in which no processor computes more than half of the vertices of $\zeta(G, \mathcal{P})$ must obey the relations*

$$F \cdot S^{d-1} = \Omega\left(|\mathcal{P}|^d\right), \quad W \cdot S^{d-2} = \Omega\left(|\mathcal{P}|^{d-1}\right).$$

PROOF. This is an application of Theorem 4.1 with $\epsilon(b) = b^{d-1}$ and $\sigma(b) = b^d$. The theorem yields

$$F = \Omega\left(b^{d-1} \cdot |\mathcal{P}|\right), \quad W = \Omega\left(b^{d-2} \cdot |\mathcal{P}|\right), \quad S = \Omega(|\mathcal{P}|/b).$$

These equations can be manipulated algebraically to obtain the conclusion. $\square$

5. LOWER BOUNDS ON LATTICE HYPERGRAPH CUTS

For any hypergraph $H = (V, E)$, we say a hyperedge $e \in E$ is **internal** to some $V' \subset V$ if $e \subset V'$. If no $e \in E$ is adjacent to (i.e., contains) a $v \in V' \subset V$, then say V' is **disconnected** from H. A $\frac{1}{q}$-**balanced (hyperedge) cut** of is a subset of E whose removal from H partitions $V = V_1 \cup V_2$ with $\min(|V_1|, |V_2|) \geq \lfloor |V|/q \rfloor$ such that all remaining (uncut) hyperedges are internal to one of the two parts.

5.1 Lattice hypergraphs

We define a d-dimensional **lattice hypergraph** $H = (V, E)$ of breadth n, with $|V| = \binom{n}{d}$ vertices and $|E| = \binom{n}{d-1}$ hyperedges. Each vertex is represented as $v_{i_1, \ldots, i_d} = (i_1, \ldots, i_d)$ for $\{i_1, \ldots, i_d\} \in \{1, \ldots, n\}^d$ with $i_1 < \cdots < i_d$. Each hyperedge connects all vertices which share $d - 1$ indices, that is $e_{j_1, \ldots, j_{d-1}}$ for $\{j_1, \ldots, j_{d-1}\} \in \{1, \ldots, n\}^{d-1}$ with $j_1 < \cdots < j_{d-1}$ includes all vertices $v_{i_1, \ldots, i_d}$ for which $\{j_1, \ldots, j_{d-1}\} \subset \{i_1, \ldots, i_d\}$. There are $n - (d-1)$ vertices per hyperedge, and each vertex appears in d hyperedges. Each hyperedge intersects $(d-1)(n - (d-1))$ other hyperedges, each at a unique vertex.

A key step in the lower bound proofs in [14] and [3] was the use of an inequality introduced by Loomis and Whitney [16]. We will use this inequality (in the following form) to prove a lower bound on the cut size of a lattice hypergraph.

---

[1]This mathematical relation can be demonstrated by a basic application of Lagrange multipliers.

THEOREM 5.1 (LOOMIS-WHITNEY). *Let V be a finite, nonempty set of d-tuples $(i_1, \ldots, i_d) \in \mathbb{N}^d$; then*

$$|V| \leq \prod_{j=1}^{d} |\pi_j(V)|^{1/(d-1)},$$

where, for $j \in \{1, \ldots, d\}$, $\pi_j \colon \mathbb{N}^d \to \mathbb{N}^{d-1}$ is the projection

$$\pi_j(i_1, \ldots, i_d) = (i_1, \ldots, i_{j-1}, i_{j+1}, \ldots, i_d).$$

THEOREM 5.2. *For $2 \leq d, q \ll n$, the minimum $\frac{1}{q}$-balanced cut of a d-dimensional lattice hypergraph $H = (V, E)$ of breadth n is of size $\epsilon_q(H) = \Omega(n^{d-1}/q^{(d-1)/d})$.*

PROOF. We prove Theorem 5.2 by induction on the dimension, d. In the base case $d = 2$, we must show that $\epsilon_q(H) = \Omega(n/\sqrt{q})$. Consider any $\frac{1}{q}$-balanced cut $Q \subset E$, which splits the vertices into two disjoint sets V_1 and V_2. Note that in 2 dimensions, every pair of hyperedges overlaps, i.e., for $i_1, i_2 \in \{1, \ldots, n\}$ with $i_1 < i_2$, $e_{i_1} \cap e_{i_2} = \{v_{i_1, i_2}\}$. If the first partition, V_1, has an internal hyperedge, then since every pair of hyperedges overlaps, V_1 is adjacent to all hyperedges in H. Therefore, every hyperedge adjacent to the other part $V_2 \subset V$ must be in the cut, Q. On the other hand, if V_1 has no internal hyperedges, then all hyperedges adjacent to V_1 must connect both parts, and thus are cut. So, without loss of generality we will assume that V_2 is disconnected after the cut. We now argue that $\Omega(n/\sqrt{q})$ hyperedges must be cut to disconnect V_2.

Since the cut is $\frac{1}{q}$-balanced, we know that $|V_2| \geq n(n-1)/(2q)$. To disconnect each $v_{i_1, i_2} \in V_2$, both adjacent hyperedges (e_{i_1} and e_{i_2}) must be cut. We can bound from below the cut size by first obtaining a lower bound on the product of the sizes of the projections $\pi_1(v_{i_1, i_2}) = i_2$ and $\pi_2(v_{i_1, i_2}) = i_1$ via the Loomis-Whitney inequality (Theorem 5.1),

$$|\pi_1(V_2)| \cdot |\pi_2(V_2)| \geq |V_2| \geq n(n-1)/(2q),$$

and then concluding

$$\epsilon_q(H) = |\pi_1(V_2) \cup \pi_2(V_2)| \geq (|\pi_1(V_2)| + |\pi_2(V_2)|)/2$$
$$\geq \sqrt{|\pi_1(V_2)||\pi_2(V_2)|} \geq \sqrt{n(n-1)/(2q)} = \Omega(n/\sqrt{q}),$$

since the size of the union of the two projections equals the number of hyperedges that must be cut to disconnect V_2.

For the inductive step, we assume that the theorem holds for dimension $d - 1$ and prove that it must also hold for dimension d, where $d \geq 3$. In d dimensions, we define a **hyperplane** $x_{k_1, \ldots, k_{d-2}}$ for each $\{k_1, \ldots, k_{d-2}\} \in \{1, \ldots, n\}^{d-2}$ with $k_1 < \cdots < k_{d-2}$ as the set of all hyperedges $e_{j_1, \ldots, j_{d-1}}$ which satisfy $\{k_1, \ldots, k_{d-2}\} \subset \{j_1, \ldots, j_{d-1}\}$. Thus, each of the $|X| = \binom{n}{d-2}$ hyperplanes contains $n - (d - 2)$ hyperedges, and each hyperedge is in $d - 1$ hyperplanes. Note that each hyperplane shares a unique hyperedge with $(d-2)(n-(d-2))$ other hyperplanes. Further, each hyperedge in a hyperplane intersects each other hyperedge in the same hyperplane in a unique vertex, and the set of all these vertices are precisely those sharing the $d - 2$ indices defining the hyperplane.

Consider any $\frac{1}{q}$-balanced hyperedge cut $Q \subset E$. Since all hyperedges which contain vertices in both V_1 and V_2 must be part of the cut Q, all vertices are either disconnected completely by the cut or remain in hyperedges which are all internal to either V_1 or V_2. Let $U_1 \subset V_1$ be the vertices contained in a hyperedge internal to V_1 and let $U_2 \subset V_2$ be the vertices contained in a hyperedge internal to V_2. Since both V_1 and V_2 contain $\lfloor n^d/q \rfloor$ vertices, either $\lfloor n^d/(2q) \rfloor$ vertices must be in internal hyperedges within both V_1 as well as V_2, that is,

case (i): $|U_1| \geq \lfloor n^d/(2q) \rfloor$ and $|U_2| \geq \lfloor n^d/(2q) \rfloor$,

or there must be $\lfloor n^d/2q \rfloor$ vertices that are disconnected completely by the cut,

case (ii): $|(V_1 \setminus U_1) \cup (V_2 \setminus U_2)| \geq \lfloor n^d/(2q) \rfloor$.

In case (i), since both U_1 and U_2 have at least $\lfloor n^d/(2q) \rfloor$ vertices, we know that there are at least $|U_1|/(n-(d-1)) \geq \lfloor n^{d-1}/(2q) \rfloor$ hyperedges W_1 which are internal to V_1 after the cut Q, and a similar set of hyperedges W_2 internal to V_2. We now obtain a lower bound on the size of the cut Q for this case by counting the hyperplanes which Q must contain. Our argument relies on the idea that if two hyperedges are in the same hyperplane, the entire hyperplane must be disconnected (all of its hyperedges must be part of the cut Q) in order to disconnect the two hyperedges. This allows us to bound the number of hyperplanes which must be disconnected in order for W_1 to be disconnected from W_2.

We define a new $(d-1)$-dimensional lattice hypergraph $H' = (E, X)$, with vertices and hyperedges equal to the hyperedges and hyperplanes of the original hypergraph H. The cut Q induces a $\frac{1}{2q}$-balanced cut on H' since it creates two disconnected partitions of hyperedges: W_1 and W_2, each of size $\lfloor n^{d-1}/(2q) \rfloor$. We can assert a lower bound on the size of any $\frac{1}{2q}$-balanced cut of H' by induction,

$$\epsilon_q(H') = \Omega\left(n^{d-2}/(2q)^{(d-2)/(d-1)}\right) = \Omega\left(n^{d-2}/q^{(d-2)/(d-1)}\right).$$

This lower bound on cut size of H' yields a lower bound on the number of hyperplanes which must be cut to disconnect the hyperedges into two balanced sets W_1 and W_2. Remembering that disconnecting each hyperplane requires cutting all $n - (d - 2)$ of its internal hyperedges (and also that each pair of hyperplanes overlap on at most one hyperedge), we conclude that the number of hyperedges cut (in Q) must be at least

$$\epsilon_q(H) \geq \frac{(n - (d - 2))}{d - 1} \epsilon_q(H') = \Omega\left(n^{d-1}/q^{(d-2)/(d-1)}\right).$$

The quantity on the right is always larger than the lower bound we are trying to prove, $\epsilon_q(H) = \Omega(n^{d-1}/q^{(d-1)/d})$, so the proof for this case is complete.

In case (ii), we know that $\lfloor n^d/(2q) \rfloor$ vertices $\bar{U} \subset V$ are disconnected by the cut (before the cut, every vertex was adjacent to d hyperedges). We define d projections,

$$\pi_j(v_{i_1, \ldots, i_d}) = (i_1, \ldots, i_{j-1}, i_{j+1}, \ldots, i_d),$$

for $j \in \{1, \ldots, d\}$ corresponding to each of d hyperedges adjacent to $v_{i_1, \ldots, i_d}$. We apply the Loomis-Whitney inequality (Theorem 5.1) to obtain a lower bound on the product of the size of the projections,

$$\prod_{j=1}^{d} |\pi_j(\bar{U})|^{1/(d-1)} \geq |\bar{U}| \geq \lfloor n^d/(2q) \rfloor,$$

and then conclude with a lower bound on the number of hyperedges in the cut of H,

$$\epsilon_q(H) \geq \left| \bigcup_{j=1}^{d} \pi_j(\bar{U}) \right| \geq \max_{j=1}^{d} |\pi_j(\bar{U})| \geq \prod_{j=1}^{d} |\pi_j(\bar{U})|^{1/d}$$
$$\geq \lfloor n^d/(2q) \rfloor^{(d-1)/d} = \Omega\left(n^{d-1}/q^{(d-1)/d}\right).$$

By induction, this lower bound holds for all $2 \leq d \ll n$. $\square$

5.2 Parent hypergraphs

In order to apply our lower bounds to applications, we consider how a given hypergraph can be transformed without increasing the minimum-cut size. We employ the idea that it is possible to merge sets of hyperedges which define connected components without increasing the size of any cut. Given a hypergraph $H = (V, E)$, a disjoint partition R of the hyperedges E defines a **parent hypergraph**, if every sub-hypergraph induced by (adjacent to) each subset of hyperedges $r_i \in R$, $H_i = (y_i, r_i)$, is connected. In particular, the parent hypergraph is $H' = (V, Y)$ where each hyperedge $y_i \in Y$ contains to all vertices adjacent to hyperedge part r_i.

We obtain lower bounds on the vertex separator size of a directed or undirected graph by constructing a parent hypergraph in which every vertex is adjacent to a constant number of hyperedges. The following theorem states this result for vertex separators of (undirected) hypergraphs, which immediately generalizes the case of undirected graphs, and also directed graphs, since in our definition of a vertex separator, all hyperedges leaving or entering one of the two parts to or from a node outside the part must be disconnected.

THEOREM 5.3. *Given a hypergraph $H = (V, E)$, consider any parent hypergraph $H' = (V, Y)$, defined by a disjoint hyperedge partition R. If the degree of each vertex in H' is at most k, the minimum $\frac{1}{q}$-balanced hyperedge cut of H' is no larger than k times the minimum size of a $\frac{1}{q}$-balanced vertex separator of H.*

PROOF. Consider any vertex-separator $S \subset V$ of H. We construct a hyperedge cut X' of H' consisting of all hyperedges adjacent to S in H'. X' is a cut of H' since for any path consisting of hyperedges $\mathcal{P} = \{y_1, y_2, \ldots\}$ in H', corresponding to parts $\{r_1, r_2, \ldots\}$, there exists a path in H consisting of hyperedges $\mathcal{Q} = \{e_{11}, e_{12}, \ldots\} \cup \{e_{21}, e_{22}, \ldots\} \cup \ldots$, where for each i, $\{e_{i1}, e_{i2}, \ldots\} \subset r_i$. Therefore, since S disconnects every path though H between two partitions of vertices, the cut X' must disconnect all such paths also. The cut X' is also $\frac{1}{q}$-balanced since the vertex separator is and the separated vertex partitions stay the same. Further, since the maximum degree of any vertex in H' is k, the cut X' is of size at most $k \cdot |S|$. □

6. APPLICATIONS

We now apply the dependency expansion analysis Section 4 to obtain lower bounds on the costs associated with a few specific numerical linear algebra algorithms. Our analysis proceeds by obtaining lower bounds on the minimum-cut size of a parent lattice hypergraph corresponding to the computation. By employing parent hypergraphs, we express all possible reduction tree summation orders. In particular, if $T = (R, E)$ is a tree in a dependency graph which sums a set of vertices $S \subset R$, each pair of vertices in S must be connected via undirected paths. Therefore, we can define a hyperedge in a parent hypergraph corresponding to this reduction tree, which contains S and ignores the intermediate vertices $R \setminus S$.

6.1 Triangular solve

First, we consider a parameterized family of dependency graphs $G_{TR}(n)$ associated with an algorithm for the triangular solve (TRSV) operation. In TRSV, we are interested in computing a vector $\mathbf{x}$ of length n, given a dense nonsingular lower-triangular matrix $\mathbf{L}$ and a vector $\mathbf{y}$, satisfying $\mathbf{L} \cdot \mathbf{x} = \mathbf{y}$, i.e., $\sum_{j=1}^{i} L_{ij} \cdot x_j = y_i$, for $i \in \{1, \ldots, n\}$. A sequential TRSV implementation is given in Algorithm 1. For convenience, we introduced the intermediate matrix $\mathbf{Z}$ (which need not be formed explicitly in practice), and corresponding intermediate 'update' vertices $\{Z_{ij} : i, j \in \{1, \ldots, n\}, j <$

Algorithm 1 Triangular solve (TRSV) algorithm

$\mathbf{x} = \text{TRSV}(\mathbf{L}, \mathbf{y}, n)$
1 **for** $i = 1$ **to** n
2   **for** $j = 1$ **to** $i - 1$
3         $Z_{ij} = L_{ij} \cdot x_j$
4      $x_i = \left(y_i - \sum_{j=1}^{i-1} Z_{ij} \right) / L_{ii}$

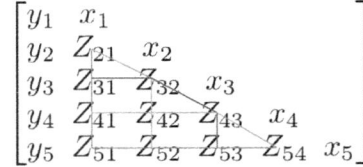

$$\begin{bmatrix} y_1 & x_1 \\ y_2 & Z_{21} & x_2 \\ y_3 & Z_{31} & Z_{32} & x_3 \\ y_4 & Z_{41} & Z_{42} & Z_{43} & x_4 \\ y_5 & Z_{51} & Z_{52} & Z_{53} & Z_{54} & x_5 \end{bmatrix}$$

Figure 3: Depiction of the hypergraph $H_{TR}(5)$ along with the inputs and outputs; each line of a different color corresponds to a hyperedge.

$i\}$. We see that the computation of Z_{ij} for $i = \{2, \ldots, n\}$ and some $j < i$ depends on the computation of x_j, which in turn influences the computations of Z_{jk} for all $k < j$.

6.1.1 Lower bounds

For fixed n, alternative orders exist for the summation on line 4, leading to multiple dependency graphs $G_{TR}(n)$. However, any order of this summation must eventually combine all partial sums; therefore, the vertices corresponding to the computation of each x_i, i.e., Z_{ij} for all $j \in \{1, \ldots, i-1\}$, must all be connected (via undirected paths) by some reduction tree. We will define a 2-dimensional lattice parent hypergraph $H_{TR}(n) = (V_{TR}(n), E_{TR}(n))$, which will allow us to obtain a communication lower bound for all possible orderings of this computation (i.e., all possible $G_{TR}(n)$), in which we will omit the output and input vertices ($\mathbf{x}$ and $\mathbf{y}$),

$$V_{TR}(n) = \{Z_{ij} : i, j \in \{1, \ldots, i-1\}, i > j\},$$
$$E_{TR}(n) = \{e_i : i \in \{1, \ldots, n\}\},$$
where $e_i = \{Z_{ij} : j \in \{1, \ldots, i-1\}\} \cup \{Z_{ki} : k \in \{i+1, \ldots, n\}\}$.

The hyperedges $E_{TR}(n)$ can be enumerated with respect to either vector $\mathbf{x}$ or $\mathbf{y}$; the ith hyperedge $e_i \in E_{TR}(n)$ includes all intermediate values on which x_i depends (Z_{ij} for $j \in \{1, \ldots, i-1\}$), or which depend on x_i (Z_{ki} for $k \in \{i+1, \ldots, n\}$). This hypergraph is depicted in Figure 3.

LEMMA 6.1. *Any vertex separator of any dependency graph $G_{TR}(n)$ which subdivides the $n(n-1)/2$ intermediate vertices $\mathbf{Z}$ into two disjoint sets of size $\lfloor n^2/(2q) \rfloor$ for some real number $2 \leq q \ll n$ must have size at least*

$$\chi_q(G_{TR}(n)) = \Omega\left(n/\sqrt{q}\right).$$

PROOF. The maximum vertex degree of the parent hypergraph $H_{TR}(n)$ of $G_{TR}(n)$ is 2, so by application of Theorem 5.3, the minimum vertex separator of $G_{TR}(n)$ is at least half the size of the hyperedge cut $H_{TR}(n)$. By Theorem 5.2, any $\frac{1}{q}$-balanced cut of a 2-dimensional lattice hypergraph is of size $\Omega(n/\sqrt{q})$. Therefore, any vertex separator must be of size at least $\chi_q(G_{TR}(n)) = \Omega(n/\sqrt{q})$. □

THEOREM 6.2. *Any parallelization of any dependency graph $G_{TR}(n)$ where two processors compute $\lfloor n^2/(2q) \rfloor$ elements of $\mathbf{Z}$*

(for some $2 \leq q \ll n$) must incur a communication cost of

$$W_{\mathrm{TR}} = \Omega\left(n/\sqrt{q}\right).$$

PROOF. Let G be any dependency graph $G_{\mathrm{TR}}(n)$ for Algorithm 1. Every vertex in G that has an outgoing edge to a vertex computed by a different processor (different color) must be communicated. Since two processors compute $\lfloor n^2/(2q) \rfloor$ vertices of $\mathbf{Z}$, the communicated set can be bounded below by the size of a $\frac{1}{q}$-balanced separator of $\mathbf{Z}$ within $G_{\mathrm{TR}}(n)$. By application of Lemma 6.1, the size of any such separator is at least $\Omega(n/\sqrt{q})$. $\square$

THEOREM 6.3. *Any parallelization of any dependency graph $G_{\mathrm{TR}}(n)$ where two of p processors compute $\lfloor n^2/(2p) \rfloor$ elements of $\mathbf{Z}$ incurs the following computation (F), bandwidth (W), and latency (S) costs, for some $b \in [1, n]$,*

$$F_{\mathrm{TR}} = \Omega\left(n \cdot b\right), \qquad W_{\mathrm{TR}} = \Omega\left(n\right), \qquad S_{\mathrm{TR}} = \Omega\left(n/b\right),$$

and furthermore, $F_{\mathrm{TR}} \cdot S_{\mathrm{TR}} = \Omega\left(n^2\right)$.

PROOF. Let G be any dependency graph $G_{\mathrm{TR}}(n)$ for Algorithm 1. We note that the computation of x_i for $i \in \{1, \ldots, n\}$ requires the computation of Z_{jk} for $j, k \in \{1, \ldots, i\}$ with $k < j$. Furthermore, no element Z_{lm} for $l, m \in \{i+1, \ldots, n\}$ with $l < m$ may be computed until x_i is computed. Consider any subpath $\mathcal{R} \subset \mathcal{P}$ of the dependency path $\mathcal{P} = \{x_1, \ldots, x_n\}$. We recall that the bubble $\zeta(G, \mathcal{R}) = (V_\zeta, E_\zeta)$ around $\mathcal{R}$ is the set of all computations that depend on an element of $\mathcal{R}$ or influence an element of $\mathcal{R}$. Evidently, if $\mathcal{R} = \{x_i, \ldots, x_j\}$, the bubble includes vertices corresponding to a subtriangle of $\mathbf{Z}$, namely, $Z_{kl} \in V_\zeta$ for $k, l \in \{i, \ldots, j\}$ with $l < k$. Therefore, $\zeta(G, \mathcal{R})$ is isomorphic to $G_{\mathrm{TRSV}}(|\mathcal{R}|)$, which implies that $|V_\zeta| = \Theta(|\mathcal{R}|^2)$ and by Lemma 6.1, we have $\chi_q(\zeta(G, \mathcal{R})) = \Omega(|\mathcal{R}|/\sqrt{q})$. Since the bubbles for TRSV are 2-dimensional we apply Corollary 4.2 with $d = 2$ to obtain the conclusion, for some $b \in [1, n]$. $\square$

6.1.2 Attainability

The lower bounds presented above for triangular solve, are attained by the communication-efficient blocked schedule suggested in Papadimitriou and Ullman [18]. In the extended technical report associated with this paper [20], we give a parallel algorithm which uses a schedule with blocking factor b to compute the triangular solve. Our algorithm is similar to the wavefront algorithm given by Heath et al. [12]. Our TRSV algorithm achieves the following costs,

$$F_{\mathrm{TR}} = O(nb), \quad W_{\mathrm{TR}} = O(n), \quad S_{\mathrm{TR}} = O(n/b),$$

which attains our communication lower bounds in Theorems 6.2 and 6.3, for any $b \in \{1, n\}$. Parallel TRSV algorithms in current numerical libraries such as Elemental [19] and ScaLAPACK [7] employ algorithms that attain our lower bound, up to an $O(\log(p))$ factor on the latency cost, due to their use of collectives for communication rather than the point-to-point communication in our wavefront TRSV algorithm.

6.2 Gaussian elimination

In this section, we show that the Gaussian elimination algorithm has 3-dimensional bubble-growth and dependency graphs which satisfy the path expansion properties necessary for the application of Corollary 4.2 with $d = 3$. We consider factorization of a symmetric positive definite matrix via Cholesky factorization (Gaussian elimination is addressed in the associated technical report [20]). We show that these factorizations of n-by-n matrices form an intermediate 3D tensor $\mathbf{Z}$ such that $Z_{ijk} \in \mathbf{Z}$ for $i > j > k \in$

$\{1, \ldots, n\}$, and Z_{ijk} depends on each Z_{lmn} for $l > m > n \in \{1, \ldots, j-1\}$. We note that fast matrix multiplication techniques such as Strassen's algorithm [23], compute a different intermediate and are outside the space of this analysis.

6.2.1 Cholesky factorization

The Cholesky factorization of a symmetric positive definite matrix $\mathbf{A}$, $\mathbf{A} = \mathbf{L} \cdot \mathbf{L}^T$, results in a lower triangular matrix $\mathbf{L}$. A simple sequential algorithm for Cholesky factorization is given in Algorithm 2. We introduced an intermediate tensor $\mathbf{Z}$, whose el-

---

Algorithm 2 Cholesky factorization algorithm

$\mathbf{L} = \mathrm{CHOLESKY}(\mathbf{A}, n)$

1 **for** $j = 1$ **to** n
2    $L_{jj} = \sqrt{A_{ij} - \sum_{k=1}^{j-1} L_{jk} \cdot L_{jk}}$
3   **for** $i = j + 1$ **to** n
4   **for** $k = 1$ **to** $j - 1$
5        $Z_{ijk} = L_{ik} \cdot L_{jk}$
6      $L_{ij} = (A_{ij} - \sum_{k=1}^{j-1} Z_{ijk})/L_{jj}$

---

ements must be computed during any execution of the Cholesky algorithm, although $\mathbf{Z}$ itself need not be stored explicitly in an actual implementation. We note that the Floyd-Warshall [11, 28] all-pairs shortest-paths graph algorithm has the same dependency structure as Cholesky for undirected graphs (and Gaussian Elimination for directed graphs), so our lower bounds may be easily extended to this case. However, alternative algorithms, in particular path-doubling, are capable of solving the all-pairs shortest-paths problem with the same asymptotic communication costs as matrix multiplication [25].

6.2.2 Lower bounds

We note that the summations on lines 2 and 6 of Algorithm 2 can be computed via any summation order (and will be computed in different orders in different parallel algorithms). This implies that the summed vertices are connected in any dependency graph $G_{\mathrm{GE}}(n)$, but the connectivity structure may be different. We define a 3-dimensional lattice parent hypergraph $H_{\mathrm{GE}}(n) = (V_{\mathrm{GE}}(n), E_{\mathrm{GE}}(n))$ for the algorithm which allows us to obtain a lower bound for any possible summation order, as

$$
\begin{aligned}
V_{\mathrm{GE}}(n) = &\{Z_{ijk} : i, j, k \in \{1, \ldots, n\}, i > j > k\}, \\
E_{\mathrm{GE}}(n) = &\{e_{i,j} : i, j \in \{1, \ldots, n\} \text{ with } i > j\} \text{ where} \\
& e_{i,j} = \{Z_{ijk} : k \in \{1, \ldots, j-1\}\} \\
& \cup \{Z_{ikj} : k \in \{j+1, \ldots, i-1\}\} \\
& \cup \{Z_{kij} : k \in \{i+1, \ldots, n\}\}.
\end{aligned}
$$

We also define hyperplanes x_i for $i \in \{1, \ldots, n\}$, where

$$x_i = e_{i,1} \cup e_{i,2} \cup \cdots \cup e_{i,i-1} \cup e_{i+1,i} \cup e_{i+2,i} \cup \cdots \cup e_{n,i}.$$

Figure 4 shows hyperplane x_{12} and hyperedge $e_{12,6}$ on $H_{\mathrm{GE}}(16)$. These hyperplanes correspond to those in the proof of Theorem 5.2.

LEMMA 6.4. *Any vertex separator S within dependency graph $G_{\mathrm{GE}}(n)$ that subdivides the intermediate vertices $\mathbf{Z}$ into two sets of size at least $\lfloor n^3/(3q) \rfloor$ (where $2 \leq q \ll n$) must have size at least*

$$\chi_q(G_{\mathrm{GE}}(n)) = \Omega\left(n^2/q^{2/3}\right).$$

PROOF. The maximum vertex degree of the parent hypergraph $H_{\mathrm{GE}}(n)$ of $G_{\mathrm{GE}}(n)$ is 3, so by application of Theorem 5.3, the

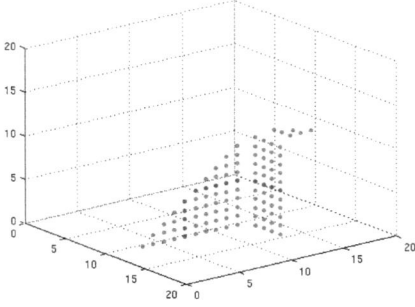

Figure 4: A hyperplane and a hyperedge in $H_{GE}(16)$.

minimum size of a $\frac{1}{q}$-balanced vertex separator of $G_{GE}(n)$ is at least one third that of a $\frac{1}{q}$-balanced hyperedge cut of $H_{GE}(n)$. By Theorem 5.2, a $\frac{1}{q}$-balanced cut of the vertices $\mathbf{Z}$ in H_{GE} is of size $\Omega(n^2/q^{2/3})$. Therefore, any vertex separator of $G_{GE}(n)$ must be of size at least $\chi_q(G_{GE}(n)) = \Omega(n^2/q^{2/3})$. $\square$

THEOREM 6.5. *Any parallelization of any dependency graph $G_{GE}(n)$, where two processors each compute $\lfloor n^3/(3q) \rfloor$ elements of $\mathbf{Z}$ (V_{GE}), must incur a communication of*

$$W_{GE} = \Omega\left(n^2/q^{2/3}\right).$$

PROOF. For any $G_{GE}(n)$, every vertex that has an outgoing edge to a vertex computed by a different processor (different color) must be communicated. Since two processors each compute $\lfloor n^3/(3q) \rfloor$ elements of $\mathbf{Z}$, the communicated set can be bounded below by the size of a $\frac{1}{q}$-balanced separator of the vertices $\mathbf{Z}$ in $G_{GE}(n)$. By Lemma 6.4, the size of any such separator is $\Omega(n^2/q^{2/3})$. $\square$

THEOREM 6.6. *Any parallelization of any dependency graph $G_{GE}(n)$ in which two of p processors compute $\lfloor n^3/(3p) \rfloor$ vertices of $\mathbf{Z}$ incurs the following computation (F), bandwidth (W), and latency (S) costs, for some $b \in [1, n]$,*

$$F_{GE} = \Omega\left(n \cdot b^2\right), \quad W_{GE} = \Omega\left(n \cdot b\right), \quad S_{GE} = \Omega\left(n/b\right),$$

and furthermore, $F_{GE} \cdot S_{GE}^2 = \Omega\left(n^3\right)$, $W_{GE} \cdot S_{GE} = \Omega\left(n^2\right)$.

PROOF. Let G be a dependency graph of $G_{GE}(n)$. We note that the computation of L_{ii} for $i \in \{1, \ldots, n\}$ requires the computation of Z_{lmk} for $l, m, k \in \{1, \ldots, i\}$ with $l > m > k$. Furthermore, no element Z_{srt} for $s, r, t \in \{i+1, \ldots, n\}$ with $s > r > t$ can be computed until L_{ii} is computed. Consider any subpath $\mathcal{R} \subset \mathcal{P}$ of the dependency path $\mathcal{P} = \{L_{11}, \ldots, L_{nn}\}$. Evidently, if $\mathcal{R} = \{L_{ii}, \ldots, L_{j+1,j+1}\}$, the bubble $\zeta(G, \mathcal{R}) = (V_\zeta, E_\zeta)$ includes vertices corresponding to a subcube of $\mathbf{Z}$, namely $Z_{klm} \in V_\zeta$ for $k, l, m \in \{i, \ldots, j\}$ with $k > l > m$. Therefore, $\zeta(G, \mathcal{R})$ is isomorphic to $G_{GE}(|\mathcal{R}|)$, which implies that $|V_\zeta| = \Theta(|\mathcal{R}|^3)$ and by Lemma 6.4, we have $\chi_q(\zeta(G, \mathcal{R})) = \Theta(|\mathcal{R}|^2/q^{2/3})$. Since we have 3-dimensional bubbles with 2-dimensional cross-sections, we apply Corollary 4.2 with $d = 3$ to obtain the conclusion, for some $b \in [1, n]$. $\square$

6.2.3 Attainability

The lower bounds presented in the previous section are attained on p processors for $b \approx n/\sqrt{p}$ by '2D algorithms', which utilize a blocked matrix layout and are employed by most standard parallel libraries, including Elemental [19] and ScaLAPACK [7]. The

BSP [17] algorithms presented by Tiskin [17] for LU factorization (without pivoting, and with pairwise pivoting [22]) and for QR factorization with Givens rotations, match the lower bounds in Theorem 6.5 and Theorem 6.6 for any $b \in [n/p^{2/3}, n/\sqrt{p}]$. Therefore, Tiskin's algorithms can lower the bandwidth cost with respect to 2D algorithms by a factor of up to $p^{1/6}$, at the cost of increasing the latency cost by the same factor. Similarly, 2.5D algorithms [21] for LU factorization (without pivoting, and with tournament pivoting [9]) also lower bandwidth cost by a factor of up to $p^{1/6}$ by sacrificing latency cost. 2.5D algorithms are practical and can improve upon the performance of standard 2D algorithms so long as the matrix is large enough to amortize synchronization overheads. Therefore, the latency-bandwidth tradeoff is of practical importance for this problem. We note that the 3D parallel LU factorization algorithm given by Irony and Toledo [13], a major motivation for the 2.5D LU algorithm, is not optimal in our model, because it does not minimize bandwidth cost along the critical path, but only communication volume.

6.3 Krylov basis computation

We consider the s-step Krylov subspace basis computation

$$\mathbf{x}^{(l)} = \mathbf{A} \cdot \mathbf{x}^{(l-1)},$$

for $l \in \{1, \ldots, s\}$ and $\mathbf{x}^{(0)}$ given as input, where the graph of the symmetric sparse matrix $\mathbf{A}$ is a $(2m+1)^d$-point stencil (with $m \geq 1$), i.e., a d-dimensional n-by-$\cdots$-by-n mesh T, and each entry in $\mathbf{A}$ represents an interaction between vertices $v_{i_1, \ldots, i_d}, w_{j_1, \ldots, j_d} \in T$, such that for $k \in \{1, \ldots, d\}$, $i_k, j_k \in \{1, \ldots, n\}$, $|j_k - i_k| \leq m$. Thus, matrix $\mathbf{A}$ and vectors $\mathbf{x}^{(l)}$, $l \in \{0, \ldots, s\}$, have dimension n^d, and $\mathbf{A}$ has $\Theta(m^d)$ nonzeros per row/column. We note that the dependency structure of this computation is analogous to direct force evaluations in particle simulations and the Ford-Fulkerson shortest-paths algorithm, which may be expressed as sparse matrix-vector multiplication, but on different algebraic semirings.

THEOREM 6.7. *Any parallel execution of an s-step Krylov subspace basis computation for a $(2m+1)^d$-point stencil, for $m \geq 1$, on a d-dimensional mesh with $d \ll s$, requires the following computational, bandwidth, and latency costs for some $b \in \{1, \ldots s\}$,*

$$F_{Kr} = \Omega\left(m^d \cdot b^d \cdot s\right), \quad W_{Kr} = \Omega\left(m^d \cdot b^{d-1} \cdot s\right), \quad S_{Kr} = \Omega\left(s/b\right).$$

and furthermore,

$$F_{Kr} \cdot S_{Kr}^d = \Omega\left(m^d \cdot s^{d+1}\right), \quad W_{Kr} \cdot S_{Kr}^{d-1} = \Omega\left(m^d \cdot s^d\right).$$

PROOF. In the following analysis, we will discard factors of d, as we assume $d \ll s$ (e.g., d is a constant), which is reasonable for most problems of interest ($d \in \{2, 3\}$), but some assumptions in this analysis may need to be revisited if more precise consideration of high-dimensional meshes is desired. We let $G_{Kr} = (V_{Kr}, E_{Kr})$ be the dependency graph of the s-step Krylov subspace basis computation defined above. We index the vertices $V_{Kr} \ni v_{i_1, \ldots, i_d, l}$ with $d+1$ coordinates, each corresponding to the computation of an intermediate vector element $x_k^{(l)}$ for $l \in \{1, \ldots, s\}$ and $k = \sum_{j=1}^d i_j n^{j-1}$, supposing the lexicographical ordering of $\{1, \ldots, n\}^d$. For each edge $(v_{i_1, \ldots, i_d}, w_{j_1, \ldots, j_d})$ in T and each $l \in \{1, \ldots, s\}$, there is an edge $(v_{i_1, \ldots, i_d, l-1}, w_{j_1, \ldots, j_d, l})$ in E_{Kr}.

Consider the following dependency path $\mathcal{P}$ and any subpath $\mathcal{R}$, where $|\mathcal{R}| = r \geq 3$,

$$\mathcal{P} = \{v_{1, \ldots, 1, 1}, \ldots, v_{1, \ldots, 1, s}\}$$
$$\mathcal{P} \supset \mathcal{R} = \{v_{1, \ldots, 1, h+1}, \ldots, v_{1, \ldots, 1, h+r}\}.$$

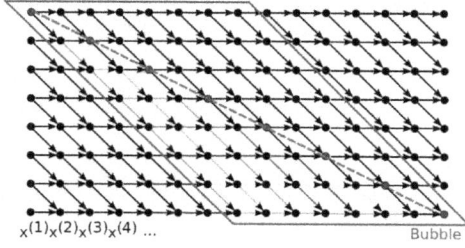

$x^{(1)}x^{(2)}x^{(3)}x^{(4)}$ ...   Bubble

Figure 5: Depiction of the bubble (blue parallelogram) along a dependency path (red dashed path) within a Krylov basis computation on a 1-dimensional mesh (2-point stencil). Edges within the bubble are colored according to the hypergraph edge to which they correspond.

The bubble $\zeta(G_{\mathrm{Kr}}, \mathcal{R}) = (V_\zeta, E_\zeta)$ includes

$$V_\zeta = \{v_{i_1,\ldots,i_d,i_{d+1}} : h+1 \leq i_{d+1} \leq h+r, \, j \in \{1,\ldots,d\},$$
$$\text{and } i_j \leq \max(1, m \cdot \min(i_{d+1} - h - 1, h + r - i_{d+1}))\}.$$

For each $(u_1, \ldots, u_{d+1}) \in \{1, \ldots, r-2\}^{d+1}$ we define the block

$$B_{u_1,\ldots,u_{d+1}} = \{v_{i_1,\ldots,i_{d+1}} \in V_\zeta :$$
$$i_j \in \{\lceil m/2 \rceil(u_j - 1) + 1, \ldots, \lceil m/2 \rceil u_j\},$$
$$j \in \{1,\ldots,d\}, i_{d+1} = u_{d+1} + h + 1\}.$$

Thus, each block should contain $\lceil m/2 \rceil^d$ vertices on the same level, u_{d+1}. We note that because the breadth of each block is $\lceil m/2 \rceil$, and the interaction distance (stencil radius) is m, every vertex in $B_{u_1,\ldots,u_j,\ldots,u_{d+1}}$ depends on every vertex in $B_{u_1,\ldots,u_j-1,\ldots,u_{d+1}-1}$ for each $j \in \{1,\ldots,d\}$, as well as on vertices $B_{u_1,\ldots,u_j,\ldots,u_{d+1}-1}$.

We now construct a DAG $G'_{\mathrm{Kr}} = (V'_{\mathrm{Kr}}, E'_{\mathrm{Kr}})$ corresponding to the connectivity of the blocks within the given bubble $\zeta(G_{\mathrm{Kr}}, \mathcal{R})$, enumerating them on a lattice of breadth $g = \lfloor (r-2)/(d+1) \rfloor$. For each $(u_1, \ldots, u_{d+1}) \in \{1, \ldots, g\}^{d+1}$, we have $w_{u_1,\ldots,u_{d+1}} \in V'_{\mathrm{Kr}}$ corresponding to block $B_{u_1,\ldots,u_d,t} \subset V_{\mathrm{Kr}}$ with $t = \sum_{j=1}^{d+1} u_j$. Each vertex $w_{i_1,\ldots,i_{d+1}}$ is connected to vertices $w_{i_1,\ldots,i_j+1,\ldots,i_{d+1}}$, for $j \in \{1,\ldots,d+1\}$, by edges in E'_{Kr}. A representative bubble is shown for $d = 1$ in Figure 5, where it is evident that the bubble vertices can be enumerated on a skewed lattice as above.

We transform G'_{Kr} into a hypergraph $H = (V_H, E_H)$, so that for $q \ll s$, a $\frac{1}{q}$-balanced separator of G'_{Kr} is proportional to a $\frac{1}{q}$-balanced hyperedge cut of H. We define $V_H = \{w_{i_1,\ldots,i_{d+1}} \in V'_{\mathrm{Kr}} : i_1 < i_2 < \cdots < i_{d+1}\}$, and the hyperedges E_H correspond to unions of vertices adjacent to disjoint subsets of edges in G'_{Kr}. In particular, we define hyperedges $e_{i_1,\ldots,i_d} \in E_H$ for $i_1, \ldots, i_d \in \{1,\ldots,g\}$ with $i_1 < \cdots < i_d$, to contain all $w_{j_1,\ldots,j_{d+1}}$ which satisfy $j_1 < \cdots < j_{d+1}$ and $\{i_1,\ldots,i_d\} \subset \{j_1,\ldots,j_{d+1}\}$. We can form these hyperedges as unions of edges in G'_{Kr},

$$e_{i_1,\ldots,i_d} \subset \bigcup_{k=1}^{i_1-1} (w_{k,i_1,\ldots,i_d}, w_{k+1,i_1,\ldots,i_d})$$
$$\cup \bigcup_{k=i_1}^{i_2-1} (w_{i_1,k,i_2\ldots,i_d}, w_{i_1,k+1,i_2,\ldots,i_d}) \cup \cdots$$
$$\cup \bigcup_{k=i_d}^{g-1} (w_{i_1,\ldots,i_d,k}, w_{i_1,\ldots,i_d,k+1})$$

where each pair of vertices in the union corresponds to a unique edge in G'_{Kr}. Because these hypergraph edges correspond to disjoint subsets of E'_{Kr}, any $\frac{1}{q}$-balanced separator of G'_{Kr} can be transformed into a $\frac{1}{q}$-balanced hyperedge cut C of H of the same size or less formed by taking the hyperedges in H to which the vertices in the separator are adjacent. Further, any such $\frac{1}{q}$-balanced separator of G'_{Kr} cannot be smaller than $\frac{1}{d+1}|C|$ because each vertex is adjacent to no more than $d+1$ edges.

We note that the hypergraph H is a lattice hypergraph of dimension $d+1$ and breadth $g = \lfloor (|\mathcal{R}| - 2)/(d+1) \rfloor$. By Theorem 5.2, its $\frac{1}{q}$-balanced hyperedge cut has size $|C| \geq \epsilon_q(H) = \Omega(g^d/q^{d/(d+1)})$. Furthermore, since the $\frac{1}{q}$-balanced separator of $\zeta(G'_{\mathrm{Kr}}, \mathcal{R})$ is at least $\frac{1}{d+1}|C|$,

$$\chi_q(\zeta(G'_{\mathrm{Kr}}, \mathcal{R})) = \Omega\left(\frac{g^d}{(d+1)q^{d/(d+1)}}\right) = \Omega(|\mathcal{R}|^d),$$

where the last bound follows since we have $d, q \ll s$.

This lower bound on edge cut size in the block graph G'_{Kr} allows us to obtain a lower bound on the size of any $\frac{1}{q}$-balanced separator of G_{Kr}, that is larger by a factor of $\Omega(m^d)$. Consider any $\frac{1}{q}$-balanced separator of G_{Kr} that separates the vertices into three disjoint subsets, the separator Q, and the parts V_1 and V_2. If two vertices $u, v \in V_{\mathrm{Kr}}$ are in two different partitions (are of different color), $u \in V_1$ and $v \in V_2$, and are in the same block, all vertices in the d adjacent blocks must have all their vertices entirely in Q, since all vertices in adjacent blocks in G'_{Kr} are adjacent to u and v in G_{Kr}. Therefore, the number of blocks which contain vertices of different color is less than $|Q|/m^d$ and therefore small with respect to $|V'_{\mathrm{Kr}}|/q$. Therefore, Q should yield $\Omega(|V'_{\mathrm{Kr}}|/q)$ blocks which contain vertices that are either in the separator or in V_1, and similarly for V_2. Now, since two blocks $B_1 \subset (V_1 \cup Q)$ and $B_2 \subset (V_2 \cup Q)$ which contain non-separator vertices of different color may not be adjacent, there must exist a separator block $B_3 \subset Q$ for any path on the lattice between B_1 and B_2. Therefore, Q also induces a separator of G'_{Kr} of size no larger than $|Q| \cdot \lceil m/2 \rceil^d$. So, we obtain the following lower bound on the size of a separator of G_{Kr}: $\chi_q(\zeta(G_{\mathrm{Kr}}, \mathcal{R})) = \Omega(m^d \cdot \chi_q(\zeta(G'_{\mathrm{Kr}}, \mathcal{R}))) = \Omega(m^d|\mathcal{R}|^d)$.

Now, the bubble size is $|V_\zeta| = \Omega(m^d|\mathcal{R}|^{d+1})$ and the total length of our main dependency path is $|\mathcal{P}| = s$. By Definition 4.1, G_{Kr} is a (ϵ, σ)-path-expander with $\epsilon(b) = m^d b^d$ and $\sigma(b) = m^d b^{d+1}$. Therefore, by application of Theorem 4.1, with $k = 3$, we obtain the following lower bounds, for some integer $b \in [3, s]$,

$$F_{\mathrm{Kr}} = \Omega\left(m^d \cdot b^d \cdot s\right), W_{\mathrm{Kr}} = \Omega\left(m^d \cdot b^{d-1} \cdot s\right), S_{\mathrm{Kr}} = \Omega\left(s/b\right).$$

$\square$

6.3.1 Attainability

A parallel communication-avoiding algorithm for computing a Krylov subspace basis, termed 'PA1', is presented in [10]. We note that although PA1 performs redundant computation to lower the parallel latency, the amount of redundant work and reduction in messages made possible by redundant work are not asymptotically significant, and thus the lower bounds of Theorem 6.7 apply. Computing an s-step Krylov subspace basis with a $(2m+1)^d$-point stencil with block size $b \in \{1, \ldots, s\}$ can be accomplished by s/b invocations of PA1 with basis size parameter b. The costs for the overall computation using PA1 are then

$$F_{\mathrm{Kr}} = O\left(m^d \cdot b^d \cdot s\right), W_{\mathrm{Kr}} = O\left(m^d \cdot b^{d-1} \cdot s\right), S_{\mathrm{Kr}} = O\left(s/b\right).$$

under the assumption $n/p^{1/d} \geq bm$. This algorithm therefore attains the lower bounds and lower bound tradeoffs of Theorem 6.7.

317

7. CONCLUSION

Our lower bounds showed that many numerical problems with lattice-like dependency structures require execution costs which are independent of the number of processors but dependent on the problem size. Architecturally, our results give lower bounds on execution time, as a function of synchronization latency (α), communication throughput (β), and arithmetic throughput (γ). The tradeoffs we derive describe the strong scaling limit of Gaussian elimination and Krylov basis computations in terms of these three quantities. In other words, we obtained lower bounds on the parallel execution time needed to solve a system of linear equations via certain numerical algorithms. As future work, we will consider Krylov basis computations (and graph algorithms) on graphs such as expanders and trees rather than just stencils (grids).

8. ACKNOWLEDGEMENTS

We thank Satish Rao, Grey Ballard, and Benjamin Lipshitz for discussions on topics related to this paper. The first author was supported by a DOE Computational Science Graduate Fellowship (DE-FG02-97ER25308). We also acknowledge support of the US DOE (grants DE-SC0003959, DE-SC0004938, DE-SC0005136, DE-SC0008700, DE-AC02-05CH11231) and DARPA (award HR0011-12-2-0016).

9. REFERENCES

[1] A. Aggarwal, A.K. Chandra, and M. Snir. Communication complexity of PRAMs. *Theoretical Computer Science*, 71(1):3 – 28, 1990.

[2] G. Ballard, J. Demmel, O. Holtz, B. Lipshitz, and O. Schwartz. Strong scaling of matrix multiplication algorithms and memory-independent communication lower bounds. In *ACM Symposium on Parallelism in Algorithms and Architectures (SPAA)*, June 2012.

[3] G. Ballard, J. Demmel, O. Holtz, and O. Schwartz. Minimizing communication in linear algebra. *SIAM J. Mat. Anal. Appl.*, 32(3), 2011.

[4] E. Bampis, C. Delorme, and J.-C. König. Optimal schedules for d-D grid graphs with communication delays. In *STACS 96*, volume 1046 of *Lecture Notes in Computer Science*, pages 655–666. Springer Berlin Heidelberg, 1996.

[5] M. A. Bender, G. S. Brodal, R. Fagerberg, R. Jacob, and E. Vicari. Optimal sparse matrix dense vector multiplication in the I/O-model. *Theory of Computing Systems*, 47(4):934–962, 2010.

[6] G. Bilardi and F. P. Preparata. Processor–time tradeoffs under bounded-speed message propagation: Part II, lower bounds. *Theory of Computing Systems*, 32(5):531–559, 1999.

[7] L. S. Blackford, J. Choi, A. Cleary, E. D'Azeuedo, J. Demmel, I. Dhillon, S. Hammarling, G. Henry, A. Petitet, K. Stanley, D. Walker, and R. C. Whaley. *ScaLAPACK user's guide*. Society for Industrial and Applied Mathematics, Philadelphia, PA, USA, 1997.

[8] D. Culler, R. Karp, D. Patterson, A. Sahay, K. E. Schauser, E. Santos, R. Subramonian, and T. von Eicken. LogP: towards a realistic model of parallel computation. In *Proceedings of the fourth ACM SIGPLAN symposium on Principles and practice of parallel programming*, PPOPP '93, pages 1–12, New York, NY, USA, 1993. ACM.

[9] J. Demmel, L. Grigori, and H. Xiang. A Communication Optimal LU Factorization Algorithm. EECS Technical Report EECS-2010-29, UC Berkeley, March 2010.

[10] J. Demmel, M. Hoemmen, M. Mohiyuddin, and K. Yelick. Avoiding communication in computing Krylov subspaces. Technical Report UCB/EECS-2007-123, EECS Dept., U.C. Berkeley, Oct 2007.

[11] R.W. Floyd. Algorithm 97: Shortest path. *Commun. ACM*, 5:345, June 1962.

[12] M.T. Heath and C.H. Romine. Parallel solution of triangular systems on distributed-memory multiprocessors. *SIAM Journal on Scientific and Statistical Computing*, 9(3):558–588, 1988.

[13] D. Irony and S. Toledo. Trading replication for communication in parallel distributed-memory dense solvers. *Parallel Processing Letters*, 71:3–28, 2002.

[14] D. Irony, S. Toledo, and A. Tiskin. Communication lower bounds for distributed-memory matrix multiplication. *Journal of Parallel and Distributed Computing*, 64(9):1017 – 1026, 2004.

[15] H. Jia-Wei and H. T. Kung. I/O complexity: The red-blue pebble game. In *Proceedings of the thirteenth annual ACM symposium on Theory of computing*, STOC '81, pages 326–333, New York, NY, USA, 1981. ACM.

[16] L.H. Loomis and H. Whitney. An inequality related to the isoperimetric inequality. *Bulletin of the AMS*, 55:961–962, 1949.

[17] W. F. McColl and A. Tiskin. Memory-efficient matrix multiplication in the BSP model. *Algorithmica*, 24:287–297, 1999.

[18] C. Papadimitriou and J. Ullman. A communication-time tradeoff. *SIAM Journal on Computing*, 16(4):639–646, 1987.

[19] J. Poulson, B. Maker, J. R. Hammond, N. A. Romero, and R. van de Geijn. Elemental: A new framework for distributed memory dense matrix computations. *ACM Transactions on Mathematical Software*, 39(2):13, 2013.

[20] E. Solomonik, E. Carson, N. Knight, and J. Demmel. Tradeoffs between synchronization, communication, and work in parallel linear algebra computations. Technical Report UCB/EECS-2014-8, EECS Department, University of California, Berkeley, Jan 2014.

[21] E. Solomonik and J. Demmel. Communication-optimal 2.5D matrix multiplication and LU factorization algorithms. In *Springer Lecture Notes in Computer Science, Proceedings of Euro-Par, Bordeaux, France*, Aug 2011.

[22] D.C. Sorensen. Analysis of pairwise pivoting in Gaussian Elimination. *Computers, IEEE Transactions on*, C-34(3):274 –278, March 1985.

[23] Volker Strassen. Gaussian elimination is not optimal. *Numerische Mathematik*, 13(4):354–356, 1969.

[24] A Tiskin. *The Design and Analysis of Bulk-Synchronous Parallel Algorithms*. PhD thesis, University of Oxford, 1998.

[25] A. Tiskin. All-pairs shortest paths computation in the BSP model. *Lecture Notes in Computer Science, Automata, Languages and Programming*, 2076:178–189, 2001.

[26] A. Tiskin. Communication-efficient parallel generic pairwise elimination. *Future Generation Computer Systems*, 23(2):179 – 188, 2007.

[27] Leslie G Valiant. A bridging model for parallel computation. *Communications of the ACM*, 33(8):103–111, 1990.

[28] S. Warshall. A theorem on boolean matrices. *J. ACM*, 9:11–12, January 1962.

Parallel Peeling Algorithms

Jiayang Jiang[*]
Harvard University
School of Engineering
and Applied Sciences
jiayangjiang@fas.harvard.edu

Michael Mitzenmacher[†]
Harvard University
School of Engineering
and Applied Sciences
michaelm@eecs.harvard.edu

Justin Thaler[‡]
Simons Institute for the
Theory of Computing
UC Berkeley
jthaler@fas.harvard.edu

ABSTRACT

The analysis of several algorithms and data structures can be framed as a *peeling process* on a random hypergraph: vertices with degree less than k are removed until there are no vertices of degree less than k left. The remaining hypergraph is known as the k-core. In this paper, we analyze parallel peeling processes, where in each round, all vertices of degree less than k are removed. It is known that, below a specific edge density threshold, the k-core is empty with high probability. We show that, with high probability, below this threshold, only $\frac{1}{\log((k-1)(r-1))} \log\log n + O(1)$ rounds of peeling are needed to obtain the empty k-core for r-uniform hypergraphs. Interestingly, we show that above this threshold, $\Omega(\log n)$ rounds of peeling are required to find the non-empty k-core. Since most algorithms and data structures aim to peel to an empty k-core, this asymmetry appears fortunate. We verify the theoretical results both with simulation and with a parallel implementation using graphics processing units (GPUs). Our implementation provides insights into how to structure parallel peeling algorithms for efficiency in practice.

1. INTRODUCTION

Consider the following *peeling process*: starting with a random hypergraph, vertices with degree less than k are repeatedly removed, together with their incident edges. (We use edges instead of hyperedges throughout the paper, as the context is clear.) This yields what is called the k-core of the hypergraph, which is the maximal subgraph where each vertex has degree at least k. It is known that the k-core is uniquely defined and does not depend on the order vertices are removed. The greedy peeling process produces sequential

[*]Supported by NSF grants CCF-0915922 and IIS-0964473.

[†]Supported in part by NSF grants CCF-0915922, IIS-0964473, and CNS-1011840. Part of this work was done while the author was visiting Microsoft Research New England.

[‡]Supported by an NSF Graduate Research Fellowship, NSF grant CCF-0915922, and a Research Fellowship from the Simons Institute for the Theory of Computing. Most of this work was performed while the author was a graduate student at Harvard University, School of Engineering and Applied Sciences.

algorithms with very fast running times, generally linear in the size of the graph. Because of its simplicity and efficiency, peeling-based approaches appear especially useful for problems involving large data sets. Indeed, this process, and variations on it, have found applications in low-density parity-check codes [14, 17], hash-based sketches [4, 9], satisfiability of random boolean formulae [3, 19], and cuckoo hashing [20]. Frequently, the question in these settings is whether or not the k-core is empty. As we discuss further below, it is known that below a specific edge density threshold $c^*_{k,r}$, the k-core is empty with high probability. This asymptotic result in fact accurately predicts practical performance quite well.

In this paper, we focus on expanding the applicability of peeling processes by examining the use of parallelism in conjunction with peeling. Peeling seems particularly amenable to parallel processing via the following simple round-based algorithm: in each round, all vertices of degree less than k and their adjacent edges are removed in parallel from the graph. The major question we study is: how many rounds are necessary before peeling is complete?

We show that, with high probability, when the edge density is a constant strictly below the threshold $c^*_{k,r}$, only $\frac{1}{\log((k-1)(r-1))} \log\log n + O(1)$ rounds of peeling are needed for r-uniform hypergraphs. (The hidden constant in the $O(1)$ term depends on the size of the "gap" between the edge density and the threshold density. We more precisely characterize this dependence later.) Specifically, we show that the fraction of vertices that remain in each round decreases doubly exponentially, in a manner similar in spirit to existing analyses of "balanced allocations" load-balancing problems [2, 15]. Interestingly, we show in contrast that at edge densities above the threshold, with high probability $\Omega(\log n)$ rounds of peeling are required to find the non-empty k-core. Since most algorithms and data structures that use peeling aim for an empty k-core, the fact that empty k-cores are faster to find in parallel than non-empty ones appears particularly fortuitous.

We then consider some of the details in implementation, focusing on the algorithmic example of Invertible Bloom Lookup Tables (IBLTs) [9]. An IBLT stores a set of keys, with each key being hashed to r cells in a table, and all keys in a cell XORed together. The IBLT defines a random hypergraph, where keys correspond to edges, and cells to vertices. As we describe later, recovering the set of keys from the IBLT corresponds to peeling on the associated hypergraph. Applications of IBLTs are further discussed in [9]; they can be used, for example, for sparse recovery [9], simple low-density parity-check codes [17], and efficient set reconciliation across communication links [7]. Our implementation demonstrates that our parallel peeling algorithm yields concrete speedups, and provides insights into how to structure parallel peeling algorithms for efficiency in practice.

Our results are closely related to work of Achlioptas and Molloy [1]. With different motivations than our own, they show that at most $O(\log n)$ rounds of peeling are needed to find the (possibly nonempty) k-core both above and below the threshold edge density $c_{k,r}^*$. Our $O(\log\log n)$ upper bound below the threshold is an exponential improvement on their $O(\log n)$ bound, while our $\Omega(\log n)$ lower bound above the threshold demonstrates the tightness of their upper bound in this regime. Perhaps surprisingly, we cannot find other analyses of parallel peeling in the literature, although early work by Karp, Luby, and Meyer auf der Heide on PRAM simulation uses an algorithm similar to peeling to obtain $O(\log\log n)$ bounds for load balancing [11], and we use other load balancing arguments [2, 21] for inspiration. We also rely heavily on the framework established by Molloy [19] for analyzing the k-core of random hypergraphs.

Subsequent to our work, Gao [8] has provided an alternative proof of an $O(\log\log n)$ upper bound on the number of rounds required to peel to an empty core when the edge density is below the threshold $c_{k,r}^*$. Her proof, short and elegant, obtains a leading constant of $\frac{1}{\log(k(r-1)/r)}$, larger than the constant $\frac{1}{\log((k-1)(r-1))}$ obtained through our more detailed analysis.

Paper Outline. Section 3 characterizes the round complexity of the peeling process when the edge density is a constant strictly below the threshold $c_{k,r}^*$, showing that the number of rounds required is $\frac{1}{\log((k-1)(r-1))}\log\log n + O(1)$. Section 4 shows that when the edge density is a constant strictly above the threshold $c_{k,r}^*$, the number of rounds required is $\Omega(\log n)$. Section 5 presents simulation results demonstrating that our theoretical analysis closely matches the empirical evolution of the peeling process. Section 6 describes our GPU-based IBLT implementation. Our IBLT implementation must deal with a fundamental issue that is inherent to *any* implementation of a parallel peeling algorithm, regardless of the application domain: the need to avoid peeling the same item multiple times. Consequently, the peeling process used in our IBLT implementation differs slightly from the one analyzed in Sections 3 and 4. In Appendix B we formally analyze this variant of the parallel peeling process, demonstrating that it terminates significantly faster than might be expected.

As discussed above, the hidden constant in the additive $O(1)$ term in the upper bound of Section 3 depends on the distance between the edge density and the threshold density $c_{k,r}^*$; we refer to this distance as ν. Section 7 extends the analysis of Section 3 to precisely characterize this dependence, demonstrating that there is an additive $\Theta(1/\sqrt{\nu})$ term in the number of rounds required. Section 8 concludes.

2. PRELIMINARIES

For constants $r \geq 2$ and c, let $G_{n,cn}^r$ denote a random hypergraph[1] with n vertices and cn edges, where each edge consists of r distinct vertices. Such hypergraphs are called *r-uniform*, and we refer to c as the *edge density* of $G_{n,cn}^r$. Previous analyses of random hypergraphs have determined the threshold values $c_{k,r}^*$ such that when $c < c_{k,r}^*$, the k-core is empty with probability $1 - o(1)$, and when $c > c_{k,r}^*$, the k-core is non-empty with probability $1 - o(1)$. Here and throughout this paper, $k, r \geq 2$, but the special (and already well understood) case of $k = r = 2$ is excluded from consid-

---

[1] When $r = 2$ we have a graph, but we may use hypergraph when speaking generally.

eration. From [19], the formula for $c_{k,r}^*$ is given by

$$c_{k,r}^* = \min_{x>0} \frac{x}{r\left(1 - e^{-x}\sum_{j=0}^{k-2}\frac{x^j}{j!}\right)^{r-1}}. \tag{1}$$

For example, we find that $c_{2,3}^* \approx 0.818$, $c_{2,4}^* \approx 0.772$ and $c_{3,3}^* \approx 1.553$.

3. BELOW THE THRESHOLD

In this section, we characterize the number of rounds required by the peeling process when the edge density c is a constant strictly below the threshold density $c_{k,r}^*$. Recall that this peeling process repeatedly removes vertices with degree less than k, together with their incident edges. We prove the following theorem.

THEOREM 3.1. *Let $k, r \geq 2$ with $k + r \geq 5$, and let c be a constant. With probability $1 - o(1)$, the parallel peeling process for the k-core in a random hypergraph $G_{n,cn}^r$ with edge density c and r-ary edges terminates after $\frac{1}{\log((k-1)(r-1))}\log\log n + O(1)$ rounds when $c < c_{k,r}^*$.*

Theorem 3.1 is tight up to an additive constant.

THEOREM 3.2. *Let $k, r \geq 2$ with $k + r \geq 5$, and let c be a constant. With probability $1 - o(1)$, the parallel peeling process for the k-core in a random hypergraph $G_{n,cn}^r$ with edge density c and r-ary edges requires $\frac{1}{\log((k-1)(r-1))}\log\log n - O(1)$ rounds to terminate when $c < c_{k,r}^*$.*

In proving Theorems 3.1 and 3.2, we begin in Section 3.1 with a high-level overview of our argument, before presenting full details of the proof in Section 3.2.

3.1 The High-Level Argument

The neighborhood of a node v in a random r-uniform hypergraph can be accurately modeled as a branching process, with a random number of edges adjacent to this vertex, and similarly a random number of edges adjacent to each of those vertices, and so on. For intuition, we assume this branching process yields a tree, and further that the number of adjacent edges is distributed according to a discrete Poisson distribution with mean rc. These assumptions are sufficiently accurate for our analysis, as we later prove. (This approach is standard; see e.g. [6, 19] for similar arguments.)

The intuition for the main result comes from considering the (tree) neighborhood of v, and applying the following algorithm: for $1 \leq i \leq t - 1$, in round i, look at all the vertices at distance $t - i$ and delete a vertex if it has fewer than $k - 1$ child edges. Finally, in round t, v is deleted if it has degree less than k. Vertex v survives after t rounds of peeling if and only if it survives after t rounds of this algorithm.

In what follows, we denote the probability that v survives after t rounds in this model by λ_t, and the probability a vertex u at distance $t - i$ from v survives i rounds by ρ_i.

Here $\rho_0 = 1$. In this idealized setting, the following relationships hold:

$$\rho_i = \Pr(\text{Poisson}(\rho_{i-1}^{r-1}rc) \geq k - 1),$$

and similarly

$$\lambda_i = \Pr(\text{Poisson}(\rho_{i-1}^{r-1}rc) \geq k). \tag{2}$$

The recursion for ρ_i arises as follows: each node u has a Poisson distributed number of descendant edges with mean rc, and each edge has $r - 1$ additional vertices that each survive $i - 1$ rounds with probability ρ_{i-1}. By the splitting property of Poisson distributions

[16, Chapter 5], the number of surviving descendant edges of u is Poisson distributed with mean $\rho_{i-1}^{r-1} rc$, and this must be at least $k-1$ for u to itself survive the ith round.

We use β_i to represent the expected number of surviving descendant edges after $i-1$ rounds:

$$\beta_i = \rho_{i-1}^{r-1} rc.$$

Then,

$$\rho_i = 1 - e^{-\beta_i} \sum_{j=0}^{k-2} \frac{\beta_i^{\ j}}{j!}, \qquad (3)$$

$$\lambda_i = 1 - e^{-\beta_i} \sum_{j=0}^{k-1} \frac{\beta_i^{\ j}}{j!}, \qquad (4)$$

$$\beta_{i+1} = \left[1 - e^{-\beta_i} \sum_{j=0}^{k-2} \frac{\beta_i^{\ j}}{j!} \right]^{r-1} rc. \qquad (5)$$

When $c < c_k^*$, which is the setting where we know the core becomes empty, we have $\lim_{t \to \infty} \rho_t = 0$, so $\lim_{t \to \infty} \beta_t = 0$. Thus, for any constant $\tau > 0$, we can choose a constant I such that $\beta_I \le \tau$.

For any $x > 0$ and $k \ge 2$, by basic calculus, we have

$$1 - e^{-x} \sum_{j=0}^{k-2} \frac{x^j}{j!} \le \frac{x^{k-1}}{(k-1)!}. \qquad (6)$$

Applying this bound to β_{I+1} gives

$$\beta_{I+1} \le \left[\frac{\beta_I^{k-1}}{(k-1)!} \right]^{r-1} rc \le \beta_I^{(k-1)(r-1)} \frac{rc}{[(k-1)!]^{r-1}}.$$

Using induction, we can show that

$$\beta_{I+t} \le \beta_I^{[(k-1)(r-1)]^t} \left[\frac{rc}{[(k-1)!]^{r-1}} \right]^{\frac{[(k-1)(r-1)]^t - 1}{(k-1)(r-1) - 1}}.$$

If $\frac{rc}{[(k-1)!]^{r-1}} \ge 1$, we can apply the upper bound

$$\beta_{I+t} \le \left[\tau \left(\frac{rc}{[(k-1)!]^{r-1}} \right)^{\frac{1}{(k-1)(r-1)-1}} \right]^{[(k-1)(r-1)]^t},$$

and if $\frac{rc}{[(k-1)!]^{r-1}} < 1$, then $\beta_{I+t} \le \tau^{[(k-1)(r-1)]^t}$. Setting

$$\tau' = \max \left(\tau \left(\frac{rc}{[(k-1)!]^{r-1}} \right)^{\frac{1}{(k-1)(r-1)-1}}, \tau \right)$$

gives

$$\beta_{I+t} \le (\tau')^{[(k-1)(r-1)]^t}. \qquad (7)$$

Pick τ such that $\tau' < 1$. By Equations (4), (6), and (7), it holds that

$$\lambda_{I+t} \le \frac{\beta_{I+t}^k}{k!} \le \frac{(\tau')^{k[(k-1)(r-1)]^t}}{k!}.$$

Solving $\frac{(\tau')^{k[(k-1)(r-1)]^t}}{k!} < n^{-2}$ gives $t > \frac{1}{\log((k-1)(r-1))} \log \log n + O(1)$. This shows that it takes $t^* = \frac{1}{\log((k-1)(r-1))} \log \log n + O(1)$ rounds for $\lambda_t n = o(1)$ in our idealized setting.

Remark: One can similarly show that with probability $1 - o(1)$ termination requires at least $\frac{1}{\log((k-1)(r-1))} \log \log n - O(1)$ rounds for any constant $c < c_{k,r}^*$ when $k + r \ge 5$ as well in the idealized setting. Starting from Equation (6), we can show

$$1 - e^{-x} \sum_{j=0}^{k-2} \frac{x^j}{j!} \ge \frac{x^{k-1}}{C(k-1)!}$$

for some constant C and sufficiently small $x > 0$. It then follows by similar arguments that

$$\beta_{I+t} \ge (\tau'')^{[(k-1)(r-1)]^t}$$

for suitable constants I and τ''. In particular, we can choose a t that is $\frac{1}{\log((k-1)(r-1))} \log \log n - O(1)$, so that the number of vertices that remain to be peeled after t rounds is still at least $n^{2/3}$ in expectation. As we show later (cf. Section 3.2.3), the fact that this expectation is large implies that the number of surviving vertices after this many rounds is bigger than 0 with probability $1 - o(1)$, in both the idealized setting considered in this overview, and in the actual random process corresponding to $G_{n,cn}^r$.

3.2 Completing the Argument

3.2.1 Preliminary Lemmas

To formalize the argument outlined in Section 3.1, we first note that instead of working in the $G_{n,cn}^r$ model, we adopt the standard approach of having each edge appear independently in the hypergraph with probability $q = cn/\binom{n}{r}$. It can be shown easily that the result in this model (which we denote by G_c^r) implies that the same result holds in the $G_{n,cn}^r$ model (see e.g. [6, 12, 19]). Here, we sketch a simple version of this standard argument for this setting.

LEMMA 3.3. *Let G_c^r be an r-uniform hypergraph on n vertices in which each edge appears independently with probability $q = cn/\binom{n}{r}$. Suppose that for all $c < c_{k,r}^*$, peeling succeeds on G_c^r in $\frac{1}{\log((k-1)(r-1))} \log \log n + O(1)$ rounds with probability $1 - o(1)$. Then peeling similarly succeeds on $G_{n,cn}^r$ in $\frac{1}{\log((k-1)(r-1))} \log \log n + O(1)$ rounds with probability $1 - o(1)$ for all $c < c_{k,r}^*$.*

PROOF. (Sketch) Let c' be a constant value (independent of n) with $c < c' < c_{k,r}^*$. With probability $1 - o(1)$, parallel peeling will succeed for the hypergraph $G_{c'}^r$ in the appropriate number of rounds. Moreover, by standard Chernoff bounds, $G_{c'}^r$ will have greater than cn edges with probability $1 - o(1)$. Since the probability that the parallel peeling algorithm succeeds after any number of rounds monotonically decreases with the addition of random edges, it holds that the success probability is also $1 - o(1)$ when the graph is chosen from $G_{n,cn}^r$. (Formally, one would first condition on the number of edges chosen on the graph $G_{c'}^r$; given the number of edges, the actual edges selected are random. Hence we can couple the choice of the first cn edges between the two graphs.) □

We will also need the following lemma, which is essentially due to Voll [22]. We provide the proof for completeness. (We have not aimed to optimize the constants.)

LEMMA 3.4. *For any constants $c, r, c_1 > 0$, there is a constant $c_2 > 0$ such that with probability $1 - 1/n$, for all vertices v in G_c^r, the neighborhood of distance $c_1 \log \log n$ around v contains at most $\log^{c_2} n$ vertices.*

PROOF. We follow the approach used in the dissertation of Voll [22, Lemma 3.3.1]. Denote by N_d the number of vertices at distance d in the neighborhood of a root vertex u. We prove inductively on d that

$$\Pr(N_d > (6cr^2)^d \log(1/\varepsilon)) \le d\varepsilon$$

for d up to $c_1 \log \log n$ and $\varepsilon = 1/n^2$. The claim then follows by a union bound over all n vertices u.

For convenience we assume $6cr \ge 1$; the argument is easily modified if this is not the case, instead proving $\Pr(N_d > r^d \log(1/\varepsilon)) \le$

$d\varepsilon$. Recall that the number of edges adjacent to u is dominated by a binomial random variable $B\left(\binom{n-1}{r-1}, q\right)$, which has mean cr. The number of vertices adjacent to u via these edges is dominated by $r-1$ times the number of edges. When $d=1$, we find that the number of neighboring edges of the root, which we denote by N_0', is at most $6cr\log(1/\varepsilon)$ with probability bounded above by

$$\binom{\binom{n-1}{r-1}}{6cr\log(1/\varepsilon)}q^{6cr\log 1/\varepsilon} \leq \left(\frac{ecr}{6cr\log(1/\varepsilon)}\right)^{6cr\log(1/\varepsilon)} \leq \varepsilon.$$

This gives an upper bound of $6cr^2\log(1/\varepsilon)$ on N_1.

For the induction, we use Chernoff bounds, noting that N_{d+1} can be bounded as follows. Conditioned on the event that $N_d \leq \log(1/\varepsilon)(6cr^2)^d$, we note the number of edges adjacent to nodes of distance d is bounded above by the sum of N_d independent binomial random variables as above, and each such edge generates at most $r-1$ nodes for N_{d+1}. Let N_d' be the number of such edges. Then we have

$$\Pr\left(N_{d+1} > (6cr^2)^{d+1}\log(1/\varepsilon)\right) \leq$$

$$\Pr\left(N_{d+1} > (6cr^2)^{d+1}\log(1/\varepsilon) \mid N_d > (6cr^2)^d\log(1/\varepsilon)\right) +$$

$$\Pr\left(N_{d+1} > (6cr^2)^{d+1}\log(1/\varepsilon) \mid N_d \leq (6cr^2)^d\log(1/\varepsilon)\right) \leq$$

$$d\varepsilon + \Pr\left(N_d' > \left((6cr^2)^d \cdot (6cr)\right)\log(1/\varepsilon) \mid N_d \leq \log(1/\varepsilon)(6cr^2)^d\right).$$

We bound the last term via a Chernoff bound, noting that the sum of the N_d independent binomial random variables $B(\binom{n-1}{r-1}, q)$ has the same distribution as the sum of $N_d\binom{n-1}{r-1}$ independent Bernoulli random variables that take value 1 with probability q. We use the Chernoff bound from [16, Theorem 4.4, part 3], which says that if X is the sum of independent 0-1 trials and $E[X] = \mu$, then for $R \geq 6\mu$,

$$\Pr(X \geq R) \leq 2^{-R}.$$

Hence,

$$\Pr\left(N_d' > \log(1/\varepsilon)\left(6cr^2\right)^d \cdot (6cr) \mid N_d \leq \log(1/\varepsilon)\left(6cr^2\right)^d\right)$$

$$\leq 2^{-\log(1/\varepsilon)(6cr^2)^d \cdot (6cr)} \leq \varepsilon,$$

completing the induction and giving the lemma. $\square$

Let E be the event that the parallel peeling process on G_c^r terminates after $\frac{1}{\log((k-1)(r-1))}\log\log n + O(1)$ rounds. Our goal is to show that $\Pr[E] = 1 - o(1)$. Let c_1 any c_2 be the constants appearing in Lemma 3.4. Let E_1 denote the event that, for all vertices v in G_c^r, the neighborhood of distance $c_1\log\log n$ around v contains at most $\log^{c_2}n$ vertices, and let $\bar{E}_1$ denote the event that E_1 does not occur.

LEMMA 3.5. *It holds that* $\Pr[E] \geq \Pr[E|E_1] - 1/n$.

PROOF. Note that

$$\Pr[E] = \Pr[E|E_1]\Pr[E_1] + \Pr[E|\bar{E}_1]\Pr[\bar{E}_1]. \tag{8}$$

By Lemma 3.4, $\Pr[E] \geq 1 - 1/n$. Hence, by Equation (8), $\Pr[E] \geq \Pr[E|E_1](1-1/n) \geq \Pr[E|E_1] - 1/n$. $\square$

Lemma 3.5 implies that, if we show that $\Pr[E|E_1] = 1 - o(1)$, then $\Pr[E] = 1 - o(1)$ as well. This is the task to which we now turn.

3.2.2 Completing the Proof of Theorem 3.1

It will help us to introduce some terminology. We will recursively refer to a vertex other than the root as *peeled* in round i if it has fewer than $k-1$ unpeeled children edges (that is, edges to children); similarly, we say that an edge e is peeled at round i if some vertex incident to e is peeled. We refer to an edge or vertex that is not peeled as *unpeeled*. At round 0, all edges and vertices begin as unpeeled. For the root, we require there to be fewer than k unpeeled children edges before it is peeled.

PROOF OF THEOREM 3.1. We analyze how the actual branching process deviates from the idealized branching process analyzed in Section 3.1, showing the deviation leads to only lower order effects. We view the branching process as generating a breadth first search (BFS) tree of depth at most $O(\log\log n)$ rooted at the initial vertex v. To clarify, breadth first search trees are defined such that once a vertex u is expanded in the breadth first search, u cannot be the child of any vertex u' in the tree that is expanded after u.

LEMMA 3.6. *When expanding a node u in the BFS tree rooted at vertex v in G_c^r, let Z_u denote the number of already expanded vertices in the BFS tree, and let $N(u)$ denote the number of child edges of u in the BFS tree. If $Z_u = polylog(n)$, then $N(u)$ is a random variable with total variation distance at most $polylog(n)/n$ from $Poisson(rc)$.*

PROOF. The number of children edges incident to u in G_c^r is a binomial random variable $B(M/q, q)$, where the mean M equals $\binom{n-Z_u-1}{r-1}q$. Since Z_u is polylogarithmic in n,

$$M = \binom{n-Z_u-1}{r-1}q = \binom{n-1}{r-1}q(1-polylog(n)/n)$$
$$= rc(1-polylog(n)/n).$$

We invoke Le Cam's Theorem [13] (see Appendix A for the statement), which bounds the total variation distance between binomial and Poisson distributions, to conclude that the total variation distance between $B(M/q, q)$ and $Poisson(M)$ is at most $Mq \leq rc(cn/\binom{n}{r}) = O(1/n^{r-1})$. Meanwhile, the total variation distance between $Poisson(M)$ and $Poisson(rc)$ is $polylog(n)/n$, and so by the triangle inequality, the total variation distance between $Poisson(rc)$ and $B(M/q, q)$ is also $polylog(n)/n$. $\square$

LEMMA 3.7. *Let $X_1(v)$ denote the random variable describing the tree of depth $i = O(\log\log n)$ rooted at v in the idealized branching process. Let $X_2(v)$ denote the random variable describing the BFS tree of depth i rooted at v in G_c^r, conditioned on event E_1 occurring. The total variation distance between $X_1(v)$ and $X_2(v)$ is at most $polylog(n)/n$.*

PROOF. We describe a standard coupling of the actual branching process and the idealized branching process. That is, we imagine running two different experiments $(Y_1(v), Y_2(v))$, with $Y_1(v)$ corresponding to the idealized branching process, and $Y_2(v)$ corresponding to the actual branching process conditioned on event E_1 occurring. The two branching processes will not be independent, yet $Y_1(v)$ and $Y_2(v)$ will have the same distribution as the idealized and actual branching processes $X_1(v)$ and $X_2(v)$ respectively. We will show that for any $i = O(\log\log n)$, with probability at least $1 - polylog(n)/n$ the two experiments *never* deviate from each other. It follows that any event that occurs in $X_1(v)$ with probability p occurs in $X_2(v)$ with probability $p \pm polylog(n)/n$, and hence the total variation distance between $X_1(v)$ and $X_2(v)$ is at most $polylog(n)/n$ as desired.

The experiments $Y_1(v)$ and $Y_2(v)$ proceed as follows. Both $Y_1(v)$ and $Y_2(v)$ begin by expanding a node v. Recall that the number of child edges of v in the idealized branching process has distribution μ_{ideal}, where μ_{ideal} denotes a discrete Poisson random variable with mean rc. Let μ_v denote the distribution of $N(v)$ in the real branching process conditioned on event E_1 occurring. Define $\alpha_v(x) = \min\{\mu_{\text{ideal}}(x), \mu_v(x)\}$.

Let γ_v denote the total variation distance between μ_{ideal} and μ_v; by Lemma 3.6, $\gamma_v \leq \text{polylog}(n)/n$. Note that $\sum_x \alpha_v(x) = 1 - \gamma_v$, and hence $\alpha'_v = \alpha_v/(1 - \gamma_v)$ is a probability distribution.

At the start of experiments $X_1(v)$ and $X_2(v)$, we toss a coin with a probability of heads equal to $1 - \gamma_v$. If it comes up heads, we choose N from the probability distribution α'_v, and set the number of child edges of v in both $Y_1(v)$ and $Y_2(v)$ to be N, and choose identical identifiers for their children uniformly at random from $[n] \setminus \{v\}$ without replacement. If it comes up tails, we choose the number of child edges of v in $Y_1(v)$ according to the probability distribution $\sigma_{\text{ideal},v}(x)$ defined via:

$$\begin{cases} \frac{\mu_{\text{ideal}}(x) - \mu_v(x)}{\gamma_v} & \text{if } \mu_{\text{ideal}}(x) > \mu_v(x) \\ 0 & \text{otherwise,} \end{cases}$$

choose the number of child edges of v in $Y_2(v)$ according to the distribution $\sigma_{\text{real},v}(x)$ defined via:

$$\begin{cases} \frac{\mu_v(x) - \mu_{\text{ideal}}(x)}{\gamma_v} & \text{if } \mu_v(x) > \mu_{\text{ideal}}(x) \\ 0 & \text{otherwise,} \end{cases}$$

and independently choose identifiers for their children at random from $[n] \setminus \{v\}$, without replacement.

Under these definitions, the number of child edges of v in $Y_1(v)$ is distributed according to μ_{ideal}, while the number of child edges of v in $Y_2(v)$ is distributed according to μ_v. That is, these quantities have the correct marginals, even though $Y_1(v)$ and $Y_2(v)$ are not independent.

If the coin came up tails, we then run $Y_1(v)$ and $Y_2(v)$ independently of each other for the remainder of the experiment. If the coin came up heads, we repeatedly expand nodes in both $X_1(v)$ and $X_2(v)$ as follows. When expanding a node u, we let μ_u denote the distribution of $N(u)$ in the real branching process, and we define α_u, γ_u, α'_u, $\sigma_{\text{ideal},u}$, and $\sigma_{\text{real},u}$ analogously. We toss a new coin with a probability of heads equal to $1 - \gamma_u$. If the new coin comes up heads, we choose N from the probability distribution α'_u and set the number of child edges of u in both $Y_1(v)$ and $Y_2(v)$ to be N, and choose identical identifiers for their children uniformly at random from $[n] \setminus T$, where T is the set of nodes already appearing in the (identical) trees. If the new coin comes up tails, we choose the number of child edges of u in $Y_1(v)$ according to $\sigma_{\text{ideal},u}$, choose the number of child edges of u in $Y_2(v)$ according to $\sigma_{\text{real},u}$, and independently choose the identifiers of the children at random from the set of nodes not already appearing in the respective tree, without replacement.

It is straightforward to check that the marginal distributions of $Y_1(v)$ and $Y_2(v)$ are the same as $X_1(v)$ and $X_2(v)$. Moreover, each time a node u is expanded in $Y_2(v)$, the processes deviate from each other with probability at most γ_u. Since $X_2(v)$ describes the actual branching process conditioned on event E_1 occurring, Lemma 3.6 guarantees that $\gamma_u \leq \text{polylog}(n)/n$ for all nodes u that are ever expanded. Moreover, at most $\text{polylog}(n)$ nodes u are ever expanded in $Y_2(v)$. By the union bound over all $\text{polylog}(n)$ nodes u ever expanded in $Y_2(v)$, it holds that $Y_1(v)$ and $Y_2(v)$ *never* deviate with probability at least $1 - \text{polylog}(n)/n$. $\quad\square$

Recall that λ_i is the probability that the root node v survives after i rounds of the idealized branching process. Let $\lambda_i^{(a)}$ denote the corresponding value in the actual branching process conditioned on event E_1 occurring. That is,

$$\lambda_i^{(a)} = \Pr[v \text{ survives } i \text{ rounds of peeling in } G_c^r | E_1]. \quad (9)$$

By symmetry, the probability on the right hand side of Equation (9) is independent of the node v.

Lemma 3.7 implies that λ_i and $\lambda_i^{(a)}$ differ by at most $\text{polylog}(n)/n$ for all $i = O(\log\log n)$, and thus

$$\lambda_{t^*}^{(a)} \leq \lambda_{t^*} + \text{polylog}(n)/n \leq \text{polylog}(n)/n.$$

It remains to improve the upper bound on $\lambda_i^{(a)}$ to $o(1/n)$, as this will allow us to apply a union bound over all the vertices v to conclude that with probability $1 - o(1)$, no vertex survives after i rounds of peeling. For expository purposes, we first show how to do this assuming the neighborhood is a tree. We then show how to handle the general case, in which vertices may be duplicated as we expand the neighborhood of the root node v. When duplicates appear, parts of our neighborhood tree expansion are no longer independent, as in our idealized analysis, but we are able to modify the analysis to cope with these dependencies.

Bounding λ_i for Trees: Assume for now that the neighborhood of the root node v is a tree. Note that for the root to be unpeeled after i rounds, there must be at least $k \geq 2$ adjacent unpeeled edges, corresponding to at least 2 (distinct, from our tree assumption) unpeeled children vertices after $i - 1$ rounds. We have shown that, conditioned on event E_1 occurring, each vertex remains unpeeled for at most $t^* = \frac{1}{\log((k-1)(r-1))} \log\log n + O(1)$ rounds with probability $O(\text{polylog}(n)/n)$. The 2 unpeeled children vertices can be chosen from the at most polylogarithmic number of children of v (the polylogarithmic bound follows from the occurrence of event E_1). This gives only $\binom{\text{polylog}(n)}{2} = \text{polylog}(n)$ possible sets of choices. Hence, via a union bound, the probability that v survives at least $t^* + 1$ rounds is bounded above by $\text{polylog}(n) \cdot (\text{polylog}(n)/n)^2 = O(\text{polylog}(n)/n^2) = o(1/n)$. We can take a union bound over all vertices for our final $1 - o(1)$ bound.

Dealing with duplicate vertices: Finally, we now explain that, with probability $1 - o(1)$, we need to worry only about a single duplicate vertex in the neighborhood for all vertices, and further that this only adds an additive constant to the number of rounds required. Conditioned on event E_1 occurring, for any fixed node v it holds that as we expand the neighborhood of v of distance $O(\log\log n)$ using breadth first search, the probability of a duplicate vertex occurring during any expansion step is only $\text{polylog}(n)/n$. As the neighborhood contains only a polylogarithmic number of vertices, the probability of having at least two duplicate vertices within the neighborhood of v is $o(1/n)$. By a union bound over all n nodes v, with probability $1 - o(1)$, *no* node v in the graph will have two duplicated vertices in the BFS tree rooted at v. We refer to this event as E_2, and we condition on this event occurring for the remainder of the proof. This conditioning does not affect our estimate of $\Pr[E|E_1]$ by more than an additive $o(1)$ factor, for the same reason conditioning on E_1 did not affect our estimate of $\Pr[E]$ by more than an additive $o(1)$ factor (cf. Lemma 3.5). Indeed,

$$\Pr[E|E_1] = \Pr[E|E_1 \cap E_2]\Pr[E_2] + \Pr[E|E_1 \cap \bar{E}_2]\Pr[\bar{E}_2]$$
$$\geq \Pr[E|E_1 \cap E_2](1 - o(1)).$$

It is therefore sufficient to show that, conditioned on event E_1 occurring, having one duplicate vertex in the neighborhood only adds a constant number of rounds to the parallel peeling process.

We first consider the case when $r \geq 3$, so that if the root remains unpeeled it has at least four (not necessarily distinct) unpeeled vertices at distance 1 from it, corresponding to the at least two edges (each with at least two other vertices, as $r \geq 3$) that prevent the root from being peeled. If we encounter a duplicate vertex, we pessimistically assume that it prevents two vertices adjacent to the root – namely, its ancestors – from being peeled. Even with this pessimistic assumption, simply adding one additional layer of expansion in the neighborhood allows the root to be peeled by round $t^* + 2$ with probability $1 - o(1/n)$, as we now show.

Consider what happens in $t^* + 2$ rounds when there is 1 duplicate vertex. As stated in the previous paragraph, for the root to remain unpeeled, it must have at least four neighbors, and at most two of these four vertices is a duplicate or has a descendant that is a duplicate. Thus, in order for the root to remain unpeeled after $t^* + 2$ rounds, at least two neighbors, u_1 and u_2, of the root must remain unpeeled after $t^* + 1$ rounds, when the neighborhoods of u_1 and u_2 for $t^* + 1$ rounds are trees. By our previous calculations, the probability that u_1 and u_2 both remain unpeeled after $t^* + 1$ rounds when their neighborhoods are trees is $O(\text{polylog}(n)/n^2)$. Thus, we take a union bound over the at most $\text{polylog}(n)$ pairs of descendants of the root, and conclude that the probability that the root survives $t^* + 2$ rounds of the peeling process is $1 - o(1/n)$.

Finally, union bounding over all nodes v in G_c^r, we conclude that *all* nodes in G_c^r are peeled after $t^* + 2$ rounds with probability $1 - o(1)$. That is, we have shown that $\Pr[E|E_1] = 1 - o(1)$.

The case where $r = 2$ and $k \geq 3$ requires a bit more care. Let us consider what happens after $t^* + 3$ rounds in this case. For the root note v to remain unpeeled, v must have at least $k \geq 3$ incident edges that remain unpeeled after $t^* + 2$ rounds of peeling. This corresponds to at least 3 (not necessarily distinct) unpeeled children of v. Thus, even if there is one duplicate vertex in the neighborhood of v, v must have at least one unpeeled child u whose neighborhood of distance $t^* + 2$ is a tree. This vertex must have at least two children (grandchildren of the root) that must remain unpeeled for $t^* + 1$ rounds. Thus, by our previous calculations, the probability that u remains unpeeled after $t^* + 2$ rounds is at most $\text{polylog}(n)/n^2$. Again we can union bound over the at most $\text{polylog}(n)$ children u of the root node v to obtain a $1 - o(1/n)$ probability that v remains unpeeled after $t^* + 3$ rounds in this case.

We have shown that $\Pr[E|E_1] = 1 - o(1)$, and by Equation (8), it follows that $\Pr[E] = 1 - o(1)$ as well.

Remark: One can obtain better than $1 - o(1)$ bounds on the probability of terminating after $\frac{1}{\log((k-1)(r-1))} \log \log n + O(1)$ rounds when $c < c_{k,r}^*$. For example, $1 - o(1/n)$ bounds are possible when $r > 3$; the argument requires considering cases for the possibility that 2 vertices are duplicated in the neighborhood around a vertex. However, one cannot hope for probability bounds of $1 - o(1/n^a)$ for an arbitrary constant a when duplicate edges may appear, as is typical for hashing applications. The probability the k-core is not empty because k edges share the same r vertices is $\Omega(n^{-kr+k+r})$ for constant k, r, and graphs with a linear number of edges, which is already $\Omega(1/n)$ for $k = 2$ and $r = 3$ or for $k = 3$ and $r = 2$.

3.2.3 Completing the Proof of Theorem 3.2

Recall that Theorem 3.2 claims that with probability $1 - o(1)$, at least $\frac{1}{\log((k-1)(r-1))} \log \log n - O(1)$ rounds of peeling are required before arriving at an empty k-core. The analysis of Section 3.1 established that, in the idealized setting, each node v remains un-

peeled after $t = \frac{1}{\log((k-1)(r-1))} \log \log n - C_1$ rounds with probability at least $n^{-1/3}$, where where C_1 is an appropriately large constant that depends on k and r. Hence, in the idealized setting, the expected number of nodes that remain unpeeled after t rounds is greater than or equal to $n^{2/3}$. We use this fact to establish that the claimed round lower bound holds in G_c^r with probability $1 - o(1)$.

The argument to bound the effects of deviations from the idealized process is substantially simpler in the context of Theorem 3.2 than in the analogous argument from Section 3.2.2. Indeed, to prove Theorem 3.1, we needed to establish that with probability $1 - o(1)$, *all* nodes in G_c^r are peeled after a suitable number of rounds. The argument of Section 3.2.2 accomplished this by establishing that, for any node v, v is peeled after t rounds with probability $1 - o(1/n)$, for an appropriate choice of $t = \frac{1}{\log((k-1)(r-1))} \log \log n + O(1)$. We then applied a union bound to conclude that this holds for all nodes with probability $1 - o(1)$. It was relatively easy to establish that v is peeled after t rounds with probability $1 - \text{polylog}(n)/n$, and most of the effort in the proof was devoted to increasing this probability to $1 - o(1/n)$, large enough to perform a union bound over all n nodes.

In contrast, to establish a *lower* bound on the number of rounds required, one merely needs to show the existence of a single node that remains unpeeled after $t = \frac{1}{\log((k-1)(r-1))} \log \log n - C_1$ rounds. Let $L_{t,\text{ideal}}$ be a random variable denoting the number of nodes that remain unpeeled after t rounds in the idealized setting of Section 3.1, and let L_t be a random variable denoting the analogous number of nodes in G_c^r. As previously mentioned, our analysis in the idealized framework (Section 3.1) shows that the expected value of $L_{t,\text{ideal}}$ is at least $n^{2/3}$ for a suitably chosen constant C_1 in the expression for t. Lemma 3.7 then implies that the expected value of L_t is at least $n^{2/3}/\text{polylog}(n)$. We now sketch an argument that L_t is concentrated around its expectation, i.e., that with probability $1 - o(1)$, $L_t = E[L_t] \pm n^{1/2}\text{polylog}(n) \geq n^{2/3}/\text{polylog}(n)$. We note that an entirely analogous argument is used later to prove Theorem 4.1 in Section 4, where the argument is given in full detail.

Let E_1 denote the event that there are $m = cn \pm O(\sqrt{n \log n})$ edges in G_c^r. Let E_2 denote the event that all nodes in G_c^r have neighbors of size at most $\log^{c_2}(n)$ for an appropriate constant c_2. By Lemma 3.4, events E_1 and E_2 both occur with probability $1 - 2/n$. We will condition on both events occurring for the duration of the argument, absorbing an additive $2/n$ into the $o(1)$ failure probability in the statement of Theorem 3.2 (note that the conditioning causes at most an $O(1)$ change in $E[L_t]$).

We consider the process of exposing the m edges of G_c^r one at a time; denote the random edges by $A_1, A_2, \ldots, A_m$. For our martingale, we consider random variables $L_t^i = E[L_t \mid A_1, \ldots, A_i]$, so $L_t^0 = E[L_t]$ and $L_t^m = L_t$. Conditioned on events E_1 and E_2 occurring, each exposed edge changes the conditional expectation of L_t by only $\log^{c_2}(n)$, so Azuma's martingale inequality[2] [16, Theorem 12.4] yields for sufficiently large n:

$$
\begin{aligned}
\Pr(|L_t - E[L_t]| \geq n^{1/2}\log^{c_2+1}(n)) &\leq 2e^{-n\log^{2c_2+2}(n)/(2m\log^{2c_2}(n))} \\
&\leq e^{-\log^{3/2}(n)} \leq 1/n.
\end{aligned}
$$

In particular, this means that with probability $1 - o(1)$ there remain unpeeled vertices in G_c^r after t rounds of peeling.

4. ABOVE THE THRESHOLD

---

[2]Formally, to cope with conditioning on events E_1 and E_2 in the application of Azuma's inequality, we must actually consider a slightly modified martingale. This technique is standard, and the details can be found in Section 4.

We now consider the case when $c > c_{k,r}^*$. We show that parallel peeling requires $\Omega(\log n)$ rounds in this case.

Molloy [19] showed that in this case there exists a $\rho > 0$ such that $\lim_{t \to \infty} \rho_t = \rho$. Similarly, $\lim_{t \to \infty} \beta_t = \beta > 0$ and $\lim_{t \to \infty} \lambda_t = \lambda > 0$. It follows that the core will have size $\lambda n + o(n)$. We examine how β_t and λ_t approach their limiting values to show that the parallel peeling algorithm takes $\Omega(\log n)$ rounds.

THEOREM 4.1. *Let $r \geq 3$ and $k \geq 2$. With probability $1 - o(1)$, the peeling process for the k-core in $G_{n,cn}^r$ terminates after $\Omega(\log n)$ rounds when $c > c_{k,r}^*$.*

PROOF. First, note that β corresponds to the fixed point

$$\beta = \left[1 - e^{-\beta} \sum_{j=0}^{k-2} \frac{\beta^j}{j!} \right]^{r-1} rc. \tag{10}$$

Let $\beta_i = \beta + \delta_i$, where $\delta_i > 0$. We begin by working in the idealized branching process model given in Section 3.1 to determine the behavior of β_i. Starting with Equation (5) and considering β_{i+1} as a function of δ_i, we obtain:

$$\beta_{i+1} = \left[1 - e^{-\beta - \delta_i} \sum_{j=0}^{k-2} \frac{(\beta + \delta_i)^j}{j!} \right]^{r-1} rc. \tag{11}$$

We now view the right hand side of Equation (11) as a function of δ_i. Denoting this function as $f(\delta_i)$, we take a Taylor series expansion around 0 and conclude that:

$$f(\delta_i) = f(0) + f'(0)\delta_i + \Theta(f''(0)\delta_i^2).$$

Equation (10) immediately implies that $f(0) = \beta$. Moreover, it can be calculated that

$$f'(0) = \frac{(r-1)\beta e^{-\beta}}{1 - e^{-\beta} \sum_{j=0}^{k-2} \frac{\beta^j}{j!}} \frac{\beta^{k-2}}{(k-2)!} \tag{12}$$

In particular, it holds that

$$0 < f'(0) < 1. \tag{13}$$

Note that while $f'(0) < 1$ can be checked explicitly, this condition also follows immediately from the convergence of the β_i values to β.

The fact that $0 < f'(0)$ is critical in our analysis. Indeed, when c is below the threshold density $c_{k,r}^*$, $\beta = 0$, and hence Equation (12) implies that $f'(0) = 0$. This is precisely why our analysis here "breaks" when $c < c_{k,r}^*$, and offers an intuitive explanation for why the number of rounds is $O(\log \log n)$ when $c < c_{k,r}^*$, but is $\Omega(\log n)$ when $c > c_{k,r}^*$.

Since $\beta_{i+1} = \beta + \delta_{i+1}$, δ_i decreases by a factor of at most $f'(0) + O(\delta_i)$ each iteration. In particular, for small enough δ_i, δ_i decreases by a factor of at most $f'(0) + \varepsilon_1$ for some $\varepsilon_1 > 0$ each iteration.

Next, we know that $\lambda = 1 - e^{-\beta} \sum_{j=0}^{k-1} \frac{\beta^j}{j!}$. Equations (4) and (13), imply that

$$\lambda_i = \lambda + \frac{e^{-\beta} \beta^{k-1}}{(k-1)!} \delta_i + O(\delta_i^2).$$

Hence, for suitably small (constant) δ_i values, in each round λ_i gets closer to λ by at most a constant factor under the idealized model. This suggests the $\Omega(\log n)$ bound. Specifically, we can choose $t = \gamma \log n$ for a suitably small constant γ so that δ_t in the idealized model remains $\Omega(n^{1-\eta})$ for a given constant $\eta < 1$. This gives that the "gap" $\lambda_t - \lambda$ is $\Omega(n^{-\eta})$, leaving an expected

$\Omega(n^{1-\eta})$ vertices still to be peeled. This number is high enough so that we can apply martingale concentration arguments, as deviations from the expectation can be made to be $o(n^{1-\eta})$ with high probability. This follows the approach of e.g. [3, 19].

To this end, note that it is straightforward to modify the argument of Lemma 3.4 to show that for a suitably small constant $c_1 > 0$, with probability $1 - O(1/n)$, for all vertices v, the neighborhood of distance $c_1 \log n$ around v contains at most n^{c_2} vertices for a suitable constant $c_2 > 0$. For suitable constants c_1, c_2, we refer to this event as E_3, and we condition on E_3 occurring for the duration of the proof.

As before, there are deviations from the idealized branching process, and we bound the effects of these deviations as follows. If we let Z_u be the number of already expanded vertices in the breadth first search when expanding a vertex u's neighborhood up to distance $c_1 \log n$, we have $Z_u \leq n^{c_2}$, so as we expand a neighborhood the probability of any collision is at most $n^{2c_2 - 1}$. Since we are proving a lower bound on the number of rounds required, we can pessimistically assume that such vertices (i.e., vertices u such that the BFS rooted at u results in a collision) will be peeled immediately – this will not affect our conclusion that $\Omega(n^{1-\eta})$ vertices remain to be peeled, as we may choose c_2 so that $n^{2c_2} = o(n^{1-\eta})$. Now we apply Azuma's martingale inequality [16, Theorem 12.4], exposing the cn edges in the graph one at a time; denote the random edges by $A_1, A_2, \ldots, A_{cn}$. We consider $t = c_1 \log n$ rounds for a c_1 that leaves a gap of $\Omega(n^\eta)$ for some small $\eta > 0$ (i.e., guarantees that $\lambda_t - \lambda > n^{-\eta}$; $\eta = 0.01$ suffices), and let X_t be the number of vertices that survive that many rounds with no duplicates in their neighborhood of depth $c_1 \log n$. Then $E[X_t] - \lambda n$ is $\Omega(n^{1-\eta})$.

For our martingale, we consider random variables $X_t^i = E[X_t \mid A_1, \ldots, A_i]$, so $X_t^0 = E[X_t]$ and $X_t^{cn} = X_t$. To cope with the conditioining on E_3, we consider the ancillary random variable Y_t^i where $Y_t^i = X_t$ as long there is no neighborhood of distance $c_1 \log n$ around any vertex v that contains at most n^{c_2} vertices among the i currently revealed edges and $Y_t^i = Y_t^{i-1}$ otherwise, for our suitably chosen constant c_2. Note $Y_t^0 = E[X_t] + O(1)$, and $\Pr(Y_t^{cn} \neq X_t^{cn})$ corresponds to the event E_3.[3] Each exposed edge changes the conditional expectation of Y_t by only $O(n^{c_2})$ vertices, so Azuma's martingale inequality yields:

$$\Pr(|Y_t - Y_t^0| \geq n^{2/3}) \leq 2e^{-n^{4/3}/(cn \cdot n^{2c_2})} \leq e^{-n^{1/6}}$$

for c_2 chosen suitably small. This implies

$$\Pr(|X_t - E[X_t]| \geq n^{2/3} + O(1)) \leq e^{-n^{1/6}} + \Pr(E_3).$$

Hence with probability $1 - o(1)$ there remain vertices to be peeled after $\Omega(\log n)$ rounds. □

Remark: As discussed in the introduction, the lower bound of Theorem 4.1 matches an $O(\log n)$ upper bound of Achiloptas and Molloy [1].

5. SIMULATION RESULTS

We implemented a simulation of the parallel peeling algorithm using the $G_{n,cn}^r$ model, in order to determine how well our theoretical analysis matches the empirical evolution of the peeling process. Our results demonstrate that the theoretical analysis matches the empirical evolution remarkably well.

To check the growth of the number of rounds as a function of n, we ran the program 1000 times for $r = 4, k = 2$ and various values of n and c, and computed the average number of rounds for the

---

[3]This method of dealing with conditioning while applying Azuma's martingale inequality is well known; see for example [5].

	$c=0.7$		$c=0.75$		$c=0.8$		$c=0.85$	
n	Failed	Rounds	Failed	Rounds	Failed	Rounds	Failed	Rounds
10000	0	12.504	0	23.352	1000	17.037	1000	10.773
20000	0	12.594	0	23.433	1000	19.028	1000	11.928
40000	0	12.791	0	23.343	1000	20.961	1000	12.992
80000	0	12.939	0	23.372	1000	22.959	1000	14.104
160000	0	12.983	0	23.421	1000	25.066	1000	15.005
320000	0	13.000	0	23.491	1000	27.089	1000	16.305
640000	0	13.000	0	23.564	1000	29.281	1000	17.334
1280000	0	13.000	0	23.716	1000	31.037	1000	18.499
2560000	0	13.000	0	23.840	1000	33.172	1000	19.570

Table 1: **Results from simulations of the parallel peeling process using** $r=4$ **and** $k=2$**, averaged over** 1000 **trials.**

peeling process to complete. For reference, $c_{2,4}^* \approx 0.772$. Table 1 shows the results.

For all the experiments, when $c < c_{2,4}^*$, all 1000 trials succeeded (empty k-core) and when $c > c_{2,4}^*$, all 1000 trials failed (non-empty k-core). For $c < c_{2,4}^*$, the average number of rounds increases very slowly with n, while for $c > c_{2,4}^*$, the average increases approximately linearly in $\log n$. This is in accord with our $O(\log \log n)$ result below the threshold and $\Omega(\log n)$ result above the threshold. The results for other values of r and k were similar.

We also tested how well the idealized values from the recurrence for λ_t (Equation (2)) approximate the fraction of vertices left after t rounds. Table 2 shows that the recurrence indeed describes the behavior of the peeling process remarkably well, both below and above the threshold. In these simulations, we used $r = 4, k = 2$ and $n = 1$ million. For each value of c, we averaged over 1000 trials.

6. GPU IMPLEMENTATION

Motivation. Using a graphics processing unit (GPU), we developed a parallel implementation for Invertible Bloom Lookup Tables (IBLTs), a data structure recently proposed by Goodrich and Mitzenmacher [9]. Two motivating applications are sparse recovery [9] and efficiently encodable and decodable error correcting codes [17]. For brevity we describe here only the sparse recovery application.

In the sparse recovery problem, N items are inserted into a set S, and subsequently all but n of the items are deleted. The goal is to recover the exact set S, using space proportional to the final number of items n, which can be much smaller than the total number of items N that were ever inserted. IBLTs achieve this roughly as follows. The IBLT maintains $O(n)$ cells, where each cell contains a key field and a checksum field. We use r hash functions $h_1, \ldots, h_r$. When an item x is inserted or deleted from S, we consider the r cells $h_1(x) \ldots h_r(x)$, and we XOR the key field of each of these cells with x, and we XOR the checksum field of each of these cells with checkSum(x), where checkSum is some simple pseudo-random function. Notice that the insertion and deletion procedures are identical.

In order to recover the set S, we iteratively look for "pure" cells – these are cells that only contain one item x in the final set S. Every time we find a pure cell whose key field is x, we recover x and delete x from S, which hopefully creates new pure cells. We continue until there are no more pure cells, or we have fully recovered the set S.

The IBLT defines a random r-uniform hypergraph G, in which vertices correspond to cells in the IBLT, and edges correspond to items in the set S. Pure cells in the IBLT correspond to vertices of degree less than $k = 2$. The IBLT recovery procedure precisely corresponds to a peeling process on G, and the recovery procedure is successful if and only if the 2-core of G is empty.

We note that this example application is similar to other applications of peeling algorithms. For example, in the setting of erasure-correcting codes [14], encoded symbols correspond to an XOR of some number of original message symbols. This naturally defines a hypergraph in which vertices correspond to encoded symbols, edges correspond to unrecovered original message symbols, and a vertex can recover a message symbol when its degree is 1. Decoding of this erasure-correcting code corresponds to peeling on the associated hypergraph (after deleting all vertices corresponding to erased codeword symbols), and full recovery of the message occurs when the 2-core is empty. Our analysis directly applies to the setting where each message symbol randomly chooses to contribute to a fixed number r of encoded symbols.

Implementation Details. Our parallel IBLT implementation consists of two stages: the insertion/deletion stage, during which items are inserted and deleted from the IBLT, and the recovery phase. Both phases can be parallelized.

One method of parallelizing the insertion/deletion phase is as follows: we devote a separate thread to each item to be inserted or deleted. A caveat is that multiple threads may try to modify a single cell at any point in time, and so we have to use atomic XOR operations, to ensure that threads trying to write to the same cell do not interfere with each other. In general, atomic operations can be a bottleneck in any parallel implementation; if t threads try to write to the same memory location, the algorithm will take at least t (serial) time steps. Nonetheless, our experiments showed this parallelization technique to be effective.

We parallelize the recovery phase as follows. We proceed in rounds, and in each round we devote a single thread to each cell in the IBLT. Each thread checks if its cell is pure, and if so it identifies the item contained in the cell, removes all r occurrences of the item from the IBLT, and marks the cell as recovered. The implementation proceeds until it reaches an iteration where no items are recovered – this can be checked by summing up (in parallel) the number of cells marked recovered after each round, and stopping when this number does not change. This procedure also requires atomic XOR operations, as two threads may simultaneously try to write to the same cell if there are two or more items $x \neq y$ recovered in the same round such that $h_i(x) = h_i(y)$ for some $1 \leq i \leq r$.

In addition, we must take care to avoid deleting an item multiple times from the IBLT. Indeed, since any item x inserted into the IBLT is placed into r cells, x might be contained in multiple pure cells at any instant, and the thread devoted to each such pure cell may try to delete x. This issue is not specific to the IBLT application: *any* implementation of the parallel peeling algorithm on a hypergraph, regardless of the application domain, must avoid peeling the same edge from the hypergraph multiple times.

To prevent this, we split the IBLT up into r subtables, and hash each item into one cell in each subtable upon insertion and dele-

	$c = 0.7$			$c = 0.85$	
t	Prediction	Experiment	t	Prediction	Experiment
1	768922	768925	1	853158	853172
2	673647	673664	2	811184	811200
3	608076	608097	3	793026	793042
4	553064	553091	4	784269	784281
5	500466	500503	5	779841	779851
6	444828	444872	6	777550	777559
7	380873	380930	7	776350	776359
8	302531	302607	8	775719	775728
9	204442	204550	9	775385	775394
10	93245	93398	10	775209	775218
11	14159	14269	11	775115	775124
12	74	78	12	775066	775074
13	0.00001	0	13	775039	775048
14	0	0	14	775025	775034
15	0	0	15	775018	775026
16	0	0	16	775014	775022
17	0	0	17	775012	775020
18	0	0	18	775011	775019
19	0	0	19	775010	775018
20	0	0	20	775010	775018

Table 2: Simulation results evaluating how well Equation (2) **approximates the number of vertices left after** t **rounds. The experiments are run using** $r = 4, k = 2, n = 1$ **million, averaged over** 1000 **trials.**

tion. When we execute the recovery algorithm, we iterate through the subtables serially (which requires r serial steps per round), processing each subtable in parallel. This ensures that an item x only gets removed from the table once, since the first time a pure cell is found containing x, x gets removed from all the other subtables.

This recovery procedure corresponds to an interesting and fundamental variant of the peeling process we analyze formally in Appendix B. In particular, one might initially expect that the number of (parallel) time steps required by our recovery procedure may be r times larger than the peeling process analyzed in Section 3, since our IBLT implementation requires r serial steps to iterate through all r subtables. However, we prove that the total number of parallel steps required by our IBLT implementation is roughly a factor of $\log_2(r-1)$ larger than the $\frac{1}{\log((k-1)(r-1))} \log\log n + O(1)$ bound proved for the peeling process of Section 3. This ensures that, in practice, the need to iterate serially through subtables does not create a significant serial bottleneck. Our analysis is connected in spirit to Vöcking's work on asymmetric load balancing [21], and we provide detailed discussion on the comparison between Theorems 3.1 and 6.1 in Appendix B.

THEOREM 6.1. (Informal) Let $r \geq$, and $\phi_{r-1} = \lim_{k \to \infty} F_{r-1}^{1/k}(k)$ be the growth rate for the Fibonacci sequence of order $r - 1$. For $c < c_{k,r}^*$, peeling with sub-tables on $G_{n,cn}^r$ terminates after $\frac{r}{r \log \phi_{r-1} + \log(k-1)} + O(1)$ sub-rounds.

We remark that while Theorem 3.1 holds for $r = 2$, $k \geq 3$, Theorem 6.1 holds only for $r \geq 3$.

Experimental Results. All of our serial code was written in C++ and all experiments were compiled with g++ using the -O3 compiler optimization flag and run on a workstation with a 64-bit Intel Xeon architecture and 48 GBs of RAM. We implemented all of our GPU code in CUDA with all compiler optimizations turned on, and ran our GPU implementation on an NVIDIA Tesla C2070 GPU with 6 GBs of device memory.

Summary of results. Relative to our serial implementation, our GPU implementation achieves 10x-12x speedups for the insertion/deletion phase, and 20x speedups for the recovery stage

when the edge density of the hypergraph is below the threshold for successful recovery (i.e. empty 2-core). When the edge density is slightly above the threshold for successful recovery, our parallel recovery implementation was only about 7x faster than our serial implementation. The reasons for this are two-fold. Firstly, above the threshold, many more rounds of the parallel peeling process were necessary before the 2-core was found. Secondly, above the threshold, less work was required of the serial implementation because fewer items were recovered; in contrast, the parallel implementation examines every cell in every round.

Our detailed experimental results are given in Tables 3 (for the case of $r = 3$ hash functions) and 4 (for the case of $r = 4$ hash functions). The timing results are averages over 10 trials each. For the GPU implementation, the reported times do count for the time to transfer data (i.e. the items to be inserted) from the CPU to the GPU.

The reported results are for a fixed IBLT size, consisting of 2^{24} cells. These results are representative for all sufficiently large input sizes: once the number of IBLT cells is larger than about 2^{19}, the runtime of our parallel implementation grows roughly linearly with the number of table cells (for any fixed table load). Here, table load refers to the ratio of the number of items in the IBLT to the number of cells in the IBLT. This corresponds to the edge density c in the corresponding hypergraph. The linear increase in runtime above a certain input size is typical, and is due to the fact that there is a finite number of threads that the GPU can launch at any one time.

7. ROUNDS AS A FUNCTION OF THE DISTANCE FROM THE THRESHOLD

Recall that the hidden constant in the $O(1)$ term of Theorem 3.1 depends on the size of the "gap" $v = c_{k,r}^* - c$ between the edge density and the threshold density. This term can be significant in practice when v is small, and in this section, we make the dependence on v explicit. Specifically, we extend the analysis of Section 3 to characterize how the growth of the number of rounds depends on $c_{k,r}^* - c$, when c is a constant with $c < c_{k,r}^*$. The proof of Theorem 7.1 below is deferred to the full version of the paper due to space constraints [10].

Table Load	No. Table Cells	% Recovered	GPU Recovery Time	Serial Recovery Time	GPU Insert Time	Serial Insert Time
0.75	16.8 million	100%	0.33 s	6.37 s	0.31 s	3.91 s
0.83	16.8 million	50.1%	0.42 s	3.64 s	0.35 s	4.34 s

Table 3: Results of our parallel and serial IBLT implementations with $r = 3$ hash functions. The table load refers to the ratio of the number of items in the IBLT to the number of cells in the IBLT.

Table Load	No. Table Cells	% Recovered	GPU Recovery Time	Serial Recovery Time	GPU Insert Time	Serial Insert Time
0.75	16.8 million	100%	0.47 s	8.37 s	0.42 s	4.55 s
0.83	16.8 million	24.6%	0.25 s	2.28 s	0.46 s	5.0 s

Table 4: Results of our parallel and serial IBLT implementations with $r = 4$ hash functions. The table load refers to the ratio of the number of items in the IBLT to the number of cells in the IBLT.

THEOREM 7.1. *Let $v = |c_{k,r}^* - c|$ for constant c with $c < c_{k,r}$. With probability $1 - o(1)$, peeling in $G_{n,cn}^r$ requires $\Theta(\sqrt{1/v}) + \frac{1}{\log((k-1)(r-1))} \log\log n$ rounds when c is below the threshold density $c_{k,r}^*$.*

8. CONCLUSION

In this paper, we analyzed parallel versions of the peeling process on random hypergraphs. We showed that when the number of edges is below the threshold edge density for the k-core to be empty, with high probability the parallel algorithm takes $O(\log\log n)$ rounds to peel the k-core to empty. In contrast, when the number of edges is above the threshold, with high probability it takes $\Omega(\log n)$ rounds for the algorithm to terminate with a non-empty k-core. We also considered some of the details of implementation and proposed a variant of the parallel algorithm that avoids a fundamental implementation issue; specifically, by using subtables, we avoid peeling the same element multiple times. We show this variant converges significantly faster than might be expected, thereby avoiding a sequential bottleneck. Our experiments confirm our theoretical results and show that in practice, peeling in parallel provides a considerable increase in efficiency over the serialized version.

9. REFERENCES

[1] D. Achlioptas and M. Molloy. The solution space geometry of random linear equations. *Random Structures and Algorithms* (to appear), 2013.

[2] Y. Azar, A. Broder, A. Karlin, and E. Upfal. Balanced allocations. *SIAM Journal of Computing* 29(1):180–200, 1999.

[3] A. Broder, A. Frieze, and E. Upfal. On the satisfiability and maximum satisfiability of random 3-CNF formulas. In *Proc. of the Fourth Annual ACM-SIAM Symposium on Discrete Algorithms*, pp. 322–330, 1993.

[4] B. Chazelle, J. Kilian, R. Rubinfeld, and A. Tal. The Bloomier filter: an efficient data structure for static support lookup tables. In *Proc. of the Fifteenth Annual ACM-SIAM Symposium on Discrete Algorithms*, pp. 30–39, 2004.

[5] F. Chung and L. Lu. Concentration inequalities and martingale inequalities: a survey. *Internet Mathematics*, 3(1):79-127, 2006.

[6] M. Dietzfelbinger, A. Goerdt, M. Mitzenmacher, A. Montanari, R. Pagh, and M. Rink. Tight thresholds for cuckoo hashing via XORSAT. In *Proc. of ICALP*, pp. 213–225, 2010.

[7] D. Eppstein, M. Goodrich, F Uyeda, and G. Varghese. What's the Difference? Efficient Set Reconciliation without Prior Context. *ACM SIGCOMM Computer Communications Review (SIGCOMM 2011)*, 41(4):218–229, 2011.

[8] P. Gao. Analysis of the parallel peeling algorithm: a short proof. *arXiv:1402.7326*, 2014.

[9] M. Goodrich and M. Mitzenmacher. Invertible Bloom Lookup Tables. In *Proc. of the 49th Allerton Conference*, pp. 792–799, 2011.

[10] J. Jiang, M. Mitzenmacher, J. Thaler. Parallel Peeling Algorithms. *CoRR abs/1302.7014*, 2013.

[11] R. Karp, M. Luby, and F. Meyer auf der Heide. Efficient PRAM simulation on a distributed memory machine. *Algorithmica*, 16(4):517–542, 1996.

[12] A. Kirsch, M. Mitzenmacher, and U. Wieder. More robust hashing: Cuckoo hashing with a stash. *SIAM Journal on Computing*, 39(4):1543-1561, 2009.

[13] L. Le Cam. An approximation theorem for the Poisson binomial distribution. Pacific Journal of Mathematics 10(4):1181-1197, 1960.

[14] M. Luby, M. Mitzenmacher, A. Shokrollahi, and D. Spielman. Efficient erasure correcting codes. *IEEE Transactions on Information Theory*, 47(2):569–584, 2001.

[15] M. Mitzenmacher. The power of two choices in randomized load balancing. *IEEE Transactions on Parallel and Distributed Systems*, 12(10):1094–1104, 2001.

[16] M. Mitzenmacher and E. Upfal. **Probability and computing: Randomized algorithms and probabilistic analysis**, 2005, Cambridge University Press.

[17] M. Mitzenmacher and G. Varghese. Biff (Bloom filter) codes: Fast error correction for large data sets. In *Proc. of the IEEE International Symposium on Information Theory*, pp. 483–487, 2012.

[18] M. Mitzenmacher and B. Vöcking. The asymptotics of selecting the shortest of two, improved. *Proc. of the 37th Annual Allerton Conference on Communication Control and Computing*, pp. 326–327, 1999.

[19] M. Molloy. The pure literal rule threshold and cores in random hypergraphs. In *Proc. of the 15th Annual ACM-SIAM Symposium on Discrete Algorithms*, pp. 672–681, 2004.

[20] A. Pagh and F. Rodler. Cuckoo hashing. Journal of Algorithms, 51(2):122–144, 2004.

[21] B. Vöcking. How asymmetry helps load balancing, *Journal of the ACM*, 50(4):568–589, 2003.

[22] U. Voll. Threshold Phenomena in Branching Trees and Sparse Random Graphs. Dissertation. Techischen Universität München. 2001.

APPENDIX

A. LE CAM'S THEOREM

Le Cam's Theorem can be stated as follows.

THEOREM A.1. *Let $X_1, X_2, \ldots, X_n$ be independent 0-1 random variables with $\Pr(X_i = 1) = p_i$. Let $\lambda = \sum_{i=1}^{n} p_i$ and $S = \sum_{i=1}^{n} X_i$. Then*

$$\sum_{k=0}^{\infty} |\Pr(S = k) - e^{-\lambda} \lambda^k / k!| < 2 \sum_{i=1}^{n} p_i^2.$$

In particular, when $p_i = \lambda/n$ for all i, we obtain that the binomial distribution converges to the Poisson distribution, with total variation distance bounded by λ^2/n.

B. PARALLEL PEELING WITH SUBTABLES

The parallel peeling process used in our GPU implementation of IBLTs in Section 6 does not precisely correspond to the one analyzed in Sections 3.2 and 4. The differences are two-fold. First, the underlying hypergraph G in our IBLT implementation is not chosen uniformly from all r-uniform hypergraphs; instead, vertices in G (i.e., IBLT cells) are partitioned into r equal-sized sets (or subtables) of size n/r, and edges are chosen at random subject to the constraint that each edge contains exactly one vertex from each set. Second, the peeling process in our GPU implementation does not attempt to peel all vertices in each round. Instead, our GPU implementation proceeds in *subrounds*, where each round consists of r subrounds. In the ith subround of a given round, we remove all the vertices of degree less than k in the ith subtable. Note that running one round of this algorithm is not equivalent to running one round of the original parallel peeling algorithm. This is because peeling the first subtable may free up new peelable vertices in the second subtable, and so on. Hence, running one round of the algorithm used in our GPU implementation may remove more vertices than running one round of the original algorithm.

In this section, we analyze the peeling process used in our GPU implementation. We can use a similar approach as above to obtain the recursion for the survival probabilities for this algorithm. Let $\rho_{i,j}$ be the probability that a vertex in the tree survives i rounds when it's in the jth subtable, with each $\rho_{0,j} = 1$. Then,

$$\rho_{i,j} = \Pr\left(\text{Poisson}\left(rc \prod_{h<j} \rho_{i,h} \prod_{h>j} \rho_{i-1,h}\right) \geq k-1\right).$$

By the same reasoning,

$$\lambda_{i,j} = \Pr\left(\text{Poisson}\left(rc \prod_{h<j} \rho_{i,h} \prod_{h>j} \rho_{i-1,h}\right) \geq k\right) \quad (14)$$

where $\lambda_{0,j} = 1$ for all j. Also, we can consider

$$\beta_{i,j} = rc \left(\prod_{h<j} \rho_{i,h}\right) \left(\prod_{h>j} \rho_{i-1,h}\right).$$

These equations differ from our original equation in a way similar to how the equations for standard multiple-choice load-balancing differ from Vöcking's asymmetric variation of multiple-choice load-balancing, where a hash table is similarly split into r subtables, each item is given one choice by hashing in each subtable, and the item is placed in the least loaded subtable, breaking ties according to some fixed ordering of the subtables [18, 21].

Motivated by this, we can show that in this variation, below the threshold, these values eventually decrease "Fibonacci exponentially", that is, with the exponent falling according to a generalized

Fibonacci sequence. We follow the same approach as outlined in Section 3.1. Let $\beta'_m = \beta_{i,j}$ where $m = (i-1)r + j$, and similarly for λ'_m and ρ'_m, so we may work in a single dimension. Let $F_{r-1}(i)$ represent the ith number in a Fibonacci sequence of order $r - 1$. Here, a Fibonacci sequence of order r is defined such that the first $r - 1$ elements in the sequence equal one, and for $i > r - 1$, the ith element is defined to be the sum of the preceding $r - 1$ terms.

We choose a constant I so that $\beta'_{I+a} \leq \phi^{F_{r-1}(a)}$ for an appropriate constant $\phi < 1$ and $0 \leq a \leq r - 1$. We inductively show that

$$\beta'_{I+t} \leq \phi^{(k-1)^{\lfloor t/r \rfloor} F_{r-1}(t)}$$

when $\frac{rc}{[(k-1)!]^{r-1}} < 1$; as in Section 3, the proof can be modified easily if $\frac{rc}{[(k-1)!]^{r-1}} > 1$ by simply choosing a different (constant) starting point I for the induction. In this case, for $t \geq r$

$$\begin{aligned}
\beta'_{I+t} &\leq \left[\prod_{I+t-r<j<I+t} \frac{(\beta'_j)^{k-1}}{(k-1)!}\right] rc \\
&\leq \frac{rc}{[(k-1)!]^{r-1}} \prod_{I+t-r<j<I+t} (\beta'_j)^{k-1} \\
&\leq \frac{rc}{[(k-1)!]^{r-1}} \prod_{I+t-r<j<I+t} \left(\phi^{F_{r-1}(j)(k-1)^{\lfloor (t-r)/r \rfloor}}\right)^{(k-1)} \\
&\leq \phi^{(k-1)^{\lfloor t/r \rfloor} F_{r-1}(t)}. \quad (15)
\end{aligned}$$

Thus, our induction yields that the exponent of ϕ in the β'_m values falls according to a generalized Fibonacci sequence of order $r - 1$, leading to an asymptotic constant factor reduction in the number of overall rounds, even as we have to work over a larger number of subrounds. Inequality (15) applies to the idealized branching process, but we can handle deviations between the idealized process and the actual process essentially as in Theorem 3.1. This yields the following variation of Theorem 3.1 for the setting of peeling with sub-tables.

THEOREM B.1. *Let $r \geq 3$ and $k \geq 2$. Let $\phi_{r-1} = \lim_{k \to \infty} F_{r-1}^{1/k}(k)$ be the asymptotic growth rate for the Fibonacci sequence of order $r - 1$. Let G be a hypergraph over n nodes with cn edges generated according to the following random process. The vertices of G are partitioned into r subsets of equal size, and the edges are generated at random subject to the constraint that each edge contains exactly one vertex from each set.*

With probability $1 - o(1)$, the peeling process for the k-core in G that uses r subrounds in each round terminates after $\frac{1}{r \log \phi_{r-1} + \log(k-1)} \log \log n + O(1)$ rounds when $c < c^*_{k,r}$.

It is worth performing a careful comparison of Theorems 3.1 and B.1. For simplicity, we will restrict the discussion to $k = 2$. This corresponds to the case where we are interested in the 2-core of the hypergraph, as in our IBLT implementation. Theorem 3.1 guarantees that the peeling process of Section 3 requires $\frac{1}{\log(r-1)} \log \log n + O(1)$. Meanwhile, Theorem B.1 guarantees that the total number of sub-rounds required by our IBLT implementation is $r \cdot \frac{1}{r \log \phi_{r-1}} \log \log n + O(1) = \frac{1}{\log \phi_{r-1}} \log \log n + O(1)$. Thus, parallel peeling with subtables takes a factor $\log(r-1)/\log(\phi_{r-1})$ more (sub)-rounds than parallel peeling without subtables.

For $r = 3$, $\phi_{r-1} \approx 1.61$ is the golden ratio, and in this case $\log(r - 1)/\log(\phi_{r-1}) \approx 1.456$. Thus, for $r = 3$ and $k = 2$, parallel peeling with sub-tables takes a factor of less than 1.5 times more (sub)-rounds than parallel peeling. In contrast, one might a priori have expected that the number of sub-rounds for peeling with sub-tables would be a factor $r = 3$ larger than in the standard peeling process, since r serial steps are required to iterate through all r subtables.

	$c = 0.7$		$c = 0.75$	
n	Failed	Subrounds	Failed	Subrounds
10000	0	26.018	0	47.732
20000	0	26.142	0	47.659
40000	0	26.273	0	47.666
80000	0	26.452	0	47.783
160000	0	26.585	0	47.769
320000	0	26.790	0	47.925
640000	0	26.957	0	48.070
1280000	0	27.006	0	48.141
2560000	0	27.012	0	48.175

Table 5: Results of simulations of peeling with subtables using $r = 4$ and $k = 2$, over 1000 trials.

As r grows, ϕ_{r-1} rapidly approaches 2 from below. For example, for $r = 4$ this quantity is approximately 1.83 and for $r = 5$ it is approximately 1.92 [21]. It follows that for large r the ratio $\log(r-1)/\log(\phi_{r-1})$ is very close to $\log_2(r-1)$.

Simulations with Subtables

We ran simulations for the parallel peeling algorithm with subtables in a similar way as the simulations in Section 5. Table 5 shows the results for the average number of subrounds. The number of subrounds is at most r times the number of rounds in the original parallel peeling algorithm, but our analysis of Section B suggests the number of subrounds should be significantly smaller. In this case, comparing Table 5 with Table 1, this factor is about 2.

We also performed simulations to determine how closely the recursion given in Equation (14) predicts the number of vertices left after peeling the jth subtable in the ith round. Denote by $\lambda'_{i,j}$ the expected fraction of vertices left in the (i,j)'th subround. Then $\lambda'_{i,j}$ is given by the following formula:

$$\lambda'_{i,j} = \frac{1}{r}\left(\sum_{h \le j} \lambda_{i,h} + \sum_{h > j} \lambda_{i-1,h}\right),$$

where the $\lambda_{i,j}$ values are given by Equation (14). The results are presented in Table 6, where the prediction column reports the values of $\lambda'_{i,j}n$. As can be seen, the prediction closely matches the number of vertices left in the simulation.

		$c = 0.7$	
i	j	Prediction	Experiment
1	1	942230	942230
1	2	876807	876803
1	3	801855	801855
1	4	714875	714878
2	1	678767	678771
2	2	643070	643080
2	3	609686	609697
2	4	581912	581919
3	1	554402	554414
3	2	527335	527341
3	3	500469	500476
3	4	472470	472475
4	1	442874	442871
4	2	410958	410956
4	3	375770	375764
4	4	336458	336447
5	1	292159	292144
5	2	242396	242374
5	3	187891	187866
5	4	131789	131776
6	1	80372	80376
6	2	40582	40600
6	3	15481	15503
6	4	3649	3666
7	1	348	354
7	2	6	6
7	3	0.003	0.008
7	4	0	0

Table 6: Results of simulations of peeling with subtables showing how well the recursion for $\lambda'_{i,j}$ approximates the number of vertices left after t rounds. The experiments are run using $r = 4, k = 2, n = 1$ million, averaged over 1000 trials.

Balanced Allocations and Double Hashing

Michael Mitzenmacher*
Harvard University
School of Engineering and Applied Sciences
michaelm@eecs.harvard.edu

ABSTRACT

With double hashing, for an item x, one generates two hash values $f(x)$ and $g(x)$, and then uses combinations $(f(x) + ig(x))$ mod n for $i = 0, 1, 2, \ldots$ to generate multiple hash values from the initial two. We show that the performance difference between double hashing and fully random hashing appears negligible in the standard balanced allocation paradigm, where each item is placed in the least loaded of d choices, as well as several related variants. We perform an empirical study, and consider multiple theoretical approaches. While several techniques can be used to show asymptotic results for the maximum load, we demonstrate how fluid limit methods explain why the behavior of double hashing and fully random hashing are essentially indistinguishable in this context.

1. INTRODUCTION

The standard balanced allocation paradigm works as follows: suppose n balls are sequentially placed into n bins, where each ball is placed in the least loaded of d uniform independent choices of the bins. Then the maximum load (that is, the maximum number of balls in a bin) is $\frac{\log \log n}{\log d} + O(1)$, much lower than the $\frac{\log n}{\log \log n}(1 + o(1))$ obtained where each ball is placed according to a single uniform choice [3].

The assumption that each ball obtains d independent uniform choices is a strong one, and a reasonable question, tackled by several other works, is how much randomness is needed for these types of results (see related work below). Here we consider a novel approach, examining balanced allocations in conjunction with *double hashing*. In the well-known technique of standard double hashing for open-addressed hash tables, the jth ball obtains two hash values, $f(j)$ and $g(j)$. For a hash table of size n, $f(j) \in [0, n-1]$ and $g(j) \in [1, n-1]$. Successive locations $h(j, k) = f(j) +$

*Supported in part by NSF grants CCF-0915922, IIS-0964473, and CNS-1011840. Part of this work was done while visiting Microsoft Research New England.

$kg(j)$ mod n, $k = 0, 1, 2, \ldots\ldots$, are tried until an empty slot is found. As discussed later in this introduction, double hashing is extremely conducive to both hardware and software implementations and is used in many deployed systems.

In our context, we use the double hashing approach somewhat differently. The jth ball again obtains two hash values $f(j)$ and $g(j)$. The d choices for the jth ball are then given by $h(j, k) = f(j) + kg(j)$ mod n, $k = 0, 1, \ldots, d-1$, and the ball is placed in the least loaded. We generally assume that $f(j)$ is uniform over $[0, n-1]$, $g(j)$ is uniform over all numbers in $[1, n-1]$ relatively prime to n, and all hash values are independent. (It is convenient to consider n a prime, or take n to be a power of 2 so that the $g(j)$ are uniformly chosen random odd numbers, to ensure the $h(j, k)$ values are distinct.)

It might appear that limiting the space of random choices available to the balls in this way might change the behavior of this random process significantly. We show that this is not the case both in theory and in practice. Specifically, by "essentially indistinguishable", we mean that, empirically, for any constant i and sufficiently large n the fraction of bins of load i is well within the difference expected by experimental variance for the two methods. Essentially indistinguishable means that in practice for even reasonable n one cannot readily distinguish the two methods. By "vanishing" we mean that, analytically, for any constant i the asymptotic fraction of bins of load i for double hashing differs only by $o(1)$ terms from fully independent choices with high probability. A related key result is that $O(\log \log n)$ bounds on the maximum load hold for double hashing as well. Surprisingly, the difference between d fully independent choices and d choices using double hashing are essentially indistinguishable for sufficiently large n and vanishing asymptotically. [1]

As an initial example of empirical results, Table 1 below shows the fraction of bins of load x for various x taken over 10000 trials, with $n = 2^{14}$ balls thrown into n bins using $d = 3$ and $d = 4$ choices, using both double hashing and fully random hash values (where for our proxy for "random" we utilize the standard approach of simply generating successive random values using the drand48 function in C initially seeded by time). Most values are given to five decimal places. The performance difference is essentially indistin-

---

[1] To be clear, we do not mean that there is *no* difference between double hashing and fully random hashing in this setting; there clearly is and we note a simple example further in the paper. As we show, analytically in the limit for large n the difference is vanishing (Theorem 8 and Corollary 9), and for finite n the results from our experiments demonstrate the difference is essentially indistinguishable (Section A).

Load	Fully Random	Double Hashing
0	0.17693	0.17691
1	0.64664	0.64670
2	0.17592	0.17589
3	0.00051	0.00051

(a) 3 choices, $n = 2^{14}$ balls and bins

Load	Fully Random	Double Hashing
0	0.14081	0.14081
1	0.71840	0.71841
2	0.14077	0.14076
3	$2.25 \cdot 10^{-5}$	$2.29 \cdot 10^{-5}$

(b) 4 choices, $n = 2^{14}$ balls and bins

Table 1: An initial example showing the performance of double hashing compared to fully random hashing. In our tables, the row with load x gives the fraction of the bins that have load x over all trials. So over 10000 trials of throwing $n = 2^{14}$ balls into 2^{14} bins using 3 choices and double hashing, the fraction of bins with load 0 was 0.17691.

guishable, well within what one would expect simply from variance from the sampling process.

More extensive empirical results appear in Appendix A. In particular, we also consider two extensions to the standard paradigm: Vöcking's extension (sometimes called d-left hashing), where the n bins are split into d subtables of size n/d laid out left to right, the d choices consist of one uniform independent choice in each subtable, and ties for the least loaded bin are broken to the left [39]; and the continuous variation, where the bins represent queues, and the balls represent customers that arrive as a Poisson process and have exponentially distributed service requirements [27]. We again find empirically that replacing fully random choices with double hashing leads to essentially indistinguishable results in practice.[2]

In this paper, we provide theoretical results explaining why this would be the case. There are multiple methods available that can yield $O(\log \log n)$ bounds on the maximum load when n balls are thrown into n bins in the setting of fully random choices. We therefore first demonstrate how some previously used methods, including the layered induction approach of [3] and the witness tree approach of [39], readily yield $O(\log \log n)$ bounds; this asymptotic behavior is, arguably, unsurprising (at least in hindsight). We then examine the key question of why the difference in empirical results is vanishing, a much stronger requirement. For the case of fully random choices, the asymptotic fraction of bins of each possible load can be determined using fluid limit methods that yield a family of differential equations describing the process behavior [27]. It is not a priori clear, however, why the method of differential equations should necessarily apply when using double hashing, and the primary result of this paper is to explain why it in fact applies. The argument depends technically on the idea that the "history" engendered by double hashing in place of d fully random hash functions has only a vanishing (that is, $o(1)$) effect on the differential equations that correspond to the limiting behavior of the bin loads. We believe this resolution suggests that double hashing will be found to obtain the same results as fully random hashing in other additional hash-based structures, which may be important in practical settings.

We argue these results are important for multiple reasons. First, we believe the fact that moving from fully random hashing to double hashing does not change performance for these particular balls and bins problems is interesting in its own right. But it also has practical applications; multiple-

choice hashing is used in several hardware systems (such as routers), and double hashing both requires less (pseudo-)randomness and is extremely conducive to implementation in hardware [11, 17]. (As we discuss below, it may also be useful in software systems.) Both the fact that double hashing does not change performance, and the fact that one can very precisely determine the performance of double hashing for load balancing simply using the same fluid limit equations as have been used under the assumption of fully random hashing, are therefore of major importance for designing systems that use multiple-choice methods (and convincing system designers to use them). Finally, as mentioned, these results suggest that using double hashing in place of fully random choices may similarly yield the same performance in other settings that make use of multiple hash functions, such as for cuckoo hashing or in error-correcting codes, offering the same potential benefits for these problems. We have explored this issue further in a subsequent (albeit already published) paper [30], where there remain further open questions. In particular, we have not yet found how to use the fluid limit analysis used here for these other problems.

Finally, it has been remarked to us that all of our arguments here apply beyond double hashing; any hashing scheme where the d choices for a ball are made so that they are pairwise independent and uniform would yield the same result by the same argument. That is, if for a given ball with d choices $h_1, h_2, \ldots, h_d$, for any distinct bins b_1 and b_2 we have for all $1 \le i, j \le d, i \ne j$:

$$\mathbf{Pr}(h_i = b_1) = 1/n \text{ and}$$

$$\mathbf{Pr}(h_i = b_1 \text{ and } h_j = b_2) = \frac{1}{\binom{n}{2}},$$

then our results apply. Unfortunately, we do not know of any actual scheme besides double hashing in practical use with these properties; hence we focus on double hashing throughout.

1.1 Related Work

The balanced allocations paradigm, or the power of two choices, has been the subject of a great deal of work, both in the discrete balls and bins setting and in the queueing theoretic setting. See, for example, the survey articles [21, 29] for references and applications.

Several recent works have considered hashing variations that utilize less randomness in place of assuming perfectly random hash functions; indeed, there is a long history of work on universal hash functions [9], and more recently minwise independent hashing [8]. Specific recent related works include results on standard one-choice balls and bins prob-

---

[2]We encourage the reader to examine these experimental results. However, because we recognize some readers are as a rule uninterested in experimental results, we have moved them to an appendix.

lems [10], hashing with linear probing with limited independence [34], and tabulation hashing [35]; other works involving balls and bins with less randomness include [15, 36]. As another example, Woelfel shows that a variation of Vöcking's results hold using simple hash functions that utilize a collection of k-wise independent hash functions for small k, and a random vector requiring $o(n)$ space [41].

Another related work in the balls and bins setting is the paper of Kenthapadi and Panigrahy [19], who consider a setting where balls are not allowed to choose any two bins, but are forced to choose two bins corresponding to an edge on an underlying random graph. In the same paper, they also show that two random choices that yield d bins are sufficient for similar $O(\log \log n)$ bounds on maximum loads that one obtains with d fully random choices, where in their case each random choice gives a contiguous block of $d/2$ bins.

Interestingly, the classical question regarding the average length of an unsuccessful search sequence for standard double hashing in an open address hash table when the table load is a constant α has been shown to be, up to lower order terms, $1/(1 - \alpha)$, showing that double hashing has essentially the same performance as random probing (where each ball would have its own random permutation of the bins to examine, in order, until finding an empty bin) when using traditional hash tables [6, 16, 24]. These results appear to have been derived using different techniques than we utilize here; it could be worthwhile to construct a general analysis that applies for both schemes.

A few papers have recently suggested using double hashing in schemes where one would use multiple hash functions and shown little or no loss in performance. For Bloom filters, Kirsch and Mitzenmacher [20], starting from the empirical analysis by Dillinger and Manolios [13], prove that using double hashing has negligible effects on Bloom filter performance. This result is closest in spirit to our current work; indeed, the type of analysis here can be used to provide an alternative argument for this phenomenon, although the case of Bloom filters is inherently simpler. Several available online implementations of Bloom filters now use this approach, suggesting that the double hashing approach can be significantly beneficial in software as well as hardware implementations.[3] Bachrach and Porat use double hashing in a variant of min-wise independent sketches [4]. The reduction in randomness stemming from using double hashing to generate multiple hash values can be useful in other contexts. For example, it is used in [33] to improve results where pairwise independent hash functions are sufficient for suitably random data; using double hashing requires fewer hash values to be generated (two in place of a larger number), which means less randomness in the data is required. Finally, in work subsequent to the original draft of this paper [30], we have empirically examined double hashing for other algorithms such as cuckoo hashing, and again found essentially no empirical difference between fully random hashing and double hashing in this and other contexts. However, theoretical results for these settings that prove this lack of difference are as of yet very limited.

Arguably, the main difference between our work and other related work is that in our setting with double hashing we

find the empirical results are essentially indistinguishable in practice, and we focus on examining this phenomenon.

2. INITIAL THEORETICAL RESULTS

We now consider formal arguments for the excellent behavior for double hashing. We begin with some simpler but coarser arguments that have been previously used in multiple-choice hashing settings, based on majorization and witness trees. While our witness tree argument dominates our majorization argument, we present both, as they may be useful in considering future variations, and they highlight how these techniques apply in these settings. In the following section, we then consider the fluid limit methodology, which best captures the result we desire here, namely that the load distributions are essentially the same with fully random hashing and double hashing. However, the fluid limit methodology captures results about the fraction of bins with load i, for every constant value i, and does not readily provide $O(\log \log n)$ bounds (without specialized additional work, which often depend on the techniques used below). The reader conversant with balanced allocation results utilizing majorization and witness trees may choose to skip this section.

2.1 A Majorization Argument

We first note that using double hashing with two choices and using random hashing with two distinct hash values per ball are equivalent. With this we can provide a simple argument, showing the seemingly obvious fact that using double hashing with $d > 2$ choices is at least as good as using 2 random choices. This in turn shows that double hashing maintains $\log \log n + O(1)$ maximum load in the standard balls and bins setting.

Our approach uses a standard majorization and coupling argument, where the coupling links the random choices made by the processes when using double hashing and using random hashing while maintaining the fidelity of both individual processes. (See, e.g., [3, 5], or [26] for more background on majorization.) Let $\vec{x} = (x_1, \ldots, x_n)$ be a vector with elements in non-increasing order, so $x_1 \geq x_2 \ldots \geq x_n$, and similarly for $\vec{y} = (y_1, \ldots, y_n)$. We say that $\vec{x}$ majorizes $\vec{y}$ if $\sum_{i=1}^{n} x_i = \sum_{i=1}^{n} y_i$ and, for $j < n$, $\sum_{i=1}^{j} x_i \geq \sum_{i=1}^{j} y_i$. For two Markovian processes X and Y, we say that X stochastically majorizes Y if there is a coupling of the processes X and Y so that at each step under the coupling the vector representing the state of X majorizes the vector representing the state of Y. We note that because we use the loads of the bins as the state, the balls and bins processes we consider are Markovian.

We make use of the following simple and standard lemma. (See, for example, [3, Lemma 3.4].)

LEMMA 1. *If $\vec{x}$ majorizes $\vec{y}$ for vectors $\vec{x}$, $\vec{y}$ of positive integers, and e_i represents a unit vector with a 1 in the ith entry and 0 elsewhere, then $\vec{x} + e_i$ majorizes $\vec{y} + e_j$ for $j \geq i$.*

THEOREM 2. *Let process X be the process where m balls are placed into n bins with two distinct random choices, and Y be the corresponding scheme with $d > 2$ choices using double hashing. Then X stochastically majorizes Y.*

PROOF. At each time step, we let $\vec{x}(t)$ and $\vec{y}(t)$ be the vectors corresponding to the loads sorted in decreasing order. We inductively claim that $\vec{x}(t)$ majorizes $\vec{y}(t)$ at all time

[3]See, for example, http://leveldb.googlecode.com/svn/trunk/util/bloom.cc, https://github.com/armon/bloomd, and http://hackage.haskell.org/packages/archive/bloomfilter/1.0/doc/html/bloomfilter.txt.

steps under the coupling of the processes where if the ath and bth bins in the sorted order for X are chosen, the ath and bth bins in the sorted order for Y are chosen as the first two choices, and then the remaining choices are determined by double hashing. That is, the d hash choices are such that the gap between successive choices is $b-a$, so the choices are a, b, $2b-a$, $3b-2a$, and so on (modulo the size of the table). Clearly $\vec{x}(0)$ majorizes $\vec{y}(0)$ as the vectors are equal. It is simple to check that this process maintains the majorization using Lemma 1, as the coordinate that increases in $\vec{y}(t)$ at each step is deeper in the sorted order than the coordinate that increases in $\vec{x}(t)$. $\square$

As two random choices stochastically majorizes d choices from double hashing under this coupling, we see that

$$\mathbf{Pr}(x_1 \geq c) \geq \mathbf{Pr}(y_1 \geq c)$$

for any value c. Since the seminal result of [3] shows that using two choices gives a maximum load of $\log \log n + O(1)$ with high probability, we therefore have this corollary.

COROLLARY 3. *The maximum load using $d > 2$ choices and double hashing for n balls and n bins is $\log \log n + O(1)$ with high probability.*

We note that, similarly, when using double hashing, we can show that using d choices stochastically majorizes using $d+1$ choices.

2.2 A Witness Tree Argument

It is well known that $d > 2$ choices performs better than 2 choices for multiple-choice hashing; while the maximum load remains $O(\log \log n)$, the constant factor depends on d, and can be important in practice. Our simple majorization argument does not provide this type of bound, so to achieve it, we next utilize the witness tree approach, following closely the work of Vöcking [39]. (See also [38] for related arguments.) While we discuss the case of insertions only, the arguments also apply in settings with deletions as well; see [39] for more details. Similarly, here we consider only the standard balls and bins setting of n balls and n bins with $d \geq 3$ being a constant, but similar results for $m = cn$ balls for some constant c can also be derived by simply changing the "base case" at the leaves of the witness tree accordingly, and similar results for Vöcking's scheme can be derived by using the "unbalanced" witness tree used by Vöcking [39] in place of the balanced one.

These methods allow us to prove statements of the following form:

THEOREM 4. *Suppose n balls are placed into n bins using the balanced allocation scheme with double hashing as described above. Then with d choices the maximum load is $\log \log n / \log d + O(d)$ with high probability.*

We note that, while Vöcking obtains a bound of $\log \log n / \log d + O(1)$, we have an $O(d)$ term that appears necessary to handle the leaves in our witness tree. (A similar issue appears to arise in [41].) For constant d these are asymptotically the same; however, an $O(1)$ additive term is more pleasing both theoretically and potentially in practice. How we deviate from Vöcking's argument is explained below.

PROOF. Following [39], we define a witness tree, which is a tree-ordered (multi)set of balls. Each node in the tree represents a ball, inserted at a certain time; the ith inserted ball corresponds to time i in the natural way. The ball represented by the root r is placed at time t, and a child node must have been inserted at a time previous to its parent. A leaf node in Vöcking's argument is *activated* if each of the d locations of the corresponding ball contains at least three balls when it is inserted. An edge (u, v) is activated if when v is the ith child of u, then the ith location of u's ball is the same as one of the locations of v's ball. A witness tree is activated if all of its leaf nodes and edges are activated.

Following Vöcking's approach, we first bound the probability that a witness tree is activated for the simpler case where the nodes of the witness trees represent distinct balls. The argument then can be generalized to deal with witness trees where the same ball may appear multiple times. As this follows straightforwardly using the technical approach in [39], we do not provide the full argument here.

We now explain where we must deviate from Vöcking's argument. The original argument utilizes the fact that most $n/3$ bins have load at least 3, deterministically. As leaf nodes in Vöcking's argument are required to have all d choices of bins have load at least 3 to be activated, a leaf node corresponding to a ball with d choices of bins is activated with probability at most 3^{-d}, and a collection of q leaf nodes are all activated with probability 3^{-dq}. However, this argument will not apply in our case, because the choices of bins are not independent when using double hashing, and depending on which bins are loaded, we can obtain very different results. For example, consider a case where the first $n/3$ bins have load at least 3. The fraction of choices using double hashing where all d bins have load at least 3 is significantly more than 3^{-d}, which would be the probability if $n/3$ bins with load 3 were randomly distributed. Indeed, for a newly placed ball j, if $f(j)$ and $g(j)$ are both less than $n/(3(d+1))$, all d choices will have load at least 3, and this occurs with probability at least $(9(d + 1)^2)^{-1}$. While such a configuration is unlikely, the deterministic argument used by Vöcking no longer applies.

We modify the argument to deal with this issue. In our double hashing setting, let us call a leaf active if either

- Some ball in the past has two or more of the bins at this leaf among its d choices.
- All the d bins chosen by this ball have previously been chosen by $4d$ previous balls.

The probability that any previous ball has hit two or more of the bins at the leaf is $O(d^4 n^{-1})$: there are $\binom{d}{2}$ pairs of bins from the d choices at the leaf; at most $d(d - 1)$ pairs of positions within the d choices where that pair could occur in any previous ball; at most n possible previous balls; and each bad choice that leads that previous ball to have a specific pair of bins in a specific pair of positions occurs with probability $1/(n(n - 1))$. Once we exclude this case, we can consider only balls that hit at most one of the d bins associated with the leaf.

For any time corresponding to a leaf, we bound the probability that any specific bin has been chosen by $4d$ or more previous balls. We note by symmetry that the probability any specific ball chooses a specific bin is d/n. The probability in question is then at most

$$\binom{n}{4d} \left(\frac{d}{n}\right)^{4d} \leq \frac{d^{4d}}{(4d)!} < \left(\frac{e}{4}\right)^d,$$

which is less than $\frac{1}{3}$ whenever $d \geq 3$. Further, once we consider the case of previous balls that choose two or more bins at this leaf separately, the events that the d bins chosen by this ball have previously been chosen by $4d$ previous balls are negatively correlated. Hence, we find the probability a specific leaf node is activated is less than 3^{-d}.

However, following [39], we need to consider a collection of q leaves and show the probability that they are all active is at most 3^{-dq}. We will do this below by using Azuma's inequality to show the fraction of choices of hash values from double hashing that lead to an activated ball is less than 3^{-d} with high probability. As balls corresponding to leaves independently choose their hash values, this result suffices.

Let S be the set of pairs of hash values that generate d values that would activate a leaf at time n. We have $\mathbb{E}[|S|] < \left(\frac{e}{4}\right)^d n(n-1) + cd^4(n-1)$ for some constant c, so $\mathbb{E}[|S|] > (3^{-d} - \gamma)n(n-1)$ for some constant γ and large enough n. Consider the Doob martingale obtained by revealing the bins for the balls one at a time. Each ball can change the final value of S by at most dn, since the bin where any ball is placed is involved in less than dn choices of pairs. Azuma's inequality (e.g., [31, Section 12.5]) then yields

$$\mathbf{Pr}(|S| > 3^{-d}n(n-1)) \leq \exp(-\delta n)$$

for a constant δ that depends on d and γ. It follows readily that the fraction of pairs of hash values that activate a leaf is at most 3^{-d} with very high probability throughout the process; by conditioning on this event, we can continue with Vöcking's argument. (The conditioning only adds an exponentially small additional probability to the probability the maximum load exceeds our bound.)

Specifically, we note for there to be a bin of load $L + 4d$, there must be an activated witness tree of depth L. We can bound the probability that some witness tree (with distinct balls) of depth L is activated. The probability an edge is activated is the probability a ball chooses a specific bin, which as previously noted is d/n. As all balls are distinct, the probability that a witness tree of m balls has all edges activated is $(d/n)^{m-1}$, and as we have shown the probability of all leaves being activated is bounded above by 3^{-dq} where $q = d^L$ is the number of leaves. Following [39], as there are at most n^m ways of choosing the balls for the witness tree, the probability that there exists an active witness tree is at most

$$
\begin{aligned}
n^m \left(\frac{d}{n}\right)^{m-1} 3^{-dq} &\leq n \cdot d^{2q} \cdot 3^{-dq} \\
&\leq n \cdot 2^{-q} \\
&= n \cdot 2^{-d^L}.
\end{aligned}
$$

Hence choosing $L \leq \log_d \log_2 n + \log_d(1 + \alpha)$ guarantees a maximum load of $L + 4d$ with probability $O(n^{-\alpha})$. □

3. THE FLUID LIMIT ARGUMENT

We now consider the fluid limit approach of [28]. (A useful survey of this approach appears in [12].) The fluid limit approach gives equations that describe the asymptotic fraction of bins with each possible integer load, and concentration around these values follows from martingale bounds (e.g., [14, 22, 42]). Values can easily be determined numerically, and prove highly accurate even for small numbers of balls and bins. We show that the same equations apply even in the

setting of double hashing, giving a theoretical justification for our empirical findings in Appendix A. This approach can be easily extended to other multiple choice processes (such as Vöcking's scheme and the queuing setting). We emphasize that the fluid limit approach does not, in itself, yield bounds of the type that the maximum load is $O(\log \log n)$ with high probability naturally; rather, it says that for any constant integer i, the fraction of bins of load i is concentrated around the value obtained by the fluid limit. One generally has to do additional work – generally similar in nature to the arguments in the proceeding sections – to obtain $O(\log \log n)$ bounds. As we already have an $O(\log \log n)$ bound from alternative techniques, here our focus is on showing the fluid limits are the same under double hashing and fully random hashing, which explains our empirical findings. (We show one could achieve an $O(\log \log n)$ bound from the results of this section – actually bound of $\log_d \log_2 n + O(1)$ – in Appendix B.)

The standard balls and bins fluid limit argument runs as follows. Let $X_i(t)$ be a random variable denoting the number of bins with load *at least* i after tn balls have been thrown; hence $X_0(0) = n$ and $X_i(0) = 0$ for all $i \geq 1$. Let $x_i(t) = X_i(t)/n$. For X_i to increase when a ball is thrown, all of its choices must have load at least $i-1$, but not all of them can have load at least i. Hence for $i \geq 1$

$$\mathbb{E}[X_i(t + 1/n) - X_i(t)] = (x_{i-1}(t))^d - (x_i(t))^d.$$

Let $\Delta(x_i) = x_i(t+1/n) - x_i(t)$ and $\Delta(t) = 1/n$. Then the above can be written as:

$$\mathbb{E}\left[\frac{\Delta(x_i)}{\Delta(t)}\right] = (x_{i-1}(t))^d - (x_i(t))^d.$$

In the limit as n grows, we can view the limiting version of the above equation as

$$\frac{dx_i}{dt} = x_{i-1}^d - x_i^d,$$

where we remove the t on the right hand side as the meaning is clear. Again, previous works [14, 22, 42] justify how the Markovian load balancing process converges to the solution of the differential equations. Specifically, it follows from Wormald's theorem [42, Theorem 1] that

$$X_i(t) = nx_i(t) + o(n)$$

with probability $1 - o(1)$, or equivalently that the fraction of balls of load i is within $o(1)$ of the result of the limiting differential equations with probability $1 - o(1)$.[4] These equations allow us to compute the limiting fraction of bins of each load numerically, and these results closely match our simulations, as for example shown in Table 2.

Given our empirical results, it is natural to conclude that these differential equations must also necessarily describe the behavior of the process when we use double hashing in place of standard hashing. The question is how can we justify this, as the equations were derived utilizing the independence of choices, which is not the case for double hashing.

We now prove that, for constant number of choices d, constant load values i, and a constant time T (corresponding to Tn total balls), the loads of the bins chosen by double

---

[4]In particular, the technical conditions corresponding to Wormald's result [42, Theorem 1] hold, and this theorem gives the appropriate convergence; we explain further in our Theorem 8.

Tail load	Fluid Limit	Fully Random	Double Hashing
≥ 1	0.8231	0.8231	0.8231
≥ 2	0.1765	0.1764	0.1764
≥ 3	0.00051	0.00051	0.00051

Table 2: 3 choices, fluid limit ($n = \infty$) vs. $n = 2^{14}$ balls and bins

hashing behave essentially the same as though the choices were independent, in that, with high probability over the entire course of the process,

$$\mathbb{E}[X_i(t + 1/n) - X_i(t)] = (x_{i-1}(t))^d - (x_i(t))^d + o(1);$$

that is, the gap is only in $o(1)$ terms. This suffices for [42, Theorem 1] (specifically condition (ii) of [42, Theorem 1] allows such $o(1)$ differences). The result is that double hashing has no effect on the fluid limit analysis. (Again, we emphasize our restriction to constant choices d, constant load values i, and constant time parameter T.) Our approach is inspired by the work of Bramson, Lue, and Prabhakar [7], who use a similar approach to obtain asymptotic independence results in the queueing setting. However, there the concern was on limiting independence in equilibrium with general service time distributions, and the choices of queues were assumed to be purely random. We show that this methodology can be applied to the double hashing setting.

LEMMA 5. *When using double hashing, with high probability over the entire course of the process,*

$$\mathbb{E}[X_i(t + 1/n) - X_i(t)] = (x_{i-1}(t))^d - (x_i(t))^d + o(1).$$

PROOF. We refer to the *ancestry list* of a bin b at time t as follows. The list begins with the balls $z_1, z_2, \ldots, z_{g(b,t)}$ that have had bin b as one of their choices, where $g(b, t)$ is the number of balls that have chosen bin b up to time t. Note that each z_i is associated with a corresponding time t_i and $d - 1$ other bin choices. For each z_i, we recursively add the list of balls that have chosen each of those $d - 1$ bins up to time t_i, and so on recursively. We also think of the bins associated with these balls as being part of the ancestry list, where the meaning is clear. It is clear that the ancestry list gives all the necessary information to determine the load of the bin b at time t (assuming the information regarding choices is presented in such a way to include how placement will occur in case of ties; e.g., the bin choices are ordered by priority). We note that the ancestry list holds more information (and more balls and bins) than the witness trees used by Vöcking (and by us in Section 2.2).

In what follows below let us assume n is prime for convenience (we explain the difference if n is not prime in footnotes). We claim that for asymptotic independence of the load among a collection of d bins at a specific time when a new ball is placed, it suffices to show that these ancestry lists are small. Specifically, we start with showing in Lemma 6 that all ancestry lists contain only $O(\log n)$ associated bins with high probability. We then show as a consequence in Lemma 7 that the ancestry lists of the bins associated with a newly placed ball have no bins in common with high probability. This last fact allows us to complete the main lemma, Lemma 5.

LEMMA 6. *The number of bins in the ancestry list of every bin after the first Tn steps is at most $O(\log n)$ with high probability.*

PROOF. We view the growth of the ancestry list as a variation of the standard branching process, by going backward in time. Let $B_0 = 1$ correspond to size of an initial ancestry list of a bin b, consisting of the bin itself. If the (Tn)th ball thrown has b as one of its d choices, then $d - 1$ additional bins are added to the ancestry list, and we then have $B_1 = d$; otherwise we have no change and $B_1 = 1$. (Note that when measuring the size of the ancestry list in bins, each bin is counted only once, even if it is associated with multiple balls.) If the $(Tn-1)$st ball thrown has a bin in the ancestry list as one of its d choices, then (at most) $d - 1$ bins are added to the ancestry list, and we set $B_2 = B_1 + d - 1$; otherwise, we have $B_2 = B_1$. We continue to add to the ancestry list with at each step $B_i = B_{i-1} + d - 1$ or $B_i = B_{i-1}$, depending on whether the $(Tn - i + 1)$st ball has one of it choices as a bin on the ancestry list, or not.

This process is *almost* equivalent to a Galton-Watson branching process where in each generation, each existing element produces 1 offspring with probability $1 - d/n$ (or equivalently, moves itself into the next generation), or produces d offspring (adding $d - 1$ new elements) with probability d/n. The one issue is that the production of offspring are not independent events; at most $d - 1$ elements are added at each step in the process. (There is also the issue that perhaps fewer than $d - 1$ elements are added when elements are added to the ancestry list; for our purposes, it is pessimistic to assume $d - 1$ offspring are produced.) Without this dependence concern, standard results on branching process would give that $E[B_{Tn}] = (1 + d(d - 1)/n)^{Tn} \leq e^{Td(d-1)}$, which is a constant. Further, we could apply (Chernoff-like) tail bounds from Karp and Zhang [18, Theorem 1], which states the following: for a supercritical finite time branching process $\{Z_n\}$ over n time steps starting with $Z_0 = 1$, with mean offspring per element $\mathbb{E}[Z_1] = \rho > 1$, and with $\mathbb{E}[e^{Z_1}] < \infty$, there exists constants c_1 and c_2 such that

$$\mathbf{Pr}(Z_n > \gamma \rho^n) < c_1 e^{-c_2 \gamma}.$$

In our setting, that would give that there exists constants c_1 and c_2 such that

$$\mathbf{Pr}(B_{Tn} > \gamma(1 + d(d - 1)/n)^{Tn}) < c_1 e^{-c_2 \gamma}.$$

This would give our desired $O(\log n)$ high probability bound on the size of the ancestry list.

To deal with this small deviation, it suffices to consider a modified Galton-Watson process where each element produces d offspring with probability d'/n; we shall see that $d' = d + 1$ suffices. Let B' be the resulting size of this Galton Walton process. From the above we have that $B' < c \log n$ with high probability for some suitable constant c.

Our original desired ancestry list process is dominated by a process where $B_i = \min(B_{i-1} + d - 1, n)$ with probability $\min(B_{i-1}d/n, 1)$ and $B_i = B_{i-1}$ otherwise, and this process is in turn dominated for values of B_i up to $c \log n$ by a Galton-Waston branching process where the constant d'

satisfies

$$1 - (1 - d'/n)^x \geq dx/n$$

for all $1 \leq x \leq c \log n$, so that at every stage the Galton-Watson process is more likely to have at least $d-1$ new offspring (and may have more). We see $d' = d+1$ suffices, as

$$1 - (1 - (d+1)/n)^x = x(d+1)/n - O(dx^2/n^2)$$

which is greater than dx/n for n sufficiently large when x is $O(\log n)$. The straightforward step by step coupling of the processes yields that

$$\mathbf{Pr}(B_{Tn} > c \log n) \leq \mathbf{Pr}(B' > c \log n),$$

giving our desired bound.

We also suggest a slightly cleaner alternative, which may prove useful for other variations: embed the branching process in a continuous time branching process. We scale time so that balls are thrown as a Poisson process of rate n per unit time over T time units. Each element therefore generates $d-1$ new offspring at time instants that are exponentially distributed with mean $1/d$ (the average time before a ball hits any bin on the ancestry list). Again, assuming $d-1$ new offspring is a pessimistic bound. If we let C_t be the number of elements at time t (starting from 1 element at time 0), it is well known (see, e.g., [2, p.108 eq. (4)], and note that generating $d-1$ new offspring is equivalent to "dieing" and generating d offspring) that for such a process,

$$\mathbb{E}[C_t] = e^{td(d-1)}.$$

In our case, we run to a fixed time T and $\mathbb{E}[C_T] = e^{Td(d-1)}$, a constant. Indeed, in this specific case, the generating function for the distribution of the number of elements is known (see, e.g., [2, p.109]), allowing us to directly apply a Chernoff bound. Specifically,

$$\mathbb{E}[s^{C_t}] = se^{-dt}[1 - (1 - e^{-d(d-1)t})s^{d-1}]^{-1/(d-1)}.$$

Hence we have

$$\begin{aligned} \mathbf{Pr}(C_T > \gamma e^{Td(d-1)}) &= \mathbf{Pr}(e^{C_T} > e^{\gamma e^{Td(d-1)}}) \\ &\leq e^{-\gamma e^{Td(d-1)}} \mathbb{E}[e^{C_T}] \\ &\leq c_3 e^{-c_4 \gamma} \end{aligned}$$

for constants c_3 and c_4 that depend on d and T. Hence, this gives that the size of the ancestry list as viewed from the setting of the continuous branching process is $O(\log n)$ with high probability.

The last concern is that running the continuous process for time Tn does not guarantee that Tn balls are thrown; this can be dealt with by thinking of the process running for a slightly longer time $T' > T$. That is, choose $T' = T + \epsilon$ for a small constant ϵ. Standard Chernoff bounds on the Poisson random variables then guarantee that at least Tn balls are then thrown with high probability, and the size of the ancestry lists are stochastically monotonically increasing with the number of balls thrown. Changing to T' time units maintains that each ancestry list is $O(\log n)$ with high probability.

Finally, by choosing the constant in the $O(\log n)$ term appropriately, we can achieve a high enough probability to apply a union bound so that this holds for all ancestry lists simultaneously with high probability. □

We now use Lemma 6 to show the following.

LEMMA 7. *The bins in the ancestry lists of the d choices are disjoint with probability $1 - \eta$ for $\eta = O(d^2 \log^2 n/n) = o(1)$.*

PROOF. Let $\mathcal{F}$ be the event that the bins are disjoint, and let $\mathcal{E}$ be the event that no pair of the d choices were previously chosen by the same ball. If $\mathcal{E}$ occurs, the ancestry lists are clearly not disjoint. Hence we wish to bound

$$\mathbf{Pr}(\mathcal{F}) \leq \mathbf{Pr}(\mathcal{E}) + \mathbf{Pr}(\mathcal{F}|\neg\mathcal{E}).$$

Consider any two of the d bins chosen by the ball being placed. Each of the up to Tn previous balls have $O(d^2)$ ways of choosing those two bins as two of their d choices (e.g., picking that bin as the 2nd and 4th choice, for example), and the probability of choosing those two bins for each possible pair of choice positions is $O(1/n^2)$.[5] There are $\binom{d}{2}$ pairs of balls, so by a union bound $\mathbf{Pr}(\mathcal{E})$ is $O(Td^4/n^2)$.

Now suppose that no pair of the d bins were previously chosen by the same ball. Suppose the bins for each of the ancestry lists of the d choices are ordered in some fixed fashion (say according to decreasing ball time, randomly permuted for each ball). We consider the probability that the ith bin in the ancestry list of one bin matches the jth bin in another. Since the lists do not share any ball in common, the jth bin in the second list matches the ith bin in the first list with probability only $O(1/n)$, as even conditioned on the value of the ith bin on the first list, the jth bin on the second list is uniform over $\Omega(n)$ possibilities.[6] We now condition on all of the d ancestry lists being of size $O(\log n)$; from Lemma 6, this can be made to occur with any inverse polynomial probability by choosing the constant factor in the $O(\log n)$ term, so we assume this bound on ancestry list sizes. In his case, the probability of a match among any of the d bins is only $O(d^2 \log^2 n/n)$ in total, where the d^2 factor is from the $\binom{d}{2}$ possible ways of choosing bins, and the $\log^2 n$ term follows the bound on the size ancestry lists. Hence $\mathbf{Pr}(\mathcal{F}|\neg\mathcal{E})$ is $O(d^2 \log^2 n/n)$, and the total probability that the ancestry lists of the d choices are *not* disjoint is $\eta = O(d^2 \log^2 n/n) = o(1)$. □

We now show that this yields the Lemma 5. To clarify this, consider bins $b_1, b_2, \ldots, b_d$ that were chosen by a ball at some time $t + 1/n$. (Recall our scaling of time.) The probability that all d bins have load at least i at that time is equivalent to the probability that each bin b_j has a corresponding ancestry list A_j showing that it has load i at some time $u_j \leq t$. Fix a collection of ancestry lists A_j, and let E_j be the event defined by "bin b_j has ancestry list A_j". If these ancestry lists have disjoint sets of bins, then the corresponding balls in each ancestry list occur at different times and have no intersecting bins, and as such

$$\mathbf{Pr}(\cap_j E_j) = \prod_j \mathbf{Pr}(E_j).$$

For constant i, t, and d, the probability that all d bins have load at least i is constant. Hence, if the probability that the

---

[5]If n is not prime, this probability is $O(1/n\phi(n))$, where ϕ is the Euler totient function counting the number of numbers less than n that are relatively prime to n. We note $\phi(n)$ is usually $\Omega(n)$ and is always $\Omega(n/\log \log n)$, so this does not affect our argument substantially.

[6]Again, for n not prime, we may use $\Omega(\phi(n))$ possibilities.

ancestry lists for the d bins intersect at any bin is $\eta = o(1)$, we have asymptotic independence. Specifically, let $\mathcal{X}$ be the set of collections of d ancestry lists for balls $b_1, b_2, \ldots, b_d$ that yield that each bin has load at least i at time t, let $\mathcal{Y}$ be the subset of collections in $\mathcal{X}$ where the d ancestry lists have no bins in common, and for a collection Z in $\mathcal{X}$ let $E_j(Z)$ be the corresponding event defined by "bin b_j has ancestry list A_j in collection Z". Then

$$
\begin{aligned}
\sum_{Z \in \mathcal{X}} \mathbf{Pr}\left(\cap_j E_j(Z)\right) &= \left[\sum_{Z \in \mathcal{Y}} \mathbf{Pr}\left(\cap_j E_j(Z)\right)\right] + o(1) \\
&= \sum_{Z \in \mathcal{Y}} \left(\prod_j \mathbf{Pr}\, E_j(Z)\right) + o(1) \\
&= \sum_{Z \in \mathcal{X}} \left(\prod_j \mathbf{Pr}\, E_j(Z)\right) + o(1).
\end{aligned}
$$

Here the first line uses that the d ancestry lists intersect somewhere with probability $o(1)$; the second lines uses that for ancestry lists in $\mathcal{Y}$ we probability of the intersection is the product of the probabilities; and the third line is again because the the collections Z in $\mathcal{X} - \mathcal{Y}$ have total probability $o(1)$. Hence up to an $o(1)$ term, the behavior is the same as if the d choices were independent (with respect to all bins having load at least i). Thus

$$
\mathbb{E}[X_i(t + 1/n) - X_i(t)] = (x_{i-1}(t))^d - (x_i(t))^d + o(1)
$$

as needed.

As a result of Lemma 5, we have the following theorem, generalizing the differential equations approach for balanced allocations to the setting of double hashing.

THEOREM 8. *Let i, d, and T be constants. Suppose Tn balls are sequentially thrown into n bins with each ball having d choices obtained from double hashing and each ball being placed in the least loaded bin (ties broken randomly). Let $X_i(T)$ be the number of bins of load at least i after the balls are thrown. Let $x_i(t)$ be determined by the family of differential equations*

$$
\frac{dx_i}{dt} = x_{i-1}^d - x_i^d,
$$

where $x_0(t) = 1$ for all time and $x_i(0) = 0$ for $i \geq 1$. Then with probability $1 - o(1)$,

$$
\frac{X_i(T)}{n} = x_i(T) + o(1).
$$

PROOF. This follows from the fact that

$$
\mathbb{E}[X_i(t + 1/n) - X_i(t)] = (x_{i-1}(t))^d - (x_i(t))^d + o(1),
$$

and applying Wormald's result [42, Theorem 1].

We remark that Theorem 1 of [42] includes other technical conditions that we briefly consider here. The first condition is that $|X_i(t + 1/n) - X_i(t)|$ is bounded by a constant; all such values here are bounded by 1. The second (and only challenging) condition exactly corresponds to our statement that $\mathbb{E}[X_i(t + 1/n) - X_i(t)] = (x_{i-1}(t))^d - (x_i(t))^d + o(1)$ over the course of the process. The third condition is our functions on the right hand side, that is $(x_{i-1}(t))^d - (x_i(t))^d$, are continuous and satisfy a Lipschitz condition on an open neighborhood containing the path of the process. These functions are continuous on the domain where all $x_i \in [0, 1]$

up to the value i being considered, and they satisfy the Lipschitz condition as

$$
\begin{aligned}
|(x_{i-1}(t))^d - (x_i(t))^d| &\leq |x_{i-1}(t) - x_i(t)| \sum_{j=0}^{d-1} (x_{i-1}(t))^j (x_i(t))^{d-1-j} \\
&\leq d|(x_{i-1}(t)) - (x_i(t))|,
\end{aligned}
$$

taking note that all x_i, x_{i-1} values are in the interval $[0, 1]$. Hence the conditions for Wormald's theorem are met. $\square$

The following corollary, based on the known fact that the result of Theorem 8 also holds in the setting of fully random hashing [28], states that the difference between fully random hashing and double hashing is vanishing.

COROLLARY 9. *Let i, d, and T be constants. Consider two processes, where in each Tn balls are sequentially thrown into n bins with each ball having d choices and each ball being placed in the least loaded bin (ties broken randomly). In one process, the d choices are fully random; in the other, the d choices are made by double hashing. Then with probability $1 - o(1)$, the fraction of bins with load i differ by an $o(1)$ additive term.*

Given the results for the differential equations, it is perhaps unsurprising that one can use these methods to obtain, for example, a maximum load of $\log \log n / \log d + O(1)$ maximum load for n balls in n bins, using the related layered induction approach of [3]. While we suggest this is not the main point (given Theorem 4), we provide further details in Appendix B.

4. CONCLUSION

We have first demonstrated empirically that using double hashing with balanced allocation processes (e.g., the power of (more than) two choices), surprisingly, does not noticeably change performance when compared with fully random hashing. We have then shown that previous methods can readily provide $O(\log \log n)$ bounds for this approach. However, explaining why the fraction of bins of load k for each k appears the same requires revisiting the fluid limit model for such processes. We have shown, interestingly, that the same family of differential equations applies for the limiting process. Our argument should extend naturally to other similar processes; for example, the analysis can similarly be made to apply in a straightforward fashion for the differential equations for Vöcking's d-left scheme [32].

This opens the door to the interesting possibility that double hashing can be suitable for other problem or analyses where this type of fluid limit analysis applies, such as low-density parity-check codes [25]. Here, however, the asymptotic independence required was aided by the fact that we were looking at the history of the process, allowing us to tie the ancestry lists to a corresponding branching process. Whether similar asymptotic independence can be derived for other problems remains to be seen. For other problems, such as cuckoo hashing, the fluid limit analysis, while an important step, may not offer a complete analysis. Even for load balancing problems, fluid limits do not straightforwardly apply for the heavily loaded case where the number of balls is superlinear in the number of bins [5], and it is unclear how double hashing performs in that setting. So again, determining more generally where double hashing can be used in place of fully random hashing without significantly changing performance may offer challenging future questions.

Acknowledgments

The author thanks George Varghese for the discussions which led to the formulation of this problem, and thanks Justin Thaler for both helpful conversations and offering several suggestions for improving the presentation of results.

5. REFERENCES

[1] N. Alon and J. Spencer. *The Probabilistic Method*, John Wiley & Sons, 1992.

[2] K. Athreya and P. Ney. *Branching Processes.* Springer-Verlag, 1972.

[3] Y. Azar, A. Broder, A. Karlin, and E. Upfal. Balanced allocations. *SIAM Journal of Computing* 29(1):180-200, 1999.

[4] Y. Bachrach and E. Porat. Fast pseudo-random fingerprints. Arxiv preprint arXiv:1009.5791, 2010.

[5] P. Berenbrink, A. Czumaj, A. Steger, and B. Vöcking. Balanced allocations: The heavily loaded case. *SIAM Journal on Computing*, 35(6):1350-1385, 2006.

[6] P. Bradford and M. Katehakis. A probabilistic study on combinatorial expanders and hashing. *SIAM Journal on Computing*, 37(1):83-111, 2007.

[7] M. Bramson, Y. Lu, and B. Prabhakar. Asymptotic independence of queues under randomized load balancing. *Queueing Systems*, 71(3):247-292, 2012.

[8] A. Broder, M. Charikar, A, Frieze, and M. Mitzenmacher. Min-wise independent permutations. *Journal of Computer and System Sciences*, 60:3, pp. 630-659, 2000.

[9] J. L. Carter and M. N. Wegman. Universal classes of hash functions. *Journal of Computer and System Sciences*, 18(2):143–154, 1979.

[10] L. Celis, O. Reingold, G. Segev, and U. Wieder. Balls and Bins: Smaller Hash Families and Faster Evaluation. In *Proc. of the 52nd Annual Symposium on Foundations of Computer Science*, pp. 599-608, 2011.

[11] ChunkStash: speeding up inline storage deduplication using flash memory. B. Debnath, S. Sengupta, and J. Li. In *Proc. of the USENIX Technical Conference*, p.16, 2010.

[12] J. Díaz and D. Mitsche. The cook-book approach to the differential equations method. *Computer Science Review*, 4(3):129-151, 2010.

[13] P.C. Dillinger and P. Manolios. Bloom Filters in Probabilistic Verification. In *Proc. of the 5th International Conference on Formal Methods in Computer-Aided Design*, pp. 367-381, 2004.

[14] S. N. Ethier and T. G. Kurtz. *Markov Processes: Characterization and Convergence.* John Wiley and Sons, 1986.

[15] P. Godfrey. Balls and bins with structure: balanced allocations on hypergraphs. In *Proc. of the Nineteenth Annual ACM-SIAM Symposium on Discrete Algorithms*, pp. 511-517, 2008.

[16] L. Guibas and E. Szemeredi. The analysis of double hashing. *Journal of Computer and System Sciences*, 16(2):226-274, 1978.

[17] G. Heileman and W. Luo. How caching affects hashing. In *Proc. of ALENEX/ANALCO*, pp. 141–154, 2005.

[18] R. Karp and Y. Zhang. Finite branching processes and AND/OR tree evaluation. ICSI Berkeley Technical Report TR-93-043. See also Bounded branching process and and/or tree evaluation. *Random Structures and Algorithms*, 7:97-116, 1995.

[19] K. Kenthapadi and R. Panigrahy. Balanced allocation on graphs. In *Proc. of the 17th Annual ACM-SIAM Symposium on Discrete Algorithms*, pp. 434-443, 2006.

[20] A. Kirsch and M. Mitzenmacher. Less hashing, same performance: Building a better Bloom filter. *Random Structures & Algorithms*, 33(2):187-218, 2008.

[21] A. Kirsch, M. Mitzenmacher and G. Varghese. Hash-Based Techniques for High-Speed Packet Processing. In *Algorithms for Next Generation Networks*, (G. Cormode and M. Thottan, eds.), pp. 181-218, Springer London, 2010.

[22] T. G. Kurtz. Solutions of Ordinary Differential Equations as Limits of Pure Jump Markov Processes. *Journal of Applied Probability* Vol. 7, 1970, pp. 49-58.

[23] L. Le Cam. An approximation theorem for the Poisson binomial distribution. *Pacific J. Math*, 10(4):1181-1197, 1960.

[24] G. Lueker and M. Molodowitch. More analysis of double hashing. *Combinatorica*, 13(1):83-96, 1993.

[25] M. Luby, M. Mitzenmacher, A. Shokrollahi, and D. Spielman. Efficient erasure correcting codes. *IEEE Transactions on Information Theory*, 47(2):569-584, 2001.

[26] A. Marshall, I. Olkin, and B. Arnold. *Inequalities: Theory of Majorization and Its Applications (2nd Edition).* Springer-Verlag, 2010.

[27] M. Mitzenmacher. The power of two choices in randomized load balancing. *IEEE Transactions on Parallel and Distributed Systems*, 12(10):1094-1104, 2001.

[28] M. Mitzenmacher. The power of two choices in randomized load balancing. Ph.D. thesis, 1996.

[29] M. Mitzenmacher, A. Richa, and R. Sitaraman. The Power of Two Choices: A Survey of Techniques and Results. In *Handbook of Randomized Computing*, (P. Pardalos, S. Rajasekaran, J. Reif, and J. Rolim, edds), pp. 255-312, Kluwer Academic Publishers, Norwell, MA, 2001.

[30] M. Mitzenmacher and J. Thaler. Peeling Arguments and Double Hashing. In *Proc. of Allerton 2012*, pp. 1118-1125.

[31] M. Mitzenmacher and E. Upfal. *Probability and computing: Randomized algorithms and probabilistic analysis*, 2005, Cambridge University Press.

[32] M. Mitzenmacher and B. Vöcking. The Asymptotics of Selecting the Shortest of Two, Improved. In *Proc. of Allerton 1999*, pp. 326-327.

[33] M. Mitzenmacher and S. Vadhan. Why Simple Hash Functions Work: Exploiting the Entropy in a Data Stream. In *Proc. of the Nineteenth Annual ACM-SIAM Symposium on Discrete Algorithms*, pp. 746-755, 2008.

[34] A. Pagh, R. Pagh, and M. Ruzic. Linear Probing with 5-wise Independence. *SIAM Review*, 53(3):547-558, 2011.

[35] M. Patrascu and M. Thorup. The power of simple tabulation hashing. In *Proc. of the 43rd Annual ACM Symposium on Theory of Computing*, pp.1-10, 2011.

[36] Y. Peres, K. Talwar, and U. Wieder. The $(1+\beta)$-choice process and weighted balls-into-bins. In *Proc. of the Twenty-First Annual ACM-SIAM Symposium on Discrete Algorithms*, pp. 1613-1619, 2010.

[37] J. Schmidt-Pruzan and E. Shamir. Component structure in the evolution of random hypergraphs. *Combinatorica*, vol. 5, pp. 81-94, 1985.

[38] T. Schickinger and A. Steger. Simplified witness tree arguments. *SOFSEM 2000: Theory and Practice of Informatics*, pp. 71–87, 2000.

[39] B. Vöcking. How asymmetry helps load balancing. *Journal of the ACM*, 50(4):568-589, 2003.

[40] N.D. Vvedenskaya, R.L. Dobrushin, and F.I. Karpelevich. Queueing system with selection of the shortest of two queues: an asymptotic approach. *Problems of Information Transmission*, 32:15–27, 1996.

[41] P. Woelfel. Asymmetric balanced allocation with simple hash functions. In *Proc. of the Seventeenth Annual ACM-SIAM Symposium on Discrete Algorithms*, pp. 424–433, 2006.

[42] N.C. Wormald. Differential equations for random processes and random graphs. *The Annals of Applied Probability*, 5(1995), pp. 1217–1235.

APPENDIX

A. EMPIRICAL RESULTS

We have done extensive simulations to test whether using double hashing in place of idealized random hashing makes a difference for several multiple choice schemes. Theoretically, of course, there is some difference; for example, the probability that k balls choose the same specified set of d bins is $O(n^{-dk})$ with fully random choices, and only $O(n^{-2k})$ with double hashing (where the order notation may hide factors that depend on d). Hence, to be clear, the best we can hope for are differences up to $o(1)$ events. Empirically, however, our experiments suggest the effects on the distribution of the loads, or in particular on the probability the maximum load exceeds some value, are all found deeply in the lower order terms. Experiments show that unless especially rare events are of special concern, we expect the two to perform similarly.

A.1 The Standard d-Choice Scheme

We first consider n balls and bins using d choices without replacement, comparing fully random choices with double hashing.[7] When using double hashing we choose an odd stride value as explained previously. All results presented are over 10000 trials. Table 3 shows the distributions of bin loads for 3 and 4 choices, averaged over all 10000 trials, for $n = 2^{16}$ and $n = 2^{18}$. (Recall $n = 2^{14}$ was shown in

---

[7]We also considered d choices with replacement, but the difference was not apparent except for very small n, so we present only results without replacement. However, we note that conversations with George Varghese regarding hardware settings with small n originally motivated our examination of this approach.

Table 1.) As can be seen, the deviations are all very small, within standard sampling error.

We may also consider the maximum load. In Table 4, we consider values of n where the maximum load is at most 3, and examine the fraction of time a load of 3 is achieved over the 10000 trials. Again, the difference between the two schemes appears small, to the point where it would be a challenge to differentiate between the two approaches.

We focus in on the case of 4 choices with 2^{18} balls and bins to examine the sample standard deviation (across 10000 trials) in Table 5. This example is representative of behavior in our other experiments. By looking at the number of bins of each load over several trials, we see the sample standard deviation is very small compared to the number of bins of a given load, whether using double hashing or fully random hashing, and again performance is similar for both.

A reasonable question is whether the same behavior occurs if the average load is larger than 1. We have tested this for several cases, and again found that empirically the behavior is essentially indistinguishable. As an example, Table 6 gives results in the case of 2^{18} balls being thrown into 2^{14} bins, for an average load of 16. Again, the differences are at the level of sampling deviations.

We note that we obtain similar results under variations of the standard d-choice scheme. For example, using Vöcking's approach of splitting in d subtables and breaking ties to the left, we obtain essentially indistinguishable load distributions with fully random hashing and double hashing. Table 7 shows results from a representative case where $d = 4$, again averaging over 10000 trials. The case of $n = 2^{18}$ is instructive; this appears very close to the threshold where bins with load 3 can appear. While there appears to be a deviation, with double hashing have some small fraction of bins with load 3, this corresponds to exactly 2 bins over the 10000 trials. Further simulations suggest that this apparent gap is less significant than it might appear; over 100000 trials, for random, the maximum load was 3 for three trials, while for double hashing, it was 3 for four trials.

In the standard queueing setting, balls arrive as a Poisson process of rate λn for $\lambda < 1$ to a bank of n first-in first-out queues, and have exponentially distributed service times with mean 1. Jobs are placed by choosing d queues and going to the queue with the fewest jobs. The asymptotic equilibrium distributions for such systems with independent, uniform choices can be found by fluid limit models [27, 40]. We ran 100 simulations of 10000 seconds, recording the average time over all packets after time 1000 (allowing the system to "burn in".) An example appears in Table 8. While double hashing performs slightly worse in these trials, the gap is far less than 0.1% in all cases.

B. EXTENDING THE FLUID LIMIT

We sketch an approach to extend the fluid limit result to provide an $O(\log \log n)$ result. In fact, we show here that for n balls being thrown into n bins via double hashing, we obtain a load of $\log \log n / \log d + O(1)$, avoiding the $O(d)$ term of Section 2.2. While this is technicality for the case of d constant, this approach could be used to obtain bounds for super-constant values of d.

The basic approach is not new, and has been used in other settings, such as [3, 28]. Essentially, we can repeat the "layered induction" approach of [3] in the setting of double hashing, making use of the results of Section 3 that the deviations

Load	Fully Random	Double Hashing
0	0.17695	0.17693
1	0.64661	0.64664
2	0.17593	0.17592
3	0.00051	0.00051

(a) 3 choices, $n = 2^{16}$ balls and bins

Load	Fully Random	Double Hashing
0	0.14081	0.14083
1	0.71841	0.71835
2	0.14076	0.14079
3	$2.32 \cdot 10^{-5}$	$2.30 \cdot 10^{-5}$

(b) 4 choices, $n = 2^{16}$ balls and bins

Load	Fully Random	Double Hashing
0	0.17696	0.17696
1	0.64658	0.64648
2	0.17595	0.17595
3	0.00051	0.00051

(c) 3 choices, $n = 2^{18}$ balls and bins

Load	Fully Random	Double Hashing
0	0.14083	0.14082
1	0.71837	0.71838
2	0.14078	0.14078
3	$2.31 \cdot 10^{-5}$	$2.32 \cdot 10^{-5}$

(d) 4 choices, $n = 2^{18}$ balls and bins

Table 3: Essentially indistinguishable differences in simulation between double hashing and fully random hashing.

n	Fully Random	Double Hashing
2^{10}	39.78	39.40
2^{11}	64.71	65.15
2^{12}	86.90	87.05
2^{13}	98.37	98.63
2^{14}	100.00	99.99
2^{15}	100.00	100.00

(a) 3 choices, fraction with maximum load 3

n	Fully Random	Double Hashing
2^{10}	2.24	2.23
2^{12}	8.91	8.52
2^{14}	30.75	31.42
2^{16}	78.23	77.72
2^{18}	99.77	99.79
2^{20}	100.00	100.00

(b) 4 choices, fraction with maximum load 3

Table 4: Comparing maximum loads. The fraction of runs with maximum load 3 is similar.

Load	min	avg	max	std.dev.
0	36522	36913.75	37308	111.06
1	187533	188322.55	189103	222.02
2	36516	36901.67	37298	110.96
3	1	6.04	17	2.42

(a) Fully random, load distribution over 10000 trials

Load	min	avg	max	std.dev.
0	36535	36916.57	37301	109.89
1	187544	188316.93	189078	219.71
2	36524	36904.45	37297	109.85
3	1	6.06	18	2.44

(b) Double hashing, load distribution over 10000 trials

Table 5: Viewing the sample standard deviation, 4 choices, 2^{18} balls and 2^{18} bins.

Load	Fully Random	Double Hashing
9	$6.10 \cdot 10^{-9}$	$6.10 \cdot 10^{-9}$
10	$1.28 \cdot 10^{-7}$	$1.71 \cdot 10^{-7}$
11	$2.50 \cdot 10^{-6}$	$2.95 \cdot 10^{-6}$
12	$4.54 \cdot 10^{-5}$	$4.51 \cdot 10^{-5}$
13	0.00076	0.00076
14	0.01254	0.01254
15	0.16885	0.16877
16	0.62220	0.62234
17	0.19482	0.19475
18	0.00079	0.00079

(a) 3 choices, 2^{18} balls and 2^{14} bins

Load	Fully Random	Double Hashing
11	$2.44 \cdot 10^{-8}$	$2.44 \cdot 10^{-8}$
12	$1.48 \cdot 10^{-6}$	$1.34 \cdot 10^{-6}$
13	$6.92 \cdot 10^{-5}$	$6.98 \cdot 10^{-4}$
14	0.00349	0.00349
15	0.13908	0.13906
16	0.71110	0.71114
17	0.14622	0.14620
18	$2.86 \cdot 10^{-5}$	$2.85 \cdot 10^{-5}$

(b) 4 choices, 2^{18} balls and 2^{14} bins

Table 6: The similarity in performance persists under higher loads.

Load	Fully Random	Double Hashing
0	0.12420	0.12421
1	0.75160	0.75158
2	0.12420	0.12421

(a) 4 choices, 2^{14} balls and bins

Load	Fully Random	Double Hashing
0	0.12421	0.12421
1	0.75159	0.75158
2	0.12421	0.12421
3		$7.63 \cdot 10^{-10}$

(b) 4 choices, 2^{18} balls and bins

Table 7: Double hashing performance with Vöcking's d-left scheme.

λ	Choices	Fully Random	Double Hashing
0.9	3	2.02805	2.02813
0.9	4	1.77788	1.77792
0.99	3	3.85967	3.86073
0.99	4	3.24347	3.24410

Table 8: $n = 2^{14}$ queues, average time

from the fully random setting are at most $o(1)$ for a suitable number of levels.

This allows us to state the following theorem:

THEOREM 10. *Suppose n balls are placed into n bins using the balanced allocation scheme with double hashing. Then with $d \geq 3$ choices (for d constant) the maximum load is $\log \log n / \log d + O(1)$ with high probability.*

PROOF. Let z_i be the number of bins of load i after all n balls have been thrown. We will follow the framework of the original balanced allocations paper [3], and start by noting that $z_6 \leq n/(2e)$. Now from the argument of Section 3, the probability that the tth ball chooses d bins all with load at least $i \geq 2$ is bounded above by $z_{i-1}^d/n^d + \eta$, where $\eta = O(d^2 \log^2 n)/n$ was determined in Lemma 5, as long as, up to that point, we can condition on all the ancestry lists being suitably small, which is a high probability event. We will denote the event that the ancestry lists are suitably small throughout the process by $\mathcal{E}_0$.

Finally, let $\beta_6 = n/(2e)$ and $\beta_i = 4\beta_{i-1}^d/n^{d-1}$ for $i \geq 6$. Let $\mathcal{E}_i$ be the event that $\mathcal{E}_0$ occurs and that $z_i \leq \beta_i$. (We choose β_i values similarly to [3] for convenience, but use the constant 4 on the right hand side whereas [3] uses the constant e to account for the extra η in our probability over just the value z_{i-1}^d/n^d.) A simple induction using the formula for β_i yields $\beta_i \leq n/e^{d^{i-6}}$ for $d \geq 3$.

Now we fix some $i > 6$ and consider random variables Y_t, where $Y_t = 1$ if the following conditions all hold: all d choices for the tth ball have load at least $i - 1$, the number of bins with load at least $i - 1$ before the ball is thrown is at most β_{i-1}, and the ancestry lists are all suitably small when the ball is thrown so the polylogarithmic bound on the "extra probability" that a ball ends up with all d choices having load at least $i - 1$ holds. Let $Y_t = 0$ otherwise. We note that the number of bins with load at least i is at most the sum of the Y_t. Let $p_i = \beta_{i-1}^d/n^d + \eta$. Conditioned on $\mathcal{E}_{i-1}$, we have

$$\mathbf{Pr}(z_i \geq k \mid \mathcal{E}_{i-1}) \leq \mathbf{Pr}(\sum_t Y_t \geq k \mid \mathcal{E}_{i-1}) \leq \frac{\mathbf{Pr}(\sum_t Y_t \geq k)}{\mathbf{Pr}(\mathcal{E}_{i-1})}.$$

Now the sum Y_t are dominated by a binomial random variable $B(n, p_i)$ of n trials, each with probability p_i of success, because of the definition of the Y_i.

As in [3], we can use the simple Chernoff bound from [1]

$$\mathbf{Pr}(B(n, p_i) \geq e p_i n) \leq e^{-p_i n}.$$

Note that, for large enough n and β_{i-1}, $e p_i n \leq 4\beta_{i-1}^d/n^d$, as η will be a lower order term. Hence for such values,

$$\mathbf{Pr}(B(n, p_i) \geq \beta_i) \leq e^{-p_i n}.$$

With these choices, we see that as long as $p_i \geq n^{-1/5}$ (note that for this value of p_i, η is indeed a lower order term),

$$\mathbf{Pr}(\neg \mathcal{E}_i \mid \mathcal{E}_{i-1}) \leq e^{-n^{4/5}}/\mathbf{Pr}(\mathcal{E}_{i-1}),$$

and using

$$\mathbf{Pr}(\neg \mathcal{E}_i) \leq \mathbf{Pr}(\neg \mathcal{E}_i \mid \mathcal{E}_{i-1})\,\mathbf{Pr}(\mathcal{E}_{i-1}) + \mathbf{Pr}(\neg \mathcal{E}_{i-1}),$$

we have

$$\mathbf{Pr}(\neg \mathcal{E}_i) \leq e^{-n^{4/5}} + \mathbf{Pr}(\neg \mathcal{E}_{i-1}).$$

Recall again that $\mathcal{E}_6$ depended on $\mathcal{E}_0$ and $z_6 \leq \beta_6 = n/(2e)$, and the latter holds with certainty.

Note that we only require $i^* = \log \log n / \log d + O(1)$ before $p_i \leq n^{-1/5}$, based on the bound for the β_i. Hence the total probability that the required events $\mathcal{E}_i$ do not hold up to this point is bounded by $\mathbf{Pr}(\neg \mathcal{E}_0) + O(\log \log n) \cdot e^{-n^{4/5}}$. Hence, as long $\mathbf{Pr}(\neg \mathcal{E}_0)$ is $1 - o(1)$ (which we argued in Section 3), we are good for loads up to i^*. After only one more round, using the same argument, we can get to the point where $z_{i^*+1} \leq n^{5/6}$, using the same Chernoff bound argument, since the expected number of bins with load at least $i^* + 1$ would be dominated by $n^{4/5}$.

From this point, one can show that the maximum load is $i^* + c$ for some constant c with high probability by continuing with a variation of the *layered induction* argument as used in [3]. If we condition on there being $n^{1-\varsigma}$ bins with load at least i' for some $i' \geq i^*$, for a ball have all d choices have bins with at least $i'+1$, it must have at least two of its bin choices have load at least i'. Even when using double hashing, for any ball, any pair of the d choices of bins are chosen independently from all possible pairs of distinct bins[8]; hence, by a union bound the probability any ball causes a bin to have load at least $i' + 1$ is at most $\binom{d}{2}n^{-2\varsigma}$, giving an expected number of bins of load at least $i' + 1$ of at most $\binom{d}{2}n^{1-2\varsigma}$. (Here this step is slightly different than the corresponding step in [3]; because of the use of double hashing in place of independent hashes, we use a union bound over the $\binom{d}{2}$ pairs of bins. This avoids the issue of the ancestry lists completely at this point of the argument, which we take advantage of once we've gotten down to a small enough number of bins to complete the argument.)

Applying the same Chernoff bounds as previously, we find $z_{i^*+2} \leq e n^{2/3}$ with high probability, $z_{i^*+3} \leq e^2 n^{1/3}$ with high probability. By a union bound, the probability of any ball having at least 2 choices with load at least $i^* + 4$ is at most $n \cdot (e^2 n^{-2/3})^2 = o(1)$, and hence $z_{i^*+4} = 0$ with probability $1 - o(1)$. Note can make the probability smaller (such as $1 - o(1/n)$) by taking a larger constant $O(1)$ term. This gives that the maximum load is $\log \log n / \log d + O(1)$ with high probability under double hashing. $\square$

---

[8]Here we again assume n is prime; if not, we need to take into account the issue that the offset is relatively prime to n.

Author Index